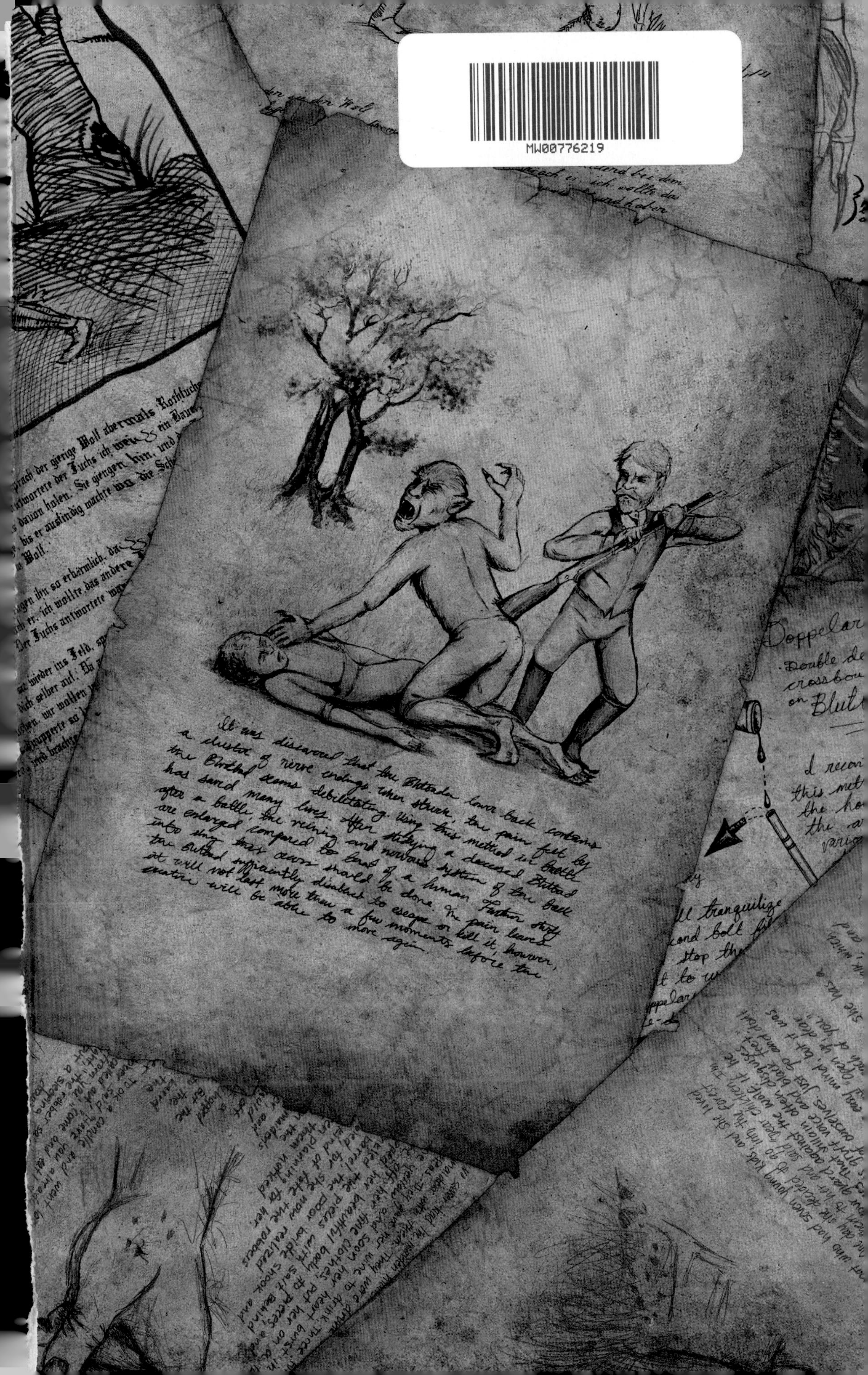
It was discovered that the Blutbaden lower back contains
a cluster of nerve endings when struck, the pain felt by
the Blutbad seems debilitating. Using this method in battle
has saved many lives. After studying a deceased Blutbad
after a battle, the veining and nervous system of the back
are enlarged compared to that of a human. Further study
into why these occurs should be done. The pain leaves
the Blutbad sufficiently disabled to escape or kill it, however,
it will not last more than a few moments before the
creature will be able to move again.

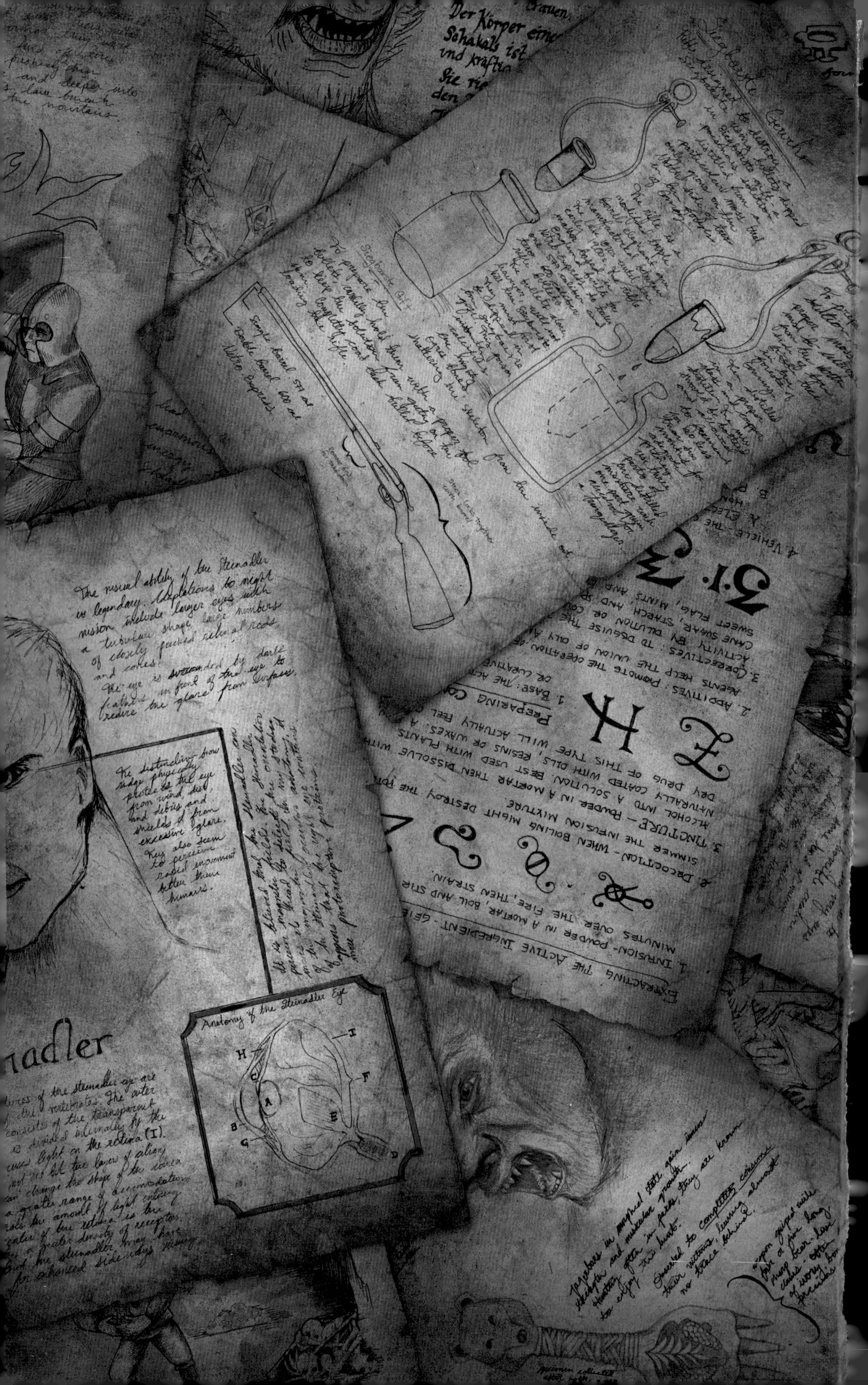

Der Körper eines
Schakals ist
und kräftig
The visual ability of the Steinadler is legendary. Adaptations to night vision include larger eyes with a tubular shape, large numbers of closely packed retinal rods and cones.
Anatomy of the Steinadler Eye
nadler

GRIMM
OMNIBUS

ORIGINAL SERIES 0-12

PLOT BY
JIM KOUF & DAVID GREENWALT

SCRIPT BY
MARC GAFFEN & KYLE MCVEY

ART BY
JOSE MALAGA (1-5, FCBD SPECIAL)
ROD RODOLFO (6-12)

COLORS BY
THIAGO DAL BELLO

LETTERS BY
MARSHALL DILLON

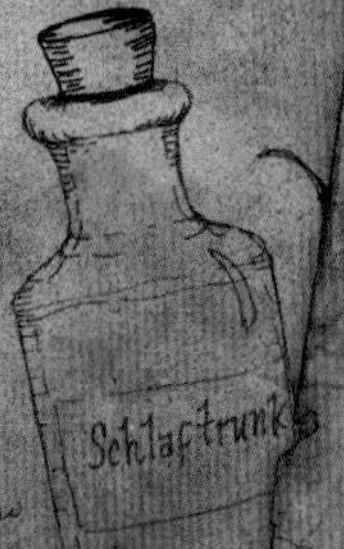

WARLOCK 1-4

WRITTEN BY
JAI NITZ

ART BY
JOSE MALAGA

COLORS BY
LISA MOORE

LETTERS BY
MARSHALL DILLON

PORTLAND, WU

WRITTEN BY
MARC GAFFEN & KYLE MCVEY

ART BY
DANIEL GOVAR

COLORS BY
KEVIN COLDEN

LETTERS BY
PATRICK BROSSEAU

COLLECTION DESIGN BY
ALEXIS PERSSON

SPECIAL THANKS TO
CHRIS LUCERO, LYNN KOUF,
KIM, NIEMI, & ED PRINCE

BASED ON THE NBC
TELEVISION SERIES GRIMM

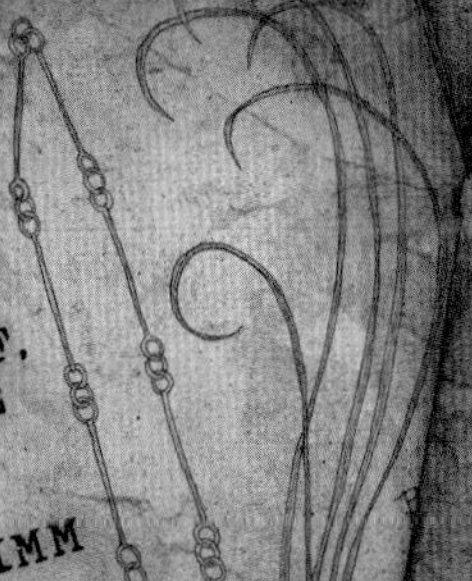

DYNAMITE

Online at www.DYNAMITE.com
On Facebook /Dynamitecomics
On Instagram /Dynamitecomics.tumblr.com
On Tumblr dynamitecomics
On Twitter @dynamitecomics
On YouTube /dynamitecomics

Nick Barrucci, CEO / Publisher
Juan Collado, President / COO

Joe Rybandt, Executive Editor
Matt Idelson, Senior Editor
Rachel Pinnelas, Associate Editor
Anthony Marques, Assistant Editor
Kevin Ketner, Editorial Assistant

Jason Ullmeyer, Art Director
Geoff Harkins, Senior Graphic Designer
Cathleen Heard, Graphic Designer
Alexis Persson, Production Artist

Chris Caniano, Digital Associate
Rachel Kilbury, Digital Assistant

Brandon Dante Primavera, V.P. of IT and Operations
Rich Young, Director of Business Development

Alan Payne, V.P. of Sales and Marketing
Keith Davidsen, Marketing Director
Pat O'Connell, Sales Manager

ISBN-10: 1-5241-0076-5   ISBN-13: 978-1-5241-0076-6

First Printing   10 9 8 7 6 5 4 3 2 1

GRIMM™ OMNIBUS, VOLUME ONE. First printing. Contains materials originally published in GRIMM #0-12, Grimm: The Warlock #1-4, and Portland, WU. Published by Dynamite Entertainment. 113 Gaither Dr., STE 205, Mt. Laurel, NJ 08054 and 121 W. 27th St., STE801, New York, NY 10001. Grimm is a trademark and copyright of Universal Network Television LLC. Licensed by NBCUniversal Television Consumer Products Group 2016. All Rights Reserved. DYNAMITE, DYNAMITE ENTERTAINMENT and its logo are © & ® 2016 Dynamite. All names, characters, events,

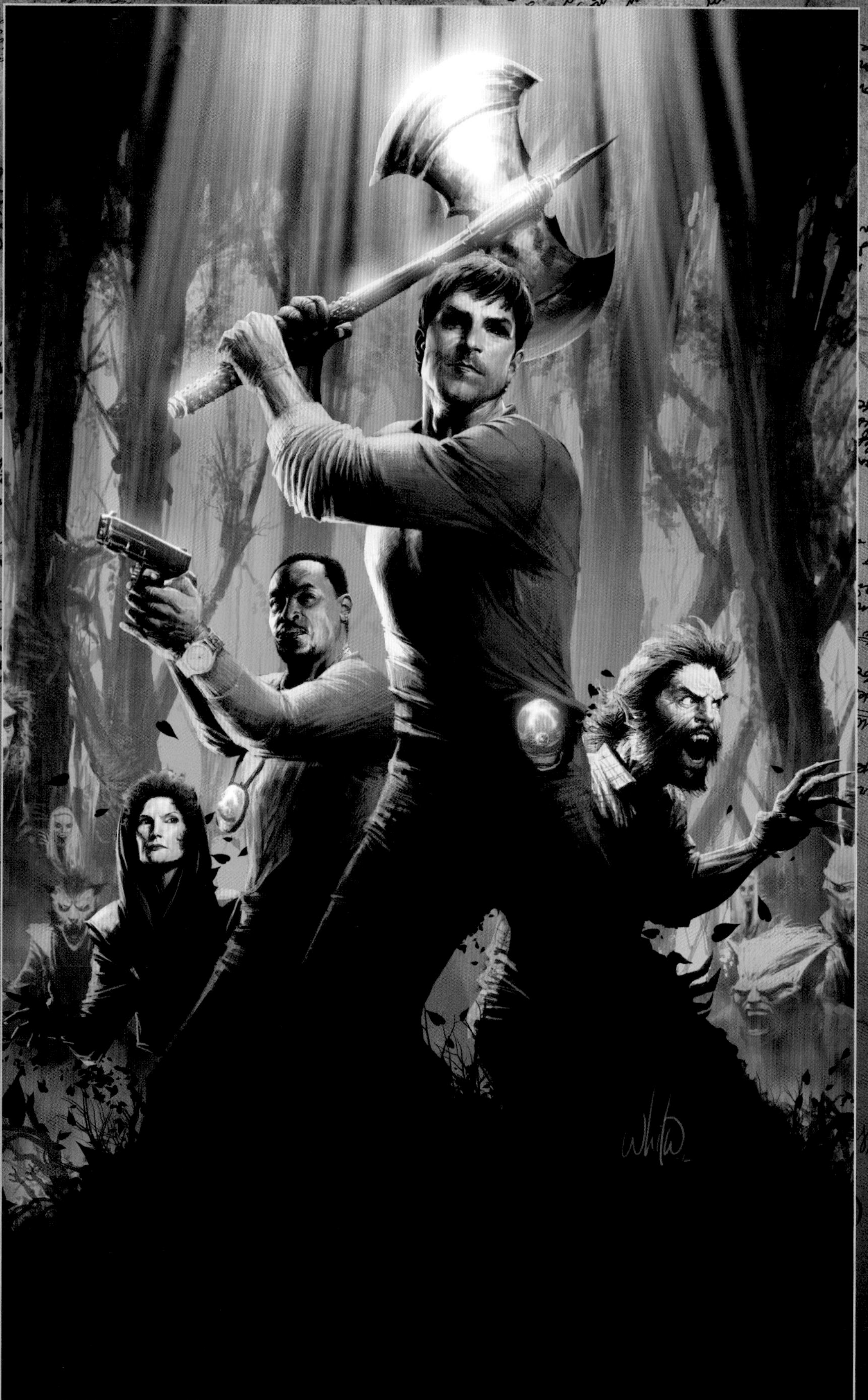

ISSUE #0 COVER

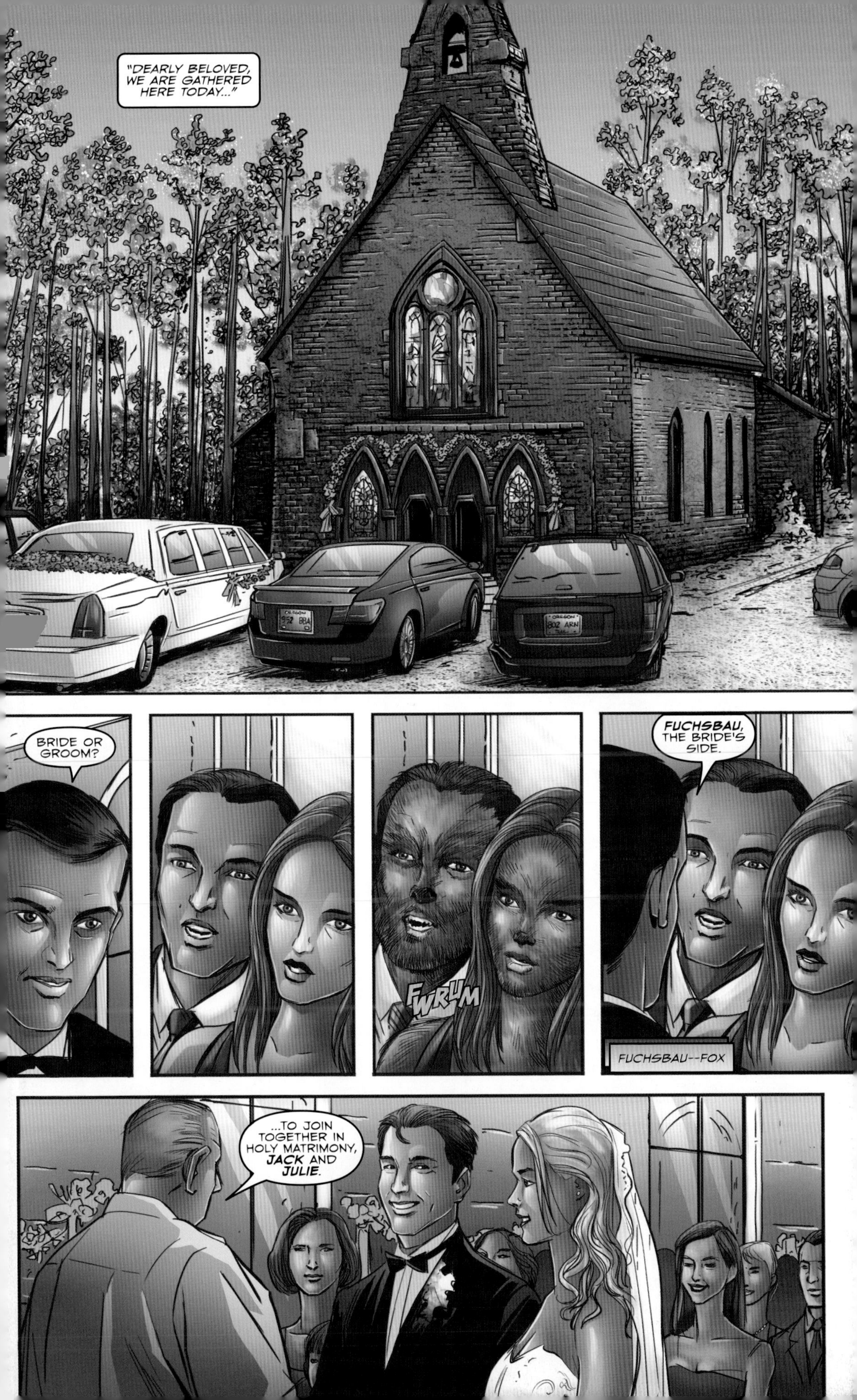
"DEARLY BELOVED, WE ARE GATHERED HERE TODAY..."
OREGON 952 BBA
OREGON 802 ARN
BRIDE OR GROOM?
FWRUM
FUCHSBAU, THE BRIDE'S SIDE.
FUCHSBAU--FOX
...TO JOIN TOGETHER IN HOLY MATRIMONY, JACK AND JULIE.

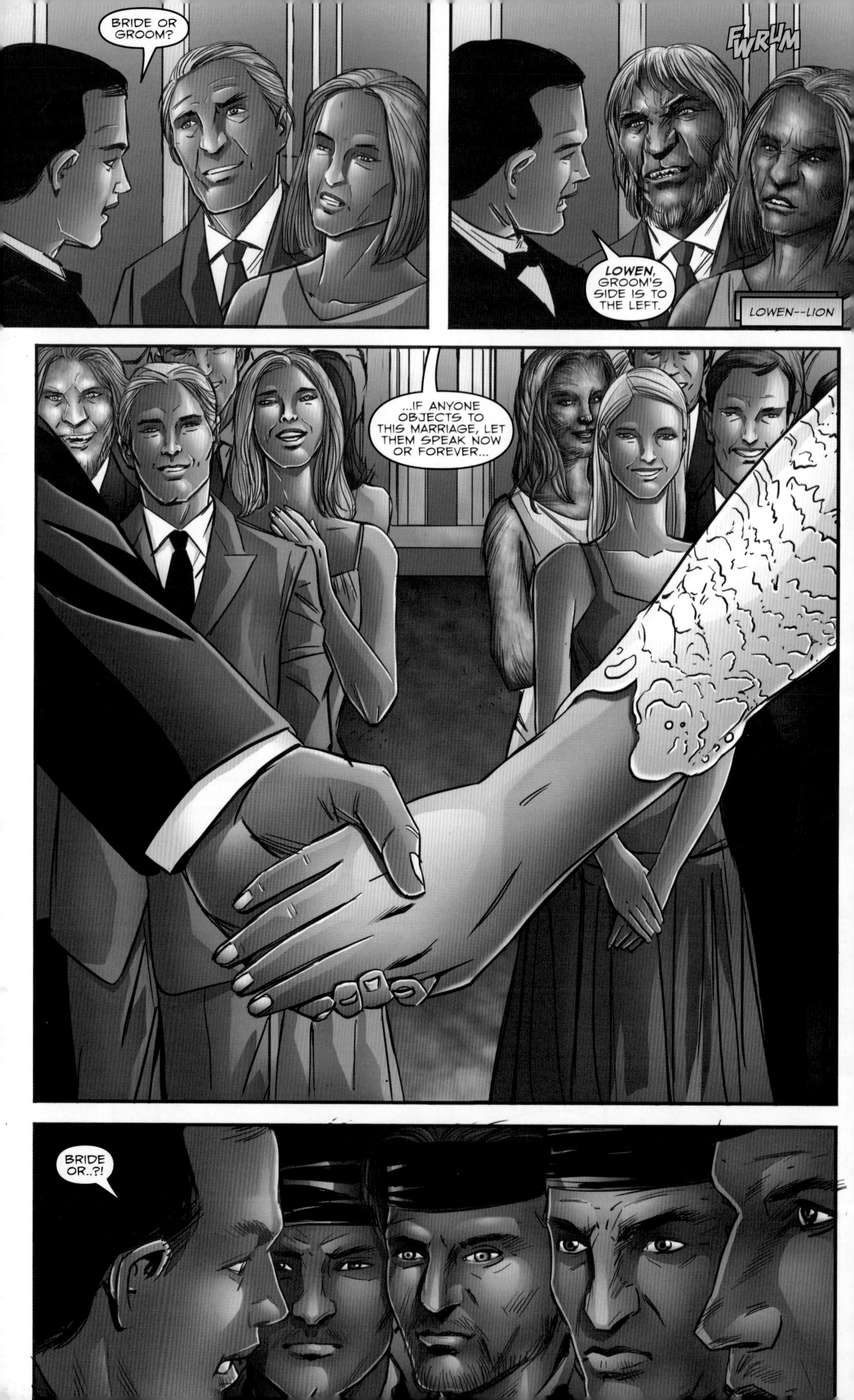

BRIDE OR GROOM?
FWRUM
LOWEN, GROOM'S SIDE IS TO THE LEFT.
LOWEN--LION
...IF ANYONE OBJECTS TO THIS MARRIAGE, LET THEM SPEAK NOW OR FOREVER...
BRIDE OR..?!

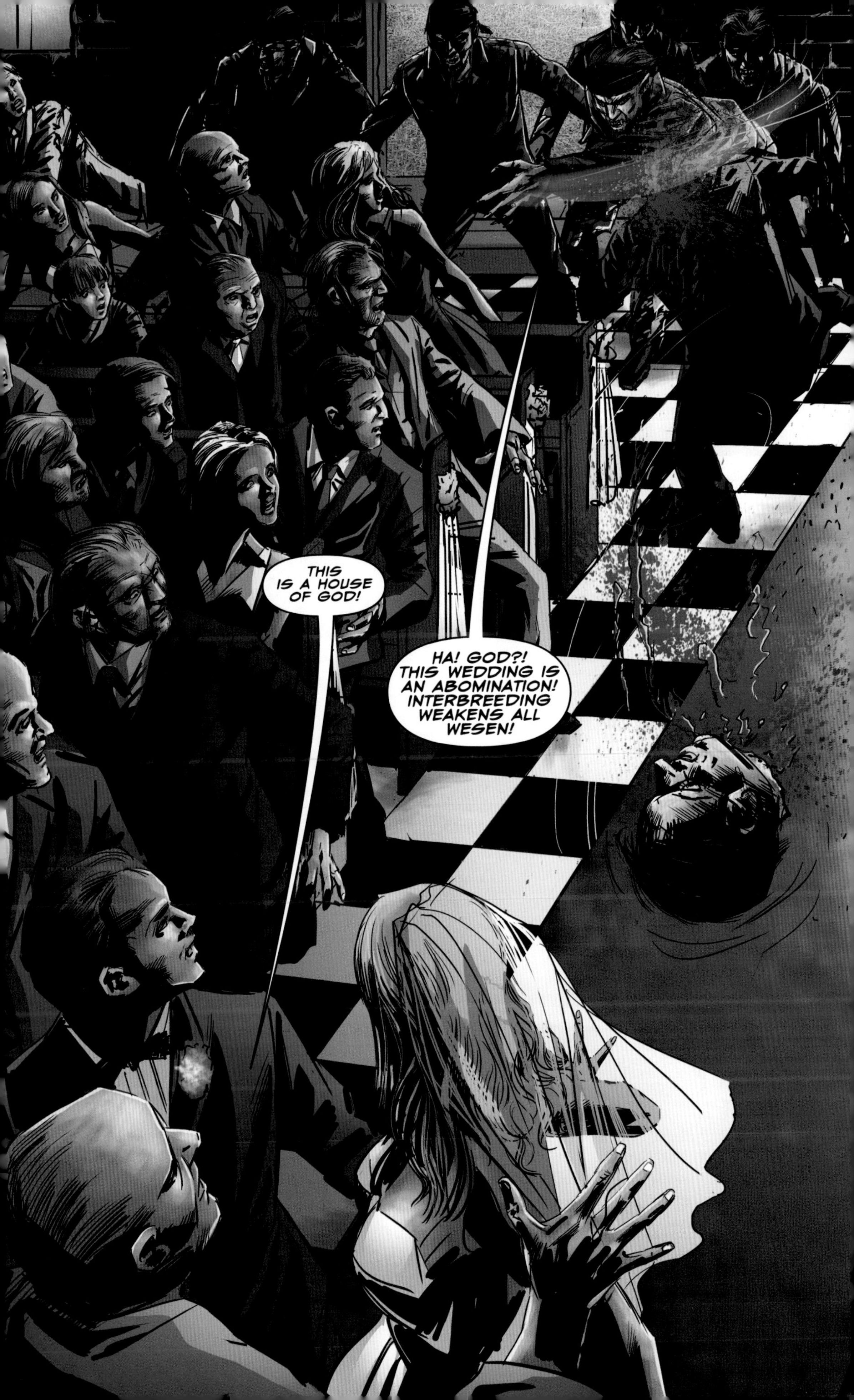
THIS IS A HOUSE OF GOD!
HA! GOD?! THIS WEDDING IS AN ABOMINATION! INTERBREEDING WEAKENS ALL WESEN!

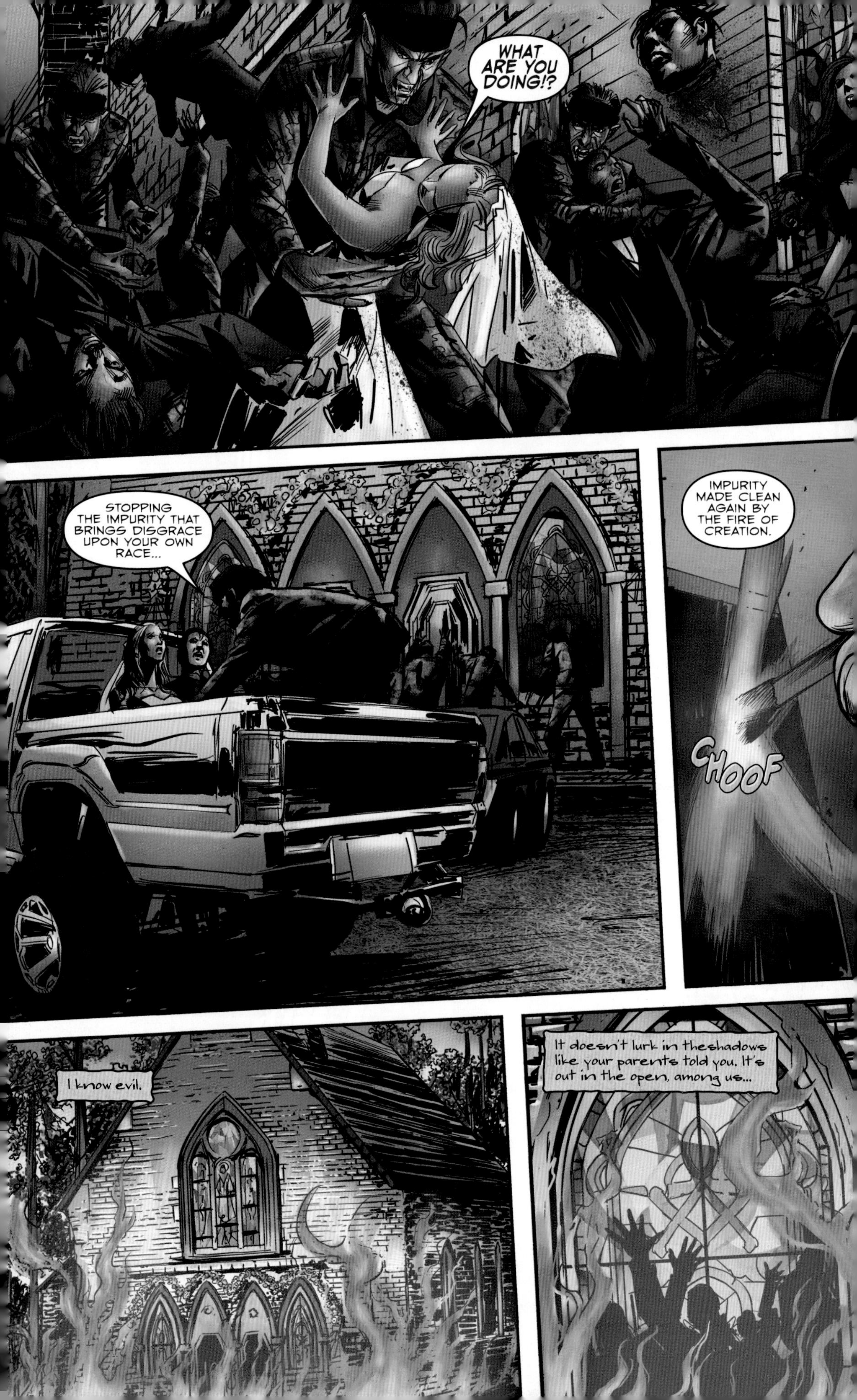
WHAT ARE YOU DOING!?
STOPPING THE IMPURITY THAT BRINGS DISGRACE UPON YOUR OWN RACE...
IMPURITY MADE CLEAN AGAIN BY THE FIRE OF CREATION.
CHOOF
I know evil.
It doesn't lurk in theshadows like your parents told you. It's out in the open, among us...

...You just need to know what you're looking for.

UNBELIEVABLE. THIS IS DISGUSTING.

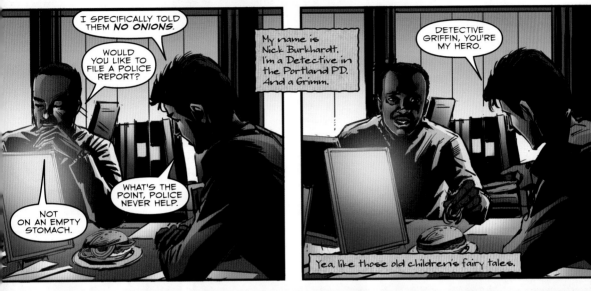

I SPECIFICALLY TOLD THEM *NO ONIONS*.

WOULD YOU LIKE TO FILE A POLICE REPORT?

My name is Nick Burkhardt. I'm a Detective in the Portland PD. And a Grimm.

DETECTIVE GRIFFIN, YOU'RE MY HERO.

NOT ON AN EMPTY STOMACH.

WHAT'S THE POINT, POLICE NEVER HELP.

Yea, like those old children's fairy tales.

Turns out they're true. Monsters are hiding among us. And I can see them when they don't want to be seen.

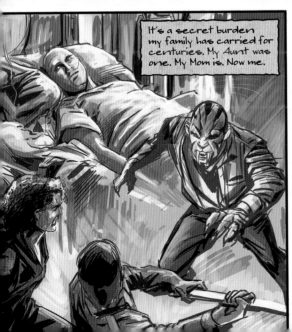

It's a secret burden my family has carried for centuries. My Aunt was one. My Mom is. Now me.

Few people know my secret. My partner Hank Griffin and my Captain among them.

MURDER AND MAYHEM AT PINE HILL CHURCH. AND NICK... IT WAS A MIXED MARRIAGE.

I know it sounds glamorous. Secret life. Creatures of the night trying to kill you. But I'm no super hero. Hell, I can't even get a sandwich without onions on it.

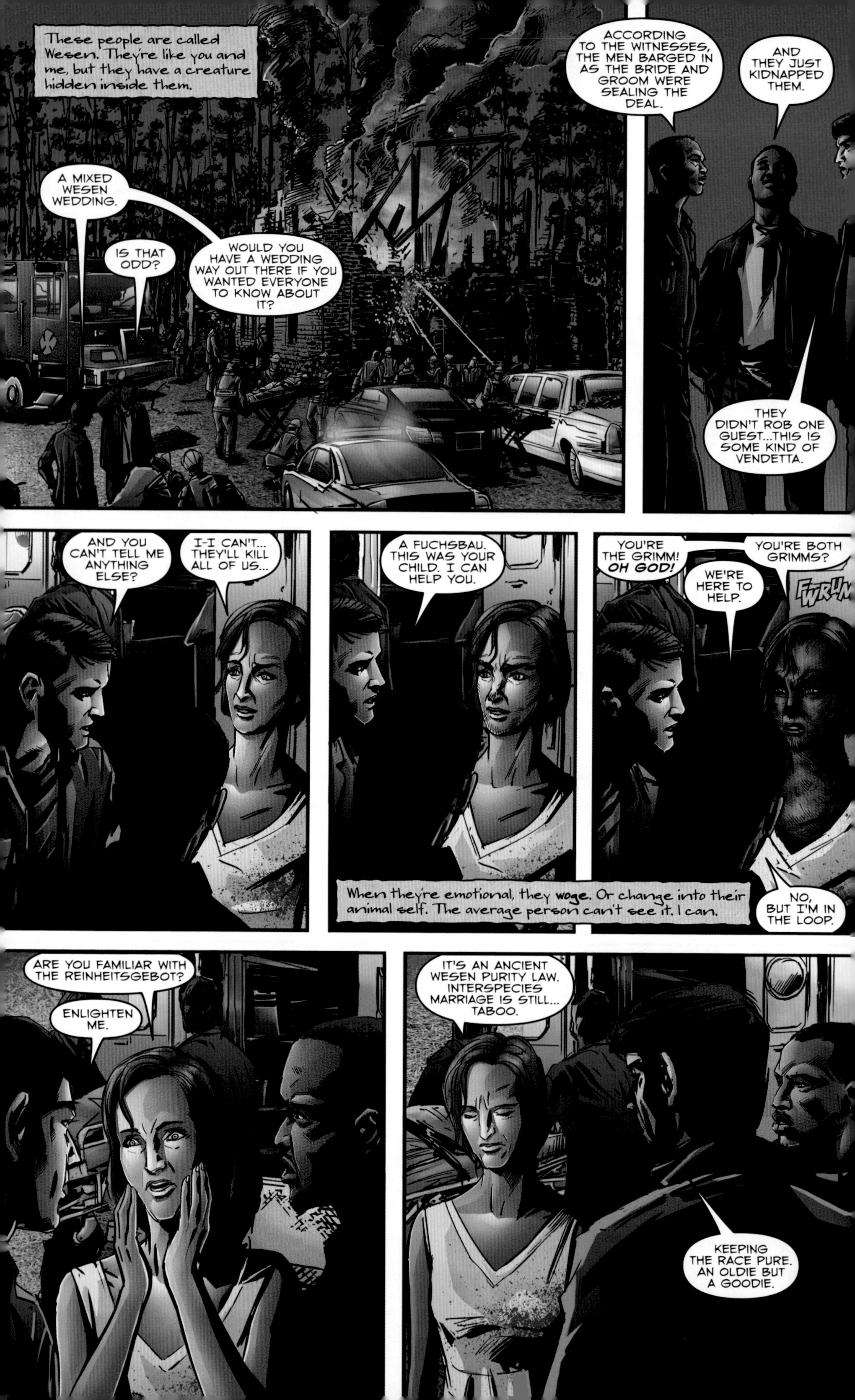
These people are called Wesen. They're like you and me, but they have a creature hidden inside them.
A MIXED WESEN WEDDING.
IS THAT ODD?
WOULD YOU HAVE A WEDDING WAY OUT THERE IF YOU WANTED EVERYONE TO KNOW ABOUT IT?
ACCORDING TO THE WITNESSES, THE MEN BARGED IN AS THE BRIDE AND GROOM WERE SEALING THE DEAL.
AND THEY JUST KIDNAPPED THEM.
THEY DIDN'T ROB ONE GUEST...THIS IS SOME KIND OF VENDETTA.
AND YOU CAN'T TELL ME ANYTHING ELSE?
I-I CAN'T... THEY'LL KILL ALL OF US...
A FUCHSBAU. THIS WAS YOUR CHILD. I CAN HELP YOU.
When they're emotional, they woge. Or change into their animal self. The average person can't see it. I can.
YOU'RE THE GRIMM! OH GOD!
WE'RE HERE TO HELP.
YOU'RE BOTH GRIMMS?
FWRUM
NO, BUT I'M IN THE LOOP.
ARE YOU FAMILIAR WITH THE REINHEITSGEBOT?
ENLIGHTEN ME.
IT'S AN ANCIENT WESEN PURITY LAW. INTERSPECIES MARRIAGE IS STILL... TABOO.
KEEPING THE RACE PURE. AN OLDIE BUT A GOODIE.

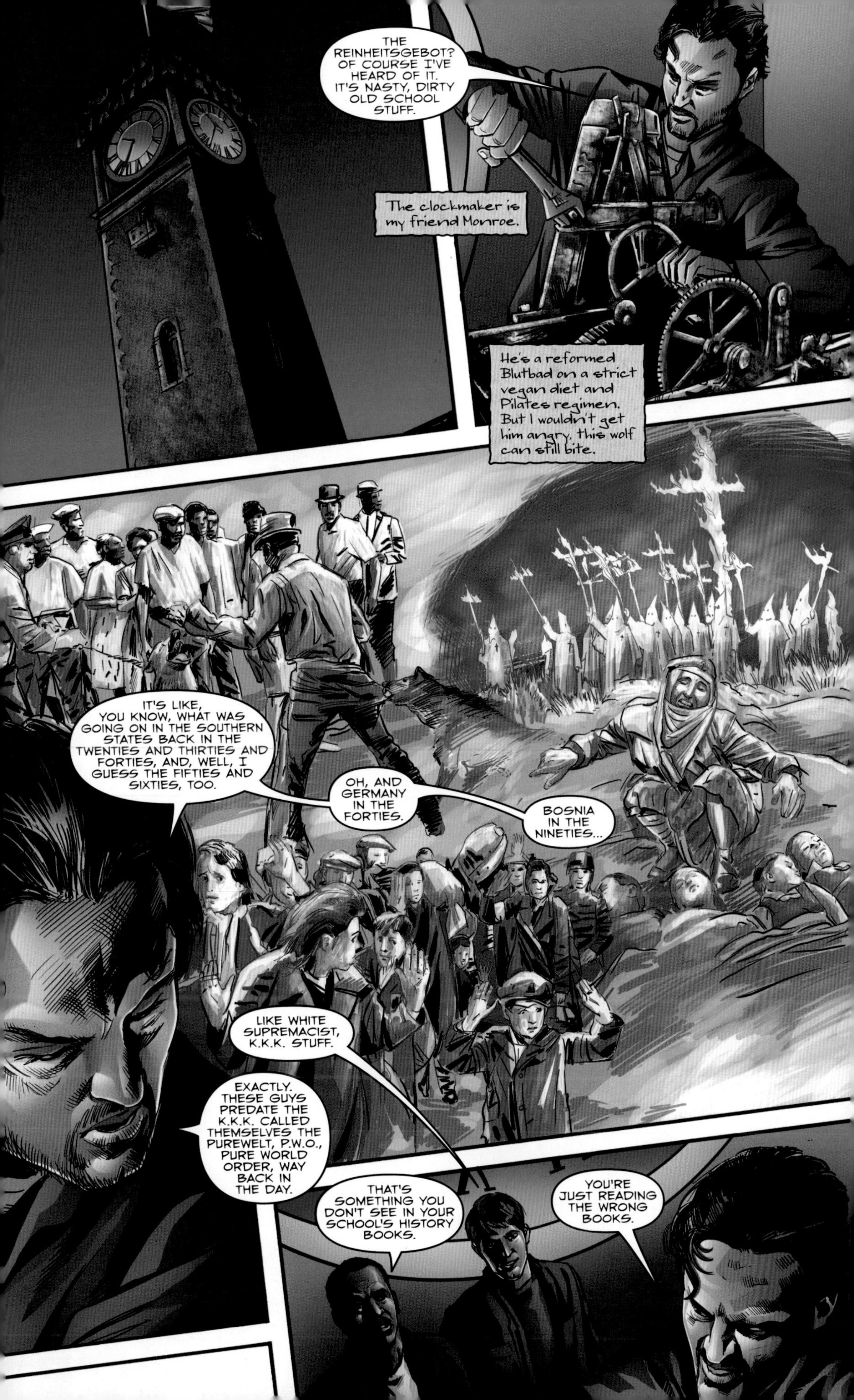
THE REINHEITSGEBOT? OF COURSE I'VE HEARD OF IT. IT'S NASTY, DIRTY OLD SCHOOL STUFF.
The clockmaker is my friend Monroe.
He's a reformed Blutbad on a strict vegan diet and Pilates regimen. But I wouldn't get him angry, this wolf can still bite.
IT'S LIKE, YOU KNOW, WHAT WAS GOING ON IN THE SOUTHERN STATES BACK IN THE TWENTIES AND THIRTIES AND FORTIES, AND, WELL, I GUESS THE FIFTIES AND SIXTIES, TOO.
OH, AND GERMANY IN THE FORTIES.
BOSNIA IN THE NINETIES...
LIKE WHITE SUPREMACIST, K.K.K. STUFF.
EXACTLY. THESE GUYS PREDATE THE K.K.K. CALLED THEMSELVES THE PUREWELT, P.W.O., PURE WORLD ORDER, WAY BACK IN THE DAY.
THAT'S SOMETHING YOU DON'T SEE IN YOUR SCHOOL'S HISTORY BOOKS.
YOU'RE JUST READING THE WRONG BOOKS.

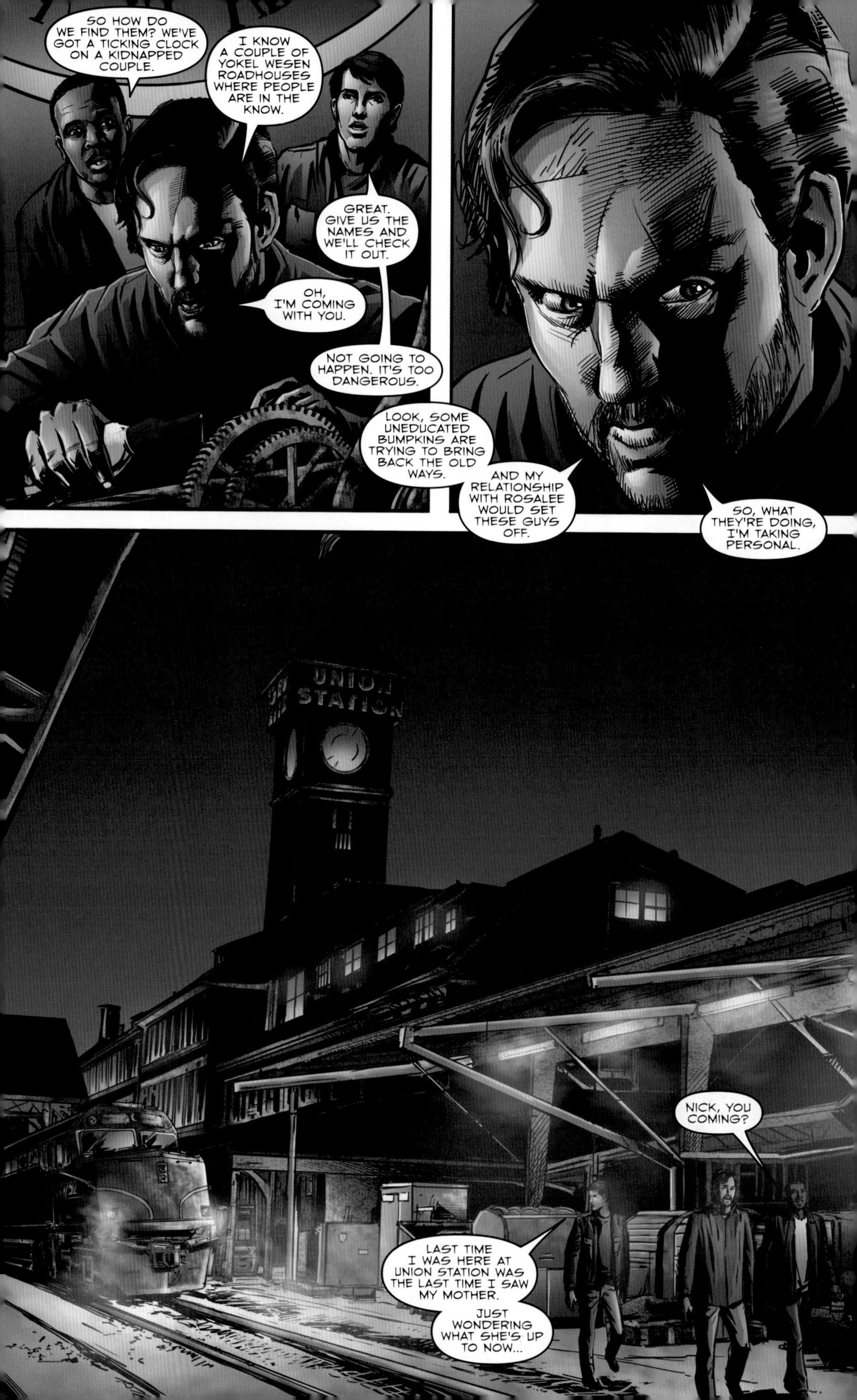
SO HOW DO WE FIND THEM? WE'VE GOT A TICKING CLOCK ON A KIDNAPPED COUPLE.
I KNOW A COUPLE OF YOKEL WESEN ROADHOUSES WHERE PEOPLE ARE IN THE KNOW.
GREAT. GIVE US THE NAMES AND WE'LL CHECK IT OUT.
OH, I'M COMING WITH YOU.
NOT GOING TO HAPPEN. IT'S TOO DANGEROUS.
LOOK, SOME UNEDUCATED BUMPKINS ARE TRYING TO BRING BACK THE OLD WAYS.
AND MY RELATIONSHIP WITH ROSALEE WOULD SET THESE GUYS OFF.
SO, WHAT THEY'RE DOING, I'M TAKING PERSONAL.
UNION STATION
NICK, YOU COMING?
LAST TIME I WAS HERE AT UNION STATION WAS THE LAST TIME I SAW MY MOTHER.
JUST WONDERING WHAT SHE'S UP TO NOW...

SOMEWHERE IN THE SWISS ALPS

The worst thing about being a Grimm...

...is you never get a moment to yourself.

Sure. The travel is a perk. But it's the simple things, like taking a nap for instance, that I miss most.

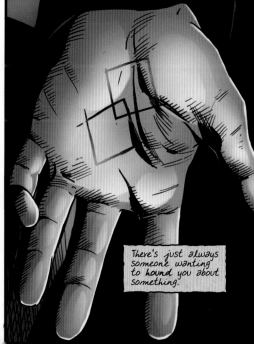

There's just always someone wanting to hound you about something.

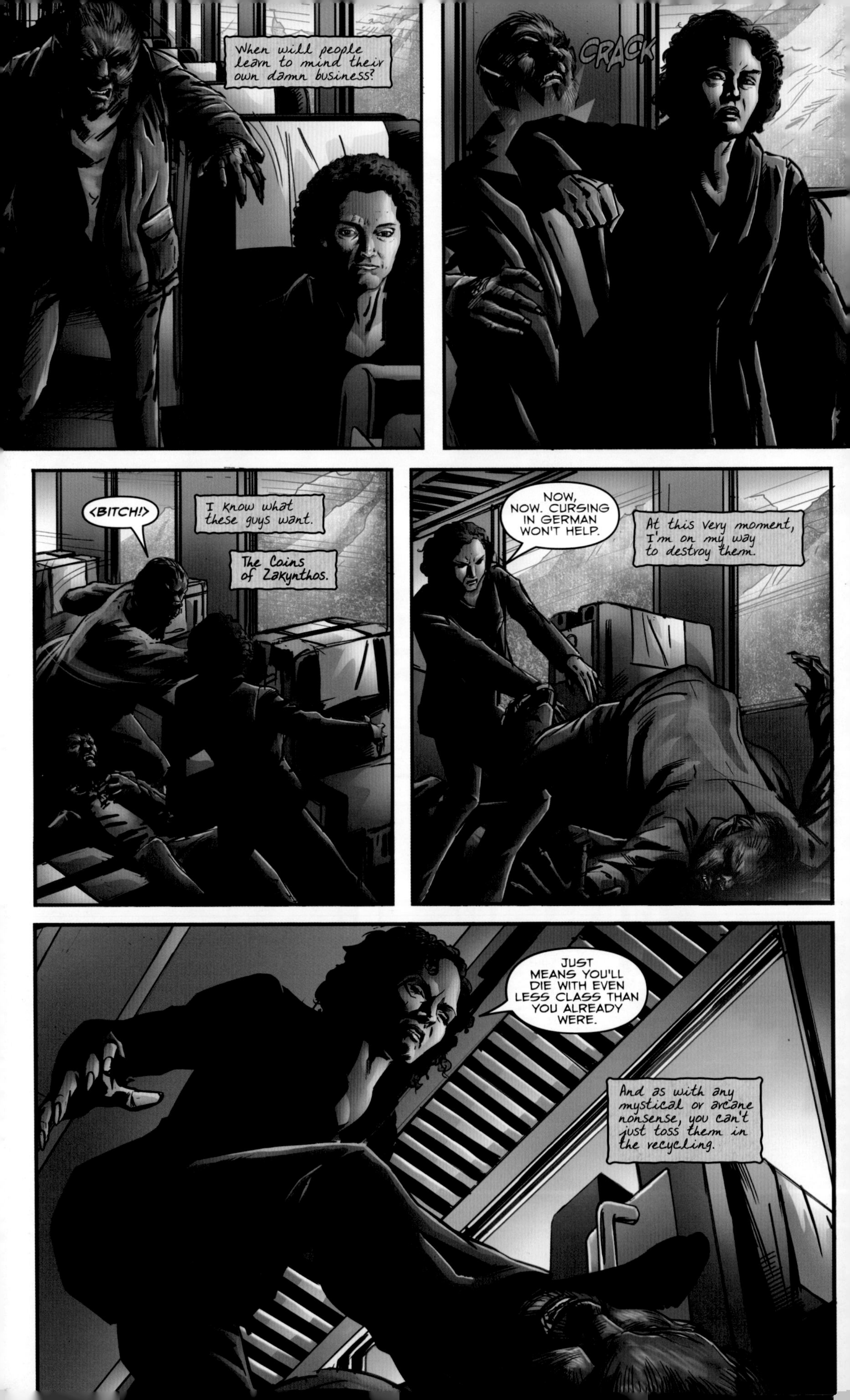
When will people learn to mind their own damn business?
CRACK
<BITCH!>
I know what these guys want.
The Coins of Zakynthos.
NOW, NOW. CURSING IN GERMAN WON'T HELP.
At this very moment, I'm on my way to destroy them.
JUST MEANS YOU'LL DIE WITH EVEN LESS CLASS THAN YOU ALREADY WERE.
And as with any mystical or arcane nonsense, you can't just toss them in the recycling.

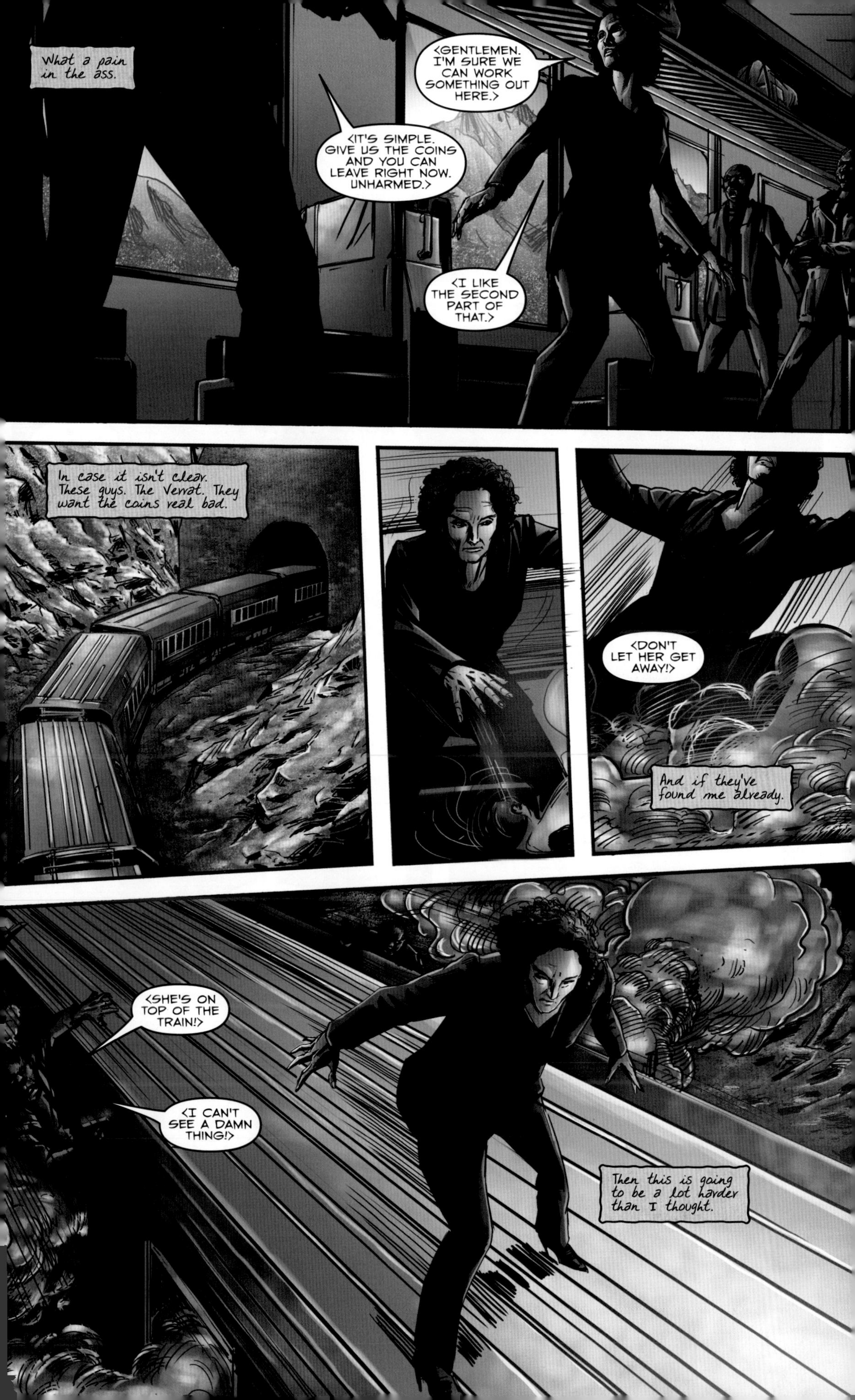
What a pain in the ass.
<GENTLEMEN. I'M SURE WE CAN WORK SOMETHING OUT HERE.>
<IT'S SIMPLE. GIVE US THE COINS AND YOU CAN LEAVE RIGHT NOW. UNHARMED.>
<I LIKE THE SECOND PART OF THAT.>
In case it isn't clear. These guys. The Verrat. They want the coins real bad.
<DON'T LET HER GET AWAY!>
And if they've found me already.
<SHE'S ON TOP OF THE TRAIN!>
<I CAN'T SEE A DAMN THING!>
Then this is going to be a lot harder than I thought.

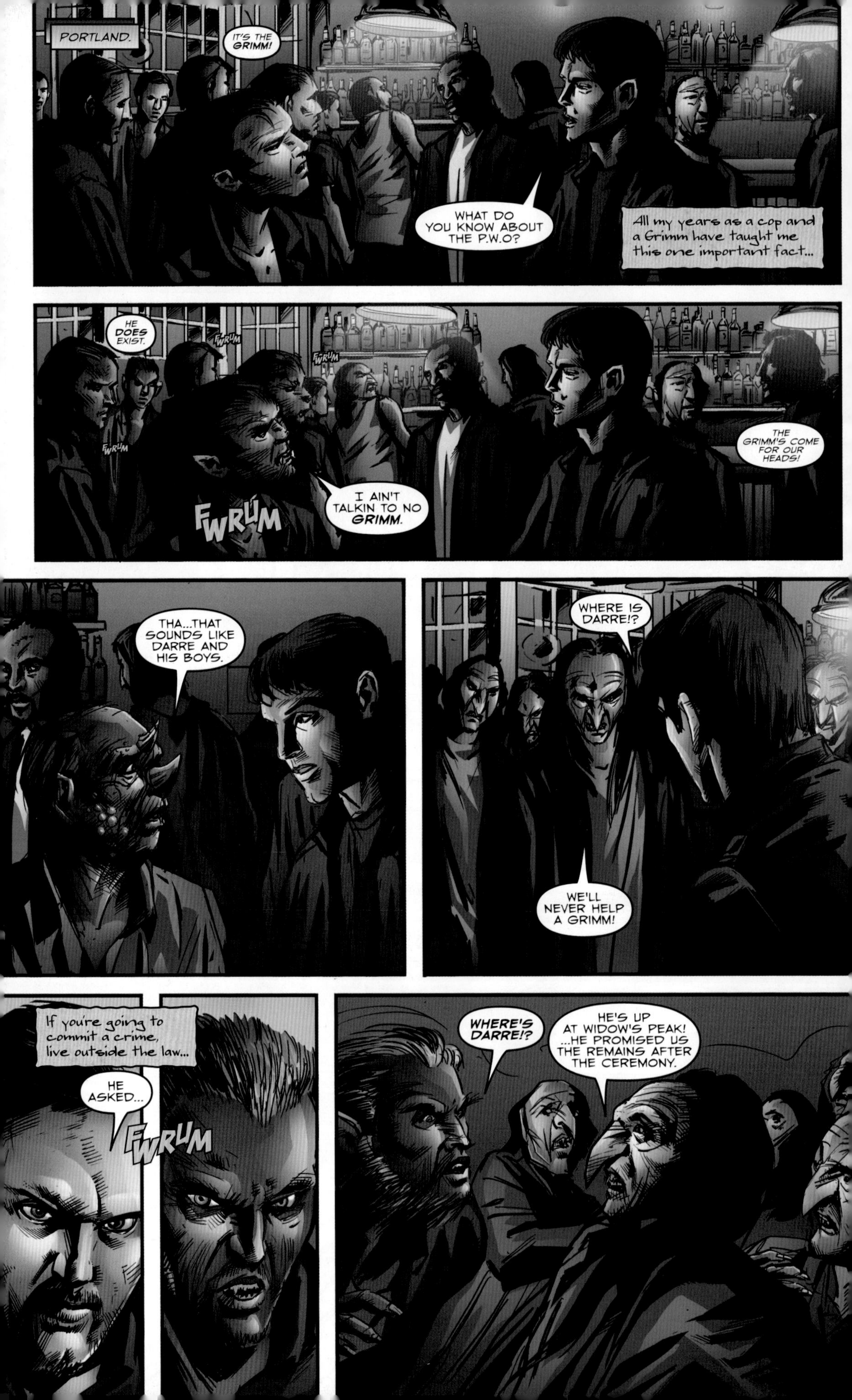
PORTLAND.
IT'S THE GRIMM!
WHAT DO YOU KNOW ABOUT THE P.W.O?
All my years as a cop and a Grimm have taught me this one important fact...
HE DOES EXIST.
FWRUM
FWRUM
FWRUM
FWRUM
I AIN'T TALKIN TO NO GRIMM.
THE GRIMM'S COME FOR OUR HEADS!
THA...THAT SOUNDS LIKE DARRE AND HIS BOYS.
WHERE IS DARRE!?
WE'LL NEVER HELP A GRIMM!
If you're going to commit a crime, live outside the law...
HE ASKED...
FWRUM
WHERE'S DARRE!?
HE'S UP AT WIDOW'S PEAK! ...HE PROMISED US THE REMAINS AFTER THE CEREMONY.

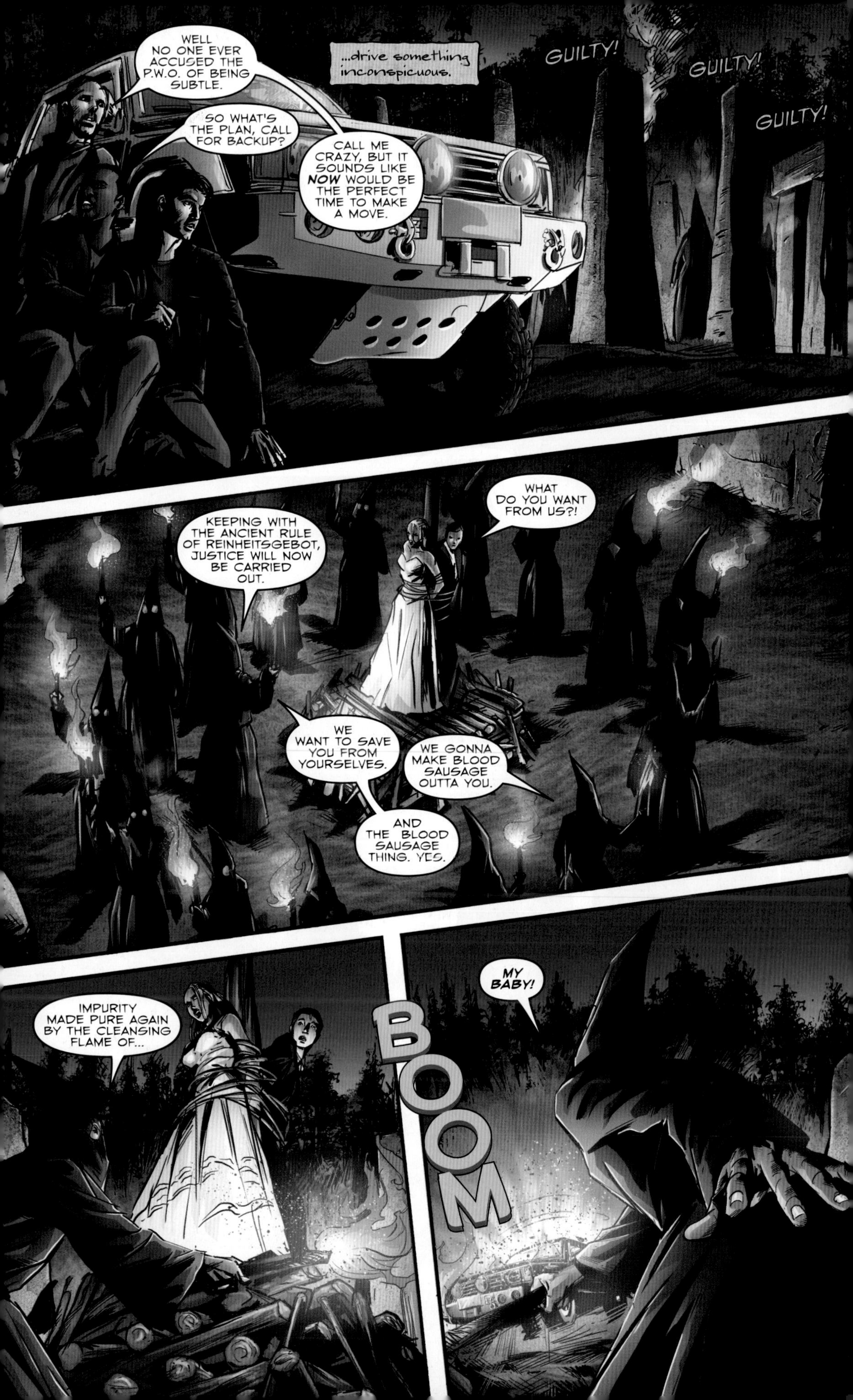
WELL NO ONE EVER ACCUSED THE P.W.O. OF BEING SUBTLE.
...drive something inconspicuous.
GUILTY!
GUILTY!
GUILTY!
SO WHAT'S THE PLAN, CALL FOR BACKUP?
CALL ME CRAZY, BUT IT SOUNDS LIKE NOW WOULD BE THE PERFECT TIME TO MAKE A MOVE.
KEEPING WITH THE ANCIENT RULE OF REINHEITSGEBOT, JUSTICE WILL NOW BE CARRIED OUT.
WHAT DO YOU WANT FROM US?!
WE WANT TO SAVE YOU FROM YOURSELVES.
WE GONNA MAKE BLOOD SAUSAGE OUTTA YOU.
AND THE BLOOD SAUSAGE THING. YES.
IMPURITY MADE PURE AGAIN BY THE CLEANSING FLAME OF...
BOOM
MY BABY!

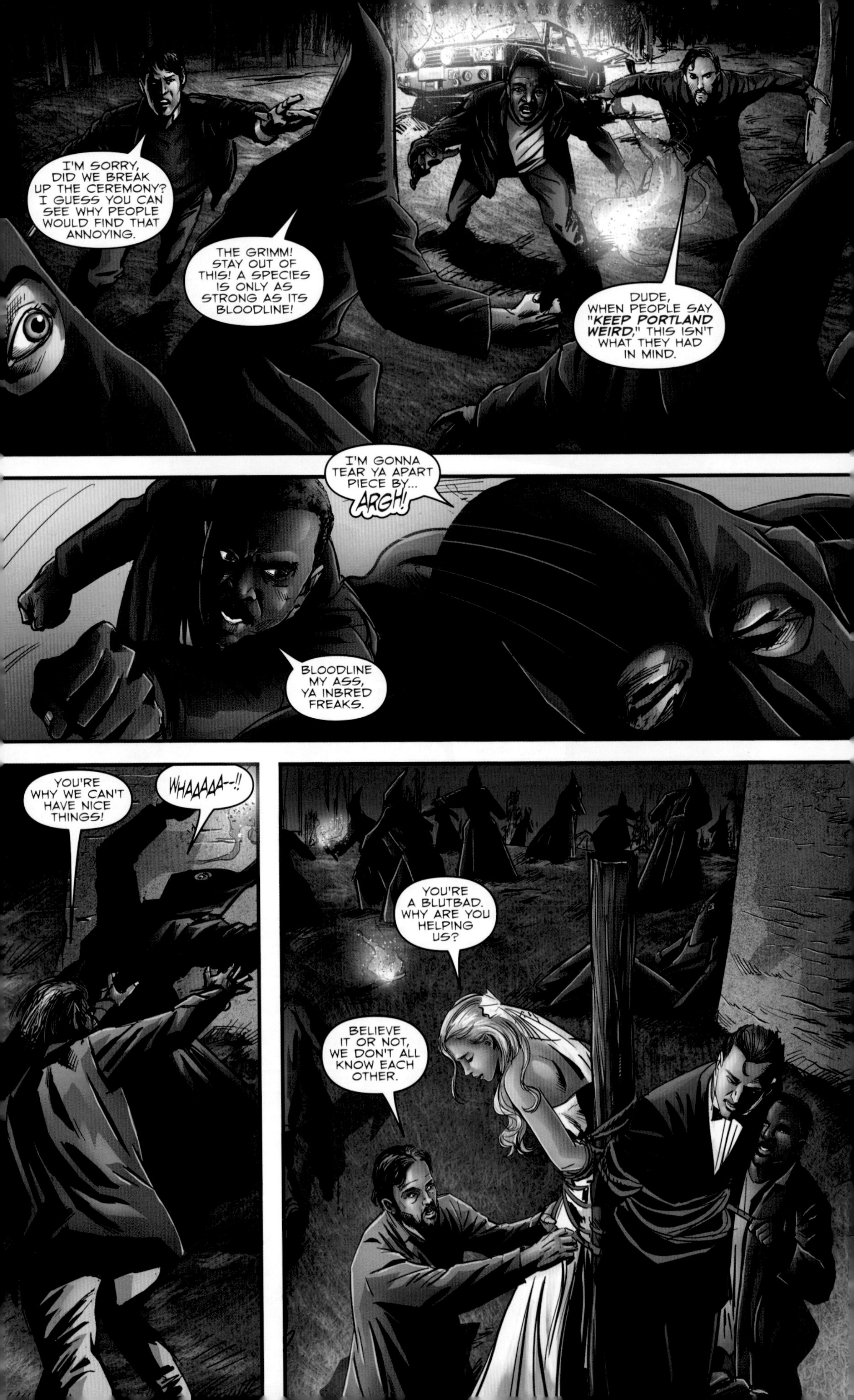
I'M SORRY, DID WE BREAK UP THE CEREMONY? I GUESS YOU CAN SEE WHY PEOPLE WOULD FIND THAT ANNOYING.
THE GRIMM! STAY OUT OF THIS! A SPECIES IS ONLY AS STRONG AS ITS BLOODLINE!
DUDE, WHEN PEOPLE SAY "*KEEP PORTLAND WEIRD*," THIS ISN'T WHAT THEY HAD IN MIND.
I'M GONNA TEAR YA APART PIECE BY... *ARGH!*
BLOODLINE MY ASS, YA INBRED FREAKS.
YOU'RE WHY WE CAN'T HAVE NICE THINGS!
WHAAAAA--!!
YOU'RE A BLUTBAD. WHY ARE YOU HELPING US?
BELIEVE IT OR NOT, WE DON'T ALL KNOW EACH OTHER.

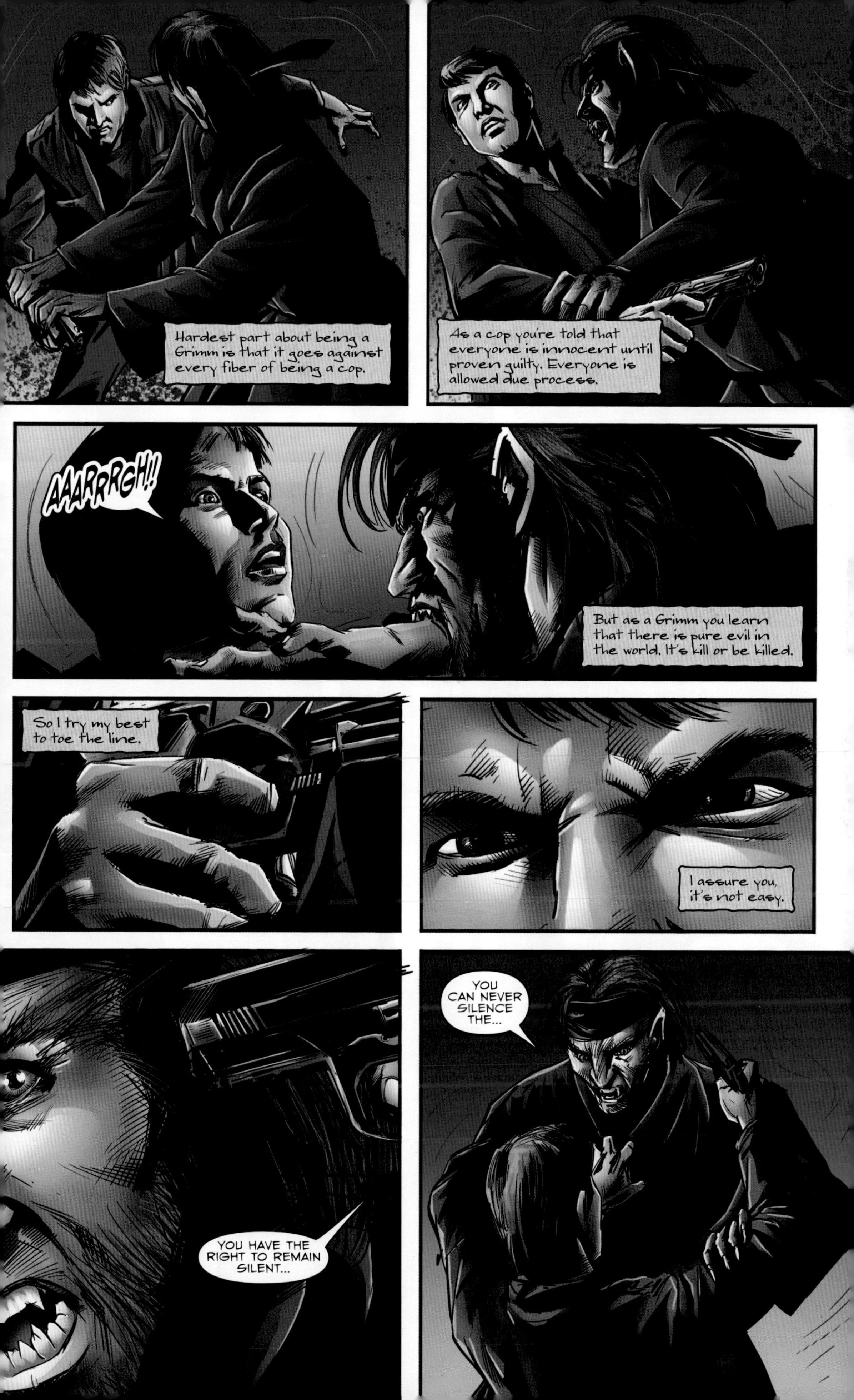
Hardest part about being a Grimm is that it goes against every fiber of being a cop.
As a cop you're told that everyone is innocent until proven guilty. Everyone is allowed due process.
AAARRRGH!!
But as a Grimm you learn that there is pure evil in the world. It's kill or be killed.
So I try my best to toe the line.
I assure you, it's not easy.
YOU HAVE THE RIGHT TO REMAIN SILENT...
YOU CAN NEVER SILENCE THE...

OOPS, GUESS YOU'RE WRONG ABOUT THAT TOO.

WAP

It can be rough. But sometimes all you need is something as simple as a proper nap to set you straight.

Which seems to rarely happen nowadays.

BZZT BZZT

BURKHARDT.

NICKY?

MOM?! WHERE ARE YOU?

VIENNA. THE VERRAT KNOW I'M IN EUROPE WITH THE COINS. I'VE HIDDEN THEM. I COULDN'T CHANCE THEM FALLING INTO THEIR HANDS AGAIN.

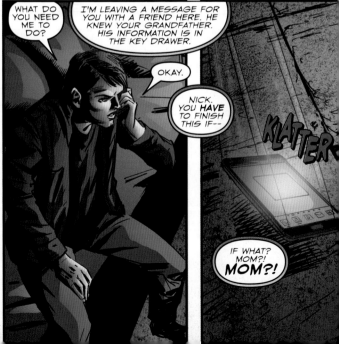

WHAT DO YOU NEED ME TO DO?

I'M LEAVING A MESSAGE FOR YOU WITH A FRIEND HERE. HE KNEW YOUR GRANDFATHER. HIS INFORMATION IS IN THE KEY DRAWER.

OKAY.

NICK. YOU HAVE TO FINISH THIS IF--

KLATTER

IF WHAT? MOM?! MOM?!

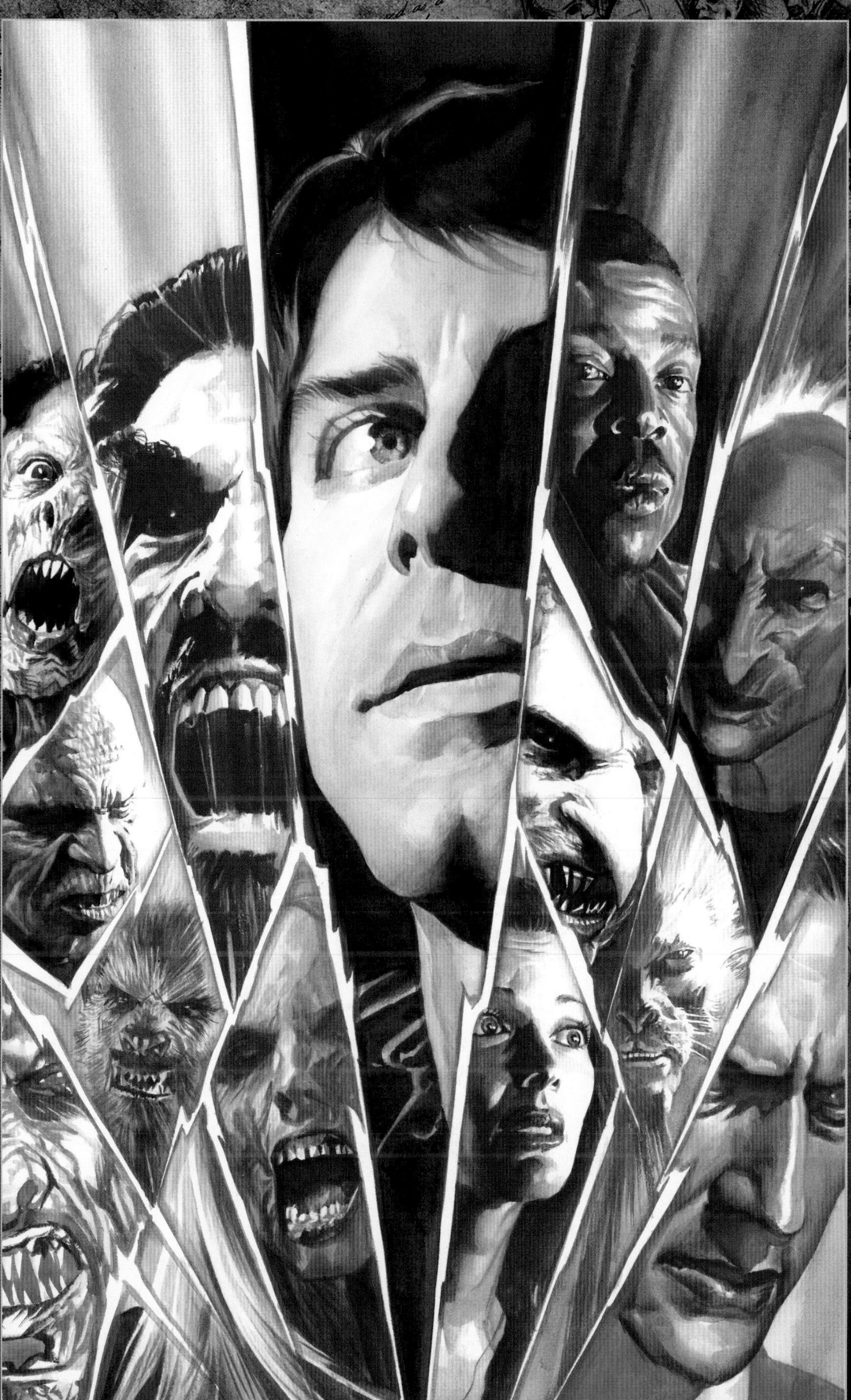

ISSUE #1 COVER

It was discovered that the Battalia lower back contains a cluster of nerve endings when struck the pain felt by the Battled seems debilitating. Using this method it could has saved many lives, after studying a deceased Battled after a battle, the relaxing and nervous system I have been are enlarged compared to that of a human, Further study into sing that seems should be done. No pain means the Battled sufficiently disabled to escape or kill it, however, it will not last more than a few minutes before the creature will be able to move again

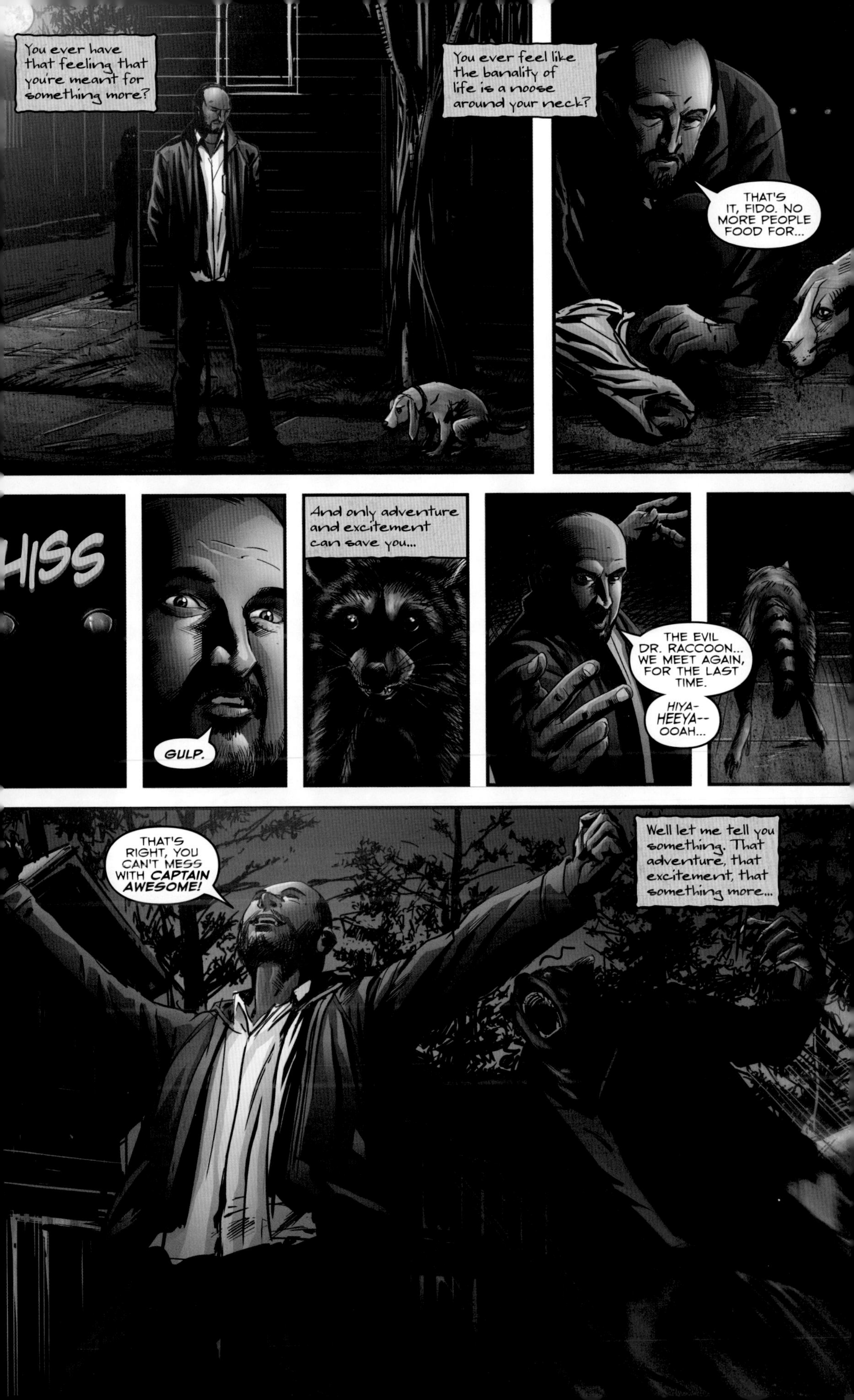
You ever have that feeling that you're meant for something more?
You ever feel like the banality of life is a noose around your neck?
THAT'S IT, FIDO. NO MORE PEOPLE FOOD FOR...
HISS
GULP.
And only adventure and excitement can save you...
THE EVIL DR. RACCOON... WE MEET AGAIN, FOR THE LAST TIME.
HIYA-HEEYA--OOAH...
THAT'S RIGHT, YOU CAN'T MESS WITH CAPTAIN AWESOME!
Well let me tell you something. That adventure, that excitement, that something more...

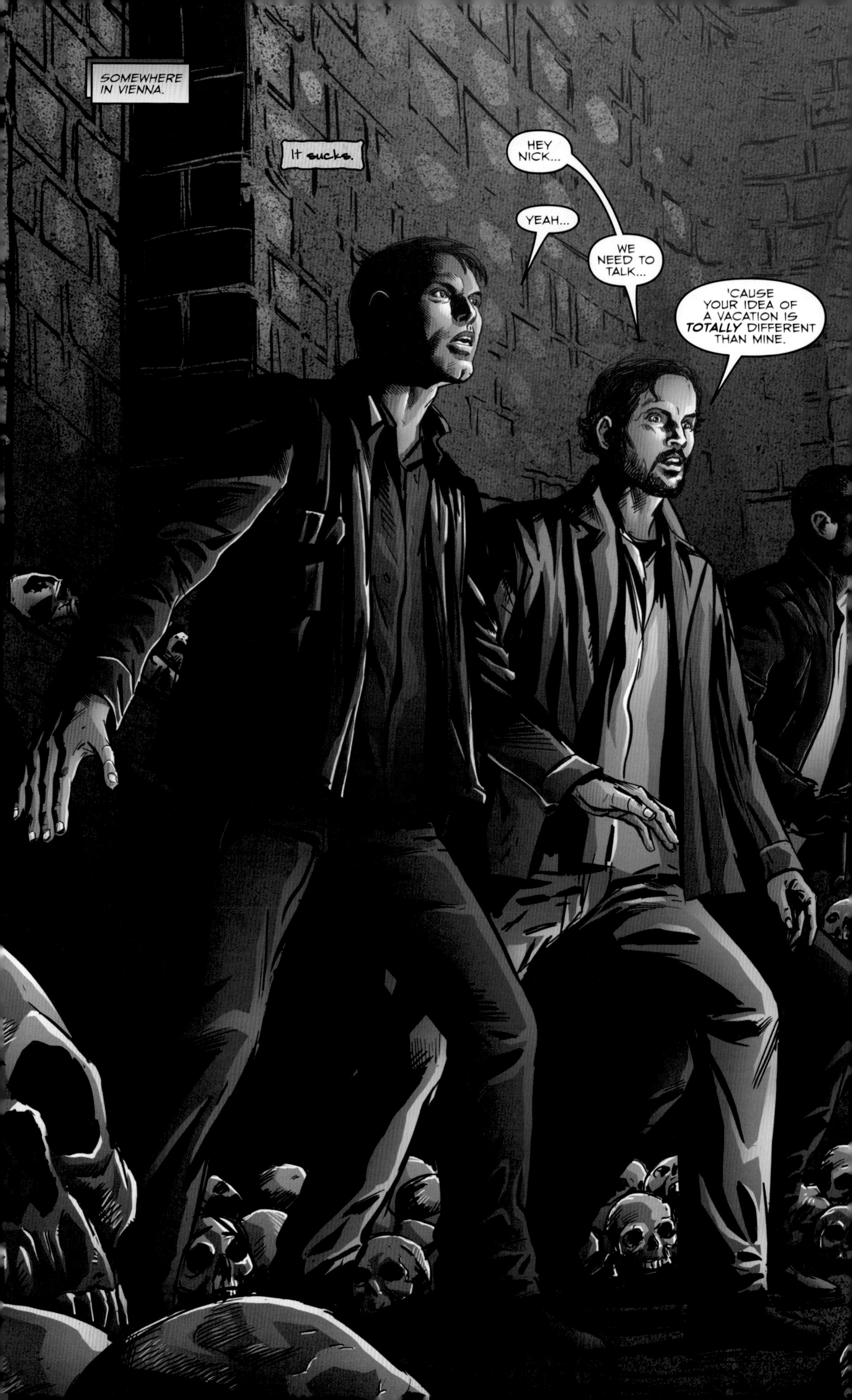
SOMEWHERE IN VIENNA.
It sucks.
HEY NICK...
YEAH...
WE NEED TO TALK...
'CAUSE YOUR IDEA OF A VACATION IS TOTALLY DIFFERENT THAN MINE.

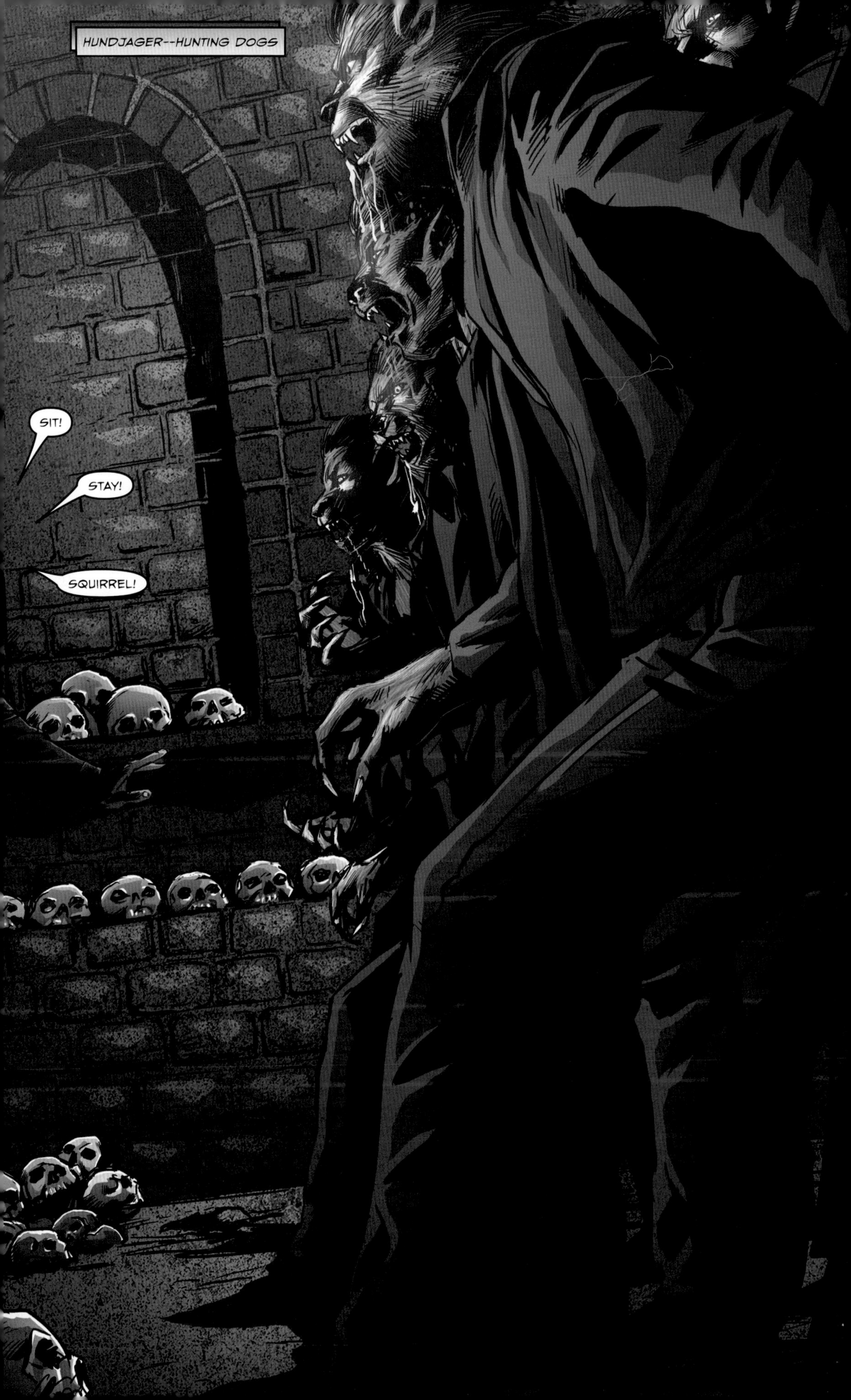
HUNDJAGER--HUNTING DOGS
SIT!
STAY!
SQUIRREL!

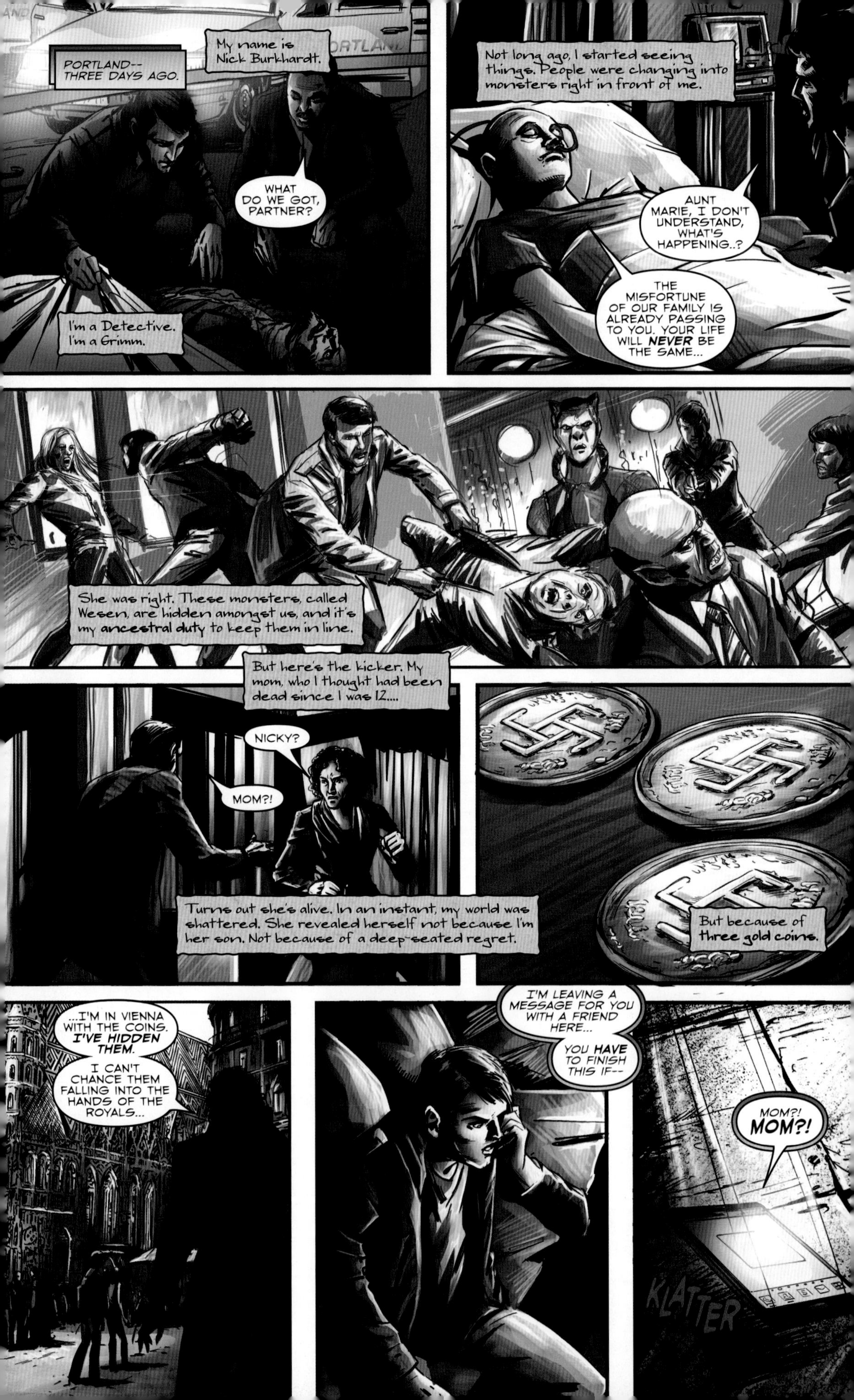

PORTLAND-- THREE DAYS AGO.
My name is Nick Burkhardt.
WHAT DO WE GOT, PARTNER?
I'm a Detective. I'm a Grimm.
Not long ago, I started seeing things. People were changing into monsters right in front of me.
AUNT MARIE, I DON'T UNDERSTAND, WHAT'S HAPPENING..?
THE MISFORTUNE OF OUR FAMILY IS ALREADY PASSING TO YOU. YOUR LIFE WILL NEVER BE THE SAME...
She was right. These monsters, called Wesen, are hidden amongst us, and it's my ancestral duty to keep them in line.
But here's the kicker. My mom, who I thought had been dead since I was 12....
NICKY?
MOM?!
Turns out she's alive. In an instant, my world was shattered. She revealed herself not because I'm her son. Not because of a deep-seated regret.
But because of three gold coins.
...I'M IN VIENNA WITH THE COINS. I'VE HIDDEN THEM.
I CAN'T CHANCE THEM FALLING INTO THE HANDS OF THE ROYALS...
I'M LEAVING A MESSAGE FOR YOU WITH A FRIEND HERE...
YOU HAVE TO FINISH THIS IF--
MOM?! MOM?!
KLATTER

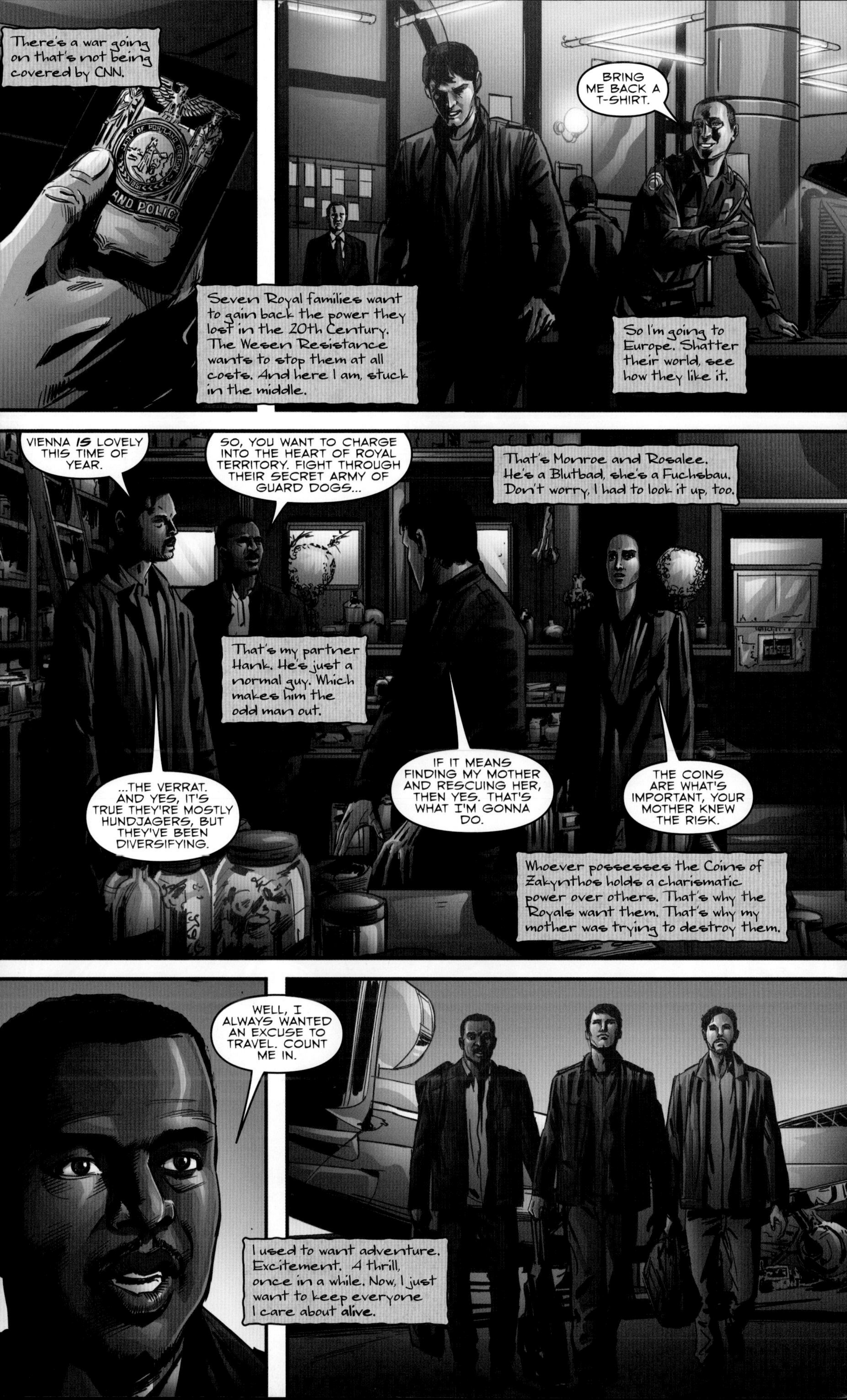
There's a war going on that's not being covered by CNN.
AND POLICE
BRING ME BACK A T-SHIRT.
Seven Royal families want to gain back the power they lost in the 20th Century. The Wesen Resistance wants to stop them at all costs. And here I am, stuck in the middle.
So I'm going to Europe. Shatter their world, see how they like it.
VIENNA IS LOVELY THIS TIME OF YEAR.
SO, YOU WANT TO CHARGE INTO THE HEART OF ROYAL TERRITORY. FIGHT THROUGH THEIR SECRET ARMY OF GUARD DOGS...
That's Monroe and Rosalee. He's a Blutbad, she's a Fuchsbau. Don't worry, I had to look it up, too.
That's my partner Hank. He's just a normal guy. Which makes him the odd man out.
...THE VERRAT. AND YES, IT'S TRUE THEY'RE MOSTLY HUNDJAGERS, BUT THEY'VE BEEN DIVERSIFYING.
IF IT MEANS FINDING MY MOTHER AND RESCUING HER, THEN YES. THAT'S WHAT I'M GONNA DO.
THE COINS ARE WHAT'S IMPORTANT, YOUR MOTHER KNEW THE RISK.
Whoever possesses the Coins of Zakynthos holds a charismatic power over others. That's why the Royals want them. That's why my mother was trying to destroy them.
WELL, I ALWAYS WANTED AN EXCUSE TO TRAVEL. COUNT ME IN.
I used to want adventure. Excitement. A thrill, once in a while. Now, I just want to keep everyone I care about alive.

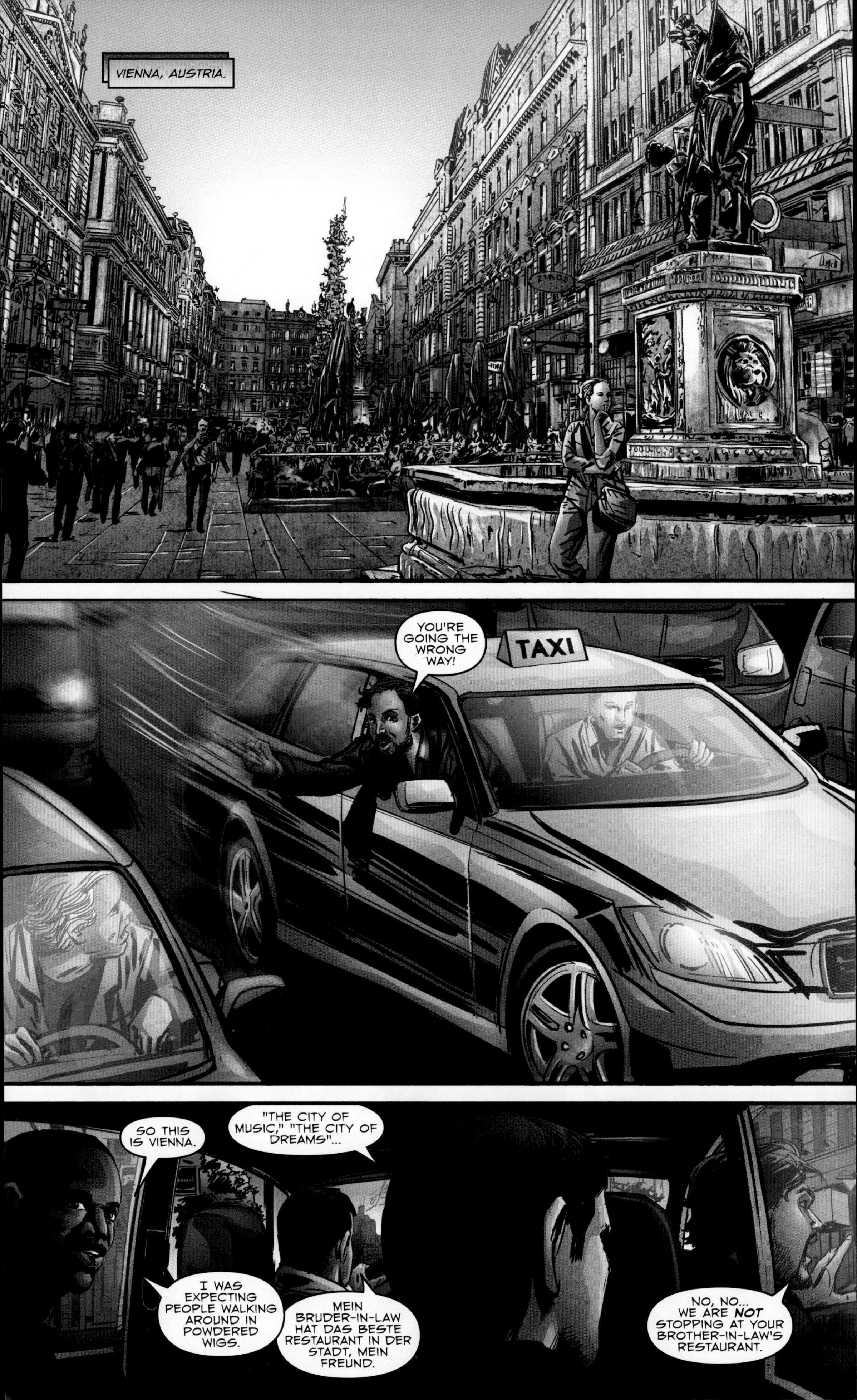
VIENNA, AUSTRIA.
YOU'RE GOING THE WRONG WAY!
TAXI
SO THIS IS VIENNA.
"THE CITY OF MUSIC," "THE CITY OF DREAMS"...
I WAS EXPECTING PEOPLE WALKING AROUND IN POWDERED WIGS.
MEIN BRUDER-IN-LAW HAT DAS BESTE RESTAURANT IN DER STADT, MEIN FREUND.
NO, NO... WE ARE *NOT* STOPPING AT YOUR BROTHER-IN-LAW'S RESTAURANT.

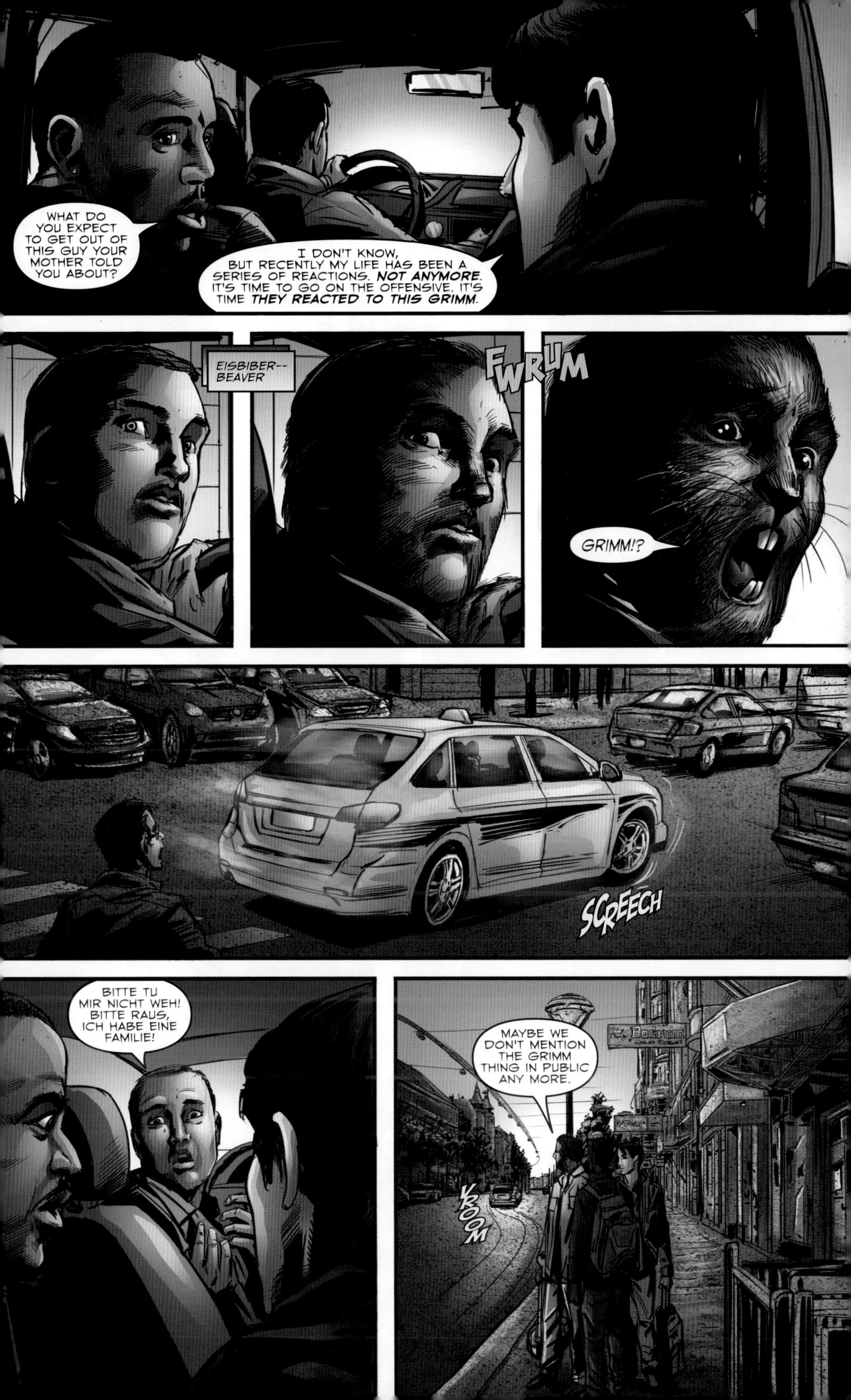
WHAT DO YOU EXPECT TO GET OUT OF THIS GUY YOUR MOTHER TOLD YOU ABOUT?
I DON'T KNOW, BUT RECENTLY MY LIFE HAS BEEN A SERIES OF REACTIONS. NOT ANYMORE. IT'S TIME TO GO ON THE OFFENSIVE. IT'S TIME THEY REACTED TO THIS GRIMM.
EISBIBER-- BEAVER
FWRUM
GRIMM!?
SCREECH
BITTE TU MIR NICHT WEH! BITTE RAUS, ICH HABE EINE FAMILIE!
MAYBE WE DON'T MENTION THE GRIMM THING IN PUBLIC ANY MORE.
VROOM

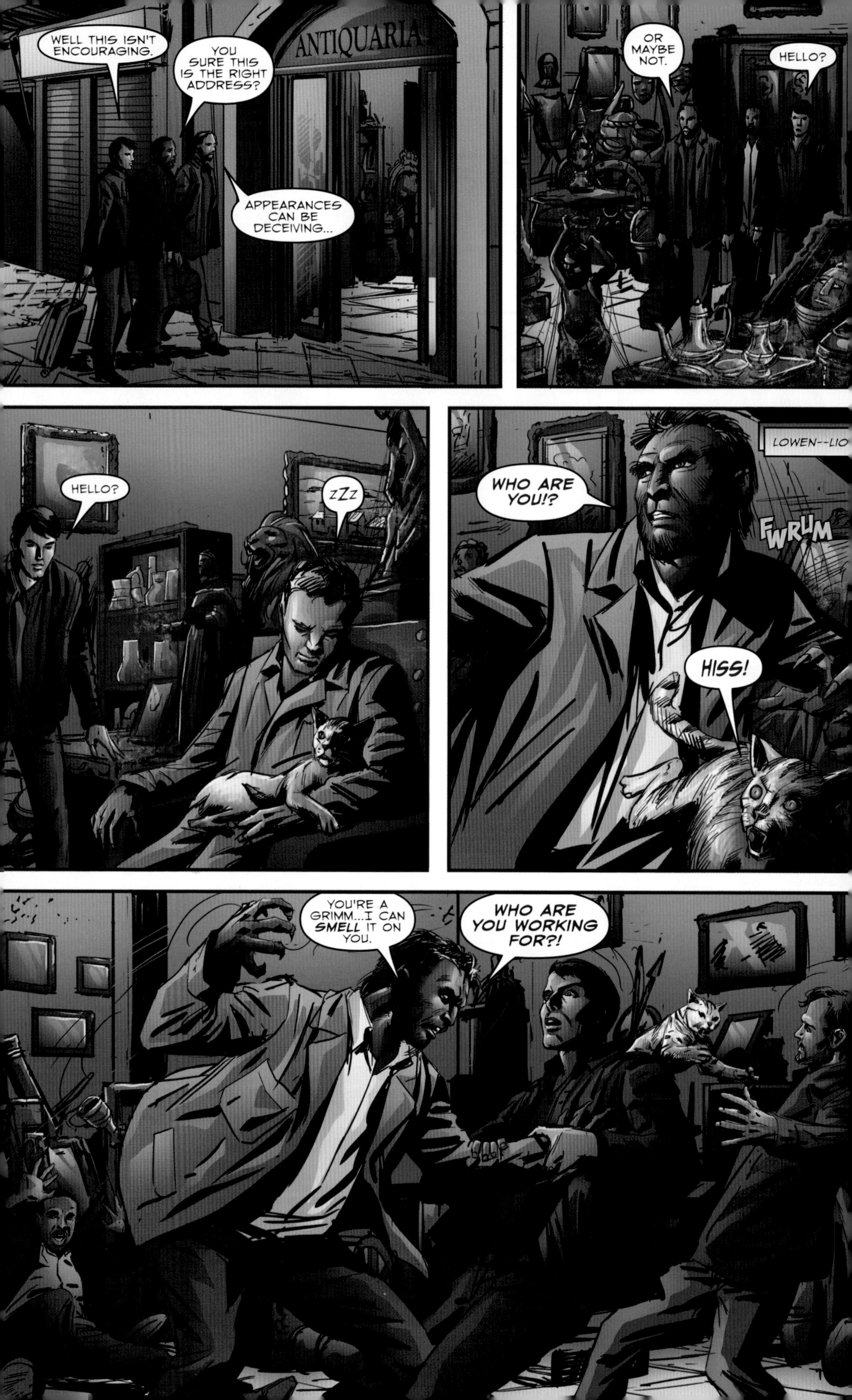
ANTIQUARIA
WELL THIS ISN'T ENCOURAGING.
YOU SURE THIS IS THE RIGHT ADDRESS?
APPEARANCES CAN BE DECEIVING...
OR MAYBE NOT.
HELLO?
HELLO?
zZz
LOWEN--LIO
WHO ARE YOU!?
FWRUM
HISS!
YOU'RE A GRIMM...I CAN SMELL IT ON YOU.
WHO ARE YOU WORKING FOR?!

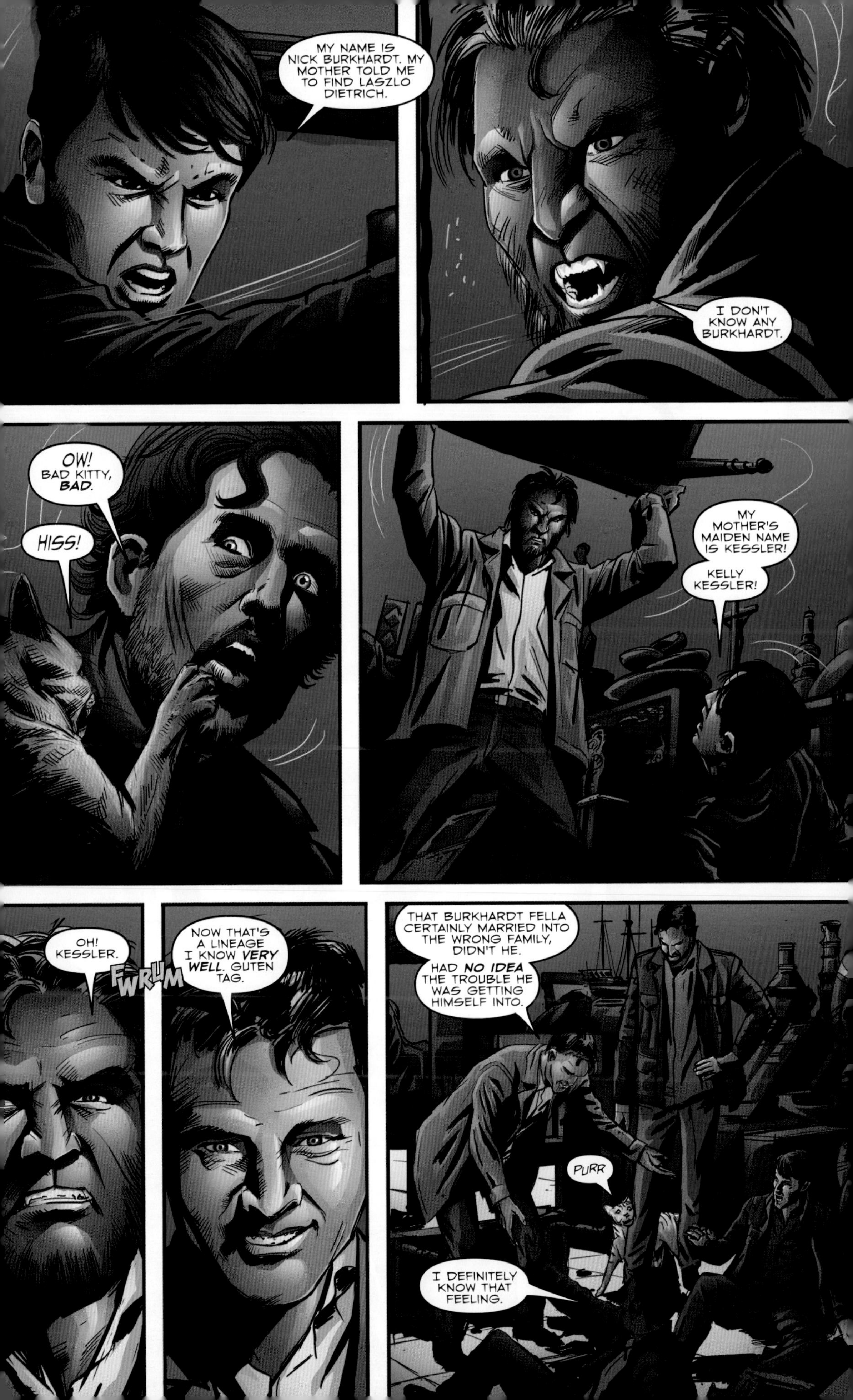

MY NAME IS NICK BURKHARDT. MY MOTHER TOLD ME TO FIND LASZLO DIETRICH.
I DON'T KNOW ANY BURKHARDT.
OW! BAD KITTY, BAD.
HISS!
MY MOTHER'S MAIDEN NAME IS KESSLER!
KELLY KESSLER!
OH! KESSLER.
FWRUM
NOW THAT'S A LINEAGE I KNOW VERY WELL. GUTEN TAG.
THAT BURKHARDT FELLA CERTAINLY MARRIED INTO THE WRONG FAMILY, DIDN'T HE.
HAD NO IDEA THE TROUBLE HE WAS GETTING HIMSELF INTO.
PURR
I DEFINITELY KNOW THAT FEELING.

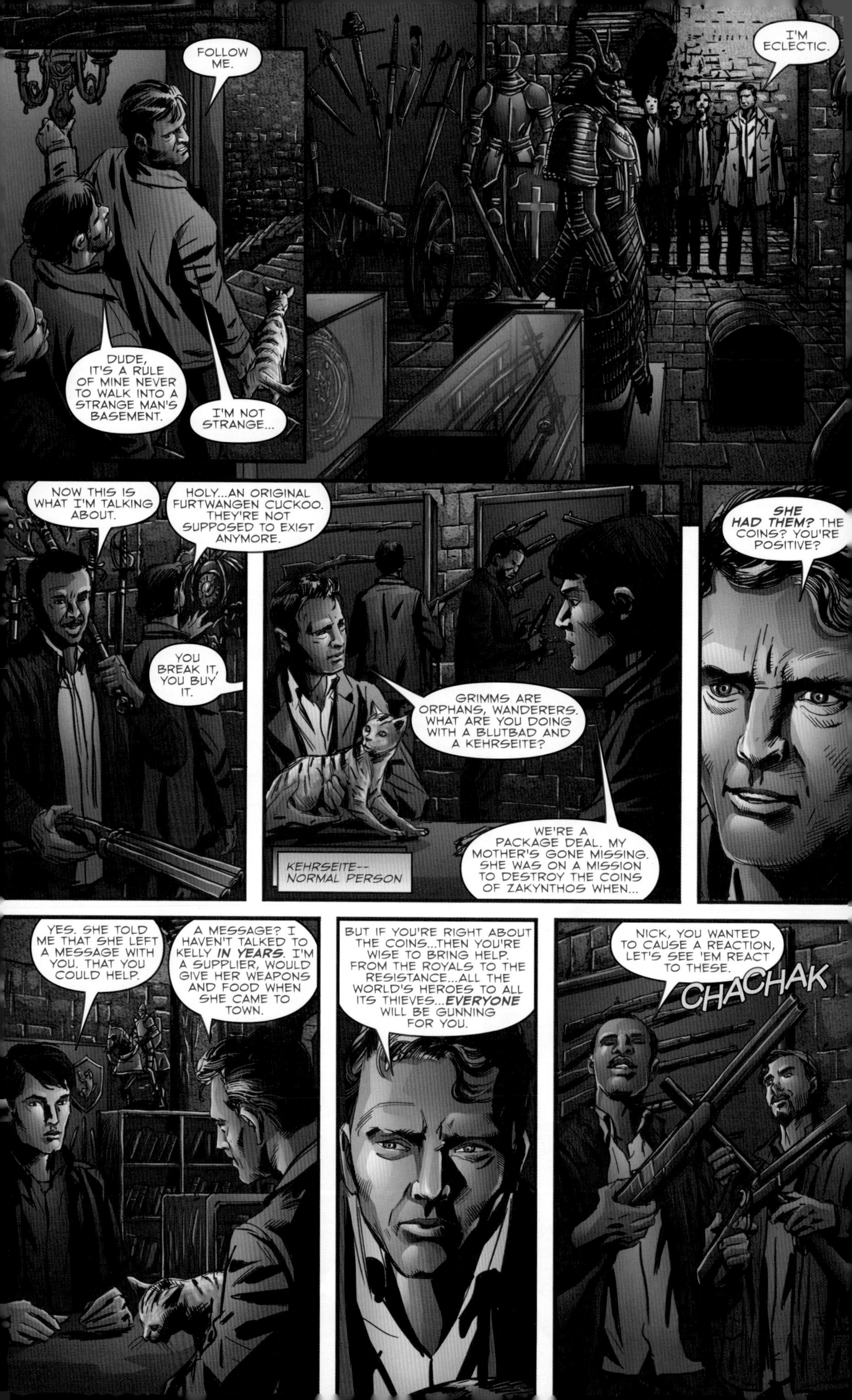
FOLLOW ME.
DUDE, IT'S A RULE OF MINE NEVER TO WALK INTO A STRANGE MAN'S BASEMENT.
I'M NOT STRANGE...
I'M ECLECTIC.
NOW THIS IS WHAT I'M TALKING ABOUT.
HOLY...AN ORIGINAL FURTWANGEN CUCKOO. THEY'RE NOT SUPPOSED TO EXIST ANYMORE.
YOU BREAK IT, YOU BUY IT.
GRIMMS ARE ORPHANS, WANDERERS. WHAT ARE YOU DOING WITH A BLUTBAD AND A KEHRSEITE?
KEHRSEITE-- NORMAL PERSON
WE'RE A PACKAGE DEAL. MY MOTHER'S GONE MISSING. SHE WAS ON A MISSION TO DESTROY THE COINS OF ZAKYNTHOS WHEN...
SHE HAD THEM? THE COINS? YOU'RE POSITIVE?
YES. SHE TOLD ME THAT SHE LEFT A MESSAGE WITH YOU. THAT YOU COULD HELP.
A MESSAGE? I HAVEN'T TALKED TO KELLY IN YEARS. I'M A SUPPLIER, WOULD GIVE HER WEAPONS AND FOOD WHEN SHE CAME TO TOWN.
BUT IF YOU'RE RIGHT ABOUT THE COINS...THEN YOU'RE WISE TO BRING HELP. FROM THE ROYALS TO THE RESISTANCE...ALL THE WORLD'S HEROES TO ALL ITS THIEVES...EVERYONE WILL BE GUNNING FOR YOU.
NICK, YOU WANTED TO CAUSE A REACTION, LET'S SEE 'EM REACT TO THESE.
CHACHAK

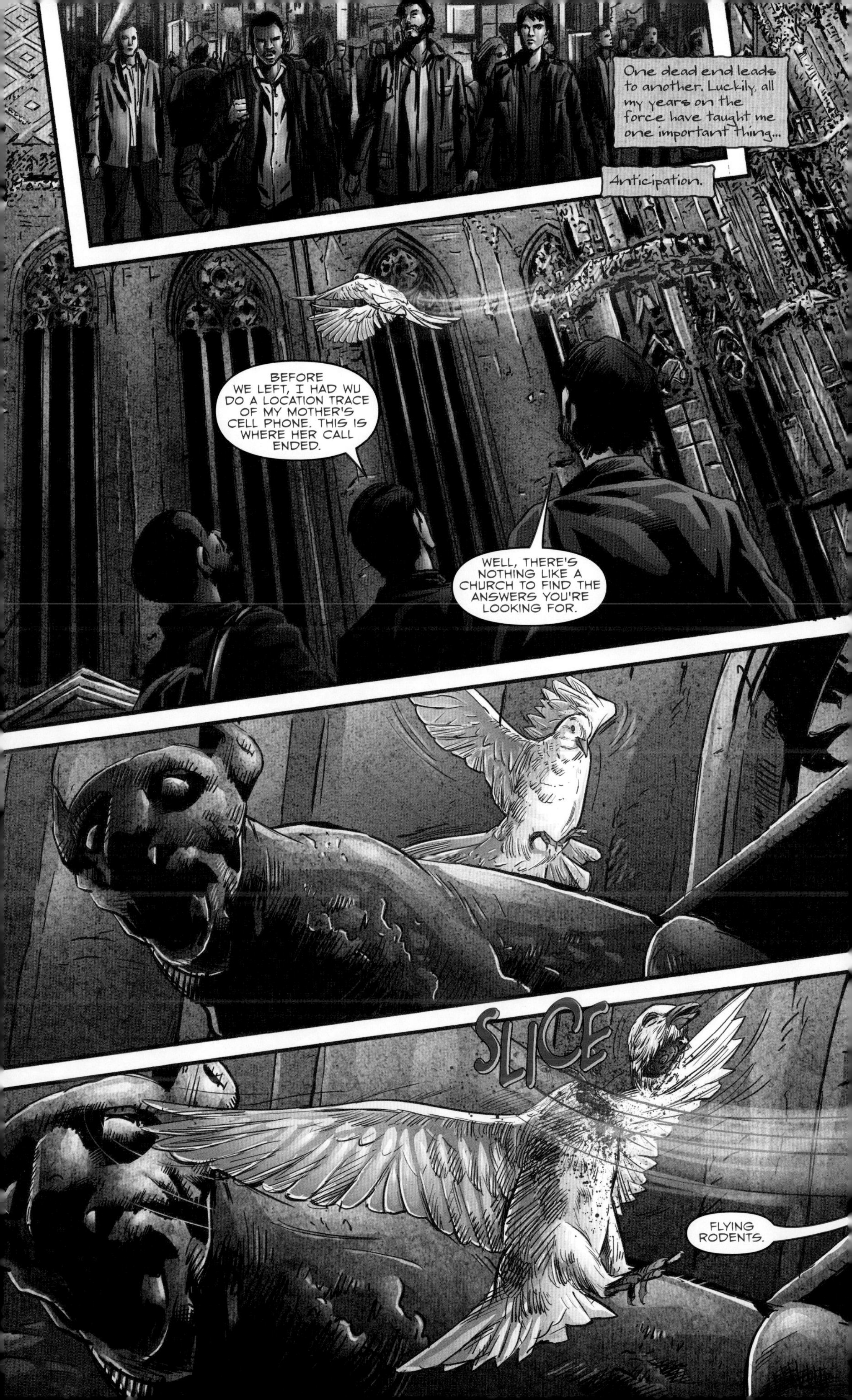
One dead end leads to another. Luckily, all my years on the force have taught me one important thing...
Anticipation.
BEFORE WE LEFT, I HAD WU DO A LOCATION TRACE OF MY MOTHER'S CELL PHONE. THIS IS WHERE HER CALL ENDED.
WELL, THERE'S NOTHING LIKE A CHURCH TO FIND THE ANSWERS YOU'RE LOOKING FOR.
SLICE
FLYING RODENTS.

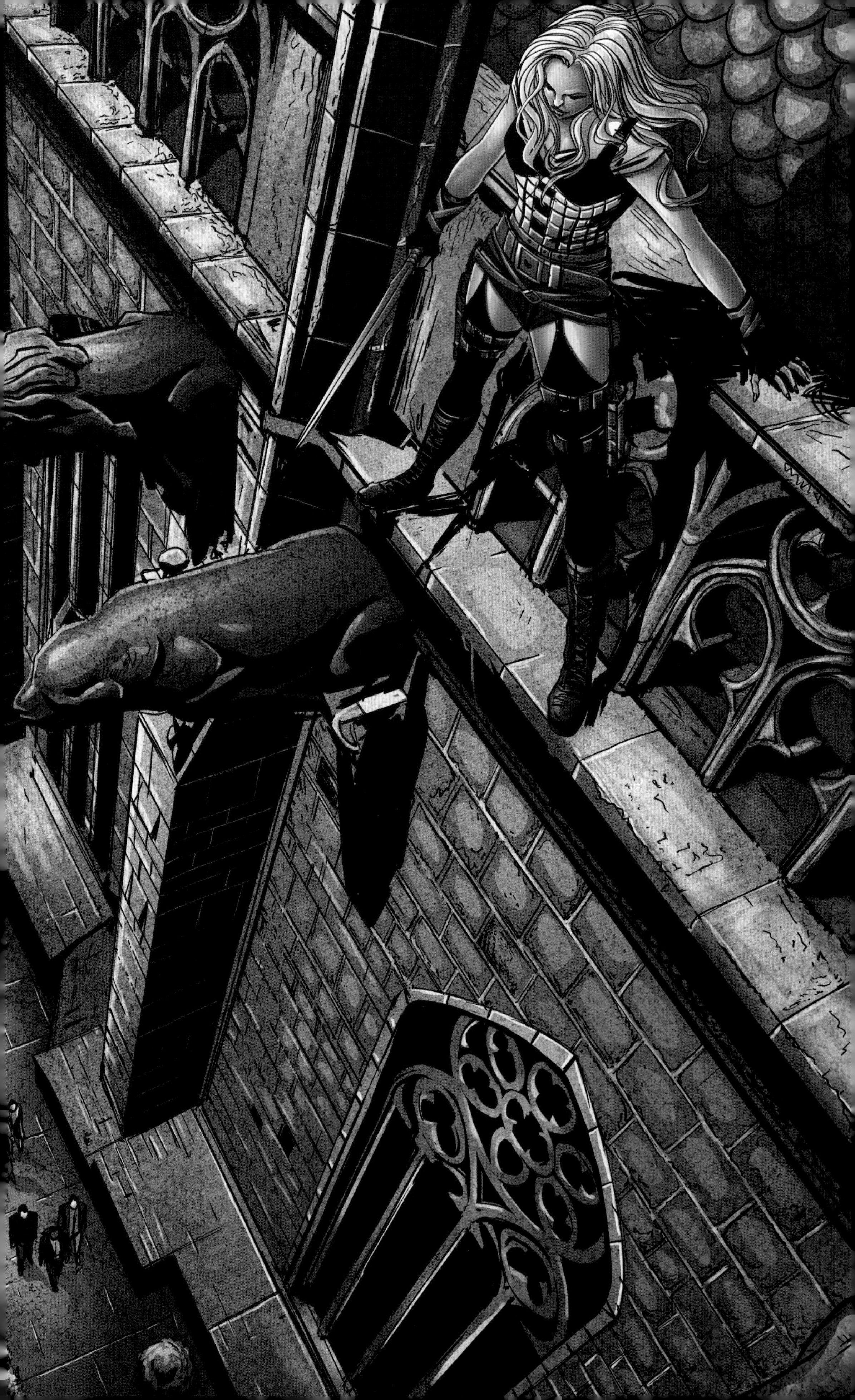

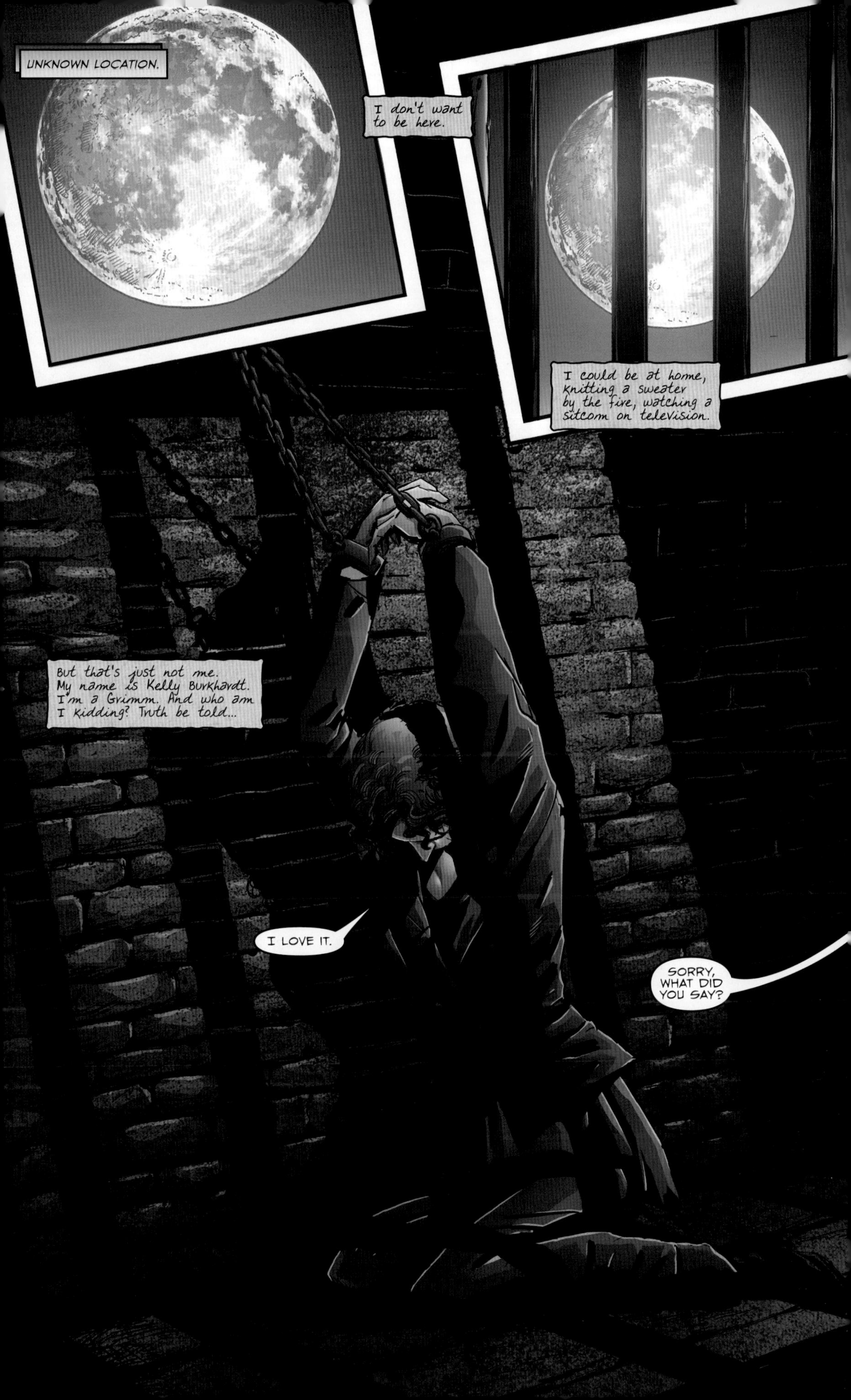
UNKNOWN LOCATION.
I don't want to be here.
I could be at home, knitting a sweater by the fire, watching a sitcom on television.
But that's just not me. My name is Kelly Burkhardt. I'm a Grimm. And who am I kidding? Truth be told...
I LOVE IT.
SORRY, WHAT DID YOU SAY?

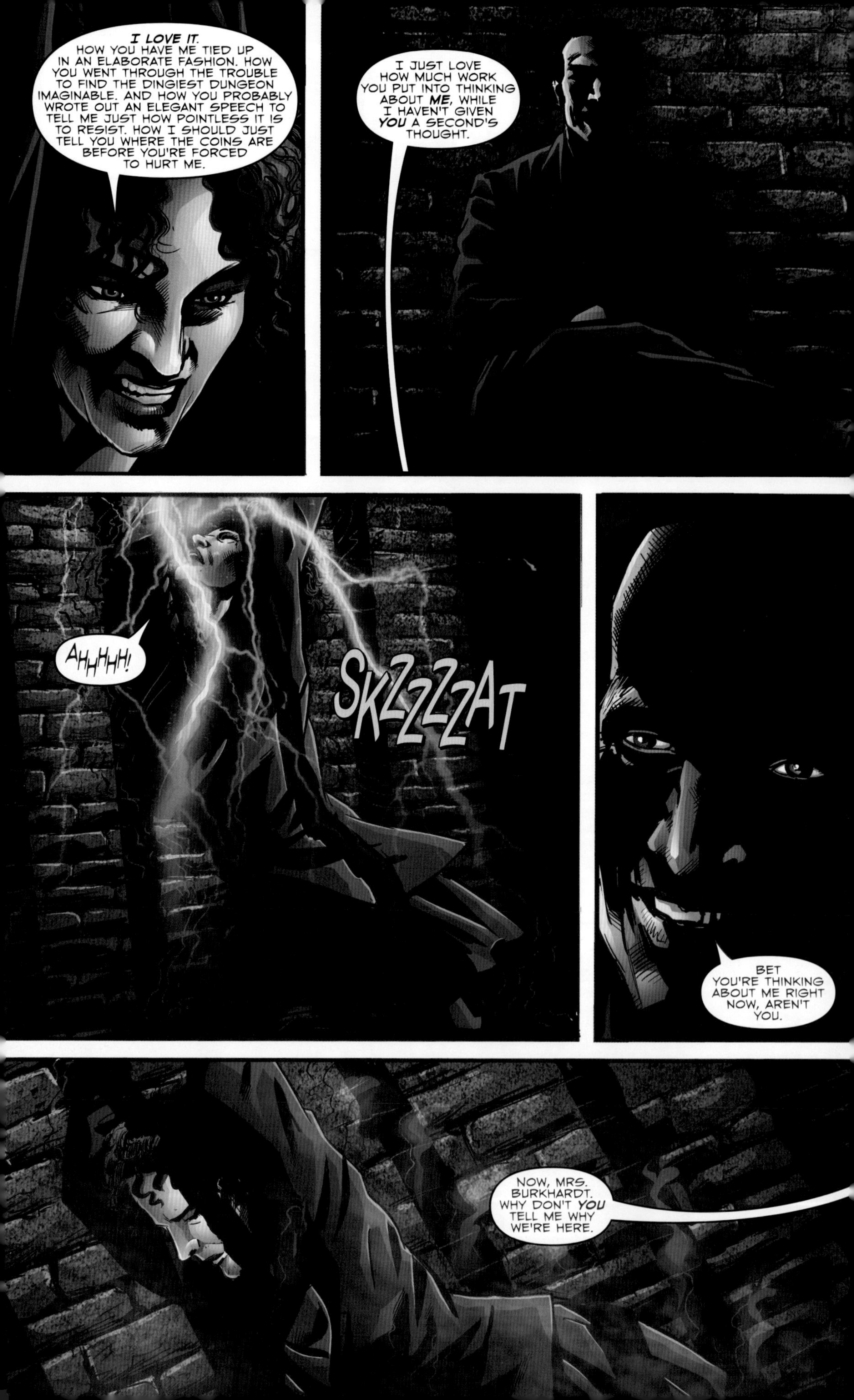
I LOVE IT. HOW YOU HAVE ME TIED UP IN AN ELABORATE FASHION. HOW YOU WENT THROUGH THE TROUBLE TO FIND THE DINGIEST DUNGEON IMAGINABLE. AND HOW YOU PROBABLY WROTE OUT AN ELEGANT SPEECH TO TELL ME JUST HOW POINTLESS IT IS TO RESIST. HOW I SHOULD JUST TELL YOU WHERE THE COINS ARE BEFORE YOU'RE FORCED TO HURT ME.
I JUST LOVE HOW MUCH WORK YOU PUT INTO THINKING ABOUT ME, WHILE I HAVEN'T GIVEN YOU A SECOND'S THOUGHT.
AHHHHH!
SKZZZZZAT
BET YOU'RE THINKING ABOUT ME RIGHT NOW, AREN'T YOU.
NOW, MRS. BURKHARDT. WHY DON'T YOU TELL ME WHY WE'RE HERE.

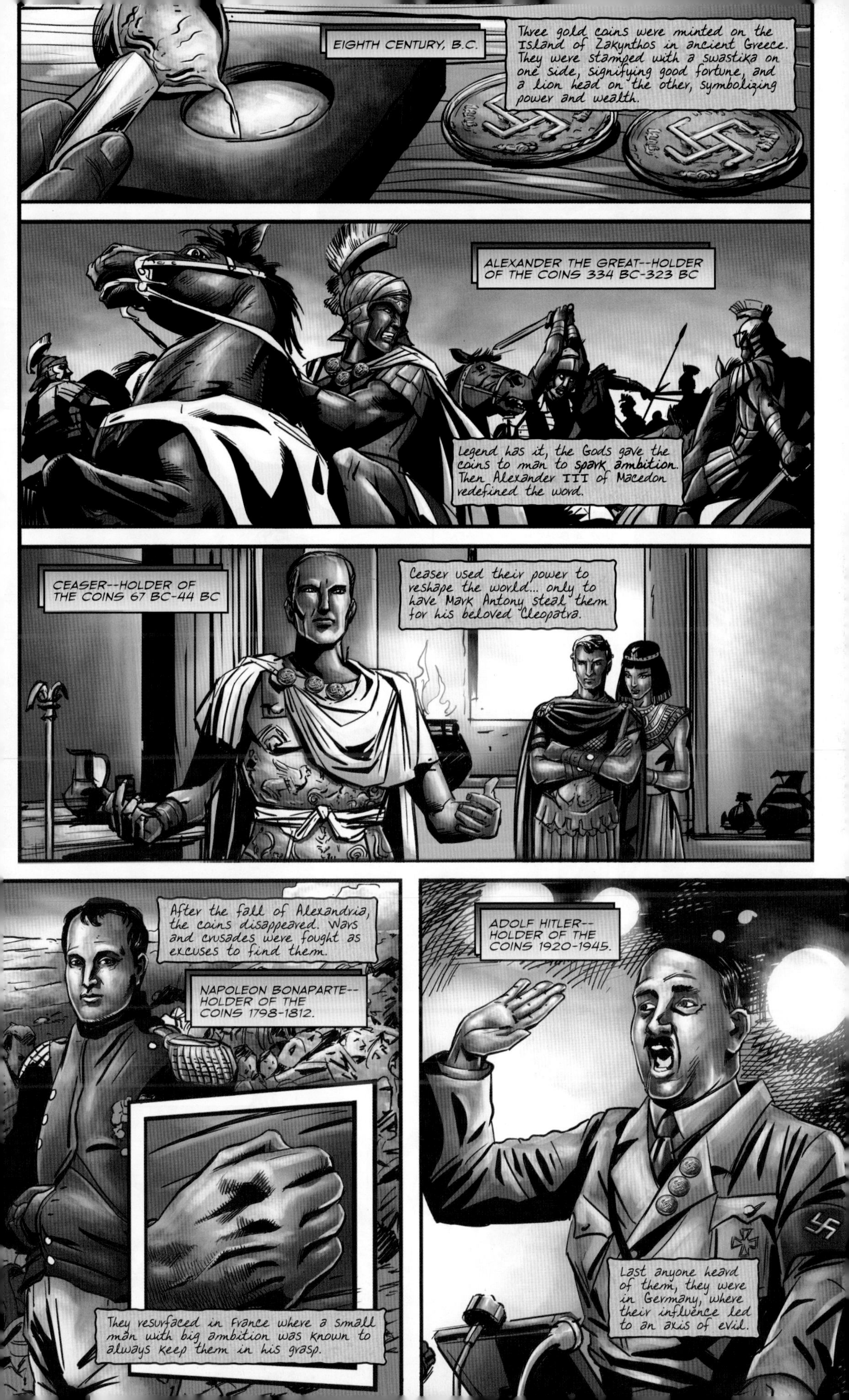
EIGHTH CENTURY, B.C.
Three gold coins were minted on the Island of Zakynthos in ancient Greece. They were stamped with a swastika on one side, signifying good fortune, and a lion head on the other, symbolizing power and wealth.
ALEXANDER THE GREAT--HOLDER OF THE COINS 334 BC-323 BC
Legend has it, the Gods gave the coins to man to spark ambition. Then Alexander III of Macedon redefined the word.
CEASER--HOLDER OF THE COINS 67 BC-44 BC
Ceaser used their power to reshape the world... only to have Mark Antony steal them for his beloved Cleopatra.
After the fall of Alexandria, the coins disappeared. Wars and crusades were fought as excuses to find them.
NAPOLEON BONAPARTE--HOLDER OF THE COINS 1798-1812.
They resurfaced in France where a small man with big ambition was known to always keep them in his grasp.
ADOLF HITLER--HOLDER OF THE COINS 1920-1945.
Last anyone heard of them, they were in Germany, where their influence led to an axis of evil.

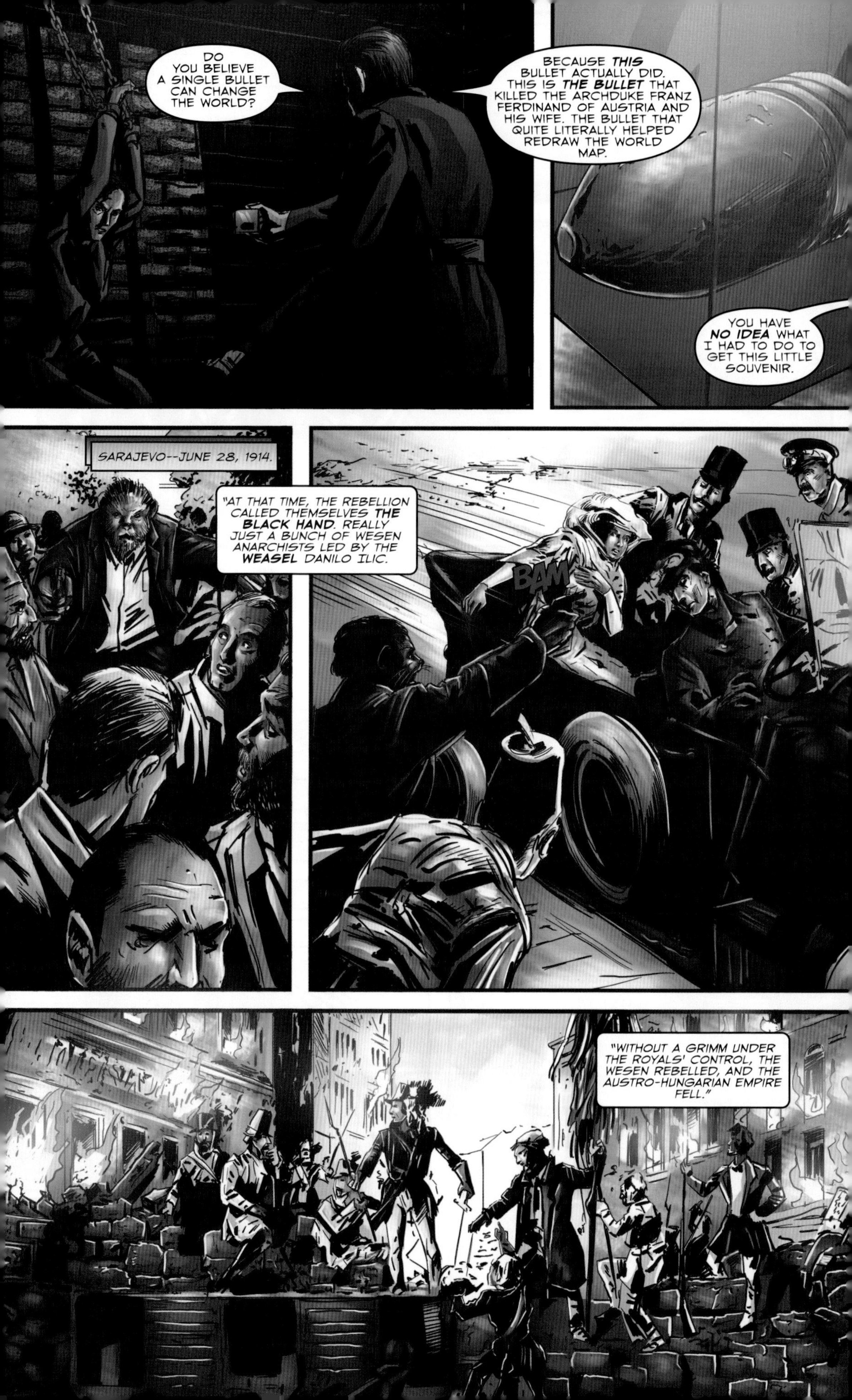
DO YOU BELIEVE A SINGLE BULLET CAN CHANGE THE WORLD?
BECAUSE THIS BULLET ACTUALLY DID. THIS IS THE BULLET THAT KILLED THE ARCHDUKE FRANZ FERDINAND OF AUSTRIA AND HIS WIFE. THE BULLET THAT QUITE LITERALLY HELPED REDRAW THE WORLD MAP.
YOU HAVE NO IDEA WHAT I HAD TO DO TO GET THIS LITTLE SOUVENIR.
SARAJEVO--JUNE 28, 1914.
"AT THAT TIME, THE REBELLION CALLED THEMSELVES THE BLACK HAND. REALLY JUST A BUNCH OF WESEN ANARCHISTS LED BY THE WEASEL DANILO ILIC.
BAM
"WITHOUT A GRIMM UNDER THE ROYALS' CONTROL, THE WESEN REBELLED, AND THE AUSTRO-HUNGARIAN EMPIRE FELL."

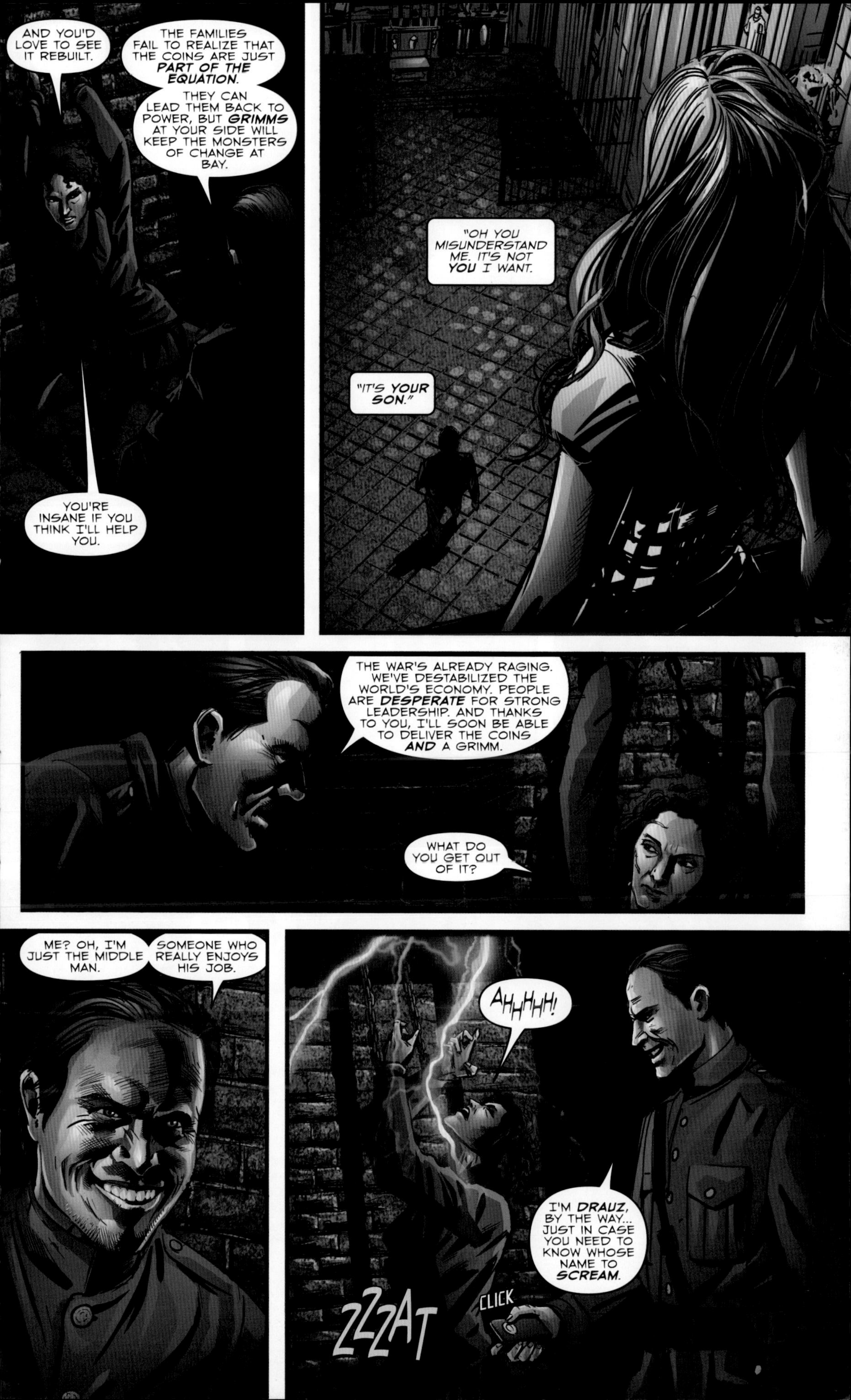
AND YOU'D LOVE TO SEE IT REBUILT.
THE FAMILIES FAIL TO REALIZE THAT THE COINS ARE JUST PART OF THE EQUATION.
THEY CAN LEAD THEM BACK TO POWER, BUT GRIMMS AT YOUR SIDE WILL KEEP THE MONSTERS OF CHANGE AT BAY.
YOU'RE INSANE IF YOU THINK I'LL HELP YOU.
"OH YOU MISUNDERSTAND ME. IT'S NOT YOU I WANT.
"IT'S YOUR SON."
THE WAR'S ALREADY RAGING. WE'VE DESTABILIZED THE WORLD'S ECONOMY. PEOPLE ARE DESPERATE FOR STRONG LEADERSHIP. AND THANKS TO YOU, I'LL SOON BE ABLE TO DELIVER THE COINS AND A GRIMM.
WHAT DO YOU GET OUT OF IT?
ME? OH, I'M JUST THE MIDDLE MAN.
SOMEONE WHO REALLY ENJOYS HIS JOB.
AHHHHH!
I'M DRAUZ, BY THE WAY... JUST IN CASE YOU NEED TO KNOW WHOSE NAME TO SCREAM.
ZZZAT
CLICK

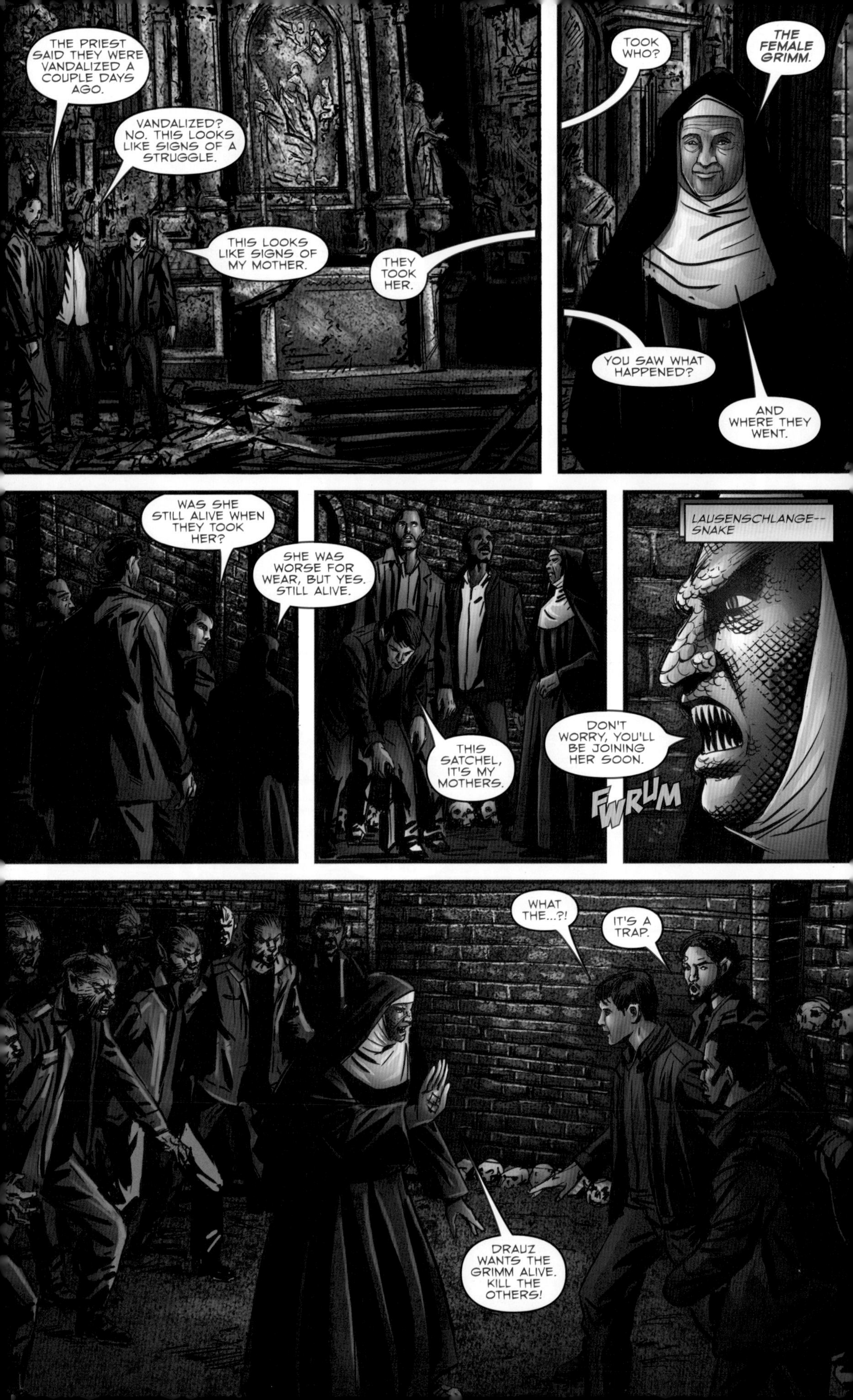
THE PRIEST SAID THEY WERE VANDALIZED A COUPLE DAYS AGO.
VANDALIZED? NO. THIS LOOKS LIKE SIGNS OF A STRUGGLE.
THIS LOOKS LIKE SIGNS OF MY MOTHER.
THEY TOOK HER.
TOOK WHO?
THE FEMALE GRIMM.
YOU SAW WHAT HAPPENED?
AND WHERE THEY WENT.
WAS SHE STILL ALIVE WHEN THEY TOOK HER?
SHE WAS WORSE FOR WEAR, BUT YES. STILL ALIVE.
THIS SATCHEL, IT'S MY MOTHERS.
LAUSENSCHLANGE-- SNAKE
DON'T WORRY, YOU'LL BE JOINING HER SOON.
FWRUM
WHAT THE...?!
IT'S A TRAP.
DRAUZ WANTS THE GRIMM ALIVE. KILL THE OTHERS!

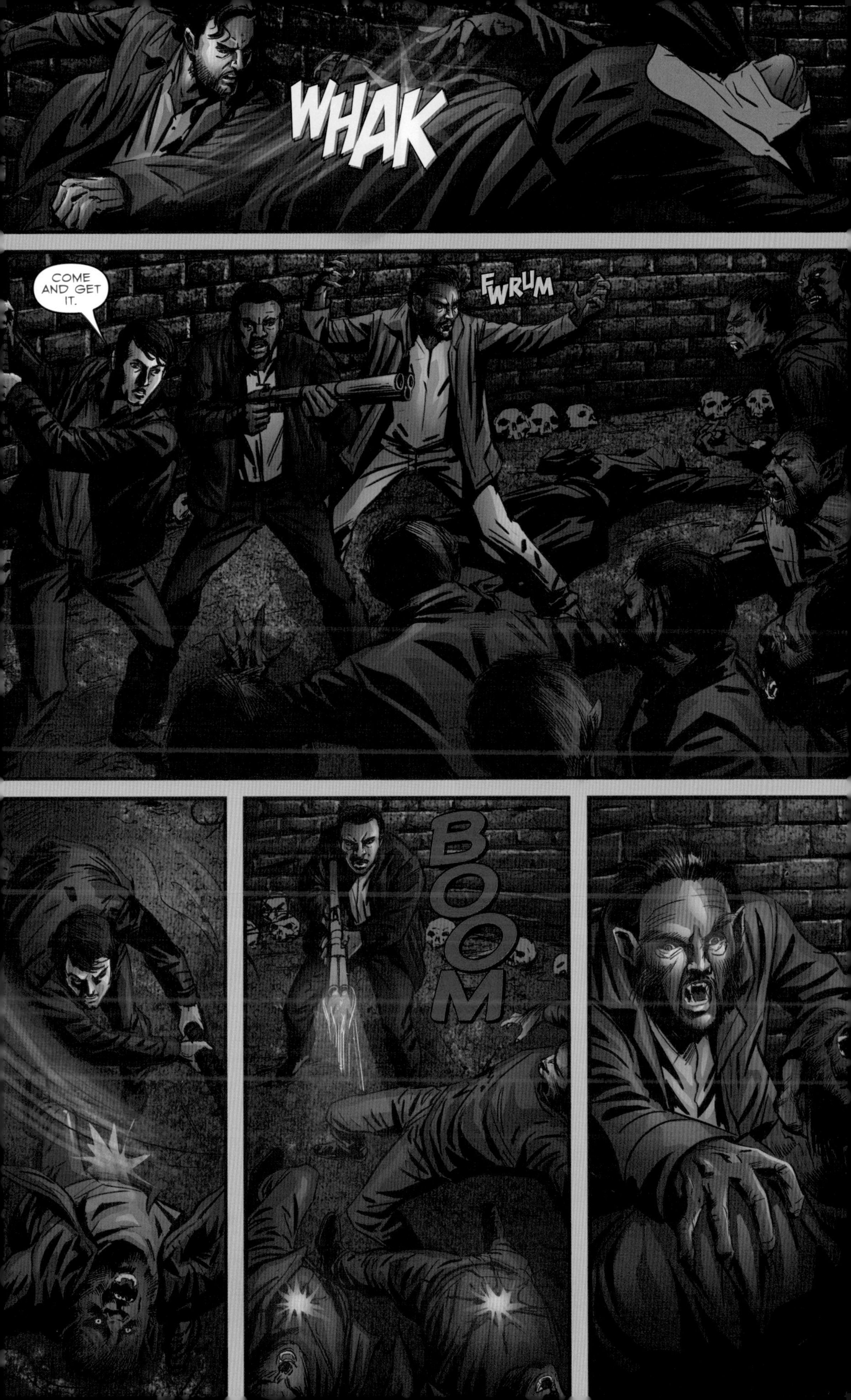
WHAK
COME AND GET IT.
FWRUM
BOOM

KROOM

DICKFELLIG--RHINO

TOLD YOU THEY WERE DIVERSIFYING.

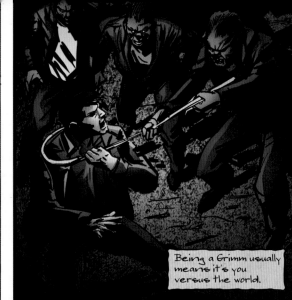

Being a Grimm usually means it's you versus the world.

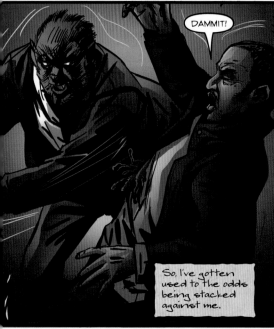

DAMMIT!

So, I've gotten used to the odds being stacked against me.

But even this is a bit much.

SNAP

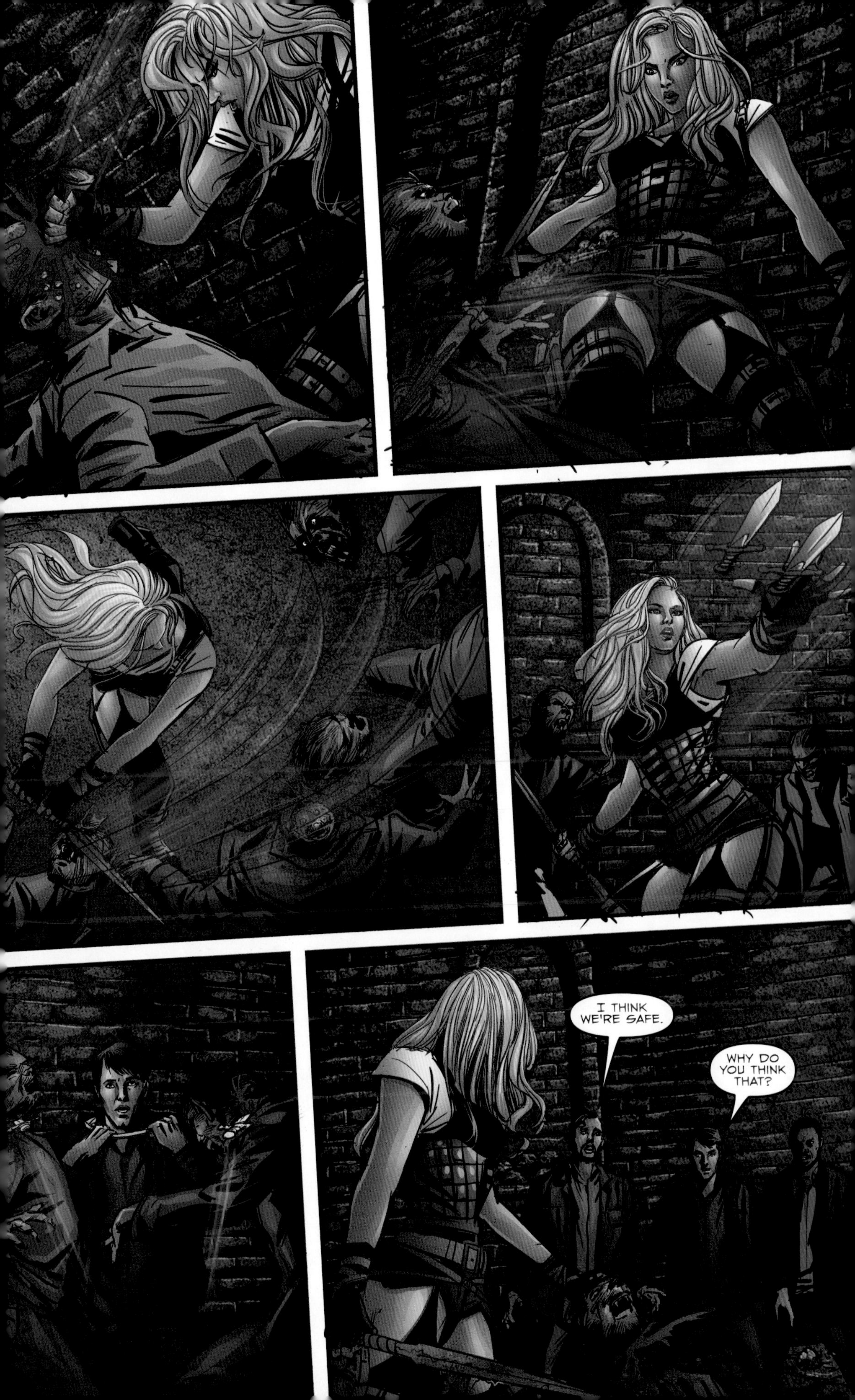
I THINK WE'RE SAFE.
WHY DO YOU THINK THAT?

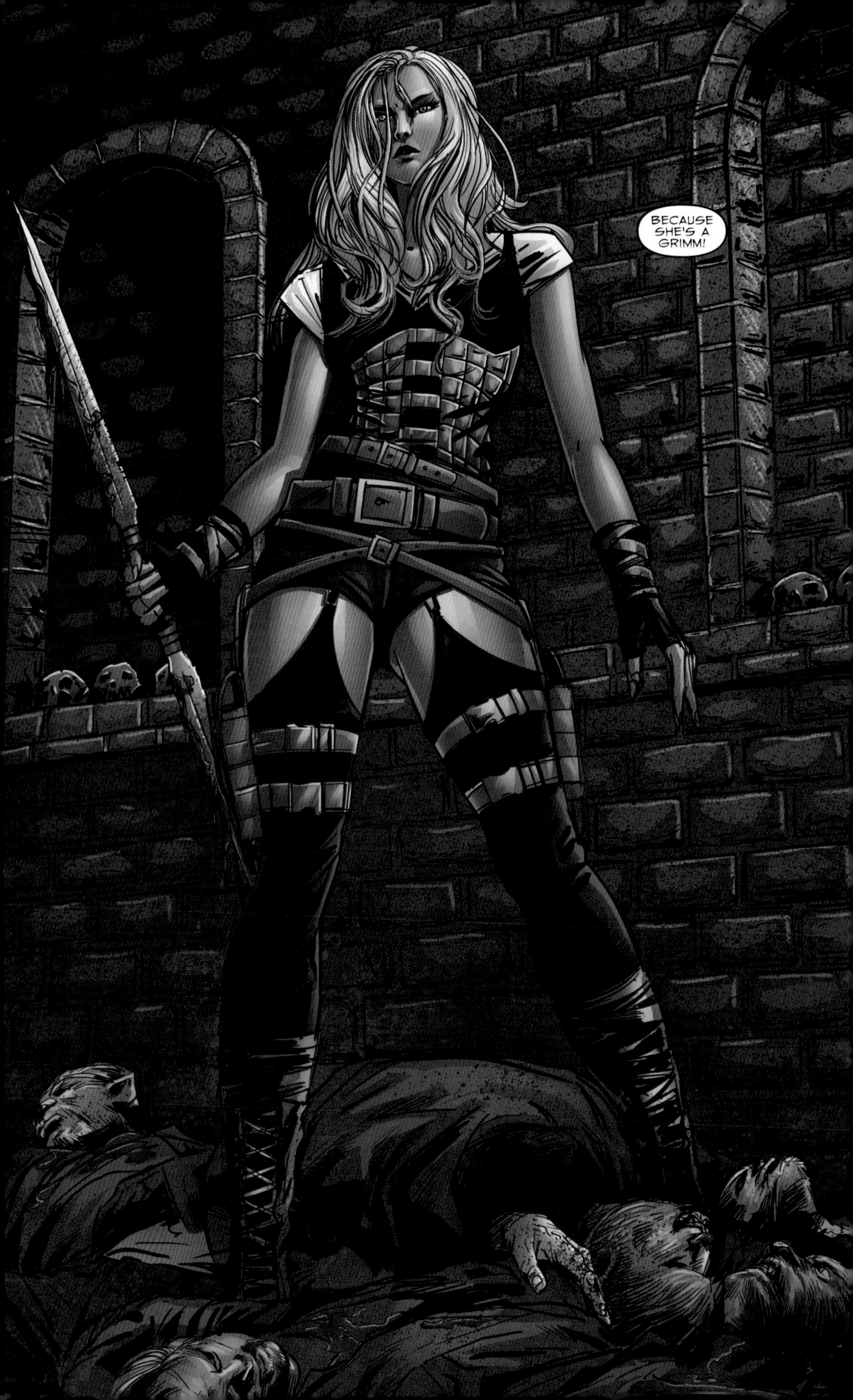
BECAUSE SHE'S A GRIMM!

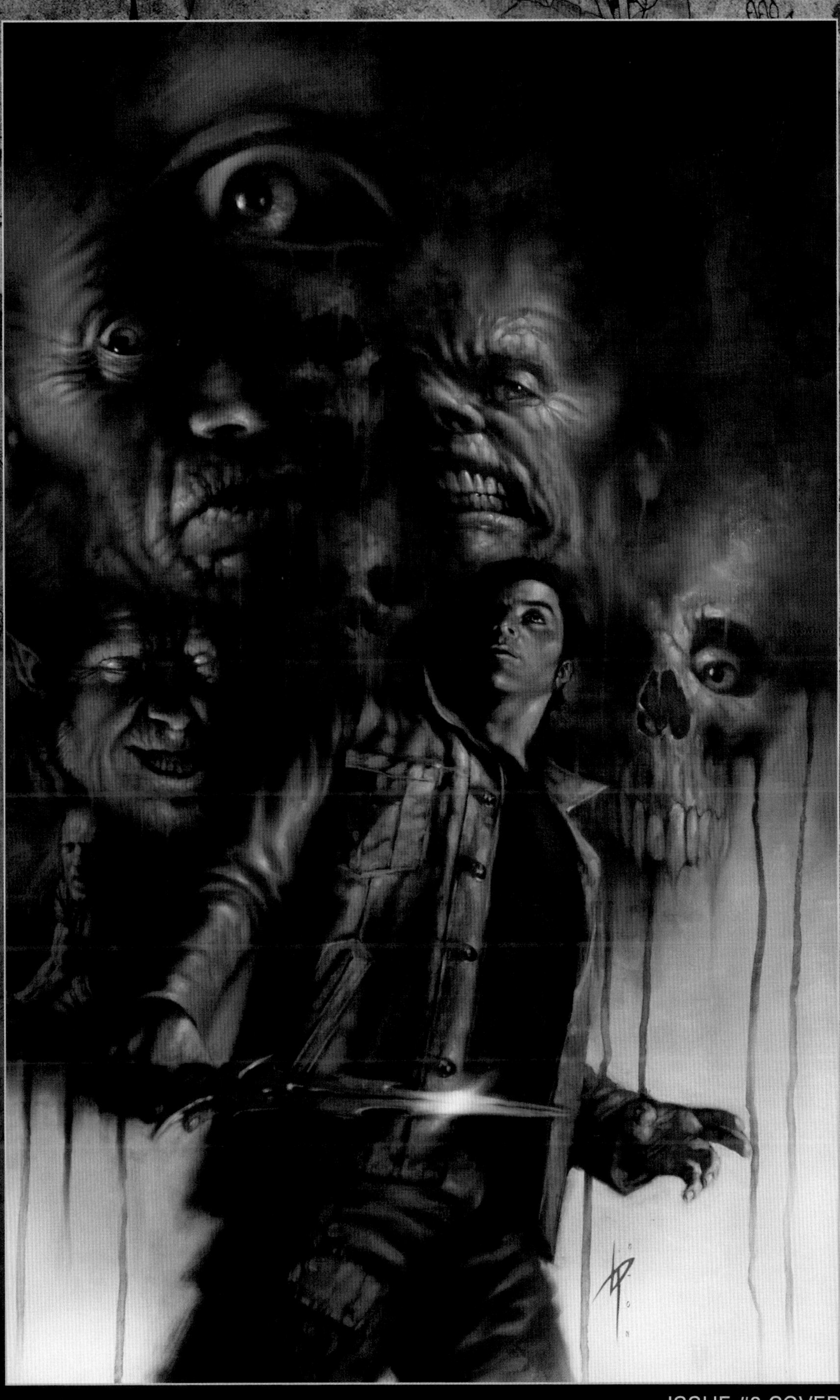

ISSUE #2 COVER

Siegbarste

I developed a serum
which calcifies the Siegbarste
bones using a moss that only
grows on the North side of
trees near the timberline.
As it is highly improbable
to administer the poison orally,
I also developed a way to propel the serum:
Siegbarst Gewehr - to propel the serum

- 14oz extract of S. gift moss
- 3gm wort powder
- 2gm powder of Magnum
- 15oz extract of lorum
- 3 tsp ground Zimis omnis
- 4 drops of rabbit blood

Finished product should
Amber in color and pure
in smell. Calcifies Siegbarste
bones - causing immediate

Siegbarste gift
(Bryophyta Sphagnopsida)

Grows on the North side
of trees near the
timberline.

(1) Harvest from evergreen variety, two
in late fall or rare occasions of
bloom in the spring.

(2) After harvest
using a mo...
until the pl...
to a fine

(3) Dilute powder with water (1 to 3 ratio)
using distillation process, reduce plant
to liquid and ferment.

Skin thickness
in Siegbarste
is significantly
thicker, on
average 10-15mm
thick. Human skin
is 2-3mm thick.

Siegbarste bone structure
and skin thickness

...cture and Skin thickness

...making it nearly impenetrable
...abnormally dense and thick
...for pain-making their
...comparison which I
...human cadaver and
...my second batch
...and density of
...to humans &
...10-15mm thick
...fatty present

Gewehr

...to destroy a
...using bullets dipped
...Siegbarste gift - a
...poisonous solution
...distilled from a
...particular moss that
...only grows on the
...North side of trees
...in the forests of
...Gimey

The rifle is a
modified triple-
...16 elephant gun

To prepare the
solution, the
proper moss
must be culti...
from the North
side of tr...
in the
forests of...
coming.

When distilled
in a proper
glass and copper
distiller the moss
should be bottled
and allowed
...

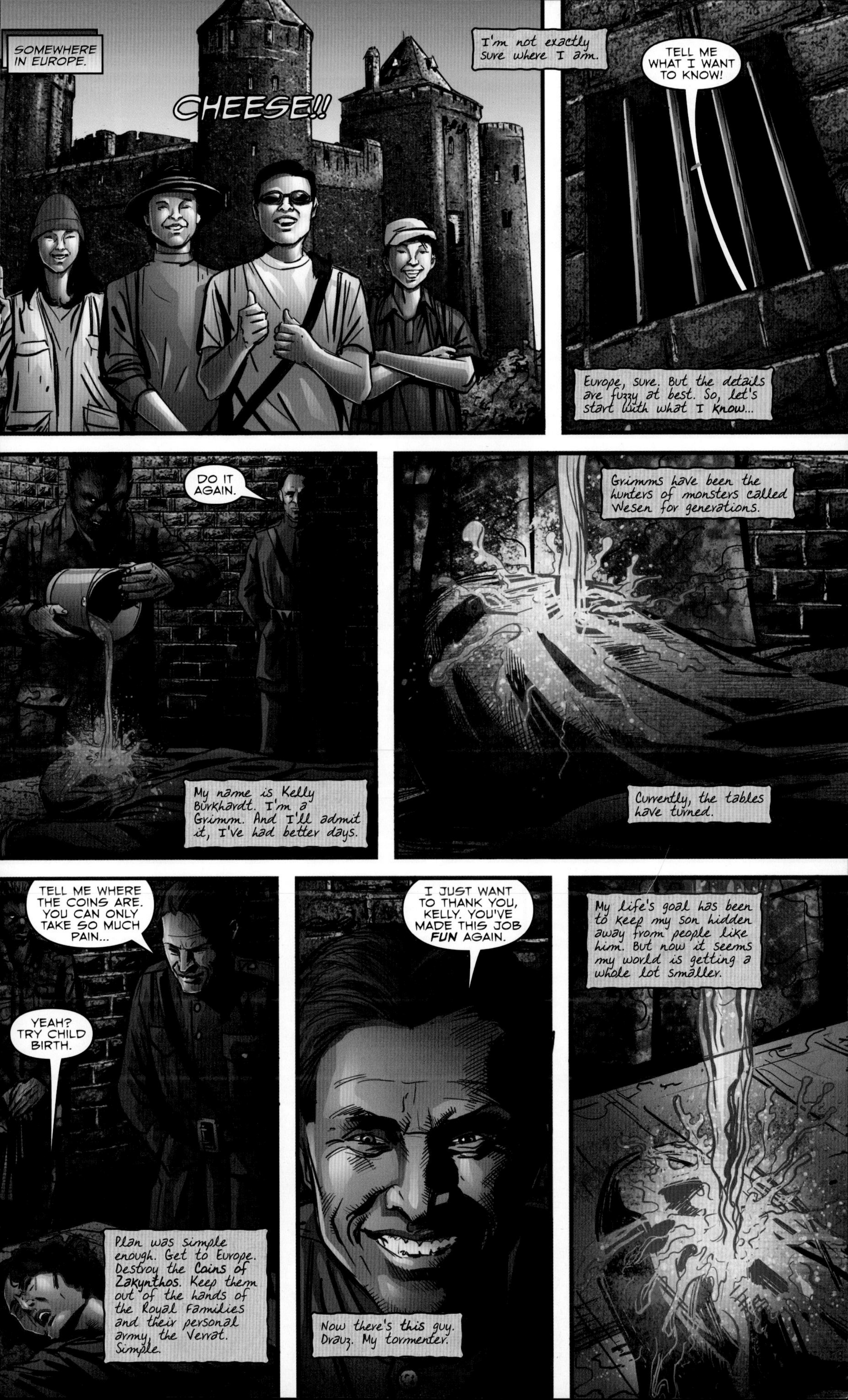

SOMEWHERE IN EUROPE.
CHEESE!!
I'm not exactly sure where I am.
TELL ME WHAT I WANT TO KNOW!
Europe, sure. But the details are fuzzy at best. So, let's start with what I know...
DO IT AGAIN.
My name is Kelly Burkhardt. I'm a Grimm. And I'll admit it, I've had better days.
Grimms have been the hunters of monsters called Wesen for generations.
Currently, the tables have turned.
TELL ME WHERE THE COINS ARE. YOU CAN ONLY TAKE SO MUCH PAIN...
YEAH? TRY CHILD BIRTH.
Plan was simple enough. Get to Europe. Destroy the Coins of Zakynthos. Keep them out of the hands of the Royal Families and their personal army, the Verrat. Simple.
I JUST WANT TO THANK YOU, KELLY. YOU'VE MADE THIS JOB FUN AGAIN.
Now there's this guy. Drauz. My tormenter.
My life's goal has been to keep my son hidden away from people like him. But now it seems my world is getting a whole lot smaller.

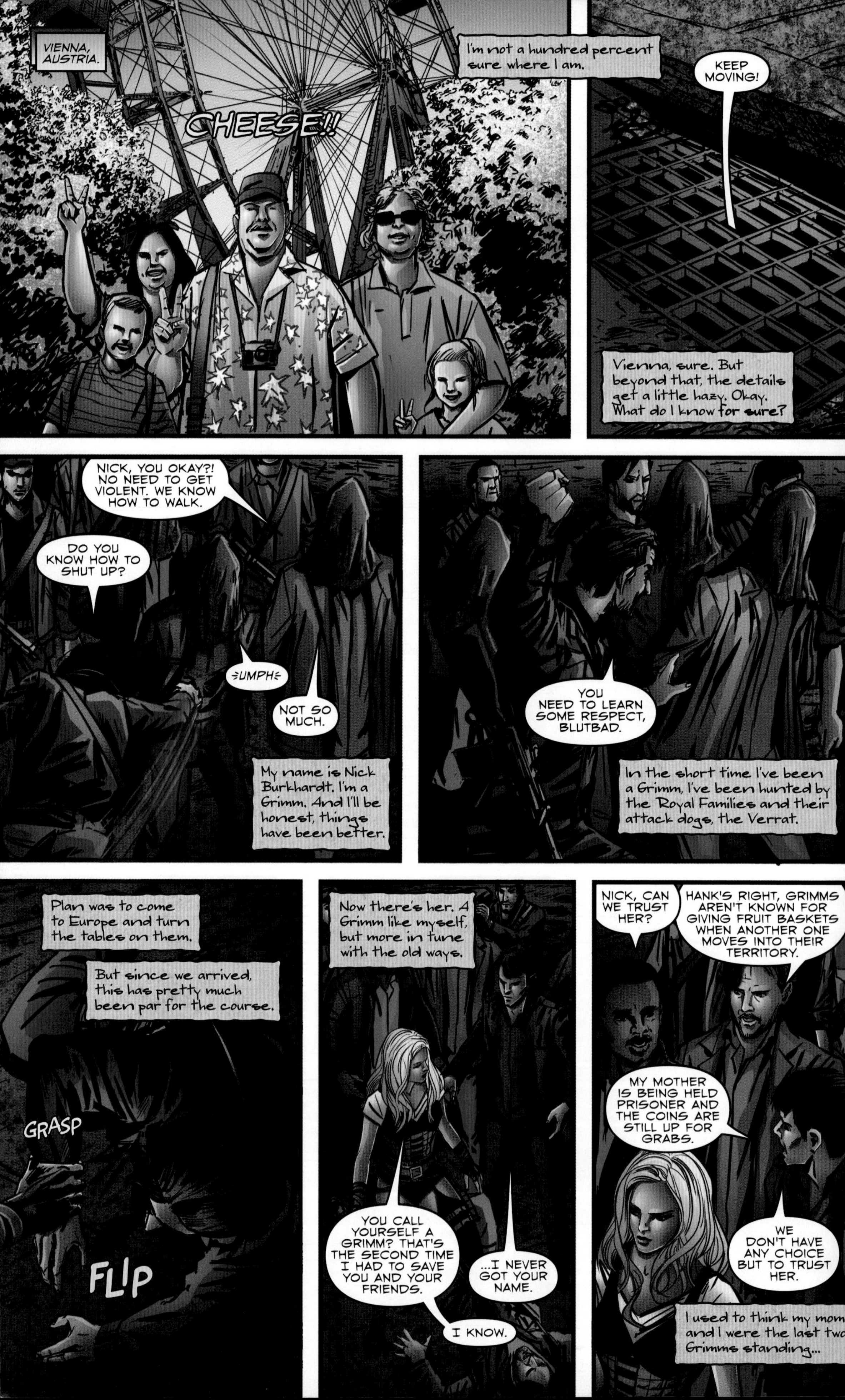
VIENNA, AUSTRIA.
I'm not a hundred percent sure where I am.
CHEESE!!
KEEP MOVING!
Vienna, sure. But beyond that, the details get a little hazy. Okay. What do I know for sure?
NICK, YOU OKAY?! NO NEED TO GET VIOLENT. WE KNOW HOW TO WALK.
DO YOU KNOW HOW TO SHUT UP?
UMPH
NOT SO MUCH.
My name is Nick Burkhardt. I'm a Grimm. And I'll be honest, things have been better.
YOU NEED TO LEARN SOME RESPECT, BLUTBAD.
In the short time I've been a Grimm, I've been hunted by the Royal Families and their attack dogs, the Verrat.
Plan was to come to Europe and turn the tables on them.
But since we arrived, this has pretty much been par for the course.
GRASP
FLIP
Now there's her. A Grimm like myself, but more in tune with the old ways.
YOU CALL YOURSELF A GRIMM? THAT'S THE SECOND TIME I HAD TO SAVE YOU AND YOUR FRIENDS.
...I NEVER GOT YOUR NAME.
I KNOW.
NICK, CAN WE TRUST HER?
HANK'S RIGHT, GRIMMS AREN'T KNOWN FOR GIVING FRUIT BASKETS WHEN ANOTHER ONE MOVES INTO THEIR TERRITORY.
MY MOTHER IS BEING HELD PRISONER AND THE COINS ARE STILL UP FOR GRABS.
WE DON'T HAVE ANY CHOICE BUT TO TRUST HER.
I used to think my mom and I were the last two Grimms standing...

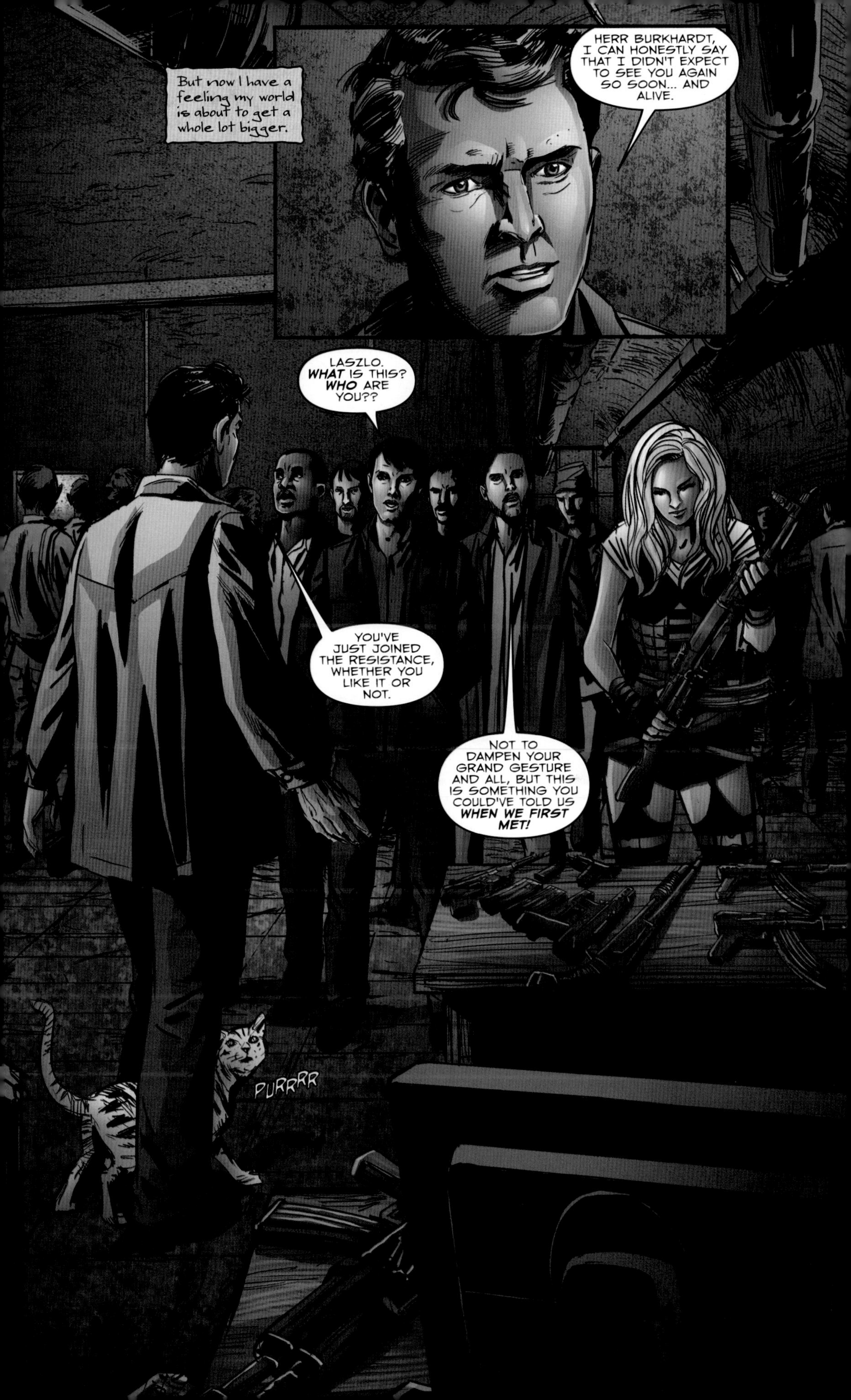
But now I have a feeling my world is about to get a whole lot bigger.
HERR BURKHARDT, I CAN HONESTLY SAY THAT I DIDN'T EXPECT TO SEE YOU AGAIN SO SOON... AND ALIVE.
LASZLO. **WHAT** IS THIS? **WHO** ARE YOU??
YOU'VE JUST JOINED THE RESISTANCE, WHETHER YOU LIKE IT OR NOT.
NOT TO DAMPEN YOUR GRAND GESTURE AND ALL, BUT THIS IS SOMETHING YOU COULD'VE TOLD US **WHEN WE FIRST MET!**
PURRRR

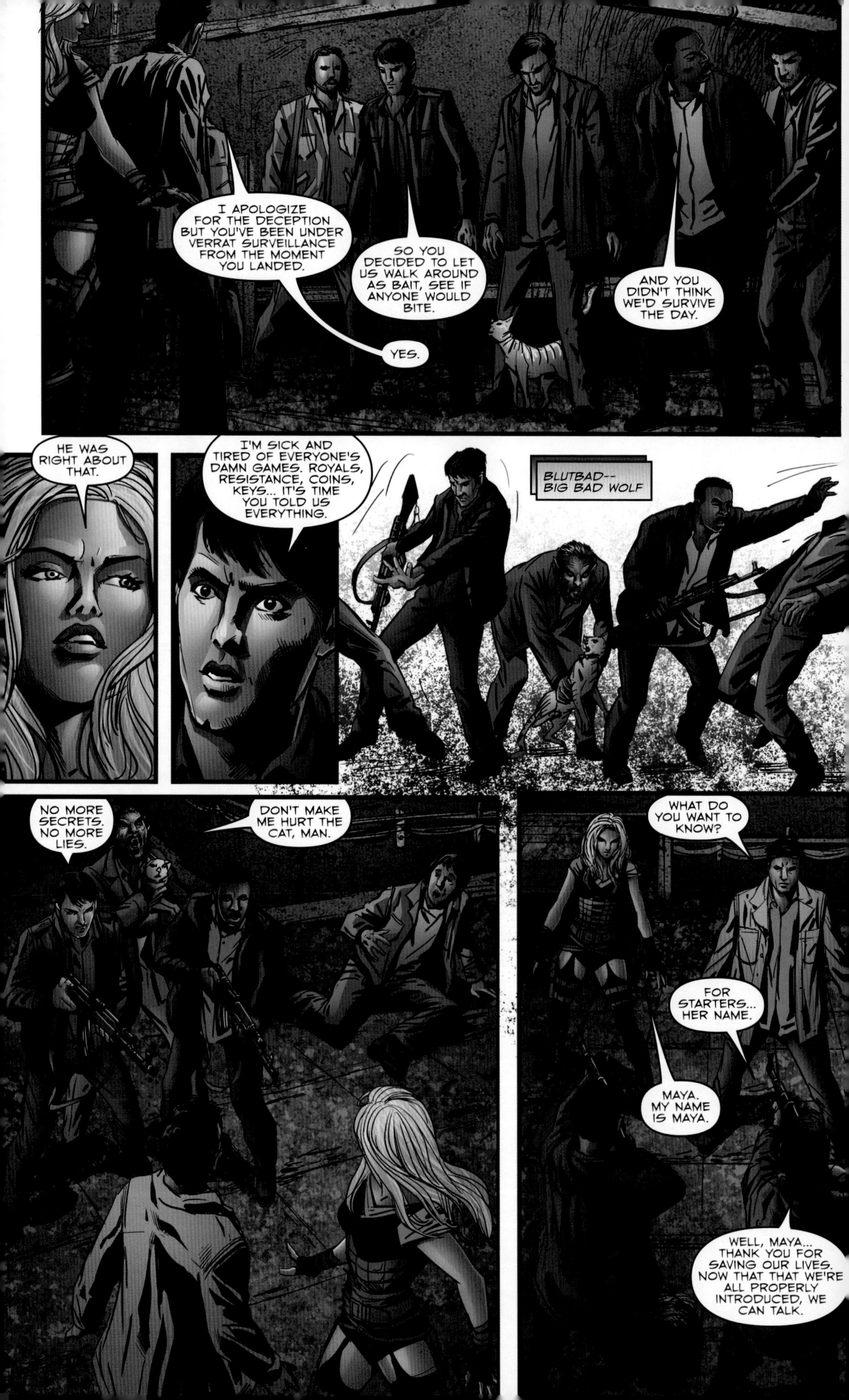
I APOLOGIZE FOR THE DECEPTION BUT YOU'VE BEEN UNDER VERRAT SURVEILLANCE FROM THE MOMENT YOU LANDED.
SO YOU DECIDED TO LET US WALK AROUND AS BAIT, SEE IF ANYONE WOULD BITE.
YES.
AND YOU DIDN'T THINK WE'D SURVIVE THE DAY.
HE WAS RIGHT ABOUT THAT.
I'M SICK AND TIRED OF EVERYONE'S DAMN GAMES. ROYALS, RESISTANCE, COINS, KEYS... IT'S TIME YOU TOLD US EVERYTHING.
BLUTBAD-- BIG BAD WOLF
NO MORE SECRETS. NO MORE LIES.
DON'T MAKE ME HURT THE CAT, MAN.
WHAT DO YOU WANT TO KNOW?
FOR STARTERS... HER NAME.
MAYA. MY NAME IS MAYA.
WELL, MAYA... THANK YOU FOR SAVING OUR LIVES. NOW THAT THAT WE'RE ALL PROPERLY INTRODUCED, WE CAN TALK.

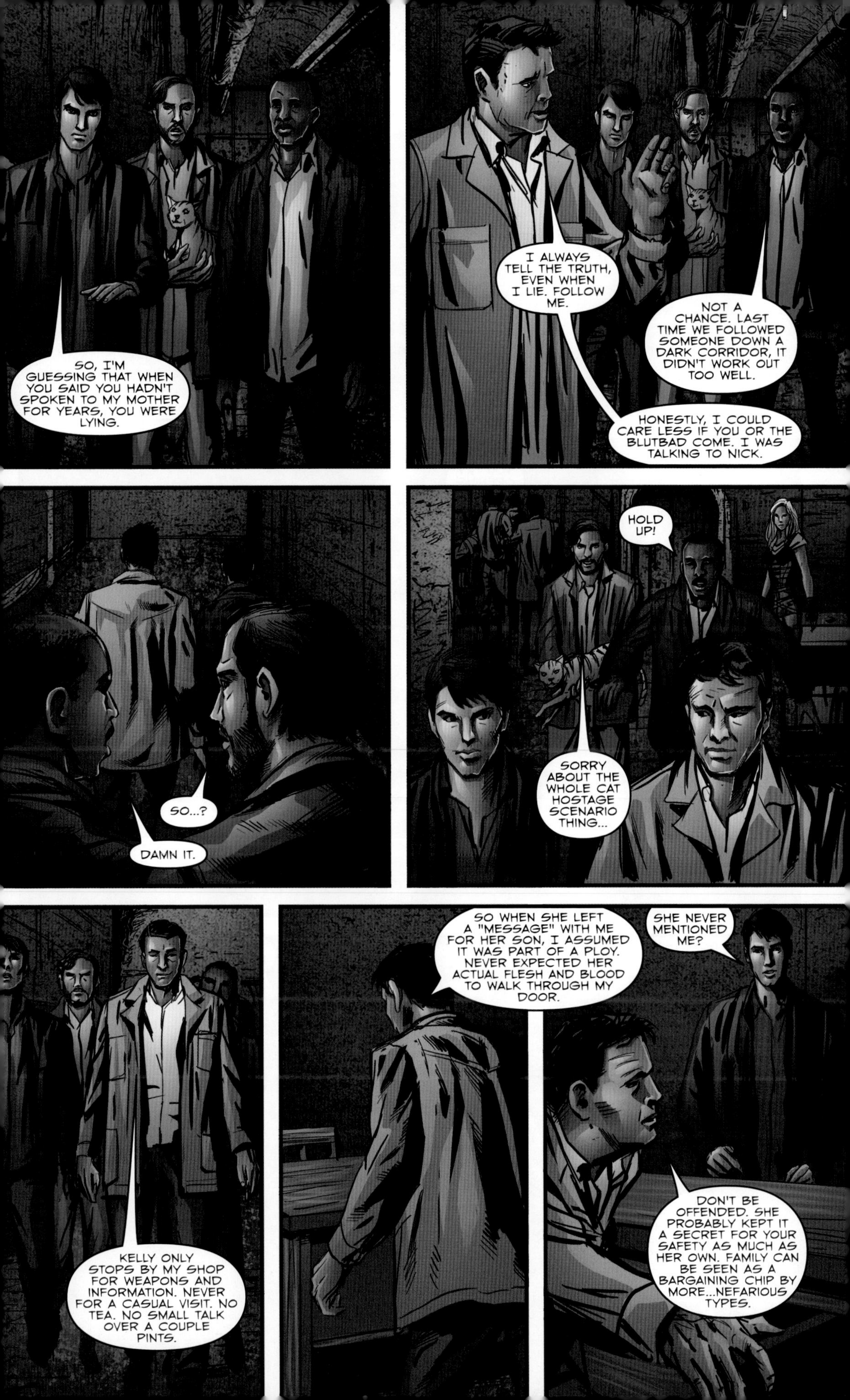

SO, I'M GUESSING THAT WHEN YOU SAID YOU HADN'T SPOKEN TO MY MOTHER FOR YEARS, YOU WERE LYING.
I ALWAYS TELL THE TRUTH, EVEN WHEN I LIE. FOLLOW ME.
NOT A CHANCE. LAST TIME WE FOLLOWED SOMEONE DOWN A DARK CORRIDOR, IT DIDN'T WORK OUT TOO WELL.
HONESTLY, I COULD CARE LESS IF YOU OR THE BLUTBAD COME. I WAS TALKING TO NICK.
SO...?
DAMN IT.
HOLD UP!
SORRY ABOUT THE WHOLE CAT HOSTAGE SCENARIO THING...
KELLY ONLY STOPS BY MY SHOP FOR WEAPONS AND INFORMATION. NEVER FOR A CASUAL VISIT. NO TEA. NO SMALL TALK OVER A COUPLE PINTS.
SO WHEN SHE LEFT A "MESSAGE" WITH ME FOR HER SON, I ASSUMED IT WAS PART OF A PLOY. NEVER EXPECTED HER ACTUAL FLESH AND BLOOD TO WALK THROUGH MY DOOR.
SHE NEVER MENTIONED ME?
DON'T BE OFFENDED. SHE PROBABLY KEPT IT A SECRET FOR YOUR SAFETY AS MUCH AS HER OWN. FAMILY CAN BE SEEN AS A BARGAINING CHIP BY MORE...NEFARIOUS TYPES.

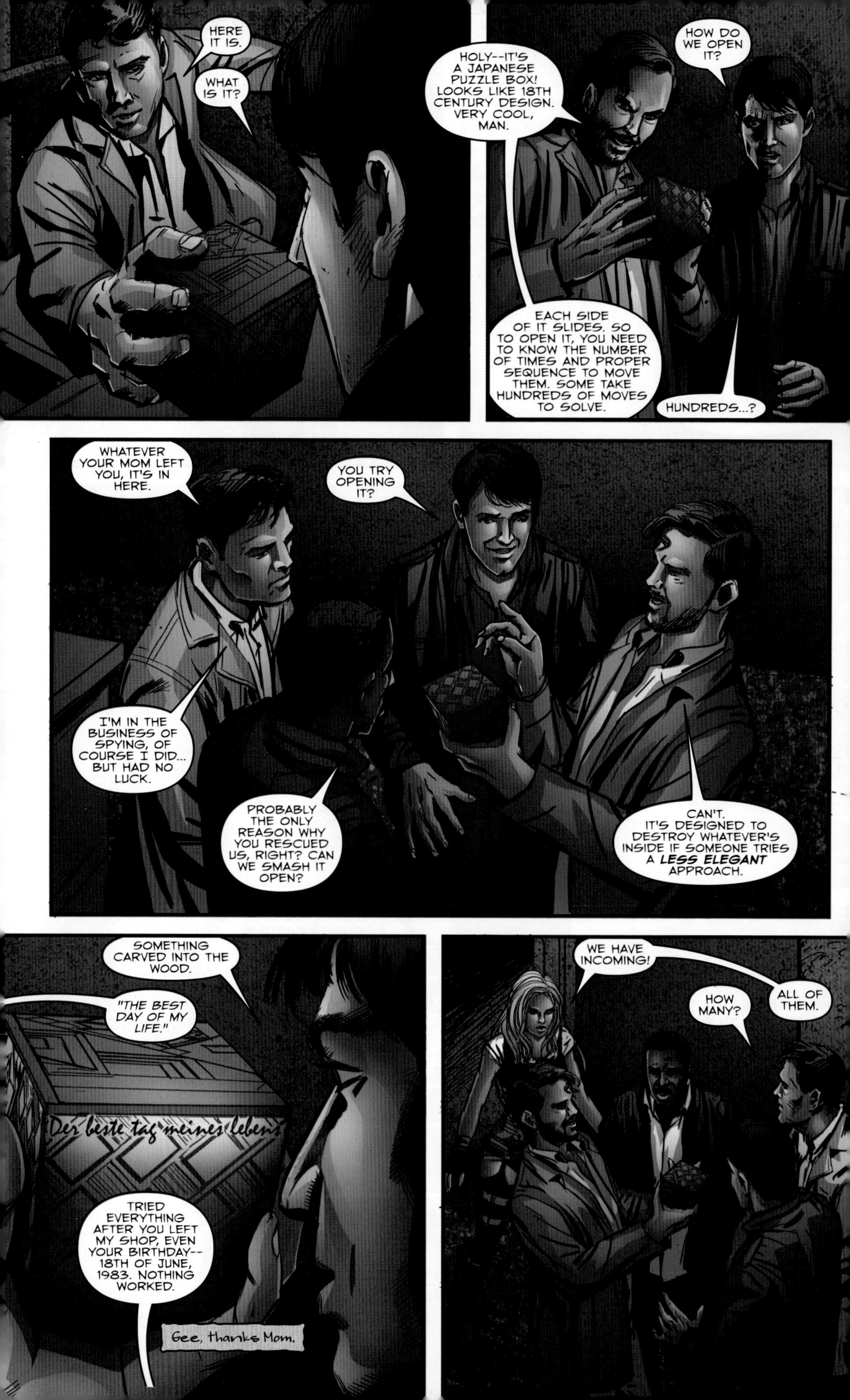
HERE IT IS.
WHAT IS IT?
HOLY--IT'S A JAPANESE PUZZLE BOX! LOOKS LIKE 18TH CENTURY DESIGN. VERY COOL, MAN.
HOW DO WE OPEN IT?
EACH SIDE OF IT SLIDES. SO TO OPEN IT, YOU NEED TO KNOW THE NUMBER OF TIMES AND PROPER SEQUENCE TO MOVE THEM. SOME TAKE HUNDREDS OF MOVES TO SOLVE.
HUNDREDS...?
WHATEVER YOUR MOM LEFT YOU, IT'S IN HERE.
YOU TRY OPENING IT?
I'M IN THE BUSINESS OF SPYING, OF COURSE I DID... BUT HAD NO LUCK.
PROBABLY THE ONLY REASON WHY YOU RESCUED US, RIGHT? CAN WE SMASH IT OPEN?
CAN'T. IT'S DESIGNED TO DESTROY WHATEVER'S INSIDE IF SOMEONE TRIES A ***LESS ELEGANT*** APPROACH.
SOMETHING CARVED INTO THE WOOD.
"THE BEST DAY OF MY LIFE."
Der beste tag meines lebens
TRIED EVERYTHING AFTER YOU LEFT MY SHOP, EVEN YOUR BIRTHDAY-- 18TH OF JUNE, 1983. NOTHING WORKED.
Gee, thanks Mom.
WE HAVE INCOMING!
HOW MANY?
ALL OF THEM.

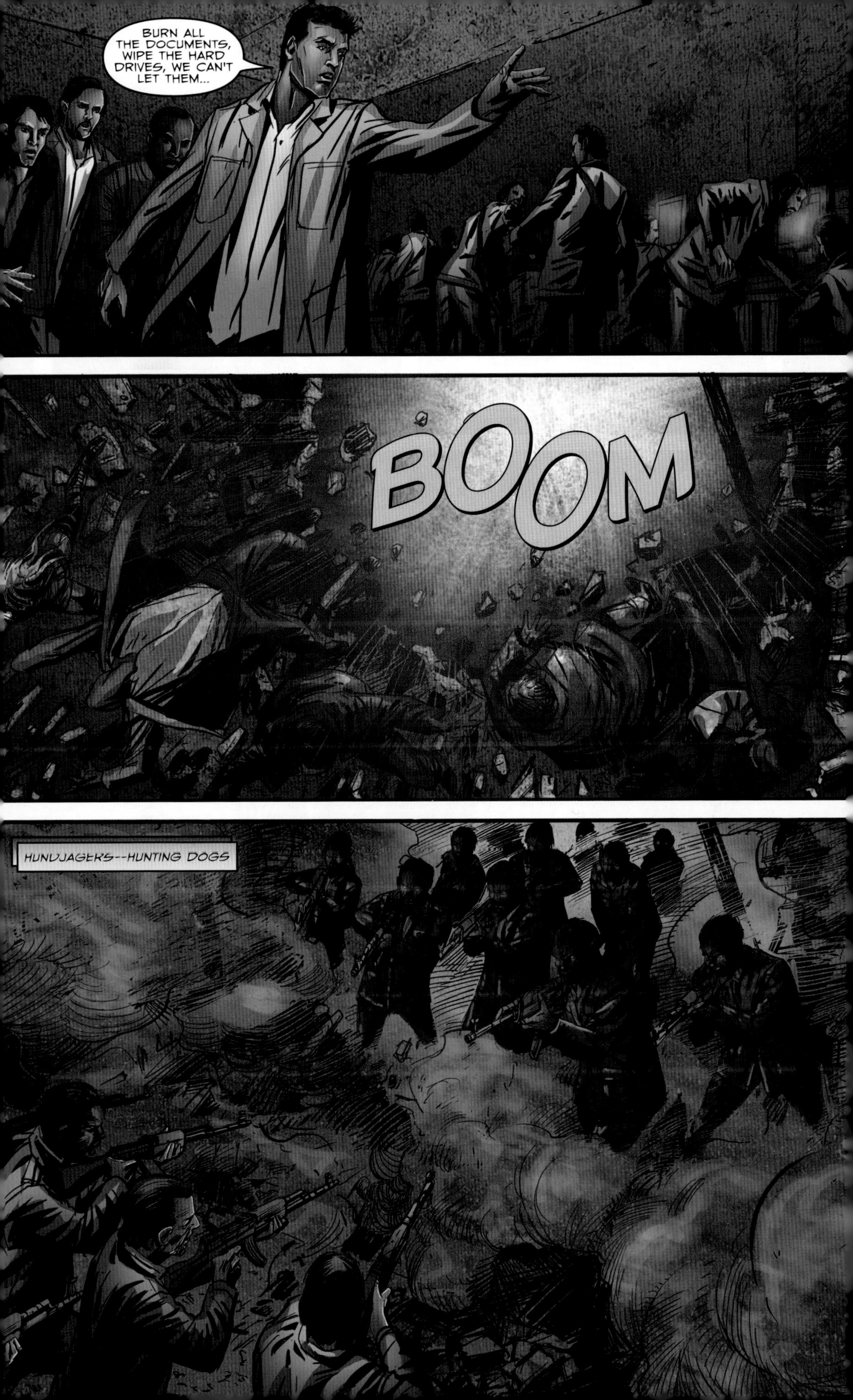
BURN ALL THE DOCUMENTS, WIPE THE HARD DRIVES, WE CAN'T LET THEM...
BOOM
HUNDJAGERS--HUNTING DOGS

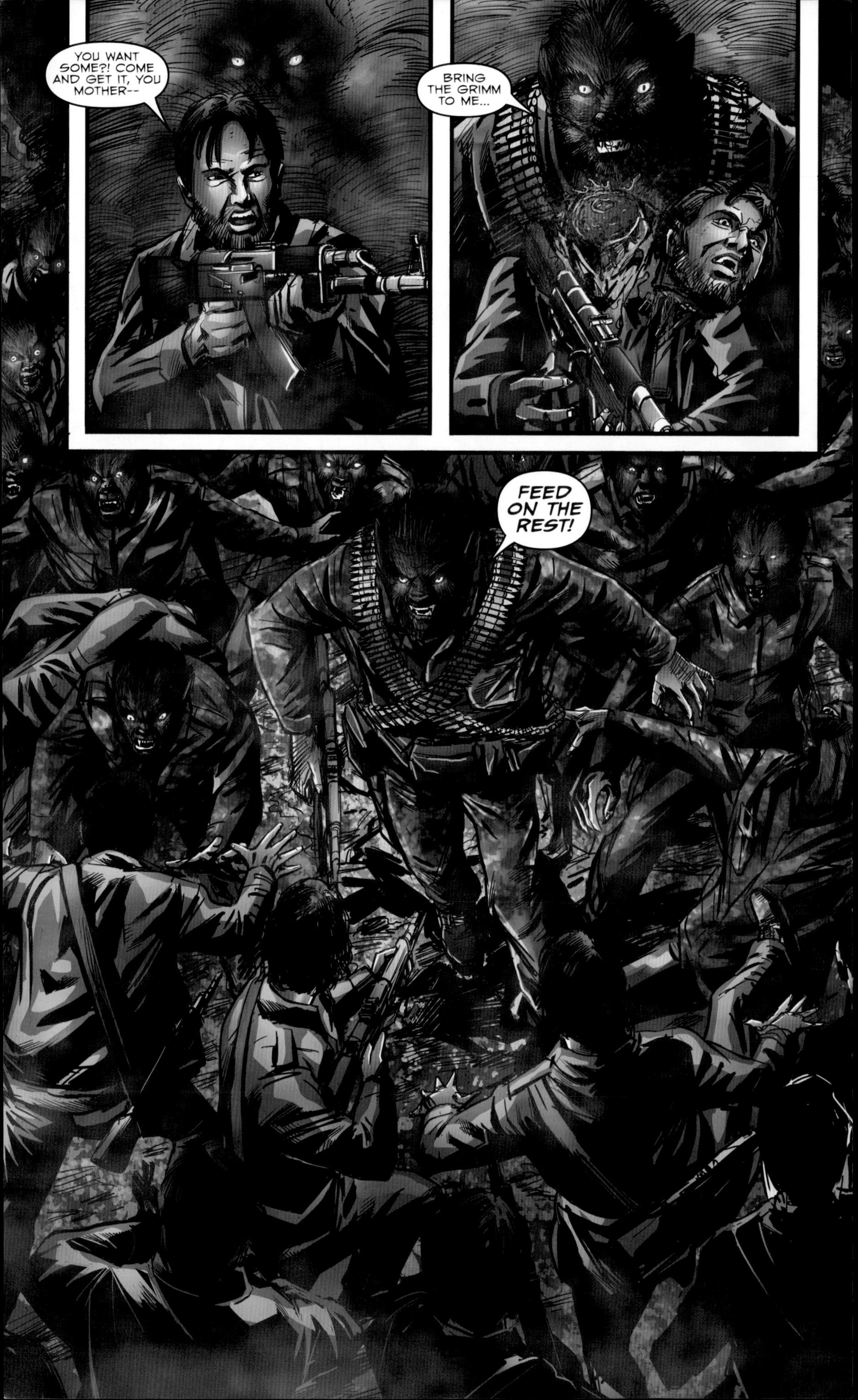
YOU WANT SOME?! COME AND GET IT, YOU MOTHER--
BRING THE GRIMM TO ME...
FEED ON THE REST!

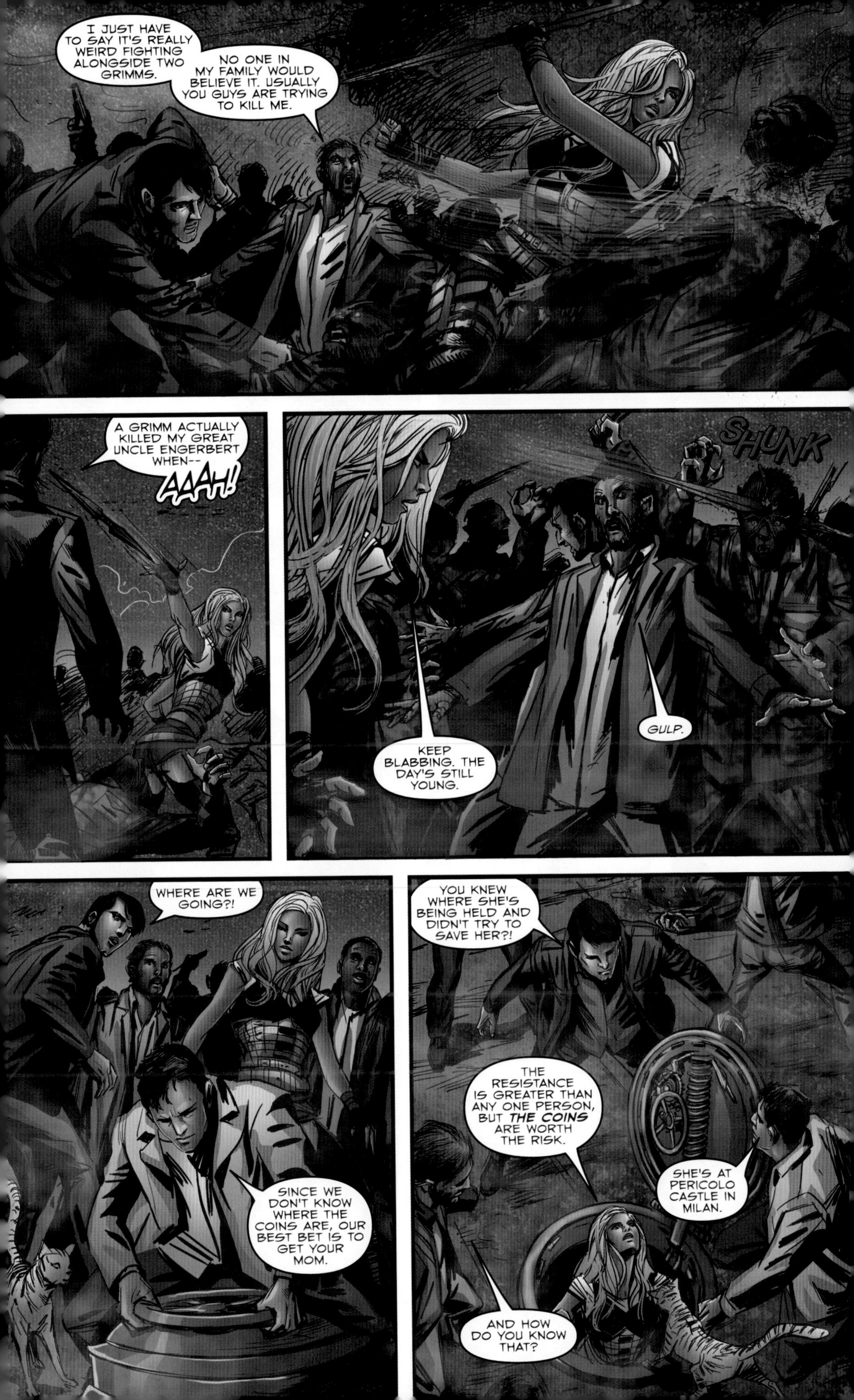
I JUST HAVE TO SAY IT'S REALLY WEIRD FIGHTING ALONGSIDE TWO GRIMMS.
NO ONE IN MY FAMILY WOULD BELIEVE IT. USUALLY YOU GUYS ARE TRYING TO KILL ME.
A GRIMM ACTUALLY KILLED MY GREAT UNCLE ENGERBERT WHEN--
AAAH!
SHUNK
KEEP BLABBING. THE DAY'S STILL YOUNG.
GULP.
WHERE ARE WE GOING?!
SINCE WE DON'T KNOW WHERE THE COINS ARE, OUR BEST BET IS TO GET YOUR MOM.
YOU KNEW WHERE SHE'S BEING HELD AND DIDN'T TRY TO SAVE HER?!
THE RESISTANCE IS GREATER THAN ANY ONE PERSON, BUT THE COINS ARE WORTH THE RISK.
SHE'S AT PERICOLO CASTLE IN MILAN.
AND HOW DO YOU KNOW THAT?

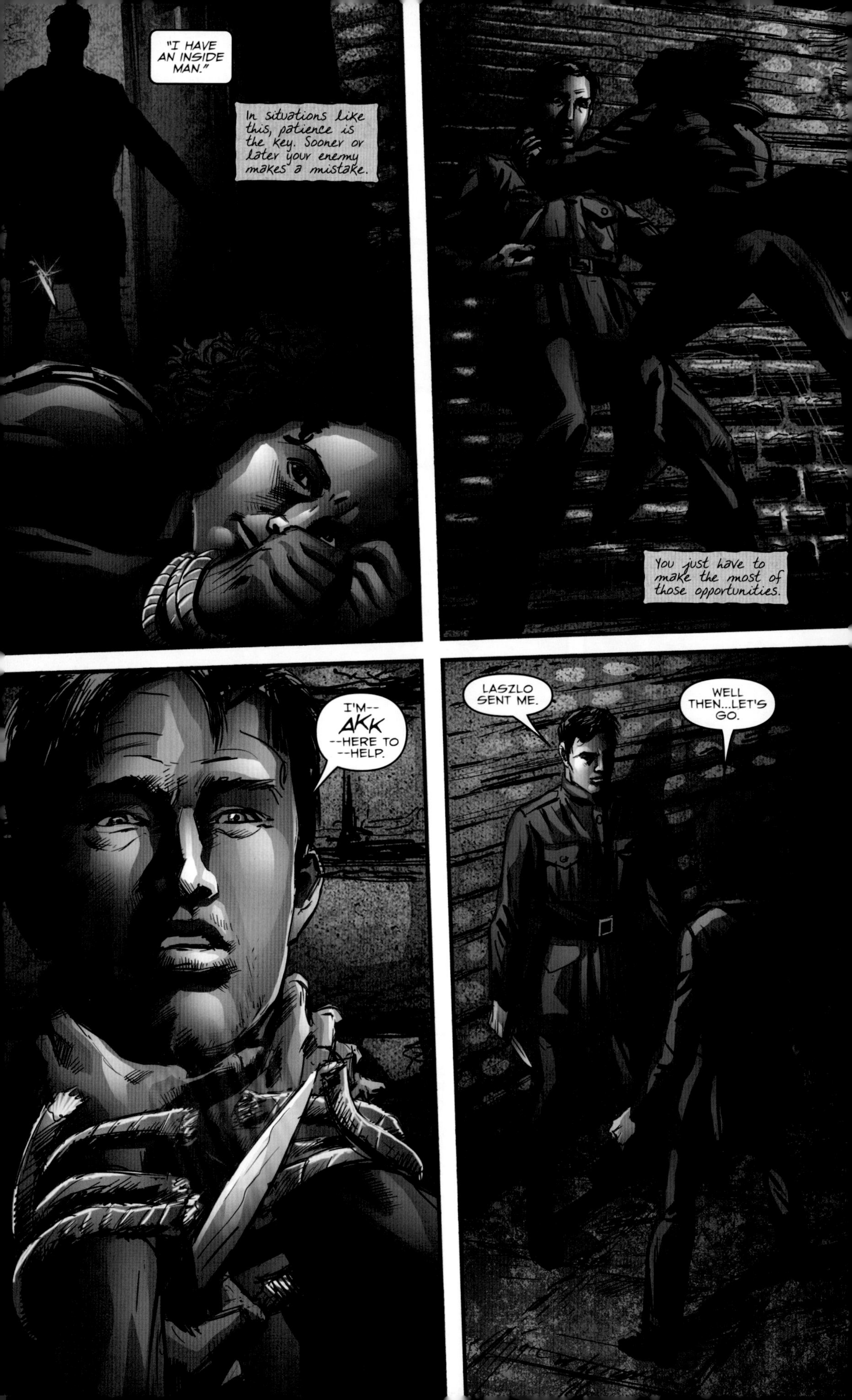
"I HAVE AN INSIDE MAN."
In situations like this, patience is the key. Sooner or later your enemy makes a mistake.
You just have to make the most of those opportunities.
I'M-- AKK --HERE TO --HELP.
LASZLO SENT ME.
WELL THEN...LET'S GO.

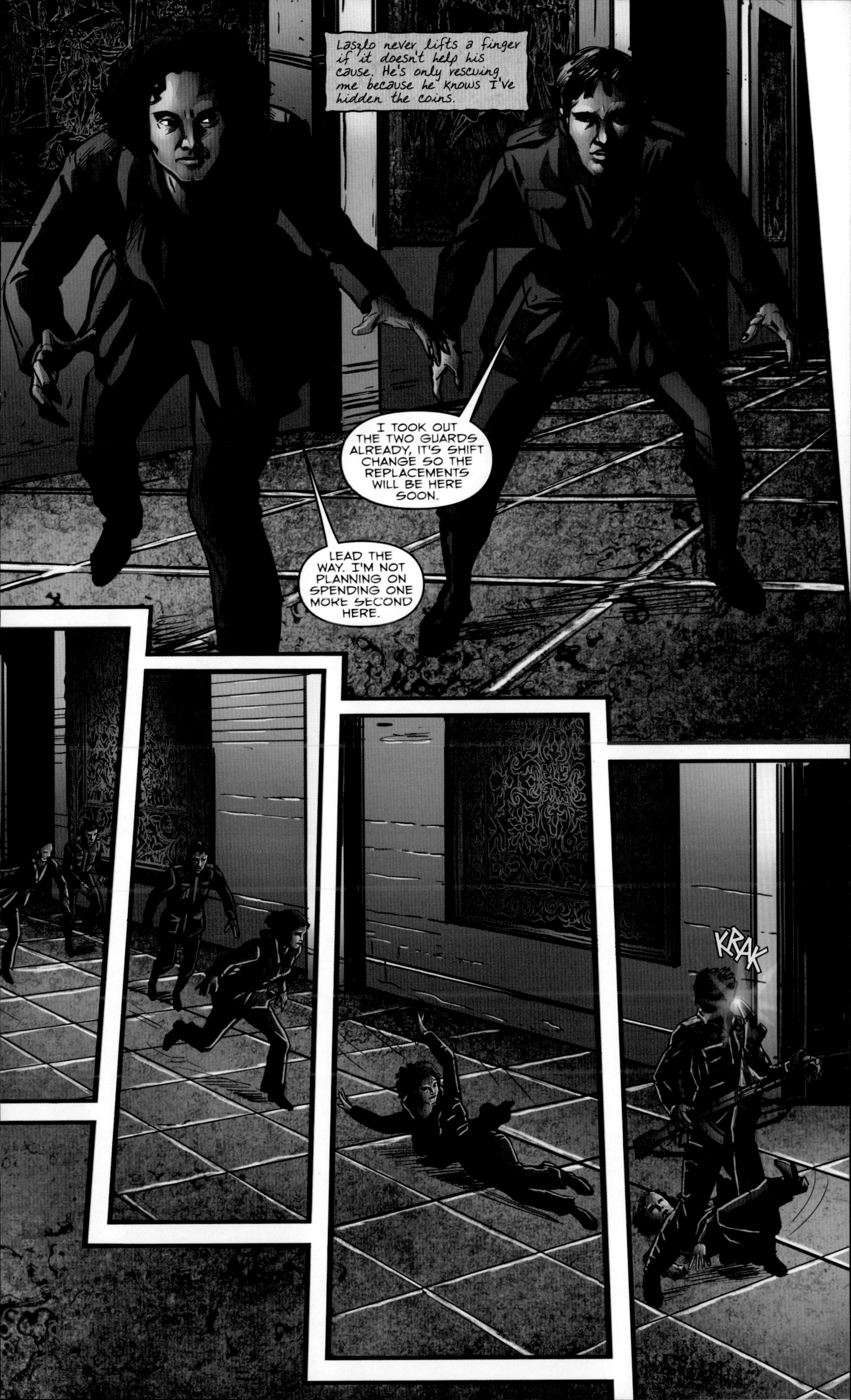
Laszlo never lifts a finger if it doesn't help his cause. He's only rescuing me because he knows I've hidden the coins.
I TOOK OUT THE TWO GUARDS ALREADY, IT'S SHIFT CHANGE SO THE REPLACEMENTS WILL BE HERE SOON.
LEAD THE WAY. I'M NOT PLANNING ON SPENDING ONE MORE SECOND HERE.
KRAK

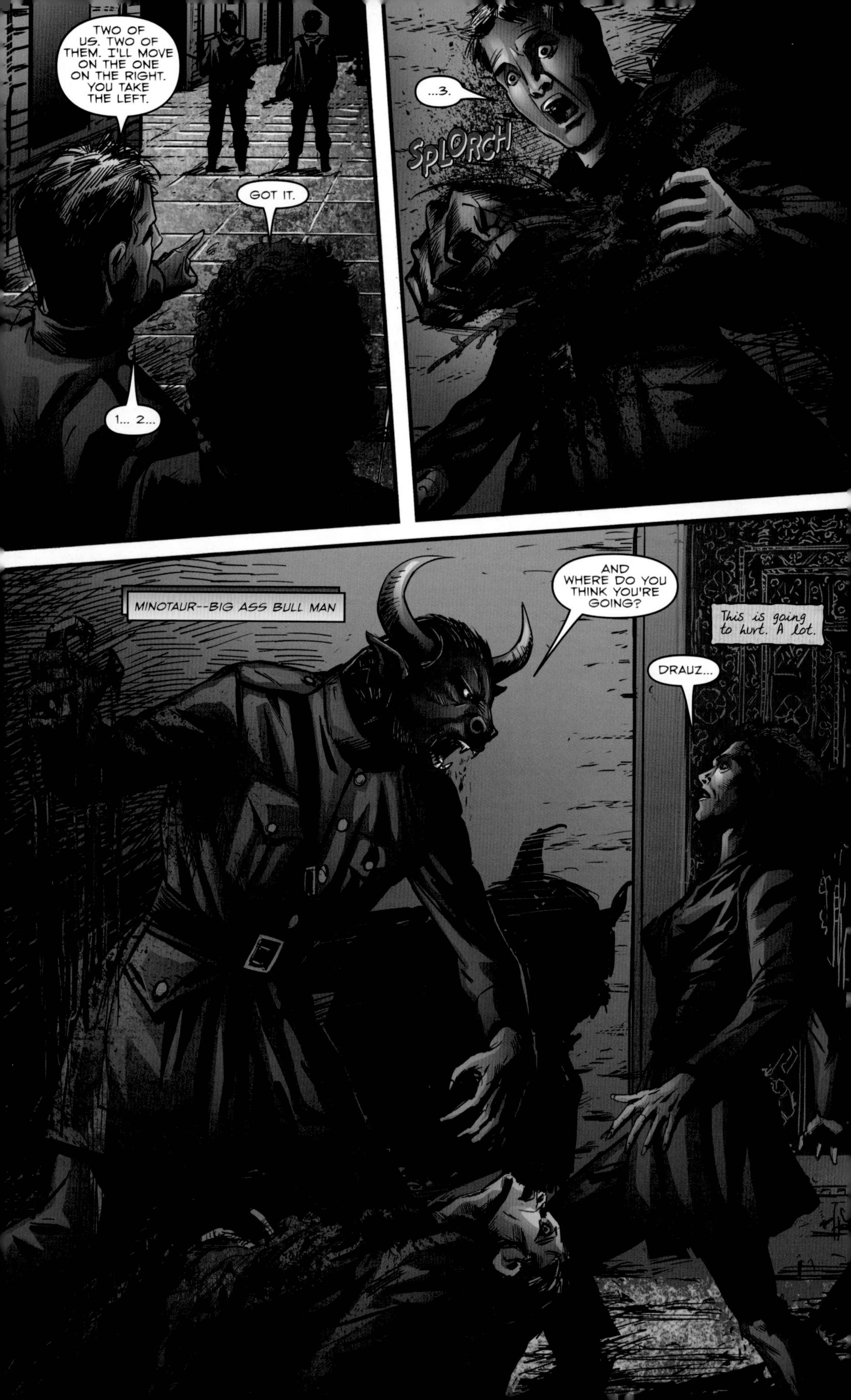
TWO OF US. TWO OF THEM. I'LL MOVE ON THE ONE ON THE RIGHT. YOU TAKE THE LEFT.
GOT IT.
1... 2...
...3.
SPLORCH
MINOTAUR--BIG ASS BULL MAN
AND WHERE DO YOU THINK YOU'RE GOING?
This is going to hurt. A lot.
DRAUZ...

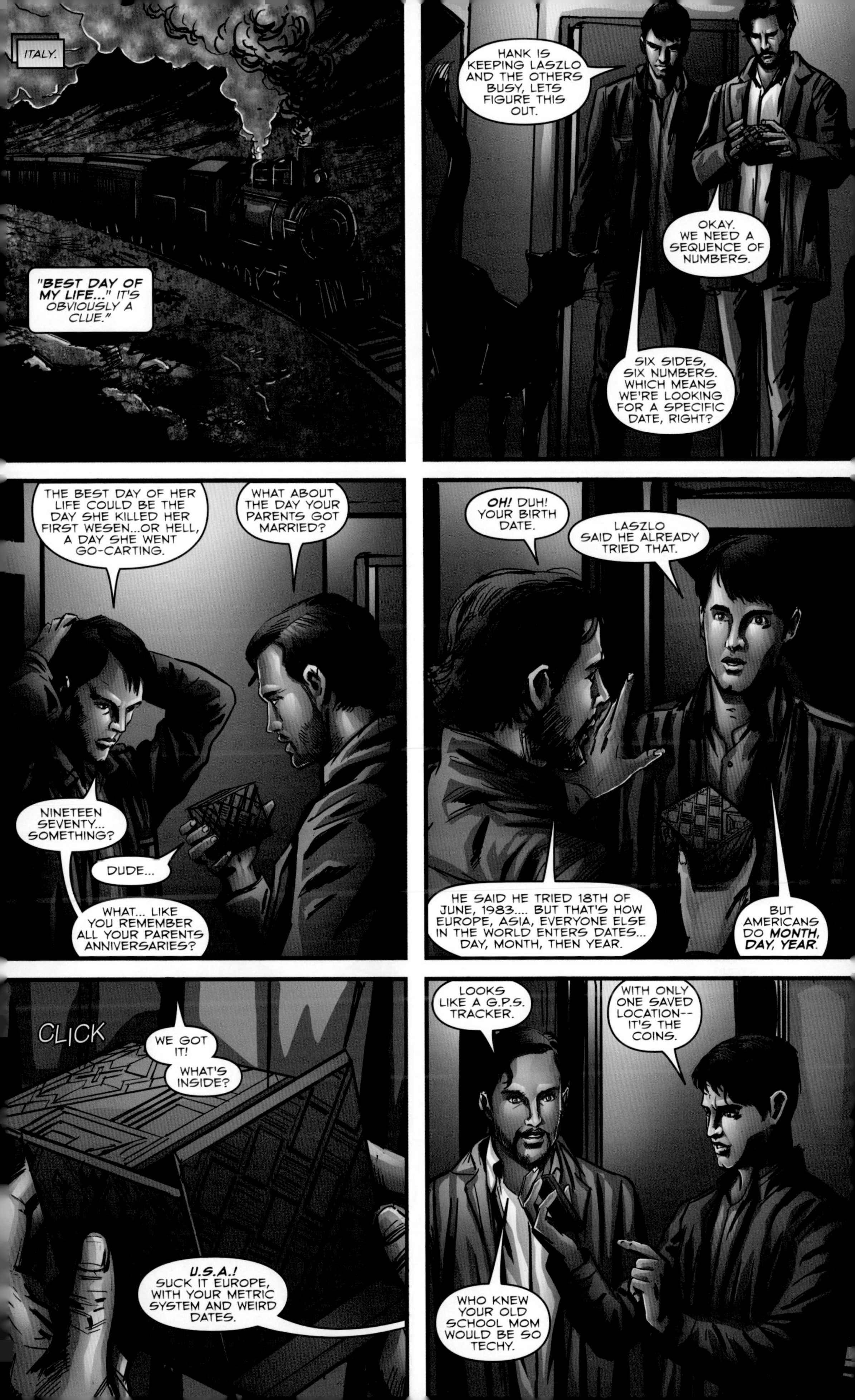
ITALY.
"BEST DAY OF MY LIFE..." IT'S OBVIOUSLY A CLUE."
HANK IS KEEPING LASZLO AND THE OTHERS BUSY, LETS FIGURE THIS OUT.
OKAY. WE NEED A SEQUENCE OF NUMBERS.
SIX SIDES, SIX NUMBERS. WHICH MEANS WE'RE LOOKING FOR A SPECIFIC DATE, RIGHT?
THE BEST DAY OF HER LIFE COULD BE THE DAY SHE KILLED HER FIRST WESEN...OR HELL, A DAY SHE WENT GO-CARTING.
WHAT ABOUT THE DAY YOUR PARENTS GOT MARRIED?
NINETEEN SEVENTY... SOMETHING?
DUDE...
WHAT... LIKE YOU REMEMBER ALL YOUR PARENTS ANNIVERSARIES?
OH! DUH! YOUR BIRTH DATE.
LASZLO SAID HE ALREADY TRIED THAT.
HE SAID HE TRIED 18TH OF JUNE, 1983.... BUT THAT'S HOW EUROPE, ASIA, EVERYONE ELSE IN THE WORLD ENTERS DATES... DAY, MONTH, THEN YEAR.
BUT AMERICANS DO MONTH, DAY, YEAR.
CLICK
WE GOT IT!
WHAT'S INSIDE?
U.S.A.! SUCK IT EUROPE, WITH YOUR METRIC SYSTEM AND WEIRD DATES.
LOOKS LIKE A G.P.S. TRACKER.
WITH ONLY ONE SAVED LOCATION-- IT'S THE COINS.
WHO KNEW YOUR OLD SCHOOL MOM WOULD BE SO TECHY.

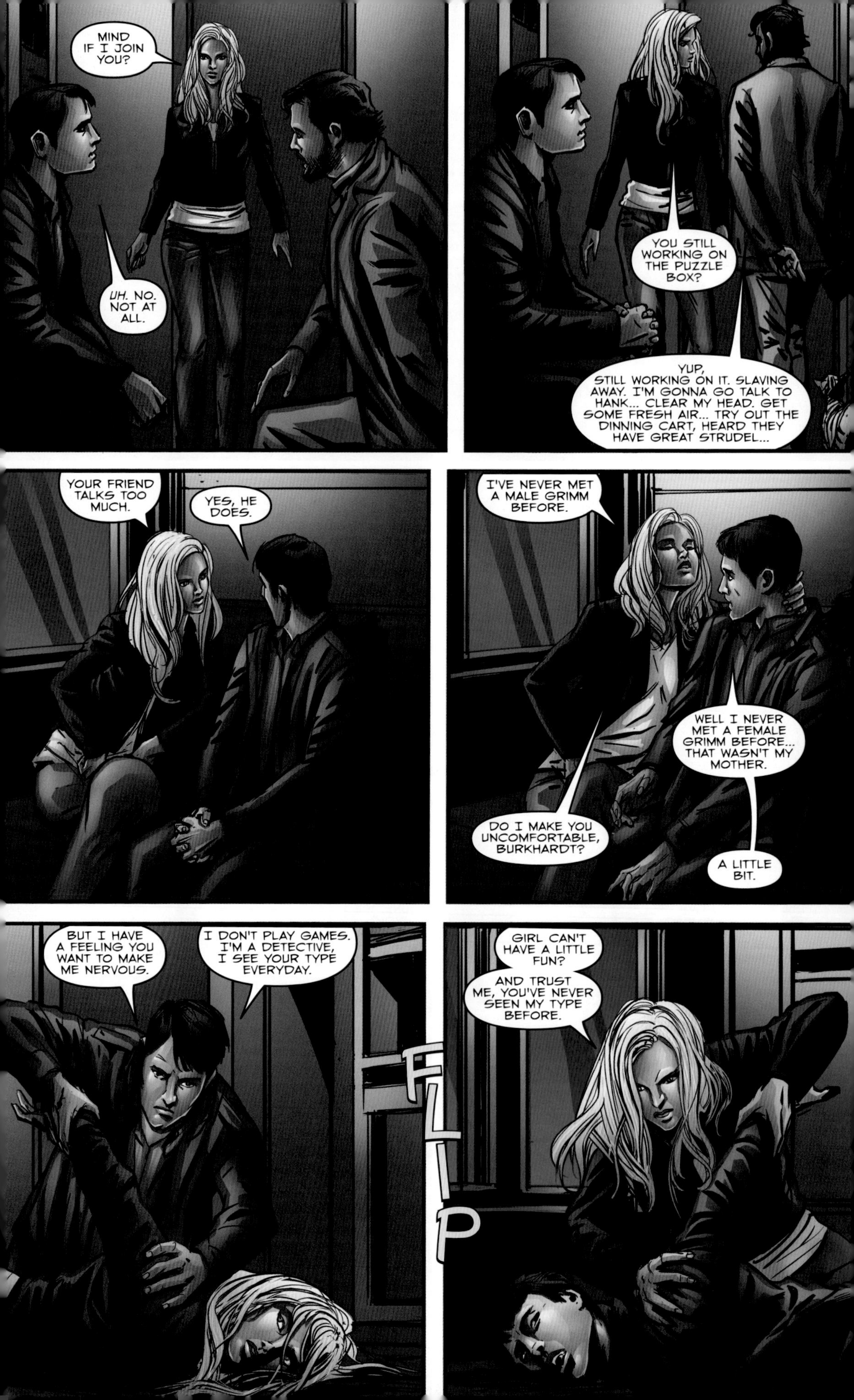
MIND IF I JOIN YOU?
UH. NO. NOT AT ALL.
YOU STILL WORKING ON THE PUZZLE BOX?
YUP, STILL WORKING ON IT. SLAVING AWAY. I'M GONNA GO TALK TO HANK... CLEAR MY HEAD. GET SOME FRESH AIR... TRY OUT THE DINNING CART, HEARD THEY HAVE GREAT STRUDEL...
YOUR FRIEND TALKS TOO MUCH.
YES, HE DOES.
I'VE NEVER MET A MALE GRIMM BEFORE.
WELL I NEVER MET A FEMALE GRIMM BEFORE... THAT WASN'T MY MOTHER.
DO I MAKE YOU UNCOMFORTABLE, BURKHARDT?
A LITTLE BIT.
BUT I HAVE A FEELING YOU WANT TO MAKE ME NERVOUS.
I DON'T PLAY GAMES. I'M A DETECTIVE, I SEE YOUR TYPE EVERYDAY.
FLIP
GIRL CAN'T HAVE A LITTLE FUN?
AND TRUST ME, YOU'VE NEVER SEEN MY TYPE BEFORE.

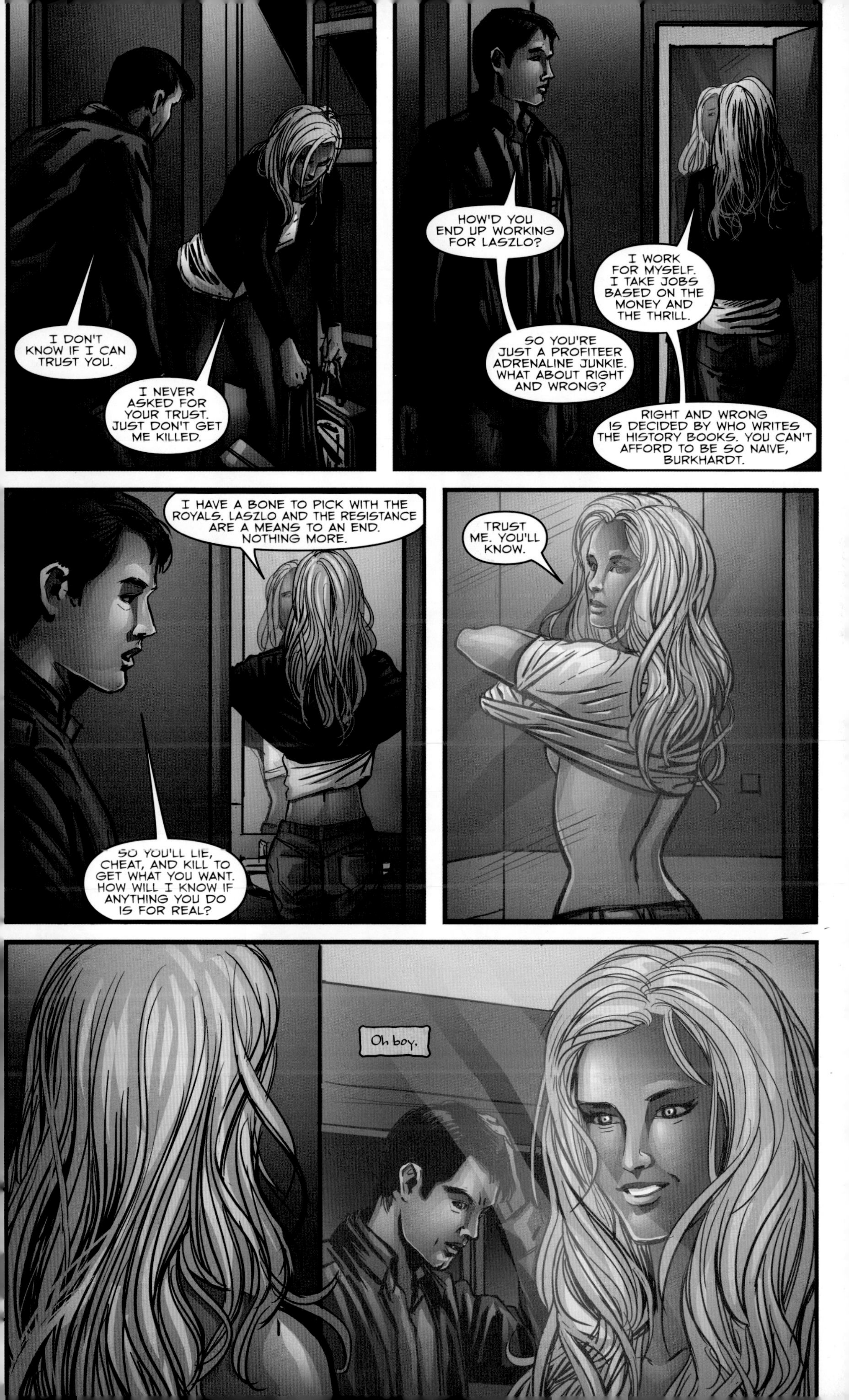
I DON'T KNOW IF I CAN TRUST YOU.
I NEVER ASKED FOR YOUR TRUST. JUST DON'T GET ME KILLED.
HOW'D YOU END UP WORKING FOR LASZLO?
I WORK FOR MYSELF. I TAKE JOBS BASED ON THE MONEY AND THE THRILL.
SO YOU'RE JUST A PROFITEER ADRENALINE JUNKIE. WHAT ABOUT RIGHT AND WRONG?
RIGHT AND WRONG IS DECIDED BY WHO WRITES THE HISTORY BOOKS. YOU CAN'T AFFORD TO BE SO NAIVE, BURKHARDT.
I HAVE A BONE TO PICK WITH THE ROYALS. LASZLO AND THE RESISTANCE ARE A MEANS TO AN END. NOTHING MORE.
SO YOU'LL LIE, CHEAT, AND KILL TO GET WHAT YOU WANT. HOW WILL I KNOW IF ANYTHING YOU DO IS FOR REAL?
TRUST ME. YOU'LL KNOW.
Oh boy.

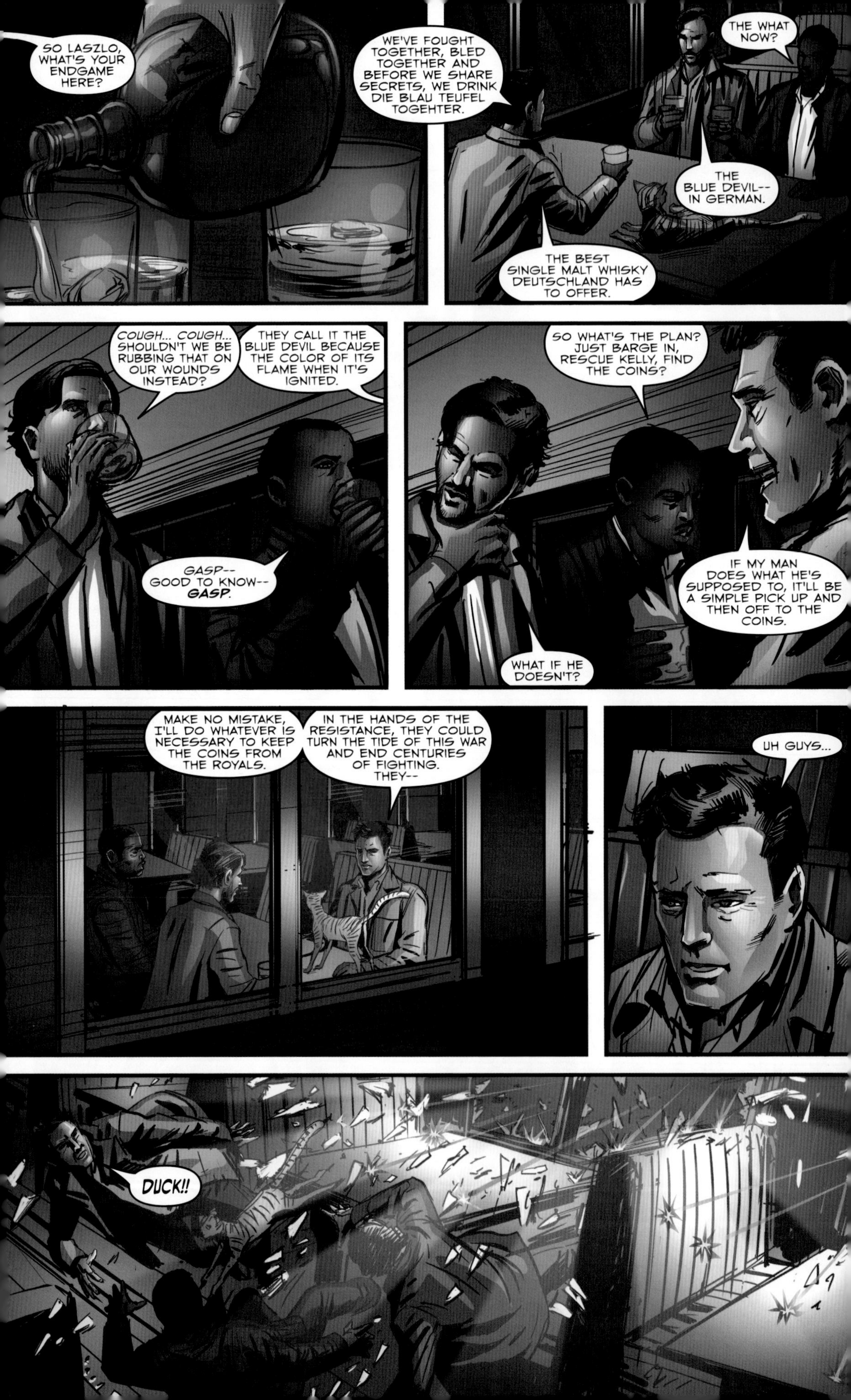
SO LASZLO, WHAT'S YOUR ENDGAME HERE?
WE'VE FOUGHT TOGETHER, BLED TOGETHER AND BEFORE WE SHARE SECRETS, WE DRINK DIE BLAU TEUFEL TOGEHTER.
THE WHAT NOW?
THE BLUE DEVIL-- IN GERMAN.
THE BEST SINGLE MALT WHISKY DEUTSCHLAND HAS TO OFFER.
COUGH... COUGH... SHOULDN'T WE BE RUBBING THAT ON OUR WOUNDS INSTEAD?
THEY CALL IT THE BLUE DEVIL BECAUSE THE COLOR OF ITS FLAME WHEN IT'S IGNITED.
GASP-- GOOD TO KNOW-- GASP.
SO WHAT'S THE PLAN? JUST BARGE IN, RESCUE KELLY, FIND THE COINS?
IF MY MAN DOES WHAT HE'S SUPPOSED TO, IT'LL BE A SIMPLE PICK UP AND THEN OFF TO THE COINS.
WHAT IF HE DOESN'T?
MAKE NO MISTAKE, I'LL DO WHATEVER IS NECESSARY TO KEEP THE COINS FROM THE ROYALS.
IN THE HANDS OF THE RESISTANCE, THEY COULD TURN THE TIDE OF THIS WAR AND END CENTURIES OF FIGHTING. THEY--
UH GUYS...
DUCK!!

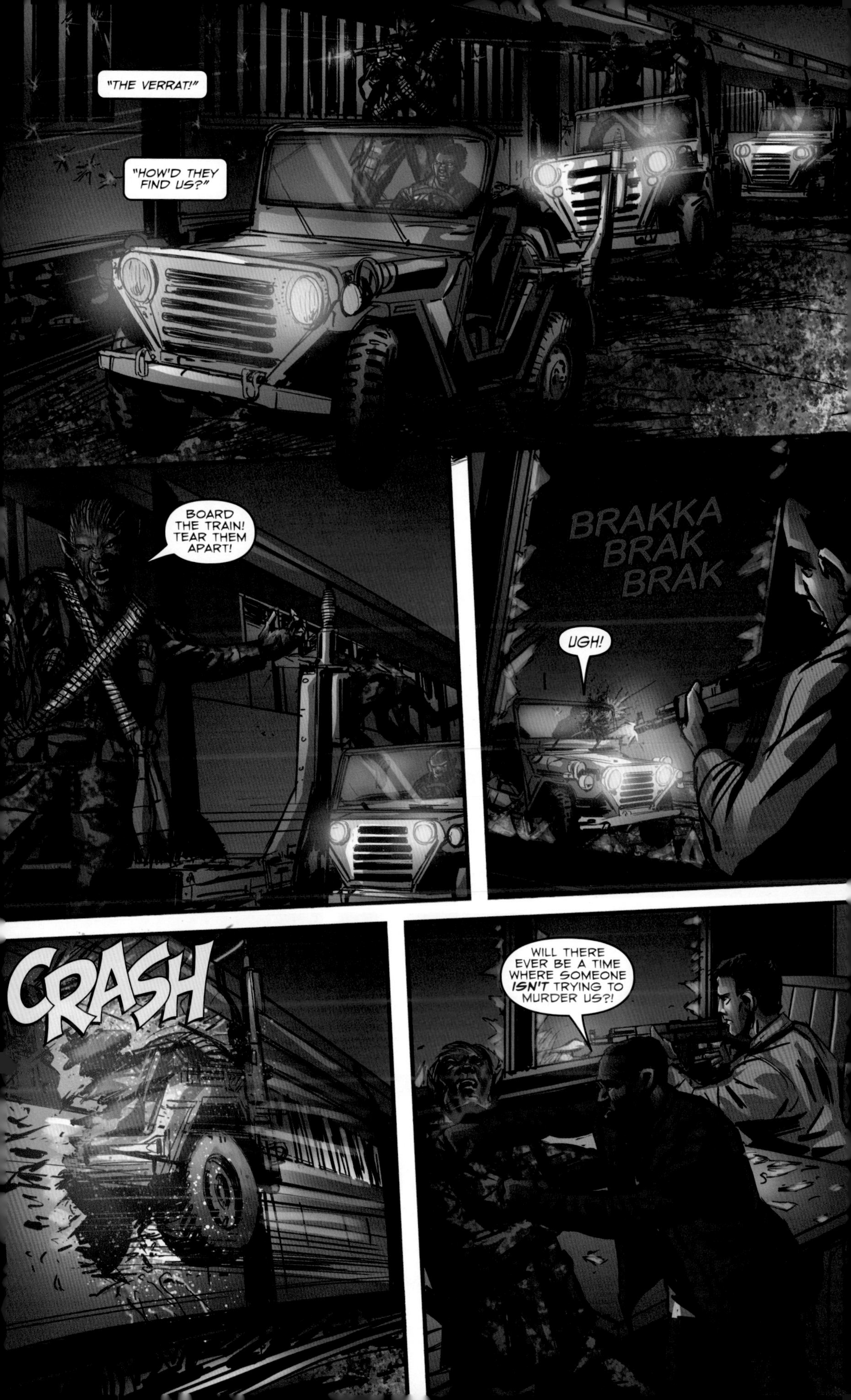
"THE VERRAT!"
"HOW'D THEY FIND US?"
BOARD THE TRAIN! TEAR THEM APART!
BRAKKA BRAK BRAK
UGH!
CRASH
WILL THERE EVER BE A TIME WHERE SOMEONE ISN'T TRYING TO MURDER US?!

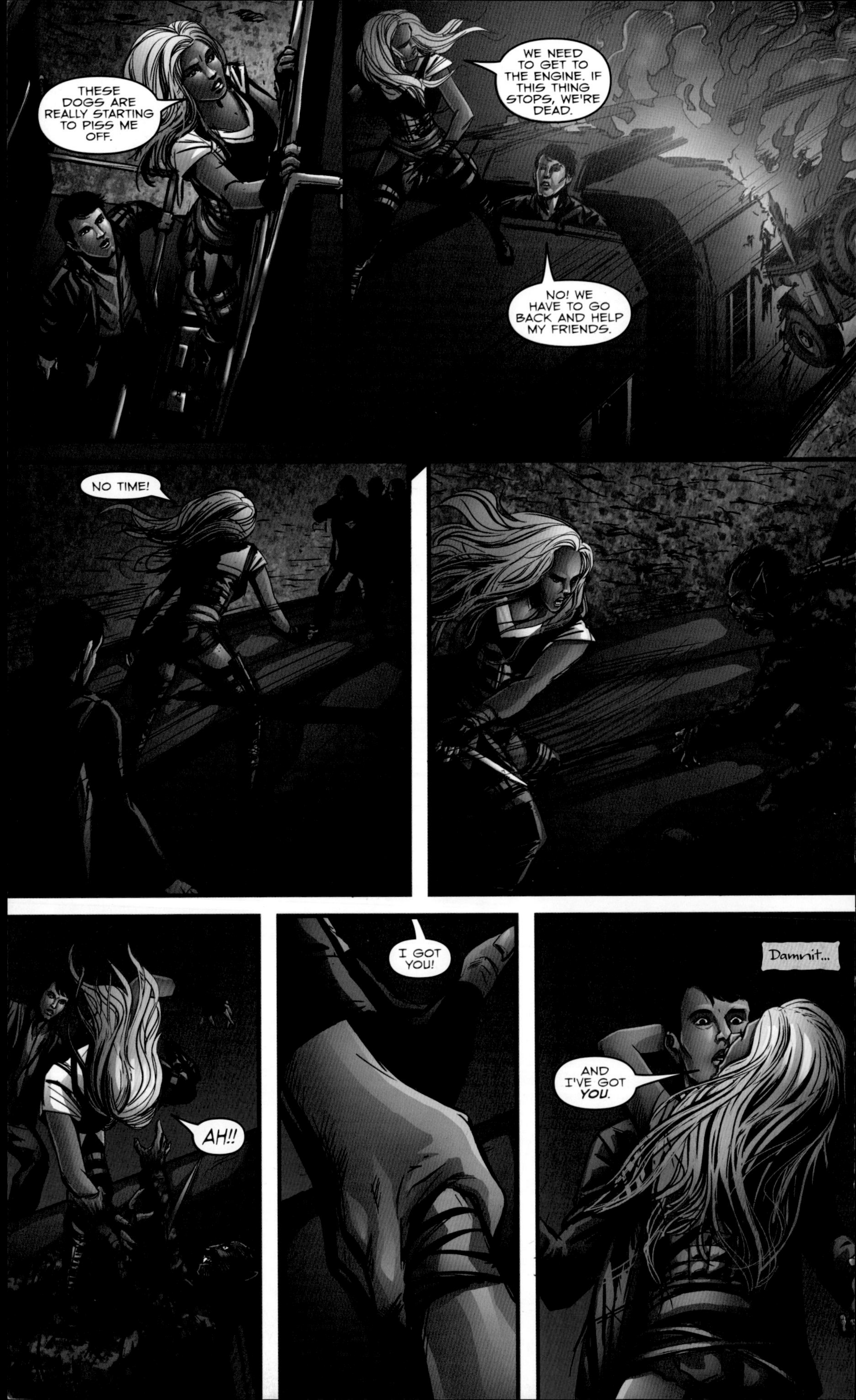
THESE DOGS ARE REALLY STARTING TO PISS ME OFF.
WE NEED TO GET TO THE ENGINE. IF THIS THING STOPS, WE'RE DEAD.
NO! WE HAVE TO GO BACK AND HELP MY FRIENDS.
NO TIME!
AH!!
I GOT YOU!
Damnit...
AND I'VE GOT YOU.

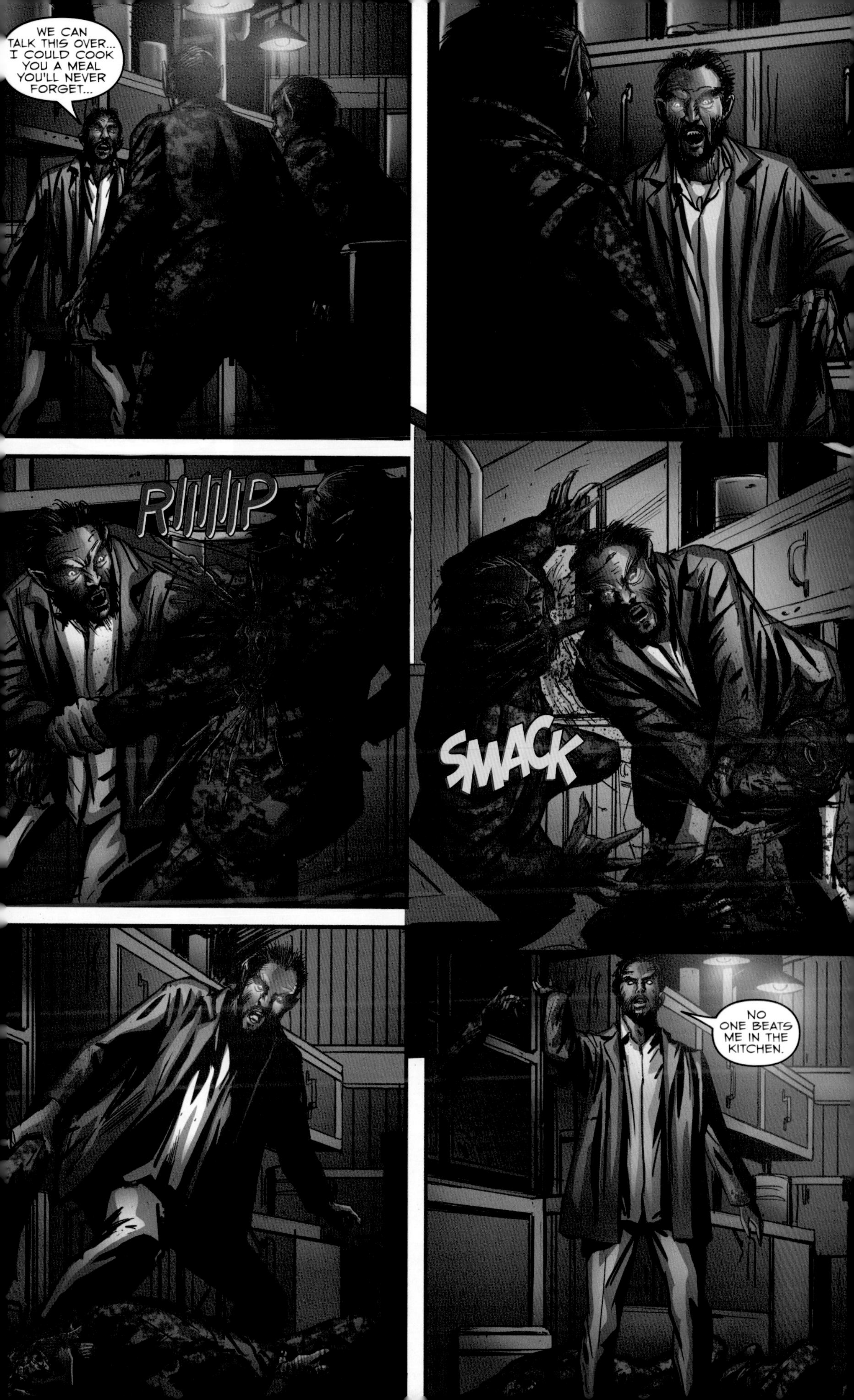
WE CAN TALK THIS OVER... I COULD COOK YOU A MEAL YOU'LL NEVER FORGET...
RIIIIP
SMACK
NO ONE BEATS ME IN THE KITCHEN.

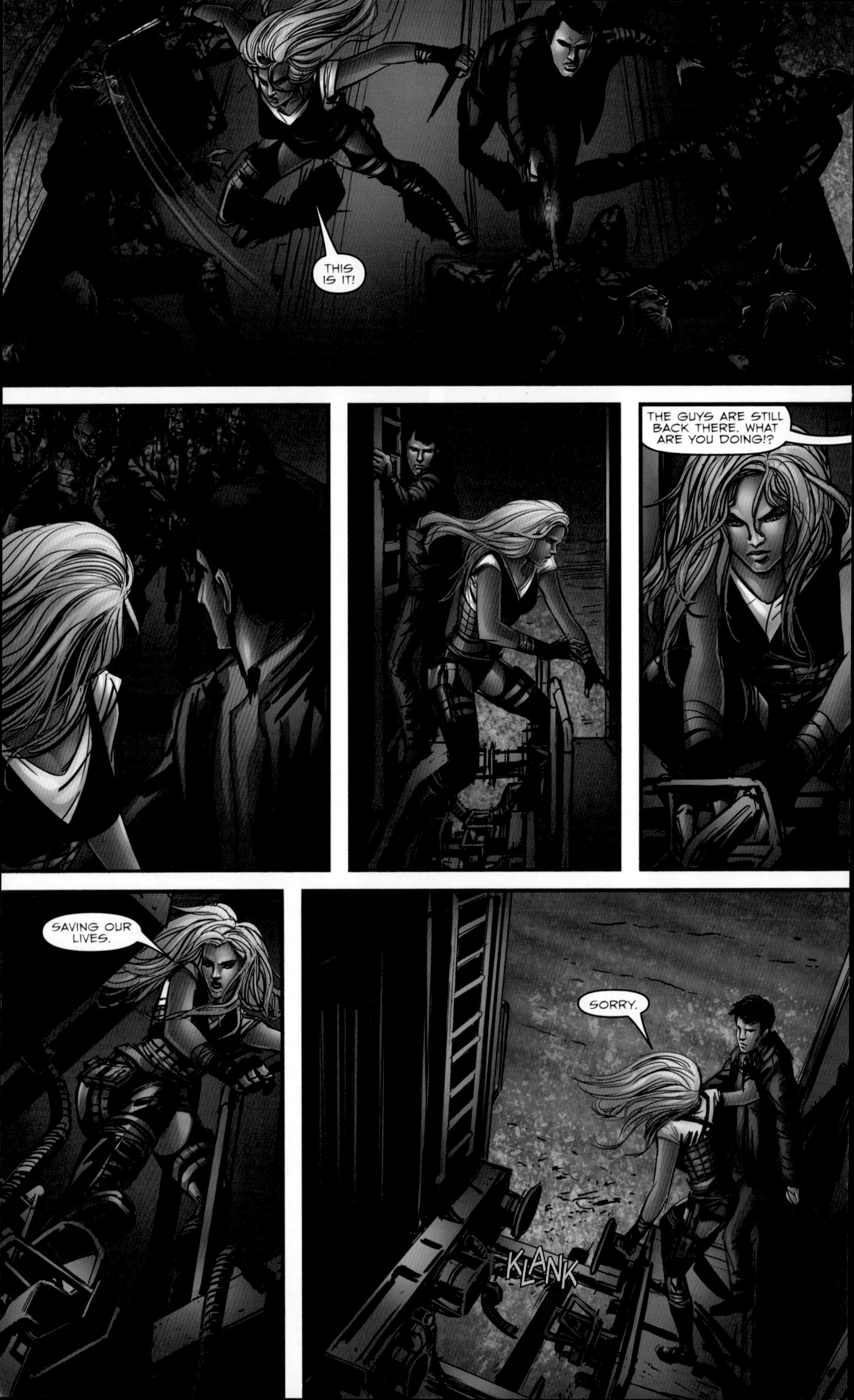
THIS IS IT!
THE GUYS ARE STILL BACK THERE. WHAT ARE YOU DOING!?
SAVING OUR LIVES.
SORRY.
KLANK

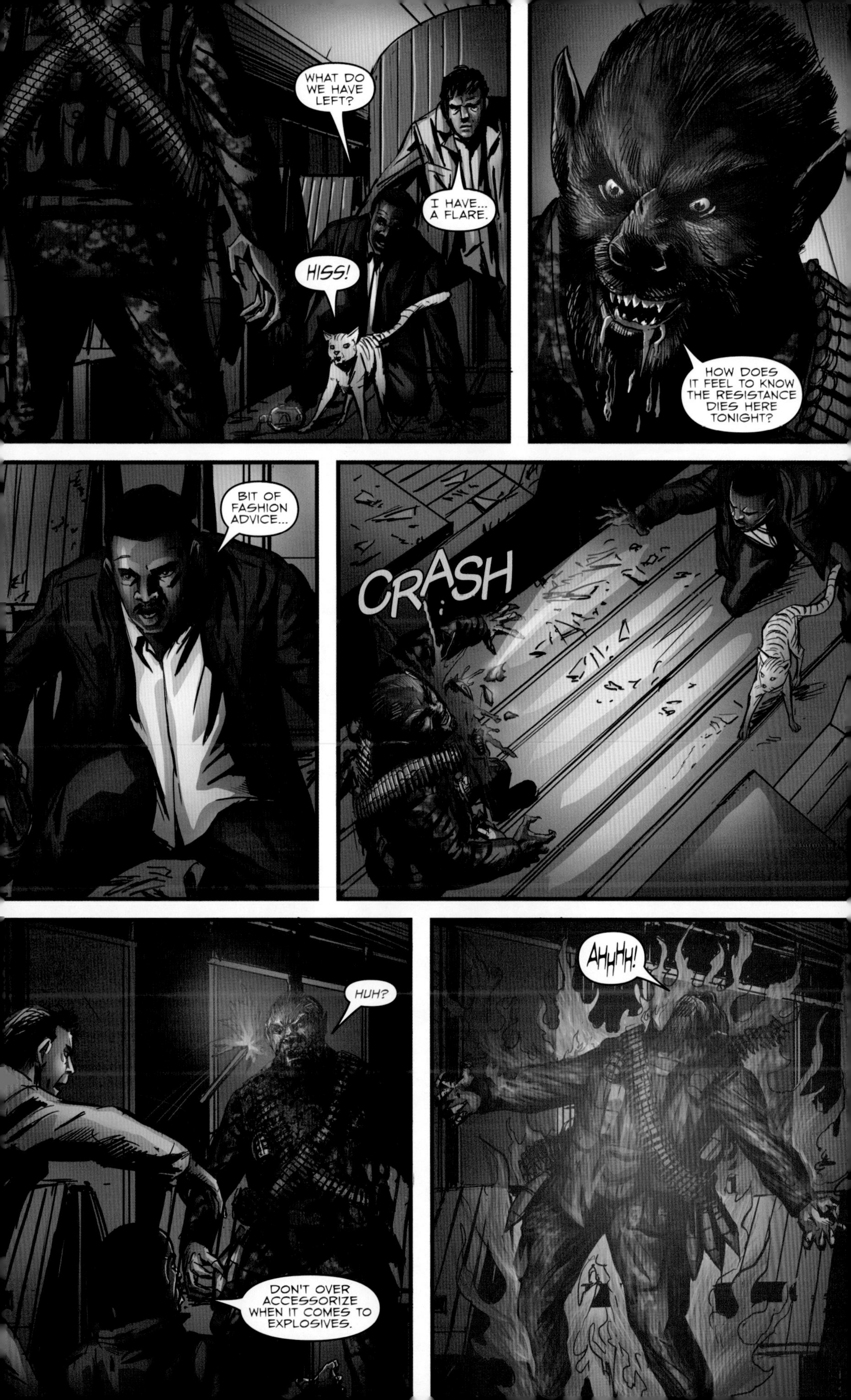
WHAT DO WE HAVE LEFT?
I HAVE... A FLARE.
HISS!
HOW DOES IT FEEL TO KNOW THE RESISTANCE DIES HERE TONIGHT?
BIT OF FASHION ADVICE...
CRASH
HUH?
DON'T OVER ACCESSORIZE WHEN IT COMES TO EXPLOSIVES.
AHHHH!

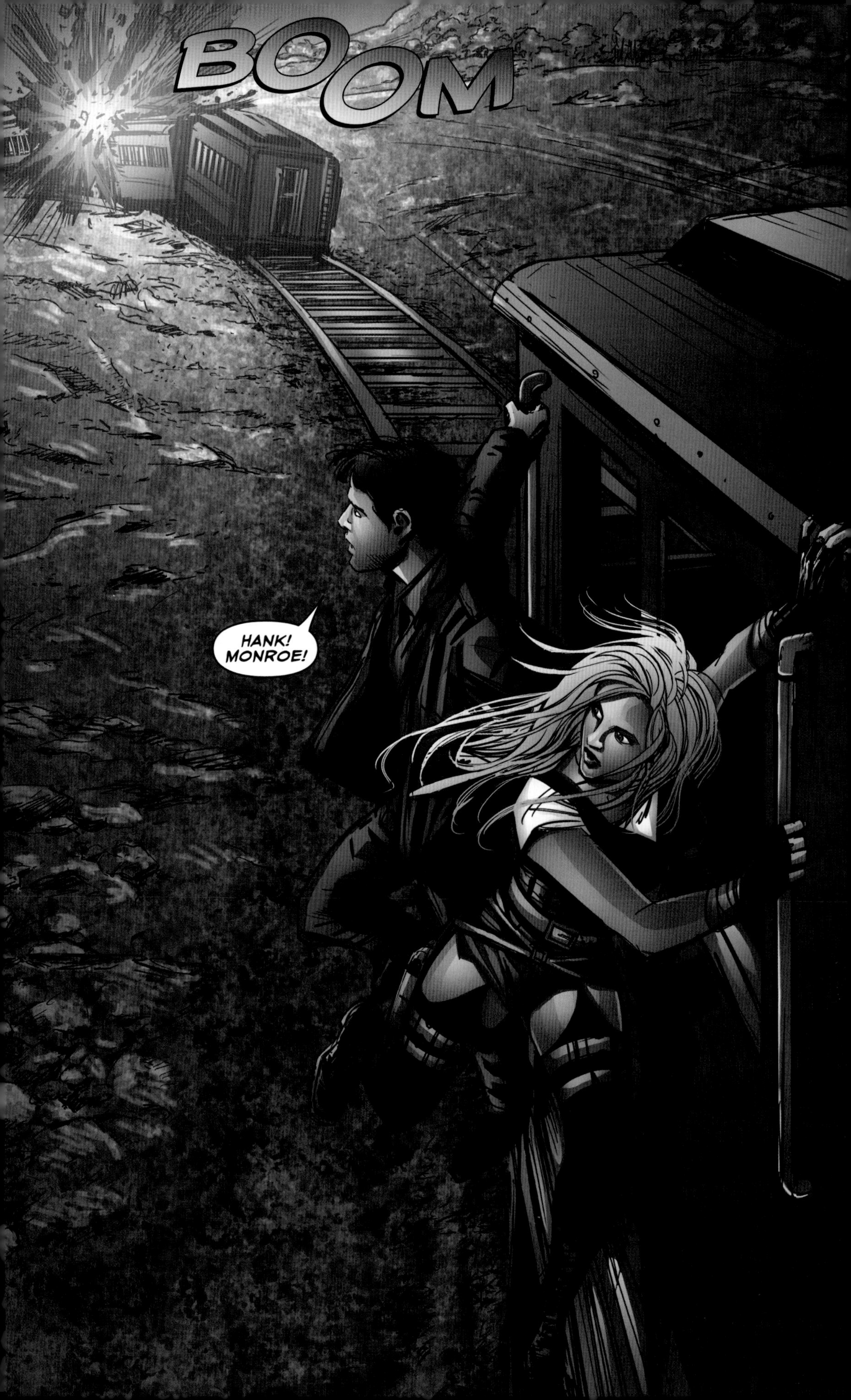
BOOM
HANK! MONROE!

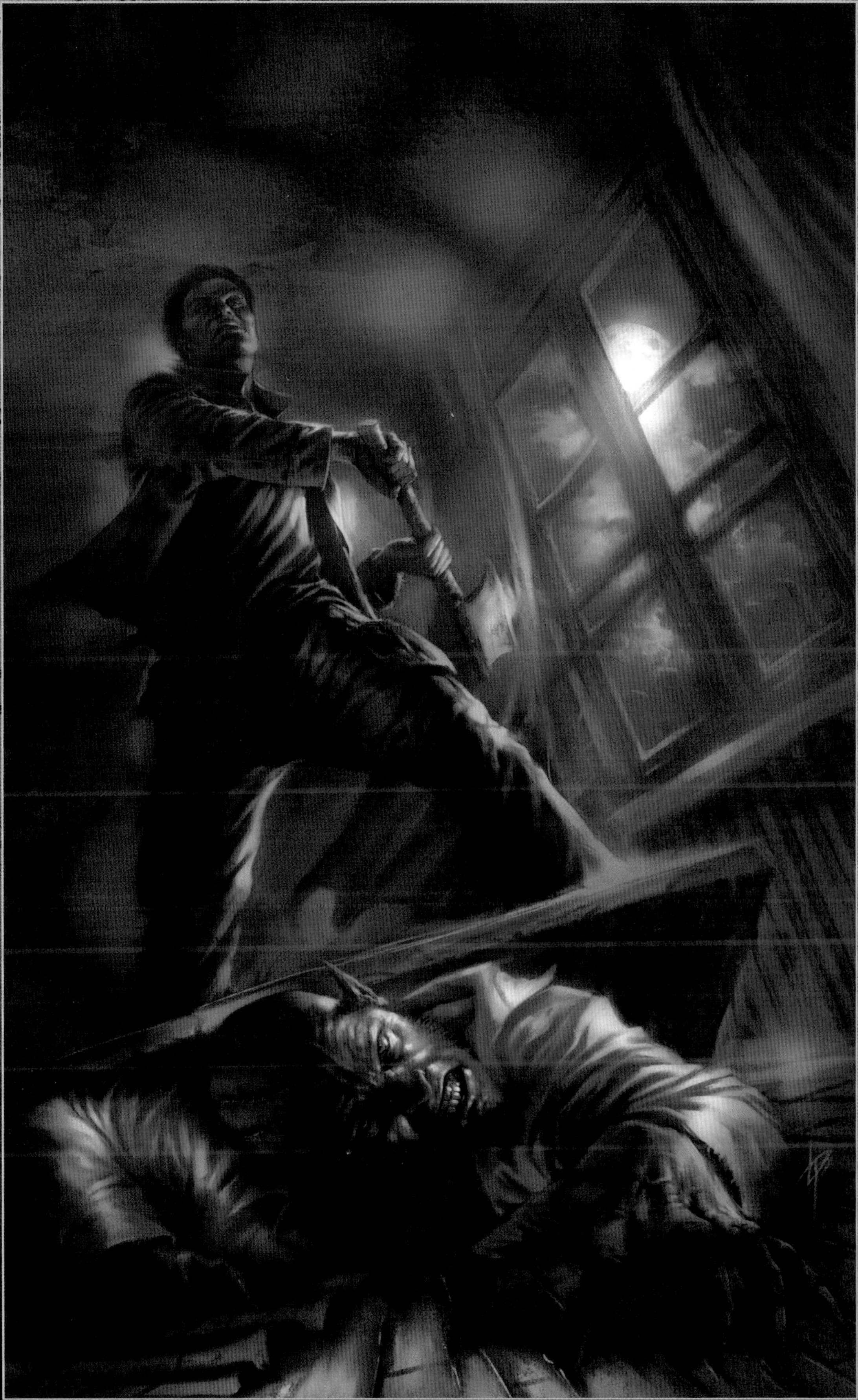

ISSUE #3 COVER

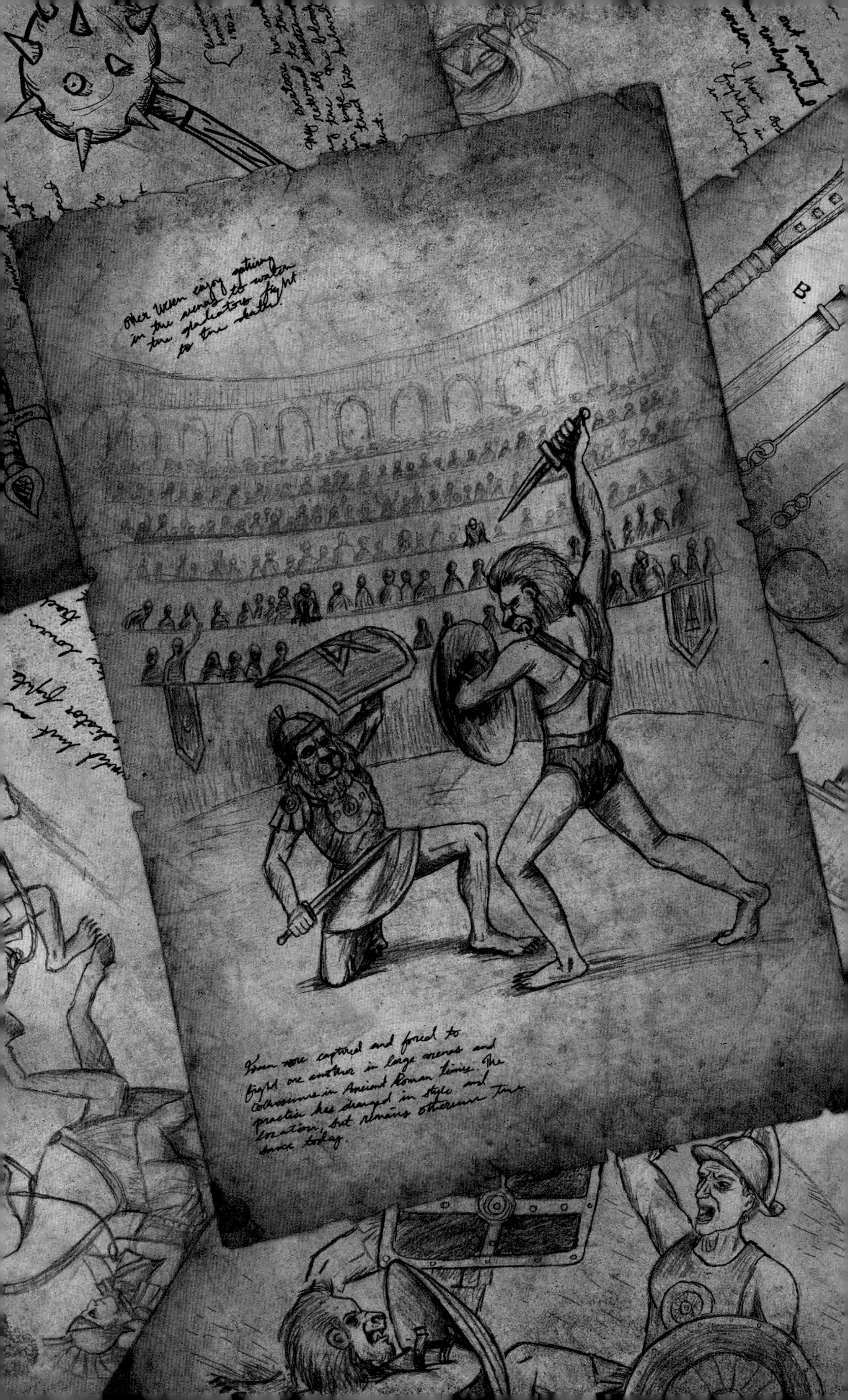
Other Weren enjoy gathering in the arenas to watch the gladiators fight to the death.
B.
Weren were captured and forced to fight one another in large arenas and Colosseums in Ancient Roman times. The practice has changed in style and location, but remains otherwise true since today.

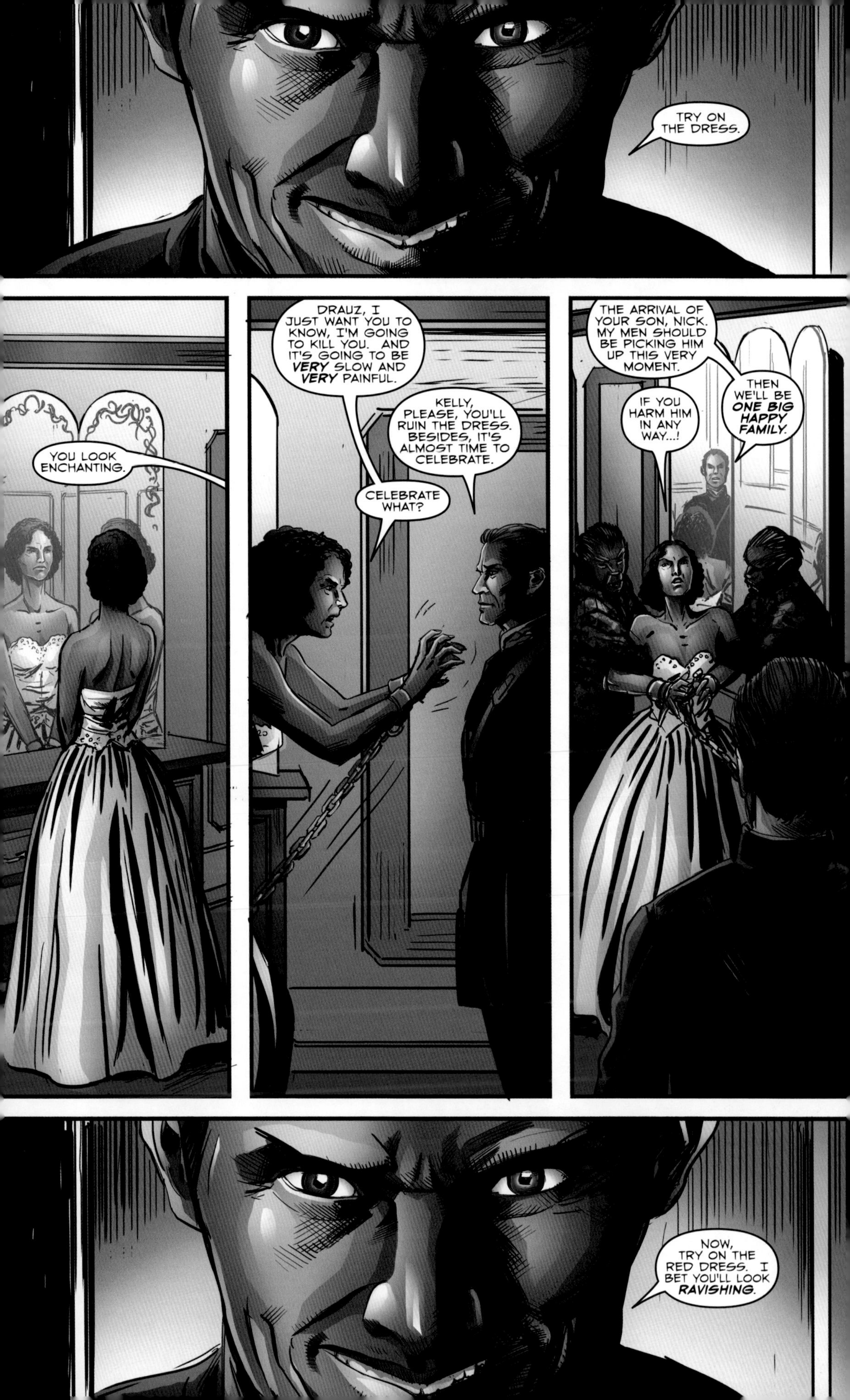
TRY ON THE DRESS.
YOU LOOK ENCHANTING.
DRAUZ, I JUST WANT YOU TO KNOW, I'M GOING TO KILL YOU. AND IT'S GOING TO BE VERY SLOW AND VERY PAINFUL.
KELLY, PLEASE, YOU'LL RUIN THE DRESS. BESIDES, IT'S ALMOST TIME TO CELEBRATE.
CELEBRATE WHAT?
THE ARRIVAL OF YOUR SON, NICK. MY MEN SHOULD BE PICKING HIM UP THIS VERY MOMENT.
IF YOU HARM HIM IN ANY WAY...!
THEN WE'LL BE ONE BIG HAPPY FAMILY.
NOW, TRY ON THE RED DRESS. I BET YOU'LL LOOK RAVISHING.

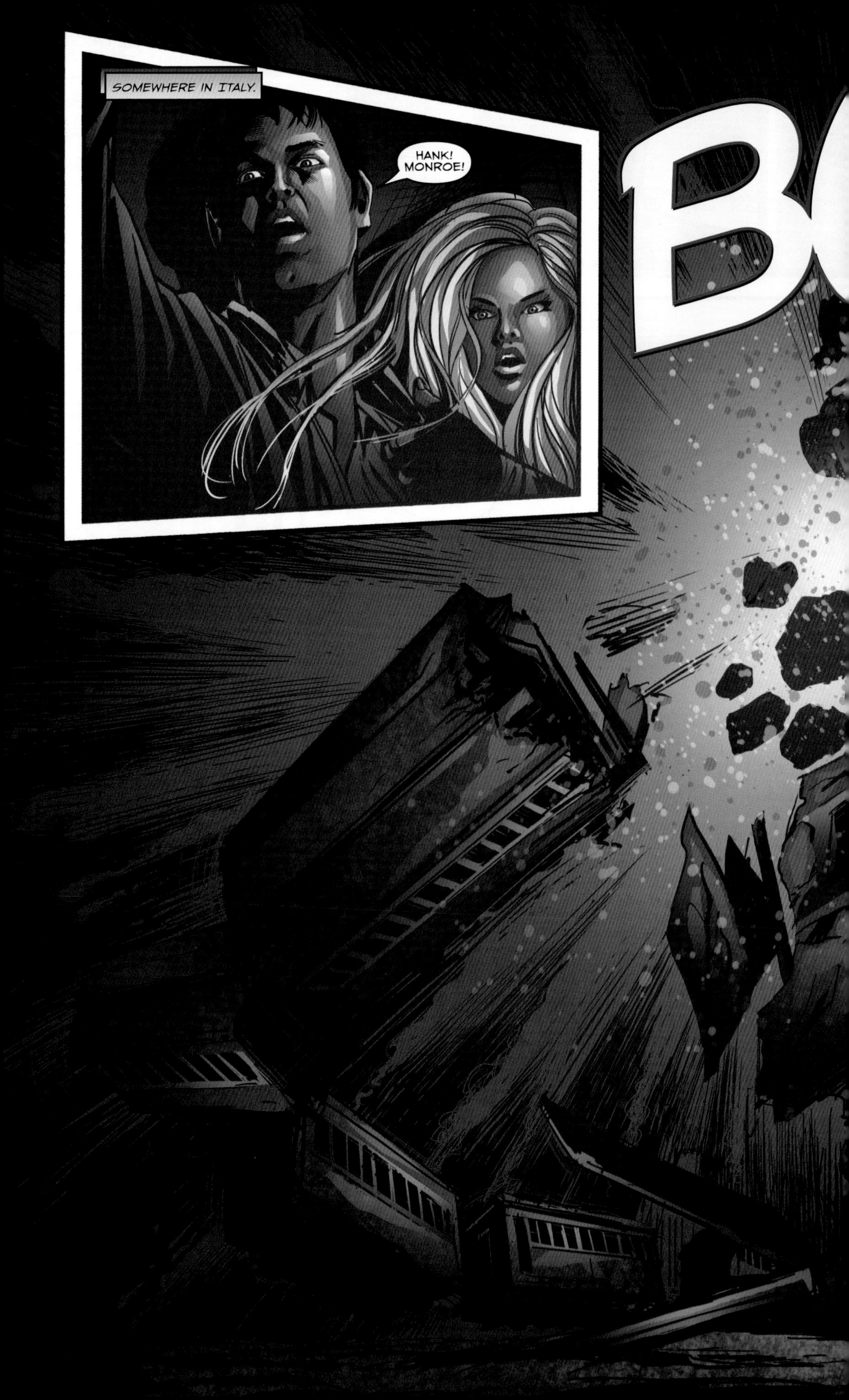
SOMEWHERE IN ITALY.
HANK! MONROE!

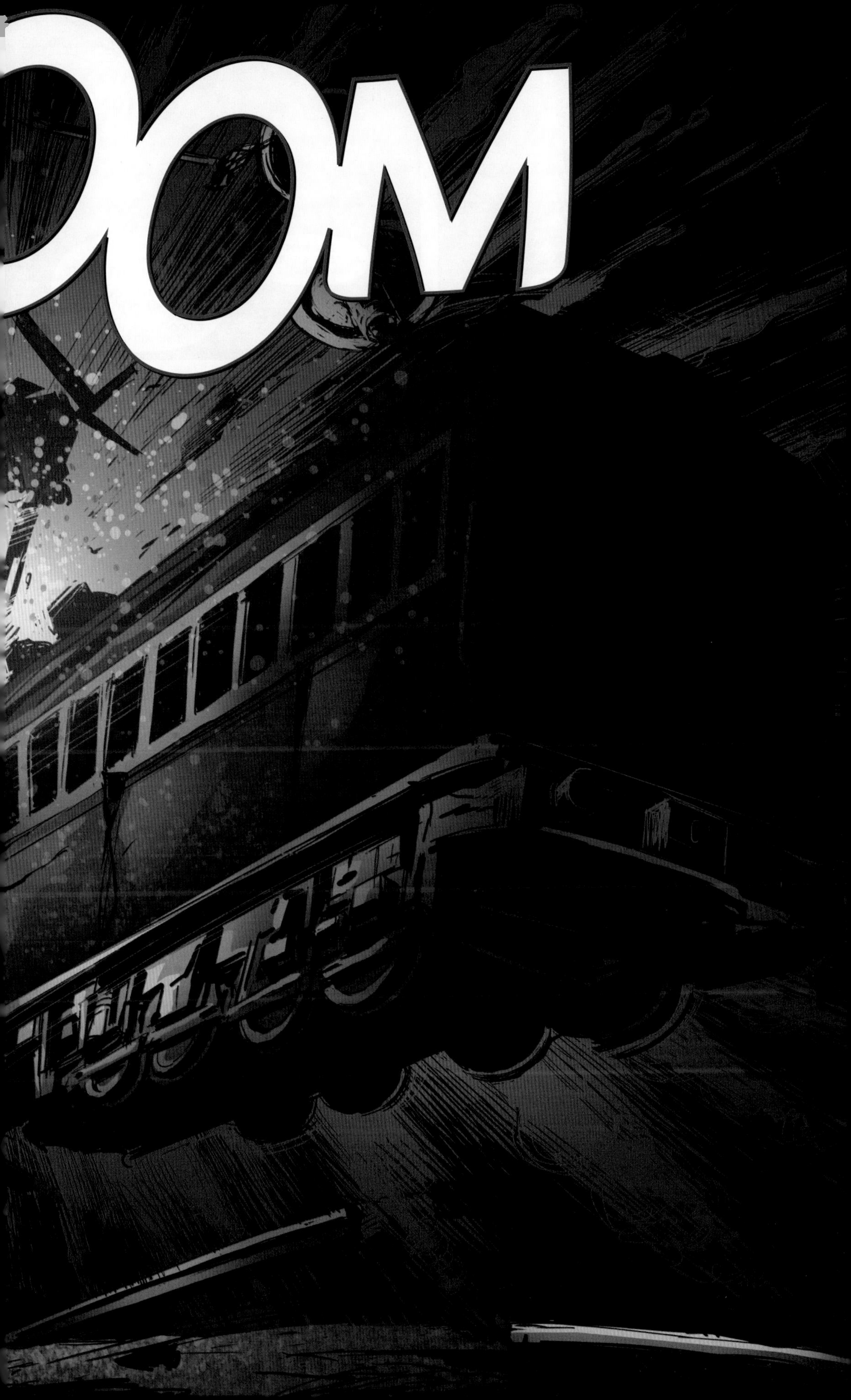
OOM

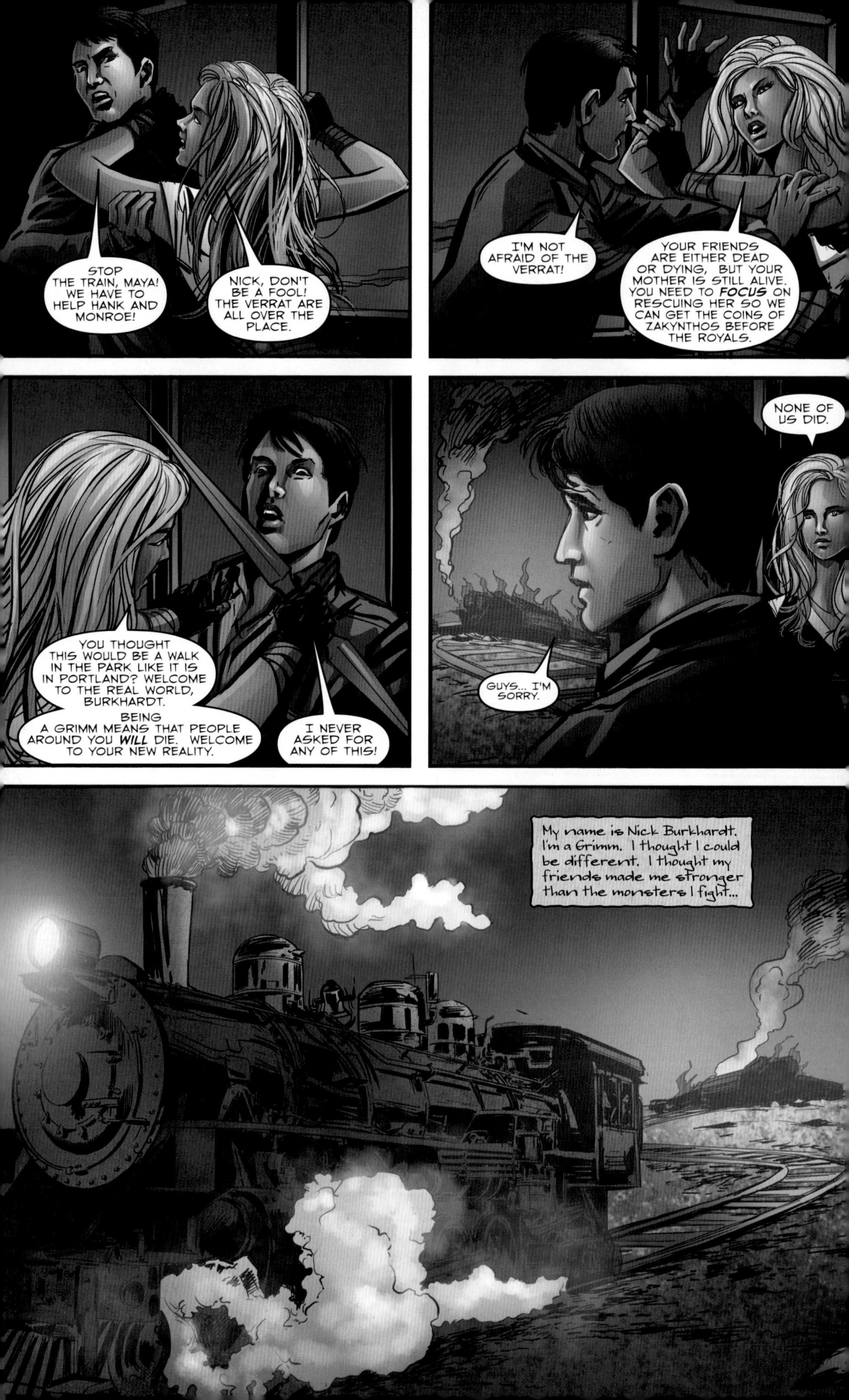
STOP THE TRAIN, MAYA! WE HAVE TO HELP HANK AND MONROE!
NICK, DON'T BE A FOOL! THE VERRAT ARE ALL OVER THE PLACE.
I'M NOT AFRAID OF THE VERRAT!
YOUR FRIENDS ARE EITHER DEAD OR DYING, BUT YOUR MOTHER IS STILL ALIVE. YOU NEED TO FOCUS ON RESCUING HER SO WE CAN GET THE COINS OF ZAKYNTHOS BEFORE THE ROYALS.
YOU THOUGHT THIS WOULD BE A WALK IN THE PARK LIKE IT IS IN PORTLAND? WELCOME TO THE REAL WORLD, BURKHARDT.
BEING A GRIMM MEANS THAT PEOPLE AROUND YOU WILL DIE. WELCOME TO YOUR NEW REALITY.
I NEVER ASKED FOR ANY OF THIS!
NONE OF US DID.
GUYS... I'M SORRY.
My name is Nick Burkhardt. I'm a Grimm. I thought I could be different. I thought my friends made me stronger than the monsters I fight...

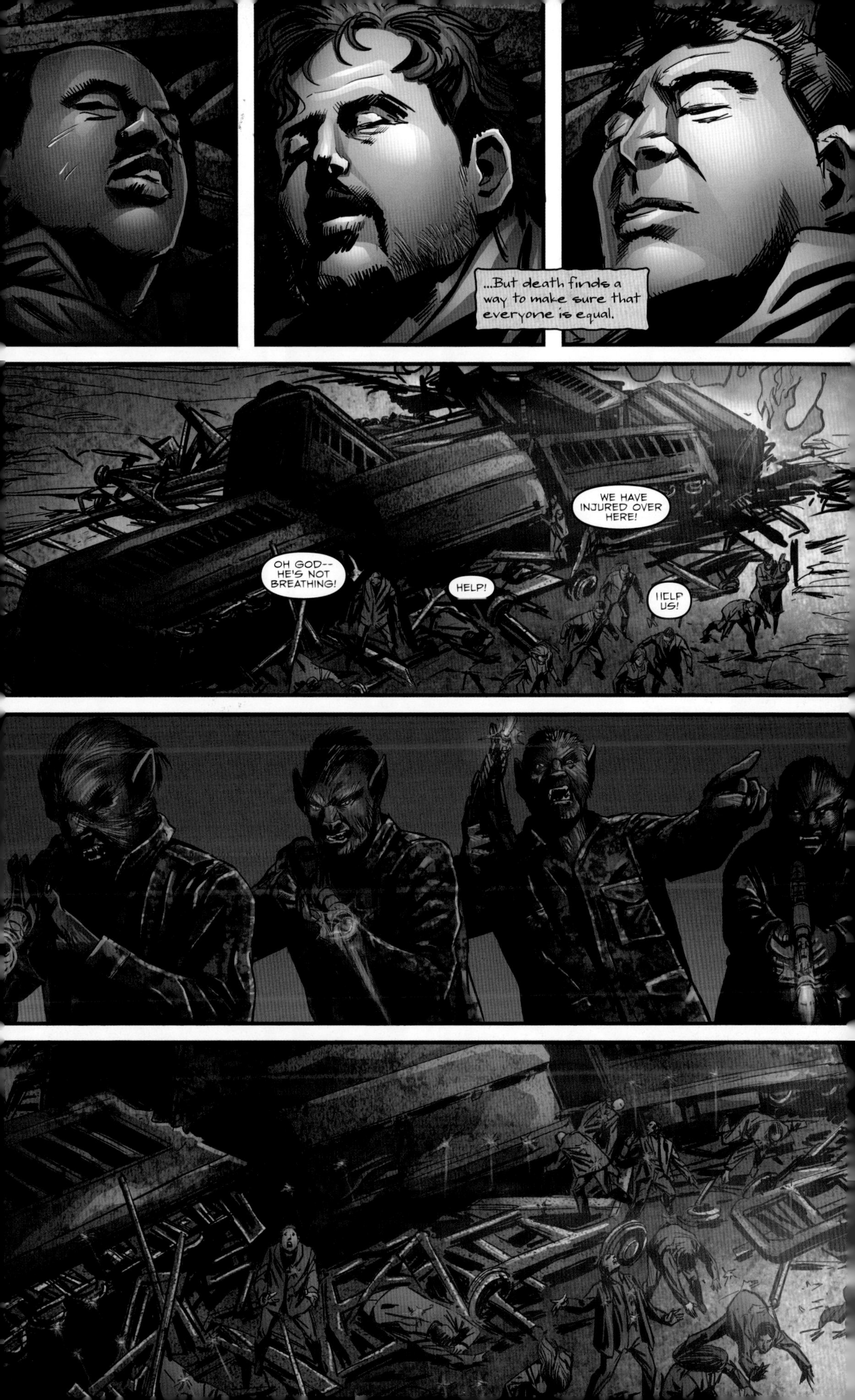
...But death finds a way to make sure that everyone is equal.
WE HAVE INJURED OVER HERE!
OH GOD-- HE'S NOT BREATHING!
HELP!
HELP US!

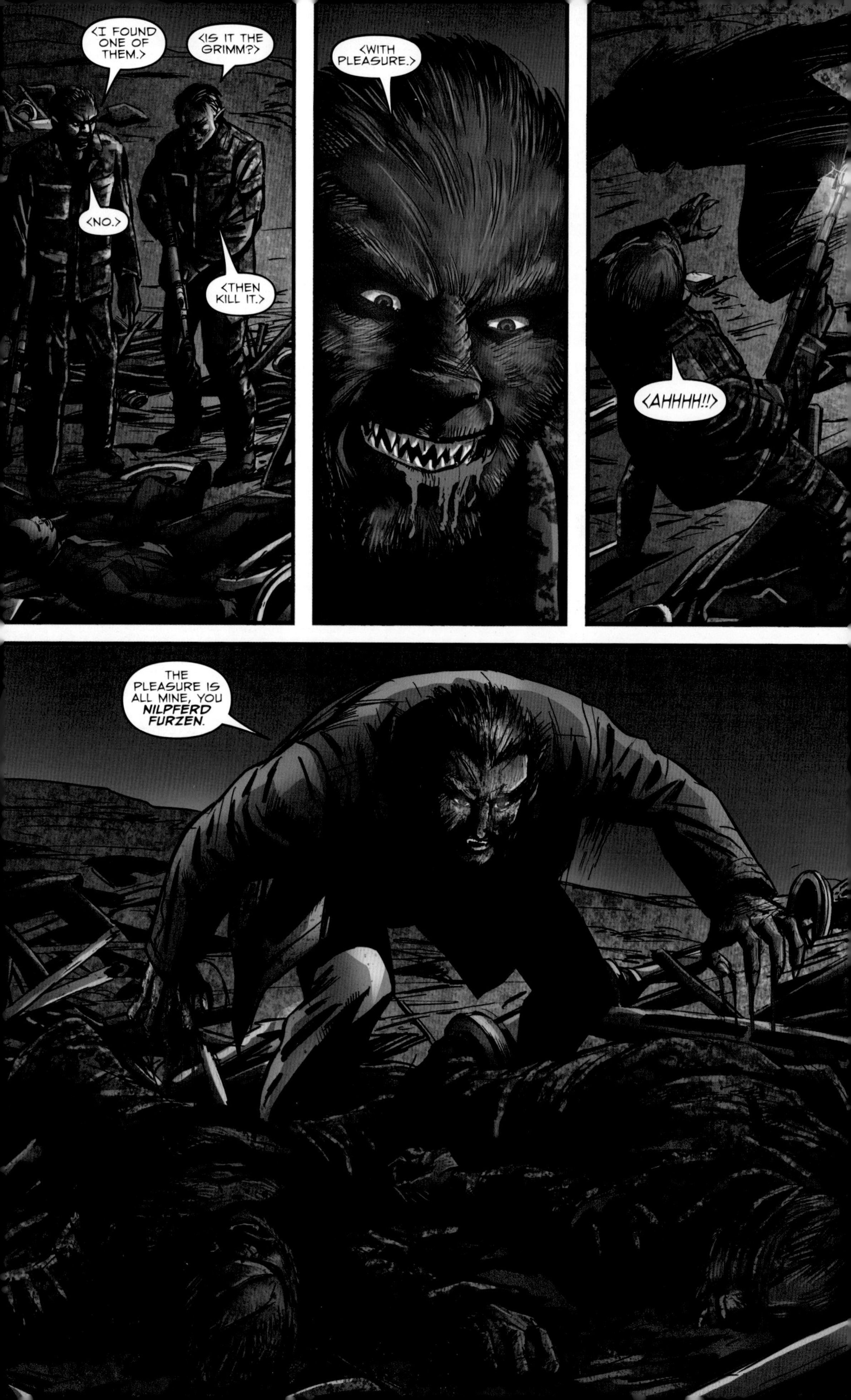
<I FOUND ONE OF THEM.>
<IS IT THE GRIMM?>
<NO.>
<THEN KILL IT.>
<WITH PLEASURE.>
<AHHHH!!>
THE PLEASURE IS ALL MINE, YOU NILPFERD FURZEN.

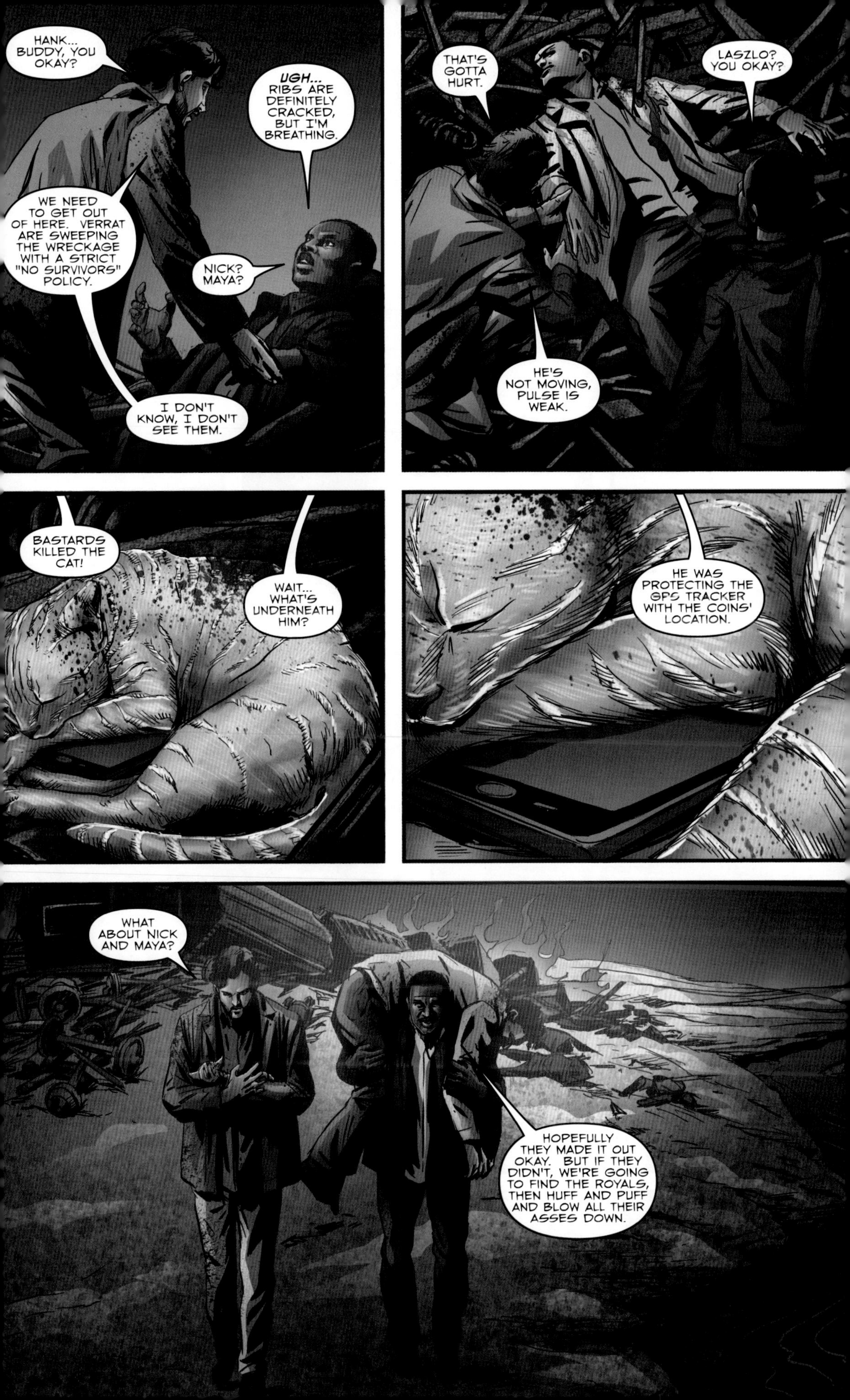
HANK... BUDDY, YOU OKAY?
UGH... RIBS ARE DEFINITELY CRACKED, BUT I'M BREATHING.
WE NEED TO GET OUT OF HERE. VERRAT ARE SWEEPING THE WRECKAGE WITH A STRICT "NO SURVIVORS" POLICY.
NICK? MAYA?
I DON'T KNOW, I DON'T SEE THEM.
THAT'S GOTTA HURT.
LASZLO? YOU OKAY?
HE'S NOT MOVING, PULSE IS WEAK.
BASTARDS KILLED THE CAT!
WAIT... WHAT'S UNDERNEATH HIM?
HE WAS PROTECTING THE GPS TRACKER WITH THE COINS' LOCATION.
WHAT ABOUT NICK AND MAYA?
HOPEFULLY THEY MADE IT OUT OKAY. BUT IF THEY DIDN'T, WE'RE GOING TO FIND THE ROYALS, THEN HUFF AND PUFF AND BLOW ALL THEIR ASSES DOWN.

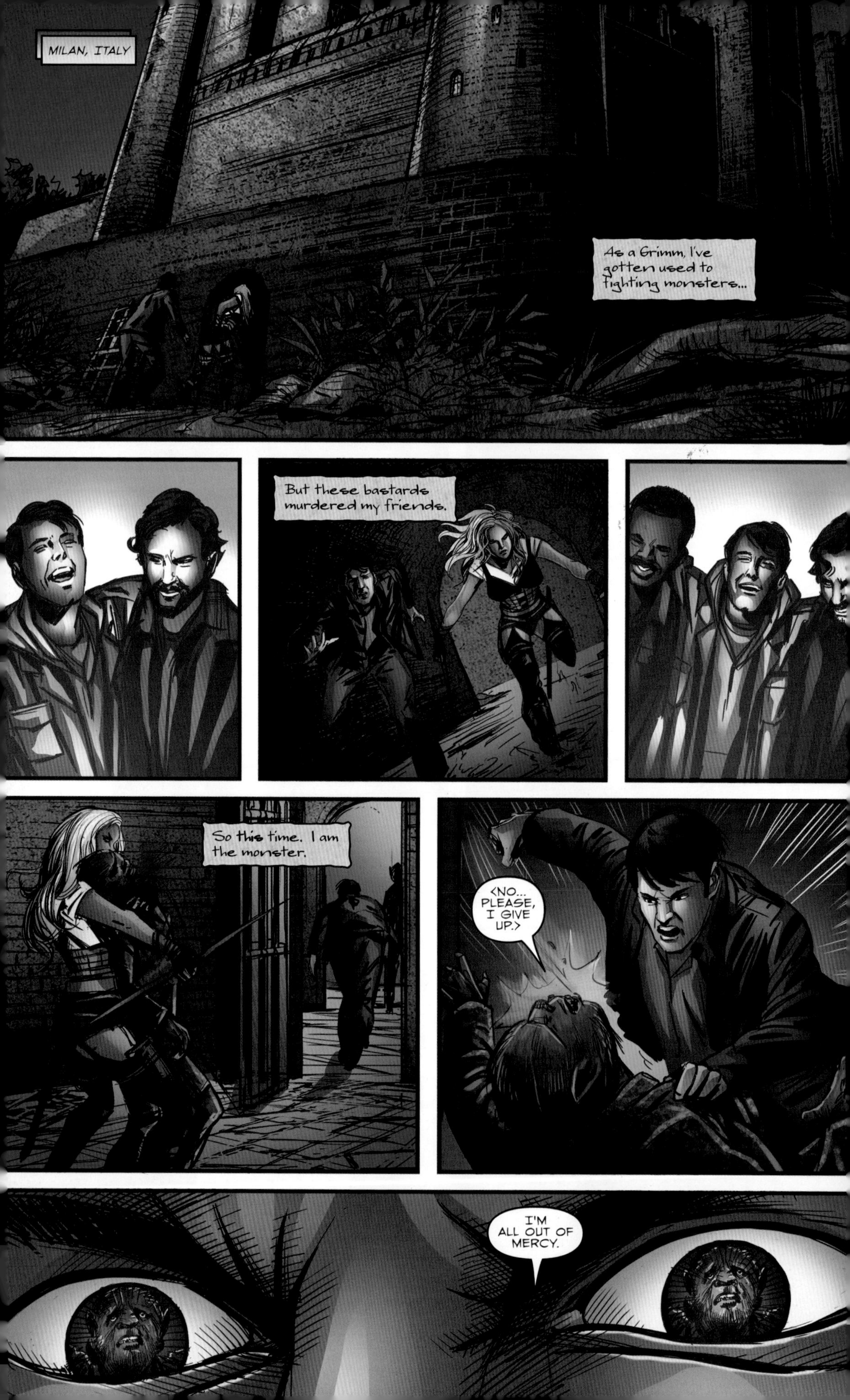
MILAN, ITALY
As a Grimm, I've gotten used to fighting monsters...
But these bastards murdered my friends.
So this time. I am the monster.
<NO... PLEASE, I GIVE UP.>
I'M ALL OUT OF MERCY.

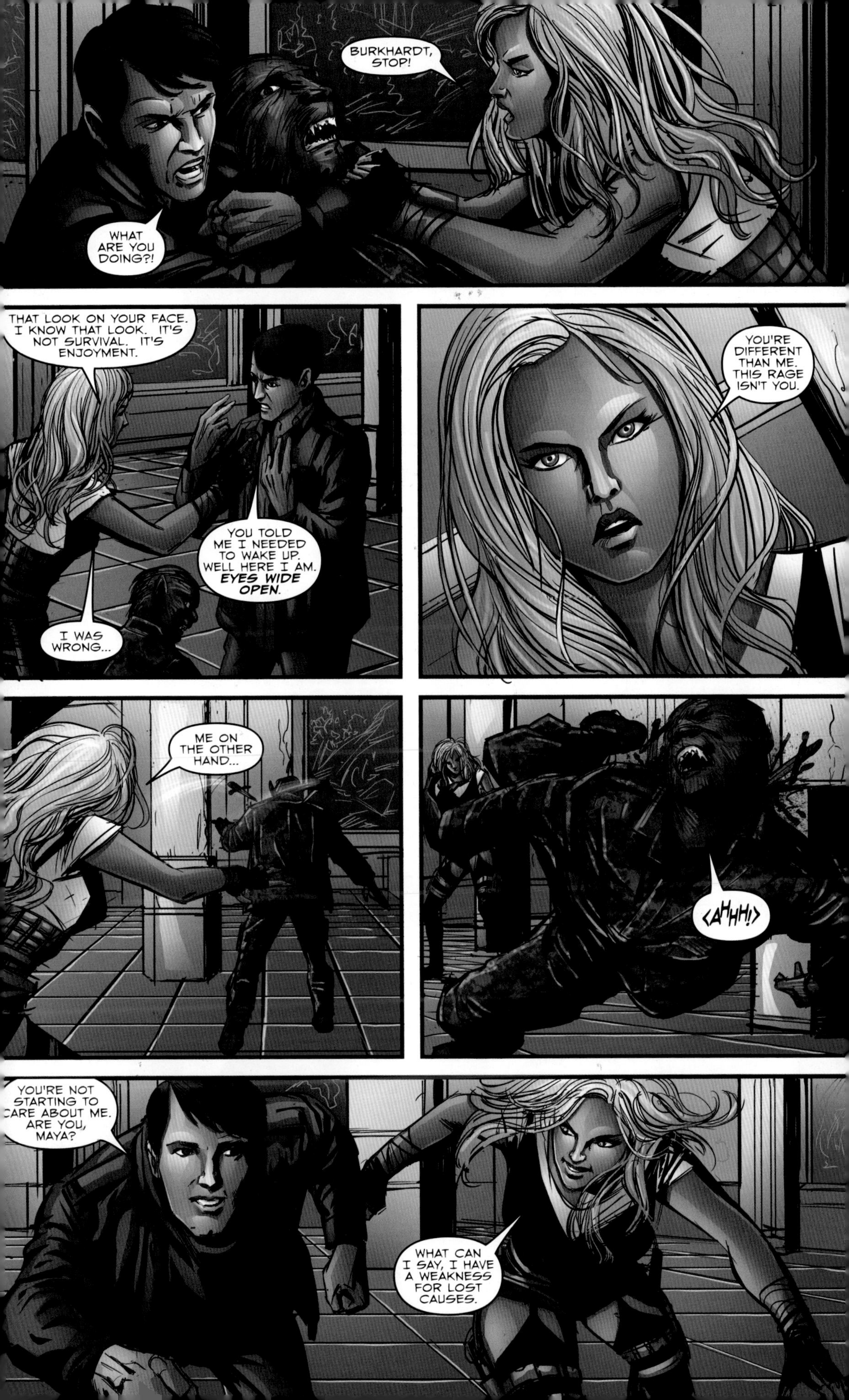
BURKHARDT, STOP!
WHAT ARE YOU DOING?!
THAT LOOK ON YOUR FACE. I KNOW THAT LOOK. IT'S NOT SURVIVAL. IT'S ENJOYMENT.
YOU TOLD ME I NEEDED TO WAKE UP. WELL HERE I AM. EYES WIDE OPEN.
I WAS WRONG...
YOU'RE DIFFERENT THAN ME. THIS RAGE ISN'T YOU.
ME ON THE OTHER HAND...
<AHHH!>
YOU'RE NOT STARTING TO CARE ABOUT ME. ARE YOU, MAYA?
WHAT CAN I SAY, I HAVE A WEAKNESS FOR LOST CAUSES.

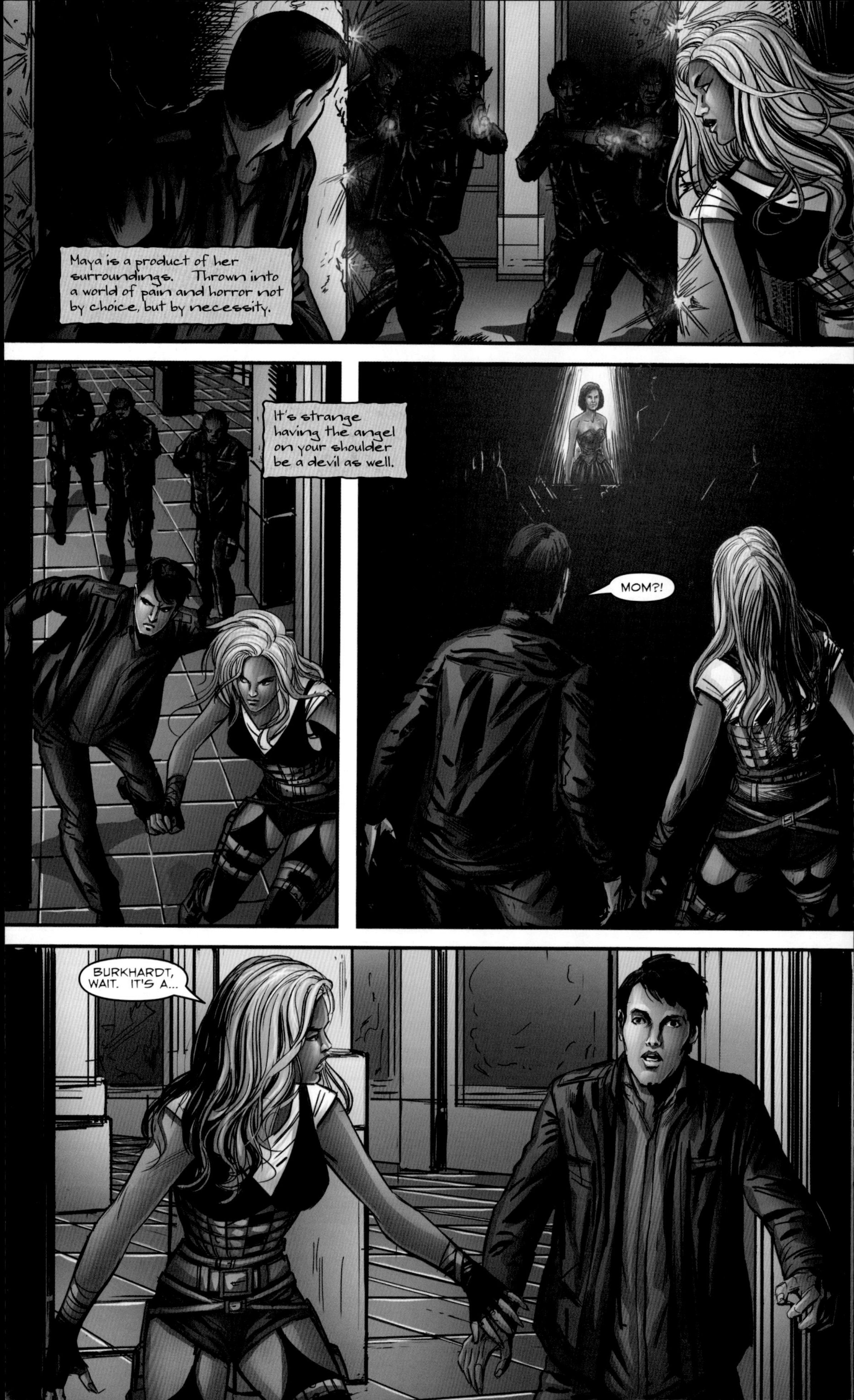
Maya is a product of her surroundings. Thrown into a world of pain and horror not by choice, but by necessity.
It's strange having the angel on your shoulder be a devil as well.
MOM?!
BURKHARDT, WAIT. IT'S A...

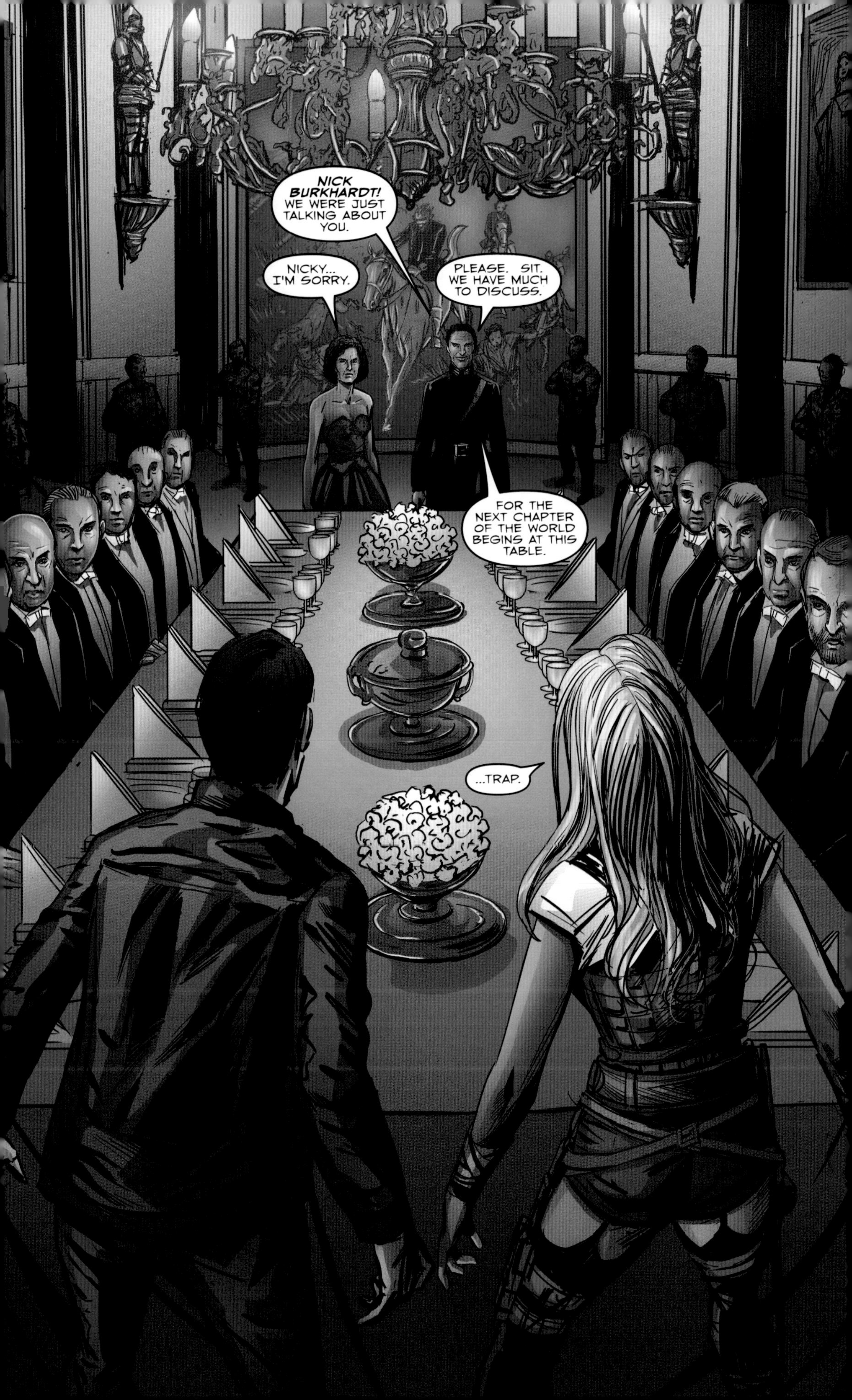

NICK BURKHARDT! WE WERE JUST TALKING ABOUT YOU.
NICKY... I'M SORRY.
PLEASE. SIT. WE HAVE MUCH TO DISCUSS.
FOR THE NEXT CHAPTER OF THE WORLD BEGINS AT THIS TABLE.
...TRAP.

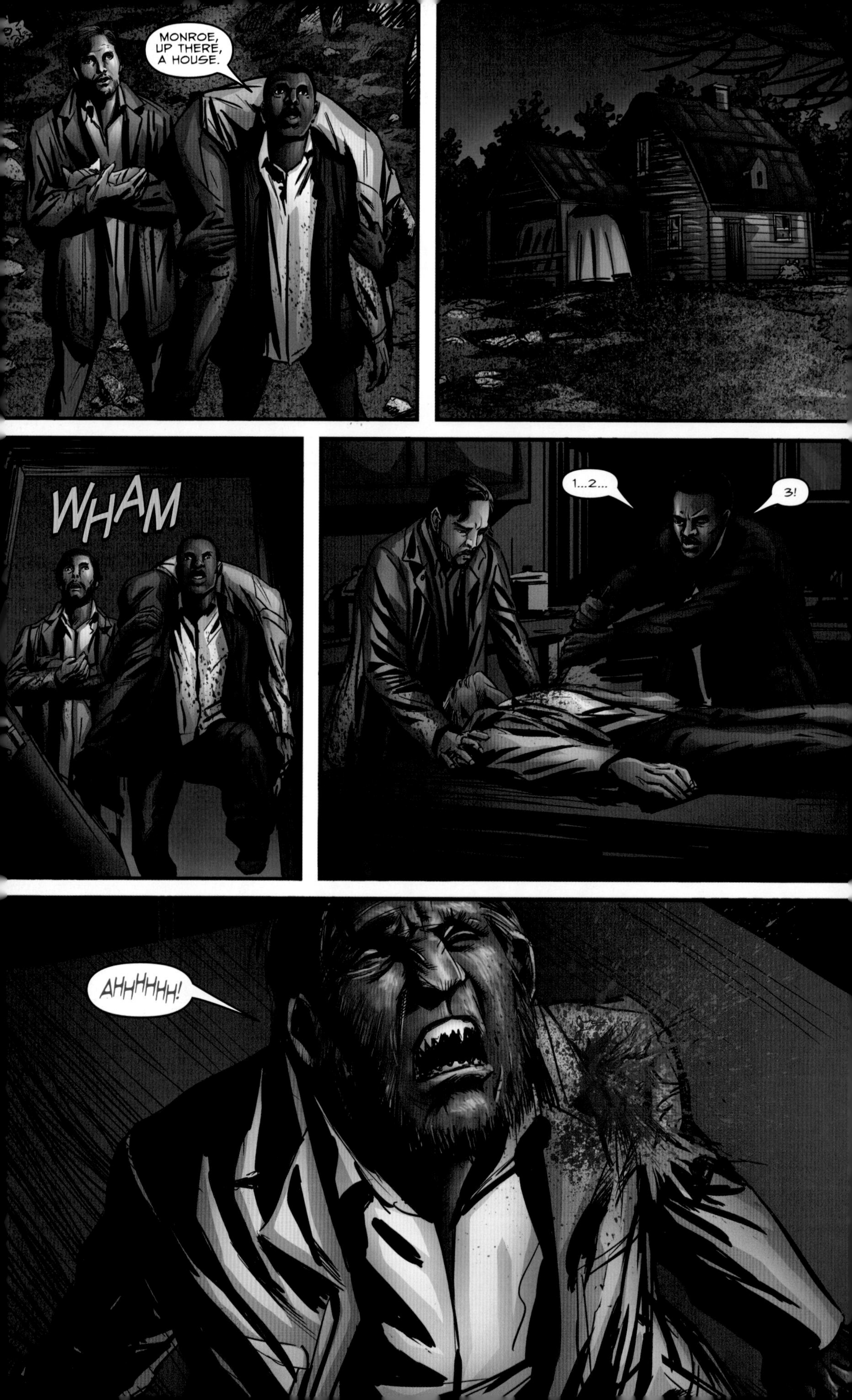
MONROE, UP THERE, A HOUSE.
WHAM
1...2...
3!
AHHHHHH!

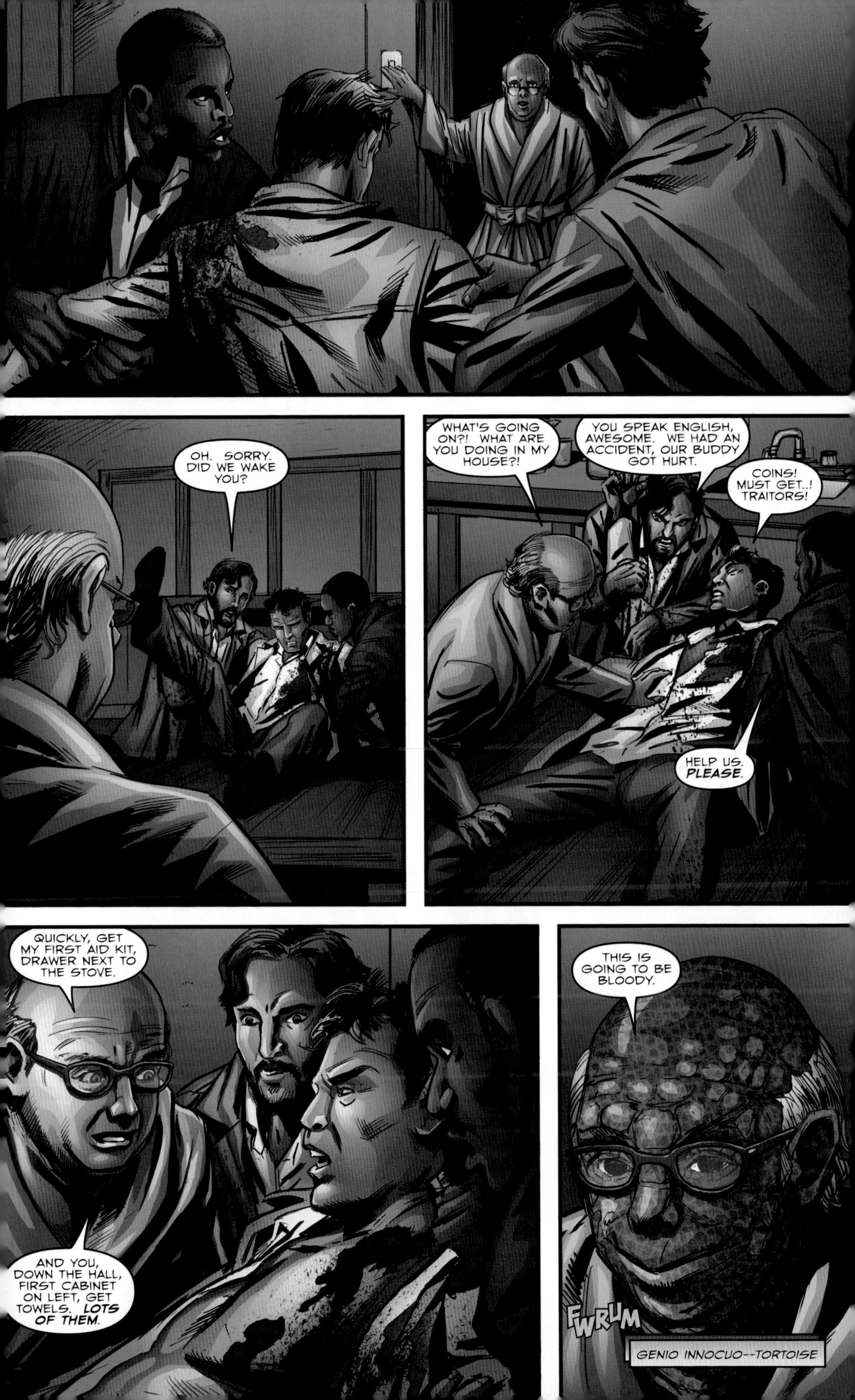
OH. SORRY. DID WE WAKE YOU?
WHAT'S GOING ON?! WHAT ARE YOU DOING IN MY HOUSE?!
YOU SPEAK ENGLISH, AWESOME. WE HAD AN ACCIDENT, OUR BUDDY GOT HURT.
COINS! MUST GET..! TRAITORS!
HELP US. *PLEASE*.
QUICKLY, GET MY FIRST AID KIT, DRAWER NEXT TO THE STOVE.
AND YOU, DOWN THE HALL, FIRST CABINET ON LEFT, GET TOWELS. ***LOTS OF THEM***.
THIS IS GOING TO BE BLOODY.
FWRUM
GENIO INNOCUO--TORTOISE

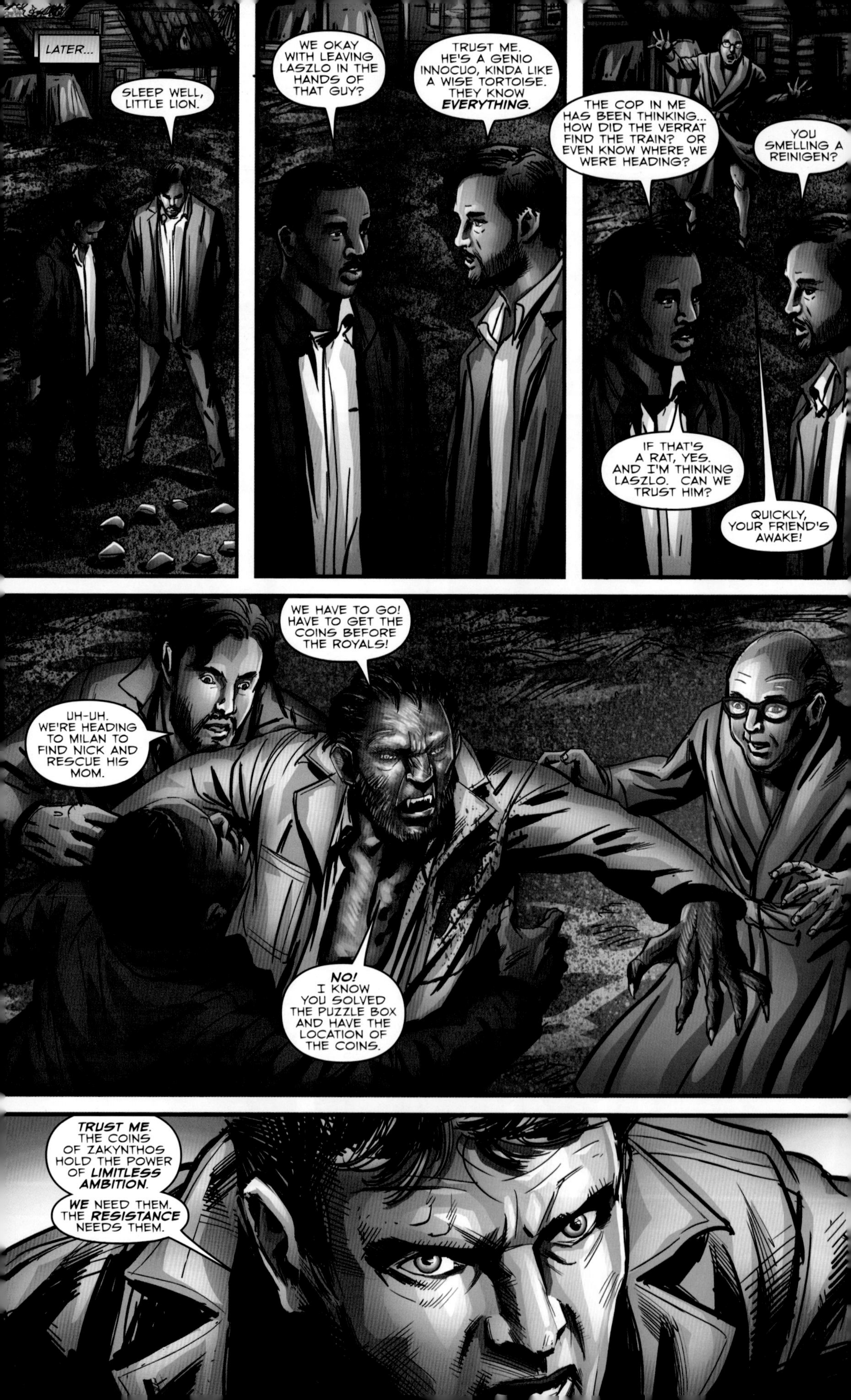
LATER...
SLEEP WELL, LITTLE LION.
WE OKAY WITH LEAVING LASZLO IN THE HANDS OF THAT GUY?
TRUST ME. HE'S A GENIO INNOCUO, KINDA LIKE A WISE TORTOISE. THEY KNOW *EVERYTHING*.
THE COP IN ME HAS BEEN THINKING... HOW DID THE VERRAT FIND THE TRAIN? OR EVEN KNOW WHERE WE WERE HEADING?
YOU SMELLING A REINIGEN?
IF THAT'S A RAT, YES. AND I'M THINKING LASZLO. CAN WE TRUST HIM?
QUICKLY, YOUR FRIEND'S AWAKE!
WE HAVE TO GO! HAVE TO GET THE COINS BEFORE THE ROYALS!
UH-UH. WE'RE HEADING TO MILAN TO FIND NICK AND RESCUE HIS MOM.
NO! I KNOW YOU SOLVED THE PUZZLE BOX AND HAVE THE LOCATION OF THE COINS.
TRUST ME. THE COINS OF ZAKYNTHOS HOLD THE POWER OF *LIMITLESS AMBITION*.
WE NEED THEM. THE *RESISTANCE* NEEDS THEM.

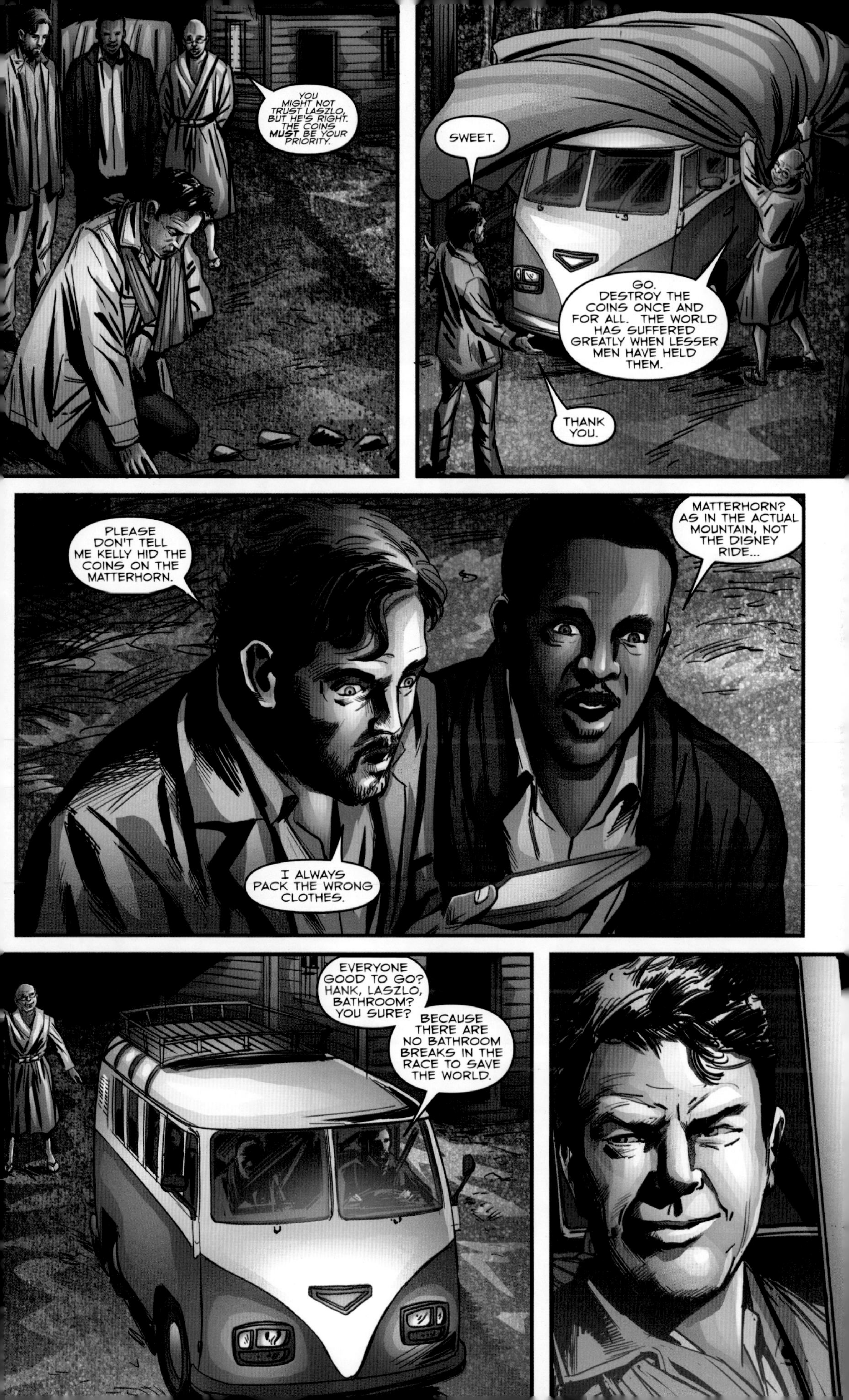
YOU MIGHT NOT TRUST LASZLO, BUT HE'S RIGHT. THE COINS **MUST** BE YOUR PRIORITY.
SWEET.
GO. DESTROY THE COINS ONCE AND FOR ALL. THE WORLD HAS SUFFERED GREATLY WHEN LESSER MEN HAVE HELD THEM.
THANK YOU.
PLEASE DON'T TELL ME KELLY HID THE COINS ON THE MATTERHORN.
MATTERHORN? AS IN THE ACTUAL MOUNTAIN, NOT THE DISNEY RIDE...
I ALWAYS PACK THE WRONG CLOTHES.
EVERYONE GOOD TO GO? HANK, LASZLO, BATHROOM? YOU SURE?
BECAUSE THERE ARE NO BATHROOM BREAKS IN THE RACE TO SAVE THE WORLD.

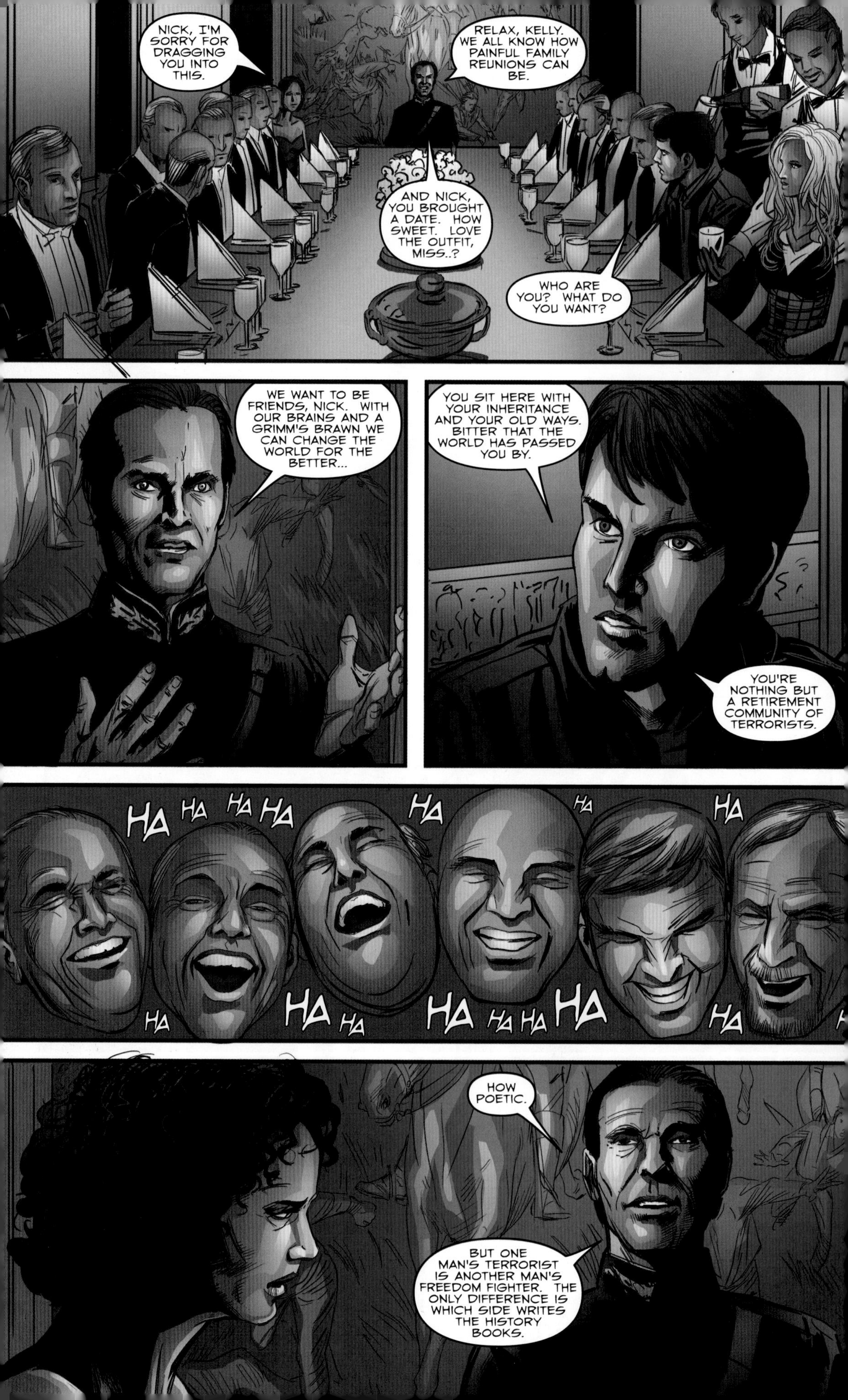

NICK, I'M SORRY FOR DRAGGING YOU INTO THIS.
RELAX, KELLY. WE ALL KNOW HOW PAINFUL FAMILY REUNIONS CAN BE.
AND NICK, YOU BROUGHT A DATE. HOW SWEET. LOVE THE OUTFIT, MISS..?
WHO ARE YOU? WHAT DO YOU WANT?
WE WANT TO BE FRIENDS, NICK. WITH OUR BRAINS AND A GRIMM'S BRAWN WE CAN CHANGE THE WORLD FOR THE BETTER...
YOU SIT HERE WITH YOUR INHERITANCE AND YOUR OLD WAYS. BITTER THAT THE WORLD HAS PASSED YOU BY.
YOU'RE NOTHING BUT A RETIREMENT COMMUNITY OF TERRORISTS.
HA HA HA HA HA HA HA
HA HA HA HA HA HA HA HA
HOW POETIC.
BUT ONE MAN'S TERRORIST IS ANOTHER MAN'S FREEDOM FIGHTER. THE ONLY DIFFERENCE IS WHICH SIDE WRITES THE HISTORY BOOKS.

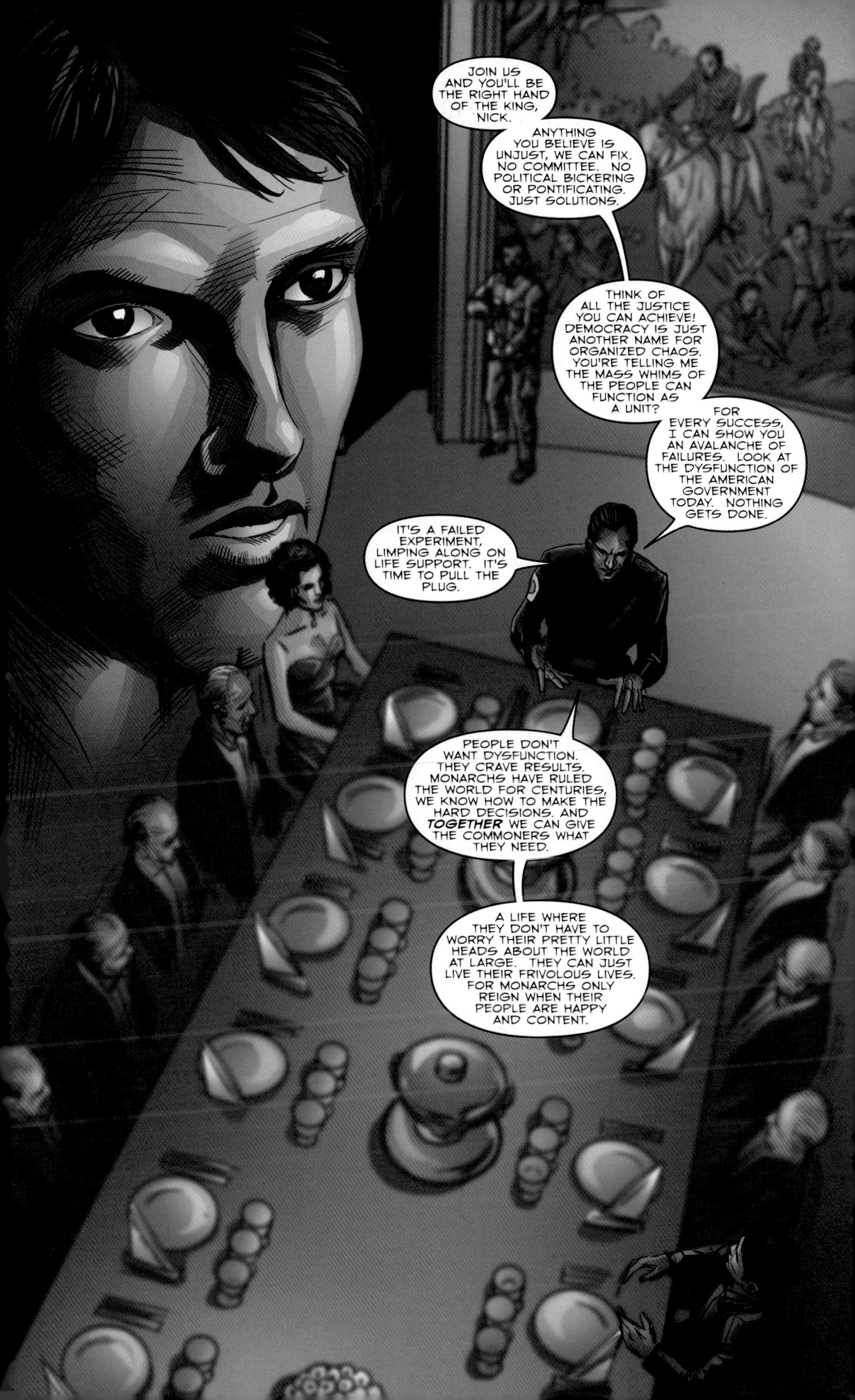
JOIN US AND YOU'LL BE THE RIGHT HAND OF THE KING, NICK.
ANYTHING YOU BELIEVE IS UNJUST, WE CAN FIX. NO COMMITTEE. NO POLITICAL BICKERING OR PONTIFICATING. JUST SOLUTIONS.
THINK OF ALL THE JUSTICE YOU CAN ACHIEVE! DEMOCRACY IS JUST ANOTHER NAME FOR ORGANIZED CHAOS. YOU'RE TELLING ME THE MASS WHIMS OF THE PEOPLE CAN FUNCTION AS A UNIT?
FOR EVERY SUCCESS, I CAN SHOW YOU AN AVALANCHE OF FAILURES. LOOK AT THE DYSFUNCTION OF THE AMERICAN GOVERNMENT TODAY. NOTHING GETS DONE.
IT'S A FAILED EXPERIMENT, LIMPING ALONG ON LIFE SUPPORT. IT'S TIME TO PULL THE PLUG.
PEOPLE DON'T WANT DYSFUNCTION. THEY CRAVE RESULTS. MONARCHS HAVE RULED THE WORLD FOR CENTURIES, WE KNOW HOW TO MAKE THE HARD DECISIONS. AND ***TOGETHER*** WE CAN GIVE THE COMMONERS WHAT THEY NEED.
A LIFE WHERE THEY DON'T HAVE TO WORRY THEIR PRETTY LITTLE HEADS ABOUT THE WORLD AT LARGE. THEY CAN JUST LIVE THEIR FRIVOLOUS LIVES. FOR MONARCHS ONLY REIGN WHEN THEIR PEOPLE ARE HAPPY AND CONTENT.

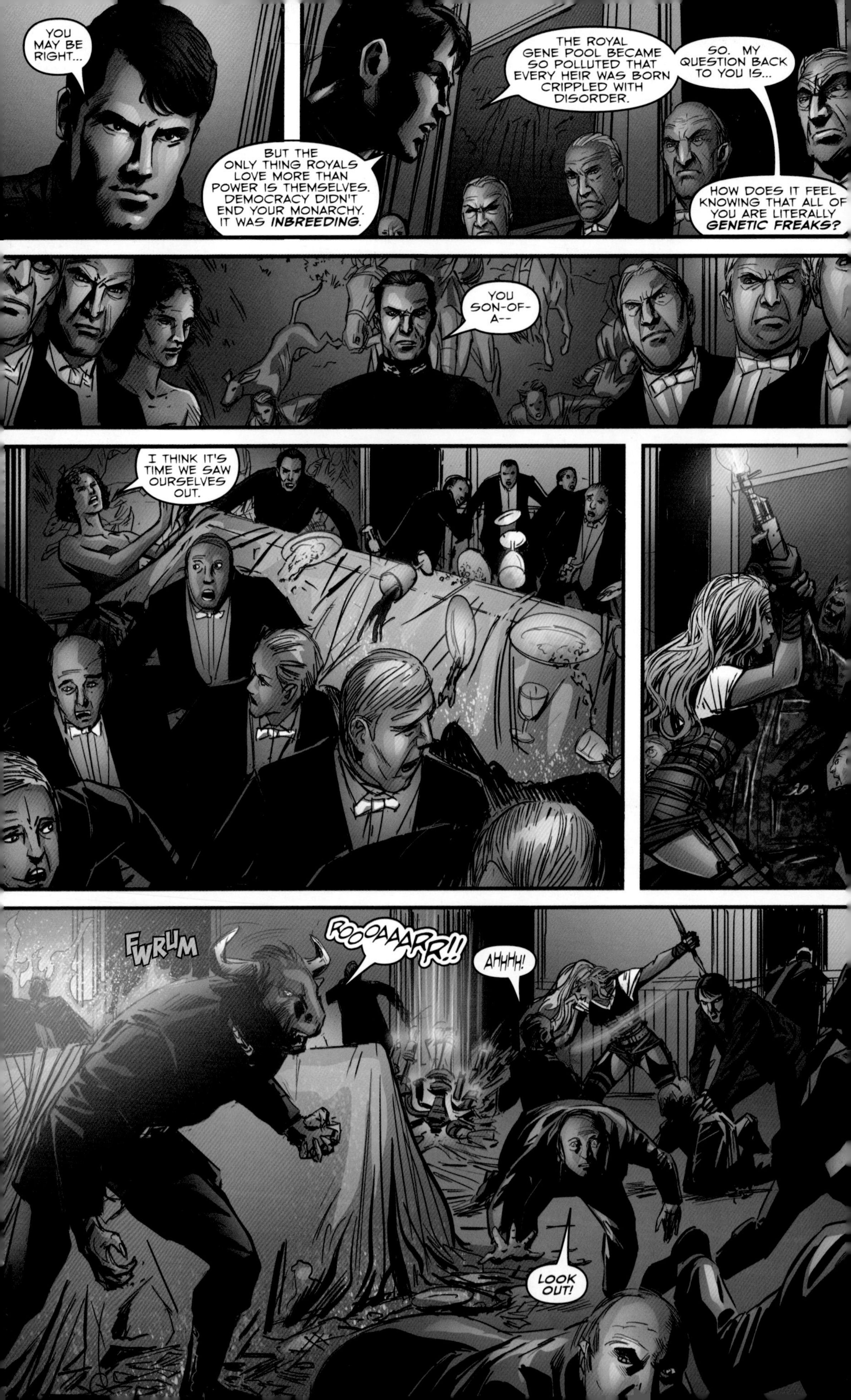
YOU MAY BE RIGHT...
BUT THE ONLY THING ROYALS LOVE MORE THAN POWER IS THEMSELVES. DEMOCRACY DIDN'T END YOUR MONARCHY. IT WAS INBREEDING.
THE ROYAL GENE POOL BECAME SO POLLUTED THAT EVERY HEIR WAS BORN CRIPPLED WITH DISORDER.
SO. MY QUESTION BACK TO YOU IS...
HOW DOES IT FEEL KNOWING THAT ALL OF YOU ARE LITERALLY GENETIC FREAKS?
YOU SON-OF-A--
I THINK IT'S TIME WE SAW OURSELVES OUT.
FWRUM
ROOOAAARR!!
AHHHH!
LOOK OUT!

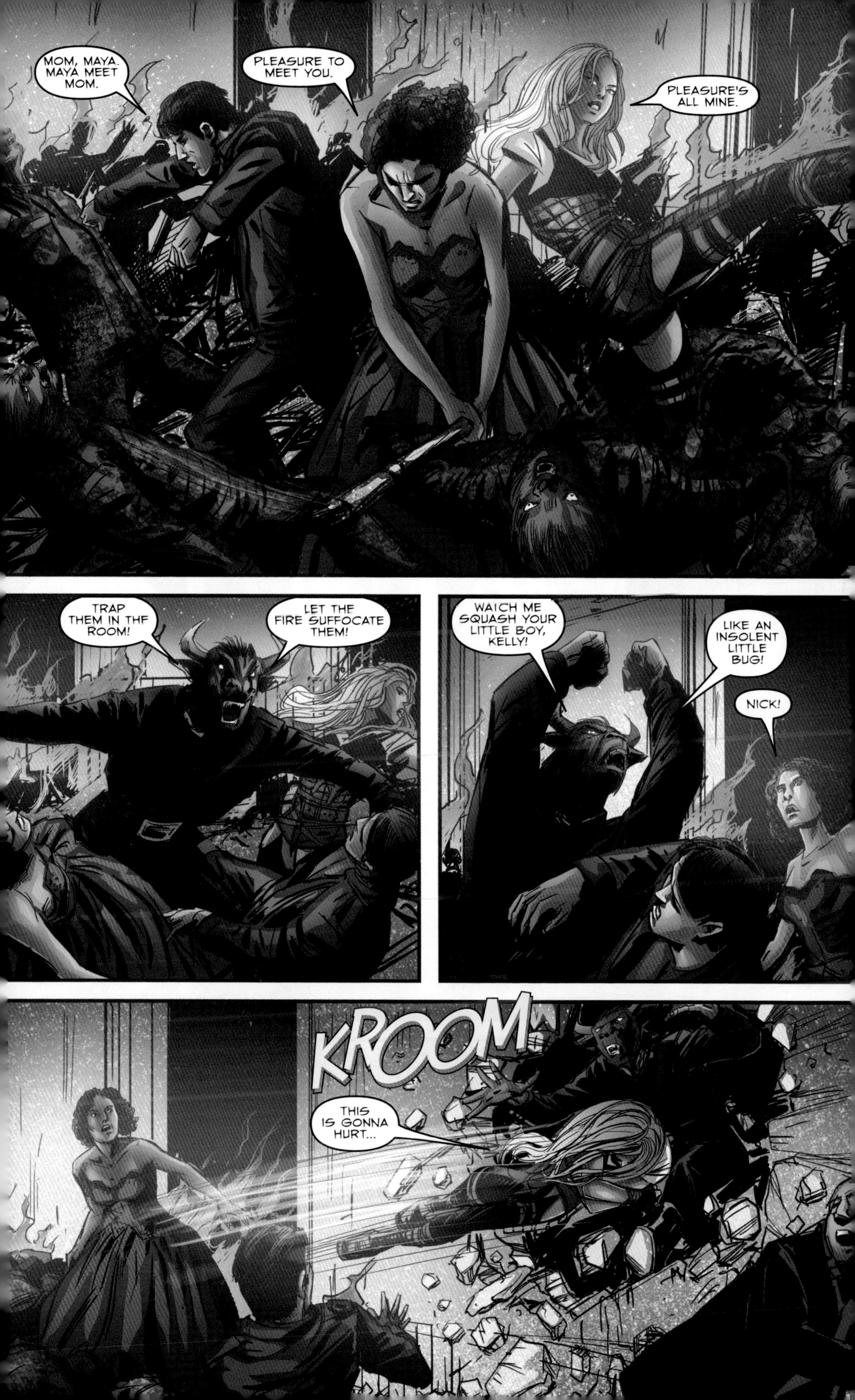
MOM, MAYA. MAYA MEET MOM.
PLEASURE TO MEET YOU.
PLEASURE'S ALL MINE.
TRAP THEM IN THF ROOM!
LET THE FIRE SUFFOCATE THEM!
WAICH ME SQUASH YOUR LITTLE BOY, KELLY!
LIKE AN INSOLENT LITTLE BUG!
NICK!
KROOM
THIS IS GONNA HURT...

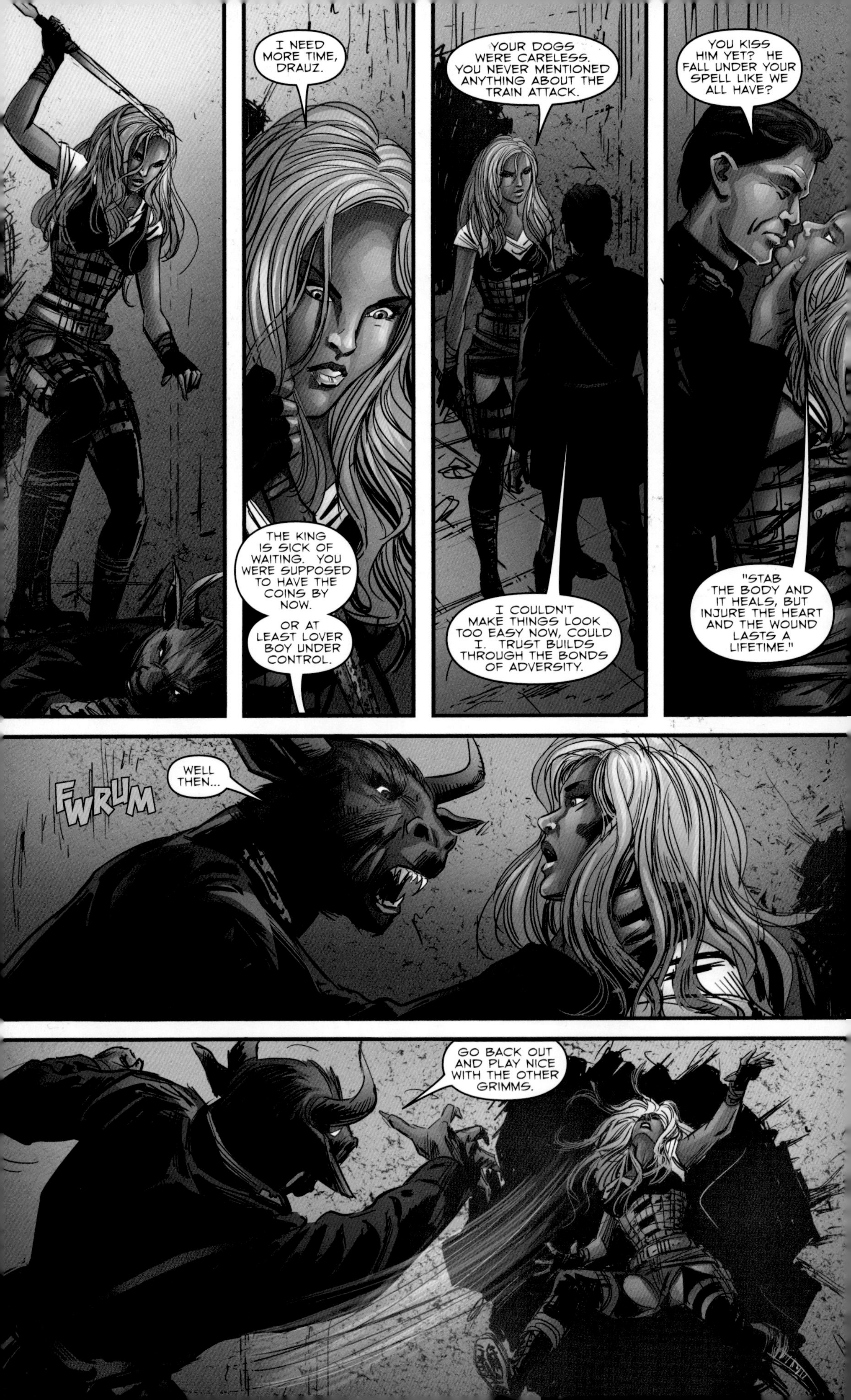
I NEED MORE TIME, DRAUZ.
THE KING IS SICK OF WAITING. YOU WERE SUPPOSED TO HAVE THE COINS BY NOW.
OR AT LEAST LOVER BOY UNDER CONTROL.
YOUR DOGS WERE CARELESS. YOU NEVER MENTIONED ANYTHING ABOUT THE TRAIN ATTACK.
I COULDN'T MAKE THINGS LOOK TOO EASY NOW, COULD I. TRUST BUILDS THROUGH THE BONDS OF ADVERSITY.
YOU KISS HIM YET? HE FALL UNDER YOUR SPELL LIKE WE ALL HAVE?
"STAB THE BODY AND IT HEALS, BUT INJURE THE HEART AND THE WOUND LASTS A LIFETIME."
FWRUM
WELL THEN...
GO BACK OUT AND PLAY NICE WITH THE OTHER GRIMMS.

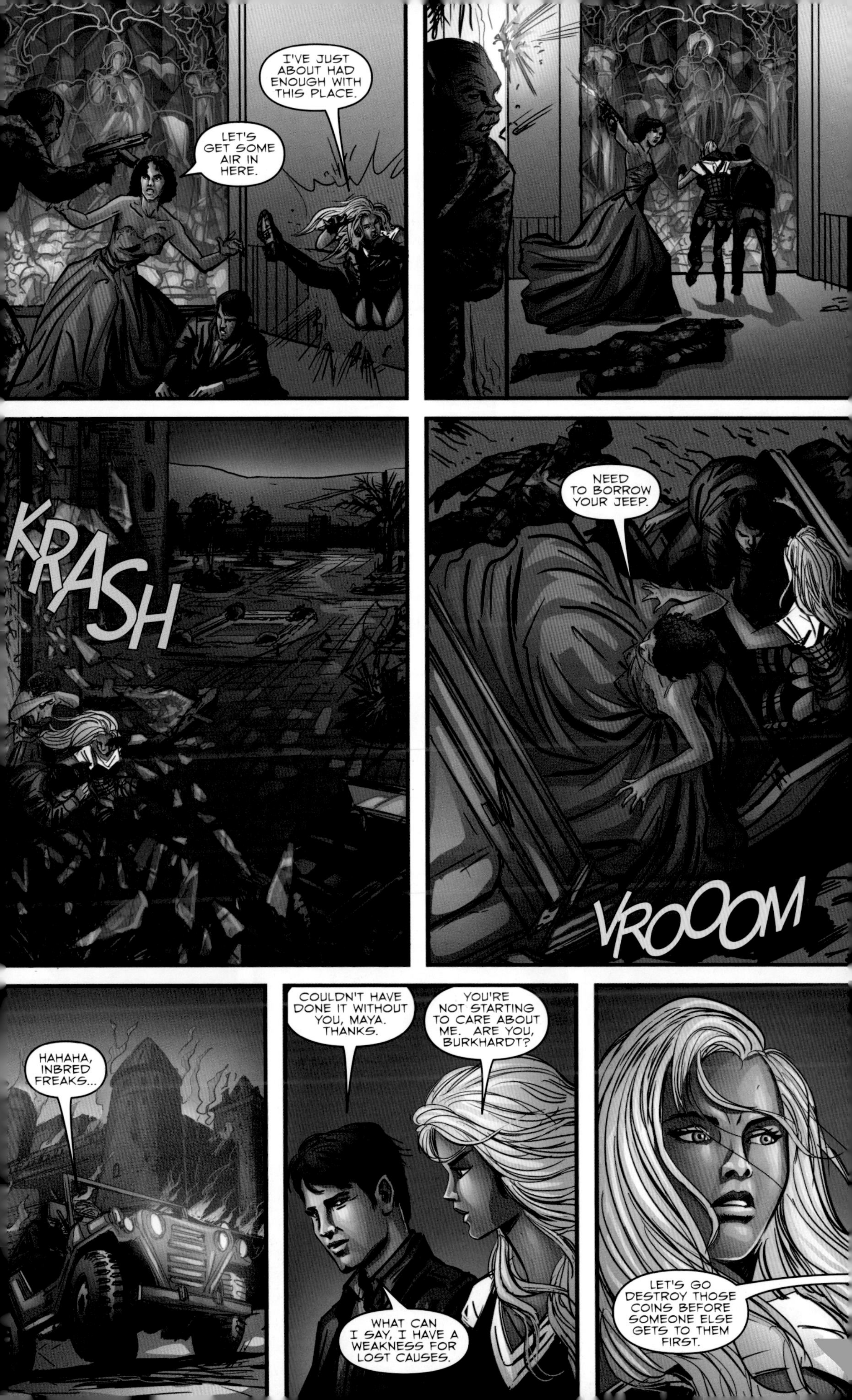
I'VE JUST ABOUT HAD ENOUGH WITH THIS PLACE.
LET'S GET SOME AIR IN HERE.
KRASH
NEED TO BORROW YOUR JEEP.
VROOOM
HAHAHA, INBRED FREAKS...
COULDN'T HAVE DONE IT WITHOUT YOU, MAYA. THANKS.
YOU'RE NOT STARTING TO CARE ABOUT ME. ARE YOU, BURKHARDT?
WHAT CAN I SAY, I HAVE A WEAKNESS FOR LOST CAUSES.
LET'S GO DESTROY THOSE COINS BEFORE SOMEONE ELSE GETS TO THEM FIRST.

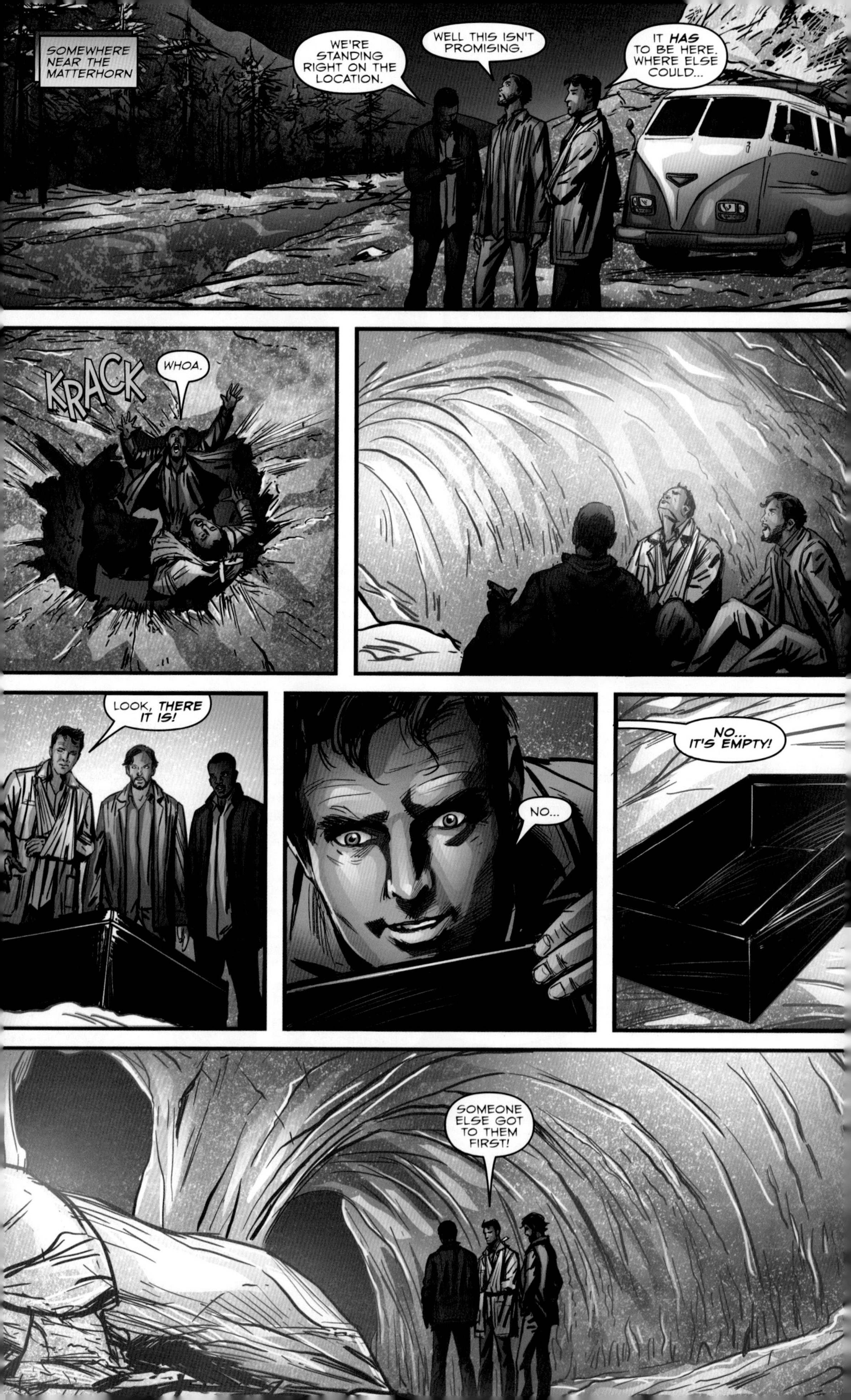
SOMEWHERE NEAR THE MATTERHORN
WE'RE STANDING RIGHT ON THE LOCATION.
WELL THIS ISN'T PROMISING.
IT HAS TO BE HERE. WHERE ELSE COULD...
KRACK
WHOA.
LOOK, THERE IT IS!
NO...
NO... IT'S EMPTY!
SOMEONE ELSE GOT TO THEM FIRST!

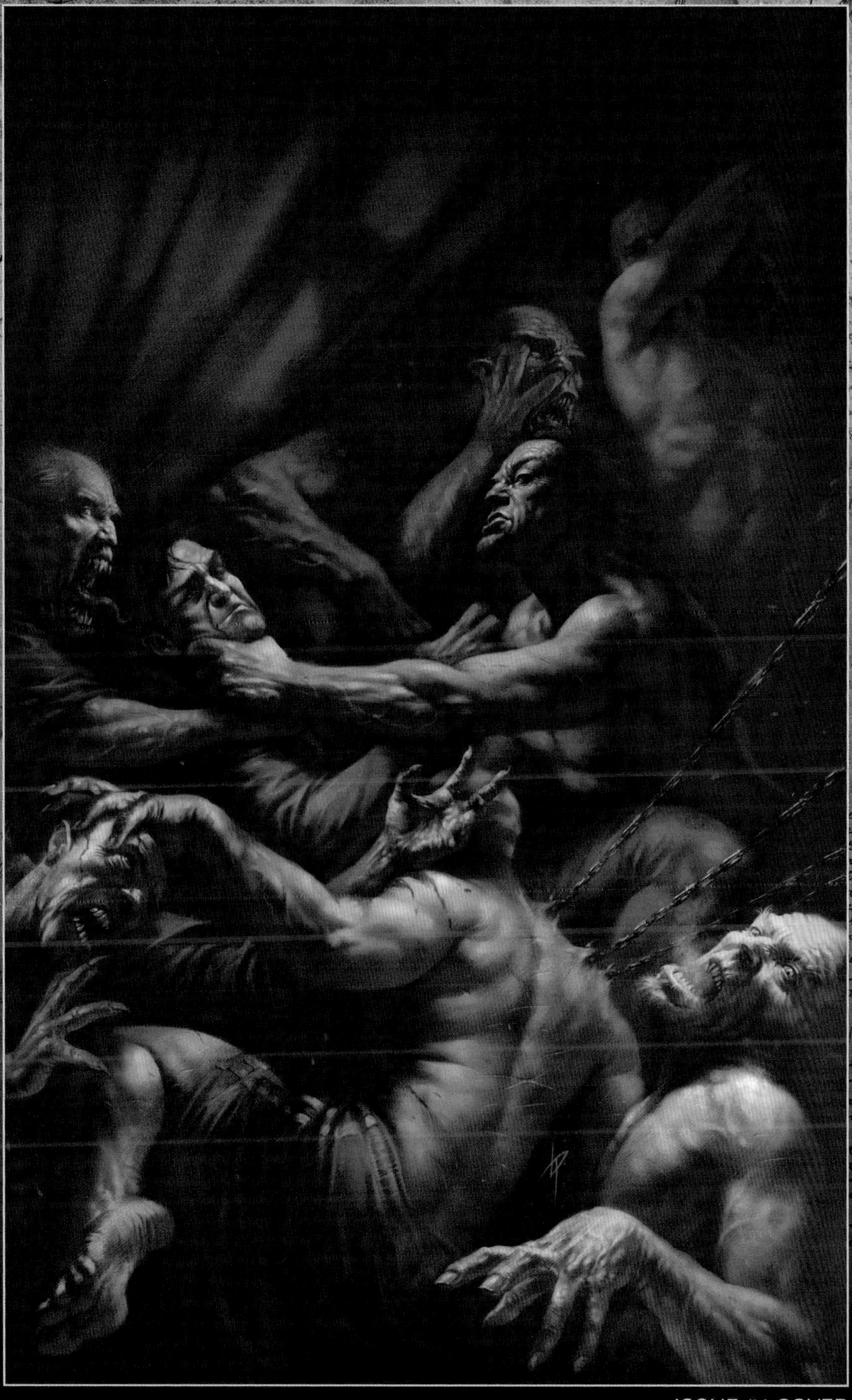

ISSUE #4 COVER
ART BY LUCIO PARRILLO

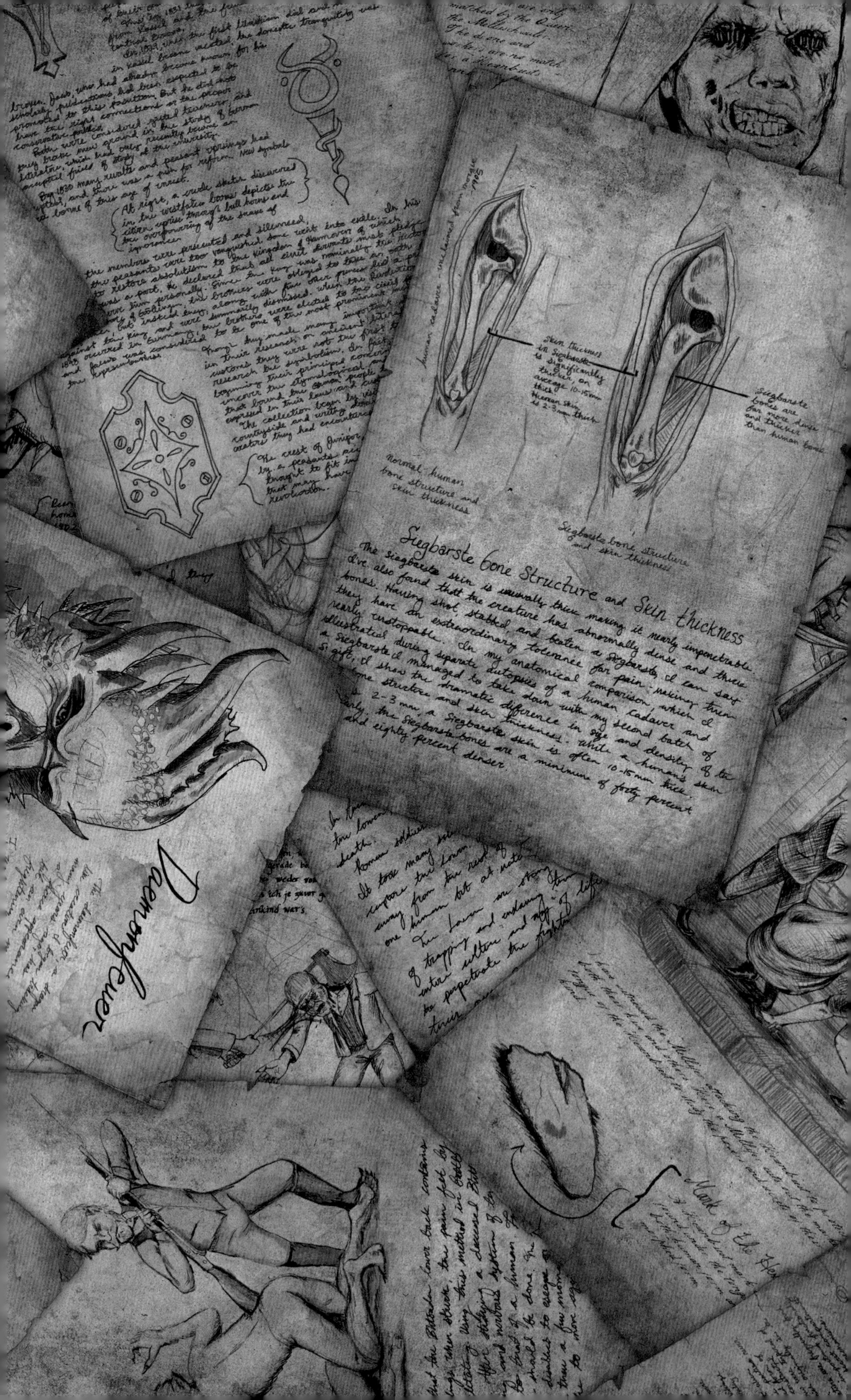
human cadaver - unclaimed from morgue 1905
Skin thickness in Siegbarste is significantly thicker, on average 10-15mm thick. Human skin is 2-3mm thick
Siegbarste bones are far more dense and thicker than human bones
Normal human bone structure and skin thickness
Siegbarste bone structure and skin thickness
Siegbarste Bone Structure and Skin thickness
The Siegbarste skin is unusually thick making it nearly impenetrable. I've also found that the creature has abnormally dense and thick bones. Having shot, stabbed, and beaten a Siegbarste, I can say they have an extraordinary tolerance for pain, making them nearly unstoppable. In my anatomical comparison, which I illustrated during separate autopsies of a human cadaver and a Siegbarste I managed to take down with my second batch of Si gift, I show the dramatic difference in size and density of the bone structure and skin thickness. While a human's skin is 2-3 mm, a Siegbarste skin is often 10-15 mm thick. And the Siegbarste bones are a minimum of forty percent and eighty percent denser.
Daemonfeuer

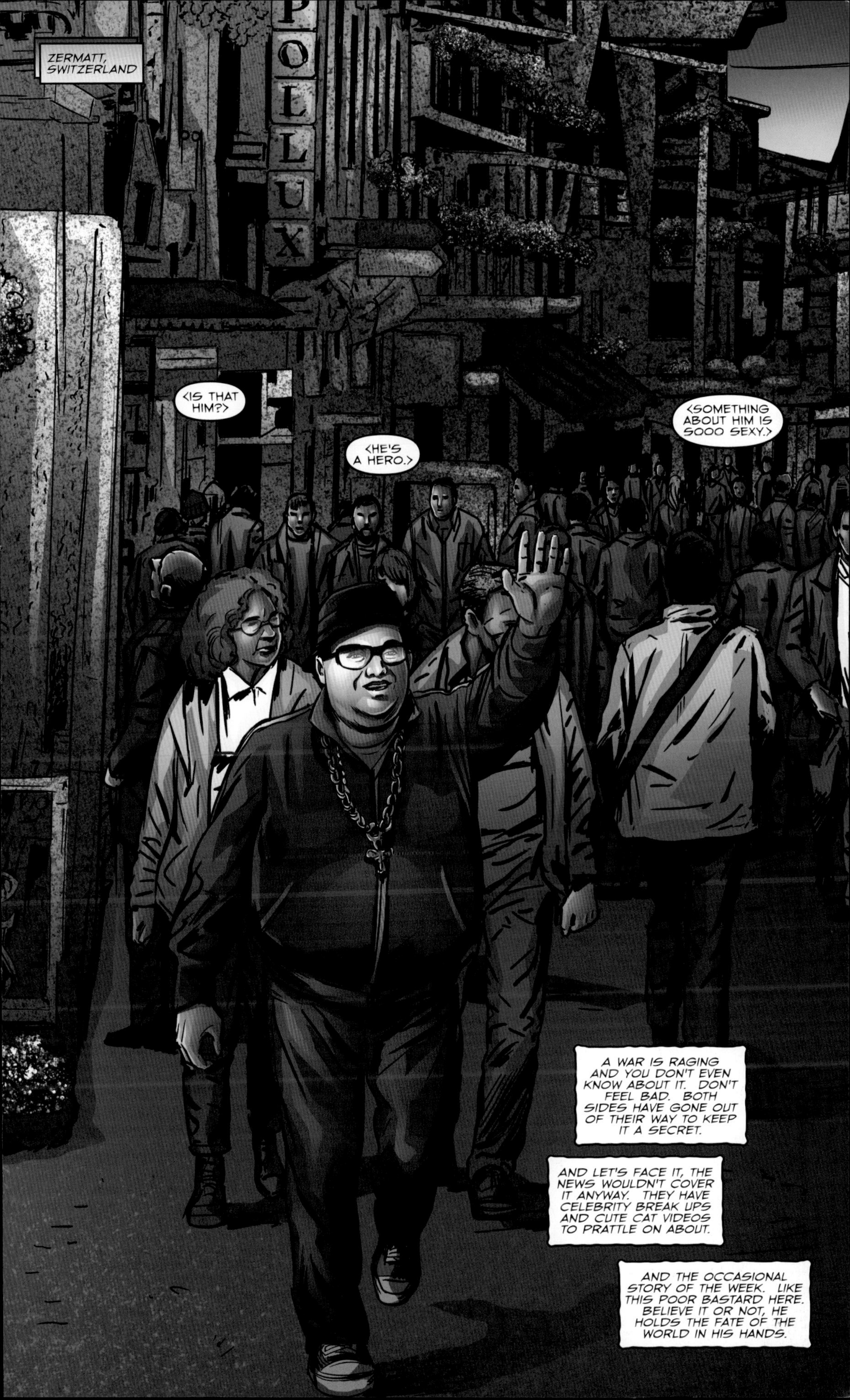
ZERMATT, SWITZERLAND
POLLUX
<IS THAT HIM?>
<HE'S A HERO.>
<SOMETHING ABOUT HIM IS SOOO SEXY.>
A WAR IS RAGING AND YOU DON'T EVEN KNOW ABOUT IT. DON'T FEEL BAD. BOTH SIDES HAVE GONE OUT OF THEIR WAY TO KEEP IT A SECRET.
AND LET'S FACE IT, THE NEWS WOULDN'T COVER IT ANYWAY. THEY HAVE CELEBRITY BREAK UPS AND CUTE CAT VIDEOS TO PRATTLE ON ABOUT.
AND THE OCCASIONAL STORY OF THE WEEK. LIKE THIS POOR BASTARD HERE. BELIEVE IT OR NOT, HE HOLDS THE FATE OF THE WORLD IN HIS HANDS.

<LOCAL HERO, GEOF DETWILER IS ONCE AGAIN IN THE NEWS TODAY...>

<THIS TIME ANNOUNCING HIS CANDIDACY FOR MAYOR.>

WAY TO GO, GEOF!

<DETWILER'S METEORIC RISE TO PROMINENCE BEGAN WHEN THIS ONCE LOWLY JANITOR DISCOVERED THE TOWN MAYOR WAS EMBEZZLING MONEY FROM THE CITY EMPLOYEE PENSION FUND.>

<DETWILER TOOK IT UPON HIMSELF TO EXPOSE THE SCANDAL, EARNING HIMSELF A HERO'S RECEPTION BY HIS FELLOW CITIZENS.>

GEOF DETWILER FOR MAYOR

<HE ATTRIBUTES HIS SUCCESS TO THE PEOPLE OF ZERMATT'S UNWAVERING SUPPORT AND HIS THREE LUCKY GOLD COINS.>

THE COINS OF ZAKYNTHOS. THEY GRANT THE MAN IN POSSESSION OF THEM AN UNNATURAL INFLUENCE OVER OTHERS. AND I NEED THEM. DESPERATELY.

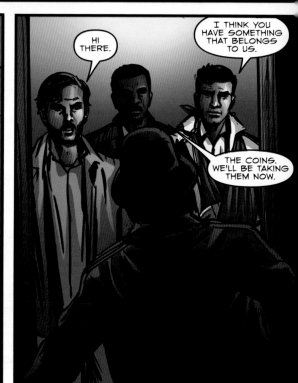

HI THERE.

I THINK YOU HAVE SOMETHING THAT BELONGS TO US.

THE COINS. WE'LL BE TAKING THEM NOW.

I...I DON'T KNOW WHAT YOU'RE TALKING ABOUT.

THE THINGS YOU'VE BEEN BLABBING ABOUT ALL OVER TV.

DUDE, WE CAN SEE THEM IN YOUR HAND.

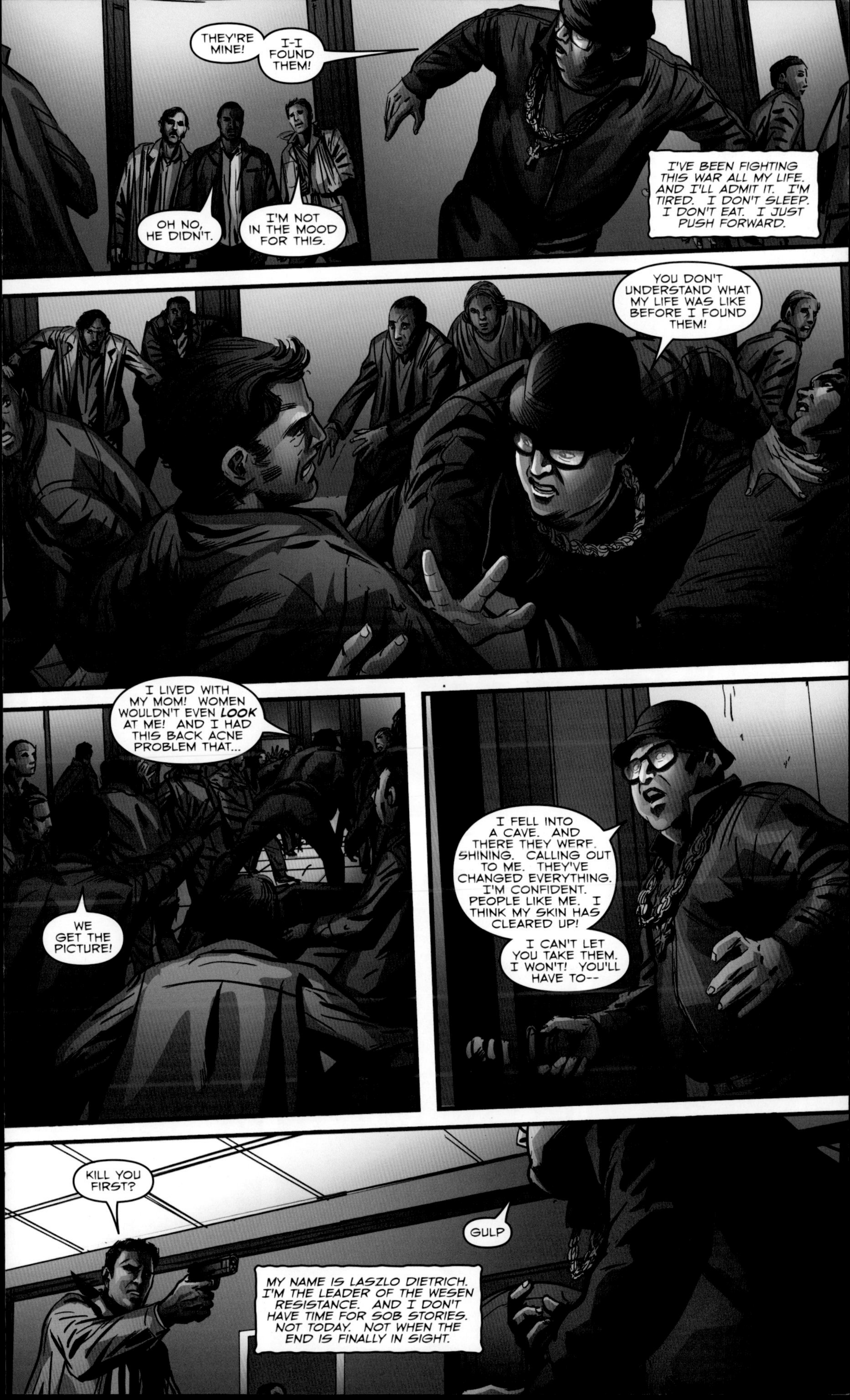
THEY'RE MINE!
I-I FOUND THEM!
OH NO, HE DIDN'T.
I'M NOT IN THE MOOD FOR THIS.
I'VE BEEN FIGHTING THIS WAR ALL MY LIFE. AND I'LL ADMIT IT. I'M TIRED. I DON'T SLEEP. I DON'T EAT. I JUST PUSH FORWARD.
YOU DON'T UNDERSTAND WHAT MY LIFE WAS LIKE BEFORE I FOUND THEM!
I LIVED WITH MY MOM! WOMEN WOULDN'T EVEN LOOK AT ME! AND I HAD THIS BACK ACNE PROBLEM THAT...
WE GET THE PICTURE!
I FELL INTO A CAVE. AND THERE THEY WERE. SHINING. CALLING OUT TO ME. THEY'VE CHANGED EVERYTHING. I'M CONFIDENT. PEOPLE LIKE ME. I THINK MY SKIN HAS CLEARED UP!
I CAN'T LET YOU TAKE THEM. I WON'T! YOU'LL HAVE TO--
KILL YOU FIRST?
GULP
MY NAME IS LASZLO DIETRICH. I'M THE LEADER OF THE WESEN RESISTANCE. AND I DON'T HAVE TIME FOR SOB STORIES. NOT TODAY. NOT WHEN THE END IS FINALLY IN SIGHT.

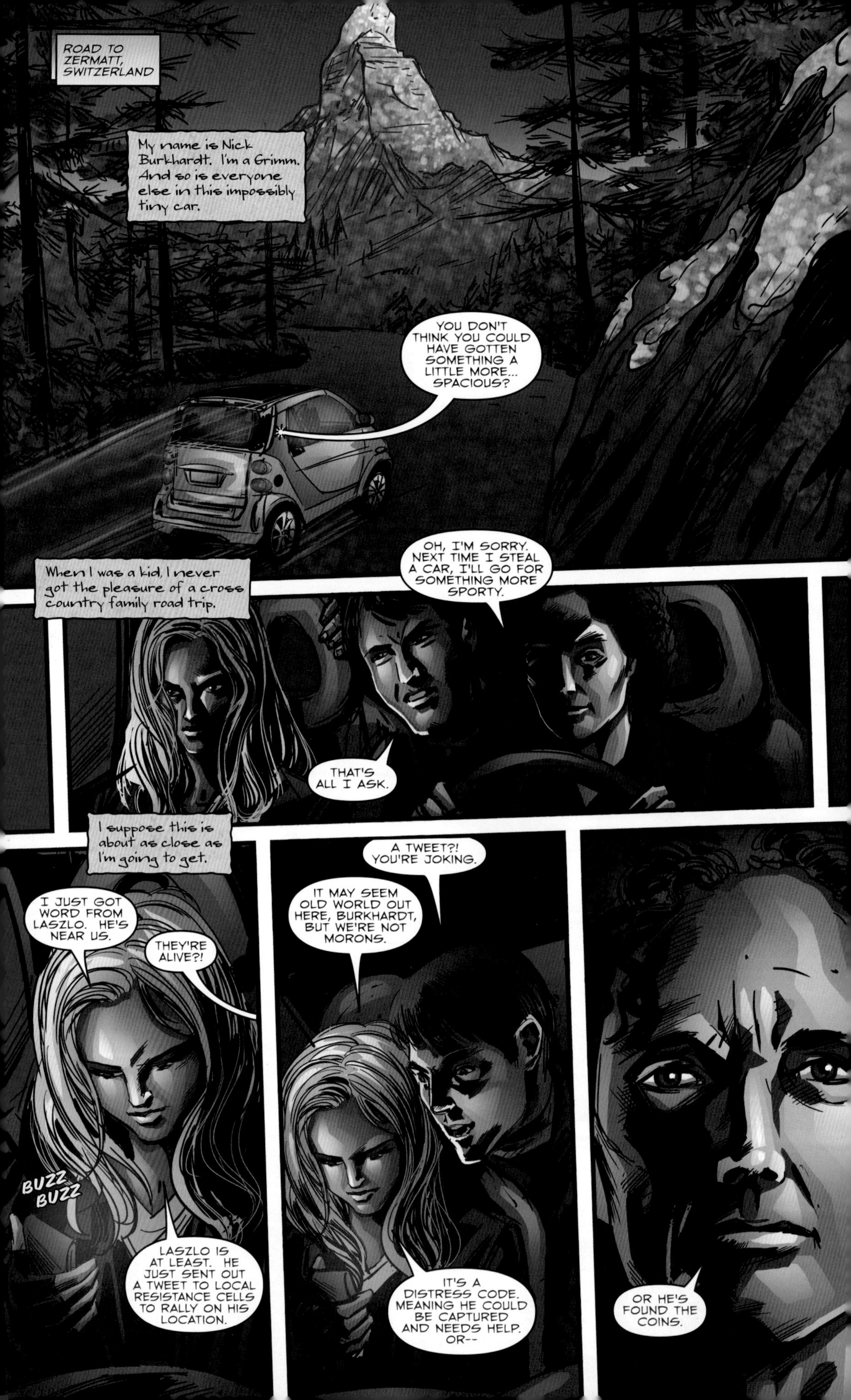
ROAD TO ZERMATT, SWITZERLAND
My name is Nick Burkhardt. I'm a Grimm. And so is everyone else in this impossibly tiny car.
YOU DON'T THINK YOU COULD HAVE GOTTEN SOMETHING A LITTLE MORE... SPACIOUS?
When I was a kid, I never got the pleasure of a cross country family road trip.
OH, I'M SORRY. NEXT TIME I STEAL A CAR, I'LL GO FOR SOMETHING MORE SPORTY.
THAT'S ALL I ASK.
I suppose this is about as close as I'm going to get.
I JUST GOT WORD FROM LASZLO. HE'S NEAR US.
THEY'RE ALIVE?!
BUZZ BUZZ
LASZLO IS AT LEAST. HE JUST SENT OUT A TWEET TO LOCAL RESISTANCE CELLS TO RALLY ON HIS LOCATION.
A TWEET?! YOU'RE JOKING.
IT MAY SEEM OLD WORLD OUT HERE, BURKHARDT, BUT WE'RE NOT MORONS.
IT'S A DISTRESS CODE. MEANING HE COULD BE CAPTURED AND NEEDS HELP. OR--
OR HE'S FOUND THE COINS.

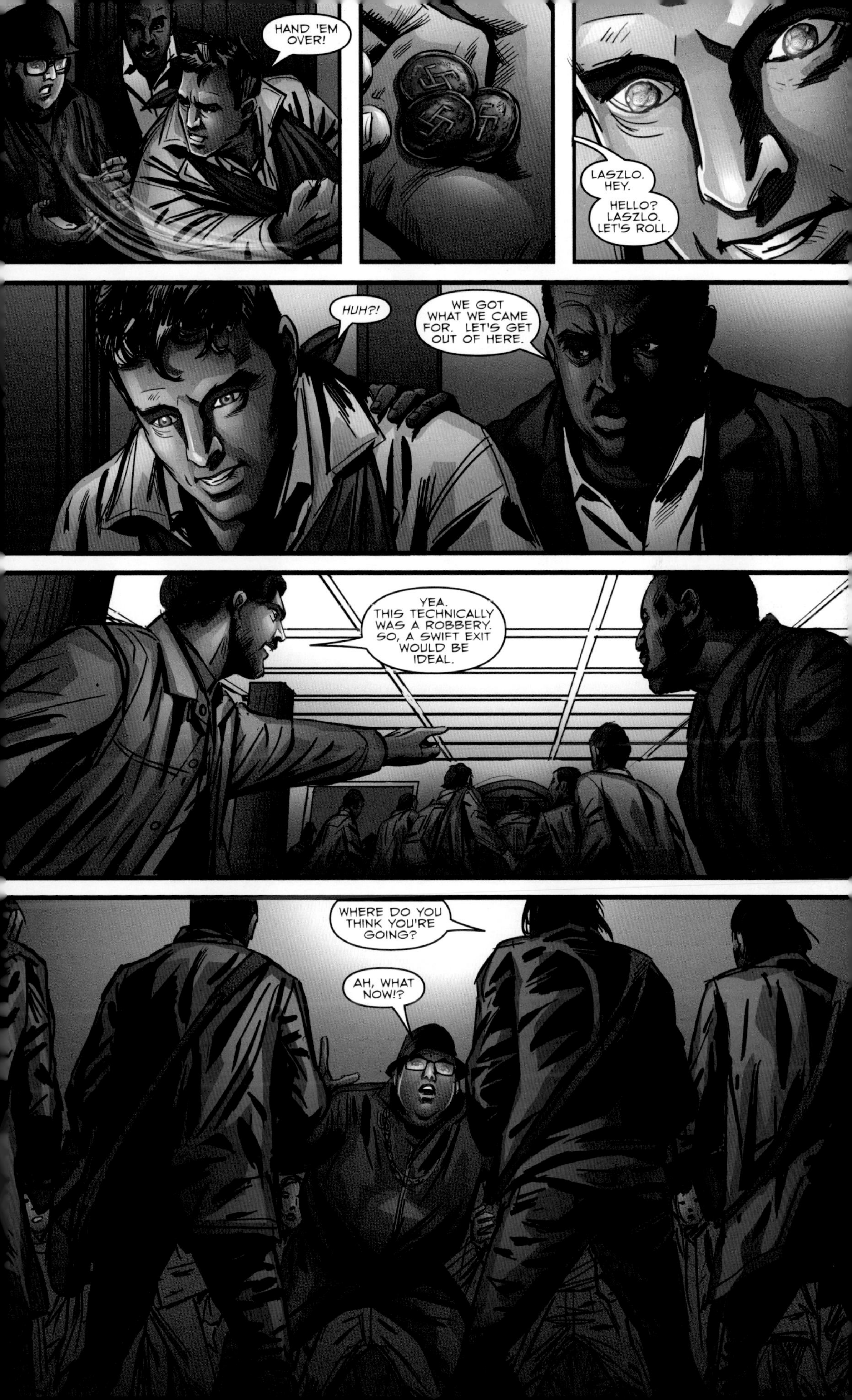
HAND 'EM OVER!
LASZLO. HEY.
HELLO? LASZLO. LET'S ROLL.
HUH?!
WE GOT WHAT WE CAME FOR. LET'S GET OUT OF HERE.
YEA. THIS TECHNICALLY WAS A ROBBERY. SO, A SWIFT EXIT WOULD BE IDEAL.
WHERE DO YOU THINK YOU'RE GOING?
AH, WHAT NOW!?

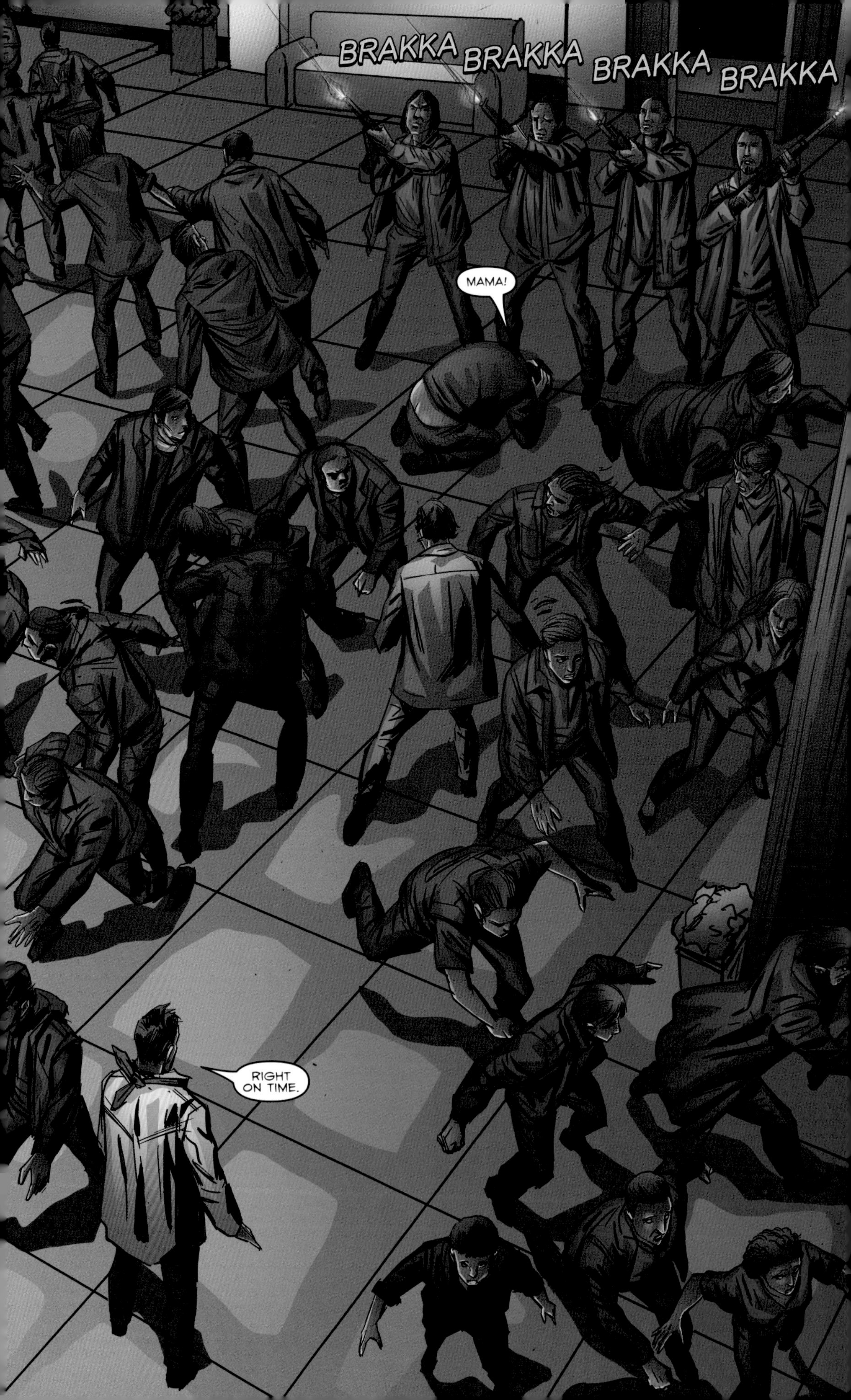
BRAKKA BRAKKA BRAKKA BRAKKA
MAMA!
RIGHT ON TIME.

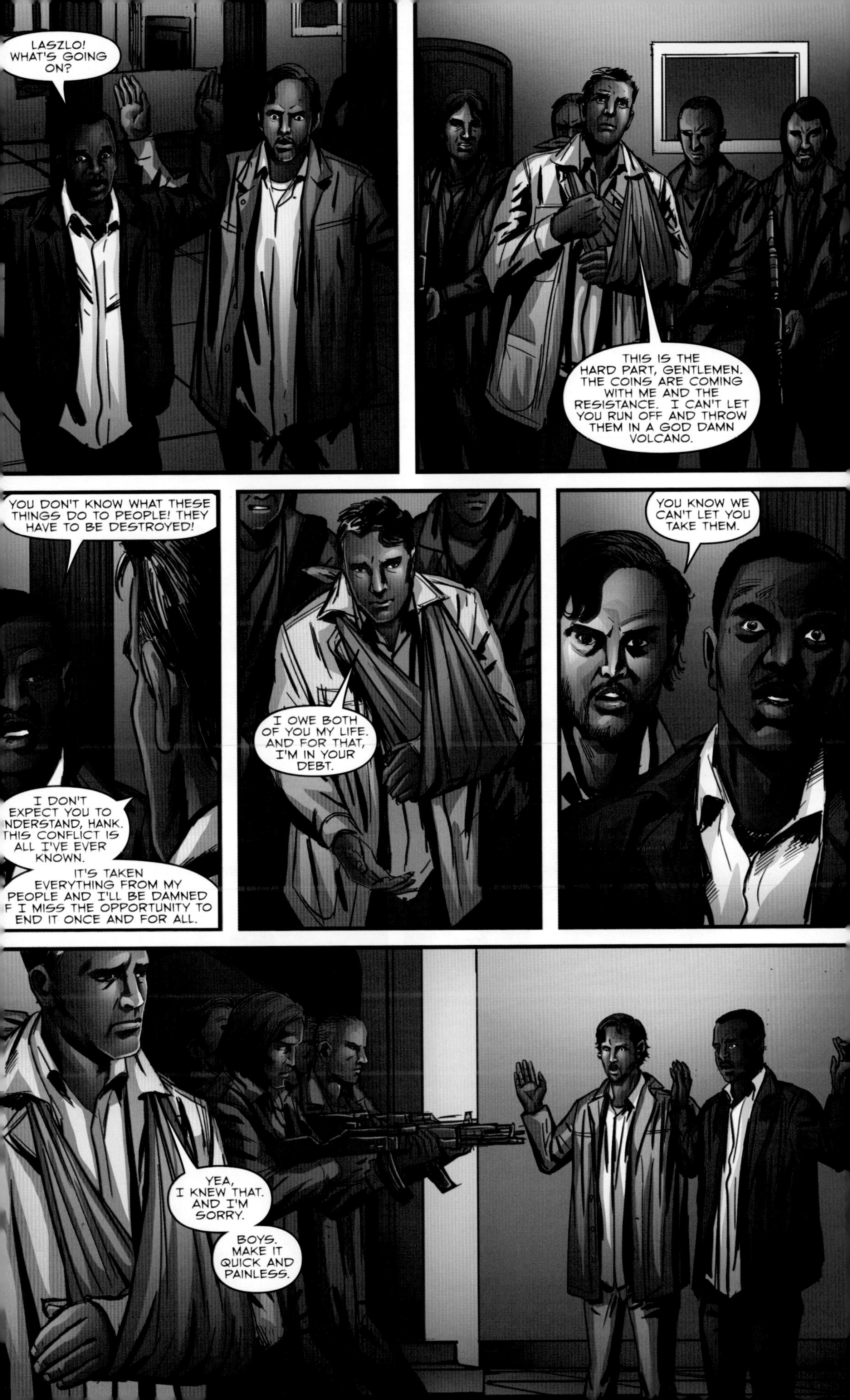
LASZLO! WHAT'S GOING ON?
THIS IS THE HARD PART, GENTLEMEN. THE COINS ARE COMING WITH ME AND THE RESISTANCE. I CAN'T LET YOU RUN OFF AND THROW THEM IN A GOD DAMN VOLCANO.
YOU DON'T KNOW WHAT THESE THINGS DO TO PEOPLE! THEY HAVE TO BE DESTROYED!
I DON'T EXPECT YOU TO NDERSTAND, HANK. THIS CONFLICT IS ALL I'VE EVER KNOWN.
IT'S TAKEN EVERYTHING FROM MY PEOPLE AND I'LL BE DAMNED F I MISS THE OPPORTUNITY TO END IT ONCE AND FOR ALL.
I OWE BOTH OF YOU MY LIFE. AND FOR THAT, I'M IN YOUR DEBT.
YOU KNOW WE CAN'T LET YOU TAKE THEM.
YEA, I KNEW THAT. AND I'M SORRY.
BOYS. MAKE IT QUICK AND PAINLESS.

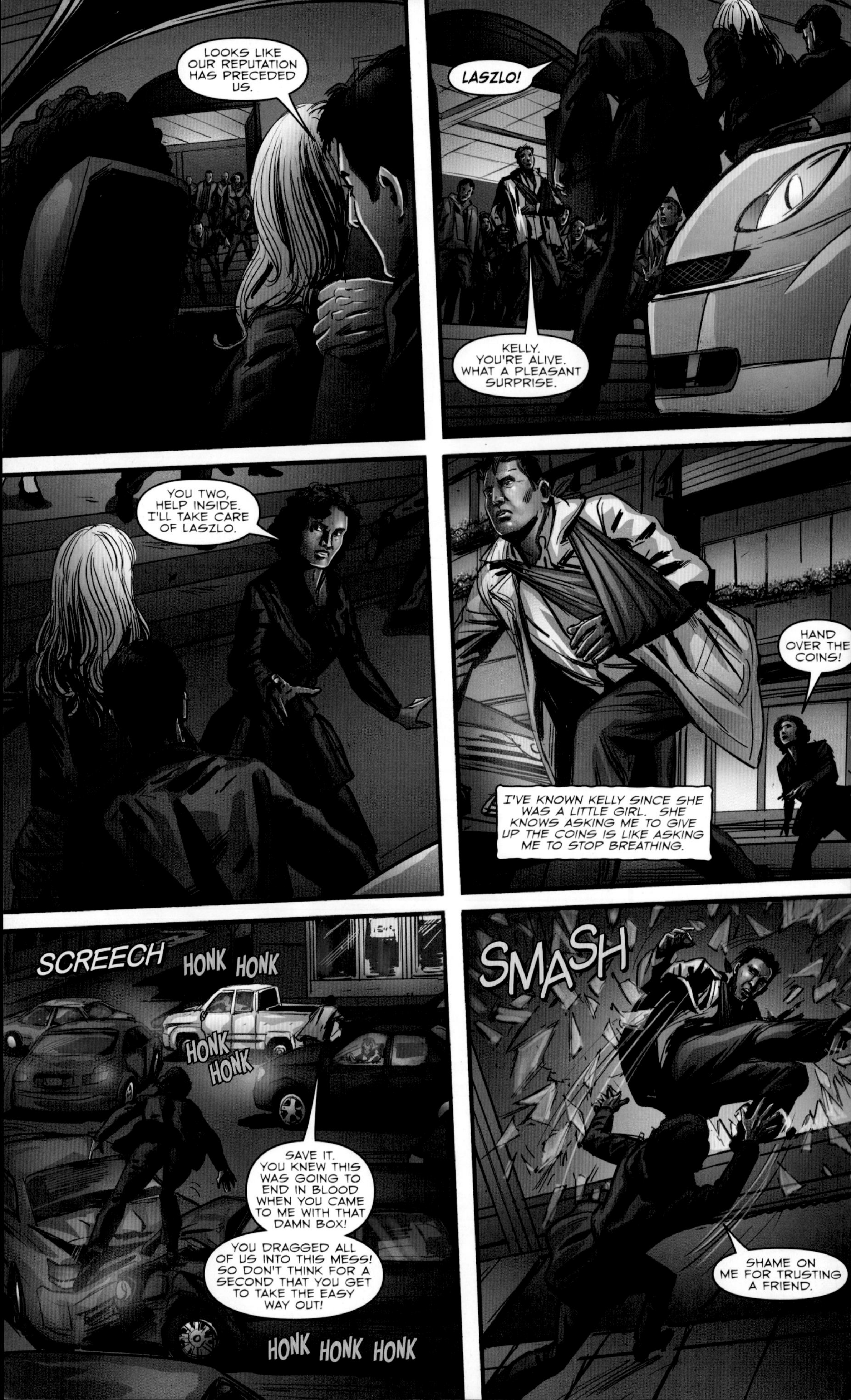
LOOKS LIKE OUR REPUTATION HAS PRECEDED US.
LASZLO!
KELLY. YOU'RE ALIVE. WHAT A PLEASANT SURPRISE.
YOU TWO, HELP INSIDE. I'LL TAKE CARE OF LASZLO.
HAND OVER THE COINS!
I'VE KNOWN KELLY SINCE SHE WAS A LITTLE GIRL. SHE KNOWS ASKING ME TO GIVE UP THE COINS IS LIKE ASKING ME TO STOP BREATHING.
SCREECH
HONK HONK
HONK HONK
SAVE IT. YOU KNEW THIS WAS GOING TO END IN BLOOD WHEN YOU CAME TO ME WITH THAT DAMN BOX!
YOU DRAGGED ALL OF US INTO THIS MESS! SO DON'T THINK FOR A SECOND THAT YOU GET TO TAKE THE EASY WAY OUT!
HONK HONK HONK
SMASH
SHAME ON ME FOR TRUSTING A FRIEND.

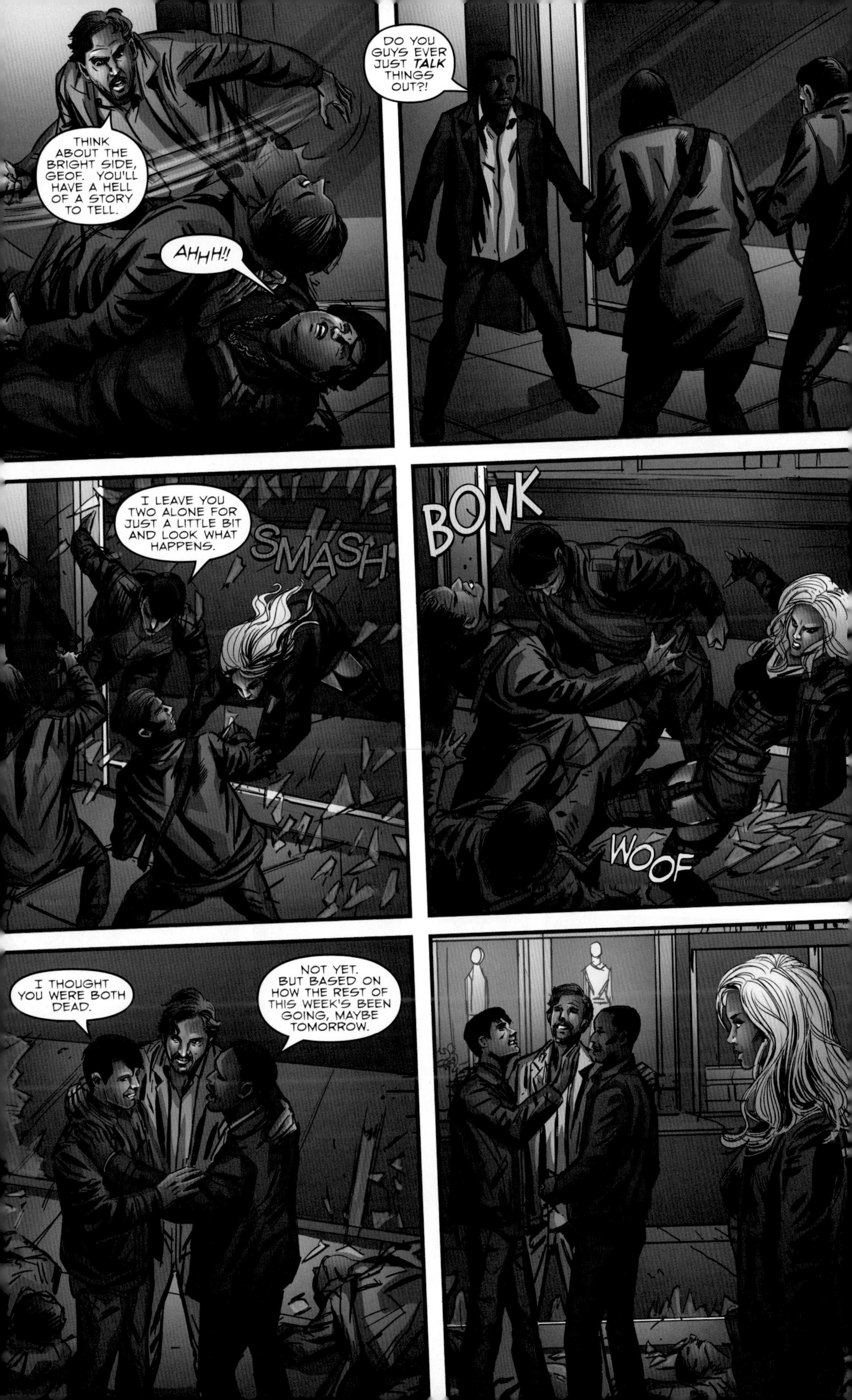
THINK ABOUT THE BRIGHT SIDE, GEOF. YOU'LL HAVE A HELL OF A STORY TO TELL.
AHHH!!
DO YOU GUYS EVER JUST TALK THINGS OUT?!
I LEAVE YOU TWO ALONE FOR JUST A LITTLE BIT AND LOOK WHAT HAPPENS.
SMASH
BONK
WOOF
I THOUGHT YOU WERE BOTH DEAD.
NOT YET. BUT BASED ON HOW THE REST OF THIS WEEK'S BEEN GOING, MAYBE TOMORROW.

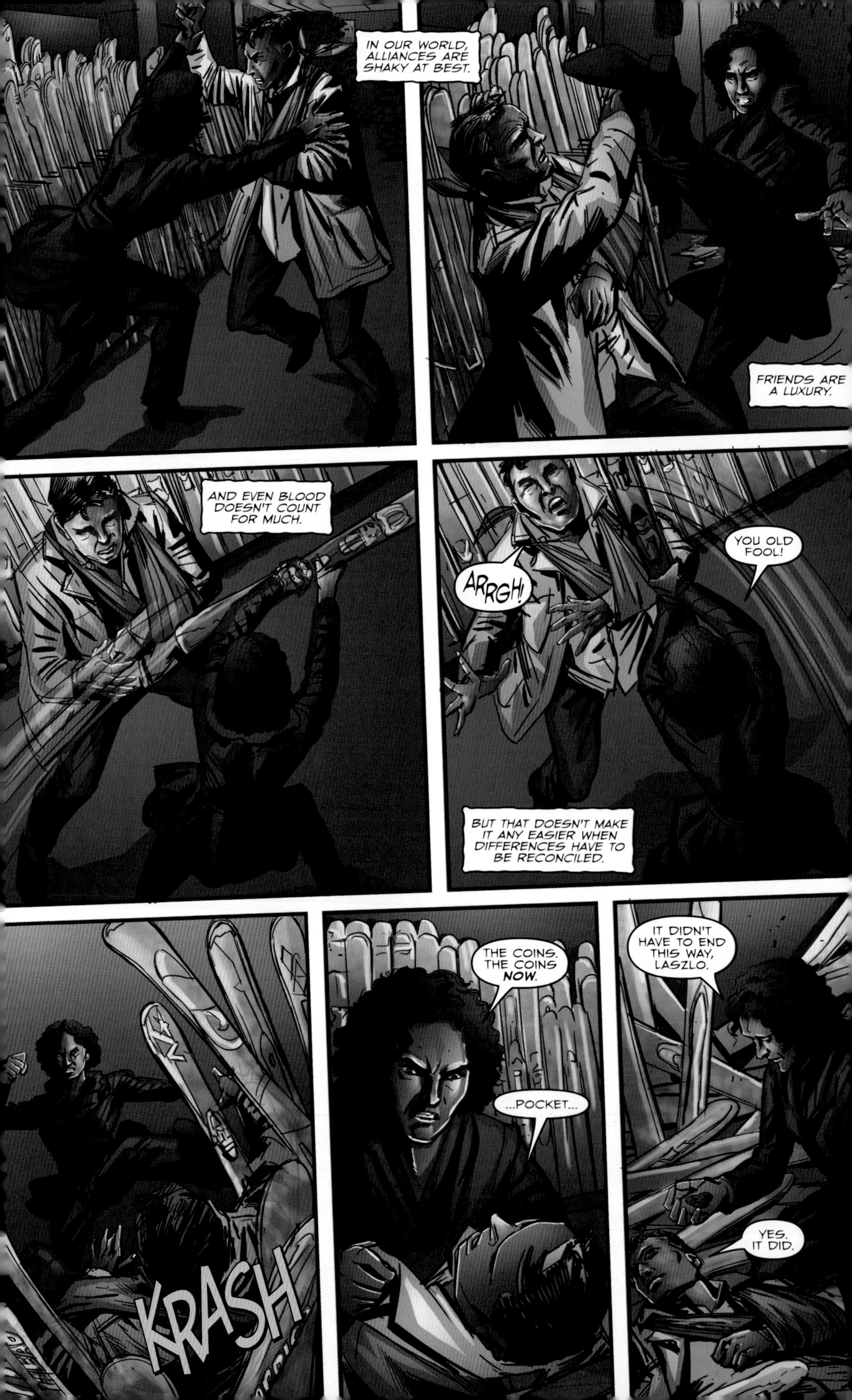
IN OUR WORLD, ALLIANCES ARE SHAKY AT BEST.
FRIENDS ARE A LUXURY.
AND EVEN BLOOD DOESN'T COUNT FOR MUCH.
ARRGH!
YOU OLD FOOL!
BUT THAT DOESN'T MAKE IT ANY EASIER WHEN DIFFERENCES HAVE TO BE RECONCILED.
KRASH
THE COINS. THE COINS NOW.
...POCKET...
IT DIDN'T HAVE TO END THIS WAY, LASZLO.
YES. IT DID.

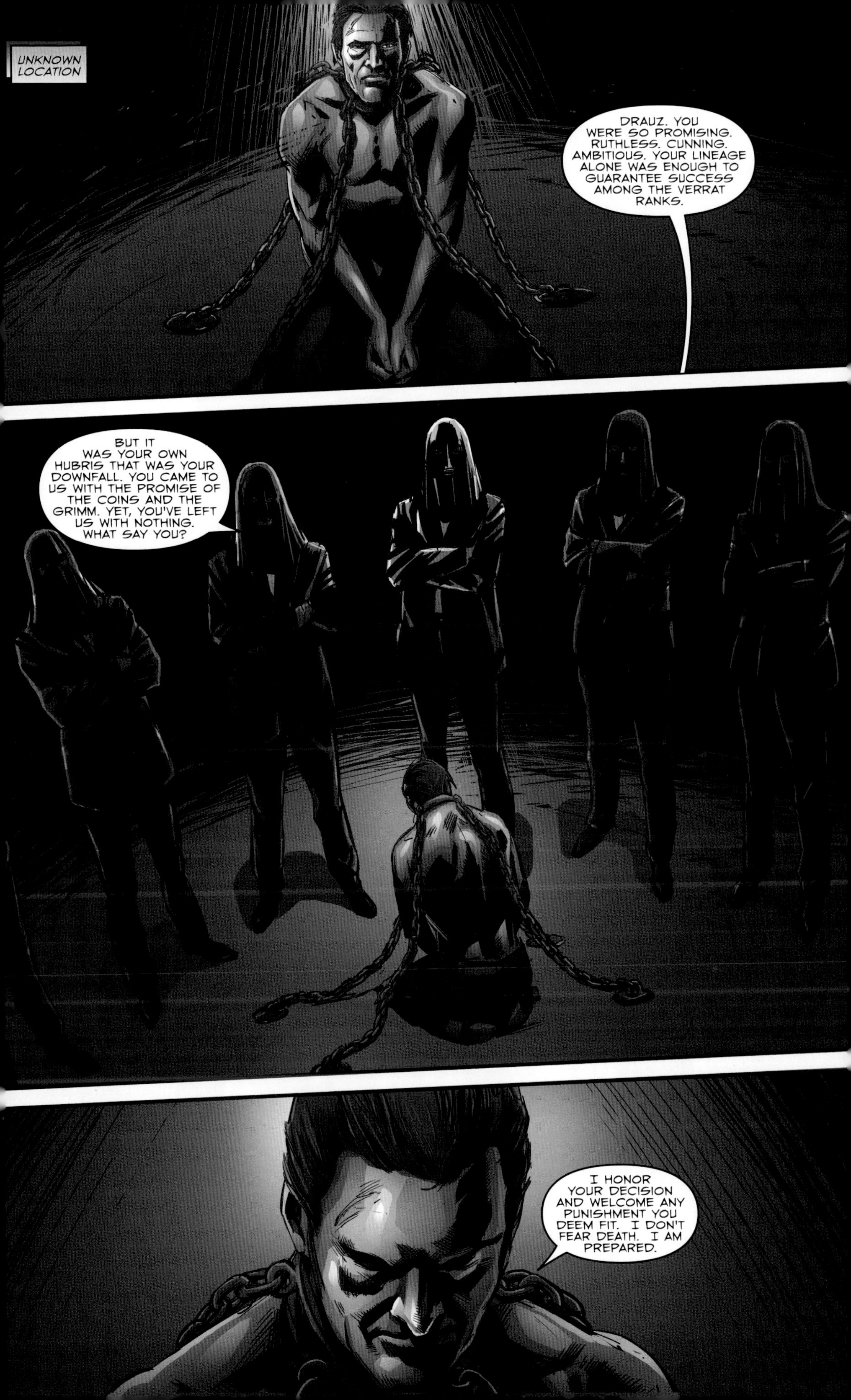
UNKNOWN LOCATION
DRAUZ. YOU WERE SO PROMISING. RUTHLESS. CUNNING. AMBITIOUS. YOUR LINEAGE ALONE WAS ENOUGH TO GUARANTEE SUCCESS AMONG THE VERRAT RANKS.
BUT IT WAS YOUR OWN HUBRIS THAT WAS YOUR DOWNFALL. YOU CAME TO US WITH THE PROMISE OF THE COINS AND THE GRIMM. YET, YOU'VE LEFT US WITH NOTHING. WHAT SAY YOU?
I HONOR YOUR DECISION AND WELCOME ANY PUNISHMENT YOU DEEM FIT. I DON'T FEAR DEATH. I AM PREPARED.

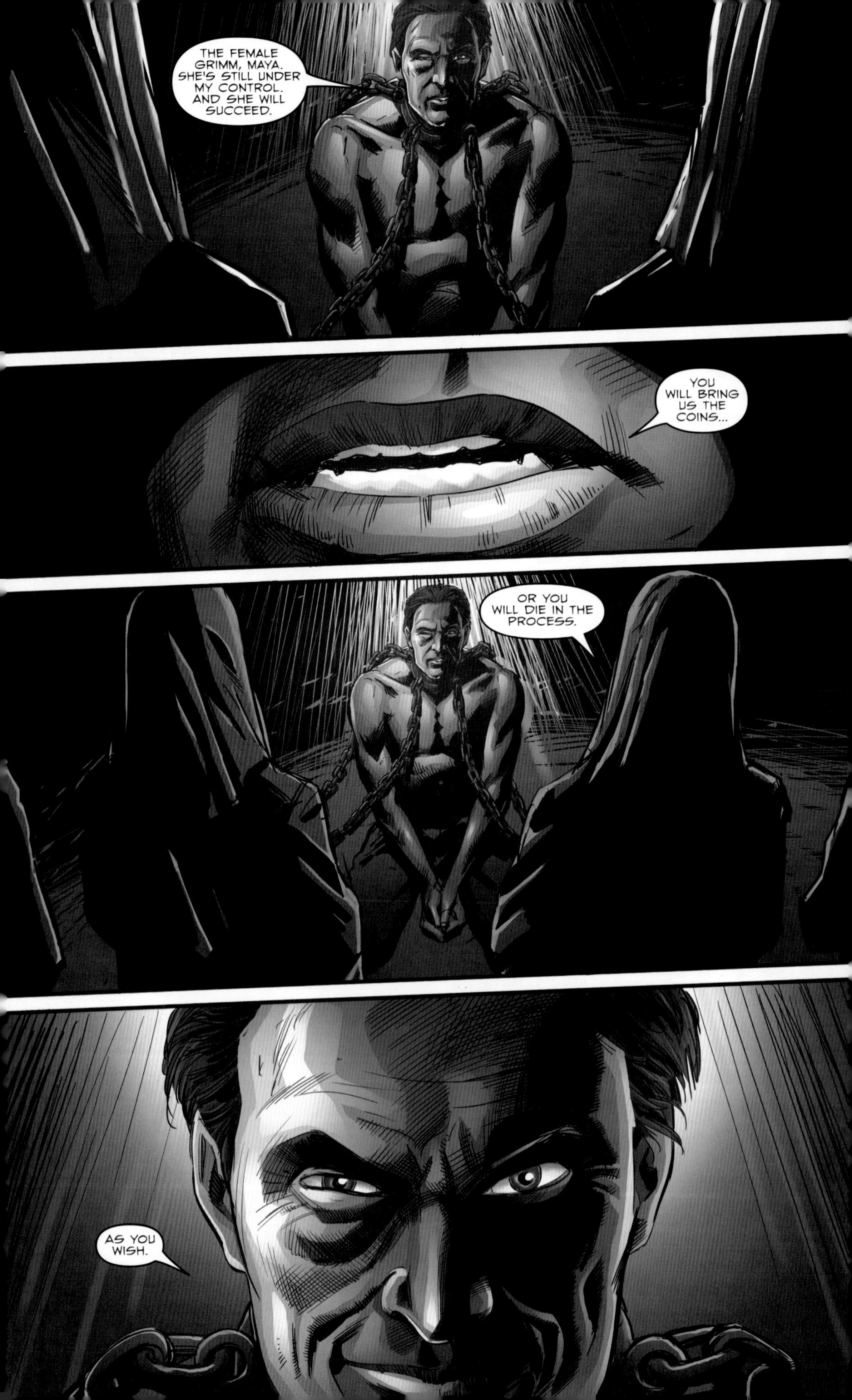
THE FEMALE GRIMM, MAYA. SHE'S STILL UNDER MY CONTROL. AND SHE WILL SUCCEED.
YOU WILL BRING US THE COINS...
OR YOU WILL DIE IN THE PROCESS.
AS YOU WISH.

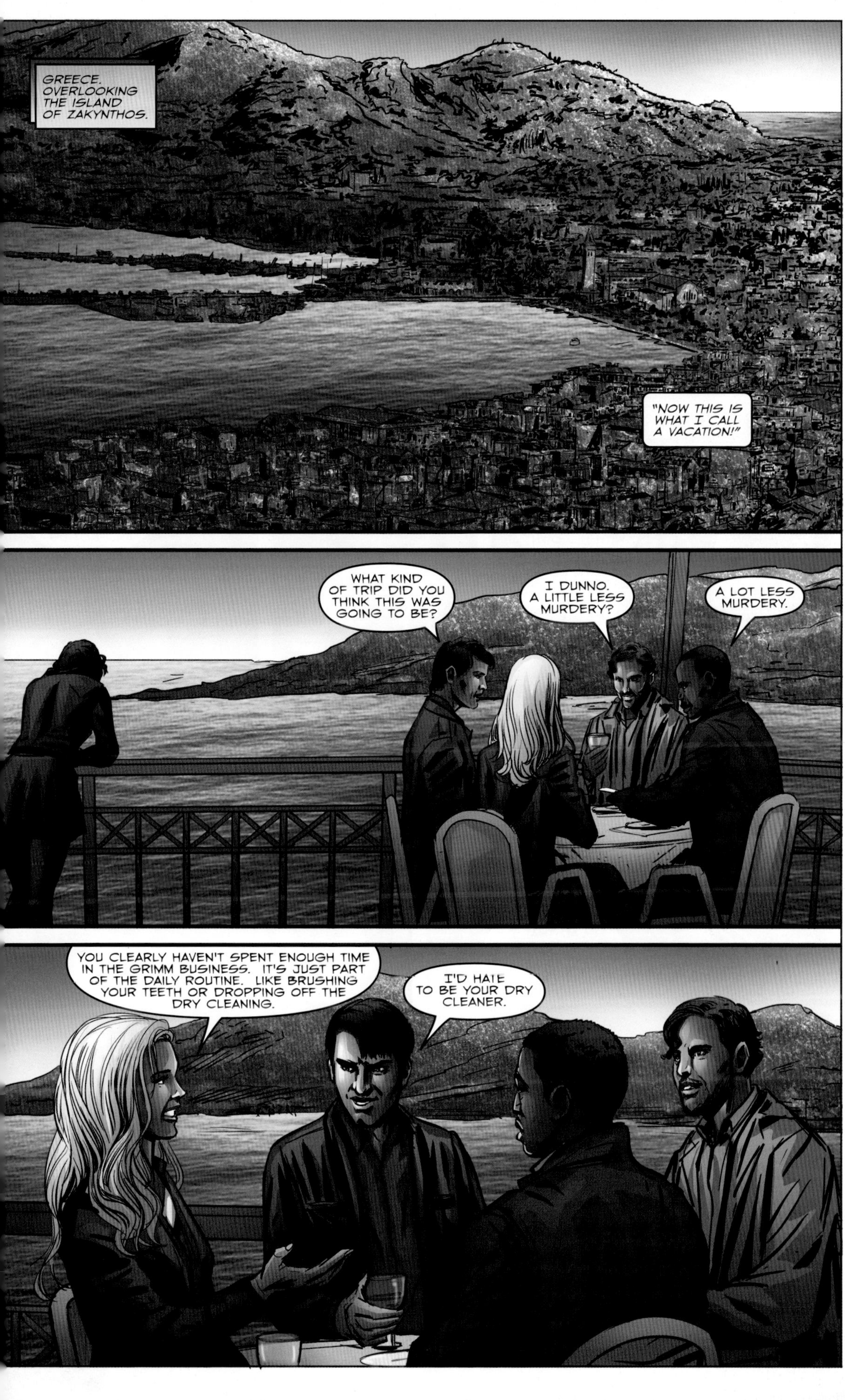
GREECE. OVERLOOKING THE ISLAND OF ZAKYNTHOS.
"NOW THIS IS WHAT I CALL A VACATION!"
WHAT KIND OF TRIP DID YOU THINK THIS WAS GOING TO BE?
I DUNNO. A LITTLE LESS MURDERY?
A LOT LESS MURDERY.
YOU CLEARLY HAVEN'T SPENT ENOUGH TIME IN THE GRIMM BUSINESS. IT'S JUST PART OF THE DAILY ROUTINE. LIKE BRUSHING YOUR TEETH OR DROPPING OFF THE DRY CLEANING.
I'D HATE TO BE YOUR DRY CLEANER.

ANYONE NEED ANYTHING? WINE?

YES, PLEASE.

I'M JUST SAYING, I DIDN'T EXPECT TO SEE MONROE LAY OUT A NUN WHILE WE WERE HERE.

WHAT?! SHE WAS LITERALLY A TERRIFYING SNAKE WOMAN.

WHATEVER THE CASE, YOU PROBABLY STILL OWE A COUPLE DOZEN HAIL MARY'S FOR THAT.

YEA WELL. MAYA STABBED A DICKFELLIG. WITH HIS OWN HORN!

AND I'D DO IT AGAIN!

JUST SAYING. IT'S A HELL OF A FIRST IMPRESSION.

BETTER SHE'S DOING THAT SORT OF STUFF TO THEM AND NOT US.

I'LL DRINK TO THAT!

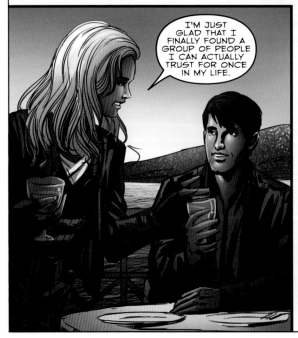

I'M JUST GLAD THAT I FINALLY FOUND A GROUP OF PEOPLE I CAN ACTUALLY TRUST FOR ONCE IN MY LIFE.

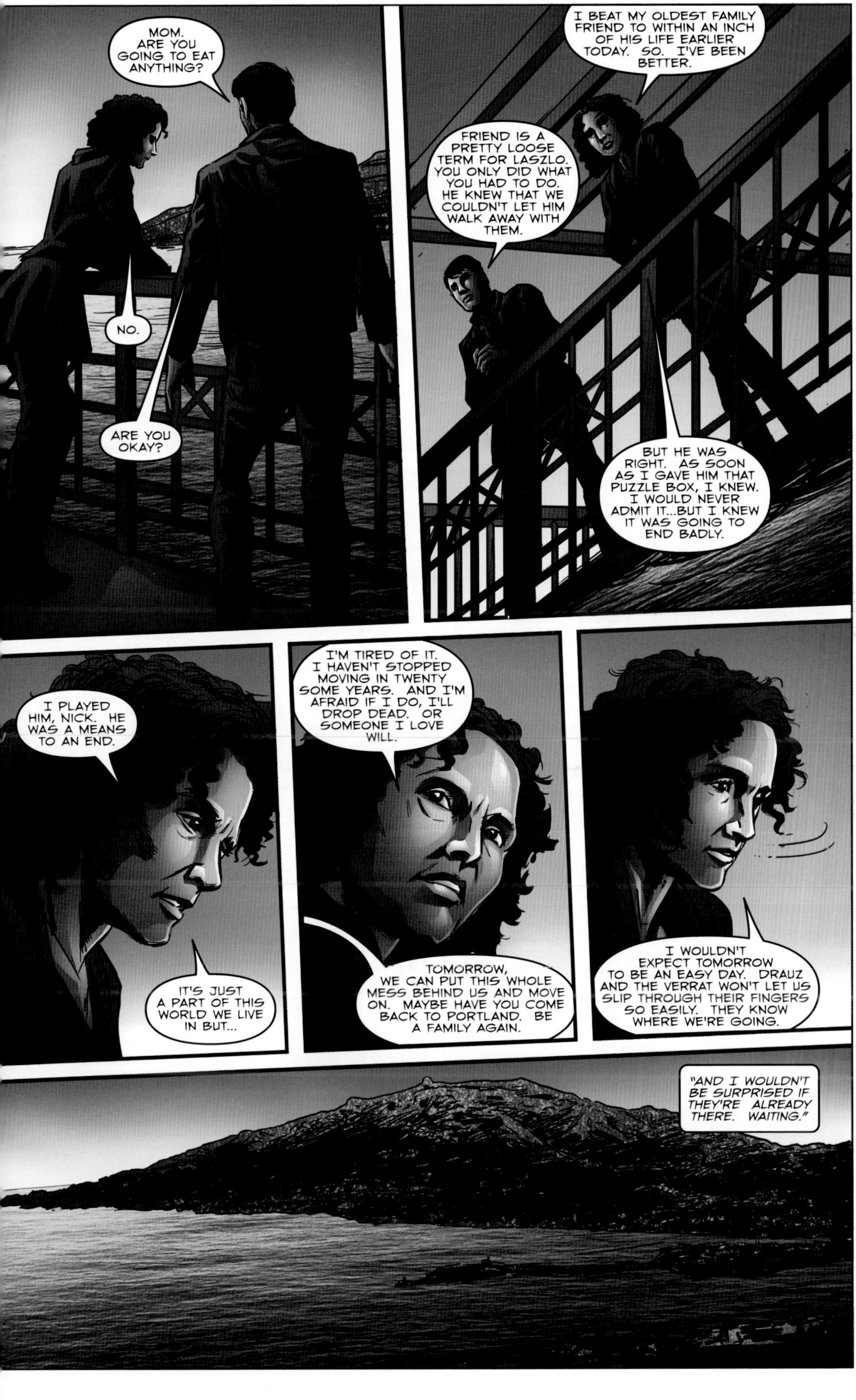
MOM. ARE YOU GOING TO EAT ANYTHING?
NO.
ARE YOU OKAY?
I BEAT MY OLDEST FAMILY FRIEND TO WITHIN AN INCH OF HIS LIFE EARLIER TODAY. SO. I'VE BEEN BETTER.
FRIEND IS A PRETTY LOOSE TERM FOR LASZLO. YOU ONLY DID WHAT YOU HAD TO DO. HE KNEW THAT WE COULDN'T LET HIM WALK AWAY WITH THEM.
BUT HE WAS RIGHT. AS SOON AS I GAVE HIM THAT PUZZLE BOX, I KNEW. I WOULD NEVER ADMIT IT...BUT I KNEW IT WAS GOING TO END BADLY.
I PLAYED HIM, NICK. HE WAS A MEANS TO AN END.
IT'S JUST A PART OF THIS WORLD WE LIVE IN BUT...
I'M TIRED OF IT. I HAVEN'T STOPPED MOVING IN TWENTY SOME YEARS. AND I'M AFRAID IF I DO, I'LL DROP DEAD. OR SOMEONE I LOVE WILL.
TOMORROW, WE CAN PUT THIS WHOLE MESS BEHIND US AND MOVE ON. MAYBE HAVE YOU COME BACK TO PORTLAND. BE A FAMILY AGAIN.
I WOULDN'T EXPECT TOMORROW TO BE AN EASY DAY. DRAUZ AND THE VERRAT WON'T LET US SLIP THROUGH THEIR FINGERS SO EASILY. THEY KNOW WHERE WE'RE GOING.
"AND I WOULDN'T BE SURPRISED IF THEY'RE ALREADY THERE. WAITING."

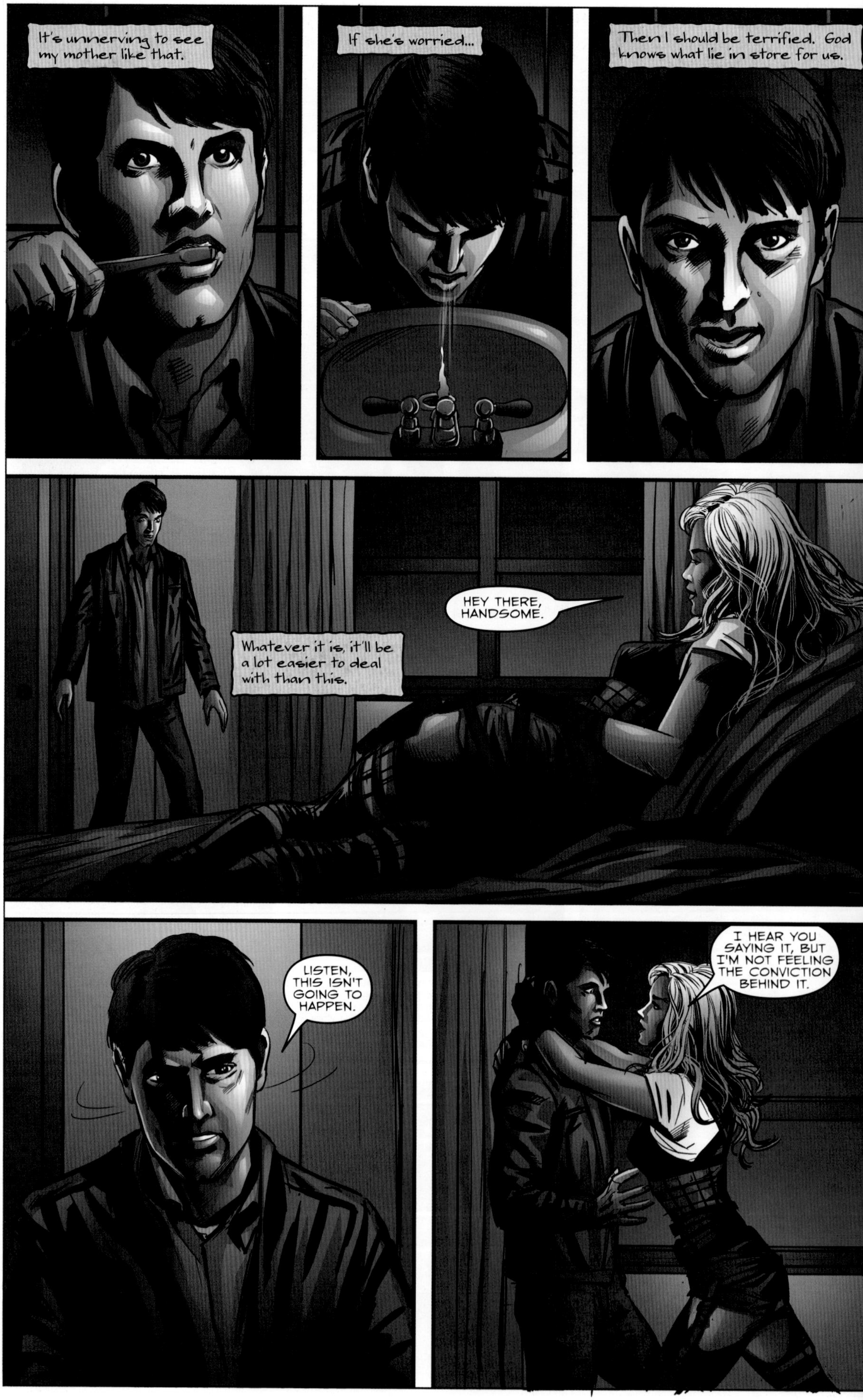
It's unnerving to see my mother like that.
If she's worried...
Then I should be terrified. God knows what lie in store for us.
HEY THERE, HANDSOME.
Whatever it is, it'll be a lot easier to deal with than this.
LISTEN, THIS ISN'T GOING TO HAPPEN.
I HEAR YOU SAYING IT, BUT I'M NOT FEELING THE CONVICTION BEHIND IT.

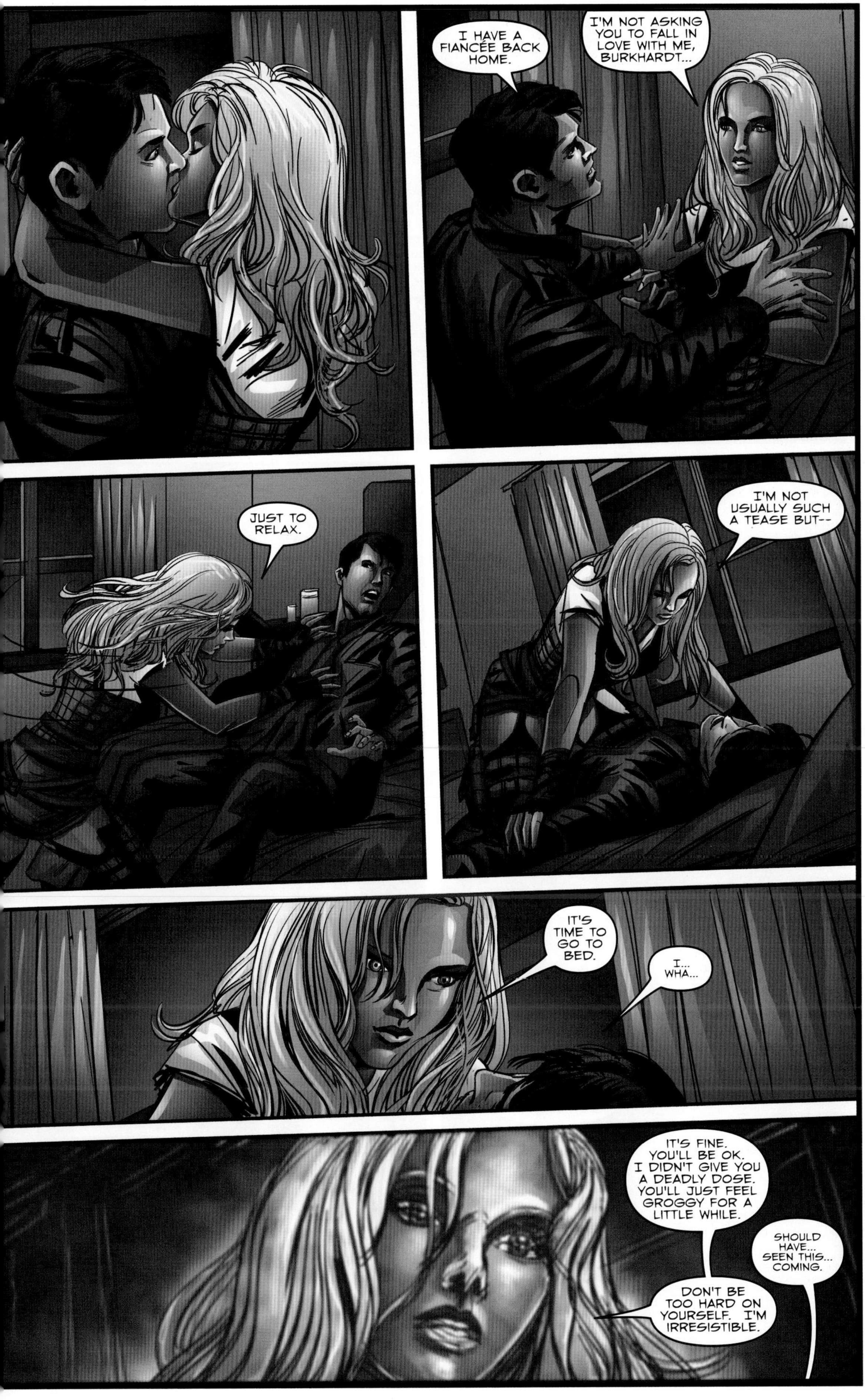
I HAVE A FIANCÉE BACK HOME.
I'M NOT ASKING YOU TO FALL IN LOVE WITH ME, BURKHARDT...
JUST TO RELAX.
I'M NOT USUALLY SUCH A TEASE BUT--
IT'S TIME TO GO TO BED.
I... WHA...
IT'S FINE. YOU'LL BE OK. I DIDN'T GIVE YOU A DEADLY DOSE. YOU'LL JUST FEEL GROGGY FOR A LITTLE WHILE.
SHOULD HAVE... SEEN THIS... COMING.
DON'T BE TOO HARD ON YOURSELF. I'M IRRESISTIBLE.

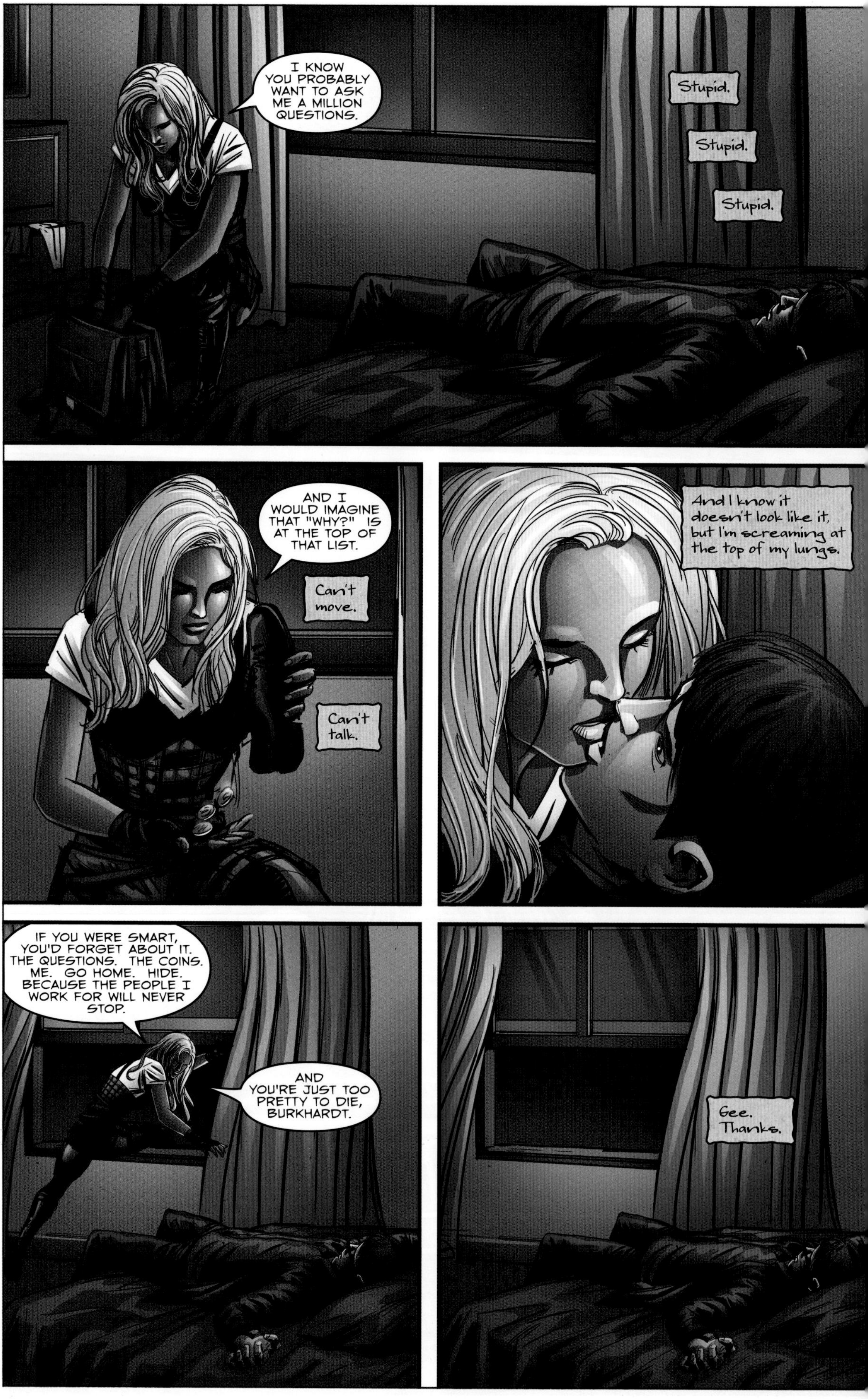
I KNOW YOU PROBABLY WANT TO ASK ME A MILLION QUESTIONS.
Stupid.
Stupid.
Stupid.
AND I WOULD IMAGINE THAT "WHY?" IS AT THE TOP OF THAT LIST.
Can't move.
Can't talk.
And I know it doesn't look like it, but I'm screaming at the top of my lungs.
IF YOU WERE SMART, YOU'D FORGET ABOUT IT. THE QUESTIONS. THE COINS. ME. GO HOME. HIDE. BECAUSE THE PEOPLE I WORK FOR WILL NEVER STOP.
AND YOU'RE JUST TOO PRETTY TO DIE, BURKHARDT.
Gee. Thanks.

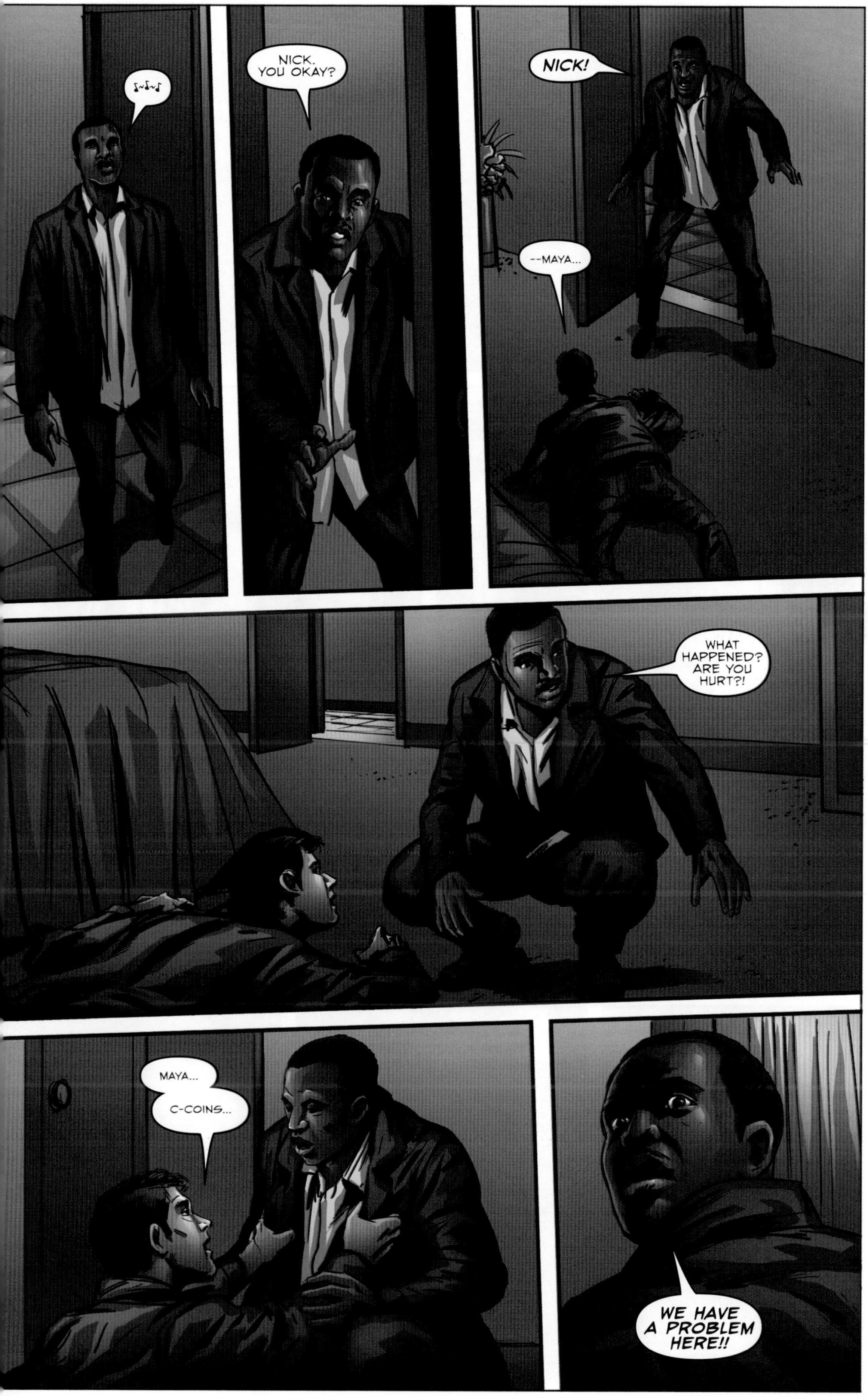
♪~♪~♪
NICK. YOU OKAY?
NICK!
--MAYA...
WHAT HAPPENED? ARE YOU HURT?!
MAYA...
C-COINS...
WE HAVE A PROBLEM HERE!!

GOING SOMEWHERE?

LASZLO--

I KNEW THERE WAS SOMETHING OFF ABOUT YOU.

I THOUGHT IT WAS THE TYPICAL GRIMM SYNDROME. ABANDONED, BROKEN GIRL.

WHOM I WAS MORE THAN HAPPY TO PROVIDE A LITTLE GUIDANCE AND PURPOSE TO.

TURNS OUT YOU'RE NOTHING MORE THAN DRAUZ' LITTLE PET.

YOU WISH IT WAS THAT SIMPLE.

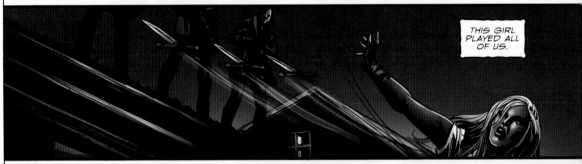

THIS GIRL PLAYED ALL OF US.

AND WHILE I MAY DISAGREE WITH KELLY ABOUT THE COINS, I KNOW THAT THEY CAN'T LEAVE WITH MAYA.

BUT I'M BEATEN.

TIRED.

OLD.

AND SHE KNOWS IT.

I'M LASZLO DIETRICH. LEADER OF THE WESEN RESISTANCE. AND I'VE LET EVERYONE I'VE EVER CARED ABOUT DOWN.

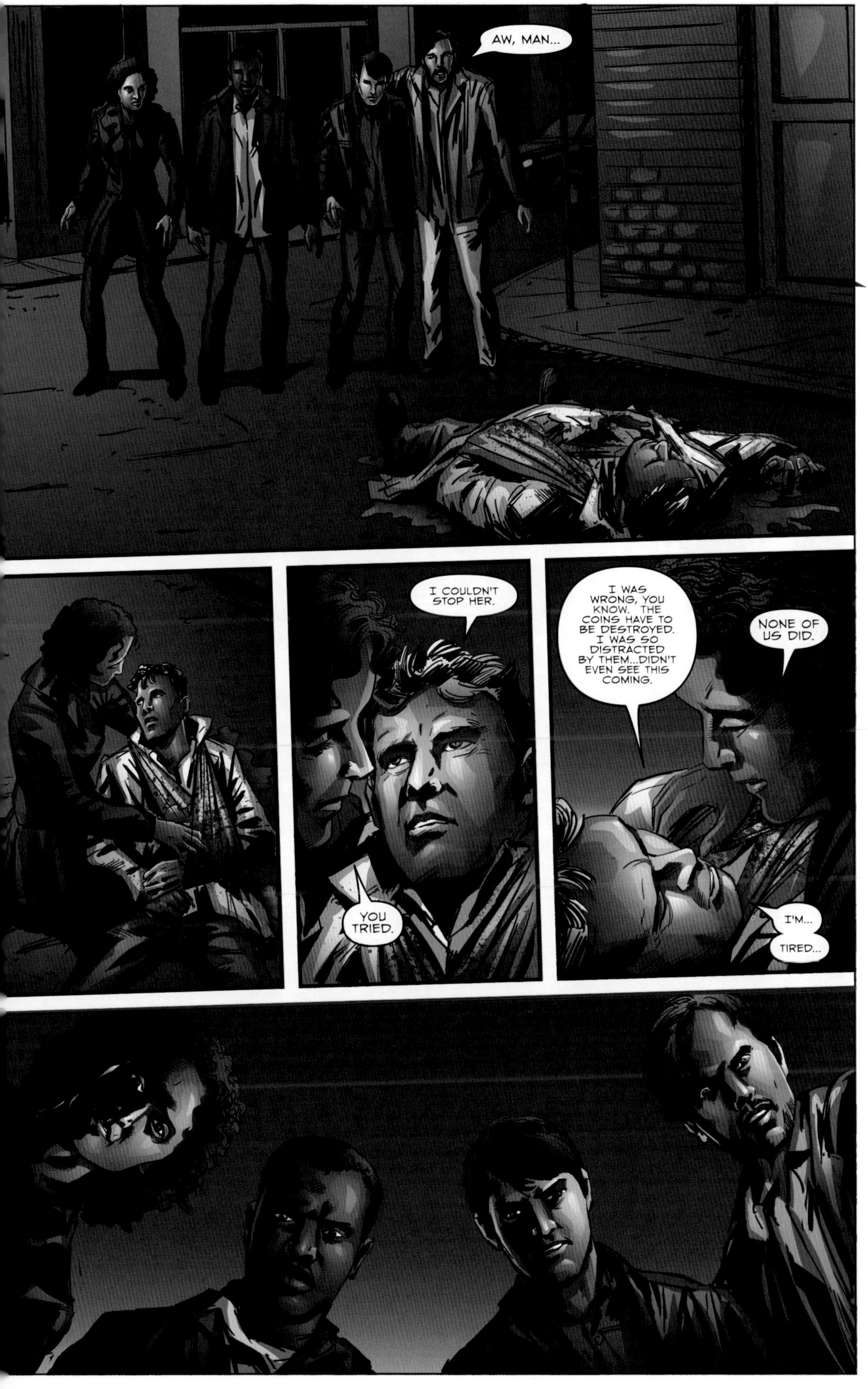
AW, MAN...
I COULDN'T STOP HER.
YOU TRIED.
I WAS WRONG, YOU KNOW. THE COINS HAVE TO BE DESTROYED. I WAS SO DISTRACTED BY THEM...DIDN'T EVEN SEE THIS COMING.
NONE OF US DID.
I'M...
TIRED...

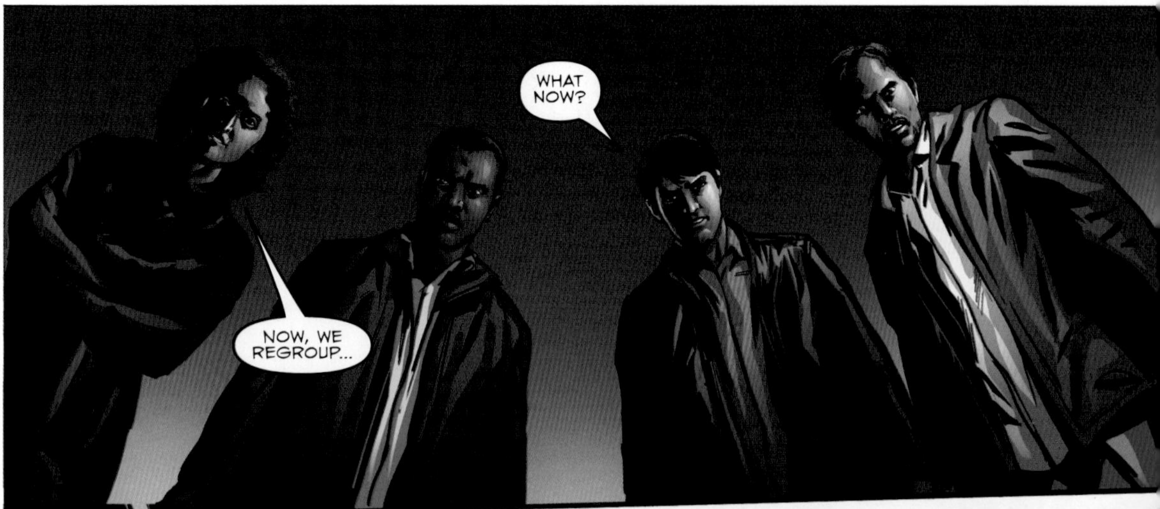
WHAT NOW?
NOW, WE REGROUP...

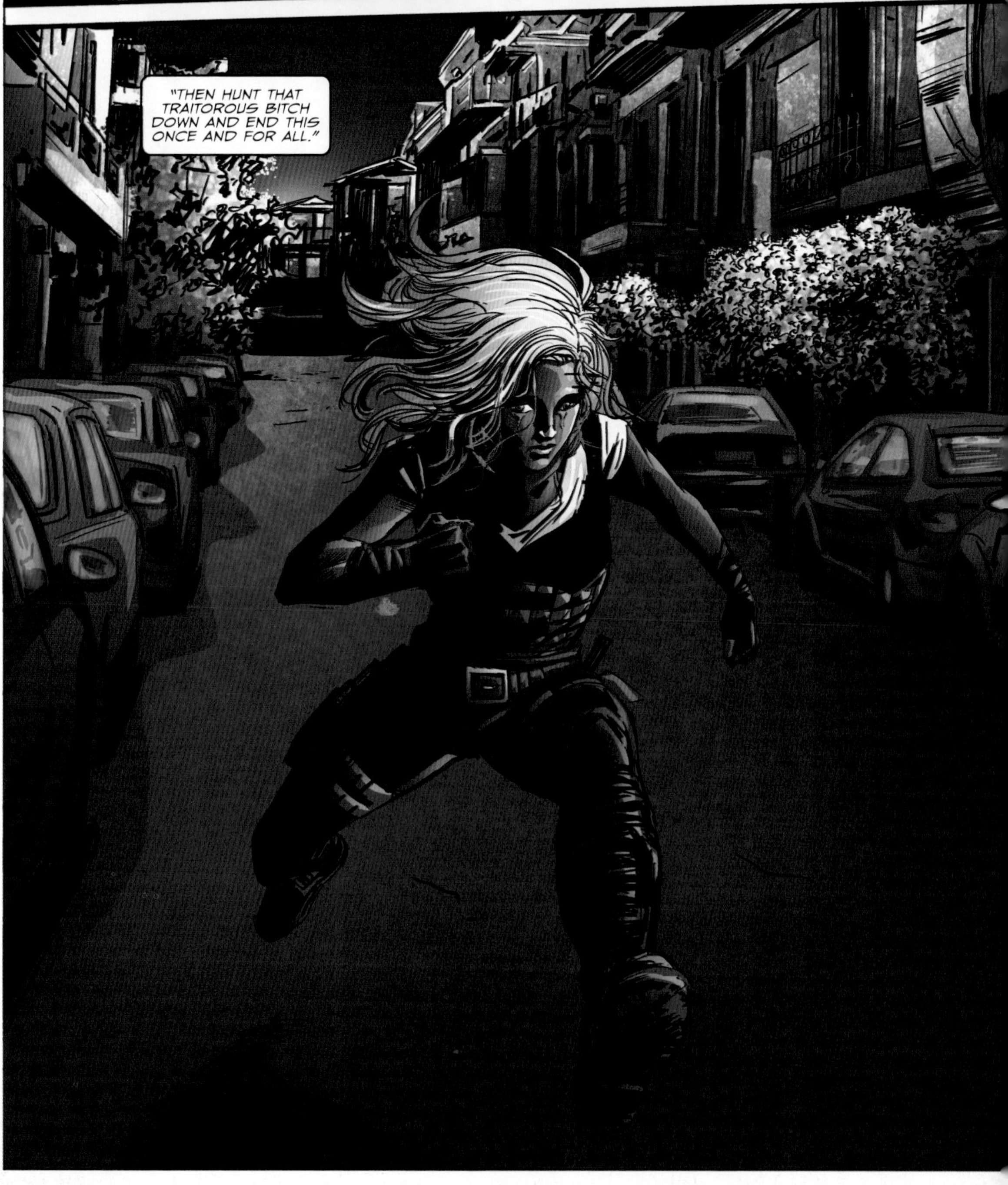
"THEN HUNT THAT TRAITOROUS BITCH DOWN AND END THIS ONCE AND FOR ALL."

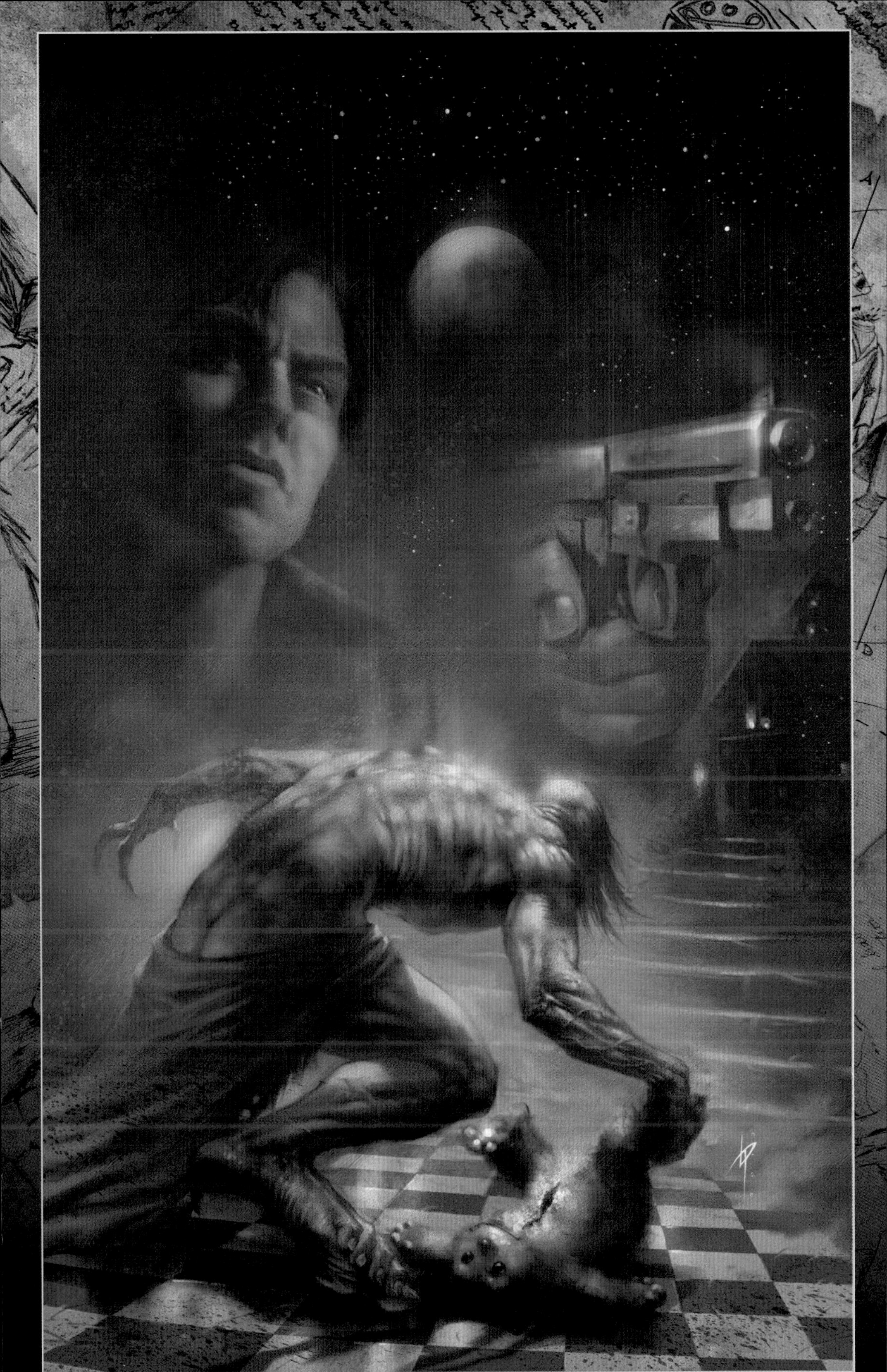

ISSUE #5 COVER

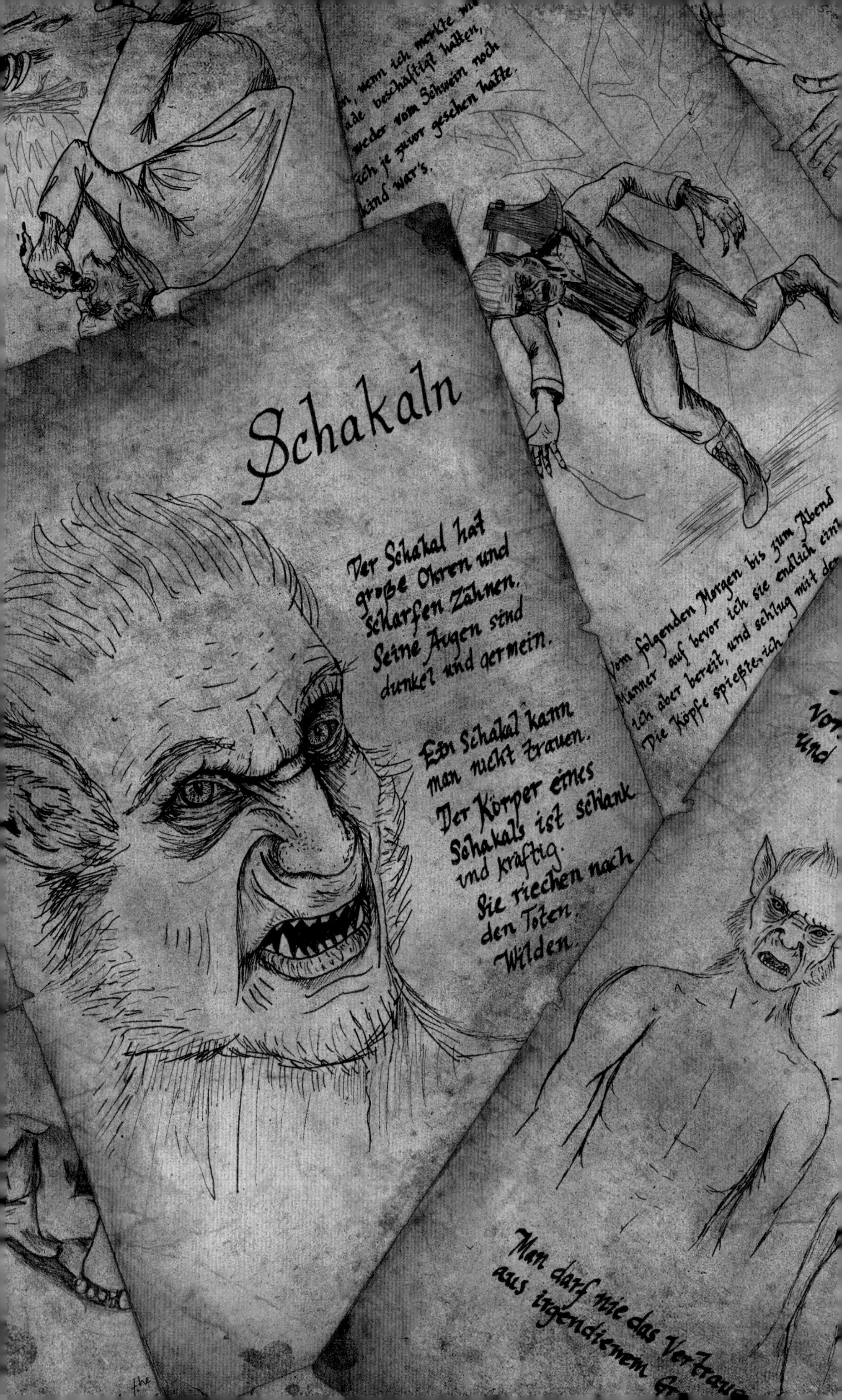

wenn ich merkte
beschäftigt hatten,
weder vom Schwein noch
ich je zuvor gesehen hatte.
kind war's.
Schakaln
Der Schakal hat
große Ohren und
scharfen Zähnen.
Seine Augen sind
dunkel und gemein.
Ein Schakal kann
man nicht trauen.
Der Körper eines
Schakals ist schlank
und kräftig.
Sie riechen nach
den Toten,
Wilden.
Vom folgenden Morgen bis zum Abend
Männer auf bevor ich sie endlich
ich aber bereit, und schlug mit de
Die Köpfe spießte, ich
und
Man darf nie das Vertrau
aus irgendeinem

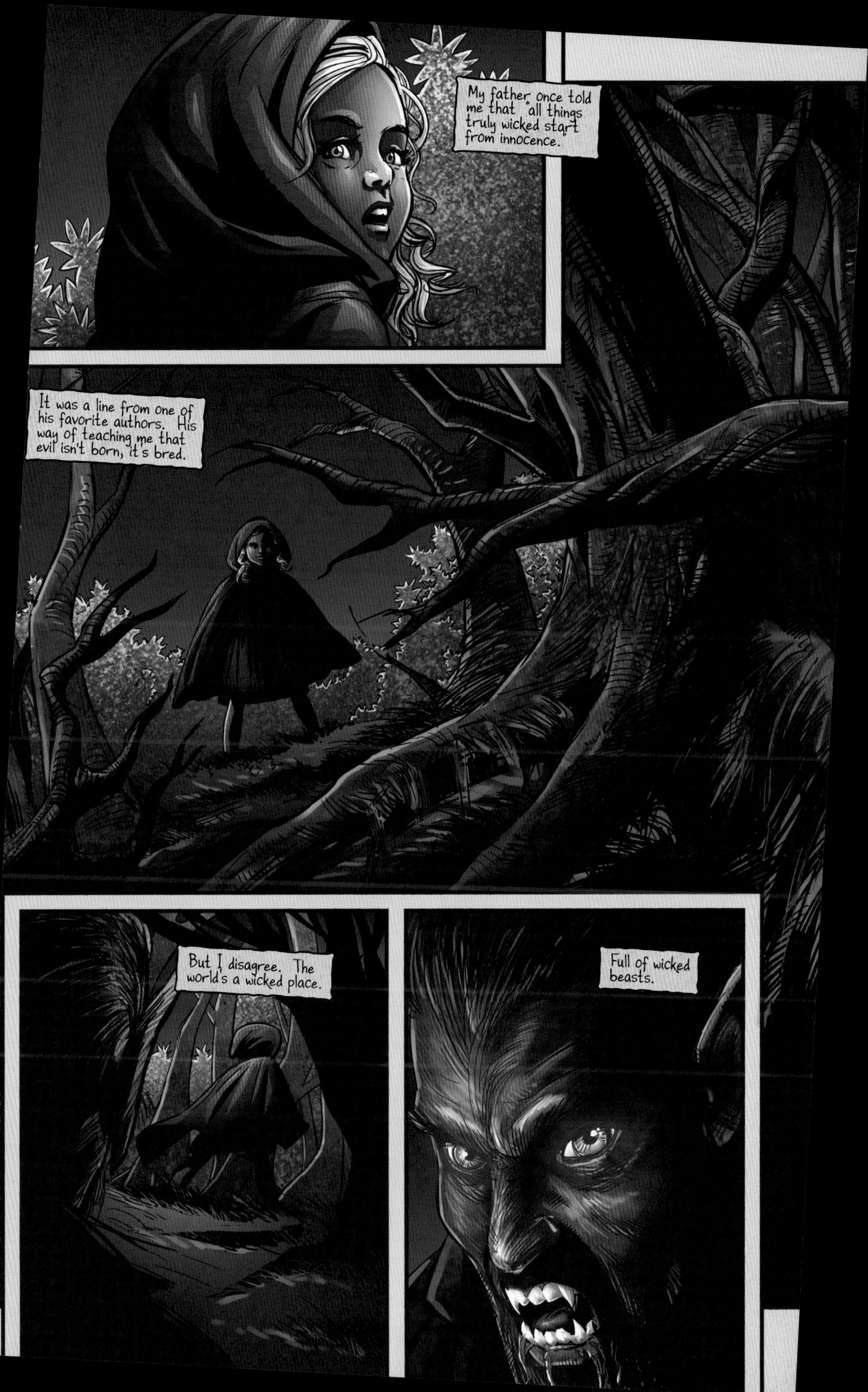
My father once told me that "all things truly wicked start from innocence."
It was a line from one of his favorite authors. His way of teaching me that evil isn't born, it's bred.
But I disagree. The world's a wicked place.
Full of wicked beasts.

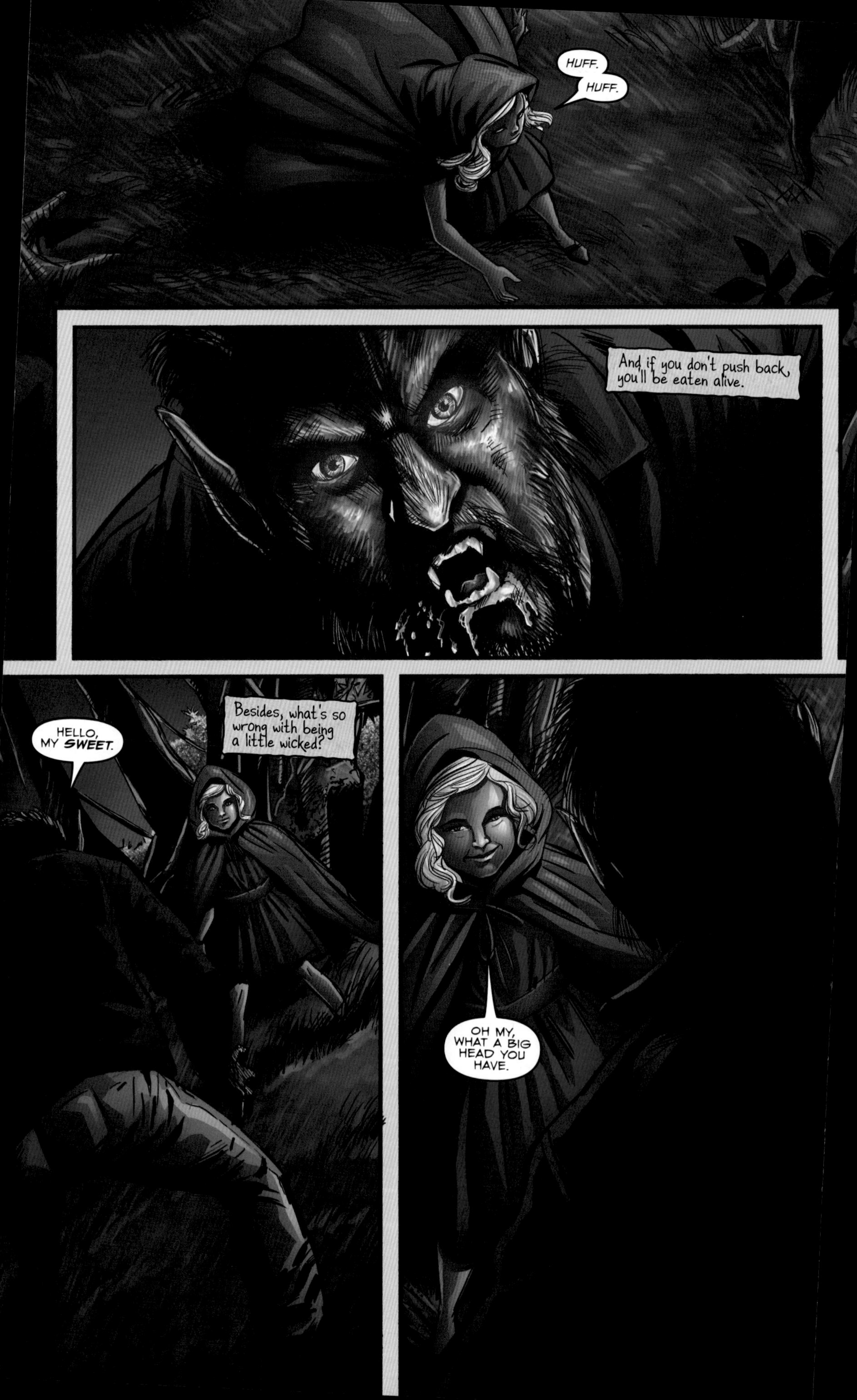
HUFF.
HUFF.
And if you don't push back, you'll be eaten alive.
HELLO, MY SWEET.
Besides, what's so wrong with being a little wicked?
OH MY, WHAT A BIG HEAD YOU HAVE.

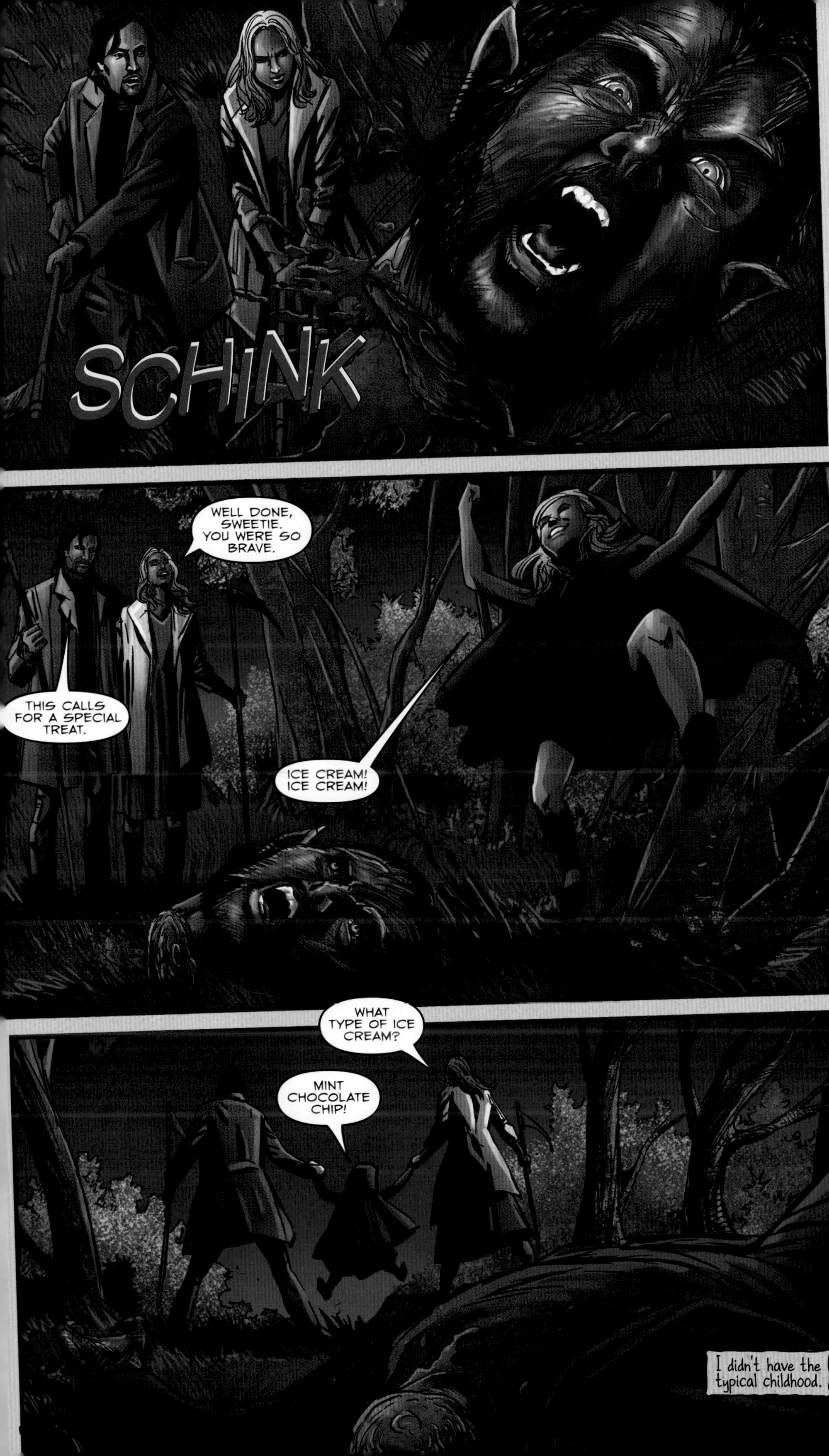
SCHINK
WELL DONE, SWEETIE. YOU WERE SO BRAVE.
THIS CALLS FOR A SPECIAL TREAT.
ICE CREAM! ICE CREAM!
WHAT TYPE OF ICE CREAM?
MINT CHOCOLATE CHIP!
I didn't have the typical childhood.

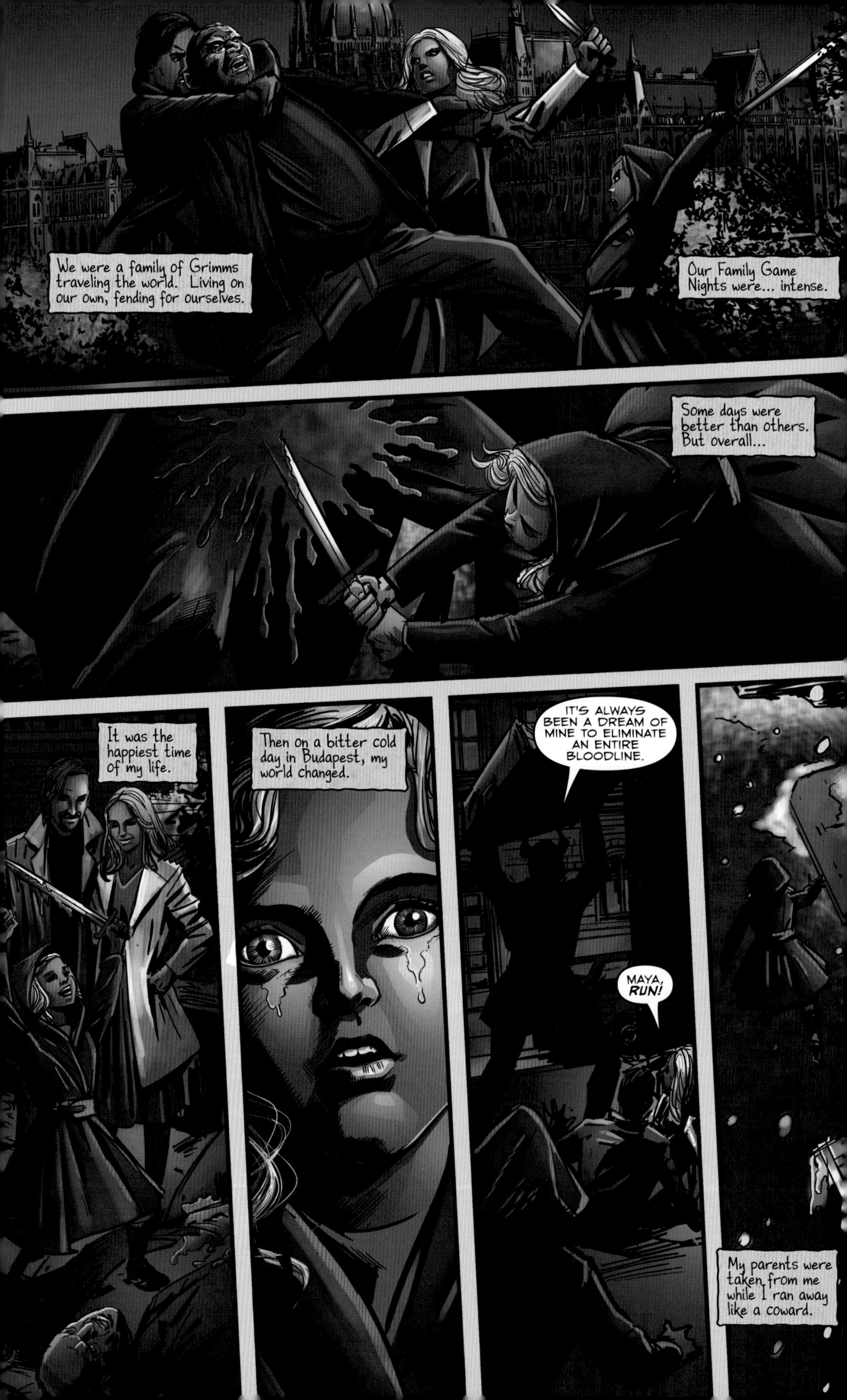

We were a family of Grimms traveling the world. Living on our own, fending for ourselves.
Our Family Game Nights were... intense.
Some days were better than others. But overall...
It was the happiest time of my life.
Then on a bitter cold day in Budapest, my world changed.
IT'S ALWAYS BEEN A DREAM OF MINE TO ELIMINATE AN ENTIRE BLOODLINE.
MAYA, RUN!
My parents were taken from me while I ran away like a coward.

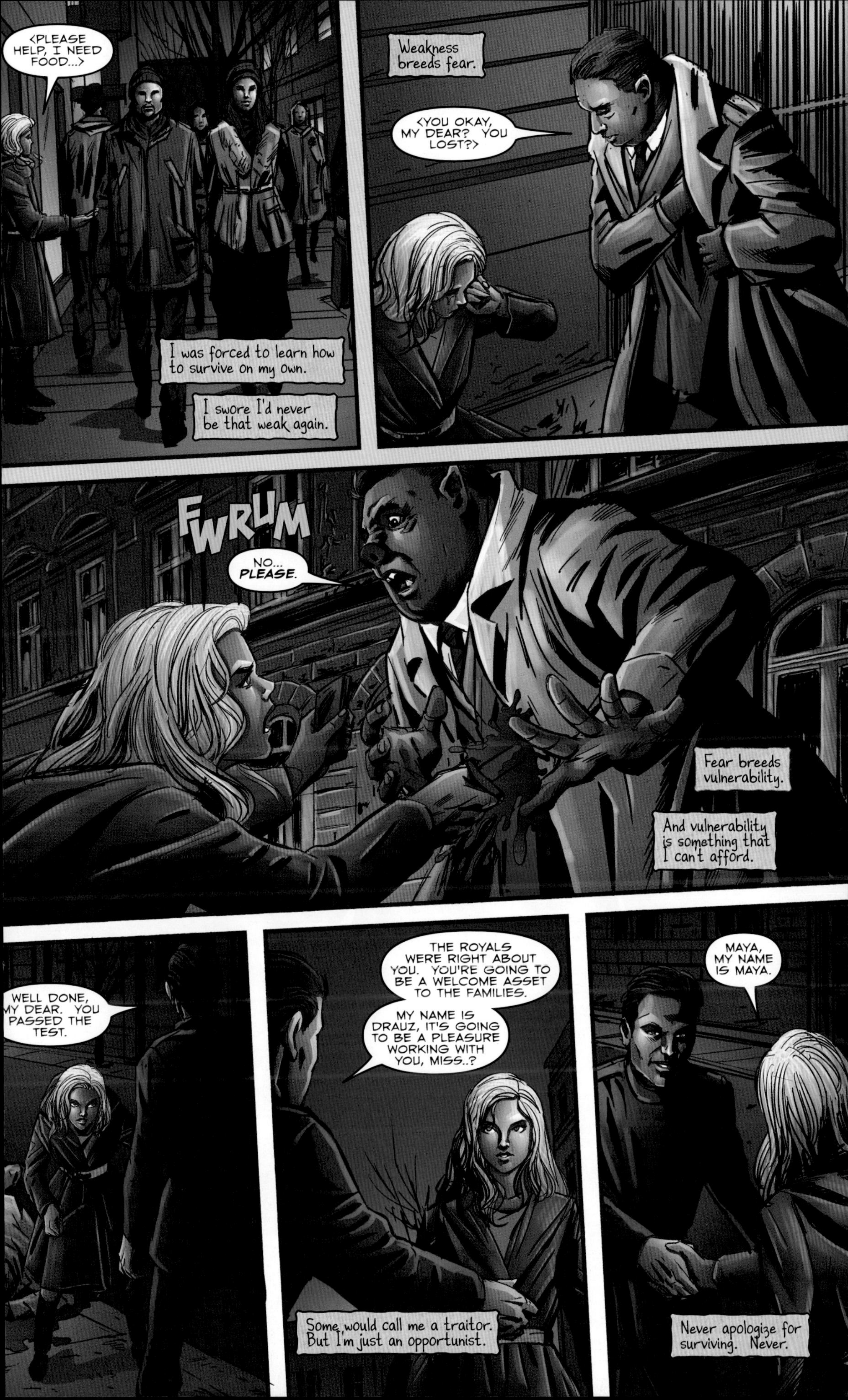
<PLEASE HELP, I NEED FOOD...>
I was forced to learn how to survive on my own.
I swore I'd never be that weak again.
Weakness breeds fear.
<YOU OKAY, MY DEAR? YOU LOST?>
FWRUM
NO... PLEASE.
Fear breeds vulnerability.
And vulnerability is something that I can't afford.
WELL DONE, MY DEAR. YOU PASSED THE TEST.
THE ROYALS WERE RIGHT ABOUT YOU. YOU'RE GOING TO BE A WELCOME ASSET TO THE FAMILIES.
MY NAME IS DRAUZ, IT'S GOING TO BE A PLEASURE WORKING WITH YOU, MISS..?
Some would call me a traitor. But I'm just an opportunist.
MAYA, MY NAME IS MAYA.
Never apologize for surviving. Never.

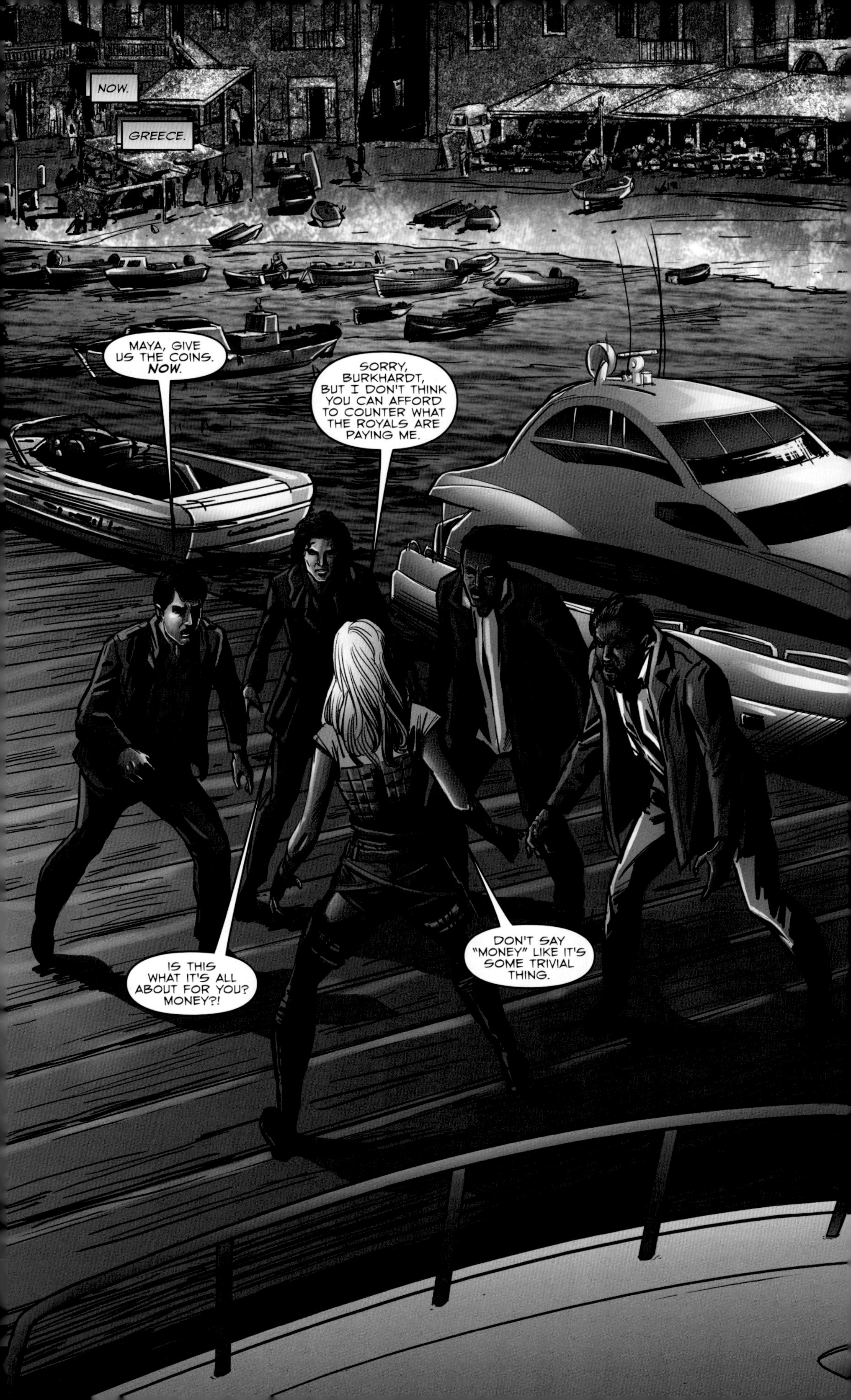
NOW.
GREECE.
MAYA, GIVE US THE COINS. **NOW.**
SORRY, BURKHARDT, BUT I DON'T THINK YOU CAN AFFORD TO COUNTER WHAT THE ROYALS ARE PAYING ME.
IS THIS WHAT IT'S ALL ABOUT FOR YOU? MONEY?!
DON'T SAY "MONEY" LIKE IT'S SOME TRIVIAL THING.

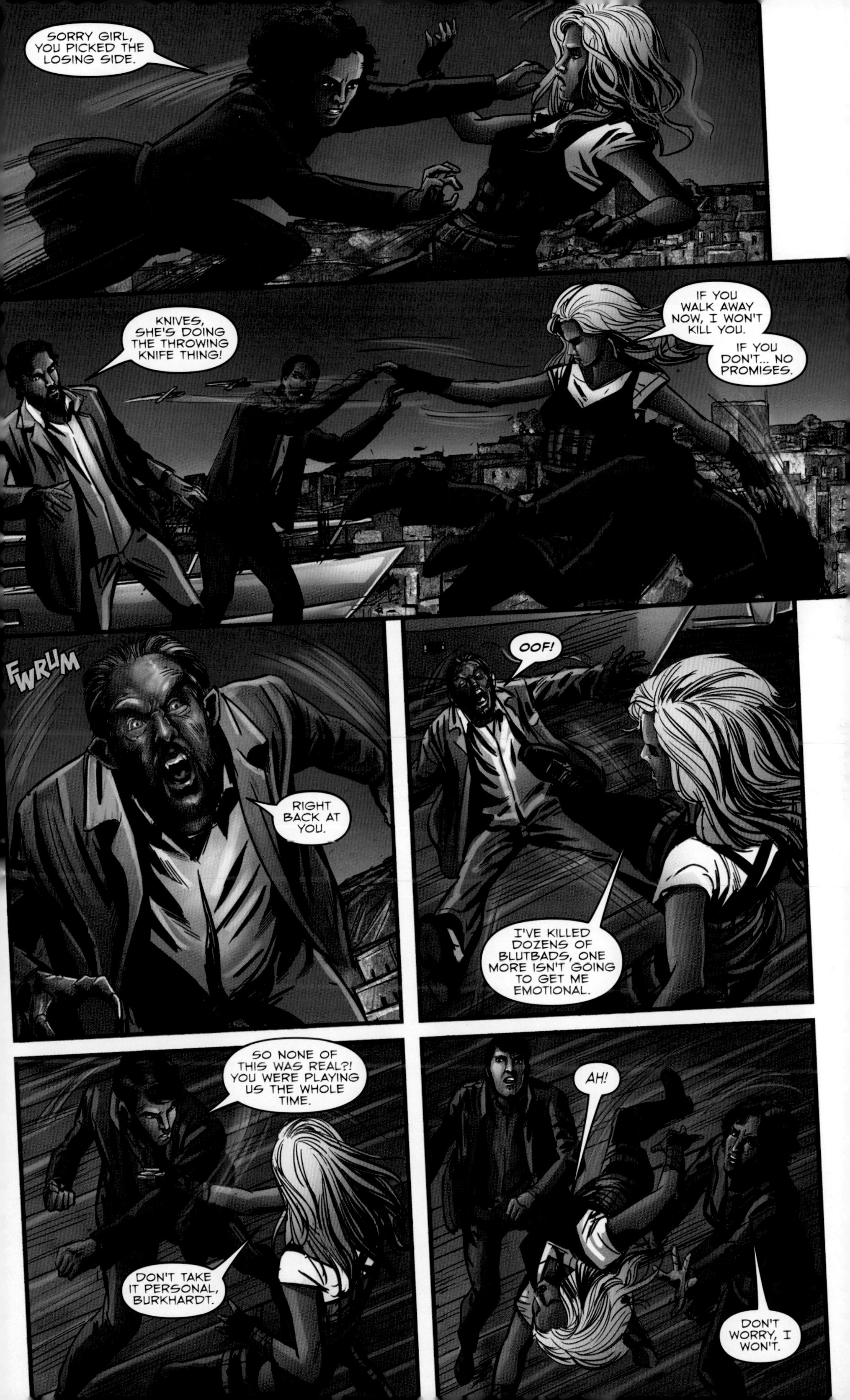
SORRY GIRL, YOU PICKED THE LOSING SIDE.
KNIVES, SHE'S DOING THE THROWING KNIFE THING!
IF YOU WALK AWAY NOW, I WON'T KILL YOU.
IF YOU DON'T... NO PROMISES.
FWRUM
RIGHT BACK AT YOU.
OOF!
I'VE KILLED DOZENS OF BLUTBADS, ONE MORE ISN'T GOING TO GET ME EMOTIONAL.
SO NONE OF THIS WAS REAL?! YOU WERE PLAYING US THE WHOLE TIME.
DON'T TAKE IT PERSONAL, BURKHARDT.
AH!
DON'T WORRY, I WON'T.

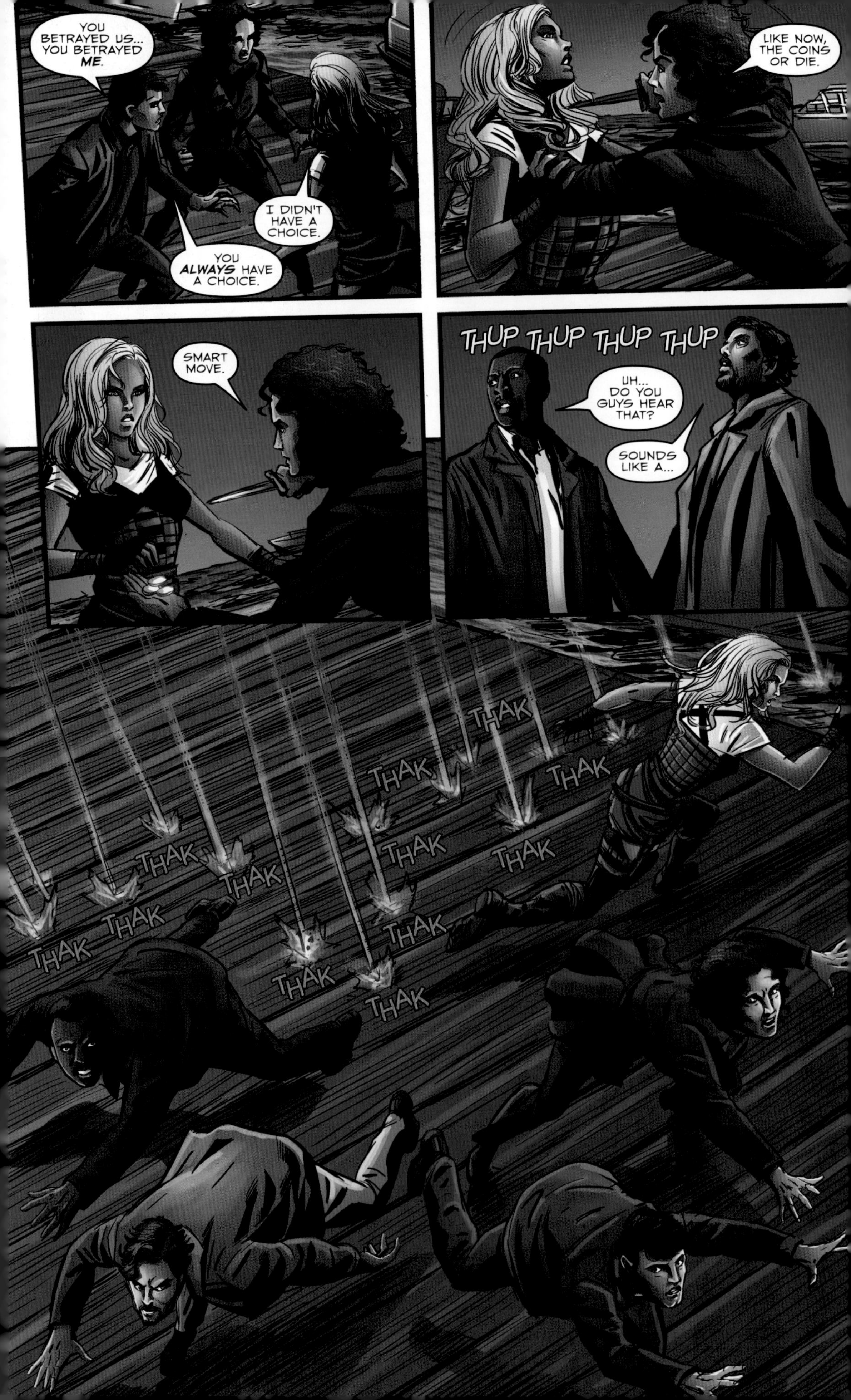
YOU BETRAYED US... YOU BETRAYED ME.
I DIDN'T HAVE A CHOICE.
YOU ALWAYS HAVE A CHOICE.
LIKE NOW, THE COINS OR DIE.
SMART MOVE.
THUP THUP THUP THUP
UH... DO YOU GUYS HEAR THAT?
SOUNDS LIKE A...
THAK
THAK
THAK
THAK
THAK
THAK
THAK
THAK
THAK
THAK
THAK
THAK
THAK

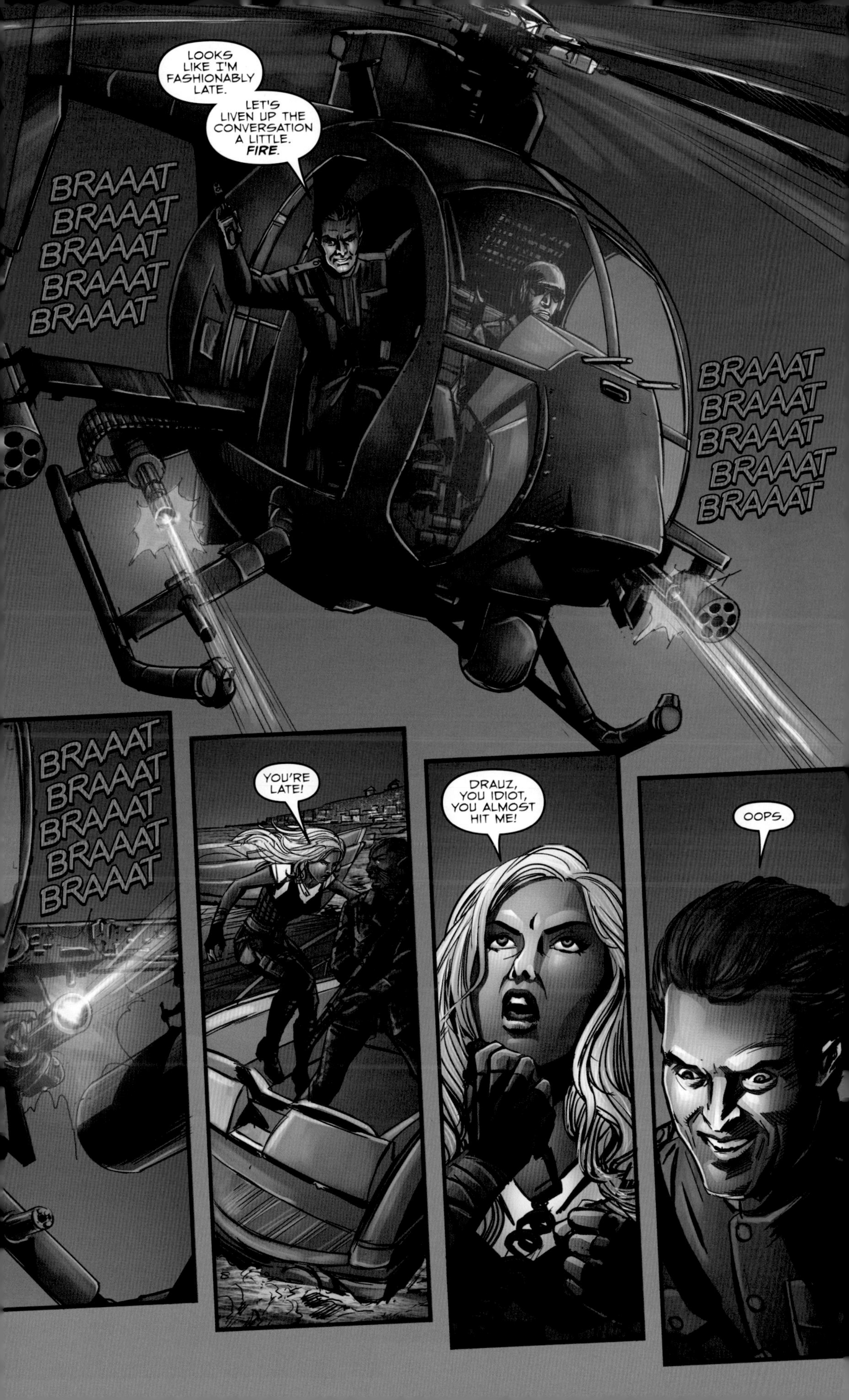
LOOKS LIKE I'M FASHIONABLY LATE.
LET'S LIVEN UP THE CONVERSATION A LITTLE. FIRE.
BRAAAT BRAAAT BRAAAT BRAAAT BRAAAT
BRAAAT BRAAAT BRAAAT BRAAAT BRAAAT
BRAAAT BRAAAT BRAAAT BRAAAT BRAAAT
YOU'RE LATE!
DRAUZ, YOU IDIOT, YOU ALMOST HIT ME!
OOPS.

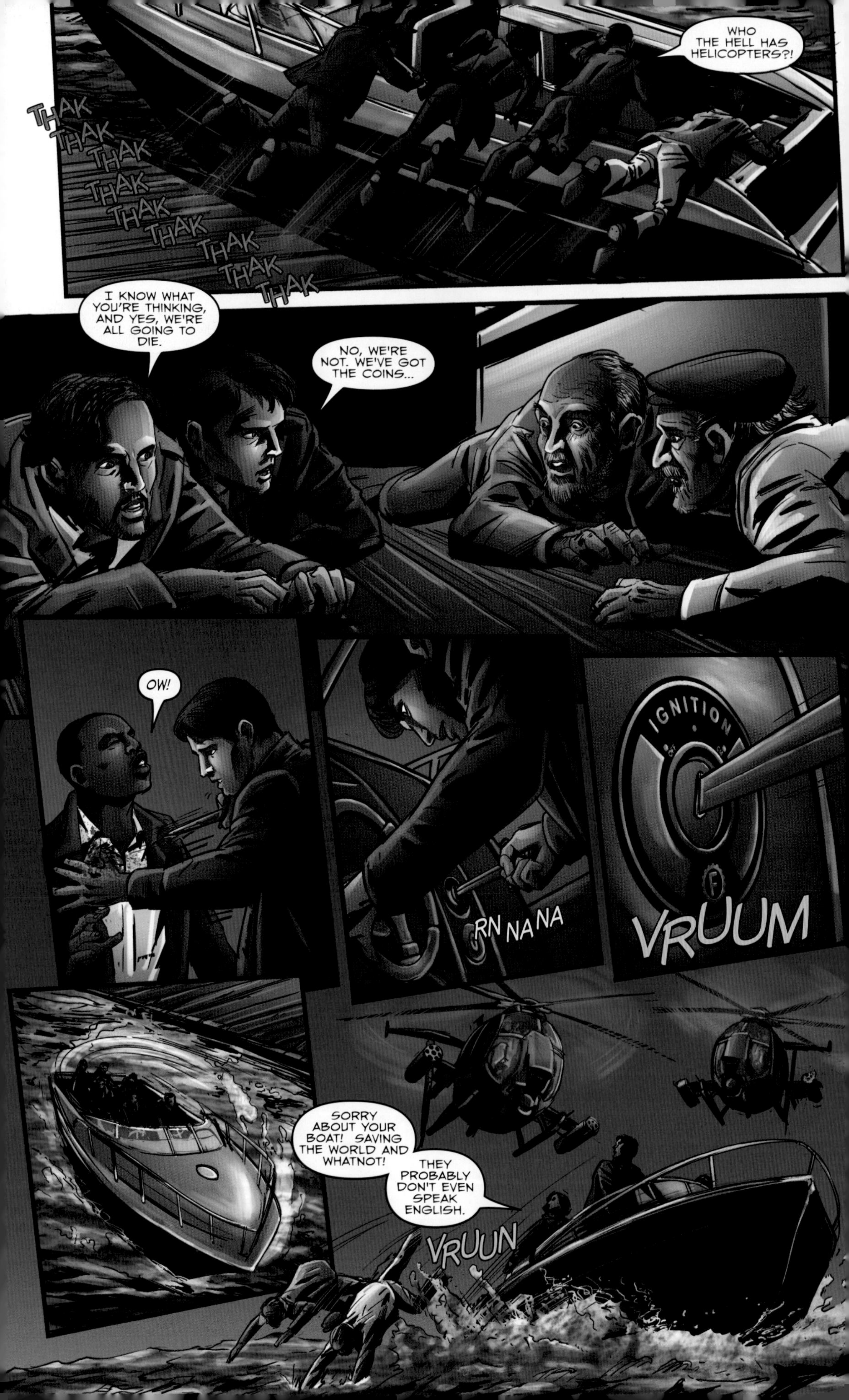
WHO THE HELL HAS HELICOPTERS?!
THAK THAK THAK THAK THAK THAK THAK THAK THAK
I KNOW WHAT YOU'RE THINKING, AND YES, WE'RE ALL GOING TO DIE.
NO, WE'RE NOT. WE'VE GOT THE COINS...
OW!
RN NA NA
IGNITION
VRUUM
SORRY ABOUT YOUR BOAT! SAVING THE WORLD AND WHATNOT!
THEY PROBABLY DON'T EVEN SPEAK ENGLISH.
VRUUN

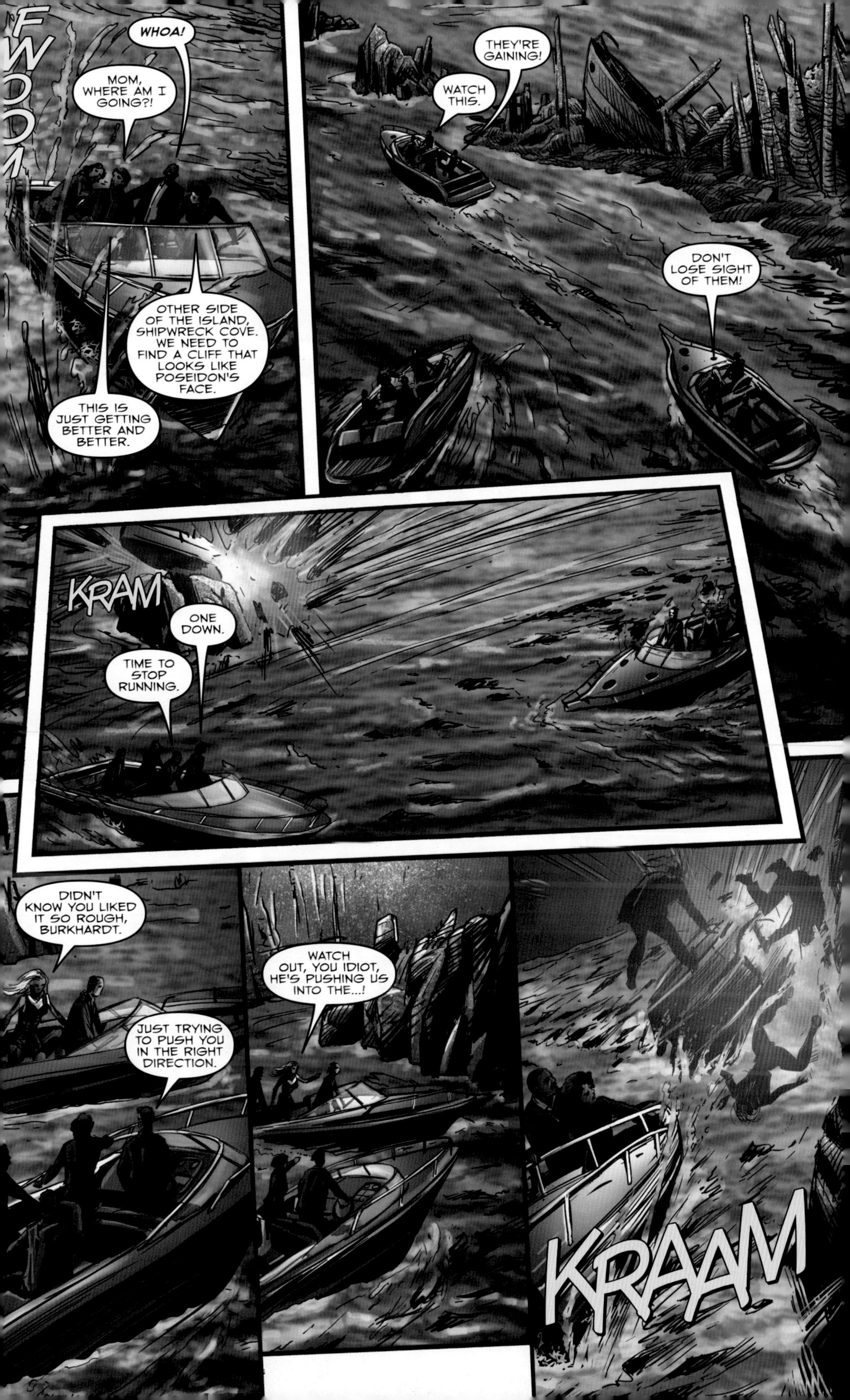
FWOOM
WHOA!
MOM, WHERE AM I GOING?!
OTHER SIDE OF THE ISLAND, SHIPWRECK COVE. WE NEED TO FIND A CLIFF THAT LOOKS LIKE POSEIDON'S FACE.
THIS IS JUST GETTING BETTER AND BETTER.
THEY'RE GAINING!
WATCH THIS.
DON'T LOSE SIGHT OF THEM!
KRAM
ONE DOWN.
TIME TO STOP RUNNING.
DIDN'T KNOW YOU LIKED IT SO ROUGH, BURKHARDT.
JUST TRYING TO PUSH YOU IN THE RIGHT DIRECTION.
WATCH OUT, YOU IDIOT, HE'S PUSHING US INTO THE...!
KRAAM

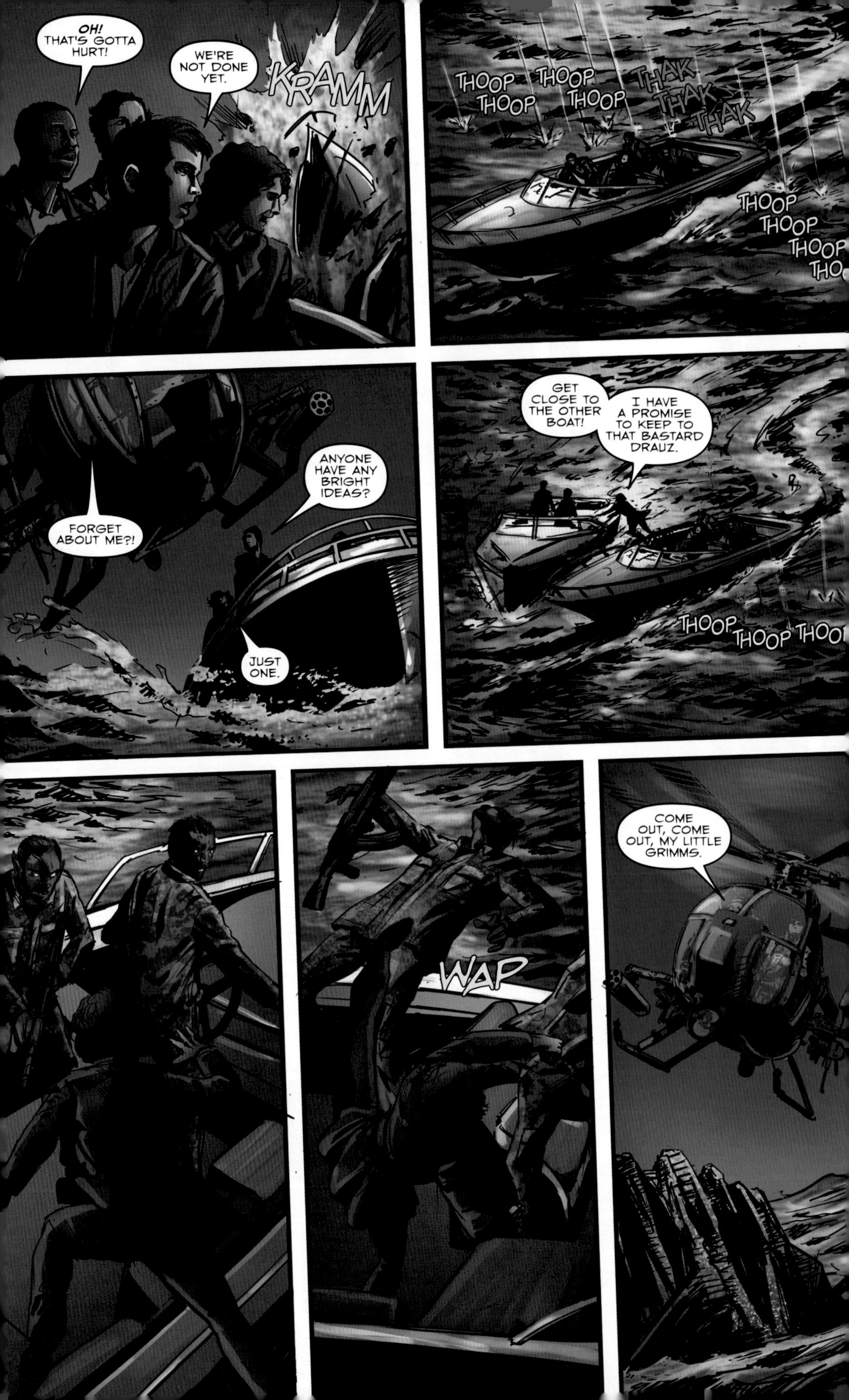
OH! THAT'S GOTTA HURT!
WE'RE NOT DONE YET.
KRAMM
THOOP THOOP THOOP THOOP THAK THAK THAK
THOOP THOOP THOOP THO
FORGET ABOUT ME?!
ANYONE HAVE ANY BRIGHT IDEAS?
JUST ONE.
GET CLOSE TO THE OTHER BOAT!
I HAVE A PROMISE TO KEEP TO THAT BASTARD DRAUZ.
THOOP THOOP THOO
WAP
COME OUT, COME OUT, MY LITTLE GRIMMS.

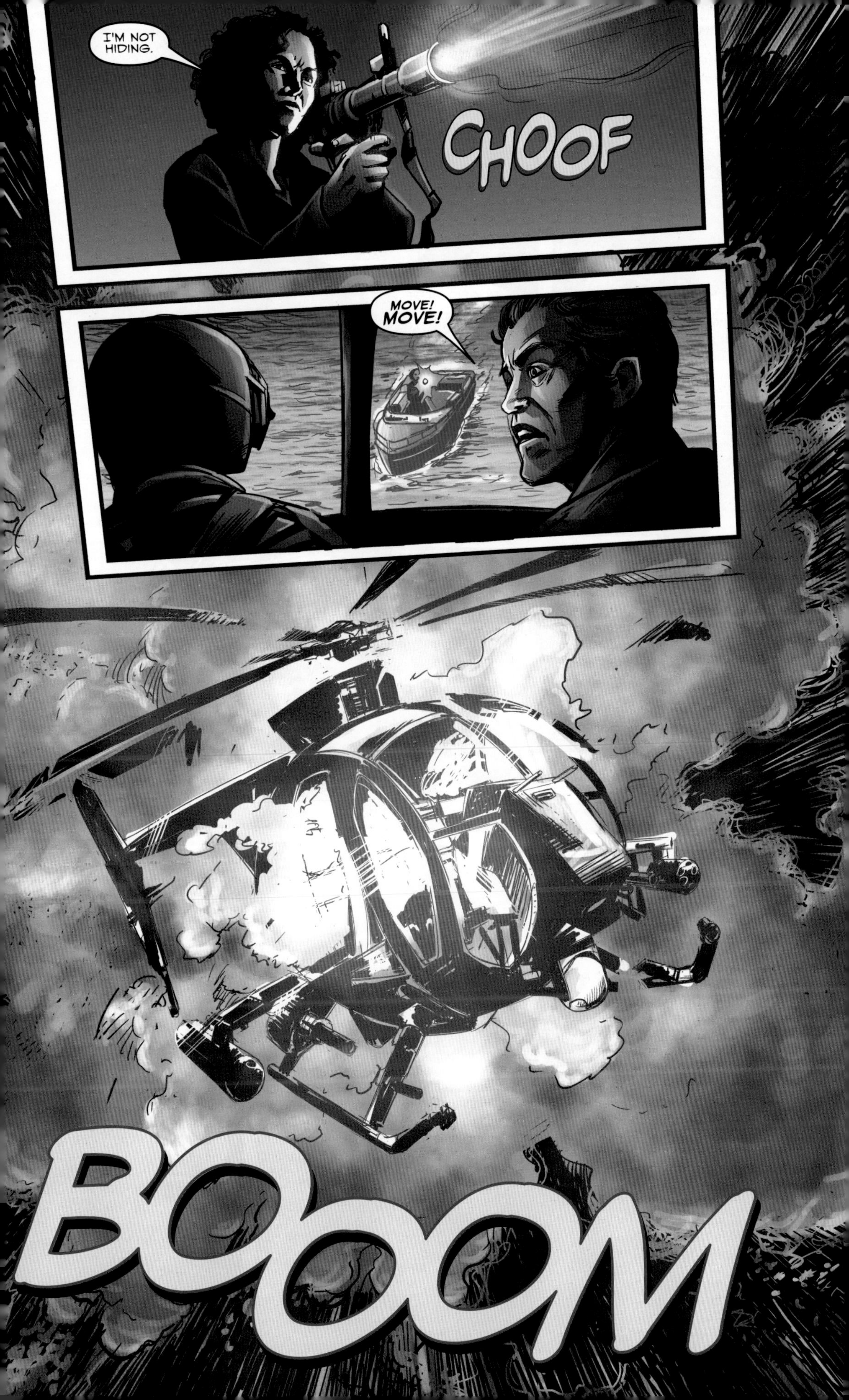
I'M NOT HIDING.
CHOOF
MOVE! MOVE!
BOOOM

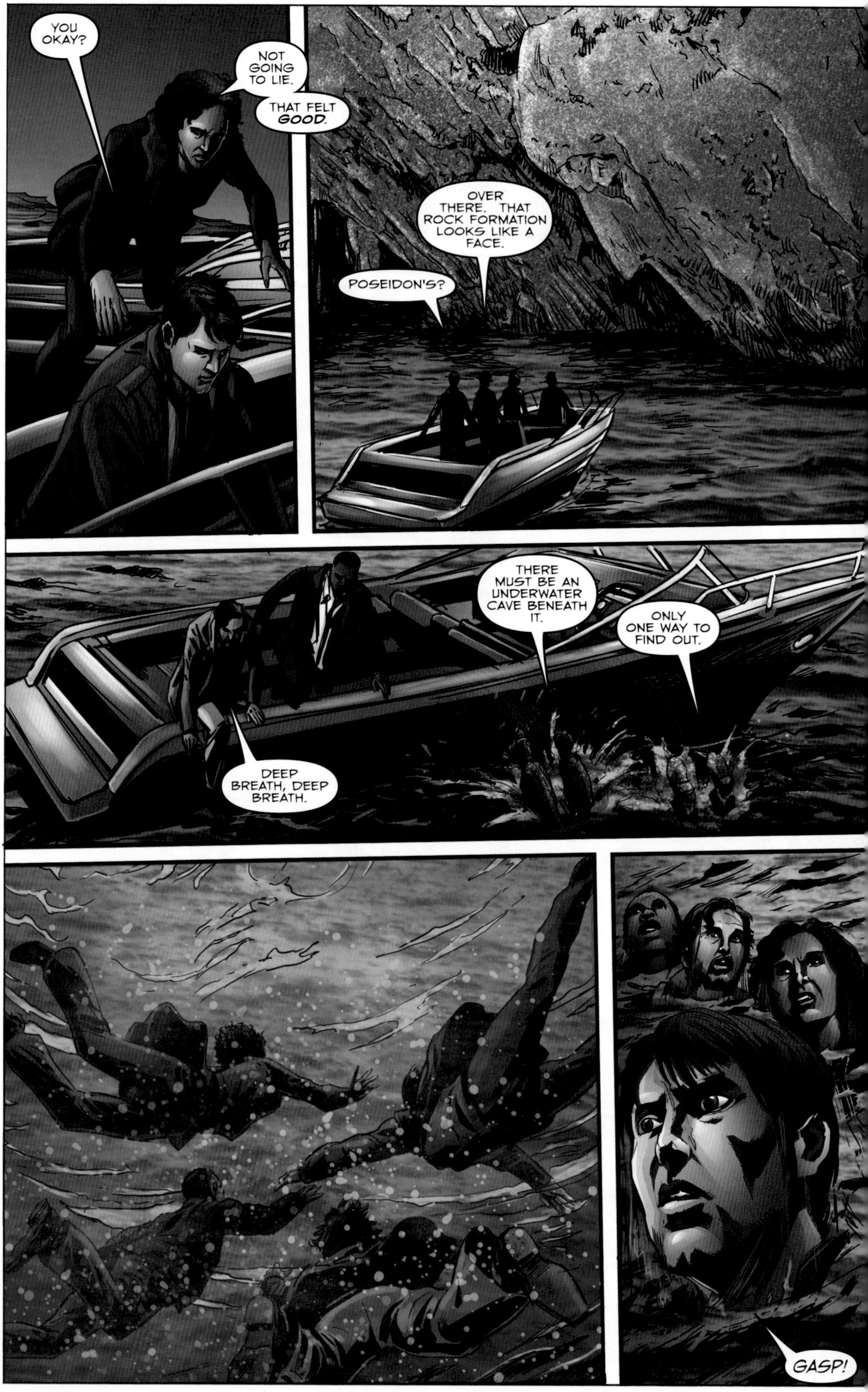
YOU OKAY?
NOT GOING TO LIE.
THAT FELT *GOOD*.
OVER THERE. THAT ROCK FORMATION LOOKS LIKE A FACE.
POSEIDON'S?
THERE MUST BE AN UNDERWATER CAVE BENEATH IT.
ONLY ONE WAY TO FIND OUT.
DEEP BREATH, DEEP BREATH.
GASP!

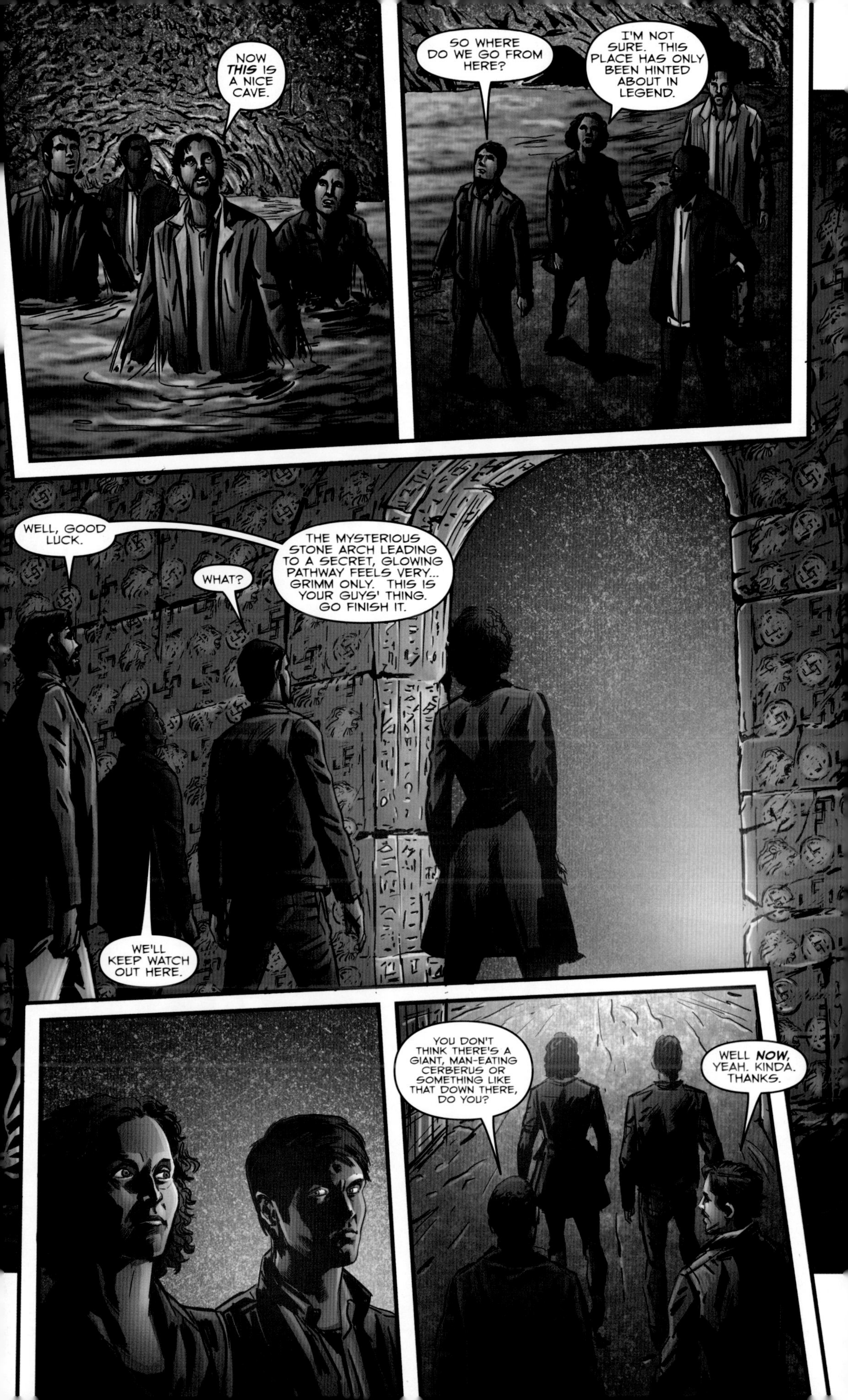
NOW *THIS* IS A NICE CAVE.
SO WHERE DO WE GO FROM HERE?
I'M NOT SURE. THIS PLACE HAS ONLY BEEN HINTED ABOUT IN LEGEND.
WELL, GOOD LUCK.
WHAT?
THE MYSTERIOUS STONE ARCH LEADING TO A SECRET, GLOWING PATHWAY FEELS VERY... GRIMM ONLY. THIS IS YOUR GUYS' THING. GO FINISH IT.
WE'LL KEEP WATCH OUT HERE.
YOU DON'T THINK THERE'S A GIANT, MAN-EATING CERBERUS OR SOMETHING LIKE THAT DOWN THERE, DO YOU?
WELL *NOW*, YEAH. KINDA. THANKS.

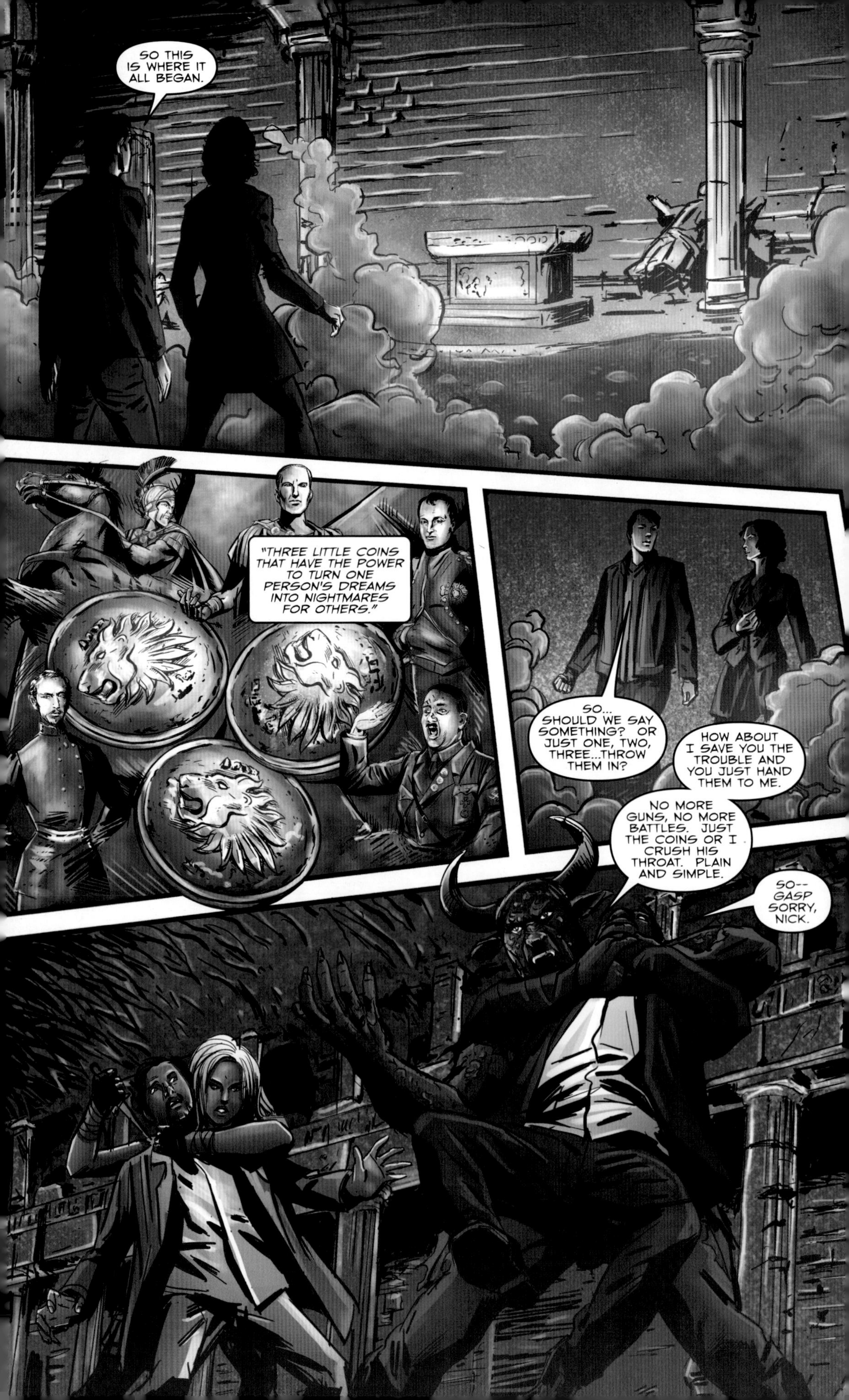
SO THIS IS WHERE IT ALL BEGAN.
"THREE LITTLE COINS THAT HAVE THE POWER TO TURN ONE PERSON'S DREAMS INTO NIGHTMARES FOR OTHERS."
SO... SHOULD WE SAY SOMETHING? OR JUST ONE, TWO, THREE...THROW THEM IN?
HOW ABOUT I SAVE YOU THE TROUBLE AND YOU JUST HAND THEM TO ME.
NO MORE GUNS, NO MORE BATTLES. JUST THE COINS OR I CRUSH HIS THROAT. PLAIN AND SIMPLE.
SO-- GASP SORRY, NICK.

YOU WANT THEM, *HERE YOU GO!!*

NO!

THEY'RE MINE... *THEY'RE MINE!*

My father used to tell me that only the most pitiful men turn their dreams into gold.

As I see Drauz scramble for the coins...

I'LL KILL ALL OF YOU!

I can see myself digging in the dirt if I thought it meant surviving another day.

DON'T JUST STAND HERE, GO HELP YOUR FRIENDS.

SERIOUSLY? YOU'VE GOT MEDICAL JOURNAL-WORTHY MOOD SWINGS, LADY.

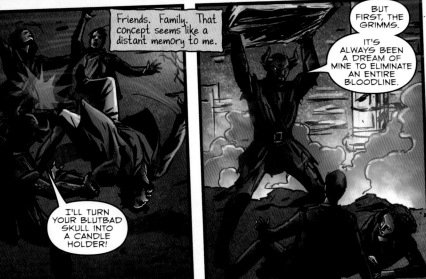

Friends. Family. That concept seems like a distant memory to me.

I'LL TURN YOUR BLUTBAD SKULL INTO A CANDLE HOLDER!

BUT FIRST, THE GRIMMS.

IT'S ALWAYS BEEN A DREAM OF MINE TO ELIMINATE AN ENTIRE BLOODLINE.

But maybe it's time I stopped living to just make it to the next day and did something worthwhile.

Something Mom and Dad would be proud of.

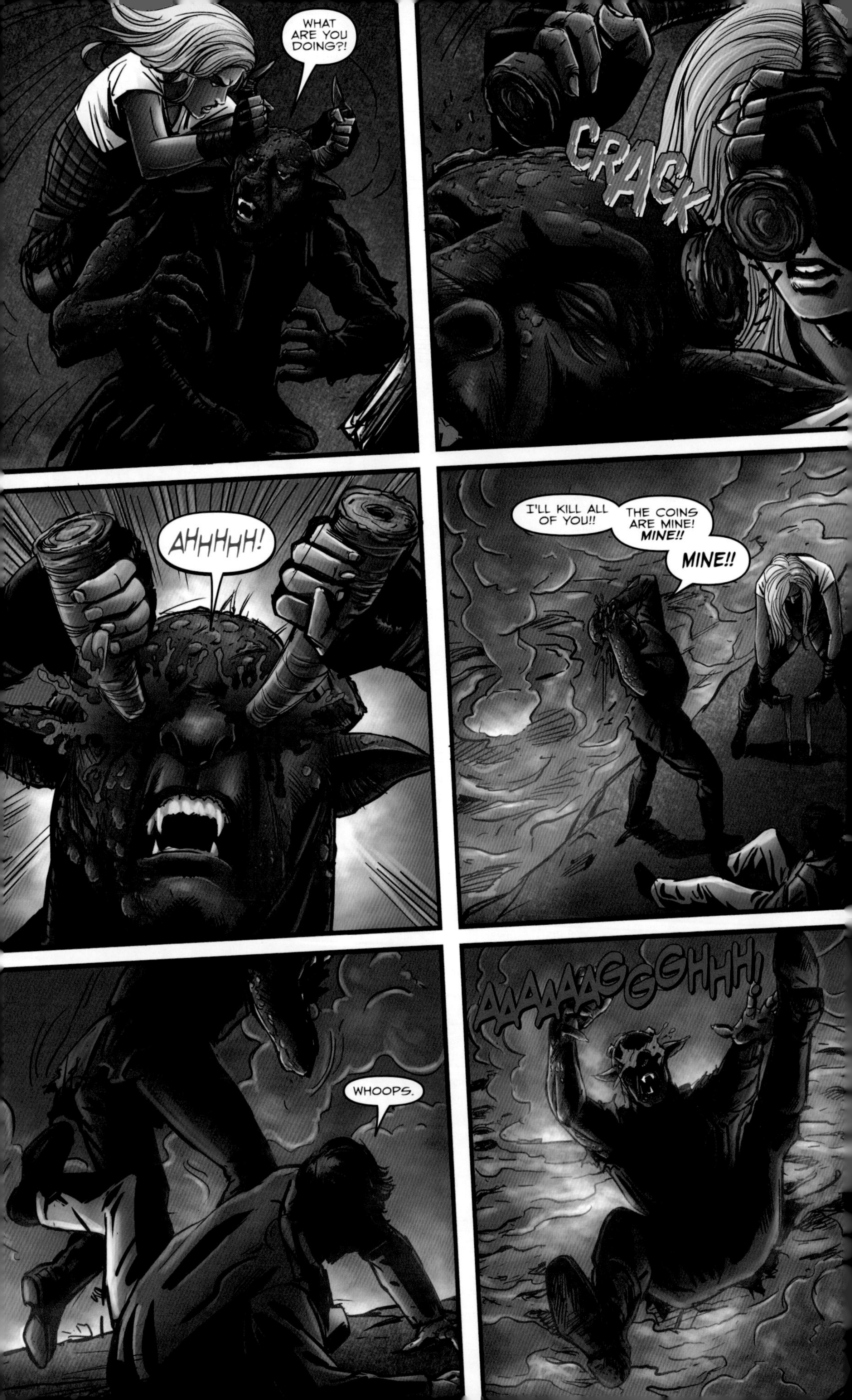
WHAT ARE YOU DOING?!
CRACK
AHHHHH!
I'LL KILL ALL OF YOU!!
THE COINS ARE MINE! MINE!!
MINE!!
WHOOPS.
AAAAAAGGGHHH!

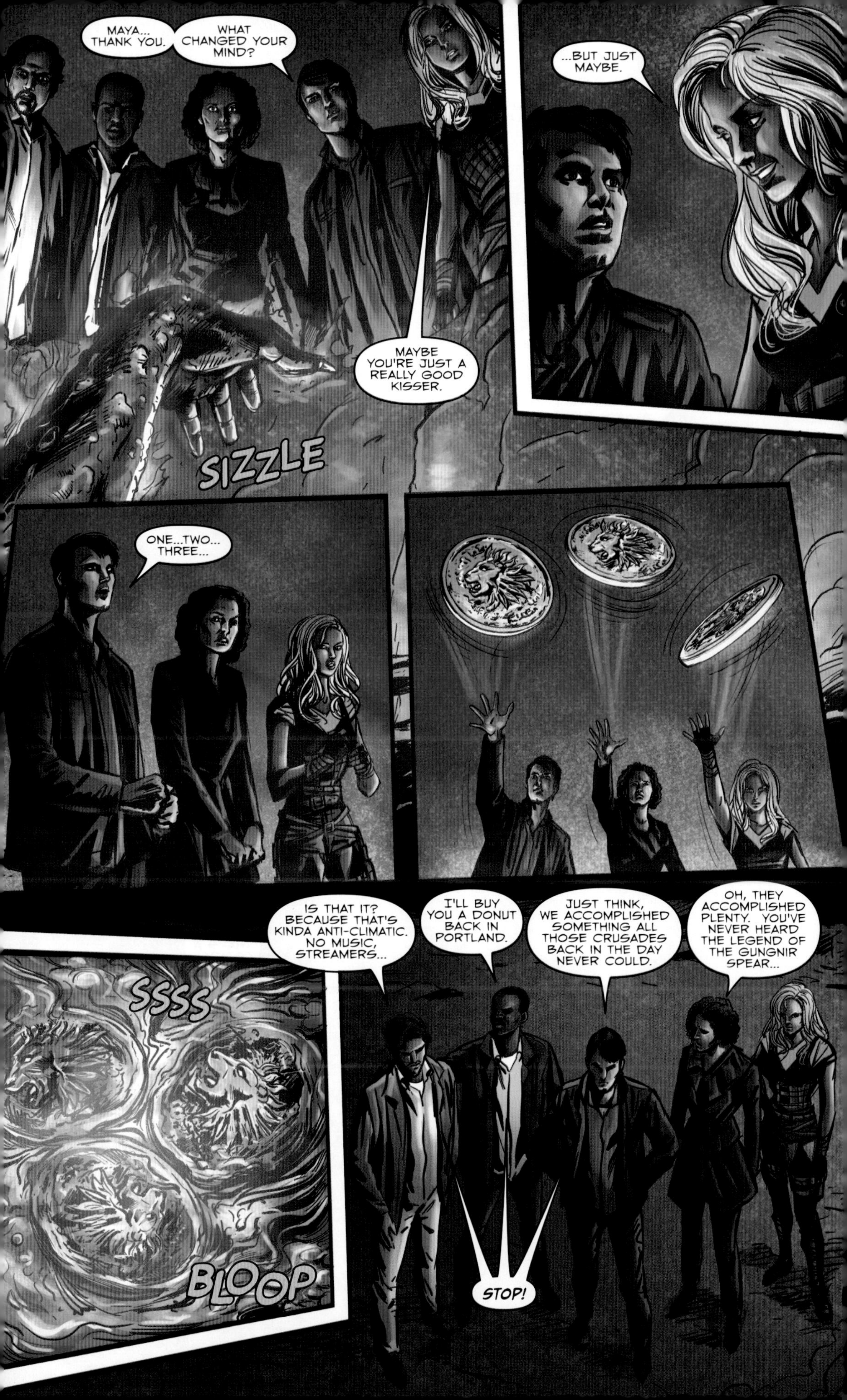
MAYA... THANK YOU.
WHAT CHANGED YOUR MIND?
MAYBE YOU'RE JUST A REALLY GOOD KISSER.
...BUT JUST MAYBE.
SIZZLE
ONE...TWO... THREE...
SSSS
BLOOP
IS THAT IT? BECAUSE THAT'S KINDA ANTI-CLIMATIC. NO MUSIC, STREAMERS...
I'LL BUY YOU A DONUT BACK IN PORTLAND.
JUST THINK, WE ACCOMPLISHED SOMETHING ALL THOSE CRUSADES BACK IN THE DAY NEVER COULD.
OH, THEY ACCOMPLISHED PLENTY. YOU'VE NEVER HEARD THE LEGEND OF THE GUNGNIR SPEAR...
STOP!

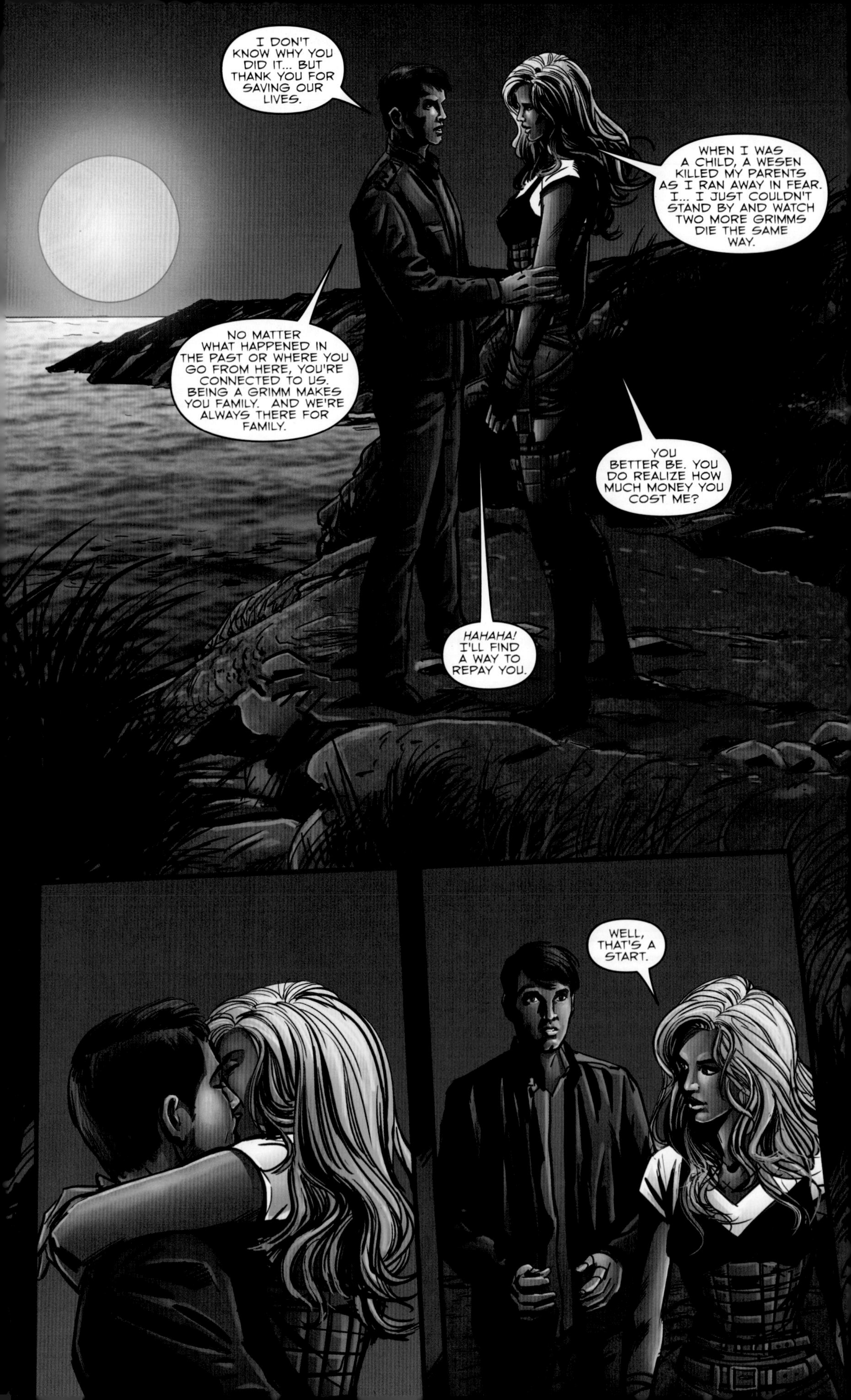
I DON'T KNOW WHY YOU DID IT... BUT THANK YOU FOR SAVING OUR LIVES.
WHEN I WAS A CHILD, A WESEN KILLED MY PARENTS AS I RAN AWAY IN FEAR. I... I JUST COULDN'T STAND BY AND WATCH TWO MORE GRIMMS DIE THE SAME WAY.
NO MATTER WHAT HAPPENED IN THE PAST OR WHERE YOU GO FROM HERE, YOU'RE CONNECTED TO US. BEING A GRIMM MAKES YOU FAMILY. AND WE'RE ALWAYS THERE FOR FAMILY.
YOU BETTER BE. YOU DO REALIZE HOW MUCH MONEY YOU COST ME?
HAHAHA! I'LL FIND A WAY TO REPAY YOU.
WELL, THAT'S A START.

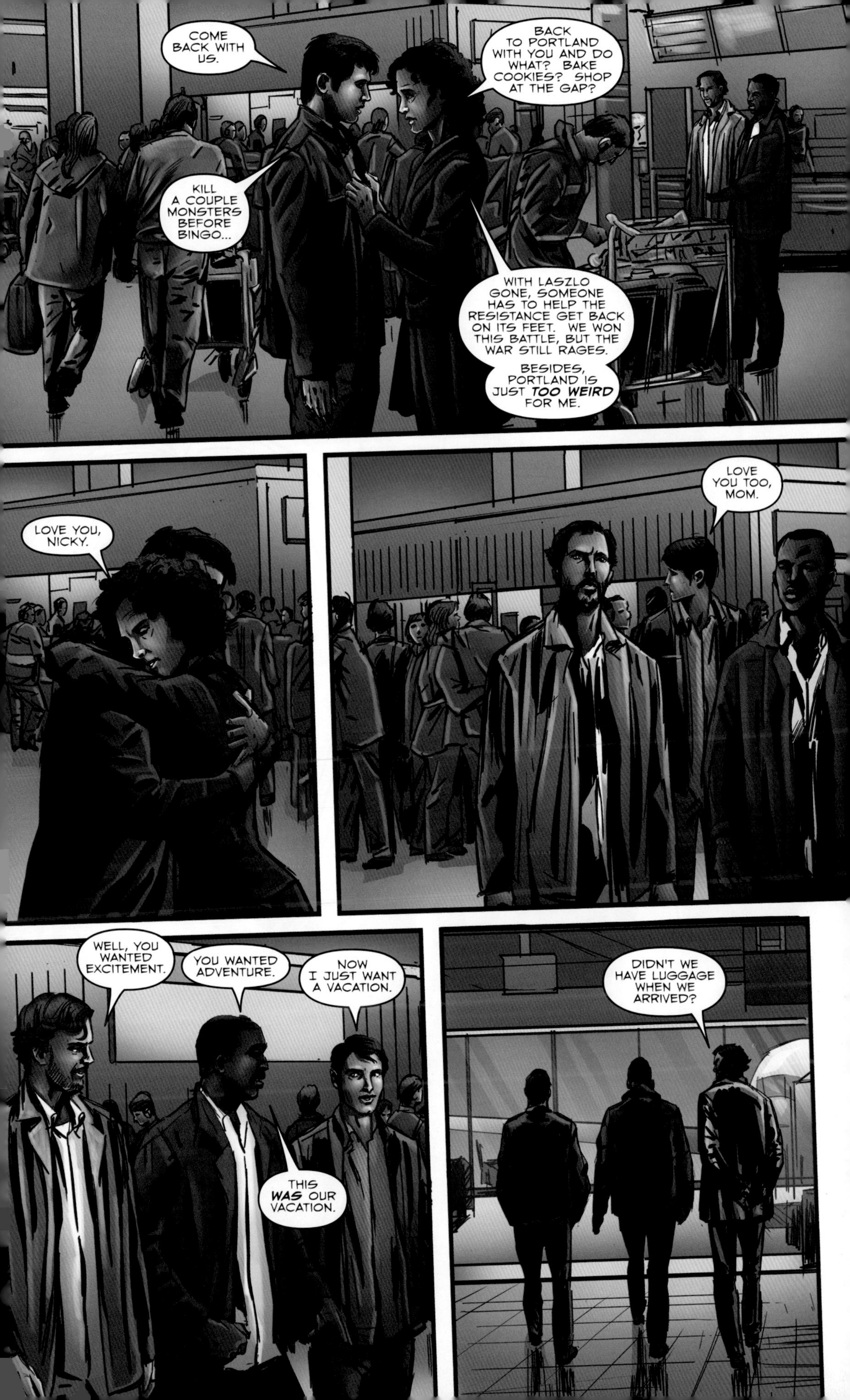
COME BACK WITH US.
BACK TO PORTLAND WITH YOU AND DO WHAT? BAKE COOKIES? SHOP AT THE GAP?
KILL A COUPLE MONSTERS BEFORE BINGO...
WITH LASZLO GONE, SOMEONE HAS TO HELP THE RESISTANCE GET BACK ON ITS FEET. WE WON THIS BATTLE, BUT THE WAR STILL RAGES.
BESIDES, PORTLAND IS JUST TOO WEIRD FOR ME.
LOVE YOU, NICKY.
LOVE YOU TOO, MOM.
WELL, YOU WANTED EXCITEMENT.
YOU WANTED ADVENTURE.
NOW I JUST WANT A VACATION.
THIS WAS OUR VACATION.
DIDN'T WE HAVE LUGGAGE WHEN WE ARRIVED?

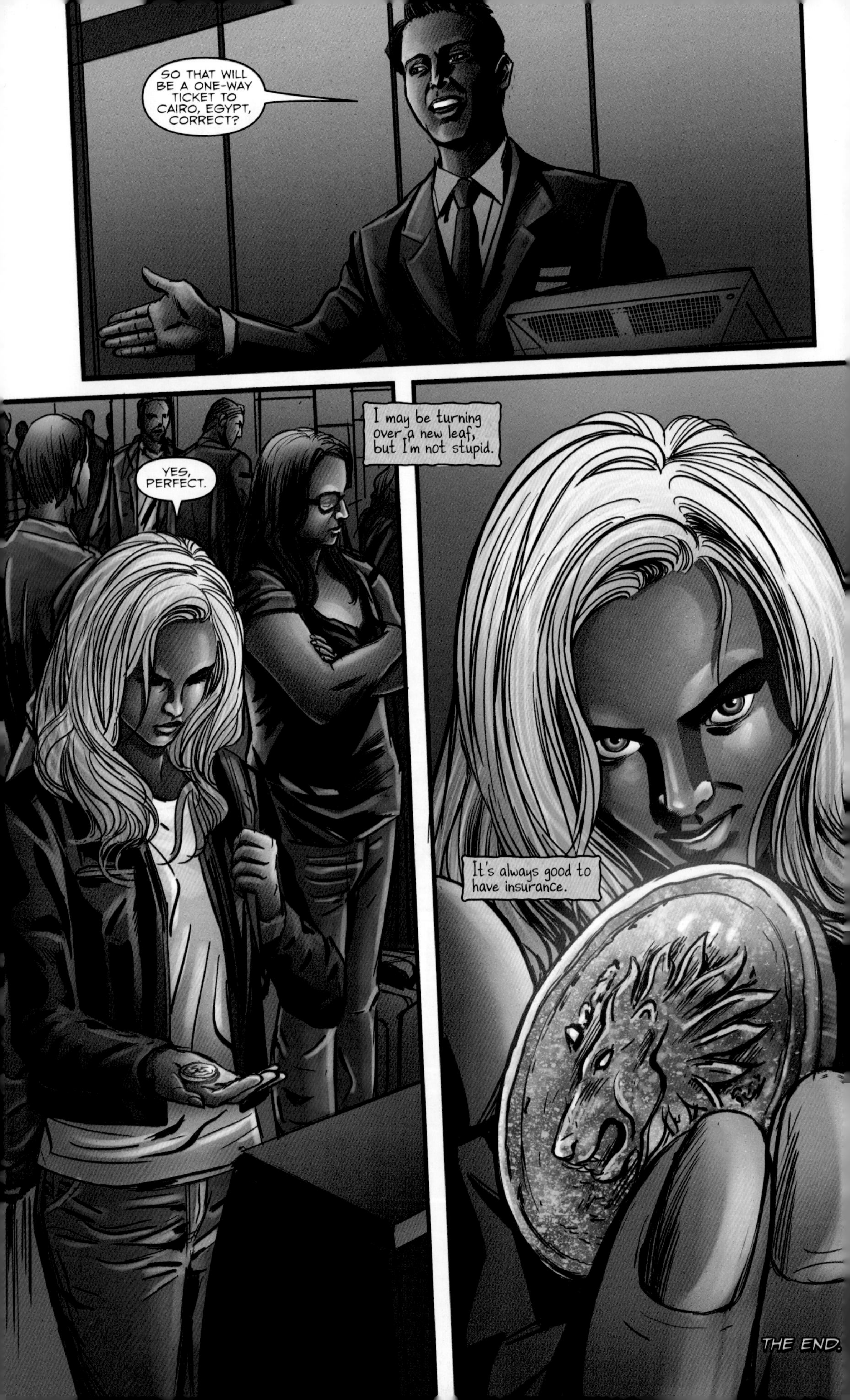
SO THAT WILL BE A ONE-WAY TICKET TO CAIRO, EGYPT, CORRECT?
YES, PERFECT.
I may be turning over a new leaf, but I'm not stupid.
It's always good to have insurance.
THE END.

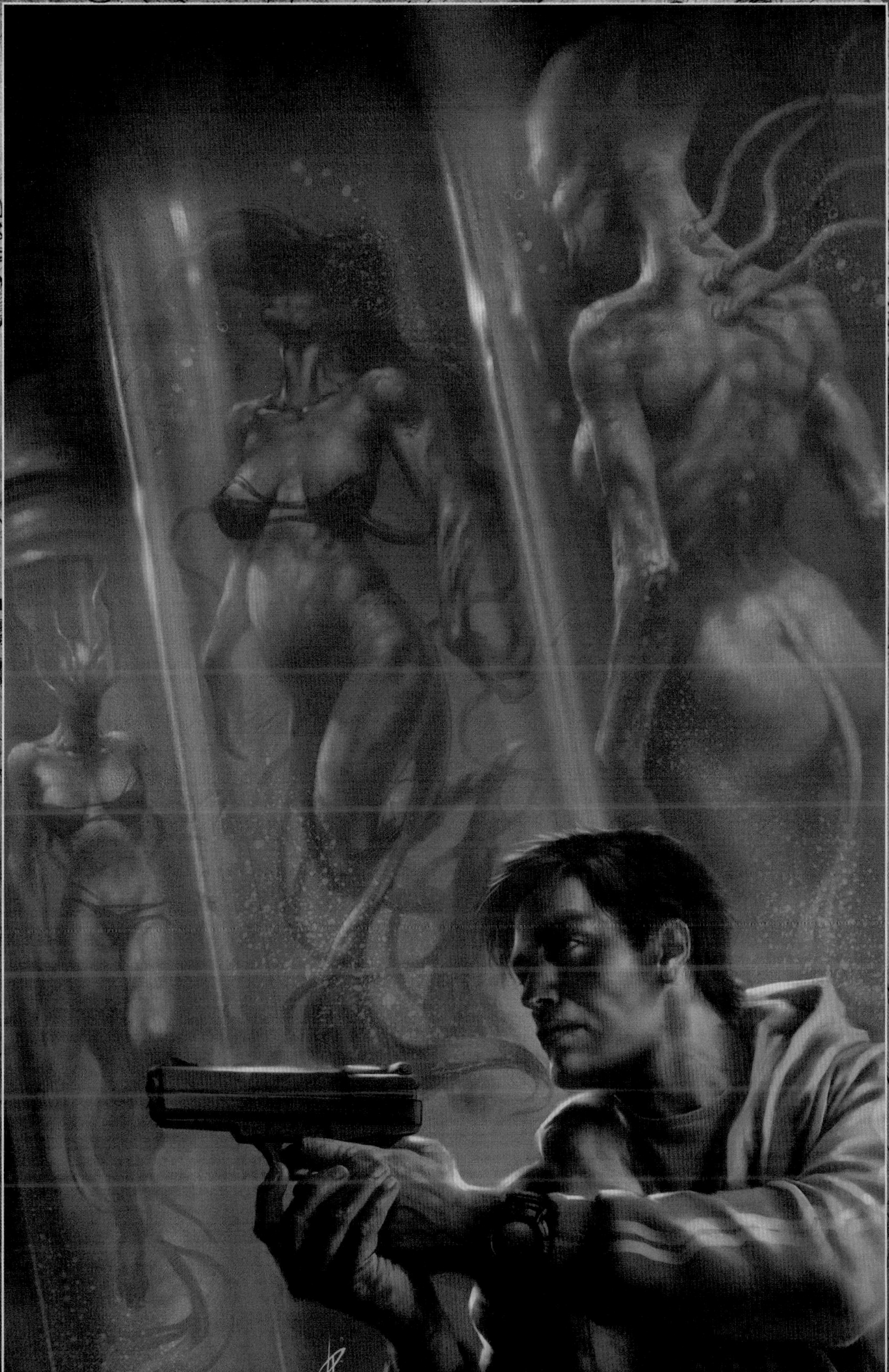

ISSUE #6 COVER
ART BY LUCIO PARRILLO

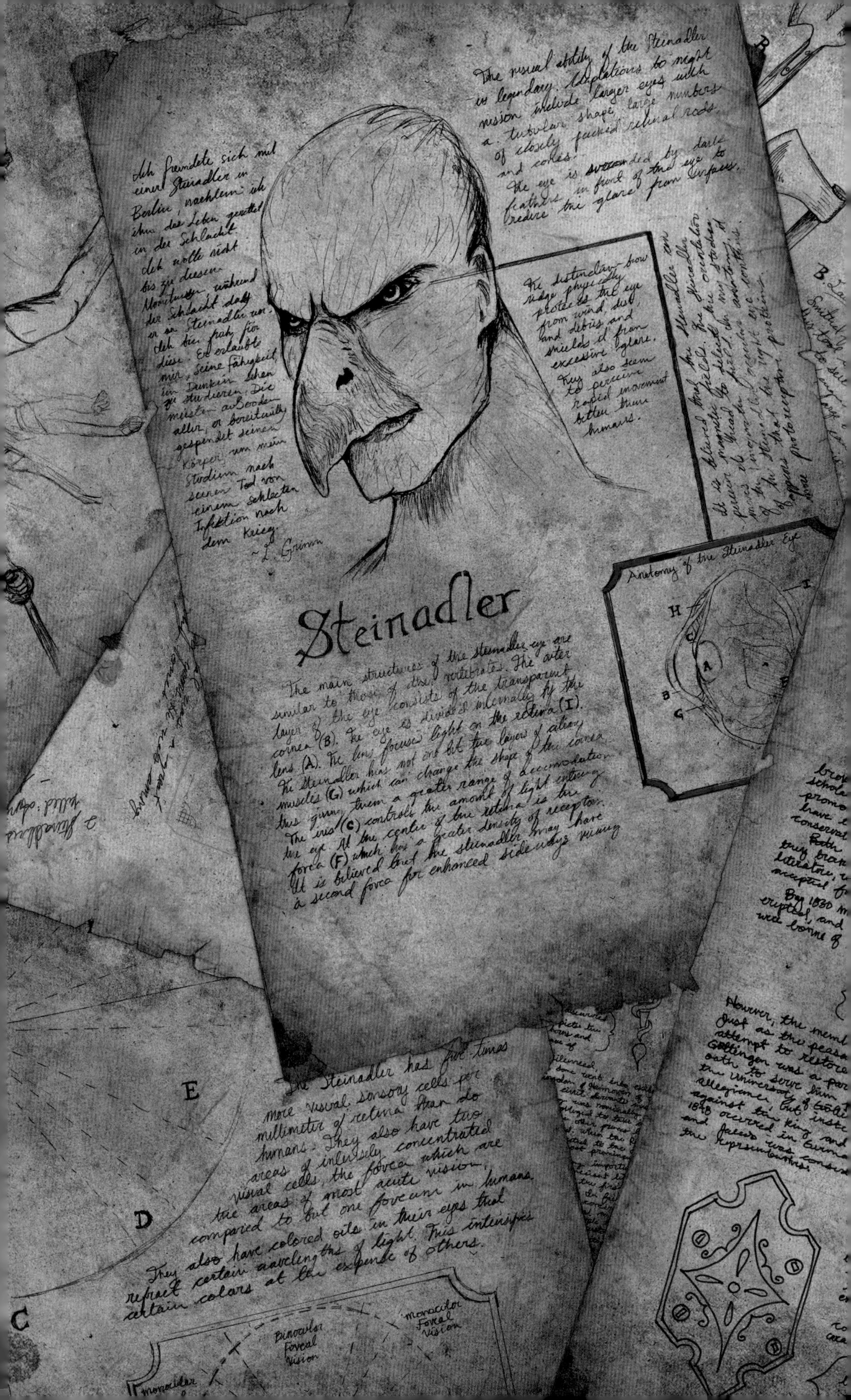
The visual ability of the Steinadler is legendary. Adaptations to night vision include larger eyes with a tubular shape, large numbers of closely packed retinal rods and cones. The eye is surrounded by dark feathers in front of the eye to reduce the glare from
Ich freundete sich mit einer Steinadler in Berlin, nachdem ich ihm das Leben gerettet in der Schlacht. Ich wollte nicht bis zu diesen Momenten während der Schlacht daß er an Steinadler war. Ich bin froh für diese. Er erlaubte mir, seine Fähigkeit im Dunkeln sehen zu studieren. Die meisten außerdem aller, er bereitwillig gespendet seinen Körper um mein Studium nach seinen Tod von einem schlechten Infektion nach dem Krieg.
~L. Grimm
The distinctive brow ridge physically protects the eye from wind, dust and debris and shields it from excessive glare. They also seem to perceive rapid movement better than humans.
Anatomy of the Steinadler Eye
H
I
C
A
B
G
F
Steinadler
The main structures of the steinadler eye are similar to those of other vertebrates. The outer layer of the eye consists of the transparent cornea (B). The eye is divided internally by the lens (A). The lens focuses light on the retina (I). The Steinadler has not one but two layers of ciliary muscles (G) which can change the shape of the cornea thus giving them a greater range of accomodation. The iris (C) controls the amount of light entering the eye. At the centre of the retina is the fovea (F) which has a greater density of receptors. It is believed that the steinadler may have a second fovea for enhanced sideways viewing
The Steinadler has five times more visual sensory cells per millimeter of retina than do humans. They also have two areas of intensely concentrated visual cells, the fovea which are the areas of most acute vision, compared to but one foveum in humans.
They also have colored oils in their eyes that refract certain wavelengths of light. This intensifies certain colors at the expense of others.
E
D
C
Binocular Foveal Vision
monocular Foveal Vision

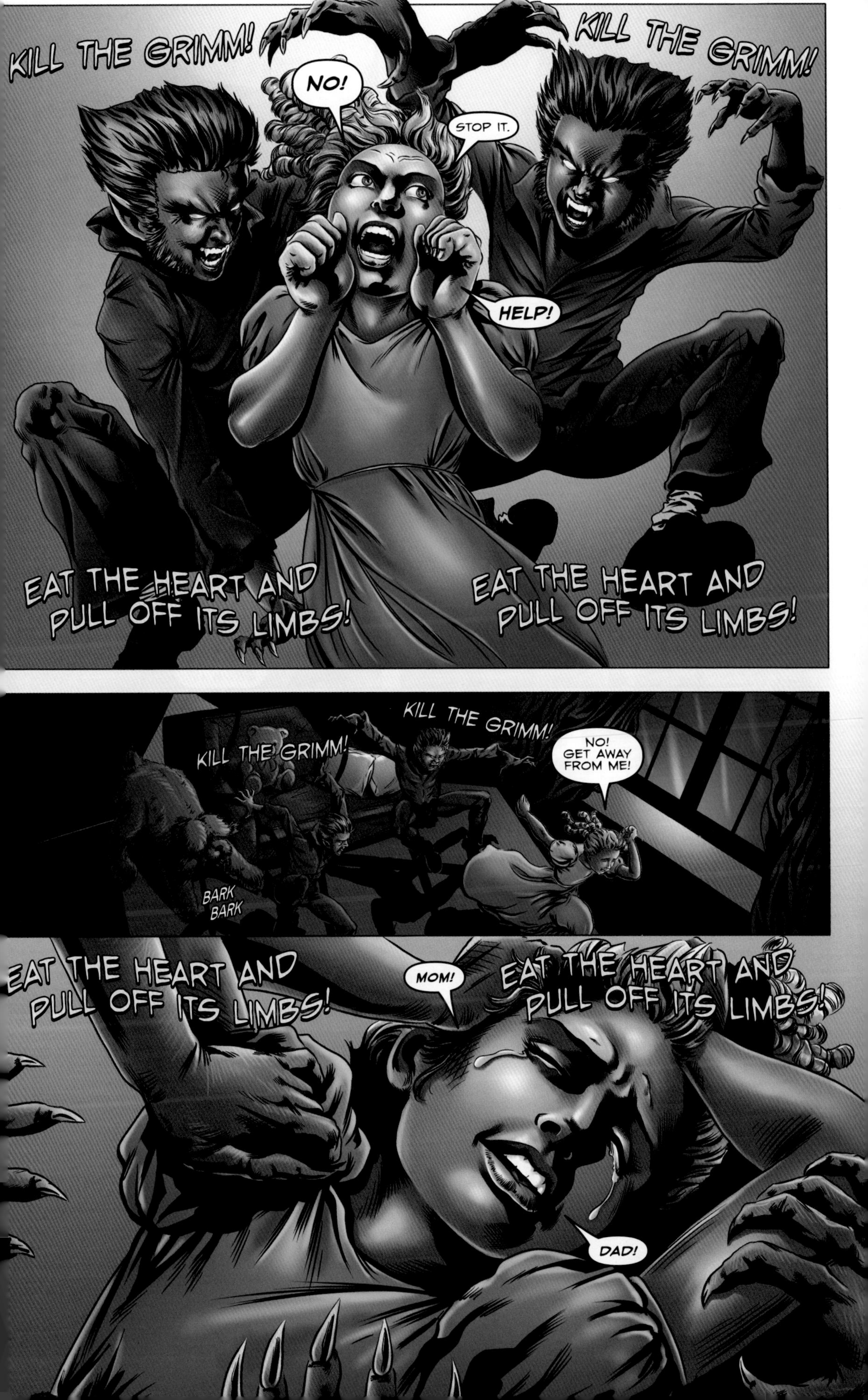
KILL THE GRIMM!
NO!
STOP IT.
KILL THE GRIMM!
HELP!
EAT THE HEART AND PULL OFF ITS LIMBS!
EAT THE HEART AND PULL OFF ITS LIMBS!
KILL THE GRIMM!
KILL THE GRIMM!
NO! GET AWAY FROM ME!
BARK BARK
EAT THE HEART AND PULL OFF ITS LIMBS!
MOM!
EAT THE HEART AND PULL OFF ITS LIMBS!
DAD!

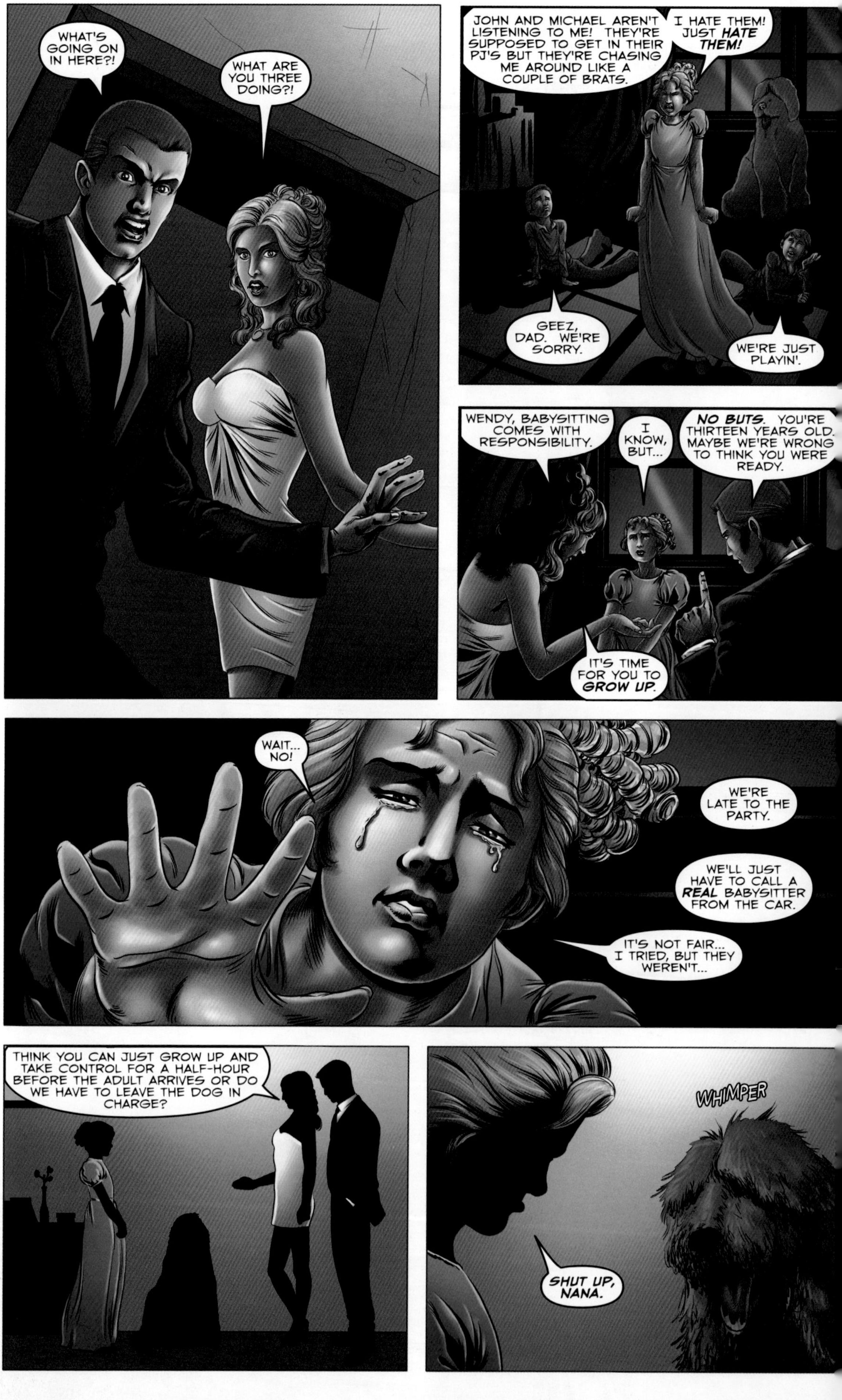
WHAT'S GOING ON IN HERE?!
WHAT ARE YOU THREE DOING?!
JOHN AND MICHAEL AREN'T LISTENING TO ME! THEY'RE SUPPOSED TO GET IN THEIR PJ'S BUT THEY'RE CHASING ME AROUND LIKE A COUPLE OF BRATS.
I HATE THEM! JUST HATE THEM!
GEEZ, DAD. WE'RE SORRY.
WE'RE JUST PLAYIN'.
WENDY, BABYSITTING COMES WITH RESPONSIBILITY.
I KNOW, BUT...
NO BUTS. YOU'RE THIRTEEN YEARS OLD. MAYBE WE'RE WRONG TO THINK YOU WERE READY.
IT'S TIME FOR YOU TO GROW UP.
WAIT... NO!
WE'RE LATE TO THE PARTY.
WE'LL JUST HAVE TO CALL A REAL BABYSITTER FROM THE CAR.
IT'S NOT FAIR... I TRIED, BUT THEY WEREN'T...
THINK YOU CAN JUST GROW UP AND TAKE CONTROL FOR A HALF-HOUR BEFORE THE ADULT ARRIVES OR DO WE HAVE TO LEAVE THE DOG IN CHARGE?
WHIMPER
SHUT UP, NANA.

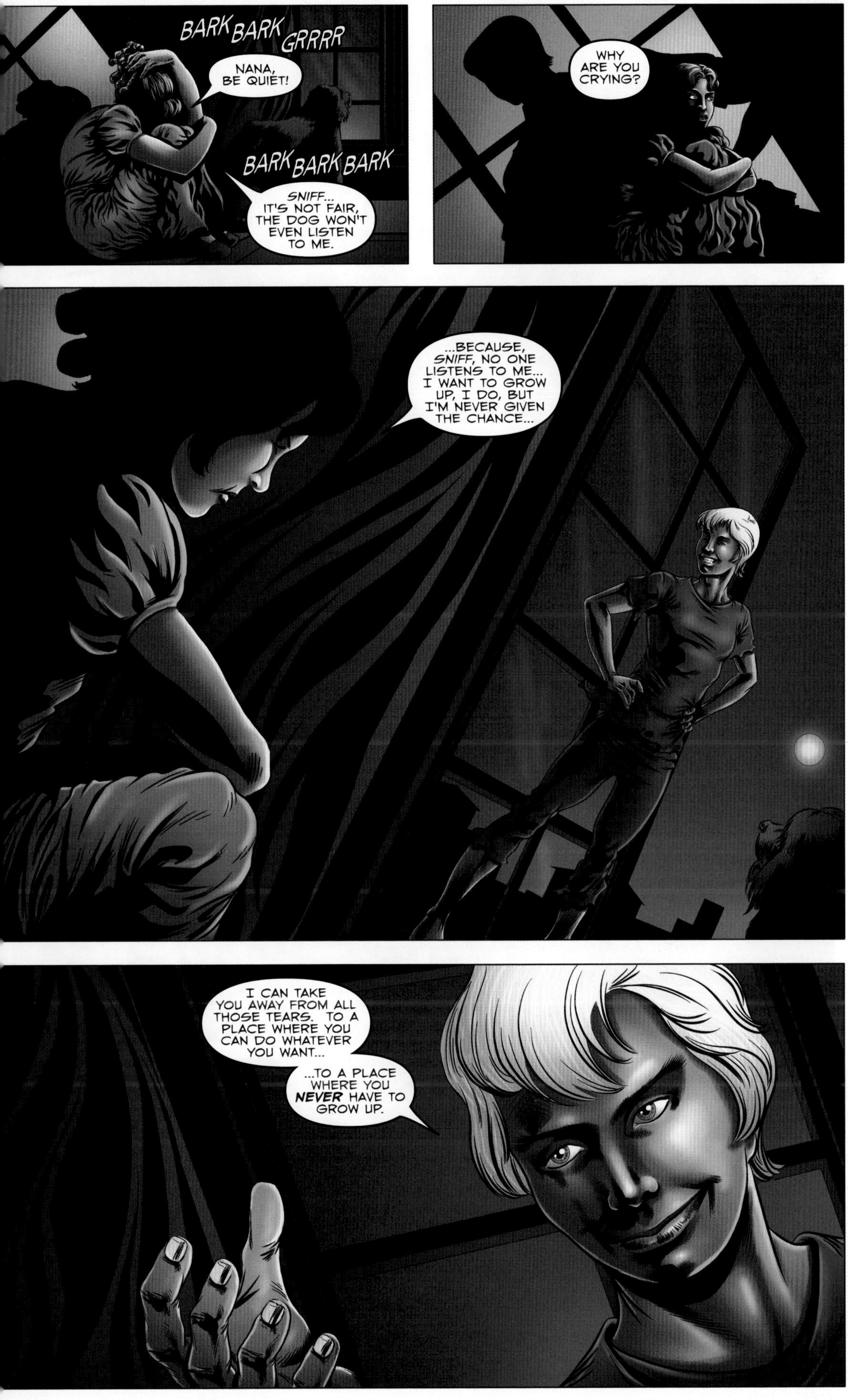
BARK BARK GRRRR
NANA, BE QUIET!
BARK BARK BARK
SNIFF... IT'S NOT FAIR, THE DOG WON'T EVEN LISTEN TO ME.
WHY ARE YOU CRYING?
...BECAUSE, SNIFF, NO ONE LISTENS TO ME... I WANT TO GROW UP, I DO, BUT I'M NEVER GIVEN THE CHANCE...
I CAN TAKE YOU AWAY FROM ALL THOSE TEARS. TO A PLACE WHERE YOU CAN DO WHATEVER YOU WANT...
...TO A PLACE WHERE YOU NEVER HAVE TO GROW UP.

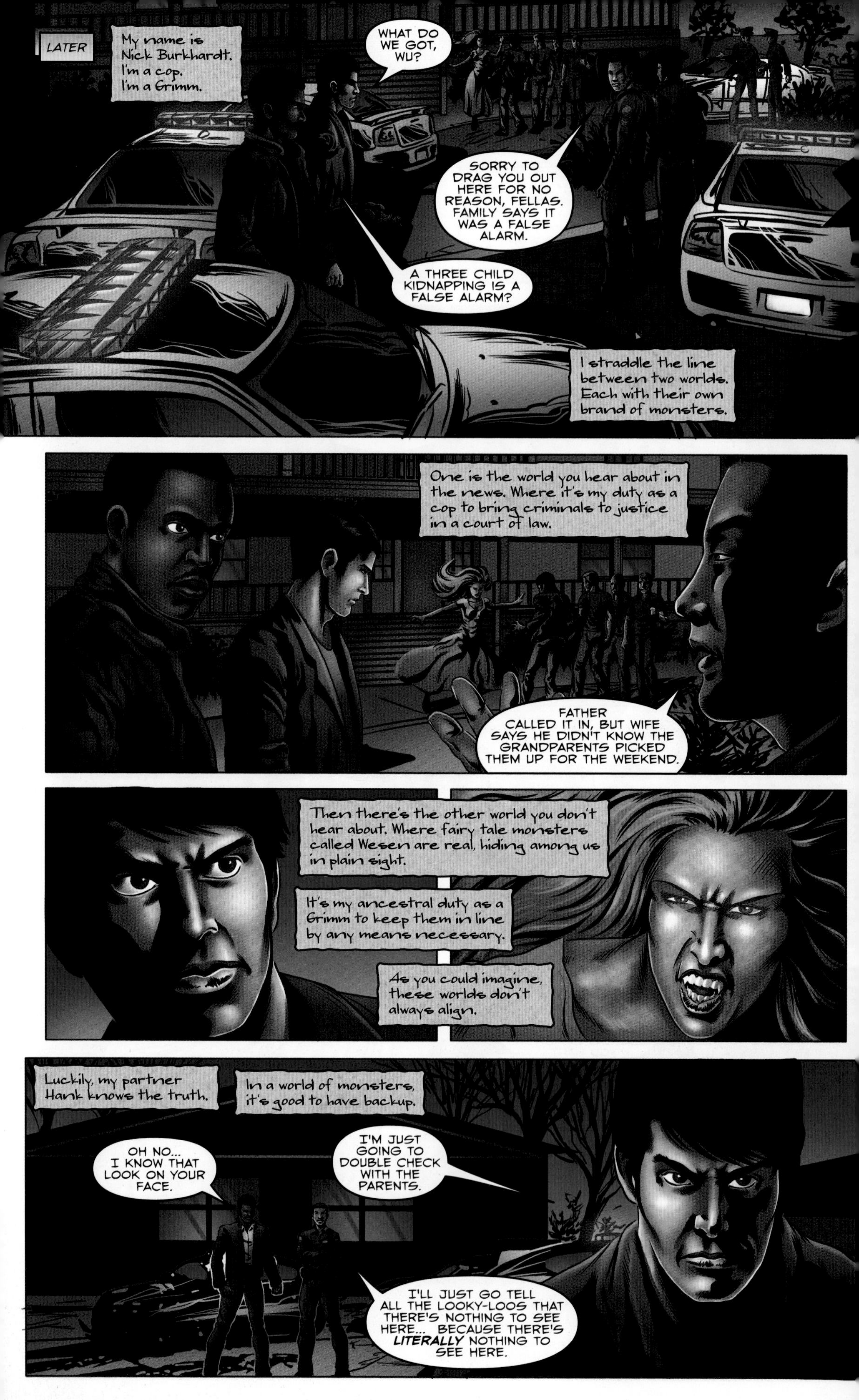
LATER
My name is Nick Burkhardt. I'm a cop. I'm a Grimm.
WHAT DO WE GOT, WU?
SORRY TO DRAG YOU OUT HERE FOR NO REASON, FELLAS. FAMILY SAYS IT WAS A FALSE ALARM.
A THREE CHILD KIDNAPPING IS A FALSE ALARM?
I straddle the line between two worlds. Each with their own brand of monsters.
One is the world you hear about in the news. Where it's my duty as a cop to bring criminals to justice in a court of law.
FATHER CALLED IT IN, BUT WIFE SAYS HE DIDN'T KNOW THE GRANDPARENTS PICKED THEM UP FOR THE WEEKEND.
Then there's the other world you don't hear about. Where fairy tale monsters called Wesen are real, hiding among us in plain sight.
It's my ancestral duty as a Grimm to keep them in line by any means necessary.
As you could imagine, these worlds don't always align.
Luckily, my partner Hank knows the truth.
In a world of monsters, it's good to have backup.
OH NO... I KNOW THAT LOOK ON YOUR FACE.
I'M JUST GOING TO DOUBLE CHECK WITH THE PARENTS.
I'LL JUST GO TELL ALL THE LOOKY-LOOS THAT THERE'S NOTHING TO SEE HERE... BECAUSE THERE'S *LITERALLY* NOTHING TO SEE HERE.

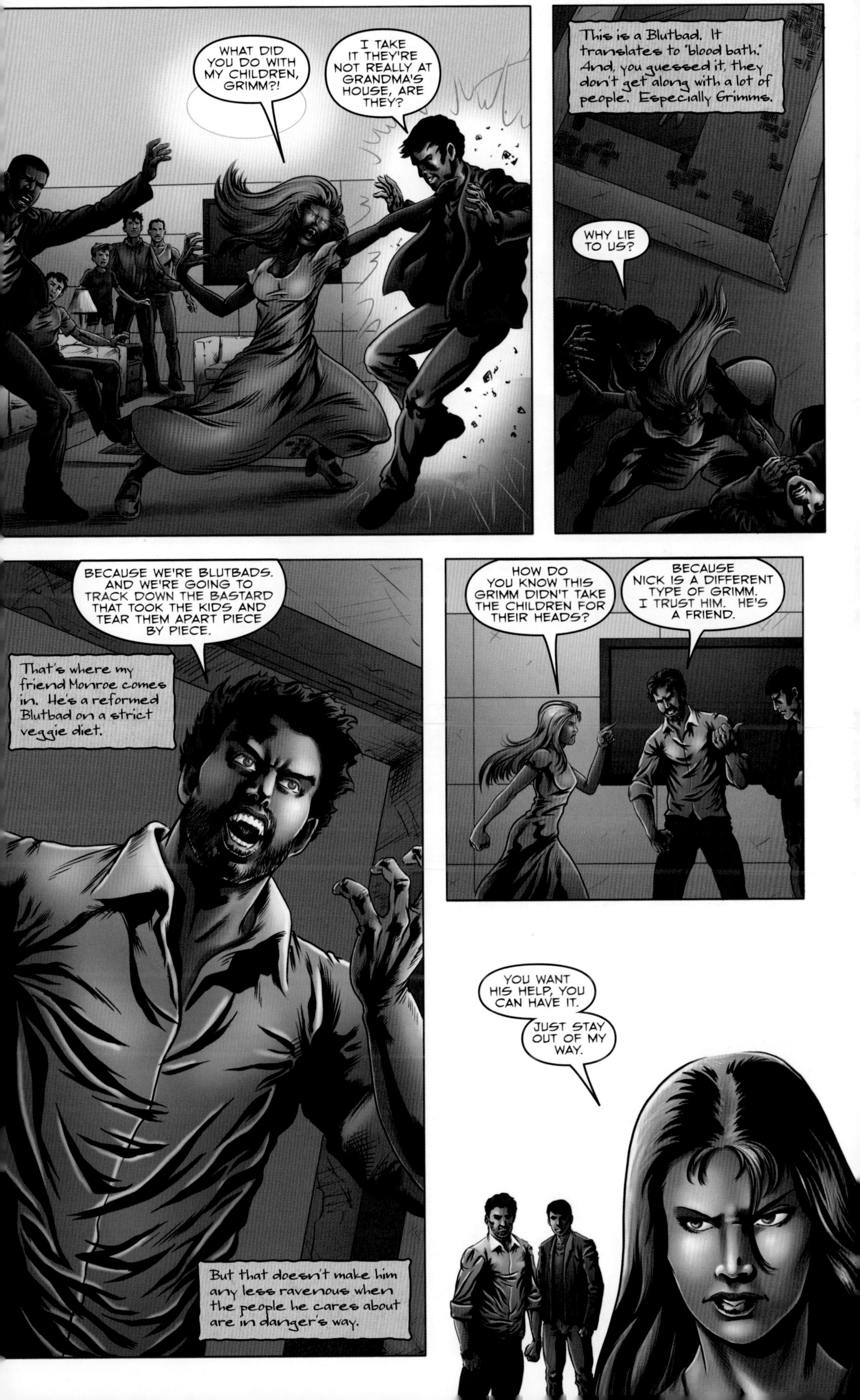
WHAT DID YOU DO WITH MY CHILDREN, GRIMM?!
I TAKE IT THEY'RE NOT REALLY AT GRANDMA'S HOUSE, ARE THEY?
This is a Blutbad. It translates to "blood bath." And, you guessed it, they don't get along with a lot of people. Especially Grimms.
WHY LIE TO US?
BECAUSE WE'RE BLUTBADS. AND WE'RE GOING TO TRACK DOWN THE BASTARD THAT TOOK THE KIDS AND TEAR THEM APART PIECE BY PIECE.
That's where my friend Monroe comes in. He's a reformed Blutbad on a strict veggie diet.
But that doesn't make him any less ravenous when the people he cares about are in danger's way.
HOW DO YOU KNOW THIS GRIMM DIDN'T TAKE THE CHILDREN FOR THEIR HEADS?
BECAUSE NICK IS A DIFFERENT TYPE OF GRIMM. I TRUST HIM. HE'S A FRIEND.
YOU WANT HIS HELP, YOU CAN HAVE IT.
JUST STAY OUT OF MY WAY.

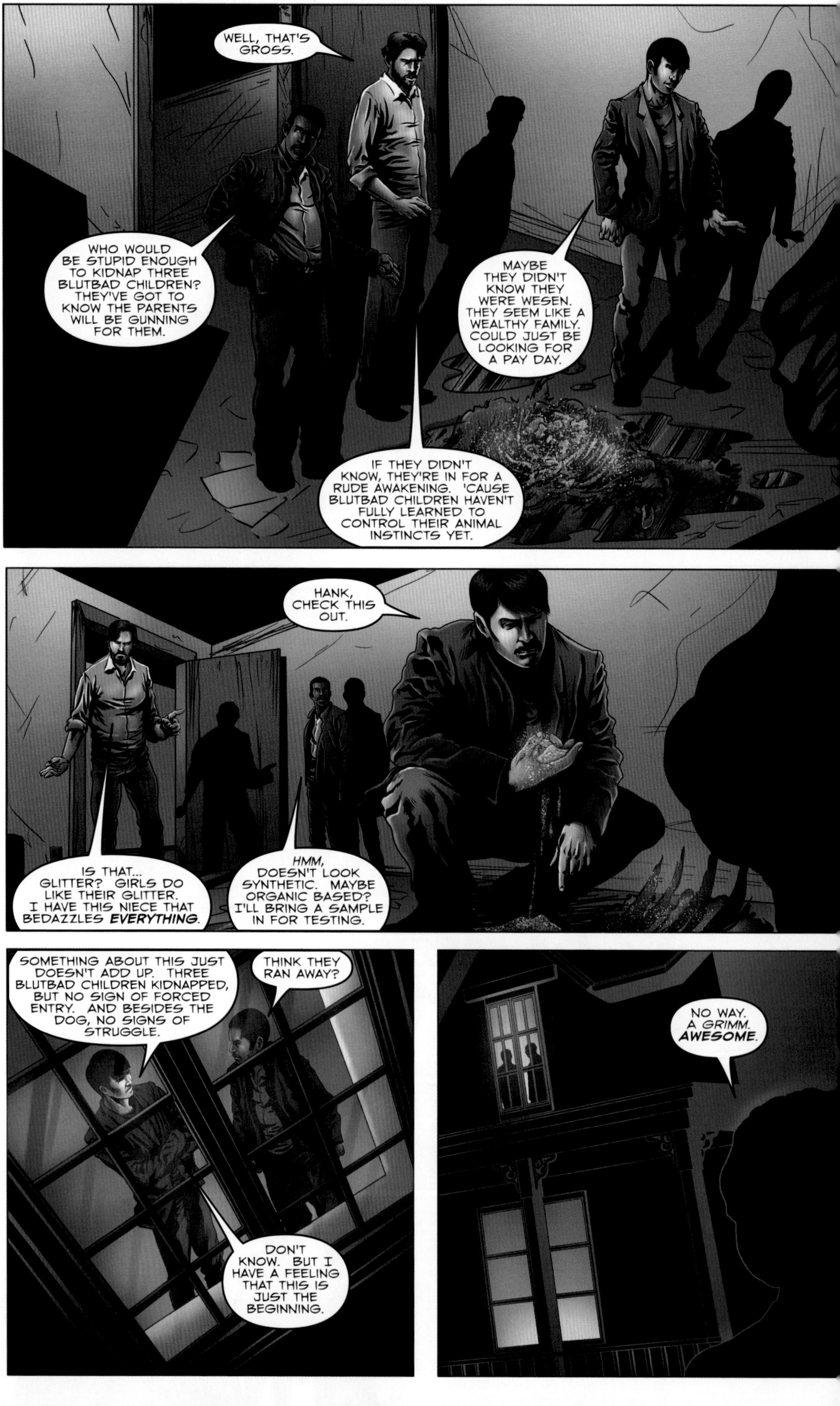
WELL, THAT'S GROSS.
WHO WOULD BE STUPID ENOUGH TO KIDNAP THREE BLUTBAD CHILDREN? THEY'VE GOT TO KNOW THE PARENTS WILL BE GUNNING FOR THEM.
MAYBE THEY DIDN'T KNOW THEY WERE WESEN. THEY SEEM LIKE A WEALTHY FAMILY. COULD JUST BE LOOKING FOR A PAY DAY.
IF THEY DIDN'T KNOW, THEY'RE IN FOR A RUDE AWAKENING. 'CAUSE BLUTBAD CHILDREN HAVEN'T FULLY LEARNED TO CONTROL THEIR ANIMAL INSTINCTS YET.
HANK, CHECK THIS OUT.
IS THAT... GLITTER? GIRLS DO LIKE THEIR GLITTER. I HAVE THIS NIECE THAT BEDAZZLES ***EVERYTHING***.
HMM, DOESN'T LOOK SYNTHETIC. MAYBE ORGANIC BASED? I'LL BRING A SAMPLE IN FOR TESTING.
SOMETHING ABOUT THIS JUST DOESN'T ADD UP. THREE BLUTBAD CHILDREN KIDNAPPED, BUT NO SIGN OF FORCED ENTRY. AND BESIDES THE DOG, NO SIGNS OF STRUGGLE.
THINK THEY RAN AWAY?
DON'T KNOW. BUT I HAVE A FEELING THAT THIS IS JUST THE BEGINNING.
NO WAY. A *GRIMM*. ***AWESOME***.

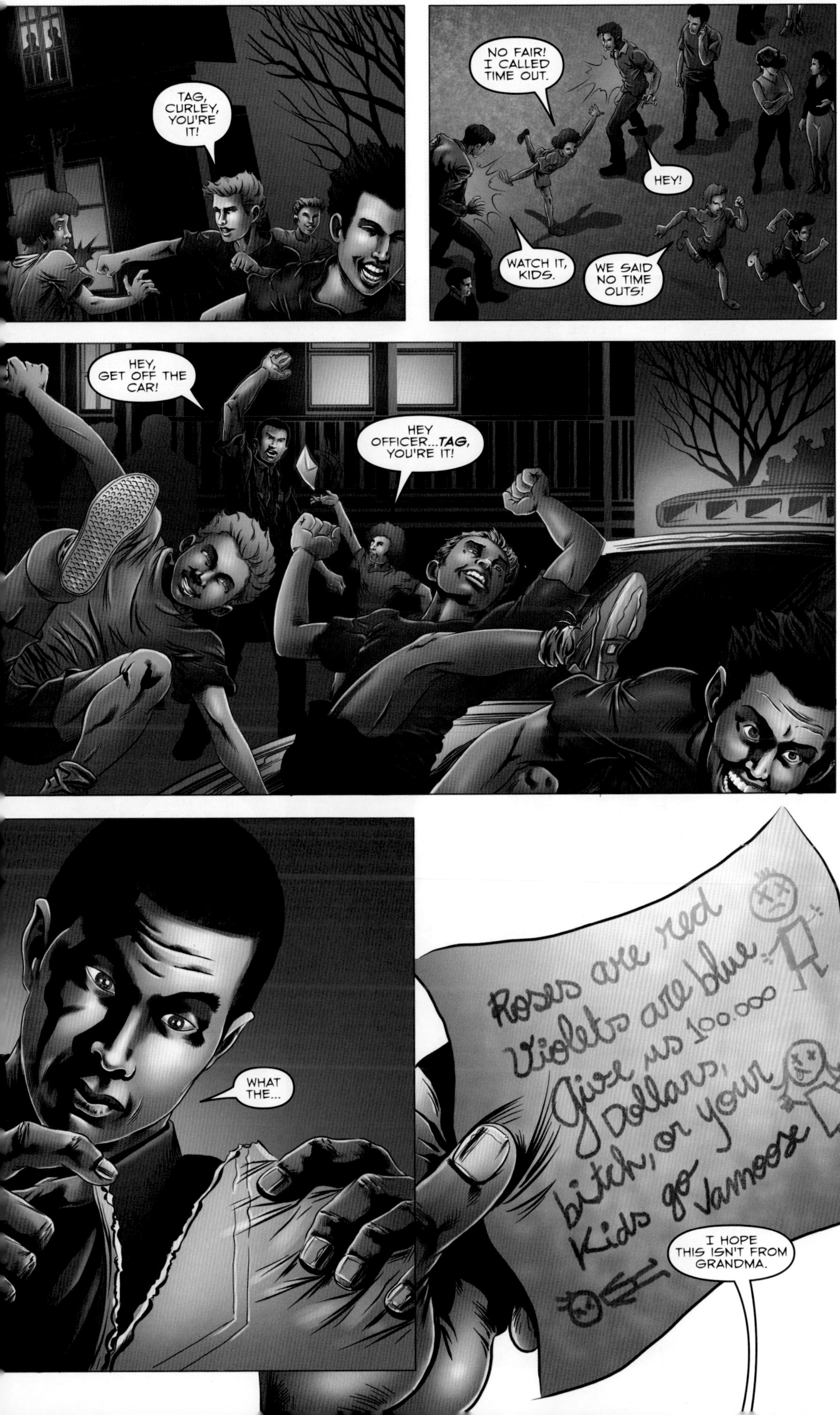
TAG, CURLEY, YOU'RE IT!
NO FAIR! I CALLED TIME OUT.
HEY!
WATCH IT, KIDS.
WE SAID NO TIME OUTS!
HEY, GET OFF THE CAR!
HEY OFFICER...TAG, YOU'RE IT!
WHAT THE...
Roses are red
Violets are blue
Give us 100.000
Dollars,
bitch, or your
Kids go Vamoose
I HOPE THIS ISN'T FROM GRANDMA.

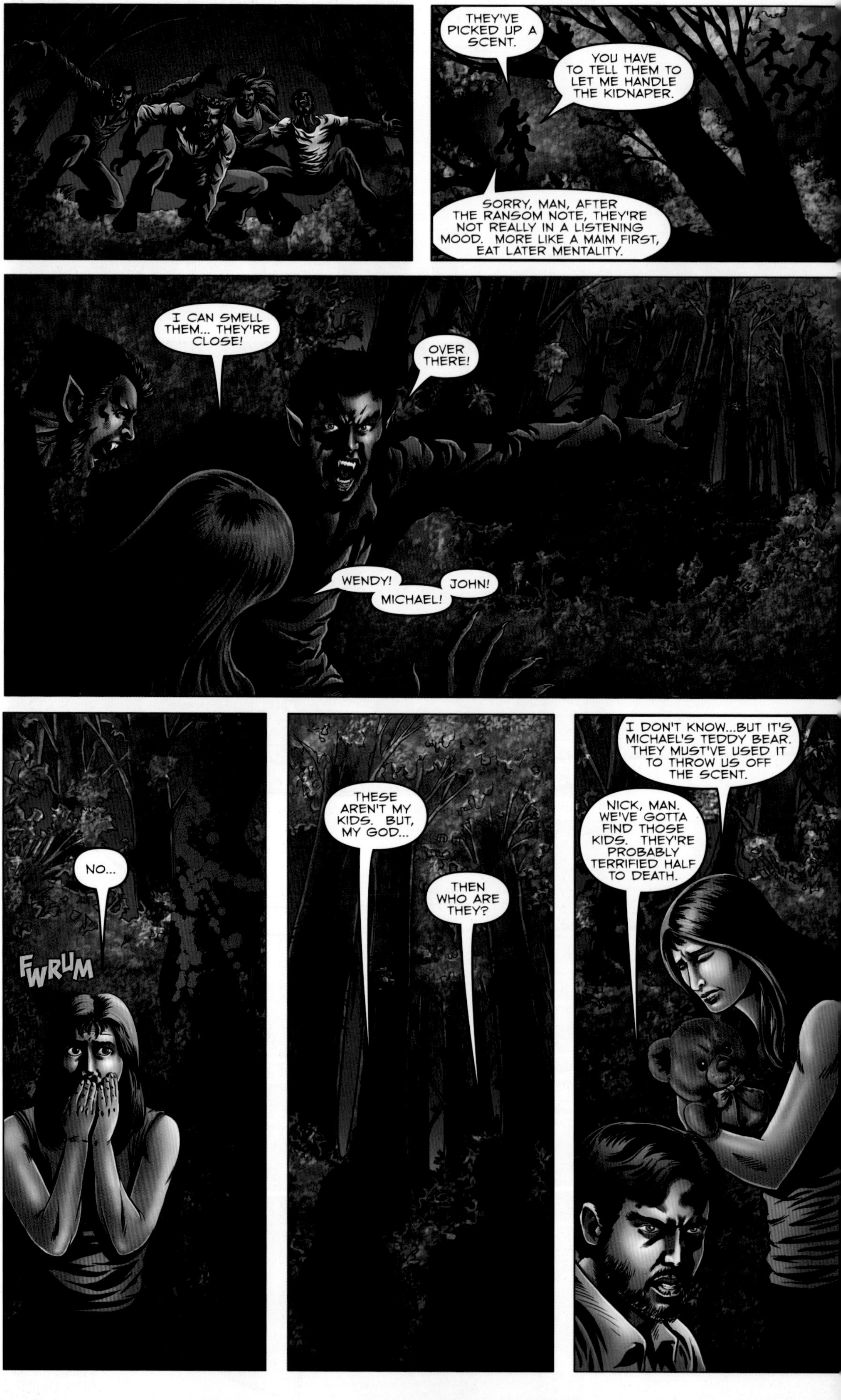
THEY'VE PICKED UP A SCENT.
YOU HAVE TO TELL THEM TO LET ME HANDLE THE KIDNAPER.
SORRY, MAN, AFTER THE RANSOM NOTE, THEY'RE NOT REALLY IN A LISTENING MOOD. MORE LIKE A MAIM FIRST, EAT LATER MENTALITY.
I CAN SMELL THEM... THEY'RE CLOSE!
OVER THERE!
WENDY!
MICHAEL!
JOHN!
NO...
FWRUM
THESE AREN'T MY KIDS. BUT, MY GOD...
THEN WHO ARE THEY?
I DON'T KNOW...BUT IT'S MICHAEL'S TEDDY BEAR. THEY MUST'VE USED IT TO THROW US OFF THE SCENT.
NICK, MAN. WE'VE GOTTA FIND THOSE KIDS. THEY'RE PROBABLY TERRIFIED HALF TO DEATH.

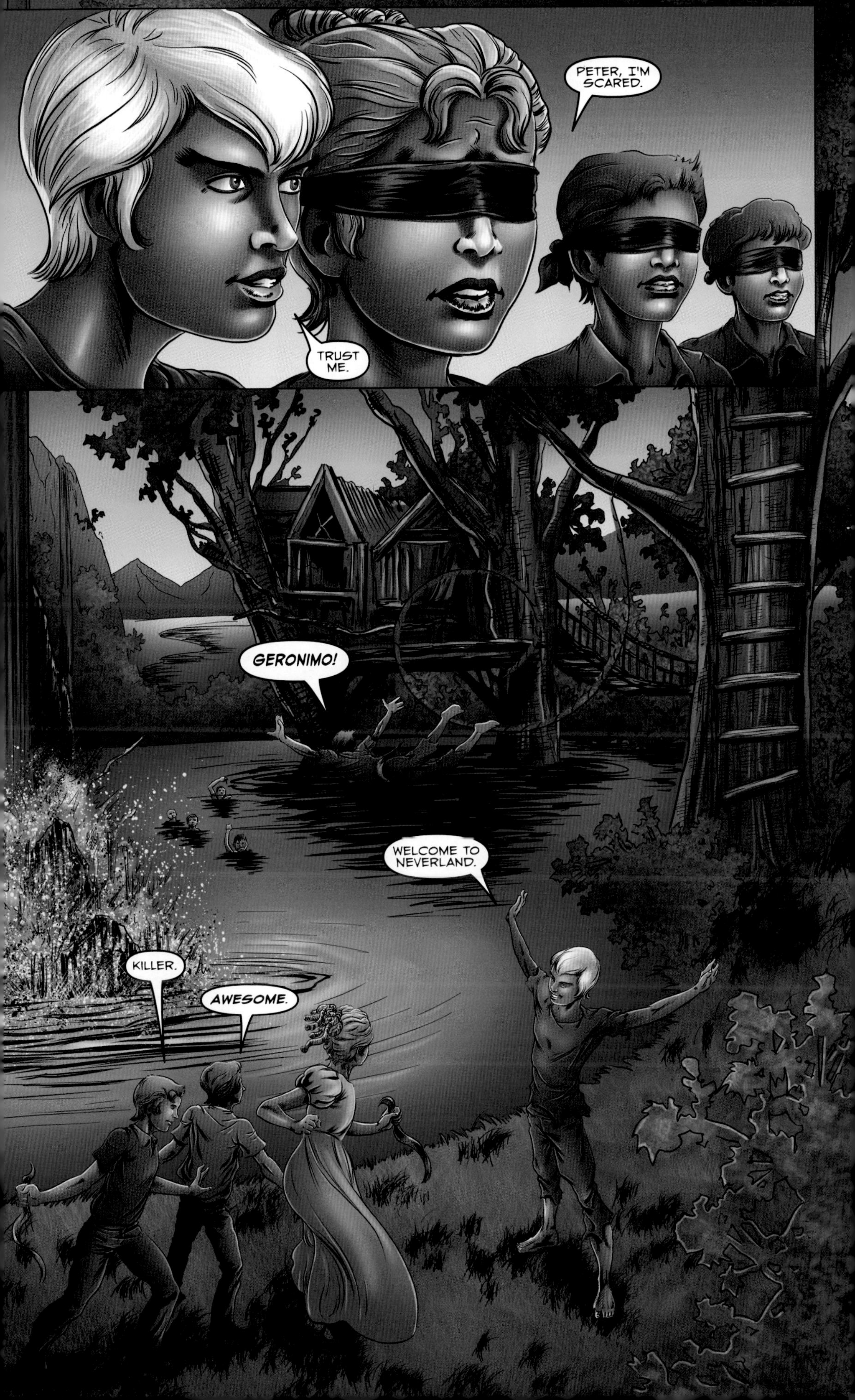
PETER, I'M SCARED.
TRUST ME.
GERONIMO!
WELCOME TO NEVERLAND.
KILLER.
AWESOME.

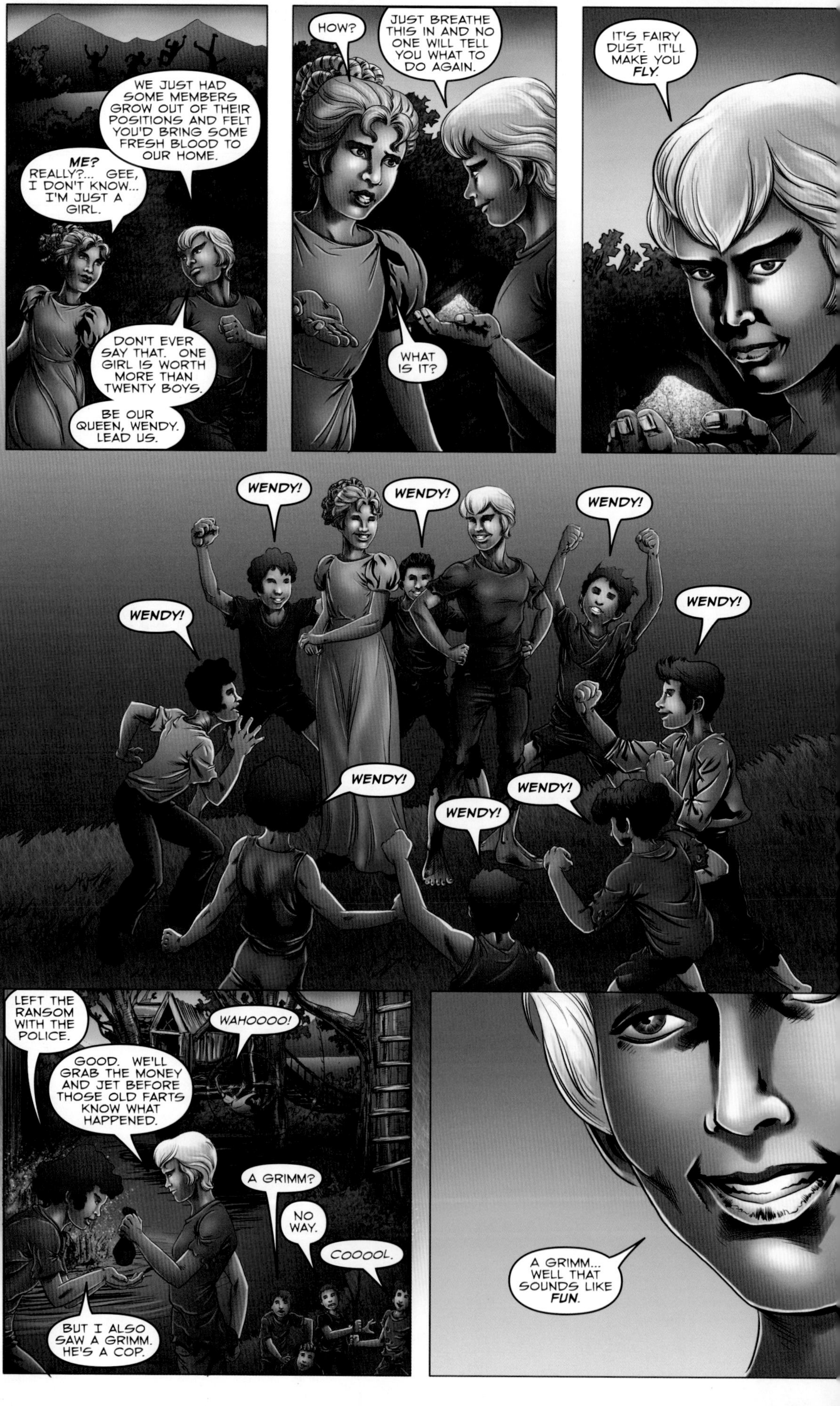
WE JUST HAD SOME MEMBERS GROW OUT OF THEIR POSITIONS AND FELT YOU'D BRING SOME FRESH BLOOD TO OUR HOME.
ME? REALLY?... GEE, I DON'T KNOW... I'M JUST A GIRL.
DON'T EVER SAY THAT. ONE GIRL IS WORTH MORE THAN TWENTY BOYS.
BE OUR QUEEN, WENDY. LEAD US.
HOW?
JUST BREATHE THIS IN AND NO ONE WILL TELL YOU WHAT TO DO AGAIN.
WHAT IS IT?
IT'S FAIRY DUST. IT'LL MAKE YOU FLY.
WENDY!
WENDY!
WENDY!
WENDY!
WENDY!
WENDY!
WENDY!
WENDY!
LEFT THE RANSOM WITH THE POLICE.
WAHOOOO!
GOOD. WE'LL GRAB THE MONEY AND JET BEFORE THOSE OLD FARTS KNOW WHAT HAPPENED.
BUT I ALSO SAW A GRIMM. HE'S A COP.
A GRIMM?
NO WAY.
COOOOL.
A GRIMM... WELL THAT SOUNDS LIKE FUN.

SO WHAT DID YOU FIND OUT?

THREE BODIES CAME BACK AS THE JAMES CHILDREN. KIDNAPPED FROM SPOKANE SIX YEARS AGO.

STORY IS EERILY SIMILAR TO THE DAVIES' KIDS DOWN TO THE NOTE WRITTEN IN CRAYON. PARENTS PAID, BUT THE KIDS WERE NEVER RETURNED.

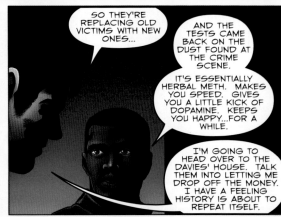

SO THEY'RE REPLACING OLD VICTIMS WITH NEW ONES...

AND THE TESTS CAME BACK ON THE DUST FOUND AT THE CRIME SCENE.

IT'S ESSENTIALLY HERBAL METH. MAKES YOU SPEED. GIVES YOU A LITTLE KICK OF DOPAMINE. KEEPS YOU HAPPY...FOR A WHILE.

I'M GOING TO HEAD OVER TO THE DAVIES' HOUSE. TALK THEM INTO LETTING ME DROP OFF THE MONEY. I HAVE A FEELING HISTORY IS ABOUT TO REPEAT ITSELF.

EAT THE HEART AND PULL OFF ITS LIMBS...

KID, WHAT'RE YOU DOING? YOU OKAY?

HEY, MISTER, WANT TO PLAY?

YOU LOST? WHERE ARE YOUR...

TAG! YOU'RE IT.

GRIMMS AREN'T ALL THAT SPECIAL. YOU'RE LAZY, FAT, AND SLOW JUST LIKE ALL GROWN UPS.

I WANT THE MONEY OR THE KIDS WILL NEVER BE SEEN AGAIN.

WHO ARE YOU?

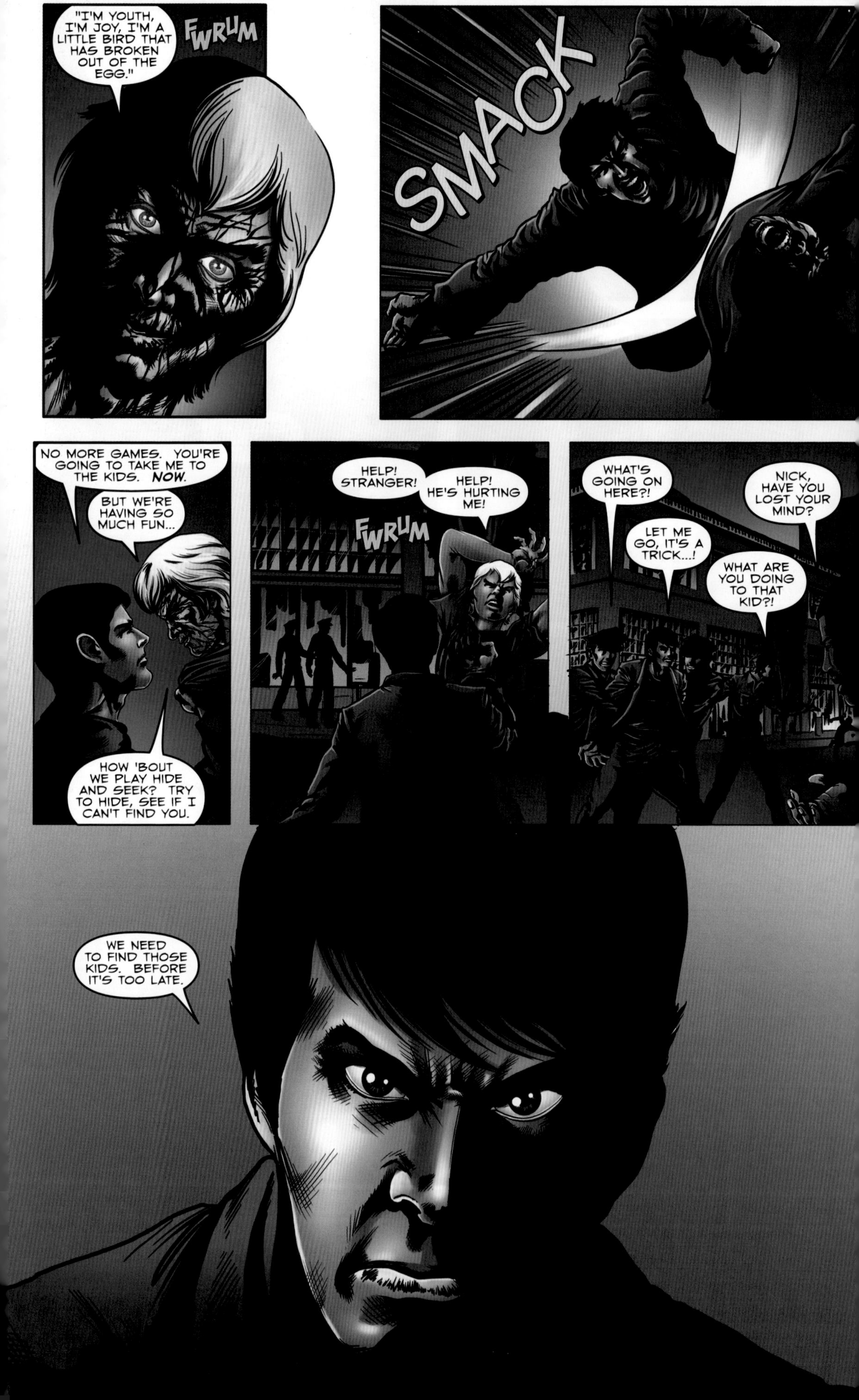
"I'M YOUTH, I'M JOY, I'M A LITTLE BIRD THAT HAS BROKEN OUT OF THE EGG."
FWRUM
SMACK
NO MORE GAMES. YOU'RE GOING TO TAKE ME TO THE KIDS. NOW.
BUT WE'RE HAVING SO MUCH FUN...
HOW 'BOUT WE PLAY HIDE AND SEEK? TRY TO HIDE, SEE IF I CAN'T FIND YOU.
HELP! STRANGER!
HELP! HE'S HURTING ME!
FWRUM
WHAT'S GOING ON HERE?!
LET ME GO, IT'S A TRICK...!
NICK, HAVE YOU LOST YOUR MIND?
WHAT ARE YOU DOING TO THAT KID?!
WE NEED TO FIND THOSE KIDS. BEFORE IT'S TOO LATE.

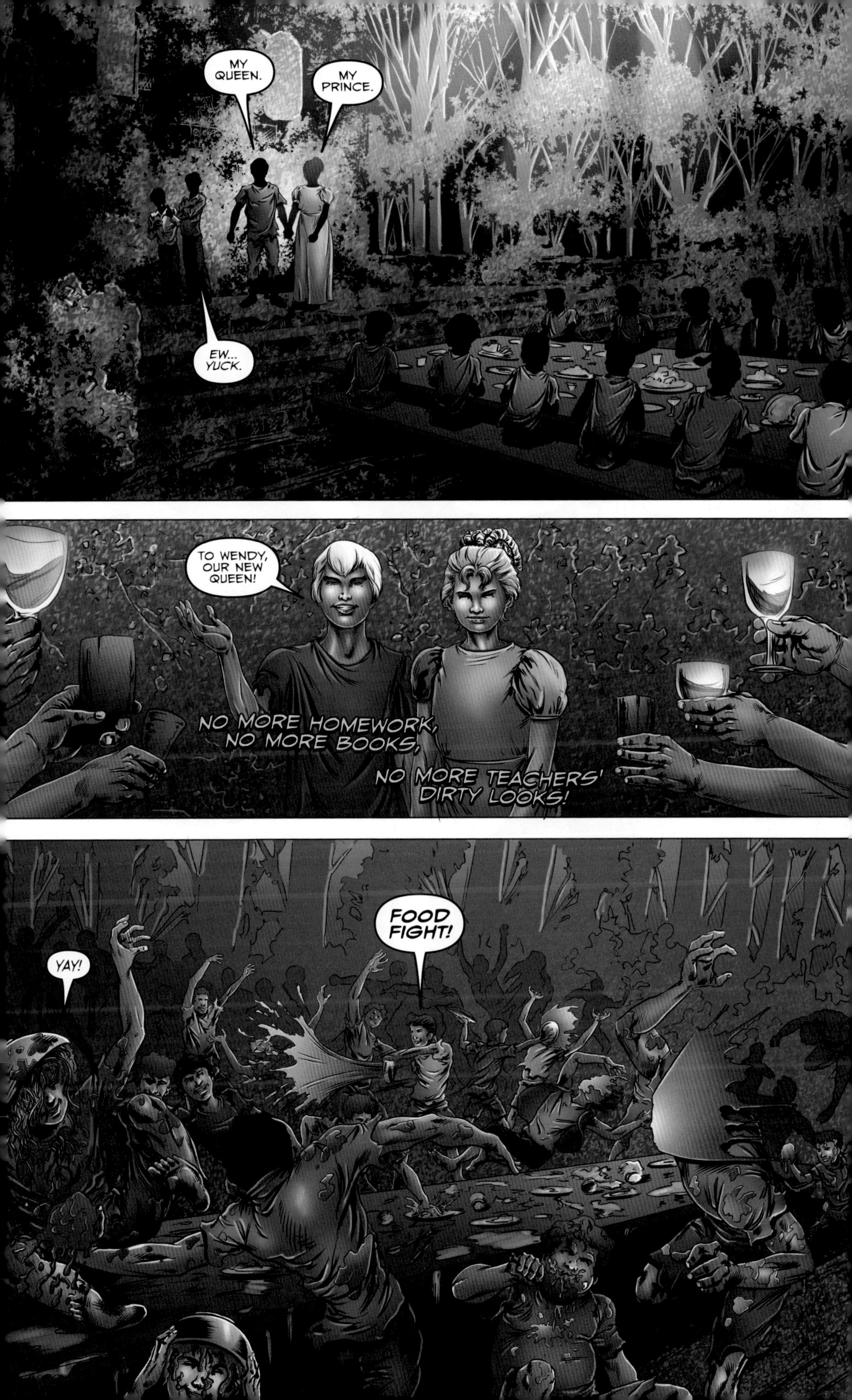
MY QUEEN.
MY PRINCE.
EW... YUCK.
TO WENDY, OUR NEW QUEEN!
NO MORE HOMEWORK, NO MORE BOOKS,
NO MORE TEACHERS' DIRTY LOOKS!
YAY!
FOOD FIGHT!

CARROT STICKS, ANYONE?

JULIETTE?

WHAT HAPPENED TO THOSE POTATO CHIPS AND PRETZELS NEXT TO THE WEAPONS CABINET?

UH, CHECK YOUR LOVE HANDLES.

THANK YOU, MONROE.

HEY, I THINK I'VE GOT SOMETHING...

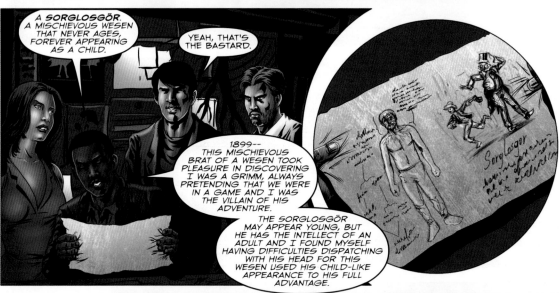

A *SORGLOSGÖR*. A MISCHIEVOUS WESEN THAT NEVER AGES, FOREVER APPEARING AS A CHILD.

YEAH, THAT'S THE BASTARD.

1899-- THIS MISCHIEVOUS BRAT OF A WESEN TOOK PLEASURE IN DISCOVERING I WAS A GRIMM, ALWAYS PRETENDING THAT WE WERE IN A GAME AND I WAS THE VILLAIN OF HIS ADVENTURE.

THE SORGLOSGÖR MAY APPEAR YOUNG, BUT HE HAS THE INTELLECT OF AN ADULT AND I FOUND MYSELF HAVING DIFFICULTIES DISPATCHING WITH HIS HEAD FOR THIS WESEN USED HIS CHILD-LIKE APPEARANCE TO HIS FULL ADVANTAGE.

FOREVER YOUNG, MUST BE NICE.

NO WAY, THINK ABOUT IT. ALWAYS TREATED LIKE A KID BUT CURSED WITH THE MIND OF AN ADULT.

ALL THE THINGS YOU CAN'T DO. SOCIETY HOLDING YOU BACK. CAN DRIVE A PERSON INSANE.

THAT'S EXACTLY WHAT THIS SORGLOSGÖR IS. *INSANE.* AND NOW IT LOOKS LIKE I'M HIS LATEST GAME.

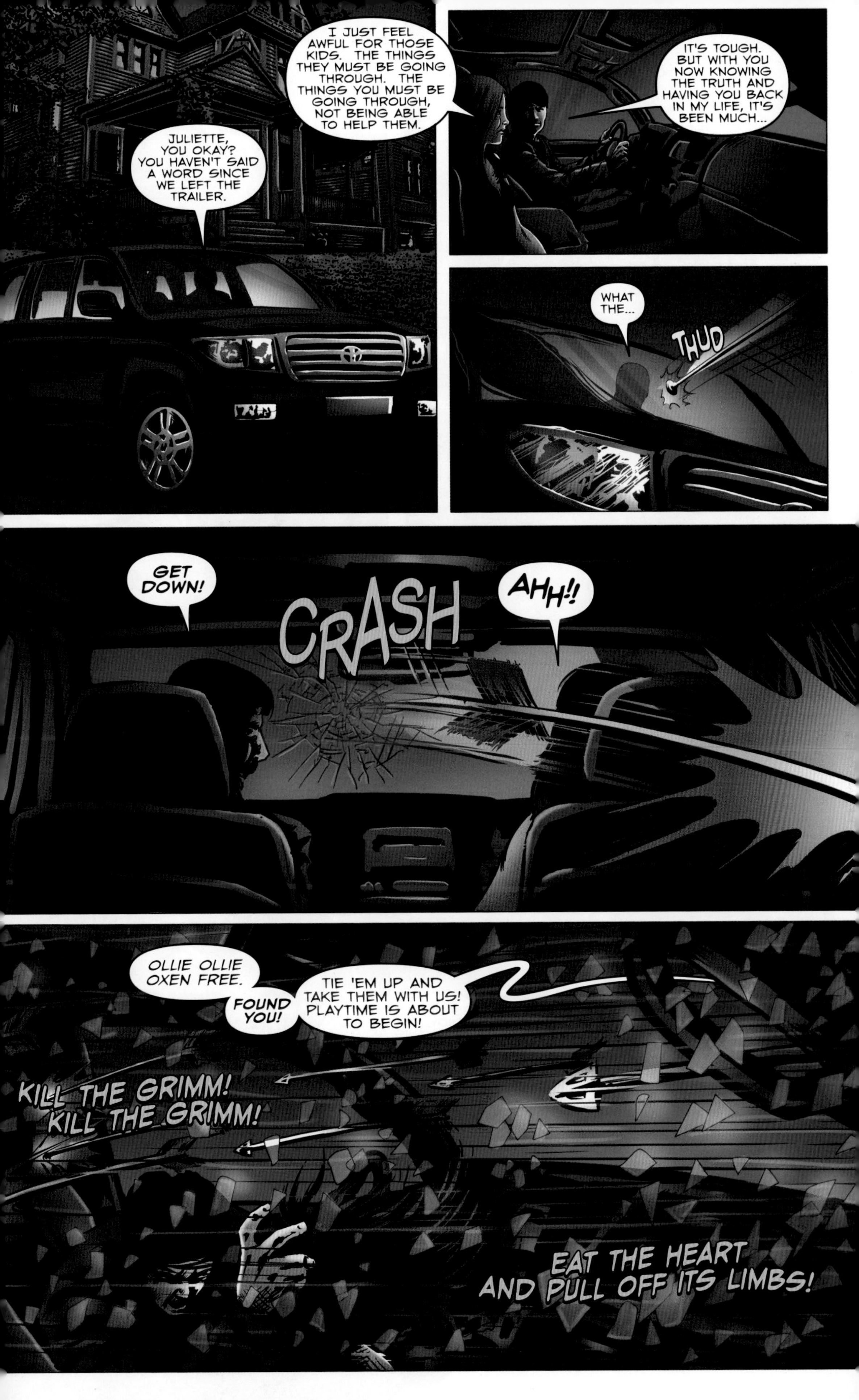
I JUST FEEL AWFUL FOR THOSE KIDS. THE THINGS THEY MUST BE GOING THROUGH. THE THINGS YOU MUST BE GOING THROUGH, NOT BEING ABLE TO HELP THEM.
JULIETTE, YOU OKAY? YOU HAVEN'T SAID A WORD SINCE WE LEFT THE TRAILER.
IT'S TOUGH. BUT WITH YOU NOW KNOWING THE TRUTH AND HAVING YOU BACK IN MY LIFE, IT'S BEEN MUCH...
WHAT THE...
THUD
GET DOWN!
CRASH
AHH!!
OLLIE OLLIE OXEN FREE.
FOUND YOU!
TIE 'EM UP AND TAKE THEM WITH US! PLAYTIME IS ABOUT TO BEGIN!
KILL THE GRIMM! KILL THE GRIMM!
EAT THE HEART AND PULL OFF ITS LIMBS!

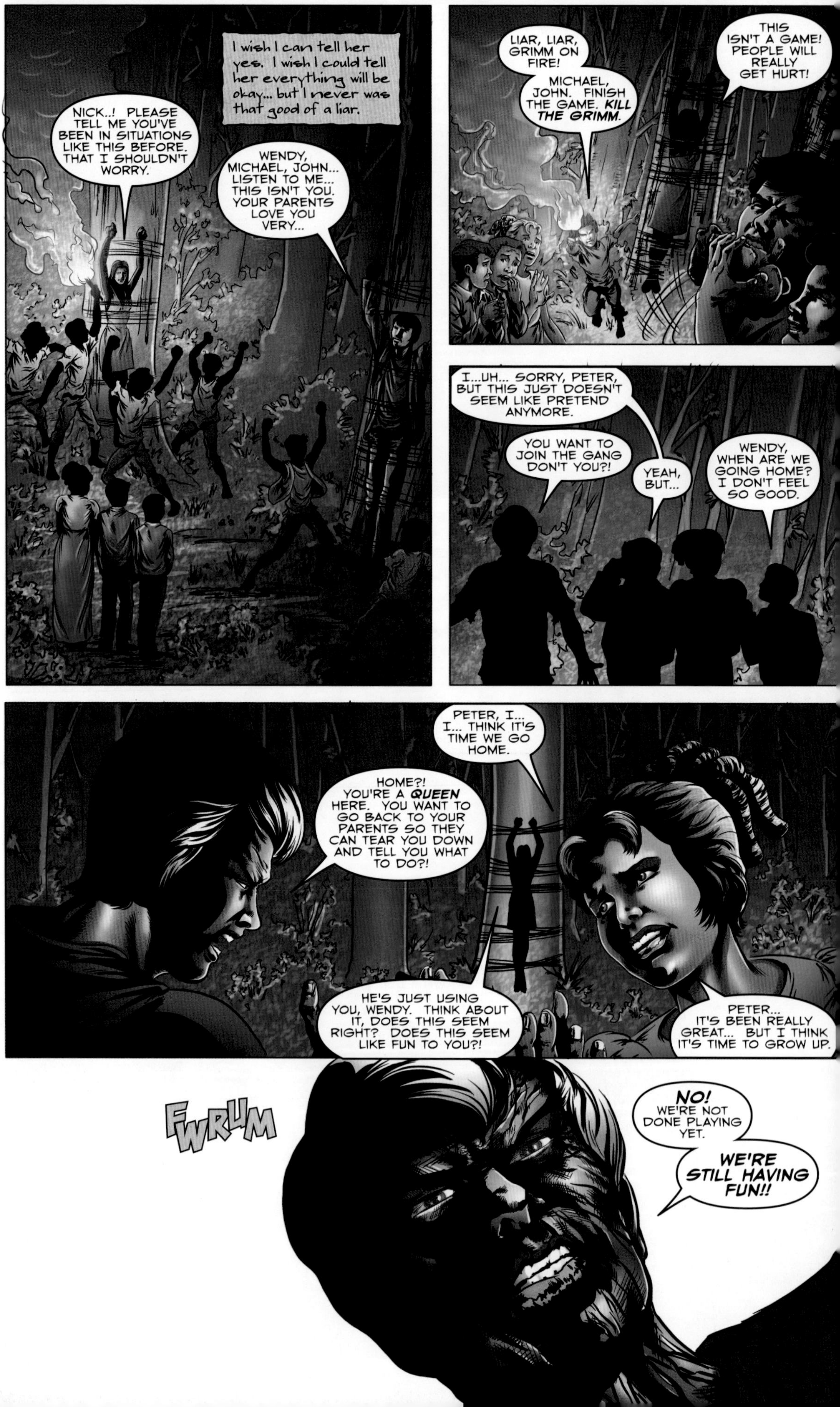

I wish I can tell her yes. I wish I could tell her everything will be okay... but I never was that good of a liar.
NICK..! PLEASE TELL ME YOU'VE BEEN IN SITUATIONS LIKE THIS BEFORE. THAT I SHOULDN'T WORRY.
WENDY, MICHAEL, JOHN... LISTEN TO ME... THIS ISN'T YOU. YOUR PARENTS LOVE YOU VERY...
LIAR, LIAR, GRIMM ON FIRE!
MICHAEL, JOHN. FINISH THE GAME. KILL THE GRIMM.
THIS ISN'T A GAME! PEOPLE WILL REALLY GET HURT!
I...UH... SORRY, PETER, BUT THIS JUST DOESN'T SEEM LIKE PRETEND ANYMORE.
YOU WANT TO JOIN THE GANG DON'T YOU?!
YEAH, BUT...
WENDY, WHEN ARE WE GOING HOME? I DON'T FEEL SO GOOD.
PETER, I... I... THINK IT'S TIME WE GO HOME.
HOME?! YOU'RE A QUEEN HERE. YOU WANT TO GO BACK TO YOUR PARENTS SO THEY CAN TEAR YOU DOWN AND TELL YOU WHAT TO DO?!
HE'S JUST USING YOU, WENDY. THINK ABOUT IT, DOES THIS SEEM RIGHT? DOES THIS SEEM LIKE FUN TO YOU?!
PETER... IT'S BEEN REALLY GREAT... BUT I THINK IT'S TIME TO GROW UP.
FWRUM
NO! WE'RE NOT DONE PLAYING YET.
WE'RE STILL HAVING FUN!!

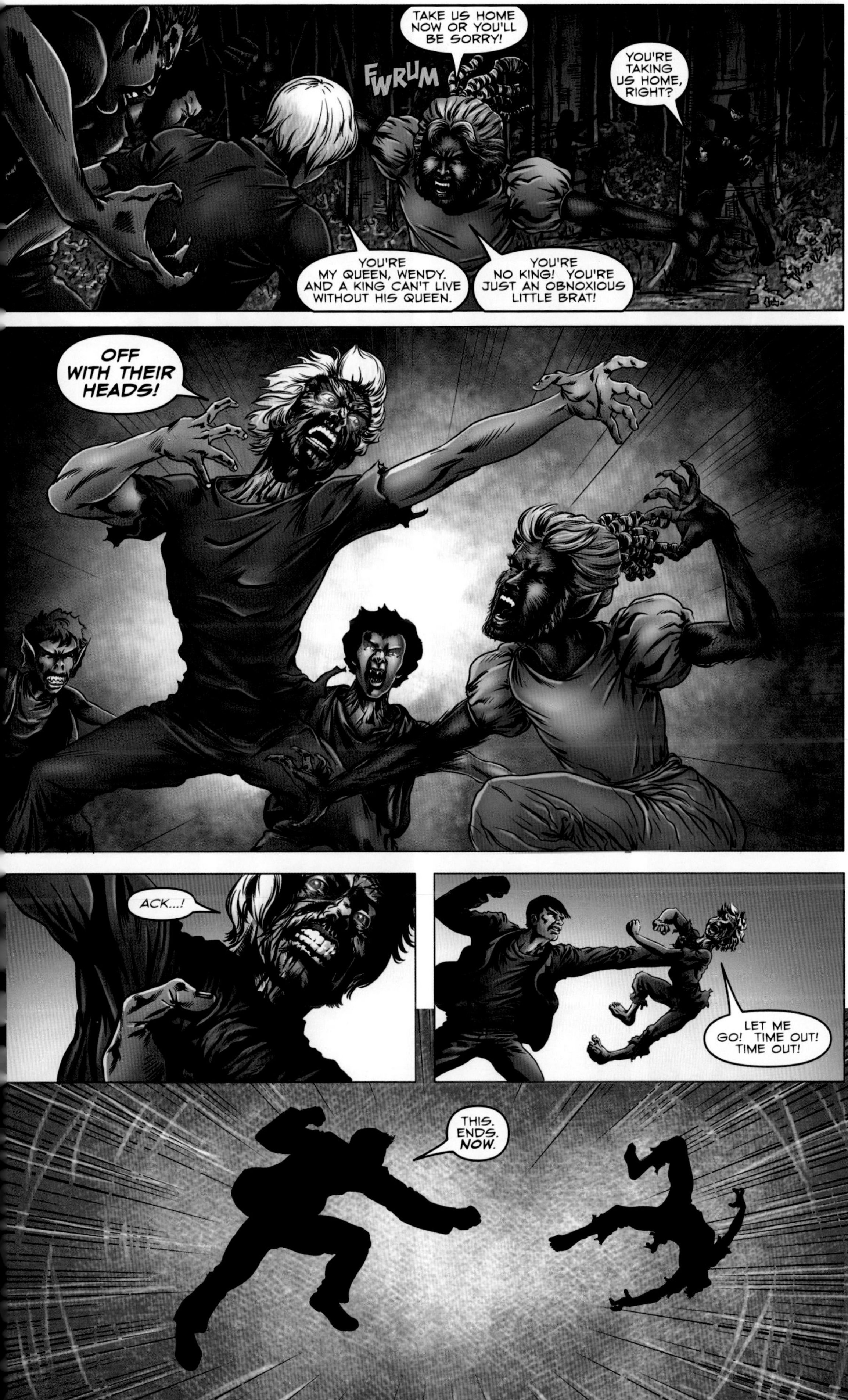
TAKE US HOME NOW OR YOU'LL BE SORRY!
FWRUM
YOU'RE TAKING US HOME, RIGHT?
YOU'RE MY QUEEN, WENDY. AND A KING CAN'T LIVE WITHOUT HIS QUEEN.
YOU'RE NO KING! YOU'RE JUST AN OBNOXIOUS LITTLE BRAT!
OFF WITH THEIR HEADS!
ACK...!
LET ME GO! TIME OUT! TIME OUT!
THIS. ENDS. NOW.

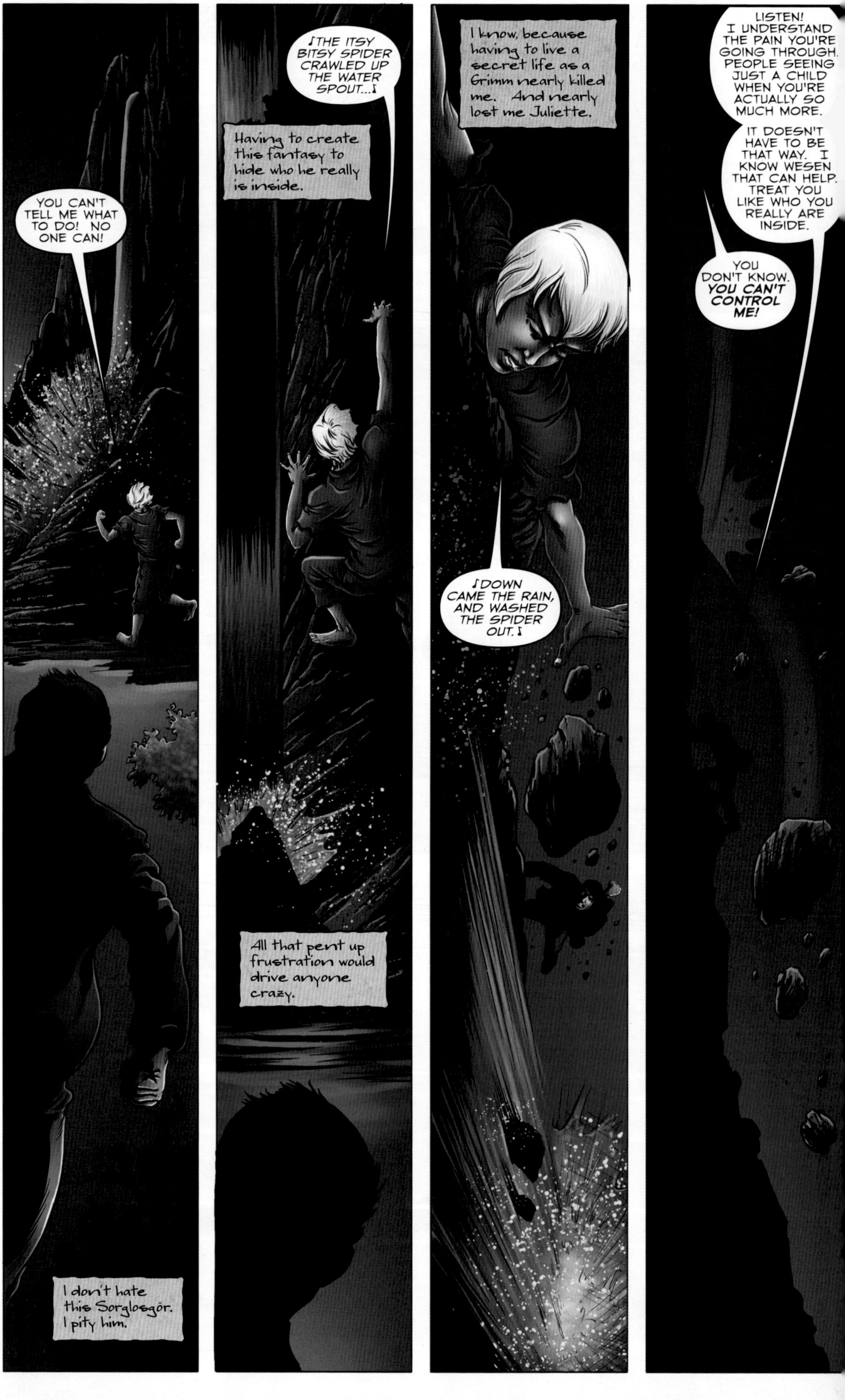
YOU CAN'T TELL ME WHAT TO DO! NO ONE CAN!
I don't hate this Sorglosgör. I pity him.
♪THE ITSY BITSY SPIDER CRAWLED UP THE WATER SPOUT...♪
Having to create this fantasy to hide who he really is inside.
All that pent up frustration would drive anyone crazy.
I know, because having to live a secret life as a Grimm nearly killed me. And nearly lost me Juliette.
♪DOWN CAME THE RAIN, AND WASHED THE SPIDER OUT.♪
LISTEN! I UNDERSTAND THE PAIN YOU'RE GOING THROUGH. PEOPLE SEEING JUST A CHILD WHEN YOU'RE ACTUALLY SO MUCH MORE.
IT DOESN'T HAVE TO BE THAT WAY. I KNOW WESEN THAT CAN HELP. TREAT YOU LIKE WHO YOU REALLY ARE INSIDE.
YOU DON'T KNOW. YOU CAN'T CONTROL ME!

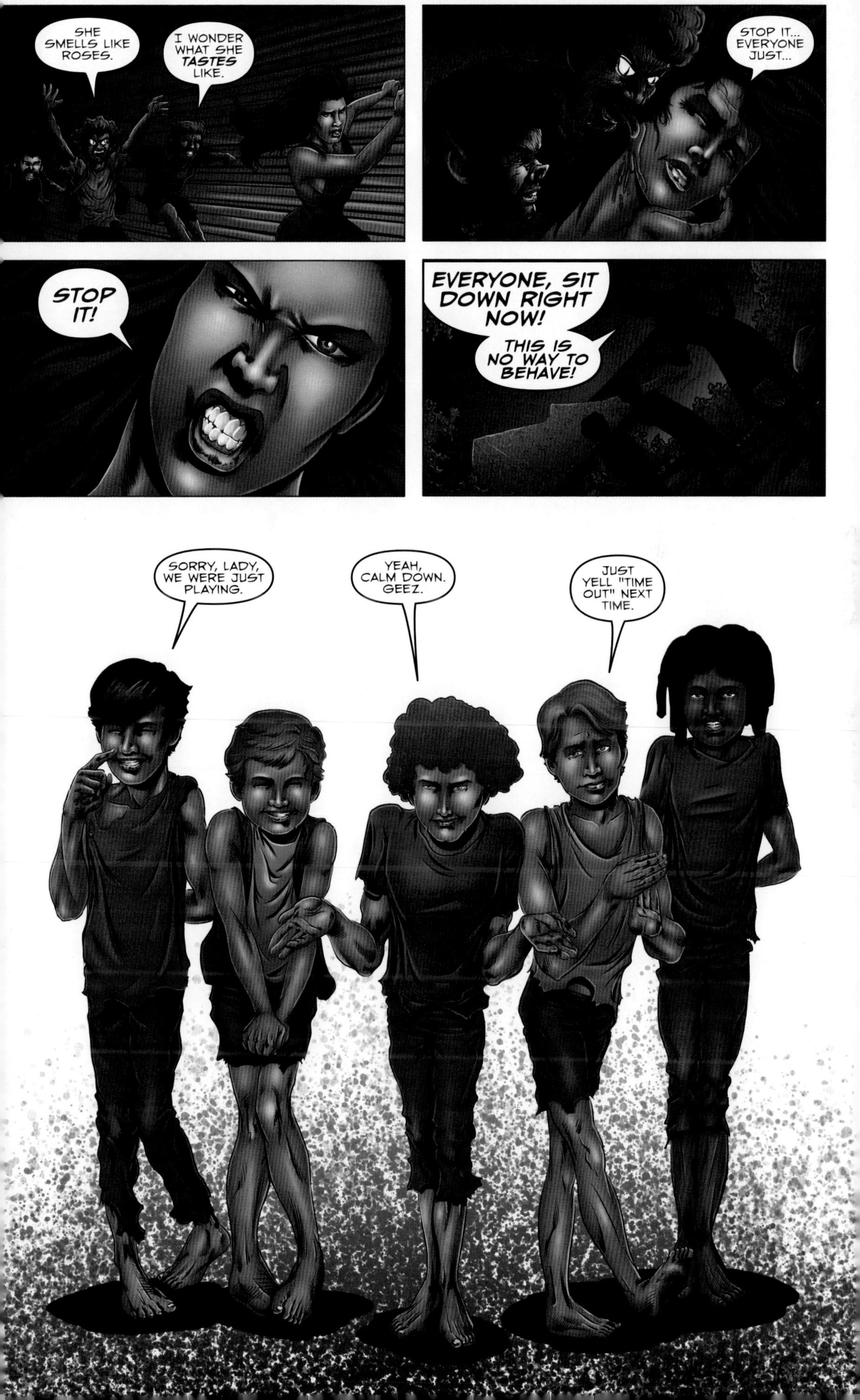
SHE SMELLS LIKE ROSES.
I WONDER WHAT SHE *TASTES* LIKE.
STOP IT... EVERYONE JUST...
STOP IT!
EVERYONE, SIT DOWN RIGHT NOW!
THIS IS NO WAY TO BEHAVE!
SORRY, LADY, WE WERE JUST PLAYING.
YEAH, CALM DOWN. GEEZ.
JUST YELL "TIME OUT" NEXT TIME.

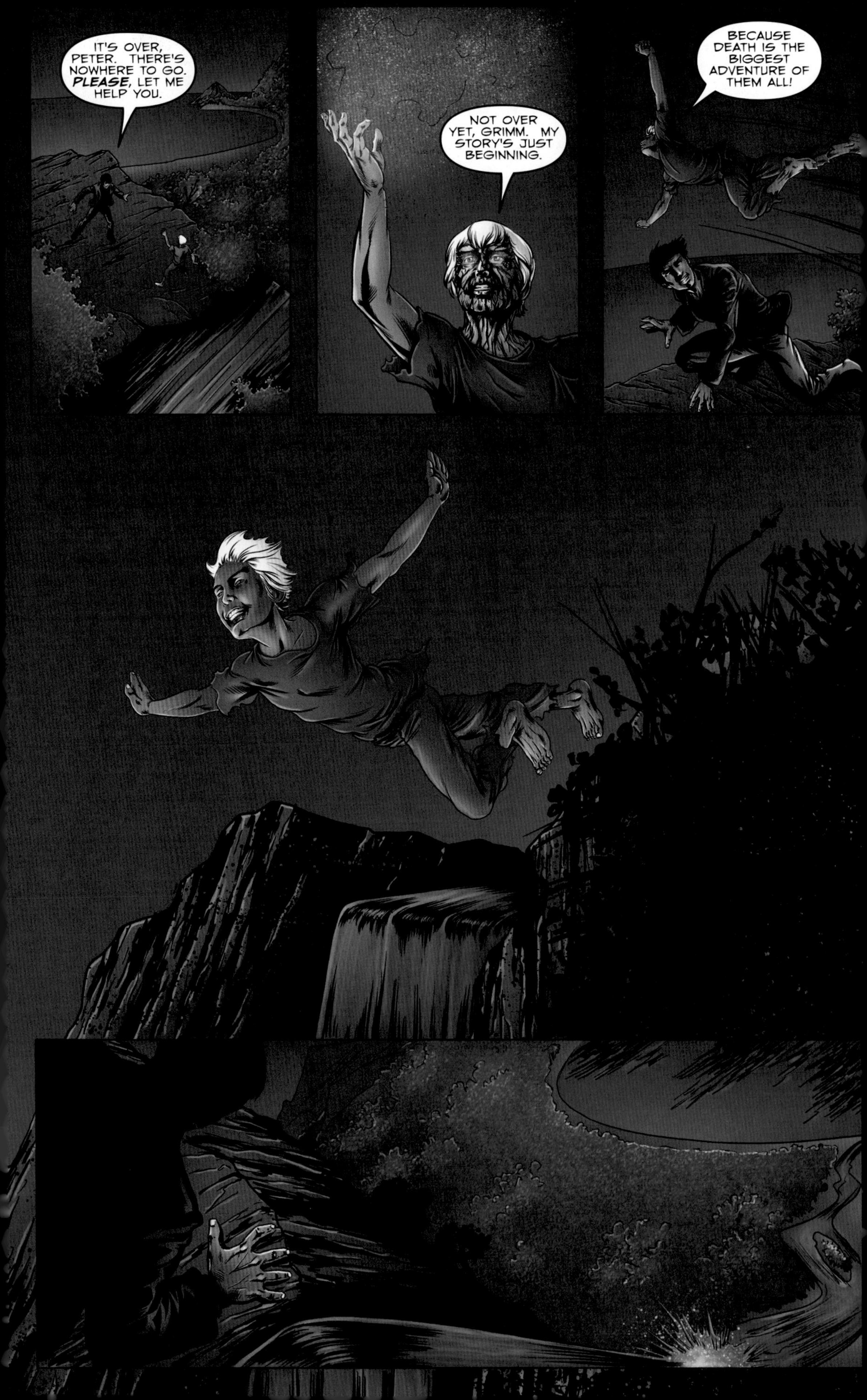
IT'S OVER, PETER. THERE'S NOWHERE TO GO. ***PLEASE***, LET ME HELP YOU.
NOT OVER YET, GRIMM. MY STORY'S JUST BEGINNING.
BECAUSE DEATH IS THE BIGGEST ADVENTURE OF THEM ALL!

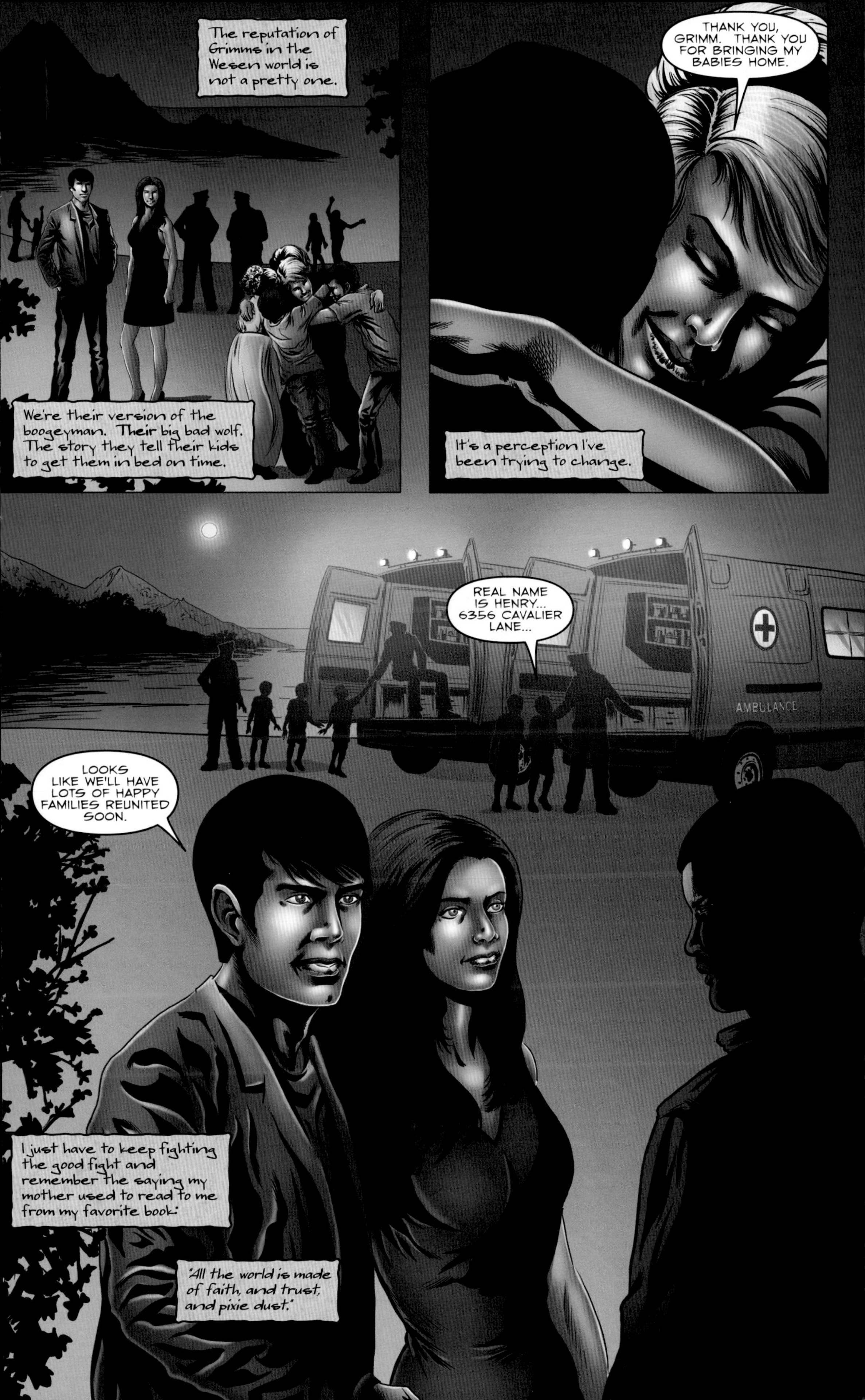
The reputation of Grimms in the Wesen world is not a pretty one.
We're their version of the boogeyman. Their big bad wolf. The story they tell their kids to get them in bed on time.
THANK YOU, GRIMM. THANK YOU FOR BRINGING MY BABIES HOME.
It's a perception I've been trying to change.
REAL NAME IS HENRY... 6356 CAVALIER LANE...
AMBULANCE
LOOKS LIKE WE'LL HAVE LOTS OF HAPPY FAMILIES REUNITED SOON.
I just have to keep fighting the good fight and remember the saying my mother used to read to me from my favorite book:
"All the world is made of faith, and trust, and pixie dust."

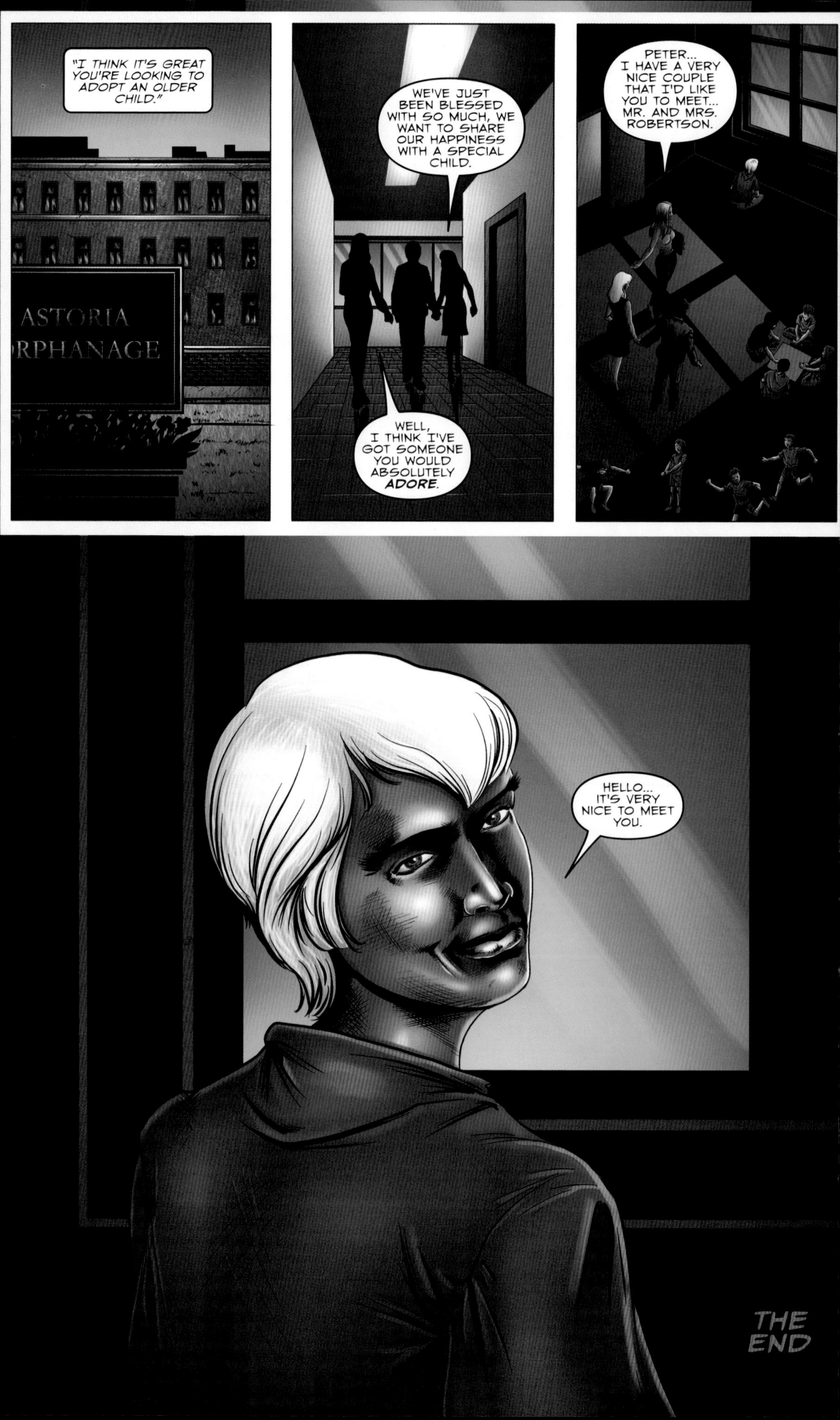
"I THINK IT'S GREAT YOU'RE LOOKING TO ADOPT AN OLDER CHILD."
ASTORIA
RPHANAGE
WE'VE JUST BEEN BLESSED WITH SO MUCH, WE WANT TO SHARE OUR HAPPINESS WITH A SPECIAL CHILD.
WELL, I THINK I'VE GOT SOMEONE YOU WOULD ABSOLUTELY ADORE.
PETER... I HAVE A VERY NICE COUPLE THAT I'D LIKE YOU TO MEET... MR. AND MRS. ROBERTSON.
HELLO... IT'S VERY NICE TO MEET YOU.
THE END

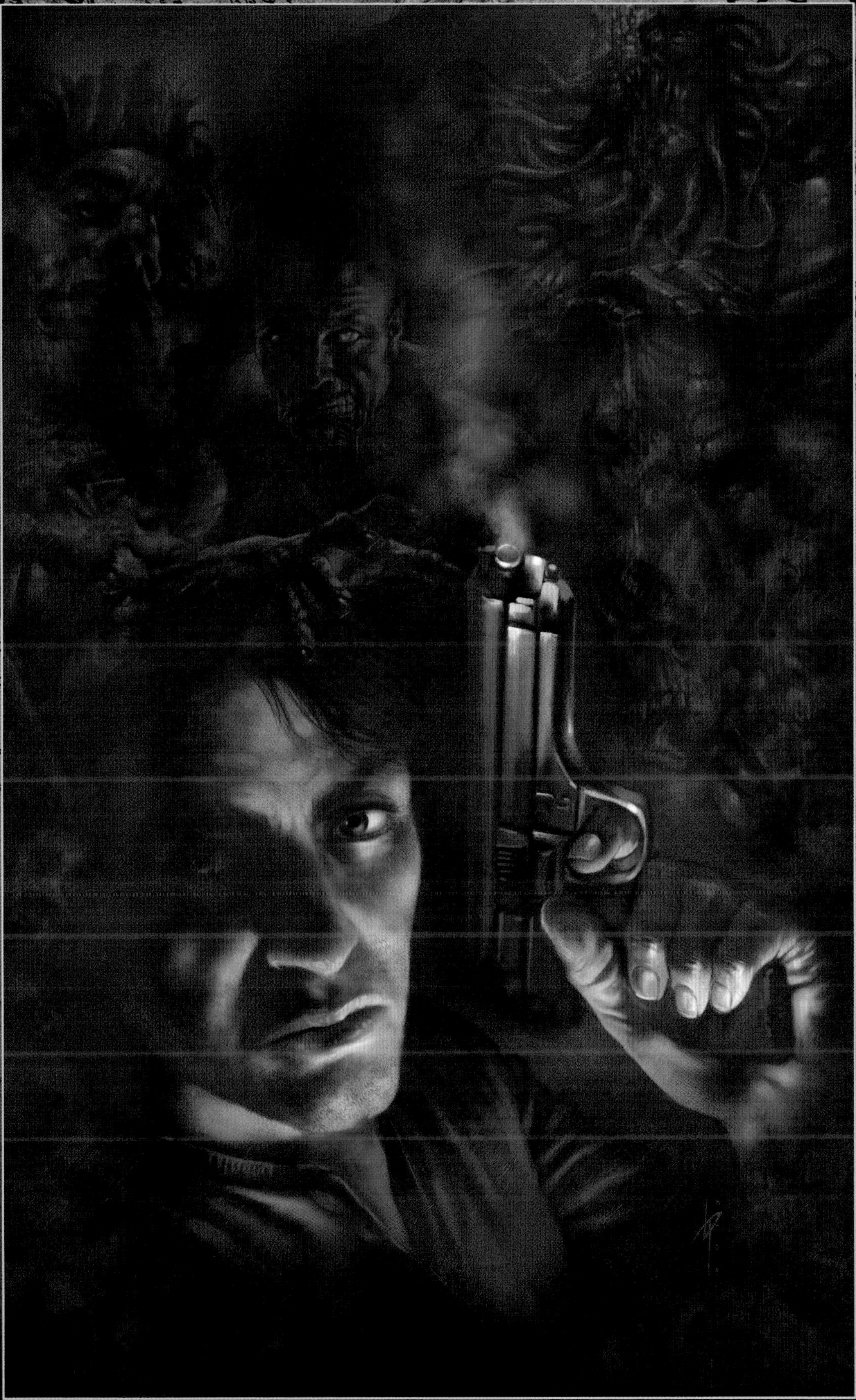

ISSUE #7 COVER
ART BY LUCIO PARRILLO

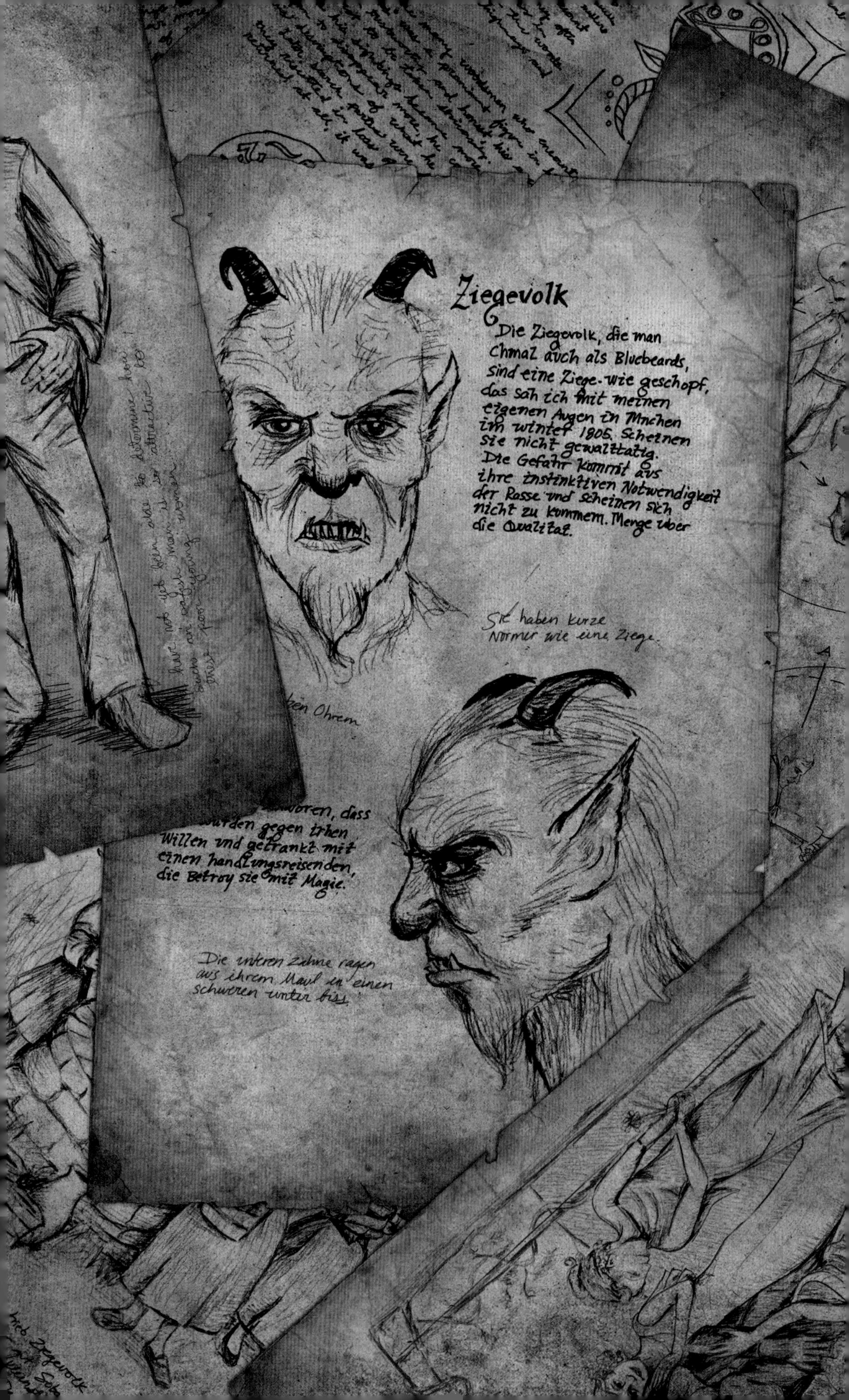
Ziegevolk
Die Ziegevolk, die man
Chmal auch als Bluebeards,
sind eine Ziege-wie geschopf,
das sah ich mit meinen
eigenen Augen in Mnchen
im winter 1805. Scheinen
sie nicht gewalttatig.
Die Gefahr kommt aus
ihre instinktiven Notwendigkeit
der Rasse und scheinen sich
nicht zu kommem. Menge uber
die Qualitat.
Sie haben kurze
Normer wie eine Ziege.
Ohrem
woren, dass
wurden gegen ihen
Willen und getrankt mit
einen handlungsreisenden,
die Betroy sie mit Magie.
Die unteren Zahne ragen
aus ihrem Maul in einen
schweren unter biss.

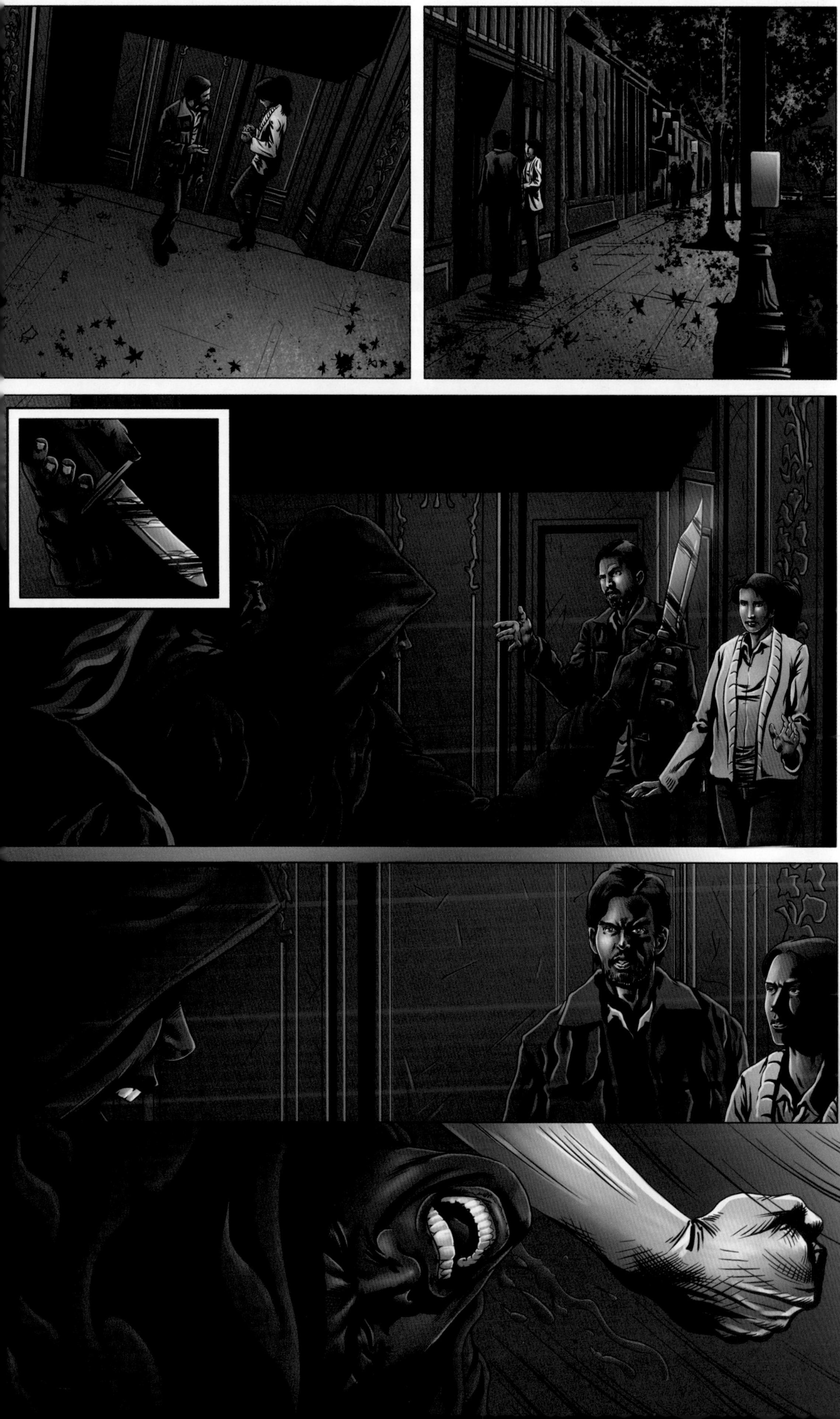

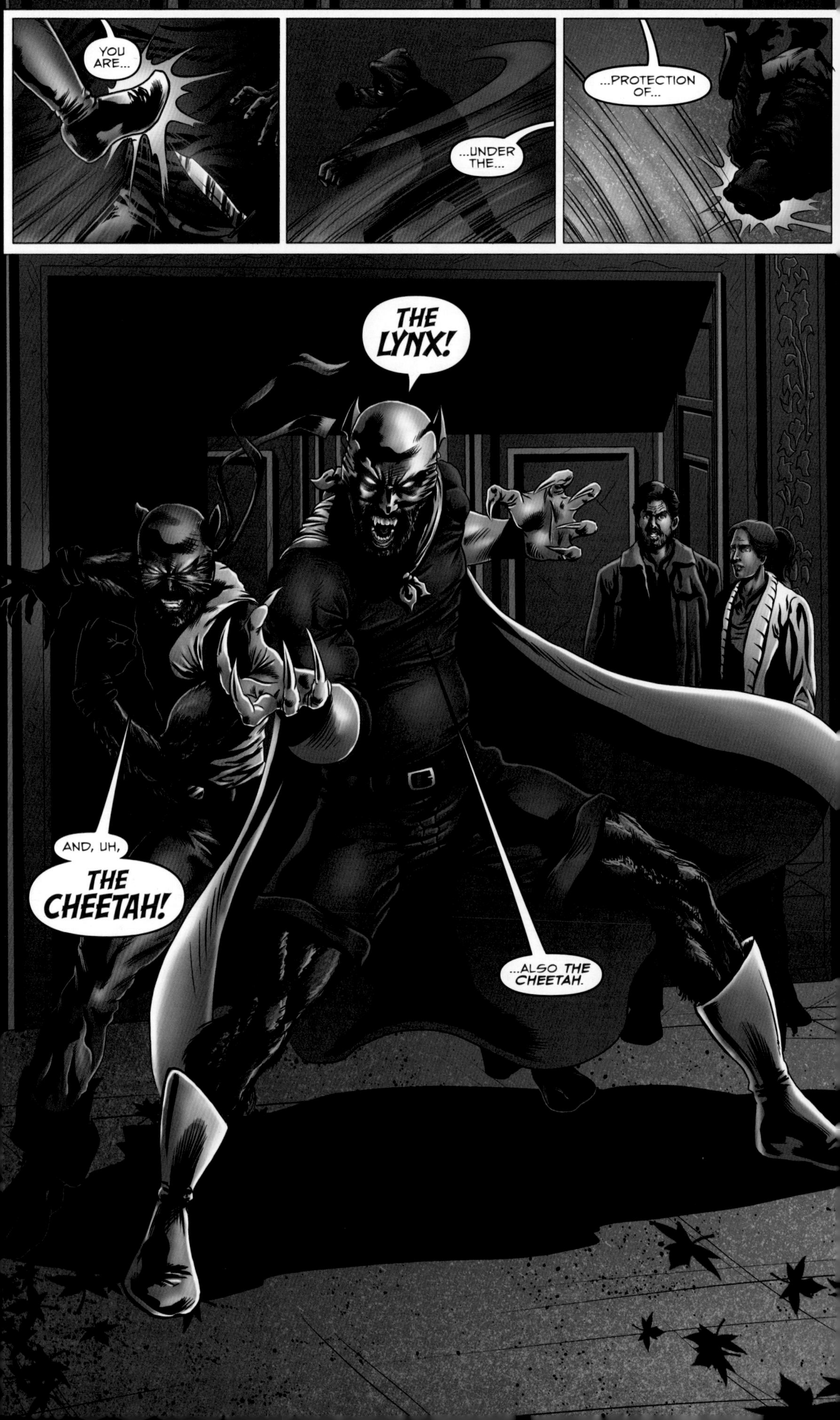
YOU ARE...
...UNDER THE...
...PROTECTION OF...
THE LYNX!
AND, UH,
THE CHEETAH!
...ALSO THE CHEETAH.

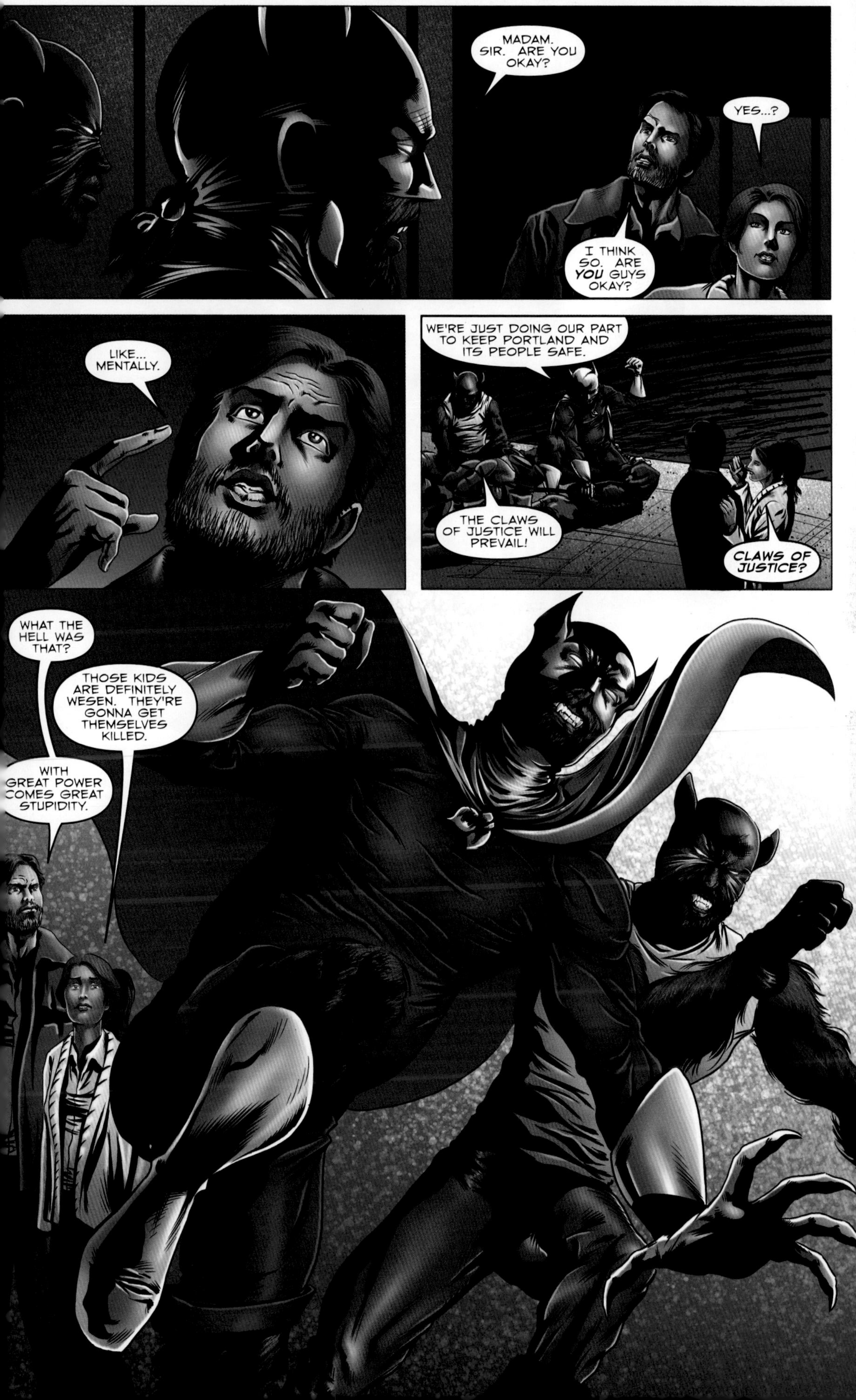

MADAM. SIR. ARE YOU OKAY?
YES...?
I THINK SO. ARE YOU GUYS OKAY?
LIKE... MENTALLY.
WE'RE JUST DOING OUR PART TO KEEP PORTLAND AND ITS PEOPLE SAFE.
THE CLAWS OF JUSTICE WILL PREVAIL!
CLAWS OF JUSTICE?
WHAT THE HELL WAS THAT?
THOSE KIDS ARE DEFINITELY WESEN. THEY'RE GONNA GET THEMSELVES KILLED.
WITH GREAT POWER COMES GREAT STUPIDITY.

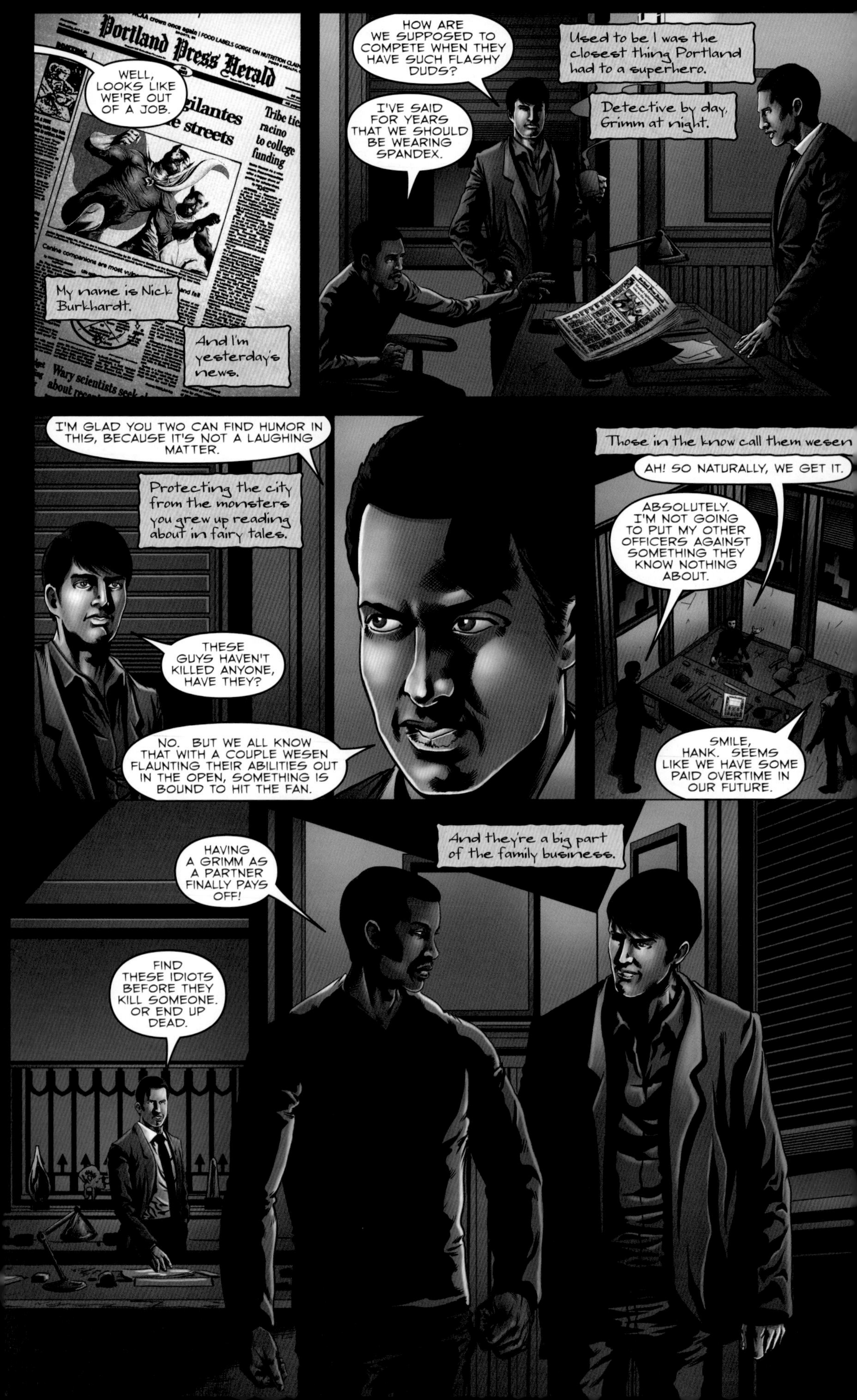

Portland Press Herald
Tribe ties racino to college funding
WELL, LOOKS LIKE WE'RE OUT OF A JOB.
My name is Nick Burkhardt.
And I'm yesterday's news.
HOW ARE WE SUPPOSED TO COMPETE WHEN THEY HAVE SUCH FLASHY DUDS?
I'VE SAID FOR YEARS THAT WE SHOULD BE WEARING SPANDEX.
Used to be I was the closest thing Portland had to a superhero.
Detective by day, Grimm at night.
I'M GLAD YOU TWO CAN FIND HUMOR IN THIS, BECAUSE IT'S NOT A LAUGHING MATTER.
Protecting the city from the monsters you grew up reading about in fairy tales.
THESE GUYS HAVEN'T KILLED ANYONE, HAVE THEY?
NO. BUT WE ALL KNOW THAT WITH A COUPLE WESEN FLAUNTING THEIR ABILITIES OUT IN THE OPEN, SOMETHING IS BOUND TO HIT THE FAN.
Those in the know call them wesen
AH! SO NATURALLY, WE GET IT.
ABSOLUTELY. I'M NOT GOING TO PUT MY OTHER OFFICERS AGAINST SOMETHING THEY KNOW NOTHING ABOUT.
SMILE, HANK. SEEMS LIKE WE HAVE SOME PAID OVERTIME IN OUR FUTURE.
HAVING A GRIMM AS A PARTNER FINALLY PAYS OFF!
And they're a big part of the family business.
FIND THESE IDIOTS BEFORE THEY KILL SOMEONE. OR END UP DEAD.

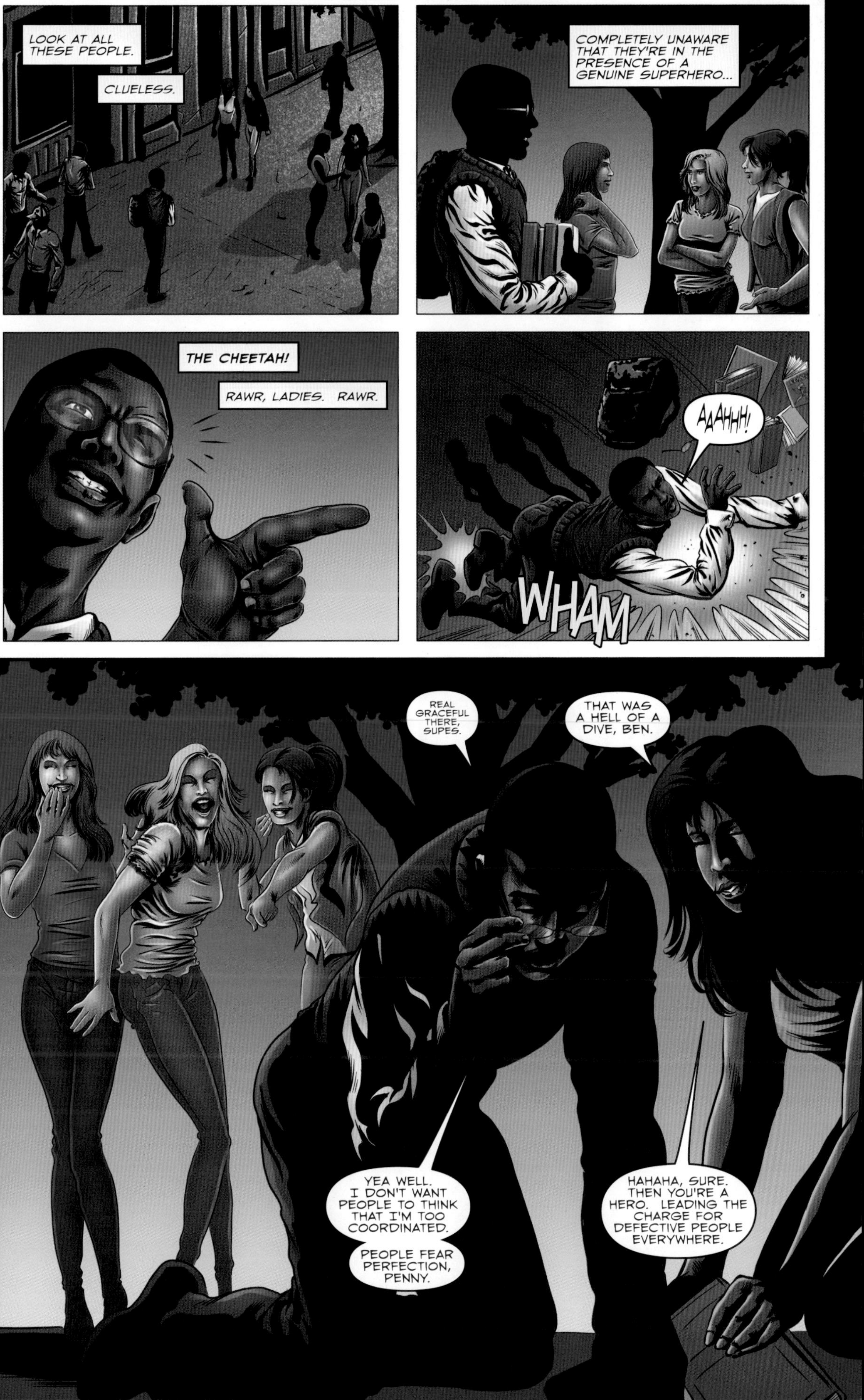
LOOK AT ALL THESE PEOPLE.
CLUELESS.
COMPLETELY UNAWARE THAT THEY'RE IN THE PRESENCE OF A GENUINE SUPERHERO...
THE CHEETAH!
RAWR, LADIES. RAWR.
AAAHHH!
WHAM
REAL GRACEFUL THERE, SUPES.
THAT WAS A HELL OF A DIVE, BEN.
YEA WELL. I DON'T WANT PEOPLE TO THINK THAT I'M TOO COORDINATED.
PEOPLE FEAR PERFECTION, PENNY.
HAHAHA, SURE. THEN YOU'RE A HERO. LEADING THE CHARGE FOR DEFECTIVE PEOPLE EVERYWHERE.

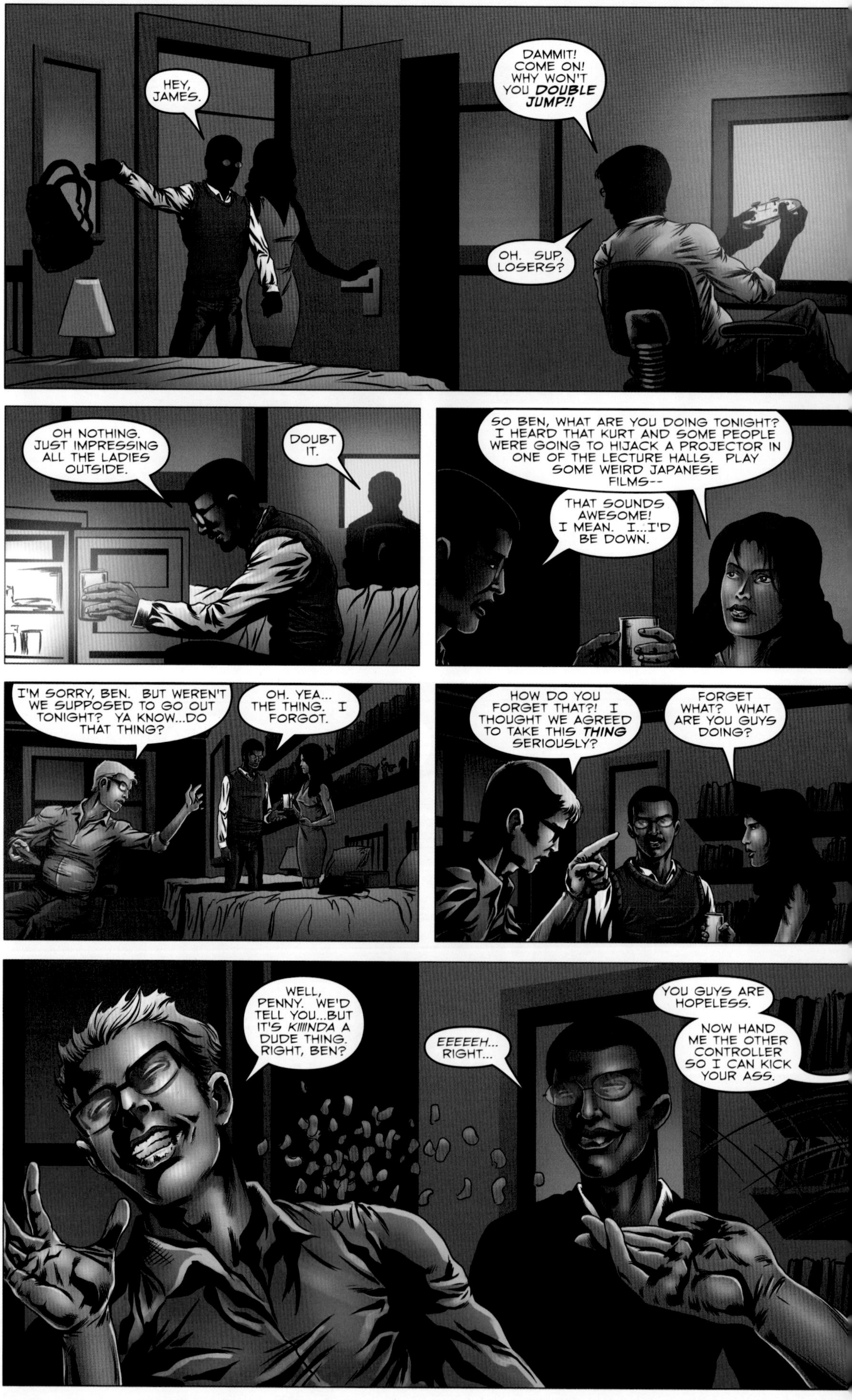
HEY, JAMES.
DAMMIT! COME ON! WHY WON'T YOU *DOUBLE JUMP!!*
OH. SUP, LOSERS?
OH NOTHING. JUST IMPRESSING ALL THE LADIES OUTSIDE.
DOUBT IT.
SO BEN, WHAT ARE YOU DOING TONIGHT? I HEARD THAT KURT AND SOME PEOPLE WERE GOING TO HIJACK A PROJECTOR IN ONE OF THE LECTURE HALLS. PLAY SOME WEIRD JAPANESE FILMS--
THAT SOUNDS AWESOME! I MEAN. I...I'D BE DOWN.
I'M SORRY, BEN. BUT WEREN'T WE SUPPOSED TO GO OUT TONIGHT? YA KNOW...DO THAT THING?
OH. YEA... THE THING. I FORGOT.
HOW DO YOU FORGET THAT?! I THOUGHT WE AGREED TO TAKE THIS *THING* SERIOUSLY?
FORGET WHAT? WHAT ARE YOU GUYS DOING?
WELL, PENNY. WE'D TELL YOU...BUT IT'S *KIIIINDA* A DUDE THING. RIGHT, BEN?
EEEEEH... RIGHT...
YOU GUYS ARE HOPELESS.
NOW HAND ME THE OTHER CONTROLLER SO I CAN KICK YOUR ASS.

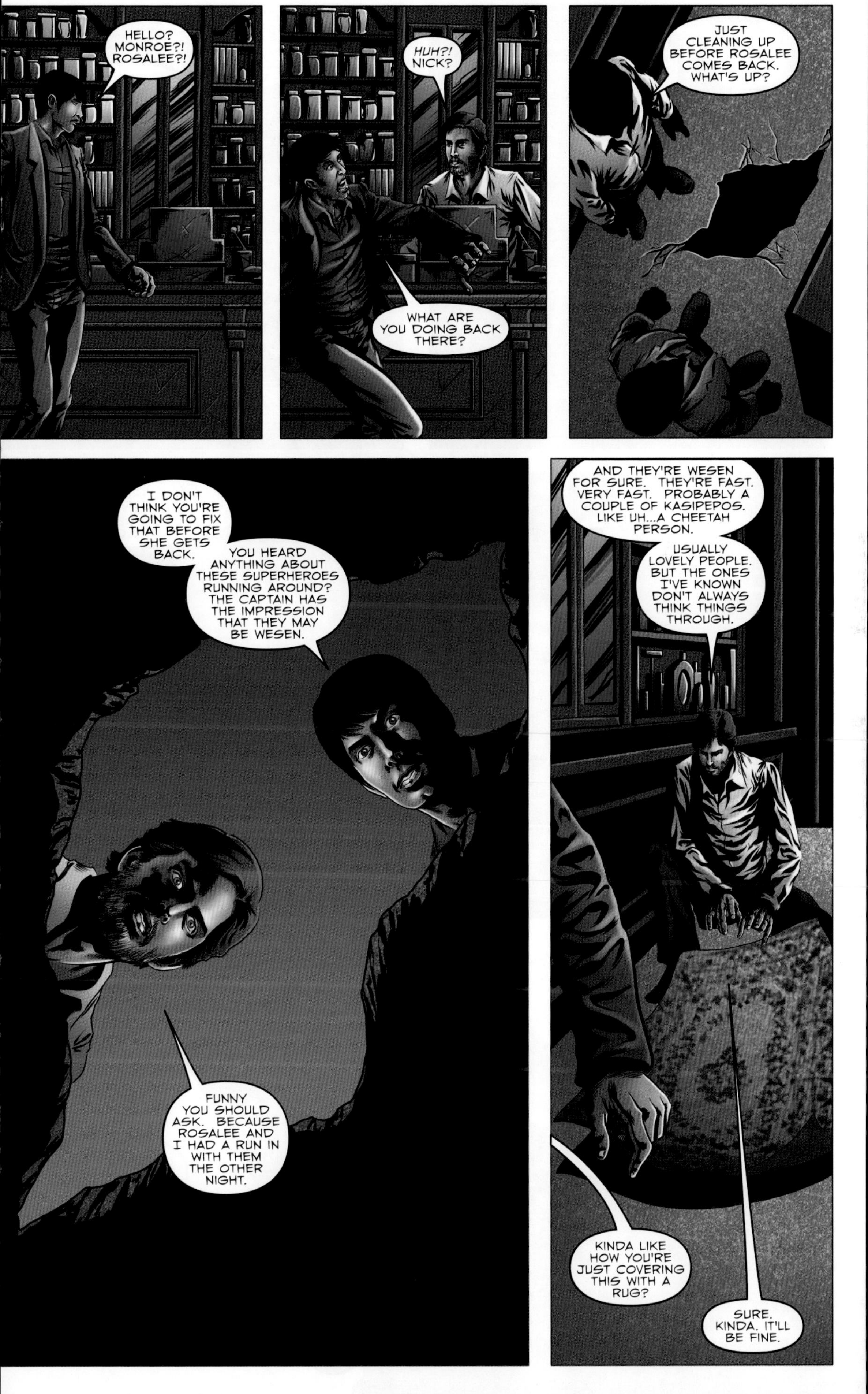
HELLO? MONROE?! ROSALEE?!
HUH?! NICK?
WHAT ARE YOU DOING BACK THERE?
JUST CLEANING UP BEFORE ROSALEE COMES BACK. WHAT'S UP?
I DON'T THINK YOU'RE GOING TO FIX THAT BEFORE SHE GETS BACK.
YOU HEARD ANYTHING ABOUT THESE SUPERHEROES RUNNING AROUND? THE CAPTAIN HAS THE IMPRESSION THAT THEY MAY BE WESEN.
FUNNY YOU SHOULD ASK. BECAUSE ROSALEE AND I HAD A RUN IN WITH THEM THE OTHER NIGHT.
AND THEY'RE WESEN FOR SURE. THEY'RE FAST. VERY FAST. PROBABLY A COUPLE OF KASIPEPOS. LIKE UH...A CHEETAH PERSON.
USUALLY LOVELY PEOPLE. BUT THE ONES I'VE KNOWN DON'T ALWAYS THINK THINGS THROUGH.
KINDA LIKE HOW YOU'RE JUST COVERING THIS WITH A RUG?
SURE. KINDA. IT'LL BE FINE.

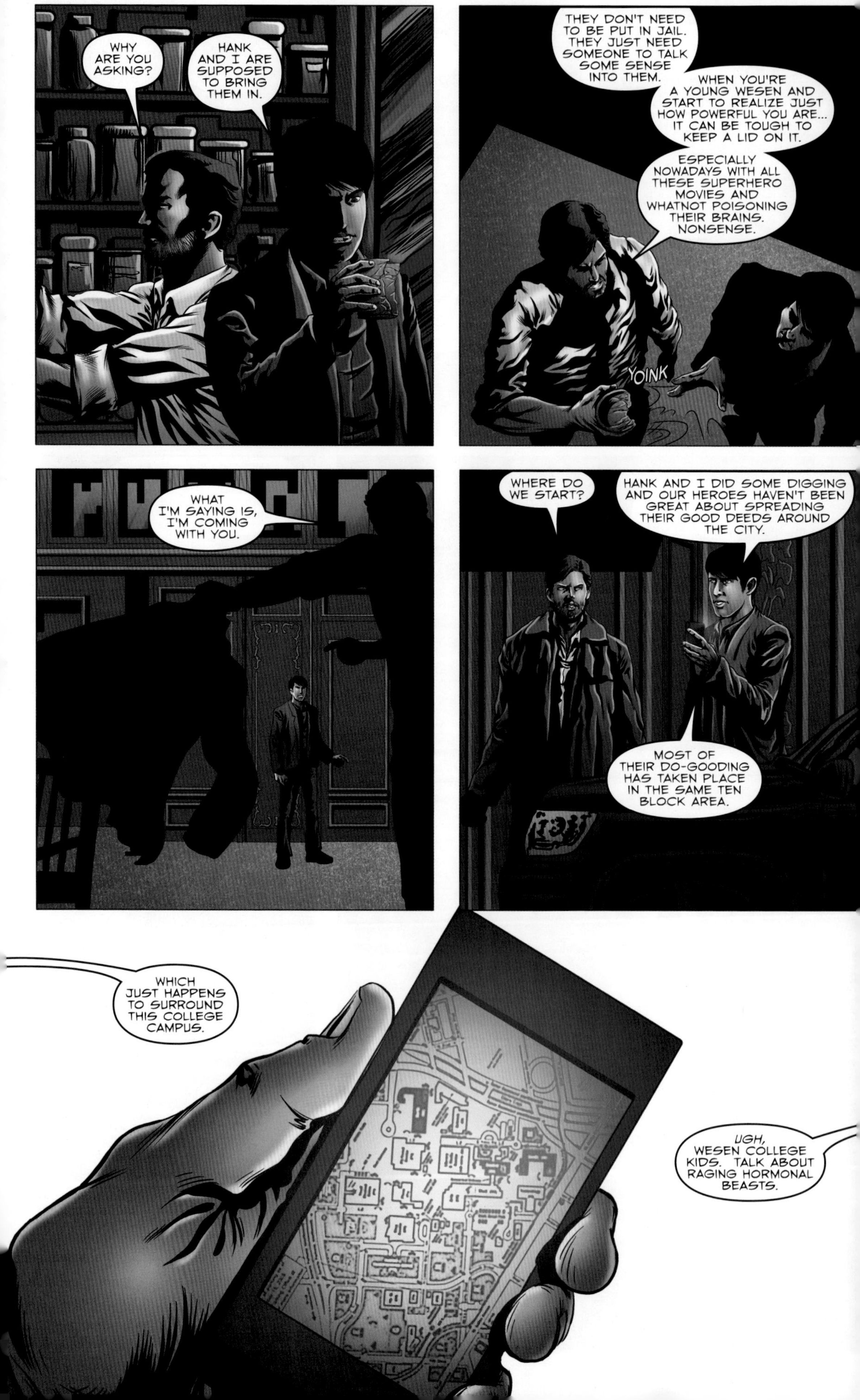
WHY ARE YOU ASKING?
HANK AND I ARE SUPPOSED TO BRING THEM IN.
THEY DON'T NEED TO BE PUT IN JAIL. THEY JUST NEED SOMEONE TO TALK SOME SENSE INTO THEM.
WHEN YOU'RE A YOUNG WESEN AND START TO REALIZE JUST HOW POWERFUL YOU ARE... IT CAN BE TOUGH TO KEEP A LID ON IT.
ESPECIALLY NOWADAYS WITH ALL THESE SUPERHERO MOVIES AND WHATNOT POISONING THEIR BRAINS. NONSENSE.
YOINK
WHAT I'M SAYING IS, I'M COMING WITH YOU.
WHERE DO WE START?
HANK AND I DID SOME DIGGING AND OUR HEROES HAVEN'T BEEN GREAT ABOUT SPREADING THEIR GOOD DEEDS AROUND THE CITY.
MOST OF THEIR DO-GOODING HAS TAKEN PLACE IN THE SAME TEN BLOCK AREA.
WHICH JUST HAPPENS TO SURROUND THIS COLLEGE CAMPUS.
UGH, WESEN COLLEGE KIDS. TALK ABOUT RAGING HORMONAL BEASTS.

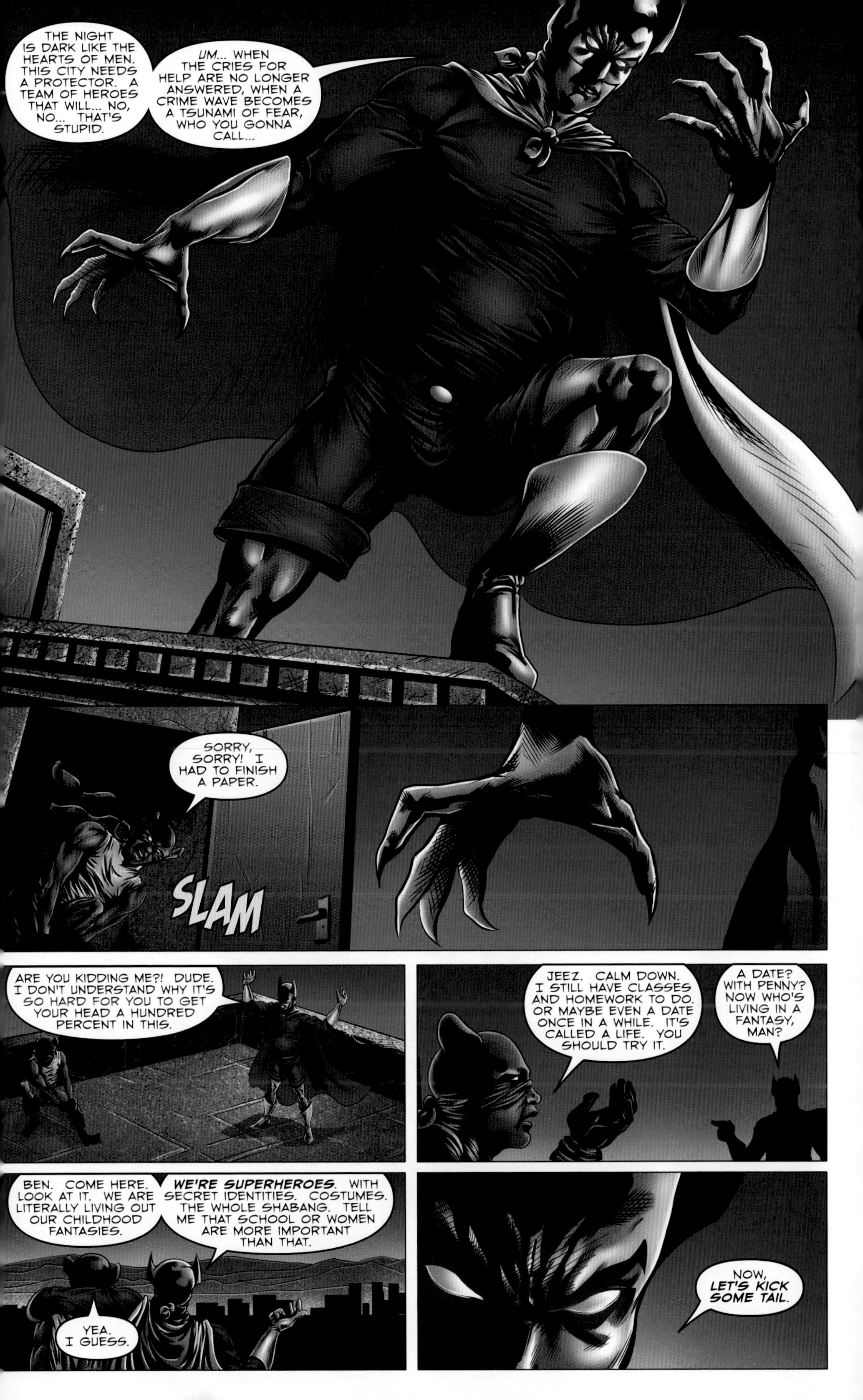
THE NIGHT IS DARK LIKE THE HEARTS OF MEN. THIS CITY NEEDS A PROTECTOR. A TEAM OF HEROES THAT WILL... NO, NO... THAT'S STUPID.
UM... WHEN THE CRIES FOR HELP ARE NO LONGER ANSWERED, WHEN A CRIME WAVE BECOMES A TSUNAMI OF FEAR, WHO YOU GONNA CALL...
SORRY, SORRY! I HAD TO FINISH A PAPER.
SLAM
ARE YOU KIDDING ME?! DUDE. I DON'T UNDERSTAND WHY IT'S SO HARD FOR YOU TO GET YOUR HEAD A HUNDRED PERCENT IN THIS.
JEEZ. CALM DOWN. I STILL HAVE CLASSES AND HOMEWORK TO DO. OR MAYBE EVEN A DATE ONCE IN A WHILE. IT'S CALLED A LIFE. YOU SHOULD TRY IT.
A DATE? WITH PENNY? NOW WHO'S LIVING IN A FANTASY, MAN?
BEN. COME HERE. LOOK AT IT. WE ARE LITERALLY LIVING OUT OUR CHILDHOOD FANTASIES.
WE'RE SUPERHEROES. WITH SECRET IDENTITIES. COSTUMES. THE WHOLE SHABANG. TELL ME THAT SCHOOL OR WOMEN ARE MORE IMPORTANT THAN THAT.
YEA. I GUESS.
NOW, LET'S KICK SOME TAIL.

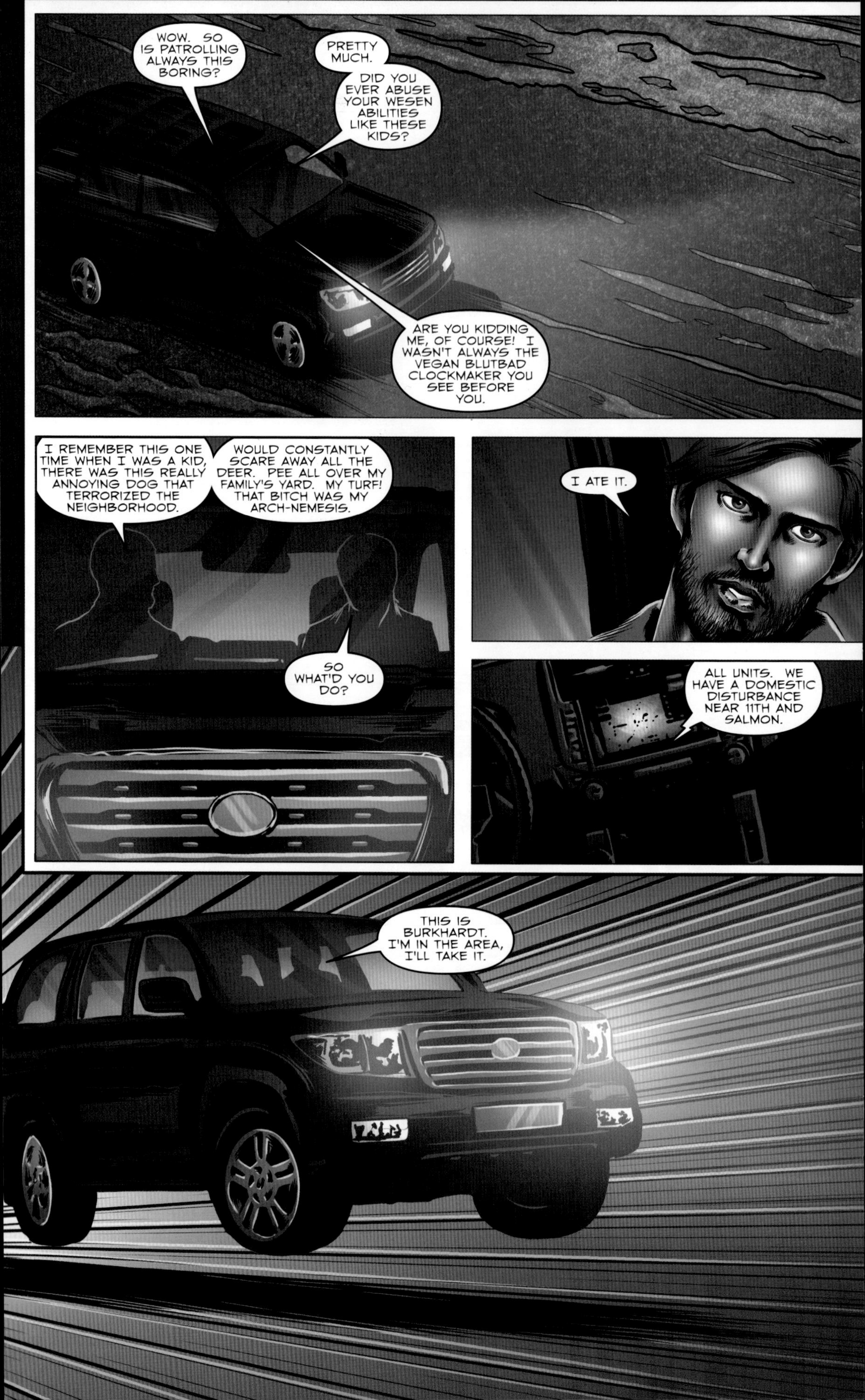
WOW. SO IS PATROLLING ALWAYS THIS BORING?
PRETTY MUCH.
DID YOU EVER ABUSE YOUR WESEN ABILITIES LIKE THESE KIDS?
ARE YOU KIDDING ME, OF COURSE! I WASN'T ALWAYS THE VEGAN BLUTBAD CLOCKMAKER YOU SEE BEFORE YOU.
I REMEMBER THIS ONE TIME WHEN I WAS A KID, THERE WAS THIS REALLY ANNOYING DOG THAT TERRORIZED THE NEIGHBORHOOD.
WOULD CONSTANTLY SCARE AWAY ALL THE DEER. PEE ALL OVER MY FAMILY'S YARD. MY TURF! THAT BITCH WAS MY ARCH-NEMESIS.
SO WHAT'D YOU DO?
I ATE IT.
ALL UNITS. WE HAVE A DOMESTIC DISTURBANCE NEAR 11TH AND SALMON.
THIS IS BURKHARDT. I'M IN THE AREA, I'LL TAKE IT.

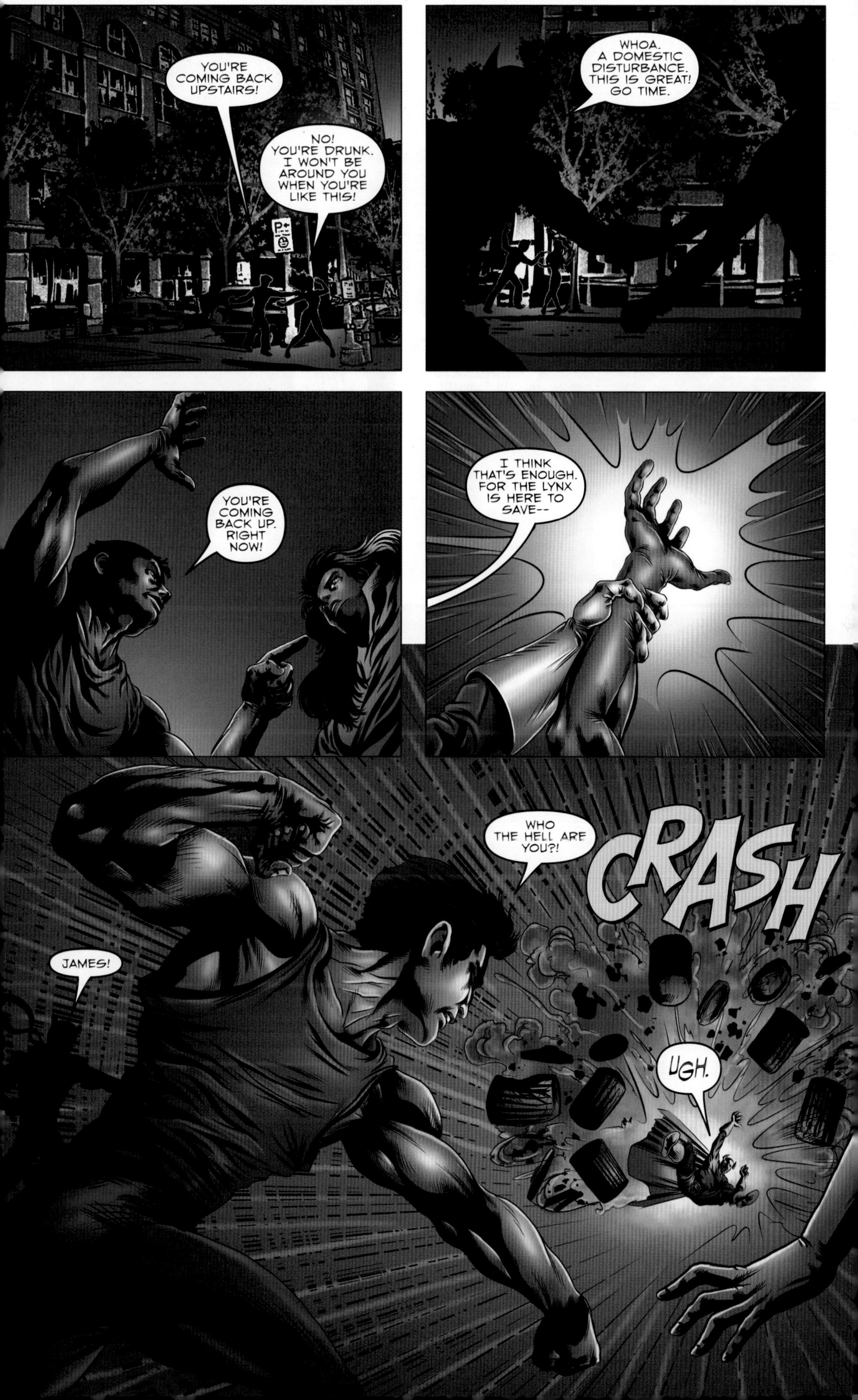
YOU'RE COMING BACK UPSTAIRS!
NO! YOU'RE DRUNK. I WON'T BE AROUND YOU WHEN YOU'RE LIKE THIS!
WHOA. A DOMESTIC DISTURBANCE. THIS IS GREAT! GO TIME.
YOU'RE COMING BACK UP. RIGHT NOW!
I THINK THAT'S ENOUGH. FOR THE LYNX IS HERE TO SAVE--
WHO THE HELL ARE YOU?!
CRASH
JAMES!
UGH.

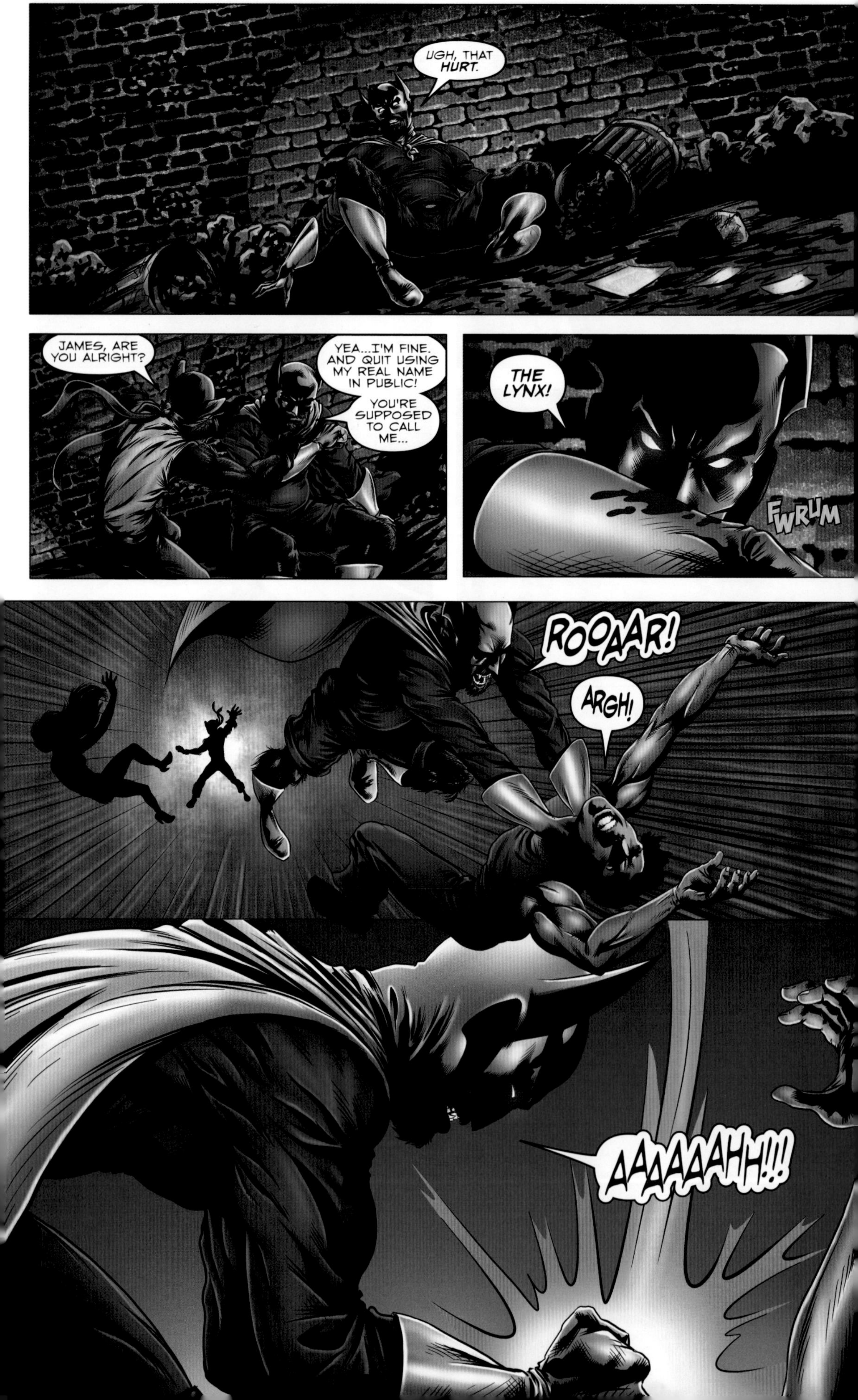
UGH, THAT HURT.
JAMES, ARE YOU ALRIGHT?
YEA...I'M FINE. AND QUIT USING MY REAL NAME IN PUBLIC!
YOU'RE SUPPOSED TO CALL ME...
THE LYNX!
FWRUM
ROOAAR!
ARGH!
AAAAAHH!!!

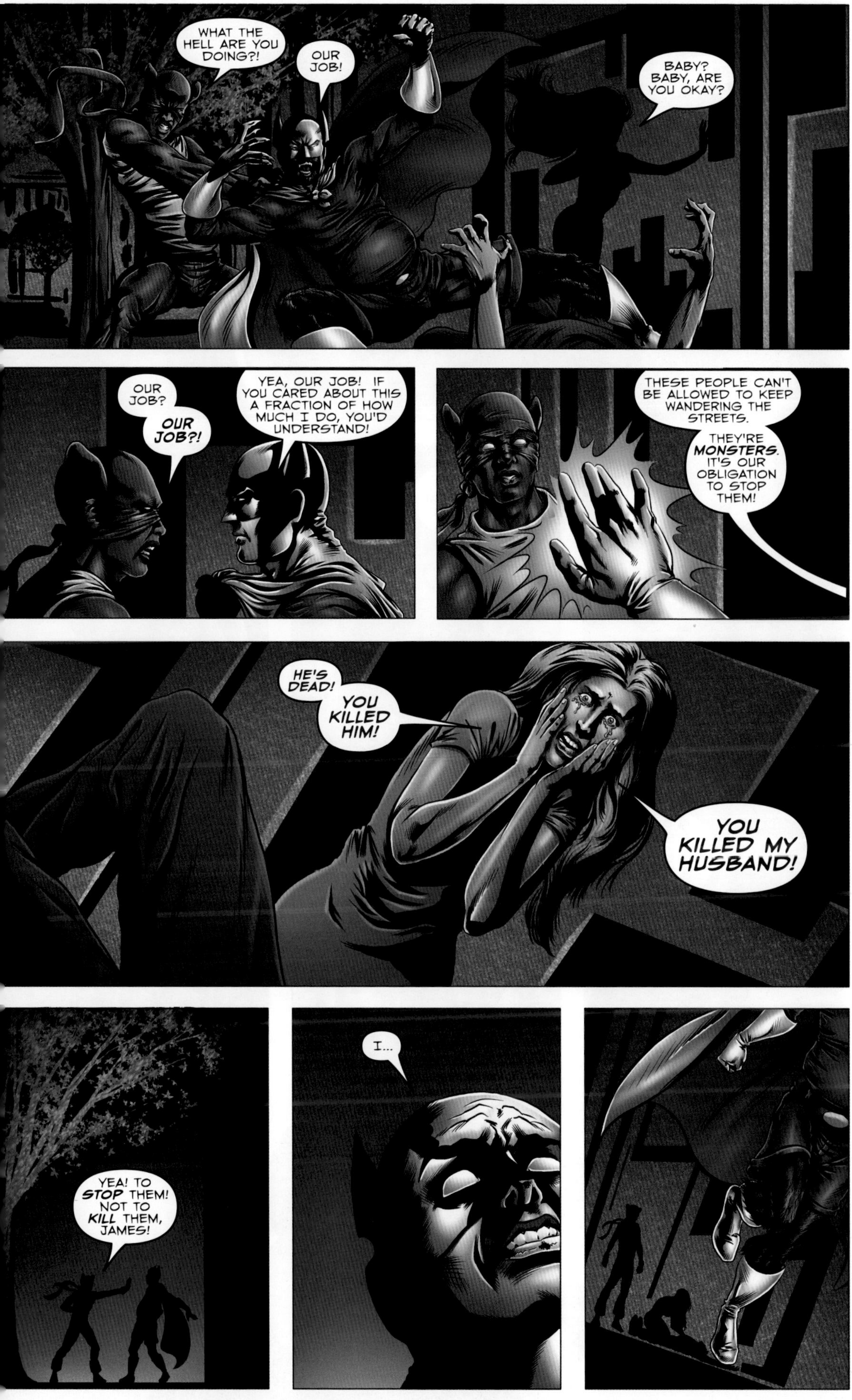
WHAT THE HELL ARE YOU DOING?!
OUR JOB!
BABY? BABY, ARE YOU OKAY?
OUR JOB? OUR JOB?!
YEA, OUR JOB! IF YOU CARED ABOUT THIS A FRACTION OF HOW MUCH I DO, YOU'D UNDERSTAND!
THESE PEOPLE CAN'T BE ALLOWED TO KEEP WANDERING THE STREETS.
THEY'RE MONSTERS. IT'S OUR OBLIGATION TO STOP THEM!
HE'S DEAD! YOU KILLED HIM!
YOU KILLED MY HUSBAND!
YEA! TO STOP THEM! NOT TO KILL THEM, JAMES!
I...

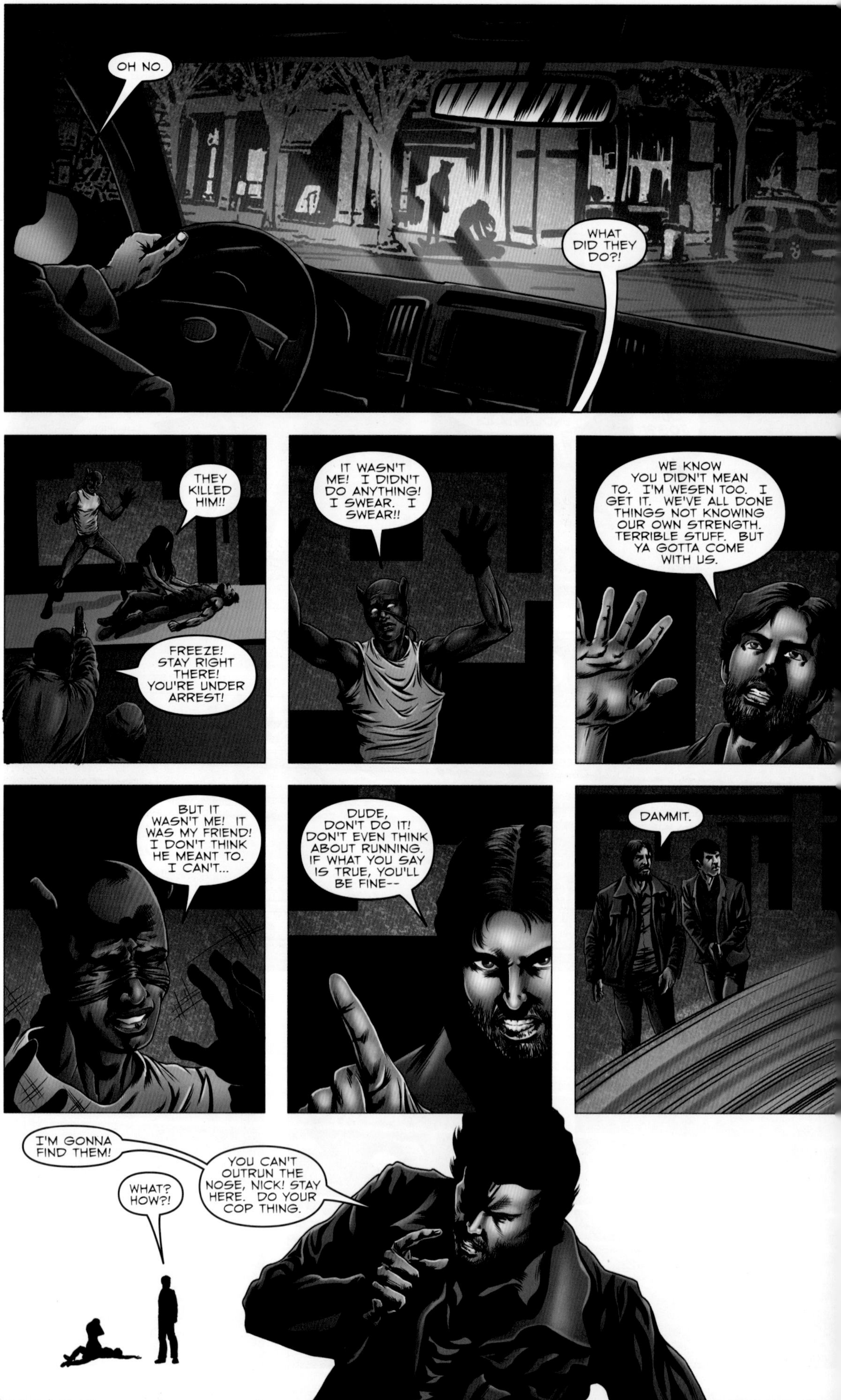
OH NO.
WHAT DID THEY DO?!
THEY KILLED HIM!!
FREEZE! STAY RIGHT THERE! YOU'RE UNDER ARREST!
IT WASN'T ME! I DIDN'T DO ANYTHING! I SWEAR. I SWEAR!!
WE KNOW YOU DIDN'T MEAN TO. I'M WESEN TOO. I GET IT. WE'VE ALL DONE THINGS NOT KNOWING OUR OWN STRENGTH. TERRIBLE STUFF. BUT YA GOTTA COME WITH US.
BUT IT WASN'T ME! IT WAS MY FRIEND! I DON'T THINK HE MEANT TO. I CAN'T...
DUDE, DON'T DO IT! DON'T EVEN THINK ABOUT RUNNING. IF WHAT YOU SAY IS TRUE, YOU'LL BE FINE--
DAMMIT.
I'M GONNA FIND THEM!
YOU CAN'T OUTRUN THE NOSE, NICK! STAY HERE. DO YOUR COP THING.
WHAT? HOW?!

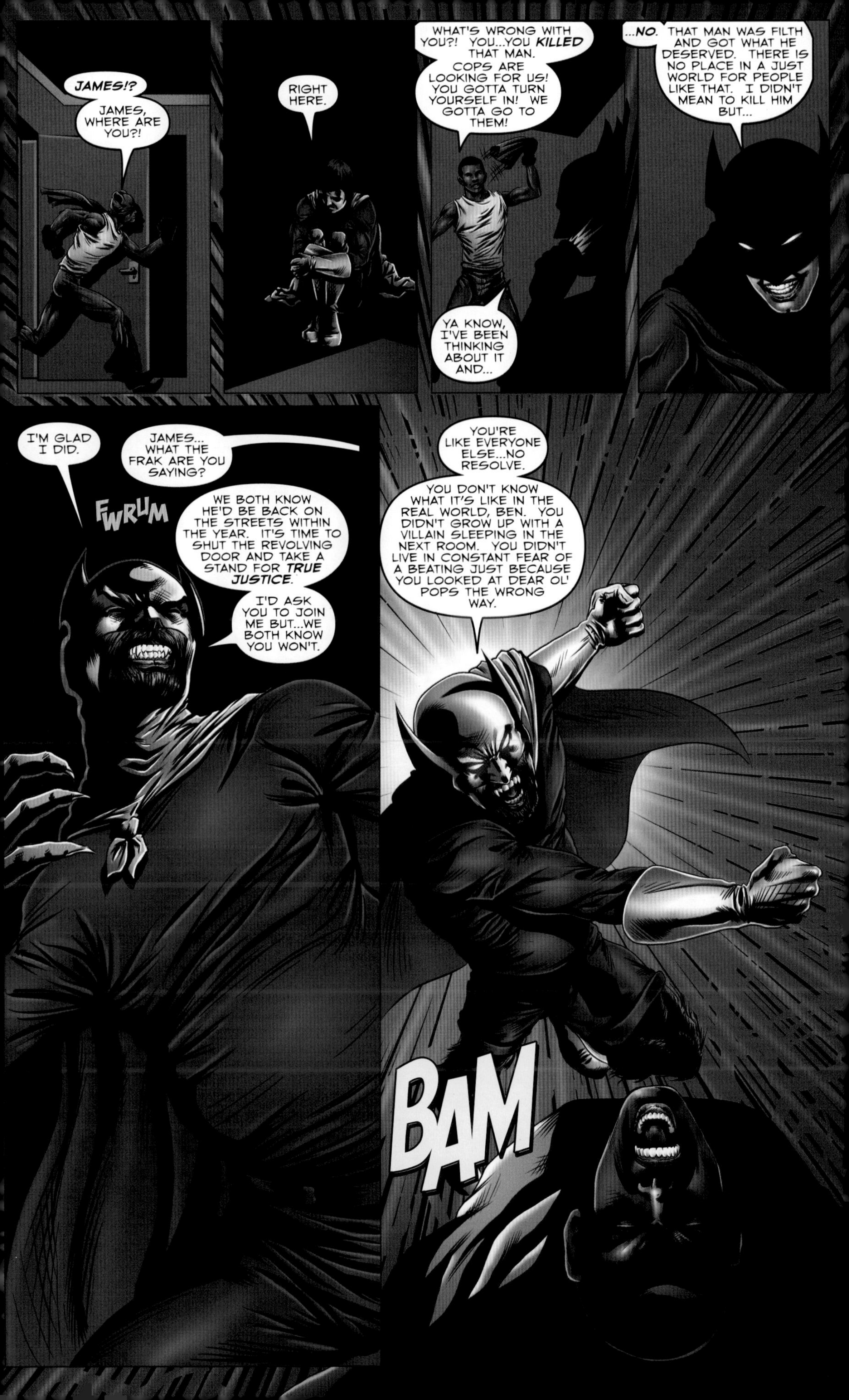
JAMES!?
JAMES, WHERE ARE YOU?!
RIGHT HERE.
WHAT'S WRONG WITH YOU?! YOU...YOU KILLED THAT MAN.
COPS ARE LOOKING FOR US! YOU GOTTA TURN YOURSELF IN! WE GOTTA GO TO THEM!
YA KNOW, I'VE BEEN THINKING ABOUT IT AND...
...NO. THAT MAN WAS FILTH AND GOT WHAT HE DESERVED. THERE IS NO PLACE IN A JUST WORLD FOR PEOPLE LIKE THAT. I DIDN'T MEAN TO KILL HIM BUT...
I'M GLAD I DID.
JAMES... WHAT THE FRAK ARE YOU SAYING?
FWRUM
WE BOTH KNOW HE'D BE BACK ON THE STREETS WITHIN THE YEAR. IT'S TIME TO SHUT THE REVOLVING DOOR AND TAKE A STAND FOR TRUE JUSTICE.
I'D ASK YOU TO JOIN ME BUT...WE BOTH KNOW YOU WON'T.
YOU'RE LIKE EVERYONE ELSE...NO RESOLVE.
YOU DON'T KNOW WHAT IT'S LIKE IN THE REAL WORLD, BEN. YOU DIDN'T GROW UP WITH A VILLAIN SLEEPING IN THE NEXT ROOM. YOU DIDN'T LIVE IN CONSTANT FEAR OF A BEATING JUST BECAUSE YOU LOOKED AT DEAR OL' POPS THE WRONG WAY.
BAM

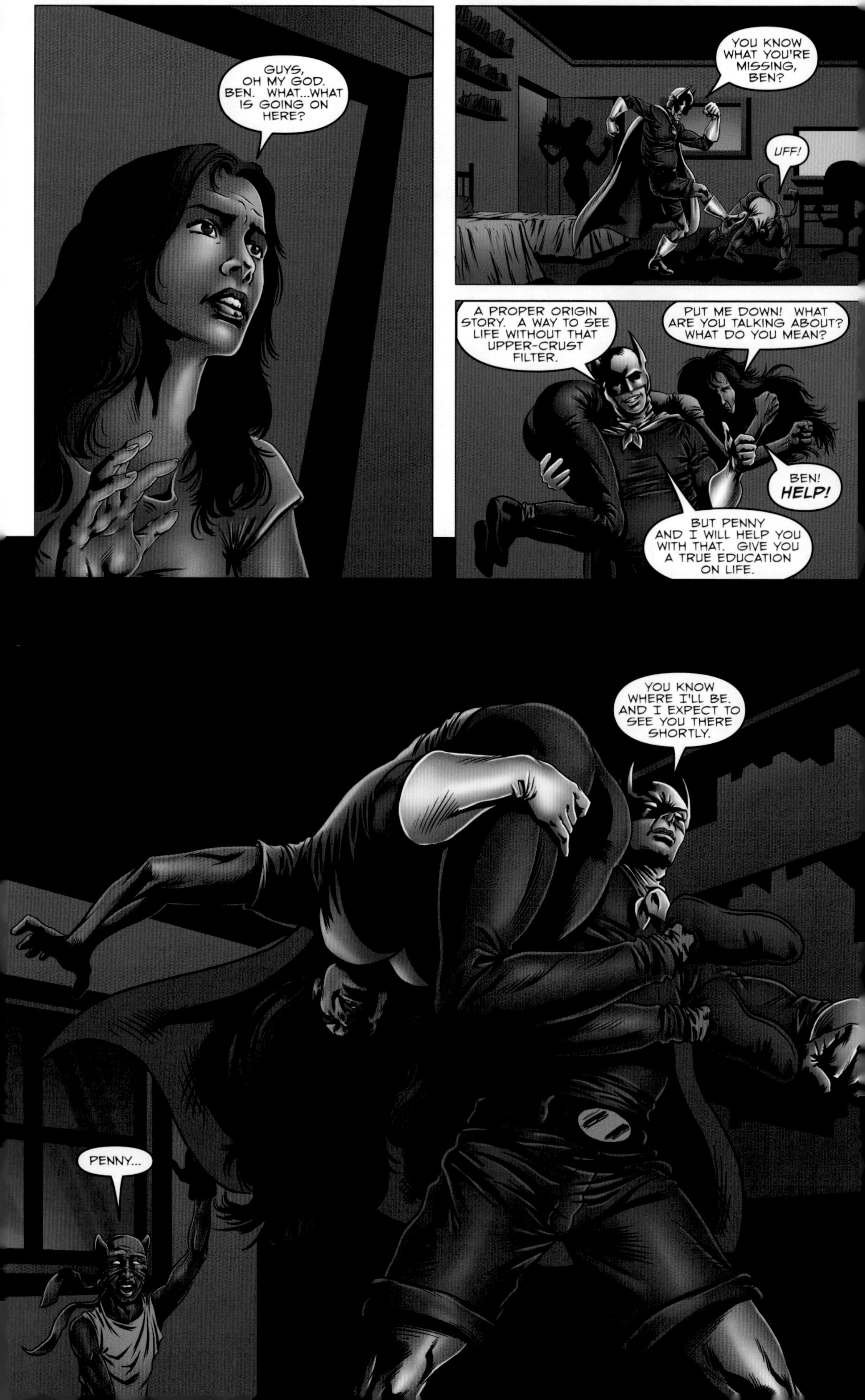
GUYS, OH MY GOD. BEN. WHAT...WHAT IS GOING ON HERE?
YOU KNOW WHAT YOU'RE MISSING, BEN?
UFF!
A PROPER ORIGIN STORY. A WAY TO SEE LIFE WITHOUT THAT UPPER-CRUST FILTER.
PUT ME DOWN! WHAT ARE YOU TALKING ABOUT? WHAT DO YOU MEAN?
BEN! HELP!
BUT PENNY AND I WILL HELP YOU WITH THAT. GIVE YOU A TRUE EDUCATION ON LIFE.
YOU KNOW WHERE I'LL BE. AND I EXPECT TO SEE YOU THERE SHORTLY.
PENNY...

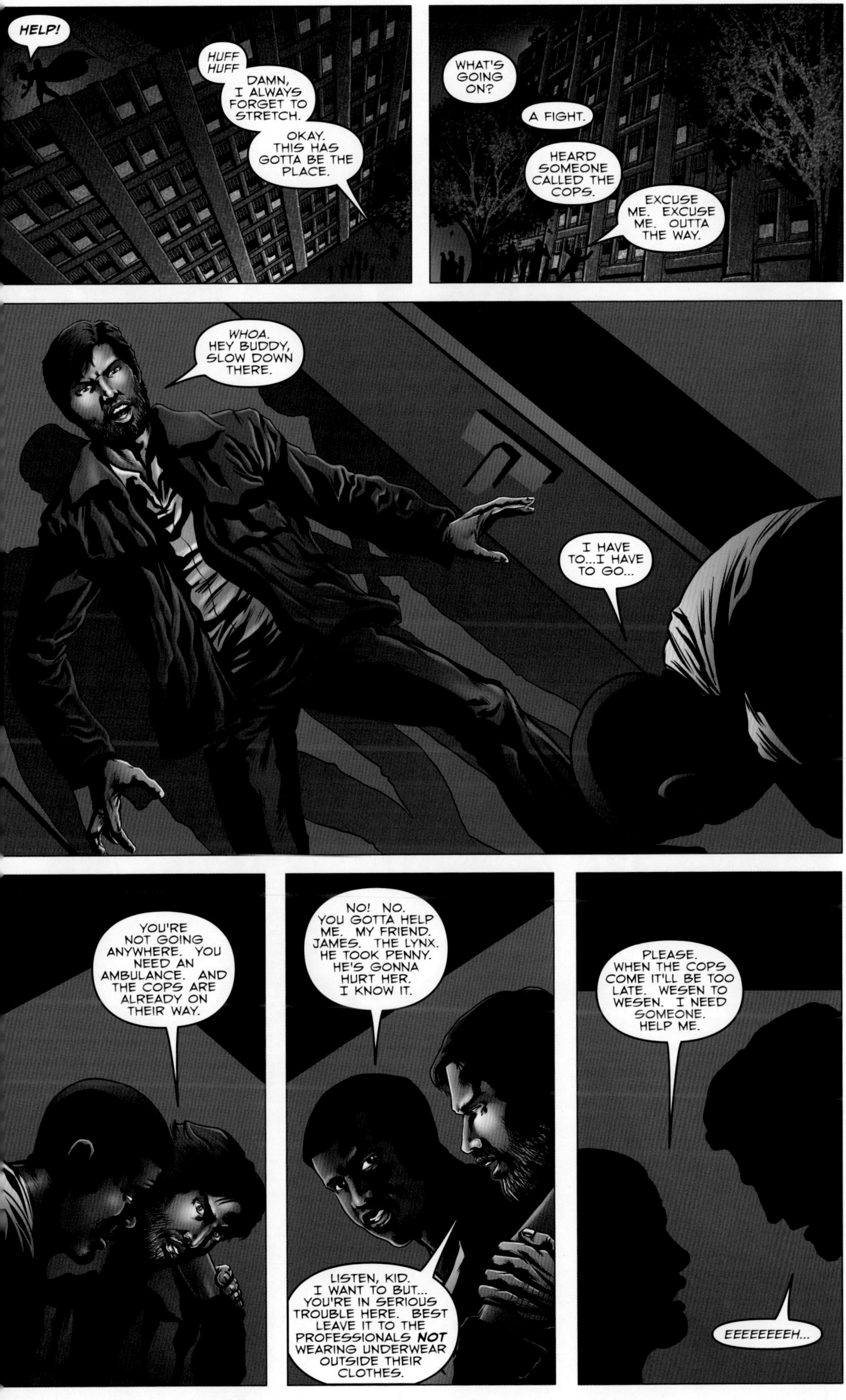
HELP!
HUFF HUFF
DAMN, I ALWAYS FORGET TO STRETCH.
OKAY. THIS HAS GOTTA BE THE PLACE.
WHAT'S GOING ON?
A FIGHT.
HEARD SOMEONE CALLED THE COPS.
EXCUSE ME. EXCUSE ME. OUTTA THE WAY.
WHOA. HEY BUDDY, SLOW DOWN THERE.
I HAVE TO...I HAVE TO GO...
YOU'RE NOT GOING ANYWHERE. YOU NEED AN AMBULANCE. AND THE COPS ARE ALREADY ON THEIR WAY.
NO! NO. YOU GOTTA HELP ME. MY FRIEND. JAMES. THE LYNX. HE TOOK PENNY. HE'S GONNA HURT HER. I KNOW IT.
LISTEN, KID. I WANT TO BUT... YOU'RE IN SERIOUS TROUBLE HERE. BEST LEAVE IT TO THE PROFESSIONALS NOT WEARING UNDERWEAR OUTSIDE THEIR CLOTHES.
PLEASE. WHEN THE COPS COME IT'LL BE TOO LATE. WESEN TO WESEN. I NEED SOMEONE. HELP ME.
EEEEEEEEH...

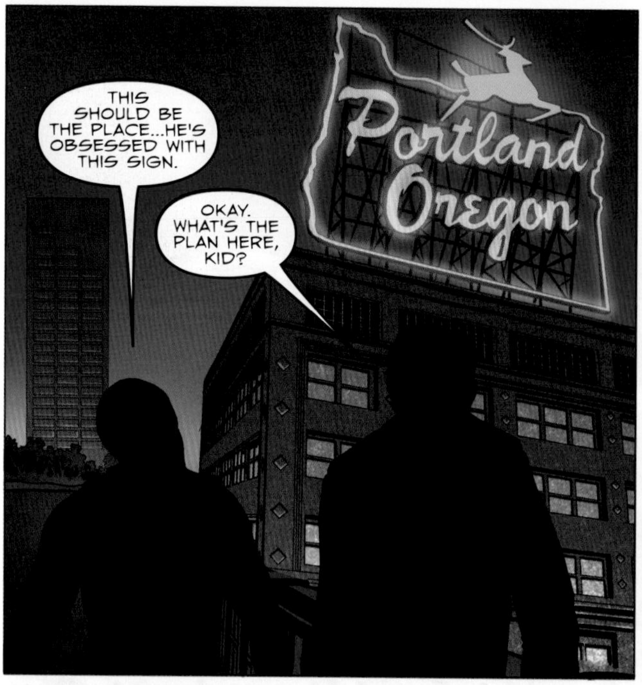
THIS SHOULD BE THE PLACE...HE'S OBSESSED WITH THIS SIGN.
Portland Oregon
OKAY. WHAT'S THE PLAN HERE, KID?

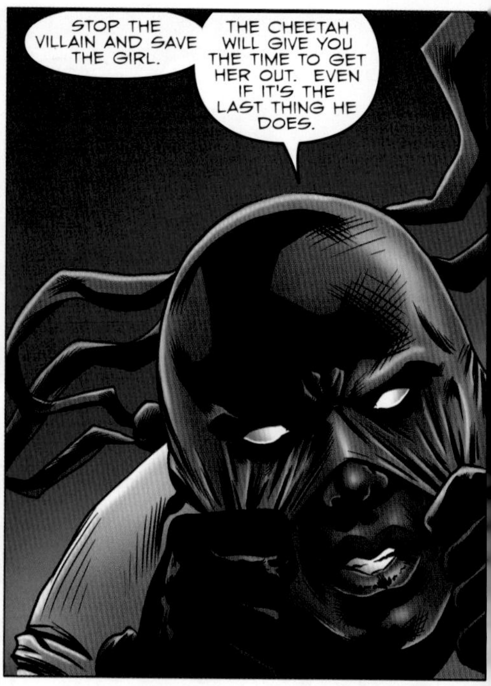
STOP THE VILLAIN AND SAVE THE GIRL.
THE CHEETAH WILL GIVE YOU THE TIME TO GET HER OUT. EVEN IF IT'S THE LAST THING HE DOES.

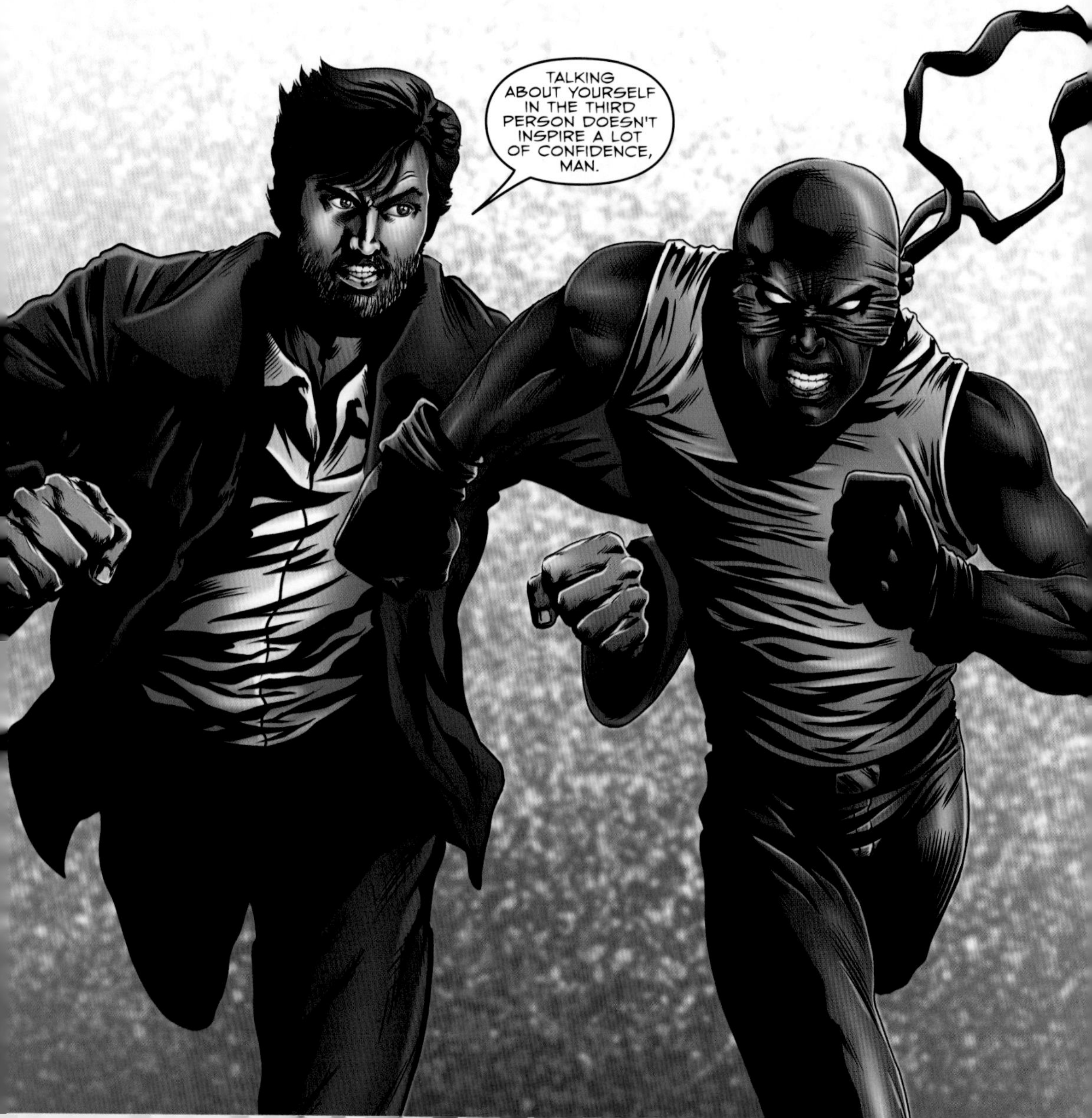
TALKING ABOUT YOURSELF IN THE THIRD PERSON DOESN'T INSPIRE A LOT OF CONFIDENCE, MAN.

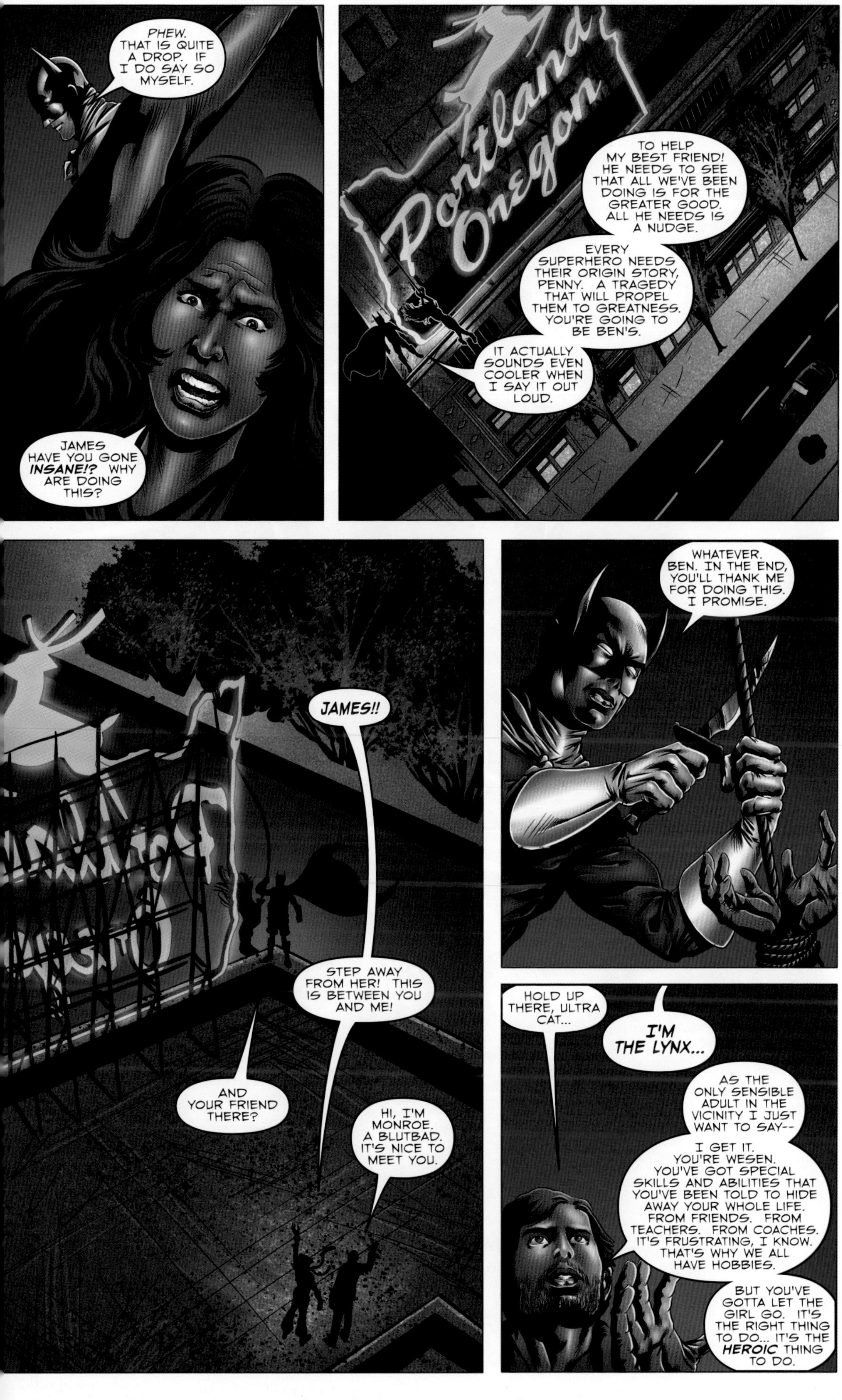
PHEW. THAT IS QUITE A DROP. IF I DO SAY SO MYSELF.
JAMES HAVE YOU GONE INSANE!? WHY ARE DOING THIS?
TO HELP MY BEST FRIEND! HE NEEDS TO SEE THAT ALL WE'VE BEEN DOING IS FOR THE GREATER GOOD. ALL HE NEEDS IS A NUDGE.
EVERY SUPERHERO NEEDS THEIR ORIGIN STORY, PENNY. A TRAGEDY THAT WILL PROPEL THEM TO GREATNESS. YOU'RE GOING TO BE BEN'S.
IT ACTUALLY SOUNDS EVEN COOLER WHEN I SAY IT OUT LOUD.
Portland Oregon
JAMES!!
STEP AWAY FROM HER! THIS IS BETWEEN YOU AND ME!
AND YOUR FRIEND THERE?
HI, I'M MONROE. A BLUTBAD. IT'S NICE TO MEET YOU.
WHATEVER. BEN. IN THE END, YOU'LL THANK ME FOR DOING THIS. I PROMISE.
HOLD UP THERE, ULTRA CAT...
I'M THE LYNX...
AS THE ONLY SENSIBLE ADULT IN THE VICINITY I JUST WANT TO SAY--
I GET IT. YOU'RE WESEN. YOU'VE GOT SPECIAL SKILLS AND ABILITIES THAT YOU'VE BEEN TOLD TO HIDE AWAY YOUR WHOLE LIFE. FROM FRIENDS. FROM TEACHERS. FROM COACHES. IT'S FRUSTRATING, I KNOW. THAT'S WHY WE ALL HAVE HOBBIES.
BUT YOU'VE GOTTA LET THE GIRL GO. IT'S THE RIGHT THING TO DO... IT'S THE HEROIC THING TO DO.

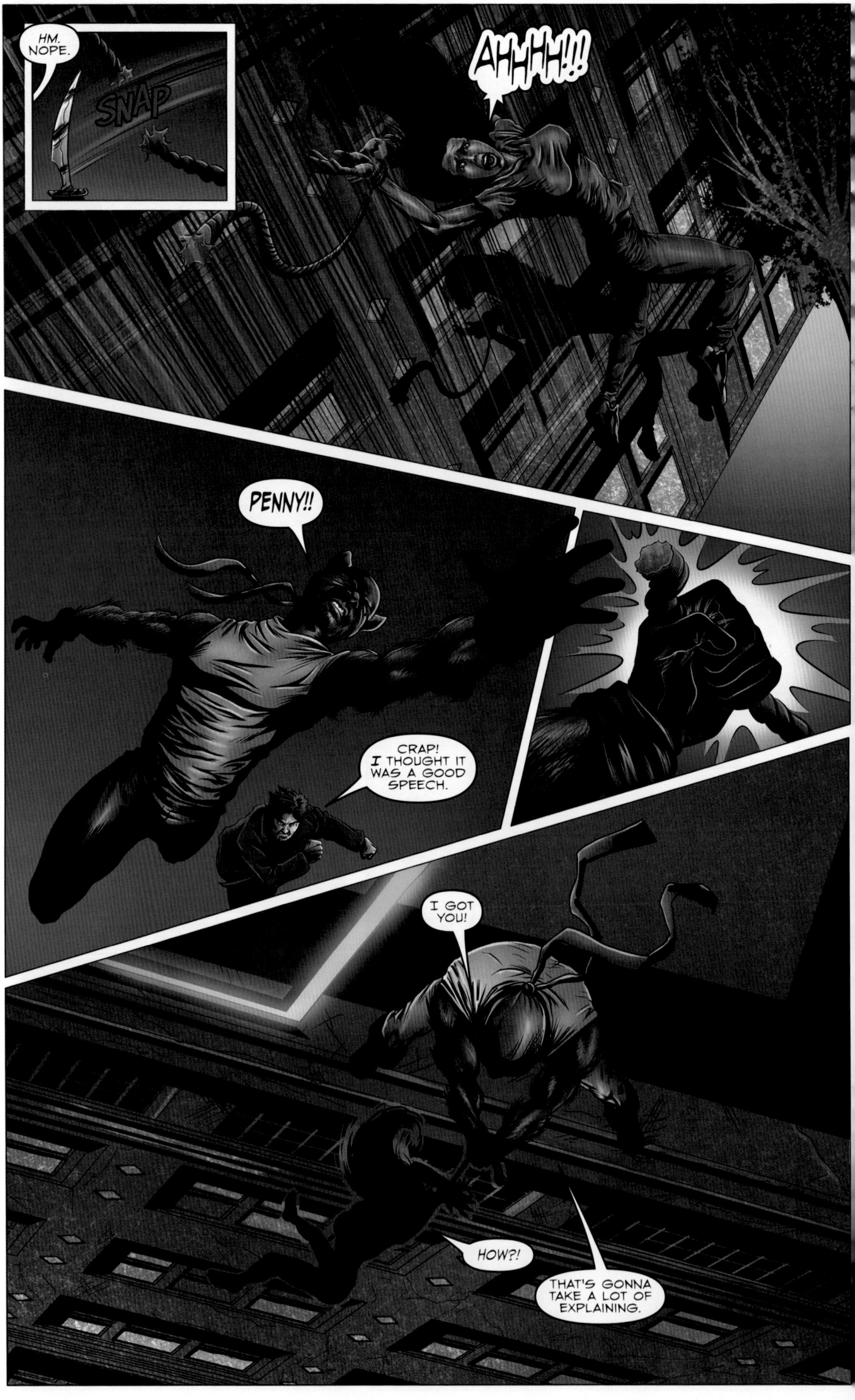
HM. NOPE.
SNAP
AHHHH!!!
PENNY!!
CRAP! I THOUGHT IT WAS A GOOD SPEECH.
I GOT YOU!
HOW?!
THAT'S GONNA TAKE A LOT OF EXPLAINING.

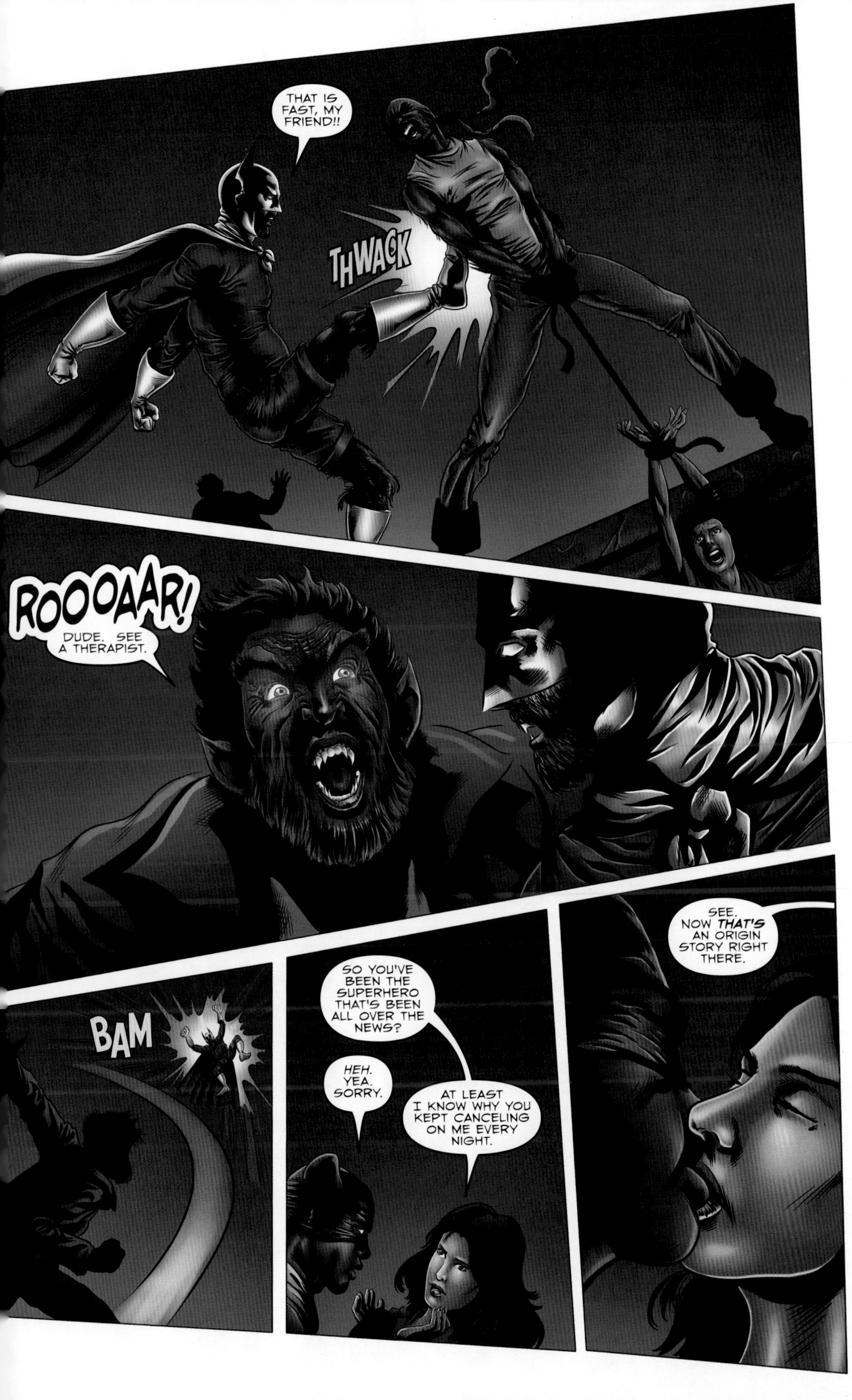
THAT IS FAST, MY FRIEND!!
THWACK
ROOOAAR!
DUDE. SEE A THERAPIST.
BAM
SO YOU'VE BEEN THE SUPERHERO THAT'S BEEN ALL OVER THE NEWS?
HEH. YEA. SORRY.
AT LEAST I KNOW WHY YOU KEPT CANCELING ON ME EVERY NIGHT.
SEE. NOW THAT'S AN ORIGIN STORY RIGHT THERE.

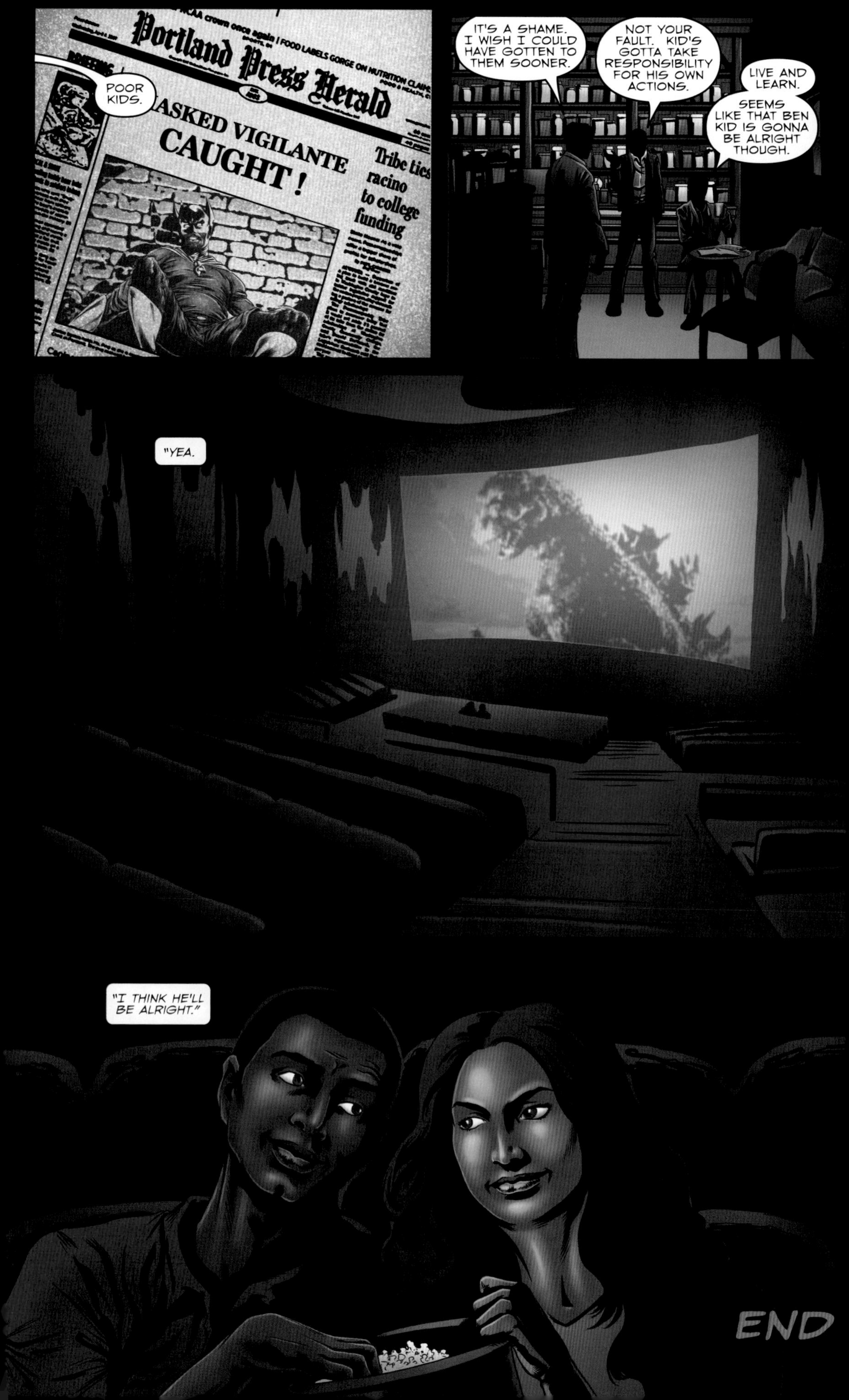
Portland Press Herald
ASKED VIGILANTE
CAUGHT!
Tribe ties racino to college funding
POOR KIDS.
IT'S A SHAME. I WISH I COULD HAVE GOTTEN TO THEM SOONER.
NOT YOUR FAULT. KID'S GOTTA TAKE RESPONSIBILITY FOR HIS OWN ACTIONS.
LIVE AND LEARN.
SEEMS LIKE THAT BEN KID IS GONNA BE ALRIGHT THOUGH.
"YEA.
"I THINK HE'LL BE ALRIGHT."
END

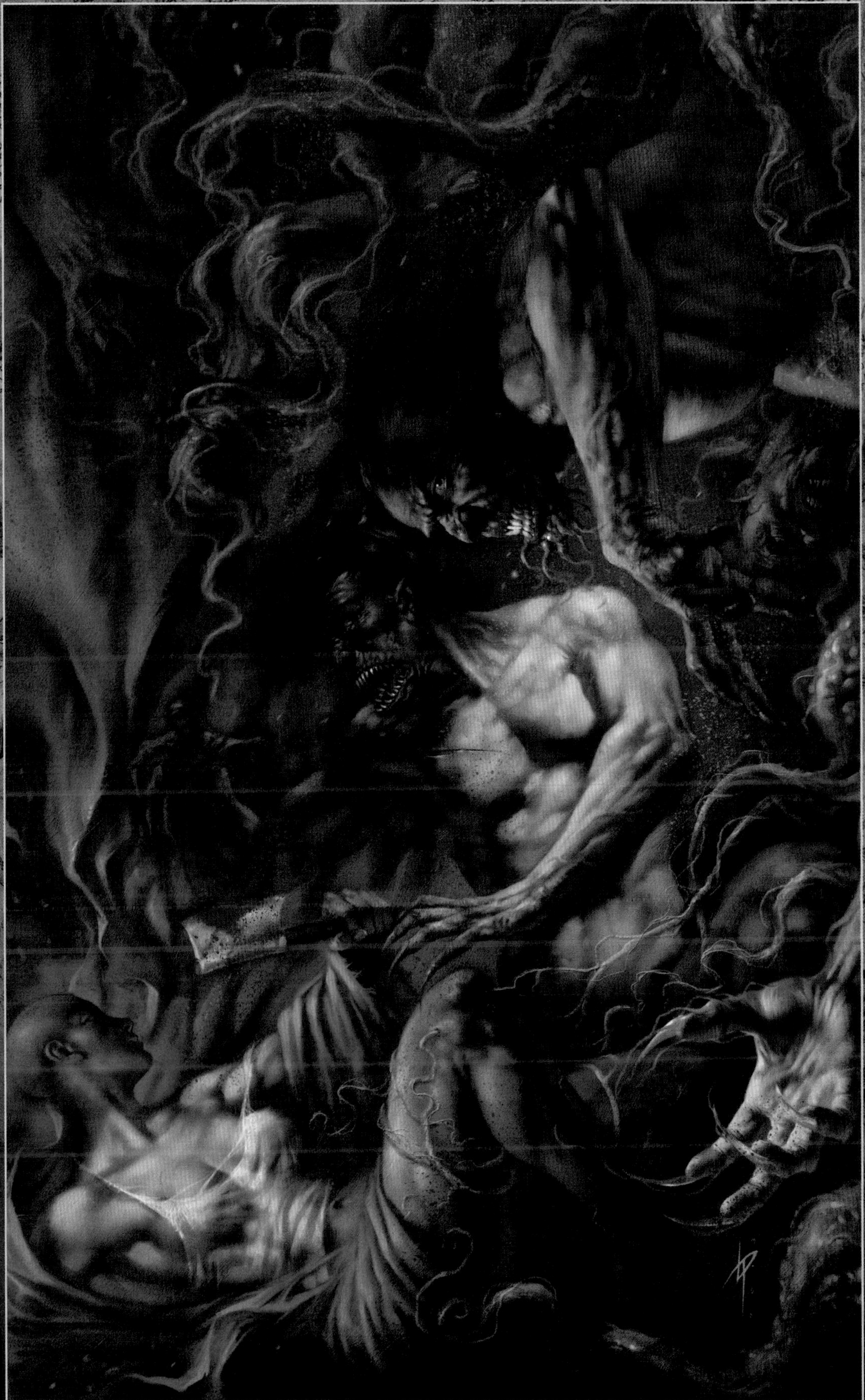

ISSUE #8 COVER

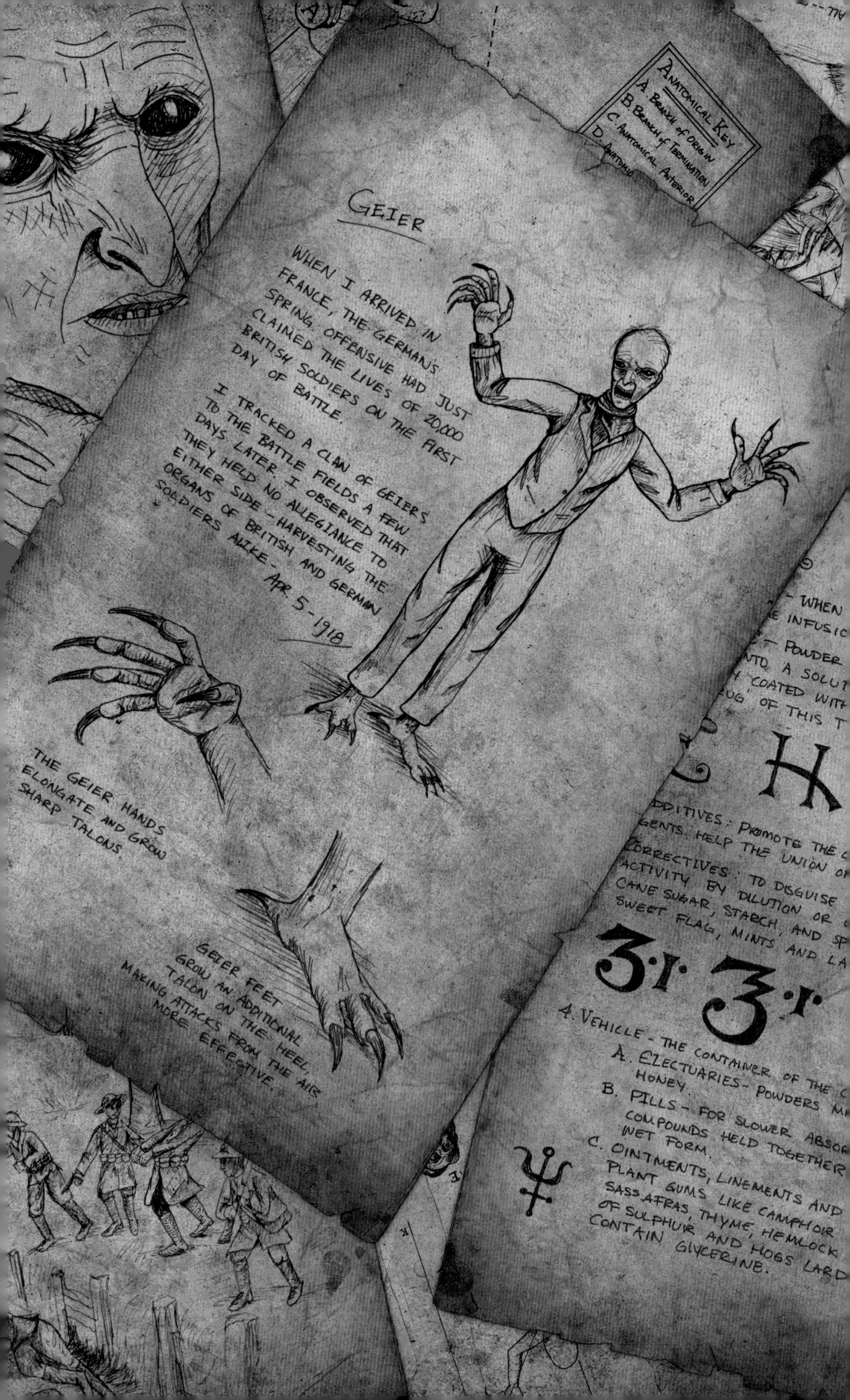
Anatomical Key
A. Branch of Origin
B. Branch of Termination
C. Anatomical Anterior
D. Anatomic
GEIER
WHEN I ARRIVED IN FRANCE, THE GERMAN'S SPRING OFFENSIVE HAD JUST CLAIMED THE LIVES OF 20,000 BRITISH SOLDIERS ON THE FIRST DAY OF BATTLE.
I TRACKED A CLAN OF GEIERS TO THE BATTLE FIELDS A FEW DAYS LATER. I OBSERVED THAT THEY HELD NO ALLEGIANCE TO EITHER SIDE - HARVESTING THE ORGANS OF BRITISH AND GERMAN SOLDIERS ALIKE -
APR. 5 - 1918
THE GEIER HANDS ELONGATE AND GROW SHARP TALONS.
GEIER FEET GROW AN ADDITIONAL TALON ON THE HEEL, MAKING ATTACKS FROM THE AIR MORE EFFECTIVE.
- WHEN
- POWDER
DDITIVES: PROMOTE THE
GENTS: HELP THE UNION OF
CORRECTIVES: TO DISGUISE
ACTIVITY BY DILUTION OR
CANE SUGAR, STARCH, AND SP
SWEET FLAG, MINTS AND LA
4. VEHICLE - THE CONTAINER OF THE C
A. ELECTUARIES - POWDERS M
HONEY.
B. PILLS - FOR SLOWER ABSOR
COMPOUNDS HELD TOGETHER
WET FORM.
C. OINTMENTS, LINEMENTS AND
PLANT GUMS LIKE CAMPHOR
SASSAFRAS, THYME, HEMLOCK
OF SULPHUR AND HOGS LARD
CONTAIN GLYCERINE.

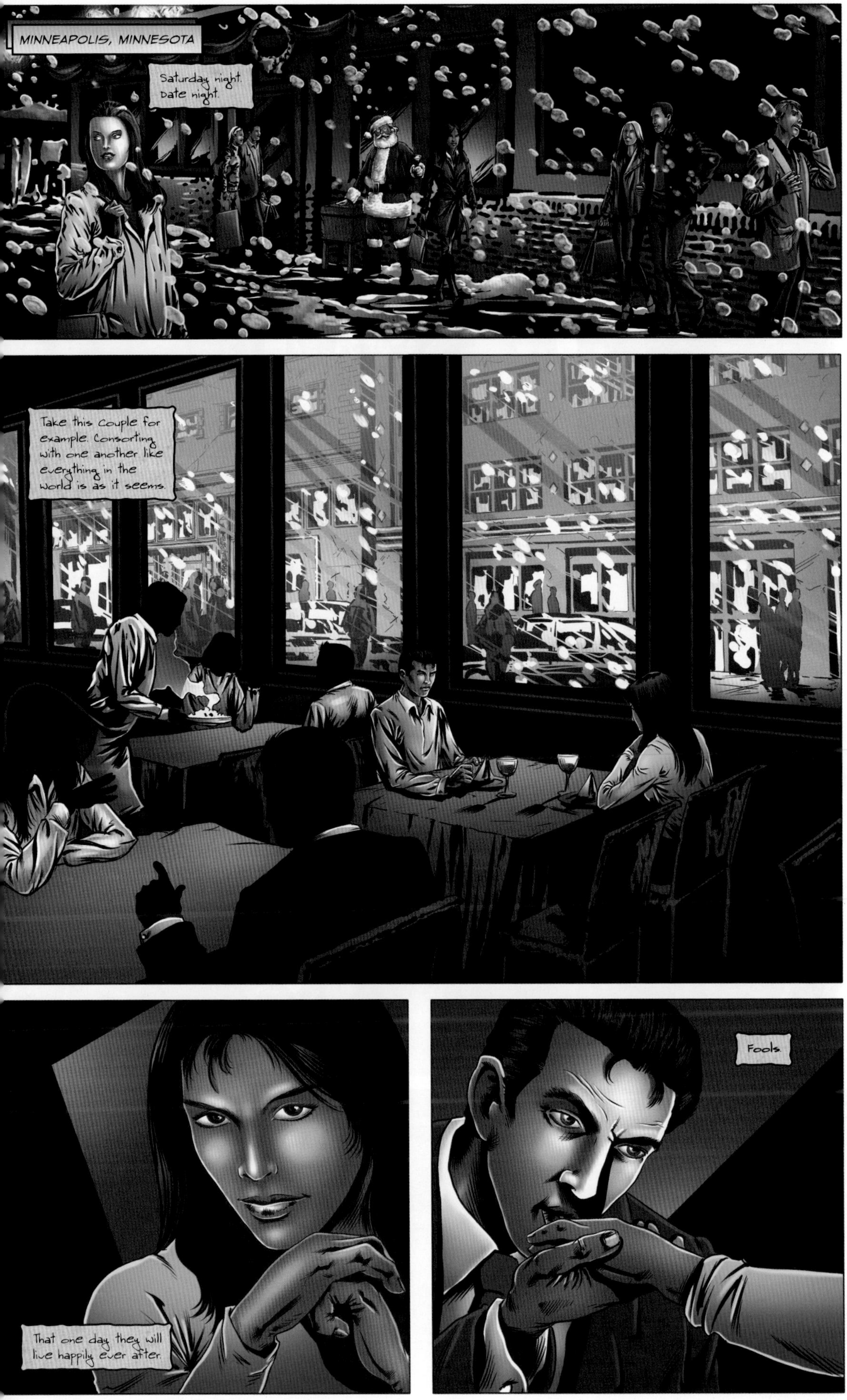
MINNEAPOLIS, MINNESOTA
Saturday night. Date night.
Take this couple for example. Consorting with one another like everything in the world is as it seems.
That one day they will live happily ever after.
Fools.

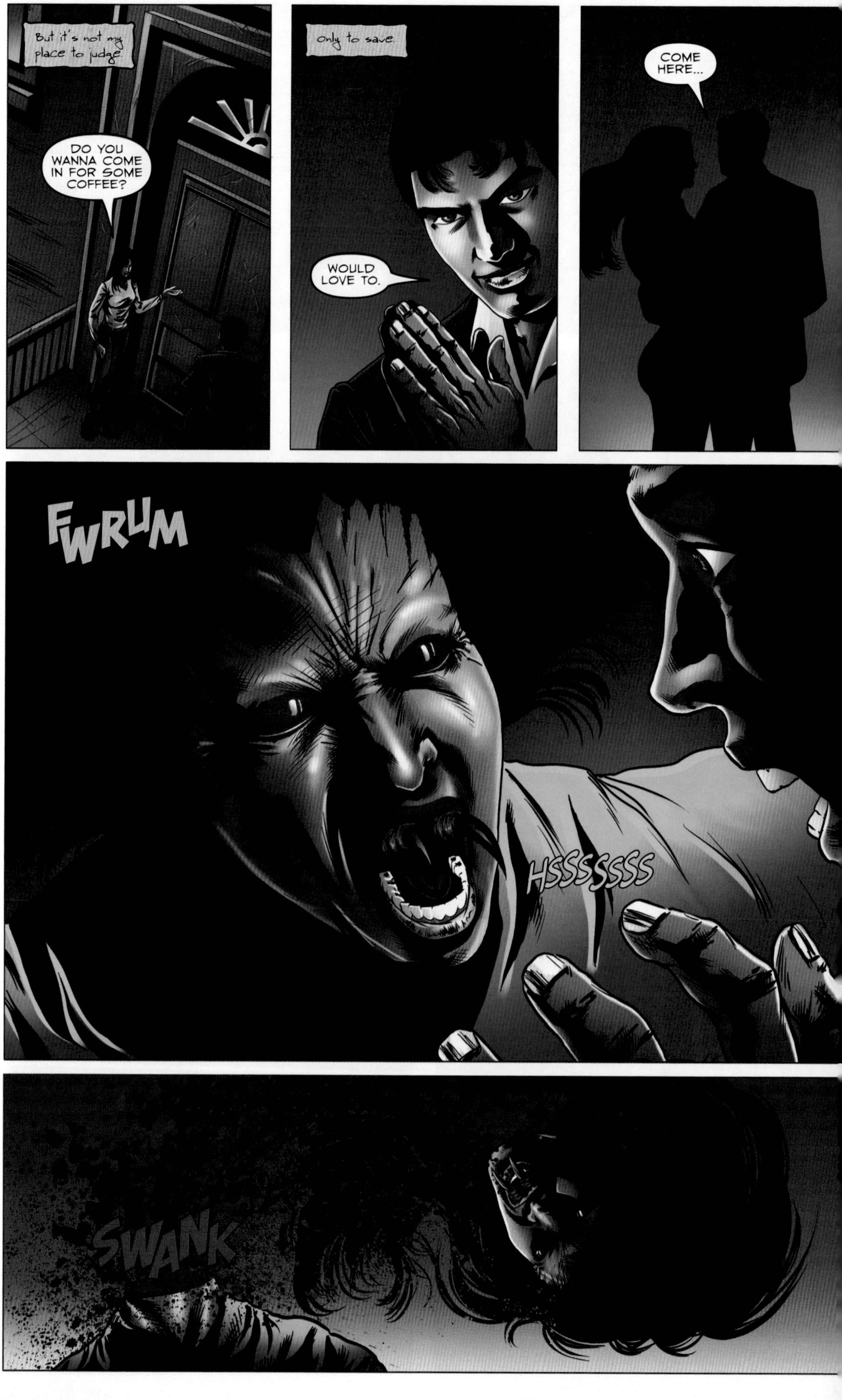
But it's not my place to judge.
DO YOU WANNA COME IN FOR SOME COFFEE?
only to save.
WOULD LOVE TO.
COME HERE...
FWRUM
HSSSSSSS
SWANK

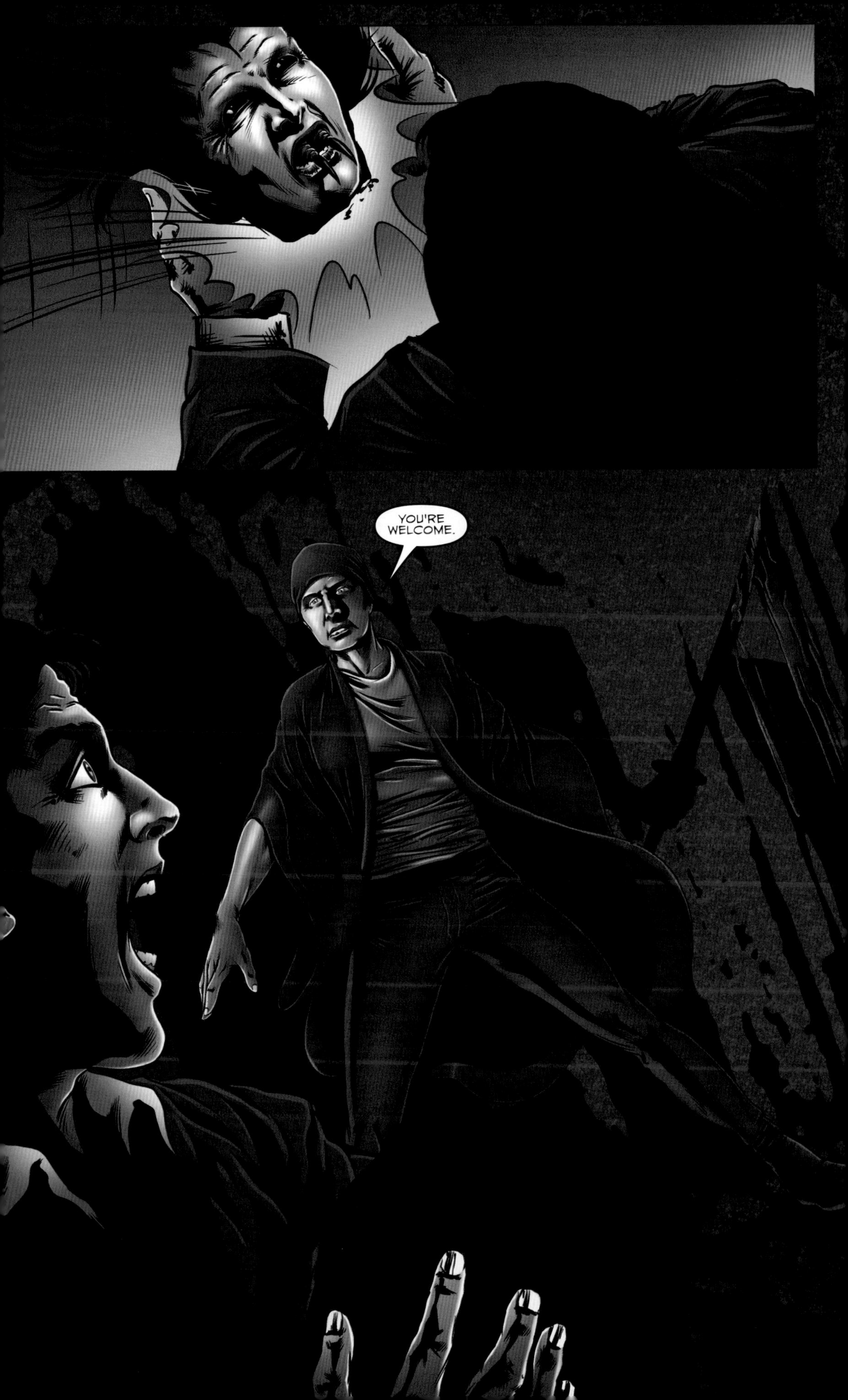
YOU'RE WELCOME.

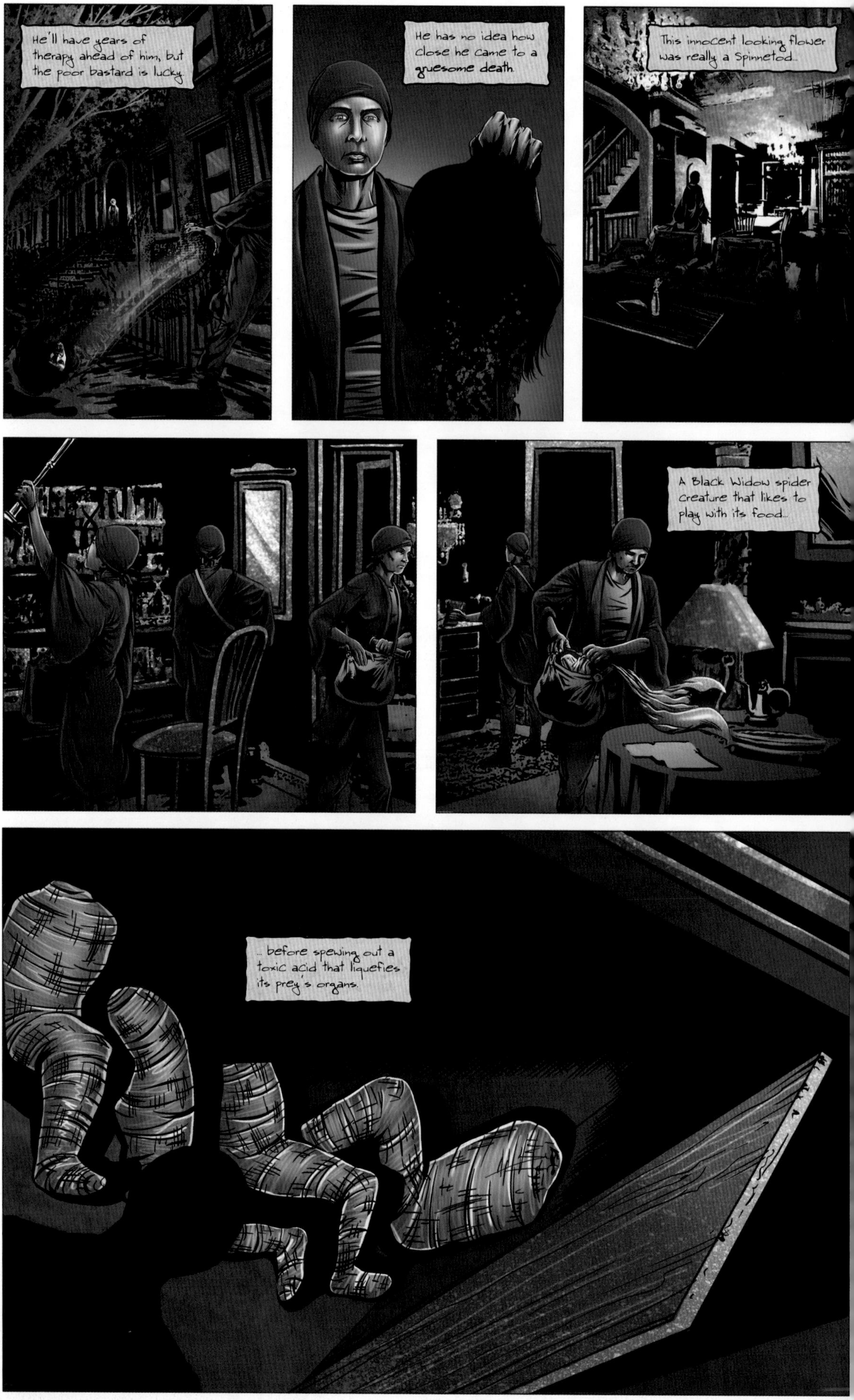
He'll have years of therapy ahead of him, but the poor bastard is lucky.
He has no idea how close he came to a gruesome death.
This innocent looking flower was really a Spinnetod...
A Black Widow spider creature that likes to play with its food...
... before spewing out a toxic acid that liquefies its prey's organs.

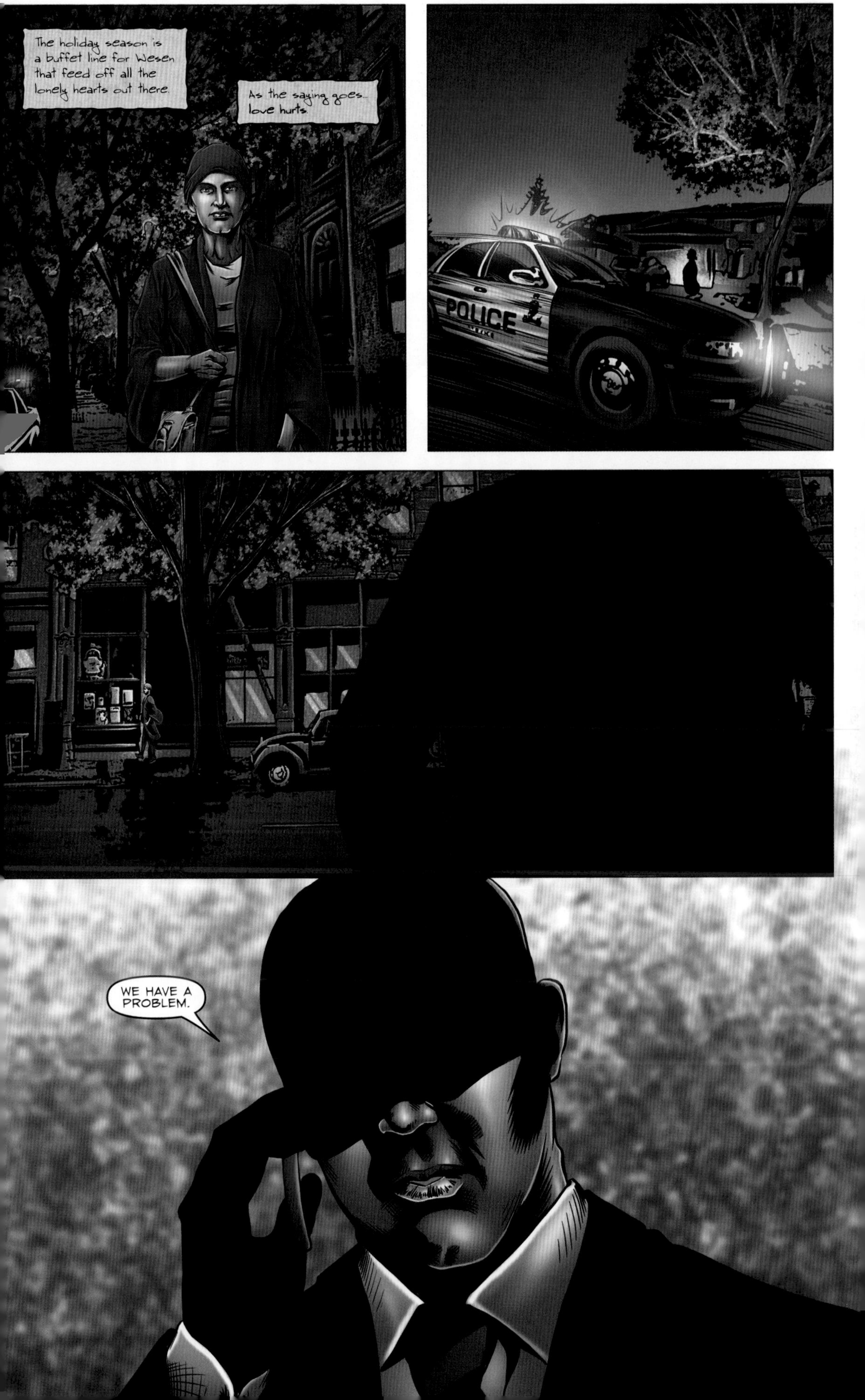
The holiday season is a buffet line for Wesen that feed off all the lonely hearts out there.
As the saying goes... love hurts.
POLICE
WE HAVE A PROBLEM.

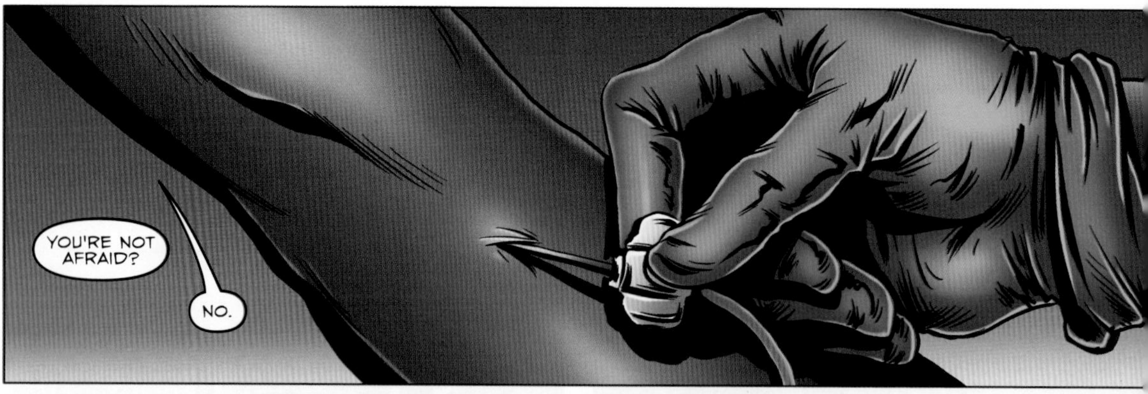
YOU'RE NOT AFRAID?
NO.

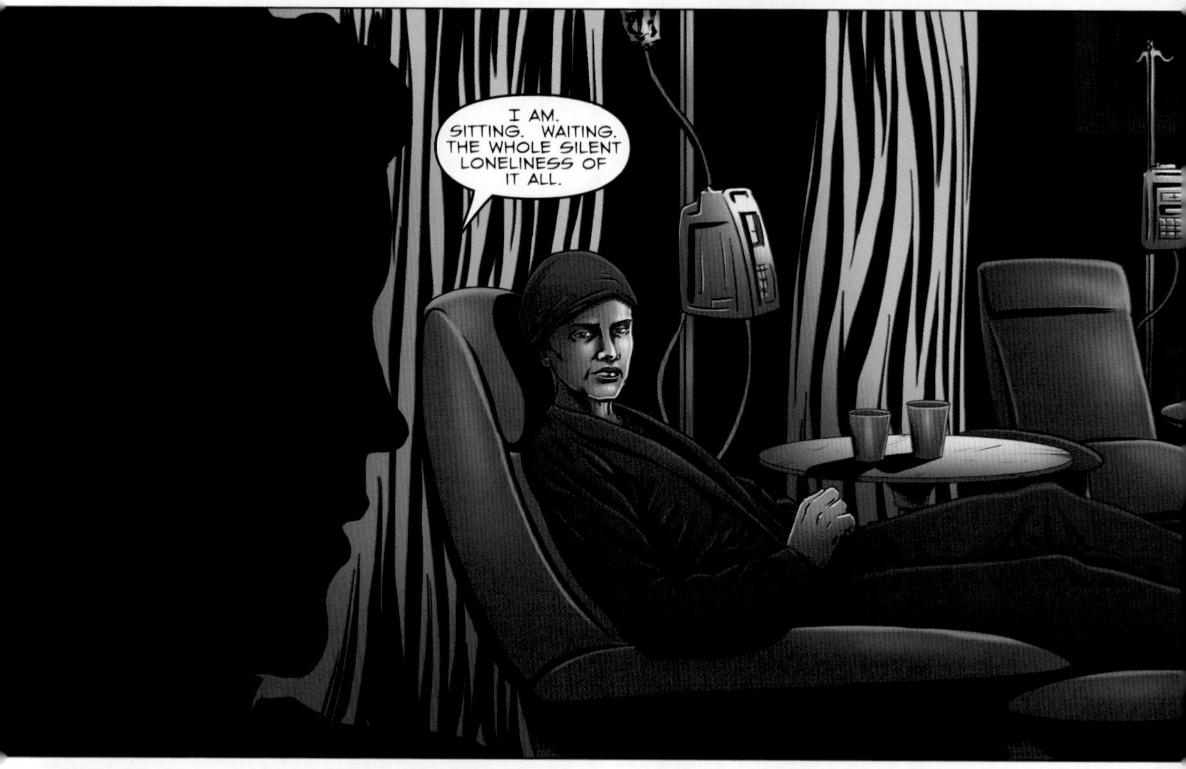
I AM. SITTING. WAITING. THE WHOLE SILENT LONELINESS OF IT ALL.

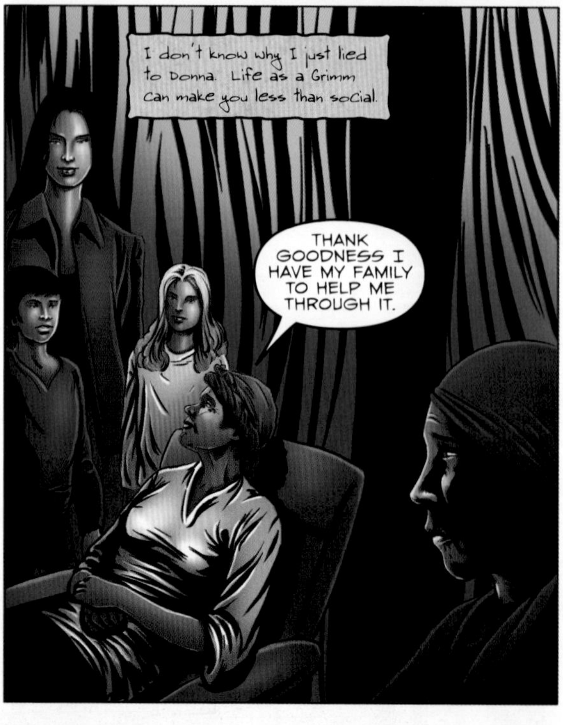
I don't know why I just lied to Donna. Life as a Grimm can make you less than social.
THANK GOODNESS I HAVE MY FAMILY TO HELP ME THROUGH IT.

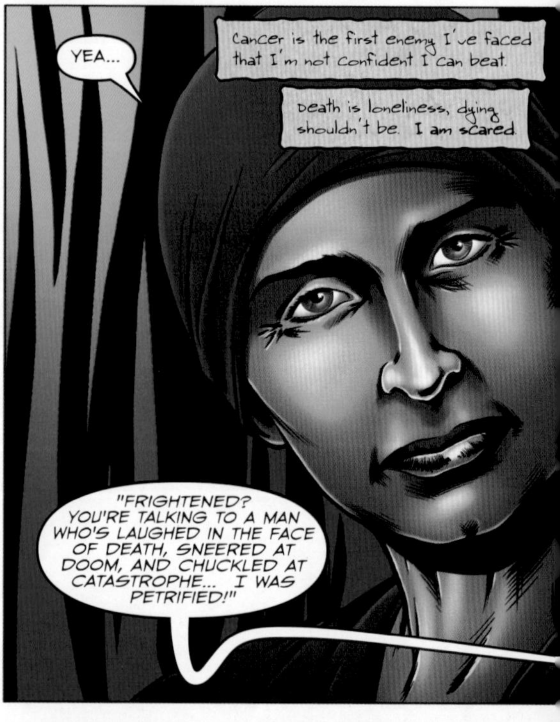
YEA...
Cancer is the first enemy I've faced that I'm not confident I can beat.
Death is loneliness, dying shouldn't be. I am scared.
"FRIGHTENED? YOU'RE TALKING TO A MAN WHO'S LAUGHED IN THE FACE OF DEATH, SNEERED AT DOOM, AND CHUCKLED AT CATASTROPHE... I WAS PETRIFIED!"

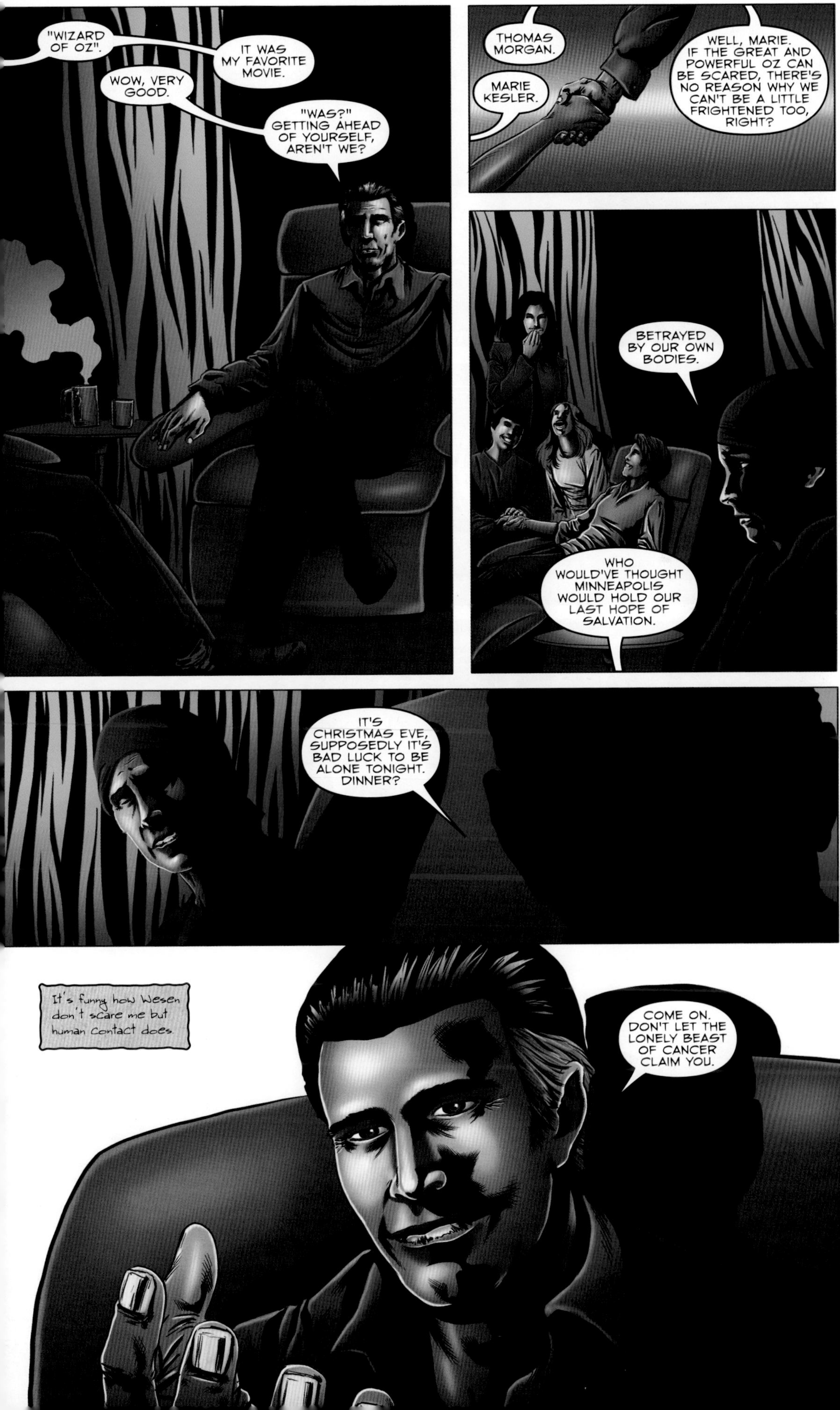
"WIZARD OF OZ".
IT WAS MY FAVORITE MOVIE.
WOW, VERY GOOD.
"WAS?" GETTING AHEAD OF YOURSELF, AREN'T WE?
THOMAS MORGAN.
MARIE KESLER.
WELL, MARIE. IF THE GREAT AND POWERFUL OZ CAN BE SCARED, THERE'S NO REASON WHY WE CAN'T BE A LITTLE FRIGHTENED TOO, RIGHT?
BETRAYED BY OUR OWN BODIES.
WHO WOULD'VE THOUGHT MINNEAPOLIS WOULD HOLD OUR LAST HOPE OF SALVATION.
IT'S CHRISTMAS EVE, SUPPOSEDLY IT'S BAD LUCK TO BE ALONE TONIGHT. DINNER?
It's funny how Wesen don't scare me but human contact does.
COME ON. DON'T LET THE LONELY BEAST OF CANCER CLAIM YOU.

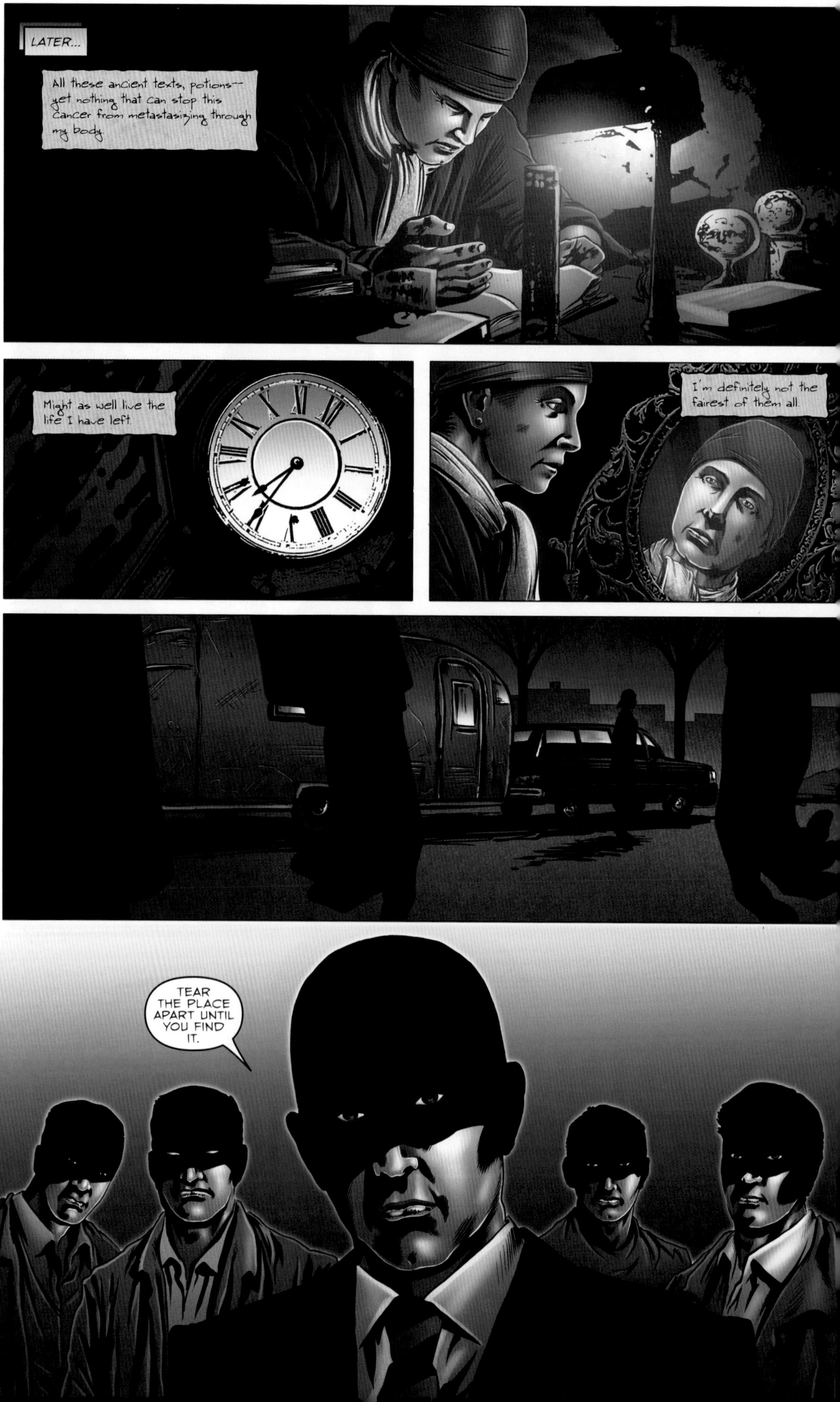
LATER...
All these ancient texts, potions--yet nothing that can stop this cancer from metastasizing through my body.
Might as well live the life I have left.
I'm definitely not the fairest of them all.
TEAR THE PLACE APART UNTIL YOU FIND IT.

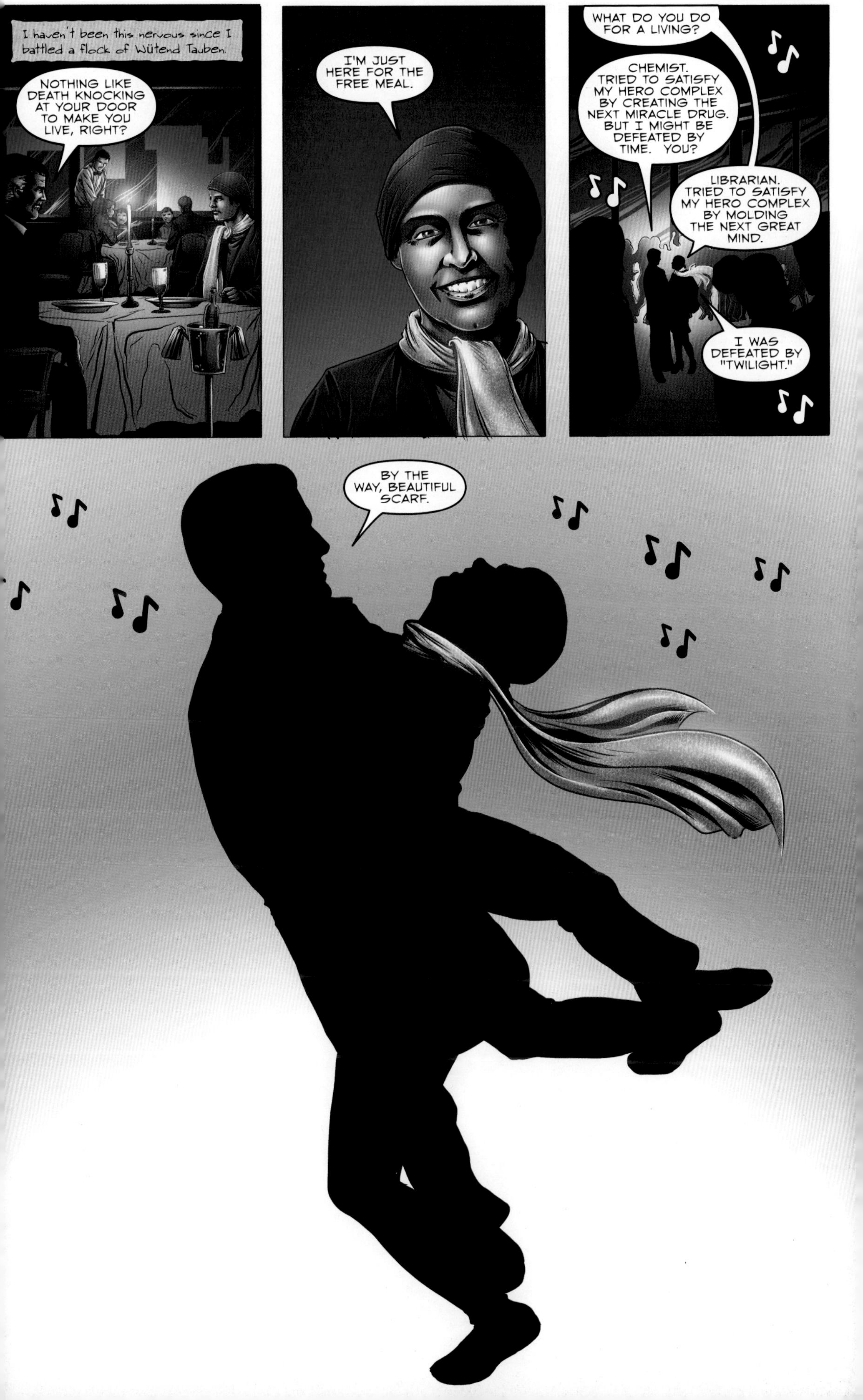
I haven't been this nervous since I battled a flock of Wütend Tauben.
NOTHING LIKE DEATH KNOCKING AT YOUR DOOR TO MAKE YOU LIVE, RIGHT?
I'M JUST HERE FOR THE FREE MEAL.
WHAT DO YOU DO FOR A LIVING?
CHEMIST. TRIED TO SATISFY MY HERO COMPLEX BY CREATING THE NEXT MIRACLE DRUG. BUT I MIGHT BE DEFEATED BY TIME. YOU?
LIBRARIAN. TRIED TO SATISFY MY HERO COMPLEX BY MOLDING THE NEXT GREAT MIND.
I WAS DEFEATED BY "TWILIGHT."
BY THE WAY, BEAUTIFUL SCARF.

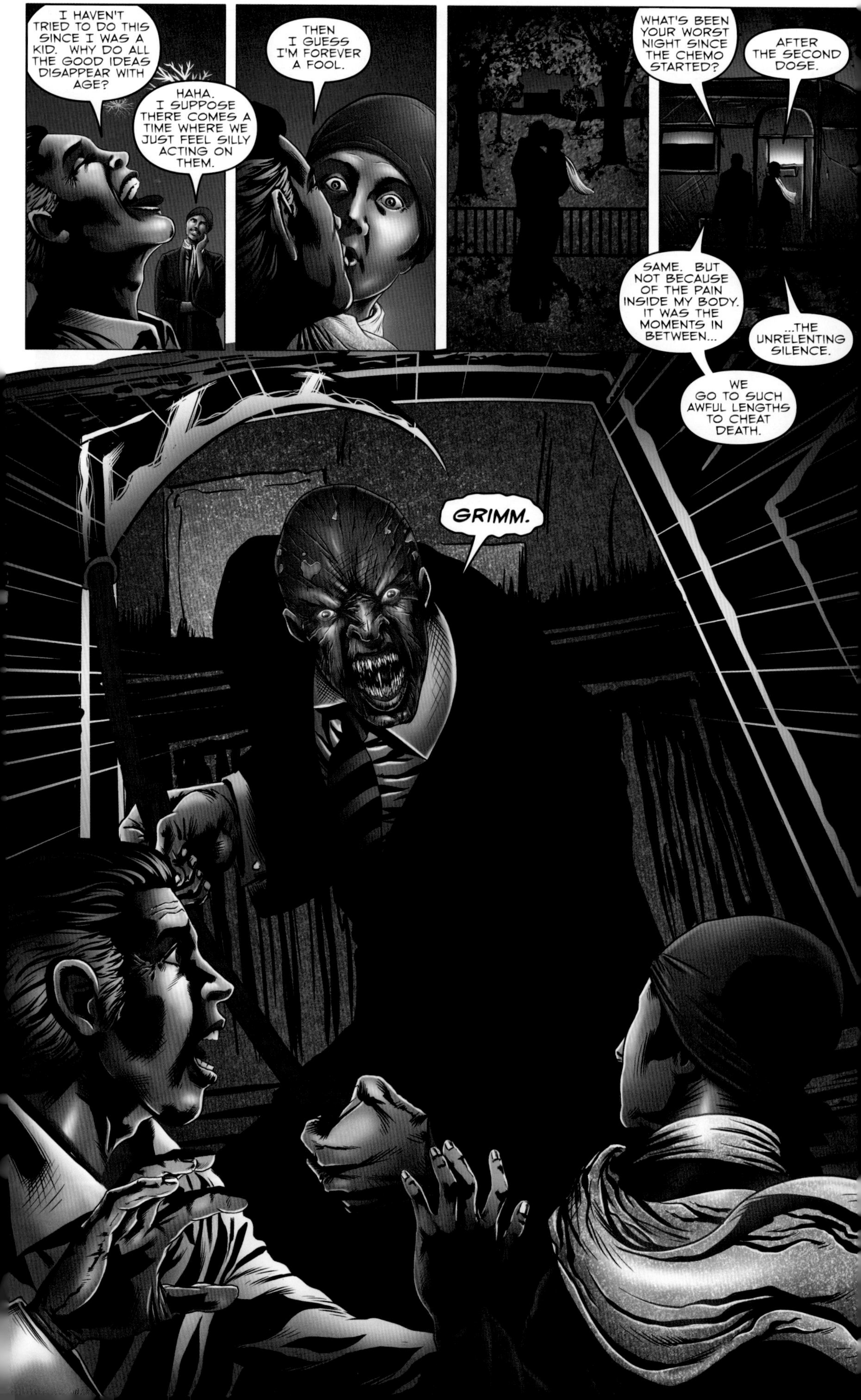
I HAVEN'T TRIED TO DO THIS SINCE I WAS A KID. WHY DO ALL THE GOOD IDEAS DISAPPEAR WITH AGE?
HAHA. I SUPPOSE THERE COMES A TIME WHERE WE JUST FEEL SILLY ACTING ON THEM.
THEN I GUESS I'M FOREVER A FOOL.
WHAT'S BEEN YOUR WORST NIGHT SINCE THE CHEMO STARTED?
AFTER THE SECOND DOSE.
SAME. BUT NOT BECAUSE OF THE PAIN INSIDE MY BODY. IT WAS THE MOMENTS IN BETWEEN...
...THE UNRELENTING SILENCE.
WE GO TO SUCH AWFUL LENGTHS TO CHEAT DEATH.
GRIMM.

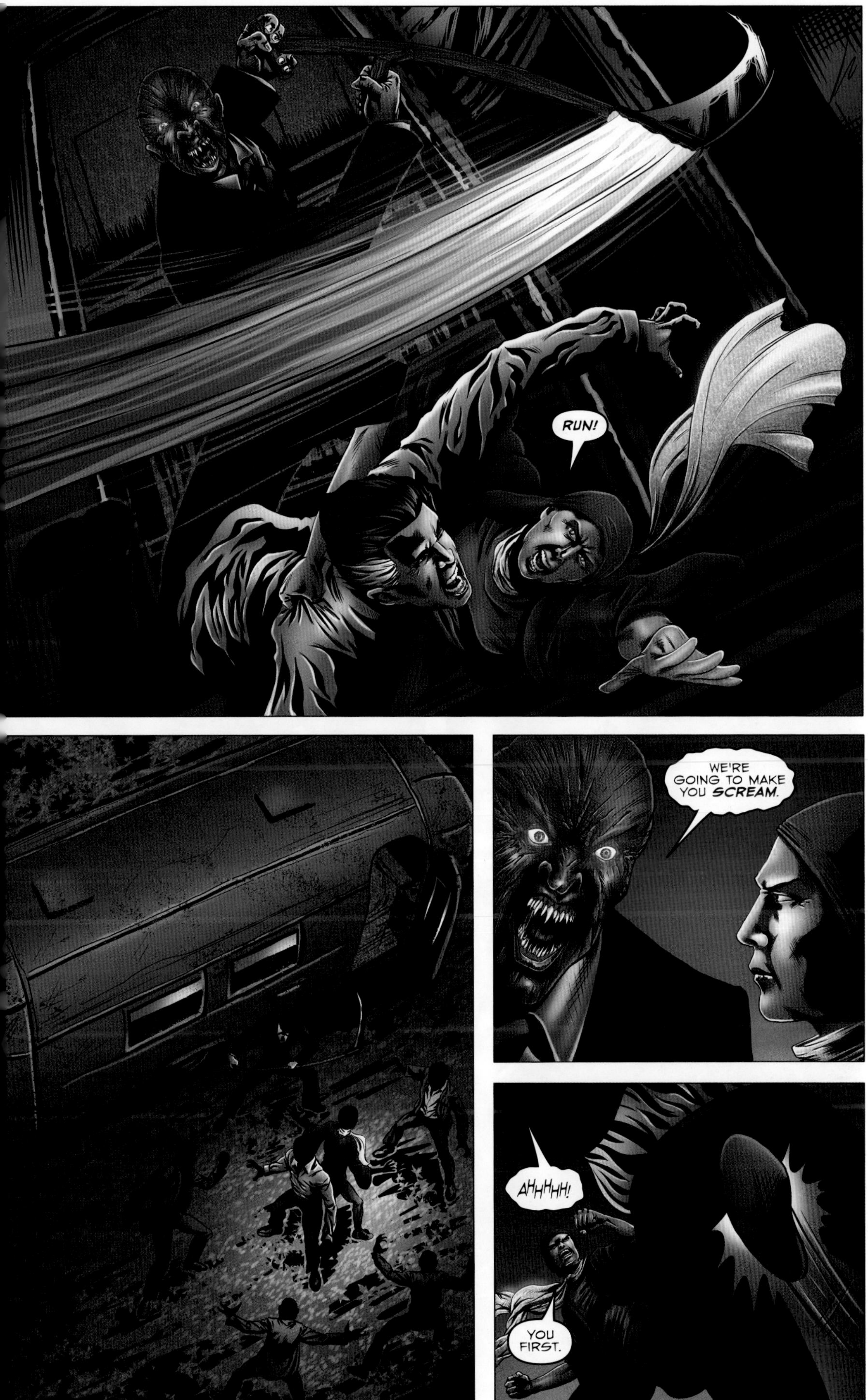

RUN!
WE'RE GOING TO MAKE YOU SCREAM.
AHHHHH!
YOU FIRST.

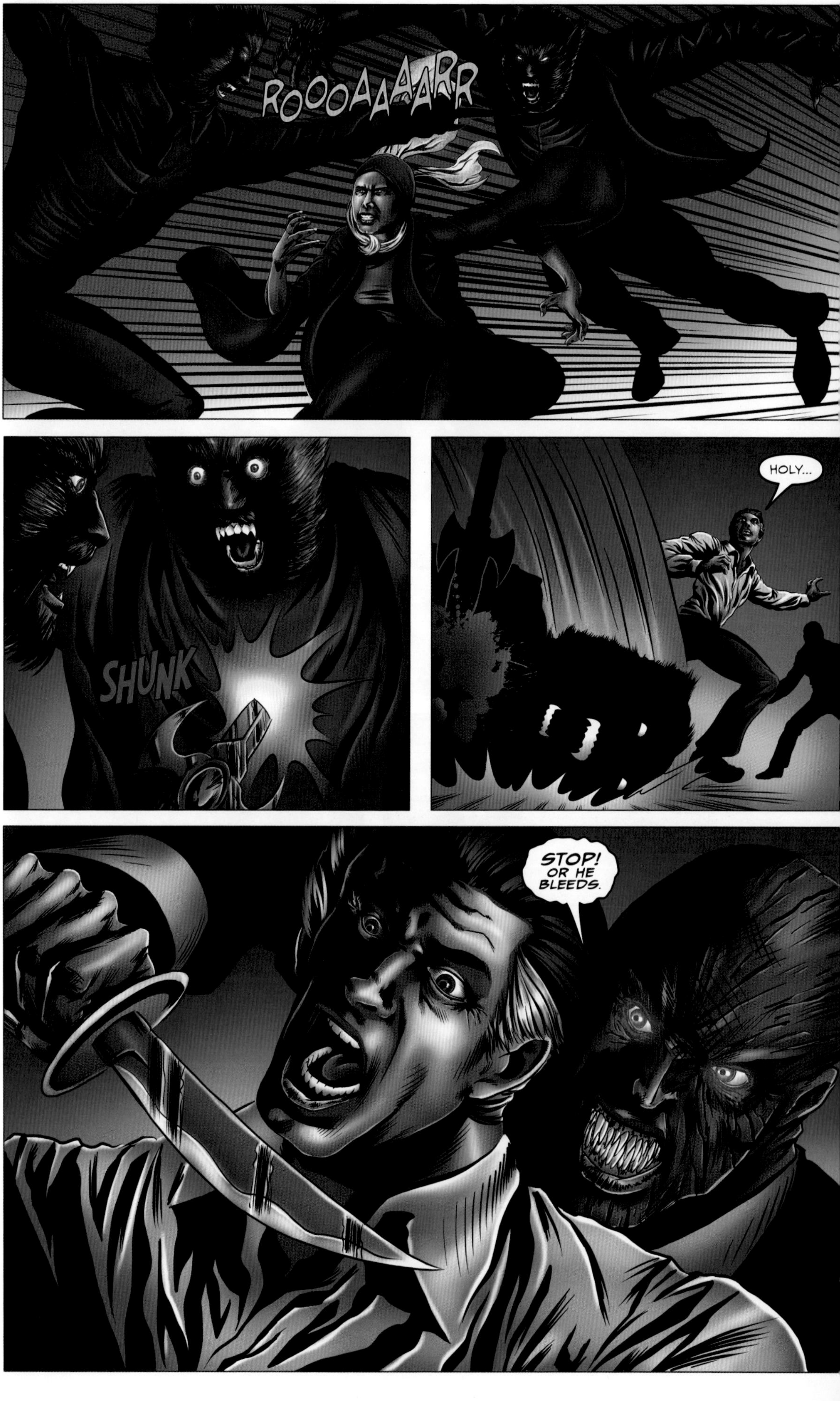
ROOOAAAARR
SHUNK
HOLY...
STOP! OR HE BLEEDS.

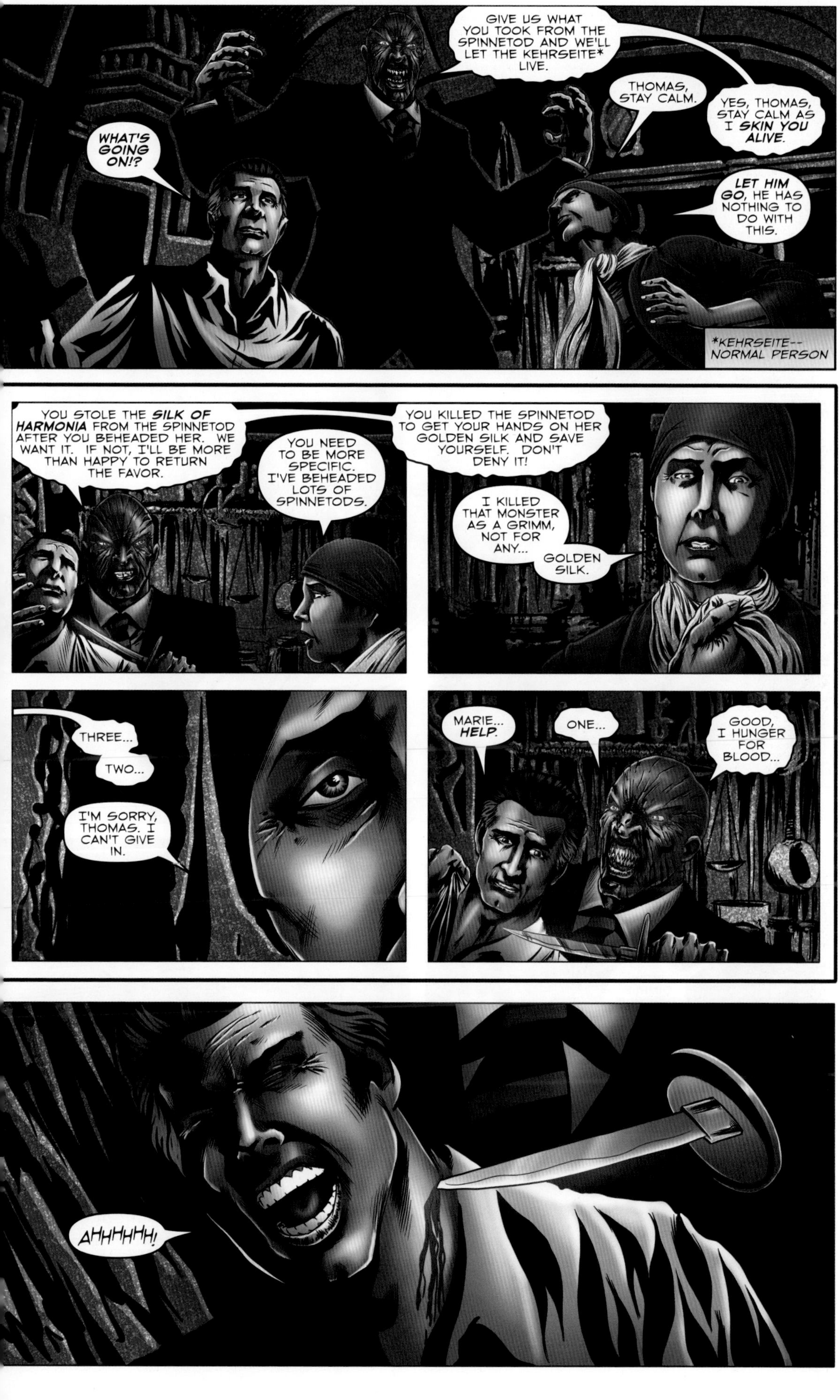
WHAT'S GOING ON!?
GIVE US WHAT YOU TOOK FROM THE SPINNETOD AND WE'LL LET THE KEHRSEITE* LIVE.
THOMAS, STAY CALM.
YES, THOMAS, STAY CALM AS I SKIN YOU ALIVE.
LET HIM GO, HE HAS NOTHING TO DO WITH THIS.
*KEHRSEITE-- NORMAL PERSON
YOU STOLE THE SILK OF HARMONIA FROM THE SPINNETOD AFTER YOU BEHEADED HER. WE WANT IT. IF NOT, I'LL BE MORE THAN HAPPY TO RETURN THE FAVOR.
YOU NEED TO BE MORE SPECIFIC. I'VE BEHEADED LOTS OF SPINNETODS.
YOU KILLED THE SPINNETOD TO GET YOUR HANDS ON HER GOLDEN SILK AND SAVE YOURSELF. DON'T DENY IT!
I KILLED THAT MONSTER AS A GRIMM, NOT FOR ANY...
GOLDEN SILK.
THREE...
TWO...
I'M SORRY, THOMAS. I CAN'T GIVE IN.
MARIE... HELP.
ONE...
GOOD, I HUNGER FOR BLOOD...
AHHHHHH!

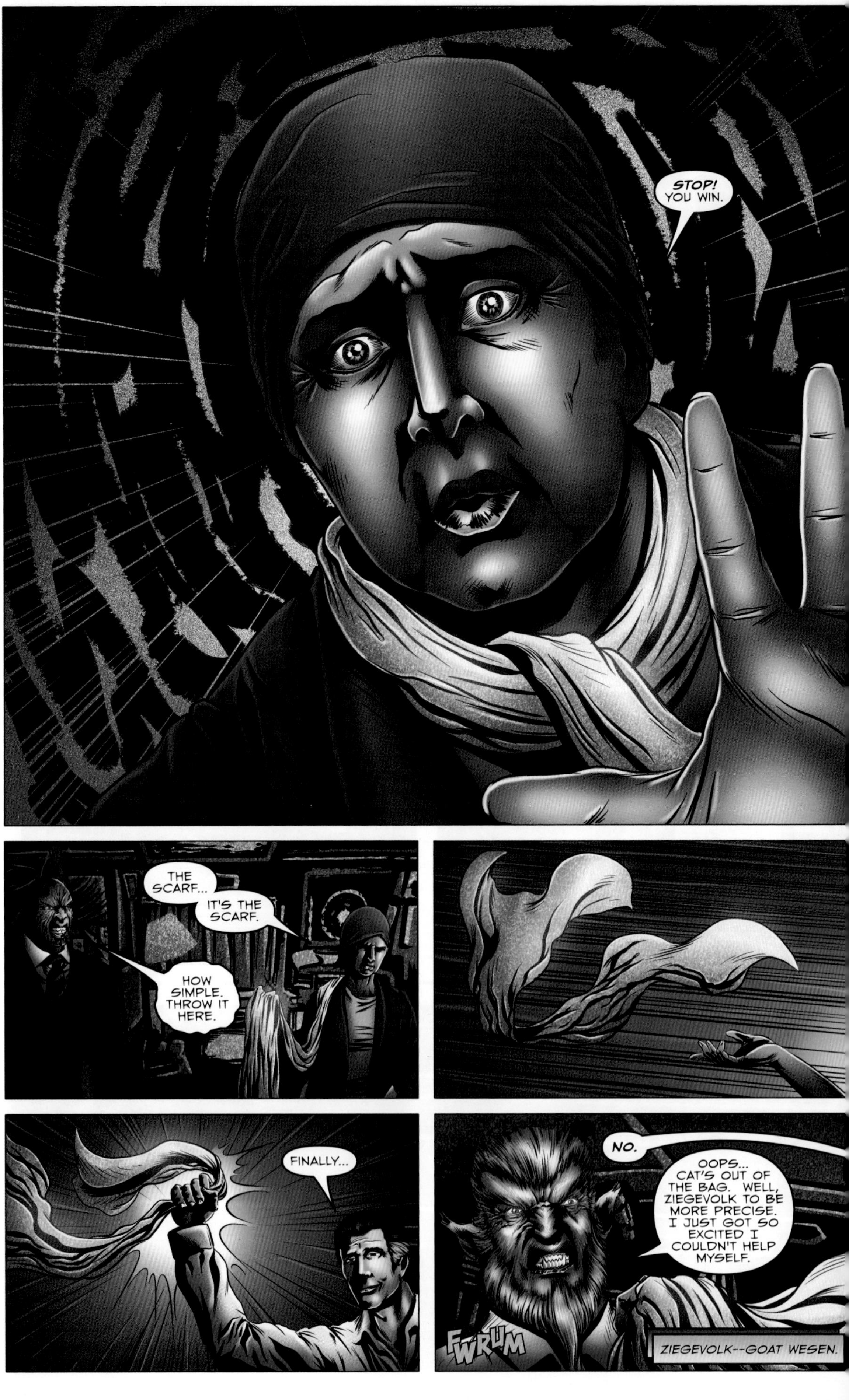
STOP! YOU WIN.
THE SCARF...
IT'S THE SCARF.
HOW SIMPLE. THROW IT HERE.
FINALLY...
NO.
OOPS... CAT'S OUT OF THE BAG. WELL, ZIEGEVOLK TO BE MORE PRECISE. I JUST GOT SO EXCITED I COULDN'T HELP MYSELF.
FWRUM
ZIEGEVOLK--GOAT WESEN.

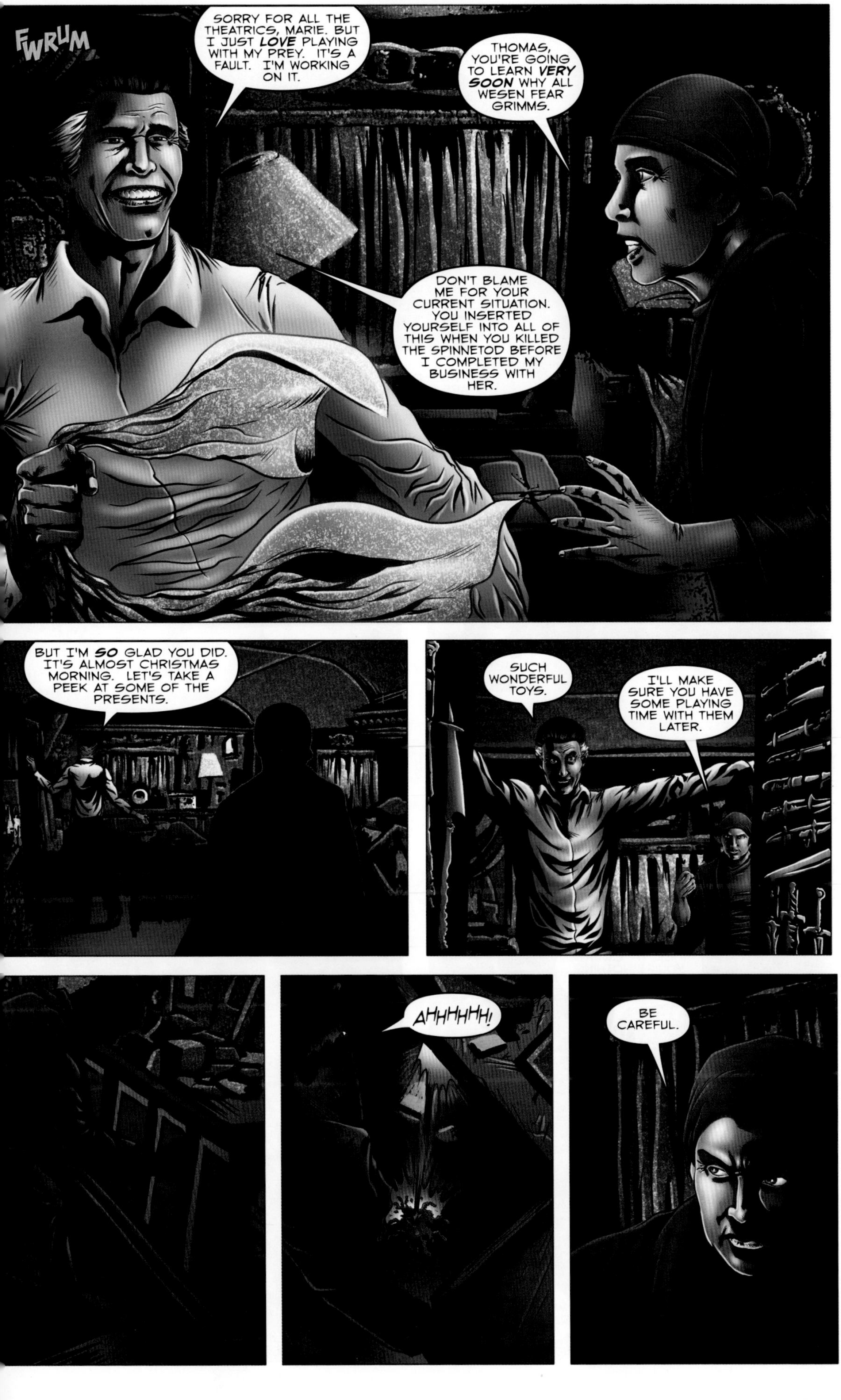
FWRUM
SORRY FOR ALL THE THEATRICS, MARIE. BUT I JUST LOVE PLAYING WITH MY PREY. IT'S A FAULT. I'M WORKING ON IT.
THOMAS, YOU'RE GOING TO LEARN VERY SOON WHY ALL WESEN FEAR GRIMMS.
DON'T BLAME ME FOR YOUR CURRENT SITUATION. YOU INSERTED YOURSELF INTO ALL OF THIS WHEN YOU KILLED THE SPINNETOD BEFORE I COMPLETED MY BUSINESS WITH HER.
BUT I'M SO GLAD YOU DID. IT'S ALMOST CHRISTMAS MORNING. LET'S TAKE A PEEK AT SOME OF THE PRESENTS.
SUCH WONDERFUL TOYS.
I'LL MAKE SURE YOU HAVE SOME PLAYING TIME WITH THEM LATER.
AHHHHHH!
BE CAREFUL.

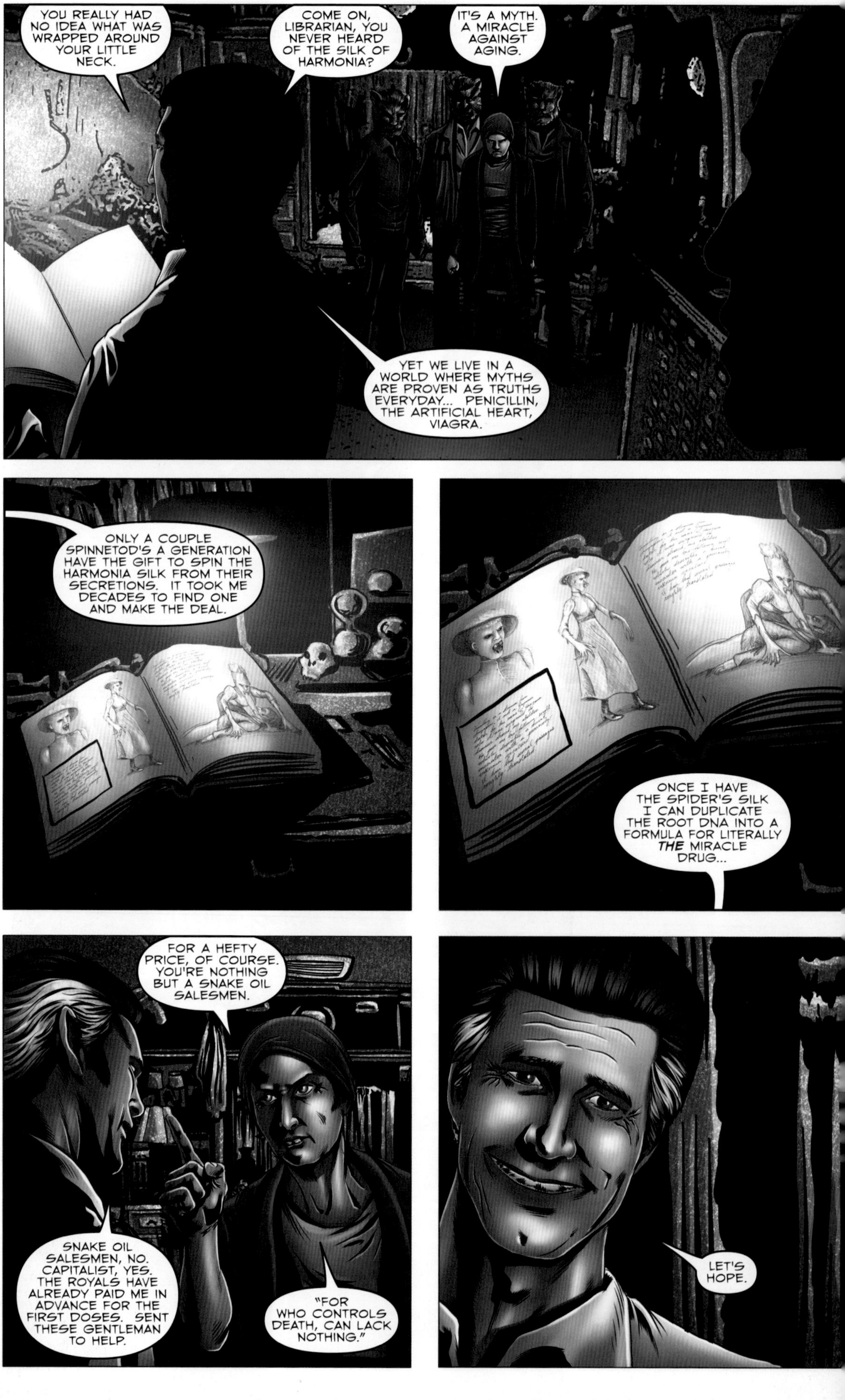
YOU REALLY HAD NO IDEA WHAT WAS WRAPPED AROUND YOUR LITTLE NECK.
COME ON, LIBRARIAN, YOU NEVER HEARD OF THE SILK OF HARMONIA?
IT'S A MYTH. A MIRACLE AGAINST AGING.
YET WE LIVE IN A WORLD WHERE MYTHS ARE PROVEN AS TRUTHS EVERYDAY... PENICILLIN, THE ARTIFICIAL HEART, VIAGRA.
ONLY A COUPLE SPINNETOD'S A GENERATION HAVE THE GIFT TO SPIN THE HARMONIA SILK FROM THEIR SECRETIONS. IT TOOK ME DECADES TO FIND ONE AND MAKE THE DEAL.
ONCE I HAVE THE SPIDER'S SILK I CAN DUPLICATE THE ROOT DNA INTO A FORMULA FOR LITERALLY THE MIRACLE DRUG...
FOR A HEFTY PRICE, OF COURSE. YOU'RE NOTHING BUT A SNAKE OIL SALESMEN.
SNAKE OIL SALESMEN, NO. CAPITALIST, YES. THE ROYALS HAVE ALREADY PAID ME IN ADVANCE FOR THE FIRST DOSES. SENT THESE GENTLEMAN TO HELP.
"FOR WHO CONTROLS DEATH, CAN LACK NOTHING."
LET'S HOPE.

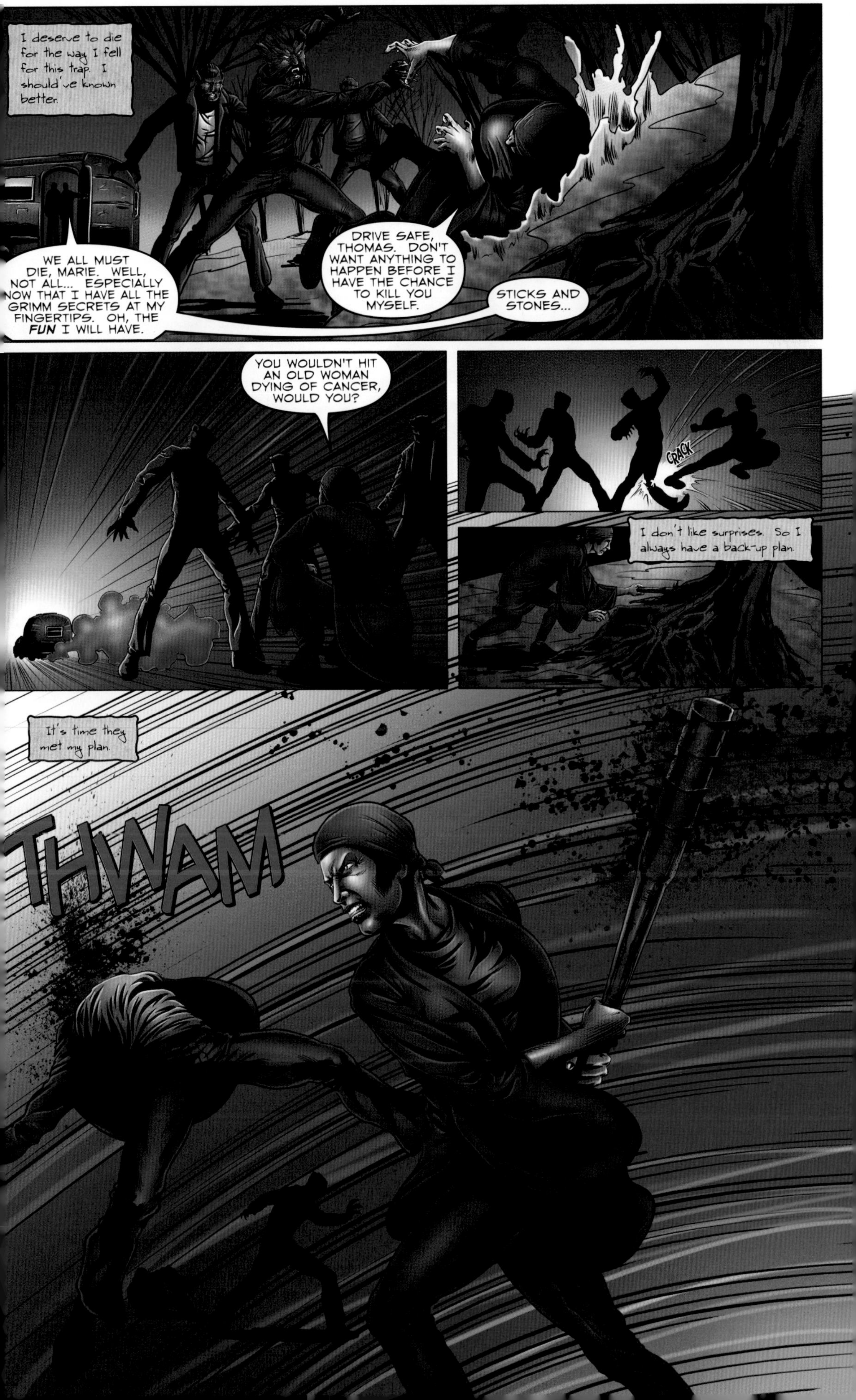
I deserve to die for the way I fell for this trap. I should've known better.
WE ALL MUST DIE, MARIE. WELL, NOT ALL... ESPECIALLY NOW THAT I HAVE ALL THE GRIMM SECRETS AT MY FINGERTIPS. OH, THE FUN I WILL HAVE.
DRIVE SAFE, THOMAS. DON'T WANT ANYTHING TO HAPPEN BEFORE I HAVE THE CHANCE TO KILL YOU MYSELF.
STICKS AND STONES...
YOU WOULDN'T HIT AN OLD WOMAN DYING OF CANCER, WOULD YOU?
CRACK
I don't like surprises. So I always have a back-up plan.
It's time they met my plan.
THWAM

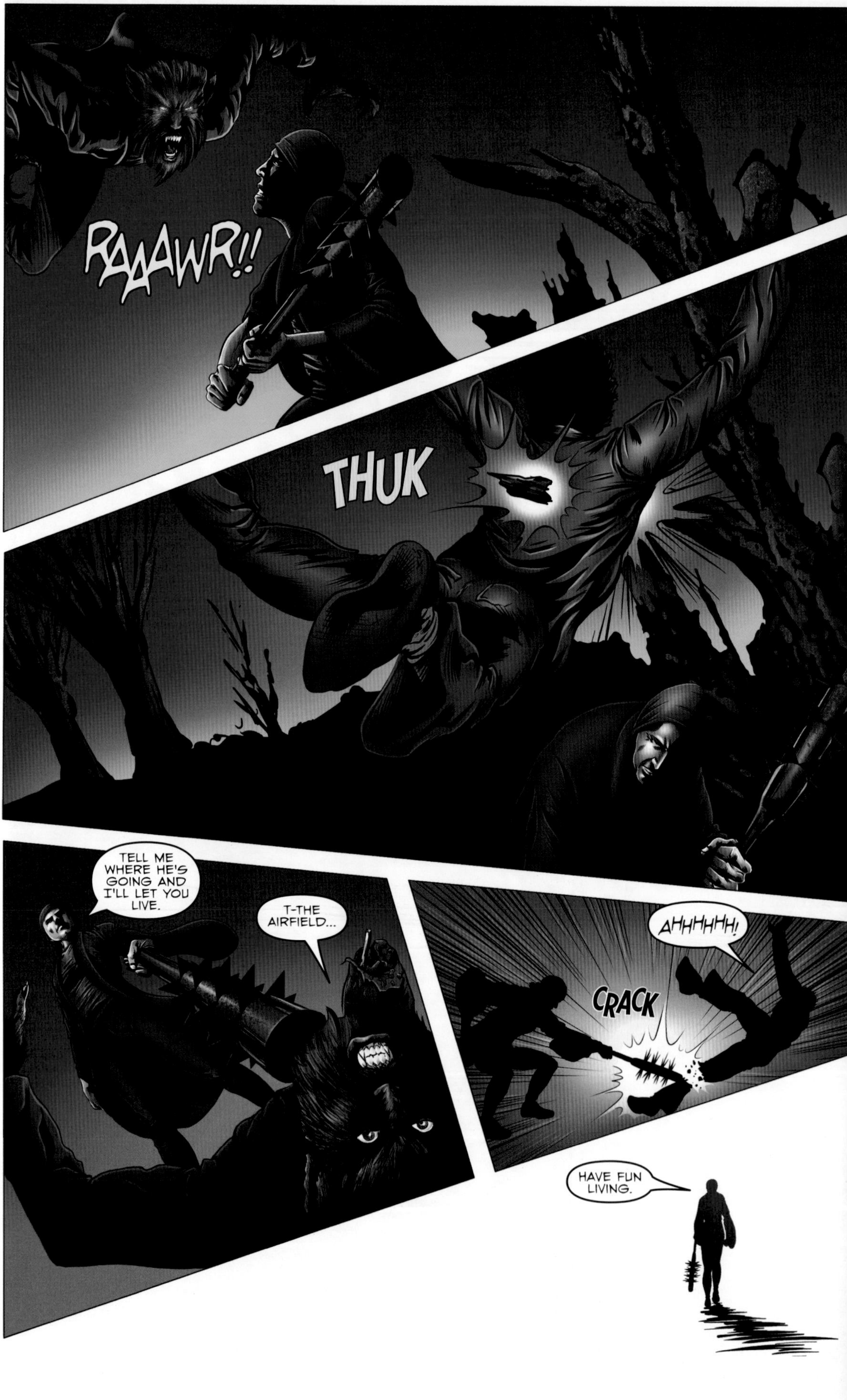
RAAAWR!!
THUK
TELL ME WHERE HE'S GOING AND I'LL LET YOU LIVE.
T-THE AIRFIELD...
AHHHHHH!
CRACK
HAVE FUN LIVING.

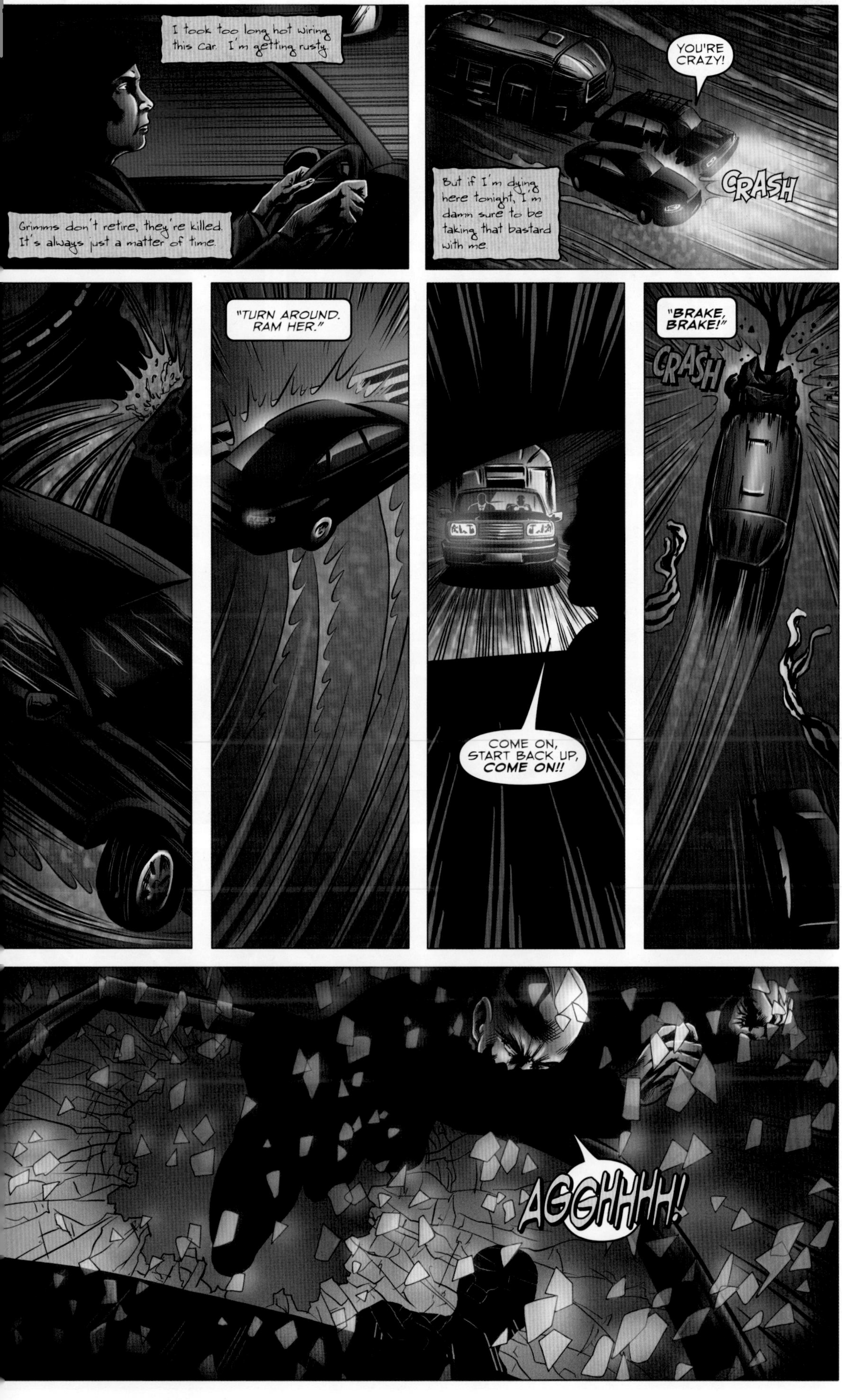

I took too long hot wiring this car. I'm getting rusty.
Grimms don't retire, they're killed. It's always just a matter of time.
YOU'RE CRAZY!
But if I'm dying here tonight, I'm damn sure to be taking that bastard with me.
CRASH
"TURN AROUND. RAM HER."
COME ON, START BACK UP, COME ON!!
"BRAKE, BRAKE!"
CRASH
AGGHHHH!

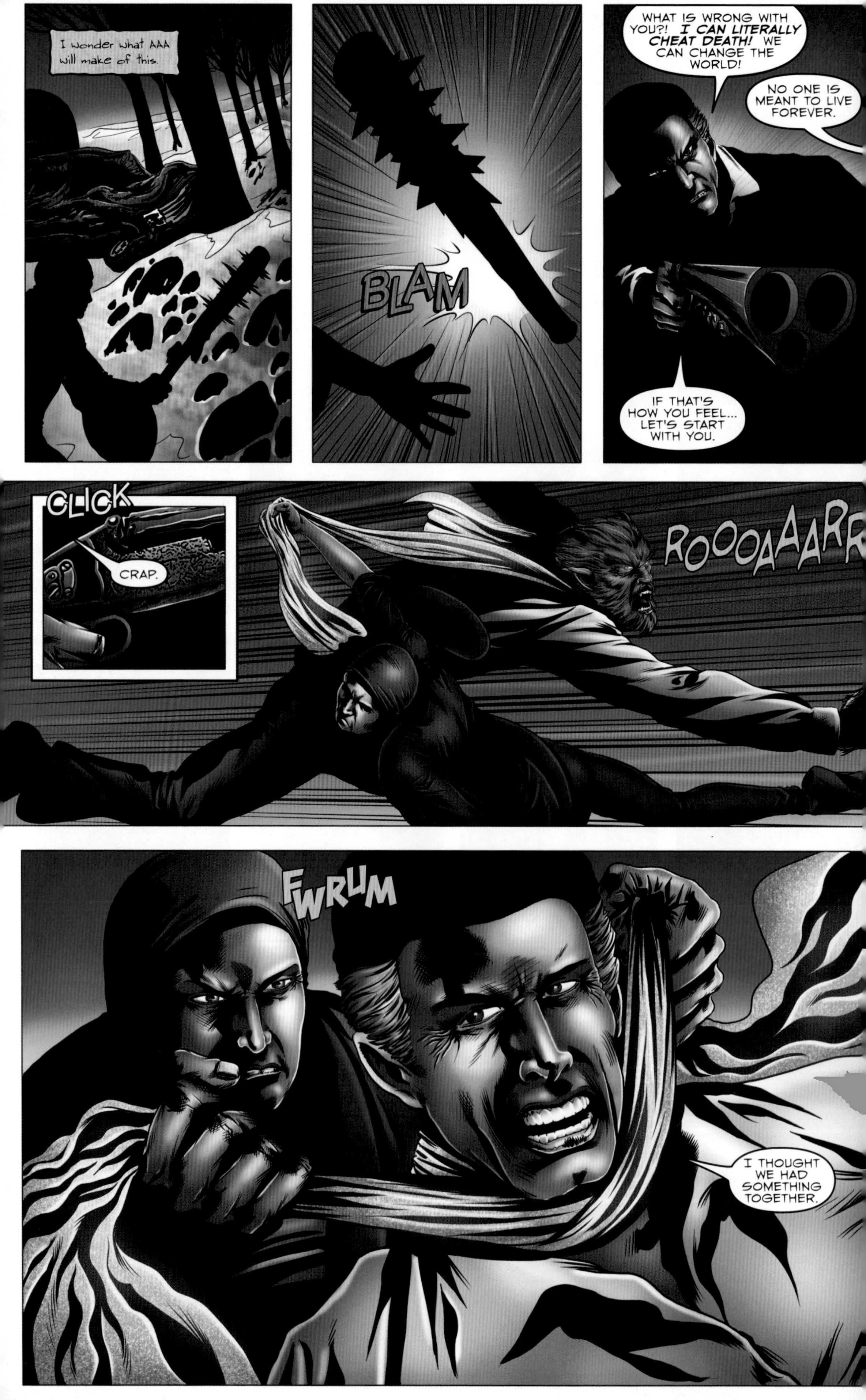
I wonder what AAA will make of this.
BLAM
WHAT IS WRONG WITH YOU?! I CAN LITERALLY CHEAT DEATH! WE CAN CHANGE THE WORLD!
NO ONE IS MEANT TO LIVE FOREVER.
IF THAT'S HOW YOU FEEL... LET'S START WITH YOU.
CLICK
CRAP.
ROOOAAARR
FWRUM
I THOUGHT WE HAD SOMETHING TOGETHER.

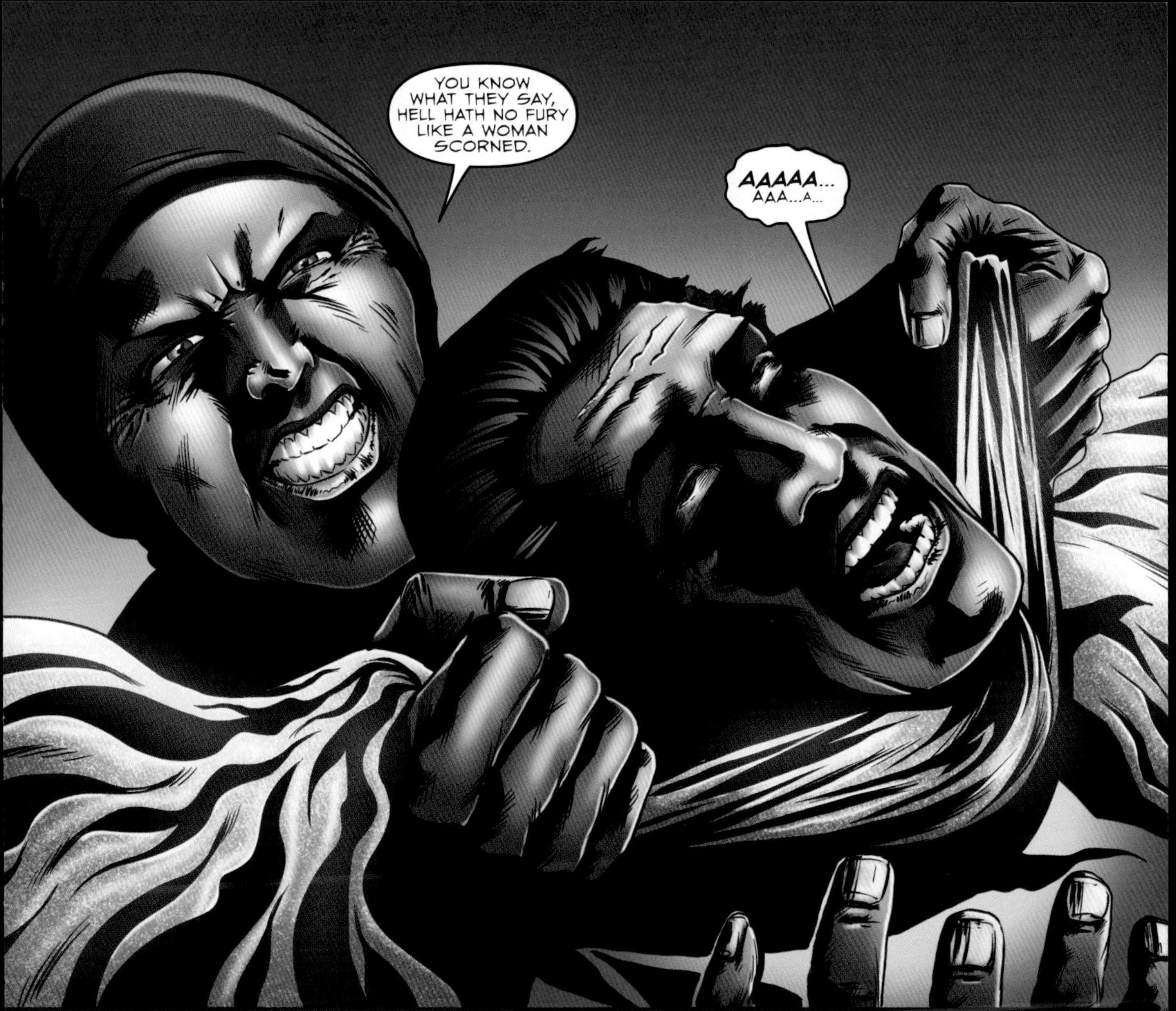
YOU KNOW WHAT THEY SAY, HELL HATH NO FURY LIKE A WOMAN SCORNED.
AAAAA... AAA...A...
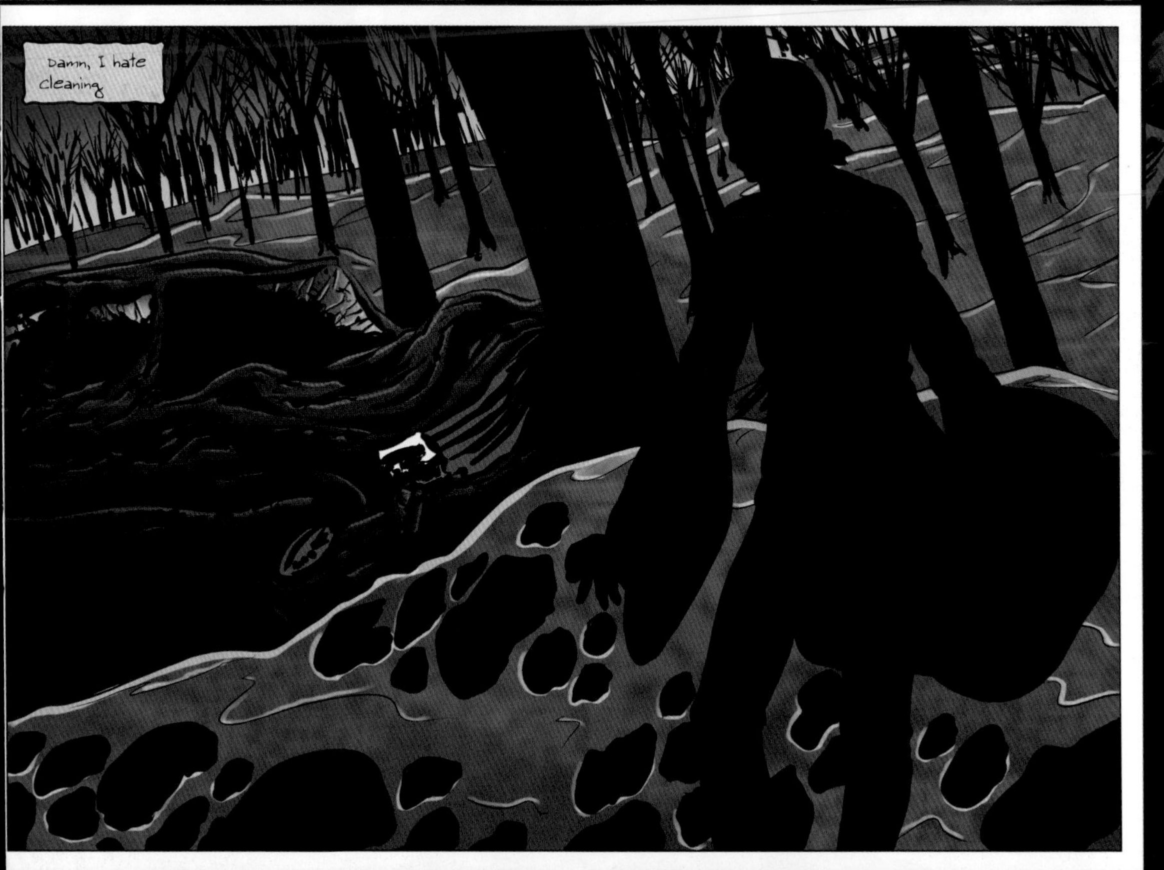
Damn, I hate cleaning.

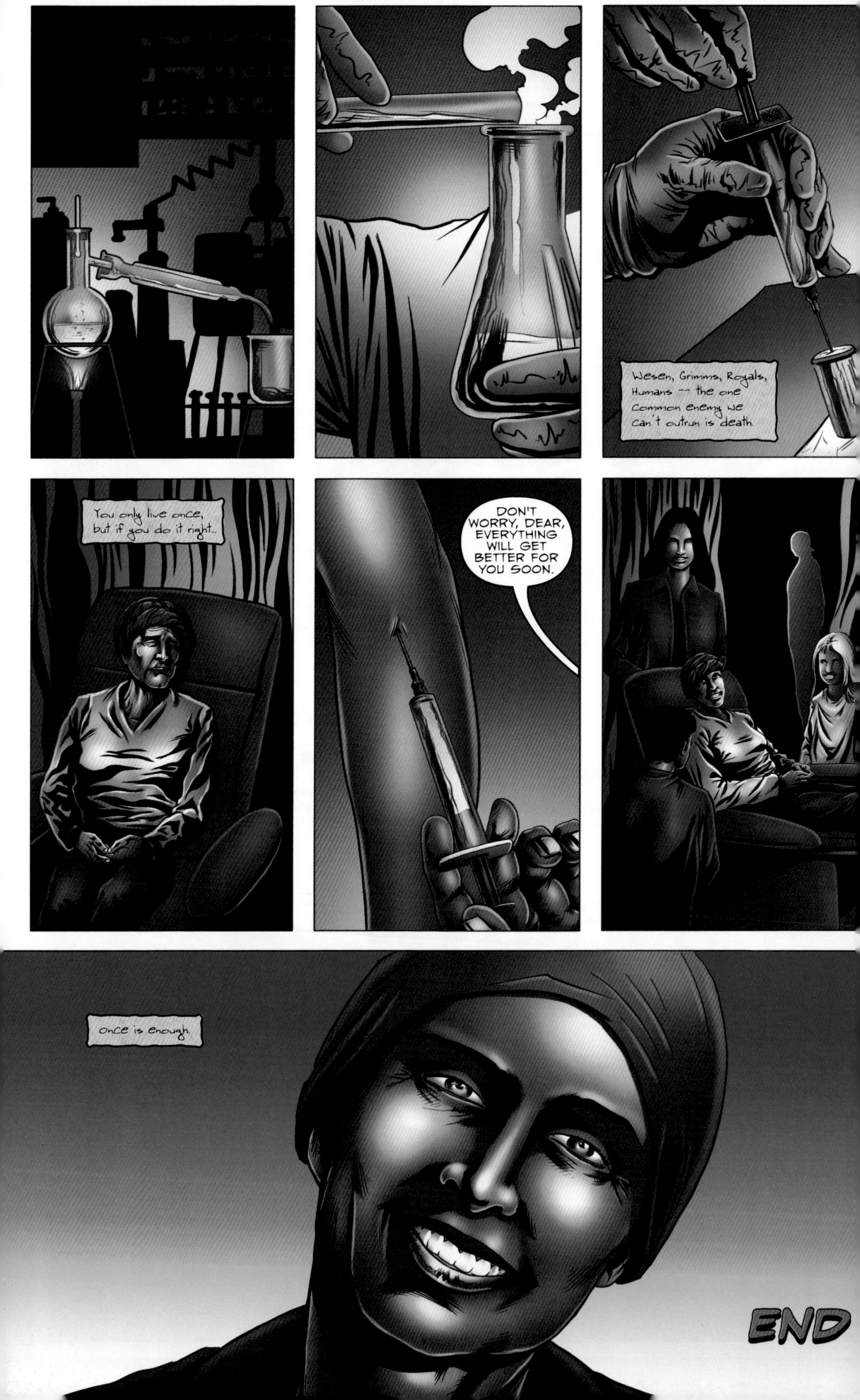
Wesen, Grimms, Royals, Humans -- the one common enemy we can't outrun is death.
You only live once, but if you do it right...
DON'T WORRY, DEAR, EVERYTHING WILL GET BETTER FOR YOU SOON.
once is enough.
END

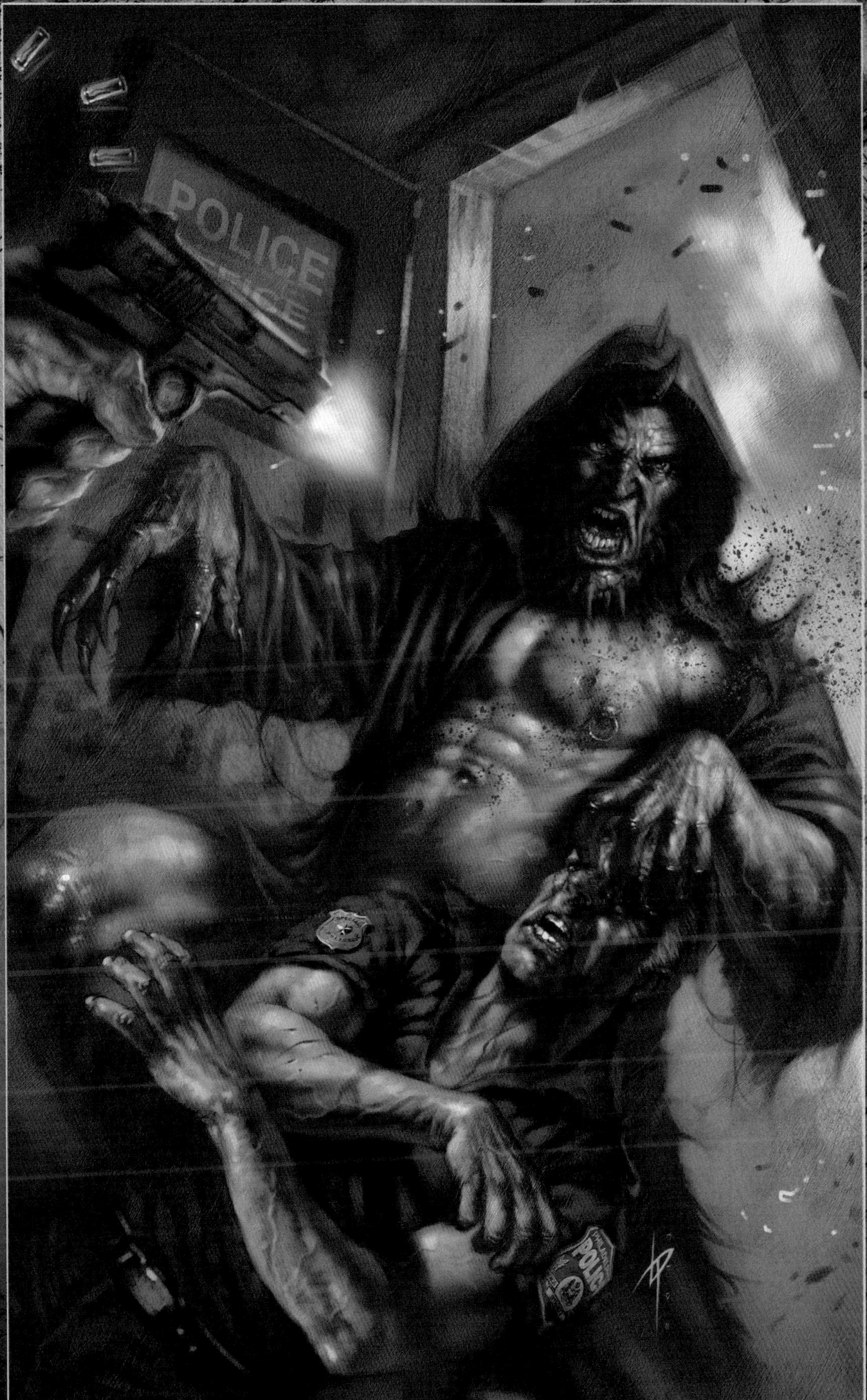
POLICE

ISSUE #9 COVER

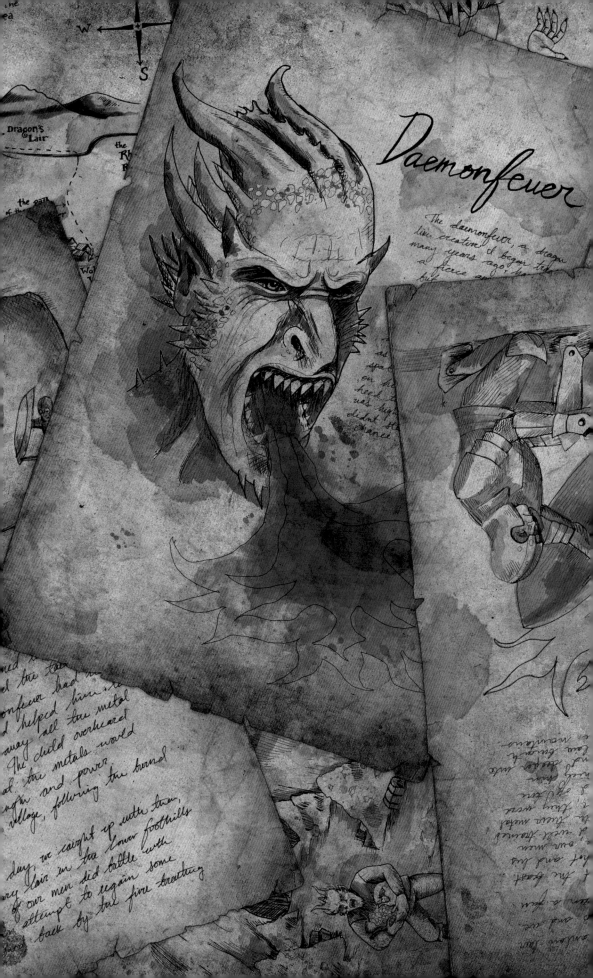

Daemonfeuer

The daemonfeur, a dragon
like creature, it began
many years ago, ...
a fierce ...
but ...

... the ...
... onfeuer had ...
d helped him ...
away all the metal
The child overheard
... of the metals would
... night and power
village, following the burned

... day, we caught up with them,
... lair in the lower foothills
of our men did battle with
... attempt to regain some
... back by the fire breathing

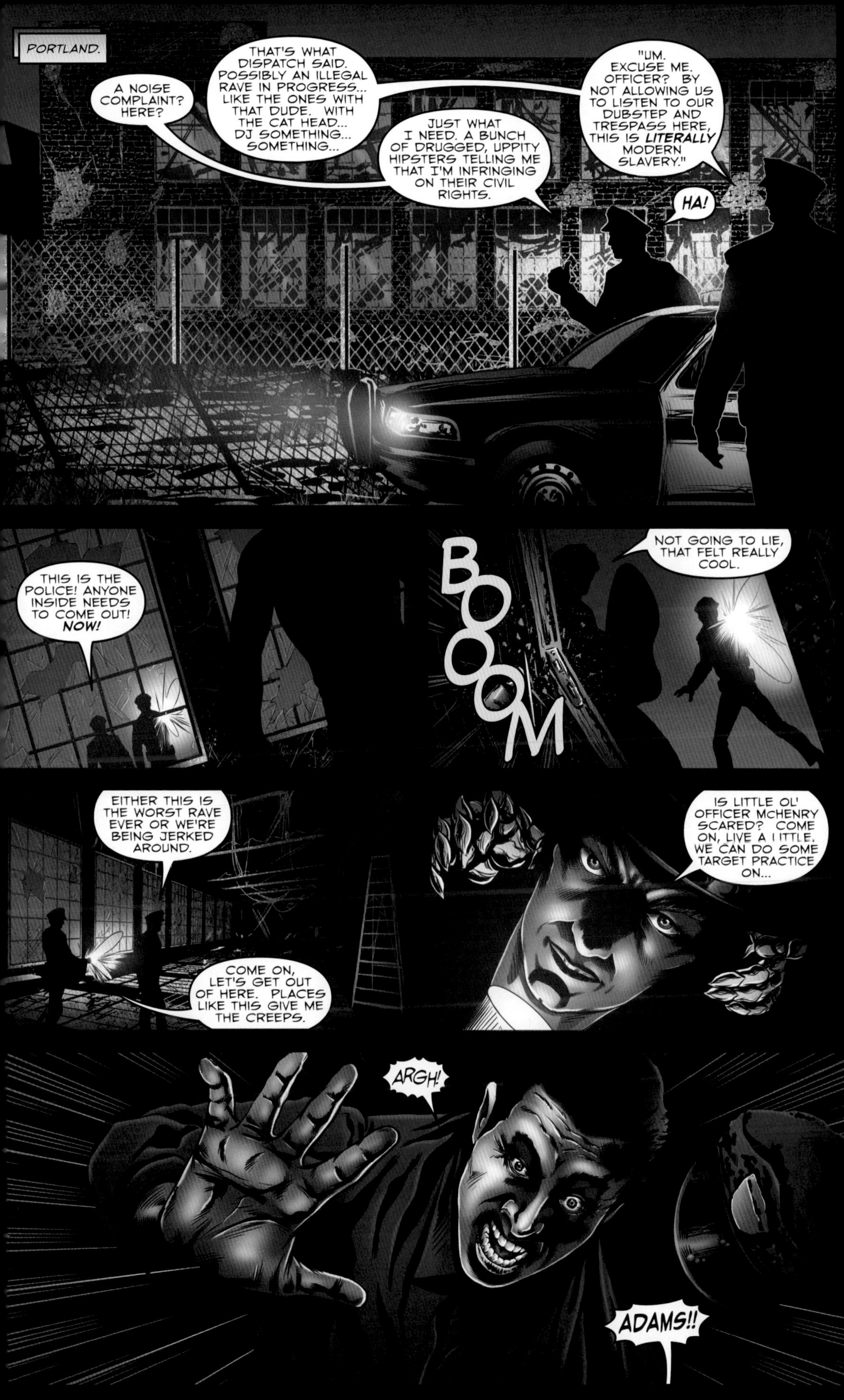
PORTLAND.
A NOISE COMPLAINT? HERE?
THAT'S WHAT DISPATCH SAID. POSSIBLY AN ILLEGAL RAVE IN PROGRESS... LIKE THE ONES WITH THAT DUDE. WITH THE CAT HEAD... DJ SOMETHING... SOMETHING...
JUST WHAT I NEED. A BUNCH OF DRUGGED, UPPITY HIPSTERS TELLING ME THAT I'M INFRINGING ON THEIR CIVIL RIGHTS.
"UM. EXCUSE ME. OFFICER? BY NOT ALLOWING US TO LISTEN TO OUR DUBSTEP AND TRESPASS HERE, THIS IS LITERALLY MODERN SLAVERY."
HA!
THIS IS THE POLICE! ANYONE INSIDE NEEDS TO COME OUT! NOW!
BOOOOM
NOT GOING TO LIE, THAT FELT REALLY COOL.
EITHER THIS IS THE WORST RAVE EVER OR WE'RE BEING JERKED AROUND.
COME ON, LET'S GET OUT OF HERE. PLACES LIKE THIS GIVE ME THE CREEPS.
IS LITTLE OL' OFFICER McHENRY SCARED? COME ON, LIVE A LITTLE. WE CAN DO SOME TARGET PRACTICE ON...
ARGH!
ADAMS!!

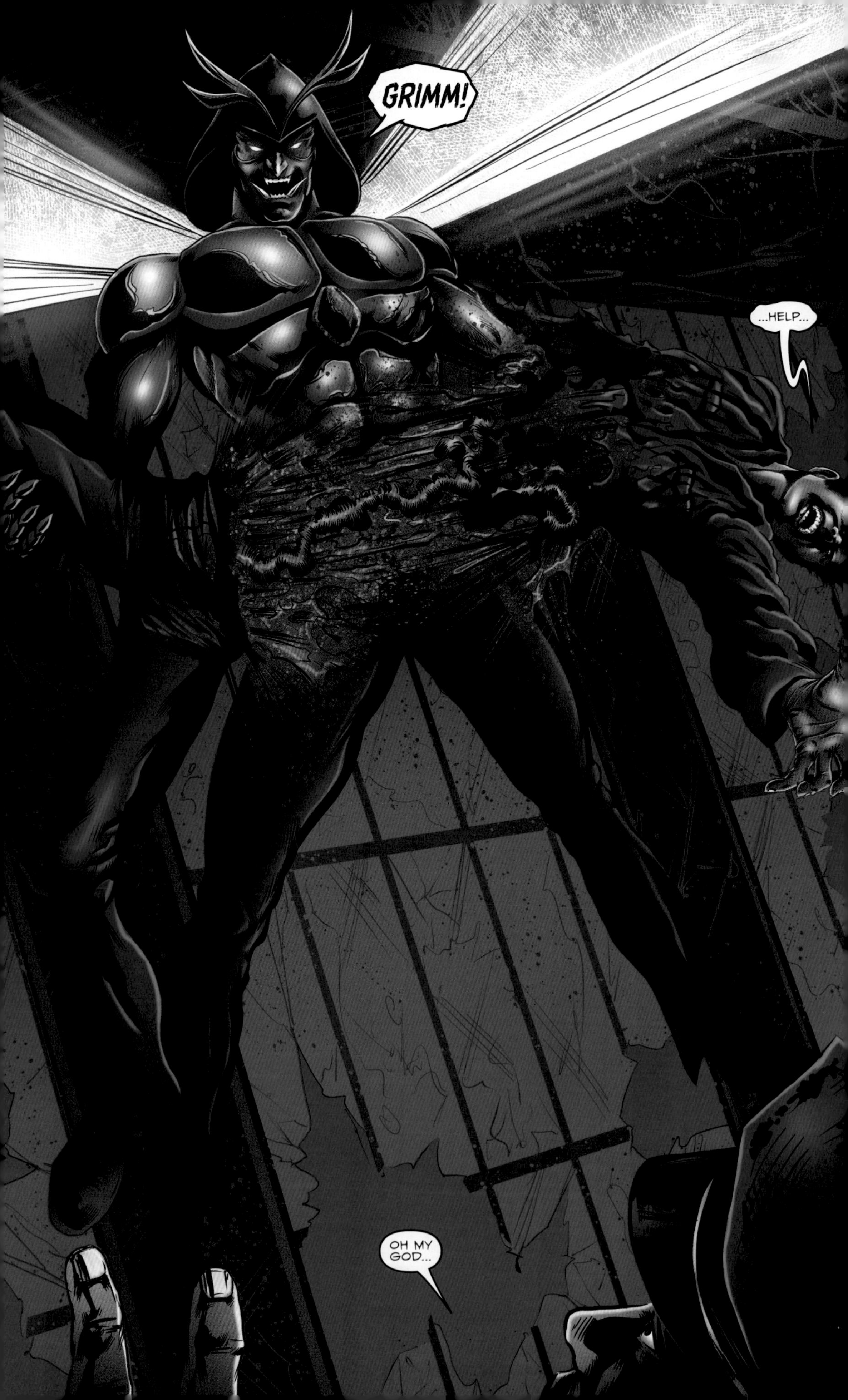
GRIMM!
...HELP...
OH MY GOD...

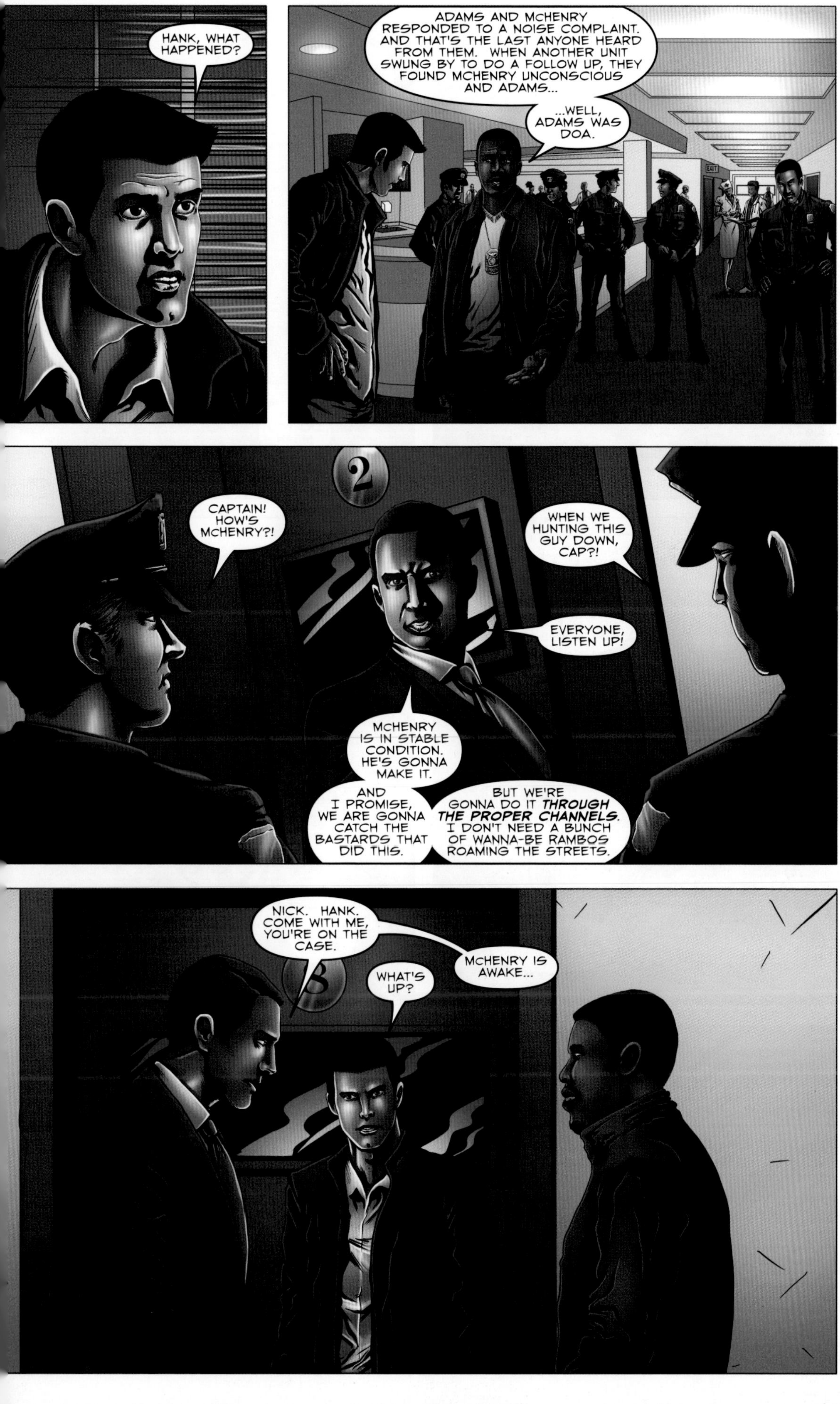
HANK, WHAT HAPPENED?
ADAMS AND McHENRY RESPONDED TO A NOISE COMPLAINT. AND THAT'S THE LAST ANYONE HEARD FROM THEM. WHEN ANOTHER UNIT SWUNG BY TO DO A FOLLOW UP, THEY FOUND MCHENRY UNCONSCIOUS AND ADAMS...
...WELL, ADAMS WAS DOA.
EXIT
2
CAPTAIN! HOW'S McHENRY?!
WHEN WE HUNTING THIS GUY DOWN, CAP?!
EVERYONE, LISTEN UP!
McHENRY IS IN STABLE CONDITION. HE'S GONNA MAKE IT.
AND I PROMISE, WE ARE GONNA CATCH THE BASTARDS THAT DID THIS.
BUT WE'RE GONNA DO IT *THROUGH THE PROPER CHANNELS*. I DON'T NEED A BUNCH OF WANNA-BE RAMBOS ROAMING THE STREETS.
3
NICK. HANK. COME WITH ME, YOU'RE ON THE CASE.
WHAT'S UP?
McHENRY IS AWAKE...

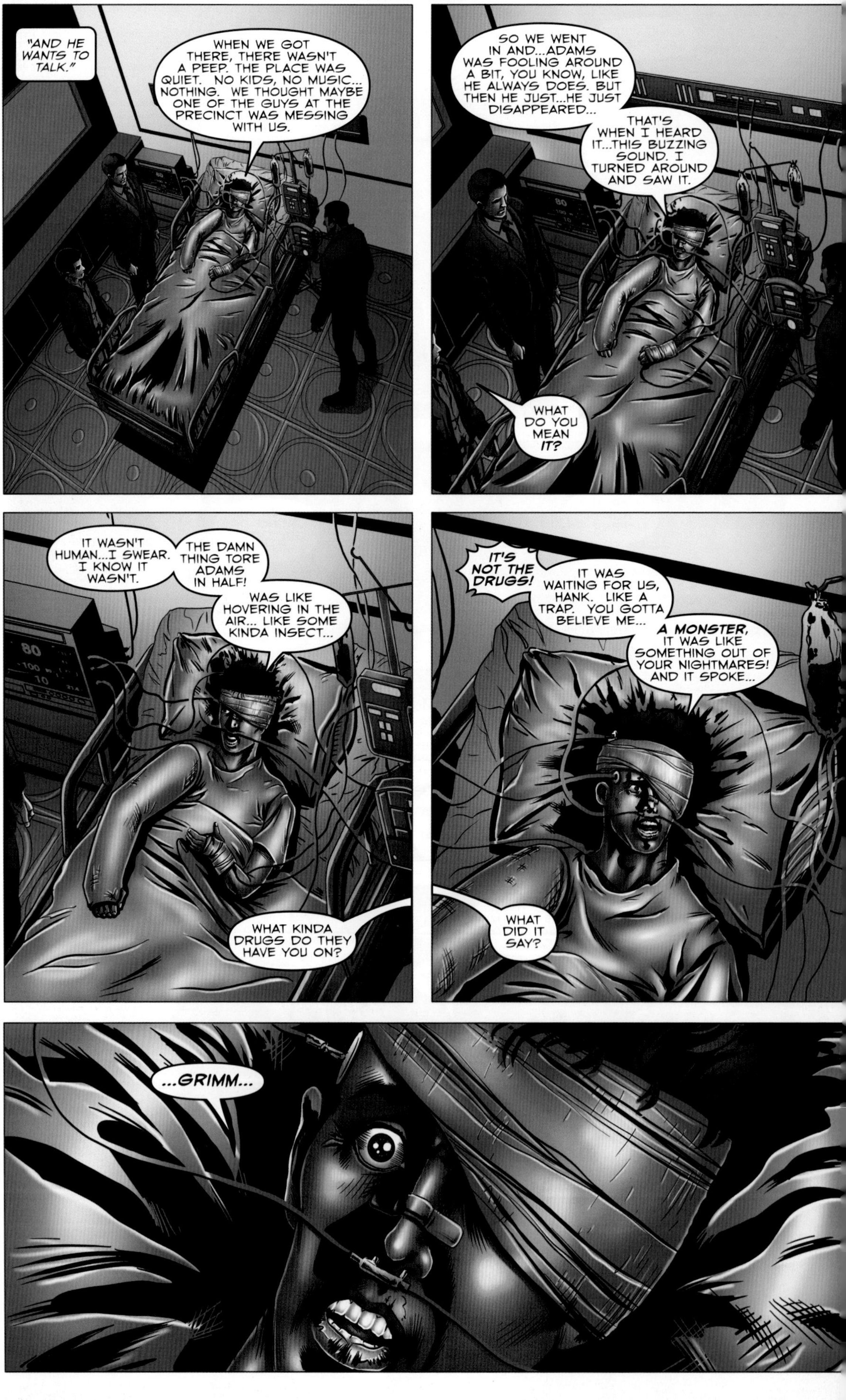
"AND HE WANTS TO TALK."
WHEN WE GOT THERE, THERE WASN'T A PEEP. THE PLACE WAS QUIET. NO KIDS, NO MUSIC... NOTHING. WE THOUGHT MAYBE ONE OF THE GUYS AT THE PRECINCT WAS MESSING WITH US.
SO WE WENT IN AND...ADAMS WAS FOOLING AROUND A BIT, YOU KNOW, LIKE HE ALWAYS DOES. BUT THEN HE JUST...HE JUST DISAPPEARED...
THAT'S WHEN I HEARD IT...THIS BUZZING SOUND. I TURNED AROUND AND SAW IT.
WHAT DO YOU MEAN IT?
IT WASN'T HUMAN...I SWEAR. I KNOW IT WASN'T.
THE DAMN THING TORE ADAMS IN HALF!
WAS LIKE HOVERING IN THE AIR... LIKE SOME KINDA INSECT...
WHAT KINDA DRUGS DO THEY HAVE YOU ON?
IT'S NOT THE DRUGS!
IT WAS WAITING FOR US, HANK. LIKE A TRAP. YOU GOTTA BELIEVE ME...
A MONSTER, IT WAS LIKE SOMETHING OUT OF YOUR NIGHTMARES! AND IT SPOKE...
WHAT DID IT SAY?
...GRIMM...

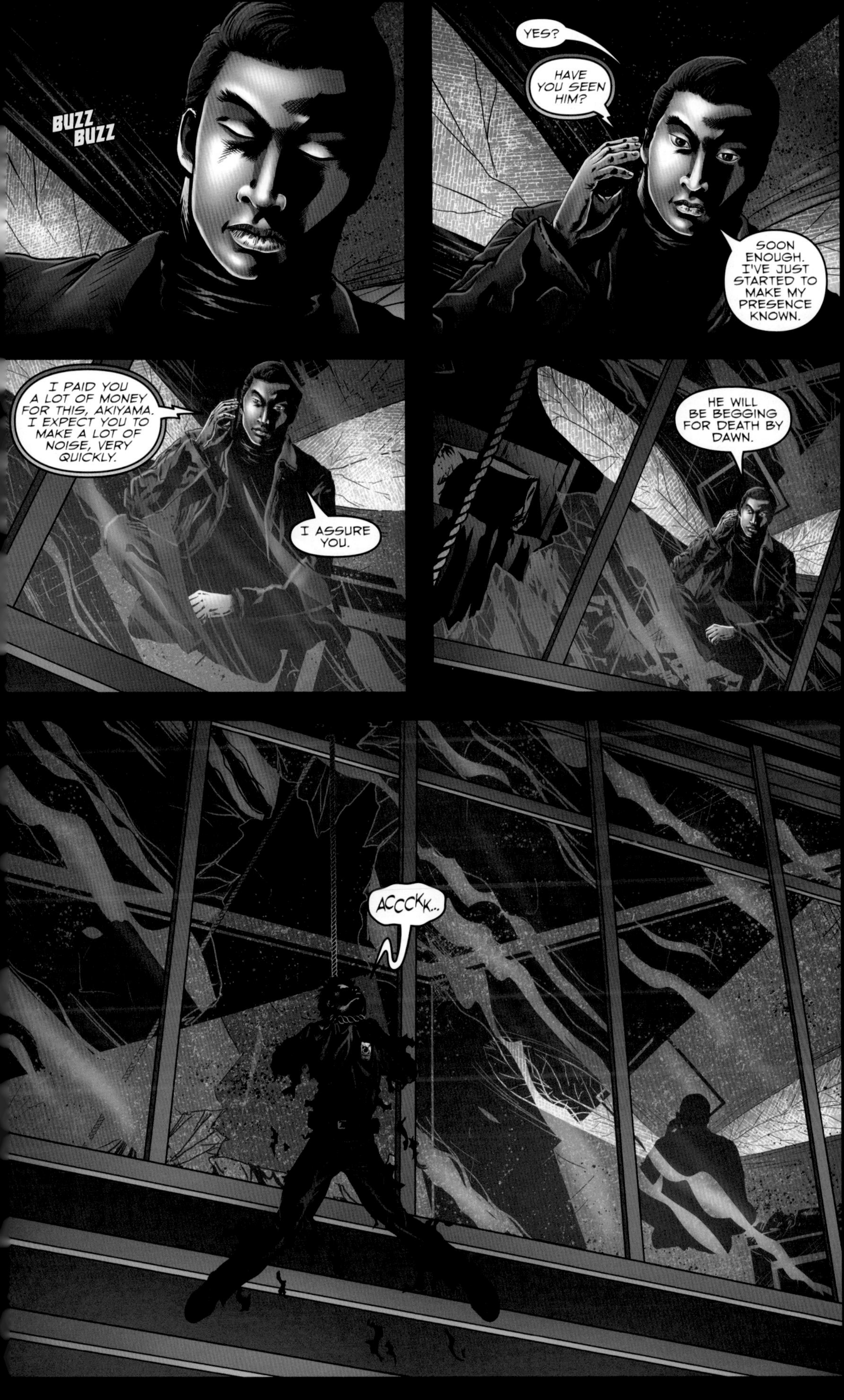
BUZZ BUZZ
YES?
HAVE YOU SEEN HIM?
SOON ENOUGH. I'VE JUST STARTED TO MAKE MY PRESENCE KNOWN.
I PAID YOU A LOT OF MONEY FOR THIS, AKIYAMA. I EXPECT YOU TO MAKE A LOT OF NOISE, VERY QUICKLY.
I ASSURE YOU.
HE WILL BE BEGGING FOR DEATH BY DAWN.
ACCCKK...

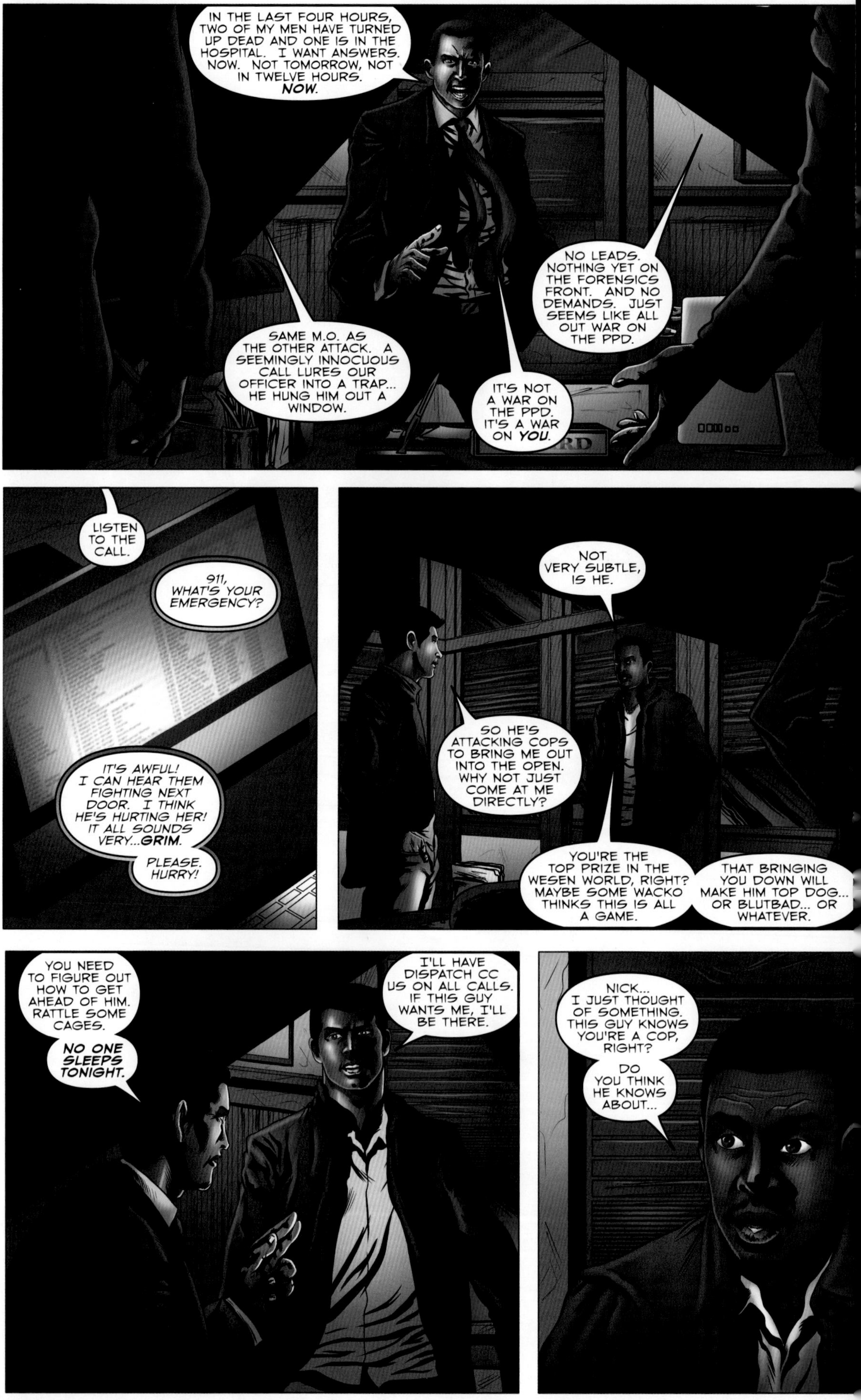
IN THE LAST FOUR HOURS, TWO OF MY MEN HAVE TURNED UP DEAD AND ONE IS IN THE HOSPITAL. I WANT ANSWERS. NOW. NOT TOMORROW, NOT IN TWELVE HOURS. NOW.
SAME M.O. AS THE OTHER ATTACK. A SEEMINGLY INNOCUOUS CALL LURES OUR OFFICER INTO A TRAP... HE HUNG HIM OUT A WINDOW.
NO LEADS. NOTHING YET ON THE FORENSICS FRONT. AND NO DEMANDS. JUST SEEMS LIKE ALL OUT WAR ON THE PPD.
IT'S NOT A WAR ON THE PPD. IT'S A WAR ON YOU.
LISTEN TO THE CALL.
911, WHAT'S YOUR EMERGENCY?
IT'S AWFUL! I CAN HEAR THEM FIGHTING NEXT DOOR. I THINK HE'S HURTING HER! IT ALL SOUNDS VERY...GRIM.
PLEASE. HURRY!
NOT VERY SUBTLE, IS HE.
SO HE'S ATTACKING COPS TO BRING ME OUT INTO THE OPEN. WHY NOT JUST COME AT ME DIRECTLY?
YOU'RE THE TOP PRIZE IN THE WESEN WORLD, RIGHT? MAYBE SOME WACKO THINKS THIS IS ALL A GAME.
THAT BRINGING YOU DOWN WILL MAKE HIM TOP DOG... OR BLUTBAD... OR WHATEVER.
YOU NEED TO FIGURE OUT HOW TO GET AHEAD OF HIM. RATTLE SOME CAGES.
NO ONE SLEEPS TONIGHT.
I'LL HAVE DISPATCH CC US ON ALL CALLS. IF THIS GUY WANTS ME, I'LL BE THERE.
NICK... I JUST THOUGHT OF SOMETHING. THIS GUY KNOWS YOU'RE A COP, RIGHT?
DO YOU THINK HE KNOWS ABOUT...

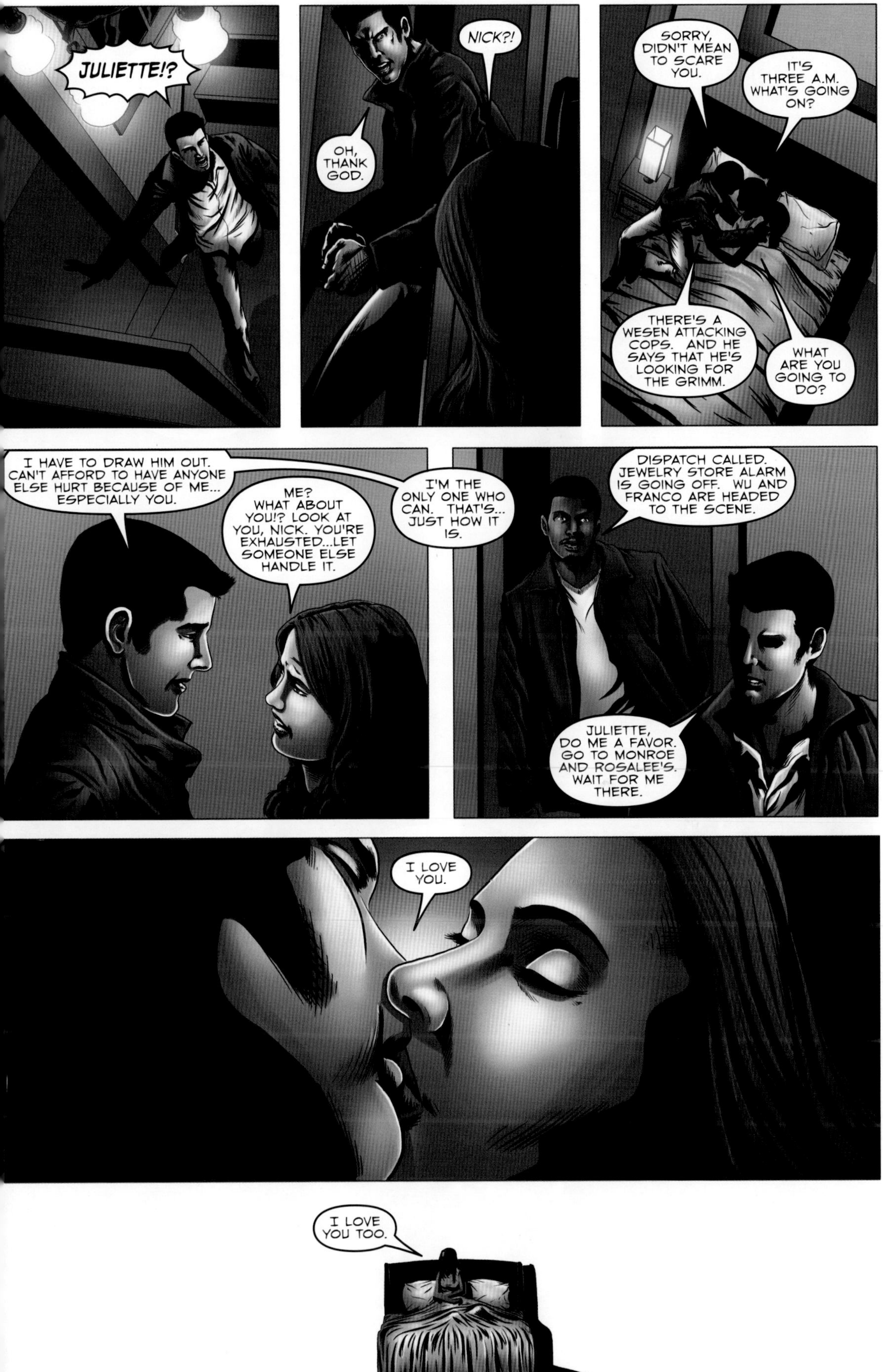
JULIETTE!?
NICK?!
OH, THANK GOD.
SORRY, DIDN'T MEAN TO SCARE YOU.
IT'S THREE A.M. WHAT'S GOING ON?
THERE'S A WESEN ATTACKING COPS. AND HE SAYS THAT HE'S LOOKING FOR THE GRIMM.
WHAT ARE YOU GOING TO DO?
I HAVE TO DRAW HIM OUT. CAN'T AFFORD TO HAVE ANYONE ELSE HURT BECAUSE OF ME... ESPECIALLY YOU.
ME? WHAT ABOUT YOU!? LOOK AT YOU, NICK. YOU'RE EXHAUSTED...LET SOMEONE ELSE HANDLE IT.
I'M THE ONLY ONE WHO CAN. THAT'S... JUST HOW IT IS.
DISPATCH CALLED. JEWELRY STORE ALARM IS GOING OFF. WU AND FRANCO ARE HEADED TO THE SCENE.
JULIETTE, DO ME A FAVOR. GO TO MONROE AND ROSALEE'S. WAIT FOR ME THERE.
I LOVE YOU.
I LOVE YOU TOO.

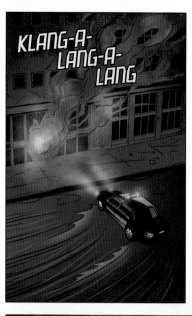

KLANG-A-
LANG-A-
LANG

WHY DO I FEEL LIKE A LITTLE PIGGY BEING LED TO THE SLAUGHTER...YOU THINK THIS IS OUR GUY?

WHOEVER IT IS, THE STANDING ORDER IS TO SURROUND AND CONTAIN. THEN WAIT FOR BACKUP.

BUT WHERE'S THE FUN IN THAT?

PORTLAND PD! FREEZE!

PUT YOUR HANDS ON YOUR HEAD AND STEP OUT INTO THE LIGHT. SLOWLY.

ARE YOU FRIENDS OF THE GRIMM?

STOP WALKING. NOW.

PUT YOUR HANDS ON YOUR HEAD!

BECAUSE I WANT YOU TO PASS A MESSAGE ON TO HIM...

TELL HIM HE'S ALREADY DEAD.

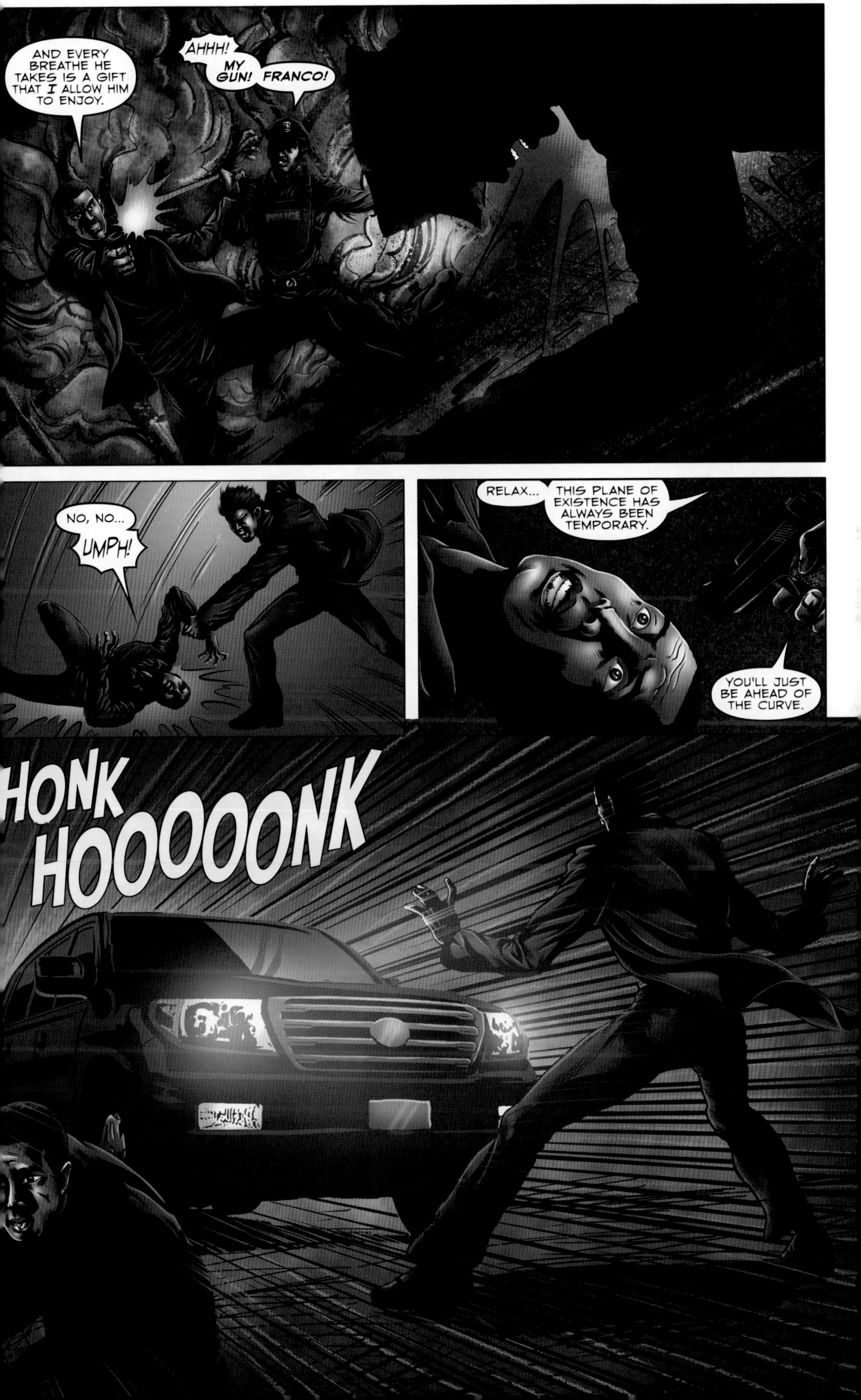

AND EVERY BREATHE HE TAKES IS A GIFT THAT I ALLOW HIM TO ENJOY.
AHHH! MY GUN!
FRANCO!
NO, NO...
UMPH!
RELAX...
THIS PLANE OF EXISTENCE HAS ALWAYS BEEN TEMPORARY.
YOU'LL JUST BE AHEAD OF THE CURVE.
HONK
HOOOOONK

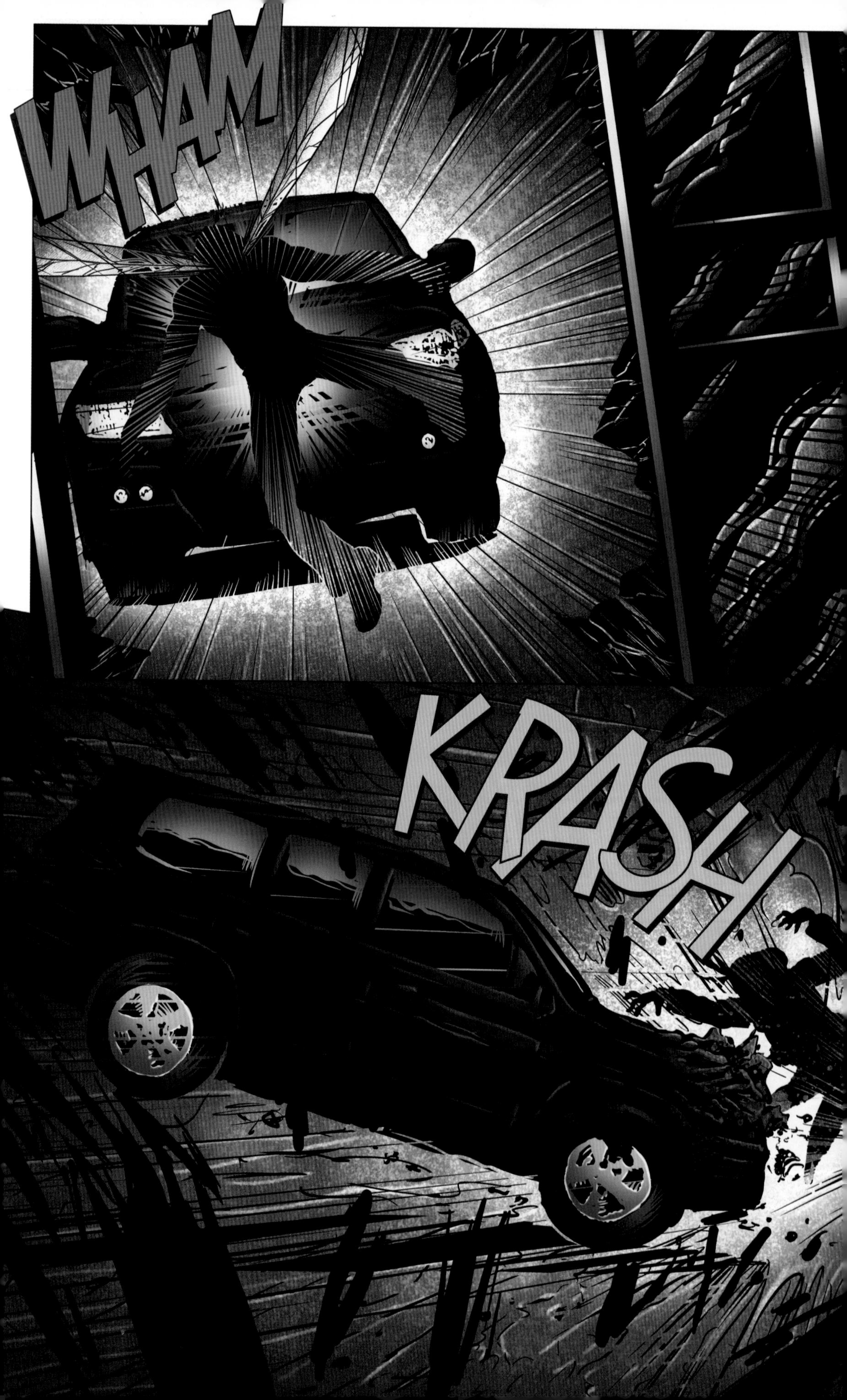
WHAM
KRASH

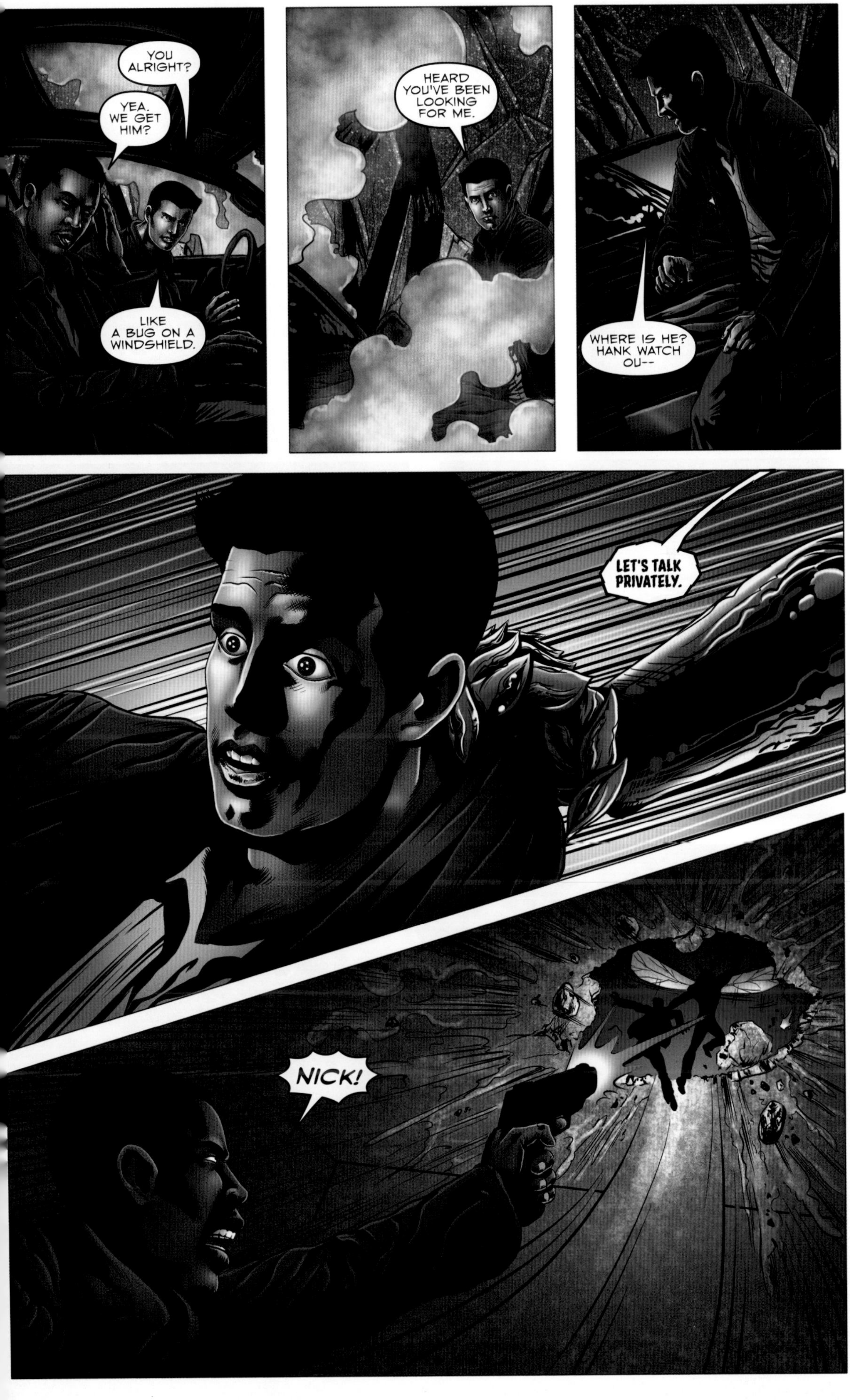
YOU ALRIGHT?
YEA. WE GET HIM?
LIKE A BUG ON A WINDSHIELD.
HEARD YOU'VE BEEN LOOKING FOR ME.
WHERE IS HE? HANK WATCH OU--
LET'S TALK PRIVATELY.
NICK!

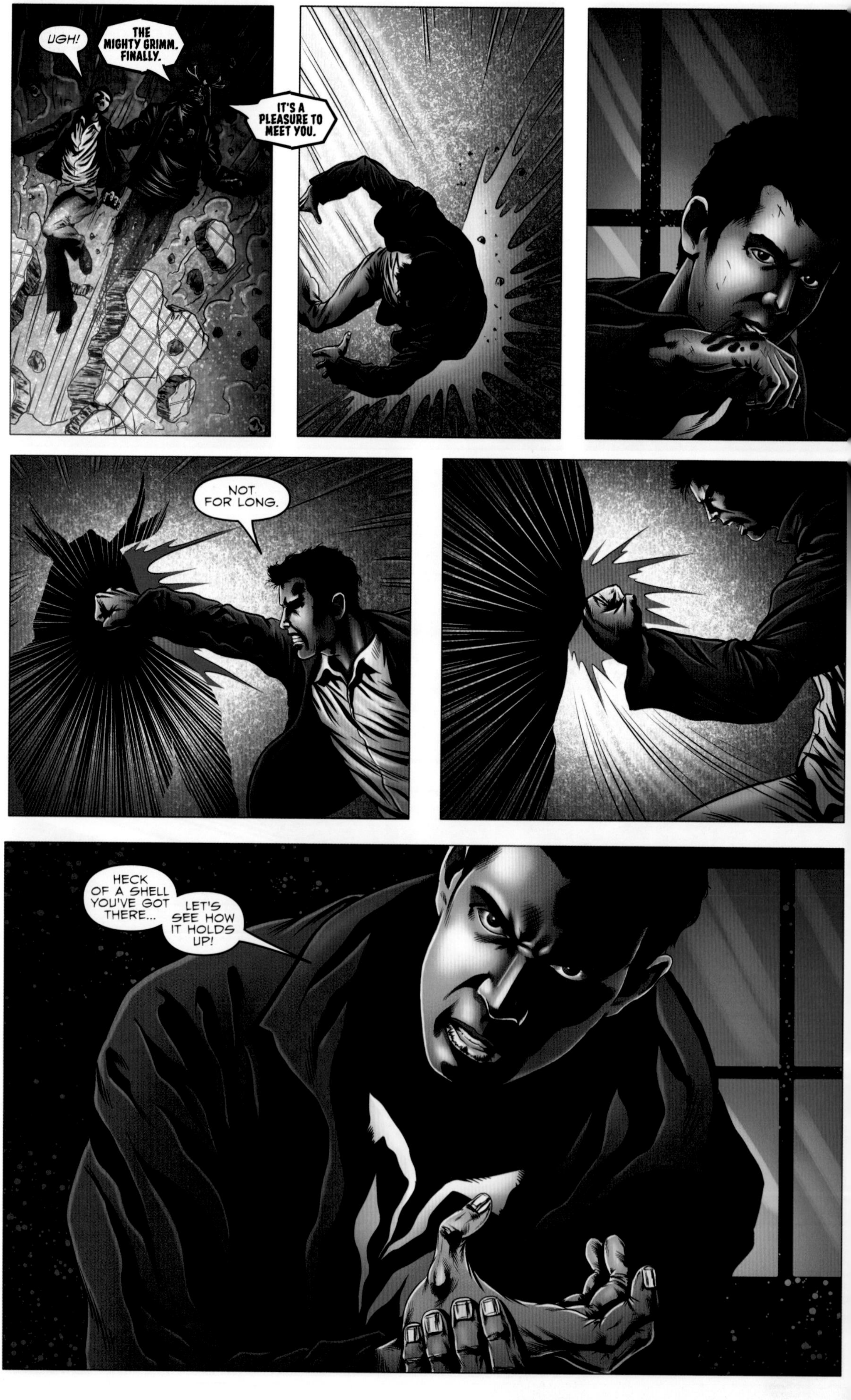
UGH!
THE MIGHTY GRIMM. FINALLY.
IT'S A PLEASURE TO MEET YOU.
NOT FOR LONG.
HECK OF A SHELL YOU'VE GOT THERE...
LET'S SEE HOW IT HOLDS UP!

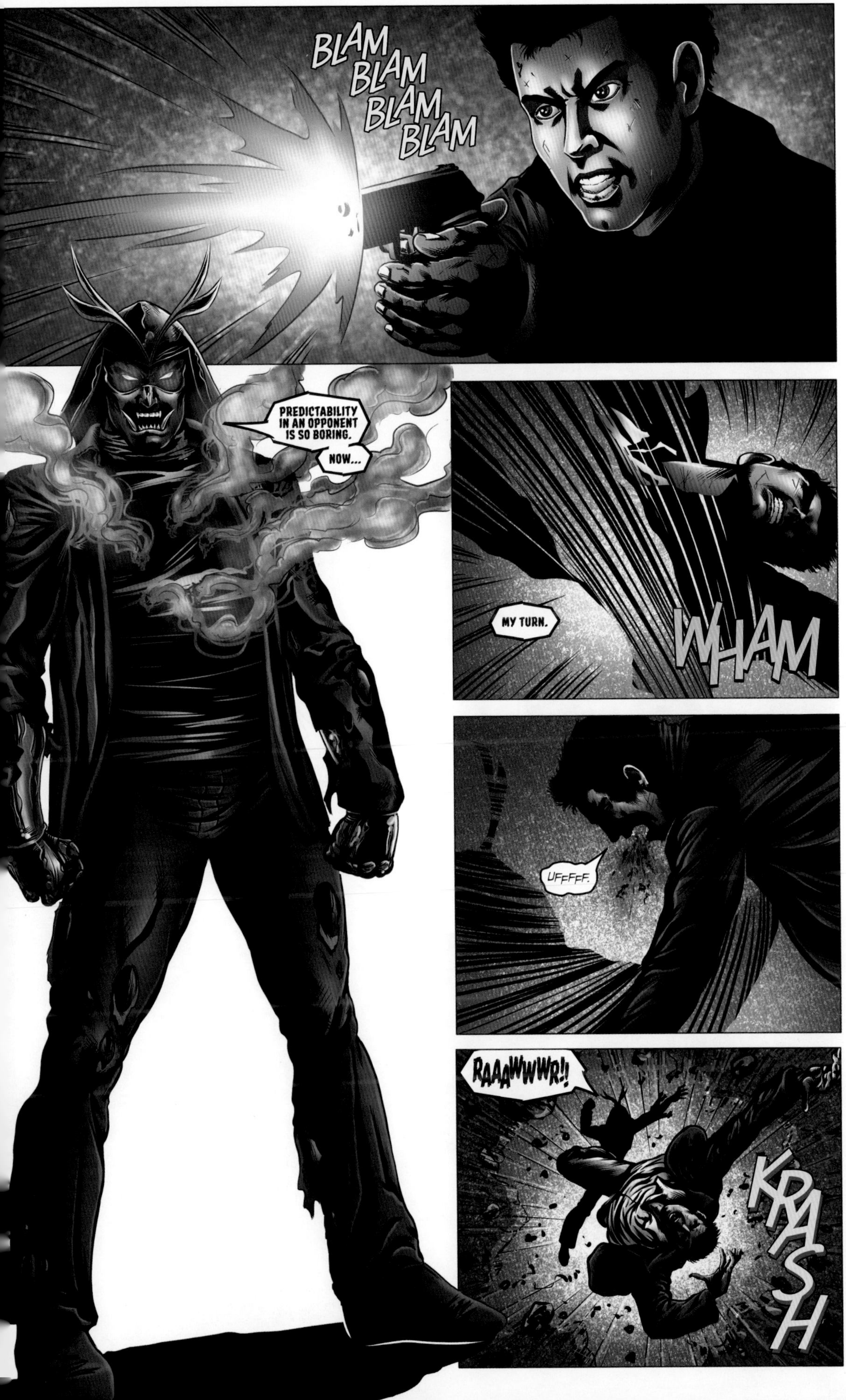
BLAM
BLAM
BLAM
BLAM
PREDICTABILITY IN AN OPPONENT IS SO BORING.
NOW...
MY TURN.
WHAM
UFFFFF.
RAAAWWWR!!
KRASH

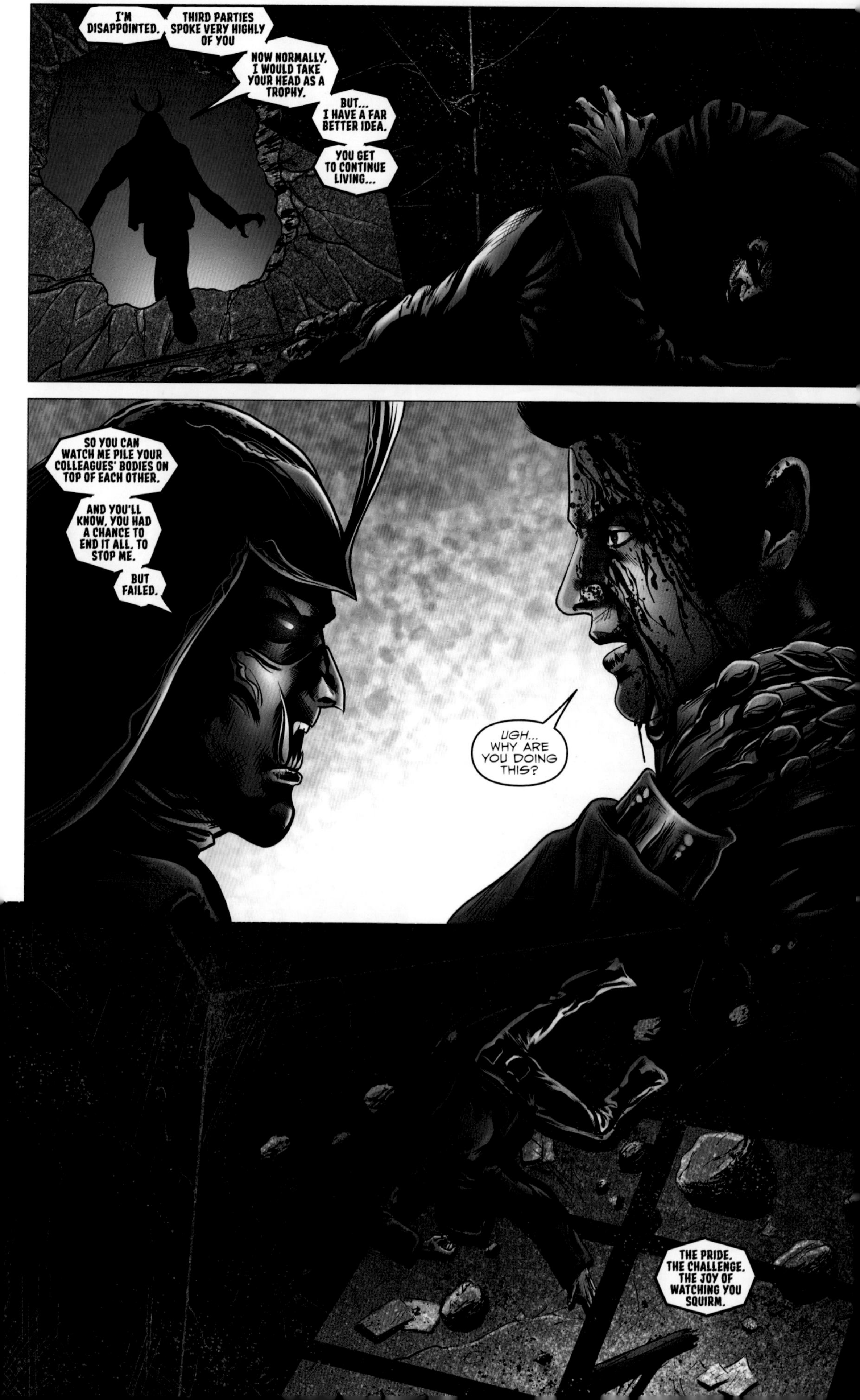
I'M DISAPPOINTED.
THIRD PARTIES SPOKE VERY HIGHLY OF YOU
NOW NORMALLY, I WOULD TAKE YOUR HEAD AS A TROPHY.
BUT... I HAVE A FAR BETTER IDEA.
YOU GET TO CONTINUE LIVING...
SO YOU CAN WATCH ME PILE YOUR COLLEAGUES' BODIES ON TOP OF EACH OTHER.
AND YOU'LL KNOW, YOU HAD A CHANCE TO END IT ALL. TO STOP ME.
BUT FAILED.
UGH... WHY ARE YOU DOING THIS?
THE PRIDE. THE CHALLENGE. THE JOY OF WATCHING YOU SQUIRM.

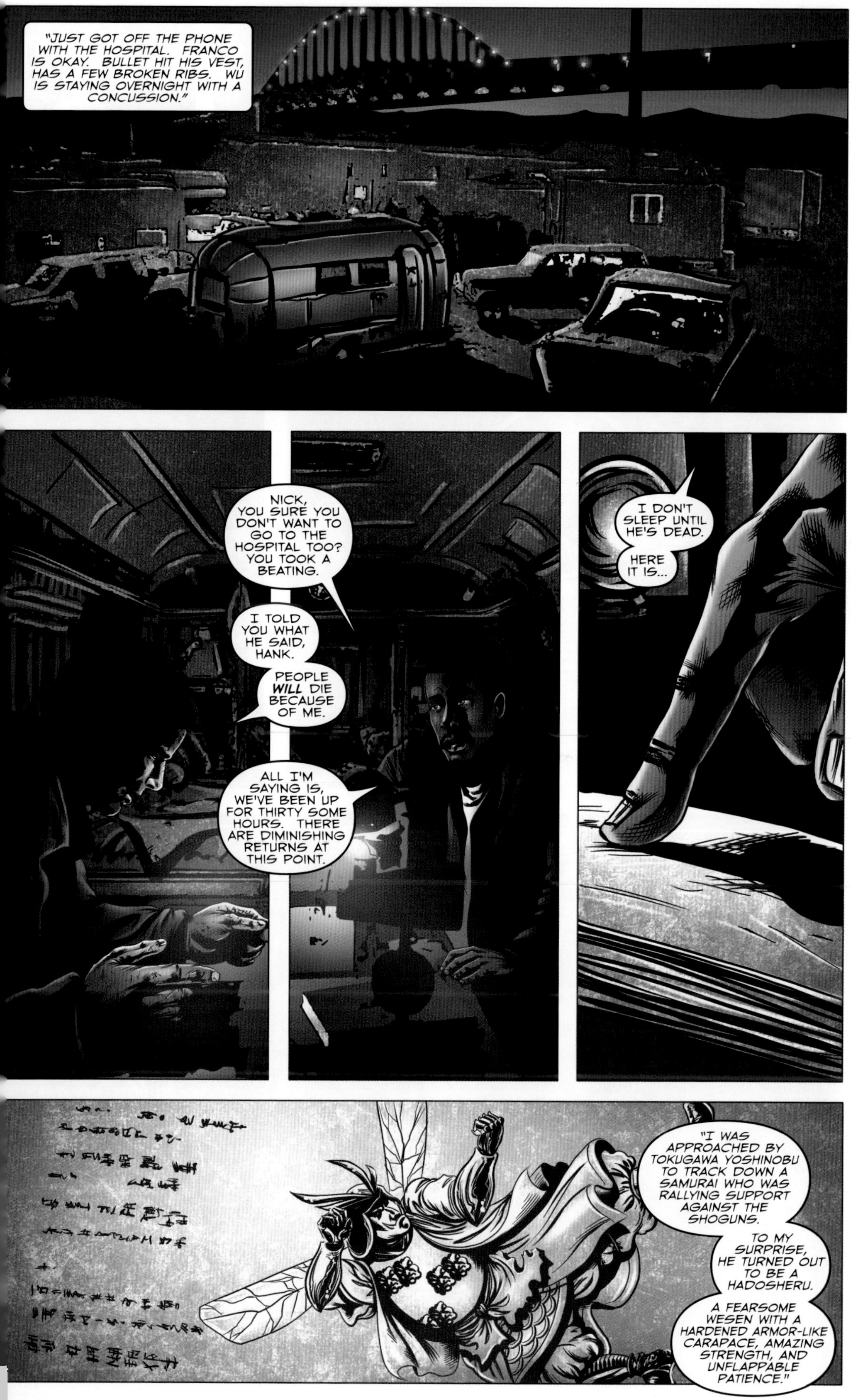
"JUST GOT OFF THE PHONE WITH THE HOSPITAL. FRANCO IS OKAY. BULLET HIT HIS VEST, HAS A FEW BROKEN RIBS. WU IS STAYING OVERNIGHT WITH A CONCUSSION."
NICK, YOU SURE YOU DON'T WANT TO GO TO THE HOSPITAL TOO? YOU TOOK A BEATING.
I TOLD YOU WHAT HE SAID, HANK.
PEOPLE WILL DIE BECAUSE OF ME.
ALL I'M SAYING IS, WE'VE BEEN UP FOR THIRTY SOME HOURS. THERE ARE DIMINISHING RETURNS AT THIS POINT.
I DON'T SLEEP UNTIL HE'S DEAD.
HERE IT IS...
"I WAS APPROACHED BY TOKUGAWA YOSHINOBU TO TRACK DOWN A SAMURAI WHO WAS RALLYING SUPPORT AGAINST THE SHOGUNS.
TO MY SURPRISE, HE TURNED OUT TO BE A HADOSHERU.
A FEARSOME WESEN WITH A HARDENED ARMOR-LIKE CARAPACE, AMAZING STRENGTH, AND UNFLAPPABLE PATIENCE."

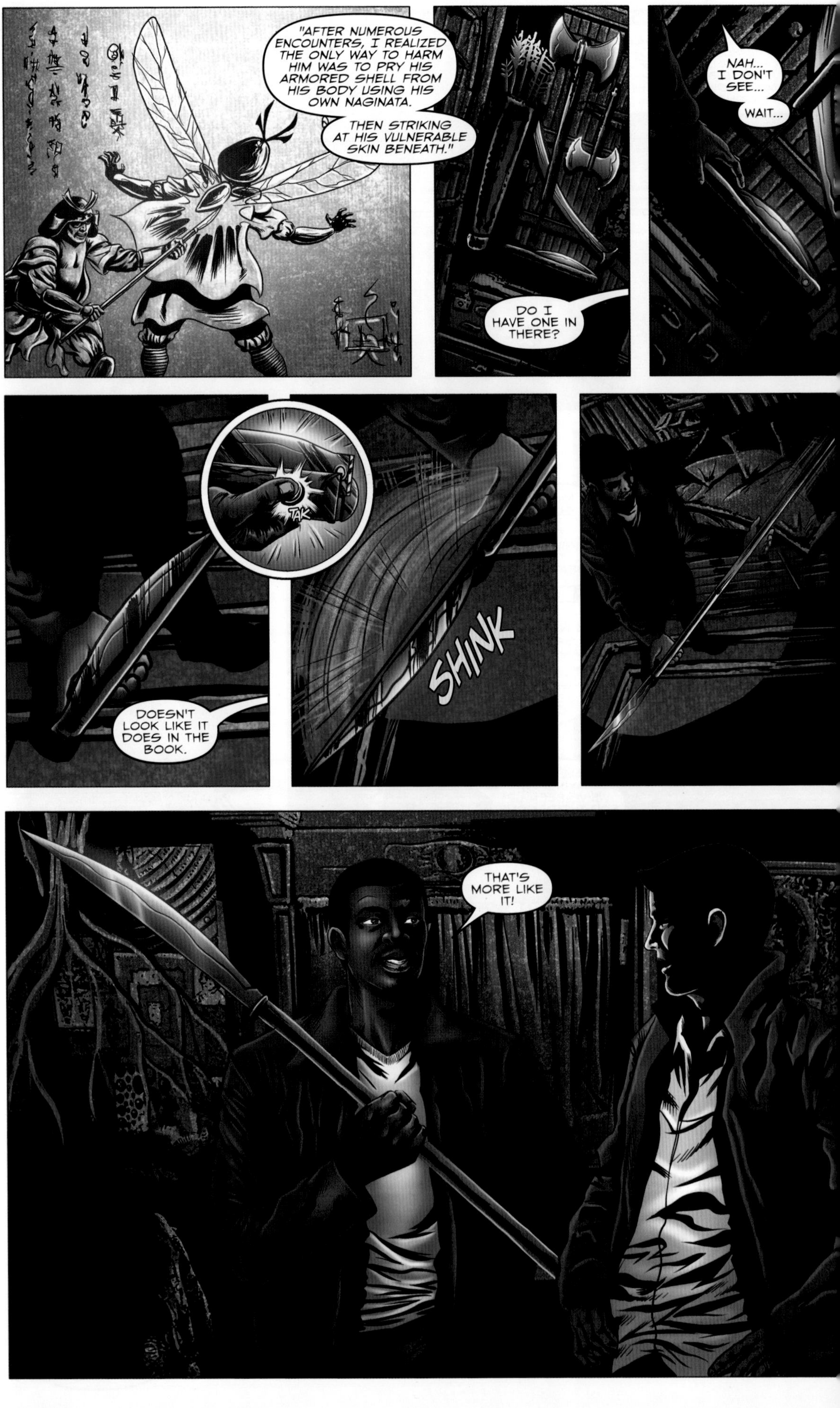
"AFTER NUMEROUS ENCOUNTERS, I REALIZED THE ONLY WAY TO HARM HIM WAS TO PRY HIS ARMORED SHELL FROM HIS BODY USING HIS OWN NAGINATA.
THEN STRIKING AT HIS VULNERABLE SKIN BENEATH."
DO I HAVE ONE IN THERE?
NAH... I DON'T SEE...
WAIT...
TAK
DOESN'T LOOK LIKE IT DOES IN THE BOOK.
SHINK
THAT'S MORE LIKE IT!

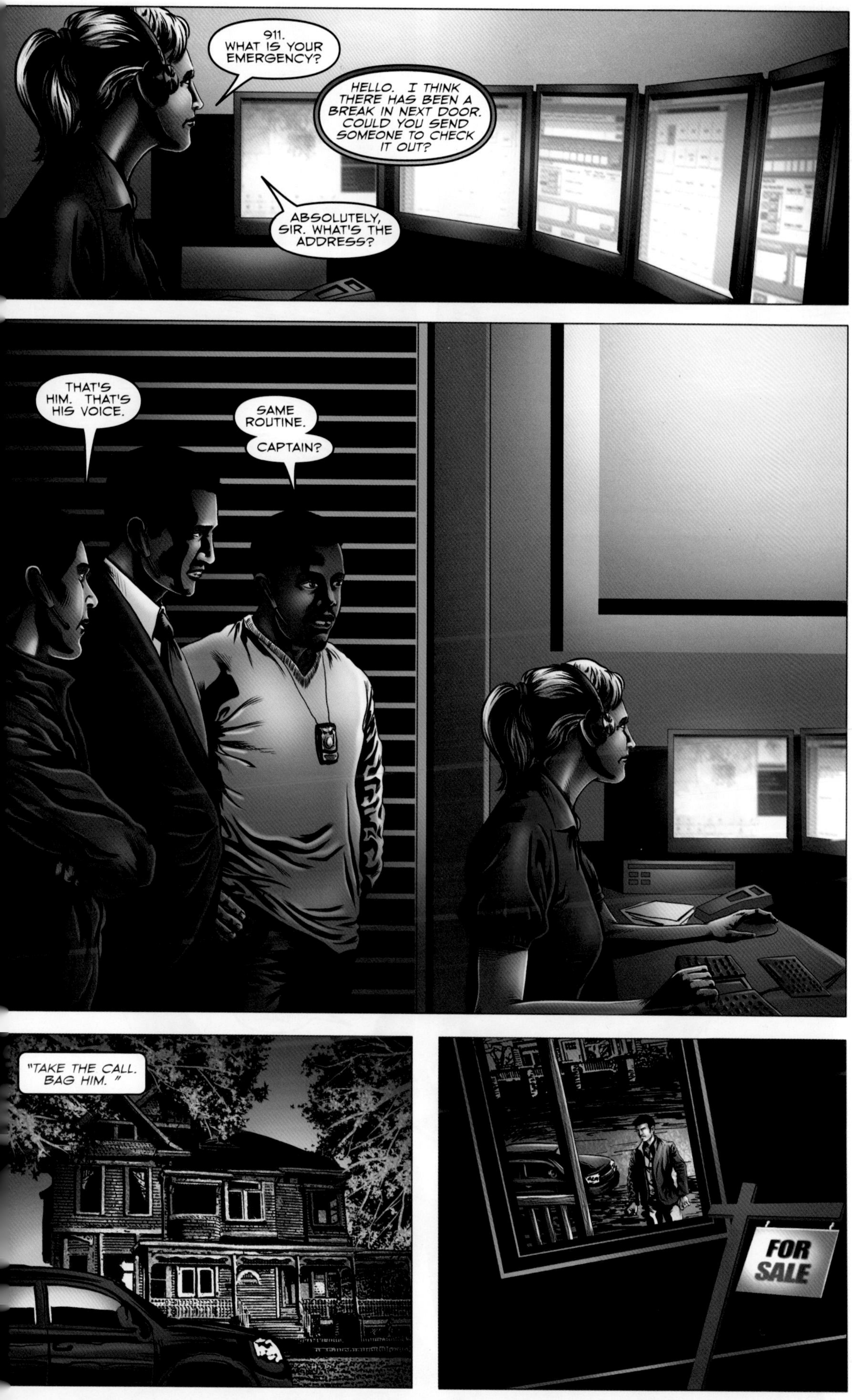
911. WHAT IS YOUR EMERGENCY?
HELLO. I THINK THERE HAS BEEN A BREAK IN NEXT DOOR. COULD YOU SEND SOMEONE TO CHECK IT OUT?
ABSOLUTELY, SIR. WHAT'S THE ADDRESS?
THAT'S HIM. THAT'S HIS VOICE.
SAME ROUTINE.
CAPTAIN?
"TAKE THE CALL. BAG HIM."
FOR SALE

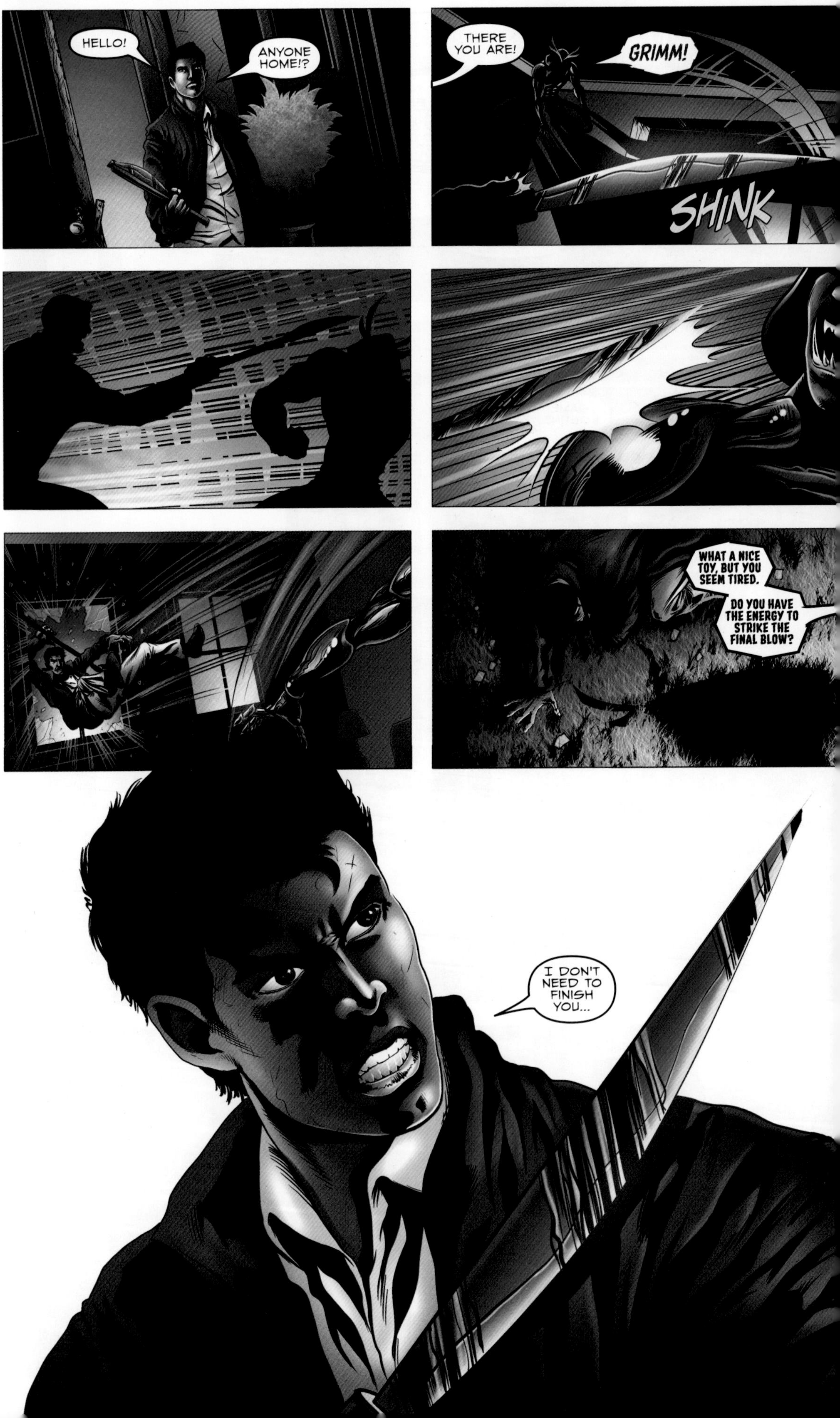

HELLO!
ANYONE HOME!?
THERE YOU ARE!
GRIMM!
SHINK
WHAT A NICE TOY, BUT YOU SEEM TIRED.
DO YOU HAVE THE ENERGY TO STRIKE THE FINAL BLOW?
I DON'T NEED TO FINISH YOU...

I JUST HAVE TO DO THE PREP WORK!

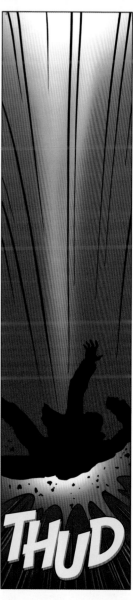

THUD

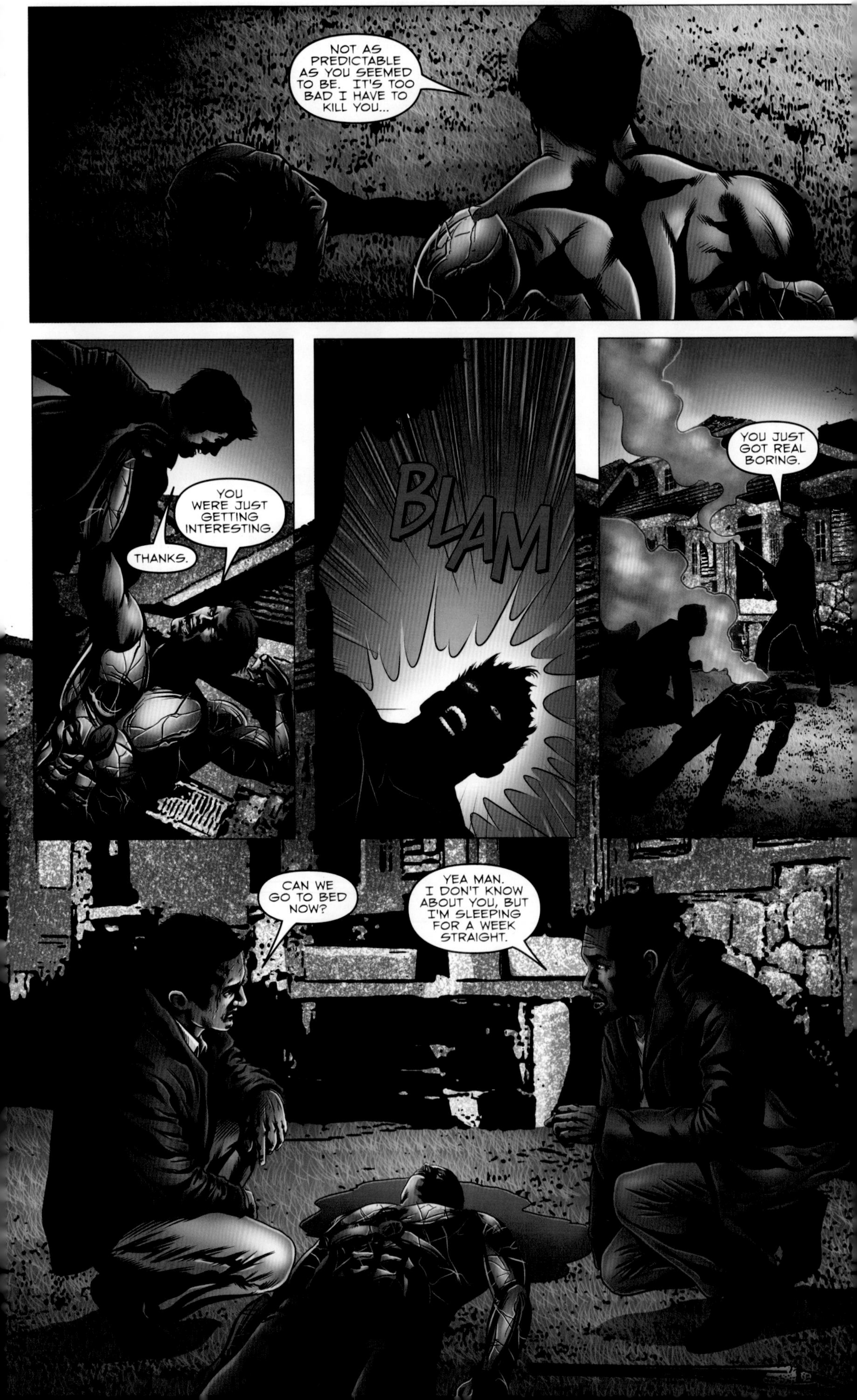
NOT AS PREDICTABLE AS YOU SEEMED TO BE. IT'S TOO BAD I HAVE TO KILL YOU...
YOU WERE JUST GETTING INTERESTING.
THANKS.
BLAM
YOU JUST GOT REAL BORING.
CAN WE GO TO BED NOW?
YEA MAN. I DON'T KNOW ABOUT YOU, BUT I'M SLEEPING FOR A WEEK STRAIGHT.

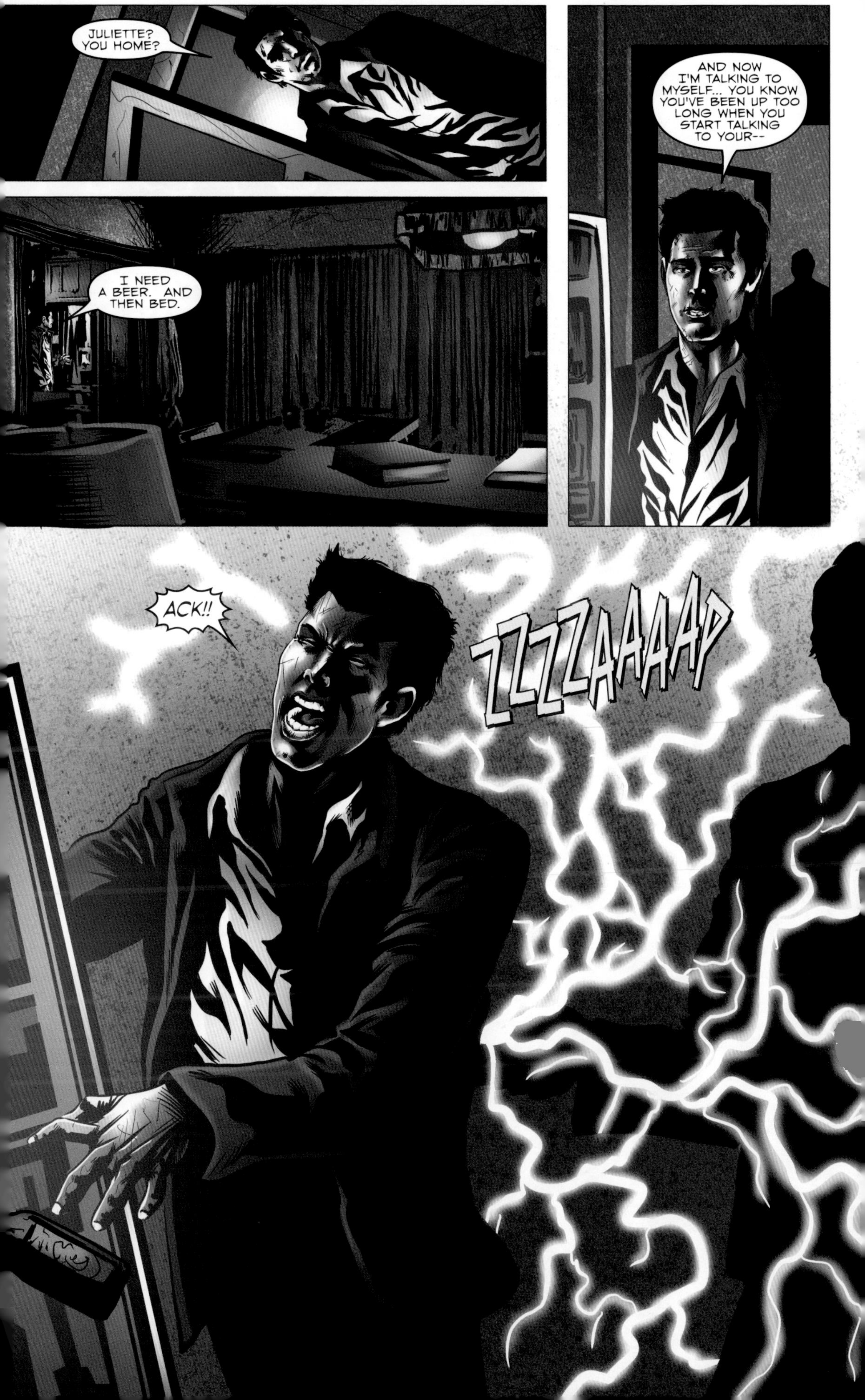
JULIETTE? YOU HOME?
I NEED A BEER. AND THEN BED.
AND NOW I'M TALKING TO MYSELF... YOU KNOW YOU'VE BEEN UP TOO LONG WHEN YOU START TALKING TO YOUR--
ACK!!
ZZZZAAAAP

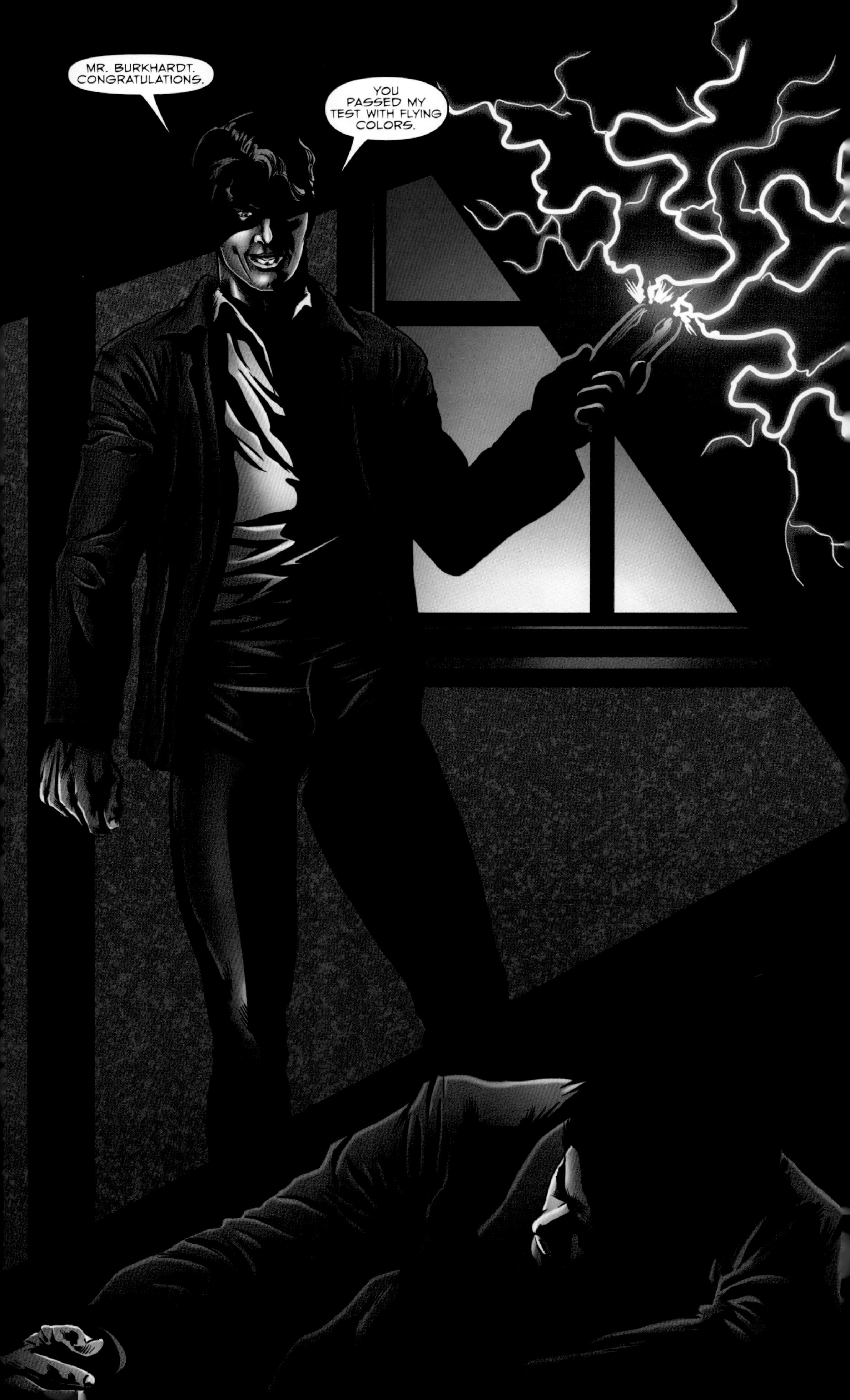
MR. BURKHARDT. CONGRATULATIONS.
YOU PASSED MY TEST WITH FLYING COLORS.

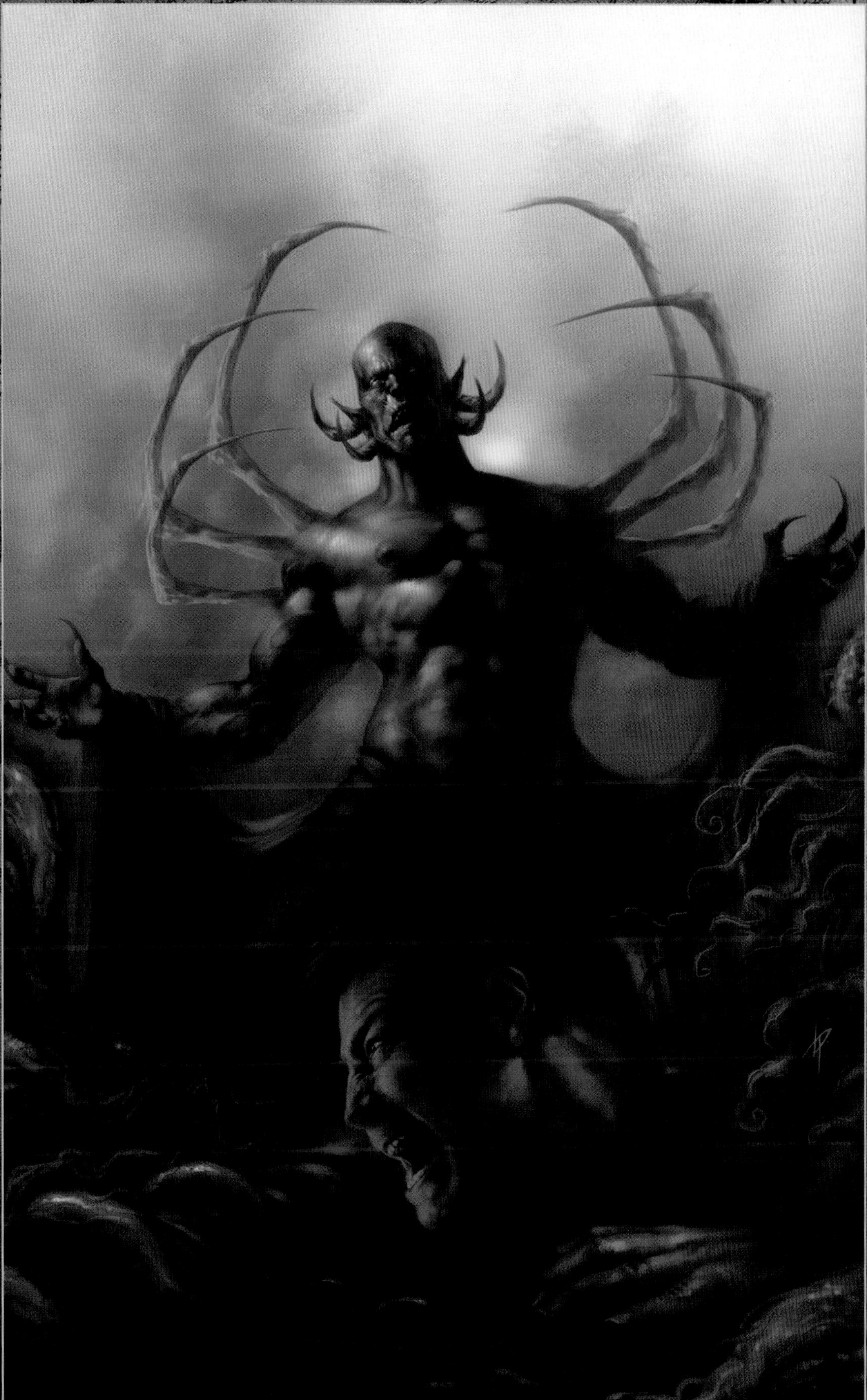

ISSUE #10 COVER
ART BY LUCIO PARRILLO

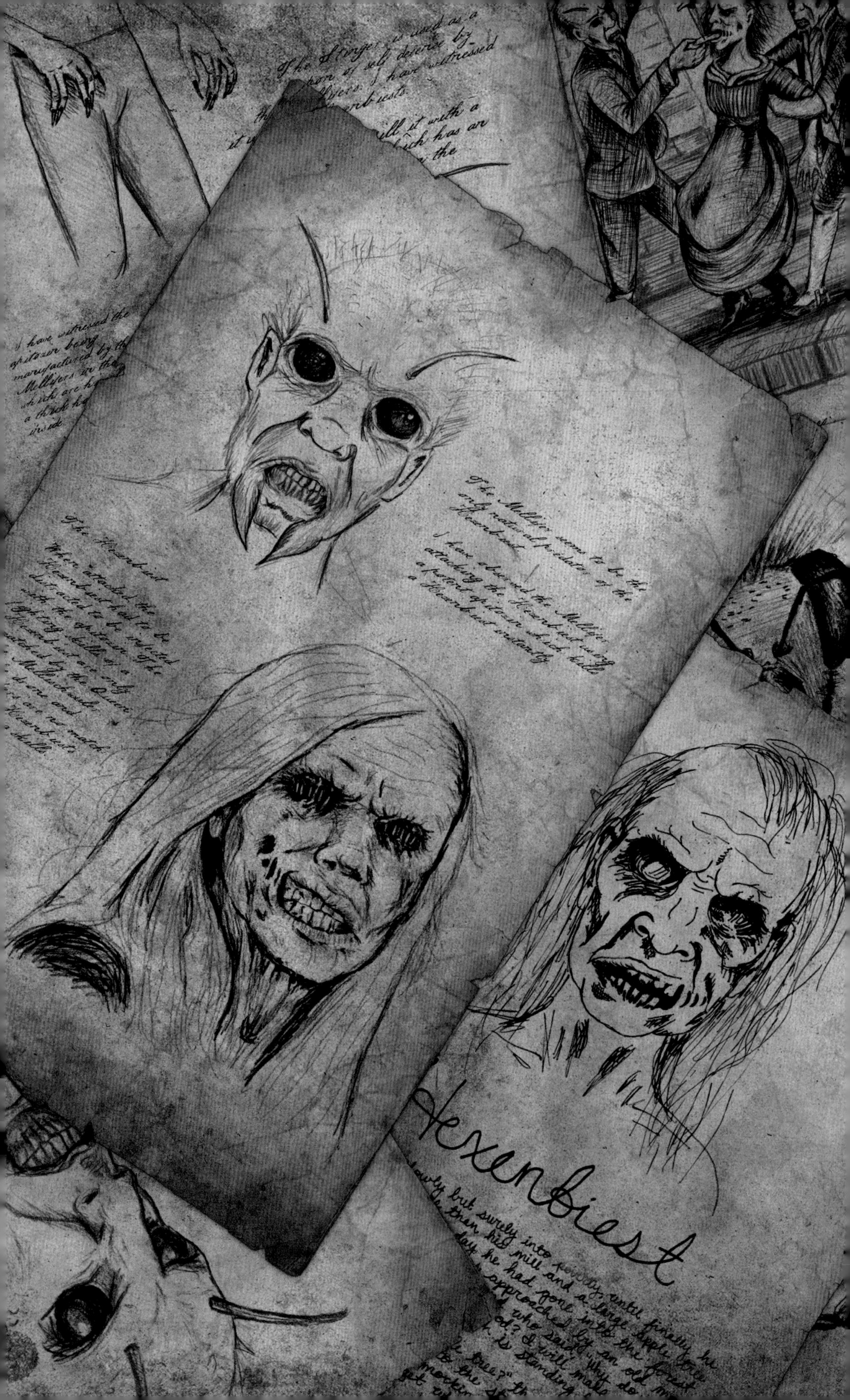
Hexenbiest

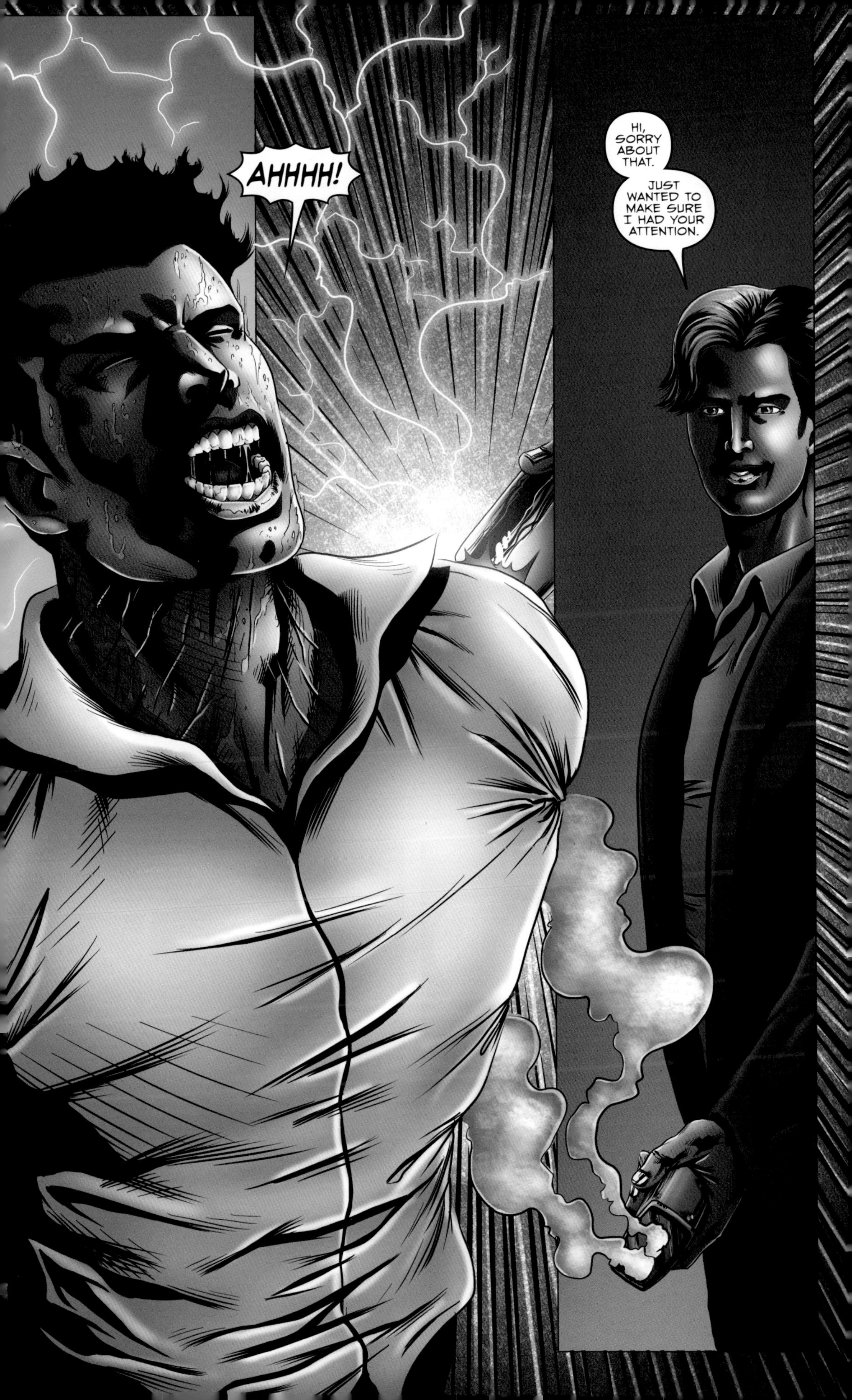
AHHHH!
HI, SORRY ABOUT THAT.
JUST WANTED TO MAKE SURE I HAD YOUR ATTENTION.

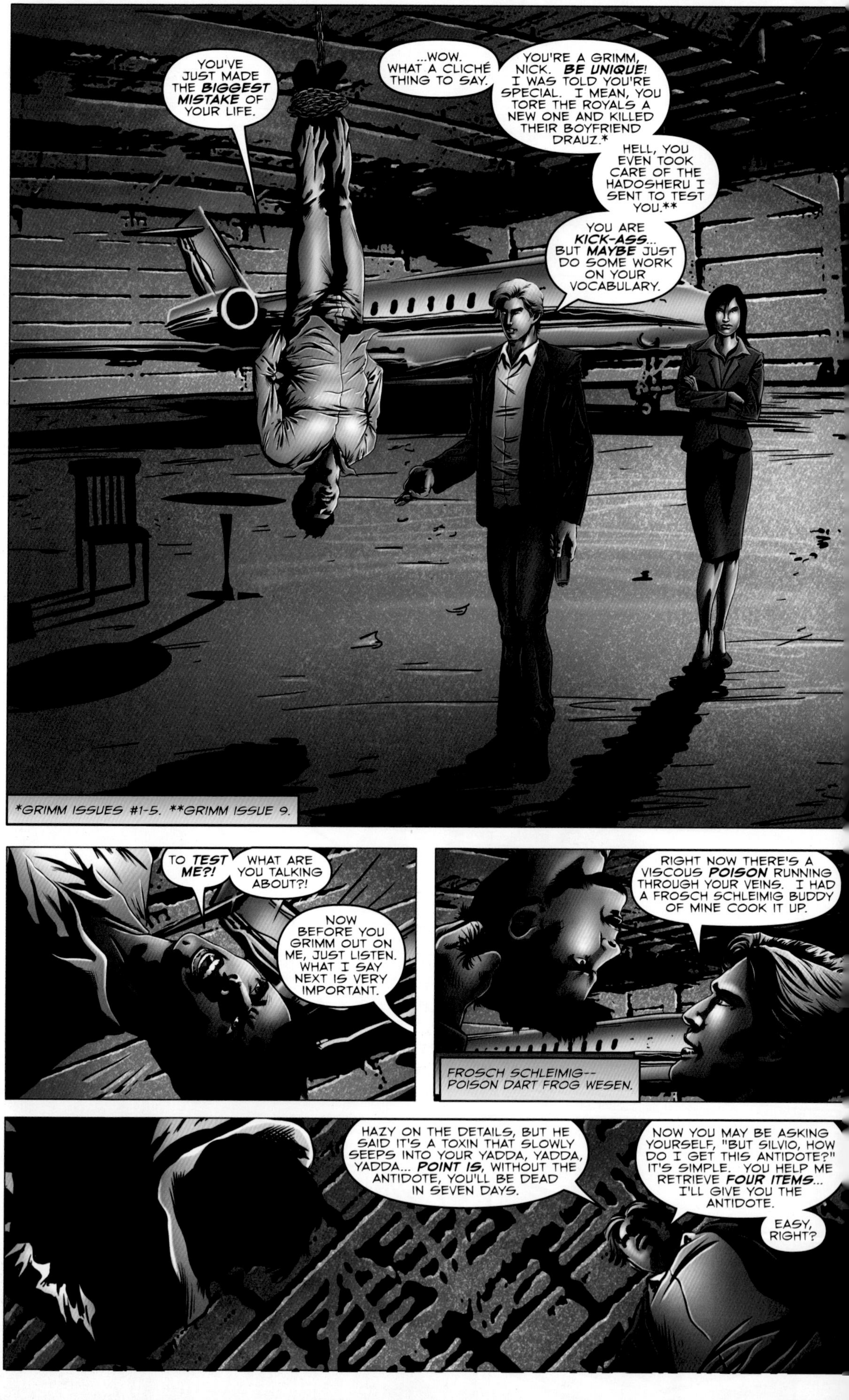
YOU'VE JUST MADE THE BIGGEST MISTAKE OF YOUR LIFE.
...WOW. WHAT A CLICHÉ THING TO SAY.
YOU'RE A GRIMM, NICK. BE UNIQUE! I WAS TOLD YOU'RE SPECIAL. I MEAN, YOU TORE THE ROYALS A NEW ONE AND KILLED THEIR BOYFRIEND DRAUZ.*
HELL, YOU EVEN TOOK CARE OF THE HADOSHERU I SENT TO TEST YOU.**
YOU ARE KICK-ASS... BUT MAYBE JUST DO SOME WORK ON YOUR VOCABULARY.
*GRIMM ISSUES #1-5. **GRIMM ISSUE 9.
TO TEST ME?!
WHAT ARE YOU TALKING ABOUT?!
NOW BEFORE YOU GRIMM OUT ON ME, JUST LISTEN. WHAT I SAY NEXT IS VERY IMPORTANT.
RIGHT NOW THERE'S A VISCOUS POISON RUNNING THROUGH YOUR VEINS. I HAD A FROSCH SCHLEIMIG BUDDY OF MINE COOK IT UP.
FROSCH SCHLEIMIG-- POISON DART FROG WESEN.
HAZY ON THE DETAILS, BUT HE SAID IT'S A TOXIN THAT SLOWLY SEEPS INTO YOUR YADDA, YADDA, YADDA... POINT IS, WITHOUT THE ANTIDOTE, YOU'LL BE DEAD IN SEVEN DAYS.
NOW YOU MAY BE ASKING YOURSELF, "BUT SILVIO, HOW DO I GET THIS ANTIDOTE?" IT'S SIMPLE. YOU HELP ME RETRIEVE FOUR ITEMS... I'LL GIVE YOU THE ANTIDOTE.
EASY, RIGHT?

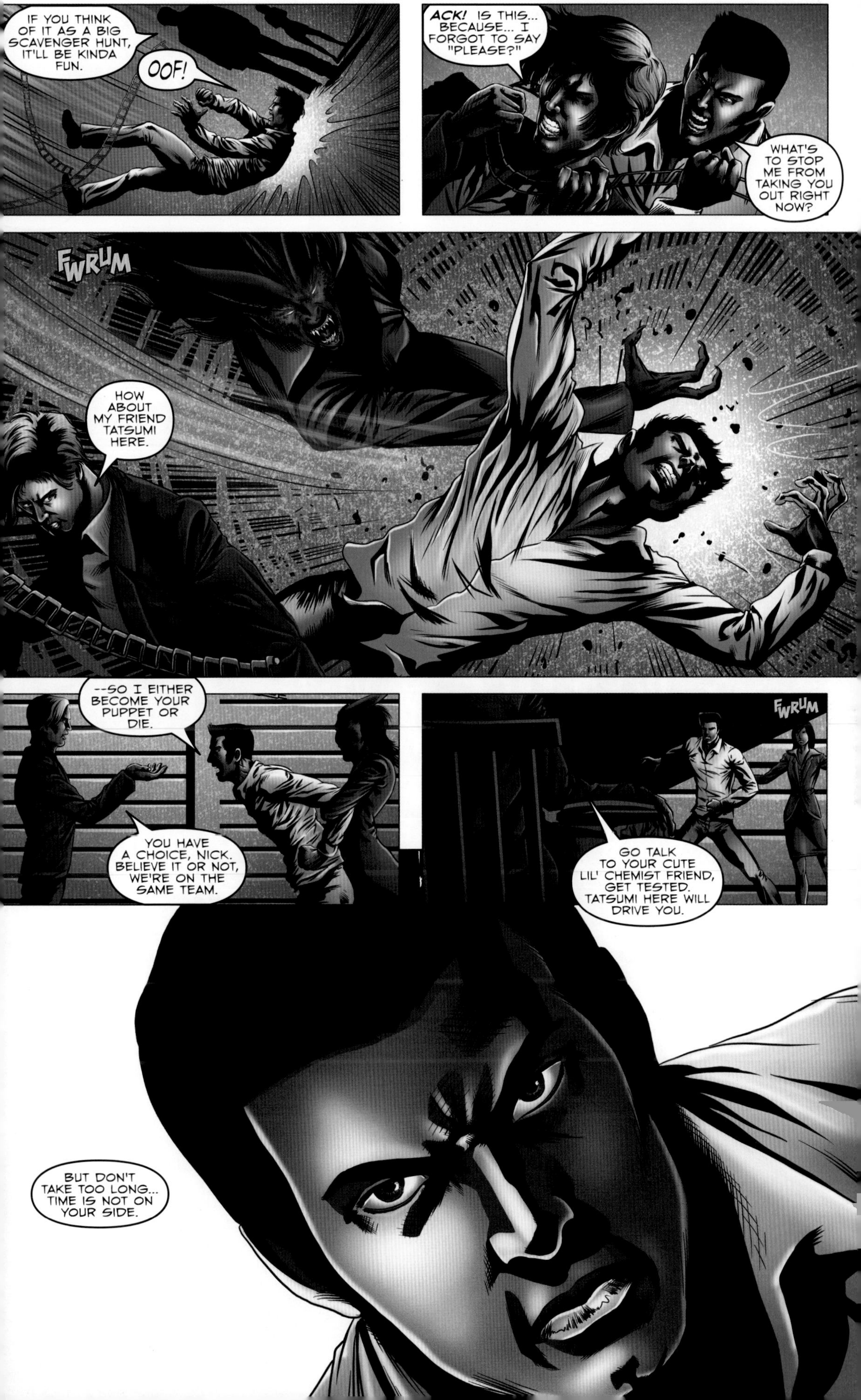
IF YOU THINK OF IT AS A BIG SCAVENGER HUNT, IT'LL BE KINDA FUN.
OOF!
ACK! IS THIS... BECAUSE... I FORGOT TO SAY "PLEASE?"
WHAT'S TO STOP ME FROM TAKING YOU OUT RIGHT NOW?
FWRUM
HOW ABOUT MY FRIEND TATSUMI HERE.
--SO I EITHER BECOME YOUR PUPPET OR DIE.
YOU HAVE A CHOICE, NICK. BELIEVE IT OR NOT, WE'RE ON THE SAME TEAM.
FWRUM
GO TALK TO YOUR CUTE LIL' CHEMIST FRIEND, GET TESTED. TATSUMI HERE WILL DRIVE YOU.
BUT DON'T TAKE TOO LONG... TIME IS NOT ON YOUR SIDE.

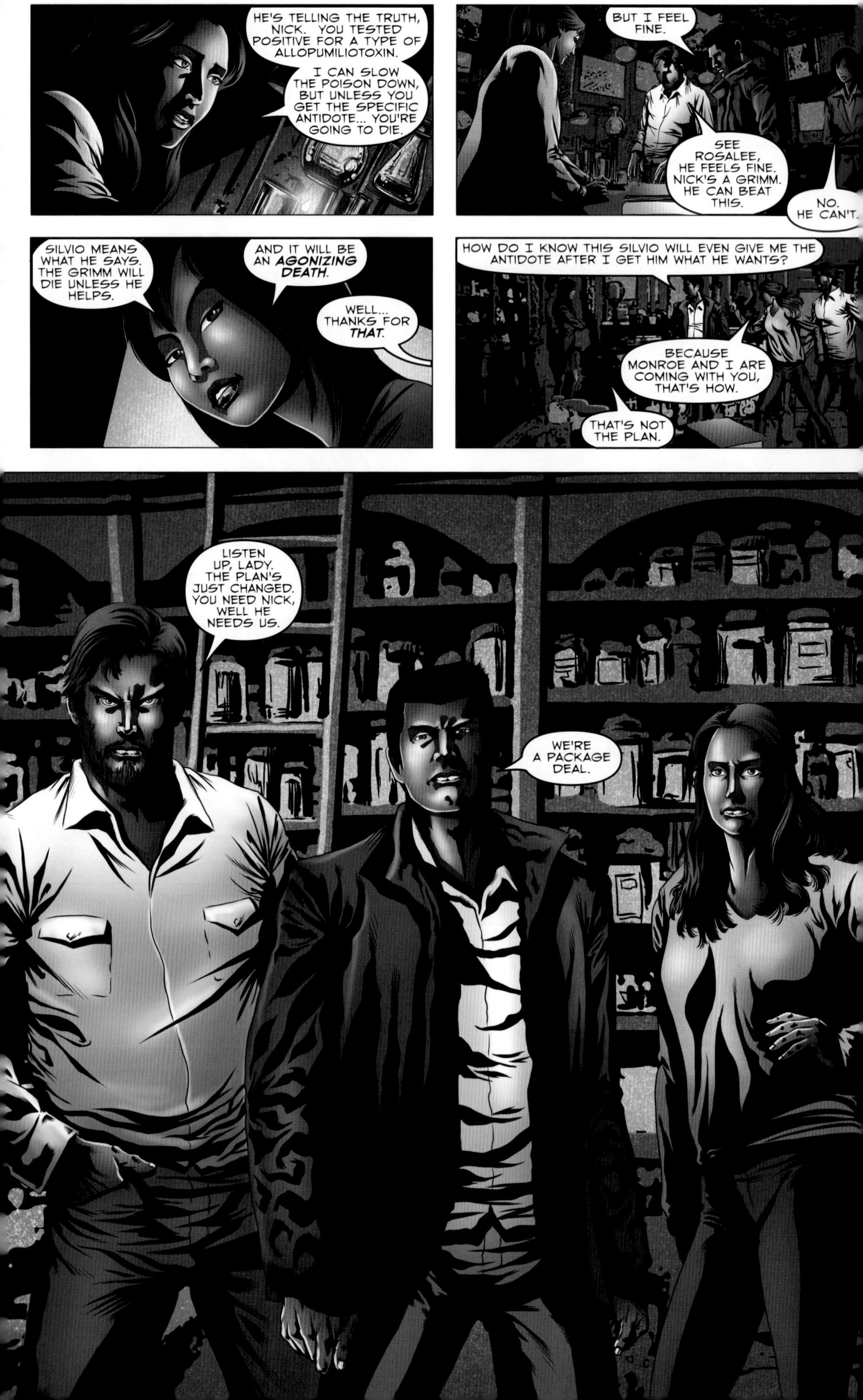
HE'S TELLING THE TRUTH, NICK. YOU TESTED POSITIVE FOR A TYPE OF ALLOPUMILIOTOXIN.
I CAN SLOW THE POISON DOWN, BUT UNLESS YOU GET THE SPECIFIC ANTIDOTE... YOU'RE GOING TO DIE.
BUT I FEEL FINE.
SEE ROSALEE, HE FEELS FINE. NICK'S A GRIMM. HE CAN BEAT THIS.
NO. HE CAN'T.
SILVIO MEANS WHAT HE SAYS. THE GRIMM WILL DIE UNLESS HE HELPS.
AND IT WILL BE AN AGONIZING DEATH.
WELL... THANKS FOR THAT.
HOW DO I KNOW THIS SILVIO WILL EVEN GIVE ME THE ANTIDOTE AFTER I GET HIM WHAT HE WANTS?
BECAUSE MONROE AND I ARE COMING WITH YOU, THAT'S HOW.
THAT'S NOT THE PLAN.
LISTEN UP, LADY. THE PLAN'S JUST CHANGED. YOU NEED NICK, WELL HE NEEDS US.
WE'RE A PACKAGE DEAL.

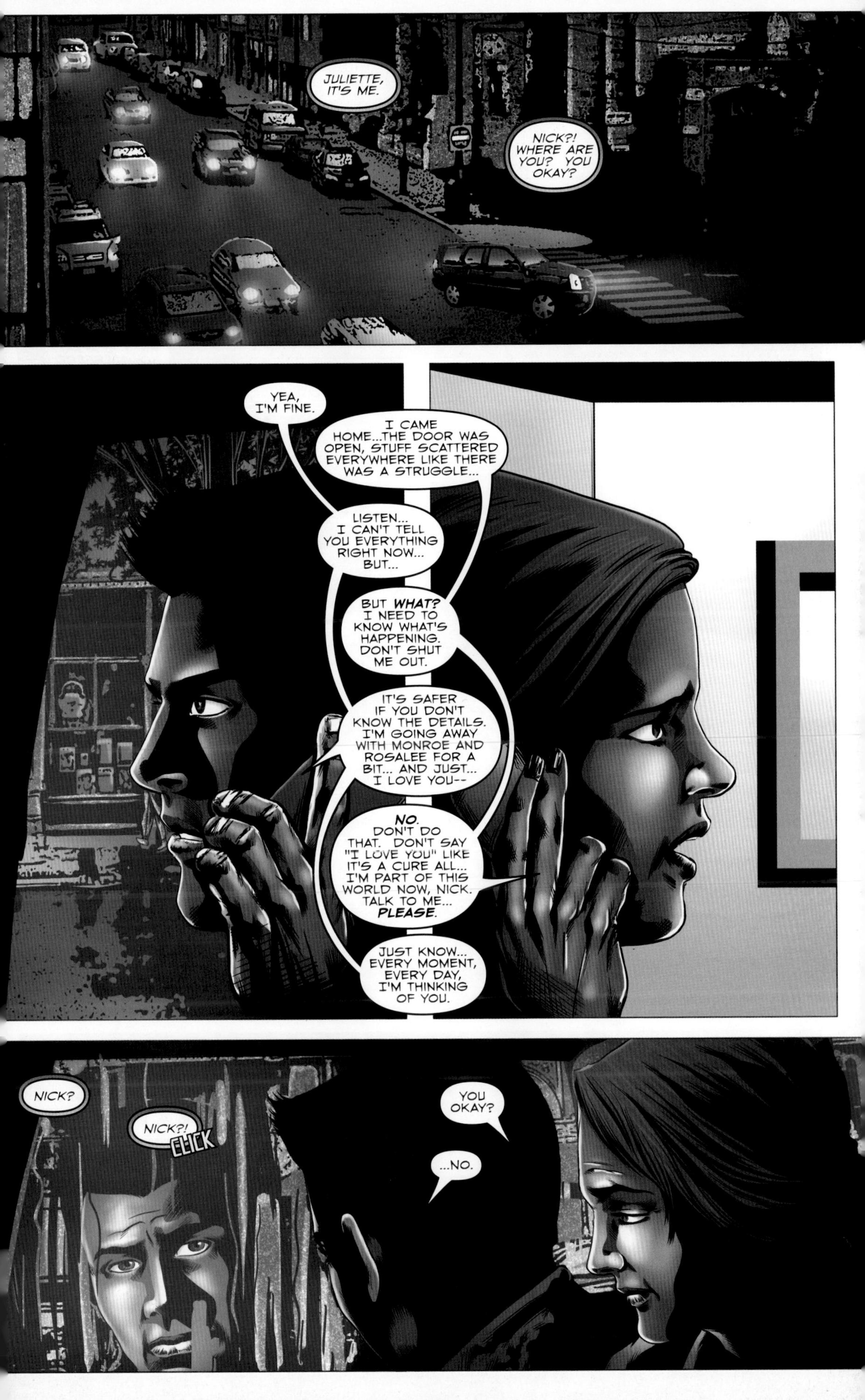

JULIETTE, IT'S ME.
NICK?! WHERE ARE YOU? YOU OKAY?
YEA, I'M FINE.
I CAME HOME...THE DOOR WAS OPEN, STUFF SCATTERED EVERYWHERE LIKE THERE WAS A STRUGGLE...
LISTEN... I CAN'T TELL YOU EVERYTHING RIGHT NOW... BUT...
BUT *WHAT?* I NEED TO KNOW WHAT'S HAPPENING. DON'T SHUT ME OUT.
IT'S SAFER IF YOU DON'T KNOW THE DETAILS. I'M GOING AWAY WITH MONROE AND ROSALEE FOR A BIT... AND JUST... I LOVE YOU--
NO. DON'T DO THAT. DON'T SAY "I LOVE YOU" LIKE IT'S A CURE ALL... I'M PART OF THIS WORLD NOW, NICK. TALK TO ME... *PLEASE*.
JUST KNOW... EVERY MOMENT, EVERY DAY, I'M THINKING OF YOU.
NICK?
NICK?!
CLICK
YOU OKAY?
...NO.

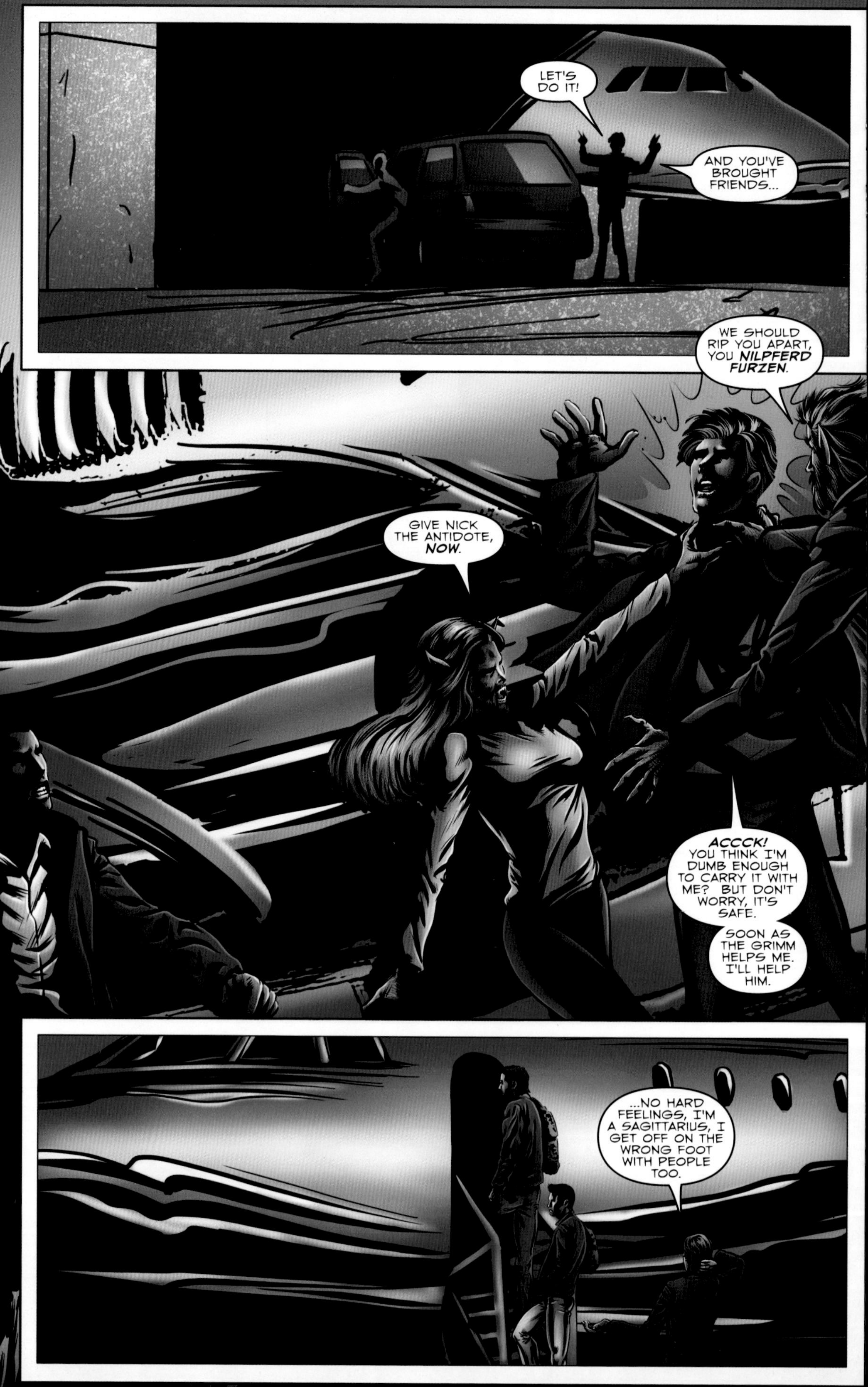
LET'S DO IT!
AND YOU'VE BROUGHT FRIENDS...
WE SHOULD RIP YOU APART, YOU NILPFERD FURZEN.
GIVE NICK THE ANTIDOTE, NOW.
ACCCK! YOU THINK I'M DUMB ENOUGH TO CARRY IT WITH ME? BUT DON'T WORRY, IT'S SAFE.
SOON AS THE GRIMM HELPS ME. I'LL HELP HIM.
...NO HARD FEELINGS, I'M A SAGITTARIUS, I GET OFF ON THE WRONG FOOT WITH PEOPLE TOO.

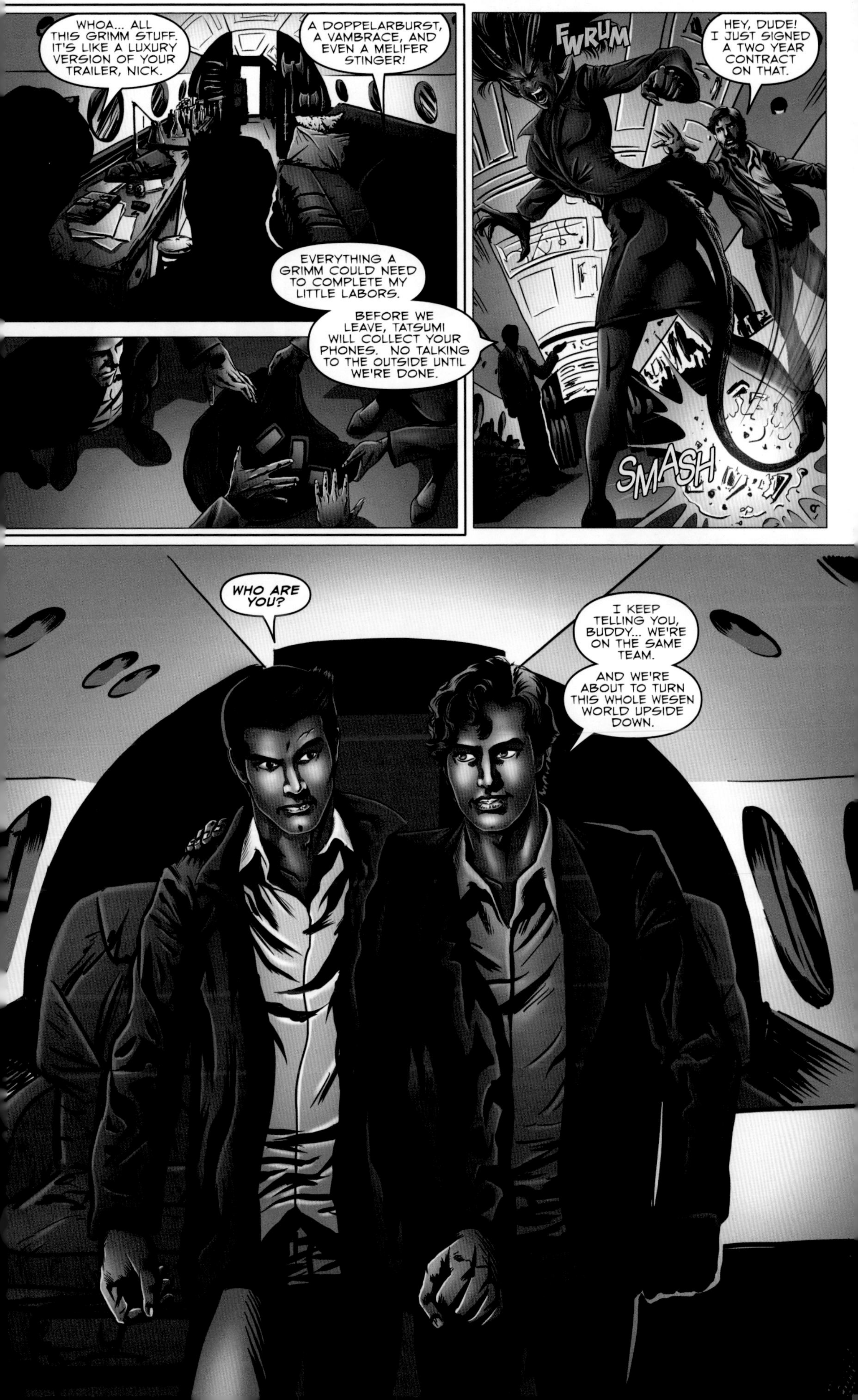
WHOA... ALL THIS GRIMM STUFF. IT'S LIKE A LUXURY VERSION OF YOUR TRAILER, NICK.
A DOPPELARBURST, A VAMBRACE, AND EVEN A MELIFER STINGER!
EVERYTHING A GRIMM COULD NEED TO COMPLETE MY LITTLE LABORS.
BEFORE WE LEAVE, TATSUMI WILL COLLECT YOUR PHONES. NO TALKING TO THE OUTSIDE UNTIL WE'RE DONE.
FWRUM
HEY, DUDE! I JUST SIGNED A TWO YEAR CONTRACT ON THAT.
SMASH
WHO ARE YOU?
I KEEP TELLING YOU, BUDDY... WE'RE ON THE SAME TEAM.
AND WE'RE ABOUT TO TURN THIS WHOLE WESEN WORLD UPSIDE DOWN.

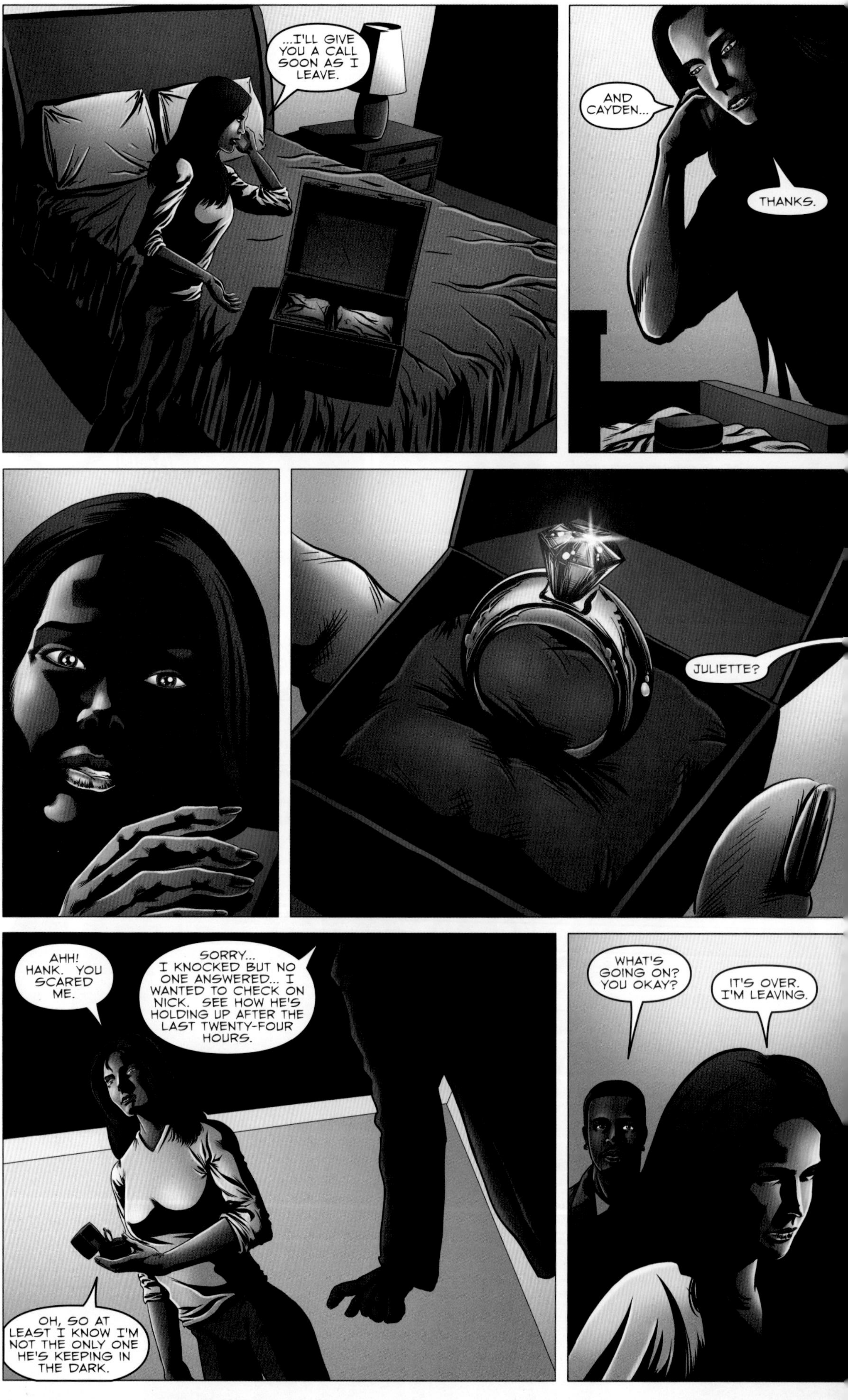
...I'LL GIVE YOU A CALL SOON AS I LEAVE.
AND CAYDEN...
THANKS.
JULIETTE?
AHH! HANK. YOU SCARED ME.
SORRY... I KNOCKED BUT NO ONE ANSWERED... I WANTED TO CHECK ON NICK. SEE HOW HE'S HOLDING UP AFTER THE LAST TWENTY-FOUR HOURS.
OH, SO AT LEAST I KNOW I'M NOT THE ONLY ONE HE'S KEEPING IN THE DARK.
WHAT'S GOING ON? YOU OKAY?
IT'S OVER. I'M LEAVING.

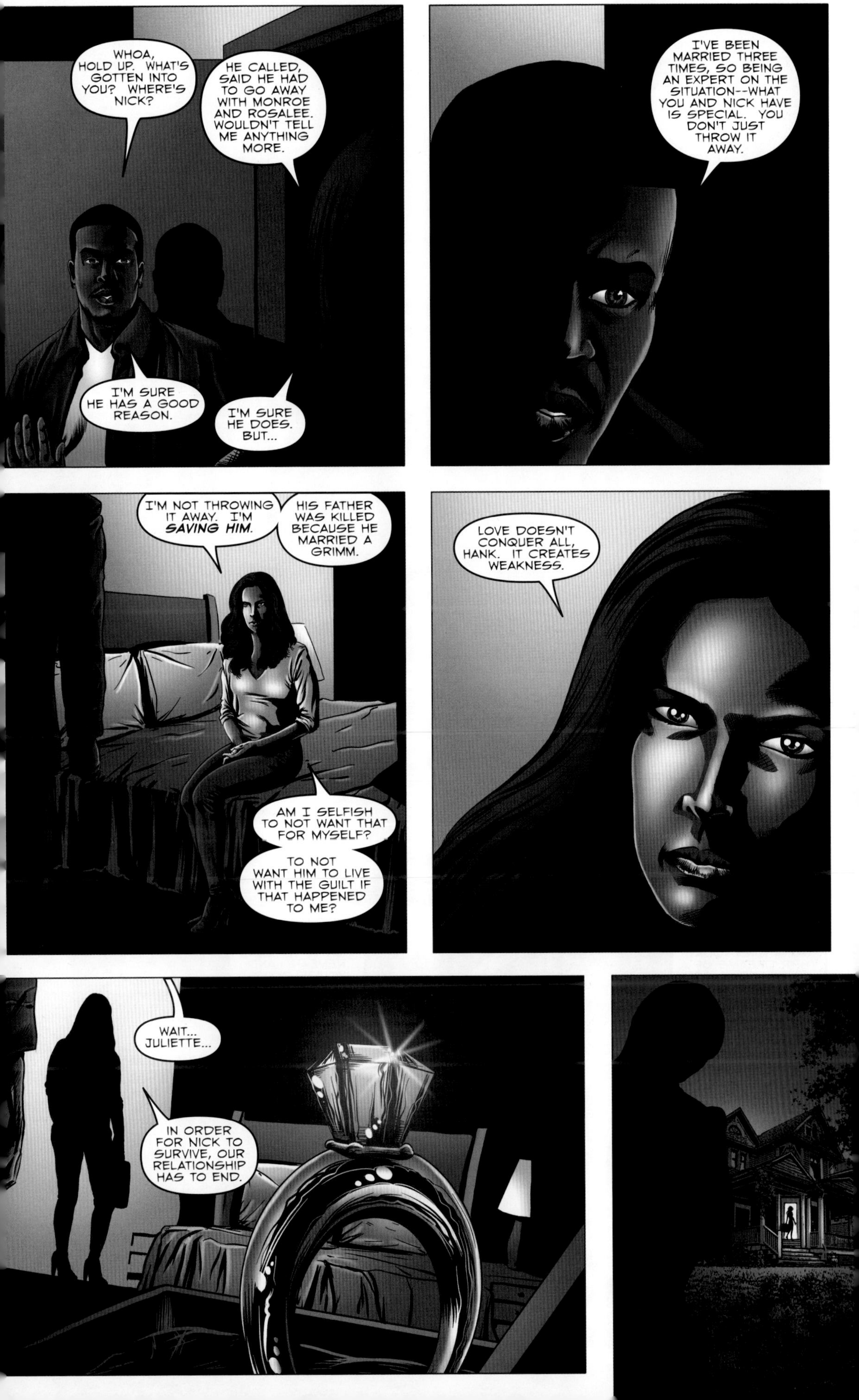
WHOA, HOLD UP. WHAT'S GOTTEN INTO YOU? WHERE'S NICK?
HE CALLED, SAID HE HAD TO GO AWAY WITH MONROE AND ROSALEE. WOULDN'T TELL ME ANYTHING MORE.
I'M SURE HE HAS A GOOD REASON.
I'M SURE HE DOES. BUT...
I'VE BEEN MARRIED THREE TIMES, SO BEING AN EXPERT ON THE SITUATION--WHAT YOU AND NICK HAVE IS SPECIAL. YOU DON'T JUST THROW IT AWAY.
I'M NOT THROWING IT AWAY. I'M *SAVING HIM*.
HIS FATHER WAS KILLED BECAUSE HE MARRIED A GRIMM.
AM I SELFISH TO NOT WANT THAT FOR MYSELF?
TO NOT WANT HIM TO LIVE WITH THE GUILT IF THAT HAPPENED TO ME?
LOVE DOESN'T CONQUER ALL, HANK. IT CREATES WEAKNESS.
WAIT... JULIETTE...
IN ORDER FOR NICK TO SURVIVE, OUR RELATIONSHIP HAS TO END.

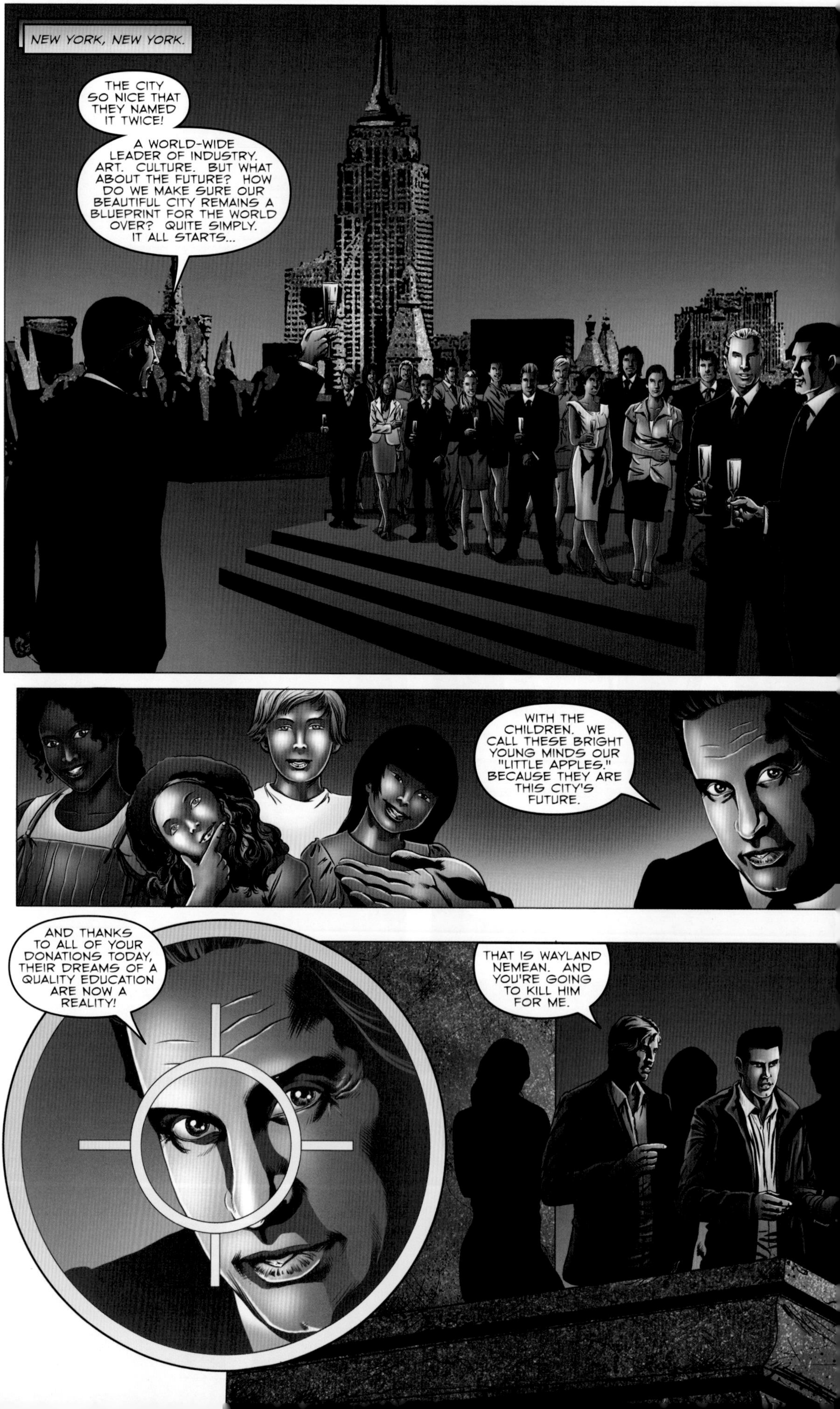
NEW YORK, NEW YORK.
THE CITY SO NICE THAT THEY NAMED IT TWICE!
A WORLD-WIDE LEADER OF INDUSTRY. ART. CULTURE. BUT WHAT ABOUT THE FUTURE? HOW DO WE MAKE SURE OUR BEAUTIFUL CITY REMAINS A BLUEPRINT FOR THE WORLD OVER? QUITE SIMPLY. IT ALL STARTS...
WITH THE CHILDREN. WE CALL THESE BRIGHT YOUNG MINDS OUR "LITTLE APPLES." BECAUSE THEY ARE THIS CITY'S FUTURE.
AND THANKS TO ALL OF YOUR DONATIONS TODAY, THEIR DREAMS OF A QUALITY EDUCATION ARE NOW A REALITY!
THAT IS WAYLAND NEMEAN. AND YOU'RE GOING TO KILL HIM FOR ME.

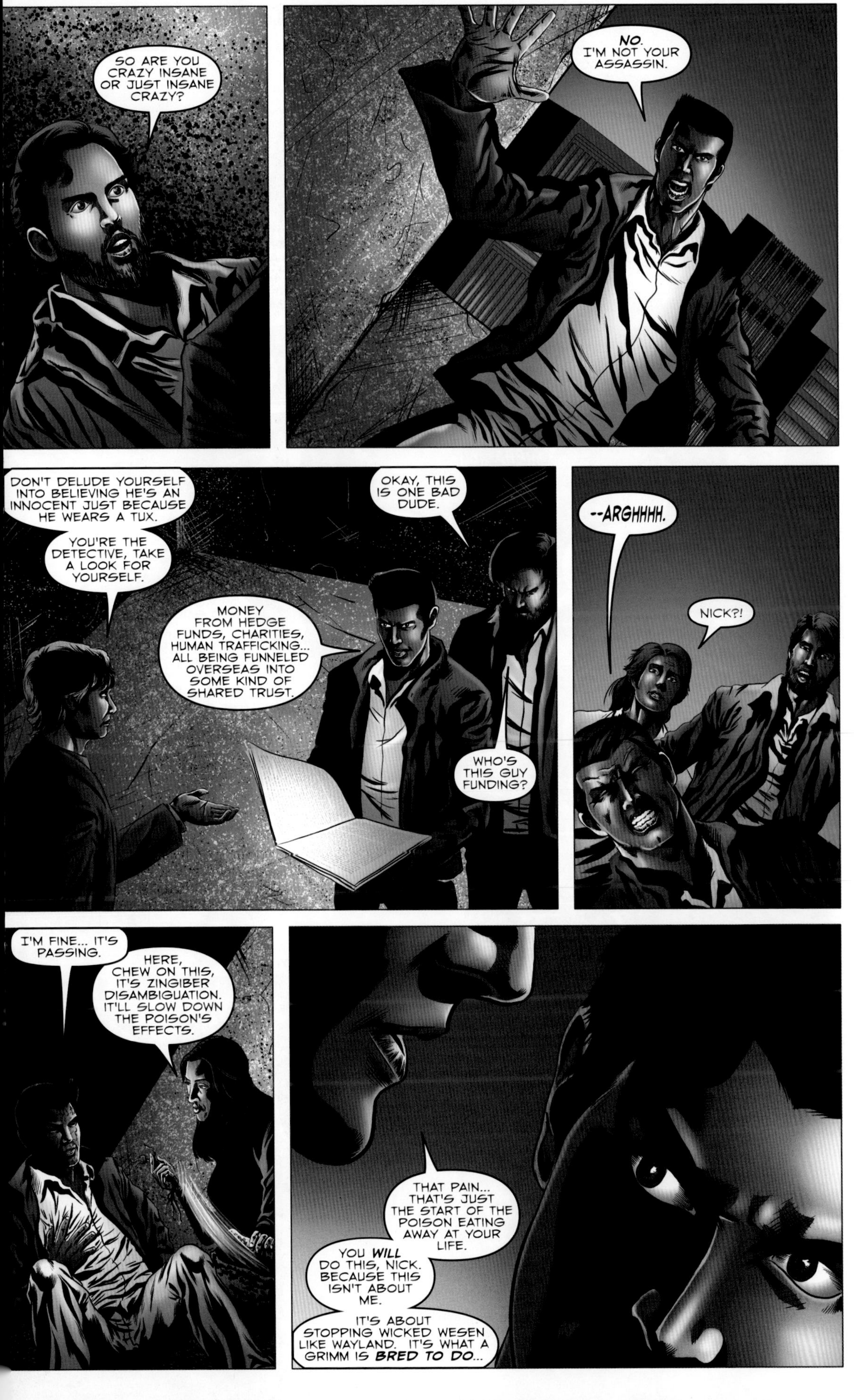

SO ARE YOU CRAZY INSANE OR JUST INSANE CRAZY?
NO. I'M NOT YOUR ASSASSIN.
DON'T DELUDE YOURSELF INTO BELIEVING HE'S AN INNOCENT JUST BECAUSE HE WEARS A TUX.
YOU'RE THE DETECTIVE, TAKE A LOOK FOR YOURSELF.
MONEY FROM HEDGE FUNDS, CHARITIES, HUMAN TRAFFICKING... ALL BEING FUNNELED OVERSEAS INTO SOME KIND OF SHARED TRUST.
OKAY, THIS IS ONE BAD DUDE.
WHO'S THIS GUY FUNDING?
--ARGHHHH.
NICK?!
I'M FINE... IT'S PASSING.
HERE, CHEW ON THIS, IT'S ZINGIBER DISAMBIGUATION. IT'LL SLOW DOWN THE POISON'S EFFECTS.
THAT PAIN... THAT'S JUST THE START OF THE POISON EATING AWAY AT YOUR LIFE.
YOU WILL DO THIS, NICK. BECAUSE THIS ISN'T ABOUT ME.
IT'S ABOUT STOPPING WICKED WESEN LIKE WAYLAND. IT'S WHAT A GRIMM IS BRED TO DO...

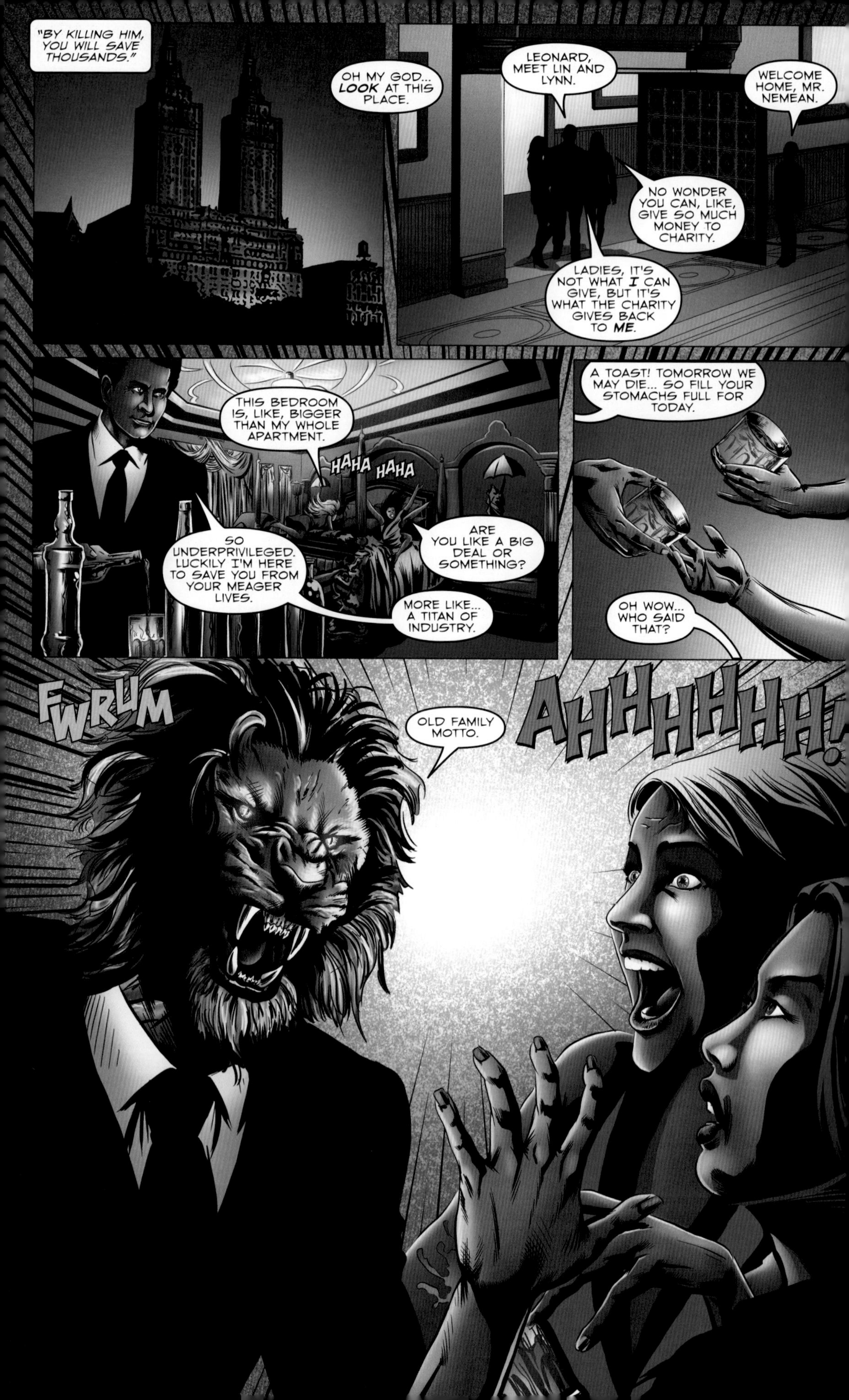
"BY KILLING HIM, YOU WILL SAVE THOUSANDS."
OH MY GOD... LOOK AT THIS PLACE.
LEONARD, MEET LIN AND LYNN.
WELCOME HOME, MR. NEMEAN.
NO WONDER YOU CAN, LIKE, GIVE SO MUCH MONEY TO CHARITY.
LADIES, IT'S NOT WHAT I CAN GIVE, BUT IT'S WHAT THE CHARITY GIVES BACK TO ME.
THIS BEDROOM IS, LIKE, BIGGER THAN MY WHOLE APARTMENT.
HAHA HAHA
SO UNDERPRIVILEGED. LUCKILY I'M HERE TO SAVE YOU FROM YOUR MEAGER LIVES.
ARE YOU LIKE A BIG DEAL OR SOMETHING?
MORE LIKE... A TITAN OF INDUSTRY.
A TOAST! TOMORROW WE MAY DIE... SO FILL YOUR STOMACHS FULL FOR TODAY.
OH WOW... WHO SAID THAT?
FWRUM
OLD FAMILY MOTTO.
AHHHHHH!

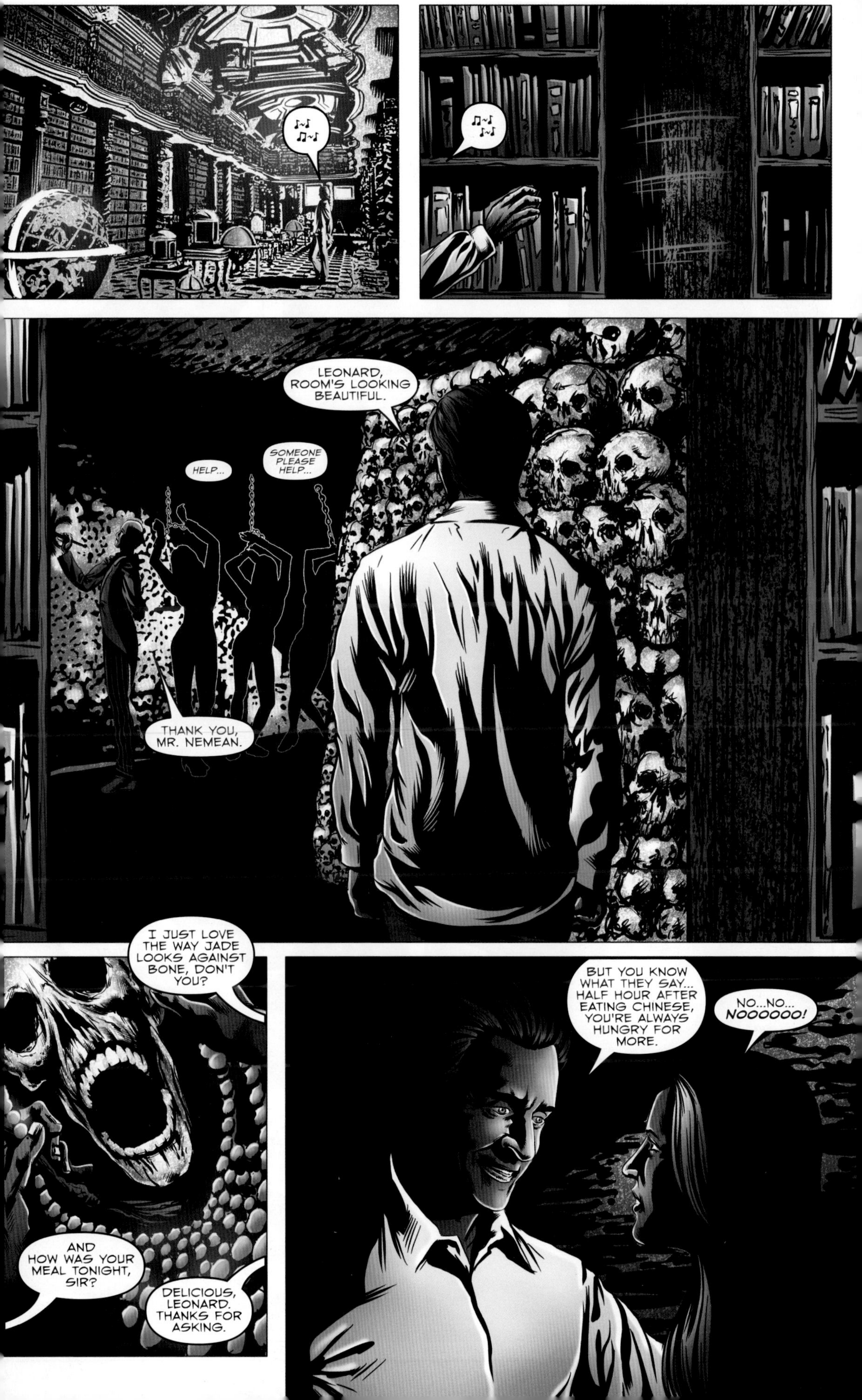
♪~♪ ♪~♪
♪~♪ ♪~♪
LEONARD, ROOM'S LOOKING BEAUTIFUL.
HELP...
SOMEONE PLEASE HELP...
THANK YOU, MR. NEMEAN.
I JUST LOVE THE WAY JADE LOOKS AGAINST BONE, DON'T YOU?
AND HOW WAS YOUR MEAL TONIGHT, SIR?
DELICIOUS, LEONARD. THANKS FOR ASKING.
BUT YOU KNOW WHAT THEY SAY... HALF HOUR AFTER EATING CHINESE, YOU'RE ALWAYS HUNGRY FOR MORE.
NO...NO... NOOOOOO!

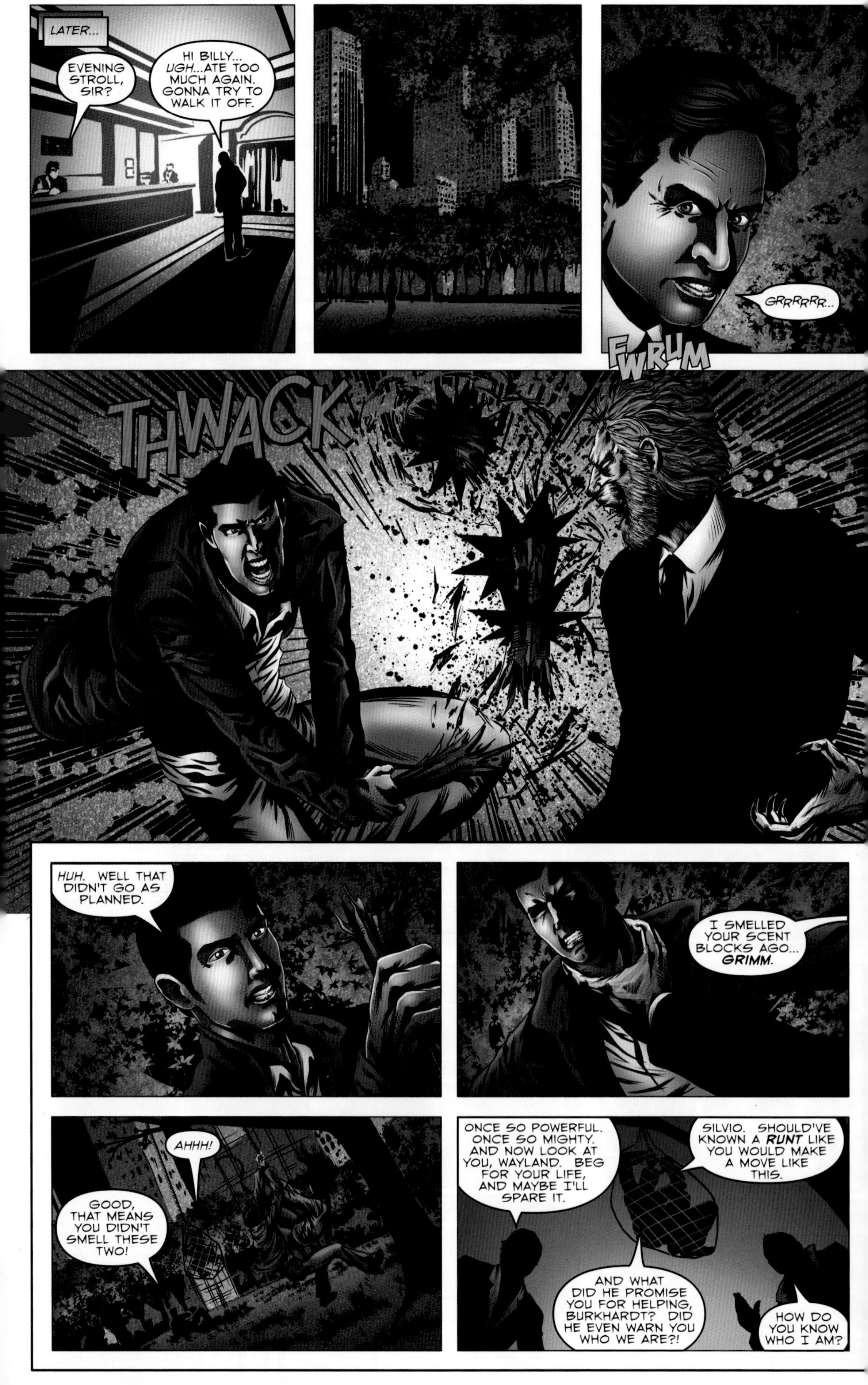
LATER...
EVENING STROLL, SIR?
HI BILLY... UGH...ATE TOO MUCH AGAIN. GONNA TRY TO WALK IT OFF.
GRRRRRR...
FWRUM
THWACK
HUH. WELL THAT DIDN'T GO AS PLANNED.
I SMELLED YOUR SCENT BLOCKS AGO... GRIMM.
AHHH!
GOOD, THAT MEANS YOU DIDN'T SMELL THESE TWO!
ONCE SO POWERFUL. ONCE SO MIGHTY. AND NOW LOOK AT YOU, WAYLAND. BEG FOR YOUR LIFE, AND MAYBE I'LL SPARE IT.
SILVIO. SHOULD'VE KNOWN A RUNT LIKE YOU WOULD MAKE A MOVE LIKE THIS.
AND WHAT DID HE PROMISE YOU FOR HELPING, BURKHARDT? DID HE EVEN WARN YOU WHO WE ARE?!
HOW DO YOU KNOW WHO I AM?

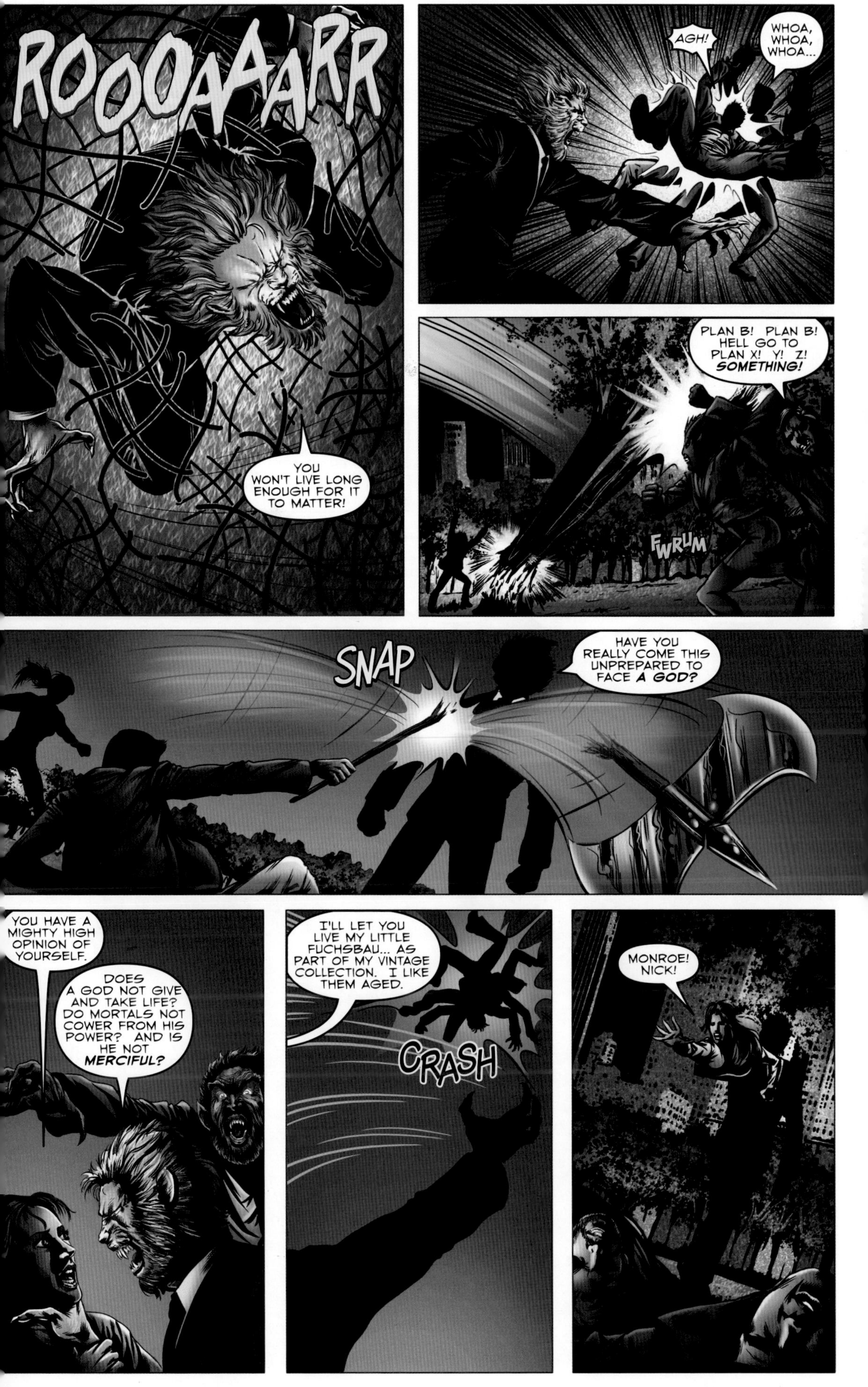
ROOOAAARR
YOU WON'T LIVE LONG ENOUGH FOR IT TO MATTER!
AGH!
WHOA, WHOA, WHOA...
PLAN B! PLAN B! HELL GO TO PLAN X! Y! Z! SOMETHING!
FWRUM
SNAP
HAVE YOU REALLY COME THIS UNPREPARED TO FACE A GOD?
YOU HAVE A MIGHTY HIGH OPINION OF YOURSELF.
DOES A GOD NOT GIVE AND TAKE LIFE? DO MORTALS NOT COWER FROM HIS POWER? AND IS HE NOT MERCIFUL?
I'LL LET YOU LIVE MY LITTLE FUCHSBAU... AS PART OF MY VINTAGE COLLECTION. I LIKE THEM AGED.
CRASH
MONROE! NICK!

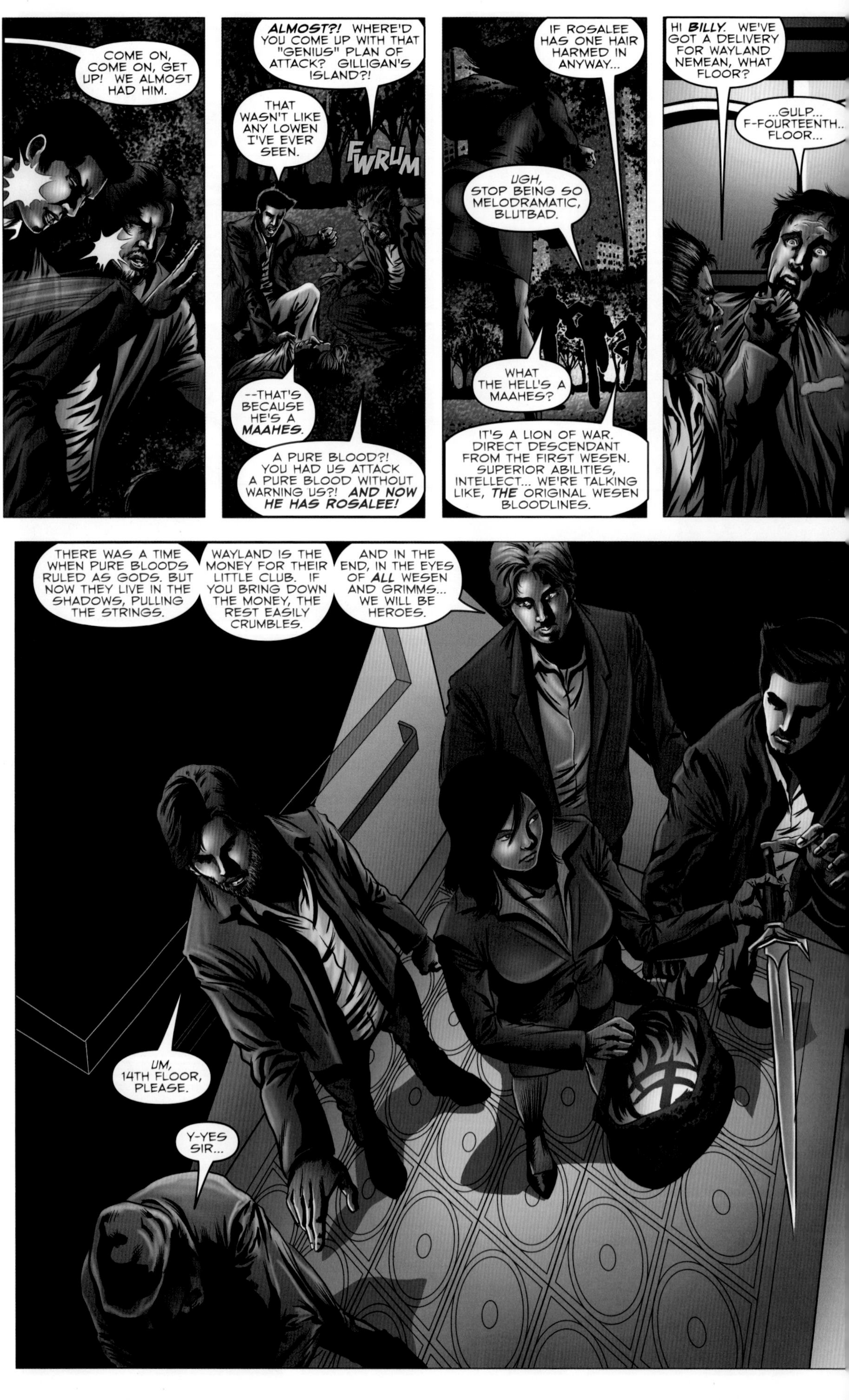
COME ON, COME ON, GET UP! WE ALMOST HAD HIM.
ALMOST?! WHERE'D YOU COME UP WITH THAT "GENIUS" PLAN OF ATTACK? GILLIGAN'S ISLAND?!
THAT WASN'T LIKE ANY LOWEN I'VE EVER SEEN.
FWRUM
--THAT'S BECAUSE HE'S A MAAHES.
A PURE BLOOD?! YOU HAD US ATTACK A PURE BLOOD WITHOUT WARNING US?! AND NOW HE HAS ROSALEE!
IF ROSALEE HAS ONE HAIR HARMED IN ANYWAY...
UGH, STOP BEING SO MELODRAMATIC, BLUTBAD.
WHAT THE HELL'S A MAAHES?
IT'S A LION OF WAR. DIRECT DESCENDANT FROM THE FIRST WESEN. SUPERIOR ABILITIES, INTELLECT... WE'RE TALKING LIKE, THE ORIGINAL WESEN BLOODLINES.
HI BILLY. WE'VE GOT A DELIVERY FOR WAYLAND NEMEAN, WHAT FLOOR?
...GULP... F-FOURTEENTH... FLOOR...
THERE WAS A TIME WHEN PURE BLOODS RULED AS GODS. BUT NOW THEY LIVE IN THE SHADOWS, PULLING THE STRINGS.
WAYLAND IS THE MONEY FOR THEIR LITTLE CLUB. IF YOU BRING DOWN THE MONEY, THE REST EASILY CRUMBLES.
AND IN THE END, IN THE EYES OF ALL WESEN AND GRIMMS... WE WILL BE HEROES.
UM, 14TH FLOOR, PLEASE.
Y-YES SIR...

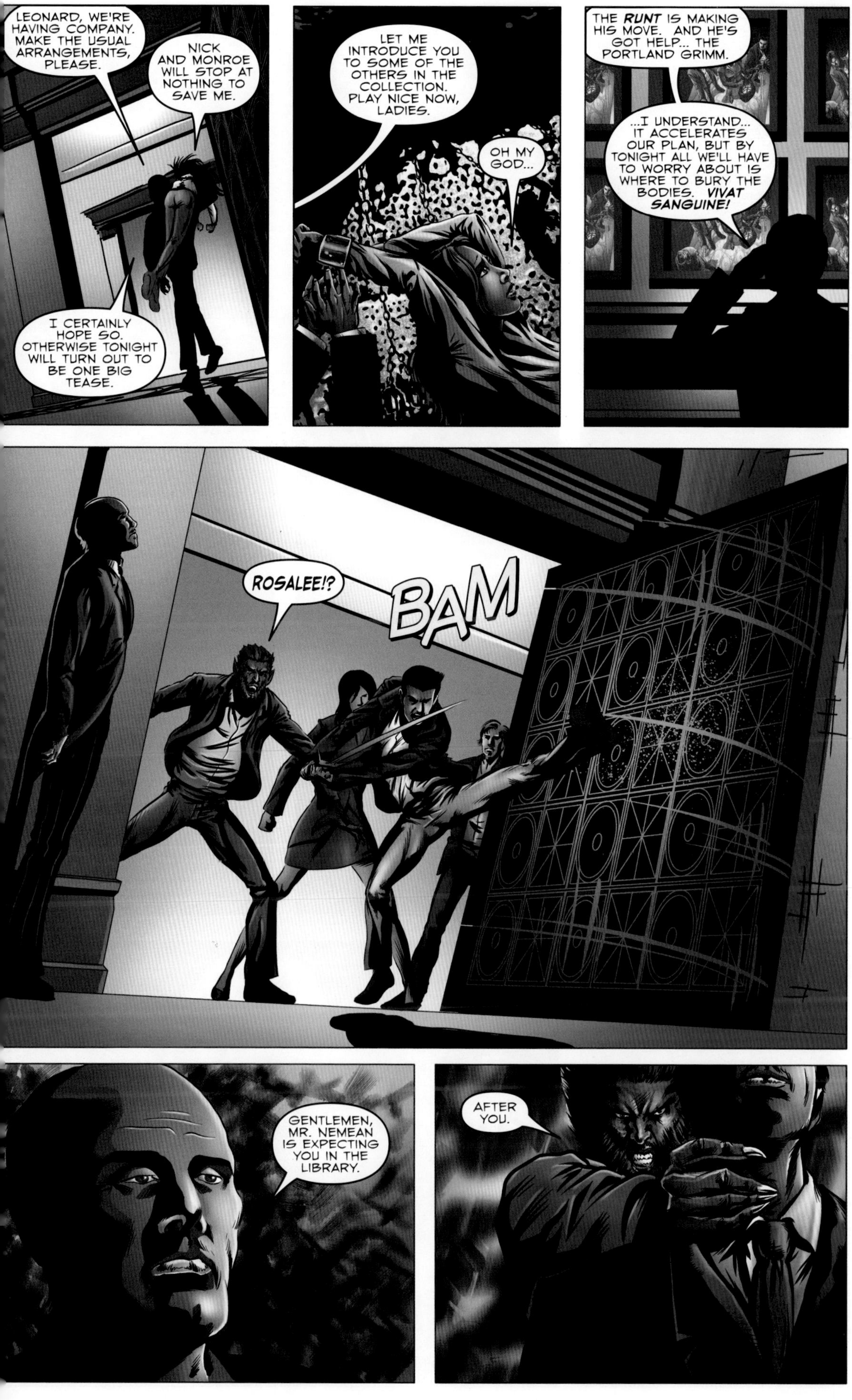
LEONARD, WE'RE HAVING COMPANY. MAKE THE USUAL ARRANGEMENTS, PLEASE.
NICK AND MONROE WILL STOP AT NOTHING TO SAVE ME.
I CERTAINLY HOPE SO. OTHERWISE TONIGHT WILL TURN OUT TO BE ONE BIG TEASE.
LET ME INTRODUCE YOU TO SOME OF THE OTHERS IN THE COLLECTION. PLAY NICE NOW, LADIES.
OH MY GOD...
THE RUNT IS MAKING HIS MOVE. AND HE'S GOT HELP... THE PORTLAND GRIMM.
...I UNDERSTAND... IT ACCELERATES OUR PLAN, BUT BY TONIGHT ALL WE'LL HAVE TO WORRY ABOUT IS WHERE TO BURY THE BODIES. VIVAT SANGUINE!
ROSALEE!?
BAM
GENTLEMEN, MR. NEMEAN IS EXPECTING YOU IN THE LIBRARY.
AFTER YOU.

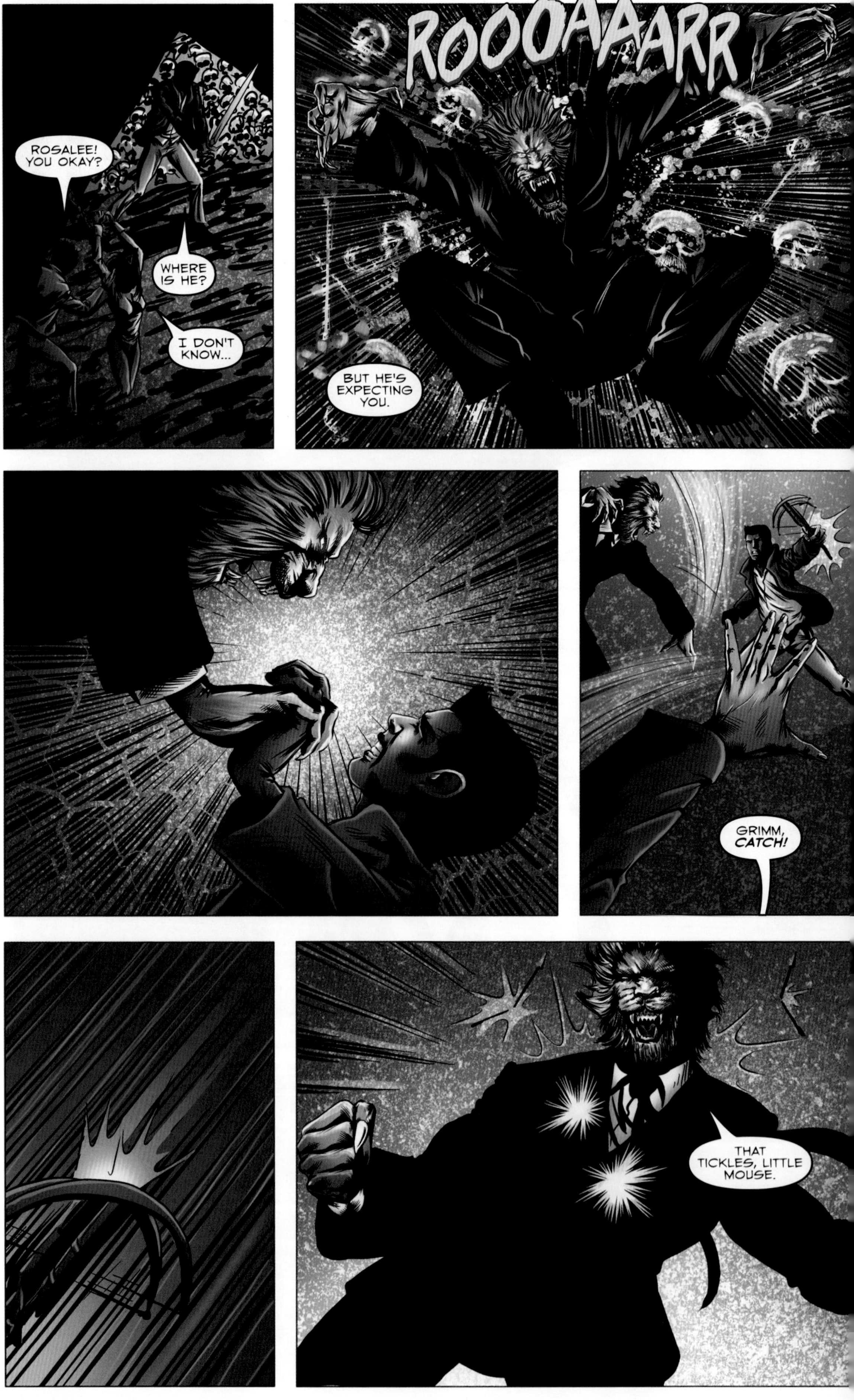
ROSALEE! YOU OKAY?
WHERE IS HE?
I DON'T KNOW...
ROOOAAARR
BUT HE'S EXPECTING YOU.
GRIMM, *CATCH!*
THAT TICKLES, LITTLE MOUSE.

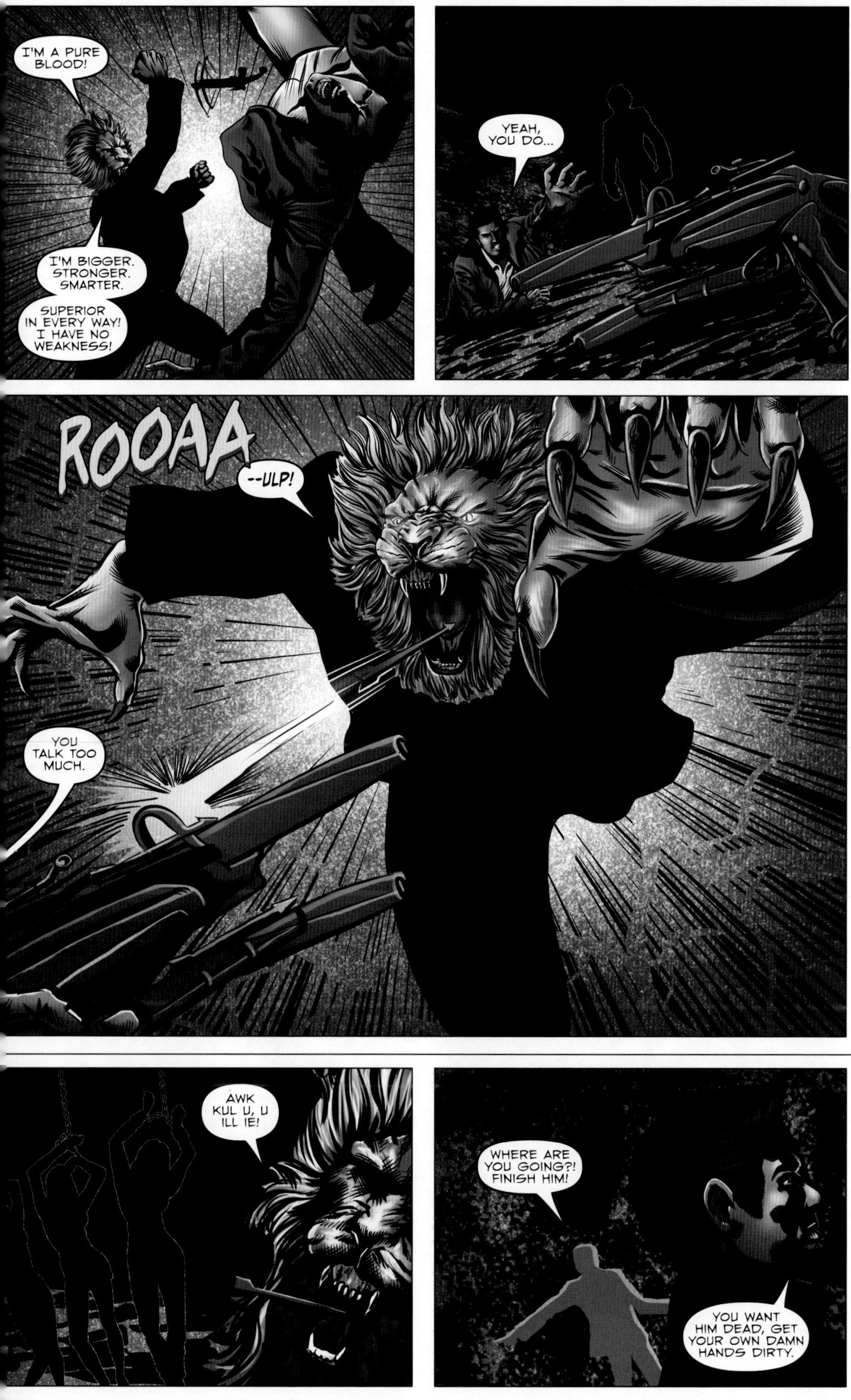
I'M A PURE BLOOD!
I'M BIGGER. STRONGER. SMARTER.
SUPERIOR IN EVERY WAY! I HAVE NO WEAKNESS!
YEAH, YOU DO...
ROOAA
--ULP!
YOU TALK TOO MUCH.
AWK KUL U, U ILL IE!
WHERE ARE YOU GOING?! FINISH HIM!
YOU WANT HIM DEAD, GET YOUR OWN DAMN HANDS DIRTY.

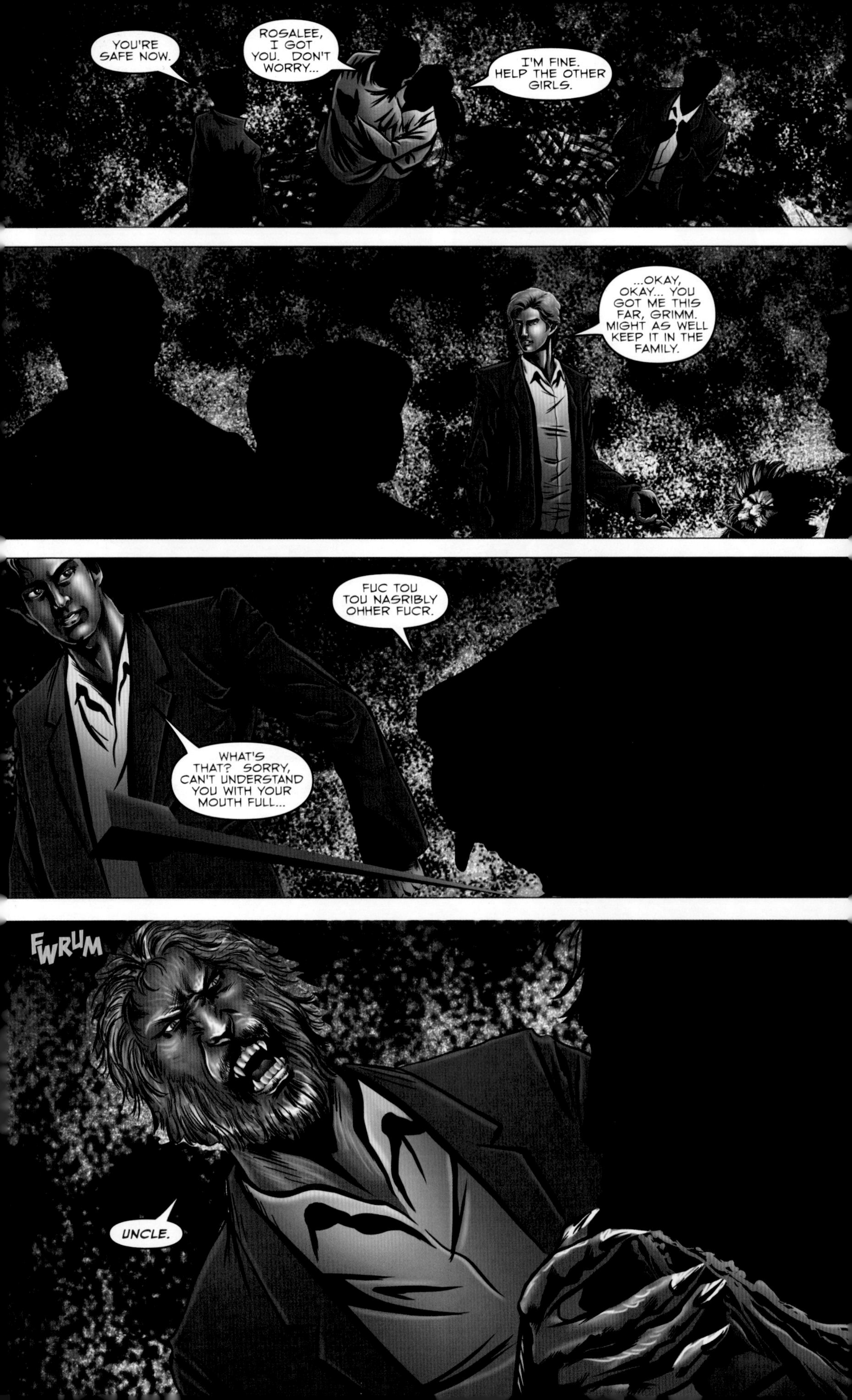
YOU'RE SAFE NOW.
ROSALEE, I GOT YOU. DON'T WORRY...
I'M FINE. HELP THE OTHER GIRLS.
...OKAY, OKAY... YOU GOT ME THIS FAR, GRIMM. MIGHT AS WELL KEEP IT IN THE FAMILY.
FUC TOU TOU NASRIBLY OHHER FUCR.
WHAT'S THAT? SORRY, CAN'T UNDERSTAND YOU WITH YOUR MOUTH FULL...
FWRUM
UNCLE.

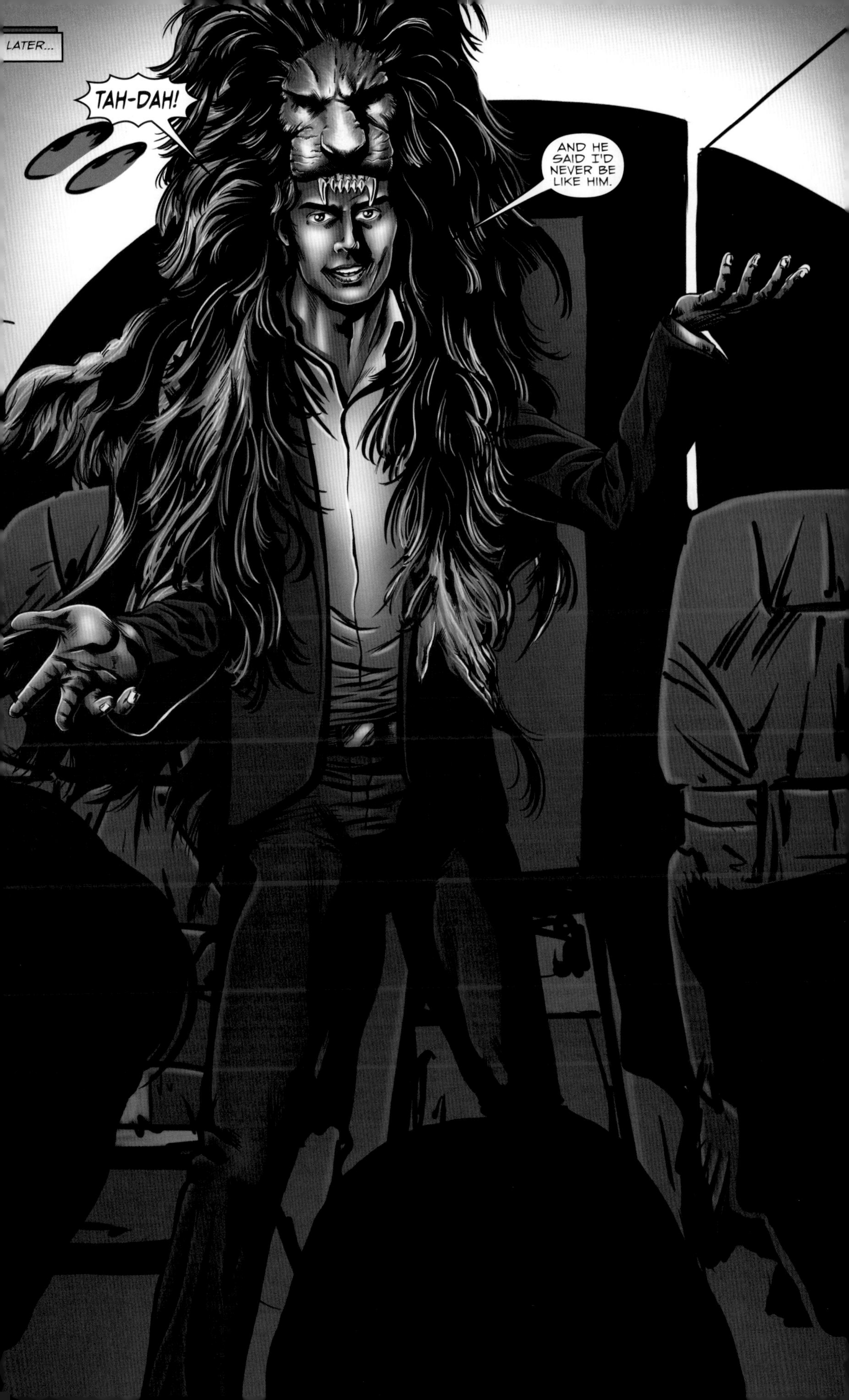
LATER...
TAH-DAH!
AND HE SAID I'D NEVER BE LIKE HIM.

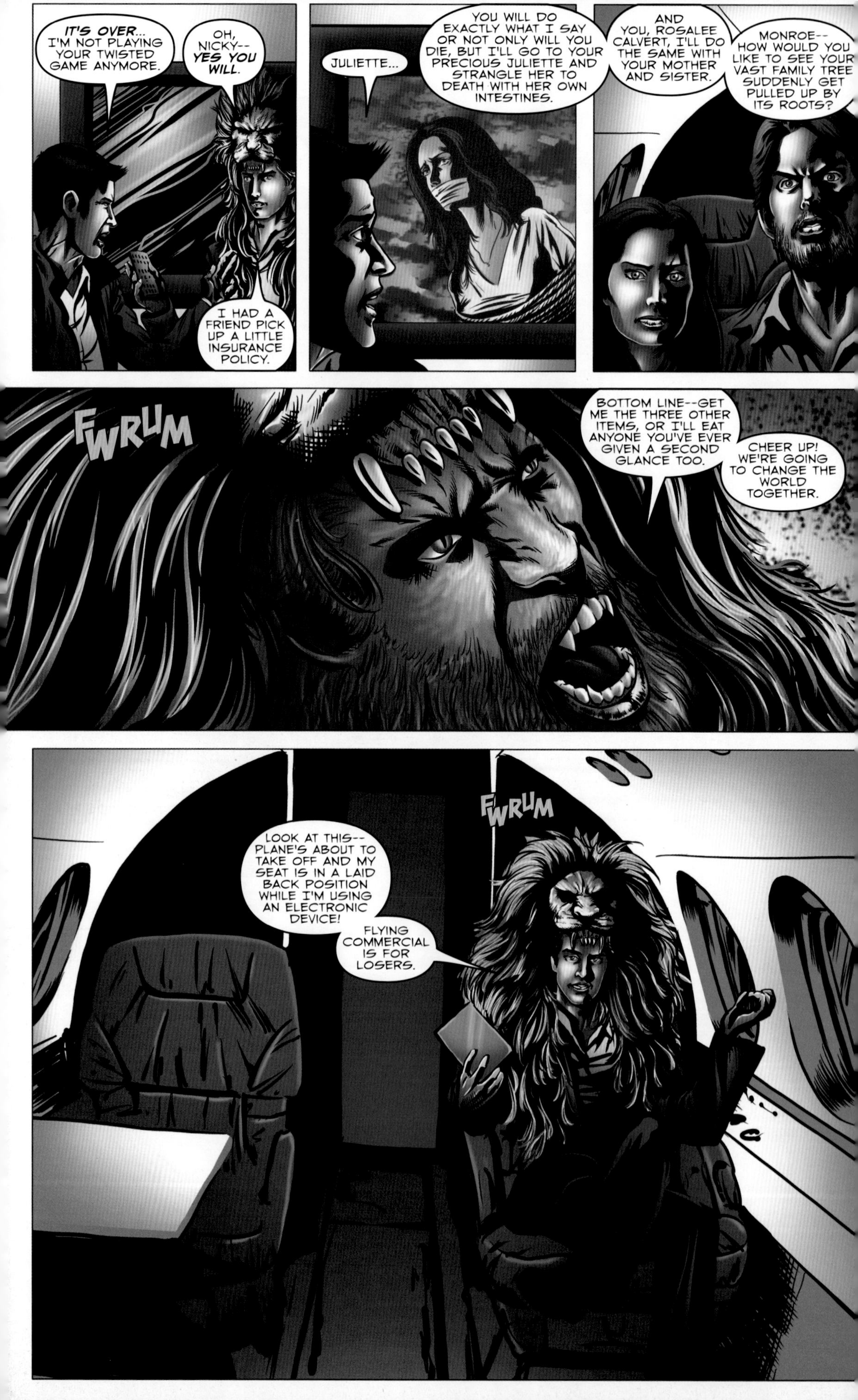
IT'S OVER... I'M NOT PLAYING YOUR TWISTED GAME ANYMORE.
OH, NICKY-- YES YOU WILL.
I HAD A FRIEND PICK UP A LITTLE INSURANCE POLICY.
JULIETTE...
YOU WILL DO EXACTLY WHAT I SAY OR NOT ONLY WILL YOU DIE, BUT I'LL GO TO YOUR PRECIOUS JULIETTE AND STRANGLE HER TO DEATH WITH HER OWN INTESTINES.
AND YOU, ROSALEE CALVERT, I'LL DO THE SAME WITH YOUR MOTHER AND SISTER.
MONROE-- HOW WOULD YOU LIKE TO SEE YOUR VAST FAMILY TREE SUDDENLY GET PULLED UP BY ITS ROOTS?
FWRUM
BOTTOM LINE--GET ME THE THREE OTHER ITEMS, OR I'LL EAT ANYONE YOU'VE EVER GIVEN A SECOND GLANCE TOO.
CHEER UP! WE'RE GOING TO CHANGE THE WORLD TOGETHER.
FWRUM
LOOK AT THIS-- PLANE'S ABOUT TO TAKE OFF AND MY SEAT IS IN A LAID BACK POSITION WHILE I'M USING AN ELECTRONIC DEVICE!
FLYING COMMERCIAL IS FOR LOSERS.

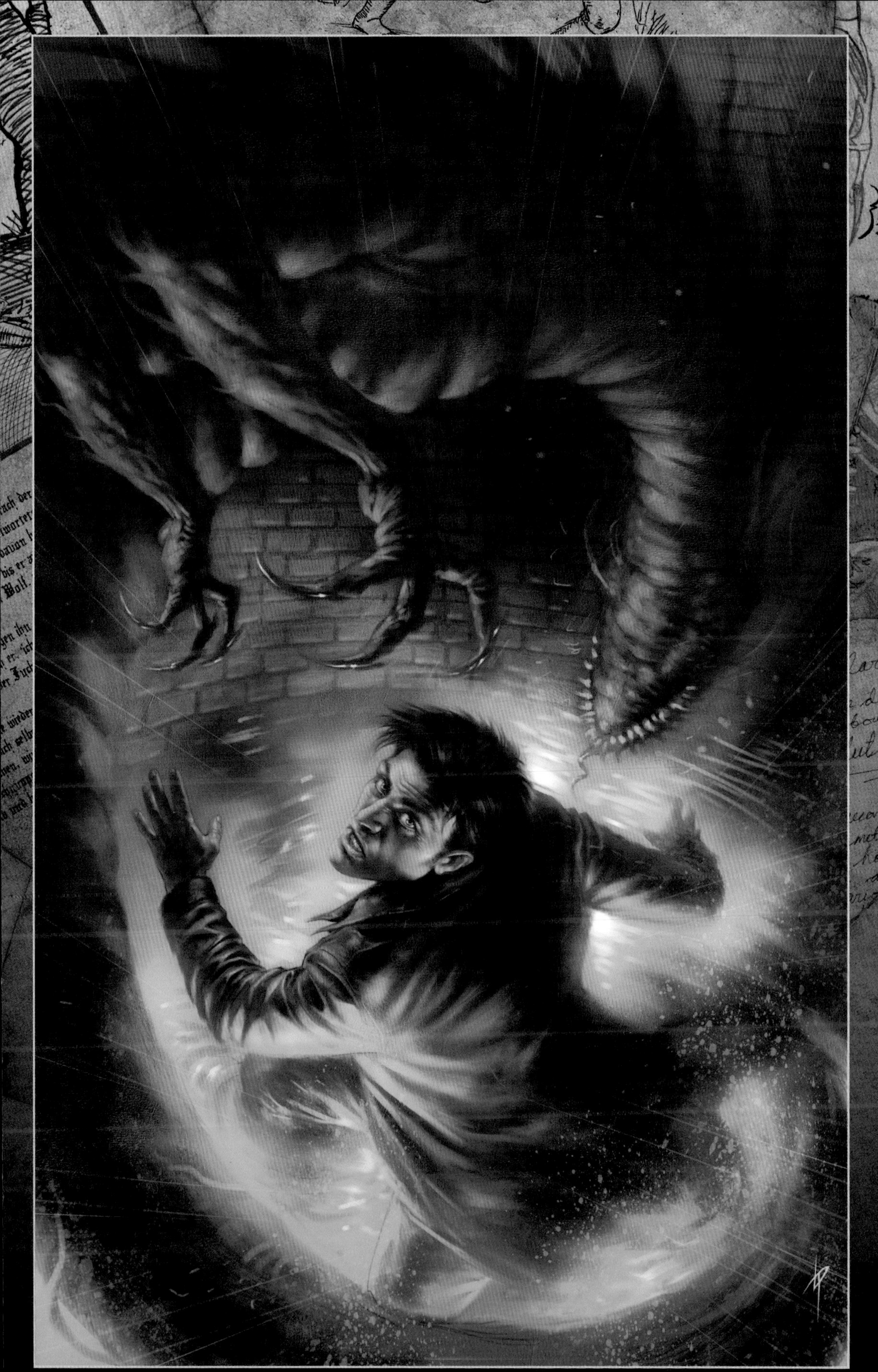

ISSUE #11 COVER

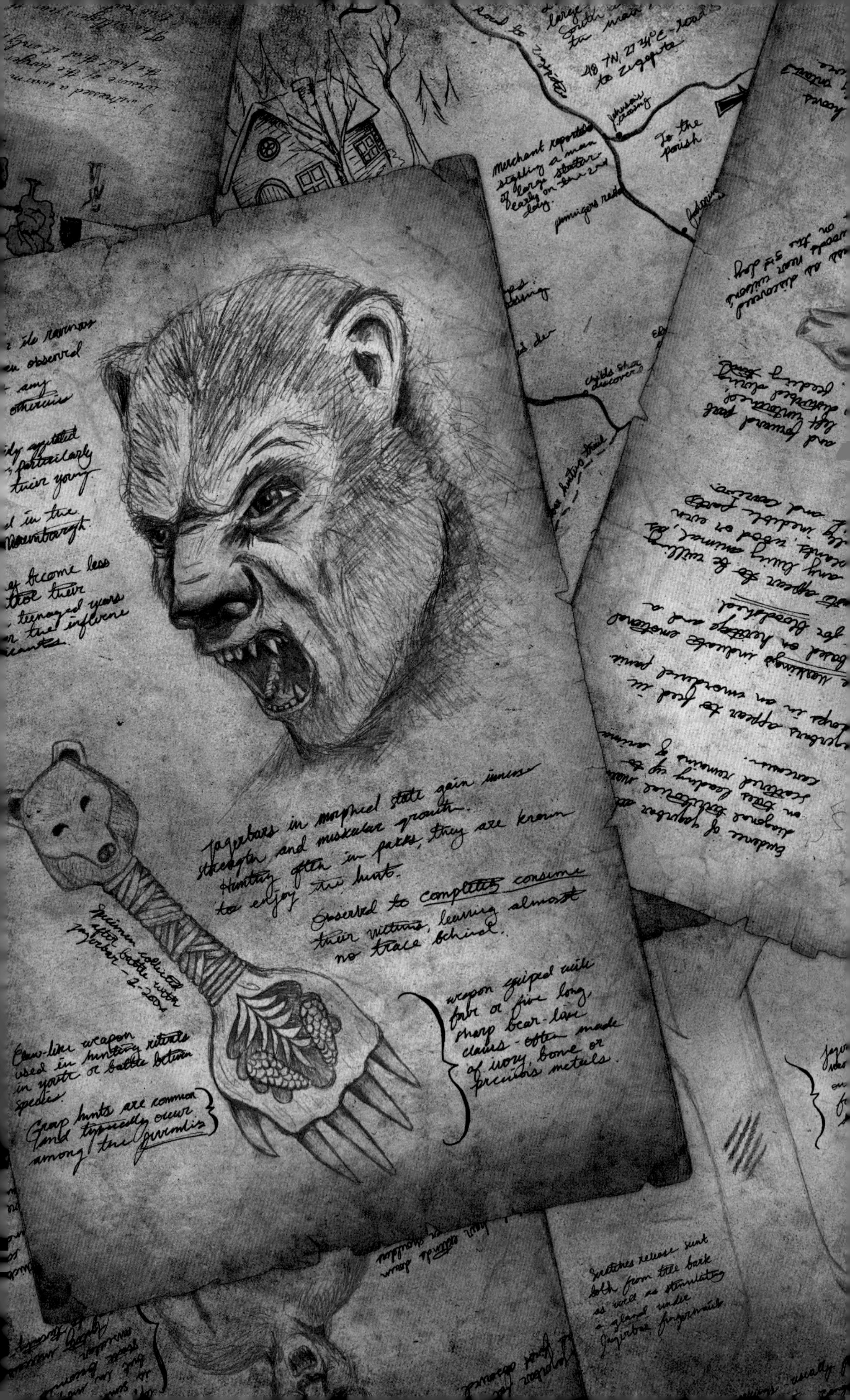

To the parish
Merchant reported sighting a man of large stature early on the 2nd day.
Jagerbars in morphed state gain immense strength and muscular growth.
Hunting often in packs, they are known to enjoy the hunt.
Observed to completely consume their victims, leaving almost no trace behind.
Specimen collected after battle with Jagerbar
weapon equipped with four or five long, sharp bear-like claws - often made of ivory bone or precious metals
Claw-like weapon used in hunting rituals in youth or battle between species
Group hunts are common and typically occur among the juveniles
Scratches release scent both from the back as well as stimulating a gland under Jagerbar fingernails

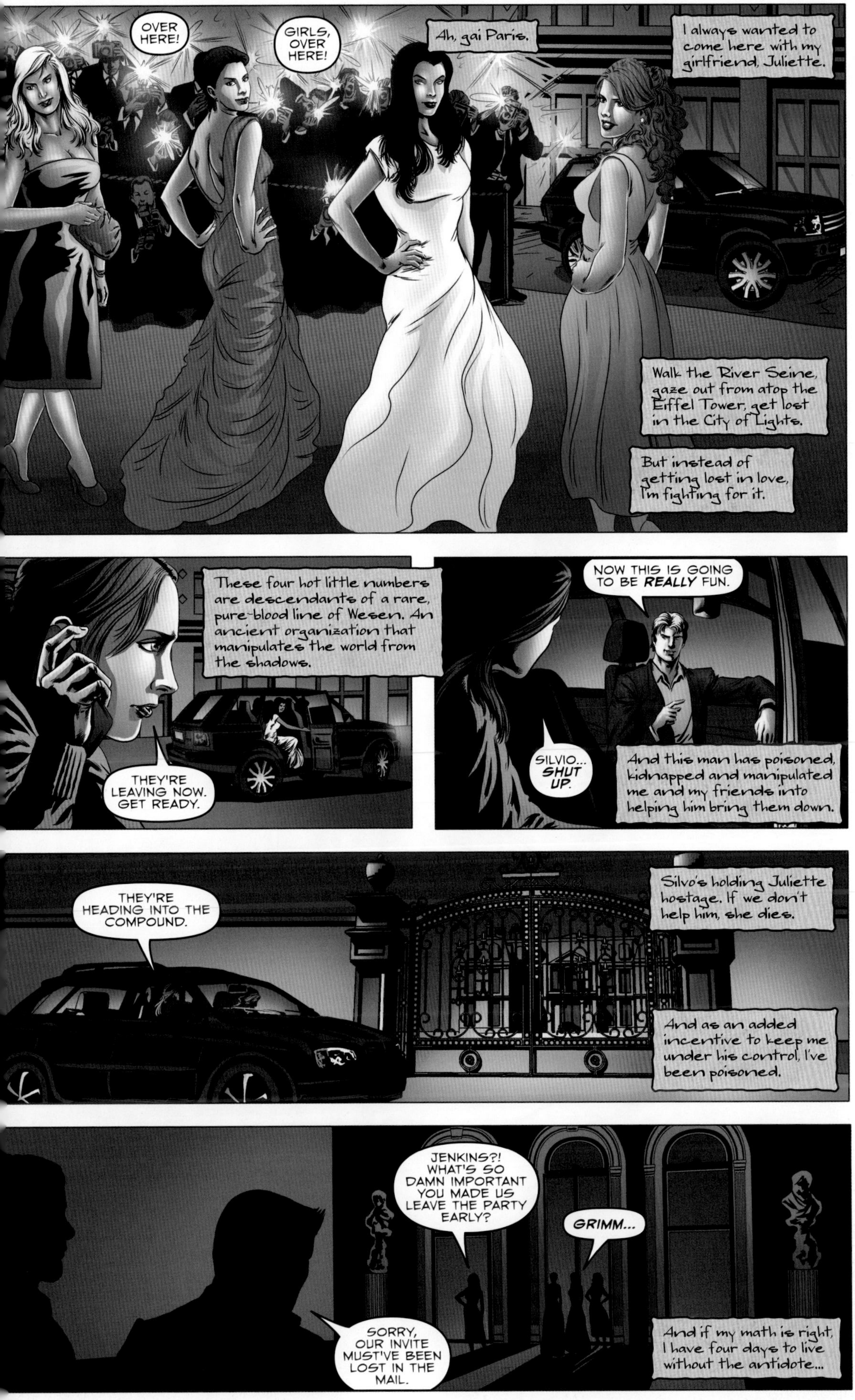
OVER HERE!
GIRLS, OVER HERE!
Ah, gai Paris.
I always wanted to come here with my girlfriend, Juliette.
Walk the River Seine, gaze out from atop the Eiffel Tower, get lost in the City of Lights.
But instead of getting lost in love, I'm fighting for it.
These four hot little numbers are descendants of a rare, pure-blood line of Wesen. An ancient organization that manipulates the world from the shadows.
THEY'RE LEAVING NOW. GET READY.
NOW THIS IS GOING TO BE REALLY FUN.
SILVIO... SHUT UP.
And this man has poisoned, kidnapped and manipulated me and my friends into helping him bring them down.
THEY'RE HEADING INTO THE COMPOUND.
Silvo's holding Juliette hostage. If we don't help him, she dies.
And as an added incentive to keep me under his control, I've been poisoned.
JENKINS?! WHAT'S SO DAMN IMPORTANT YOU MADE US LEAVE THE PARTY EARLY?
GRIMM...
SORRY, OUR INVITE MUST'VE BEEN LOST IN THE MAIL.
And if my math is right, I have four days to live without the antidote...

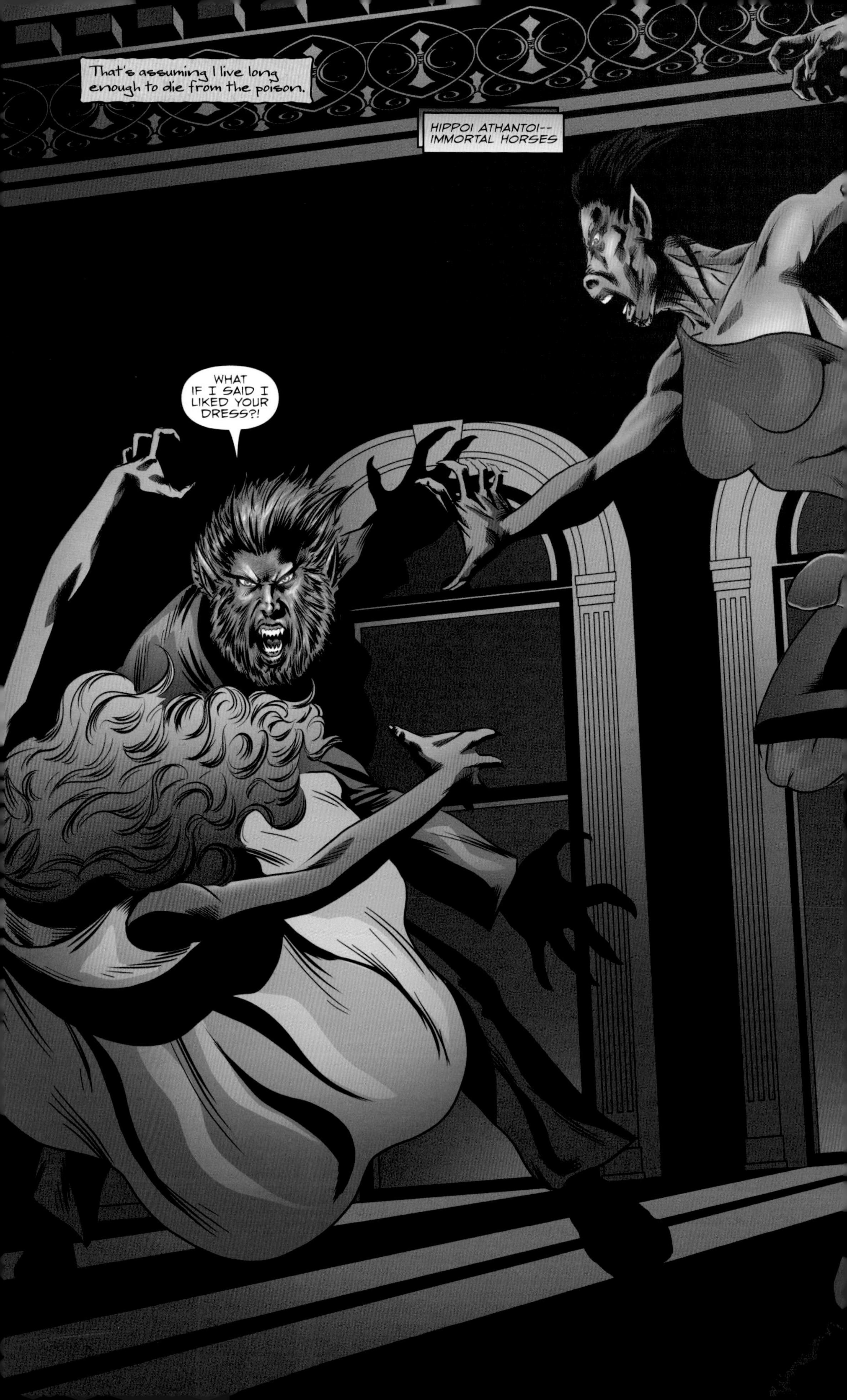

That's assuming I live long enough to die from the poison.
HIPPOI ATHANTOI--IMMORTAL HORSES
WHAT IF I SAID I LIKED YOUR DRESS?!

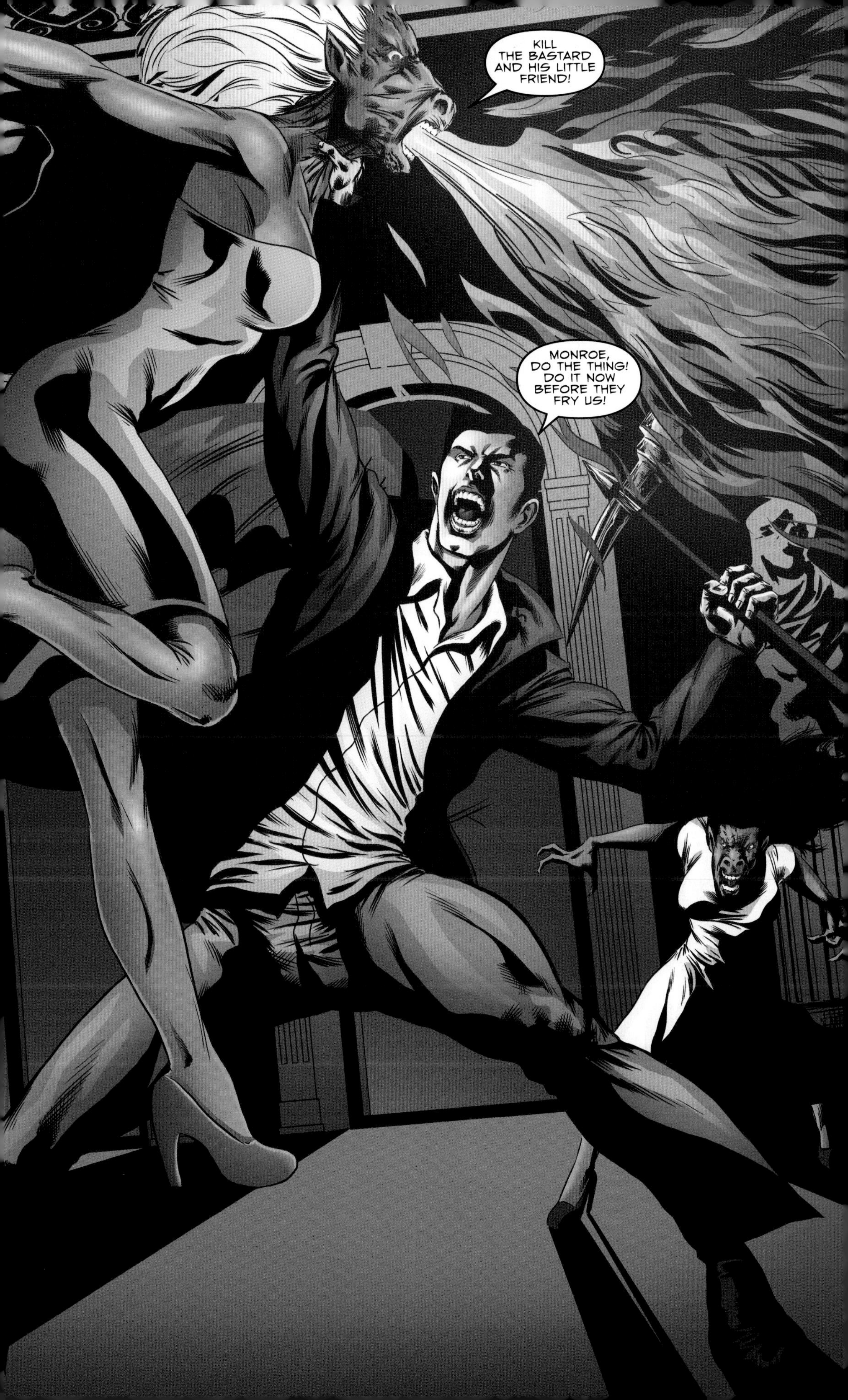
KILL THE BASTARD AND HIS LITTLE FRIEND!
MONROE, DO THE THING! DO IT NOW BEFORE THEY FRY US!

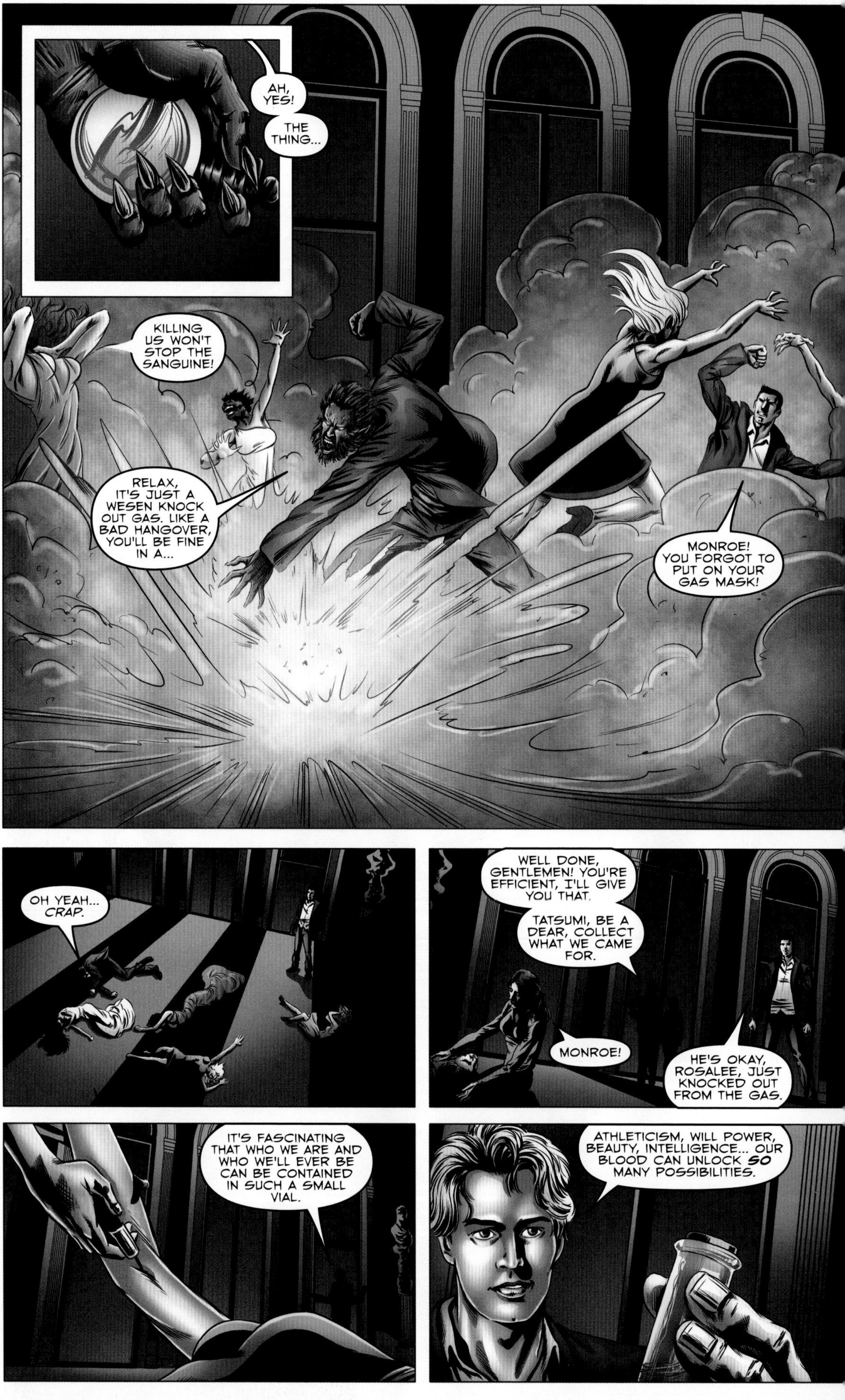
AH, YES!
THE THING...
KILLING US WON'T STOP THE SANGUINE!
RELAX, IT'S JUST A WESEN KNOCK OUT GAS. LIKE A BAD HANGOVER, YOU'LL BE FINE IN A...
MONROE! YOU FORGOT TO PUT ON YOUR GAS MASK!
OH YEAH... *CRAP.*
WELL DONE, GENTLEMEN! YOU'RE EFFICIENT, I'LL GIVE YOU THAT.
TATSUMI, BE A DEAR, COLLECT WHAT WE CAME FOR.
MONROE!
HE'S OKAY, ROSALEE, JUST KNOCKED OUT FROM THE GAS.
IT'S FASCINATING THAT WHO WE ARE AND WHO WE'LL EVER BE CAN BE CONTAINED IN SUCH A SMALL VIAL.
ATHLETICISM, WILL POWER, BEAUTY, INTELLIGENCE... OUR BLOOD CAN UNLOCK *SO* MANY POSSIBILITIES.

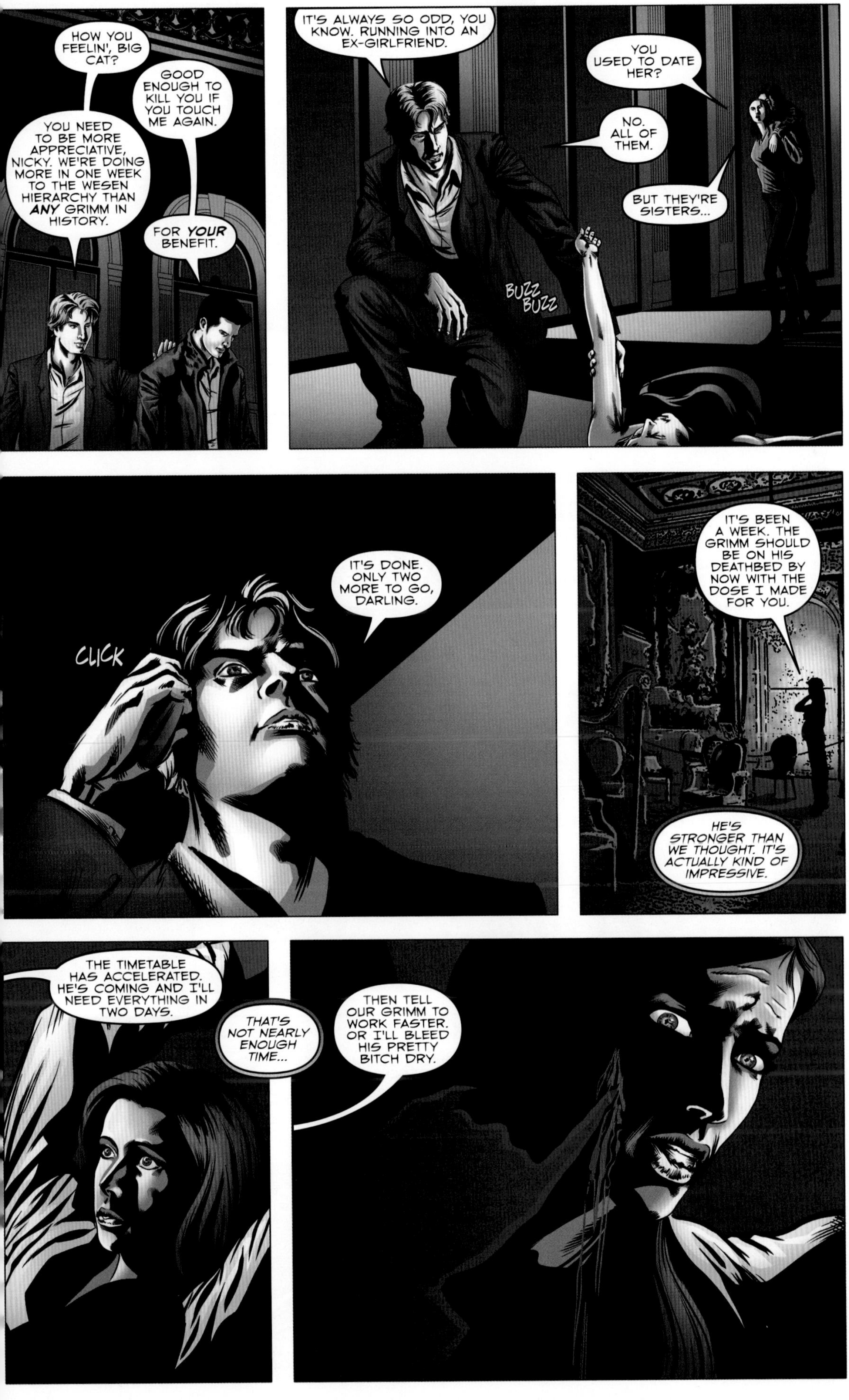
HOW YOU FEELIN', BIG CAT?
GOOD ENOUGH TO KILL YOU IF YOU TOUCH ME AGAIN.
YOU NEED TO BE MORE APPRECIATIVE, NICKY. WE'RE DOING MORE IN ONE WEEK TO THE WESEN HIERARCHY THAN ANY GRIMM IN HISTORY.
FOR YOUR BENEFIT.
IT'S ALWAYS SO ODD, YOU KNOW. RUNNING INTO AN EX-GIRLFRIEND.
YOU USED TO DATE HER?
NO. ALL OF THEM.
BUT THEY'RE SISTERS...
BUZZ BUZZ
CLICK
IT'S DONE. ONLY TWO MORE TO GO, DARLING.
IT'S BEEN A WEEK. THE GRIMM SHOULD BE ON HIS DEATHBED BY NOW WITH THE DOSE I MADE FOR YOU.
HE'S STRONGER THAN WE THOUGHT. IT'S ACTUALLY KIND OF IMPRESSIVE.
THE TIMETABLE HAS ACCELERATED. HE'S COMING AND I'LL NEED EVERYTHING IN TWO DAYS.
THAT'S NOT NEARLY ENOUGH TIME...
THEN TELL OUR GRIMM TO WORK FASTER. OR I'LL BLEED HIS PRETTY BITCH DRY.

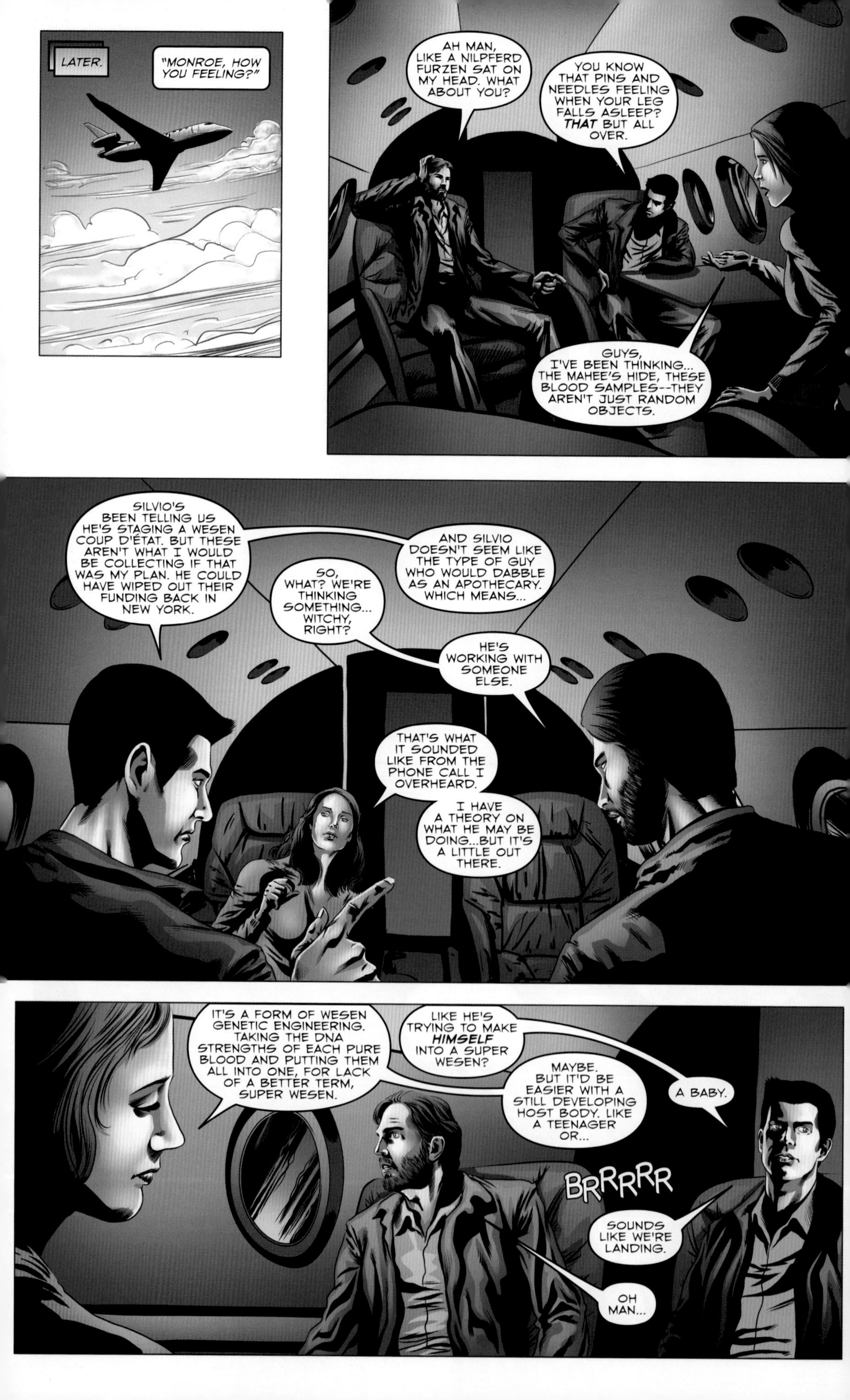
LATER.
"MONROE, HOW YOU FEELING?"
AH MAN, LIKE A NILPFERD FURZEN SAT ON MY HEAD. WHAT ABOUT YOU?
YOU KNOW THAT PINS AND NEEDLES FEELING WHEN YOUR LEG FALLS ASLEEP? THAT BUT ALL OVER.
GUYS, I'VE BEEN THINKING... THE MAHEE'S HIDE, THESE BLOOD SAMPLES--THEY AREN'T JUST RANDOM OBJECTS.
SILVIO'S BEEN TELLING US HE'S STAGING A WESEN COUP D'ÉTAT. BUT THESE AREN'T WHAT I WOULD BE COLLECTING IF THAT WAS MY PLAN. HE COULD HAVE WIPED OUT THEIR FUNDING BACK IN NEW YORK.
AND SILVIO DOESN'T SEEM LIKE THE TYPE OF GUY WHO WOULD DABBLE AS AN APOTHECARY. WHICH MEANS...
SO, WHAT? WE'RE THINKING SOMETHING... WITCHY, RIGHT?
HE'S WORKING WITH SOMEONE ELSE.
THAT'S WHAT IT SOUNDED LIKE FROM THE PHONE CALL I OVERHEARD.
I HAVE A THEORY ON WHAT HE MAY BE DOING...BUT IT'S A LITTLE OUT THERE.
IT'S A FORM OF WESEN GENETIC ENGINEERING. TAKING THE DNA STRENGTHS OF EACH PURE BLOOD AND PUTTING THEM ALL INTO ONE, FOR LACK OF A BETTER TERM, SUPER WESEN.
LIKE HE'S TRYING TO MAKE HIMSELF INTO A SUPER WESEN?
MAYBE. BUT IT'D BE EASIER WITH A STILL DEVELOPING HOST BODY. LIKE A TEENAGER OR...
A BABY.
BRRRRR
SOUNDS LIKE WE'RE LANDING.
OH MAN...

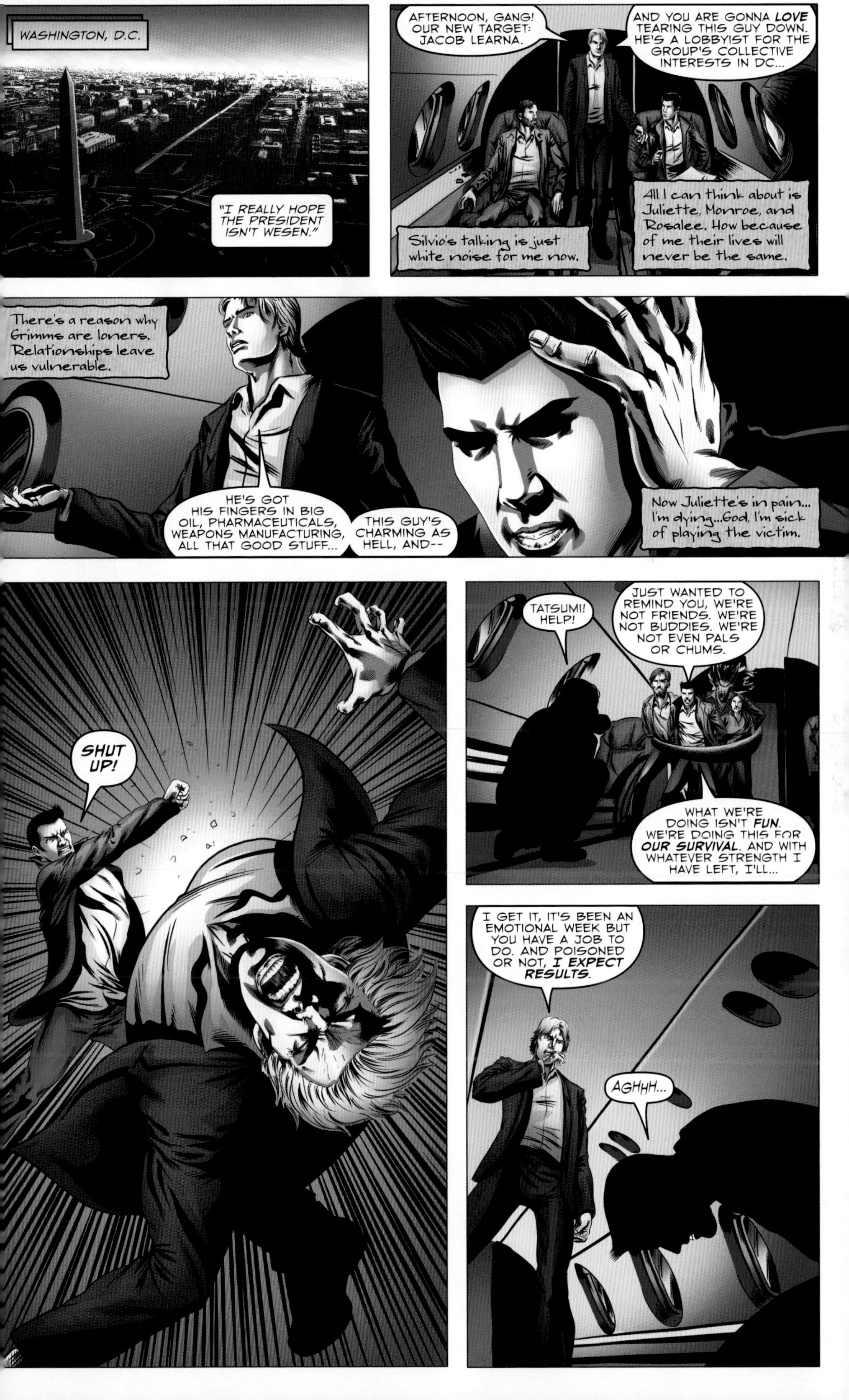
WASHINGTON, D.C.
"I REALLY HOPE THE PRESIDENT ISN'T WESEN."
AFTERNOON, GANG! OUR NEW TARGET: JACOB LEARNA.
AND YOU ARE GONNA LOVE TEARING THIS GUY DOWN. HE'S A LOBBYIST FOR THE GROUP'S COLLECTIVE INTERESTS IN DC...
Silvio's talking is just white noise for me now.
All I can think about is Juliette, Monroe, and Rosalee. How because of me their lives will never be the same.
There's a reason why Grimms are loners. Relationships leave us vulnerable.
HE'S GOT HIS FINGERS IN BIG OIL, PHARMACEUTICALS, WEAPONS MANUFACTURING, ALL THAT GOOD STUFF...
THIS GUY'S CHARMING AS HELL, AND--
Now Juliette's in pain... I'm dying...God, I'm sick of playing the victim.
SHUT UP!
TATSUMI! HELP!
JUST WANTED TO REMIND YOU, WE'RE NOT FRIENDS. WE'RE NOT BUDDIES. WE'RE NOT EVEN PALS OR CHUMS.
WHAT WE'RE DOING ISN'T FUN. WE'RE DOING THIS FOR OUR SURVIVAL. AND WITH WHATEVER STRENGTH I HAVE LEFT, I'LL...
I GET IT, IT'S BEEN AN EMOTIONAL WEEK BUT YOU HAVE A JOB TO DO. AND POISONED OR NOT, I EXPECT RESULTS.
AGHHH...

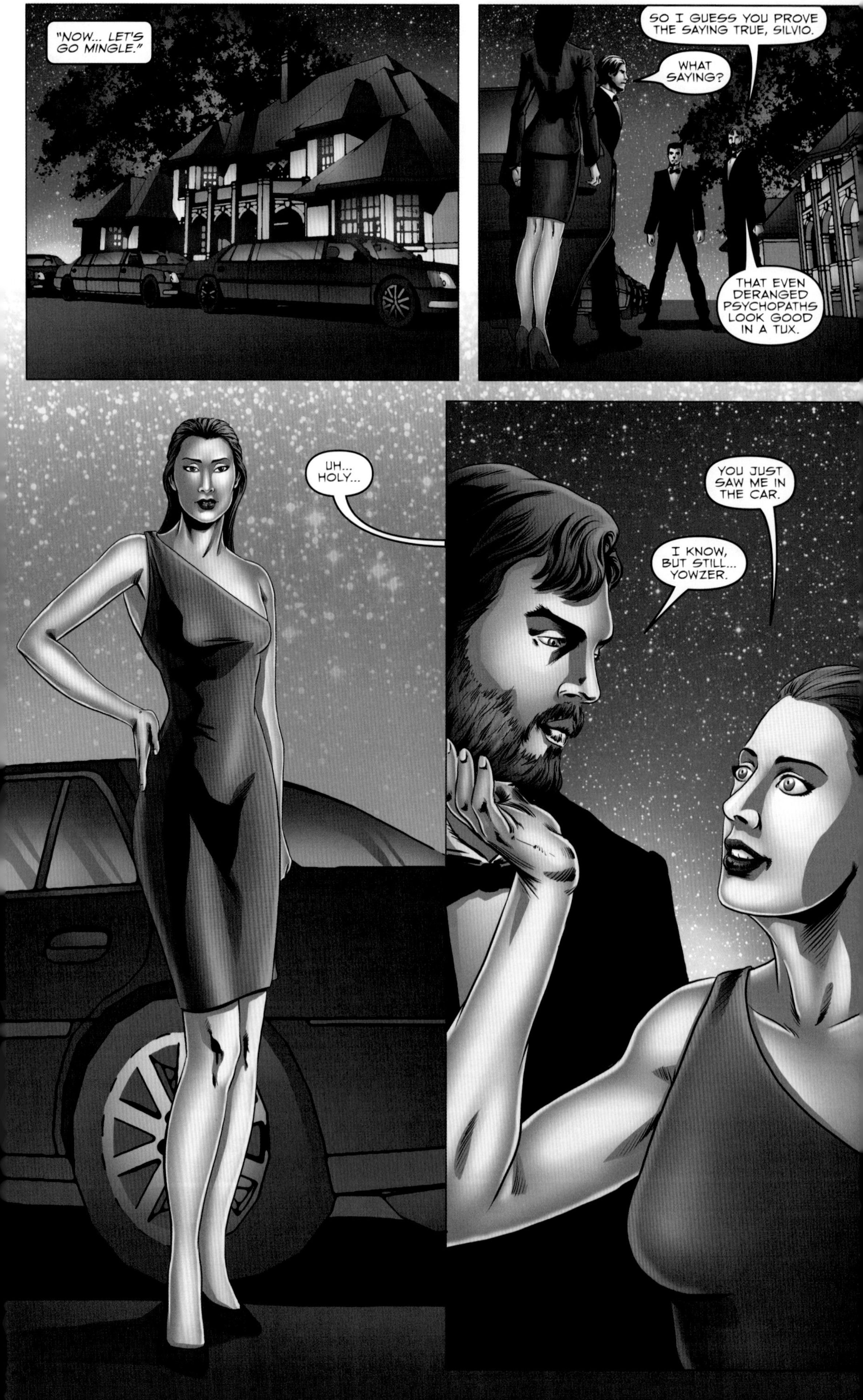
"NOW... LET'S GO MINGLE."
SO I GUESS YOU PROVE THE SAYING TRUE, SILVIO.
WHAT SAYING?
THAT EVEN DERANGED PSYCHOPATHS LOOK GOOD IN A TUX.
UH... HOLY...
YOU JUST SAW ME IN THE CAR.
I KNOW, BUT STILL... YOWZER.

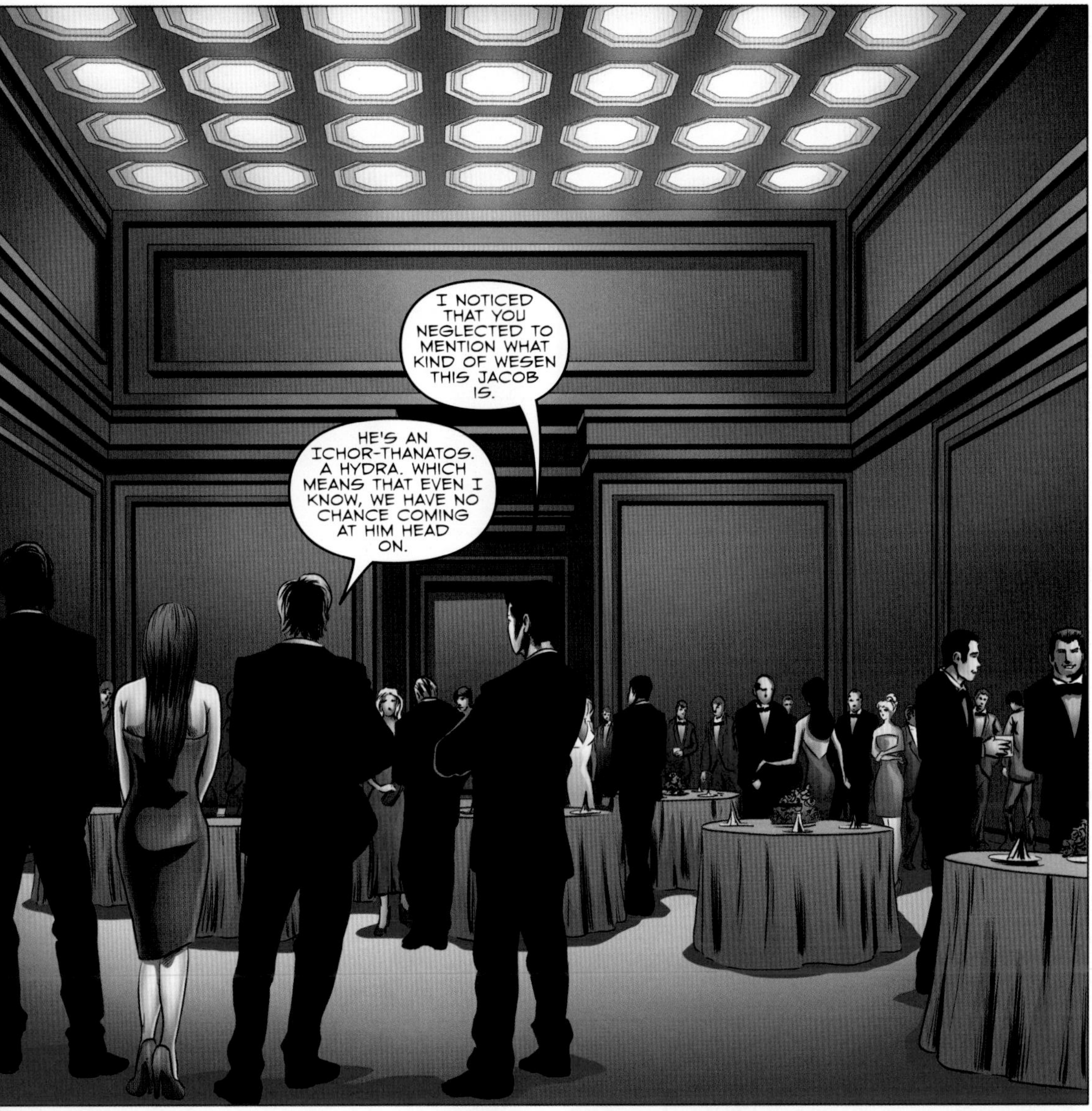
I NOTICED THAT YOU NEGLECTED TO MENTION WHAT KIND OF WESEN THIS JACOB IS.
HE'S AN ICHOR-THANATOS. A HYDRA. WHICH MEANS THAT EVEN I KNOW, WE HAVE NO CHANCE COMING AT HIM HEAD ON.

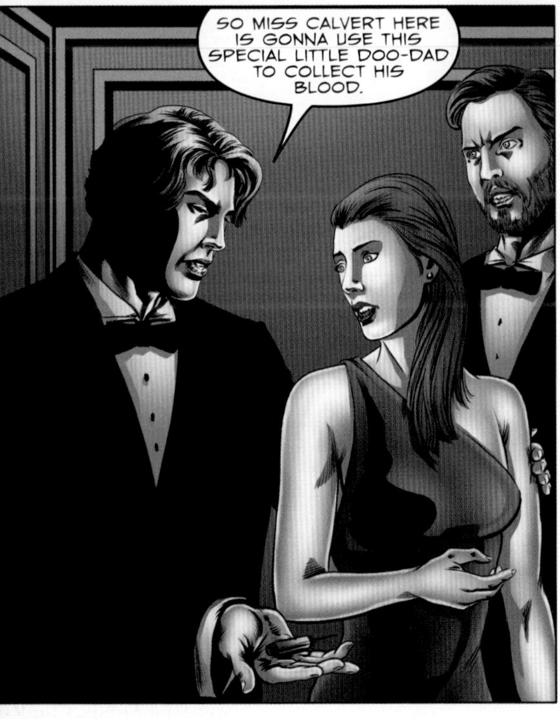
SO MISS CALVERT HERE IS GONNA USE THIS SPECIAL LITTLE DOO-DAD TO COLLECT HIS BLOOD.

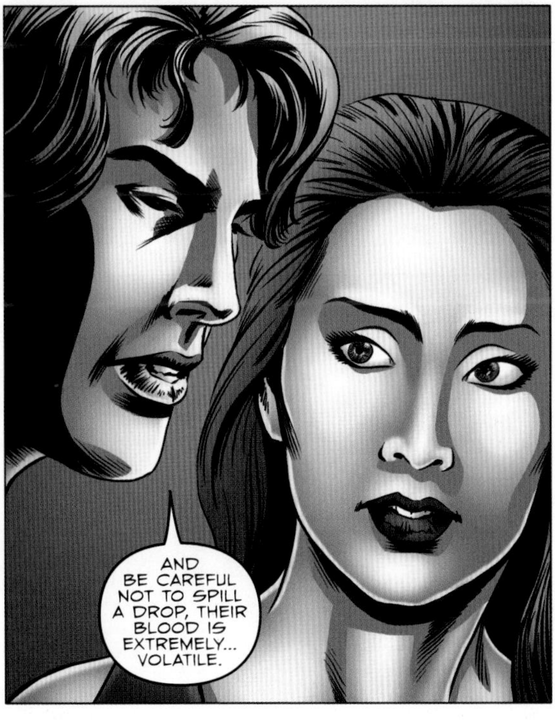
AND BE CAREFUL NOT TO SPILL A DROP, THEIR BLOOD IS EXTREMELY... VOLATILE.

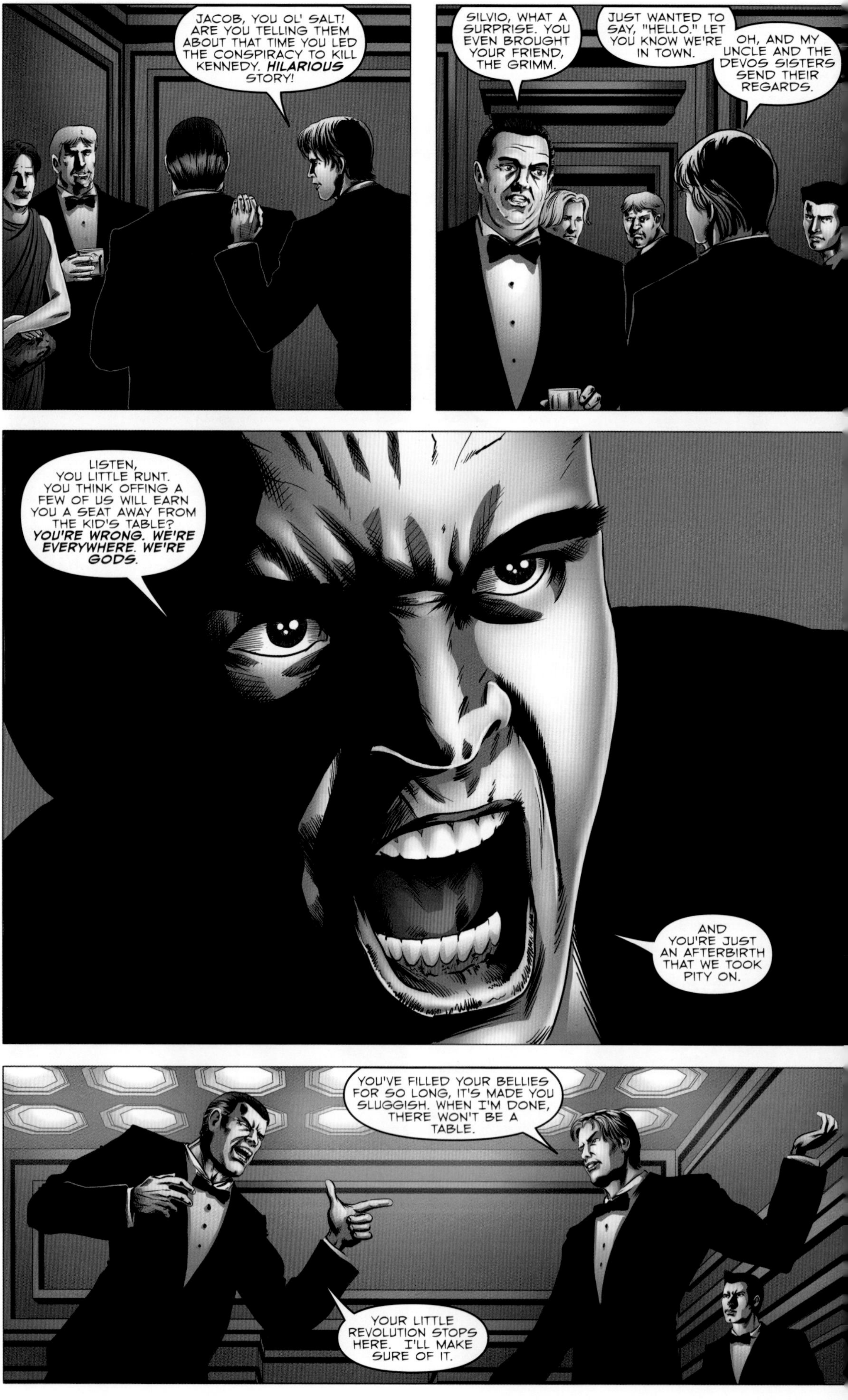
JACOB, YOU OL' SALT! ARE YOU TELLING THEM ABOUT THAT TIME YOU LED THE CONSPIRACY TO KILL KENNEDY. HILARIOUS STORY!
SILVIO, WHAT A SURPRISE. YOU EVEN BROUGHT YOUR FRIEND, THE GRIMM.
JUST WANTED TO SAY, "HELLO." LET YOU KNOW WE'RE IN TOWN.
OH, AND MY UNCLE AND THE DEVOS SISTERS SEND THEIR REGARDS.
LISTEN, YOU LITTLE RUNT. YOU THINK OFFING A FEW OF US WILL EARN YOU A SEAT AWAY FROM THE KID'S TABLE? YOU'RE WRONG. WE'RE EVERYWHERE. WE'RE GODS.
AND YOU'RE JUST AN AFTERBIRTH THAT WE TOOK PITY ON.
YOU'VE FILLED YOUR BELLIES FOR SO LONG, IT'S MADE YOU SLUGGISH. WHEN I'M DONE, THERE WON'T BE A TABLE.
YOUR LITTLE REVOLUTION STOPS HERE. I'LL MAKE SURE OF IT.

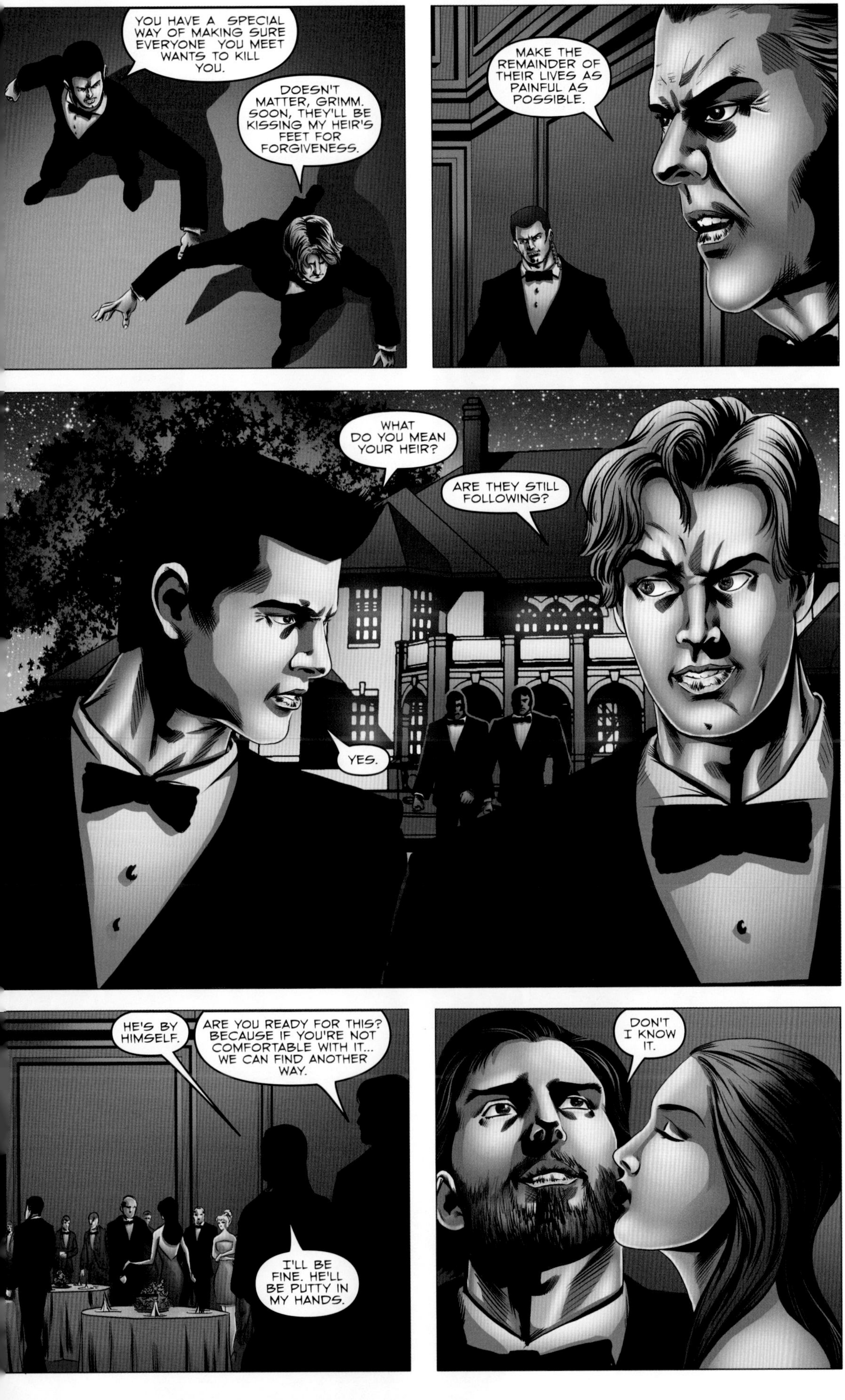

YOU HAVE A SPECIAL WAY OF MAKING SURE EVERYONE YOU MEET WANTS TO KILL YOU.
DOESN'T MATTER, GRIMM. SOON, THEY'LL BE KISSING MY HEIR'S FEET FOR FORGIVENESS.
MAKE THE REMAINDER OF THEIR LIVES AS PAINFUL AS POSSIBLE.
WHAT DO YOU MEAN YOUR HEIR?
ARE THEY STILL FOLLOWING?
YES.
HE'S BY HIMSELF.
ARE YOU READY FOR THIS? BECAUSE IF YOU'RE NOT COMFORTABLE WITH IT... WE CAN FIND ANOTHER WAY.
I'LL BE FINE. HE'LL BE PUTTY IN MY HANDS.
DON'T I KNOW IT.

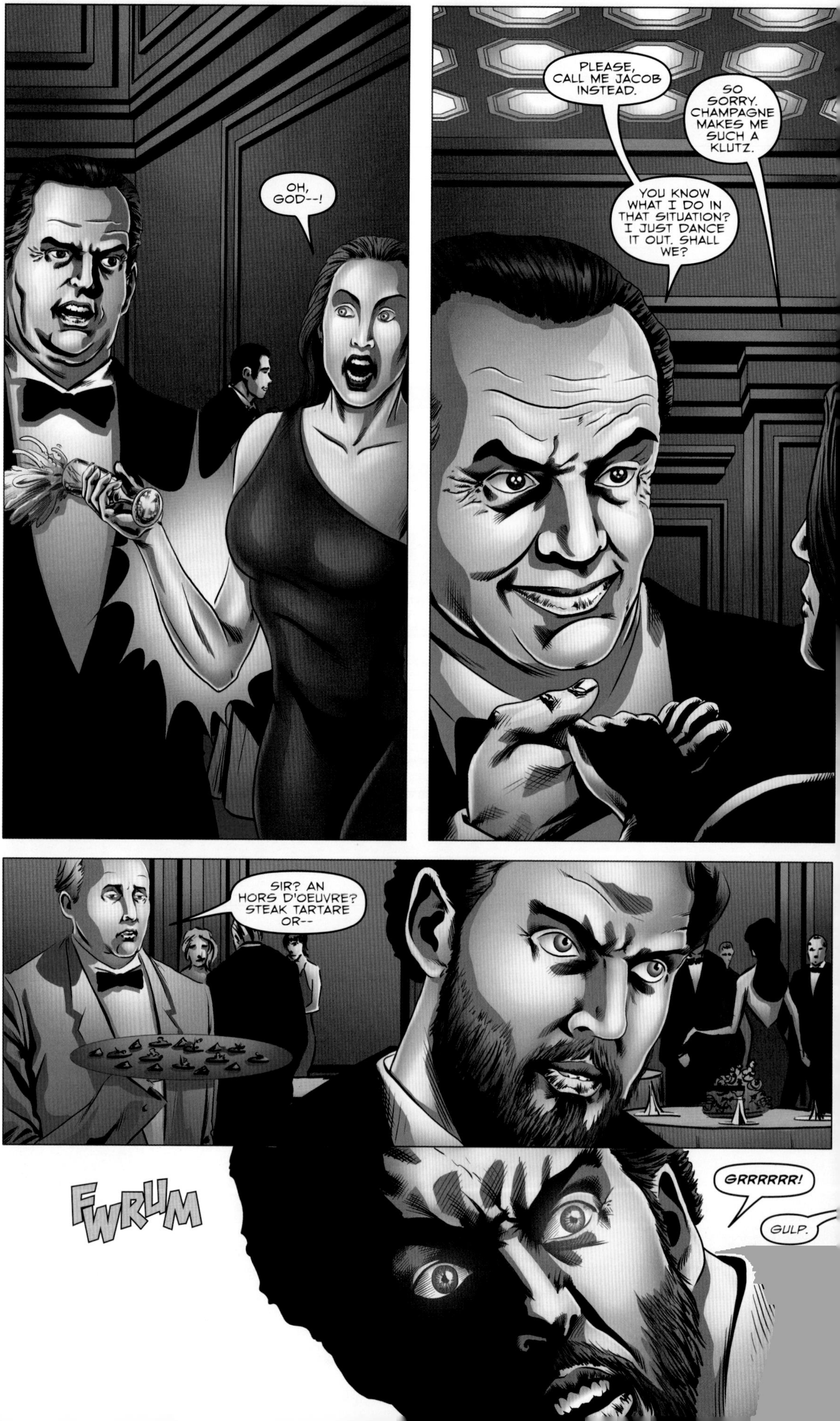
OH, GOD--!
PLEASE, CALL ME JACOB INSTEAD.
SO SORRY. CHAMPAGNE MAKES ME SUCH A KLUTZ.
YOU KNOW WHAT I DO IN THAT SITUATION? I JUST DANCE IT OUT. SHALL WE?
SIR? AN HORS D'OEUVRE? STEAK TARTARE OR--
FWRUM
GRRRRRR!
GULP.

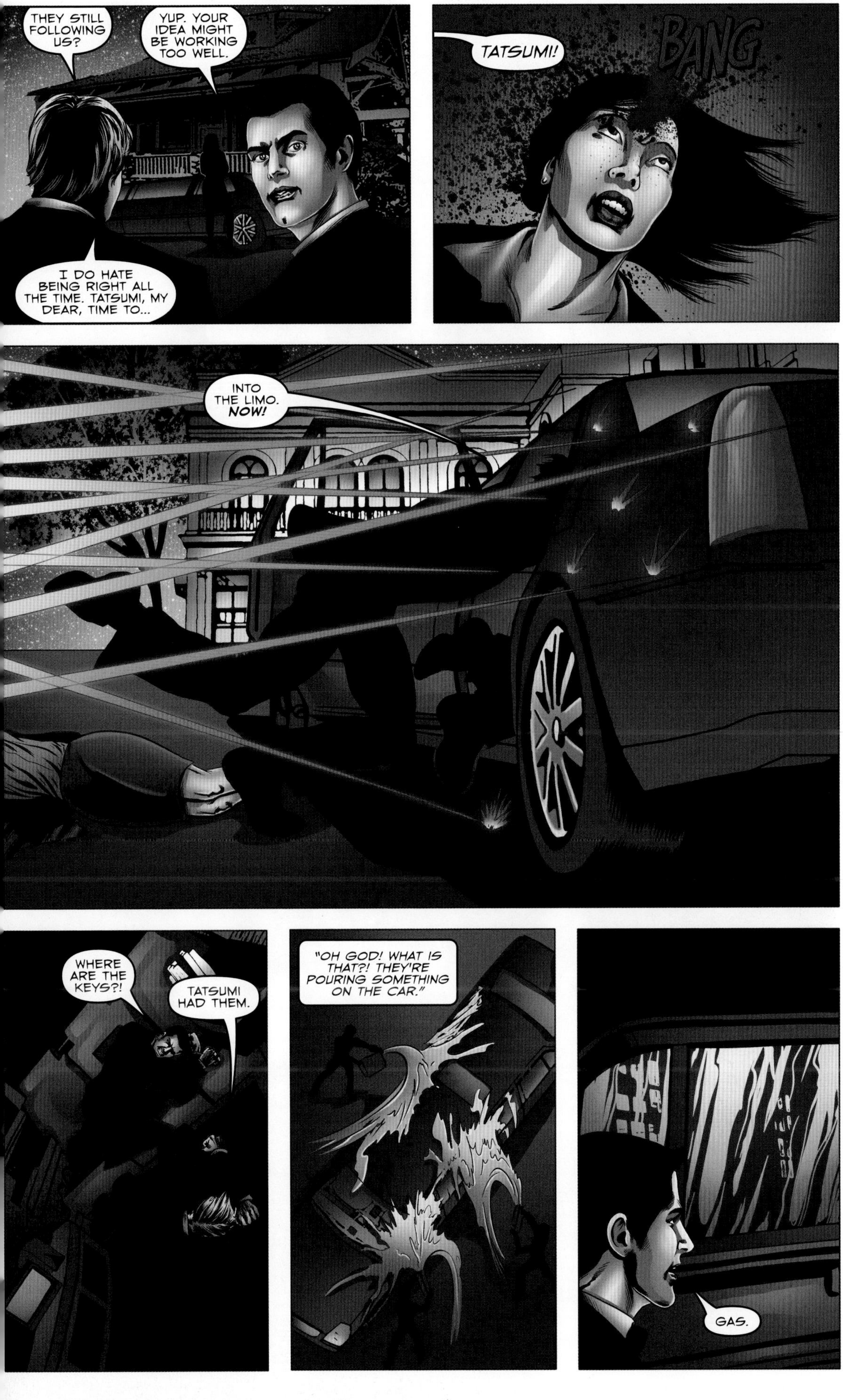
THEY STILL FOLLOWING US?
YUP. YOUR IDEA MIGHT BE WORKING TOO WELL.
I DO HATE BEING RIGHT ALL THE TIME. TATSUMI, MY DEAR, TIME TO...
TATSUMI!
BANG
INTO THE LIMO. NOW!
WHERE ARE THE KEYS?!
TATSUMI HAD THEM.
"OH GOD! WHAT IS THAT?! THEY'RE POURING SOMETHING ON THE CAR."
GAS.

"DO SOMETHING! USE YOUR GRIMM POWERS!"
"GRIMM POWERS? YOU REALLY ARE AN IDIOT."
FWRUM
VIVAT SANGUINE!
VROOM
ALMOST HAVE IT...
"GO, GO, GO!"

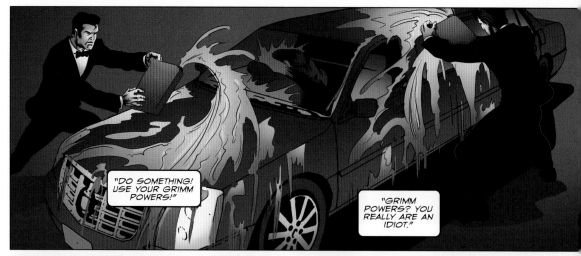

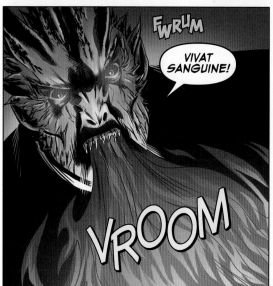

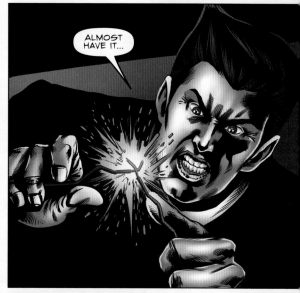

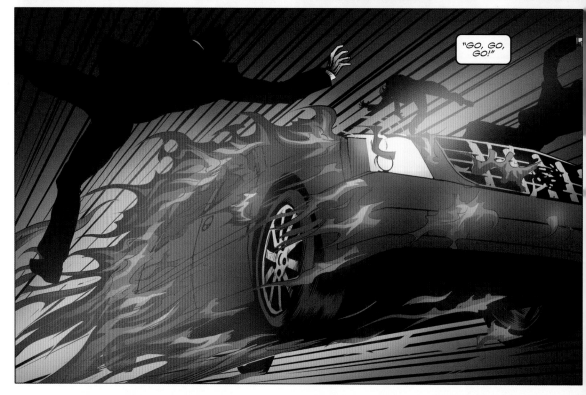

YOU'RE A WONDERFUL DANCER FOR BEING SUCH A KLUTZ, MISS...
JONES. AND YOU'RE NOT SO BAD YOURSELF.
UGH. A DIP. GUY'S NOT EVEN IN TIME WITH THE DAMN MUSIC.
YOU KNOW, YOU'RE THE BEST PART OF THIS EVENING SO FAR. WHAT DO YOU SAY WE GET OUT OF HERE?
MOVING A BIT FAST.
I KNOW WHAT I WANT WHEN I SEE IT.
GOOD, BECAUSE SO DO I.
OW!
MY KIND OF WOMAN.

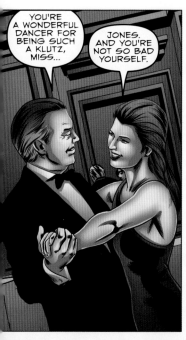

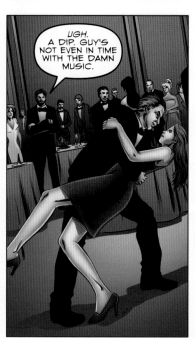

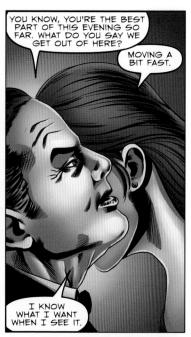

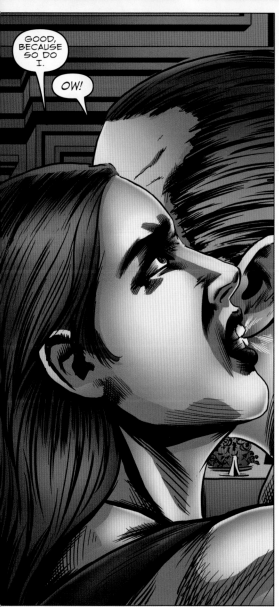

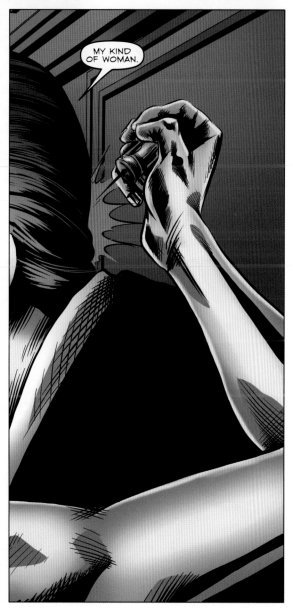

THAT ABOUT DOES IT.

KLANG -A-LANG

UNDERCOVER FIREMAN. EVERYONE MUST LEAVE THE BUILDING, PLEASE FOLLOW ME.

KLANG-A-LANG KLANG-A-LANG KLANG-A-LANG KLANG-A-LANG

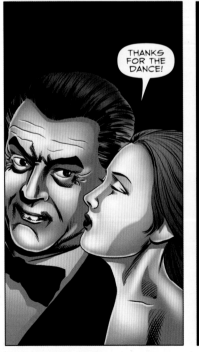

THANKS FOR THE DANCE!

SON OF A--

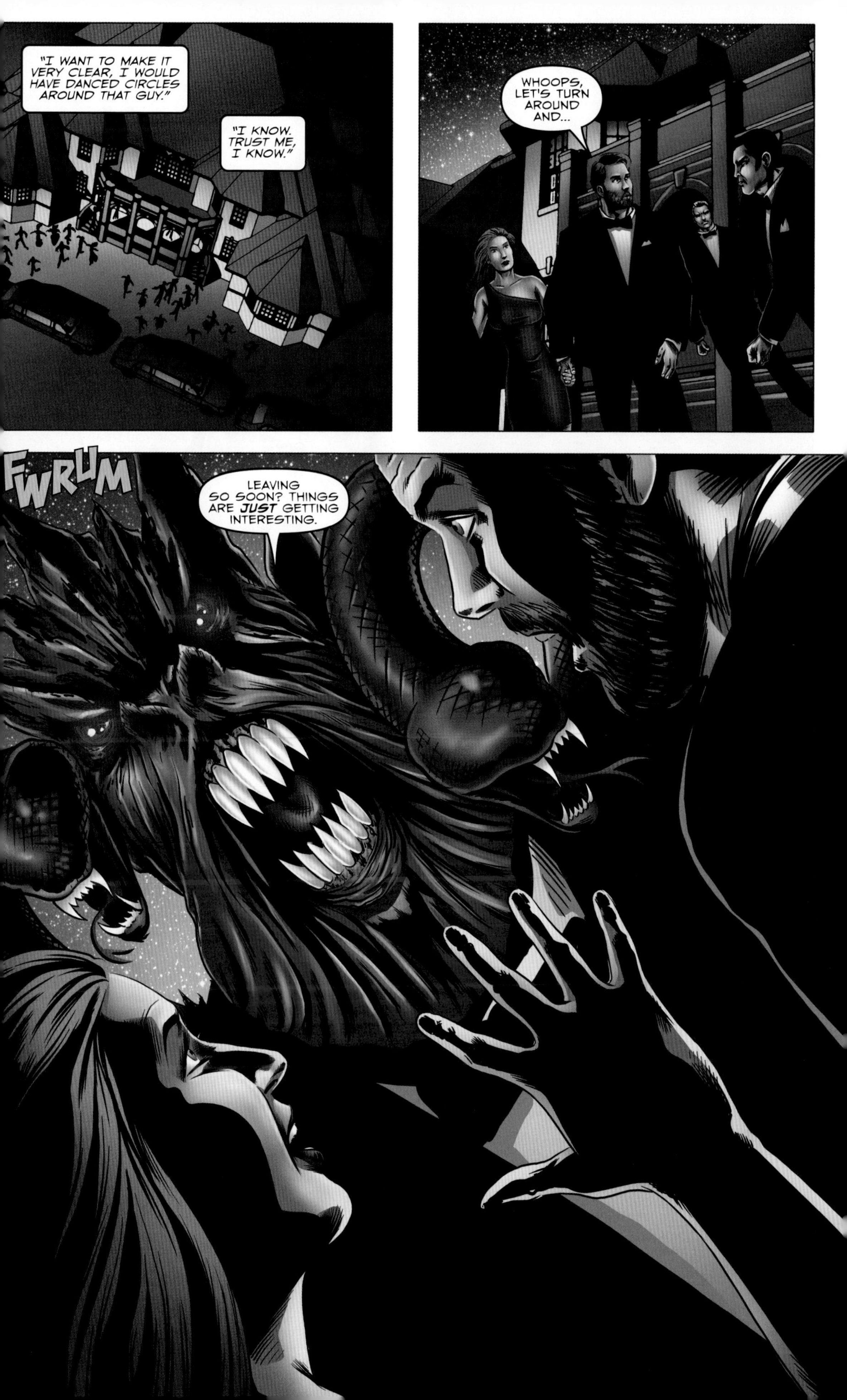
"I WANT TO MAKE IT VERY CLEAR, I WOULD HAVE DANCED CIRCLES AROUND THAT GUY."
"I KNOW. TRUST ME, I KNOW."
WHOOPS, LET'S TURN AROUND AND...
FWRUM
LEAVING SO SOON? THINGS ARE **JUST** GETTING INTERESTING.

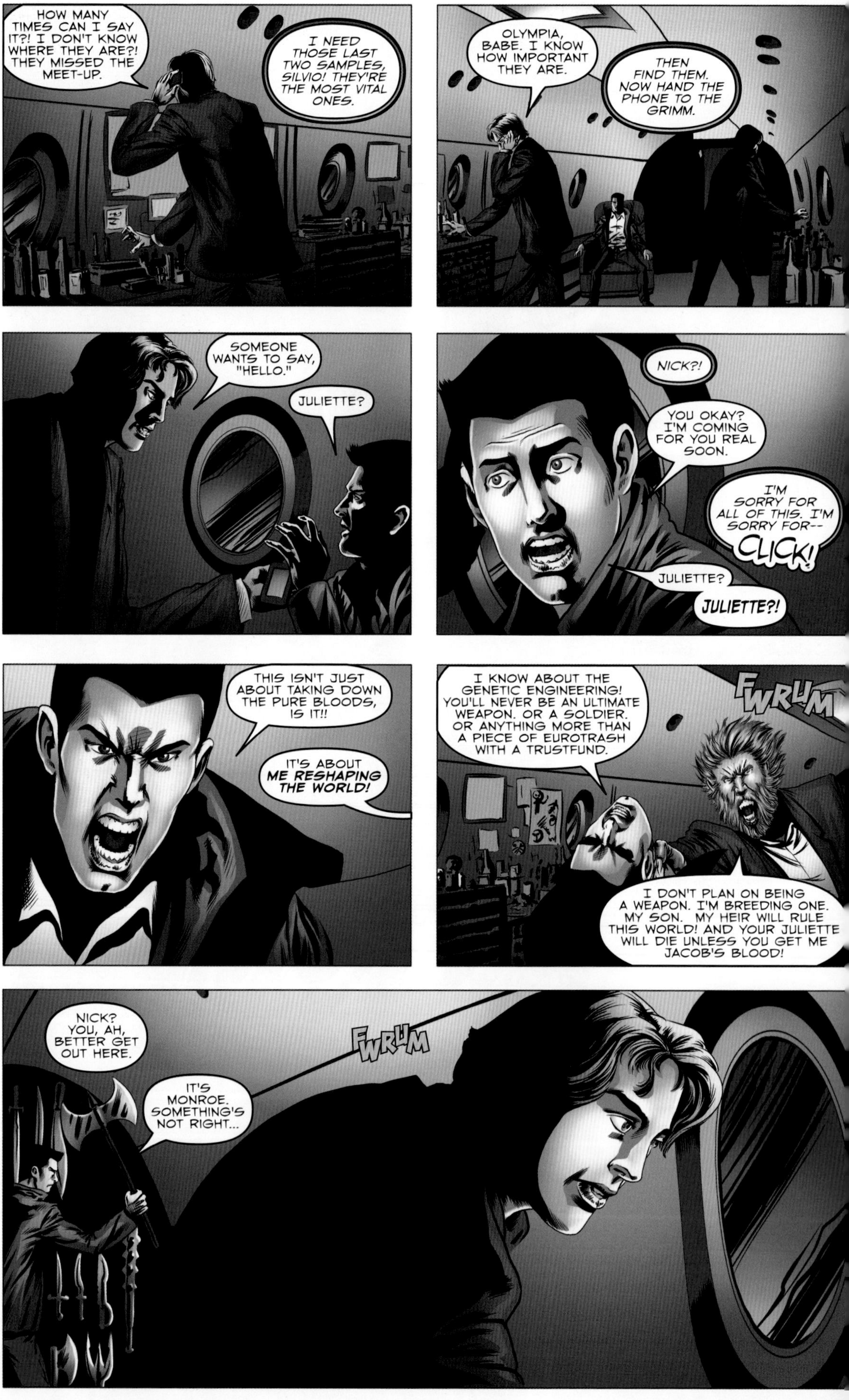
HOW MANY TIMES CAN I SAY IT?! I DON'T KNOW WHERE THEY ARE?! THEY MISSED THE MEET-UP.
I NEED THOSE LAST TWO SAMPLES, SILVIO! THEY'RE THE MOST VITAL ONES.
OLYMPIA, BABE. I KNOW HOW IMPORTANT THEY ARE.
THEN FIND THEM. NOW HAND THE PHONE TO THE GRIMM.
SOMEONE WANTS TO SAY, "HELLO."
JULIETTE?
NICK?!
YOU OKAY? I'M COMING FOR YOU REAL SOON.
I'M SORRY FOR ALL OF THIS. I'M SORRY FOR--
CLICK!
JULIETTE?
JULIETTE?!
THIS ISN'T JUST ABOUT TAKING DOWN THE PURE BLOODS, IS IT!!
IT'S ABOUT ME RESHAPING THE WORLD!
I KNOW ABOUT THE GENETIC ENGINEERING! YOU'LL NEVER BE AN ULTIMATE WEAPON. OR A SOLDIER. OR ANYTHING MORE THAN A PIECE OF EUROTRASH WITH A TRUSTFUND.
FWRUM
I DON'T PLAN ON BEING A WEAPON. I'M BREEDING ONE. MY SON. MY HEIR WILL RULE THIS WORLD! AND YOUR JULIETTE WILL DIE UNLESS YOU GET ME JACOB'S BLOOD!
NICK? YOU, AH, BETTER GET OUT HERE.
FWRUM
IT'S MONROE. SOMETHING'S NOT RIGHT...

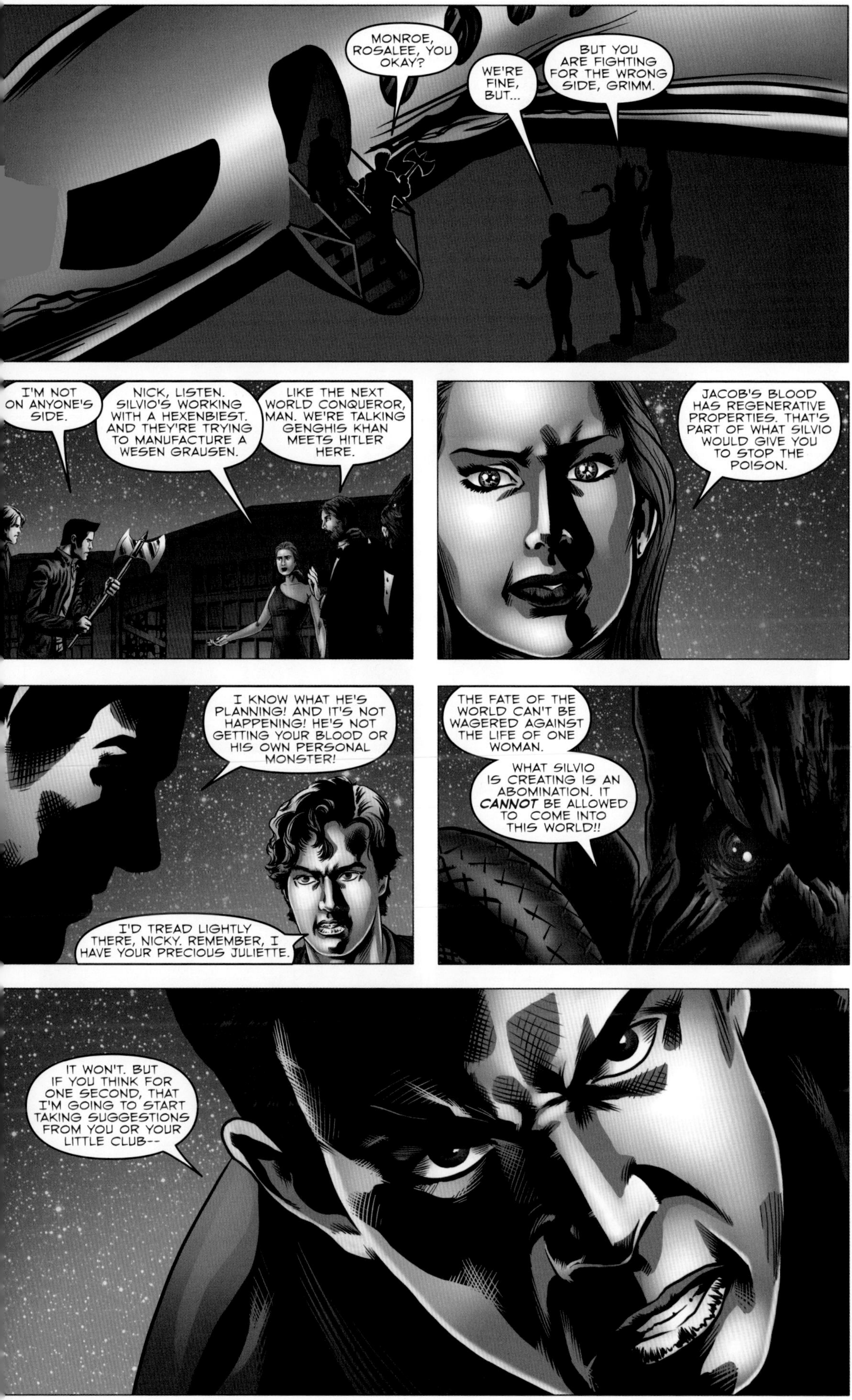
MONROE, ROSALEE, YOU OKAY?
WE'RE FINE, BUT...
BUT YOU ARE FIGHTING FOR THE WRONG SIDE, GRIMM.
I'M NOT ON ANYONE'S SIDE.
NICK, LISTEN. SILVIO'S WORKING WITH A HEXENBIEST. AND THEY'RE TRYING TO MANUFACTURE A WESEN GRAUSEN.
LIKE THE NEXT WORLD CONQUEROR, MAN. WE'RE TALKING GENGHIS KHAN MEETS HITLER HERE.
JACOB'S BLOOD HAS REGENERATIVE PROPERTIES. THAT'S PART OF WHAT SILVIO WOULD GIVE YOU TO STOP THE POISON.
I KNOW WHAT HE'S PLANNING! AND IT'S NOT HAPPENING! HE'S NOT GETTING YOUR BLOOD OR HIS OWN PERSONAL MONSTER!
I'D TREAD LIGHTLY THERE, NICKY. REMEMBER, I HAVE YOUR PRECIOUS JULIETTE.
THE FATE OF THE WORLD CAN'T BE WAGERED AGAINST THE LIFE OF ONE WOMAN.
WHAT SILVIO IS CREATING IS AN ABOMINATION. IT CANNOT BE ALLOWED TO COME INTO THIS WORLD!!
IT WON'T. BUT IF YOU THINK FOR ONE SECOND, THAT I'M GOING TO START TAKING SUGGESTIONS FROM YOU OR YOUR LITTLE CLUB--

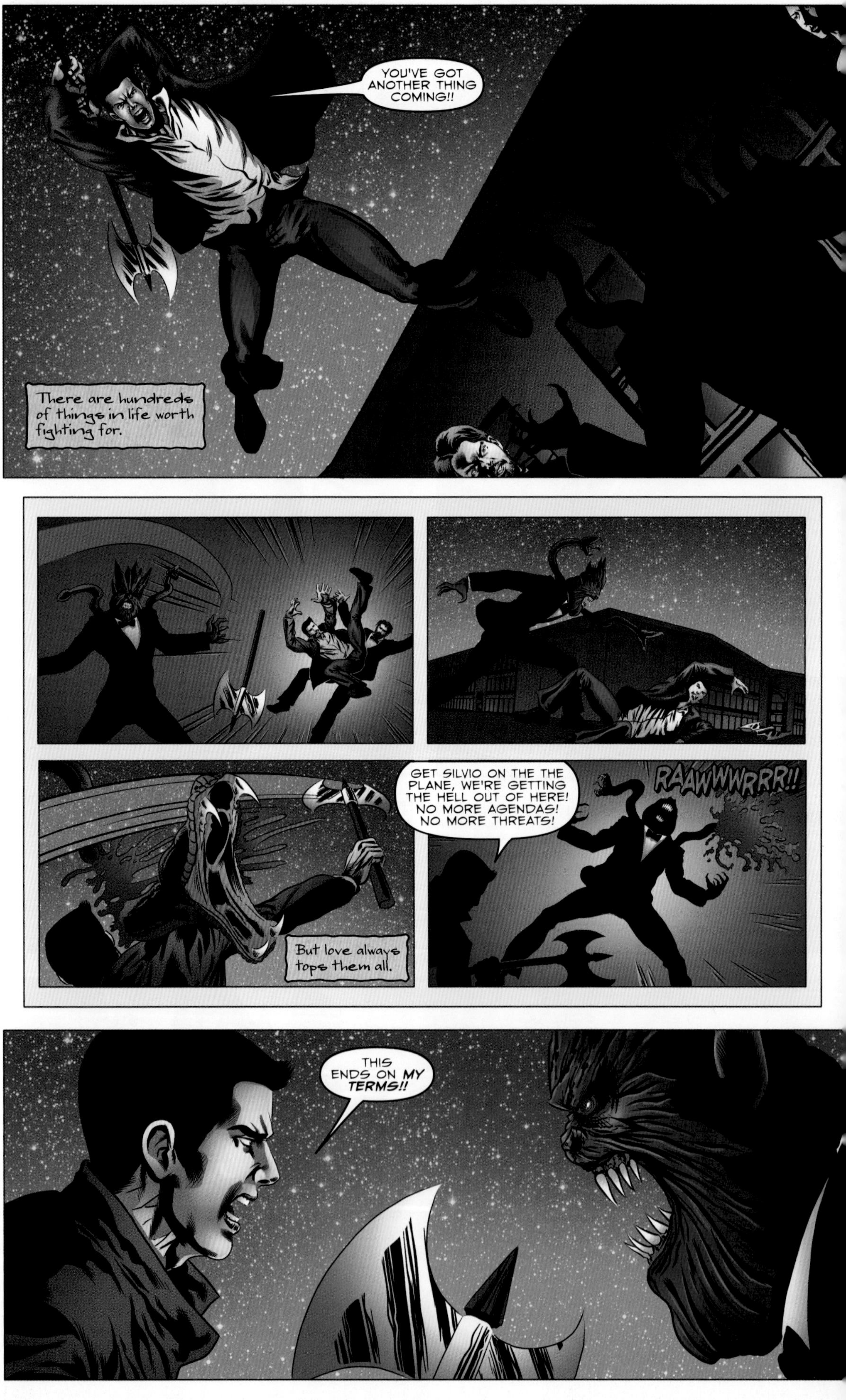
YOU'VE GOT ANOTHER THING COMING!!
There are hundreds of things in life worth fighting for.
But love always tops them all.
GET SILVIO ON THE THE PLANE, WE'RE GETTING THE HELL OUT OF HERE! NO MORE AGENDAS! NO MORE THREATS!
RAAWWWRRR!!
THIS ENDS ON MY TERMS!!

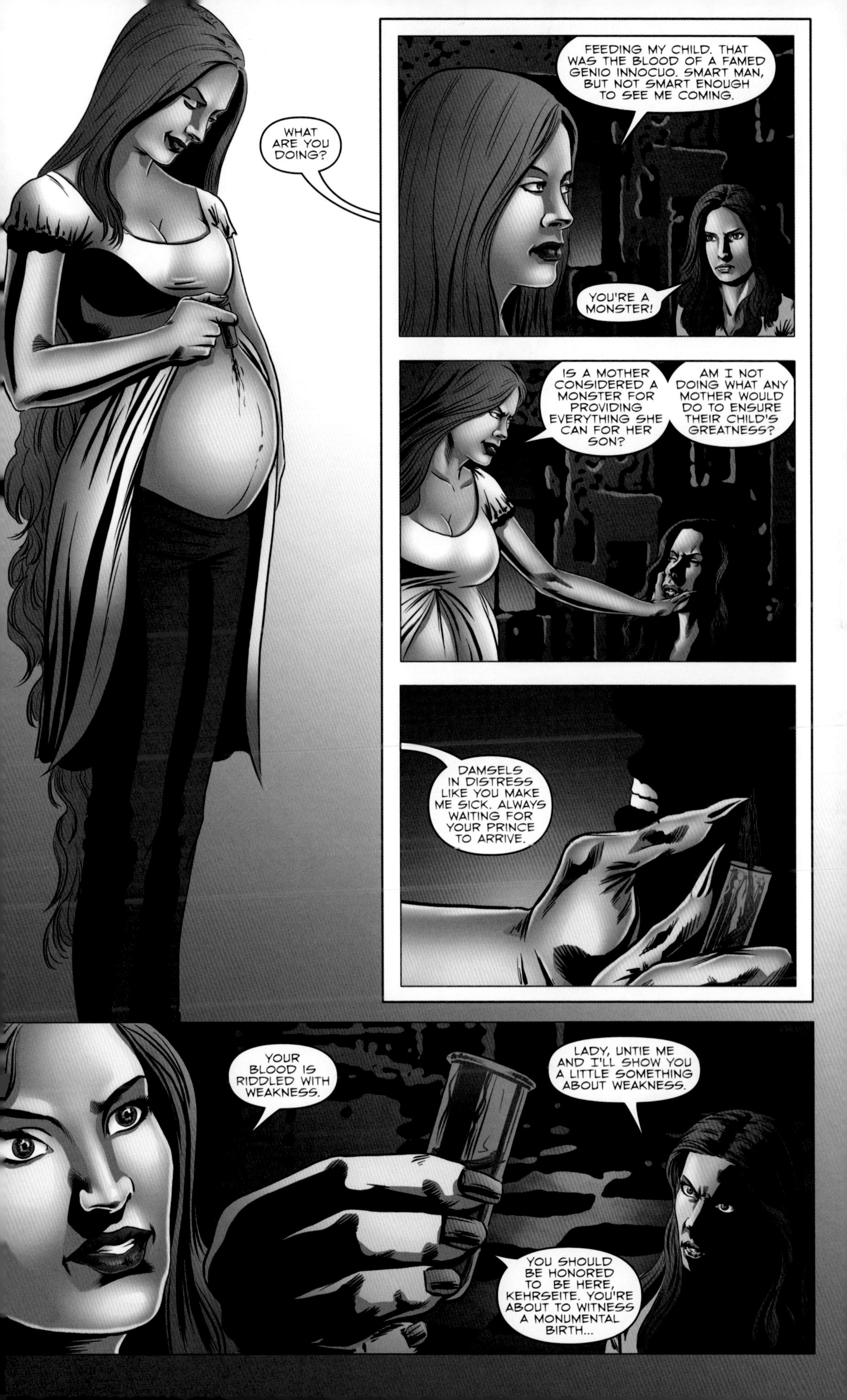
WHAT ARE YOU DOING?
FEEDING MY CHILD. THAT WAS THE BLOOD OF A FAMED GENIO INNOCUO. SMART MAN, BUT NOT SMART ENOUGH TO SEE ME COMING.
YOU'RE A MONSTER!
IS A MOTHER CONSIDERED A MONSTER FOR PROVIDING EVERYTHING SHE CAN FOR HER SON?
AM I NOT DOING WHAT ANY MOTHER WOULD DO TO ENSURE THEIR CHILD'S GREATNESS?
DAMSELS IN DISTRESS LIKE YOU MAKE ME SICK. ALWAYS WAITING FOR YOUR PRINCE TO ARRIVE.
YOUR BLOOD IS RIDDLED WITH WEAKNESS.
LADY, UNTIE ME AND I'LL SHOW YOU A LITTLE SOMETHING ABOUT WEAKNESS.
YOU SHOULD BE HONORED TO BE HERE, KEHRSEITE. YOU'RE ABOUT TO WITNESS A MONUMENTAL BIRTH...

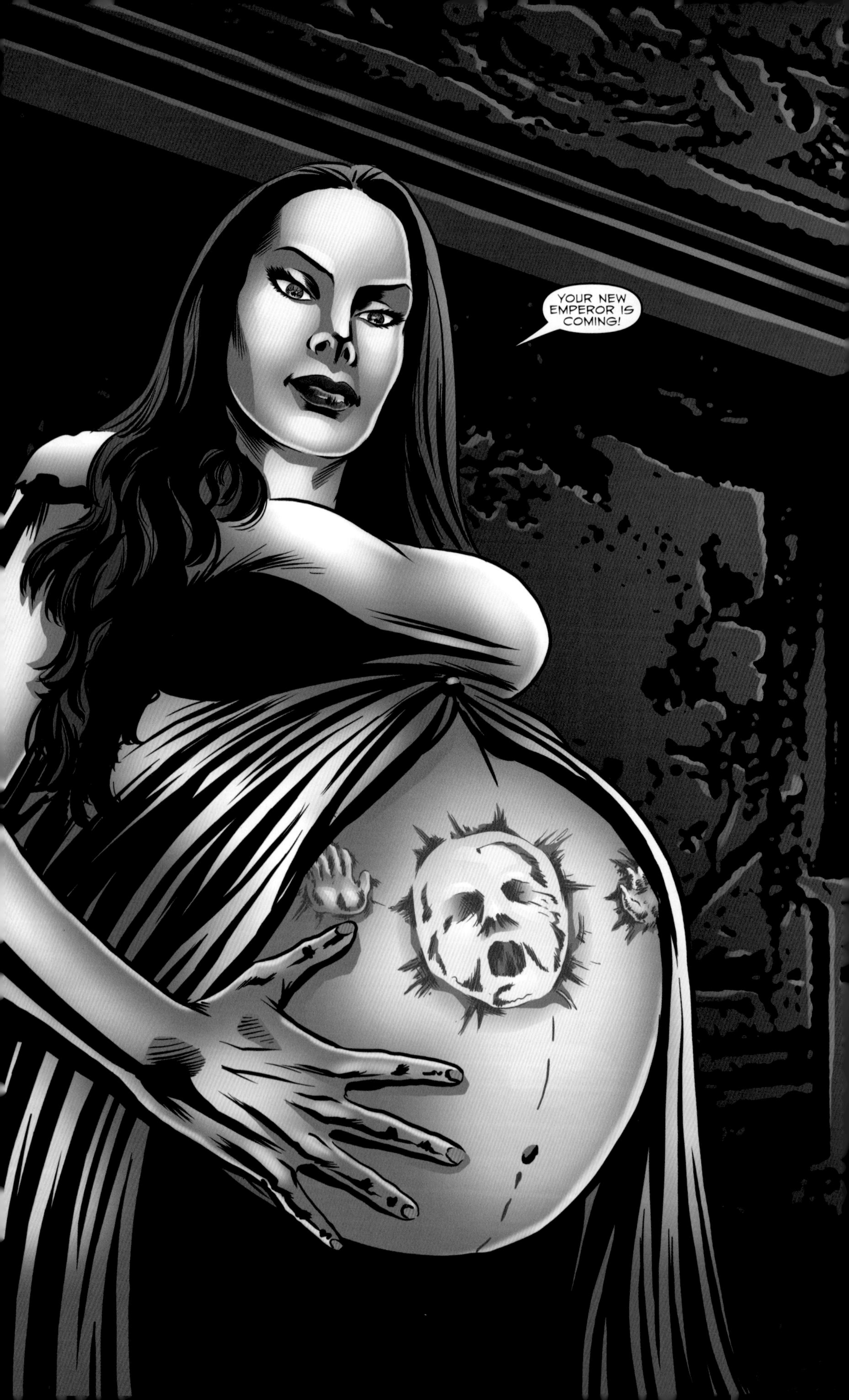
YOUR NEW EMPEROR IS COMING!

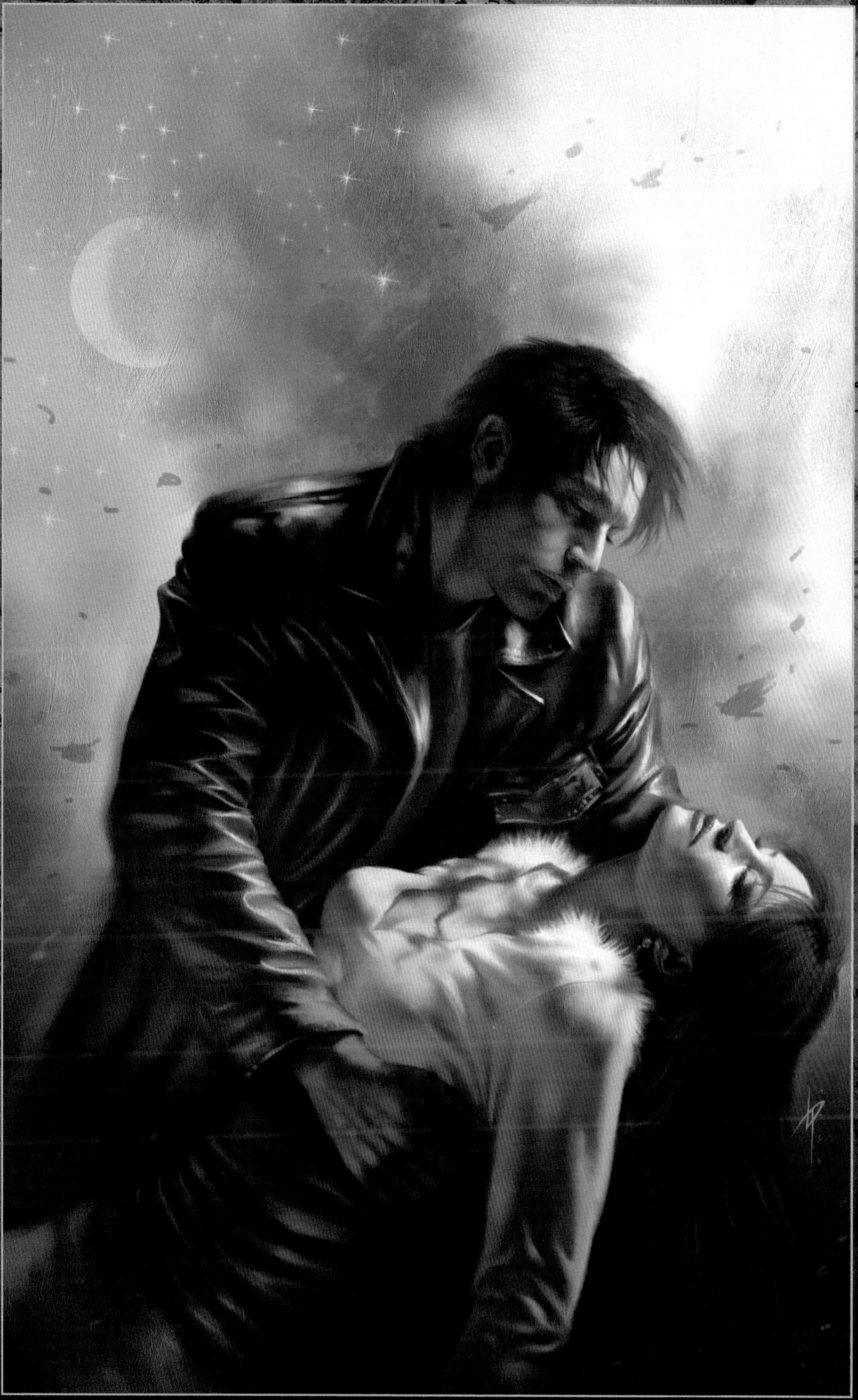

ISSUE #12 COVER
ART BY LUCIO PARRILLO

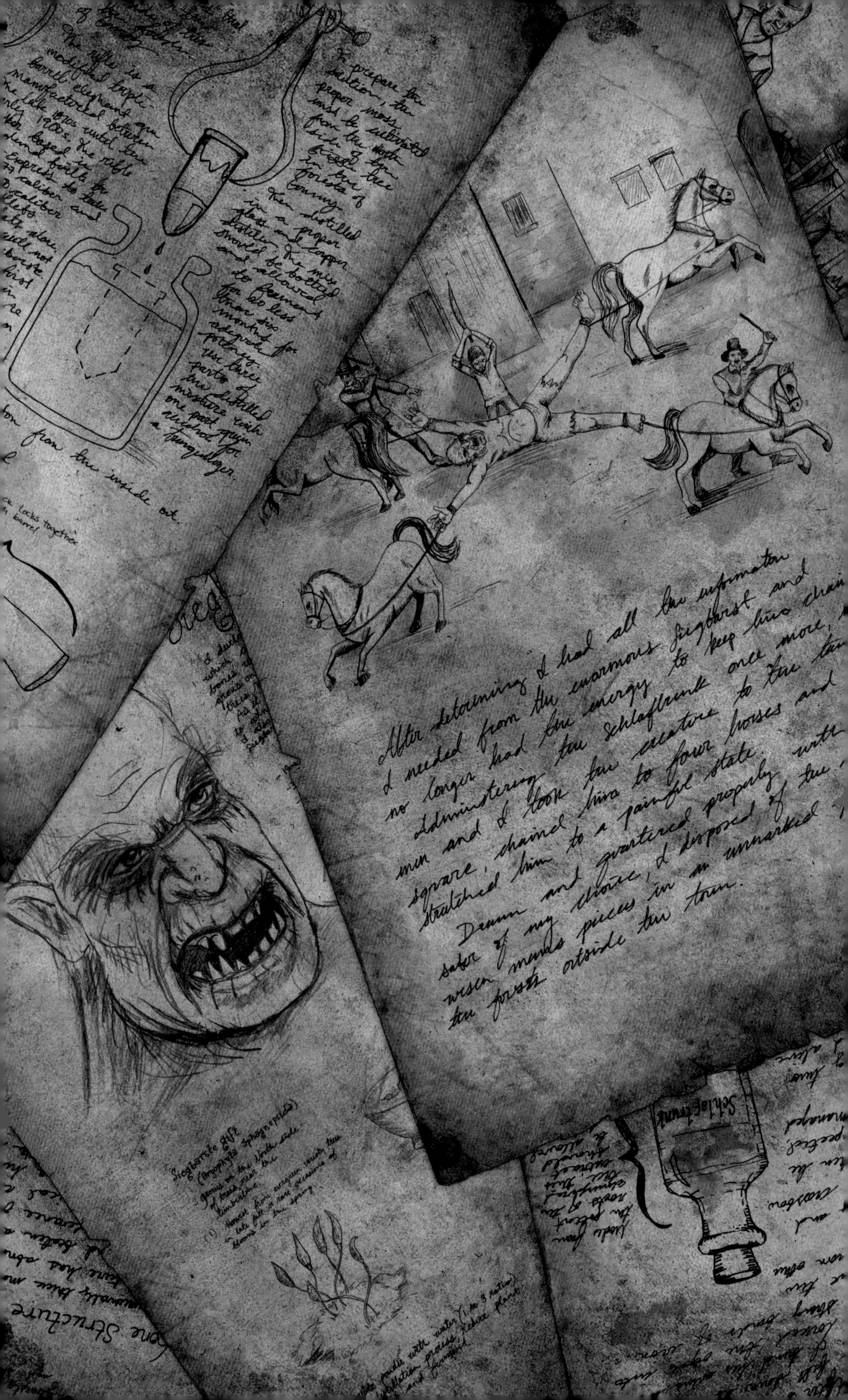
After returning I had all the information
I needed from the enormous Siegbarst and
no longer had the energy to keep him chain
Administering the Schlaftrunk once more,
men and I took the creature to the tow
square, chained him to four horses and
stretched him to a painful state.
Drawn and quartered properly with
saber of my choice, I disposed of the
wesen man's pieces in an unmarked
the forests outside the town.

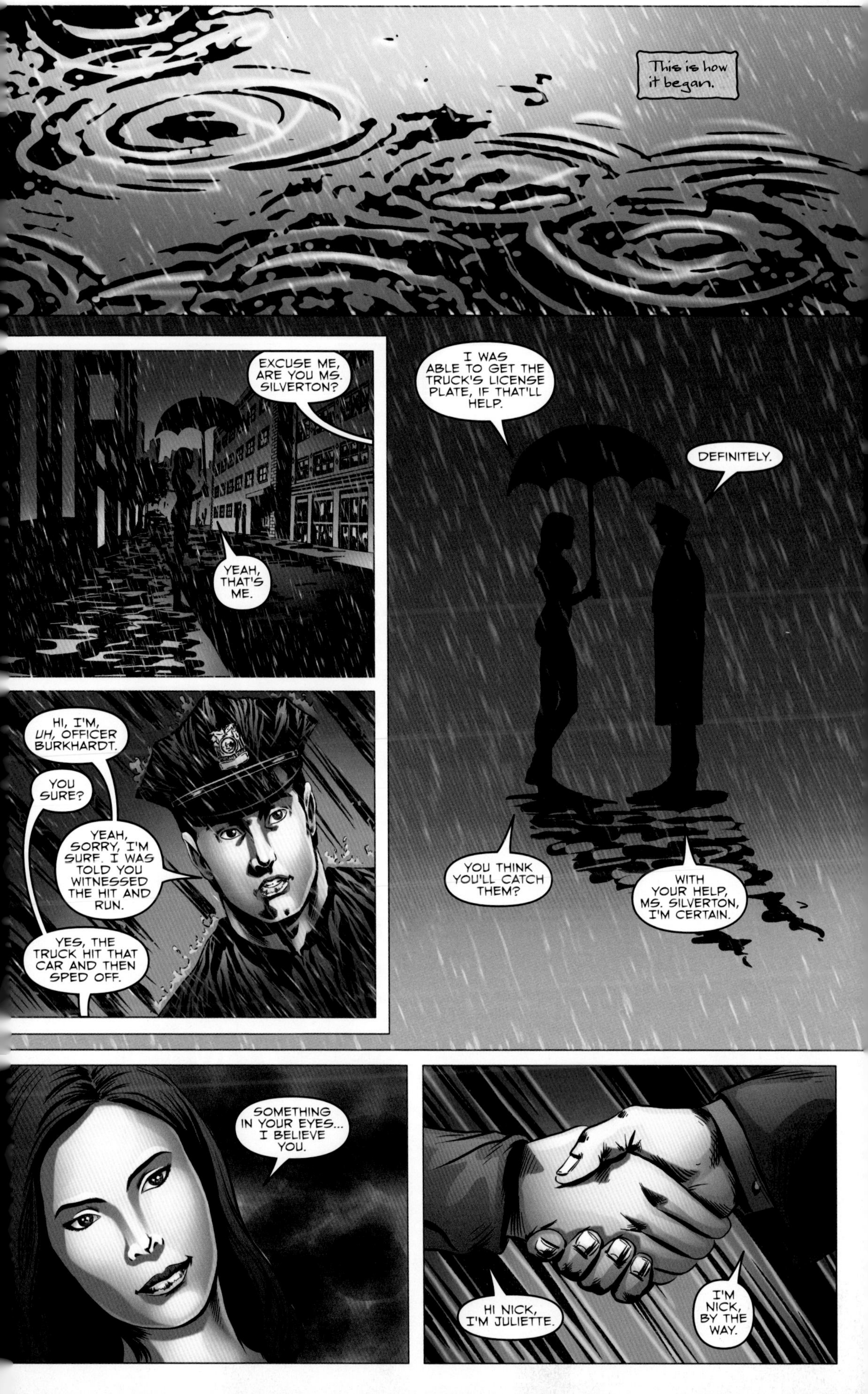

This is how it began.
EXCUSE ME, ARE YOU MS. SILVERTON?
YEAH, THAT'S ME.
HI, I'M, UH, OFFICER BURKHARDT.
YOU SURE?
YEAH, SORRY, I'M SURF. I WAS TOLD YOU WITNESSED THE HIT AND RUN.
YES, THE TRUCK HIT THAT CAR AND THEN SPED OFF.
I WAS ABLE TO GET THE TRUCK'S LICENSE PLATE, IF THAT'LL HELP.
DEFINITELY.
YOU THINK YOU'LL CATCH THEM?
WITH YOUR HELP, MS. SILVERTON, I'M CERTAIN.
SOMETHING IN YOUR EYES... I BELIEVE YOU.
I'M NICK, BY THE WAY.
HI NICK, I'M JULIETTE.

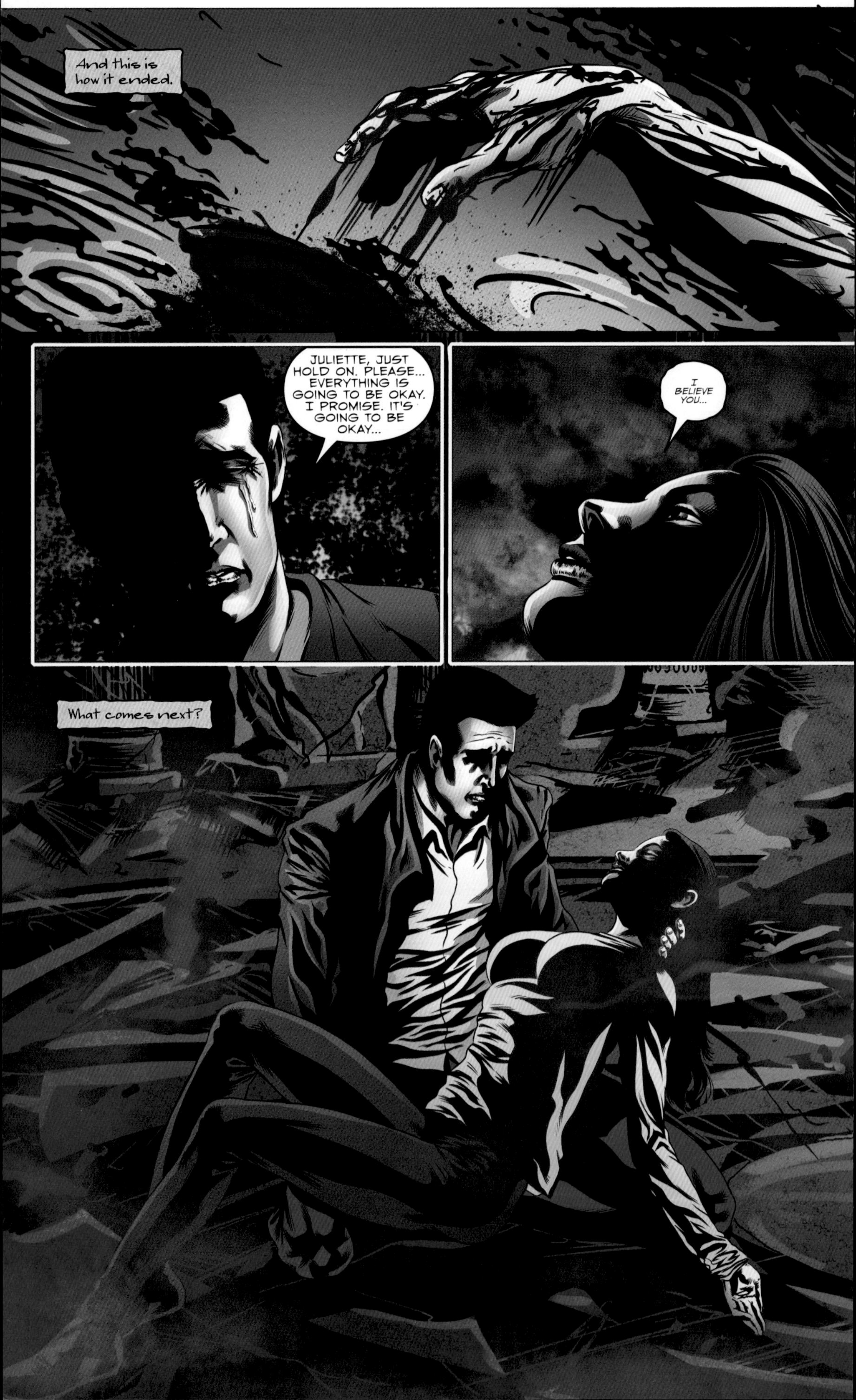
And this is how it ended.
JULIETTE, JUST HOLD ON. PLEASE... EVERYTHING IS GOING TO BE OKAY. I PROMISE. IT'S GOING TO BE OKAY...
I BELIEVE YOU...
What comes next?

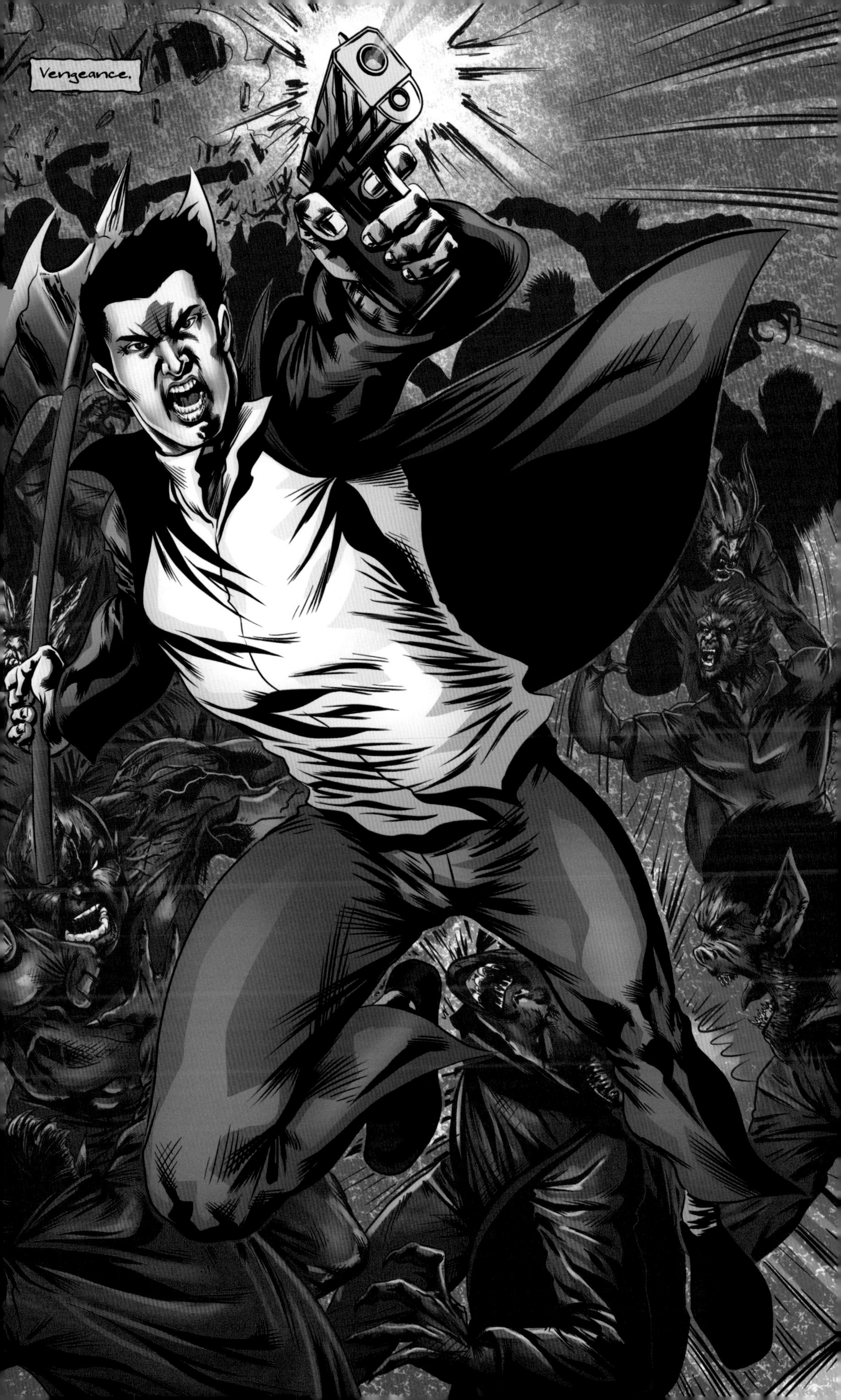
Vengeance.

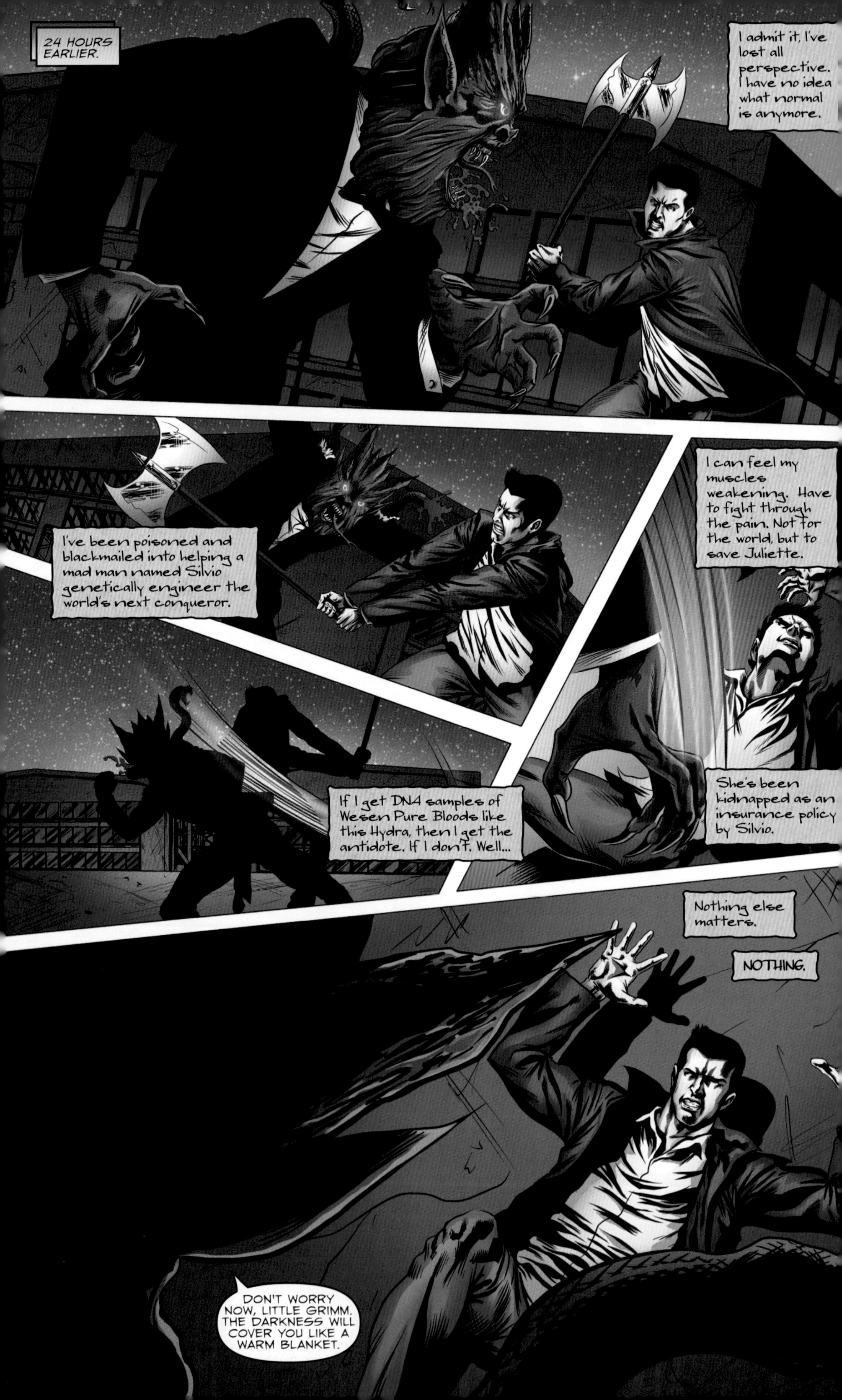
24 HOURS EARLIER.
I admit it, I've lost all perspective. I have no idea what normal is anymore.
I've been poisoned and blackmailed into helping a mad man named Silvio genetically engineer the world's next conqueror.
If I get DNA samples of Wesen Pure Bloods like this Hydra, then I get the antidote. If I don't. Well...
I can feel my muscles weakening. Have to fight through the pain. Not for the world, but to save Juliette.
She's been kidnapped as an insurance policy by Silvio.
Nothing else matters.
NOTHING.
DON'T WORRY NOW, LITTLE GRIMM. THE DARKNESS WILL COVER YOU LIKE A WARM BLANKET.

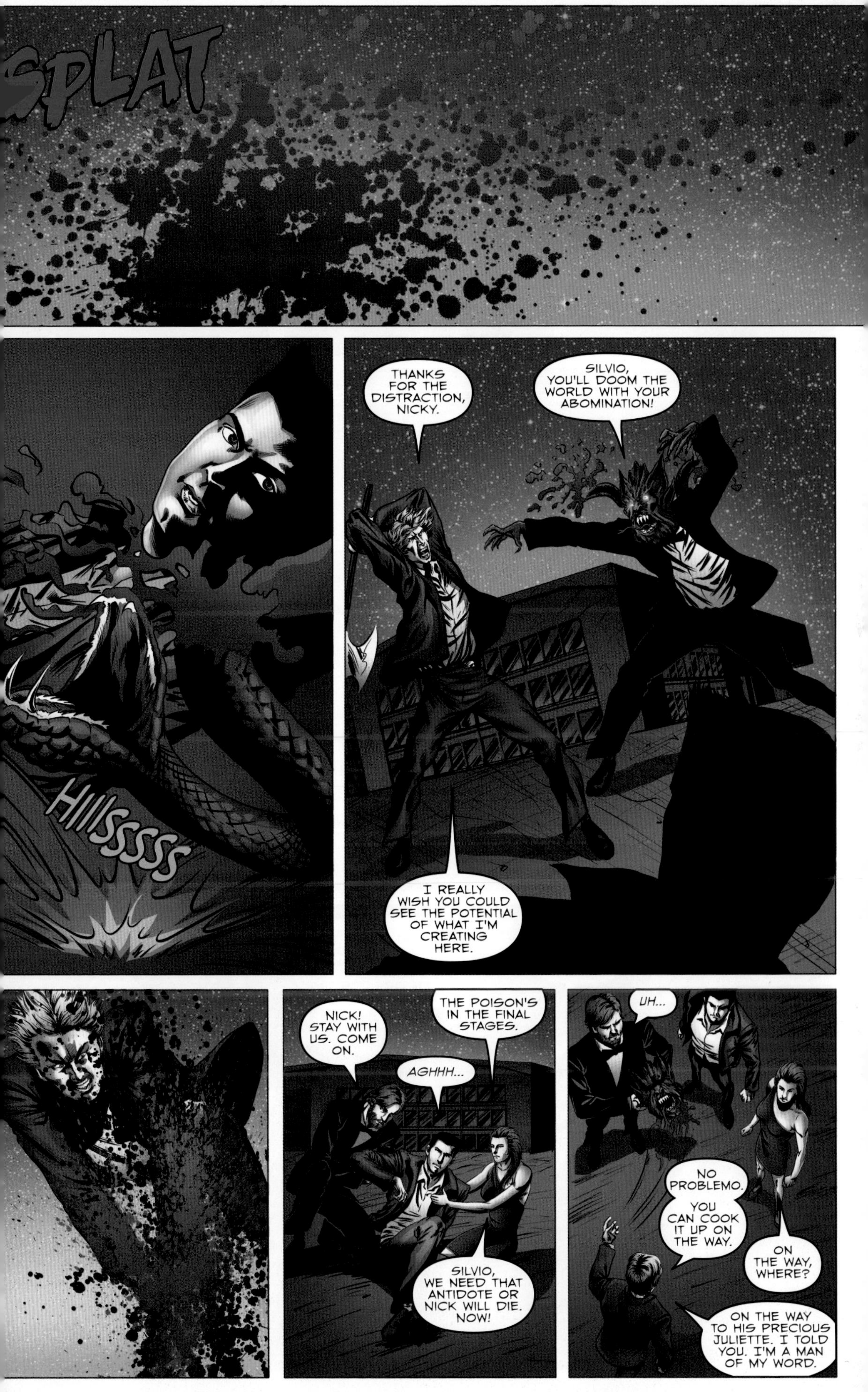
SPLAT
HIISSSSS
THANKS FOR THE DISTRACTION, NICKY.
SILVIO, YOU'LL DOOM THE WORLD WITH YOUR ABOMINATION!
I REALLY WISH YOU COULD SEE THE POTENTIAL OF WHAT I'M CREATING HERE.
NICK! STAY WITH US. COME ON.
THE POISON'S IN THE FINAL STAGES.
AGHHH...
SILVIO, WE NEED THAT ANTIDOTE OR NICK WILL DIE. NOW!
UH...
NO PROBLEMO.
YOU CAN COOK IT UP ON THE WAY.
ON THE WAY, WHERE?
ON THE WAY TO HIS PRECIOUS JULIETTE. I TOLD YOU. I'M A MAN OF MY WORD.

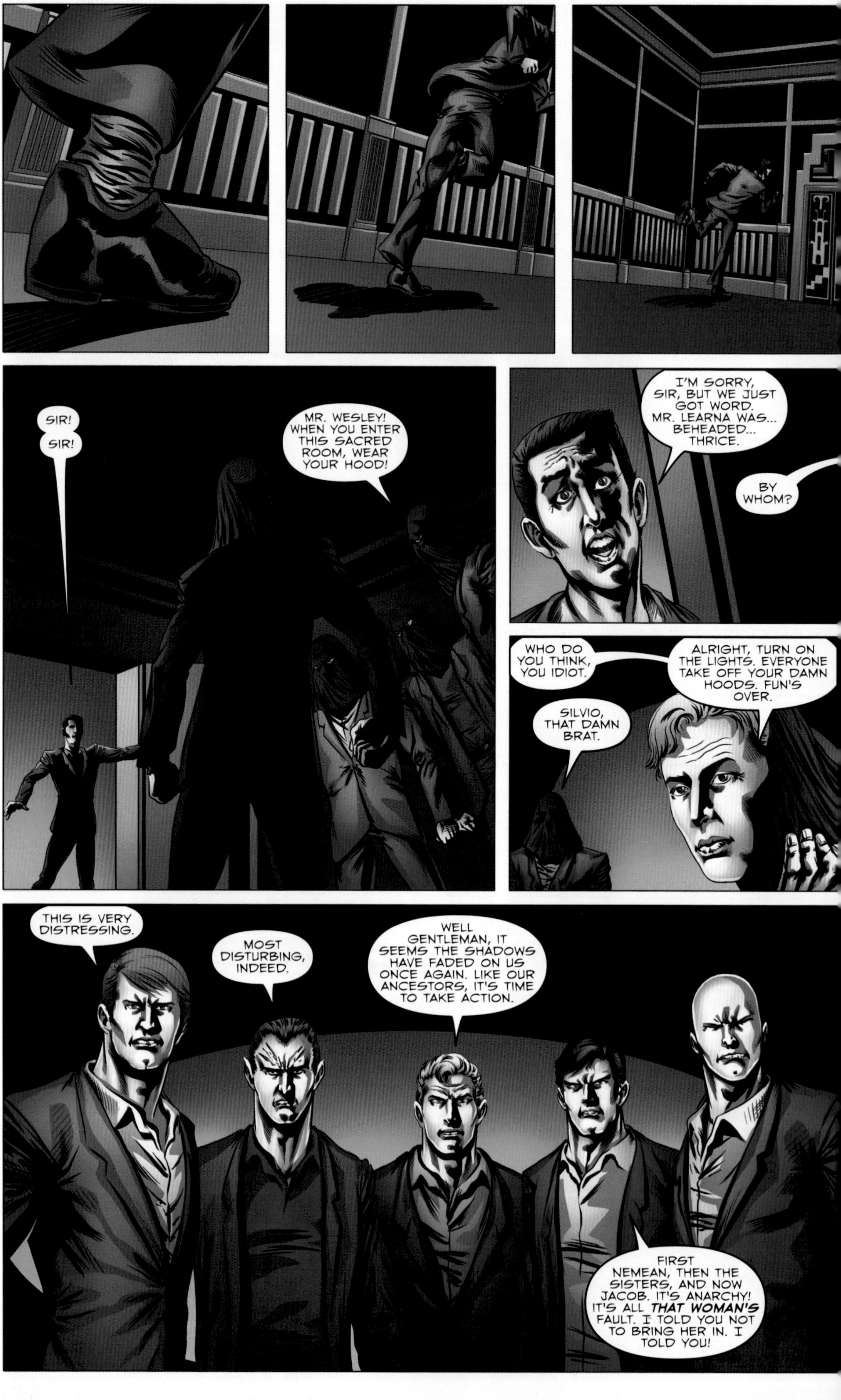
SIR!
SIR!
MR. WESLEY! WHEN YOU ENTER THIS SACRED ROOM, WEAR YOUR HOOD!
I'M SORRY, SIR, BUT WE JUST GOT WORD. MR. LEARNA WAS... BEHEADED... THRICE.
BY WHOM?
WHO DO YOU THINK, YOU IDIOT.
SILVIO, THAT DAMN BRAT.
ALRIGHT, TURN ON THE LIGHTS. EVERYONE TAKE OFF YOUR DAMN HOODS. FUN'S OVER.
THIS IS VERY DISTRESSING.
MOST DISTURBING, INDEED.
WELL GENTLEMAN, IT SEEMS THE SHADOWS HAVE FADED ON US ONCE AGAIN. LIKE OUR ANCESTORS, IT'S TIME TO TAKE ACTION.
FIRST NEMEAN, THEN THE SISTERS, AND NOW JACOB. IT'S ANARCHY! IT'S ALL ***THAT WOMAN'S*** FAULT. I TOLD YOU NOT TO BRING HER IN. I TOLD YOU!

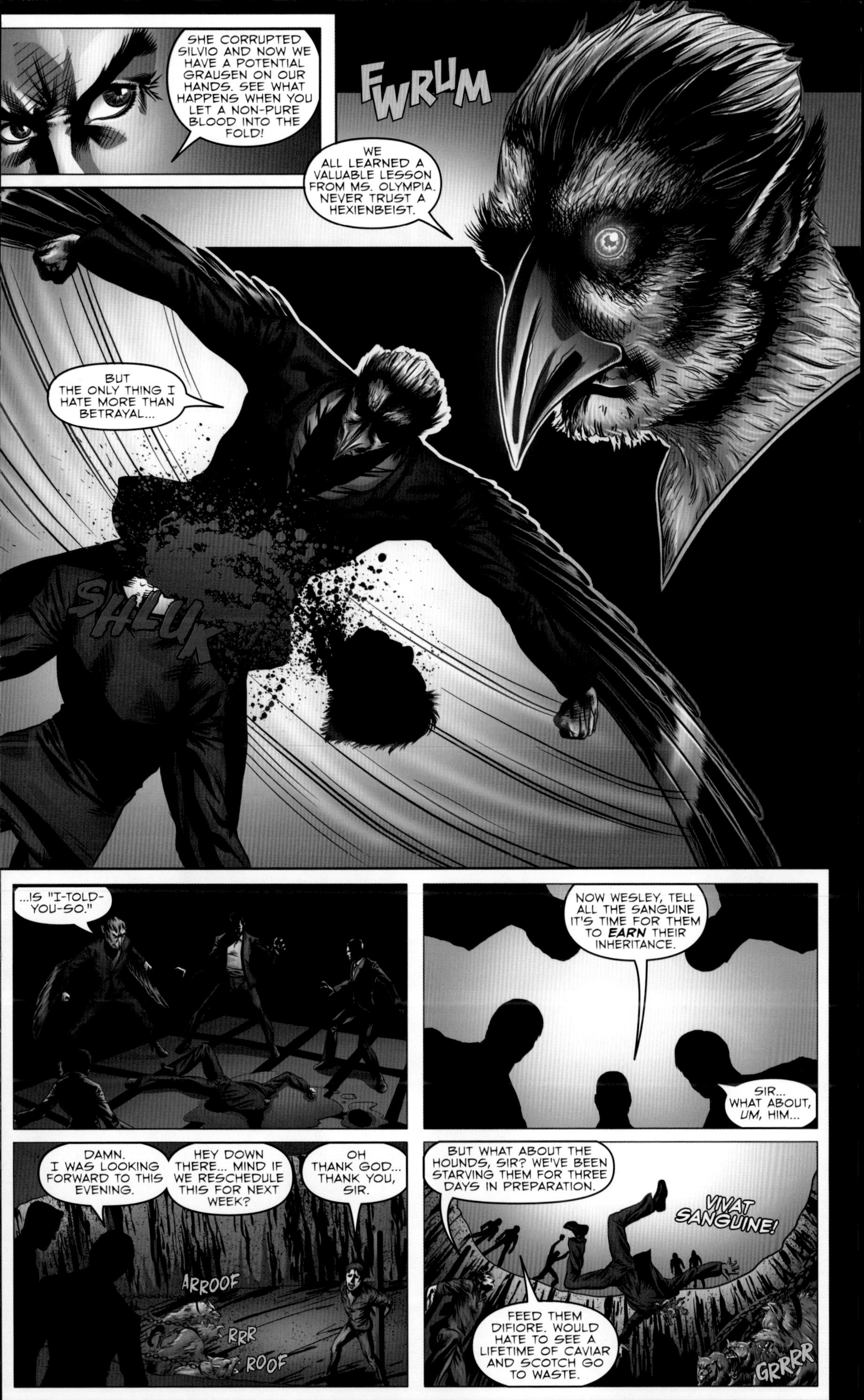
SHE CORRUPTED SILVIO AND NOW WE HAVE A POTENTIAL GRAUSEN ON OUR HANDS. SEE WHAT HAPPENS WHEN YOU LET A NON-PURE BLOOD INTO THE FOLD!
FWRUM
WE ALL LEARNED A VALUABLE LESSON FROM MS. OLYMPIA. NEVER TRUST A HEXIENBEIST.
BUT THE ONLY THING I HATE MORE THAN BETRAYAL...
SHLUK
...IS "I-TOLD-YOU-SO."
NOW WESLEY, TELL ALL THE SANGUINE IT'S TIME FOR THEM TO **EARN** THEIR INHERITANCE.
SIR... WHAT ABOUT, *UM*, HIM...
DAMN. I WAS LOOKING FORWARD TO THIS EVENING.
HEY DOWN THERE... MIND IF WE RESCHEDULE THIS FOR NEXT WEEK?
OH THANK GOD... THANK YOU, SIR.
ARROOF
RRR
ROOF
BUT WHAT ABOUT THE HOUNDS, SIR? WE'VE BEEN STARVING THEM FOR THREE DAYS IN PREPARATION.
VIVAT SANGUINE!
FEED THEM DIFIORE. WOULD HATE TO SEE A LIFETIME OF CAVIAR AND SCOTCH GO TO WASTE.
GRRRR

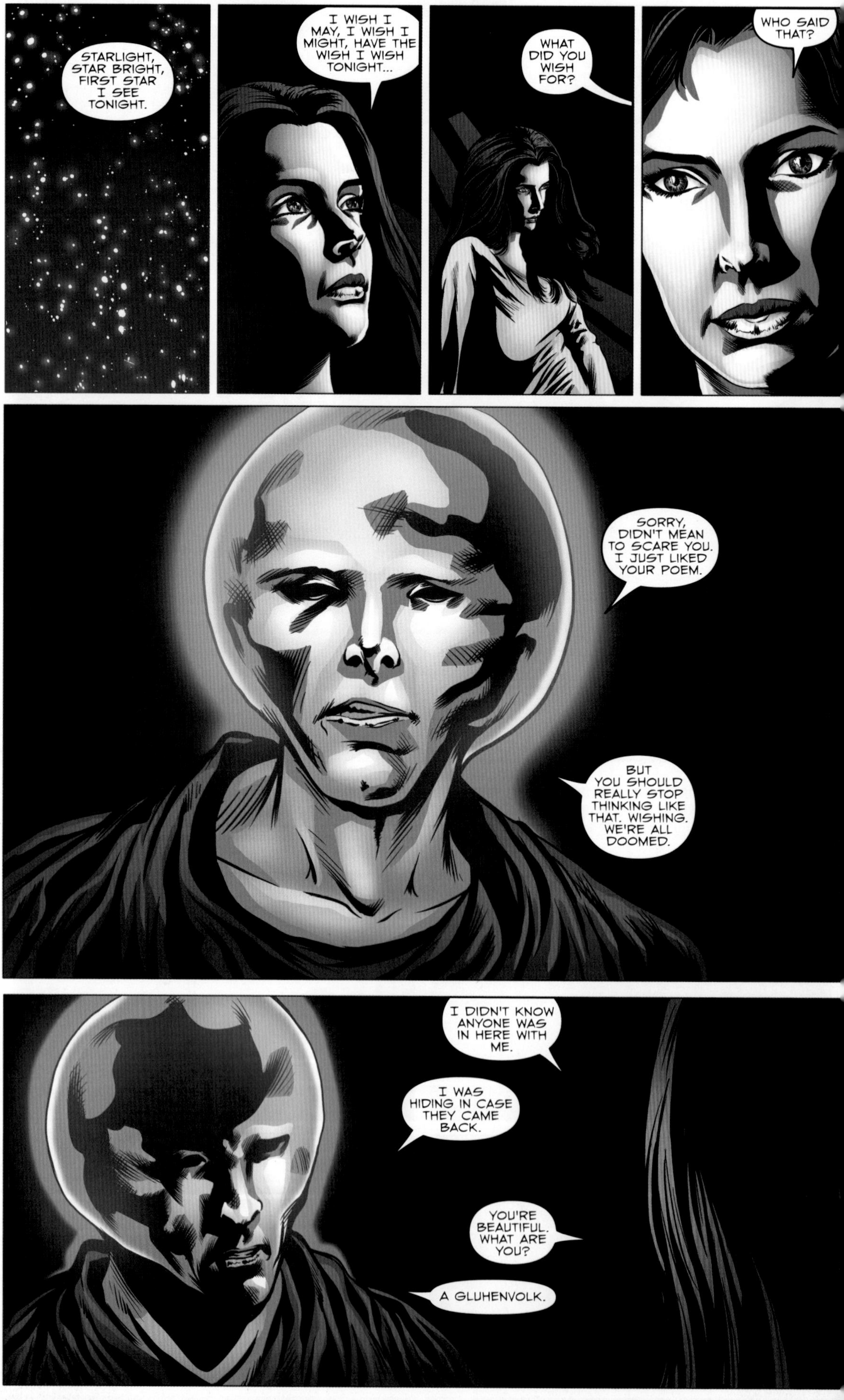
STARLIGHT, STAR BRIGHT, FIRST STAR I SEE TONIGHT.
I WISH I MAY, I WISH I MIGHT, HAVE THE WISH I WISH TONIGHT...
WHAT DID YOU WISH FOR?
WHO SAID THAT?
SORRY, DIDN'T MEAN TO SCARE YOU. I JUST LIKED YOUR POEM.
BUT YOU SHOULD REALLY STOP THINKING LIKE THAT. WISHING. WE'RE ALL DOOMED.
I DIDN'T KNOW ANYONE WAS IN HERE WITH ME.
I WAS HIDING IN CASE THEY CAME BACK.
YOU'RE BEAUTIFUL. WHAT ARE YOU?
A GLUHENVOLK.

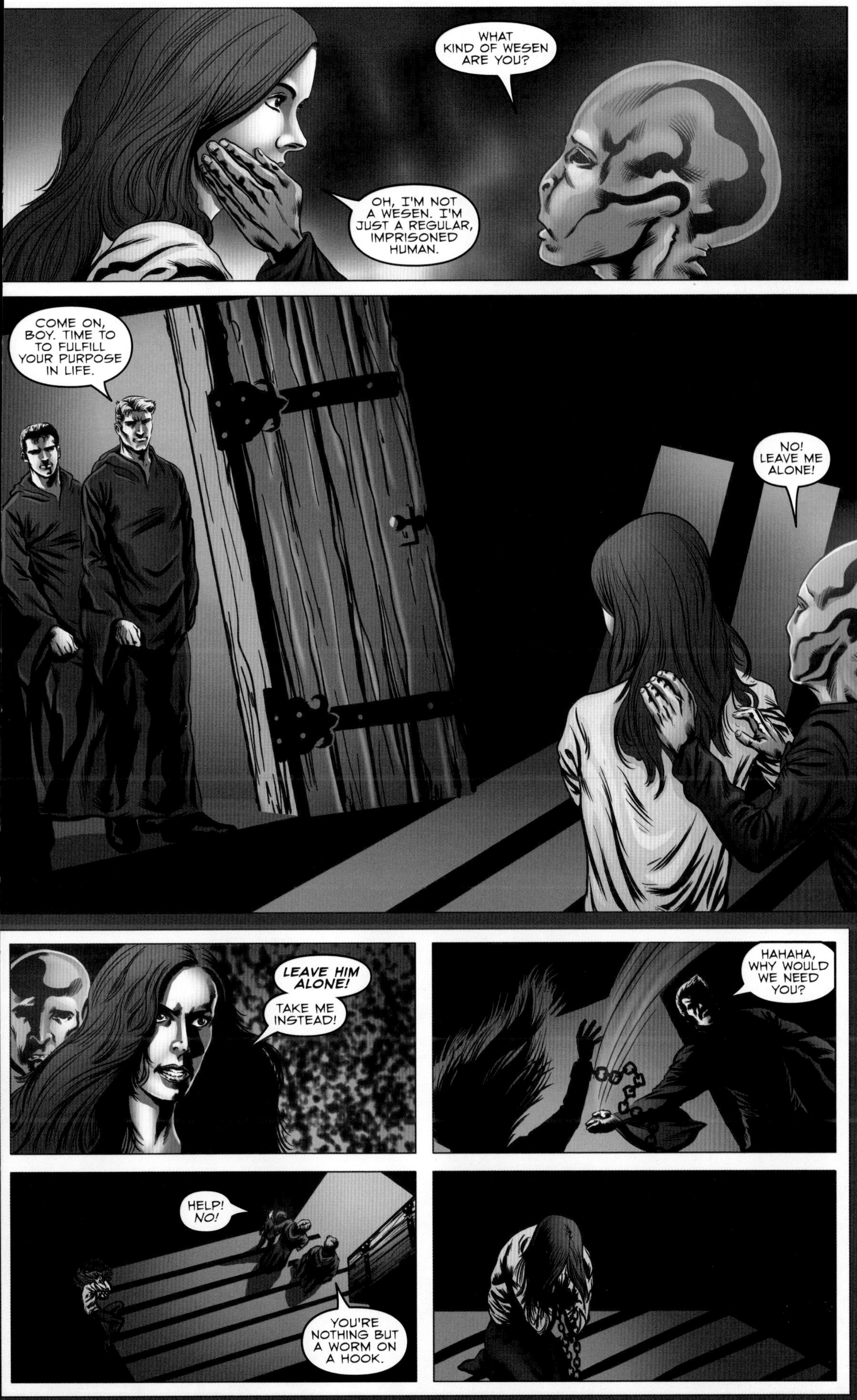
WHAT KIND OF WESEN ARE YOU?
OH, I'M NOT A WESEN. I'M JUST A REGULAR, IMPRISONED HUMAN.
COME ON, BOY. TIME TO TO FULFILL YOUR PURPOSE IN LIFE.
NO! LEAVE ME ALONE!
LEAVE HIM ALONE!
TAKE ME INSTEAD!
HAHAHA, WHY WOULD WE NEED YOU?
HELP! NO!
YOU'RE NOTHING BUT A WORM ON A HOOK.

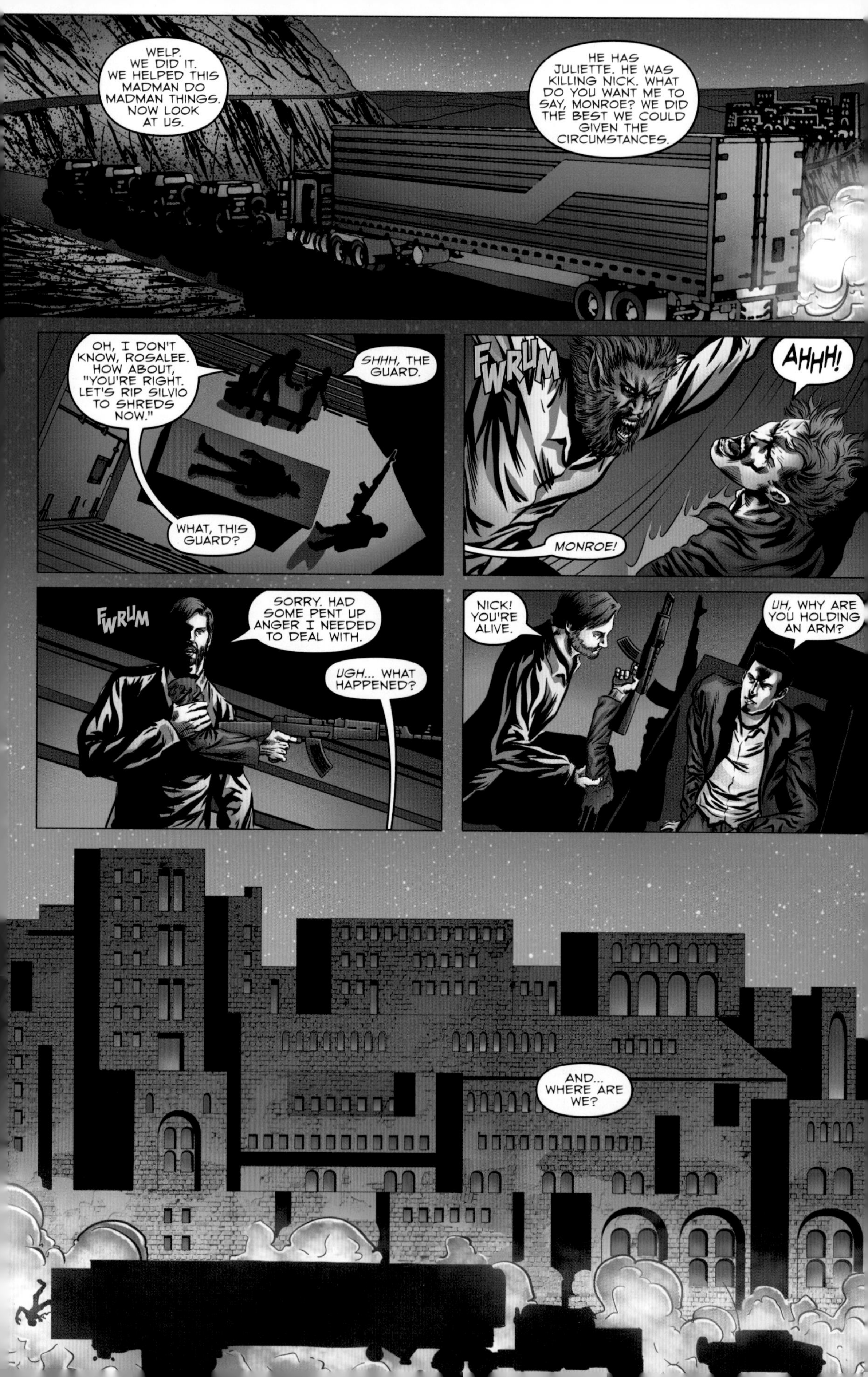
WELP. WE DID IT. WE HELPED THIS MADMAN DO MADMAN THINGS. NOW LOOK AT US.
HE HAS JULIETTE. HE WAS KILLING NICK. WHAT DO YOU WANT ME TO SAY, MONROE? WE DID THE BEST WE COULD GIVEN THE CIRCUMSTANCES.
OH, I DON'T KNOW, ROSALEE. HOW ABOUT, "YOU'RE RIGHT. LET'S RIP SILVIO TO SHREDS NOW."
SHHH, THE GUARD.
WHAT, THIS GUARD?
FWRUM
AHHH!
MONROE!
FWRUM
SORRY. HAD SOME PENT UP ANGER I NEEDED TO DEAL WITH.
UGH... WHAT HAPPENED?
NICK! YOU'RE ALIVE.
UH, WHY ARE YOU HOLDING AN ARM?
AND... WHERE ARE WE?

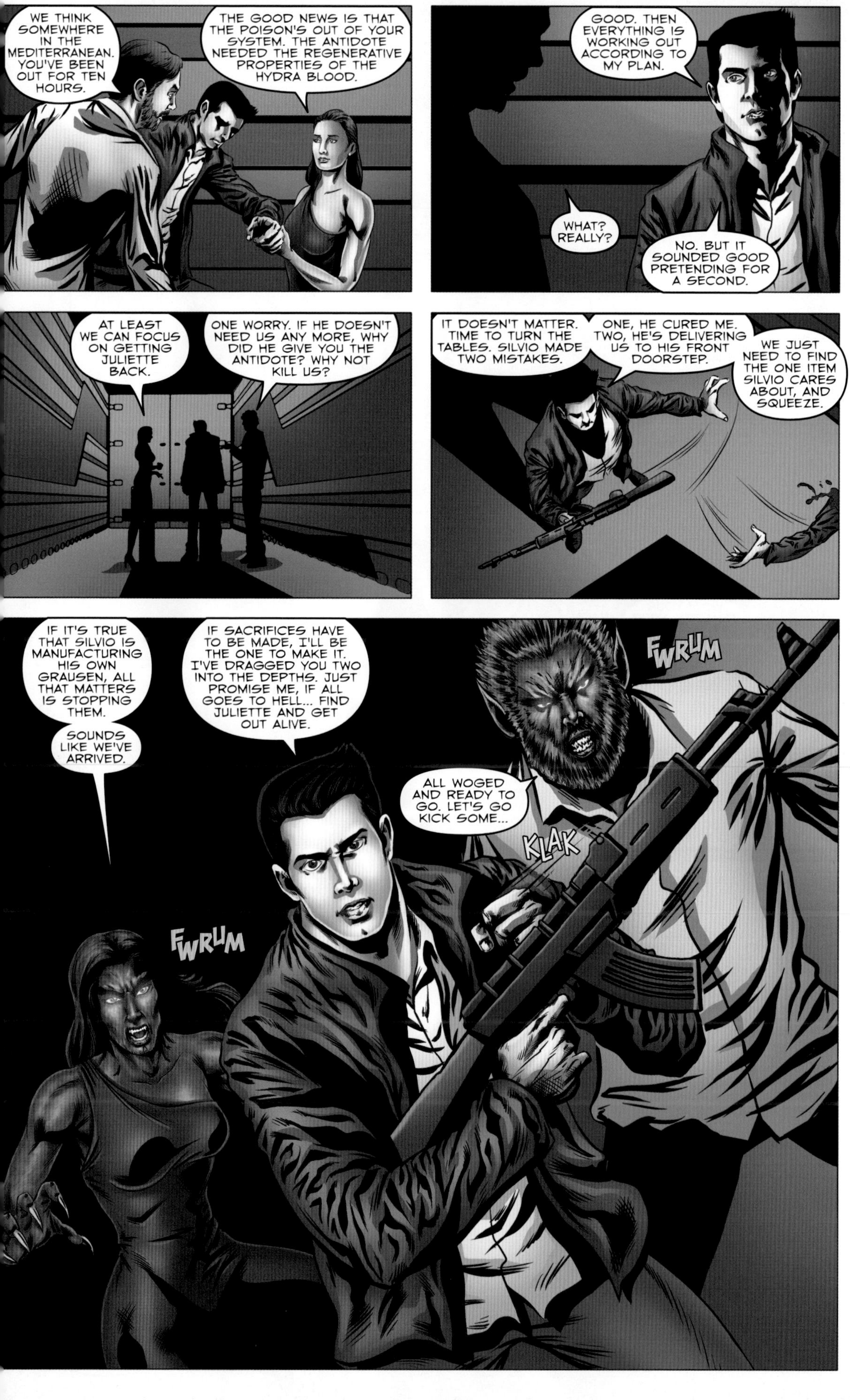
WE THINK SOMEWHERE IN THE MEDITERRANEAN. YOU'VE BEEN OUT FOR TEN HOURS.
THE GOOD NEWS IS THAT THE POISON'S OUT OF YOUR SYSTEM. THE ANTIDOTE NEEDED THE REGENERATIVE PROPERTIES OF THE HYDRA BLOOD.
GOOD. THEN EVERYTHING IS WORKING OUT ACCORDING TO MY PLAN.
WHAT? REALLY?
NO. BUT IT SOUNDED GOOD PRETENDING FOR A SECOND.
AT LEAST WE CAN FOCUS ON GETTING JULIETTE BACK.
ONE WORRY. IF HE DOESN'T NEED US ANY MORE, WHY DID HE GIVE YOU THE ANTIDOTE? WHY NOT KILL US?
IT DOESN'T MATTER. TIME TO TURN THE TABLES. SILVIO MADE TWO MISTAKES.
ONE, HE CURED ME. TWO, HE'S DELIVERING US TO HIS FRONT DOORSTEP.
WE JUST NEED TO FIND THE ONE ITEM SILVIO CARES ABOUT, AND SQUEEZE.
IF IT'S TRUE THAT SILVIO IS MANUFACTURING HIS OWN GRAUSEN, ALL THAT MATTERS IS STOPPING THEM.
SOUNDS LIKE WE'VE ARRIVED.
IF SACRIFICES HAVE TO BE MADE, I'LL BE THE ONE TO MAKE IT. I'VE DRAGGED YOU TWO INTO THE DEPTHS. JUST PROMISE ME, IF ALL GOES TO HELL... FIND JULIETTE AND GET OUT ALIVE.
FWRUM
ALL WOGED AND READY TO GO. LET'S GO KICK SOME...
KLAK
FWRUM

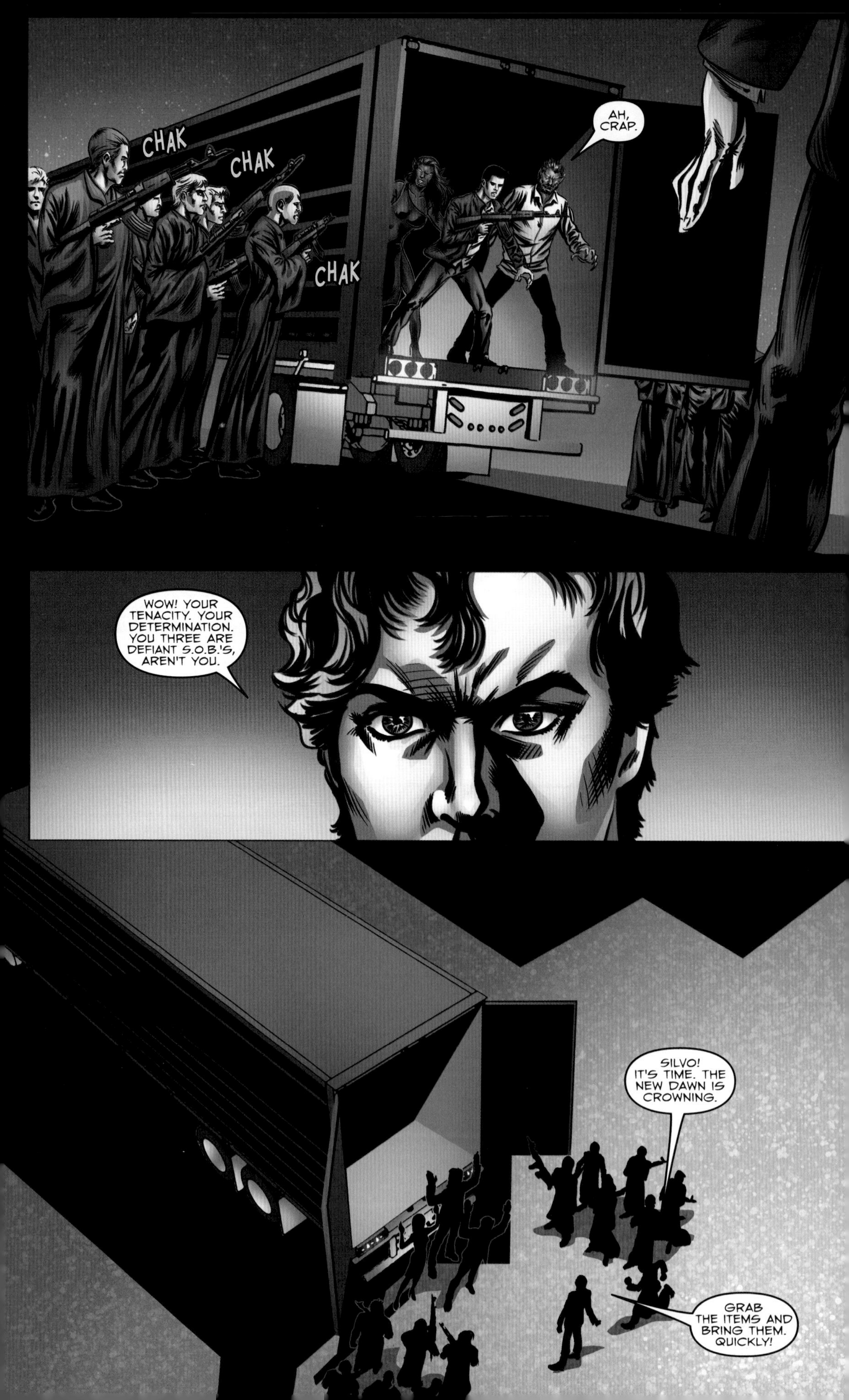
CHAK
CHAK
CHAK
AH, CRAP.
WOW! YOUR TENACITY. YOUR DETERMINATION. YOU THREE ARE DEFIANT S.O.B.'S, AREN'T YOU.
SILVO! IT'S TIME. THE NEW DAWN IS CROWNING.
GRAB THE ITEMS AND BRING THEM. QUICKLY!

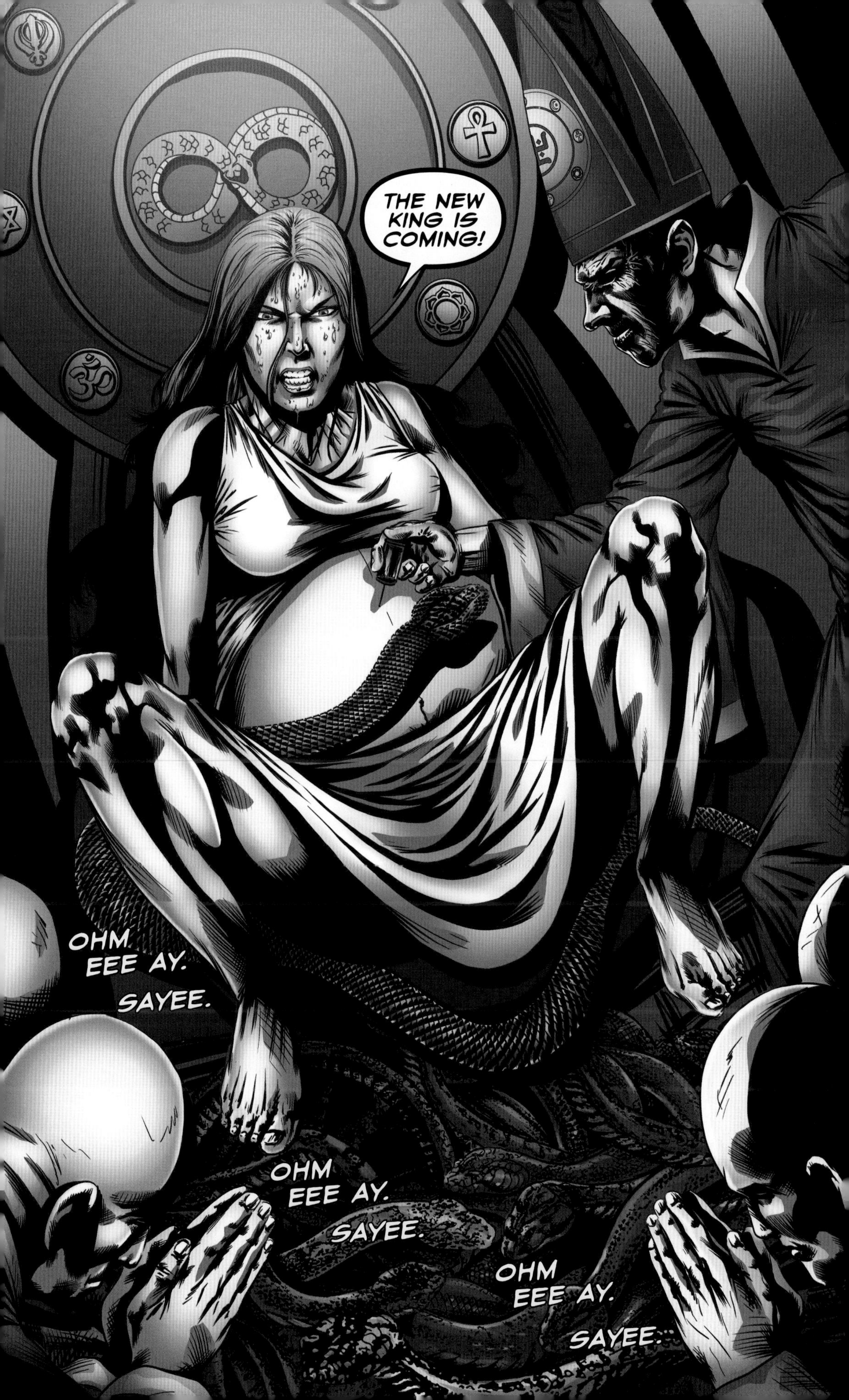
THE NEW KING IS COMING!
OHM EEE AY.
SAYEE.
OHM EEE AY.
SAYEE.
OHM EEE AY.
SAYEE.

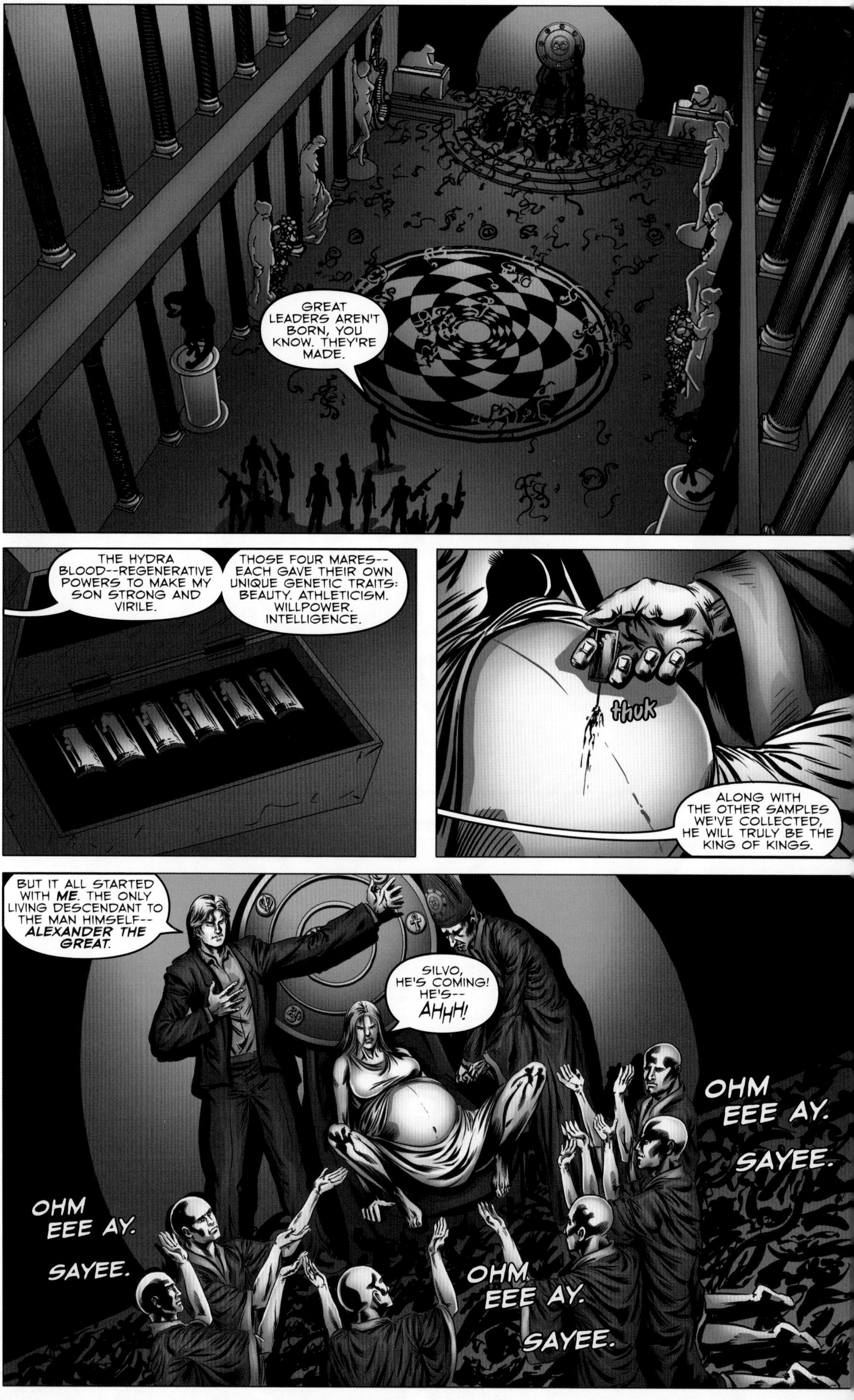
GREAT LEADERS AREN'T BORN, YOU KNOW. THEY'RE MADE.
THE HYDRA BLOOD--REGENERATIVE POWERS TO MAKE MY SON STRONG AND VIRILE.
THOSE FOUR MARES--EACH GAVE THEIR OWN UNIQUE GENETIC TRAITS: BEAUTY. ATHLETICISM. WILLPOWER. INTELLIGENCE.
thuk
ALONG WITH THE OTHER SAMPLES WE'VE COLLECTED, HE WILL TRULY BE THE KING OF KINGS.
BUT IT ALL STARTED WITH ME. THE ONLY LIVING DESCENDANT TO THE MAN HIMSELF-- ALEXANDER THE GREAT.
SILVO, HE'S COMING! HE'S-- AHHH!
OHM EEE AY.
SAYEE.
OHM EEE AY.
SAYEE.
OHM EEE AY.
SAYEE.

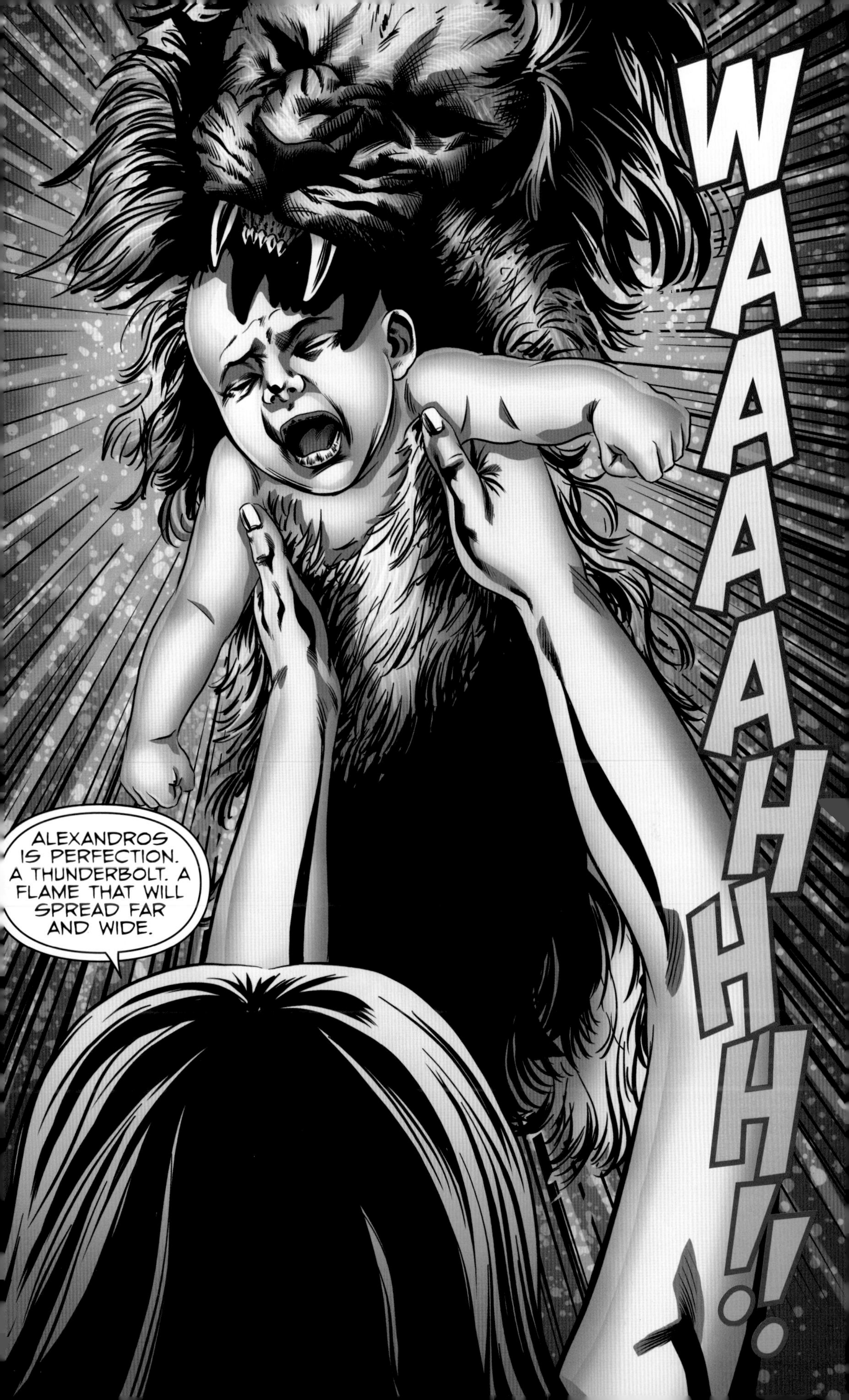
WAAAAAHHHH!!
ALEXANDROS IS PERFECTION. A THUNDERBOLT. A FLAME THAT WILL SPREAD FAR AND WIDE.

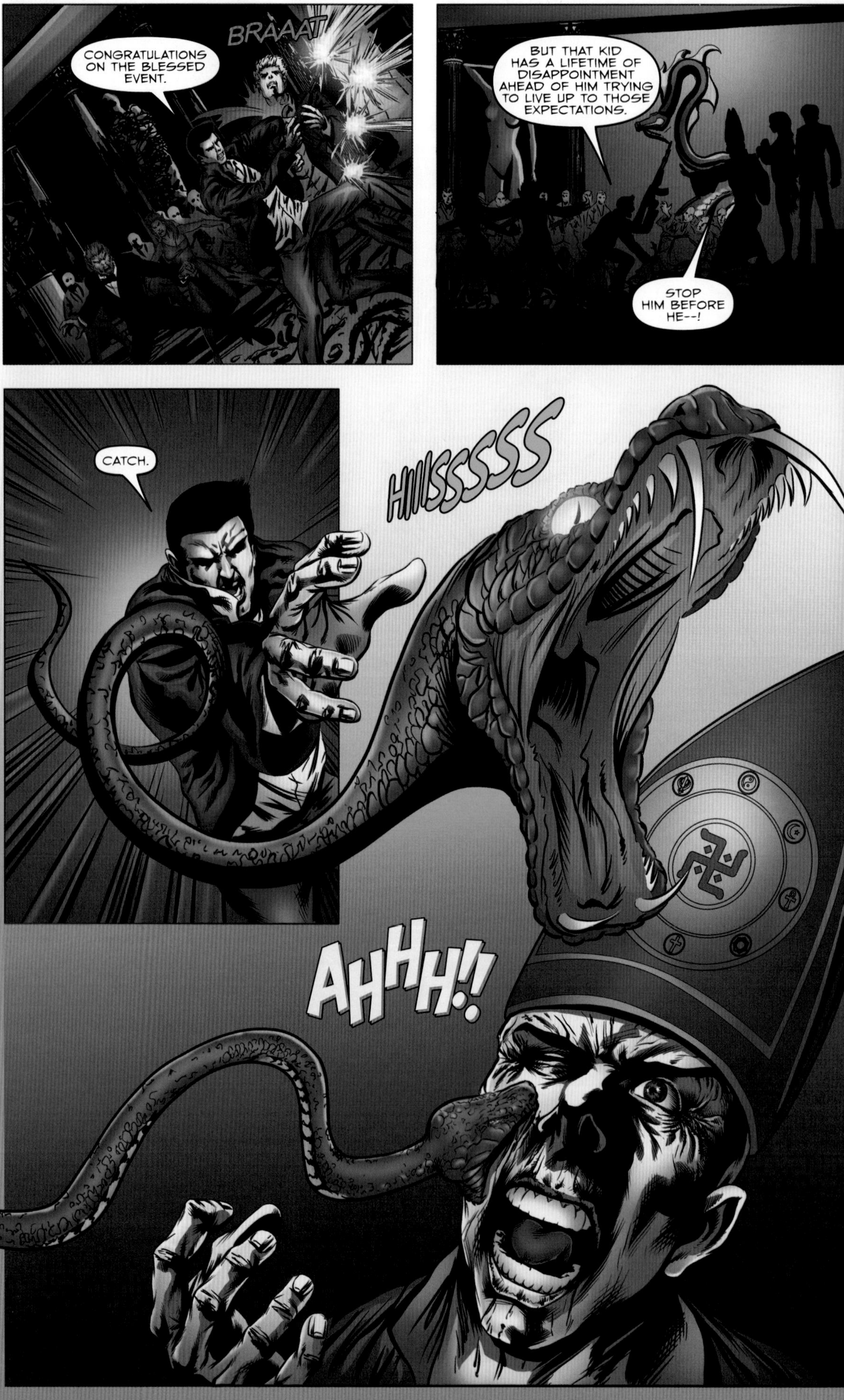
BRAAAT
CONGRATULATIONS ON THE BLESSED EVENT.
BUT THAT KID HAS A LIFETIME OF DISAPPOINTMENT AHEAD OF HIM TRYING TO LIVE UP TO THOSE EXPECTATIONS.
STOP HIM BEFORE HE--!
CATCH.
HIISSSSS
AHHH!!

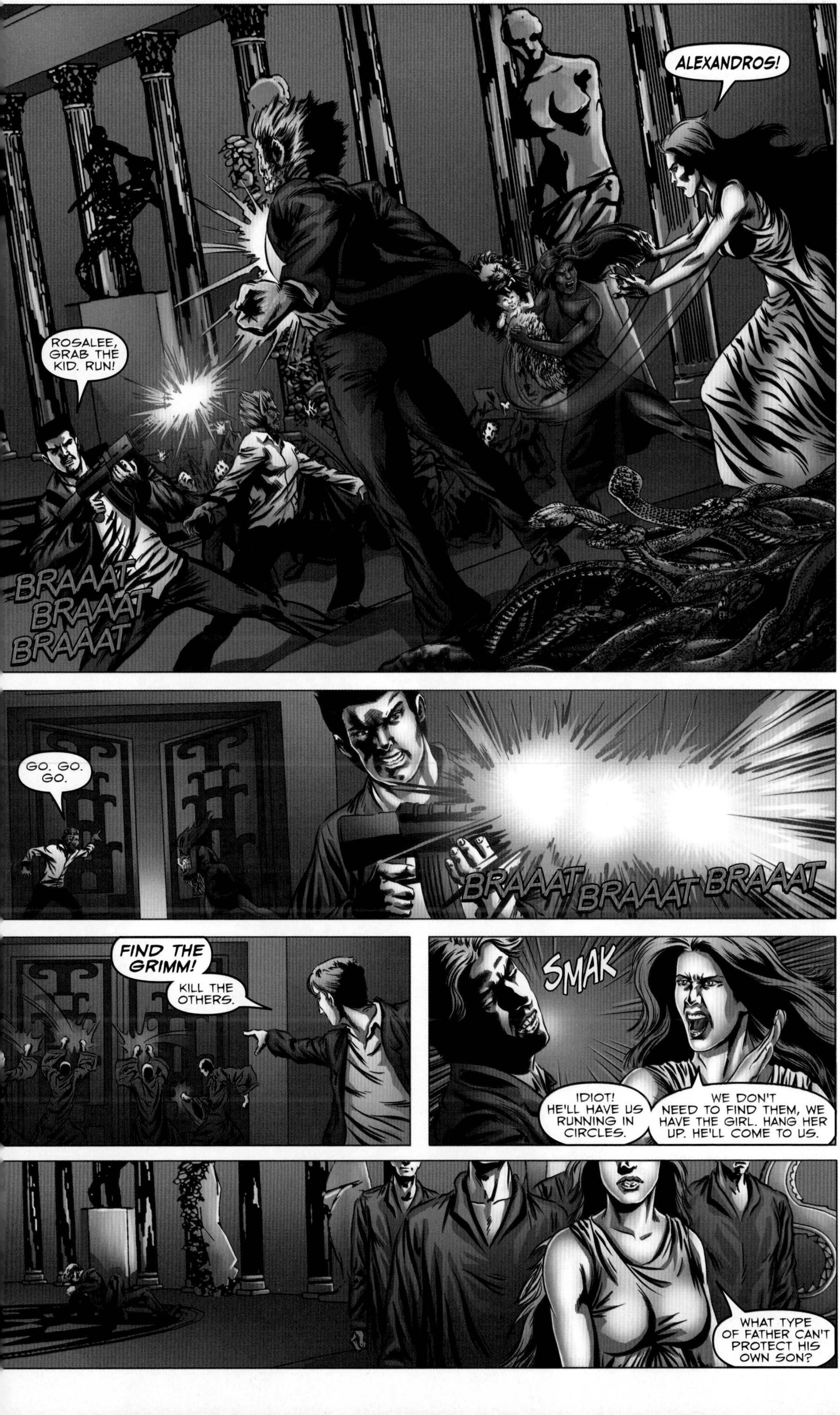
ALEXANDROS!
ROSALEE, GRAB THE KID. RUN!
BRAAAT BRAAAT BRAAAT
GO. GO. GO.
BRAAAT BRAAAT BRAAAT
FIND THE GRIMM!
KILL THE OTHERS.
SMAK
IDIOT! HE'LL HAVE US RUNNING IN CIRCLES.
WE DON'T NEED TO FIND THEM, WE HAVE THE GIRL. HANG HER UP. HE'LL COME TO US.
WHAT TYPE OF FATHER CAN'T PROTECT HIS OWN SON?

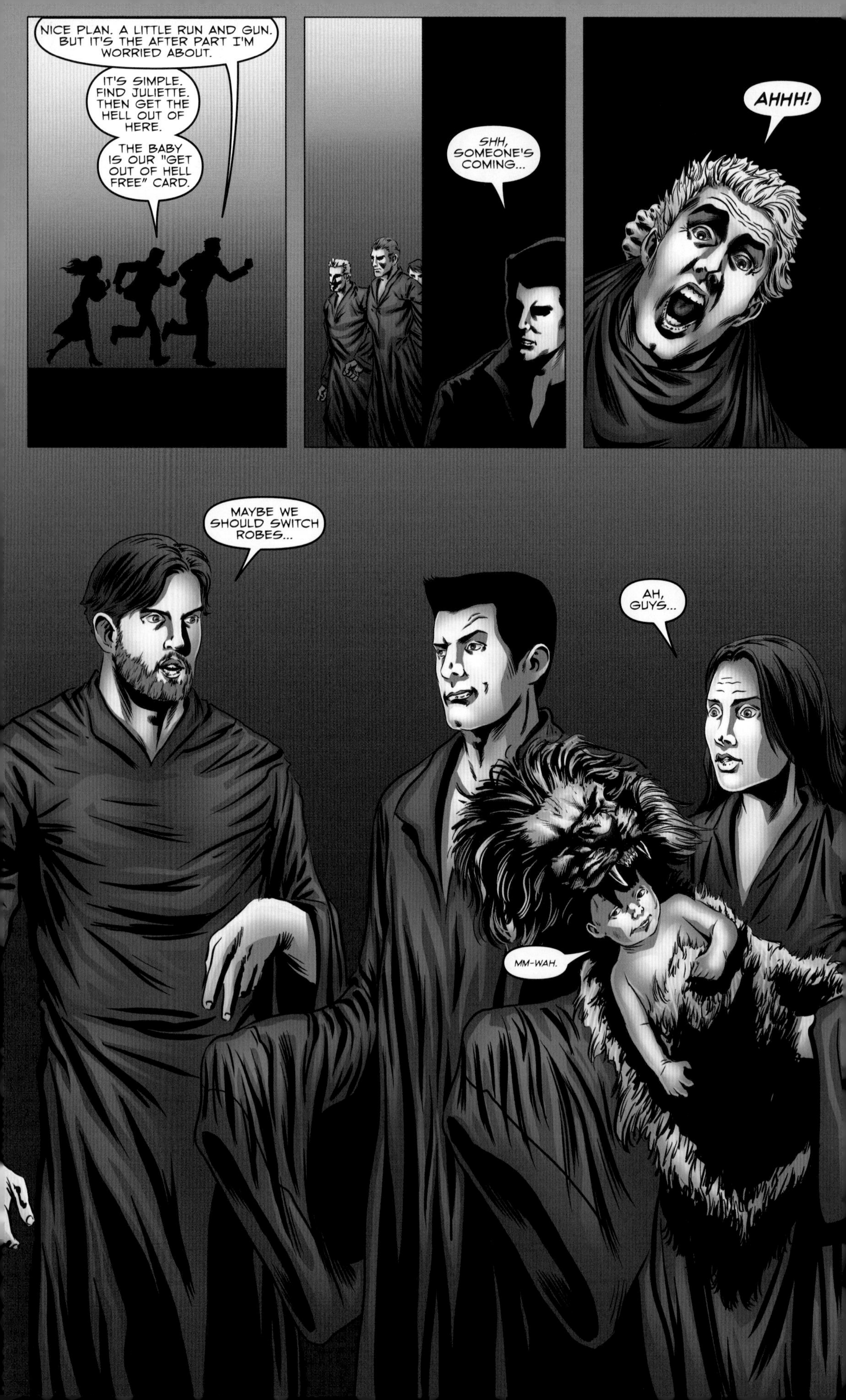
NICE PLAN. A LITTLE RUN AND GUN. BUT IT'S THE AFTER PART I'M WORRIED ABOUT.
IT'S SIMPLE. FIND JULIETTE. THEN GET THE HELL OUT OF HERE.
THE BABY IS OUR "GET OUT OF HELL FREE" CARD.
SHH, SOMEONE'S COMING...
AHHH!
MAYBE WE SHOULD SWITCH ROBES...
AH, GUYS...
MM-WAH.

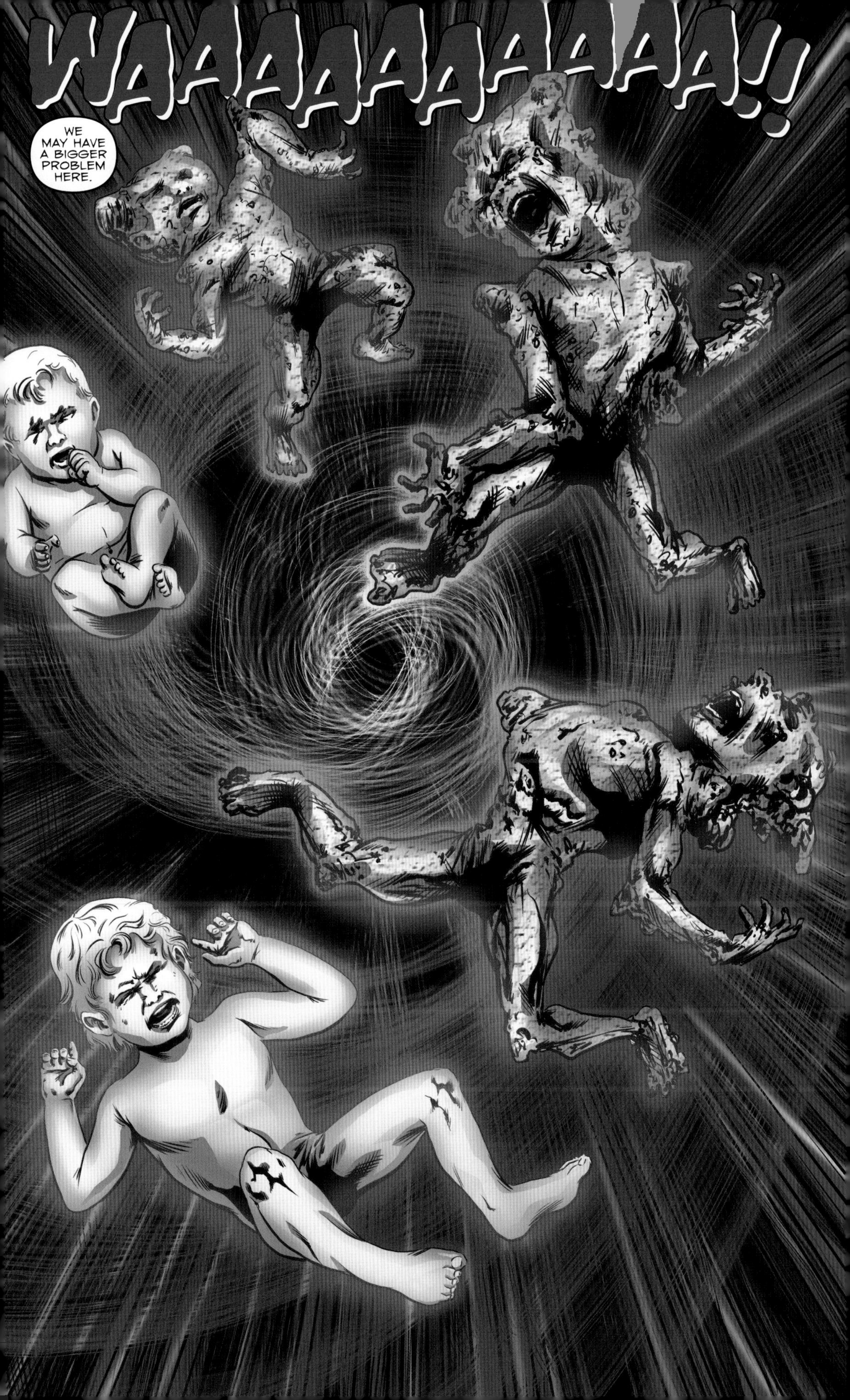
WAAAAAAAAAA!!
WE MAY HAVE A BIGGER PROBLEM HERE.

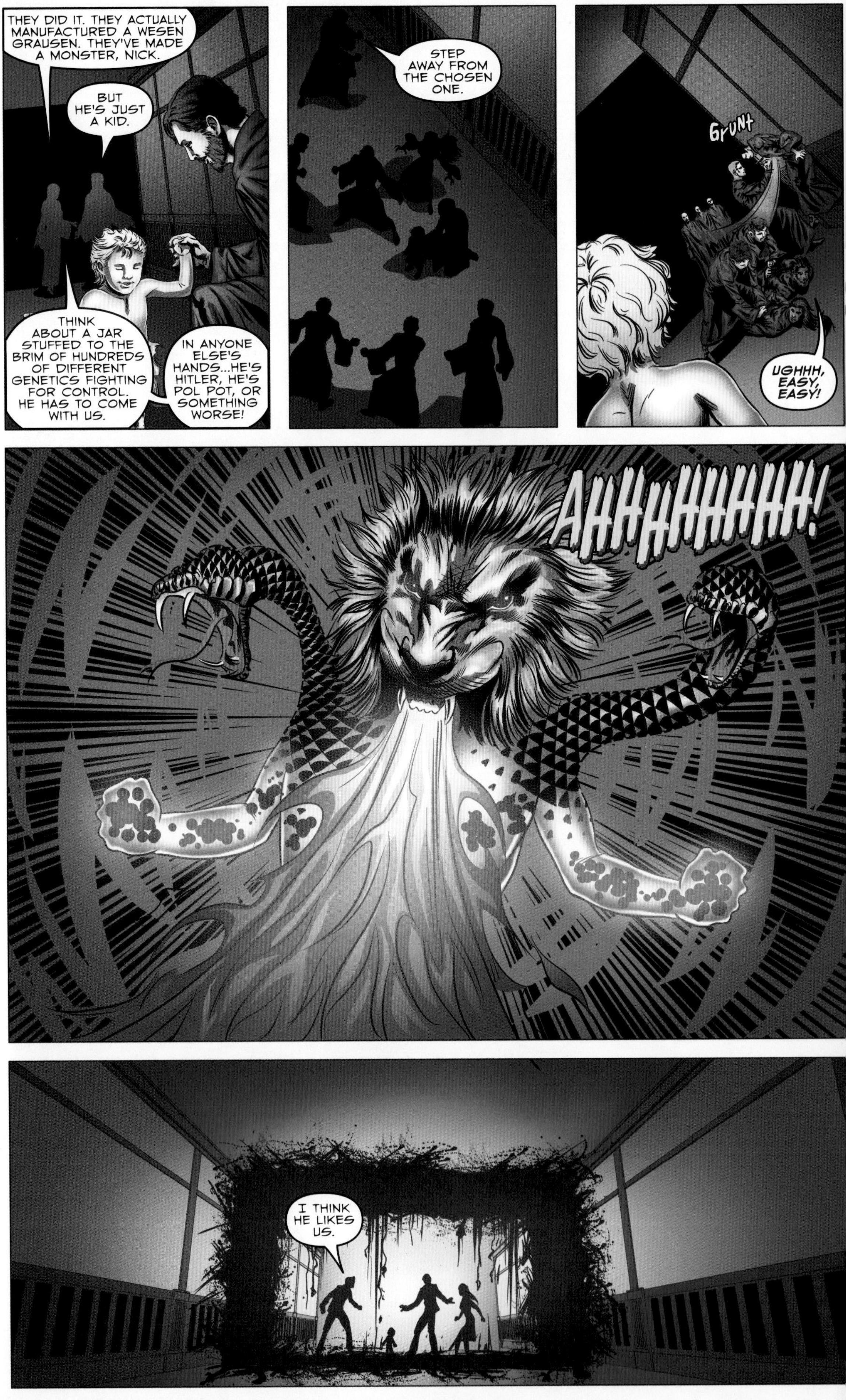
THEY DID IT. THEY ACTUALLY MANUFACTURED A WESEN GRAUSEN. THEY'VE MADE A MONSTER, NICK.
BUT HE'S JUST A KID.
THINK ABOUT A JAR STUFFED TO THE BRIM OF HUNDREDS OF DIFFERENT GENETICS FIGHTING FOR CONTROL. HE HAS TO COME WITH US.
IN ANYONE ELSE'S HANDS...HE'S HITLER, HE'S POL POT, OR SOMETHING WORSE!
STEP AWAY FROM THE CHOSEN ONE.
GRUNT
UGHHH, EASY, EASY!
AHHHHHHHH!
I THINK HE LIKES US.

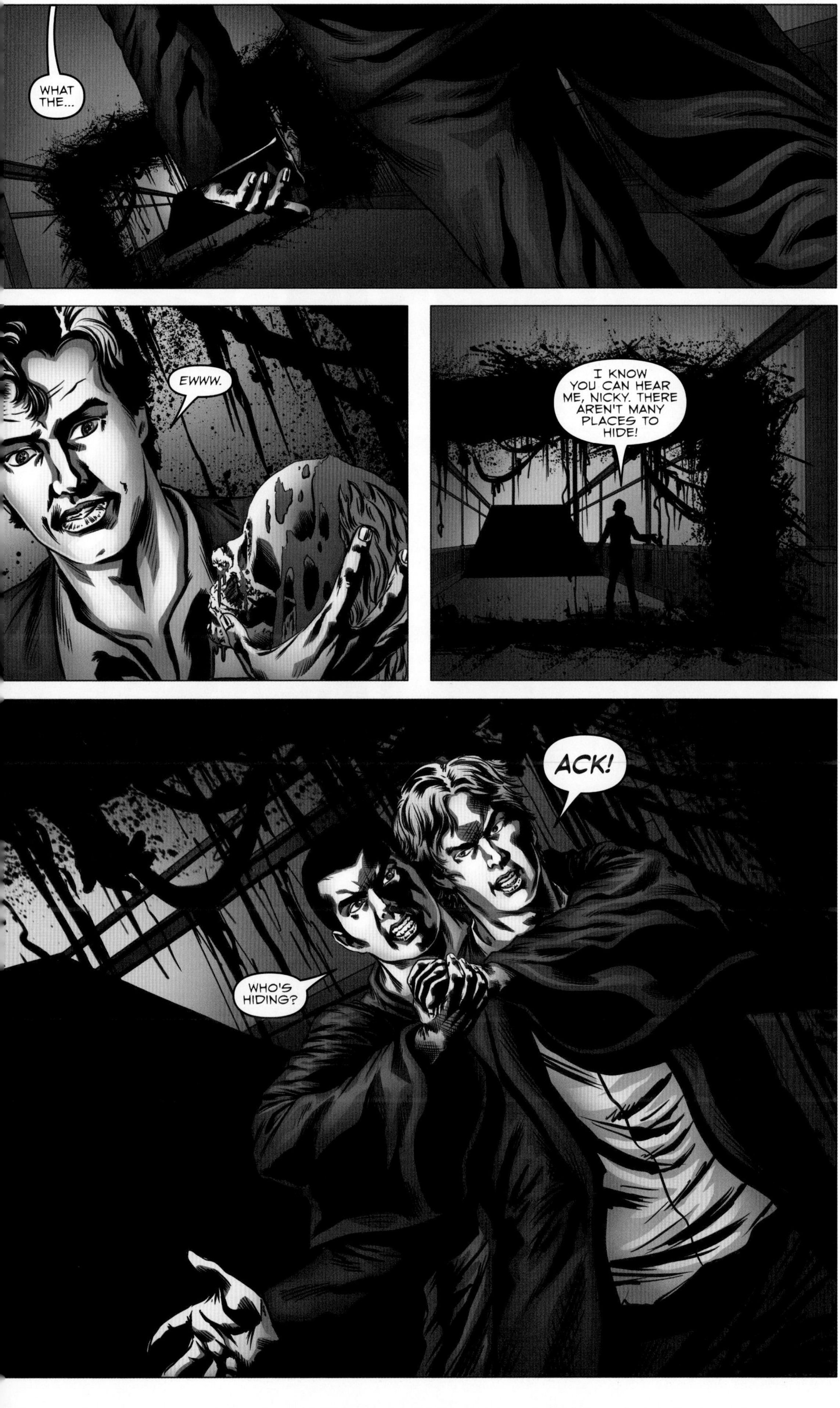
WHAT THE...
EWWW.
I KNOW YOU CAN HEAR ME, NICKY. THERE AREN'T MANY PLACES TO HIDE!
ACK!
WHO'S HIDING?

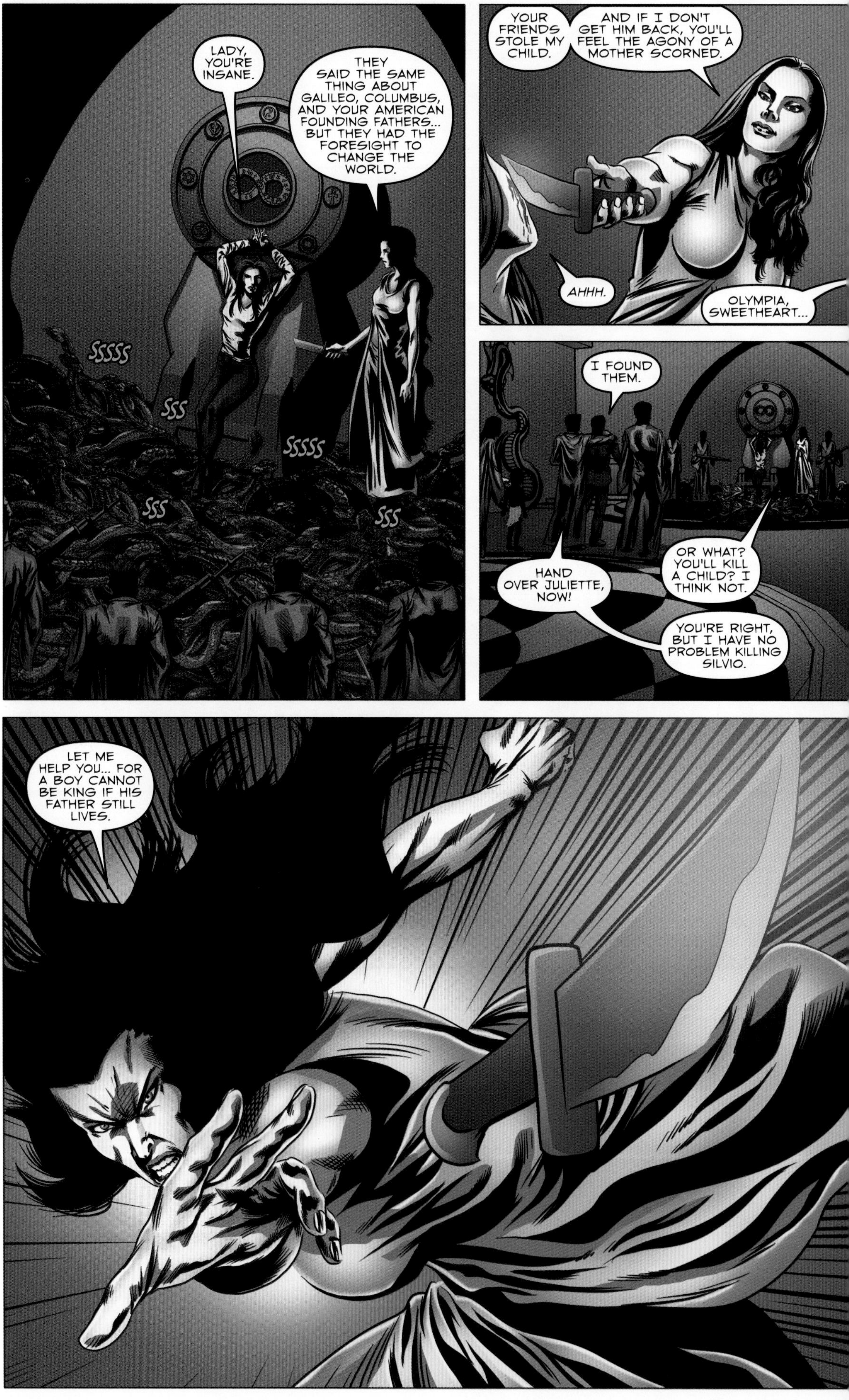
LADY, YOU'RE INSANE.
THEY SAID THE SAME THING ABOUT GALILEO, COLUMBUS, AND YOUR AMERICAN FOUNDING FATHERS... BUT THEY HAD THE FORESIGHT TO CHANGE THE WORLD.
SSSSS
SSS
SSSSS
SSS
SSS
YOUR FRIENDS STOLE MY CHILD.
AND IF I DON'T GET HIM BACK, YOU'LL FEEL THE AGONY OF A MOTHER SCORNED.
AHHH.
OLYMPIA, SWEETHEART...
I FOUND THEM.
HAND OVER JULIETTE, NOW!
OR WHAT? YOU'LL KILL A CHILD? I THINK NOT.
YOU'RE RIGHT, BUT I HAVE NO PROBLEM KILLING SILVIO.
LET ME HELP YOU... FOR A BOY CANNOT BE KING IF HIS FATHER STILL LIVES.

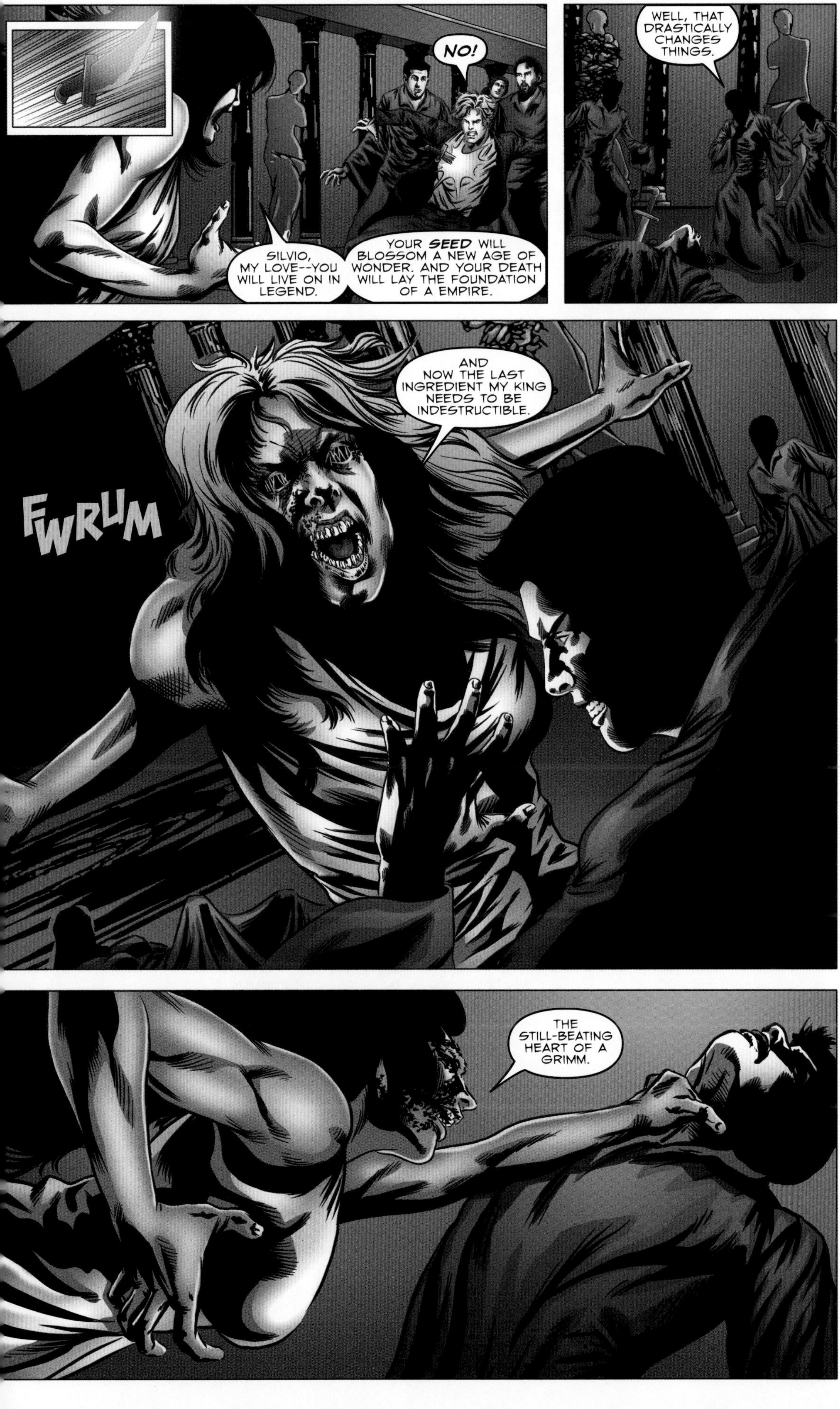
NO!
SILVIO, MY LOVE--YOU WILL LIVE ON IN LEGEND.
YOUR SEED WILL BLOSSOM A NEW AGE OF WONDER. AND YOUR DEATH WILL LAY THE FOUNDATION OF A EMPIRE.
WELL, THAT DRASTICALLY CHANGES THINGS.
AND NOW THE LAST INGREDIENT MY KING NEEDS TO BE INDESTRUCTIBLE.
FWRUM
THE STILL-BEATING HEART OF A GRIMM.

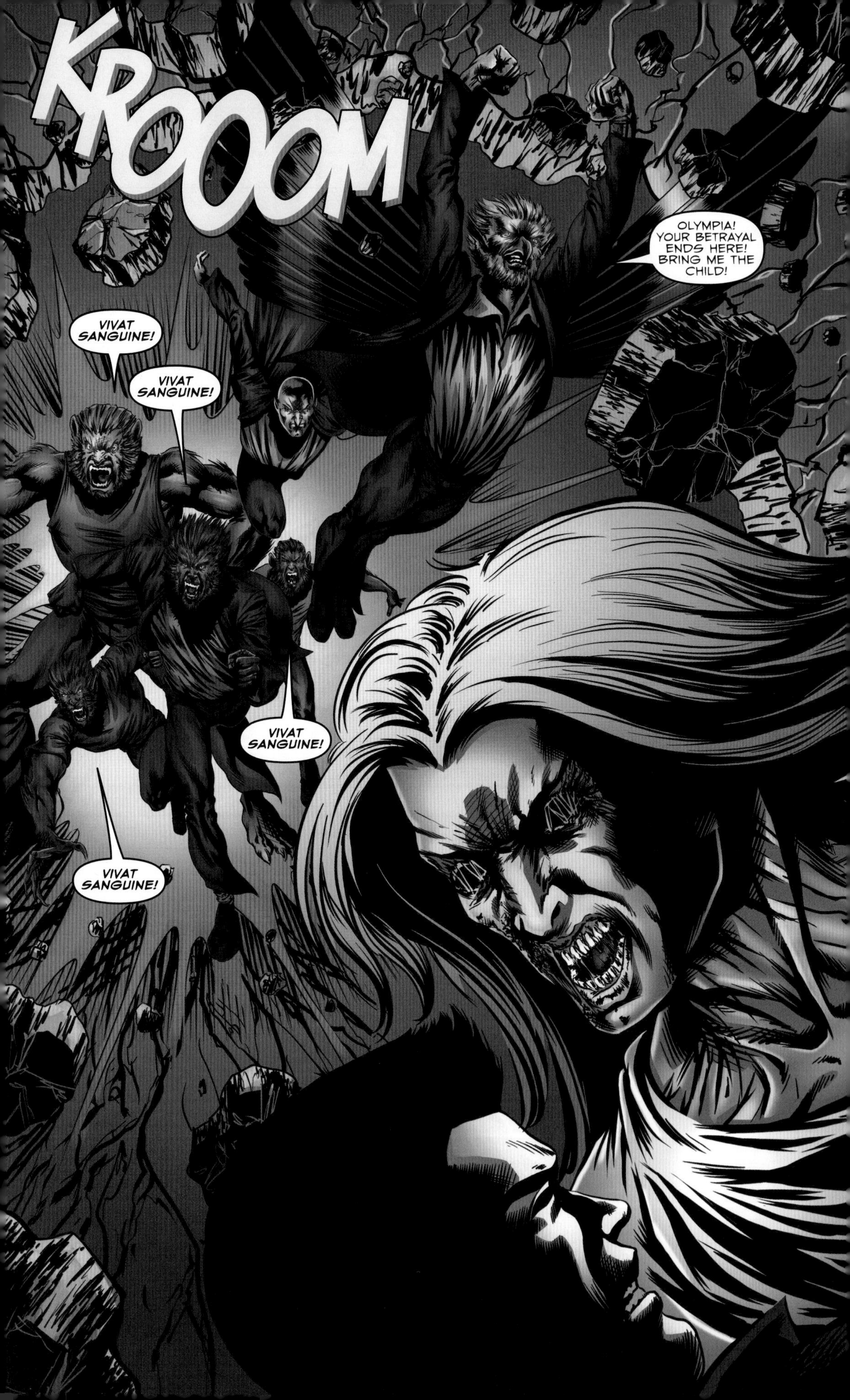
KROOOM
OLYMPIA! YOUR BETRAYAL ENDS HERE! BRING ME THE CHILD!
VIVAT SANGUINE!
VIVAT SANGUINE!
VIVAT SANGUINE!
VIVAT SANGUINE!

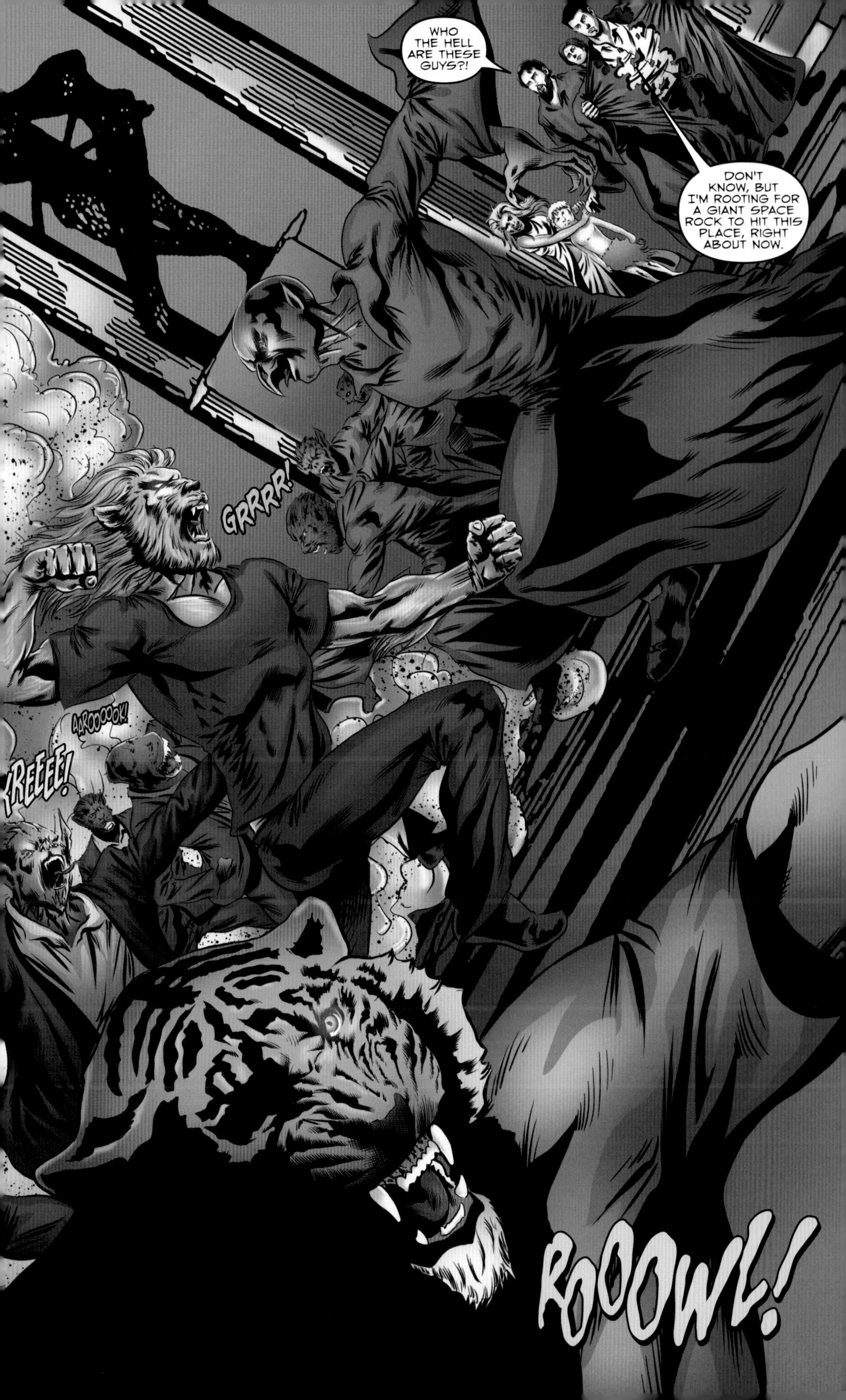
WHO THE HELL ARE THESE GUYS?!
DON'T KNOW, BUT I'M ROOTING FOR A GIANT SPACE ROCK TO HIT THIS PLACE, RIGHT ABOUT NOW.
GRRRR!
AAROOOOK!
REEEE!
ROOOWL!

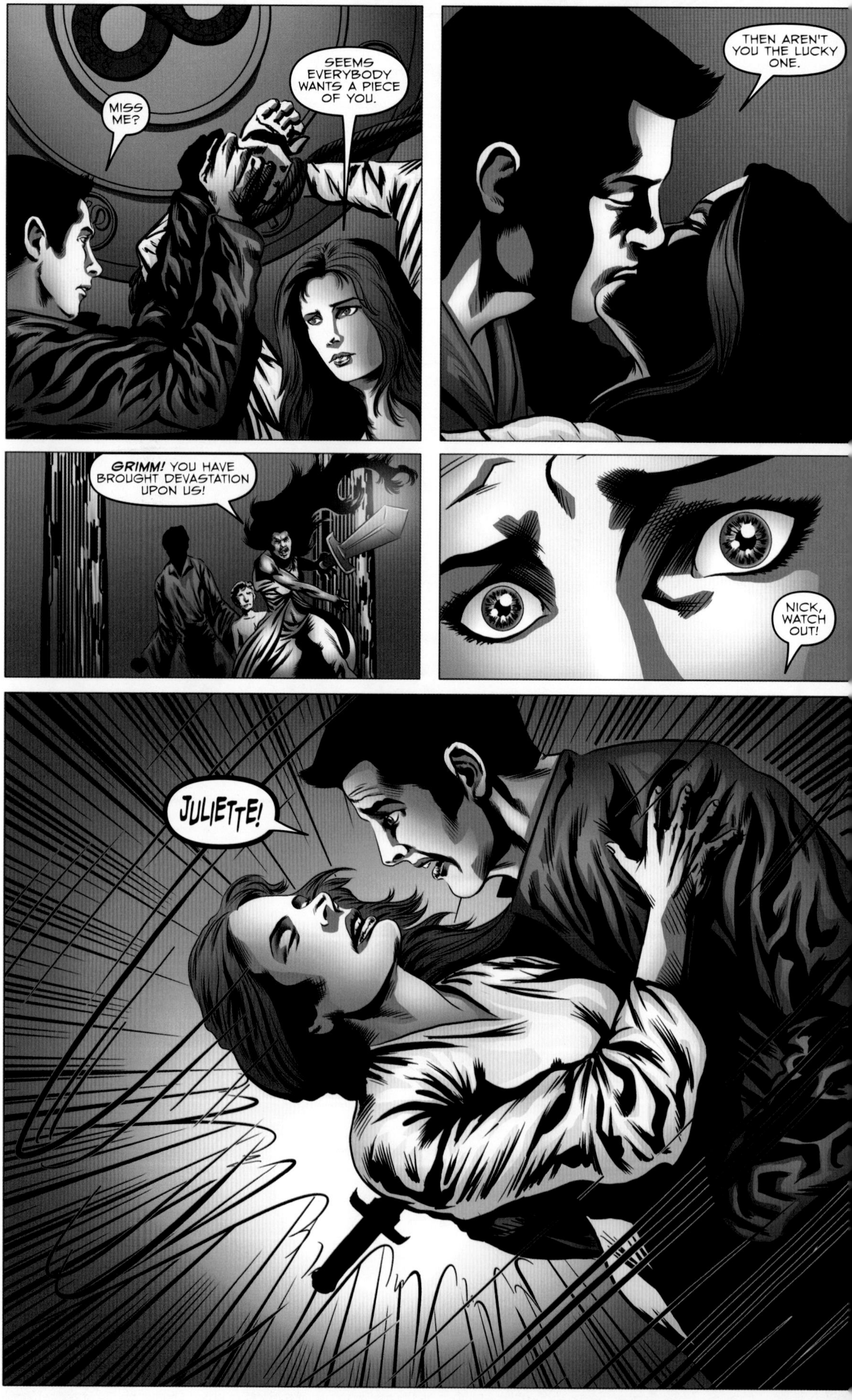
MISS ME?
SEEMS EVERYBODY WANTS A PIECE OF YOU.
THEN AREN'T YOU THE LUCKY ONE.
GRIMM! YOU HAVE BROUGHT DEVASTATION UPON US!
NICK, WATCH OUT!
JULIETTE!

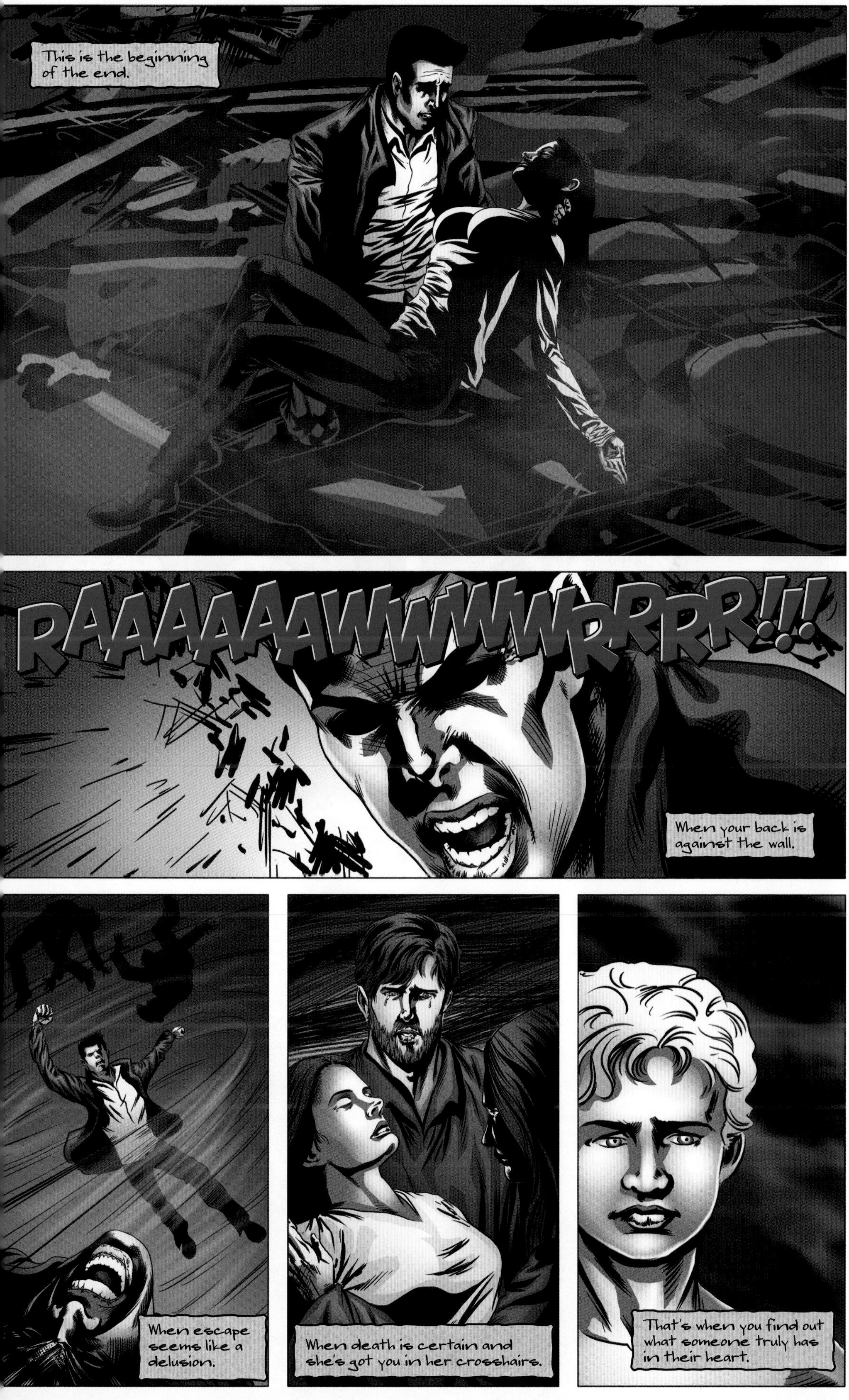
This is the beginning of the end.
RAAAAAAWWWWRRRR!!!
When your back is against the wall.
When escape seems like a delusion.
When death is certain and she's got you in her crosshairs.
That's when you find out what someone truly has in their heart.

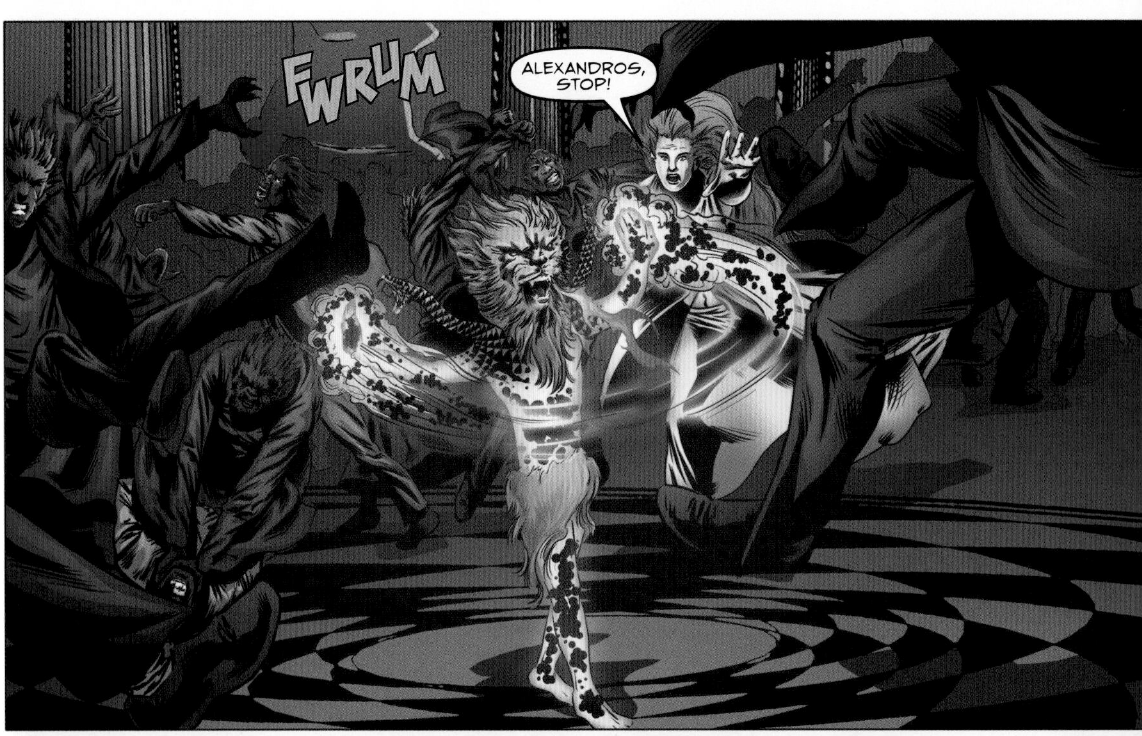
FWRUM
ALEXANDROS, STOP!

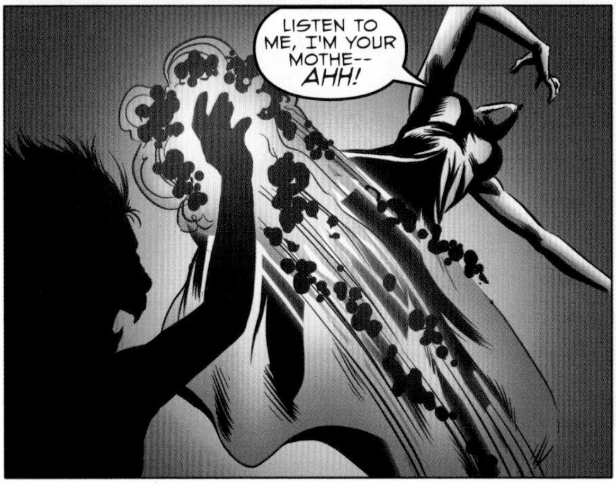
LISTEN TO ME, I'M YOUR MOTHE-- AHH!

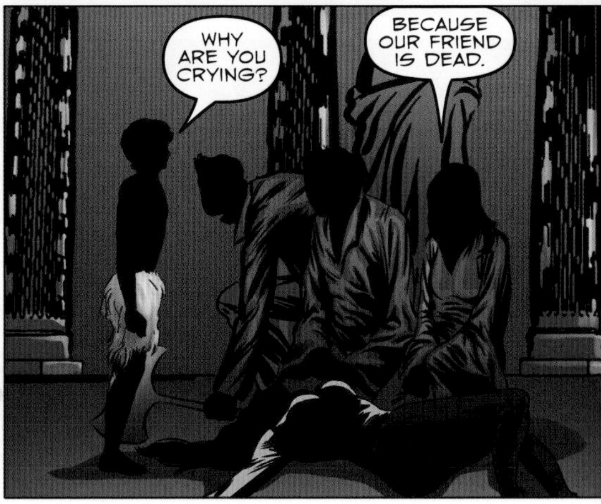
WHY ARE YOU CRYING?
BECAUSE OUR FRIEND IS DEAD.

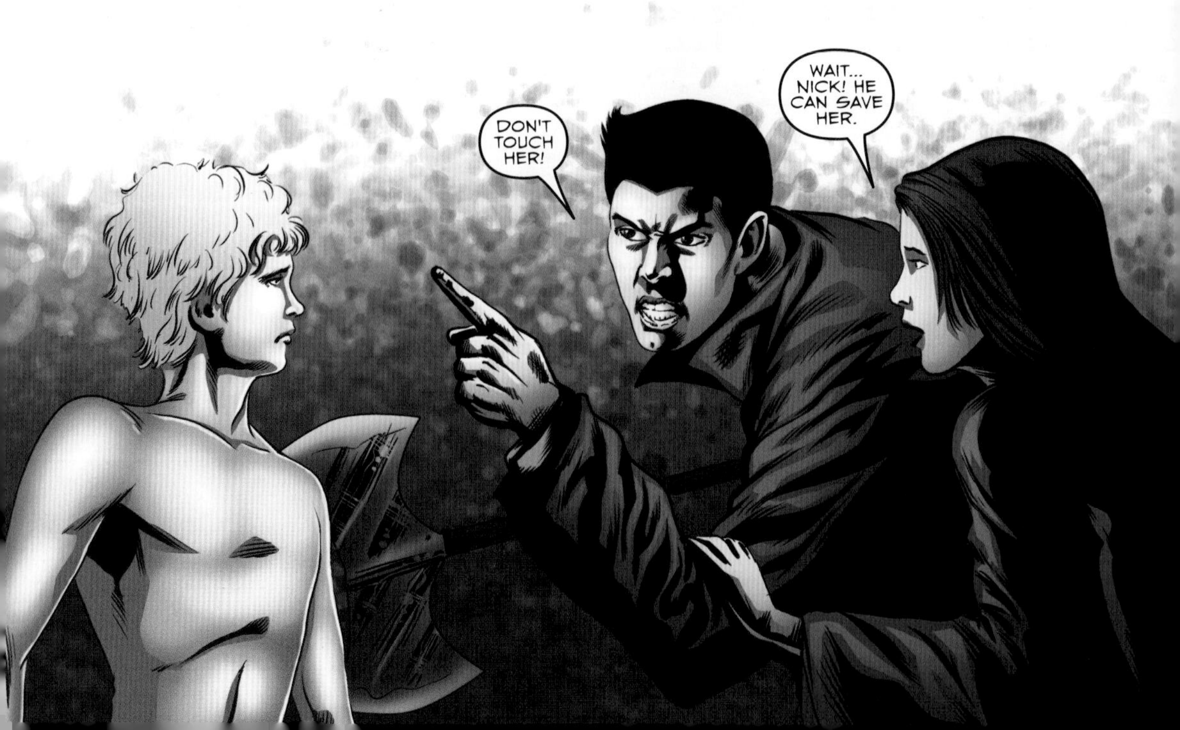
DON'T TOUCH HER!
WAIT... NICK! HE CAN SAVE HER.

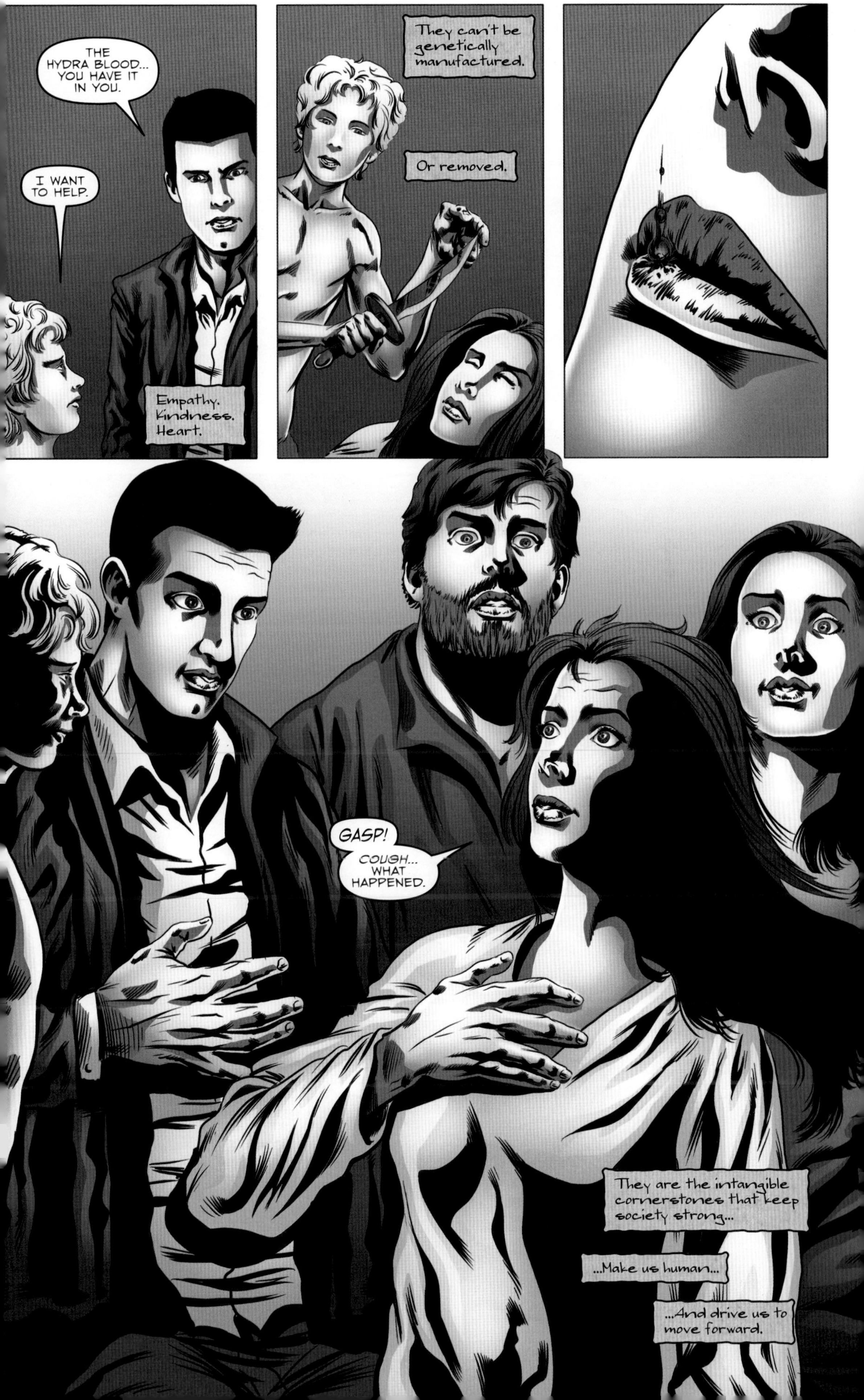

THE HYDRA BLOOD... YOU HAVE IT IN YOU.
I WANT TO HELP.
Empathy. Kindness. Heart.
They can't be genetically manufactured.
Or removed.
GASP!
COUGH... WHAT HAPPENED.
They are the intangible cornerstones that keep society strong...
...Make us human...
...And drive us to move forward.

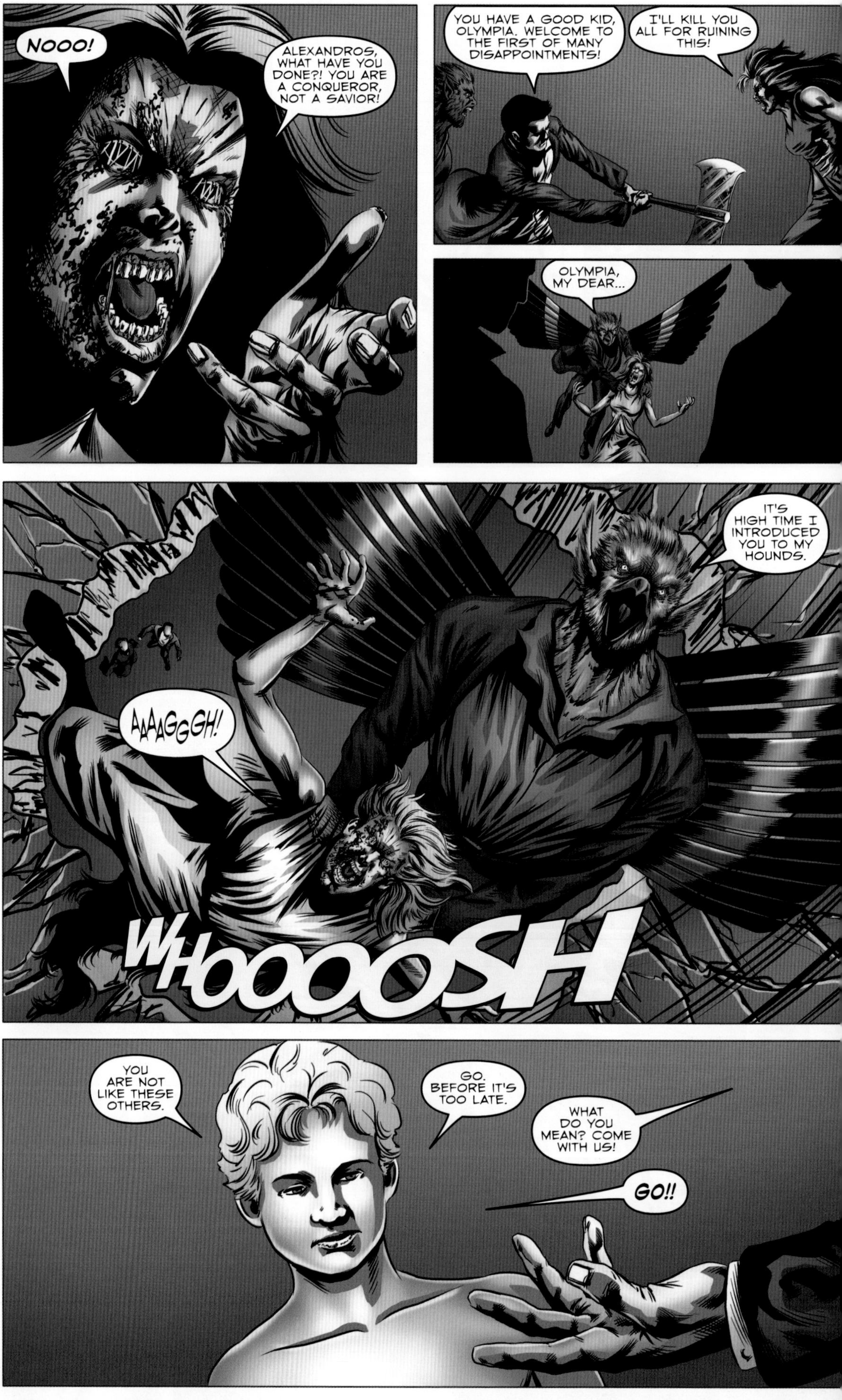
NOOO!
ALEXANDROS, WHAT HAVE YOU DONE?! YOU ARE A CONQUEROR, NOT A SAVIOR!
YOU HAVE A GOOD KID, OLYMPIA. WELCOME TO THE FIRST OF MANY DISAPPOINTMENTS!
I'LL KILL YOU ALL FOR RUINING THIS!
OLYMPIA, MY DEAR...
IT'S HIGH TIME I INTRODUCED YOU TO MY HOUNDS.
AAAAGGGH!
WHOOOOOSH
YOU ARE NOT LIKE THESE OTHERS.
GO. BEFORE IT'S TOO LATE.
WHAT DO YOU MEAN? COME WITH US!
GO!!

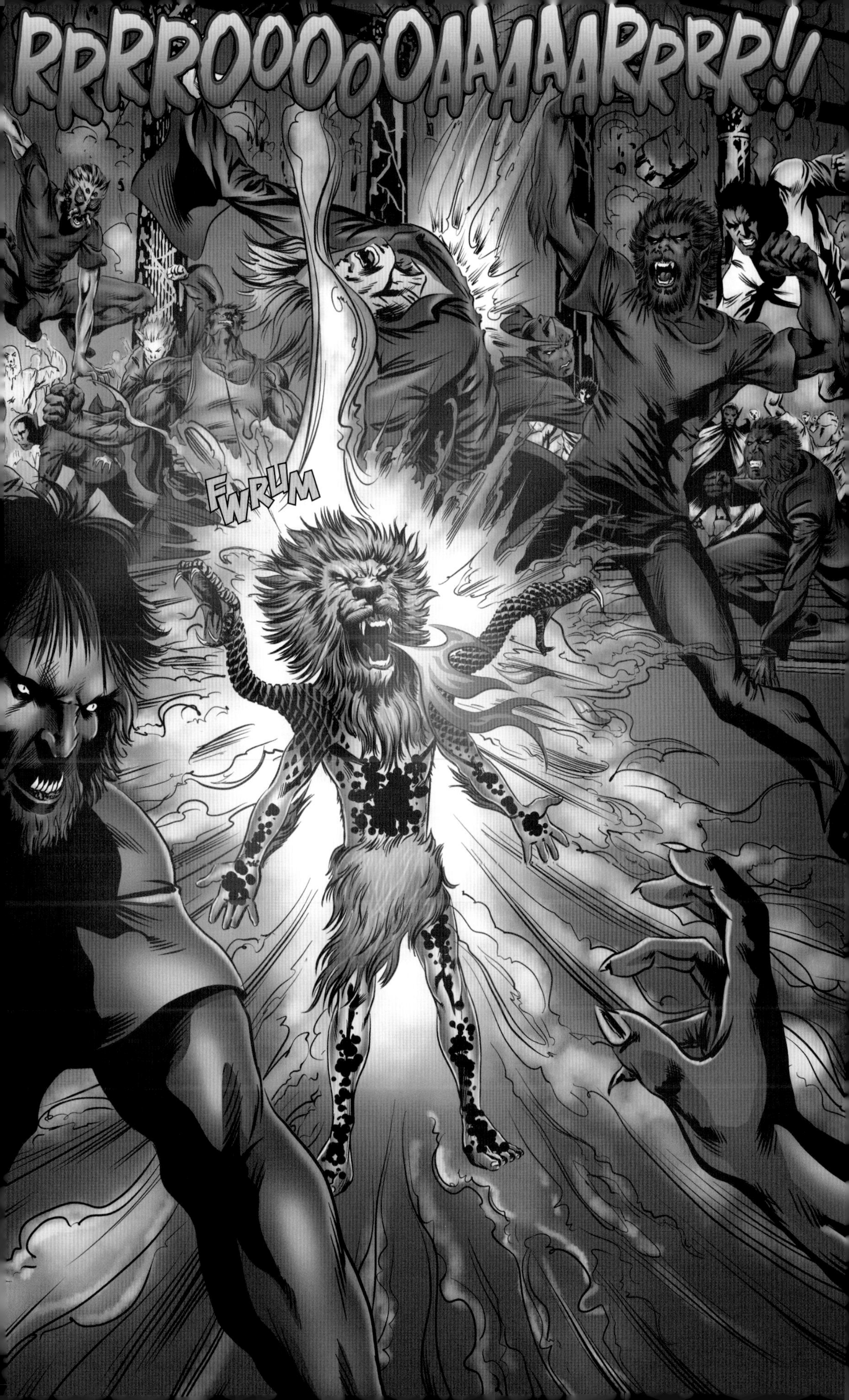
RRRROOOOOAAAAARRRR!!
FWRUM

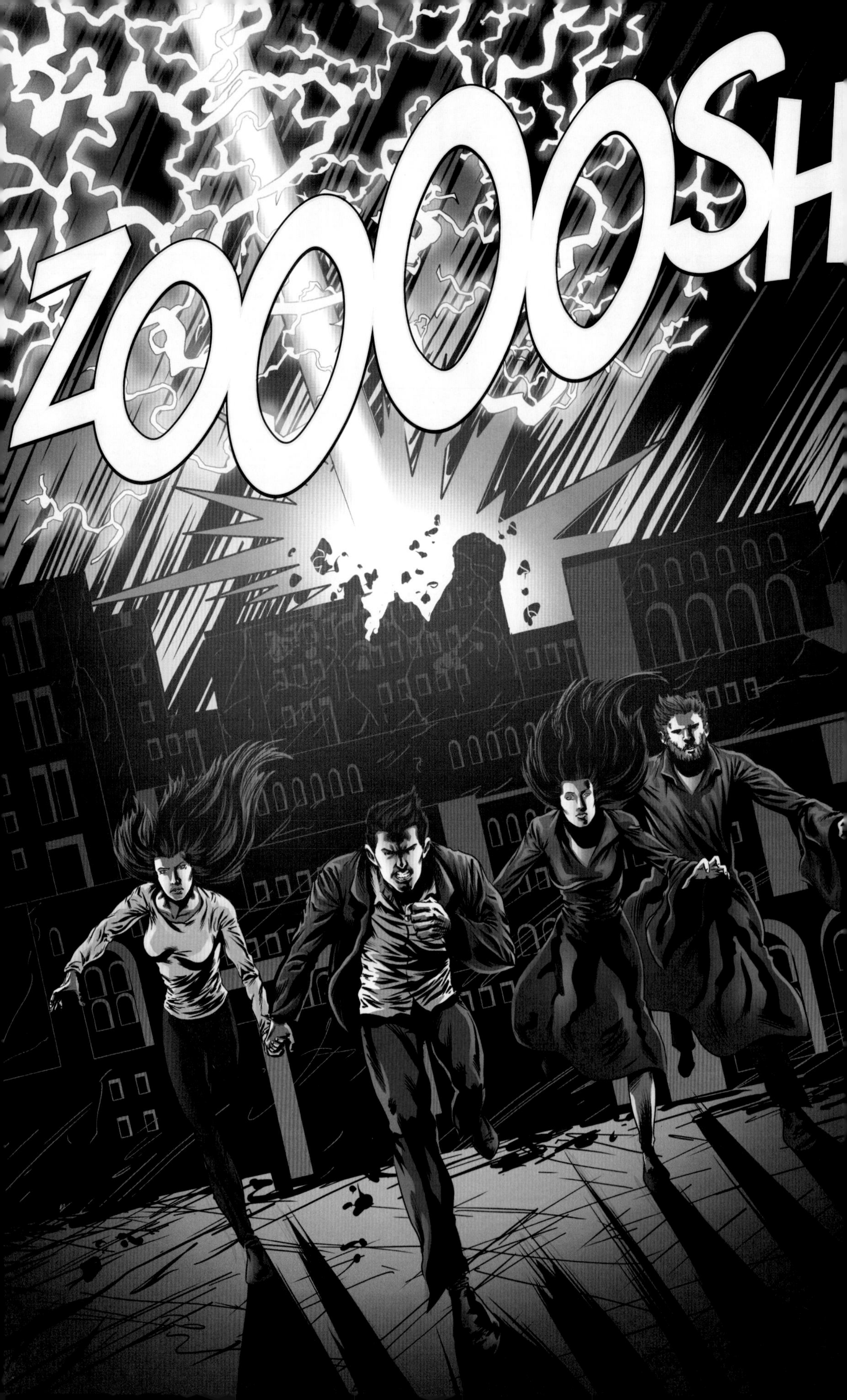
ZOOOOOSH

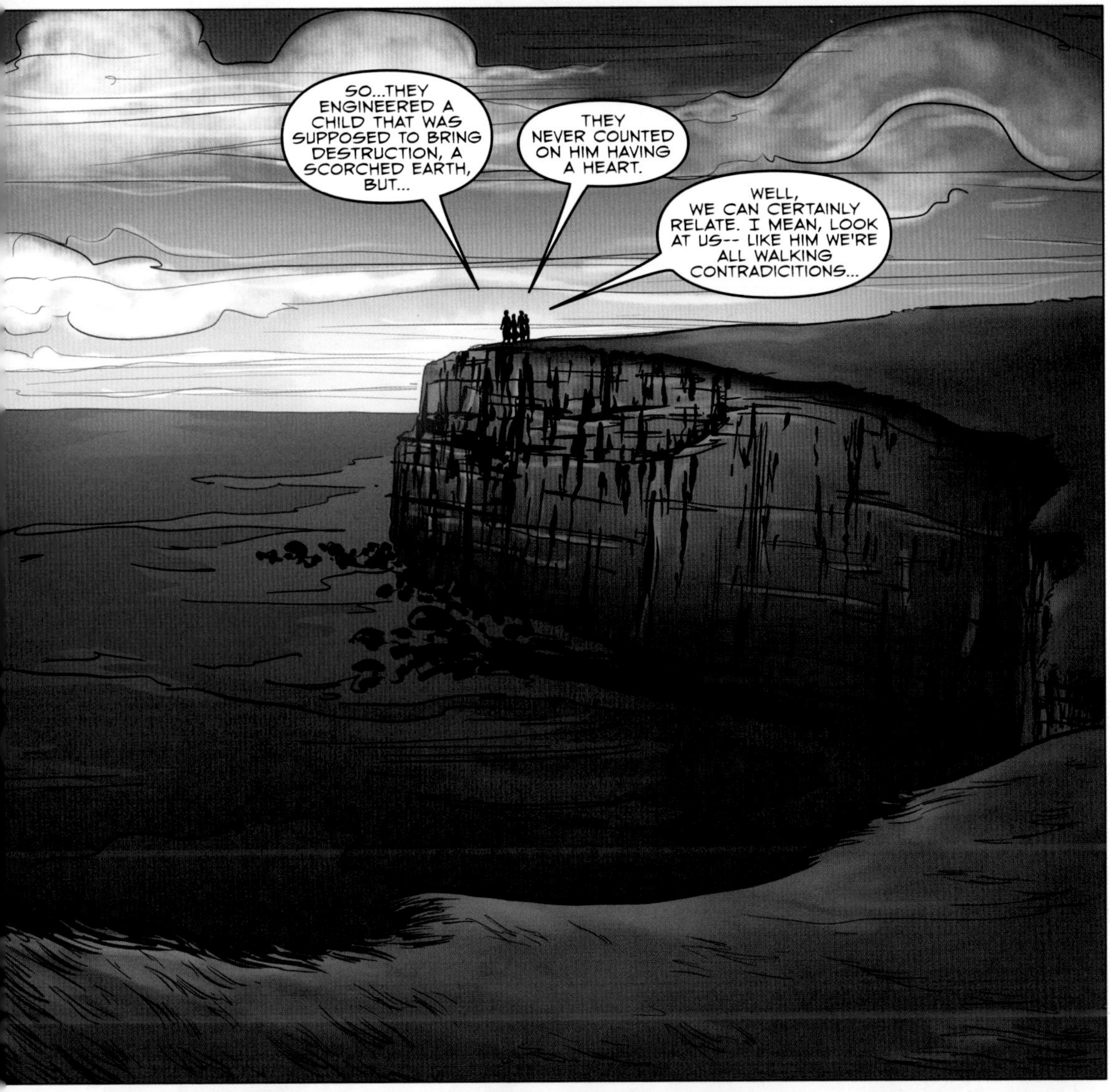
SO...THEY ENGINEERED A CHILD THAT WAS SUPPOSED TO BRING DESTRUCTION, A SCORCHED EARTH, BUT...
THEY NEVER COUNTED ON HIM HAVING A HEART.
WELL, WE CAN CERTAINLY RELATE. I MEAN, LOOK AT US-- LIKE HIM WE'RE ALL WALKING CONTRADICITIONS...

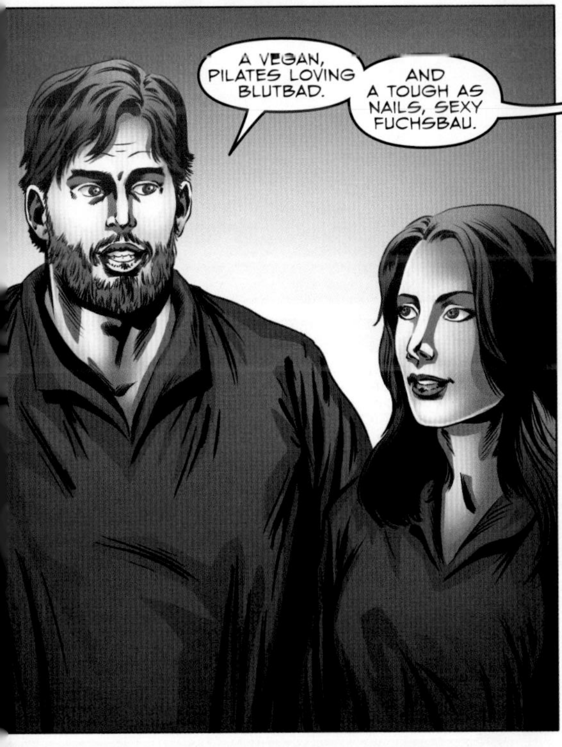
A VEGAN, PILATES LOVING BLUTBAD.
AND A TOUGH AS NAILS, SEXY FUCHSBAU.

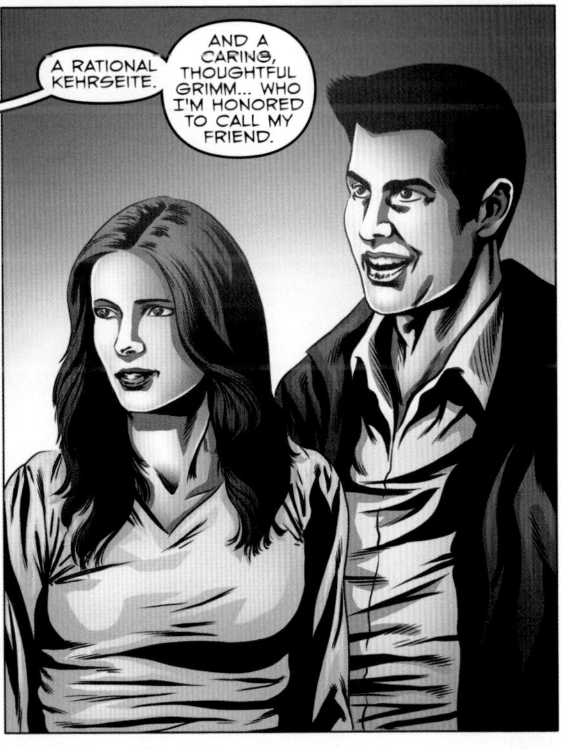
A RATIONAL KEHRSEITE.
AND A CARING, THOUGHTFUL GRIMM... WHO I'M HONORED TO CALL MY FRIEND.

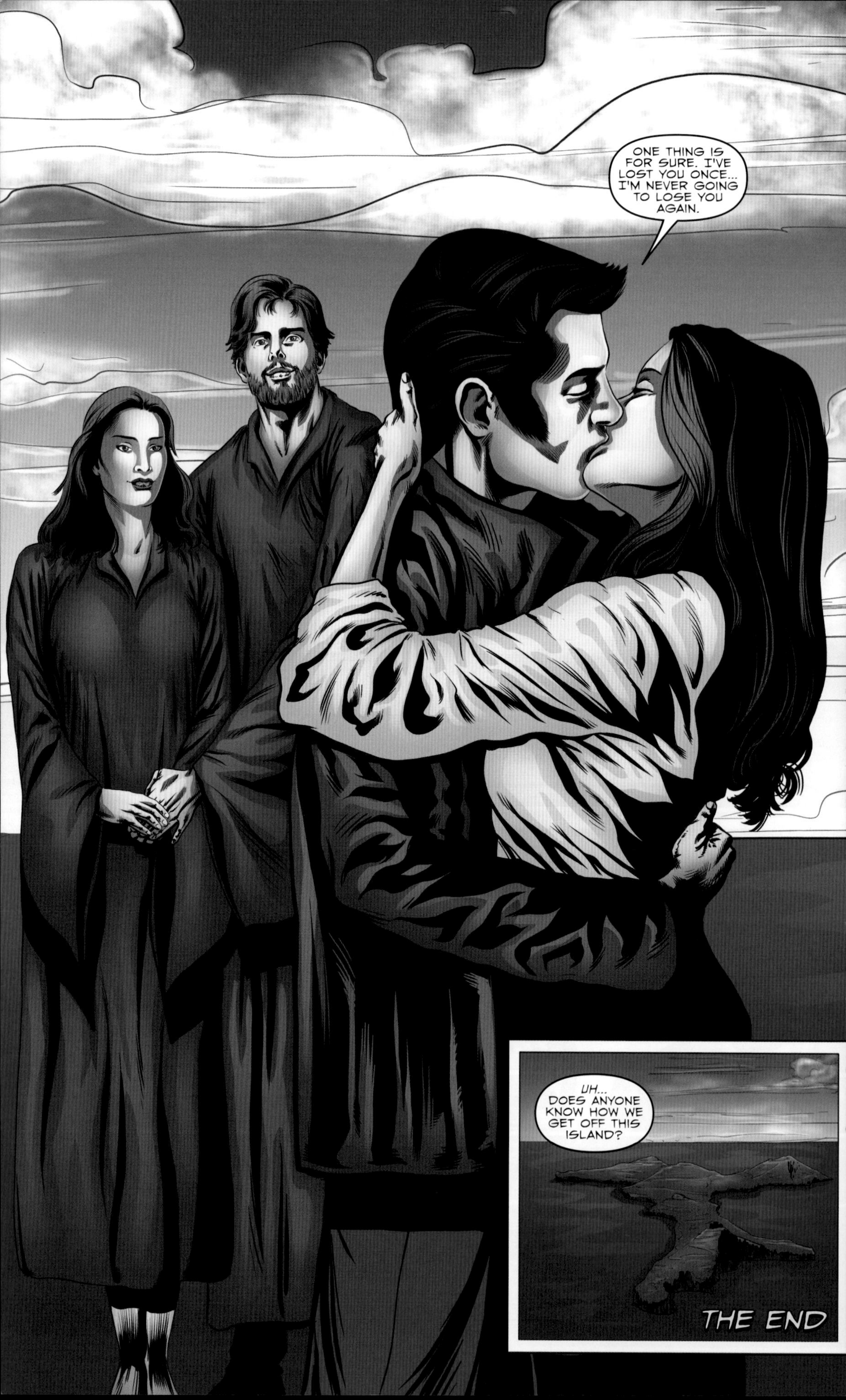
ONE THING IS FOR SURE. I'VE LOST YOU ONCE... I'M NEVER GOING TO LOSE YOU AGAIN.
UH... DOES ANYONE KNOW HOW WE GET OFF THIS ISLAND?
THE END

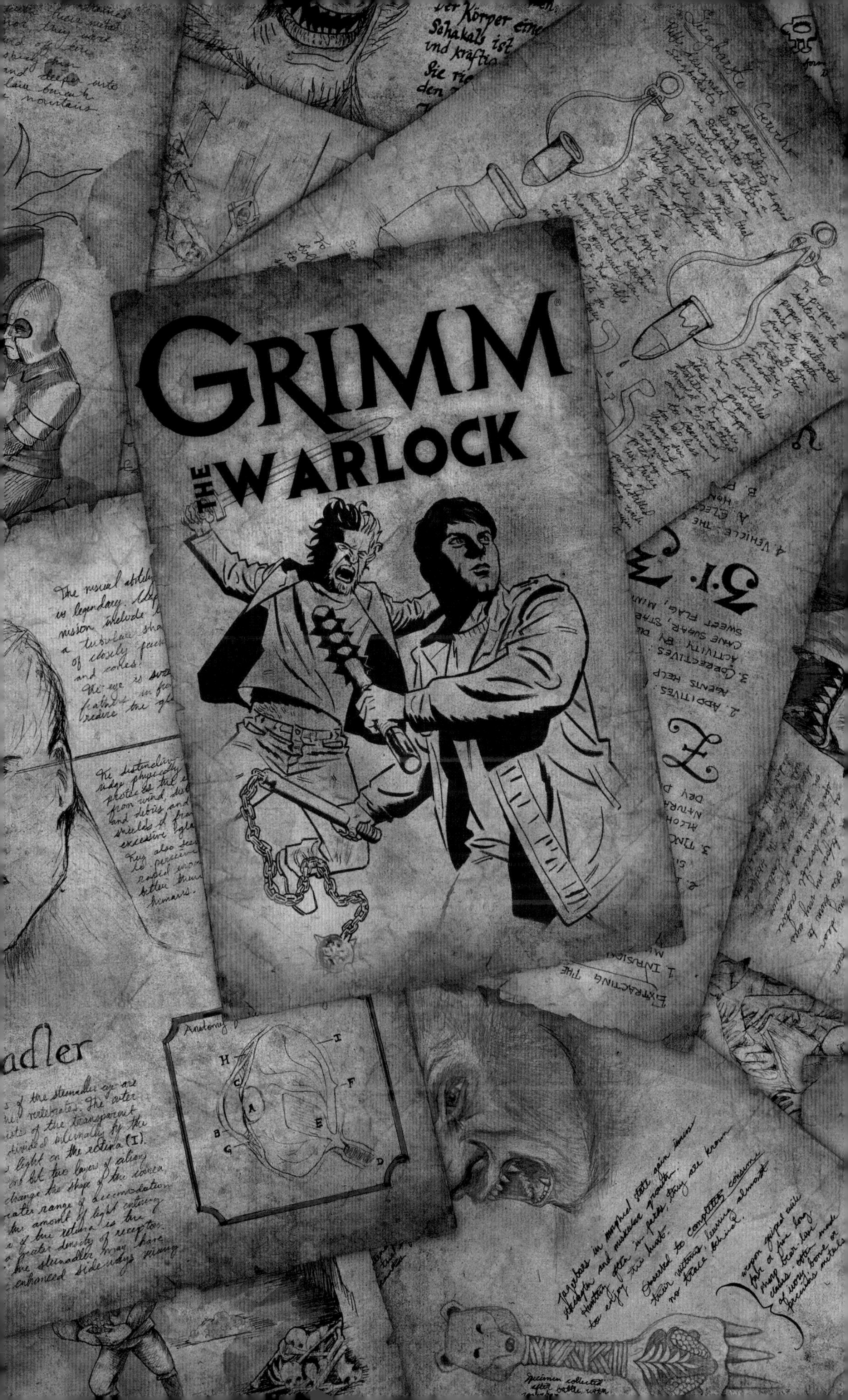
GRIMM
THE WARLOCK

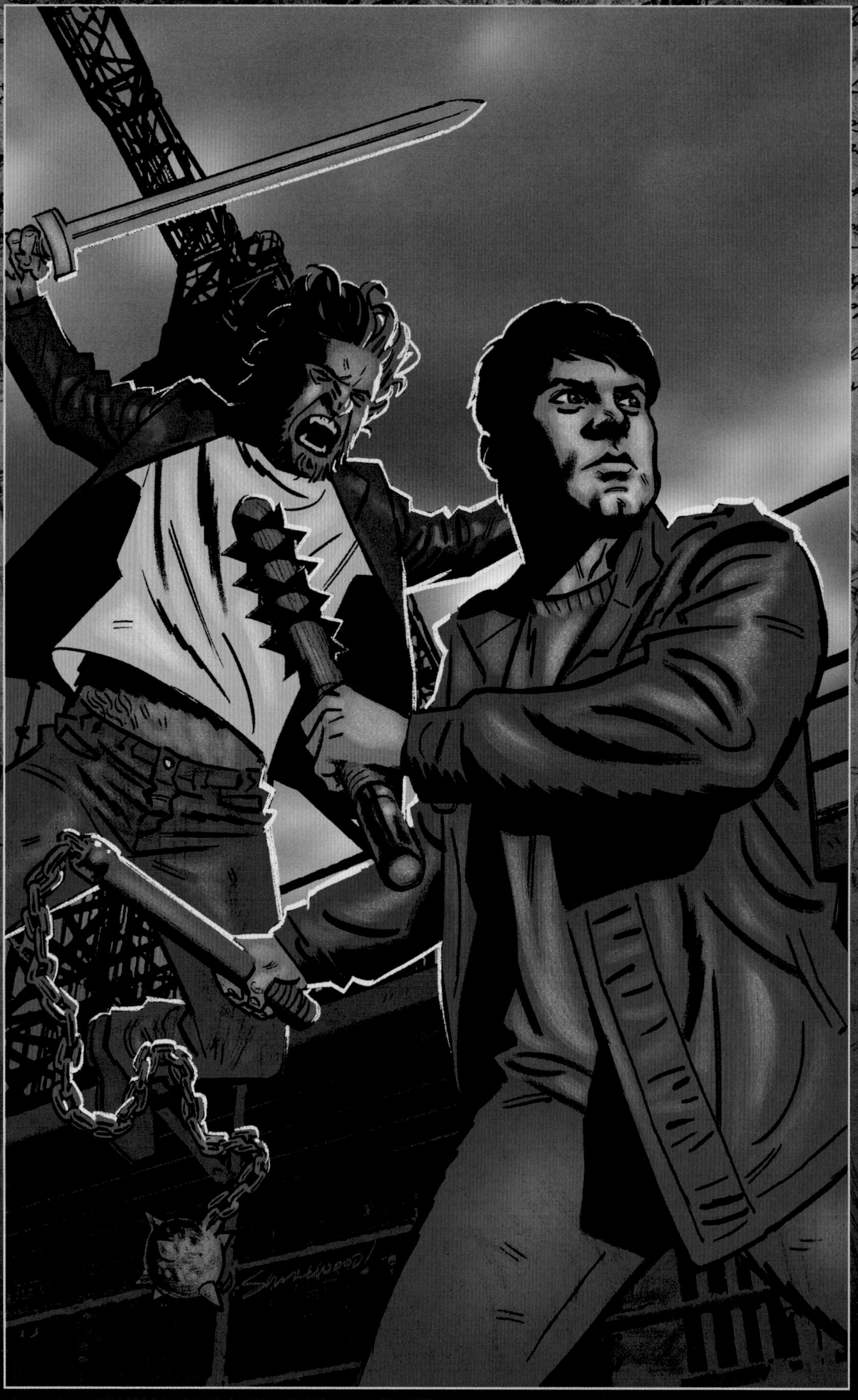

GRIMM: THE WARLOCK ISSUE #1 COVER

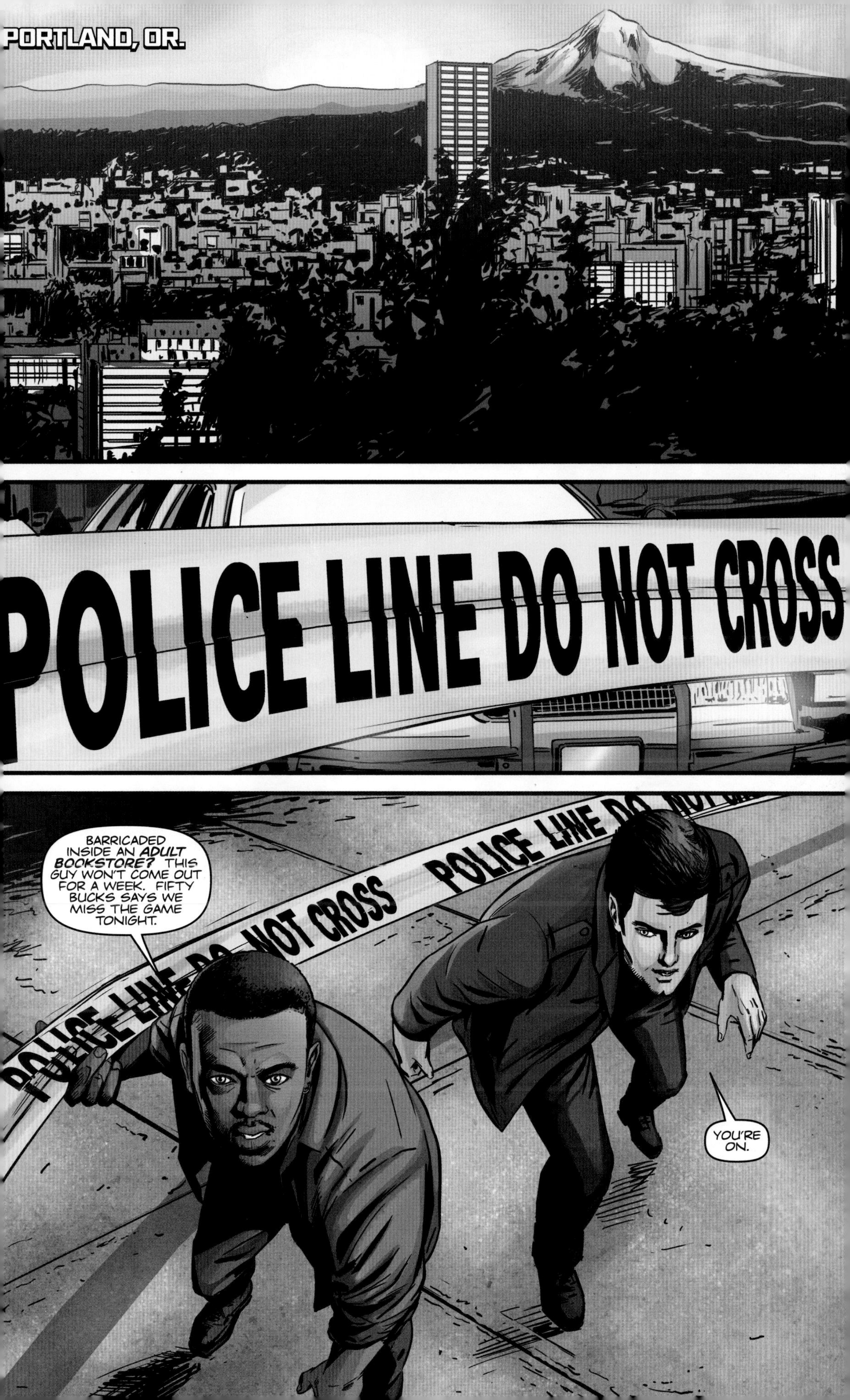
PORTLAND, OR.
POLICE LINE DO NOT CROSS
BARRICADED INSIDE AN ADULT BOOKSTORE? THIS GUY WON'T COME OUT FOR A WEEK. FIFTY BUCKS SAYS WE MISS THE GAME TONIGHT.
YOU'RE ON.

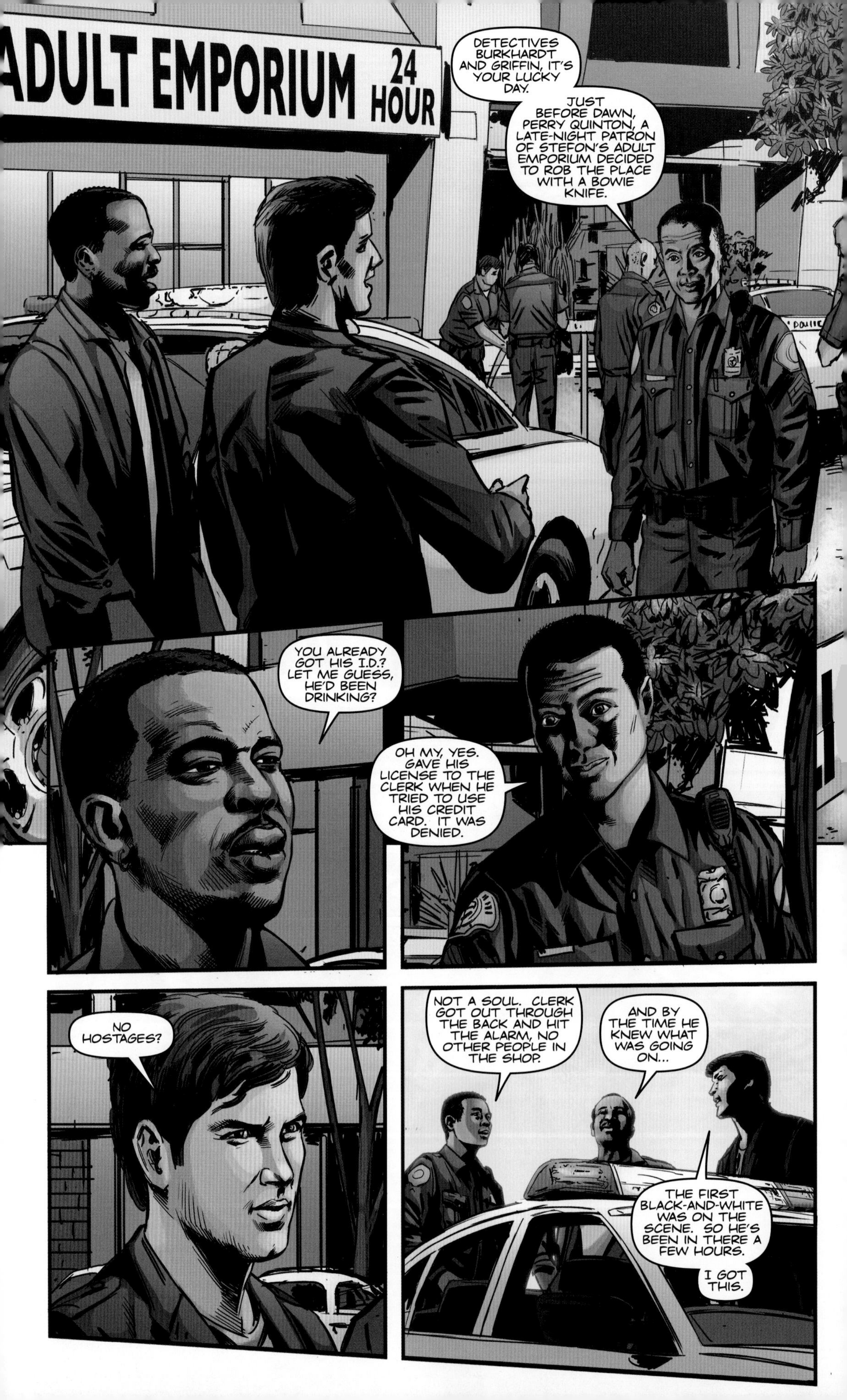
ADULT EMPORIUM 24 HOUR
DETECTIVES BURKHARDT AND GRIFFIN, IT'S YOUR LUCKY DAY.
JUST BEFORE DAWN, PERRY QUINTON, A LATE-NIGHT PATRON OF STEFON'S ADULT EMPORIUM DECIDED TO ROB THE PLACE WITH A BOWIE KNIFE.
YOU ALREADY GOT HIS I.D.? LET ME GUESS, HE'D BEEN DRINKING?
OH MY, YES. GAVE HIS LICENSE TO THE CLERK WHEN HE TRIED TO USE HIS CREDIT CARD. IT WAS DENIED.
NO HOSTAGES?
NOT A SOUL. CLERK GOT OUT THROUGH THE BACK AND HIT THE ALARM, NO OTHER PEOPLE IN THE SHOP.
AND BY THE TIME HE KNEW WHAT WAS GOING ON...
THE FIRST BLACK-AND-WHITE WAS ON THE SCENE. SO HE'S BEEN IN THERE A FEW HOURS.
I GOT THIS.

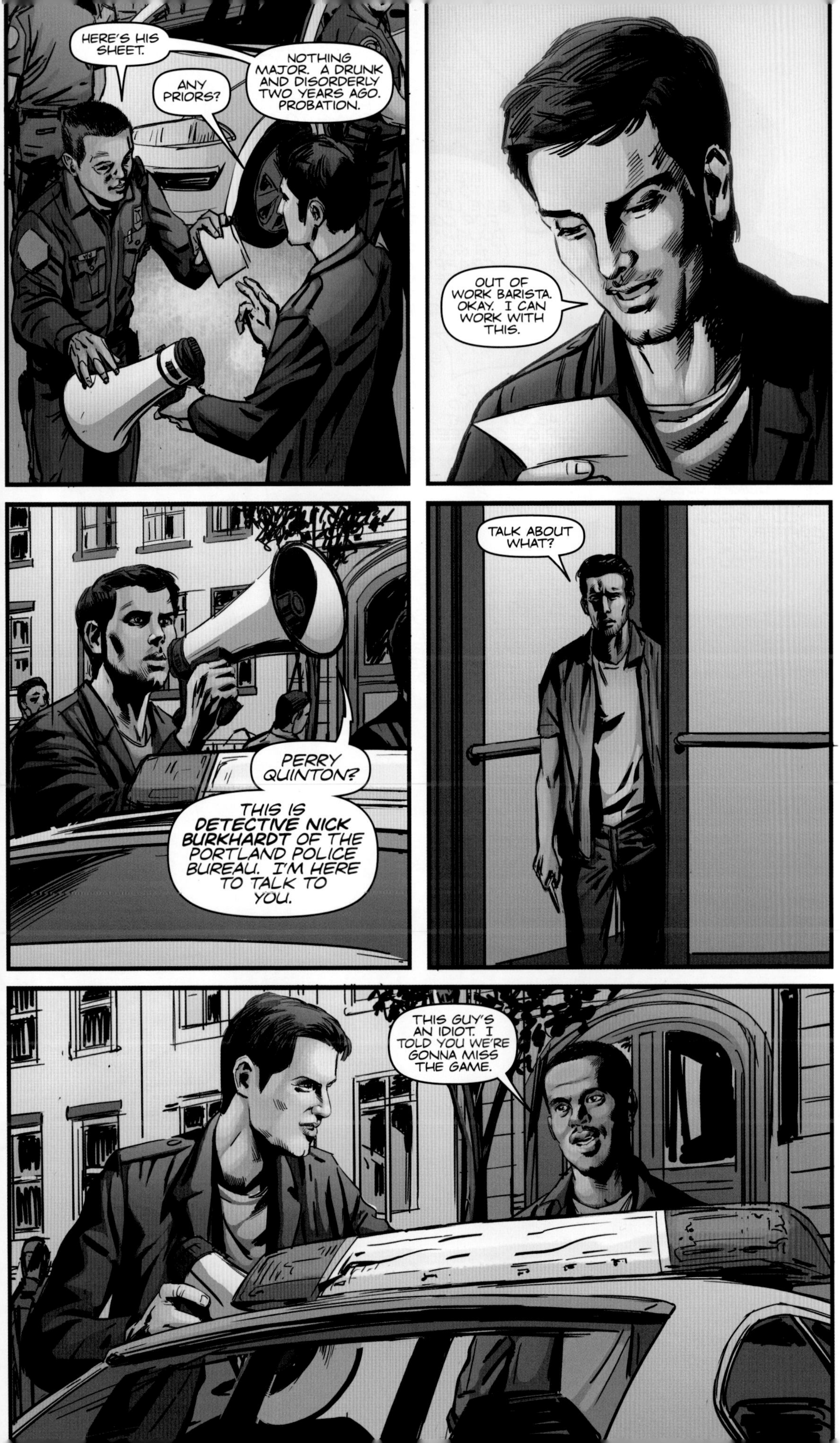
HERE'S HIS SHEET.
ANY PRIORS?
NOTHING MAJOR. A DRUNK AND DISORDERLY TWO YEARS AGO. PROBATION.
OUT OF WORK BARISTA. OKAY. I CAN WORK WITH THIS.
PERRY QUINTON?
THIS IS **DETECTIVE NICK BURKHARDT** OF THE PORTLAND POLICE BUREAU. I'M HERE TO TALK TO YOU.
TALK ABOUT WHAT?
THIS GUY'S AN IDIOT. I TOLD YOU WE'RE GONNA MISS THE GAME.

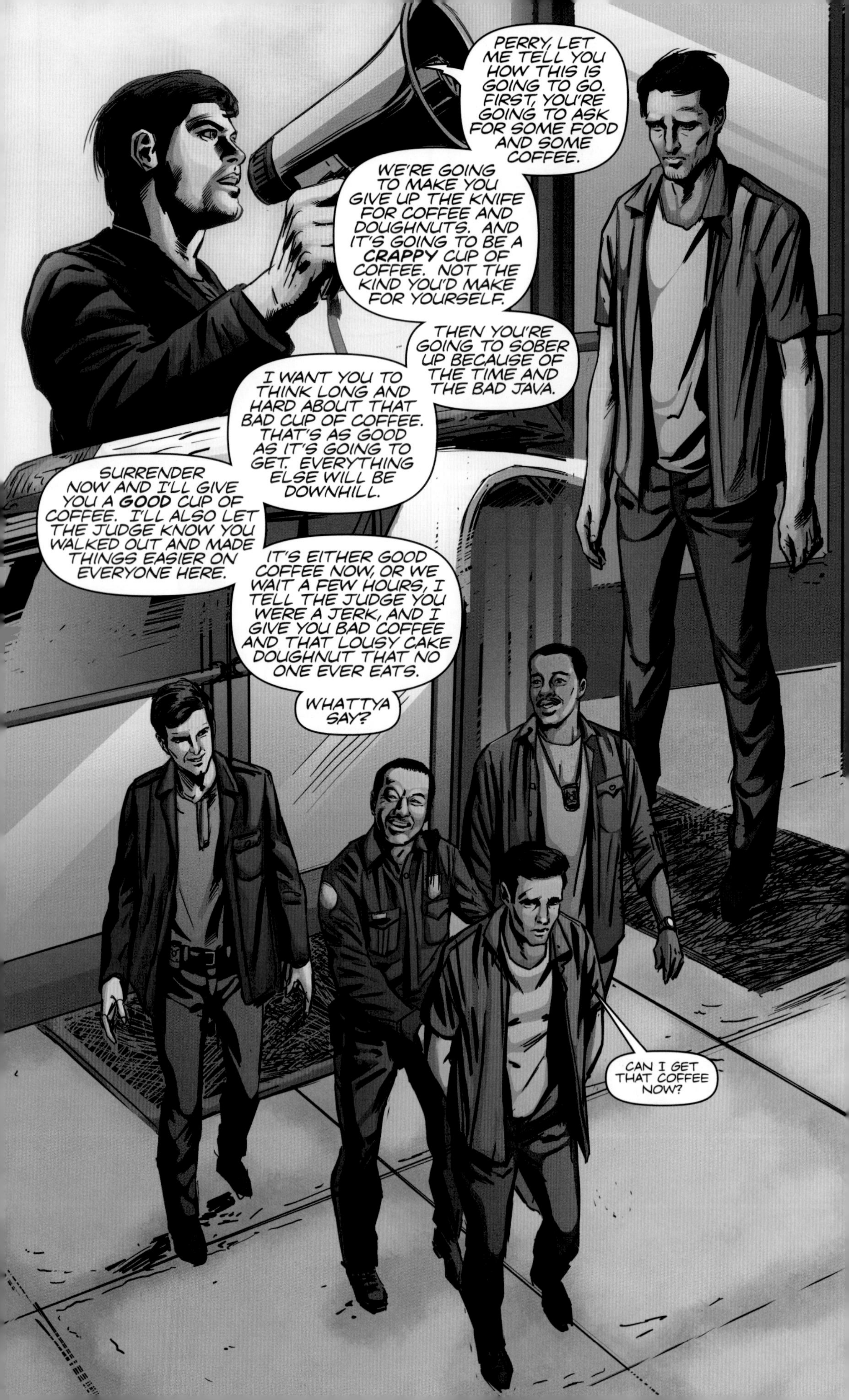

PERRY, LET ME TELL YOU HOW THIS IS GOING TO GO. FIRST, YOU'RE GOING TO ASK FOR SOME FOOD AND SOME COFFEE.
WE'RE GOING TO MAKE YOU GIVE UP THE KNIFE FOR COFFEE AND DOUGHNUTS. AND IT'S GOING TO BE A **CRAPPY** CUP OF COFFEE. NOT THE KIND YOU'D MAKE FOR YOURSELF.
THEN YOU'RE GOING TO SOBER UP BECAUSE OF THE TIME AND THE BAD JAVA.
I WANT YOU TO THINK LONG AND HARD ABOUT THAT BAD CUP OF COFFEE. THAT'S AS GOOD AS IT'S GOING TO GET. EVERYTHING ELSE WILL BE DOWNHILL.
SURRENDER NOW AND I'LL GIVE YOU A **GOOD** CUP OF COFFEE. I'LL ALSO LET THE JUDGE KNOW YOU WALKED OUT AND MADE THINGS EASIER ON EVERYONE HERE.
IT'S EITHER GOOD COFFEE NOW, OR WE WAIT A FEW HOURS, I TELL THE JUDGE YOU WERE A JERK, AND I GIVE YOU BAD COFFEE AND THAT LOUSY CAKE DOUGHNUT THAT NO ONE EVER EATS.
WHATTYA SAY?
CAN I GET THAT COFFEE NOW?

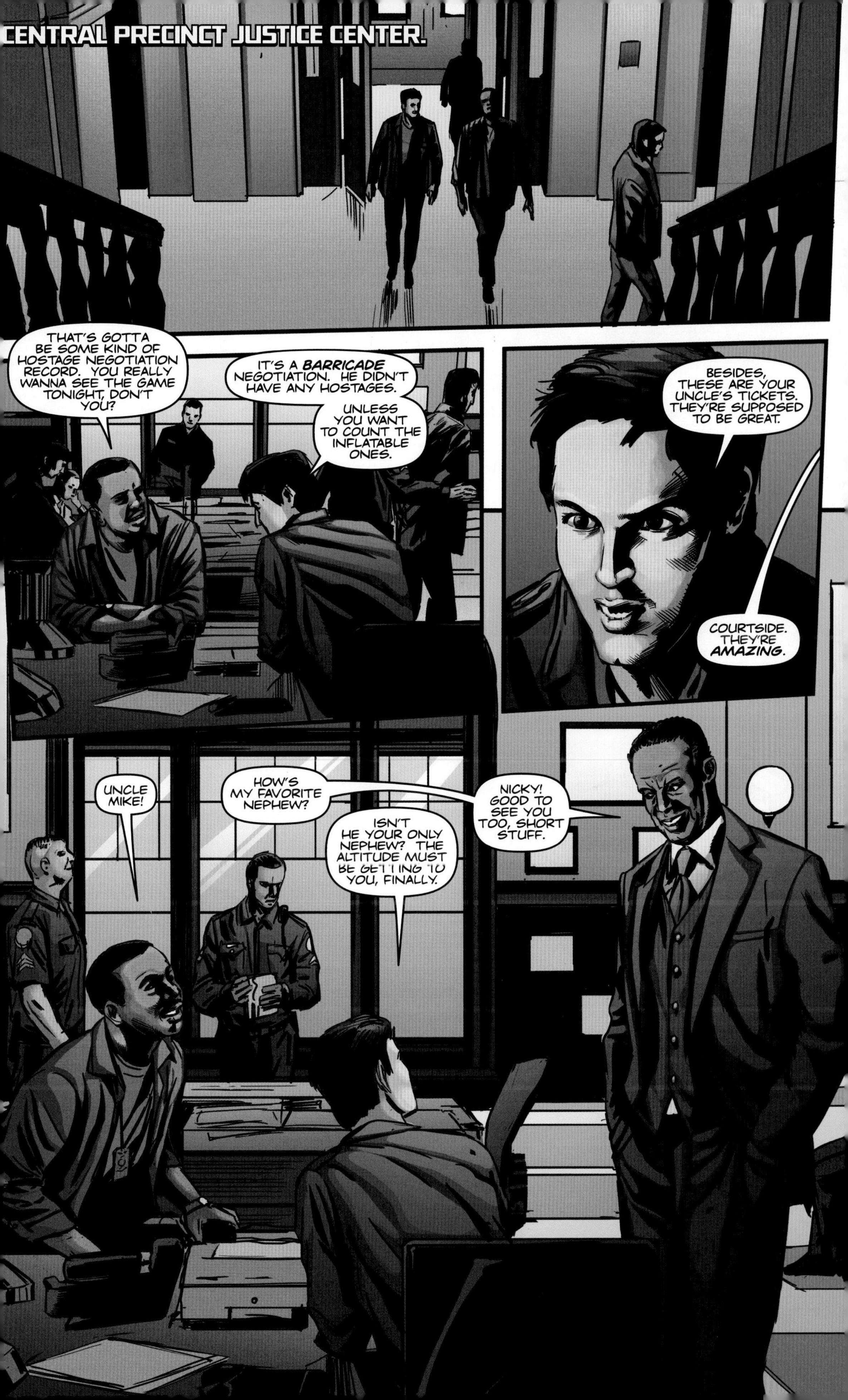
CENTRAL PRECINCT JUSTICE CENTER.
THAT'S GOTTA BE SOME KIND OF HOSTAGE NEGOTIATION RECORD. YOU REALLY WANNA SEE THE GAME TONIGHT, DON'T YOU?
IT'S A *BARRICADE* NEGOTIATION. HE DIDN'T HAVE ANY HOSTAGES.
UNLESS YOU WANT TO COUNT THE INFLATABLE ONES.
BESIDES, THESE ARE YOUR UNCLE'S TICKETS. THEY'RE SUPPOSED TO BE GREAT.
COURTSIDE. THEY'RE *AMAZING*.
UNCLE MIKE!
HOW'S MY FAVORITE NEPHEW?
NICKY! GOOD TO SEE YOU TOO, SHORT STUFF.
ISN'T HE YOUR ONLY NEPHEW? THE ALTITUDE MUST BE GETTING TO YOU, FINALLY.

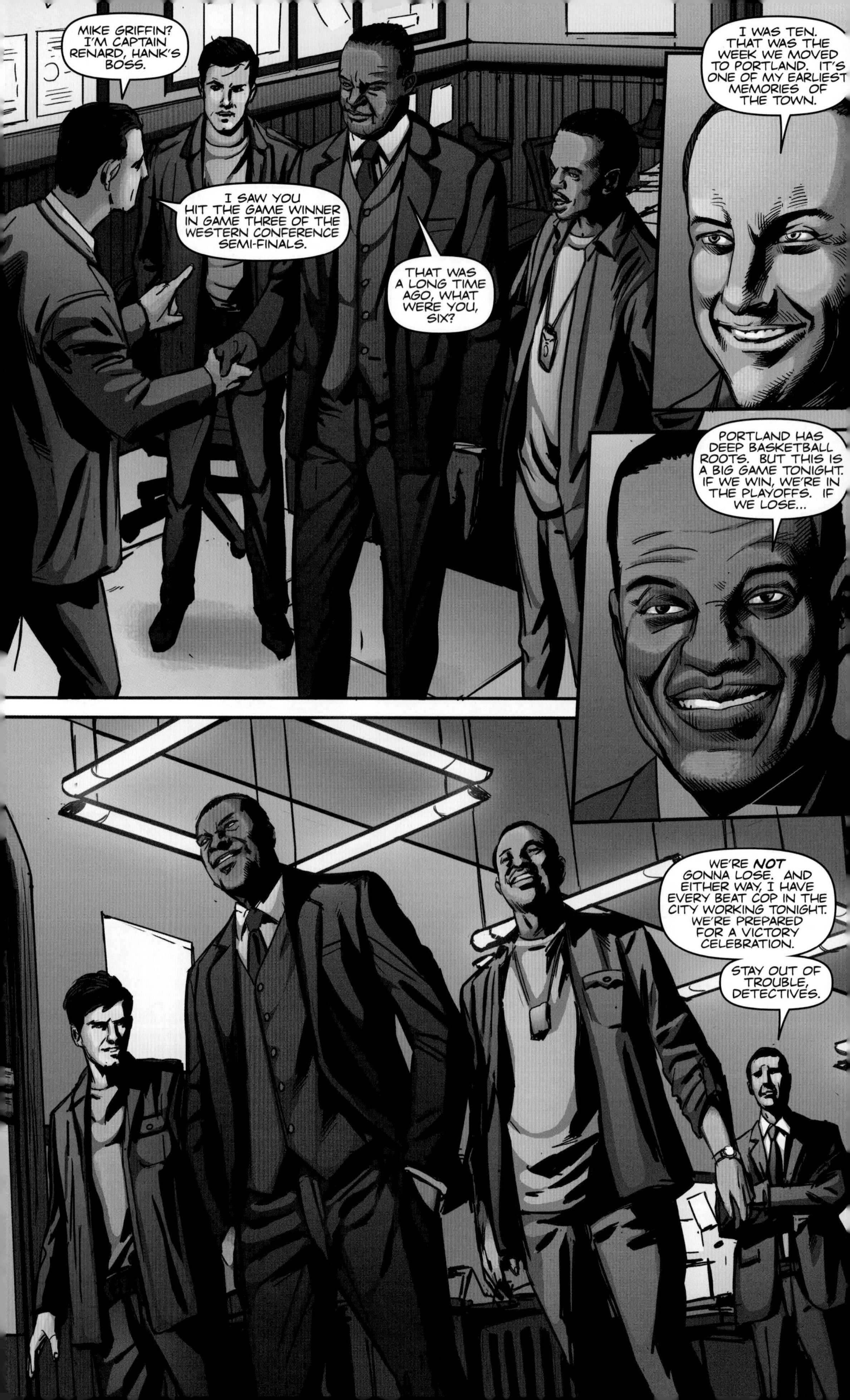
MIKE GRIFFIN? I'M CAPTAIN RENARD, HANK'S BOSS.
I SAW YOU HIT THE GAME WINNER IN GAME THREE OF THE WESTERN CONFERENCE SEMI-FINALS.
THAT WAS A LONG TIME AGO, WHAT WERE YOU, SIX?
I WAS TEN. THAT WAS THE WEEK WE MOVED TO PORTLAND. IT'S ONE OF MY EARLIEST MEMORIES OF THE TOWN.
PORTLAND HAS DEEP BASKETBALL ROOTS. BUT THIS IS A BIG GAME TONIGHT. IF WE WIN, WE'RE IN THE PLAYOFFS. IF WE LOSE...
WE'RE ***NOT*** GONNA LOSE. AND EITHER WAY, I HAVE EVERY BEAT COP IN THE CITY WORKING TONIGHT. WE'RE PREPARED FOR A VICTORY CELEBRATION.
STAY OUT OF TROUBLE, DETECTIVES.

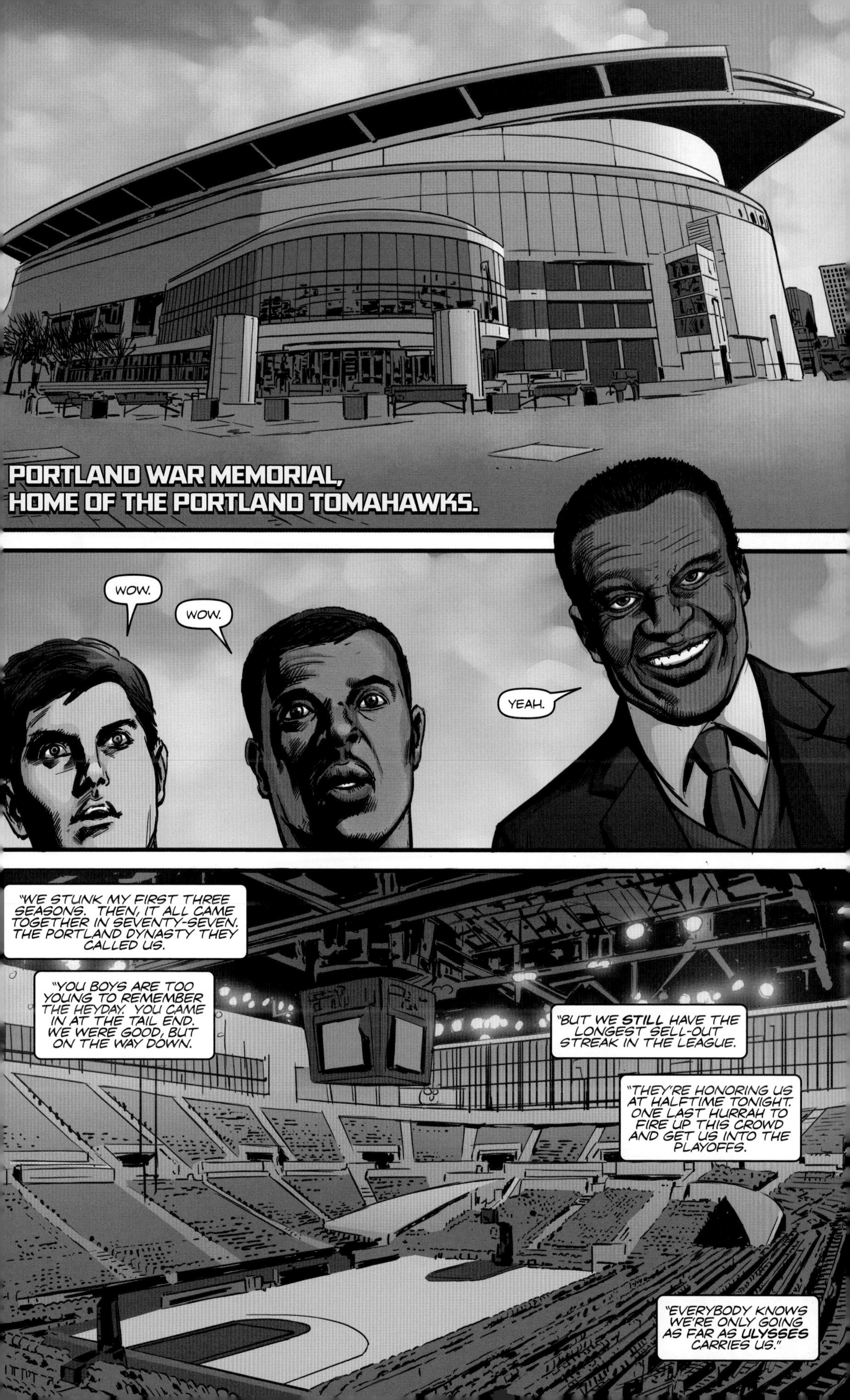
PORTLAND WAR MEMORIAL, HOME OF THE PORTLAND TOMAHAWKS.
WOW.
WOW.
YEAH.
"WE STUNK MY FIRST THREE SEASONS. THEN, IT ALL CAME TOGETHER IN SEVENTY-SEVEN. THE PORTLAND DYNASTY THEY CALLED US.
"YOU BOYS ARE TOO YOUNG TO REMEMBER THE HEYDAY. YOU CAME IN AT THE TAIL END. WE WERE GOOD, BUT ON THE WAY DOWN.
"BUT WE STILL HAVE THE LONGEST SELL-OUT STREAK IN THE LEAGUE.
"THEY'RE HONORING US AT HALFTIME TONIGHT. ONE LAST HURRAH TO FIRE UP THIS CROWD AND GET US INTO THE PLAYOFFS.
"EVERYBODY KNOWS WE'RE ONLY GOING AS FAR AS ULYSSES CARRIES US."

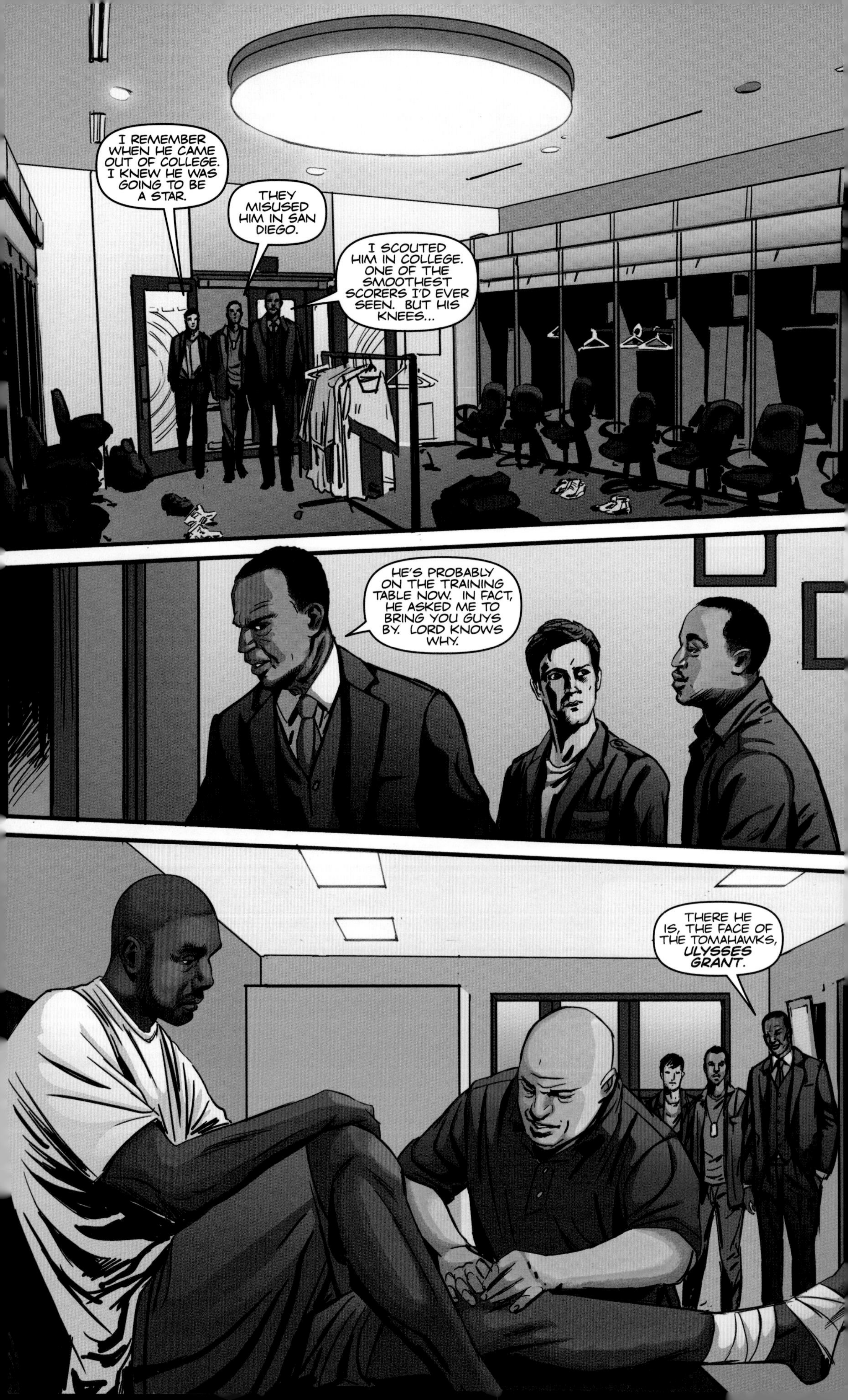
I REMEMBER WHEN HE CAME OUT OF COLLEGE. I KNEW HE WAS GOING TO BE A STAR.
THEY MISUSED HIM IN SAN DIEGO.
I SCOUTED HIM IN COLLEGE. ONE OF THE SMOOTHEST SCORERS I'D EVER SEEN. BUT HIS KNEES...
HE'S PROBABLY ON THE TRAINING TABLE NOW. IN FACT, HE ASKED ME TO BRING YOU GUYS BY. LORD KNOWS WHY.
THERE HE IS, THE FACE OF THE TOMAHAWKS, ULYSSES GRANT.

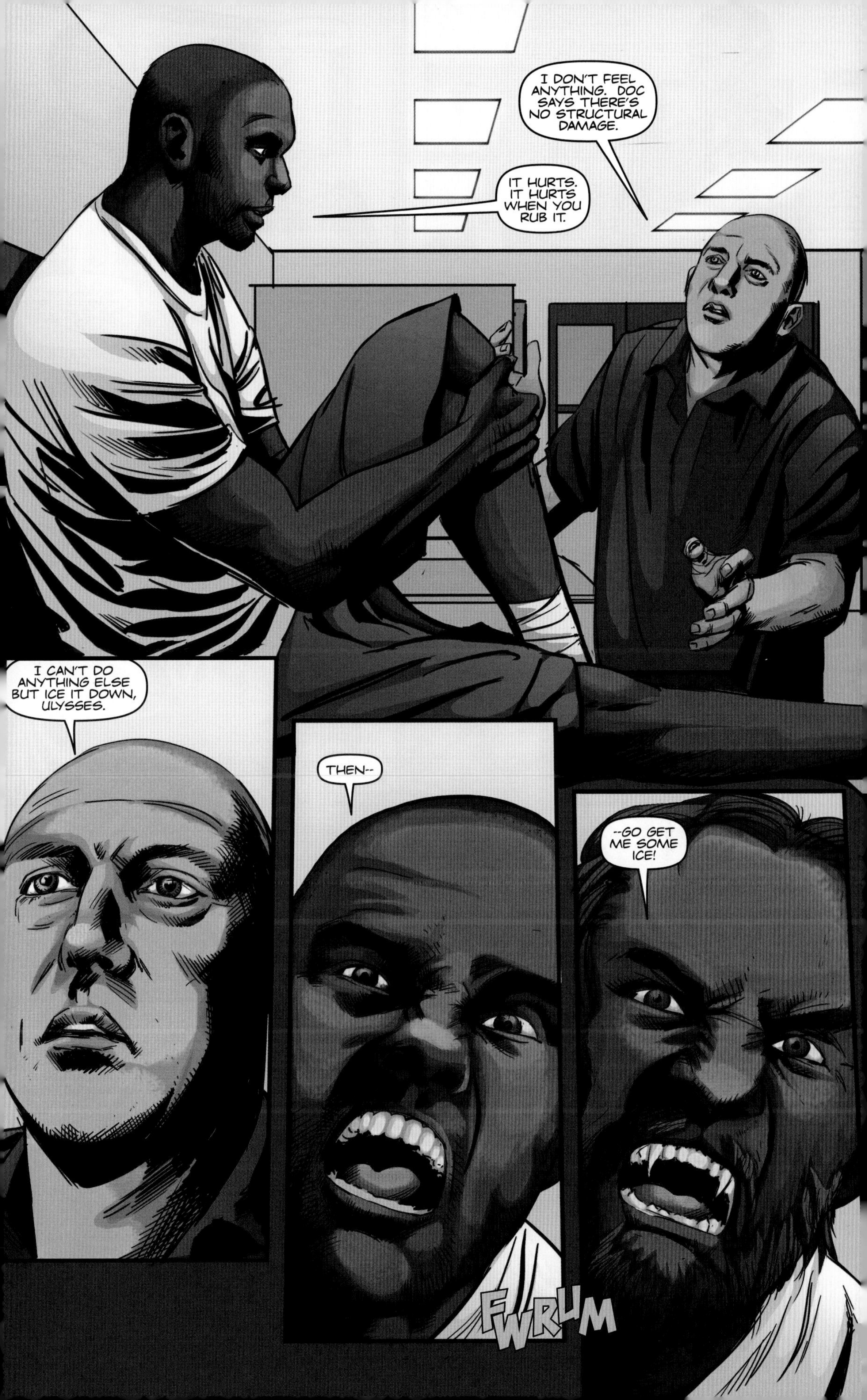
I DON'T FEEL ANYTHING. DOC SAYS THERE'S NO STRUCTURAL DAMAGE.
IT HURTS. IT HURTS WHEN YOU RUB IT.
I CAN'T DO ANYTHING ELSE BUT ICE IT DOWN, ULYSSES.
THEN--
--GO GET ME SOME ICE!
FWRUM

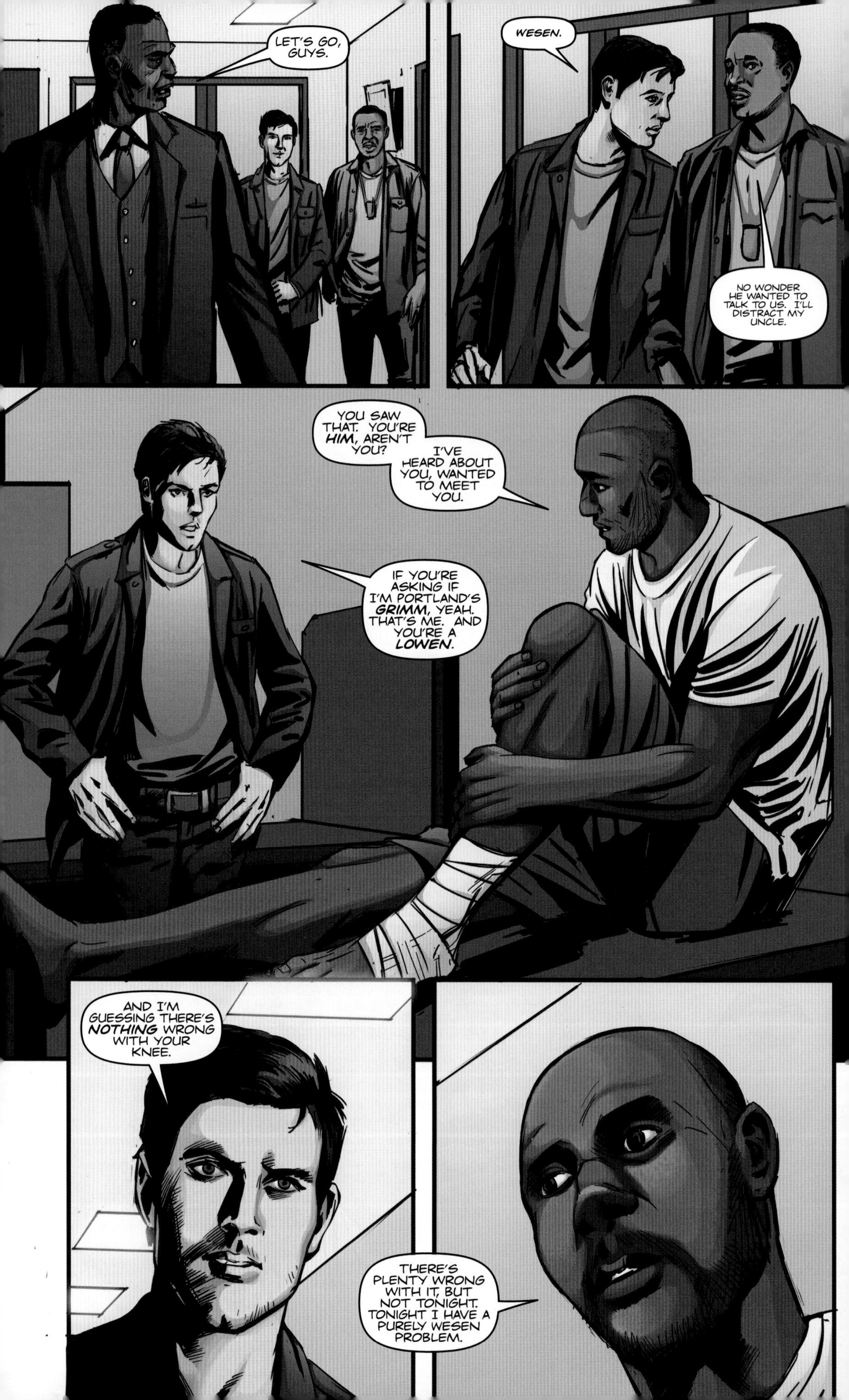
LET'S GO, GUYS.
WESEN.
NO WONDER HE WANTED TO TALK TO US. I'LL DISTRACT MY UNCLE.
YOU SAW THAT. YOU'RE HIM, AREN'T YOU?
I'VE HEARD ABOUT YOU, WANTED TO MEET YOU.
IF YOU'RE ASKING IF I'M PORTLAND'S GRIMM, YEAH. THAT'S ME. AND YOU'RE A LOWEN.
AND I'M GUESSING THERE'S NOTHING WRONG WITH YOUR KNEE.
THERE'S PLENTY WRONG WITH IT, BUT NOT TONIGHT. TONIGHT I HAVE A PURELY WESEN PROBLEM.

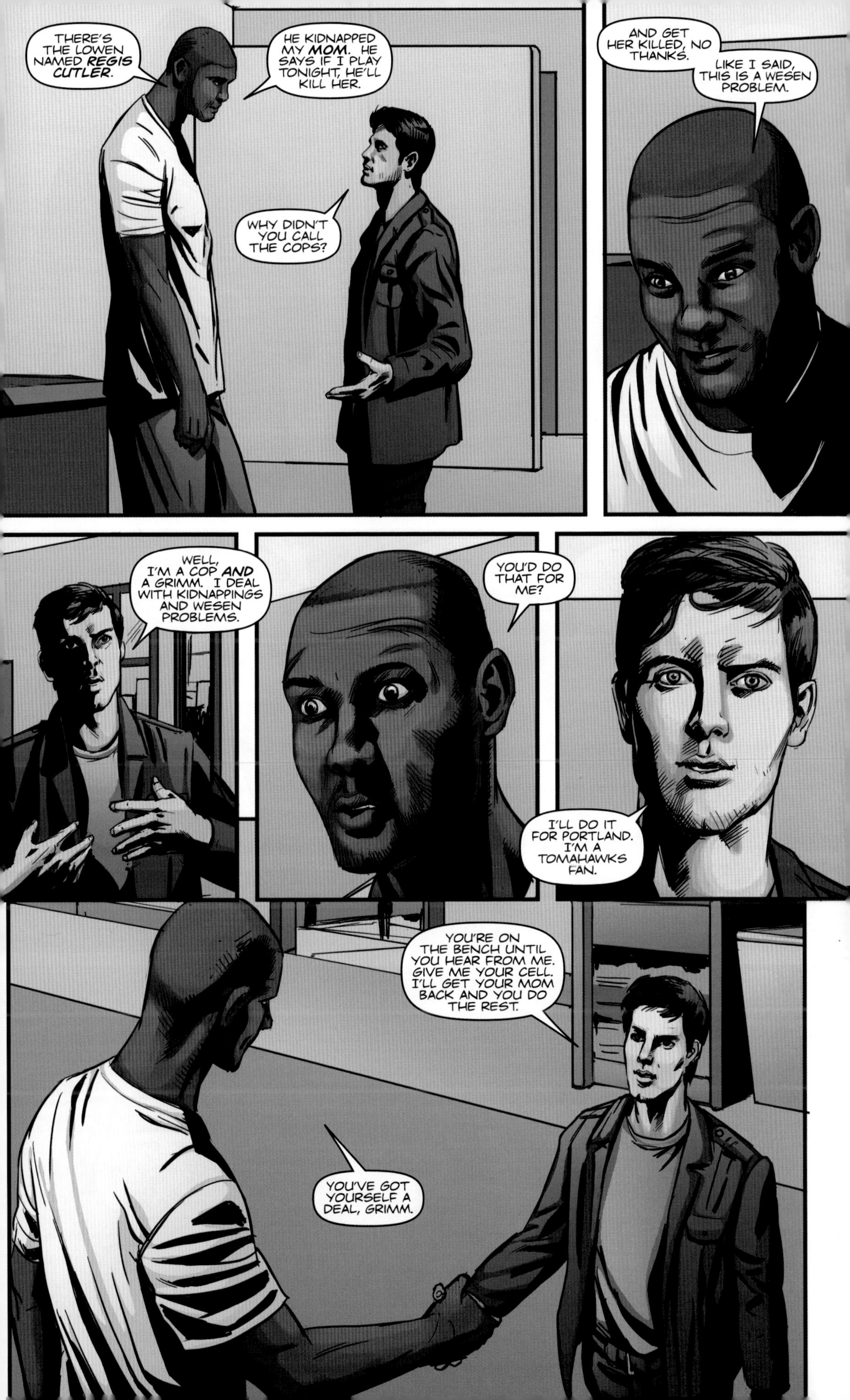
THERE'S THE LOWEN NAMED **REGIS CUTLER**.
HE KIDNAPPED MY **MOM**. HE SAYS IF I PLAY TONIGHT, HE'LL KILL HER.
WHY DIDN'T YOU CALL THE COPS?
AND GET HER KILLED, NO THANKS.
LIKE I SAID, THIS IS A WESEN PROBLEM.
WELL, I'M A COP **AND** A GRIMM. I DEAL WITH KIDNAPPINGS AND WESEN PROBLEMS.
YOU'D DO THAT FOR ME?
I'LL DO IT FOR PORTLAND. I'M A TOMAHAWKS FAN.
YOU'RE ON THE BENCH UNTIL YOU HEAR FROM ME. GIVE ME YOUR CELL. I'LL GET YOUR MOM BACK AND YOU DO THE REST.
YOU'VE GOT YOURSELF A DEAL, GRIMM.

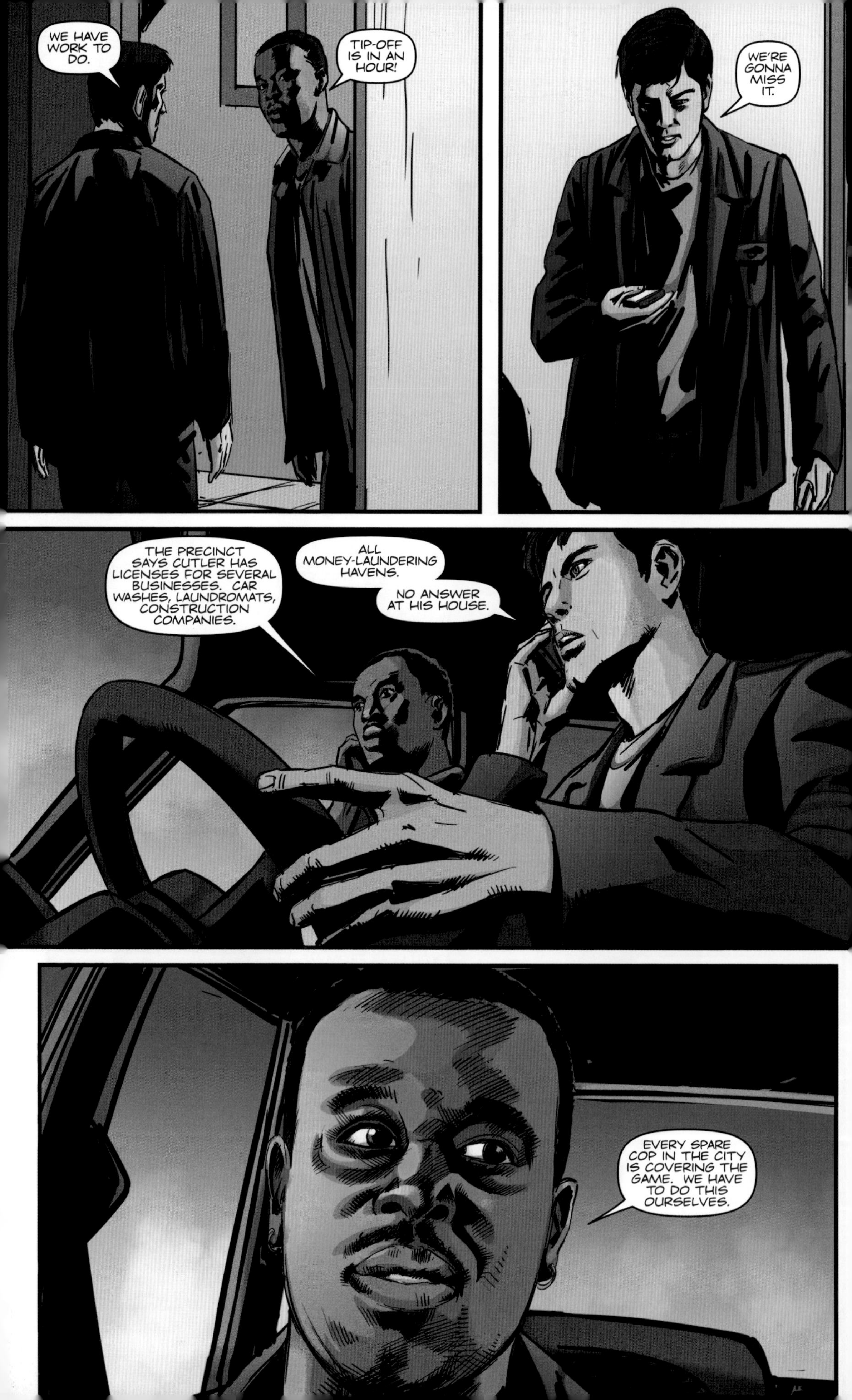
WE HAVE WORK TO DO.
TIP-OFF IS IN AN HOUR!
WE'RE GONNA MISS IT.
THE PRECINCT SAYS CUTLER HAS LICENSES FOR SEVERAL BUSINESSES. CAR WASHES, LAUNDROMATS, CONSTRUCTION COMPANIES.
ALL MONEY-LAUNDERING HAVENS.
NO ANSWER AT HIS HOUSE.
EVERY SPARE COP IN THE CITY IS COVERING THE GAME. WE HAVE TO DO THIS OURSELVES.

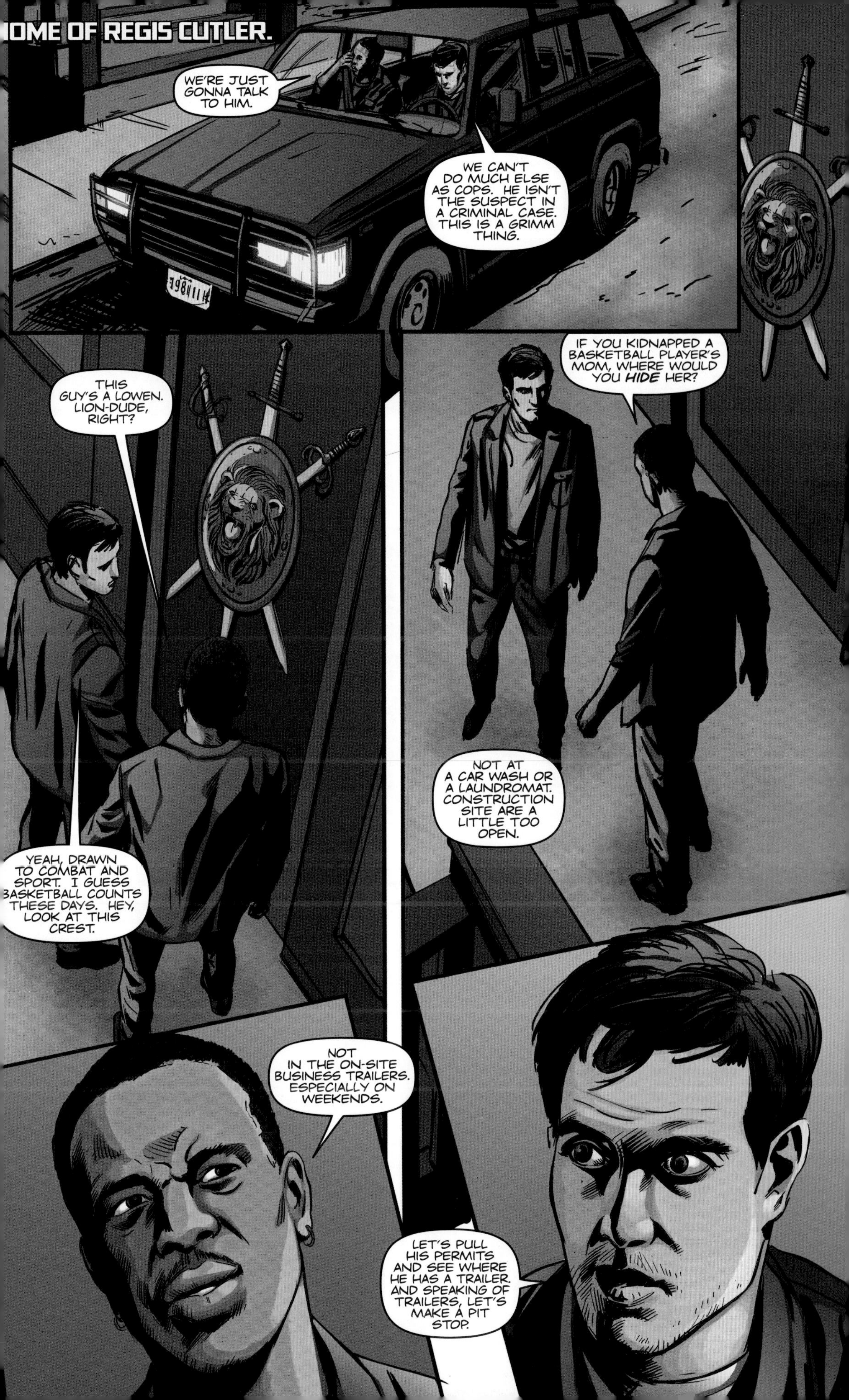
OME OF REGIS CUTLER.
WE'RE JUST GONNA TALK TO HIM.
WE CAN'T DO MUCH ELSE AS COPS. HE ISN'T THE SUSPECT IN A CRIMINAL CASE. THIS IS A GRIMM THING.
THIS GUY'S A LOWEN. LION-DUDE, RIGHT?
YEAH, DRAWN TO COMBAT AND SPORT. I GUESS BASKETBALL COUNTS THESE DAYS. HEY, LOOK AT THIS CREST.
IF YOU KIDNAPPED A BASKETBALL PLAYER'S MOM, WHERE WOULD YOU *HIDE* HER?
NOT AT A CAR WASH OR A LAUNDROMAT. CONSTRUCTION SITE ARE A LITTLE TOO OPEN.
NOT IN THE ON-SITE BUSINESS TRAILERS. ESPECIALLY ON WEEKENDS.
LET'S PULL HIS PERMITS AND SEE WHERE HE HAS A TRAILER. AND SPEAKING OF TRAILERS, LET'S MAKE A PIT STOP.

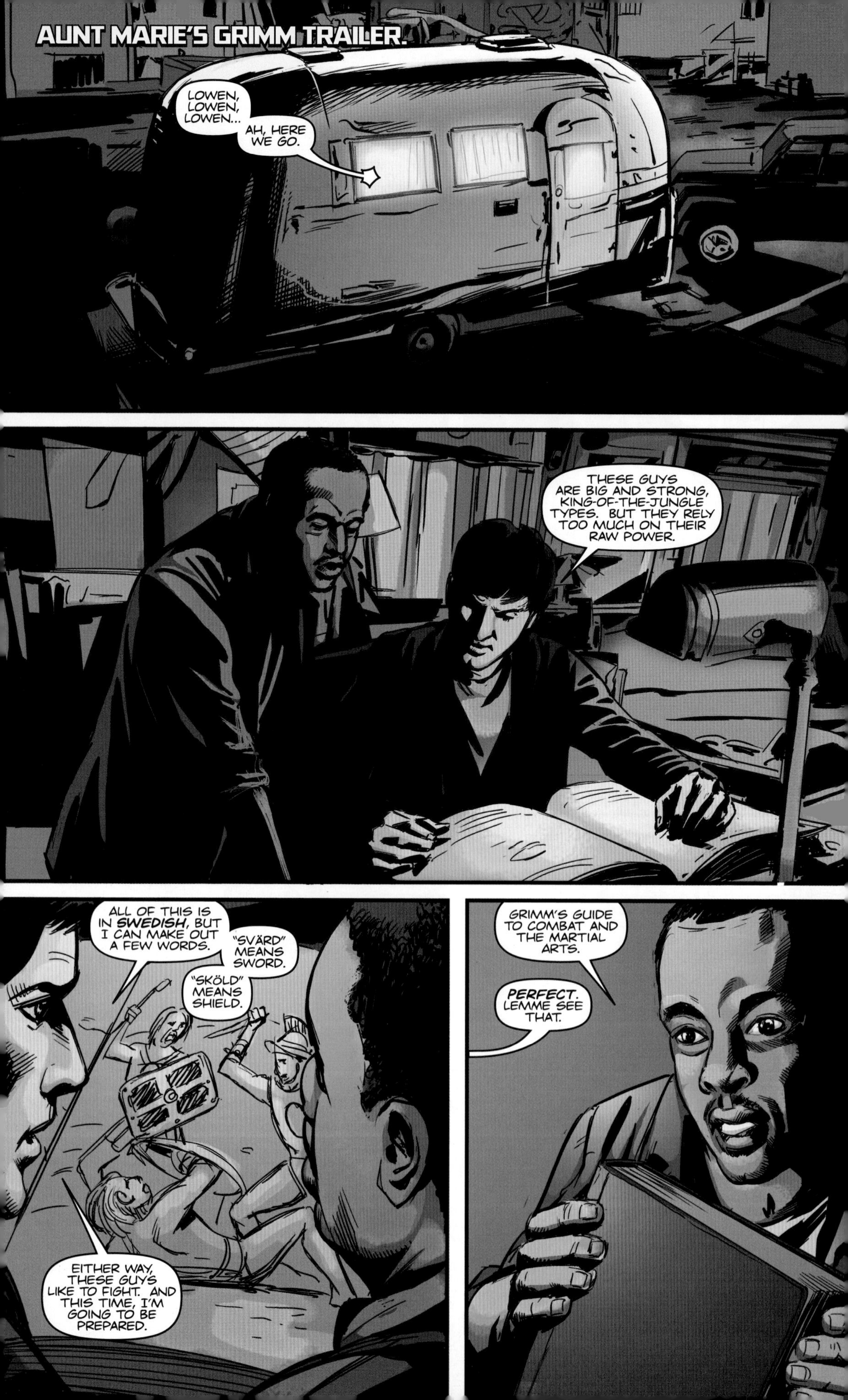
AUNT MARIE'S GRIMM TRAILER.
LOWEN, LOWEN, LOWEN...
AH, HERE WE GO.
THESE GUYS ARE BIG AND STRONG, KING-OF-THE-JUNGLE TYPES. BUT THEY RELY TOO MUCH ON THEIR RAW POWER.
ALL OF THIS IS IN SWEDISH, BUT I CAN MAKE OUT A FEW WORDS.
"SVÄRD" MEANS SWORD.
"SKÖLD" MEANS SHIELD.
EITHER WAY, THESE GUYS LIKE TO FIGHT. AND THIS TIME, I'M GOING TO BE PREPARED.
GRIMM'S GUIDE TO COMBAT AND THE MARTIAL ARTS.
PERFECT. LEMME SEE THAT.

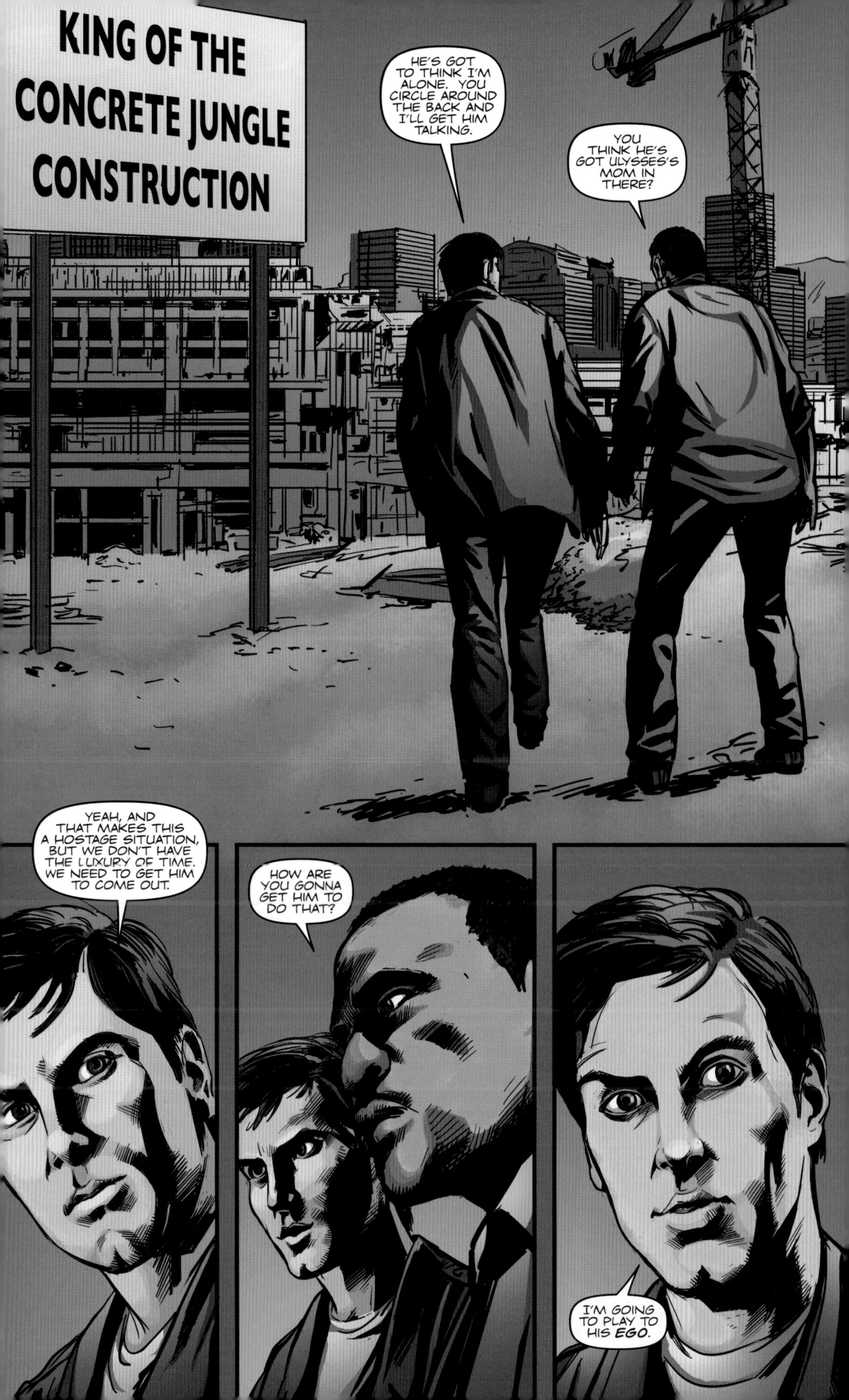
KING OF THE CONCRETE JUNGLE CONSTRUCTION
HE'S GOT TO THINK I'M ALONE. YOU CIRCLE AROUND THE BACK AND I'LL GET HIM TALKING.
YOU THINK HE'S GOT ULYSSES'S MOM IN THERE?
YEAH, AND THAT MAKES THIS A HOSTAGE SITUATION, BUT WE DON'T HAVE THE LUXURY OF TIME. WE NEED TO GET HIM TO COME OUT.
HOW ARE YOU GONNA GET HIM TO DO THAT?
I'M GOING TO PLAY TO HIS *EGO*.

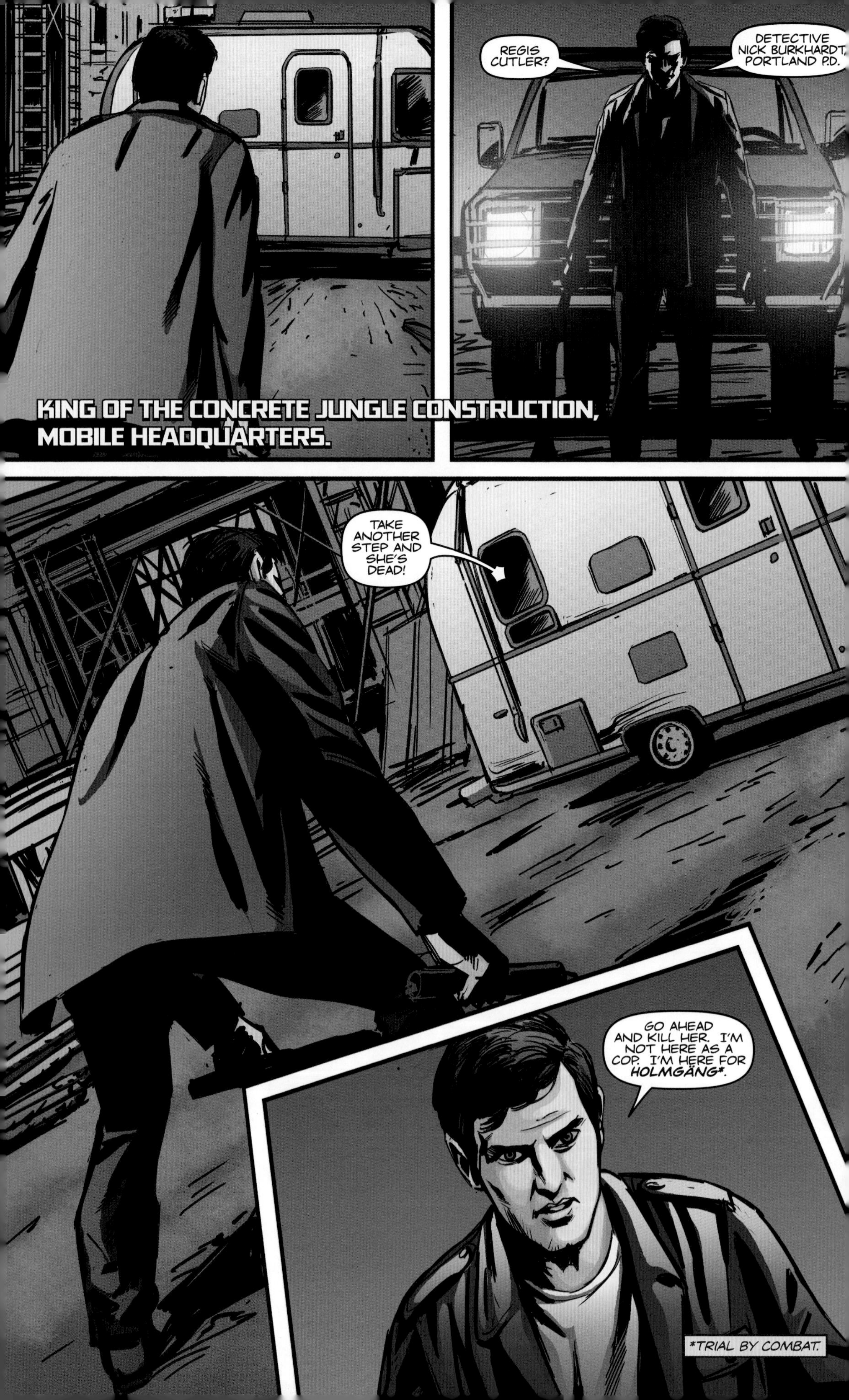
KING OF THE CONCRETE JUNGLE CONSTRUCTION, MOBILE HEADQUARTERS.
REGIS CUTLER?
DETECTIVE NICK BURKHARDT, PORTLAND P.D.
TAKE ANOTHER STEP AND SHE'S DEAD!
GO AHEAD AND KILL HER. I'M NOT HERE AS A COP. I'M HERE FOR HOLMGÅNG*.
*TRIAL BY COMBAT.

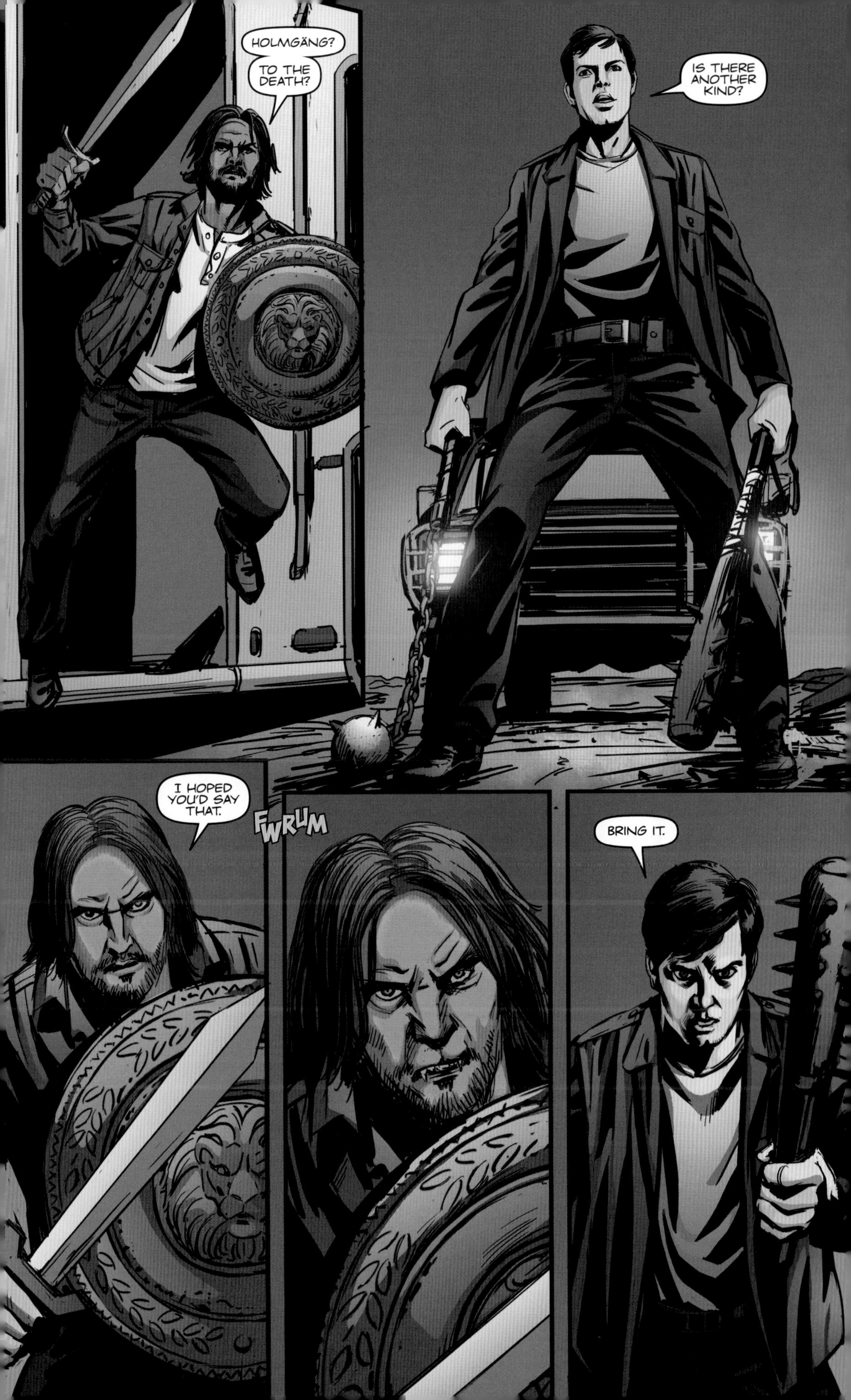
HOLMGÄNG?
TO THE DEATH?
IS THERE ANOTHER KIND?
I HOPED YOU'D SAY THAT.
FWRUM
BRING IT.

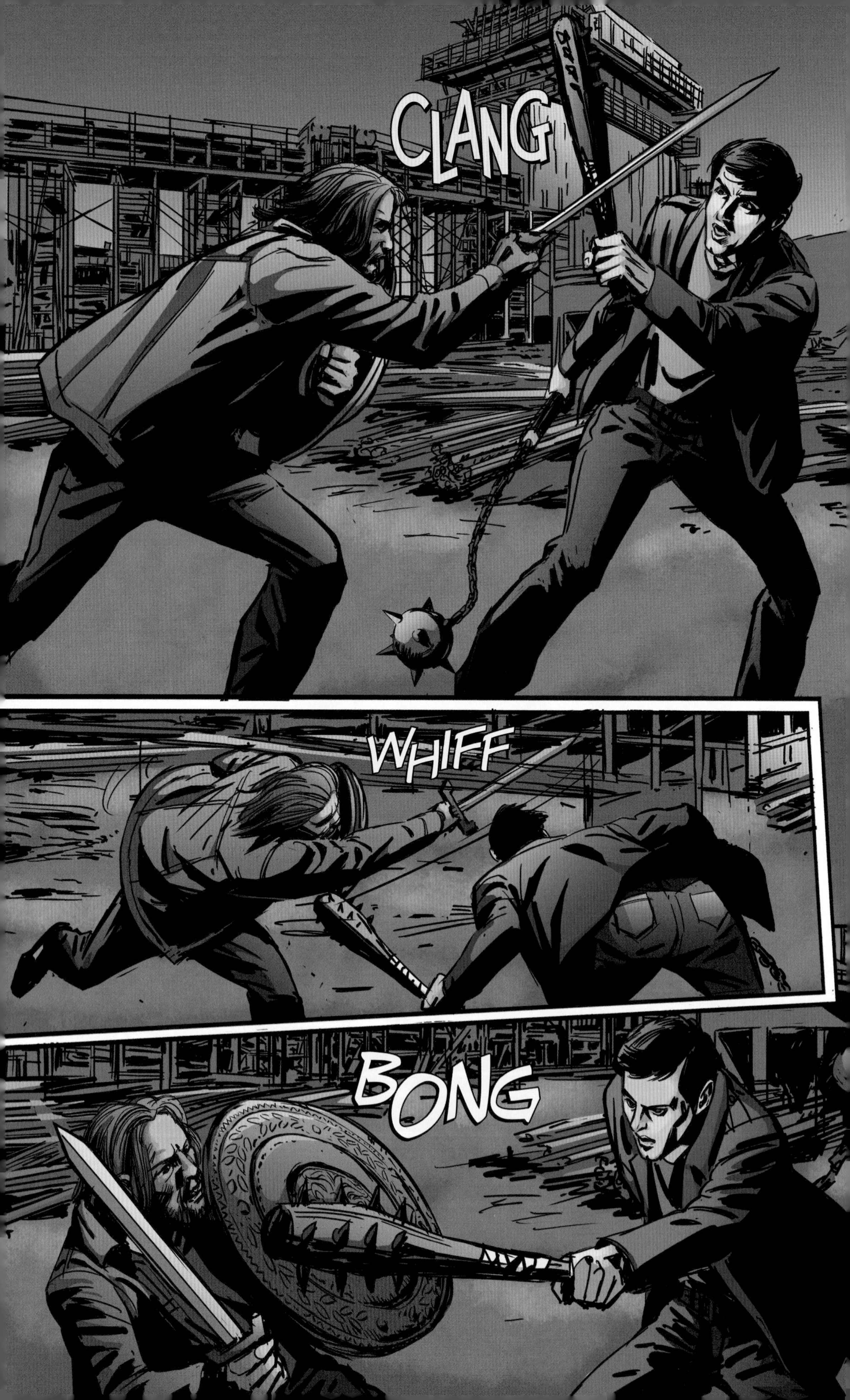
CLANG
WHIFF
BONG

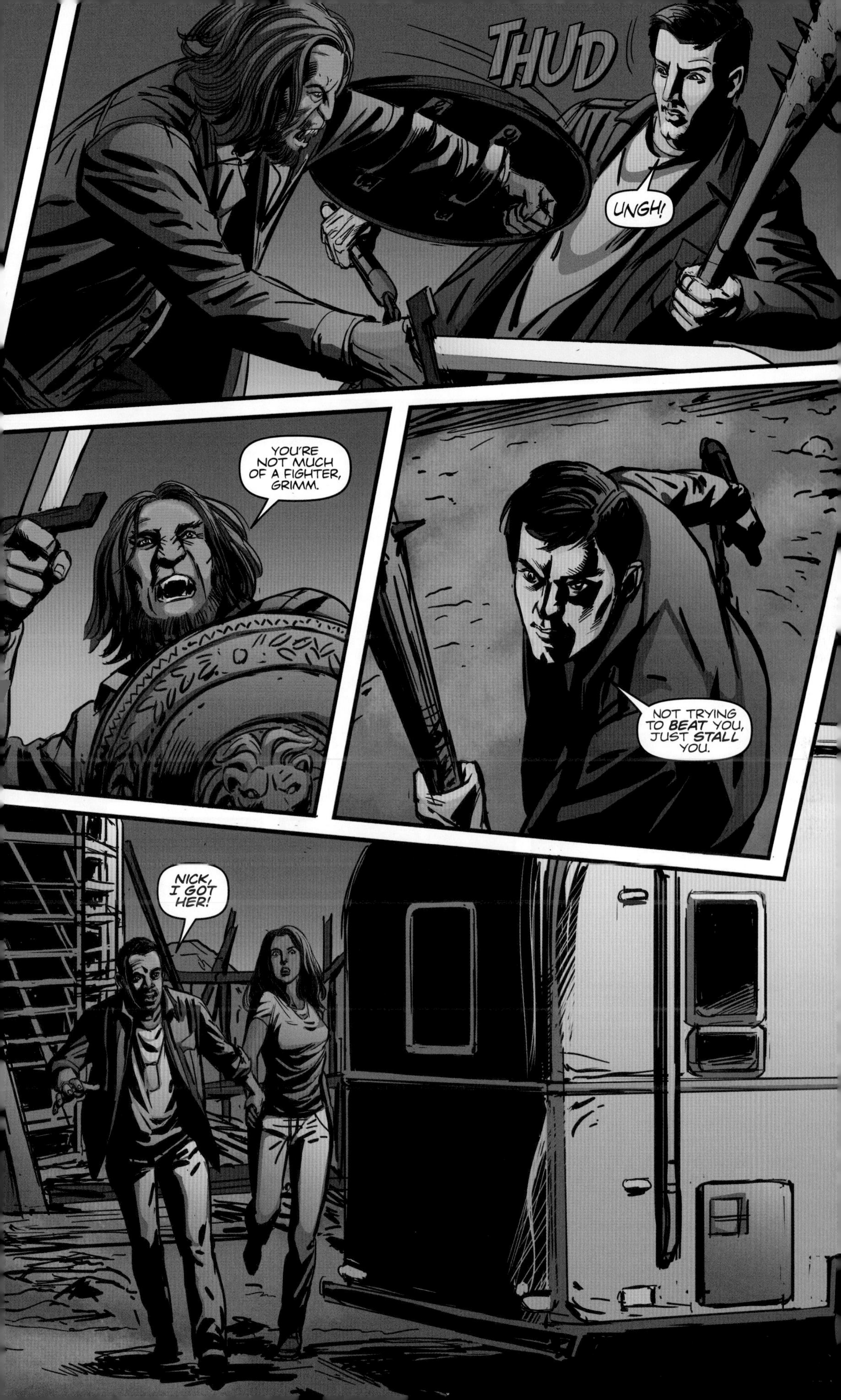
THUD
UNGH!
YOU'RE NOT MUCH OF A FIGHTER, GRIMM.
NOT TRYING TO BEAT YOU, JUST STALL YOU.
NICK, I GOT HER!

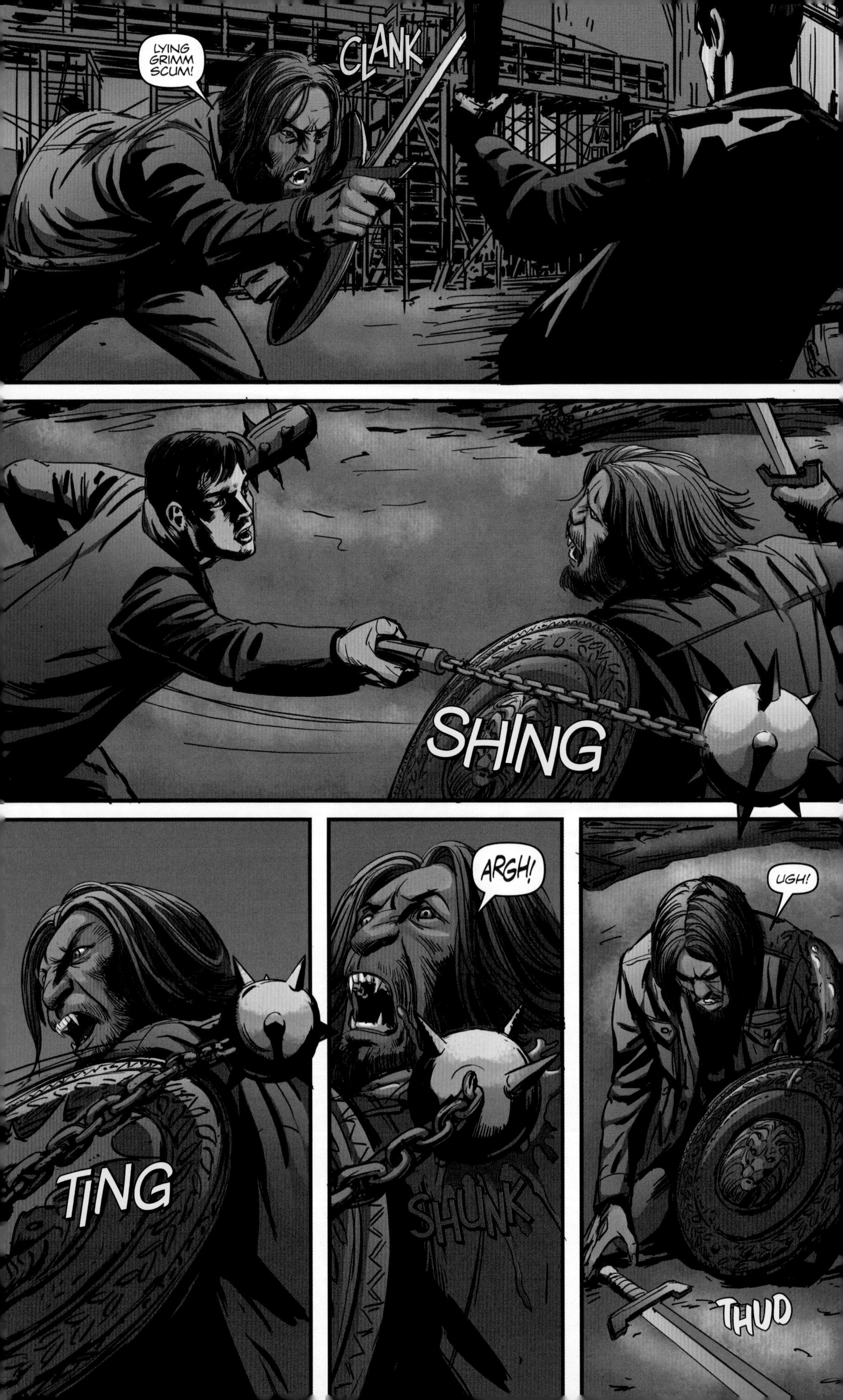
LYING GRIMM SCUM!
CLANK
SHING
TING
ARGH!
SHUNK
UGH!
THUD

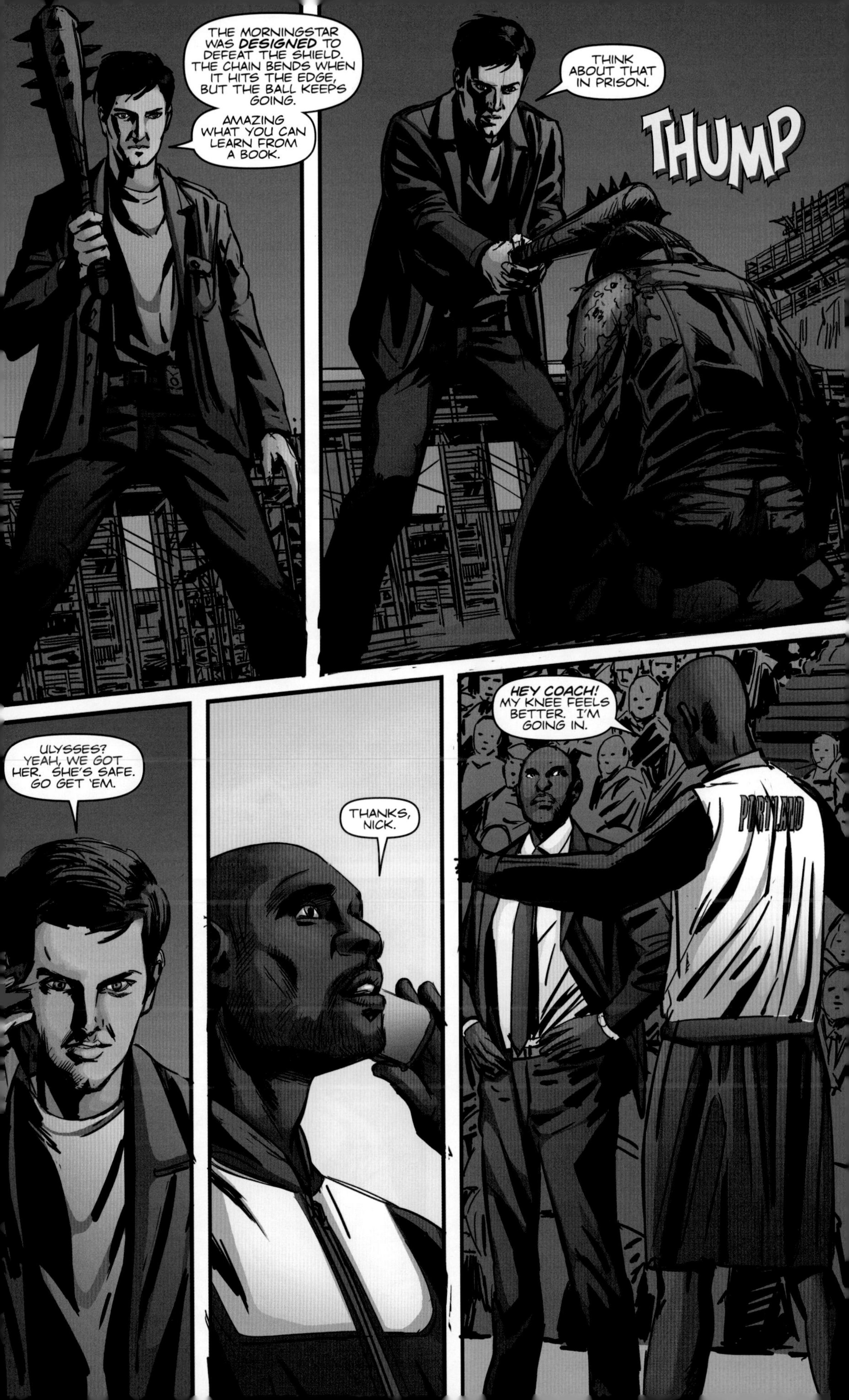
THE MORNINGSTAR WAS DESIGNED TO DEFEAT THE SHIELD. THE CHAIN BENDS WHEN IT HITS THE EDGE, BUT THE BALL KEEPS GOING.
AMAZING WHAT YOU CAN LEARN FROM A BOOK.
THINK ABOUT THAT IN PRISON.
THUMP
ULYSSES? YEAH, WE GOT HER. SHE'S SAFE. GO GET 'EM.
THANKS, NICK.
HEY COACH! MY KNEE FEELS BETTER. I'M GOING IN.

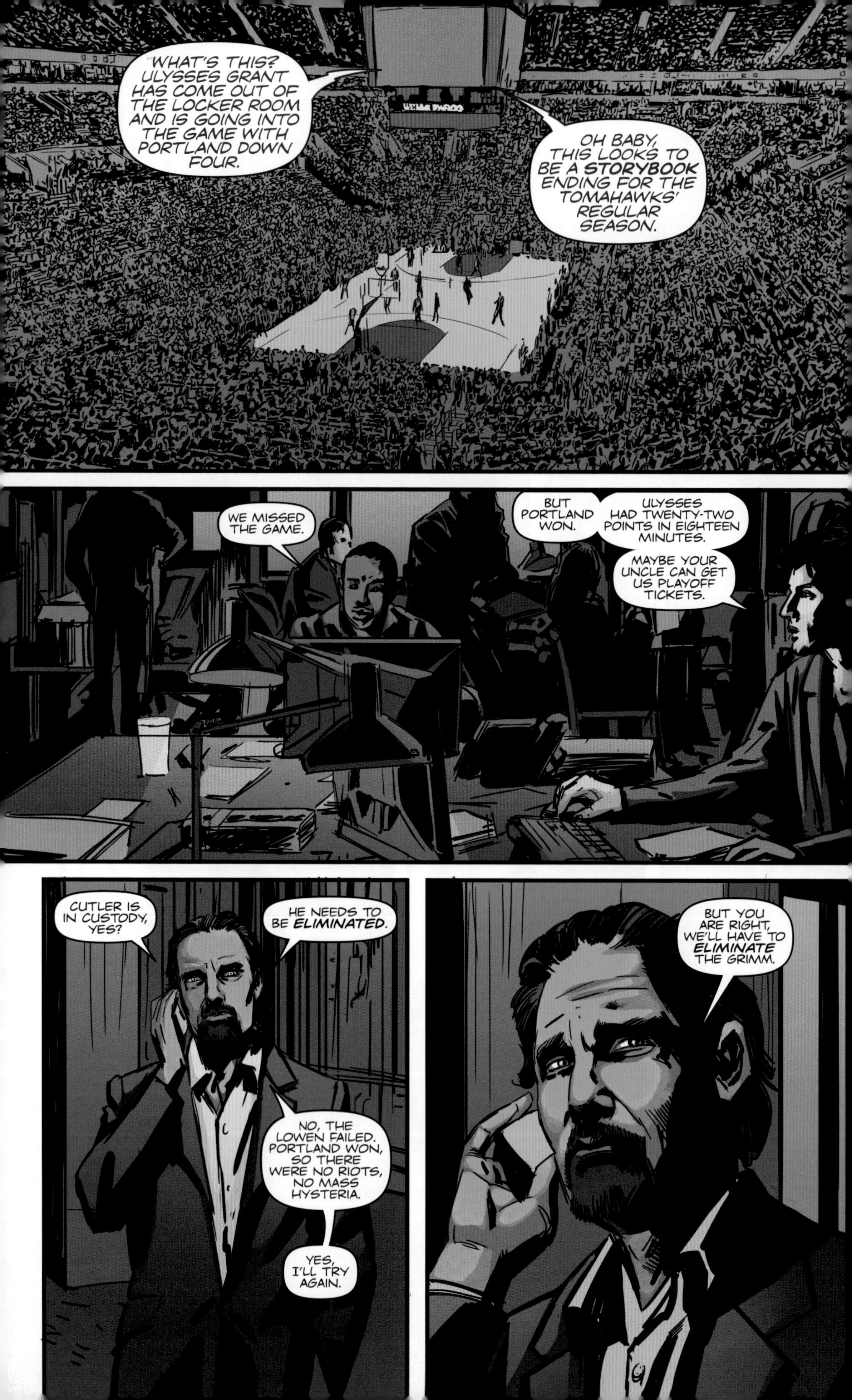
WHAT'S THIS? ULYSSES GRANT HAS COME OUT OF THE LOCKER ROOM AND IS GOING INTO THE GAME WITH PORTLAND DOWN FOUR.
OH BABY, THIS LOOKS TO BE A **STORYBOOK** ENDING FOR THE TOMAHAWKS' REGULAR SEASON.
WE MISSED THE GAME.
BUT PORTLAND WON.
ULYSSES HAD TWENTY-TWO POINTS IN EIGHTEEN MINUTES.
MAYBE YOUR UNCLE CAN GET US PLAYOFF TICKETS.
CUTLER IS IN CUSTODY, YES?
HE NEEDS TO BE ***ELIMINATED***.
NO, THE LOWEN FAILED. PORTLAND WON, SO THERE WERE NO RIOTS, NO MASS HYSTERIA.
YES, I'LL TRY AGAIN.
BUT YOU ARE RIGHT, WE'LL HAVE TO ***ELIMINATE*** THE GRIMM.

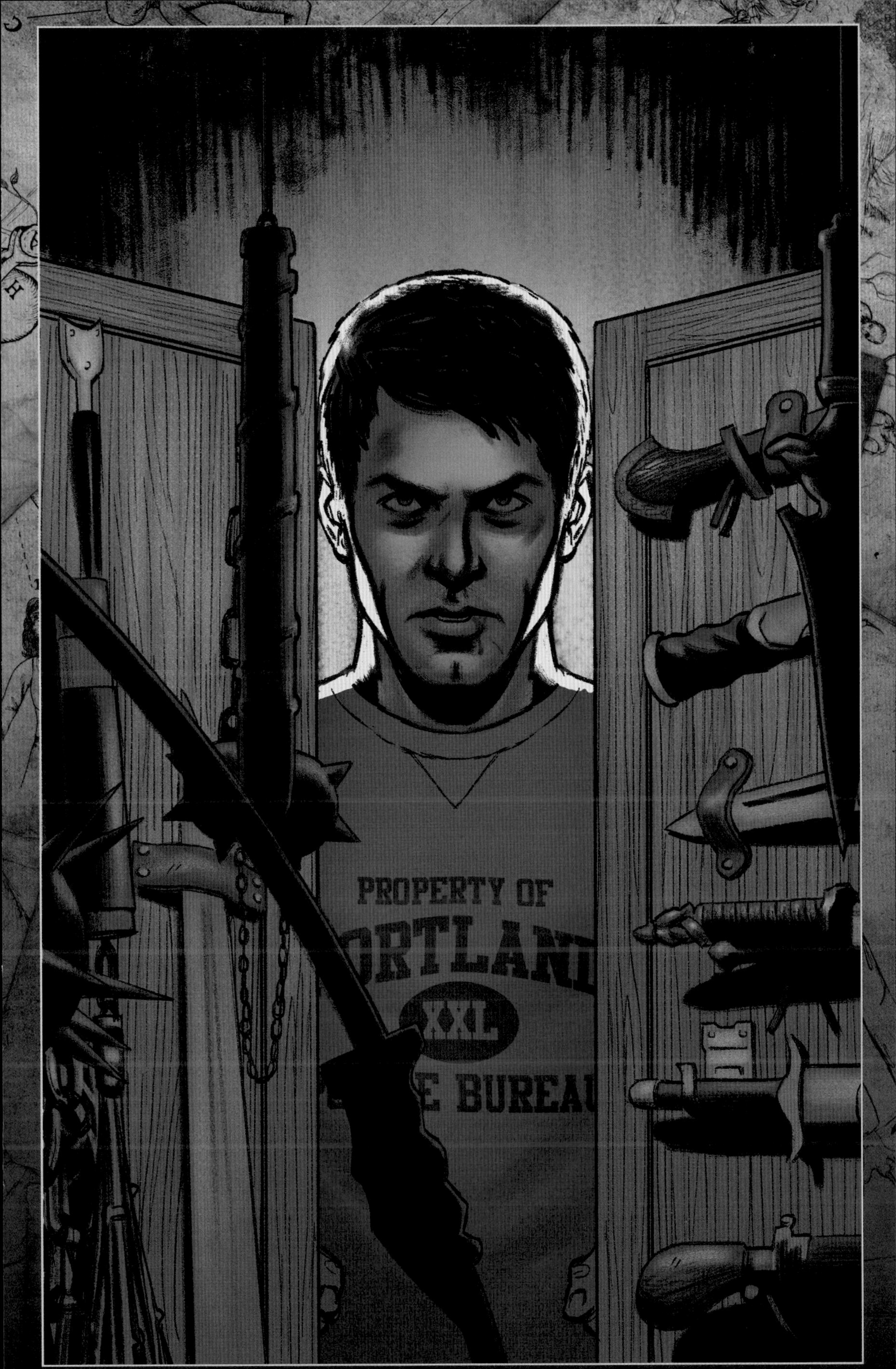
PROPERTY OF
XXL

GRIMM: THE WARLOCK ISSUE #2 COVER

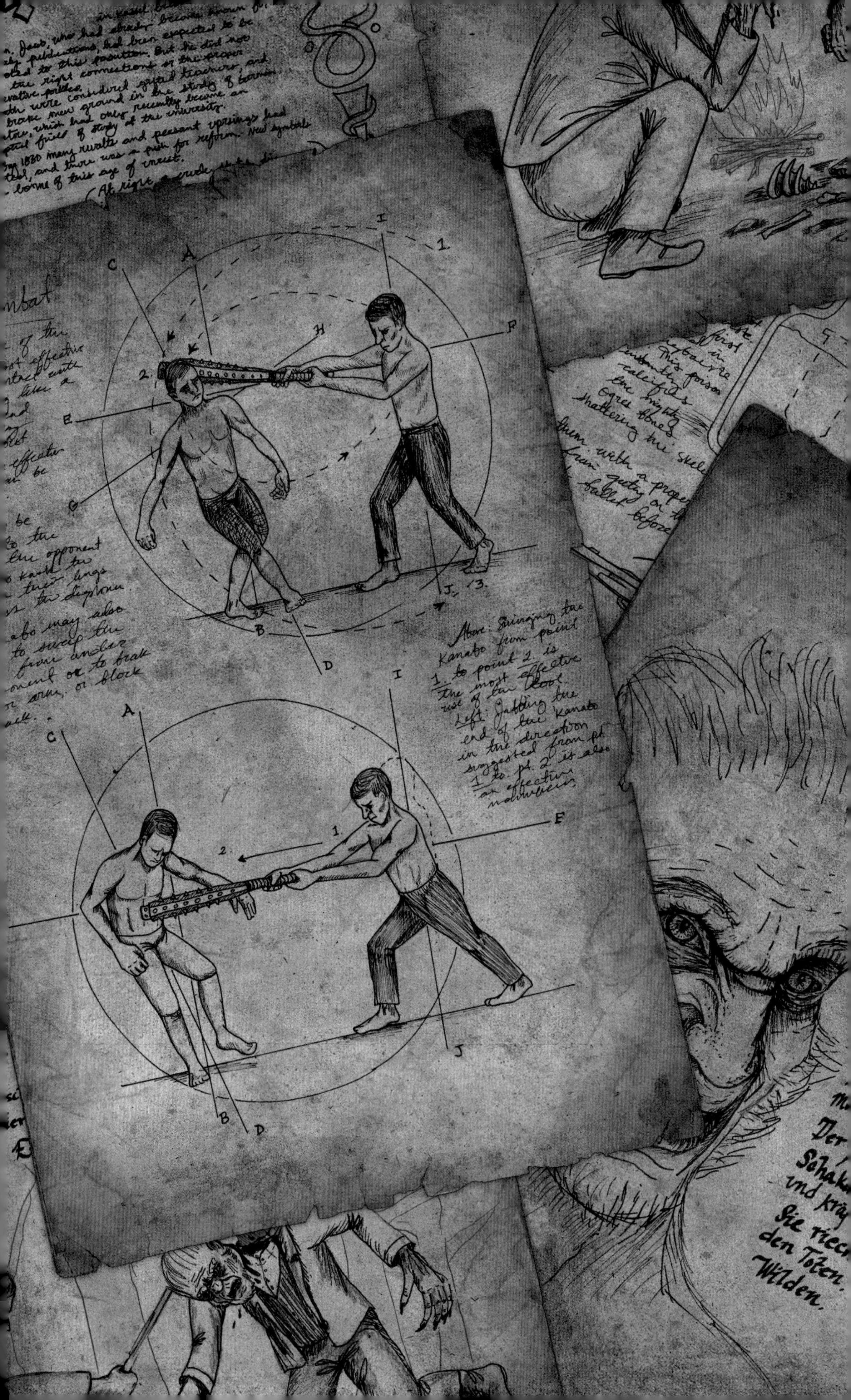
Above: Swinging the Kanabo from point 1. to point 2. is the most effective use of the tool.
Left: Jabbing the end of the Kanabo in the direction suggested from pt. 1 to pt. 2 is also an effective maneuver.
A
B
C
D
E
F
G
H
I
J
1.
2.
3.
At right, a crude
Der
Schak
und kr
Sie riec
den Toten.
Wilden.

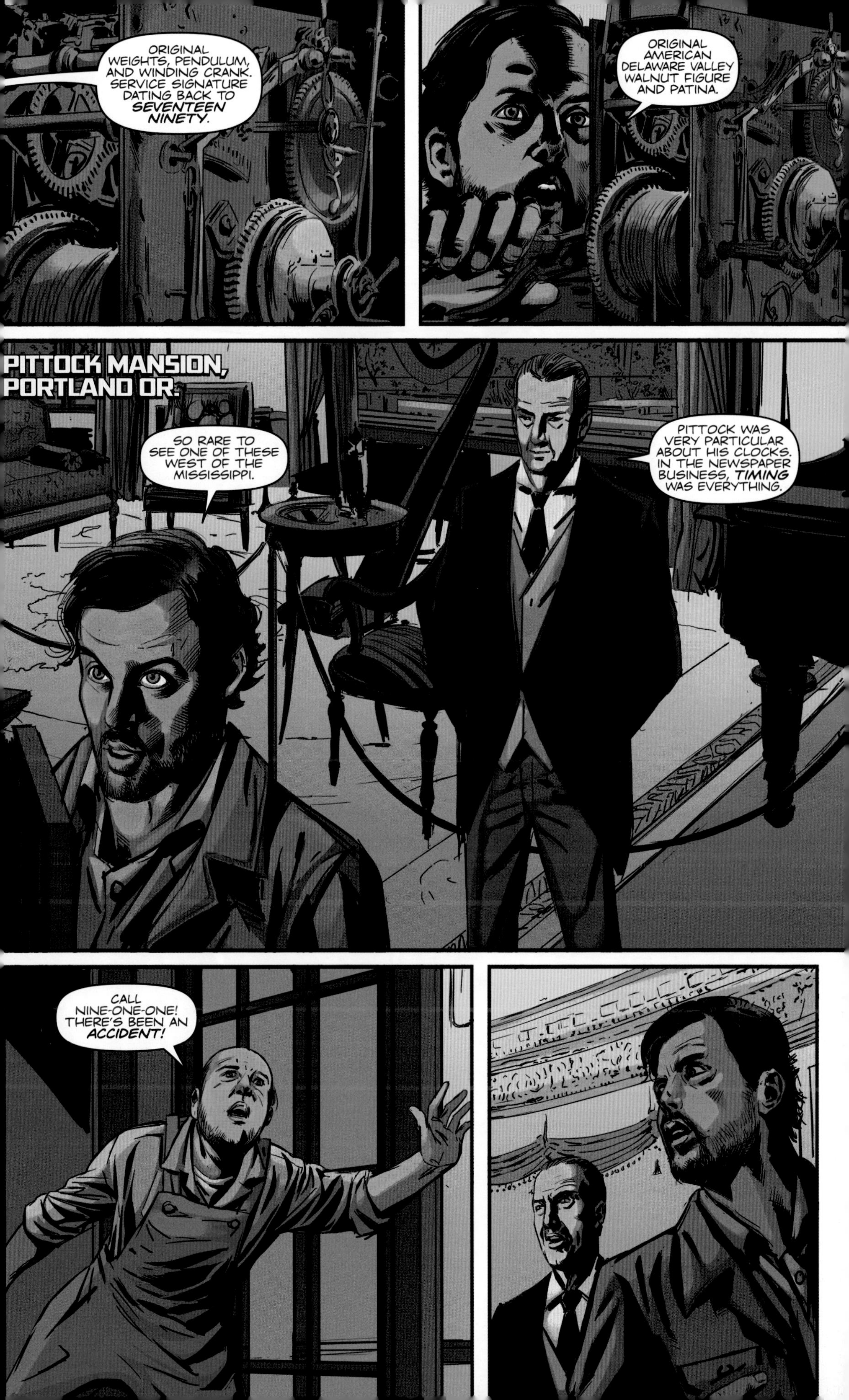
ORIGINAL WEIGHTS, PENDULUM, AND WINDING CRANK. SERVICE SIGNATURE DATING BACK TO SEVENTEEN NINETY.
ORIGINAL AMERICAN DELAWARE VALLEY WALNUT FIGURE AND PATINA.
PITTOCK MANSION, PORTLAND OR.
SO RARE TO SEE ONE OF THESE WEST OF THE MISSISSIPPI.
PITTOCK WAS VERY PARTICULAR ABOUT HIS CLOCKS. IN THE NEWSPAPER BUSINESS, TIMING WAS EVERYTHING.
CALL NINE-ONE-ONE! THERE'S BEEN AN ACCIDENT!

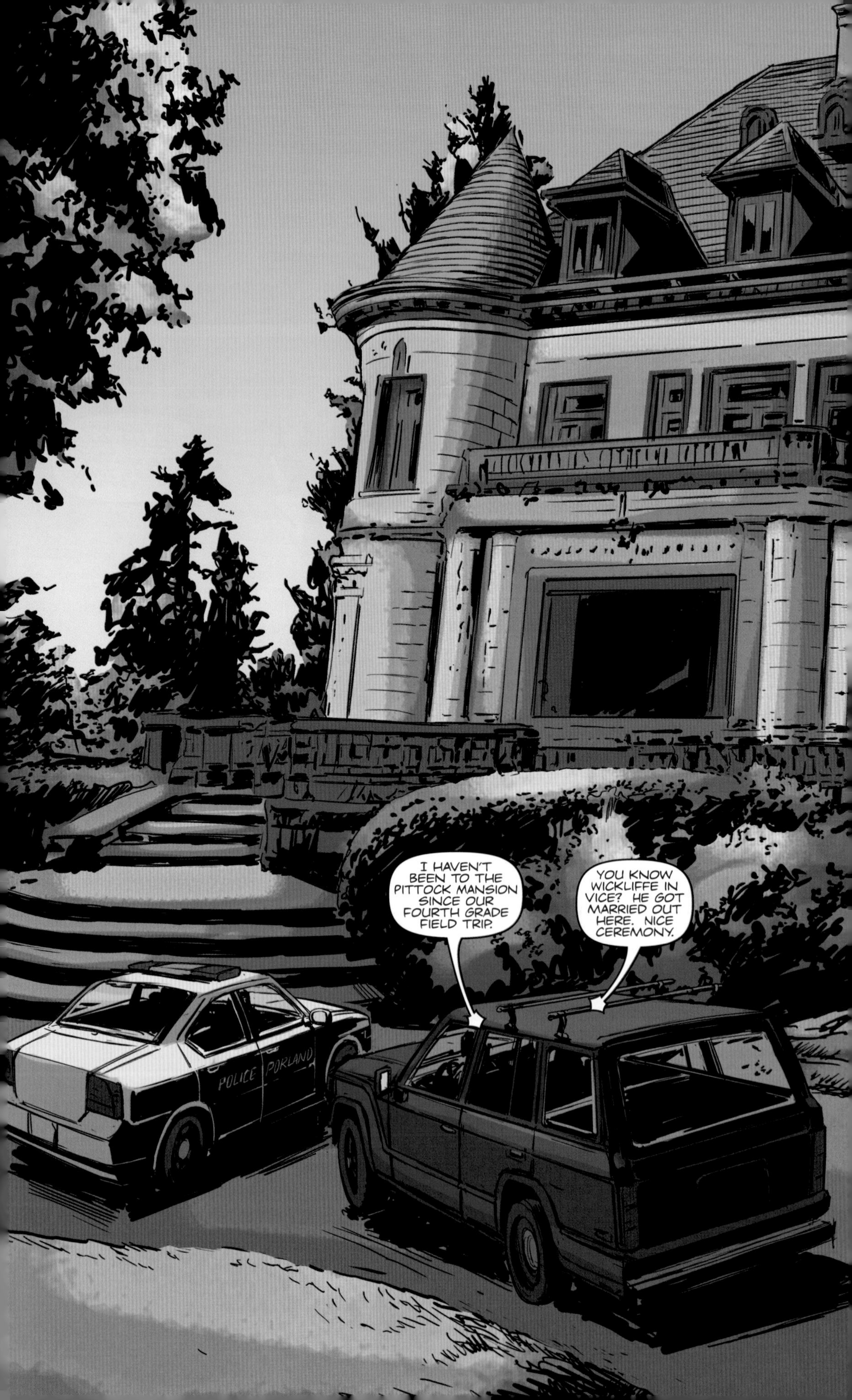
I HAVEN'T BEEN TO THE PITTOCK MANSION SINCE OUR FOURTH GRADE FIELD TRIP.
YOU KNOW WICKLIFFE IN VICE? HE GOT MARRIED OUT HERE. NICE CEREMONY.
POLICE PORLAND

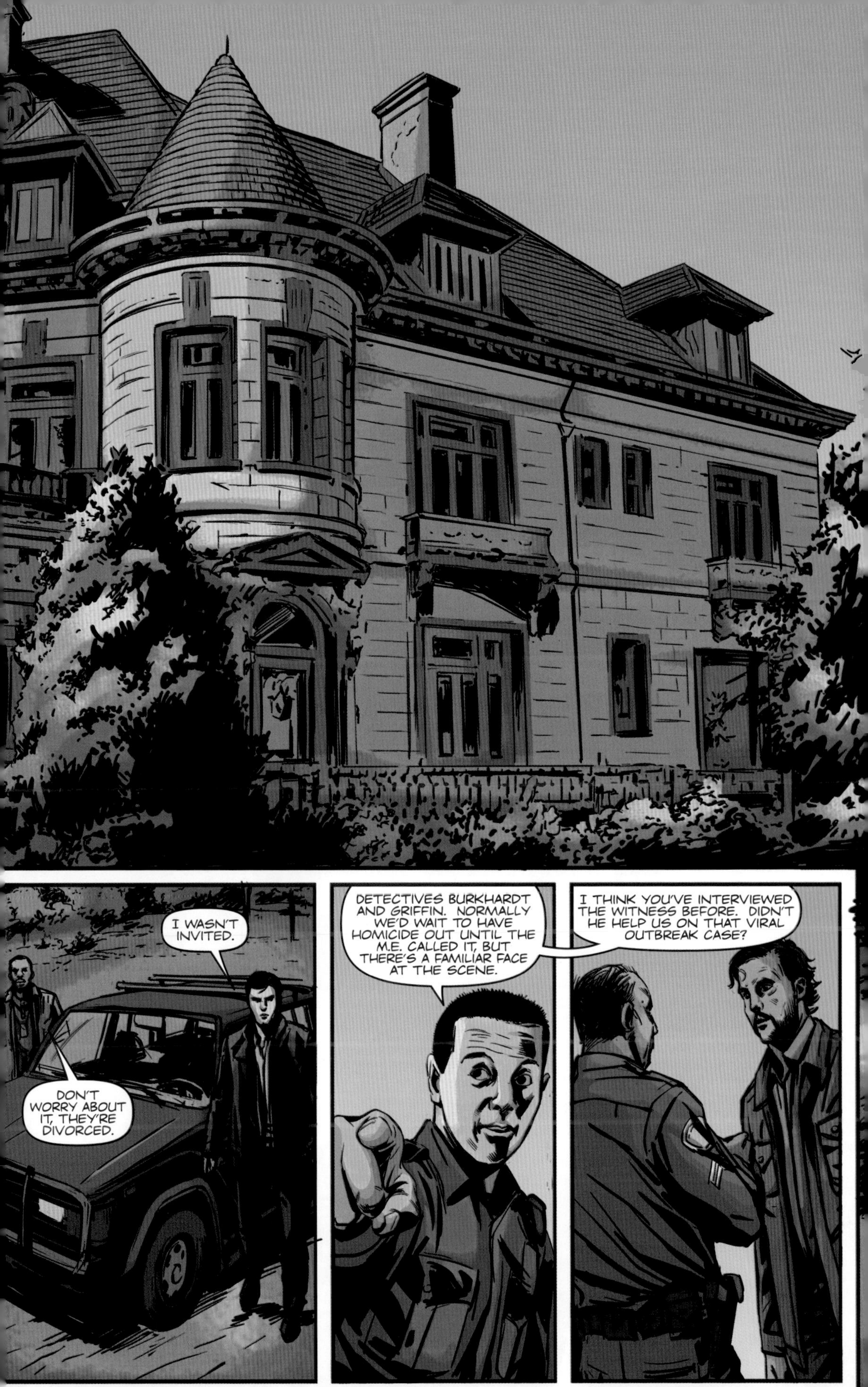
I WASN'T INVITED.
DON'T WORRY ABOUT IT, THEY'RE DIVORCED.
DETECTIVES BURKHARDT AND GRIFFIN. NORMALLY WE'D WAIT TO HAVE HOMICIDE OUT UNTIL THE M.E. CALLED IT, BUT THERE'S A FAMILIAR FACE AT THE SCENE.
I THINK YOU'VE INTERVIEWED THE WITNESS BEFORE. DIDN'T HE HELP US ON THAT VIRAL OUTBREAK CASE?

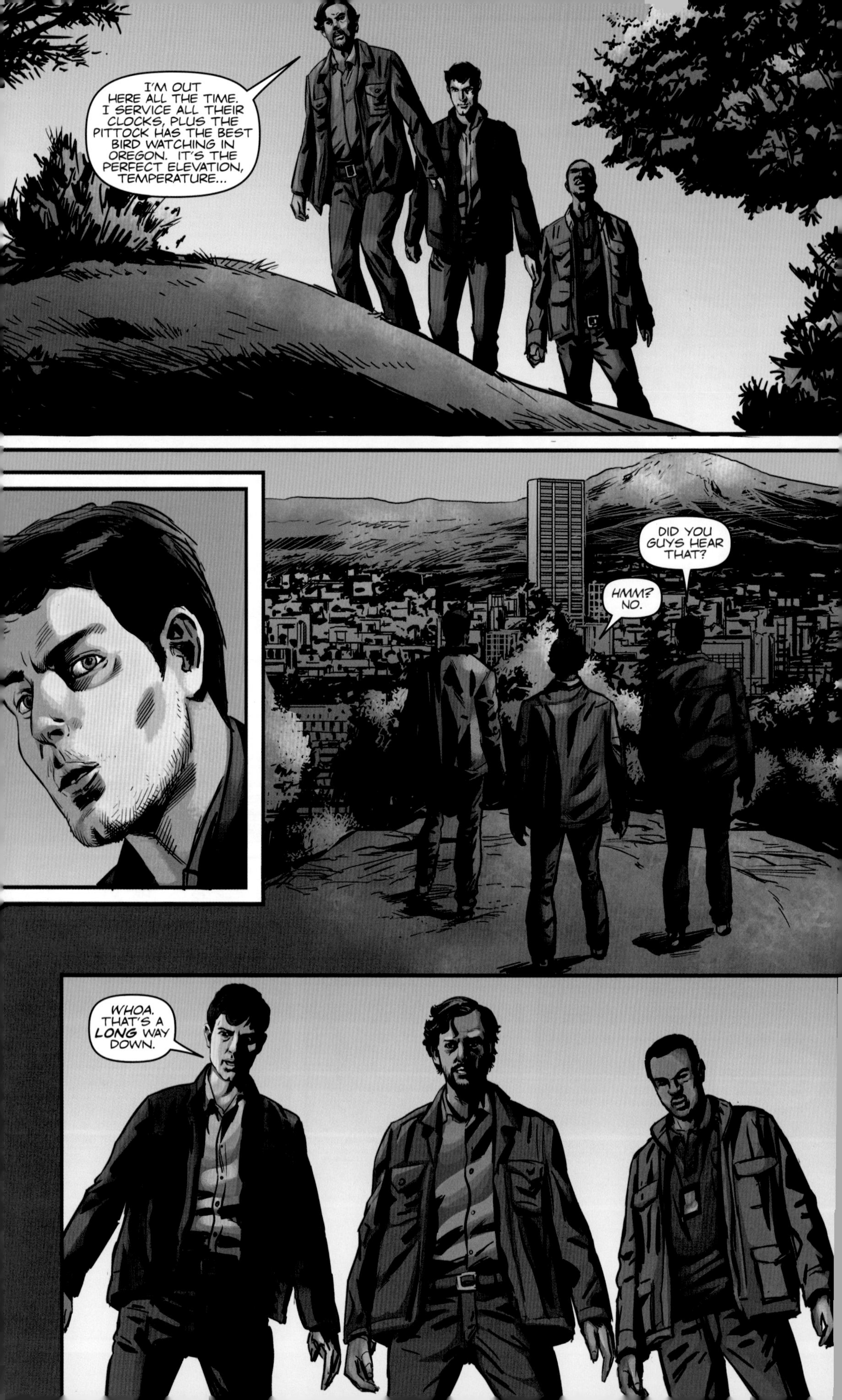
I'M OUT HERE ALL THE TIME. I SERVICE ALL THEIR CLOCKS, PLUS THE PITTOCK HAS THE BEST BIRD WATCHING IN OREGON. IT'S THE PERFECT ELEVATION, TEMPERATURE...
DID YOU GUYS HEAR THAT?
HMM? NO.
WHOA. THAT'S A **LONG** WAY DOWN.

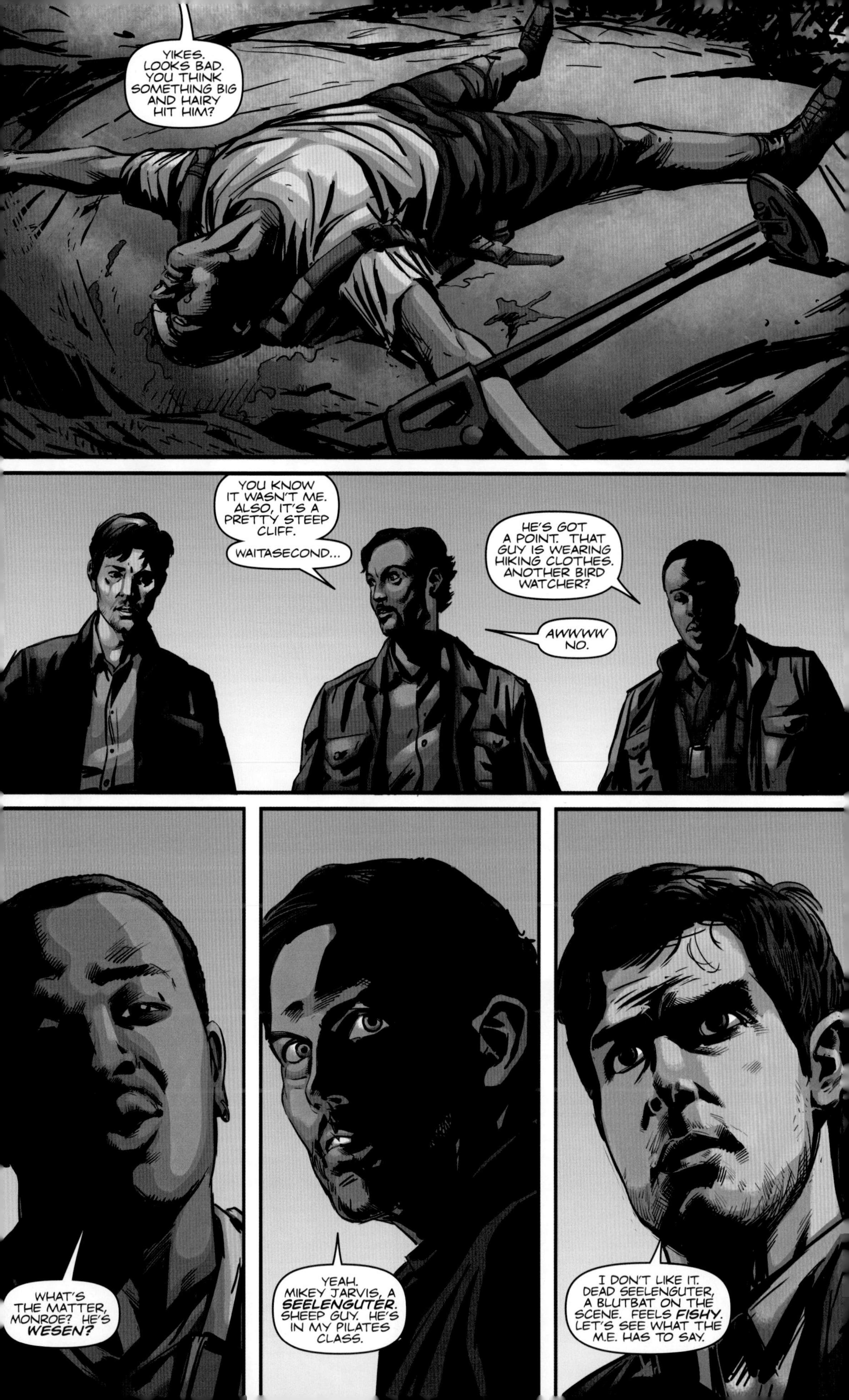
YIKES. LOOKS BAD. YOU THINK SOMETHING BIG AND HAIRY HIT HIM?
YOU KNOW IT WASN'T ME. ALSO, IT'S A PRETTY STEEP CLIFF.
WAITASECOND...
HE'S GOT A POINT. THAT GUY IS WEARING HIKING CLOTHES. ANOTHER BIRD WATCHER?
AWWWW NO.
WHAT'S THE MATTER, MONROE? HE'S WESEN?
YEAH. MIKEY JARVIS, A SEELENGUTER. SHEEP GUY. HE'S IN MY PILATES CLASS.
I DON'T LIKE IT. DEAD SEELENGUTER, A BLUTBAT ON THE SCENE. FEELS FISHY. LET'S SEE WHAT THE M.E. HAS TO SAY.

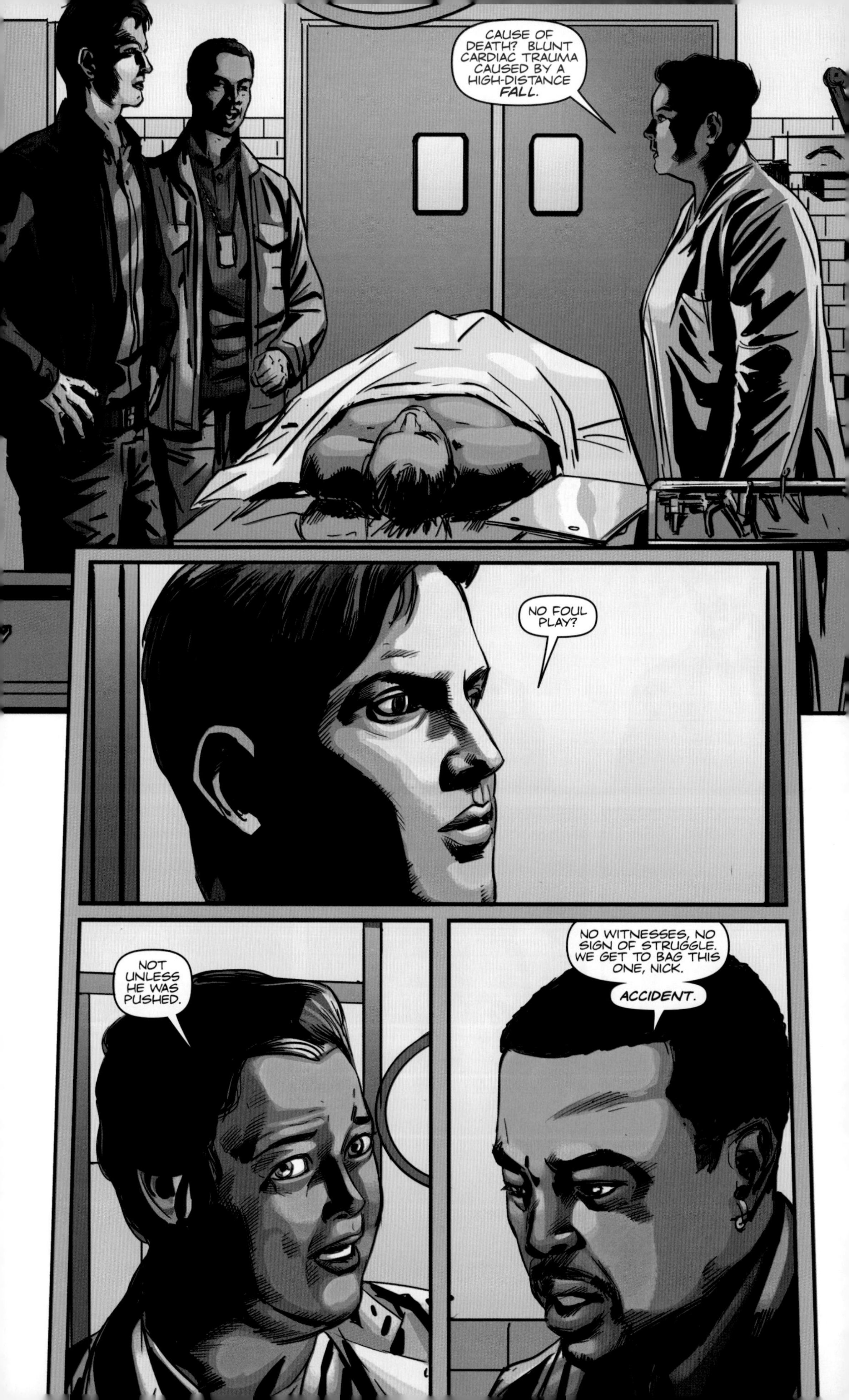
CAUSE OF DEATH? BLUNT CARDIAC TRAUMA CAUSED BY A HIGH-DISTANCE FALL.
NO FOUL PLAY?
NOT UNLESS HE WAS PUSHED.
NO WITNESSES, NO SIGN OF STRUGGLE. WE GET TO BAG THIS ONE, NICK.
ACCIDENT.

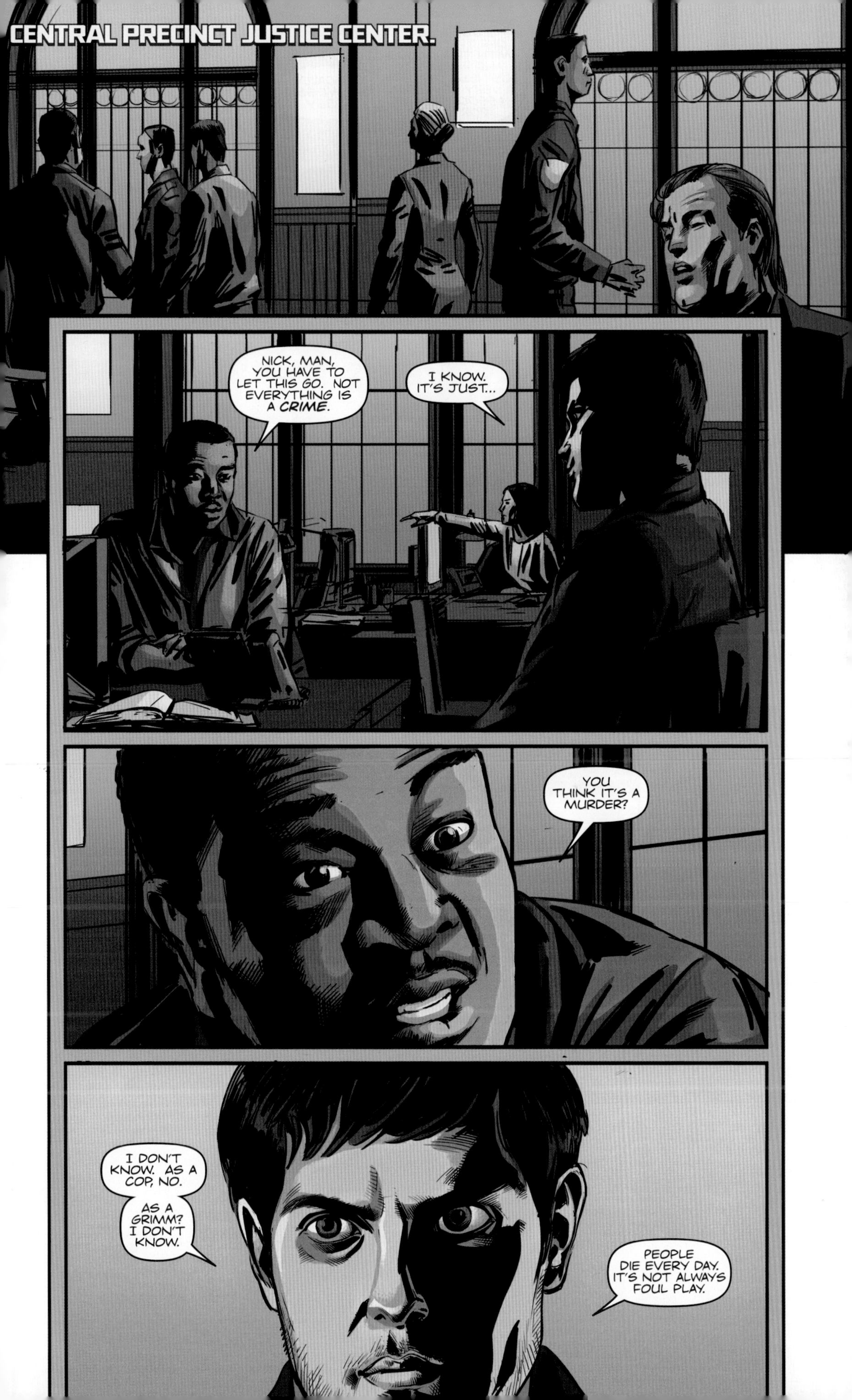
CENTRAL PRECINCT JUSTICE CENTER.
NICK, MAN, YOU HAVE TO LET THIS GO. NOT EVERYTHING IS A CRIME.
I KNOW. IT'S JUST...
YOU THINK IT'S A MURDER?
I DON'T KNOW. AS A COP, NO.
AS A GRIMM? I DON'T KNOW.
PEOPLE DIE EVERY DAY. IT'S NOT ALWAYS FOUL PLAY.

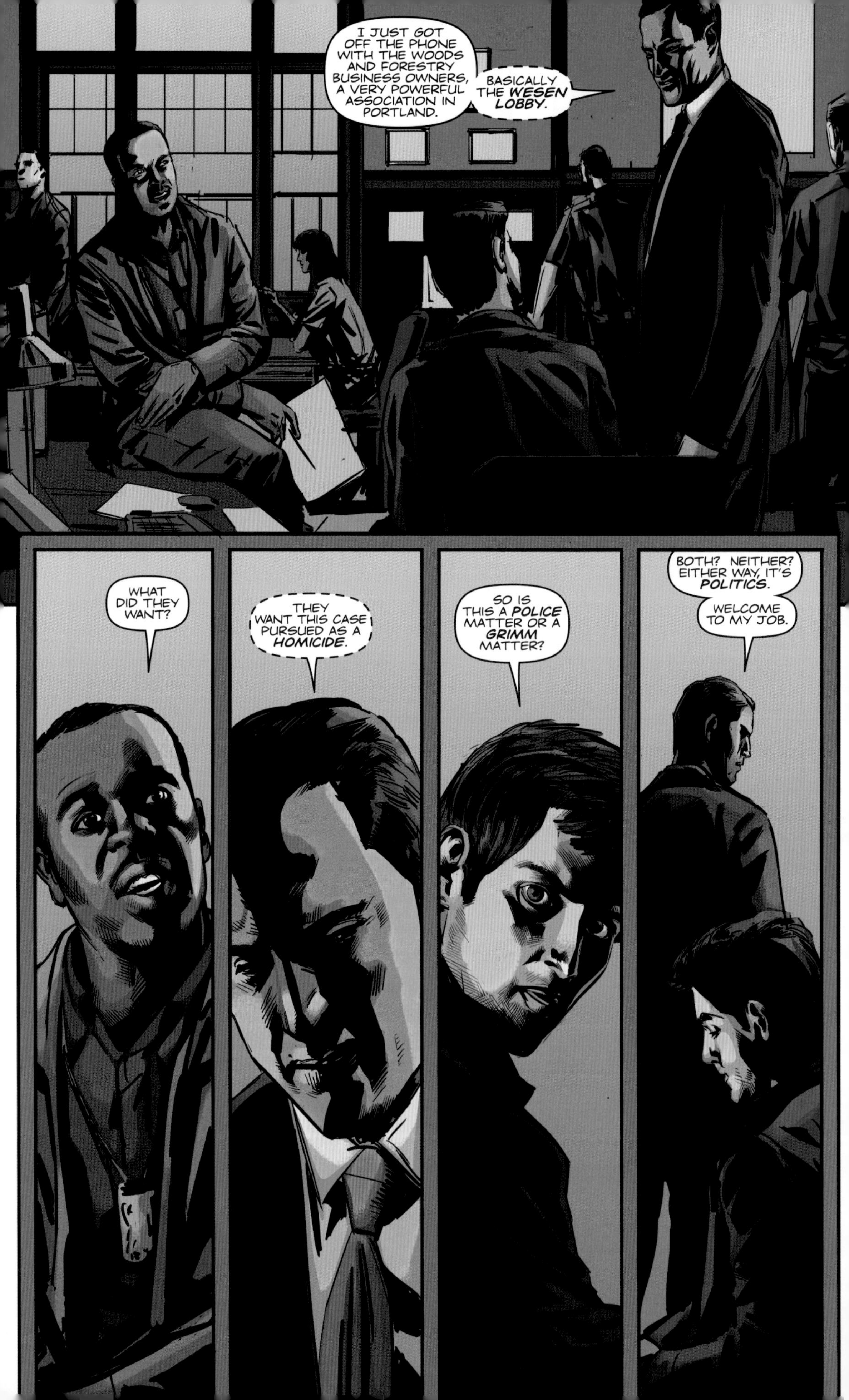
I JUST GOT OFF THE PHONE WITH THE WOODS AND FORESTRY BUSINESS OWNERS, A VERY POWERFUL ASSOCIATION IN PORTLAND.
BASICALLY THE **WESEN LOBBY**.
WHAT DID THEY WANT?
THEY WANT THIS CASE PURSUED AS A **HOMICIDE**.
SO IS THIS A **POLICE** MATTER OR A **GRIMM** MATTER?
BOTH? NEITHER? EITHER WAY, IT'S **POLITICS**.
WELCOME TO MY JOB.

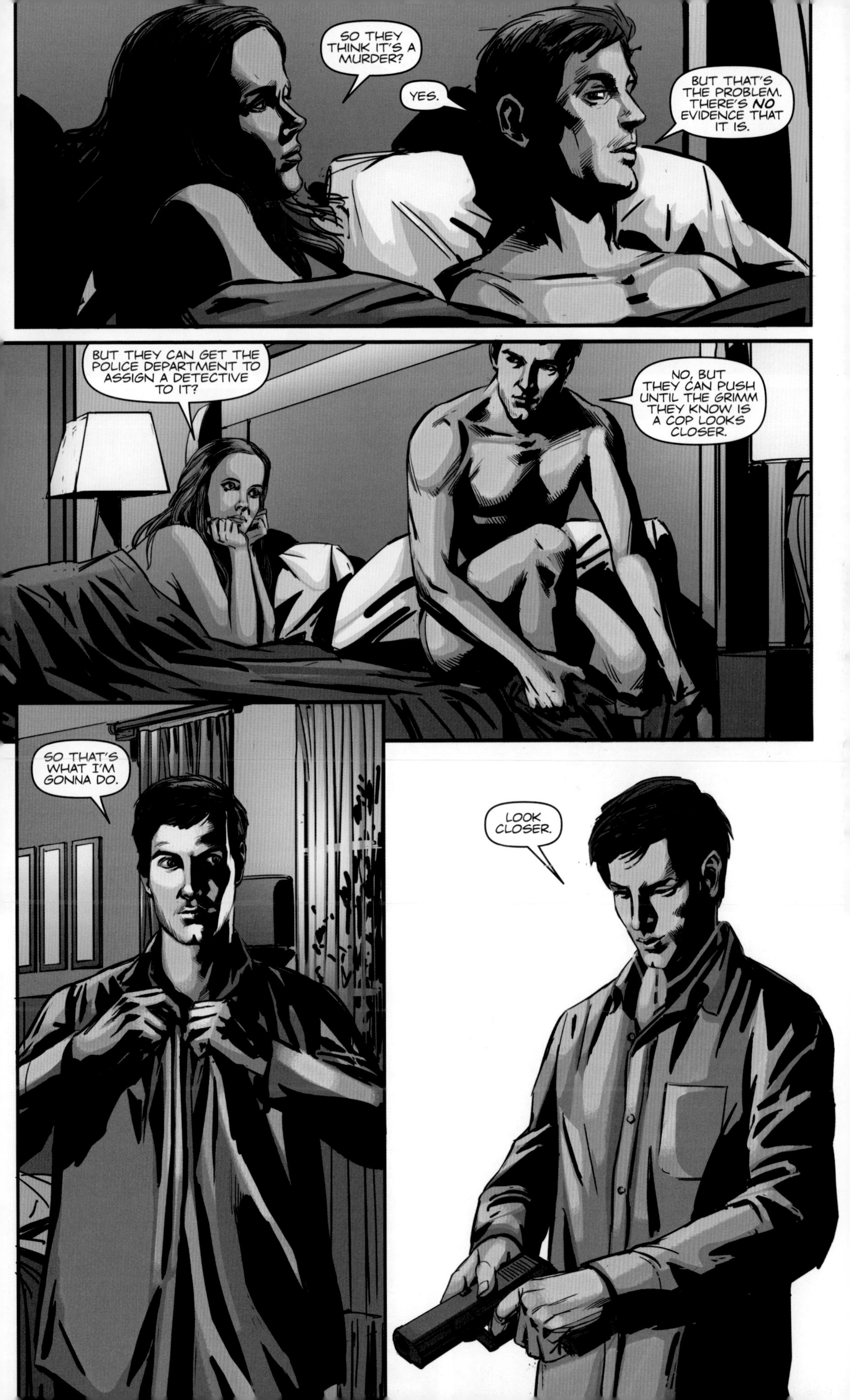
SO THEY THINK IT'S A MURDER?
YES.
BUT THAT'S THE PROBLEM. THERE'S NO EVIDENCE THAT IT IS.
BUT THEY CAN GET THE POLICE DEPARTMENT TO ASSIGN A DETECTIVE TO IT?
NO, BUT THEY CAN PUSH UNTIL THE GRIMM THEY KNOW IS A COP LOOKS CLOSER.
SO THAT'S WHAT I'M GONNA DO.
LOOK CLOSER.

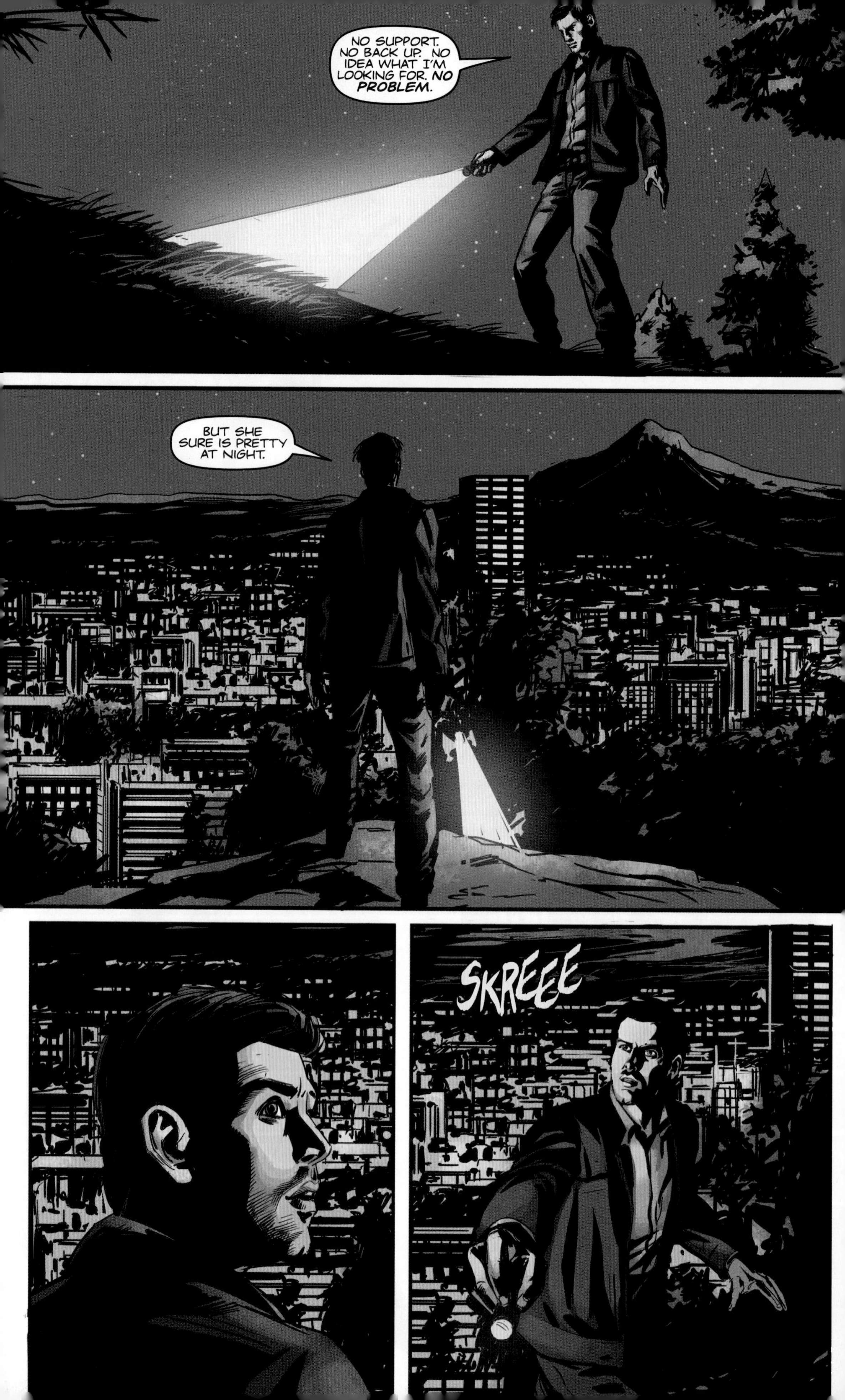
NO SUPPORT. NO BACK UP. NO IDEA WHAT I'M LOOKING FOR. NO PROBLEM.
BUT SHE SURE IS PRETTY AT NIGHT.
SKREEE

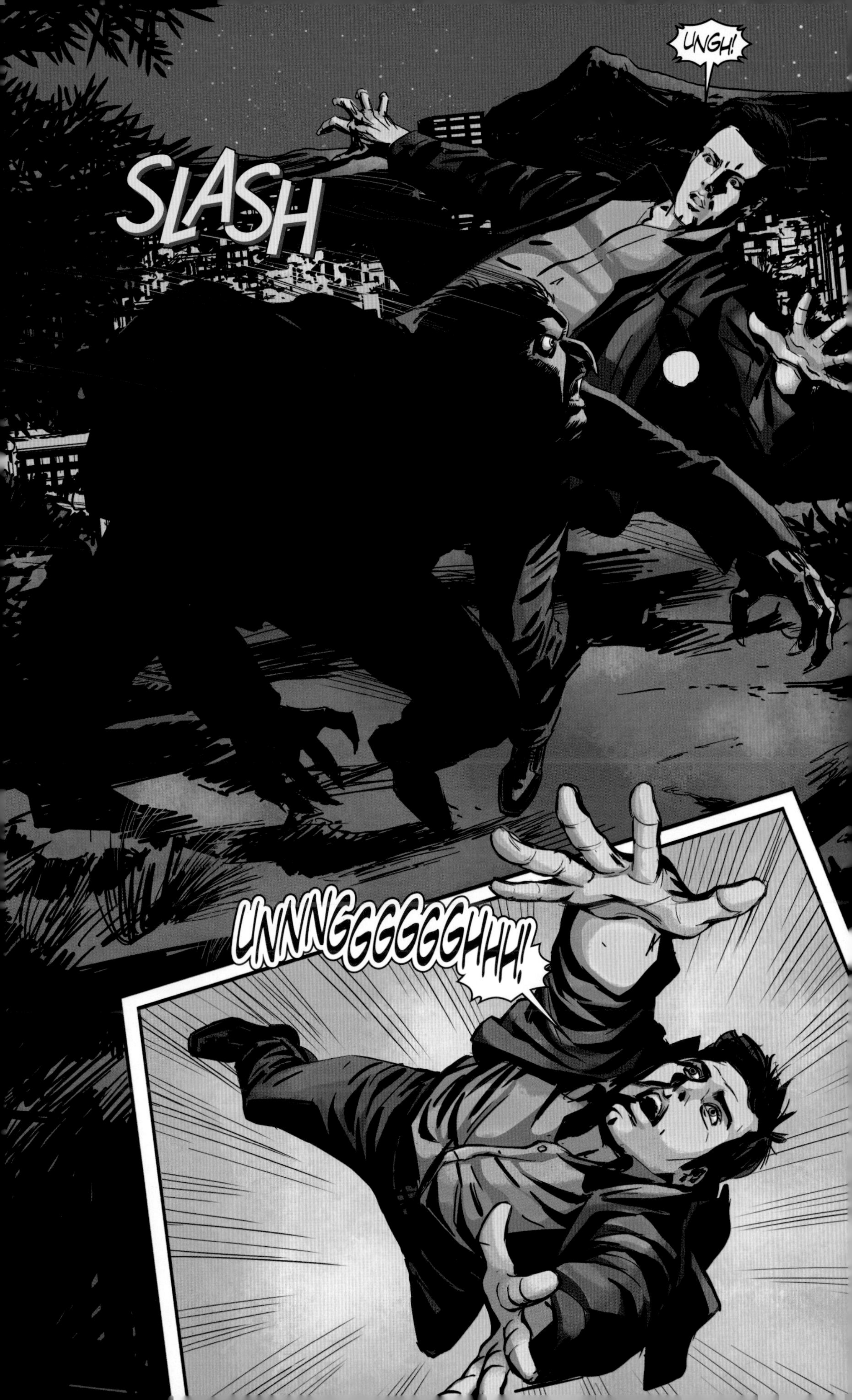
UNGH!
SLASH
UNNNGGGGGGHHH!

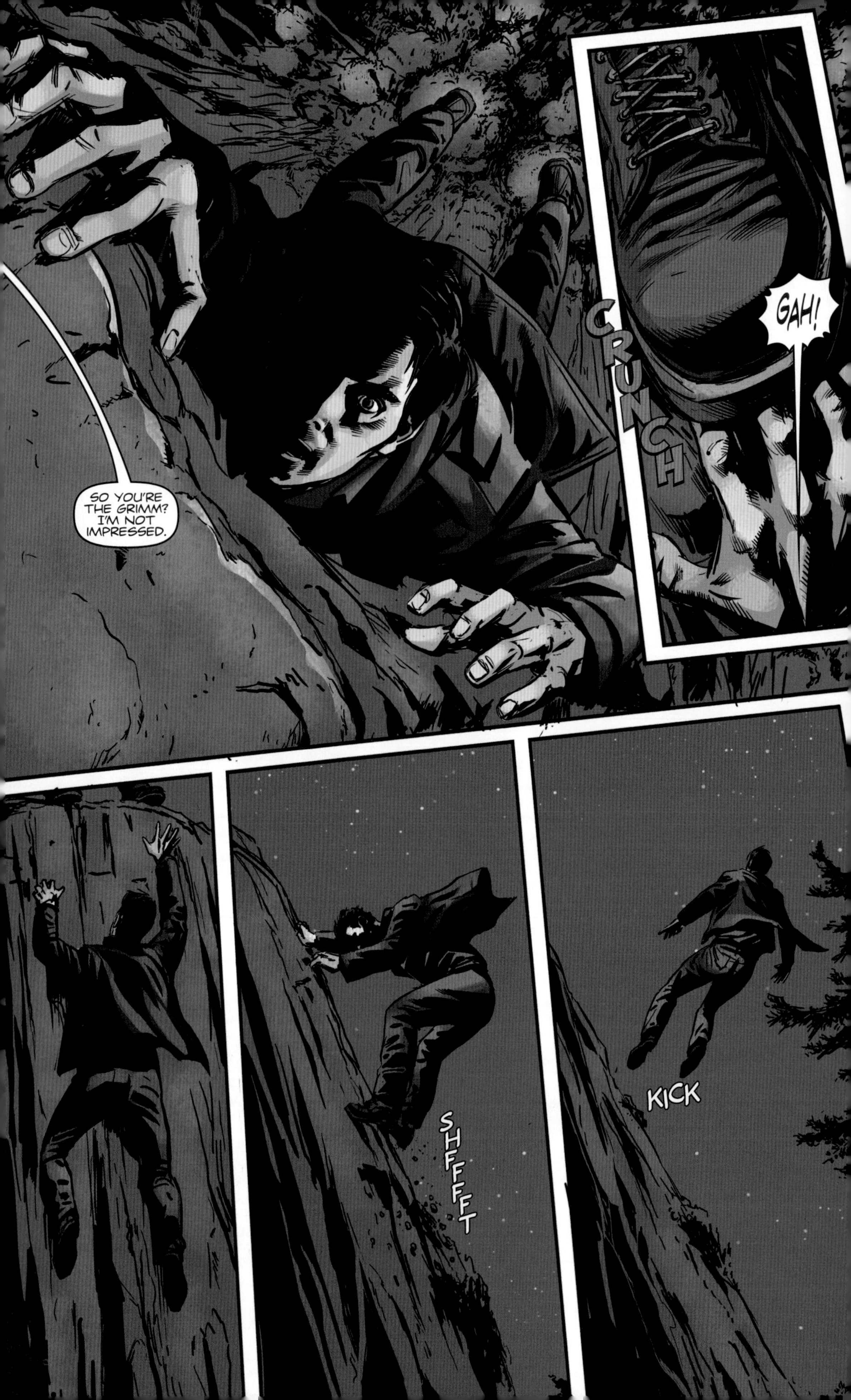
SO YOU'RE THE GRIMM? I'M NOT IMPRESSED.
CRUNCH
GAH!
SHFFFFT
KICK

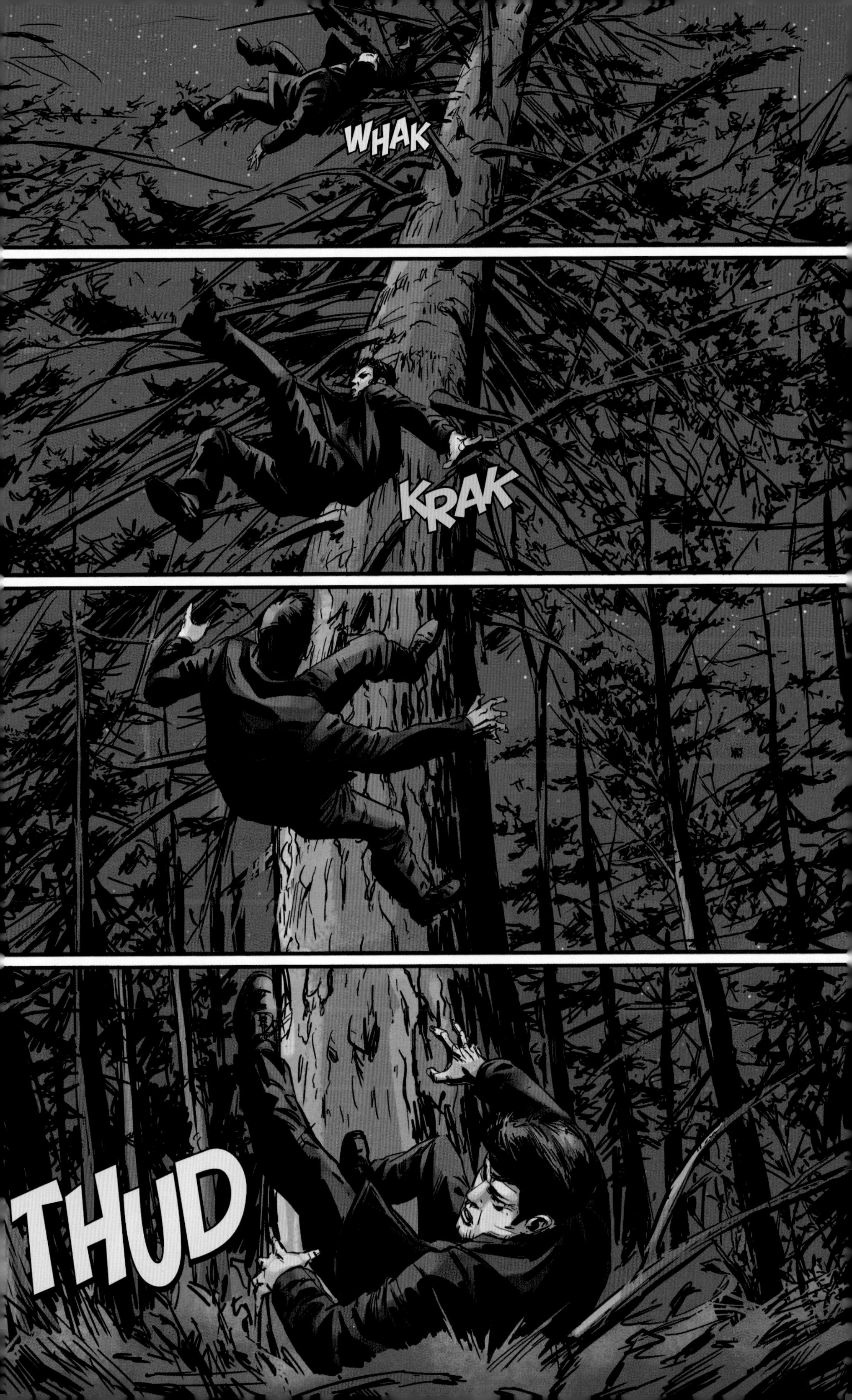
WHAK
KRAK
THUD

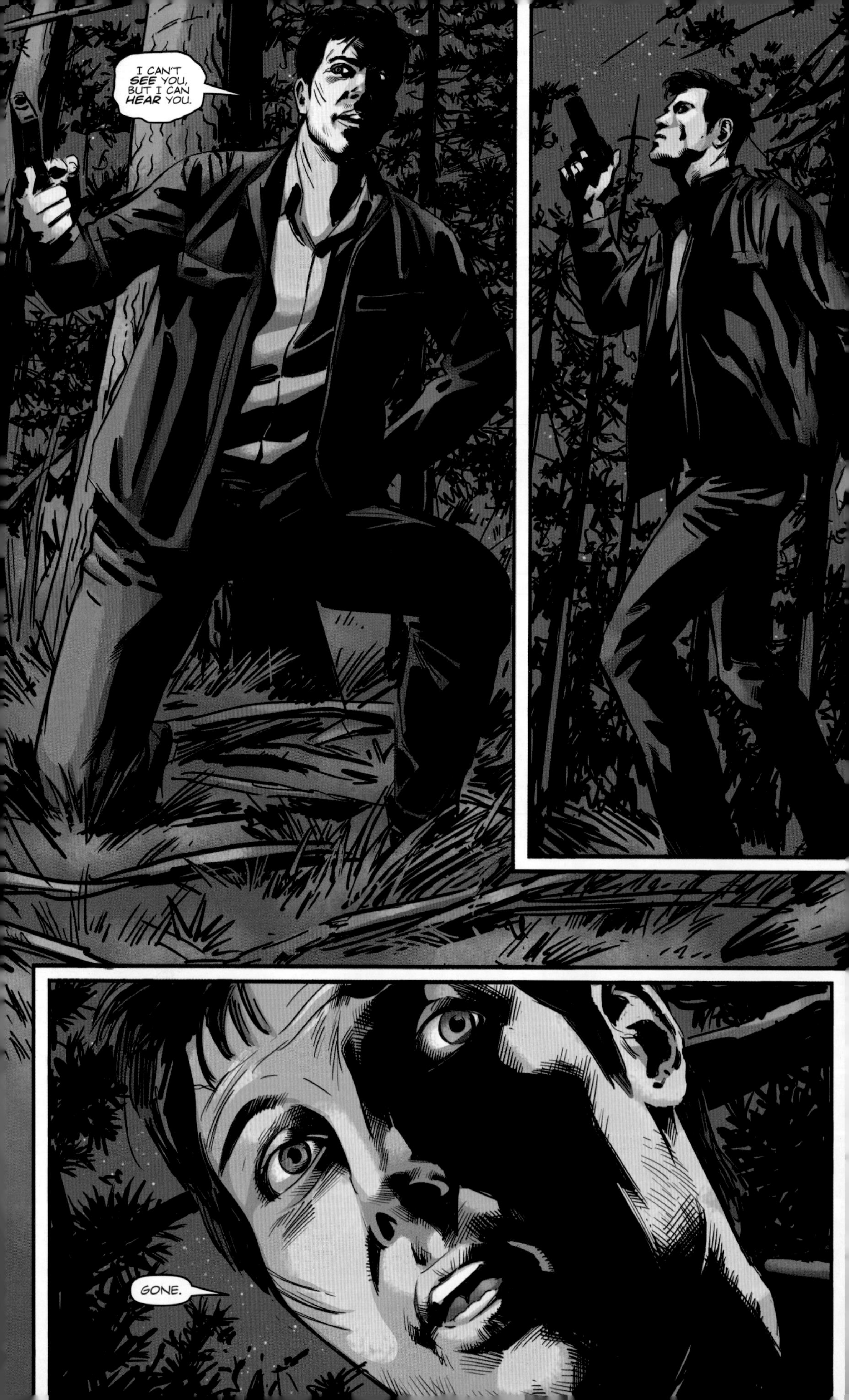
I CAN'T SEE YOU, BUT I CAN HEAR YOU.
GONE.

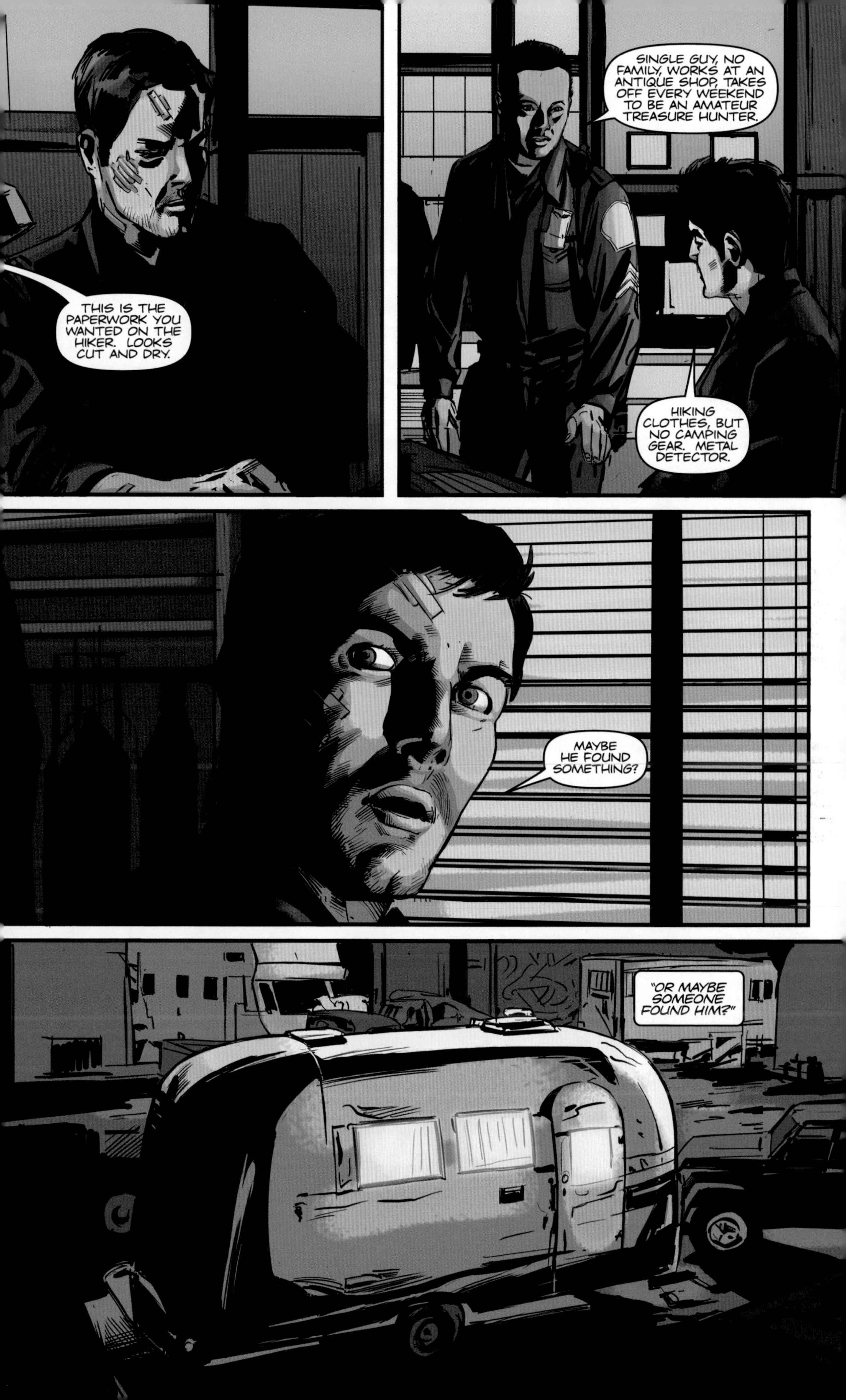
THIS IS THE PAPERWORK YOU WANTED ON THE HIKER. LOOKS CUT AND DRY.
SINGLE GUY, NO FAMILY, WORKS AT AN ANTIQUE SHOP, TAKES OFF EVERY WEEKEND TO BE AN AMATEUR TREASURE HUNTER.
HIKING CLOTHES, BUT NO CAMPING GEAR. METAL DETECTOR.
MAYBE HE FOUND SOMETHING?
"OR MAYBE SOMEONE FOUND HIM?"

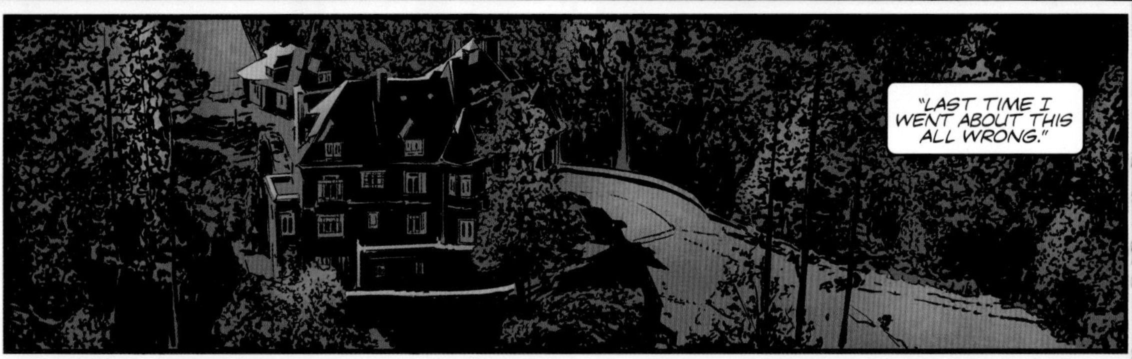
"LAST TIME I WENT ABOUT THIS ALL WRONG."

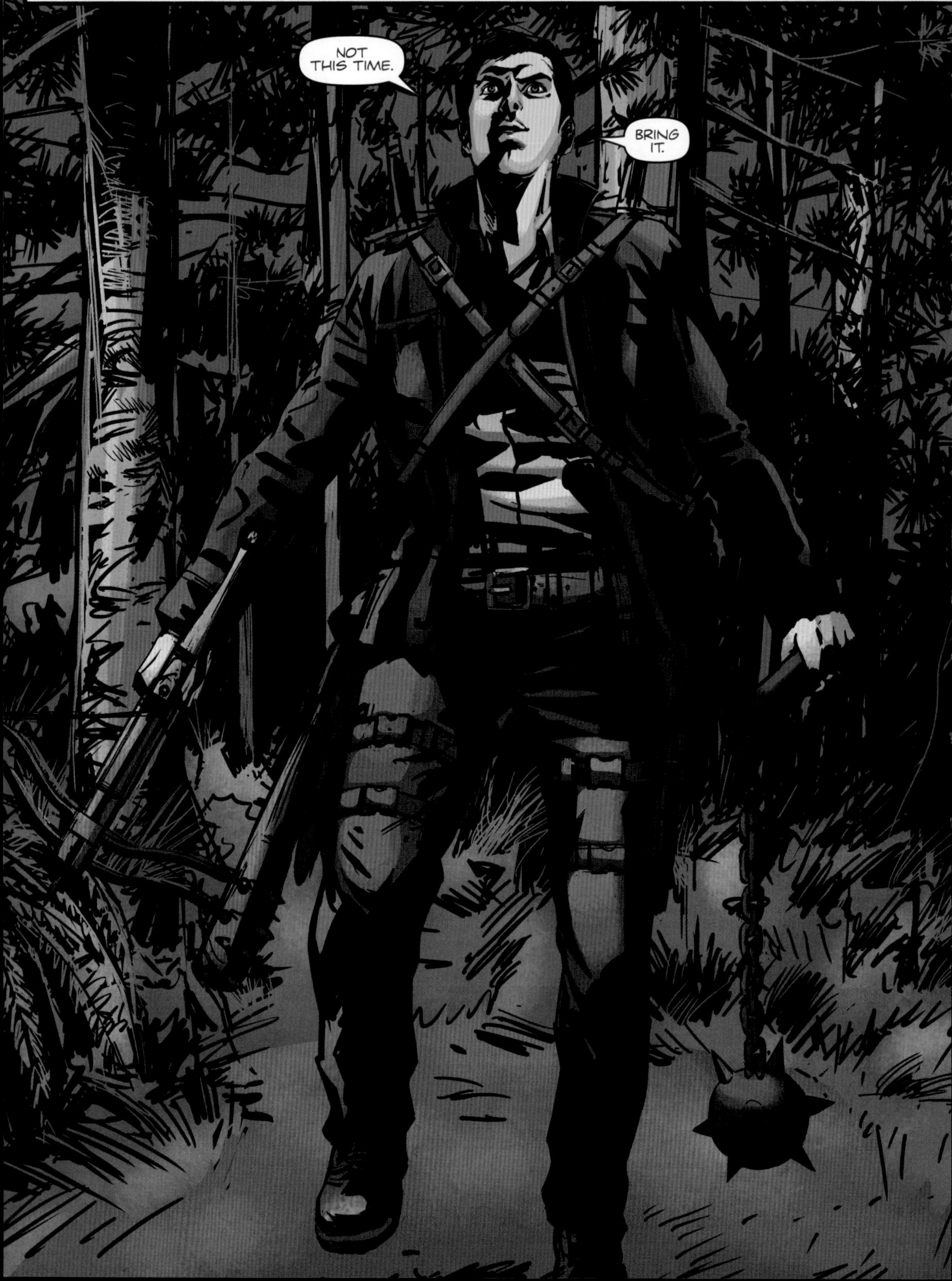
NOT THIS TIME.
BRING IT.

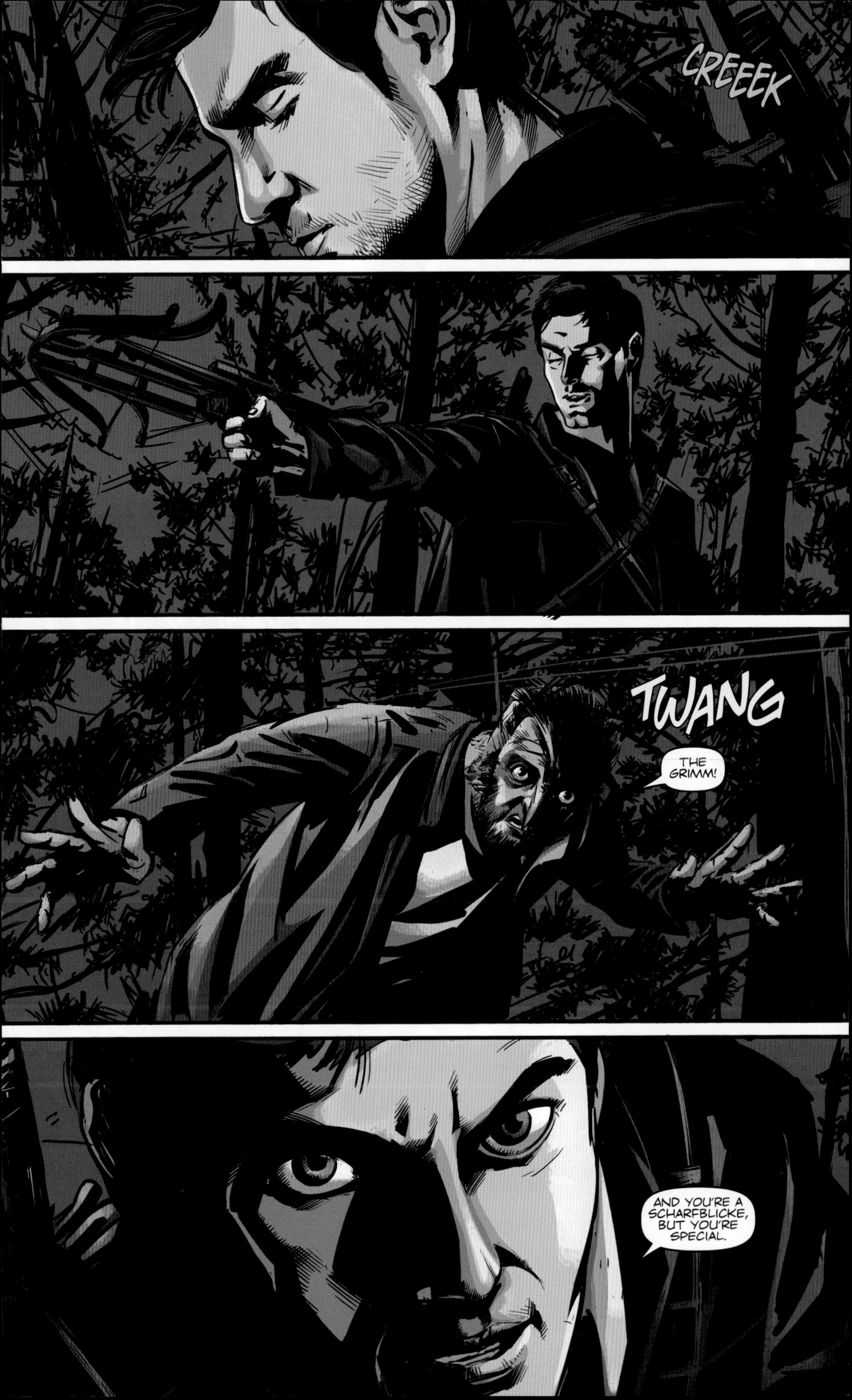
CREEEK
TWANG
THE GRIMM!
AND YOU'RE A SCHARFBLICKE, BUT YOU'RE SPECIAL.

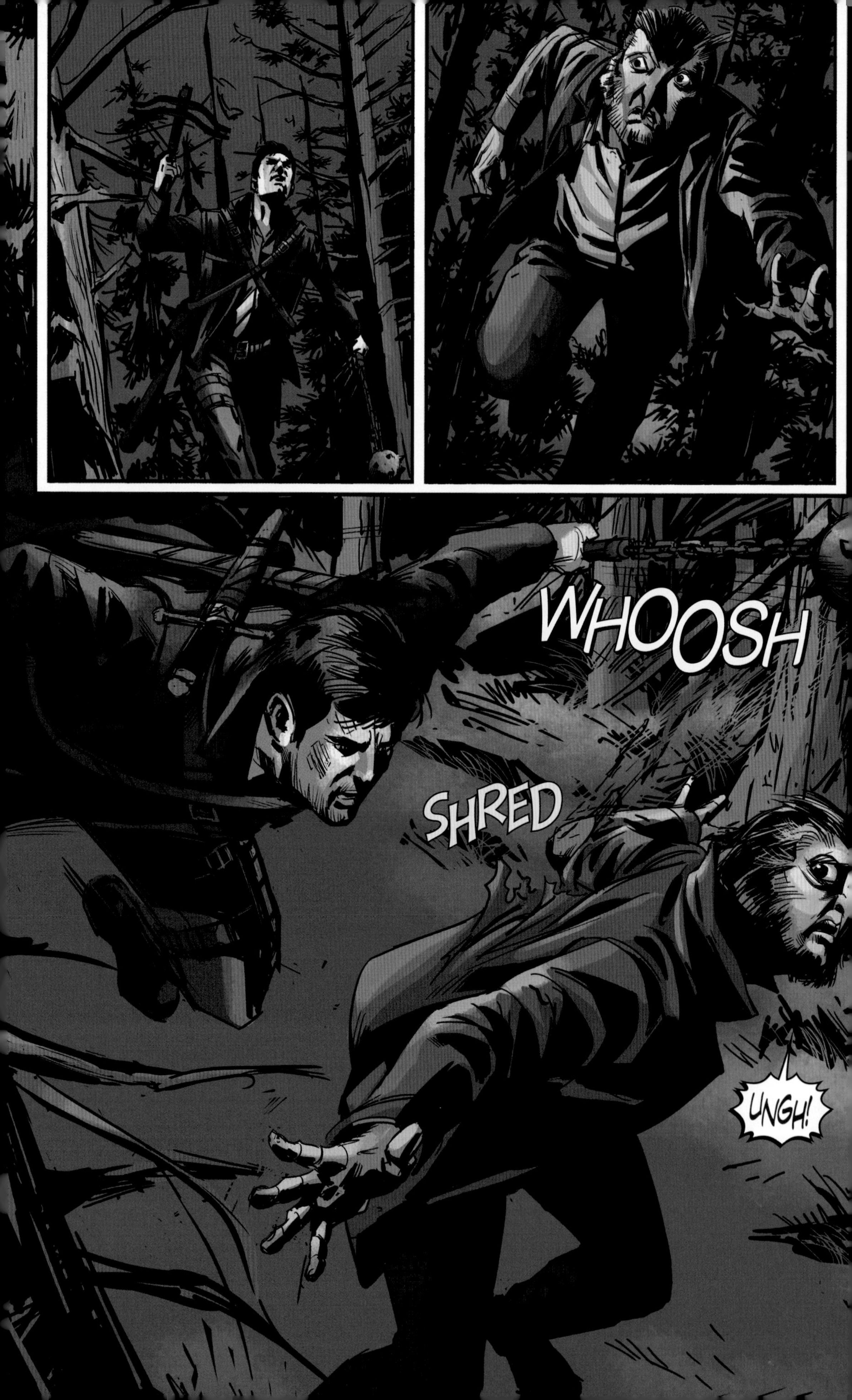
WHOOSH
SHRED
UNGH!

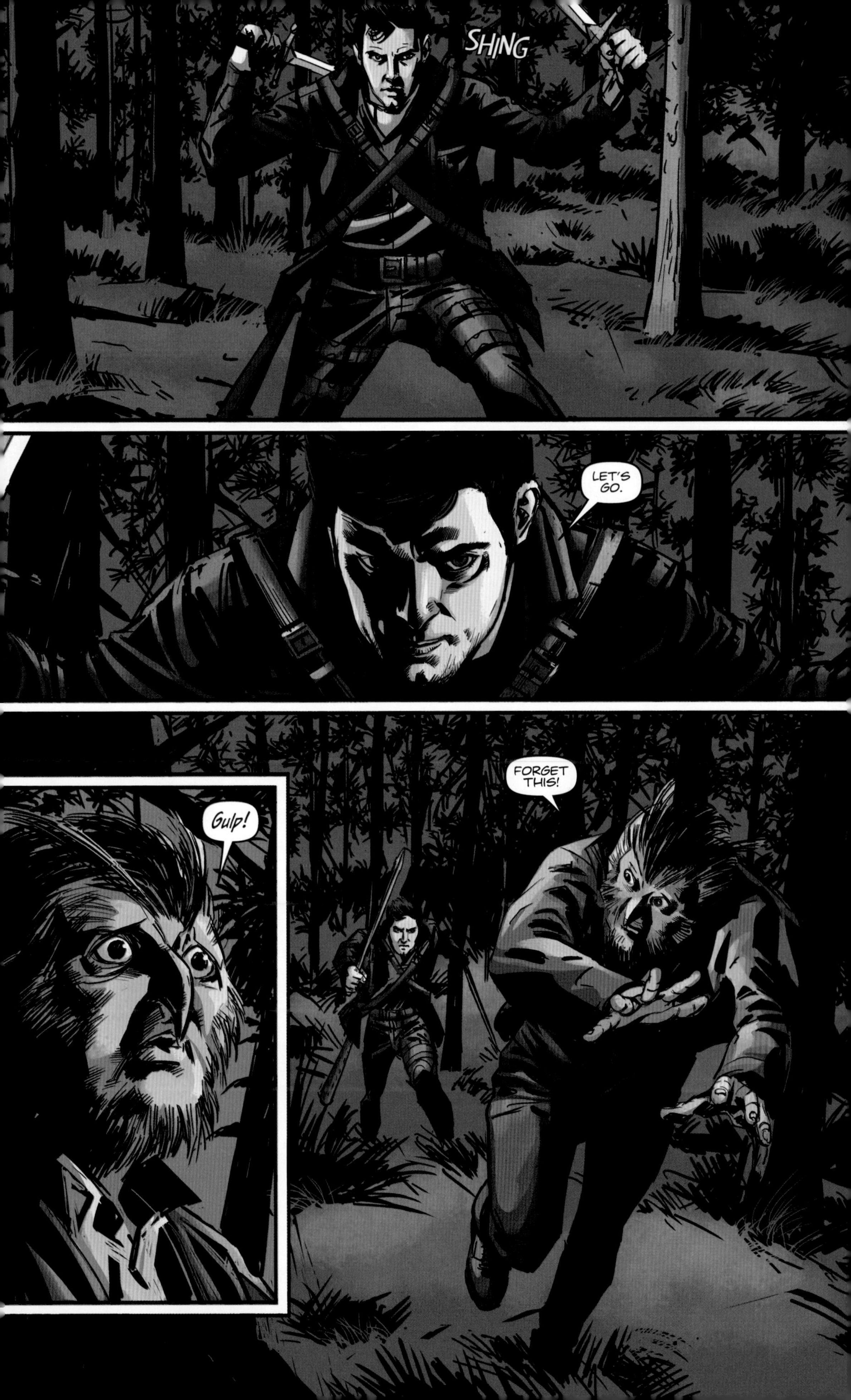
SHING
LET'S GO.
Gulp!
FORGET THIS!

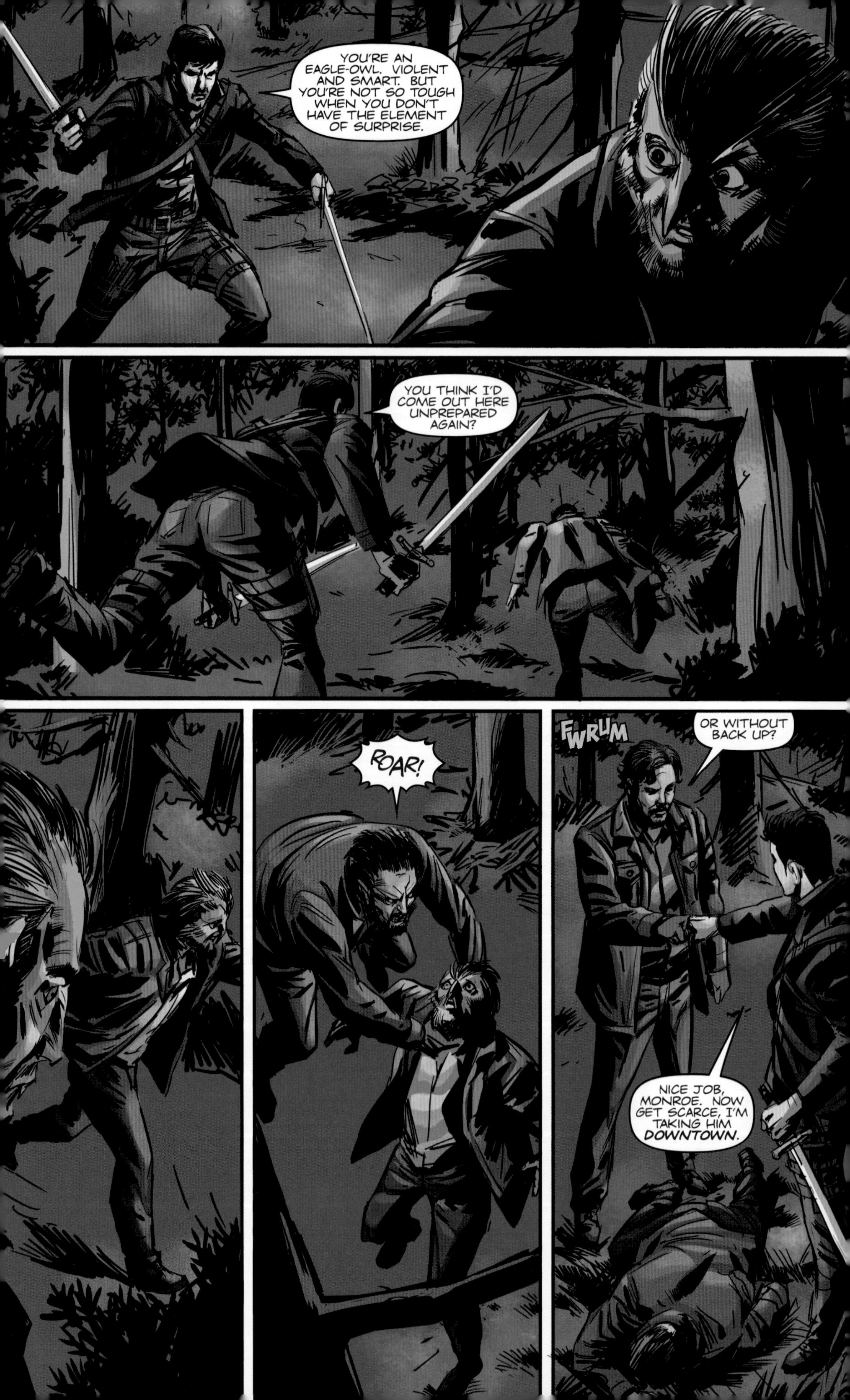
YOU'RE AN EAGLE-OWL. VIOLENT AND SMART. BUT YOU'RE NOT SO TOUGH WHEN YOU DON'T HAVE THE ELEMENT OF SURPRISE.
YOU THINK I'D COME OUT HERE UNPREPARED AGAIN?
ROAR!
FWRUM
OR WITHOUT BACK UP?
NICE JOB, MONROE. NOW GET SCARCE, I'M TAKING HIM DOWNTOWN.

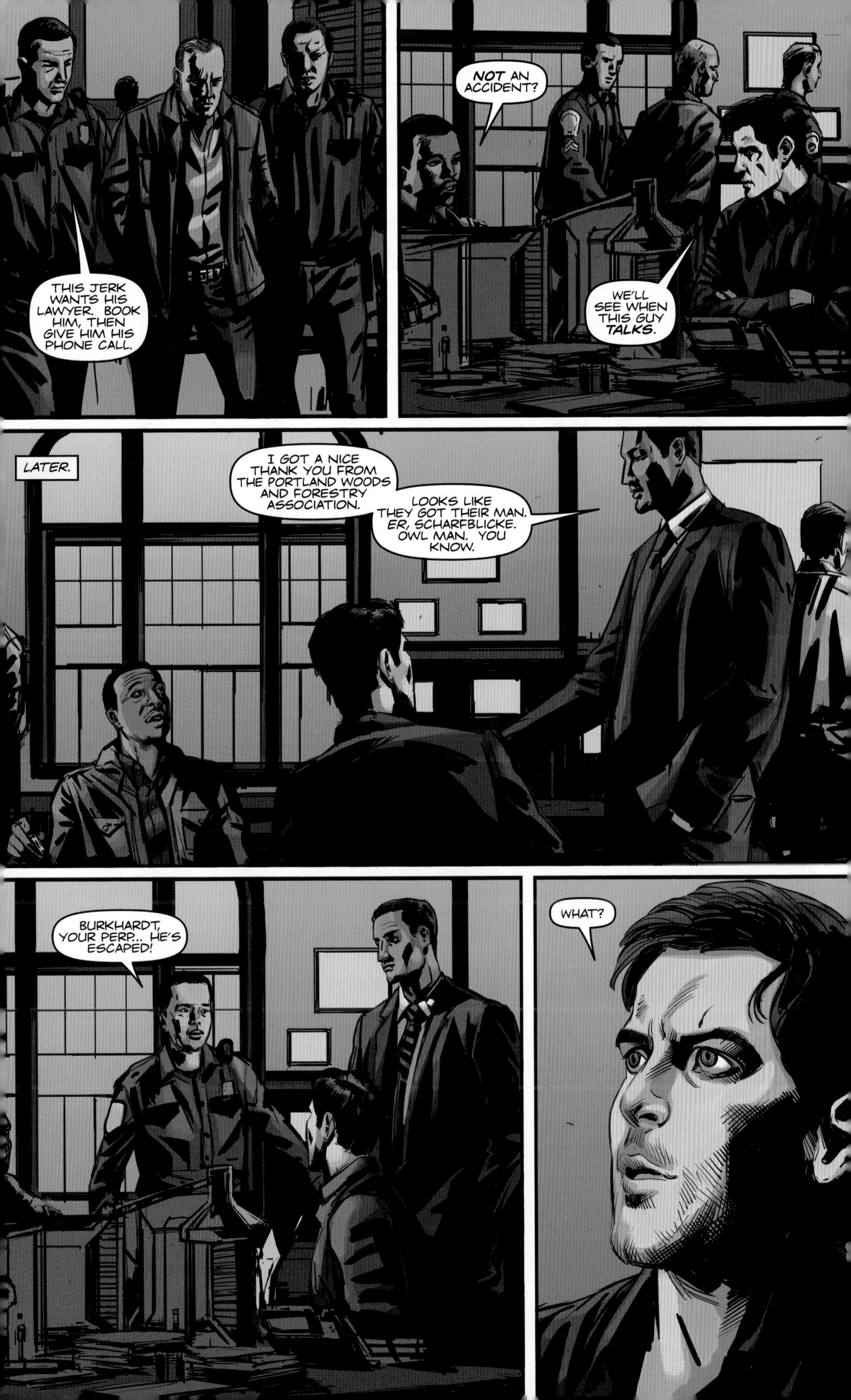
THIS JERK WANTS HIS LAWYER. BOOK HIM, THEN GIVE HIM HIS PHONE CALL.
NOT AN ACCIDENT?
WE'LL SEE WHEN THIS GUY TALKS.
LATER.
I GOT A NICE THANK YOU FROM THE PORTLAND WOODS AND FORESTRY ASSOCIATION.
LOOKS LIKE THEY GOT THEIR MAN. ER, SCHARFBLICKE. OWL MAN. YOU KNOW.
BURKHARDT, YOUR PERP... HE'S ESCAPED!
WHAT?

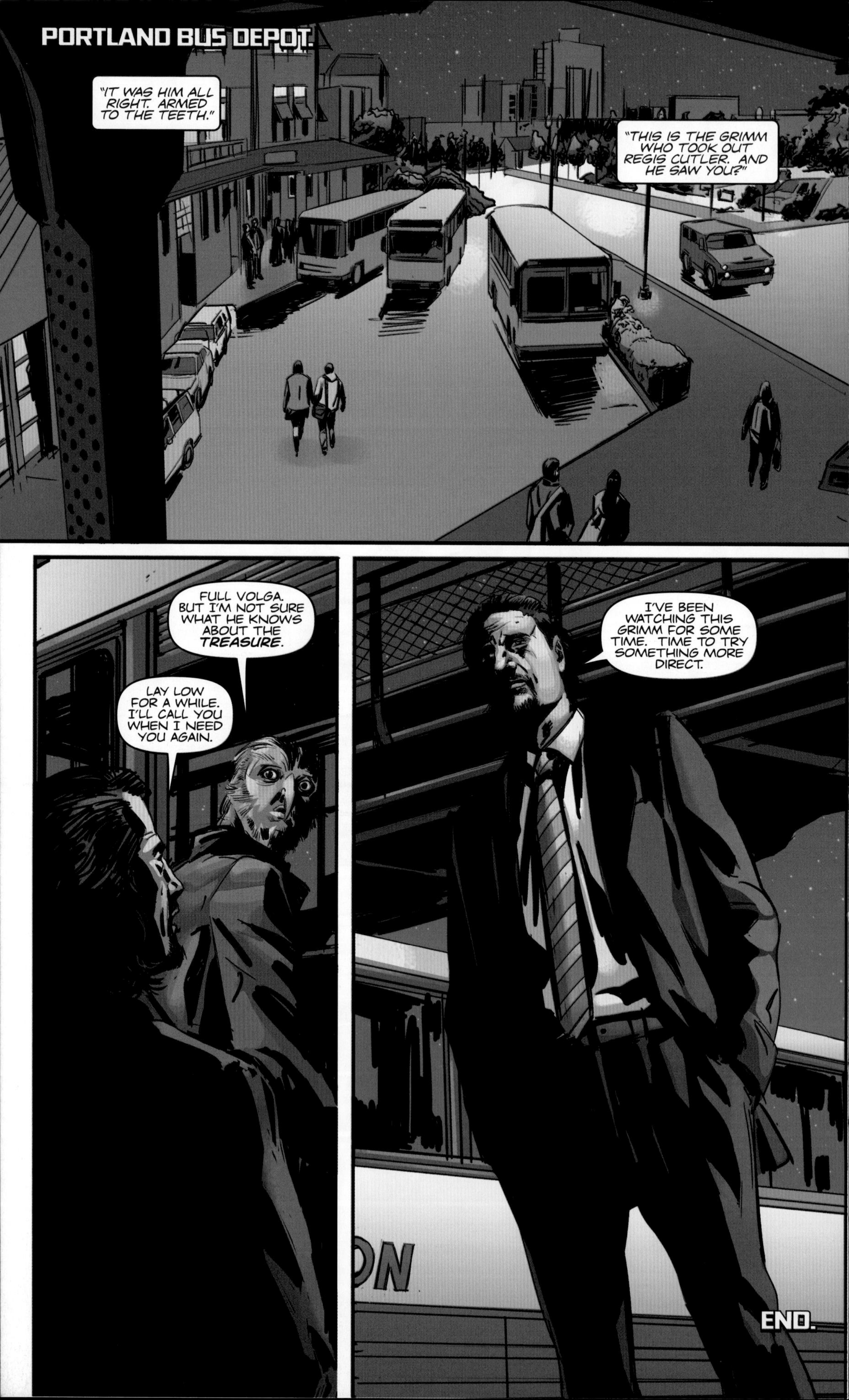
PORTLAND BUS DEPOT.
"IT WAS HIM ALL RIGHT. ARMED TO THE TEETH."
"THIS IS THE GRIMM WHO TOOK OUT REGIS CUTLER. AND HE SAW YOU?"
FULL VOLGA. BUT I'M NOT SURE WHAT HE KNOWS ABOUT THE TREASURE.
LAY LOW FOR A WHILE. I'LL CALL YOU WHEN I NEED YOU AGAIN.
I'VE BEEN WATCHING THIS GRIMM FOR SOME TIME. TIME TO TRY SOMETHING MORE DIRECT.
END.

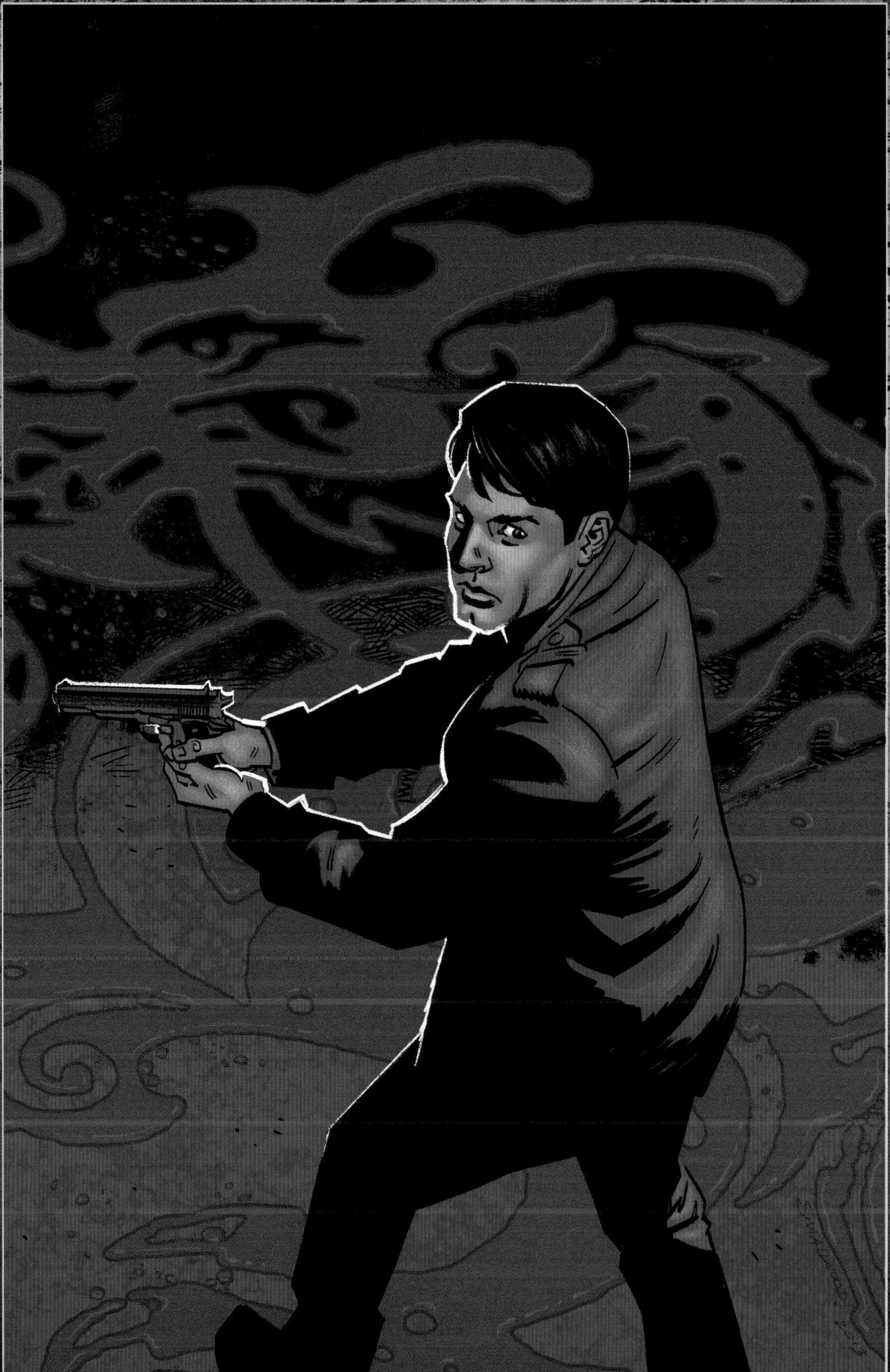

GRIMM: THE WARLOCK ISSUE #3 COVER
ART BY GREG SMALLWOOD

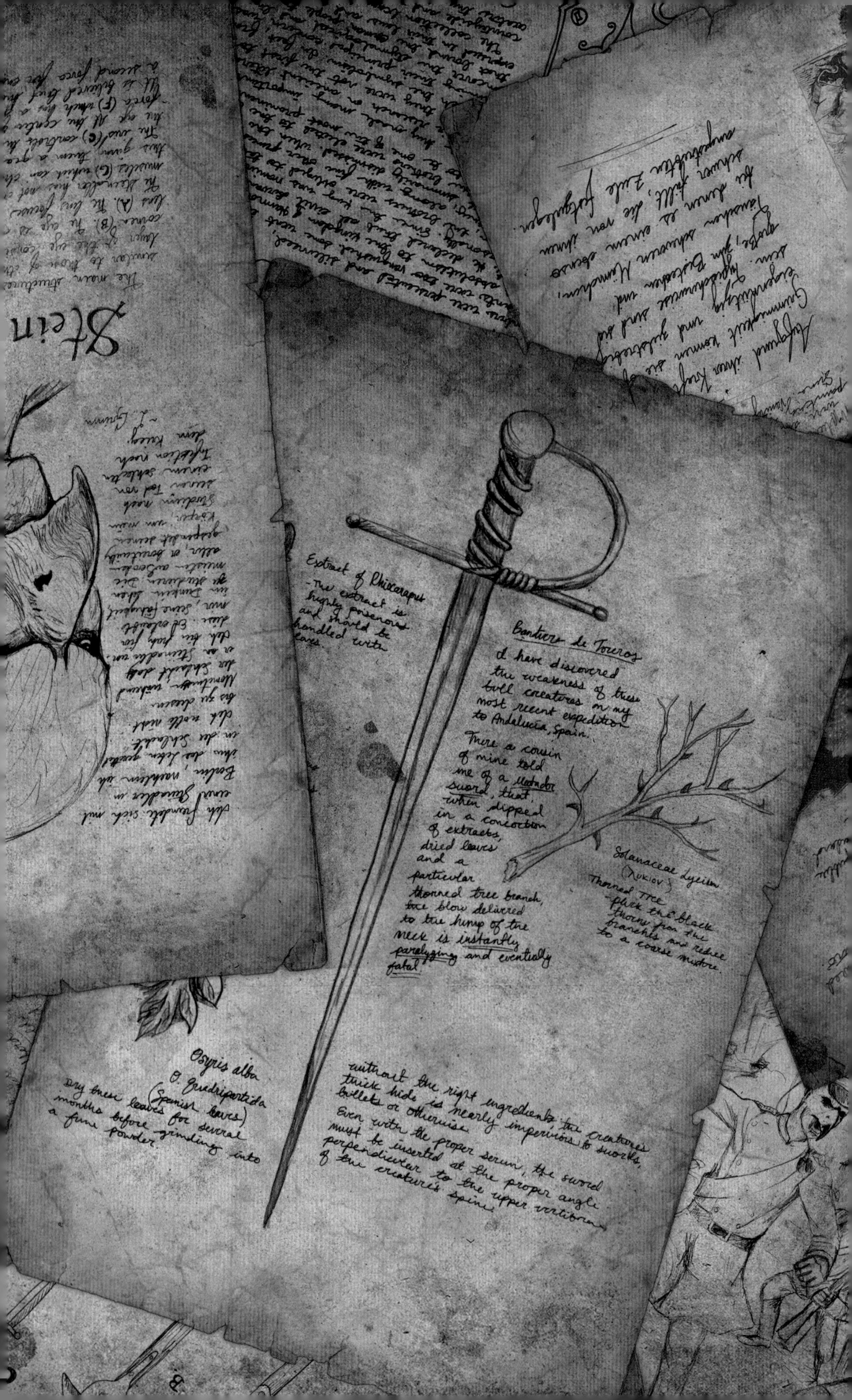
Extract of Rhixarapus
-The extract is highly poisonous and should be handled with care.
Banticro de Toreros
I have discovered the weakness of these bull creatures on my most recent expedition to Andalucia, Spain.
There a cousin of mine told me of a Matador sword, that, when dipped in a concoction of extracts, dried leaves and a particular thorned tree branch, the blow delivered to the hump of the neck is instantly paralyzing and eventually fatal.
Solanaceae Lycium
(Λυκιον)
Thorned Tree
-pluck the black thorns from the branches and reduce to a coarse mixture.
Osyris alba
O. Quadripartida
(Spanish leaves)
Dry these leaves for several months before grinding into a fine powder.
without the right ingredients, the creature's thick hide is nearly impervious to swords, billets or otherwise.
Even with the proper serum, the sword must be inserted at the proper angle perpendicular to the upper vertibrae of the creature's spine.
Stein

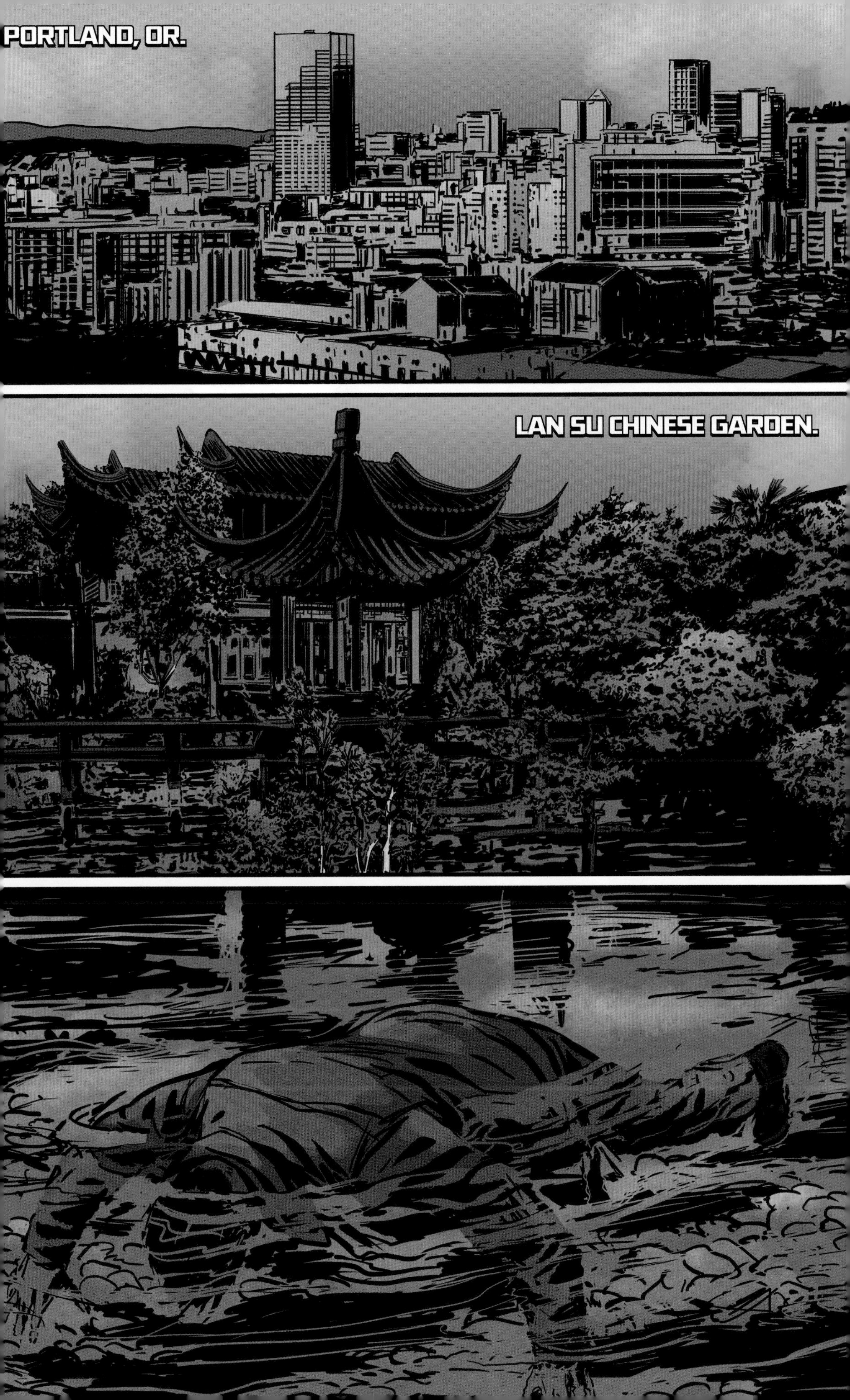
PORTLAND, OR.
LAN SU CHINESE GARDEN.

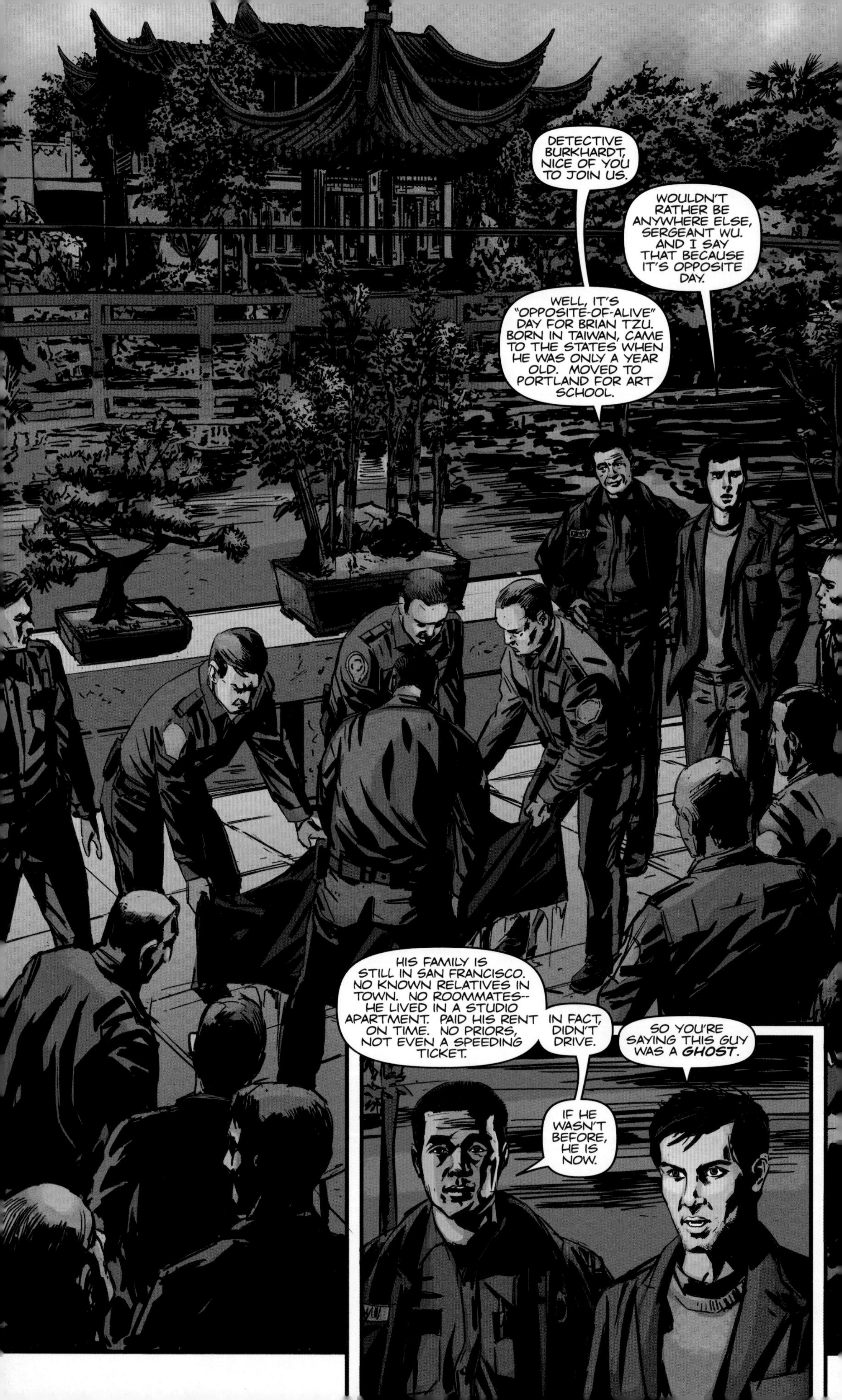
DETECTIVE BURKHARDT, NICE OF YOU TO JOIN US.
WOULDN'T RATHER BE ANYWHERE ELSE, SERGEANT WU. AND I SAY THAT BECAUSE IT'S OPPOSITE DAY.
WELL, IT'S "OPPOSITE-OF-ALIVE" DAY FOR BRIAN TZU. BORN IN TAIWAN, CAME TO THE STATES WHEN HE WAS ONLY A YEAR OLD. MOVED TO PORTLAND FOR ART SCHOOL.
HIS FAMILY IS STILL IN SAN FRANCISCO. NO KNOWN RELATIVES IN TOWN. NO ROOMMATES-- HE LIVED IN A STUDIO APARTMENT. PAID HIS RENT ON TIME. NO PRIORS, NOT EVEN A SPEEDING TICKET.
IN FACT, DIDN'T DRIVE.
SO YOU'RE SAYING THIS GUY WAS A GHOST.
IF HE WASN'T BEFORE, HE IS NOW.

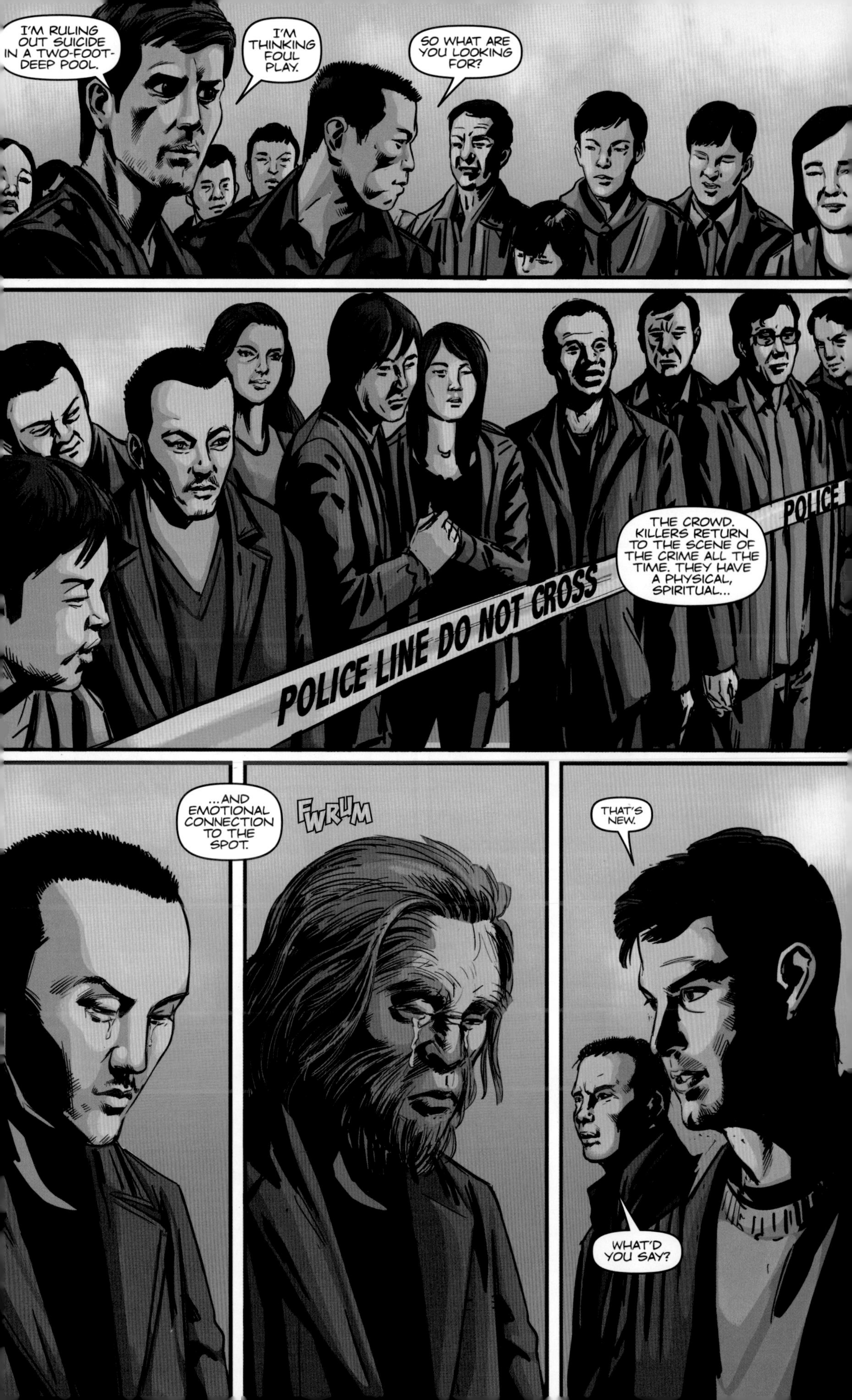
I'M RULING OUT SUICIDE IN A TWO-FOOT-DEEP POOL.
I'M THINKING FOUL PLAY.
SO WHAT ARE YOU LOOKING FOR?
POLICE LINE DO NOT CROSS
POLICE
THE CROWD. KILLERS RETURN TO THE SCENE OF THE CRIME ALL THE TIME. THEY HAVE A PHYSICAL, SPIRITUAL...
...AND EMOTIONAL CONNECTION TO THE SPOT.
FWRUM
THAT'S NEW.
WHAT'D YOU SAY?

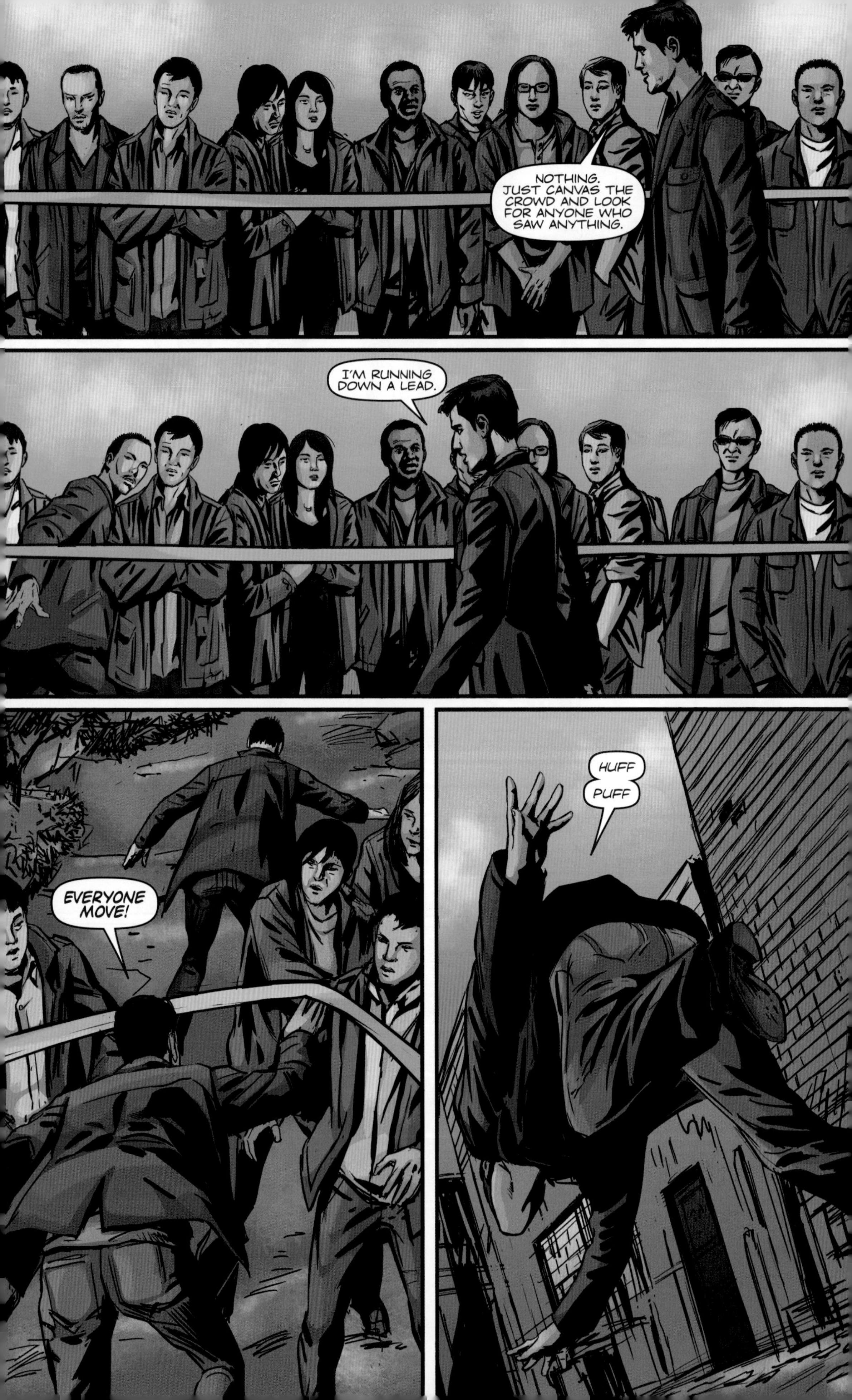
NOTHING. JUST CANVAS THE CROWD AND LOOK FOR ANYONE WHO SAW ANYTHING.
I'M RUNNING DOWN A LEAD.
EVERYONE MOVE!
HUFF
PUFF

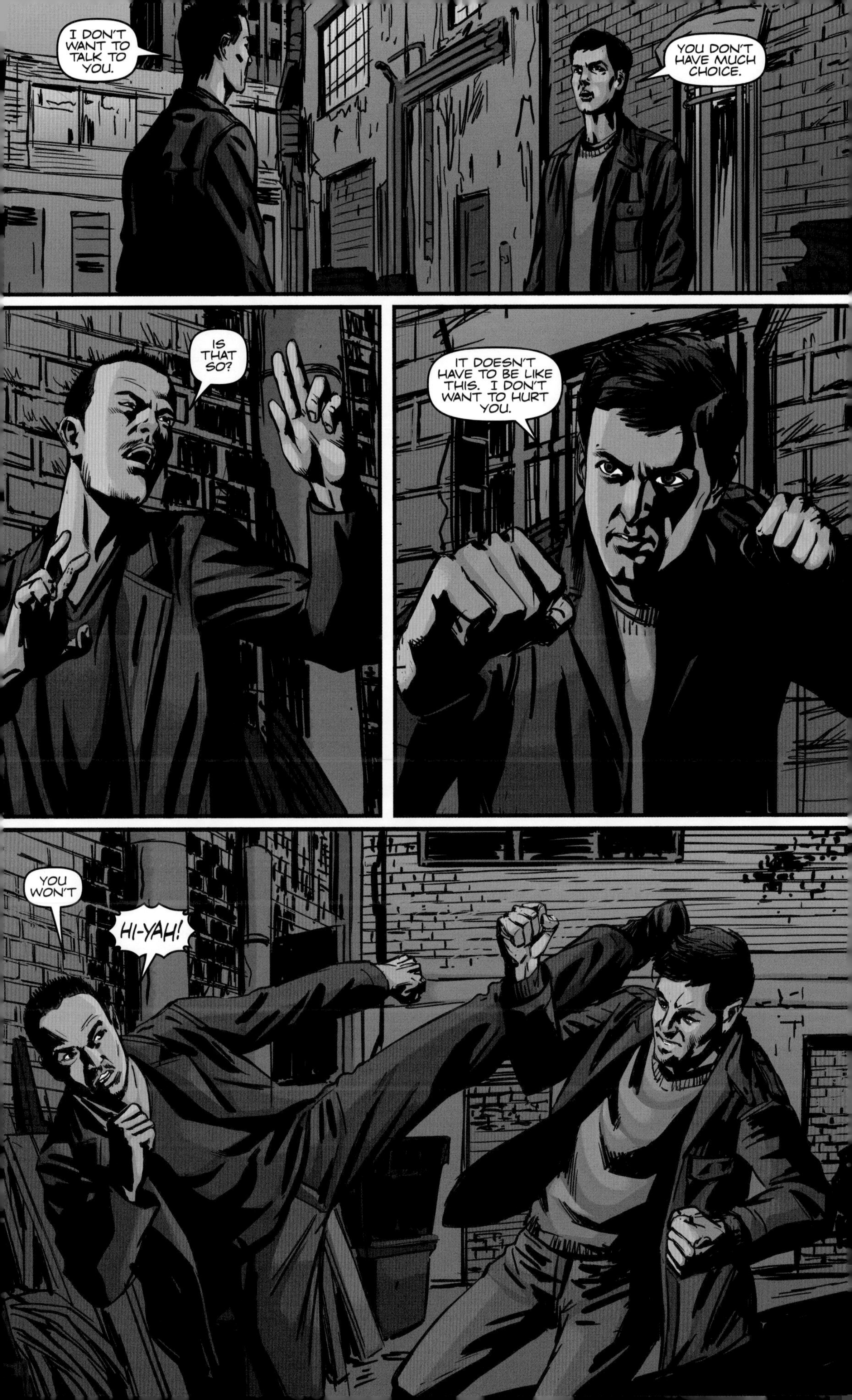
I DON'T WANT TO TALK TO YOU.
YOU DON'T HAVE MUCH CHOICE.
IS THAT SO?
IT DOESN'T HAVE TO BE LIKE THIS. I DON'T WANT TO HURT YOU.
YOU WON'T
HI-YAH!

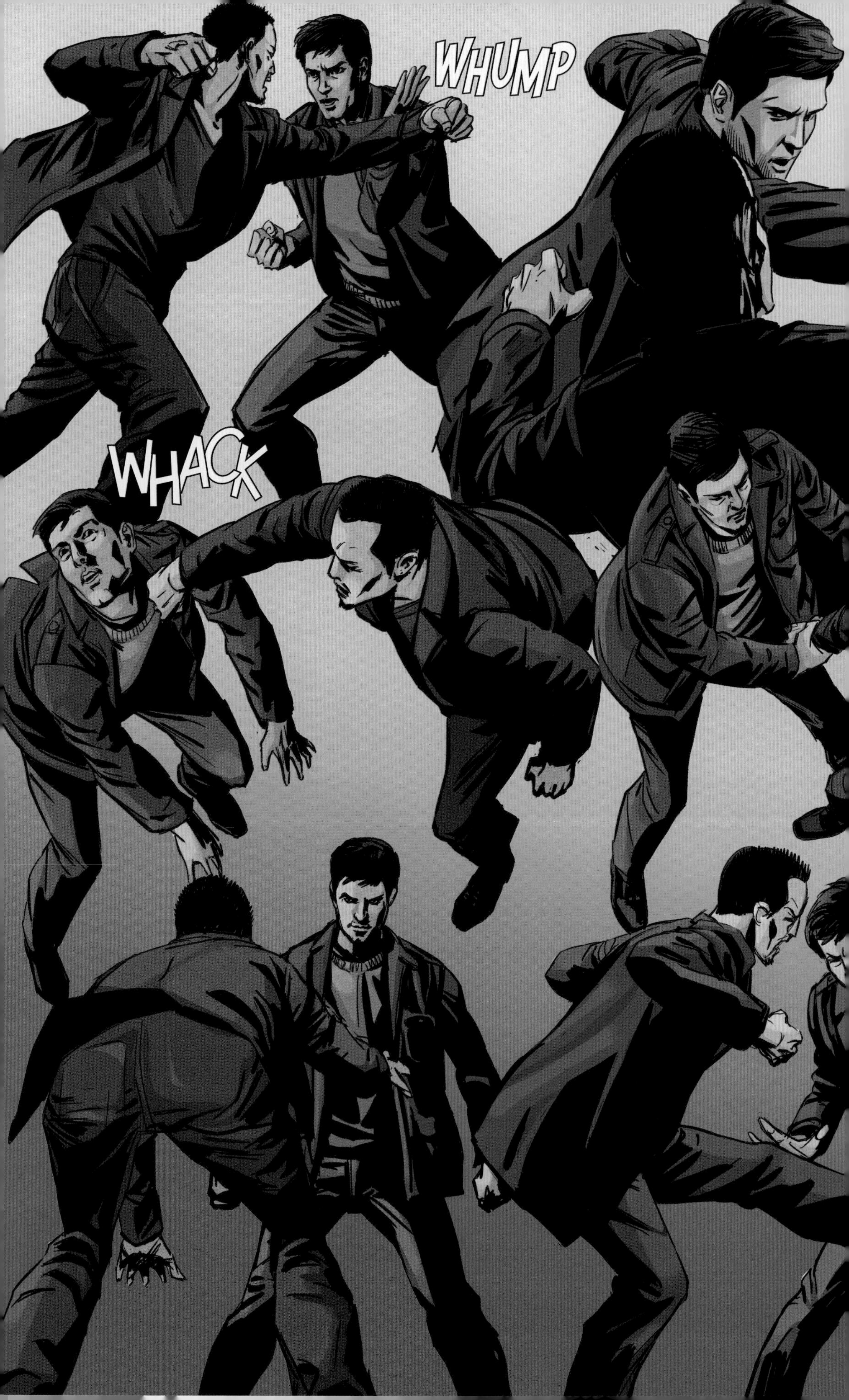
WHUMP
WHACK

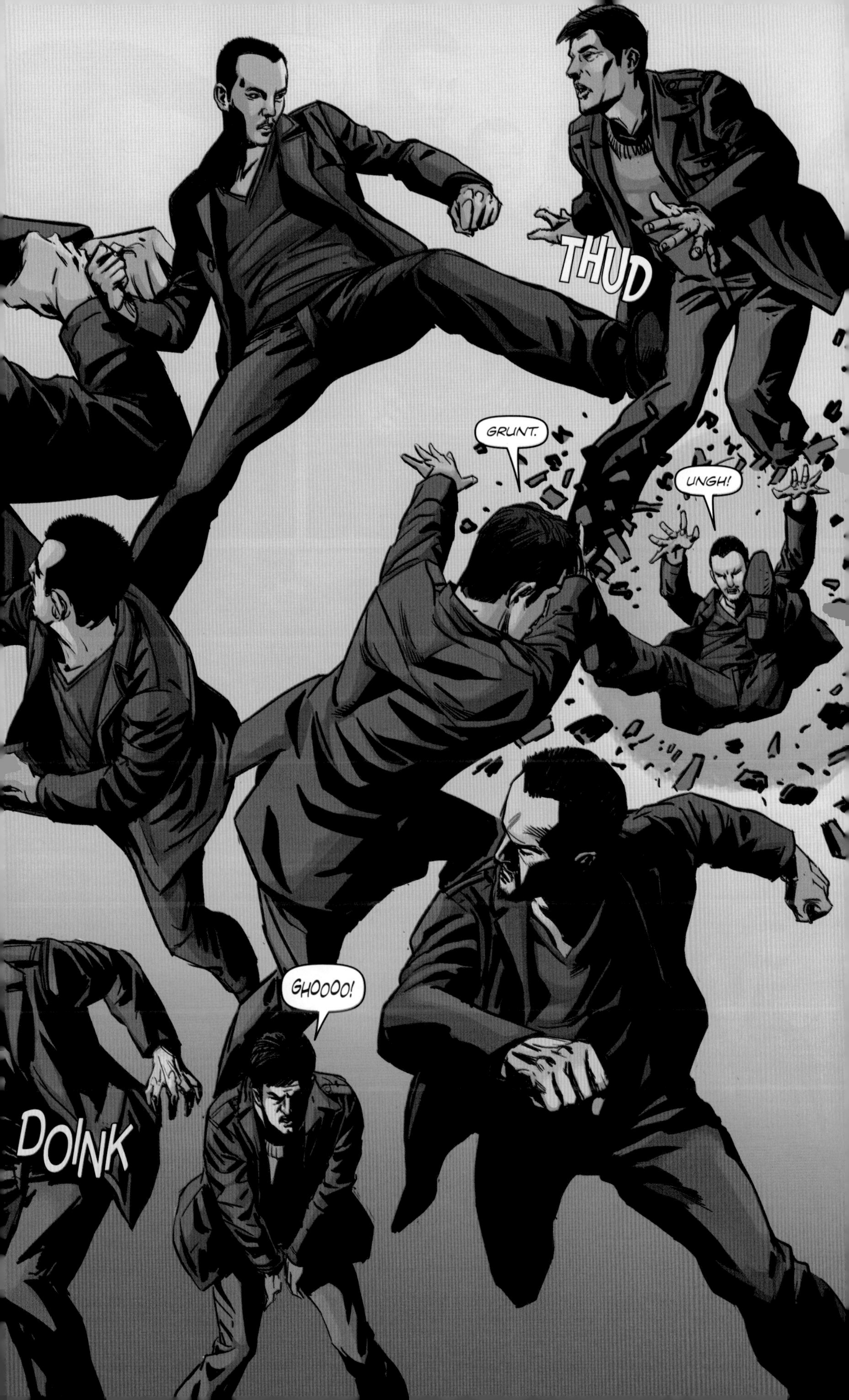
THUD
GRUNT.
UNGH!
GHOOOO!
DOINK

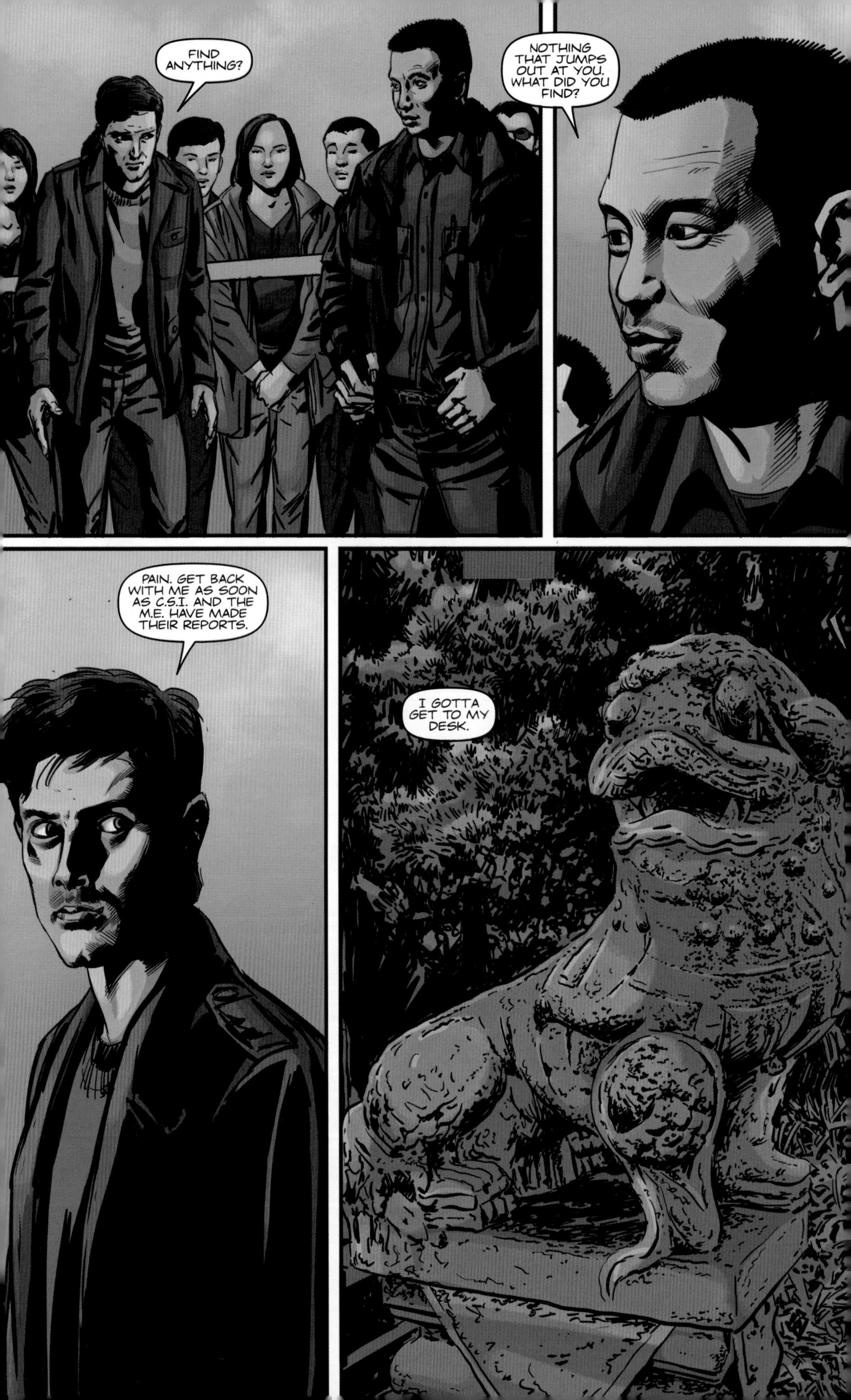
FIND ANYTHING?
NOTHING THAT JUMPS OUT AT YOU. WHAT DID YOU FIND?
PAIN. GET BACK WITH ME AS SOON AS C.S.I. AND THE M.E. HAVE MADE THEIR REPORTS.
I GOTTA GET TO MY DESK.

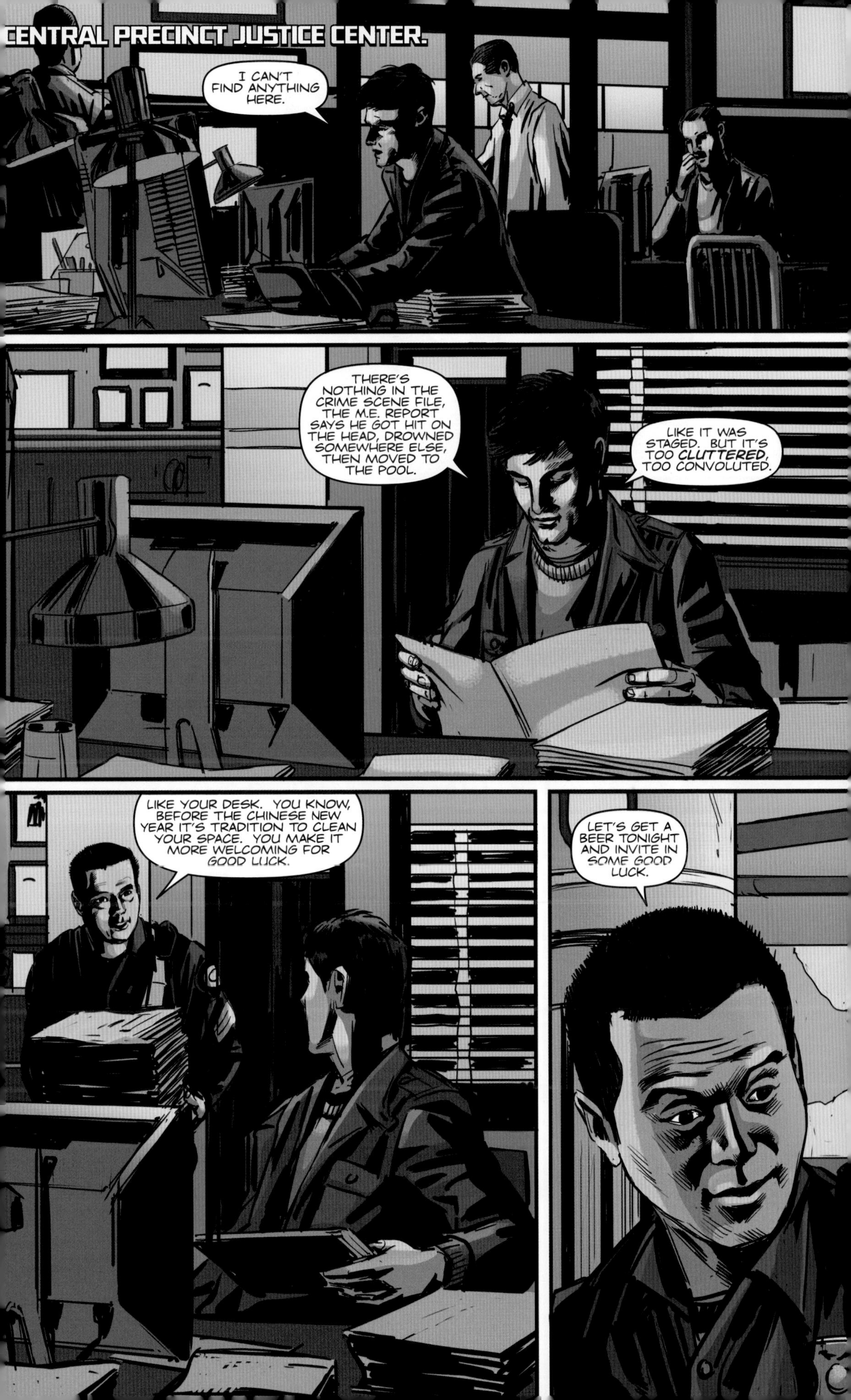
CENTRAL PRECINCT JUSTICE CENTER.
I CAN'T FIND ANYTHING HERE.
THERE'S NOTHING IN THE CRIME SCENE FILE, THE M.E. REPORT SAYS HE GOT HIT ON THE HEAD, DROWNED SOMEWHERE ELSE, THEN MOVED TO THE POOL.
LIKE IT WAS STAGED. BUT IT'S TOO CLUTTERED, TOO CONVOLUTED.
LIKE YOUR DESK. YOU KNOW, BEFORE THE CHINESE NEW YEAR IT'S TRADITION TO CLEAN YOUR SPACE. YOU MAKE IT MORE WELCOMING FOR GOOD LUCK.
LET'S GET A BEER TONIGHT AND INVITE IN SOME GOOD LUCK.

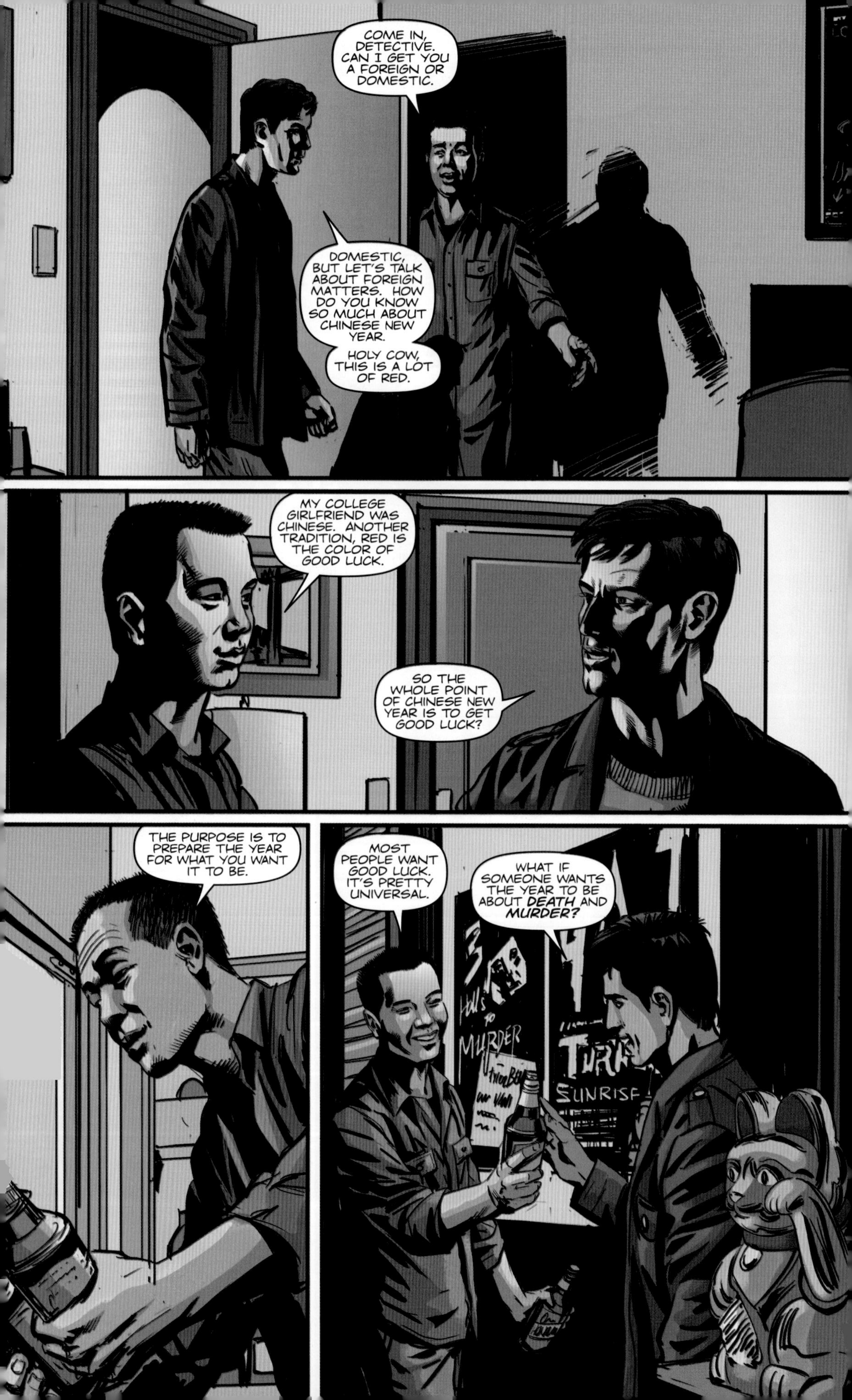
COME IN, DETECTIVE. CAN I GET YOU A FOREIGN OR DOMESTIC.
DOMESTIC, BUT LET'S TALK ABOUT FOREIGN MATTERS. HOW DO YOU KNOW SO MUCH ABOUT CHINESE NEW YEAR.
HOLY COW, THIS IS A LOT OF RED.
MY COLLEGE GIRLFRIEND WAS CHINESE. ANOTHER TRADITION, RED IS THE COLOR OF GOOD LUCK.
SO THE WHOLE POINT OF CHINESE NEW YEAR IS TO GET GOOD LUCK?
THE PURPOSE IS TO PREPARE THE YEAR FOR WHAT YOU WANT IT TO BE.
MOST PEOPLE WANT GOOD LUCK. IT'S PRETTY UNIVERSAL.
WHAT IF SOMEONE WANTS THE YEAR TO BE ABOUT *DEATH* AND *MURDER?*
MURDER
SUNRISE

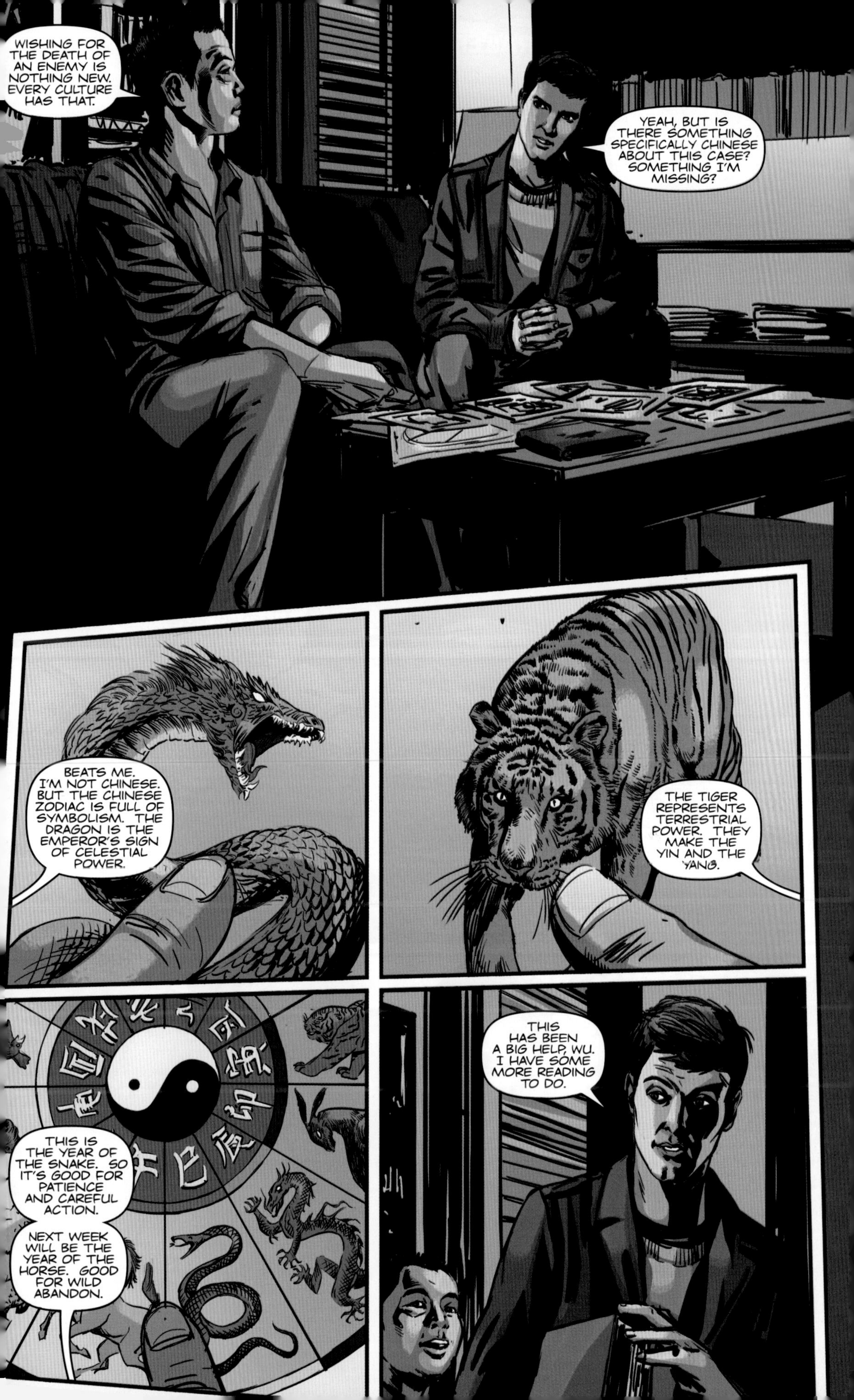
WISHING FOR THE DEATH OF AN ENEMY IS NOTHING NEW. EVERY CULTURE HAS THAT.
YEAH, BUT IS THERE SOMETHING SPECIFICALLY CHINESE ABOUT THIS CASE? SOMETHING I'M MISSING?
BEATS ME. I'M NOT CHINESE. BUT THE CHINESE ZODIAC IS FULL OF SYMBOLISM. THE DRAGON IS THE EMPEROR'S SIGN OF CELESTIAL POWER.
THE TIGER REPRESENTS TERRESTRIAL POWER. THEY MAKE THE YIN AND THE YANG.
THIS IS THE YEAR OF THE SNAKE. SO IT'S GOOD FOR PATIENCE AND CAREFUL ACTION.
NEXT WEEK WILL BE THE YEAR OF THE HORSE. GOOD FOR WILD ABANDON.
THIS HAS BEEN A BIG HELP, WU. I HAVE SOME MORE READING TO DO.

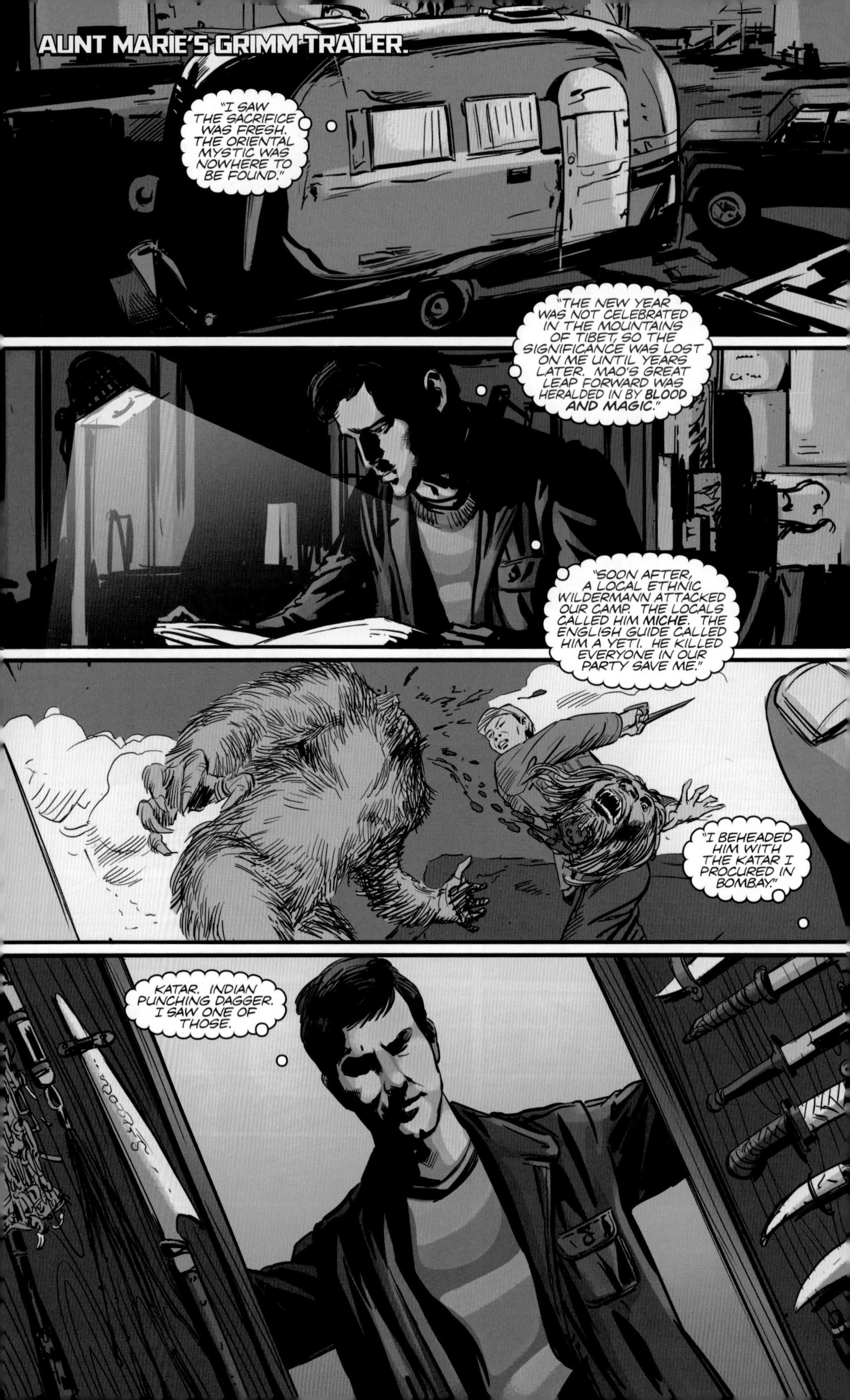
AUNT MARIE'S GRIMM TRAILER.
"I SAW THE SACRIFICE WAS FRESH. THE ORIENTAL MYSTIC WAS NOWHERE TO BE FOUND."
"THE NEW YEAR WAS NOT CELEBRATED IN THE MOUNTAINS OF TIBET, SO THE SIGNIFICANCE WAS LOST ON ME UNTIL YEARS LATER. MAO'S GREAT LEAP FORWARD WAS HERALDED IN BY BLOOD AND MAGIC."
"SOON AFTER, A LOCAL ETHNIC WILDERMANN ATTACKED OUR CAMP. THE LOCALS CALLED HIM MICHE. THE ENGLISH GUIDE CALLED HIM A YETI. HE KILLED EVERYONE IN OUR PARTY SAVE ME."
"I BEHEADED HIM WITH THE KATAR I PROCURED IN BOMBAY."
KATAR. INDIAN PUNCHING DAGGER. I SAW ONE OF THOSE.

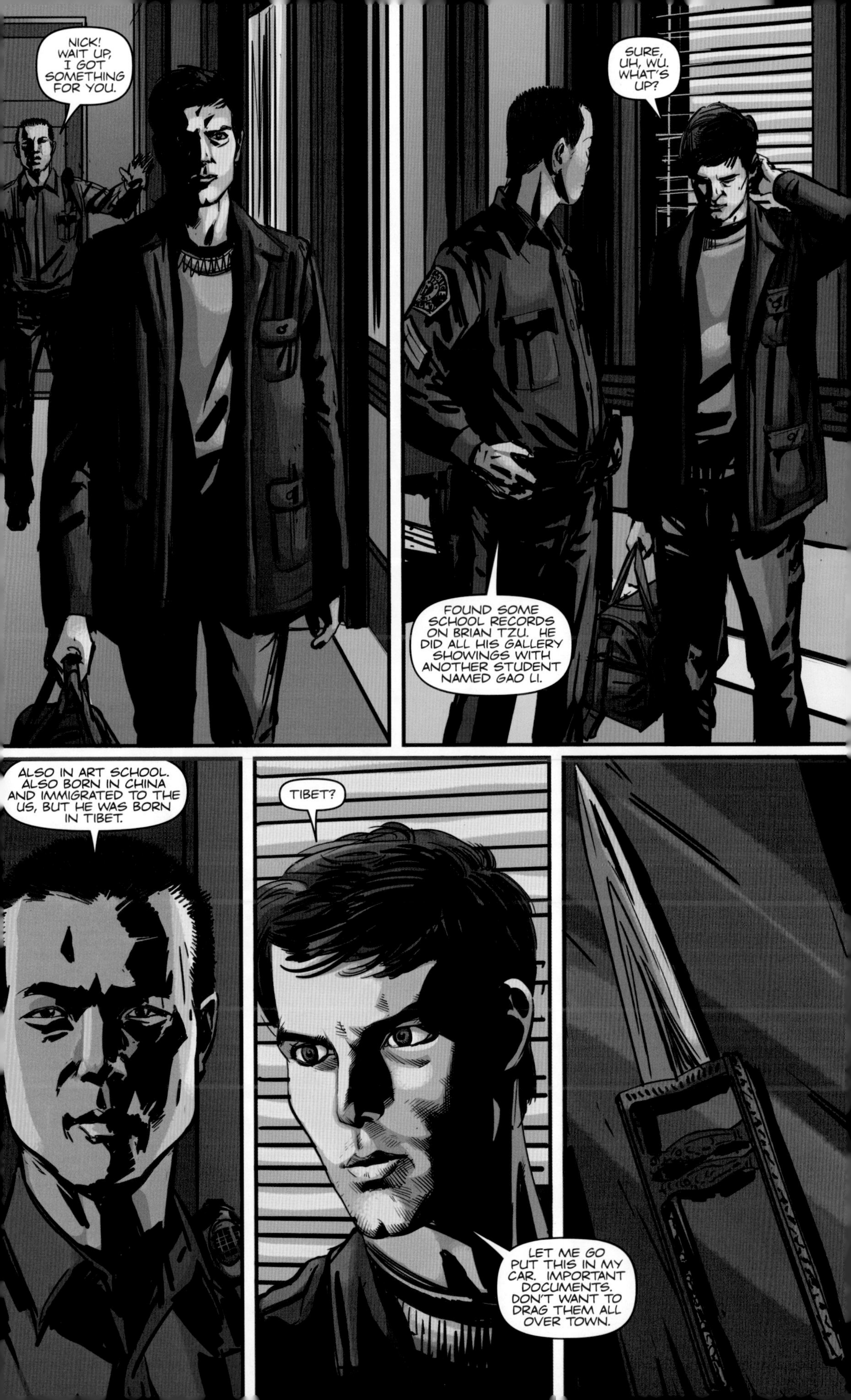
NICK! WAIT UP, I GOT SOMETHING FOR YOU.
SURE, UH, WU. WHAT'S UP?
FOUND SOME SCHOOL RECORDS ON BRIAN TZU. HE DID ALL HIS GALLERY SHOWINGS WITH ANOTHER STUDENT NAMED GAO LI.
ALSO IN ART SCHOOL. ALSO BORN IN CHINA AND IMMIGRATED TO THE US, BUT HE WAS BORN IN TIBET.
TIBET?
LET ME GO PUT THIS IN MY CAR. IMPORTANT DOCUMENTS. DON'T WANT TO DRAG THEM ALL OVER TOWN.

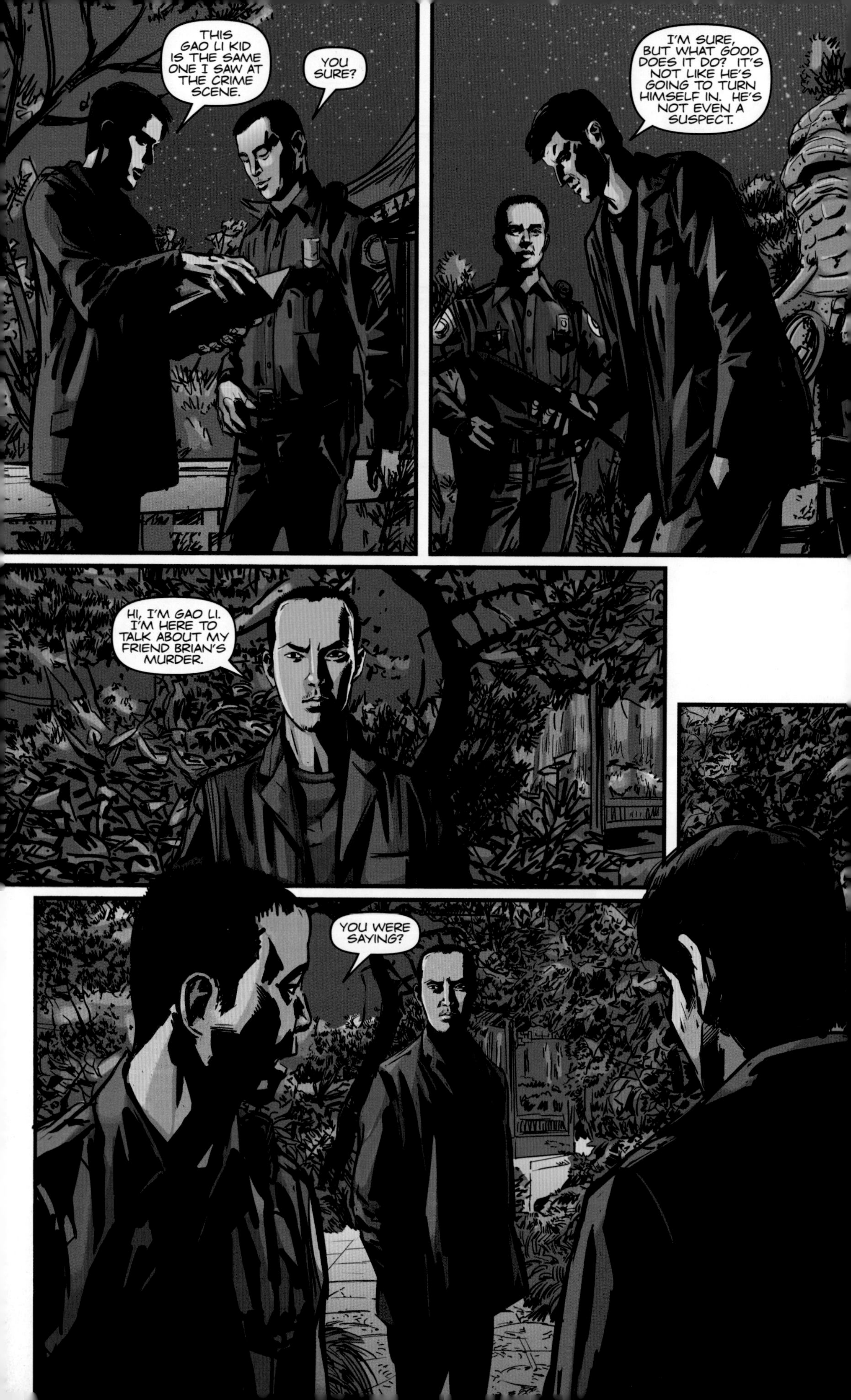

THIS GAO LI KID IS THE SAME ONE I SAW AT THE CRIME SCENE.
YOU SURE?
I'M SURE, BUT WHAT GOOD DOES IT DO? IT'S NOT LIKE HE'S GOING TO TURN HIMSELF IN. HE'S NOT EVEN A SUSPECT.
HI, I'M GAO LI. I'M HERE TO TALK ABOUT MY FRIEND BRIAN'S MURDER.
YOU WERE SAYING?

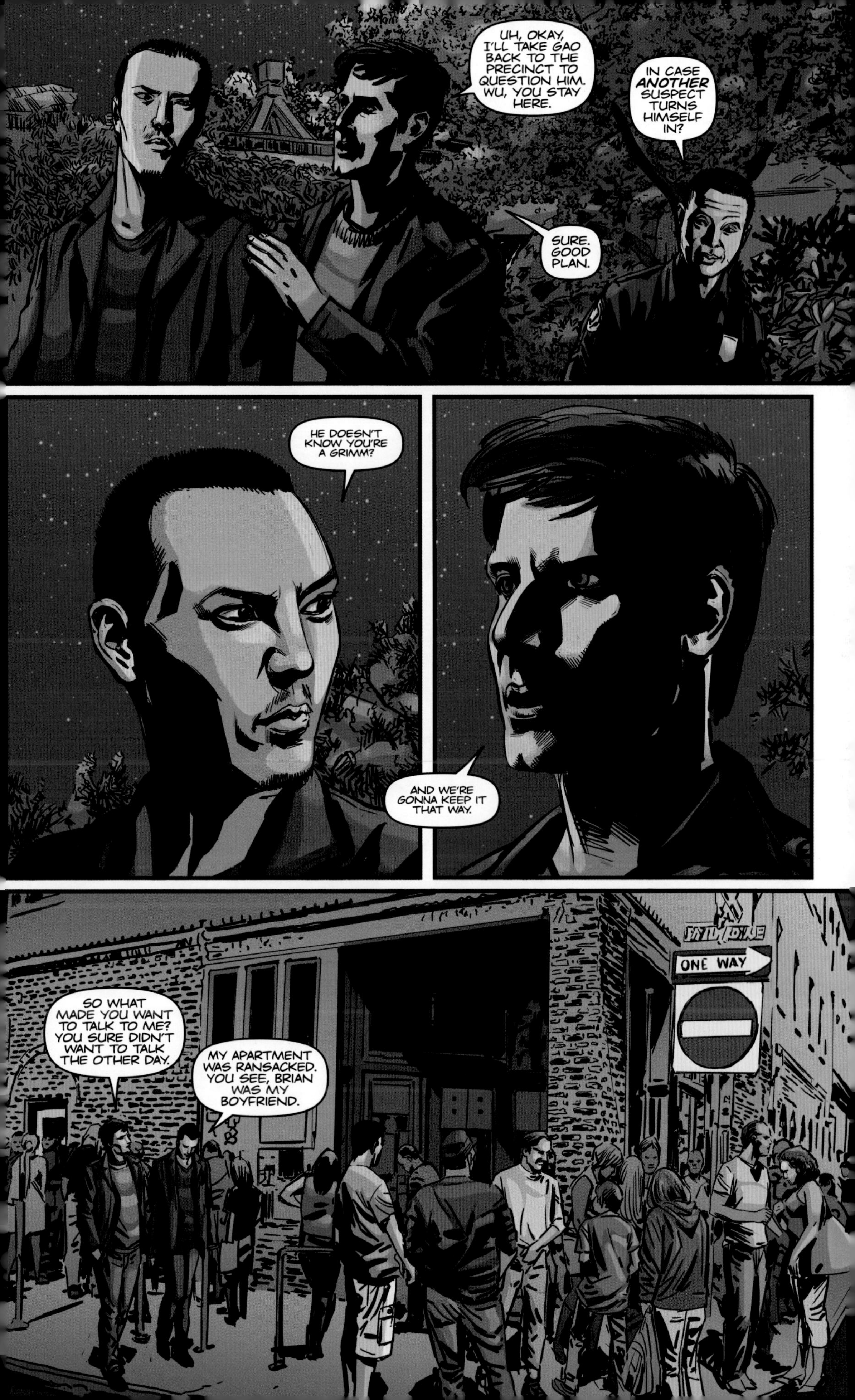
UH, OKAY, I'LL TAKE GAO BACK TO THE PRECINCT TO QUESTION HIM. WU, YOU STAY HERE.
IN CASE ANOTHER SUSPECT TURNS HIMSELF IN?
SURE. GOOD PLAN.
HE DOESN'T KNOW YOU'RE A GRIMM?
AND WE'RE GONNA KEEP IT THAT WAY.
ONE WAY
SO WHAT MADE YOU WANT TO TALK TO ME? YOU SURE DIDN'T WANT TO TALK THE OTHER DAY.
MY APARTMENT WAS RANSACKED. YOU SEE, BRIAN WAS MY BOYFRIEND.

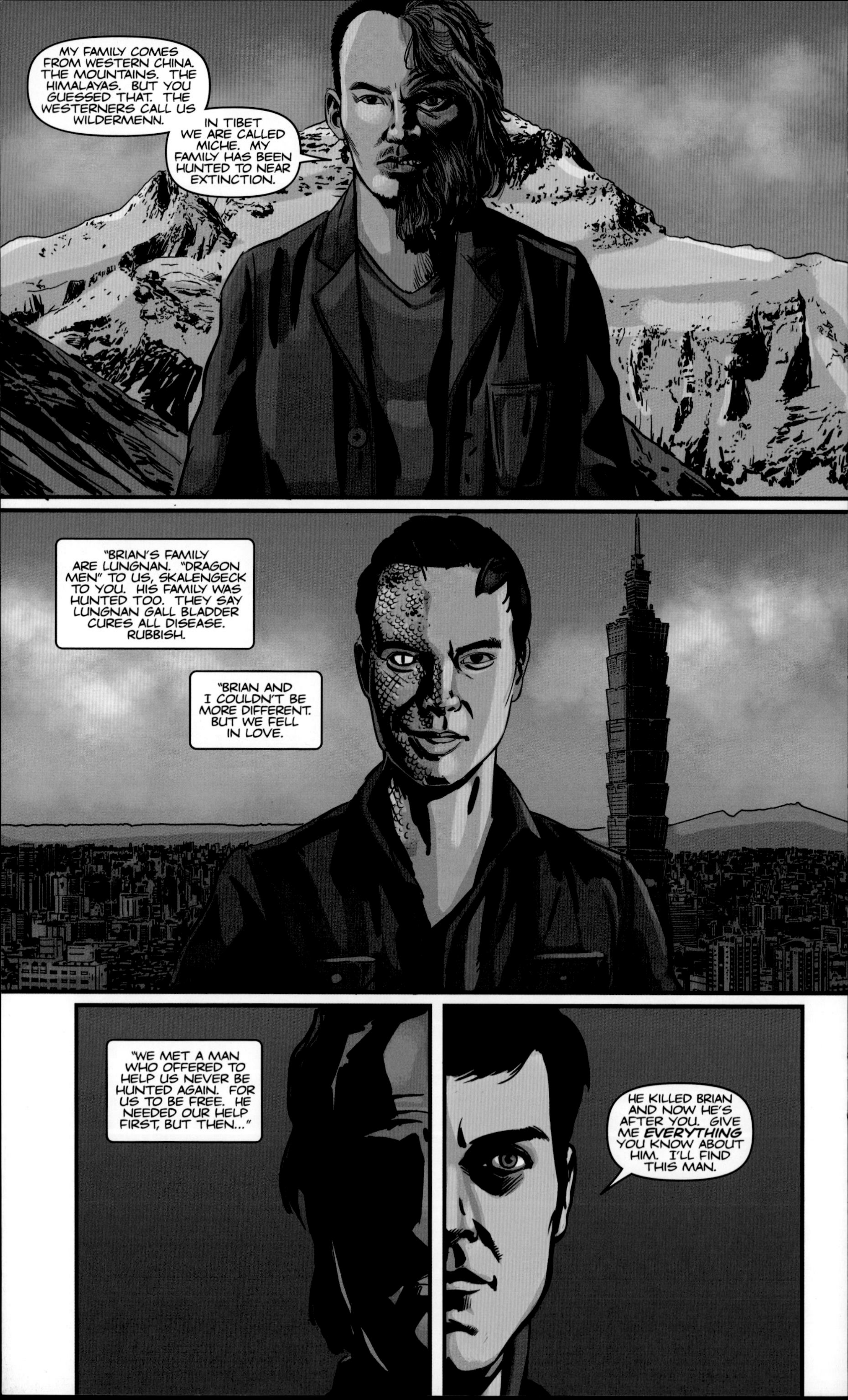
MY FAMILY COMES FROM WESTERN CHINA. THE MOUNTAINS. THE HIMALAYAS. BUT YOU GUESSED THAT. THE WESTERNERS CALL US WILDERMENN.
IN TIBET WE ARE CALLED MICHE. MY FAMILY HAS BEEN HUNTED TO NEAR EXTINCTION.
"BRIAN'S FAMILY ARE LUNGNAN. "DRAGON MEN" TO US, SKALENGECK TO YOU. HIS FAMILY WAS HUNTED TOO. THEY SAY LUNGNAN GALL BLADDER CURES ALL DISEASE. RUBBISH.
"BRIAN AND I COULDN'T BE MORE DIFFERENT. BUT WE FELL IN LOVE.
"WE MET A MAN WHO OFFERED TO HELP US NEVER BE HUNTED AGAIN. FOR US TO BE FREE. HE NEEDED OUR HELP FIRST, BUT THEN..."
HE KILLED BRIAN AND NOW HE'S AFTER YOU. GIVE ME *EVERYTHING* YOU KNOW ABOUT HIM. I'LL FIND THIS MAN.

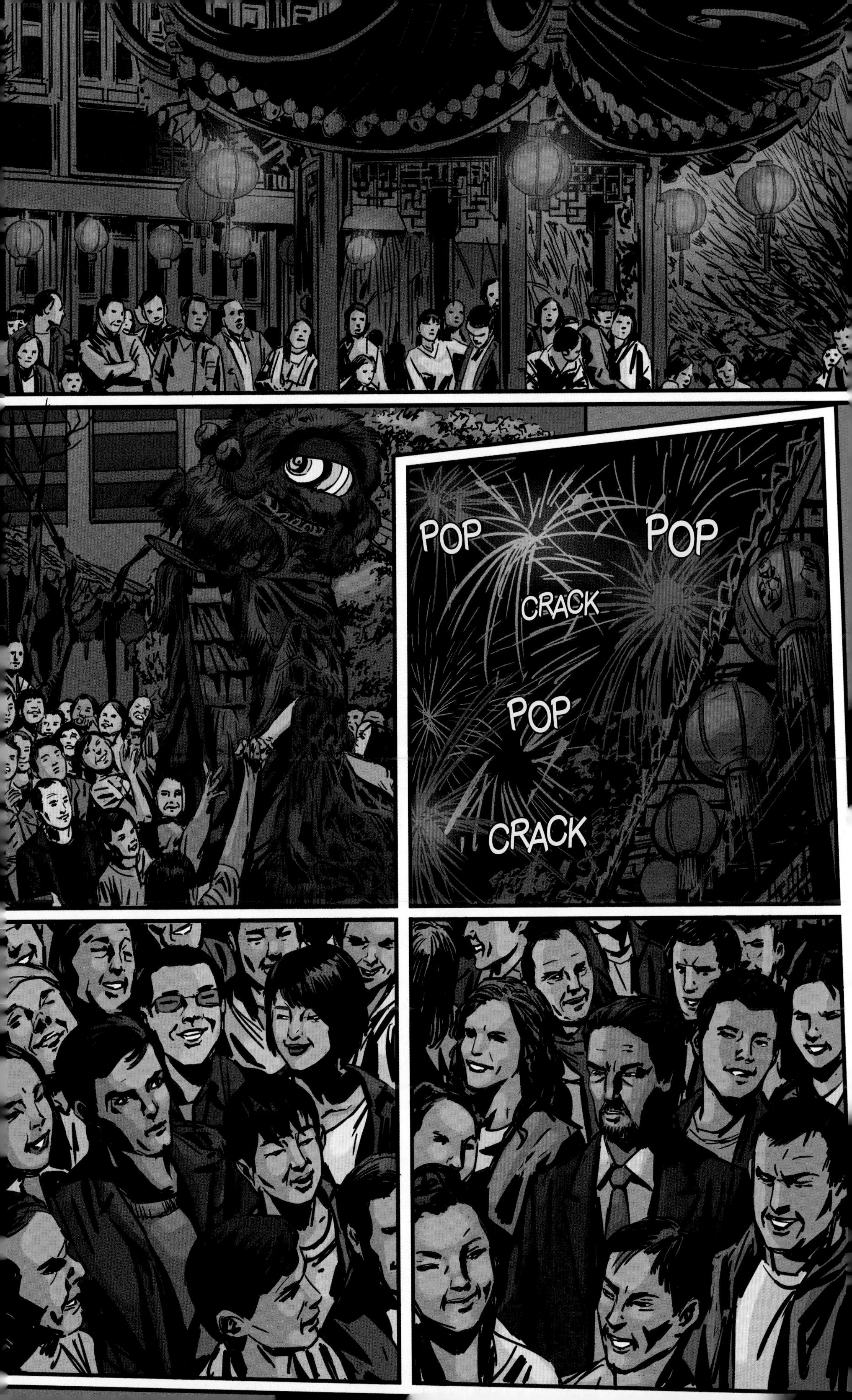
POP
POP
CRACK
POP
CRACK

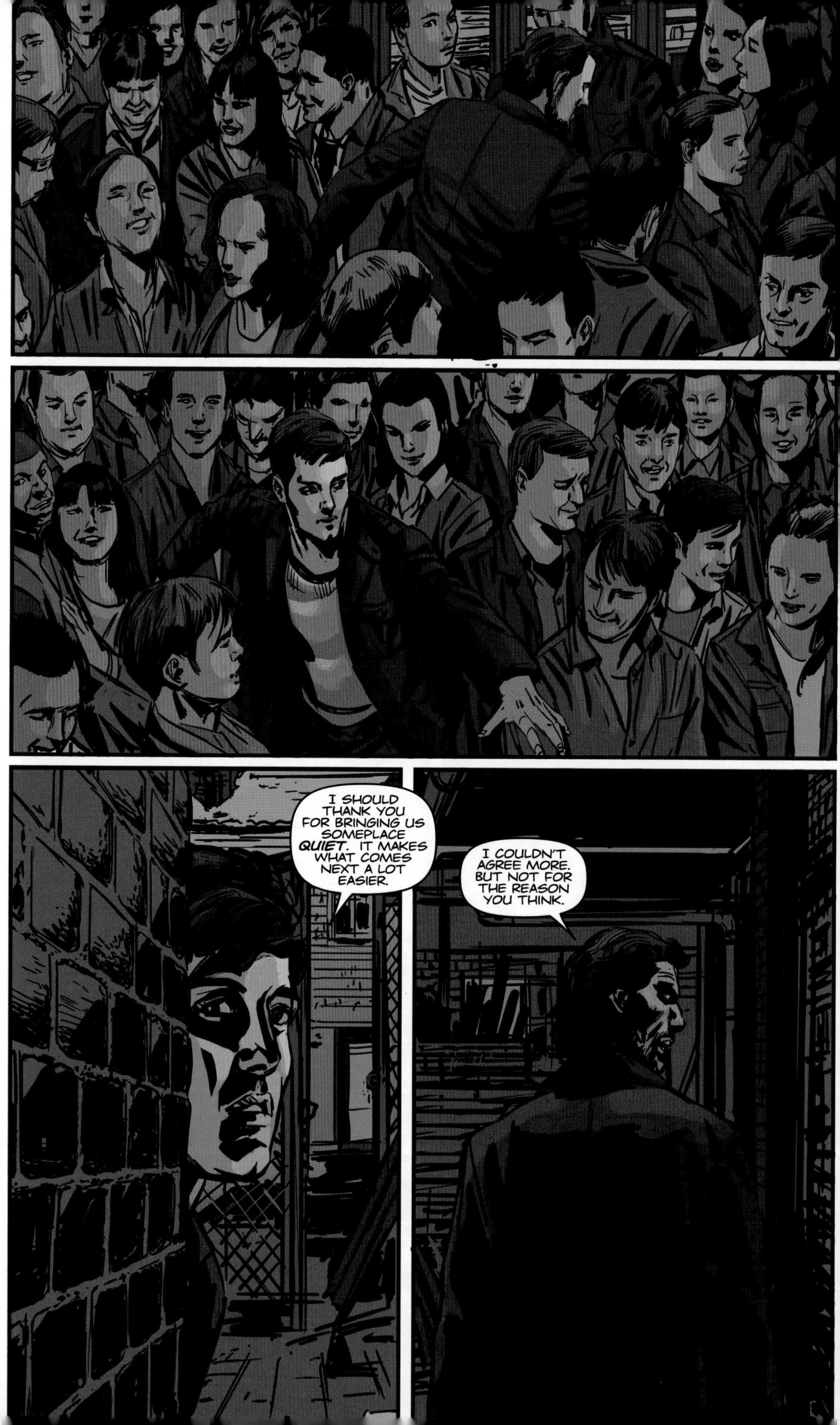
I SHOULD THANK YOU FOR BRINGING US SOMEPLACE QUIET. IT MAKES WHAT COMES NEXT A LOT EASIER.
I COULDN'T AGREE MORE. BUT NOT FOR THE REASON YOU THINK.

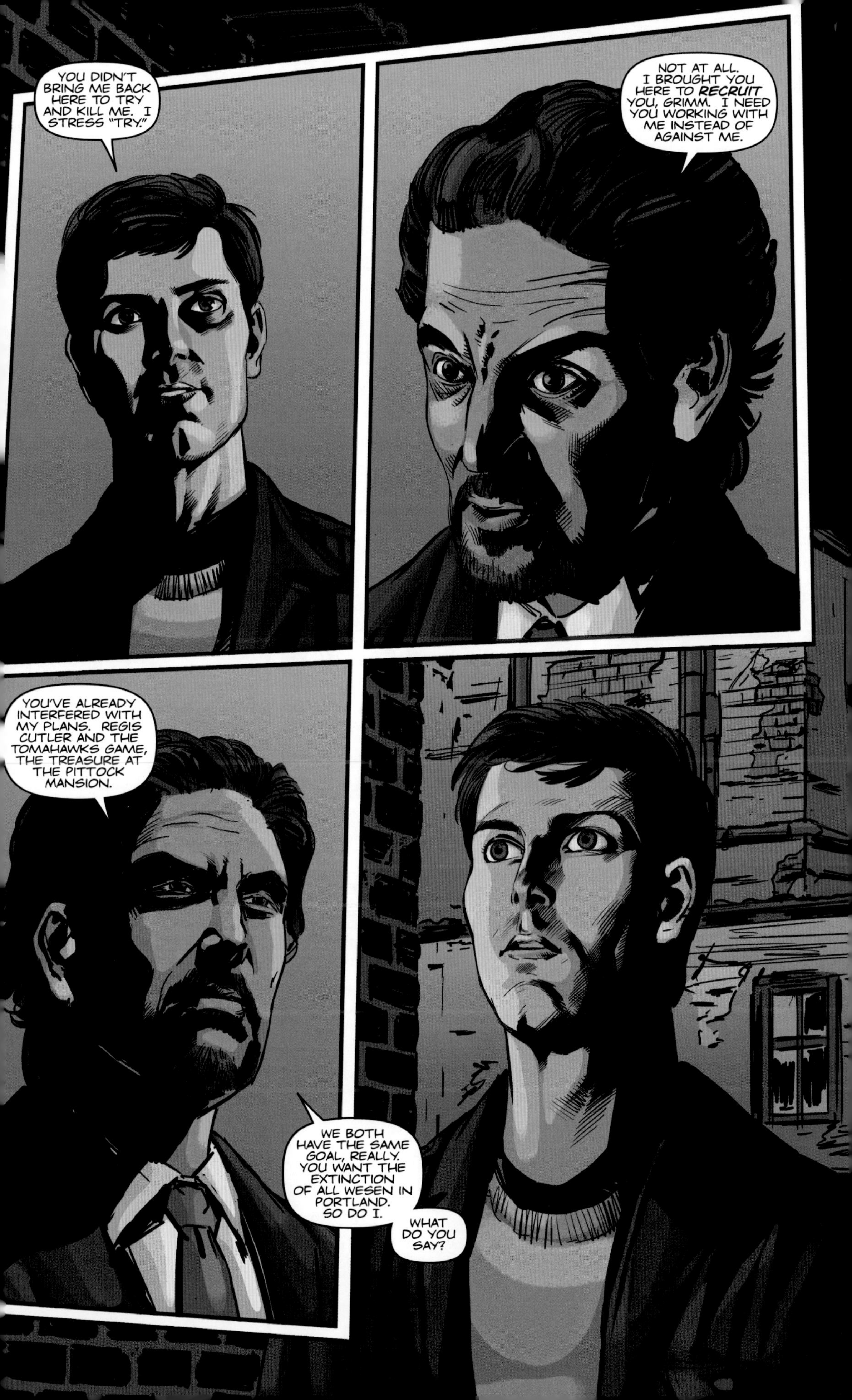
YOU DIDN'T BRING ME BACK HERE TO TRY AND KILL ME. I STRESS "TRY."
NOT AT ALL. I BROUGHT YOU HERE TO RECRUIT YOU, GRIMM. I NEED YOU WORKING WITH ME INSTEAD OF AGAINST ME.
YOU'VE ALREADY INTERFERED WITH MY PLANS. REGIS CUTLER AND THE TOMAHAWKS GAME, THE TREASURE AT THE PITTOCK MANSION.
WE BOTH HAVE THE SAME GOAL, REALLY. YOU WANT THE EXTINCTION OF ALL WESEN IN PORTLAND. SO DO I.
WHAT DO YOU SAY?

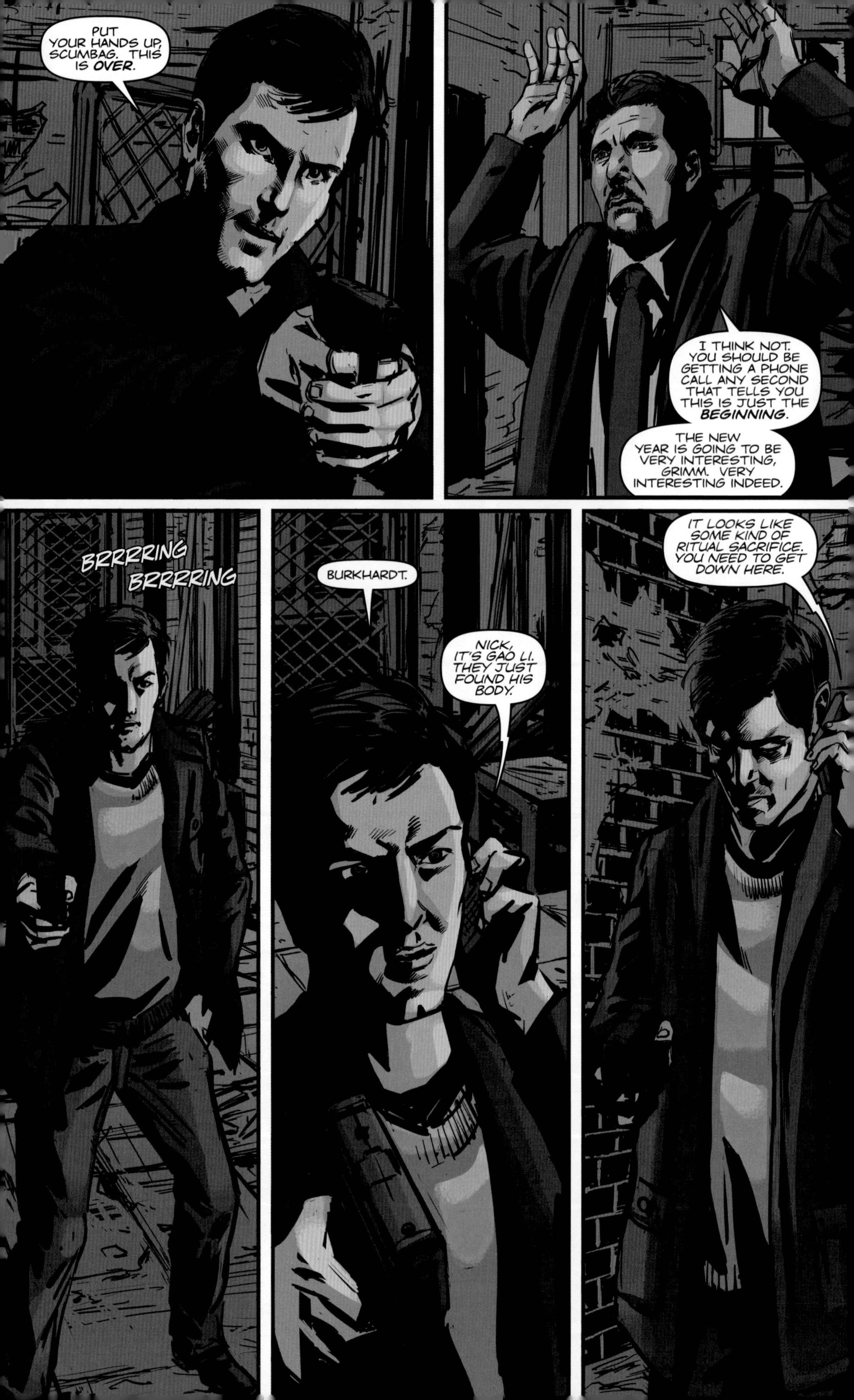
PUT YOUR HANDS UP, SCUMBAG. THIS IS **OVER**.
I THINK NOT. YOU SHOULD BE GETTING A PHONE CALL ANY SECOND THAT TELLS YOU THIS IS JUST THE **BEGINNING**.
THE NEW YEAR IS GOING TO BE VERY INTERESTING, GRIMM. VERY INTERESTING INDEED.
BRRRRING
BRRRRING
BURKHARDT.
NICK, IT'S GAO LI. THEY JUST FOUND HIS BODY.
IT LOOKS LIKE SOME KIND OF RITUAL SACRIFICE. YOU NEED TO GET DOWN HERE.

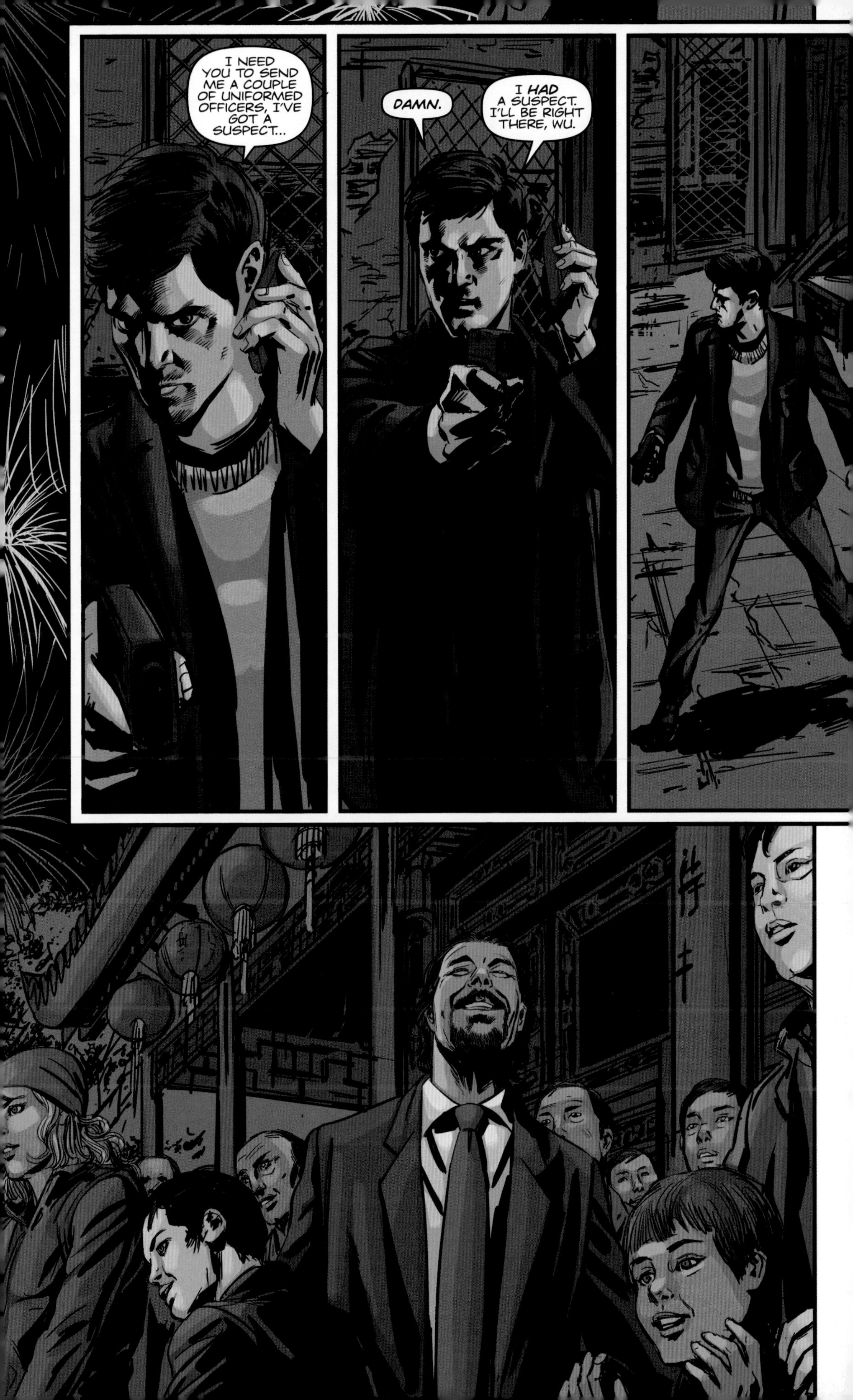
I NEED YOU TO SEND ME A COUPLE OF UNIFORMED OFFICERS, I'VE GOT A SUSPECT...
DAMN.
I HAD A SUSPECT. I'LL BE RIGHT THERE, WU.

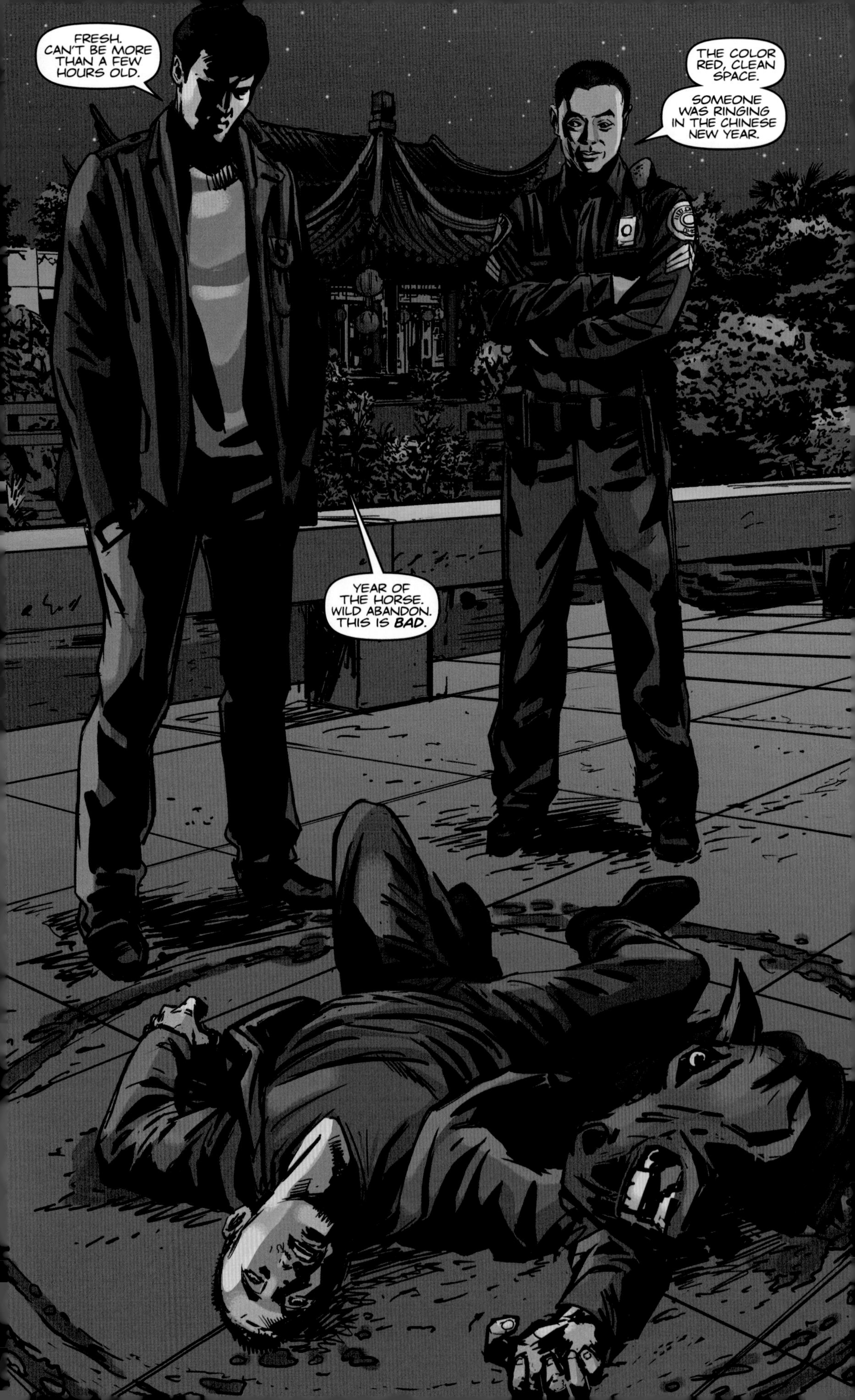
FRESH. CAN'T BE MORE THAN A FEW HOURS OLD.
THE COLOR RED, CLEAN SPACE.
SOMEONE WAS RINGING IN THE CHINESE NEW YEAR.
YEAR OF THE HORSE. WILD ABANDON. THIS IS BAD.

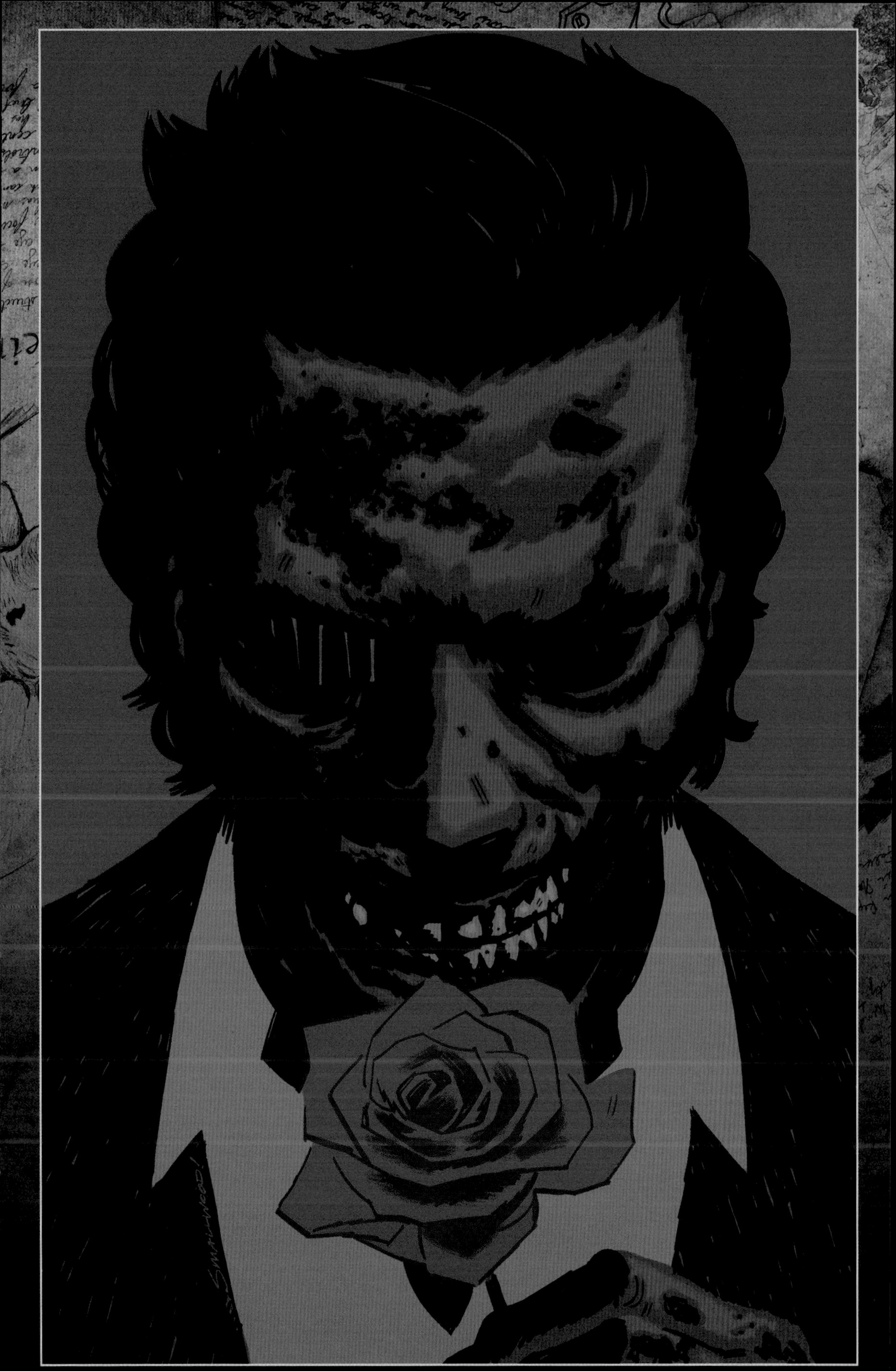

GRIMM: THE WARLOCK ISSUE #4 COVER

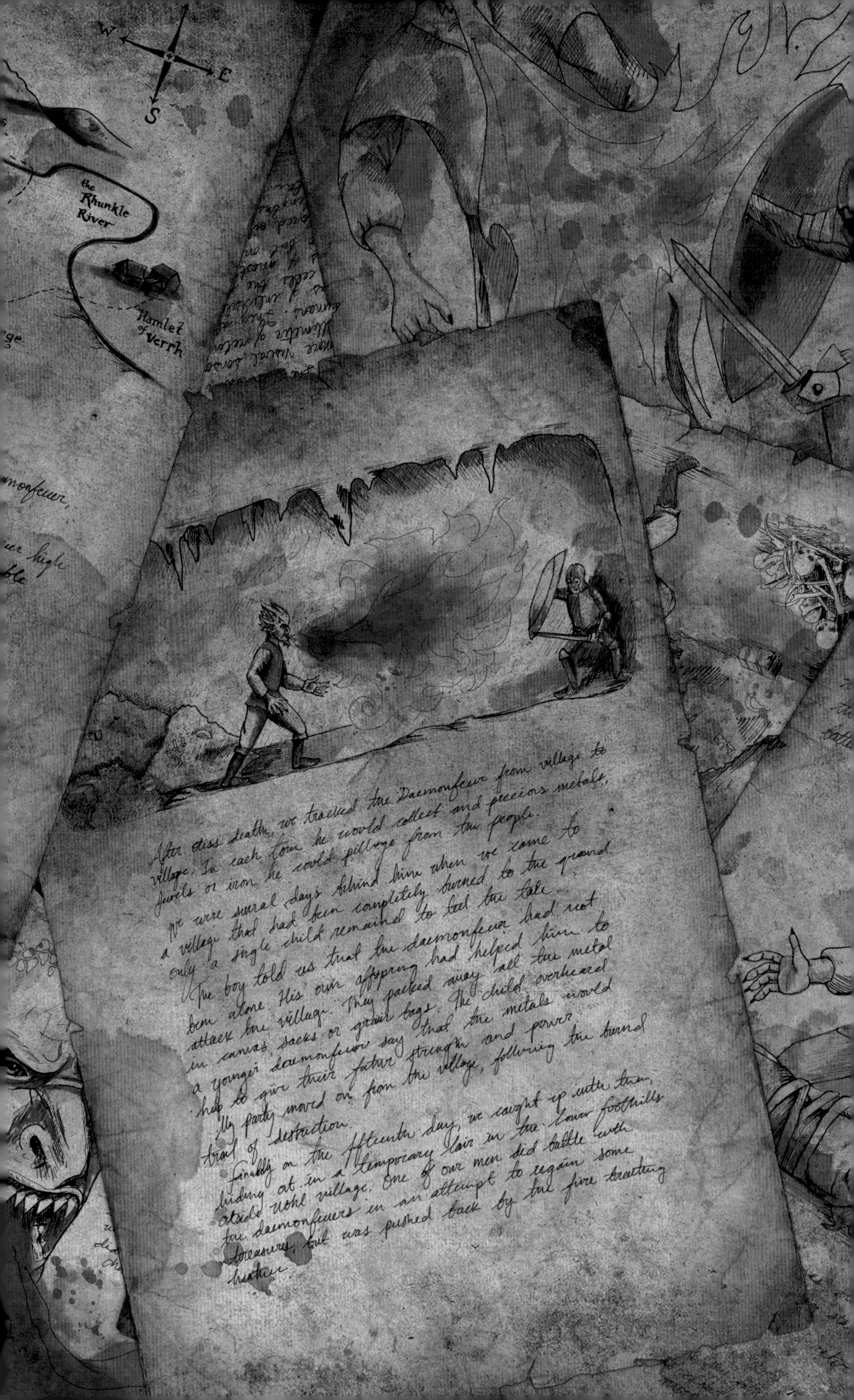
W
E
S
the Rhunkle River
Hamlet of Verrh

After Sliss death, we tracked the Daemonfeuer from village to village. In each town he would collect and precious metals, jewels or iron he could pillage from the people.

We were several days behind him when we came to a village that had been completely burned to the ground. Only a single child remained to tell the tale.

The boy told us that the daemonfeuer had not been alone. His own offspring had helped him to attack the village. They packed away all the metal in canvas sacks or grain bags. The child overheard a younger daemonfeuer say that the metals would help to give their father strength and power.

My party moved on from the village, following the burned trail of destruction.

Finally on the fifteenth day, we caught up with them hiding out in a temporary lair in the lower foothills outside Uohl village. One of our men did battle with the daemonfeuers in an attempt to regain some treasures, but was pushed back by the fire breathing heathen

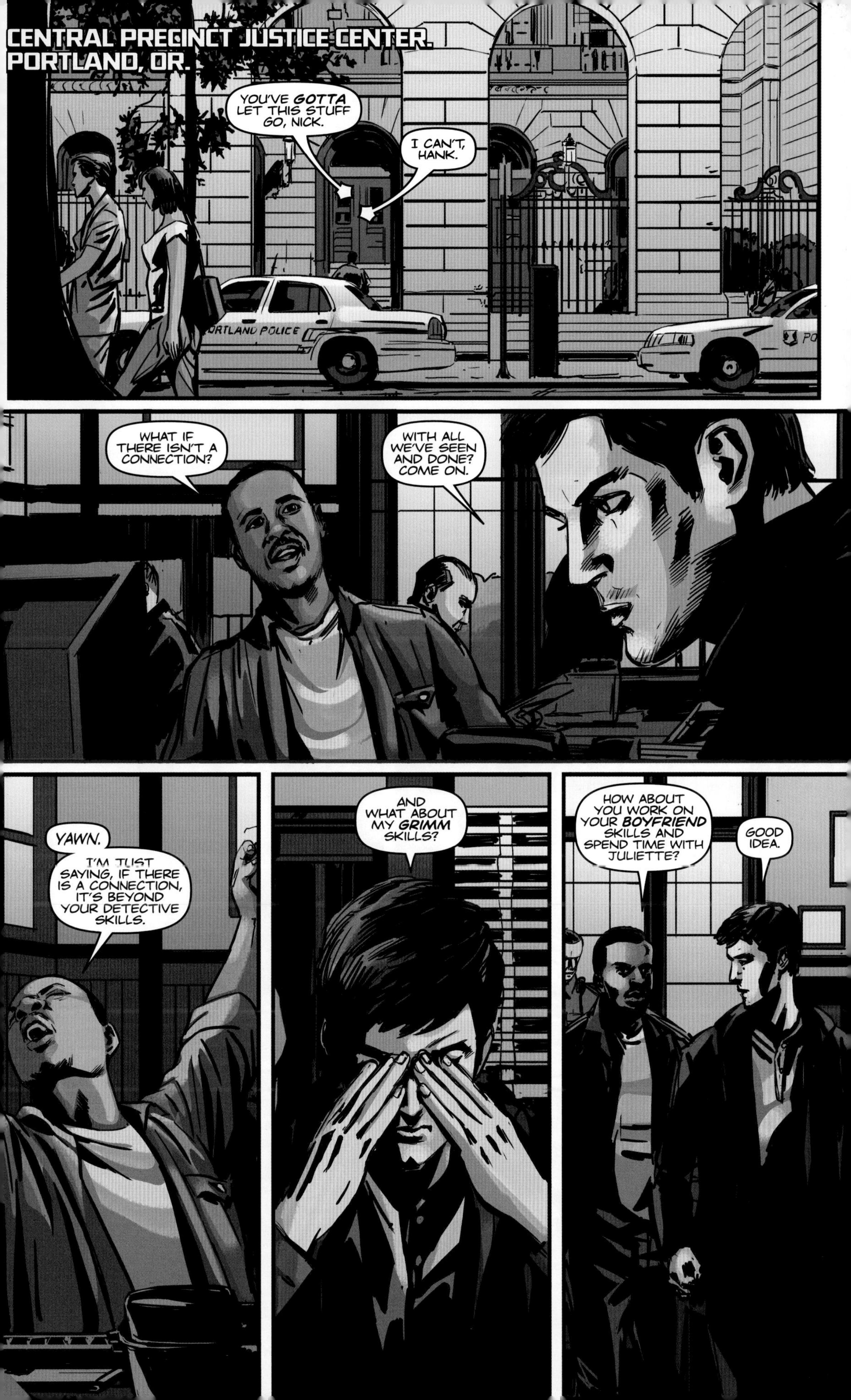
CENTRAL PRECINCT JUSTICE CENTER.
PORTLAND, OR.
YOU'VE GOTTA LET THIS STUFF GO, NICK.
I CAN'T, HANK.
PORTLAND POLICE
WHAT IF THERE ISN'T A CONNECTION?
WITH ALL WE'VE SEEN AND DONE? COME ON.
YAWN.
I'M JUST SAYING, IF THERE IS A CONNECTION, IT'S BEYOND YOUR DETECTIVE SKILLS.
AND WHAT ABOUT MY GRIMM SKILLS?
HOW ABOUT YOU WORK ON YOUR BOYFRIEND SKILLS AND SPEND TIME WITH JULIETTE?
GOOD IDEA.

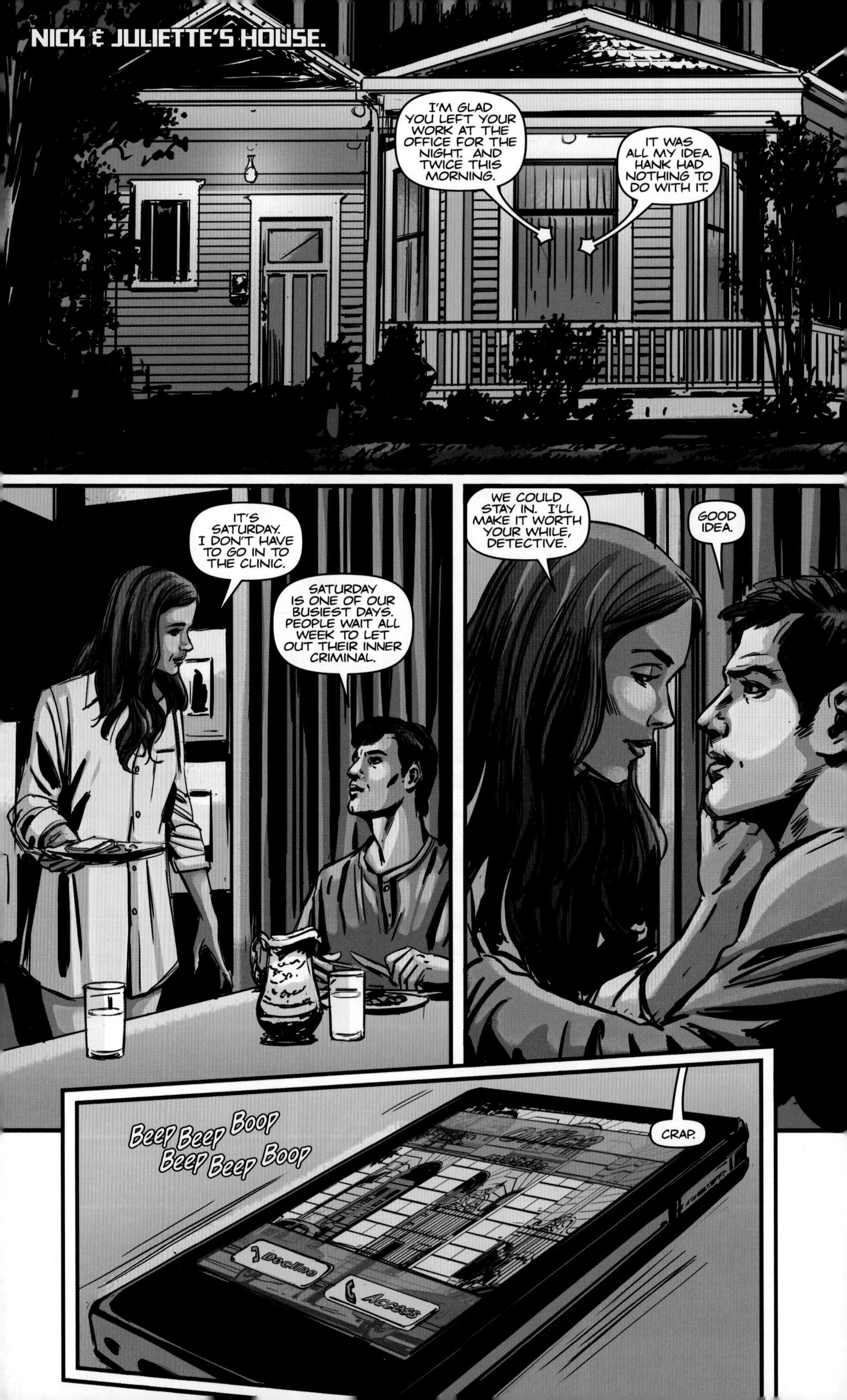
NICK & JULIETTE'S HOUSE.
I'M GLAD YOU LEFT YOUR WORK AT THE OFFICE FOR THE NIGHT. AND TWICE THIS MORNING.
IT WAS ALL MY IDEA. HANK HAD NOTHING TO DO WITH IT.
IT'S SATURDAY. I DON'T HAVE TO GO IN TO THE CLINIC.
SATURDAY IS ONE OF OUR BUSIEST DAYS. PEOPLE WAIT ALL WEEK TO LET OUT THEIR INNER CRIMINAL.
WE COULD STAY IN. I'LL MAKE IT WORTH YOUR WHILE, DETECTIVE.
GOOD IDEA.
Beep Beep Boop
Beep Beep Boop
CRAP.
Decline

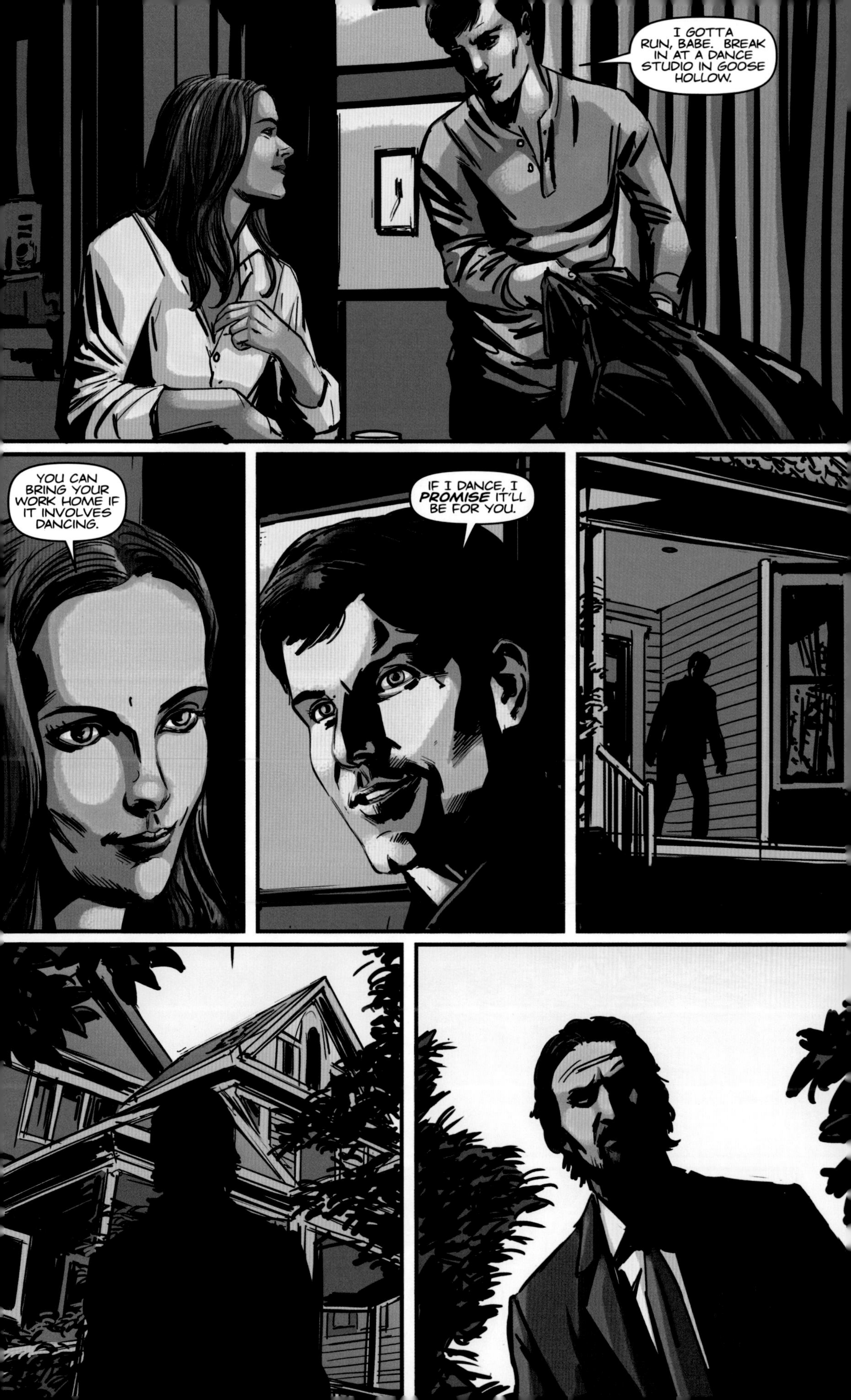
I GOTTA RUN, BABE. BREAK IN AT A DANCE STUDIO IN GOOSE HOLLOW.
YOU CAN BRING YOUR WORK HOME IF IT INVOLVES DANCING.
IF I DANCE, I *PROMISE* IT'LL BE FOR YOU.

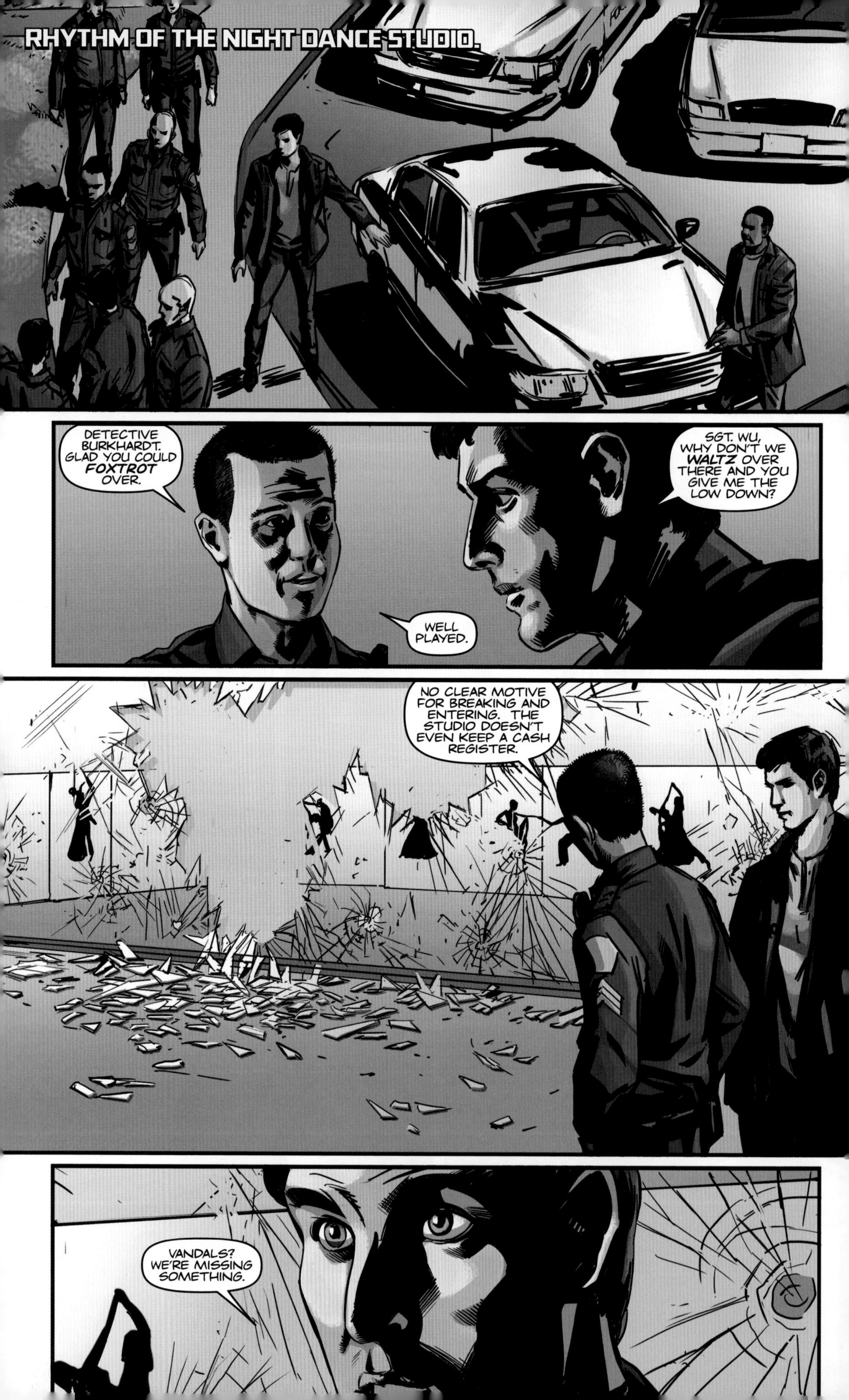
RHYTHM OF THE NIGHT DANCE STUDIO.
DETECTIVE BURKHARDT. GLAD YOU COULD FOXTROT OVER.
SGT. WU, WHY DON'T WE WALTZ OVER THERE AND YOU GIVE ME THE LOW DOWN?
WELL PLAYED.
NO CLEAR MOTIVE FOR BREAKING AND ENTERING. THE STUDIO DOESN'T EVEN KEEP A CASH REGISTER.
VANDALS? WE'RE MISSING SOMETHING.

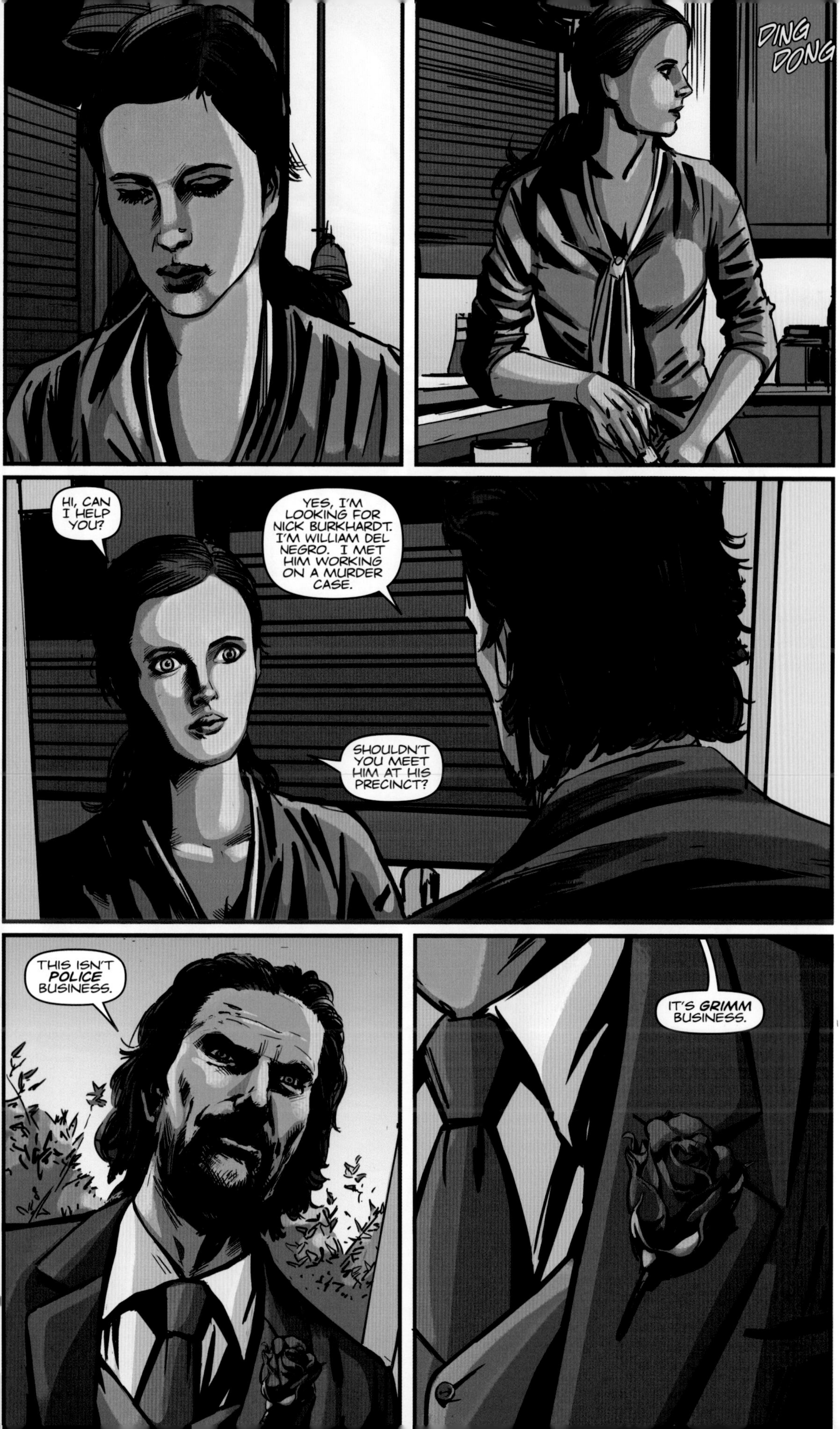
DING DONG
HI, CAN I HELP YOU?
YES, I'M LOOKING FOR NICK BURKHARDT. I'M WILLIAM DEL NEGRO. I MET HIM WORKING ON A MURDER CASE.
SHOULDN'T YOU MEET HIM AT HIS PRECINCT?
THIS ISN'T POLICE BUSINESS.
IT'S GRIMM BUSINESS.

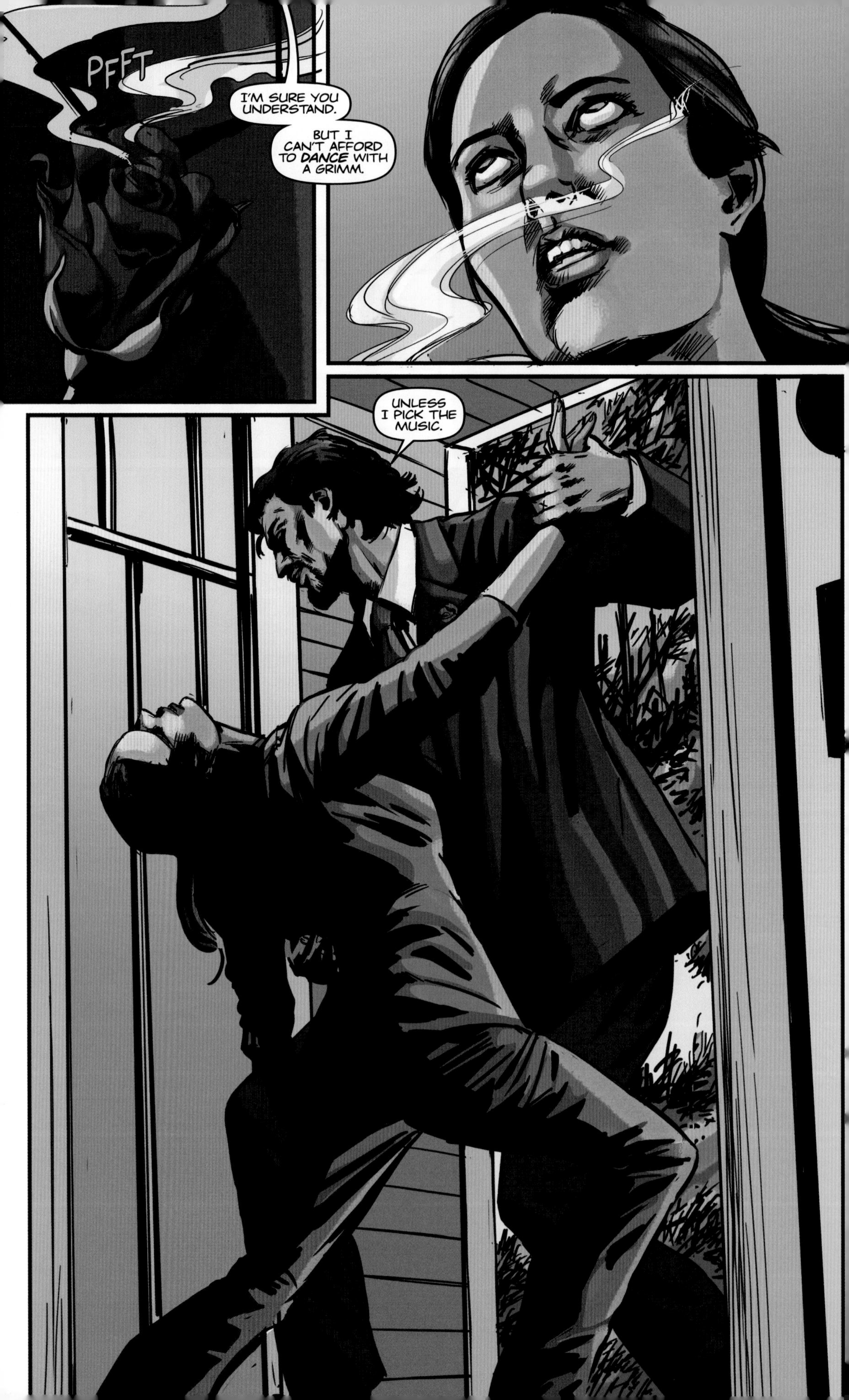
PFFT
I'M SURE YOU UNDERSTAND.
BUT I CAN'T AFFORD TO DANCE WITH A GRIMM.
UNLESS I PICK THE MUSIC.

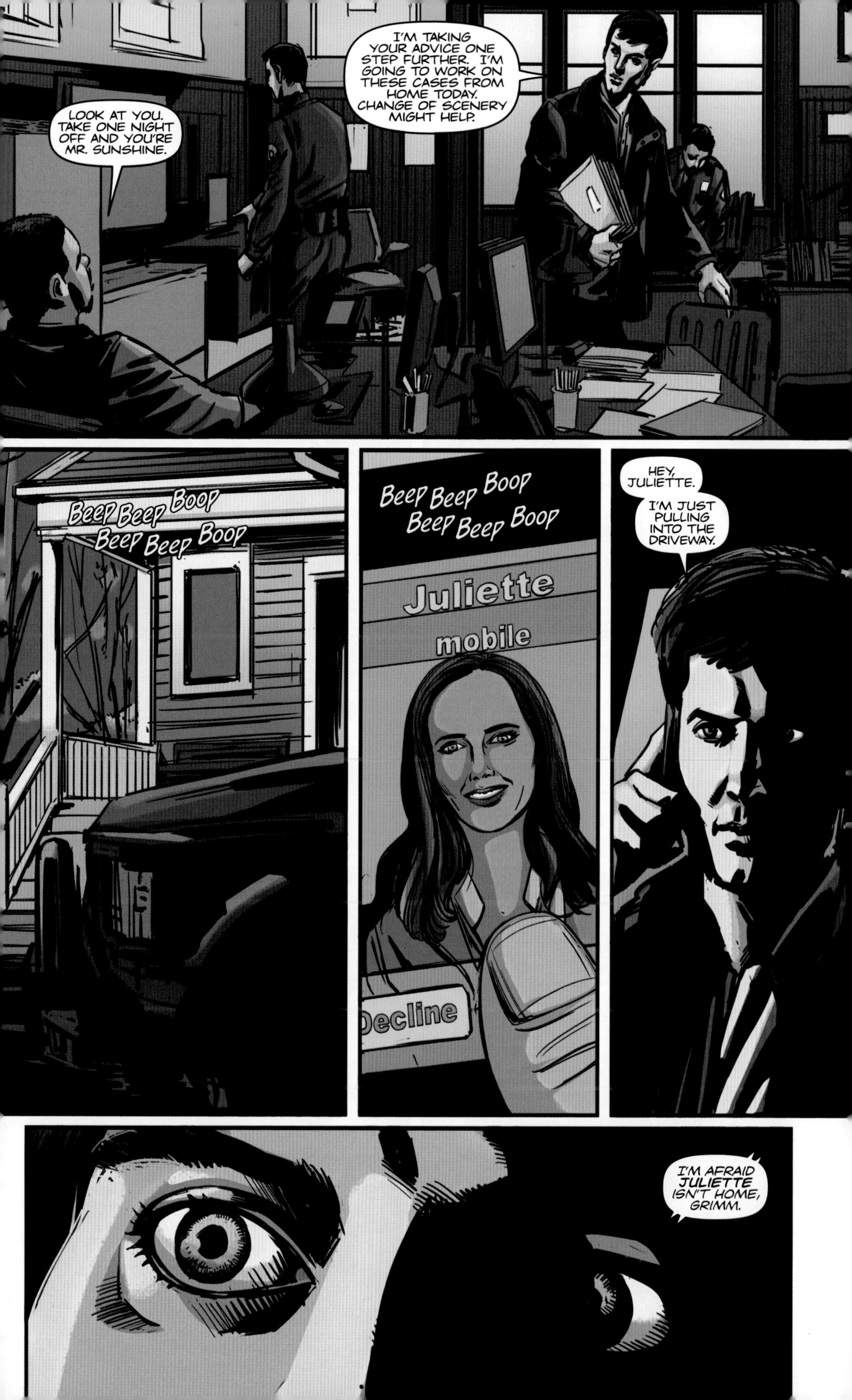
LOOK AT YOU. TAKE ONE NIGHT OFF AND YOU'RE MR. SUNSHINE.
I'M TAKING YOUR ADVICE ONE STEP FURTHER. I'M GOING TO WORK ON THESE CASES FROM HOME TODAY. CHANGE OF SCENERY MIGHT HELP.
Beep Beep Boop Beep Beep Boop
Beep Beep Boop Beep Beep Boop
Juliette
mobile
Decline
HEY, JULIETTE.
I'M JUST PULLING INTO THE DRIVEWAY.
I'M AFRAID JULIETTE ISN'T HOME, GRIMM.

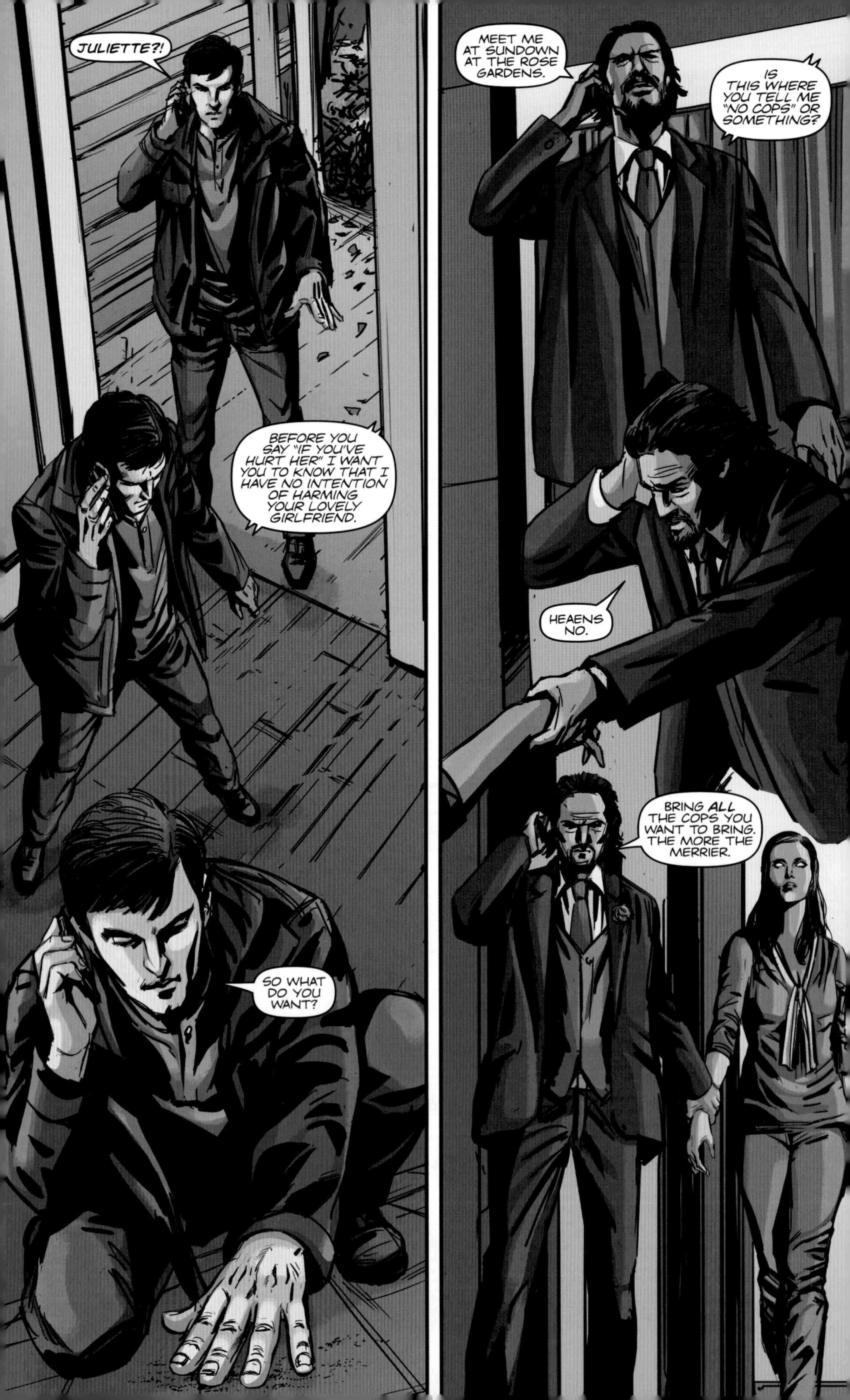
JULIETTE?!
BEFORE YOU SAY "IF YOU'VE HURT HER" I WANT YOU TO KNOW THAT I HAVE NO INTENTION OF HARMING YOUR LOVELY GIRLFRIEND.
SO WHAT DO YOU WANT?
MEET ME AT SUNDOWN AT THE ROSE GARDENS.
IS THIS WHERE YOU TELL ME "NO COPS" OR SOMETHING?
HEAENS NO.
BRING **ALL** THE COPS YOU WANT TO BRING. THE MORE THE MERRIER.

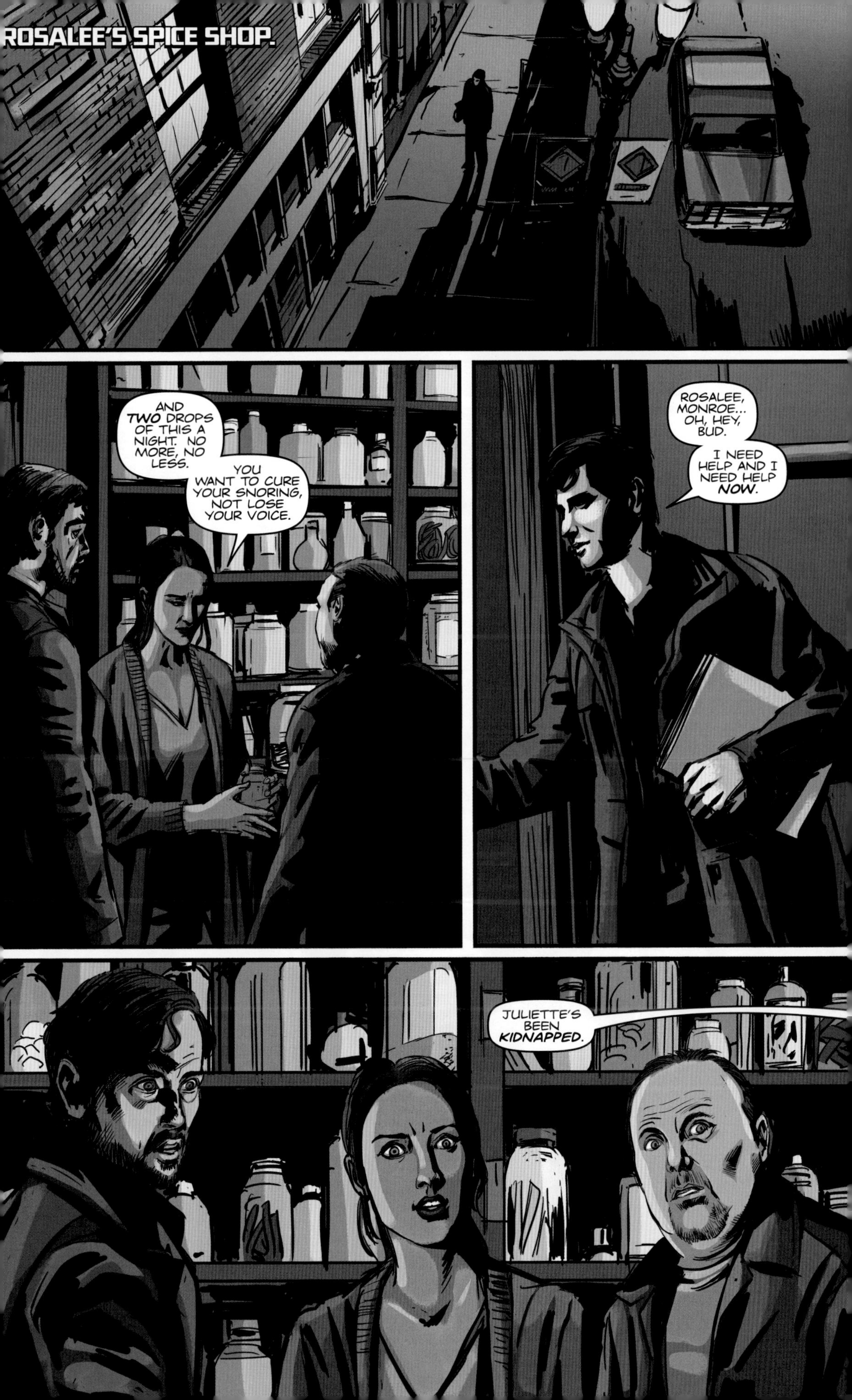
ROSALEE'S SPICE SHOP.
AND TWO DROPS OF THIS A NIGHT. NO MORE, NO LESS.
YOU WANT TO CURE YOUR SNORING, NOT LOSE YOUR VOICE.
ROSALEE, MONROE... OH, HEY, BUD.
I NEED HELP AND I NEED HELP NOW.
JULIETTE'S BEEN KIDNAPPED.

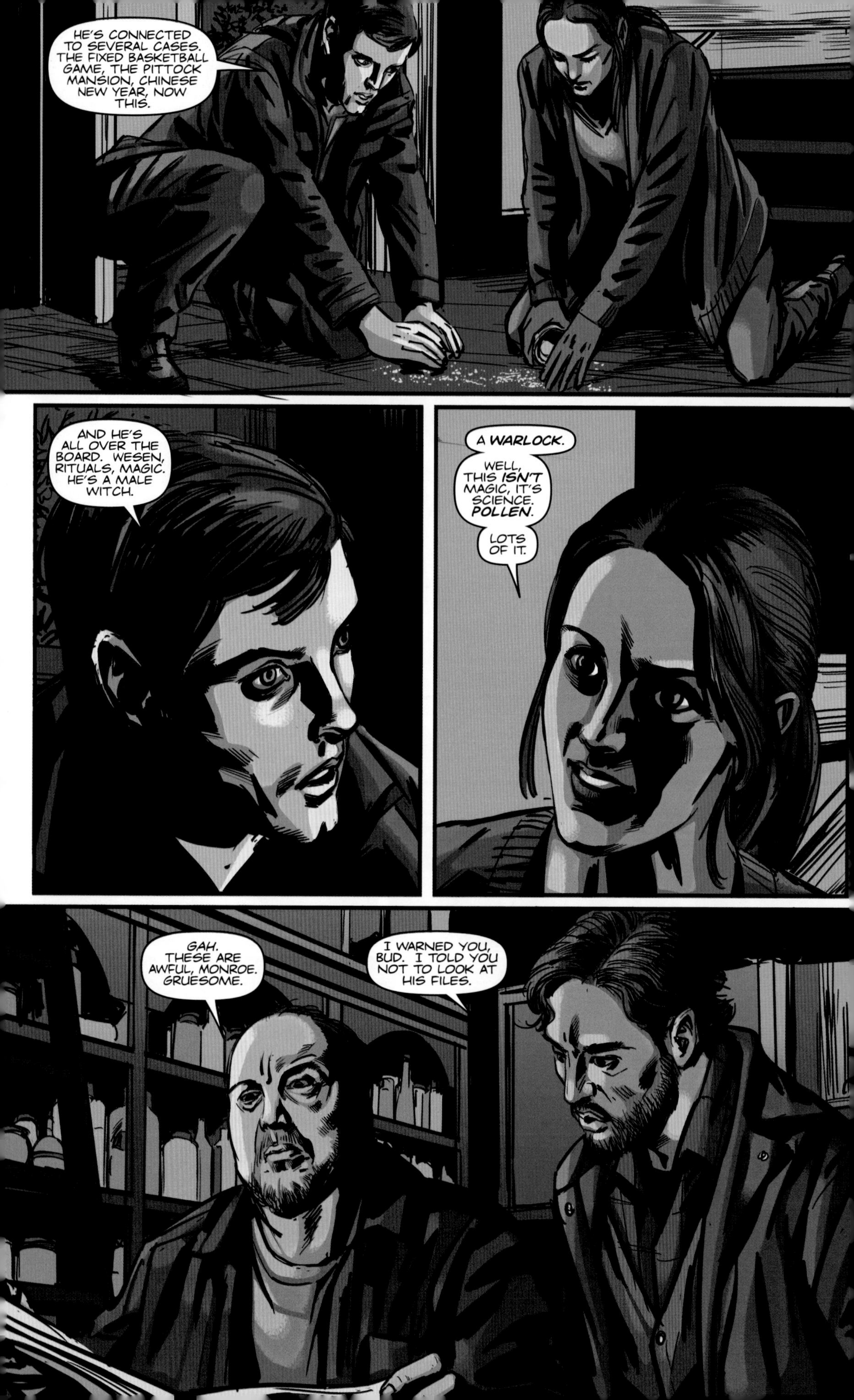
HE'S CONNECTED TO SEVERAL CASES. THE FIXED BASKETBALL GAME, THE PITTOCK MANSION, CHINESE NEW YEAR, NOW THIS.
AND HE'S ALL OVER THE BOARD. WESEN, RITUALS, MAGIC. HE'S A MALE WITCH.
A WARLOCK.
WELL, THIS ISN'T MAGIC, IT'S SCIENCE. POLLEN.
LOTS OF IT.
GAH. THESE ARE AWFUL, MONROE. GRUESOME.
I WARNED YOU, BUD. I TOLD YOU NOT TO LOOK AT HIS FILES.

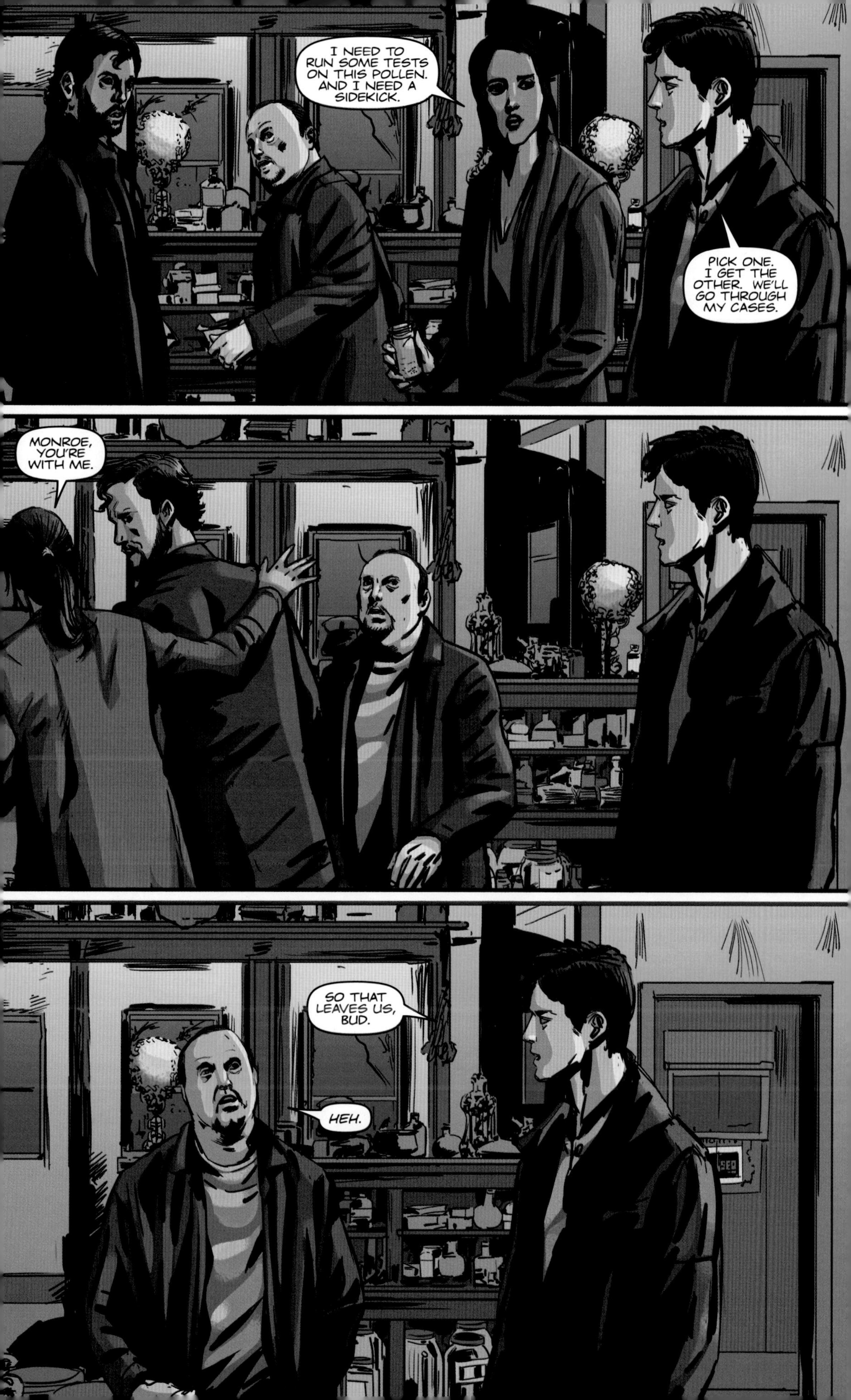
I NEED TO RUN SOME TESTS ON THIS POLLEN. AND I NEED A SIDEKICK.
PICK ONE. I GET THE OTHER. WE'LL GO THROUGH MY CASES.
MONROE, YOU'RE WITH ME.
SO THAT LEAVES US, BUD.
HEH.

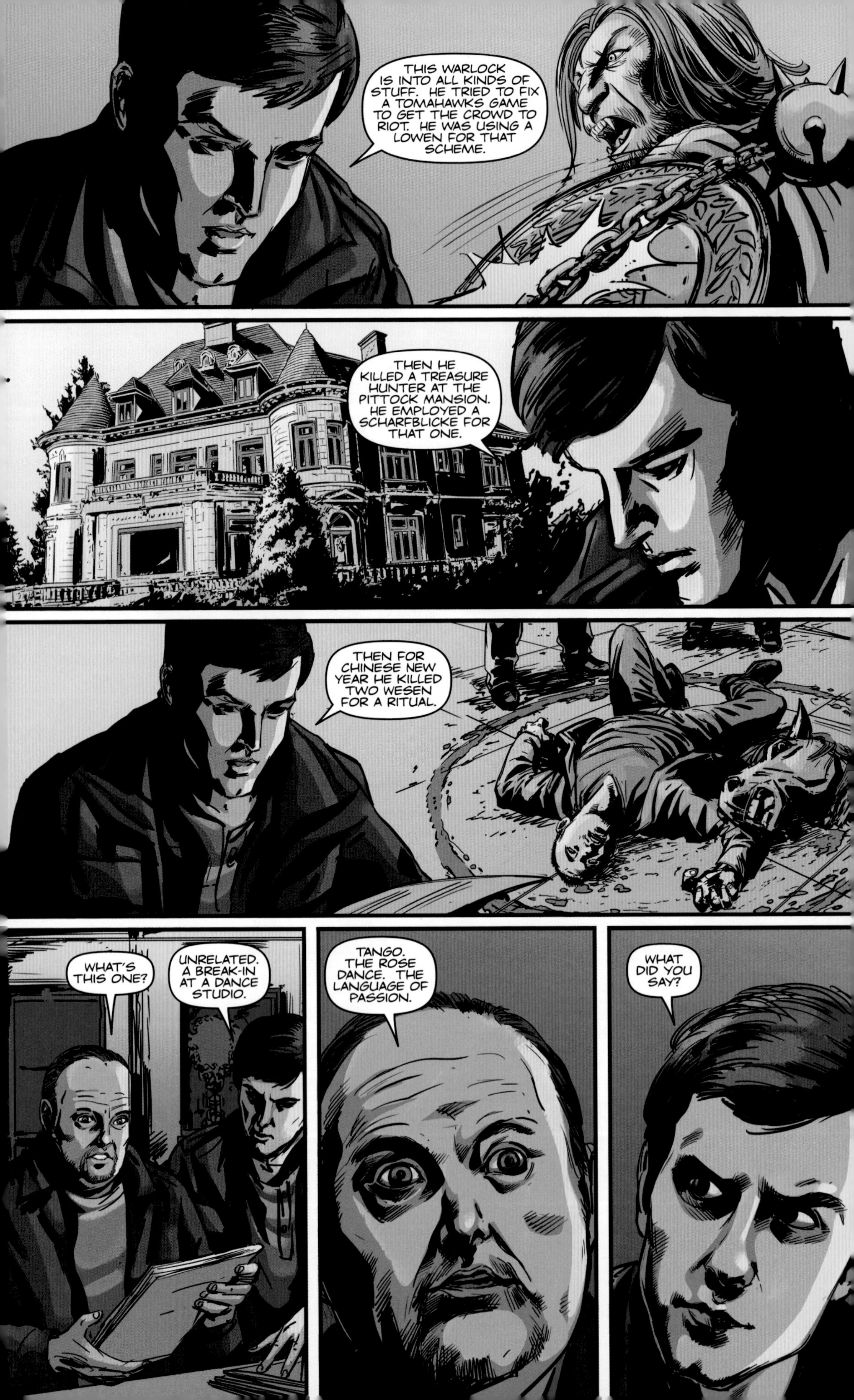
THIS WARLOCK IS INTO ALL KINDS OF STUFF. HE TRIED TO FIX A TOMAHAWKS GAME TO GET THE CROWD TO RIOT. HE WAS USING A LOWEN FOR THAT SCHEME.
THEN HE KILLED A TREASURE HUNTER AT THE PITTOCK MANSION. HE EMPLOYED A SCHARFBLICKE FOR THAT ONE.
THEN FOR CHINESE NEW YEAR HE KILLED TWO WESEN FOR A RITUAL.
WHAT'S THIS ONE?
UNRELATED. A BREAK-IN AT A DANCE STUDIO.
TANGO. THE ROSE DANCE. THE LANGUAGE OF PASSION.
WHAT DID YOU SAY?

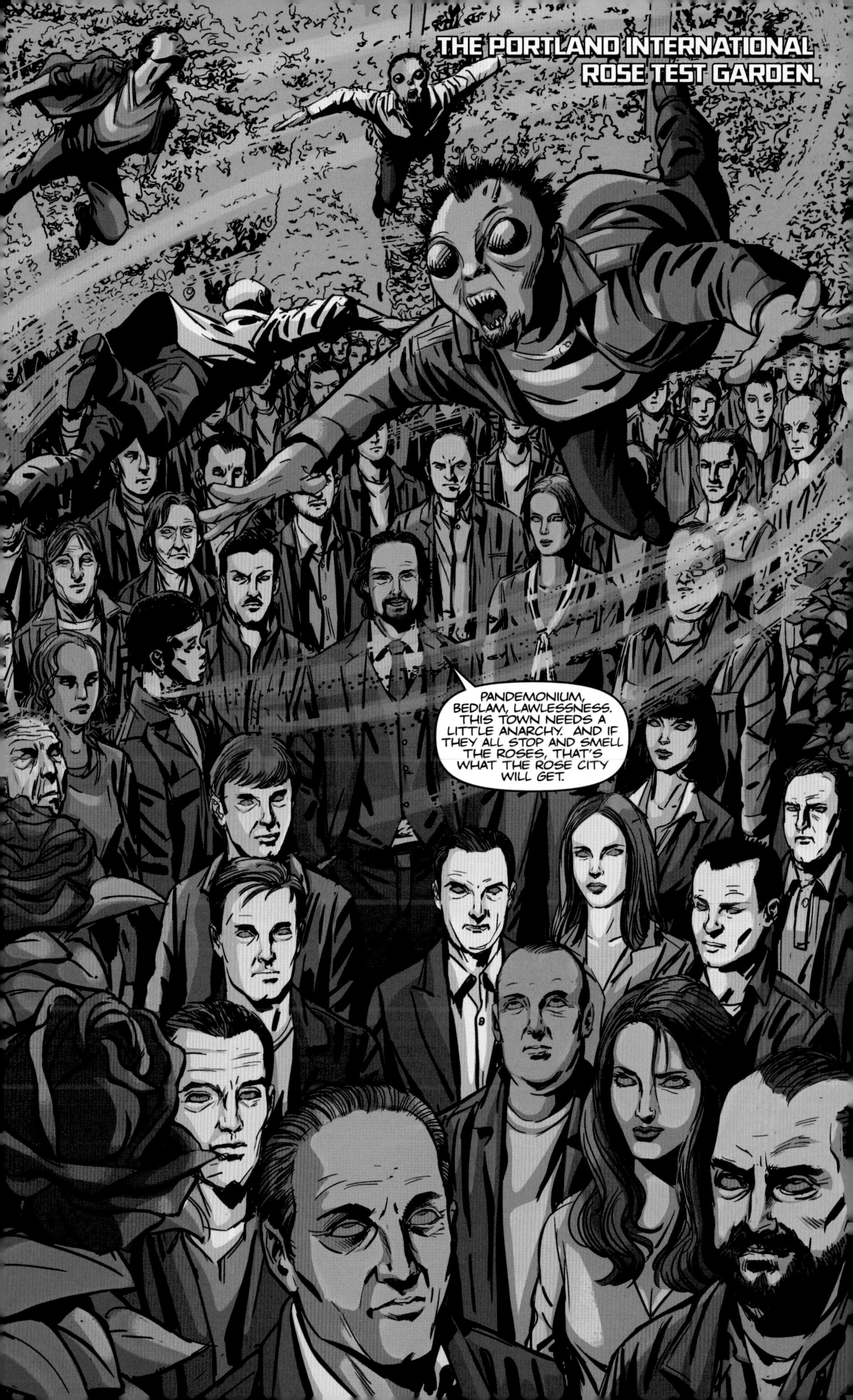

THE PORTLAND INTERNATIONAL ROSE TEST GARDEN.
PANDEMONIUM, BEDLAM, LAWLESSNESS. THIS TOWN NEEDS A LITTLE ANARCHY. AND IF THEY ALL STOP AND SMELL THE ROSES, THAT'S WHAT THE ROSE CITY WILL GET.

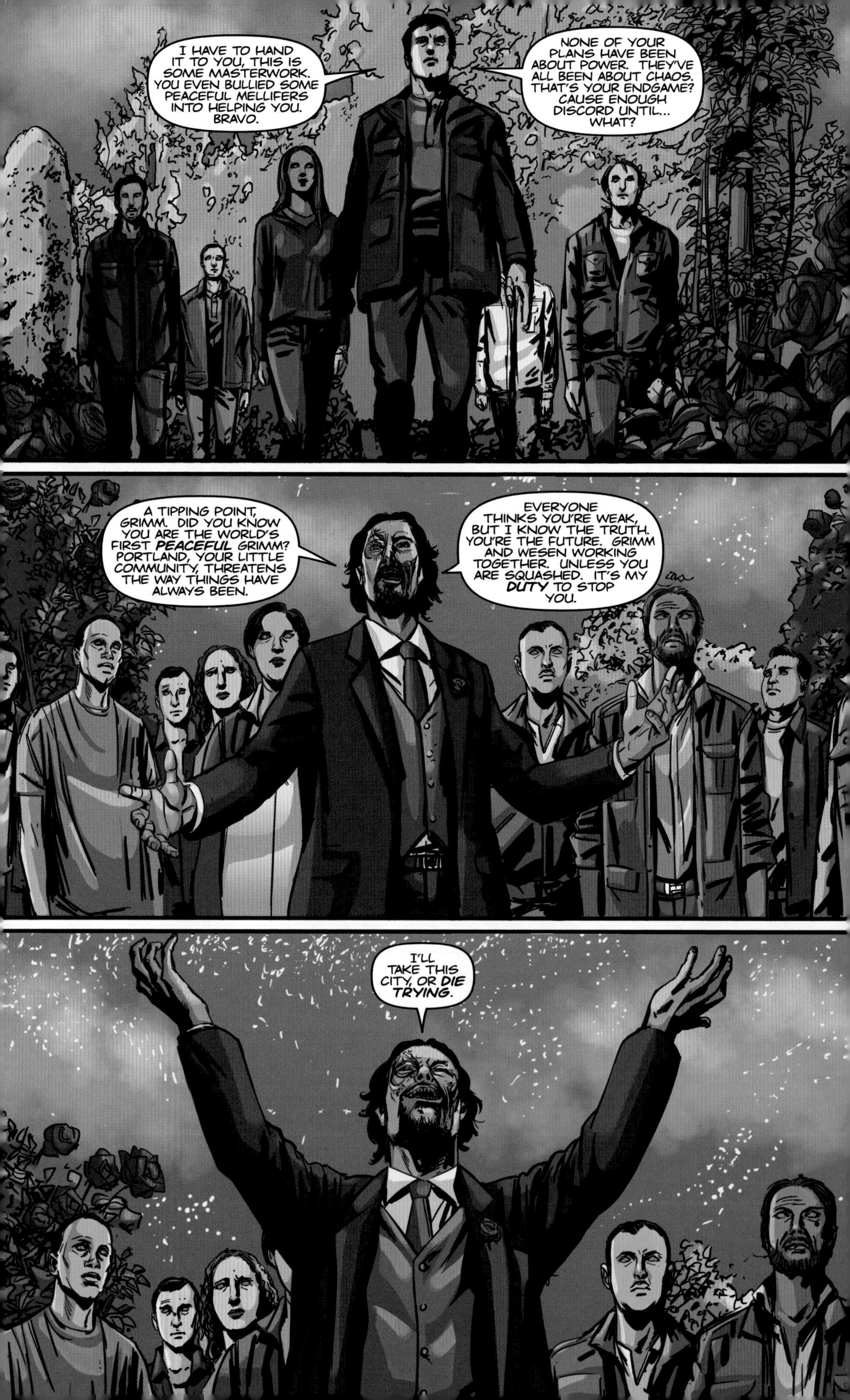
I HAVE TO HAND IT TO YOU, THIS IS SOME MASTERWORK. YOU EVEN BULLIED SOME PEACEFUL MELLIFERS INTO HELPING YOU. BRAVO.
NONE OF YOUR PLANS HAVE BEEN ABOUT POWER. THEY'VE ALL BEEN ABOUT CHAOS. THAT'S YOUR ENDGAME? CAUSE ENOUGH DISCORD UNTIL... WHAT?
A TIPPING POINT, GRIMM. DID YOU KNOW YOU ARE THE WORLD'S FIRST PEACEFUL GRIMM? PORTLAND, YOUR LITTLE COMMUNITY, THREATENS THE WAY THINGS HAVE ALWAYS BEEN.
EVERYONE THINKS YOU'RE WEAK, BUT I KNOW THE TRUTH. YOU'RE THE FUTURE. GRIMM AND WESEN WORKING TOGETHER. UNLESS YOU ARE SQUASHED. IT'S MY DUTY TO STOP YOU.
I'LL TAKE THIS CITY, OR DIE TRYING.

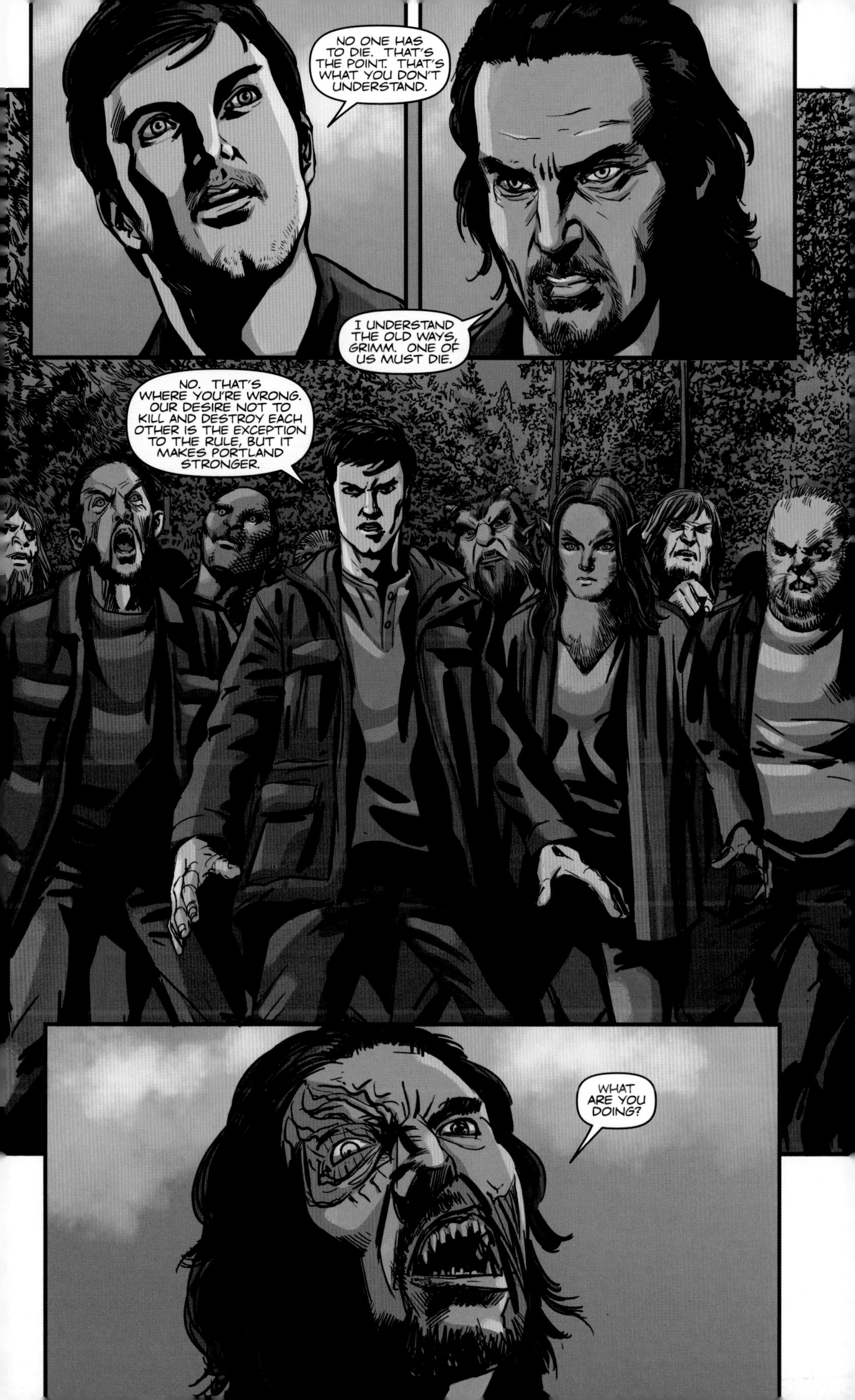
NO ONE HAS TO DIE. THAT'S THE POINT. THAT'S WHAT YOU DON'T UNDERSTAND.
I UNDERSTAND THE OLD WAYS, GRIMM. ONE OF US MUST DIE.
NO. THAT'S WHERE YOU'RE WRONG. OUR DESIRE NOT TO KILL AND DESTROY EACH OTHER IS THE EXCEPTION TO THE RULE, BUT IT MAKES PORTLAND STRONGER.
WHAT ARE YOU DOING?

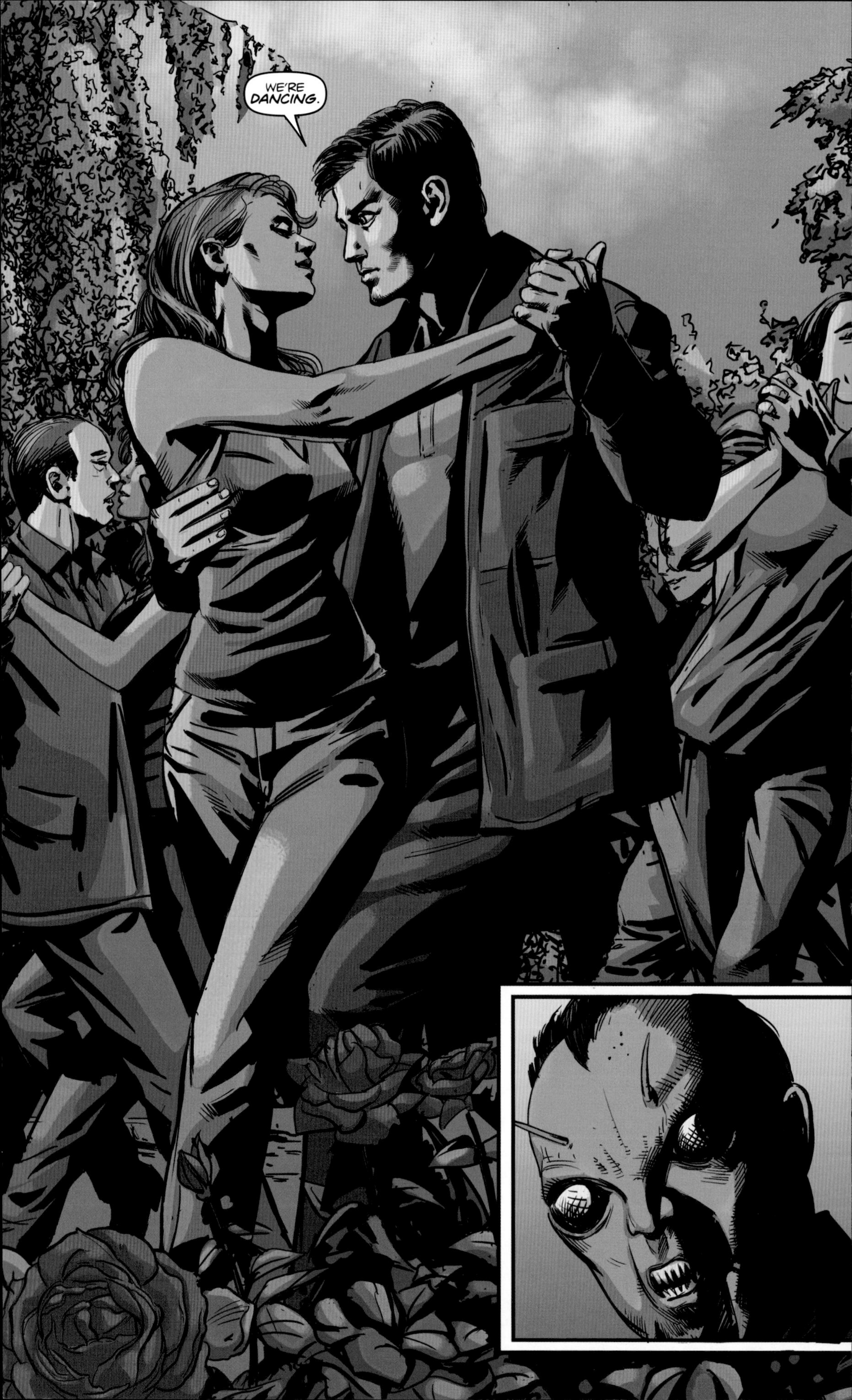
WE'RE DANCING.

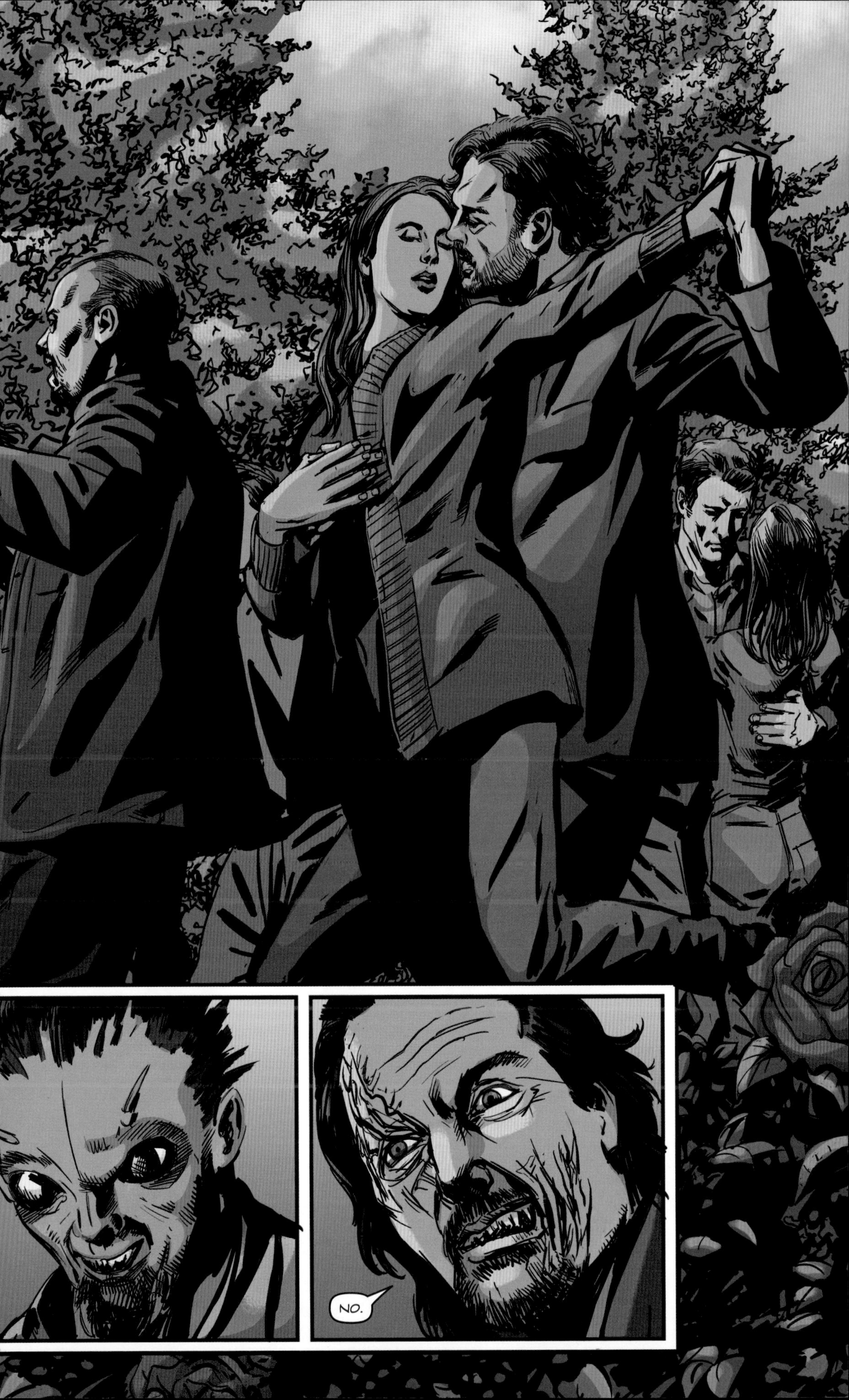
NO.

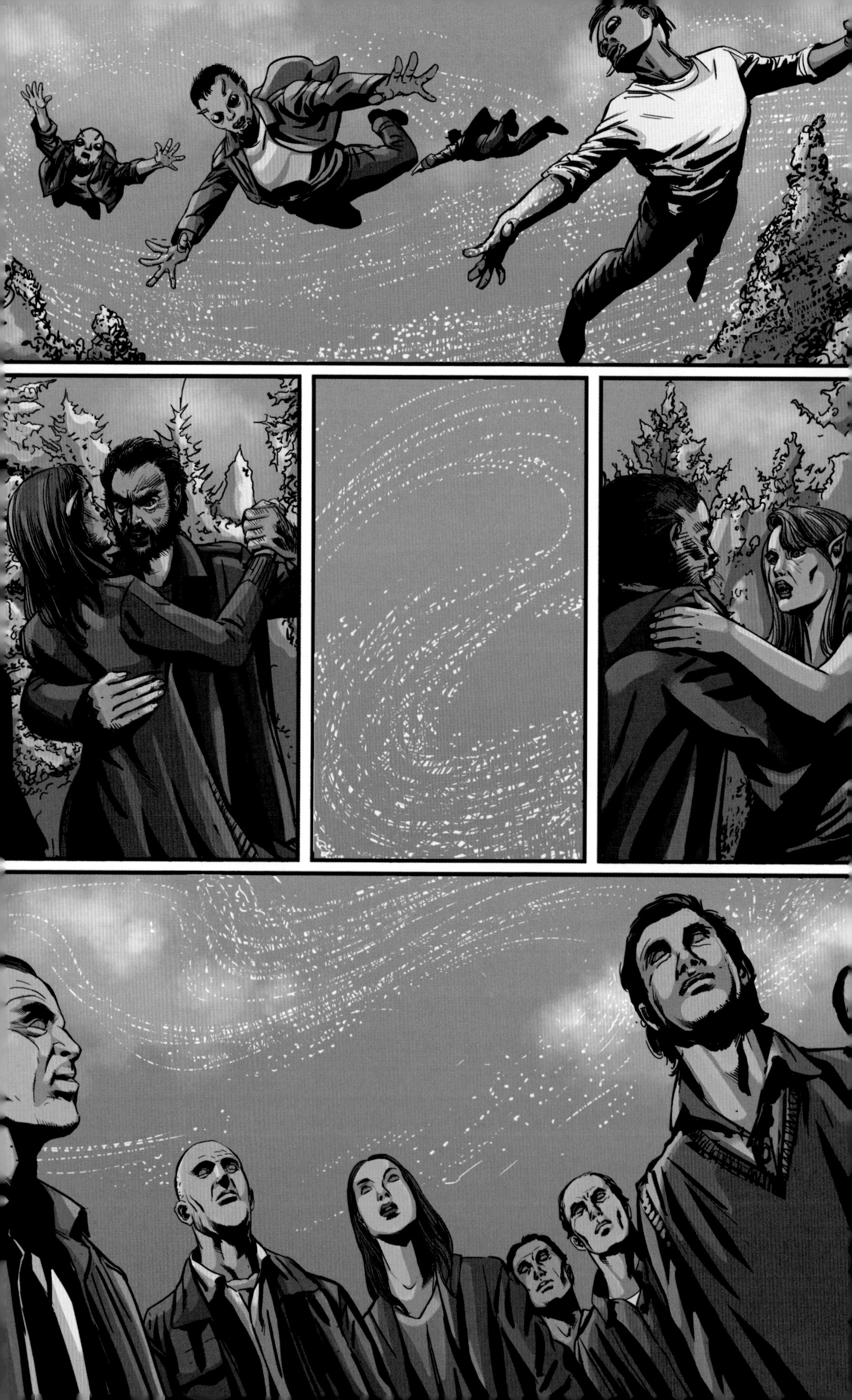

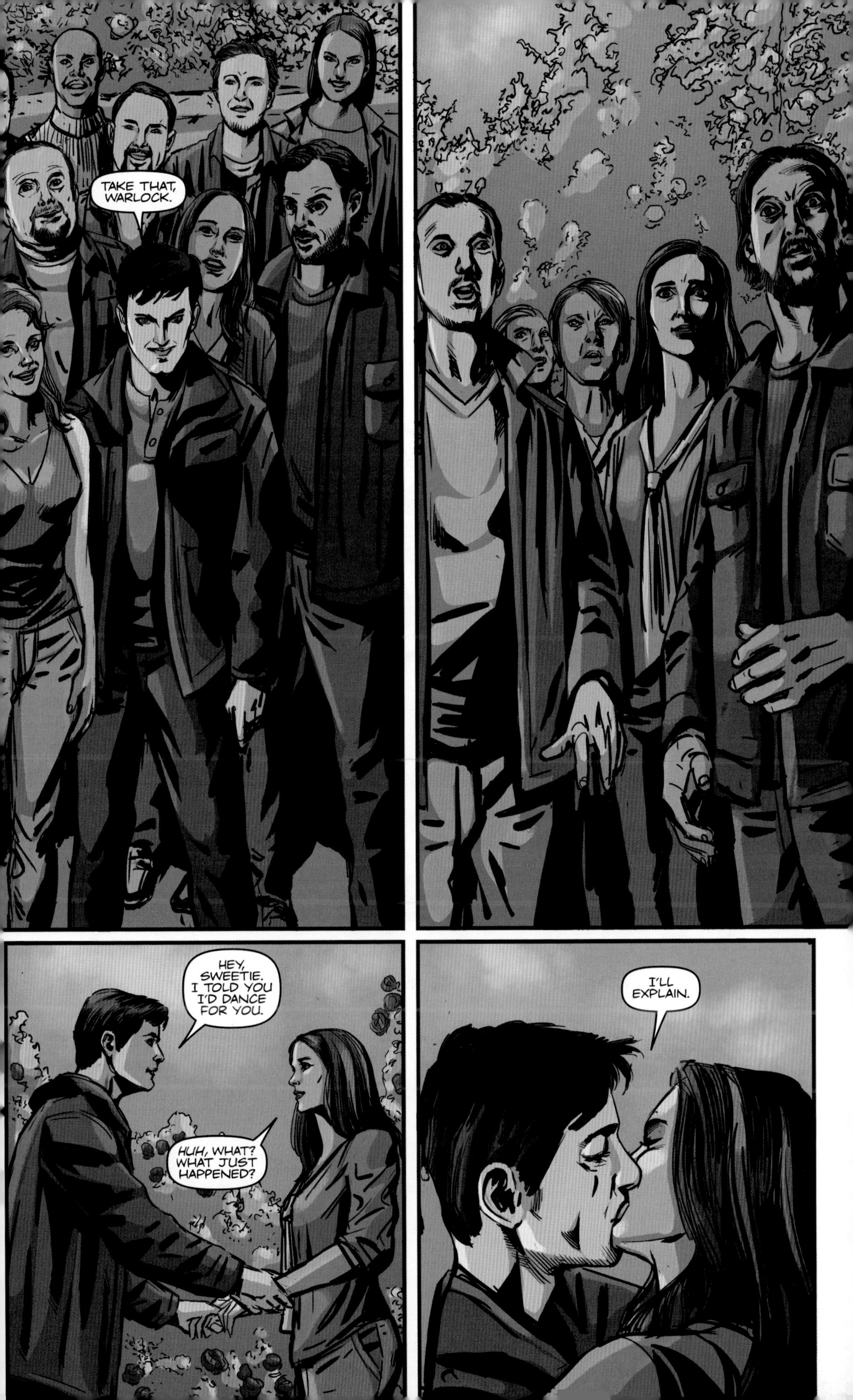
TAKE THAT, WARLOCK.
HEY, SWEETIE. I TOLD YOU I'D DANCE FOR YOU.
HUH, WHAT? WHAT JUST HAPPENED?
I'LL EXPLAIN.

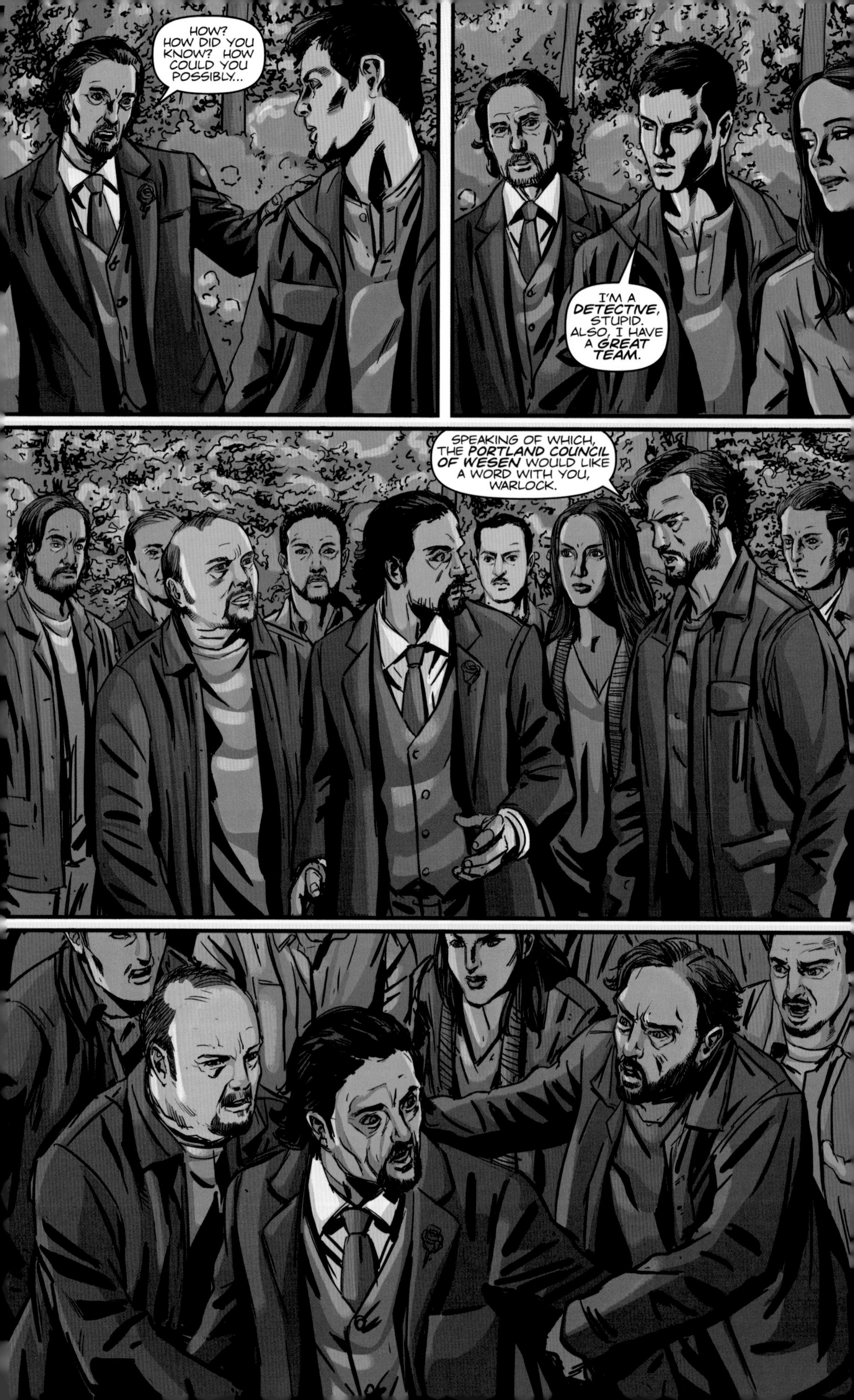
HOW? HOW DID YOU KNOW? HOW COULD YOU POSSIBLY...
I'M A **DETECTIVE**, STUPID. ALSO, I HAVE A **GREAT TEAM**.
SPEAKING OF WHICH, THE **PORTLAND COUNCIL OF WESEN** WOULD LIKE A WORD WITH YOU, WARLOCK.

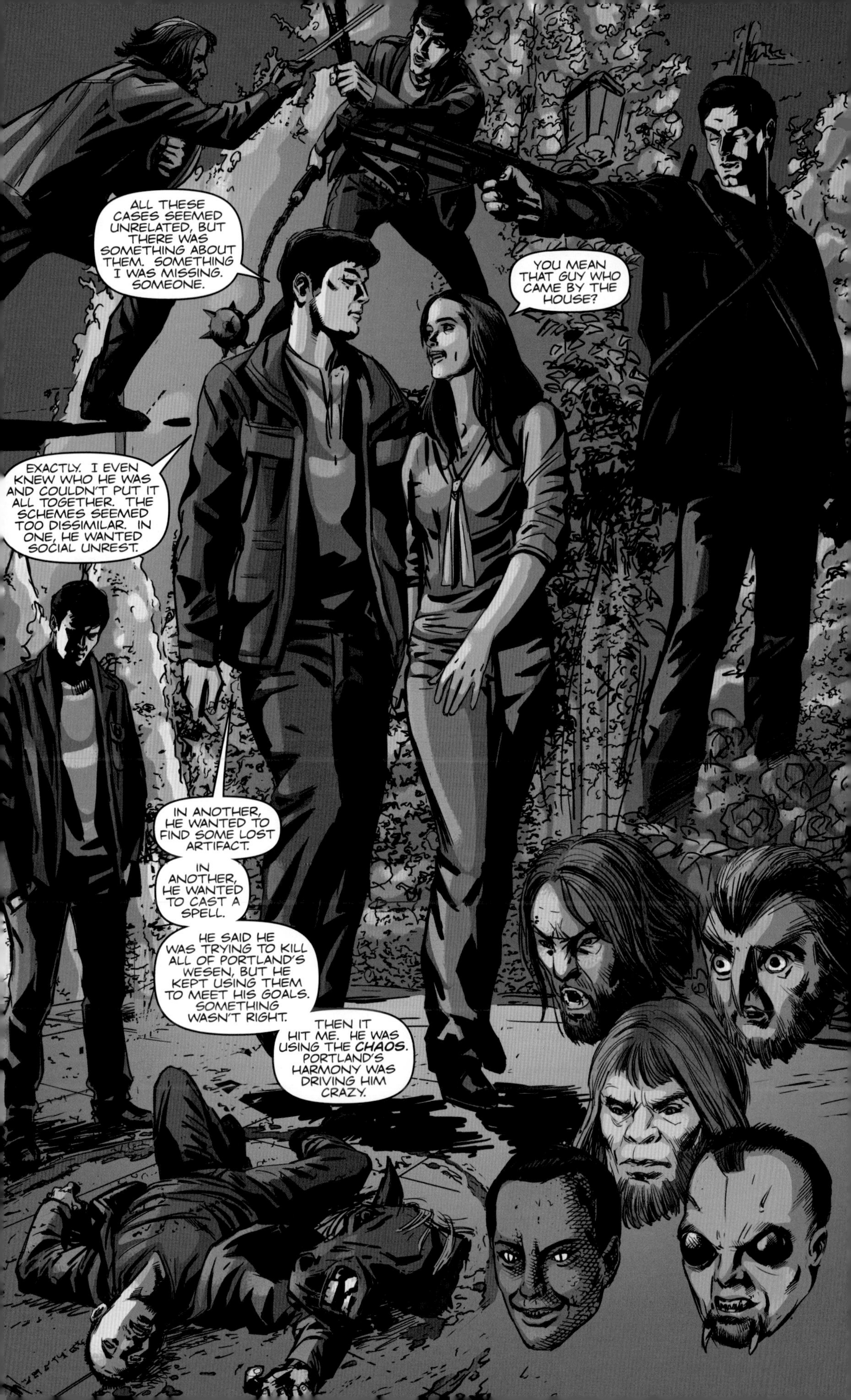
ALL THESE CASES SEEMED UNRELATED, BUT THERE WAS SOMETHING ABOUT THEM. SOMETHING I WAS MISSING. SOMEONE.
YOU MEAN THAT GUY WHO CAME BY THE HOUSE?
EXACTLY. I EVEN KNEW WHO HE WAS AND COULDN'T PUT IT ALL TOGETHER. THE SCHEMES SEEMED TOO DISSIMILAR. IN ONE, HE WANTED SOCIAL UNREST.
IN ANOTHER, HE WANTED TO FIND SOME LOST ARTIFACT.
IN ANOTHER, HE WANTED TO CAST A SPELL.
HE SAID HE WAS TRYING TO KILL ALL OF PORTLAND'S WESEN, BUT HE KEPT USING THEM TO MEET HIS GOALS. SOMETHING WASN'T RIGHT.
THEN IT HIT ME. HE WAS USING THE CHAOS. PORTLAND'S HARMONY WAS DRIVING HIM CRAZY.

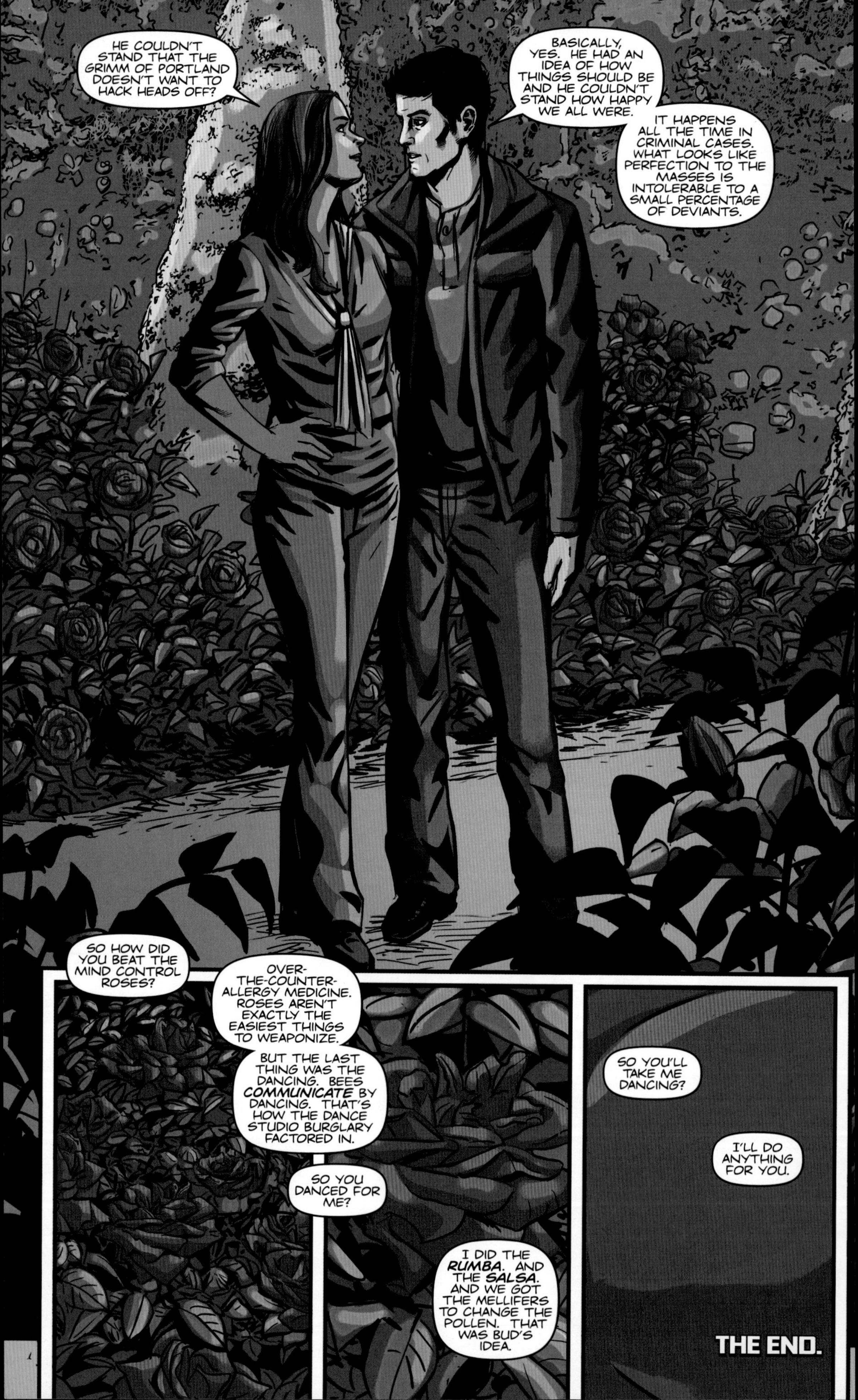
HE COULDN'T STAND THAT THE GRIMM OF PORTLAND DOESN'T WANT TO HACK HEADS OFF?
BASICALLY, YES. HE HAD AN IDEA OF HOW THINGS SHOULD BE AND HE COULDN'T STAND HOW HAPPY WE ALL WERE.
IT HAPPENS ALL THE TIME IN CRIMINAL CASES. WHAT LOOKS LIKE PERFECTION TO THE MASSES IS INTOLERABLE TO A SMALL PERCENTAGE OF DEVIANTS.
SO HOW DID YOU BEAT THE MIND CONTROL ROSES?
OVER-THE-COUNTER-ALLERGY MEDICINE. ROSES AREN'T EXACTLY THE EASIEST THINGS TO WEAPONIZE.
BUT THE LAST THING WAS THE DANCING. BEES ***COMMUNICATE*** BY DANCING. THAT'S HOW THE DANCE STUDIO BURGLARY FACTORED IN.
SO YOU DANCED FOR ME?
I DID THE ***RUMBA***. AND THE ***SALSA***. AND WE GOT THE MELLIFERS TO CHANGE THE POLLEN. THAT WAS BUD'S IDEA.
SO YOU'LL TAKE ME DANCING?
I'LL DO ANYTHING FOR YOU.
THE END.

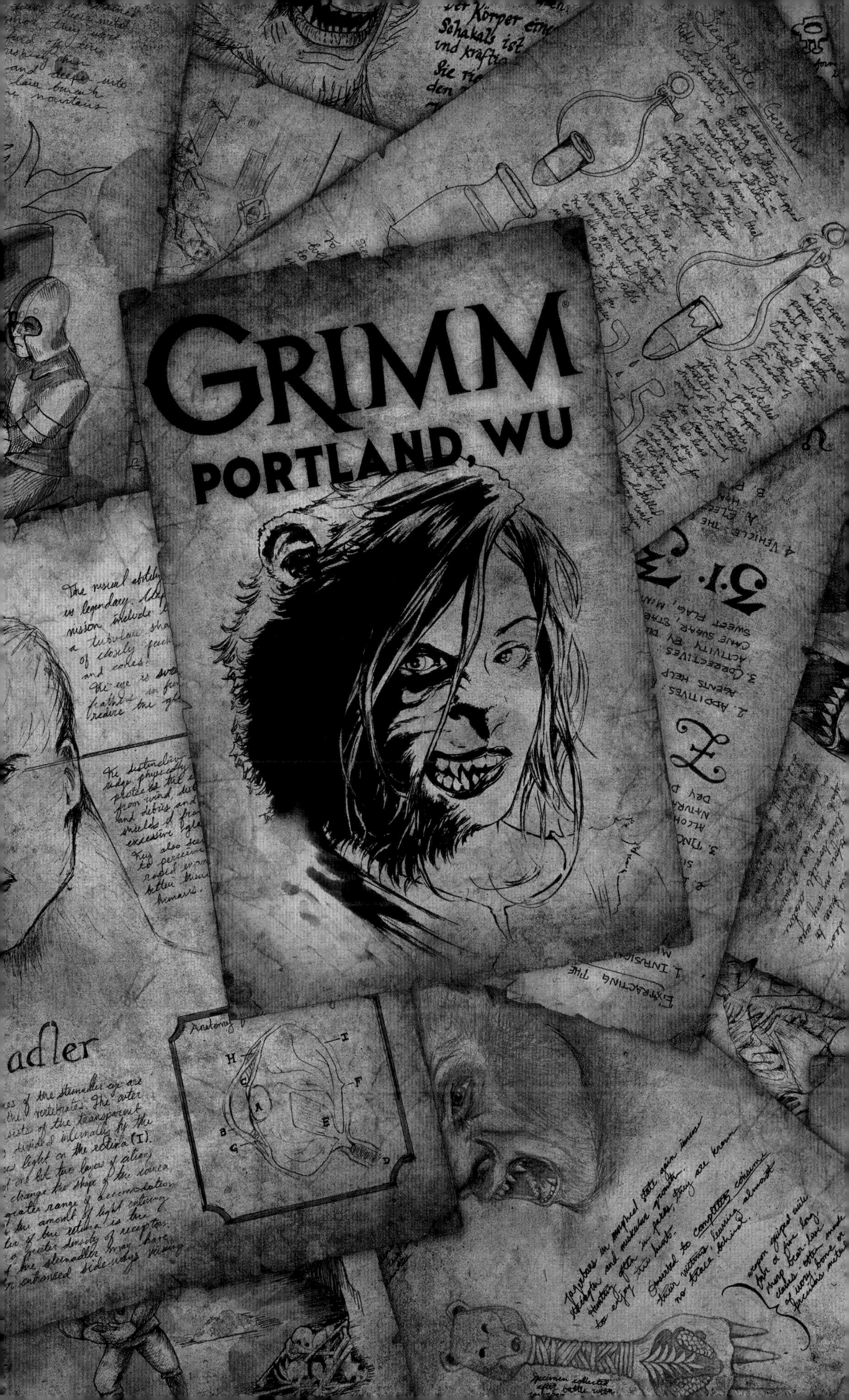
GRIMM®
PORTLAND, WU

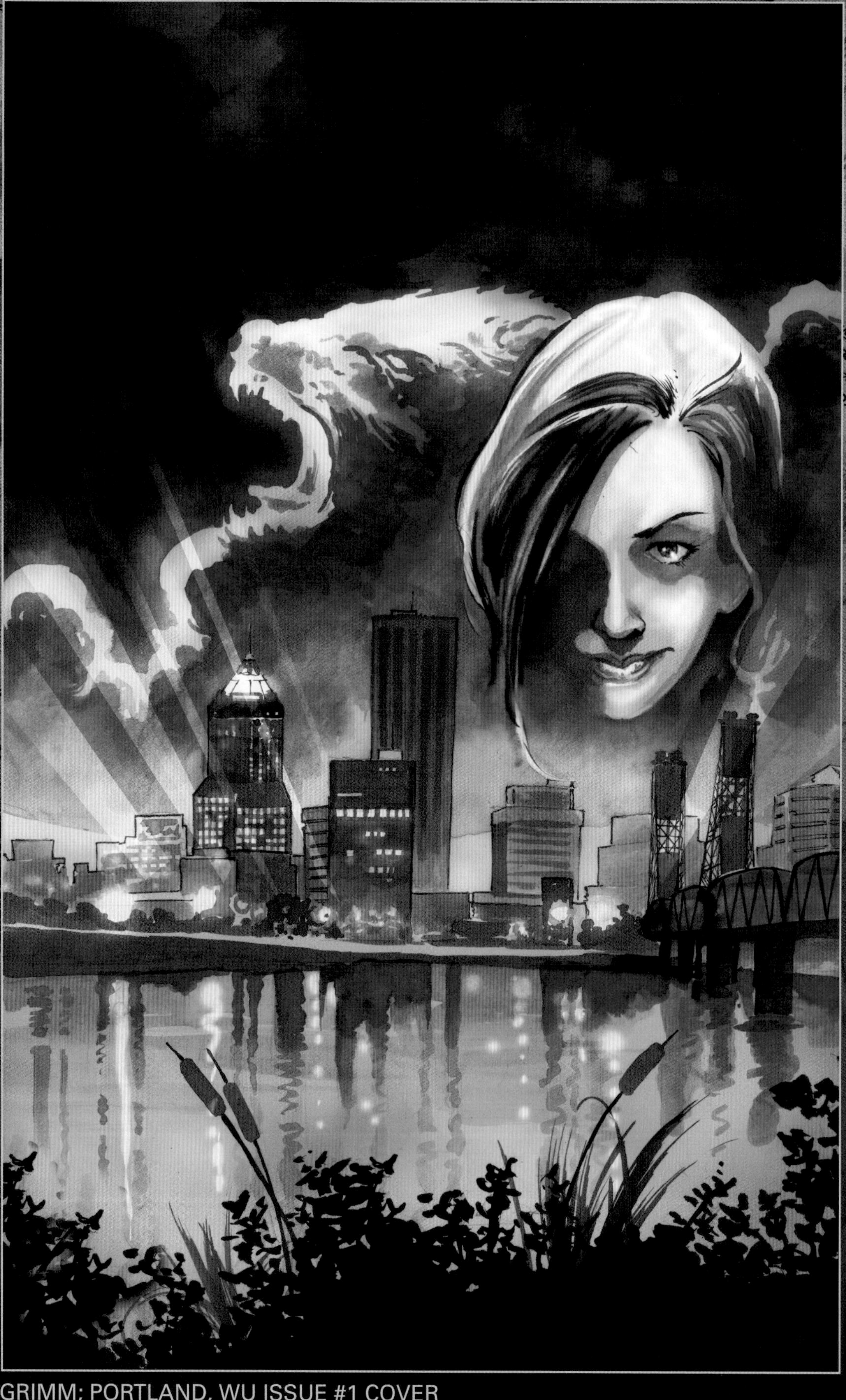

GRIMM; PORTLAND, WU ISSUE #1 COVER
ART BY DANIEL GOVER

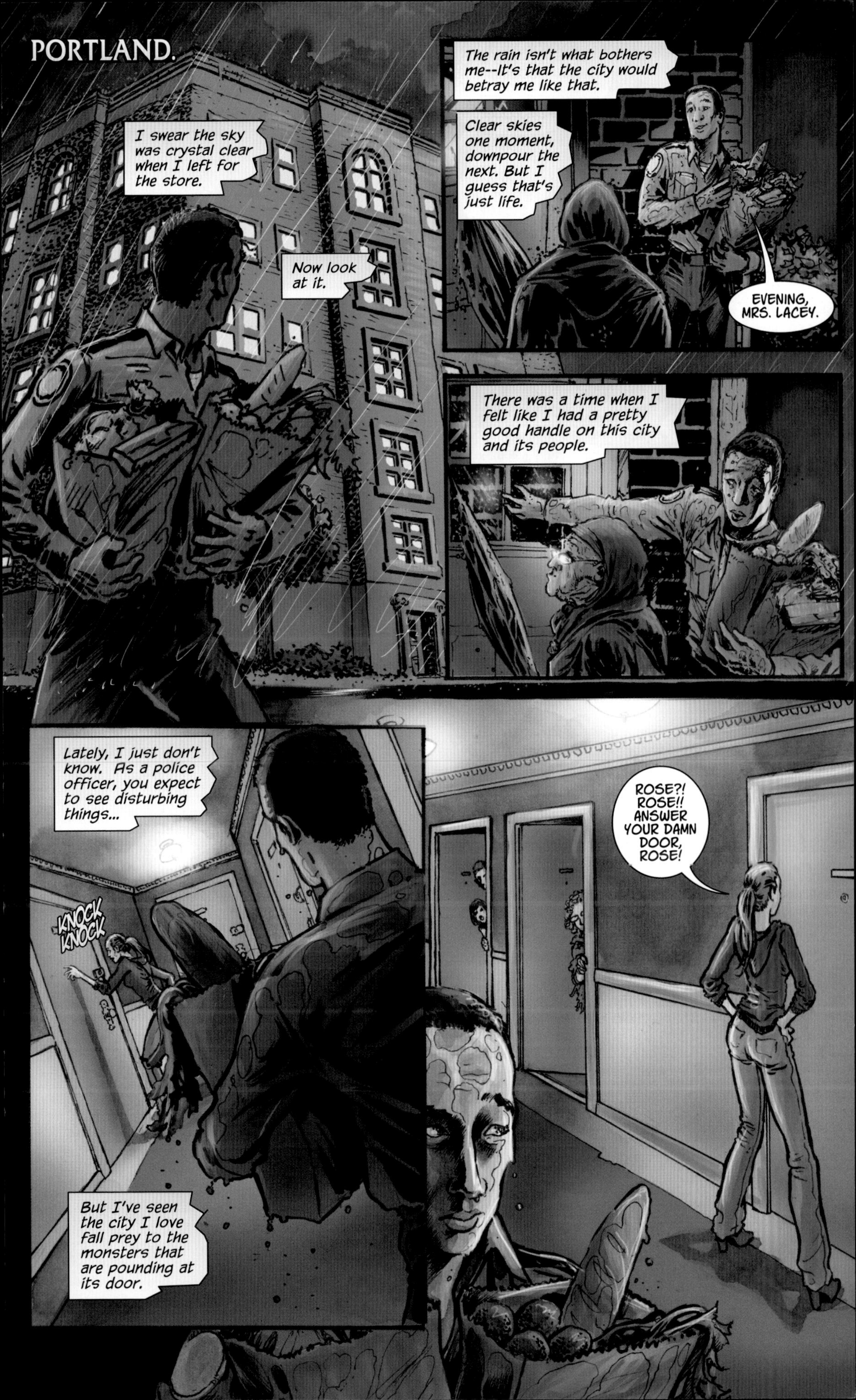
PORTLAND.
I swear the sky was crystal clear when I left for the store.
Now look at it.
The rain isn't what bothers me--It's that the city would betray me like that.
Clear skies one moment, downpour the next. But I guess that's just life.
EVENING, MRS. LACEY.
There was a time when I felt like I had a pretty good handle on this city and its people.
Lately, I just don't know. As a police officer, you expect to see disturbing things...
KNOCK KNOCK
ROSE?! ROSE!! ANSWER YOUR DAMN DOOR, ROSE!
But I've seen the city I love fall prey to the monsters that are pounding at its door.

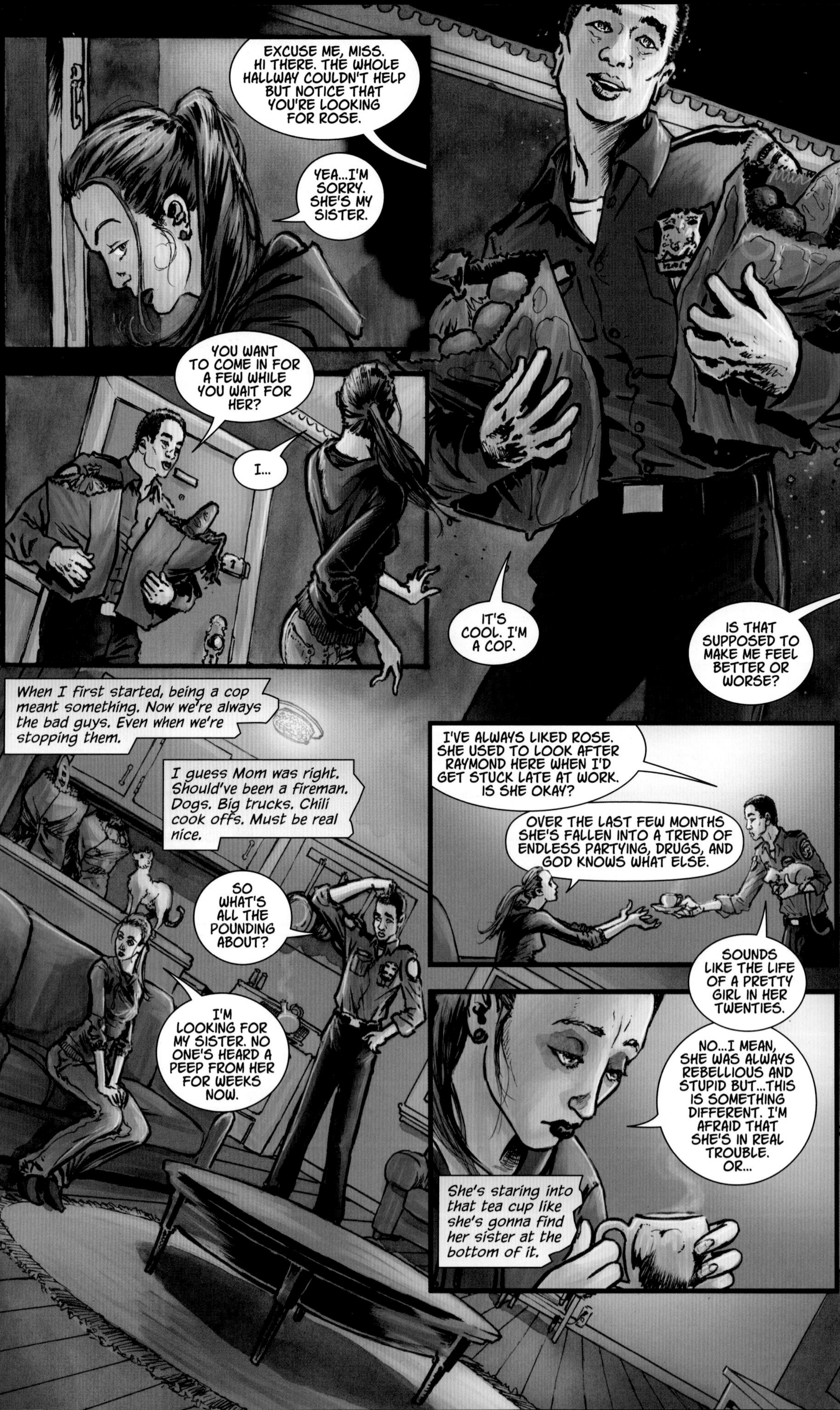
EXCUSE ME, MISS. HI THERE. THE WHOLE HALLWAY COULDN'T HELP BUT NOTICE THAT YOU'RE LOOKING FOR ROSE.
YEA...I'M SORRY. SHE'S MY SISTER.
YOU WANT TO COME IN FOR A FEW WHILE YOU WAIT FOR HER?
I...
IT'S COOL. I'M A COP.
IS THAT SUPPOSED TO MAKE ME FEEL BETTER OR WORSE?
When I first started, being a cop meant something. Now we're always the bad guys. Even when we're stopping them.
I guess Mom was right. Should've been a fireman. Dogs. Big trucks. Chili cook offs. Must be real nice.
SO WHAT'S ALL THE POUNDING ABOUT?
I'M LOOKING FOR MY SISTER. NO ONE'S HEARD A PEEP FROM HER FOR WEEKS NOW.
I'VE ALWAYS LIKED ROSE. SHE USED TO LOOK AFTER RAYMOND HERE WHEN I'D GET STUCK LATE AT WORK. IS SHE OKAY?
OVER THE LAST FEW MONTHS SHE'S FALLEN INTO A TREND OF ENDLESS PARTYING, DRUGS, AND GOD KNOWS WHAT ELSE.
SOUNDS LIKE THE LIFE OF A PRETTY GIRL IN HER TWENTIES.
NO...I MEAN, SHE WAS ALWAYS REBELLIOUS AND STUPID BUT...THIS IS SOMETHING DIFFERENT. I'M AFRAID THAT SHE'S IN REAL TROUBLE. OR...
She's staring into that tea cup like she's gonna find her sister at the bottom of it.

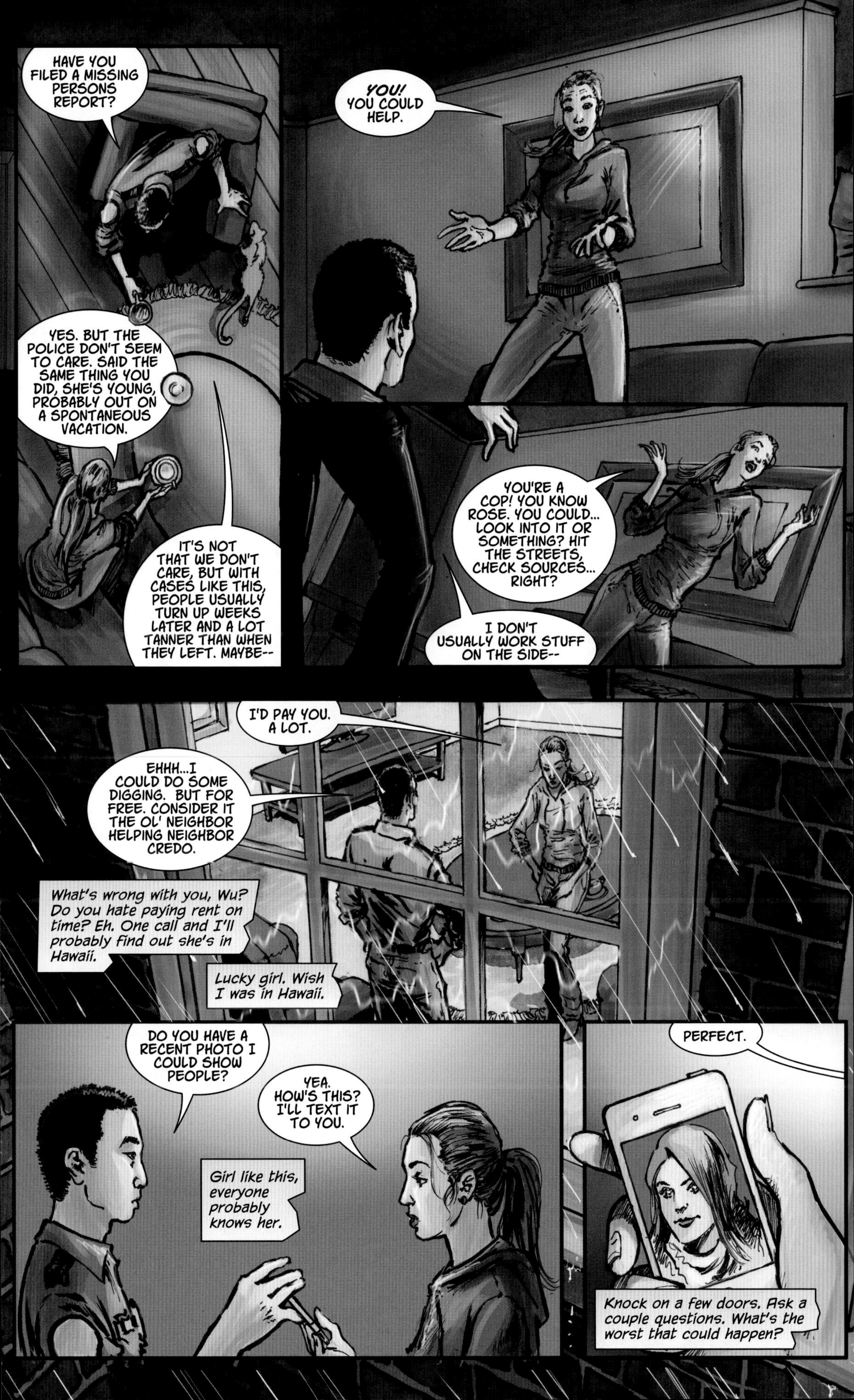
HAVE YOU FILED A MISSING PERSONS REPORT?
YES. BUT THE POLICE DON'T SEEM TO CARE. SAID THE SAME THING YOU DID, SHE'S YOUNG, PROBABLY OUT ON A SPONTANEOUS VACATION.
IT'S NOT THAT WE DON'T CARE, BUT WITH CASES LIKE THIS, PEOPLE USUALLY TURN UP WEEKS LATER AND A LOT TANNER THAN WHEN THEY LEFT. MAYBE--
YOU! YOU COULD HELP.
YOU'RE A COP! YOU KNOW ROSE. YOU COULD... LOOK INTO IT OR SOMETHING? HIT THE STREETS, CHECK SOURCES... RIGHT?
I DON'T USUALLY WORK STUFF ON THE SIDE--
I'D PAY YOU. A LOT.
EHHH...I COULD DO SOME DIGGING. BUT FOR FREE. CONSIDER IT THE OL' NEIGHBOR HELPING NEIGHBOR CREDO.
What's wrong with you, Wu? Do you hate paying rent on time? Eh. One call and I'll probably find out she's in Hawaii.
Lucky girl. Wish I was in Hawaii.
DO YOU HAVE A RECENT PHOTO I COULD SHOW PEOPLE?
YEA. HOW'S THIS? I'LL TEXT IT TO YOU.
Girl like this, everyone probably knows her.
PERFECT.
Knock on a few doors. Ask a couple questions. What's the worst that could happen?

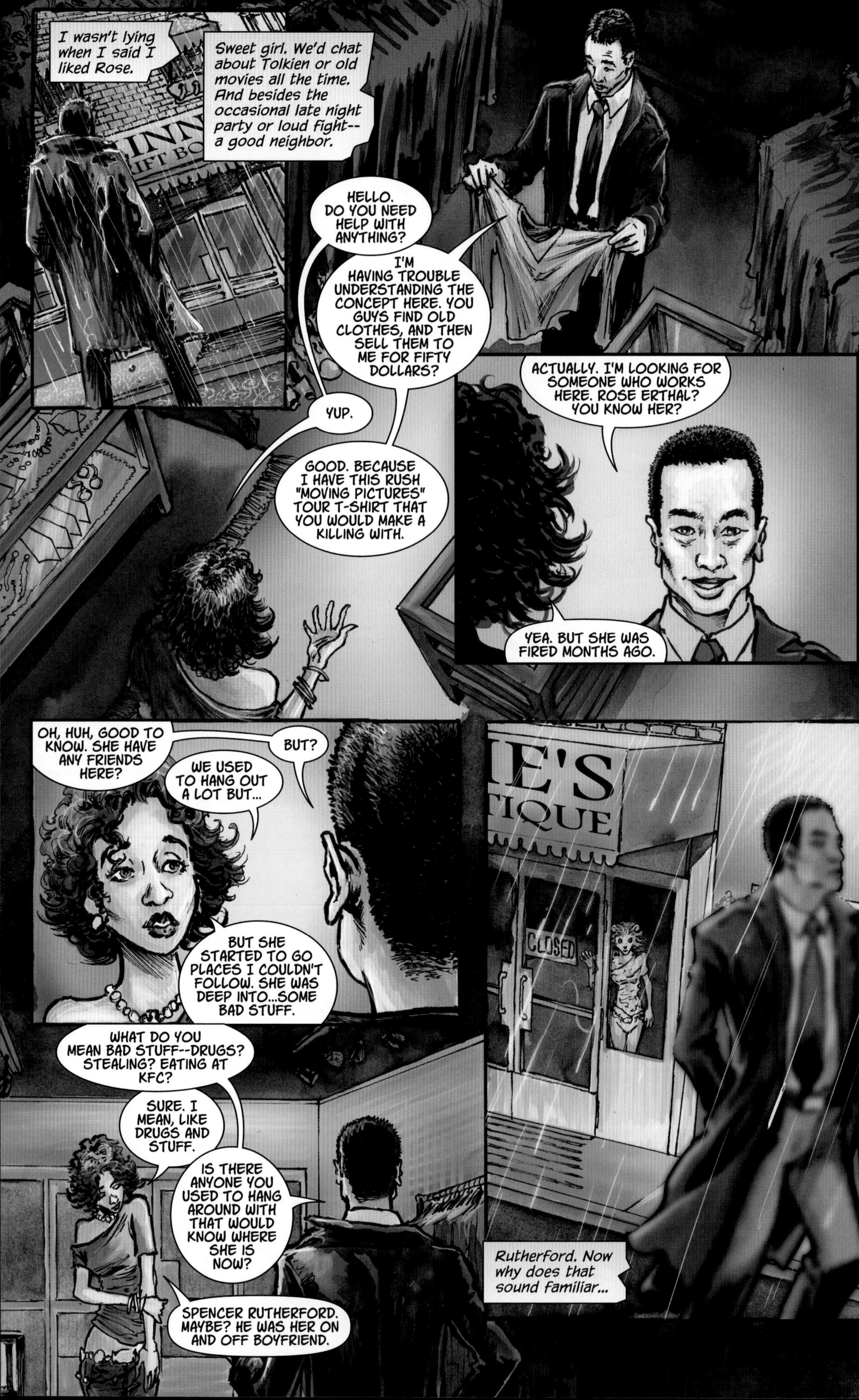
I wasn't lying when I said I liked Rose.
Sweet girl. We'd chat about Tolkien or old movies all the time. And besides the occasional late night party or loud fight--a good neighbor.
INN
IFT BO
HELLO. DO YOU NEED HELP WITH ANYTHING?
I'M HAVING TROUBLE UNDERSTANDING THE CONCEPT HERE. YOU GUYS FIND OLD CLOTHES, AND THEN SELL THEM TO ME FOR FIFTY DOLLARS?
YUP.
GOOD. BECAUSE I HAVE THIS RUSH "MOVING PICTURES" TOUR T-SHIRT THAT YOU WOULD MAKE A KILLING WITH.
ACTUALLY. I'M LOOKING FOR SOMEONE WHO WORKS HERE. ROSE ERTHAL? YOU KNOW HER?
YEA. BUT SHE WAS FIRED MONTHS AGO.
OH, HUH, GOOD TO KNOW. SHE HAVE ANY FRIENDS HERE?
WE USED TO HANG OUT A LOT BUT...
BUT?
BUT SHE STARTED TO GO PLACES I COULDN'T FOLLOW. SHE WAS DEEP INTO...SOME BAD STUFF.
WHAT DO YOU MEAN BAD STUFF--DRUGS? STEALING? EATING AT KFC?
SURE. I MEAN, LIKE DRUGS AND STUFF.
IS THERE ANYONE YOU USED TO HANG AROUND WITH THAT WOULD KNOW WHERE SHE IS NOW?
SPENCER RUTHERFORD. MAYBE? HE WAS HER ON AND OFF BOYFRIEND.
IE'S
TIQUE
CLOSED
Rutherford. Now why does that sound familiar...

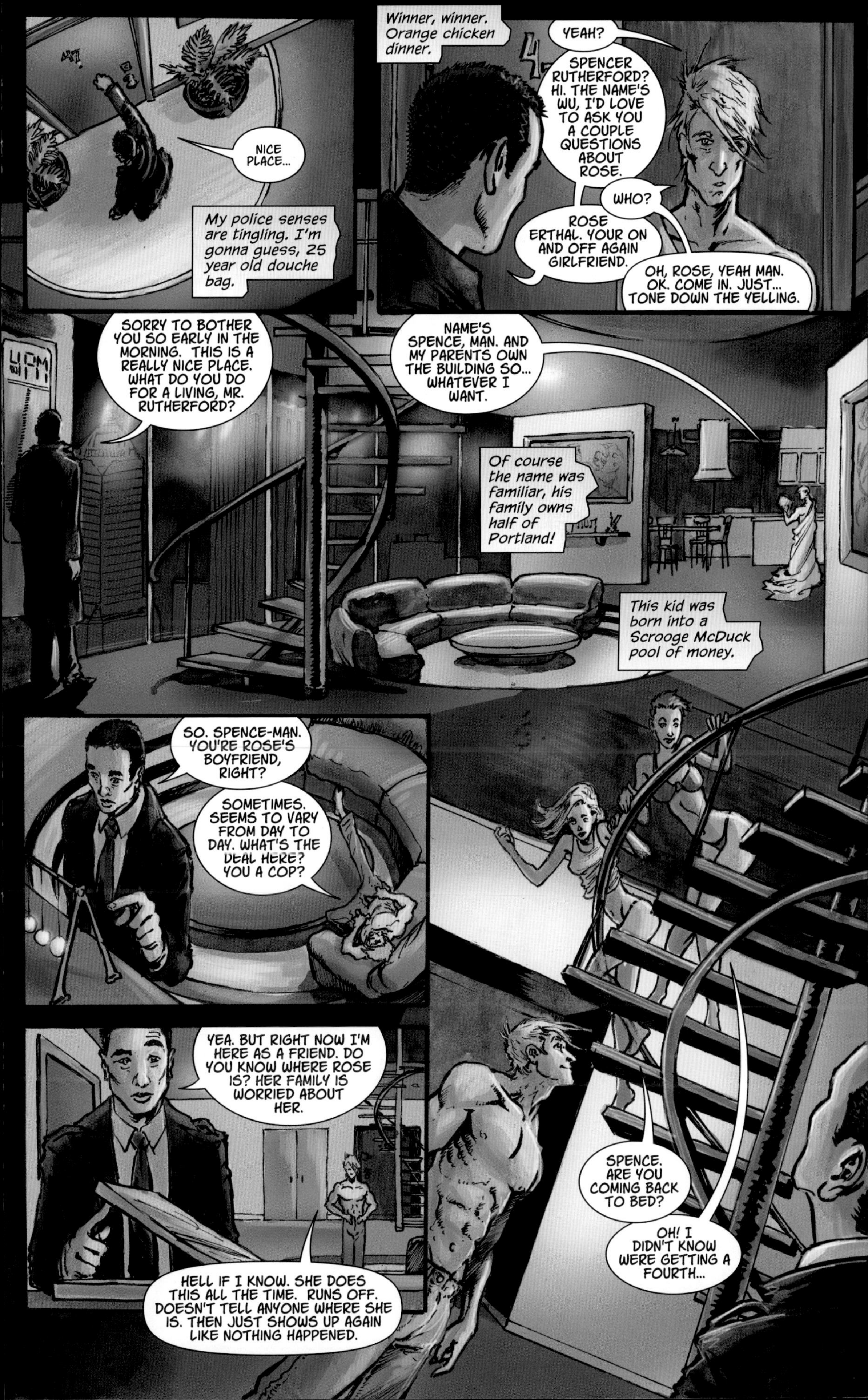
NICE PLACE...
My police senses are tingling. I'm gonna guess, 25 year old douche bag.
Winner, winner. Orange chicken dinner.
YEAH?
SPENCER RUTHERFORD? HI. THE NAME'S WU, I'D LOVE TO ASK YOU A COUPLE QUESTIONS ABOUT ROSE.
WHO?
ROSE ERTHAL. YOUR ON AND OFF AGAIN GIRLFRIEND.
OH, ROSE, YEAH MAN. OK. COME IN. JUST... TONE DOWN THE YELLING.
SORRY TO BOTHER YOU SO EARLY IN THE MORNING. THIS IS A REALLY NICE PLACE. WHAT DO YOU DO FOR A LIVING, MR. RUTHERFORD?
NAME'S SPENCE, MAN. AND MY PARENTS OWN THE BUILDING SO... WHATEVER I WANT.
Of course the name was familiar, his family owns half of Portland!
This kid was born into a Scrooge McDuck pool of money.
SO. SPENCE-MAN. YOU'RE ROSE'S BOYFRIEND, RIGHT?
SOMETIMES. SEEMS TO VARY FROM DAY TO DAY. WHAT'S THE DEAL HERE? YOU A COP?
YEA. BUT RIGHT NOW I'M HERE AS A FRIEND. DO YOU KNOW WHERE ROSE IS? HER FAMILY IS WORRIED ABOUT HER.
HELL IF I KNOW. SHE DOES THIS ALL THE TIME. RUNS OFF. DOESN'T TELL ANYONE WHERE SHE IS. THEN JUST SHOWS UP AGAIN LIKE NOTHING HAPPENED.
SPENCE. ARE YOU COMING BACK TO BED?
OH! I DIDN'T KNOW WERE GETTING A FOURTH...

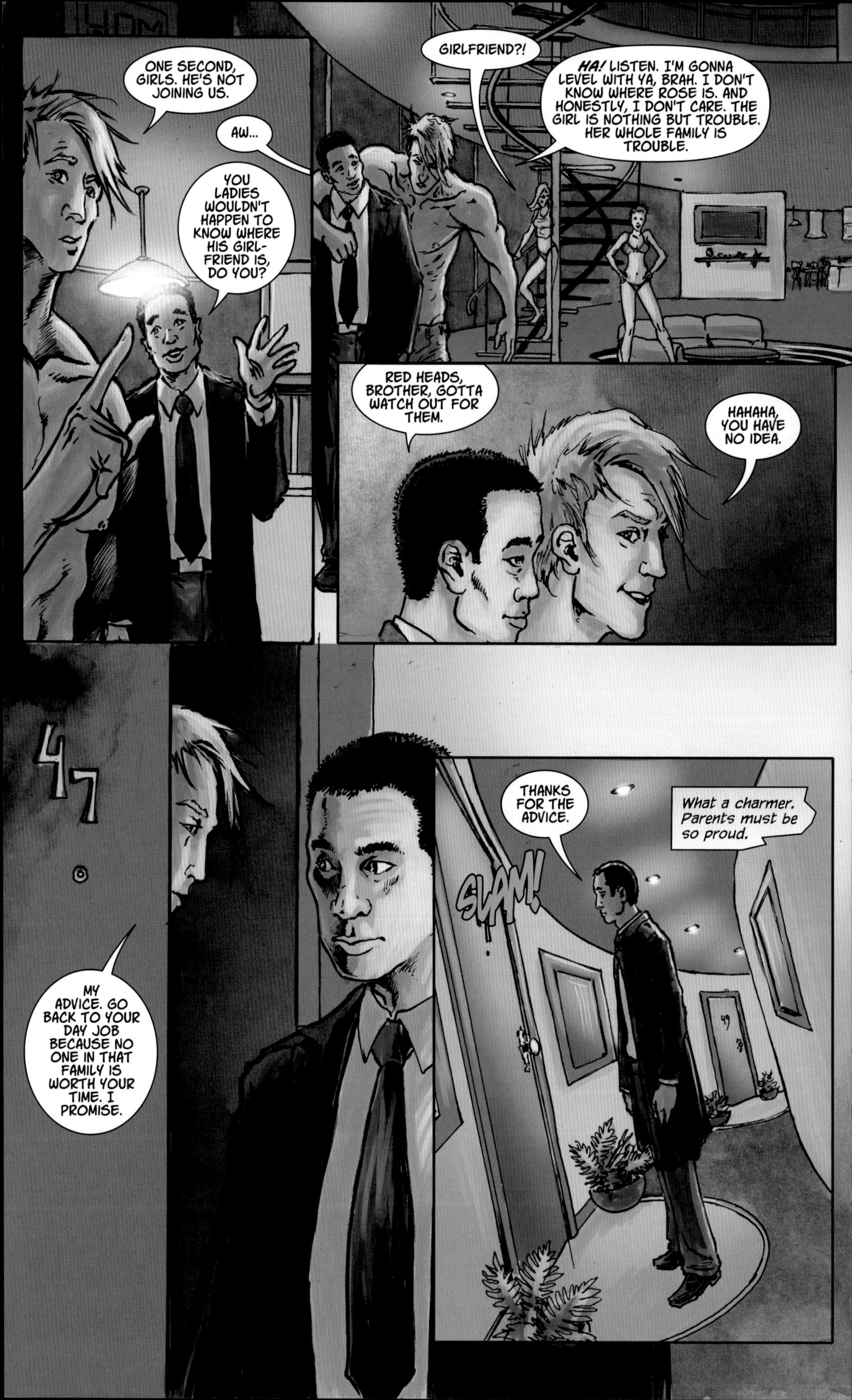

ONE SECOND, GIRLS. HE'S NOT JOINING US.
AW...
YOU LADIES WOULDN'T HAPPEN TO KNOW WHERE HIS GIRL-FRIEND IS, DO YOU?
GIRLFRIEND?!
HA! LISTEN. I'M GONNA LEVEL WITH YA, BRAH. I DON'T KNOW WHERE ROSE IS. AND HONESTLY, I DON'T CARE. THE GIRL IS NOTHING BUT TROUBLE. HER WHOLE FAMILY IS TROUBLE.
RED HEADS, BROTHER, GOTTA WATCH OUT FOR THEM.
HAHAHA, YOU HAVE NO IDEA.
47
MY ADVICE. GO BACK TO YOUR DAY JOB BECAUSE NO ONE IN THAT FAMILY IS WORTH YOUR TIME. I PROMISE.
SLAM!
THANKS FOR THE ADVICE.
What a charmer. Parents must be so proud.

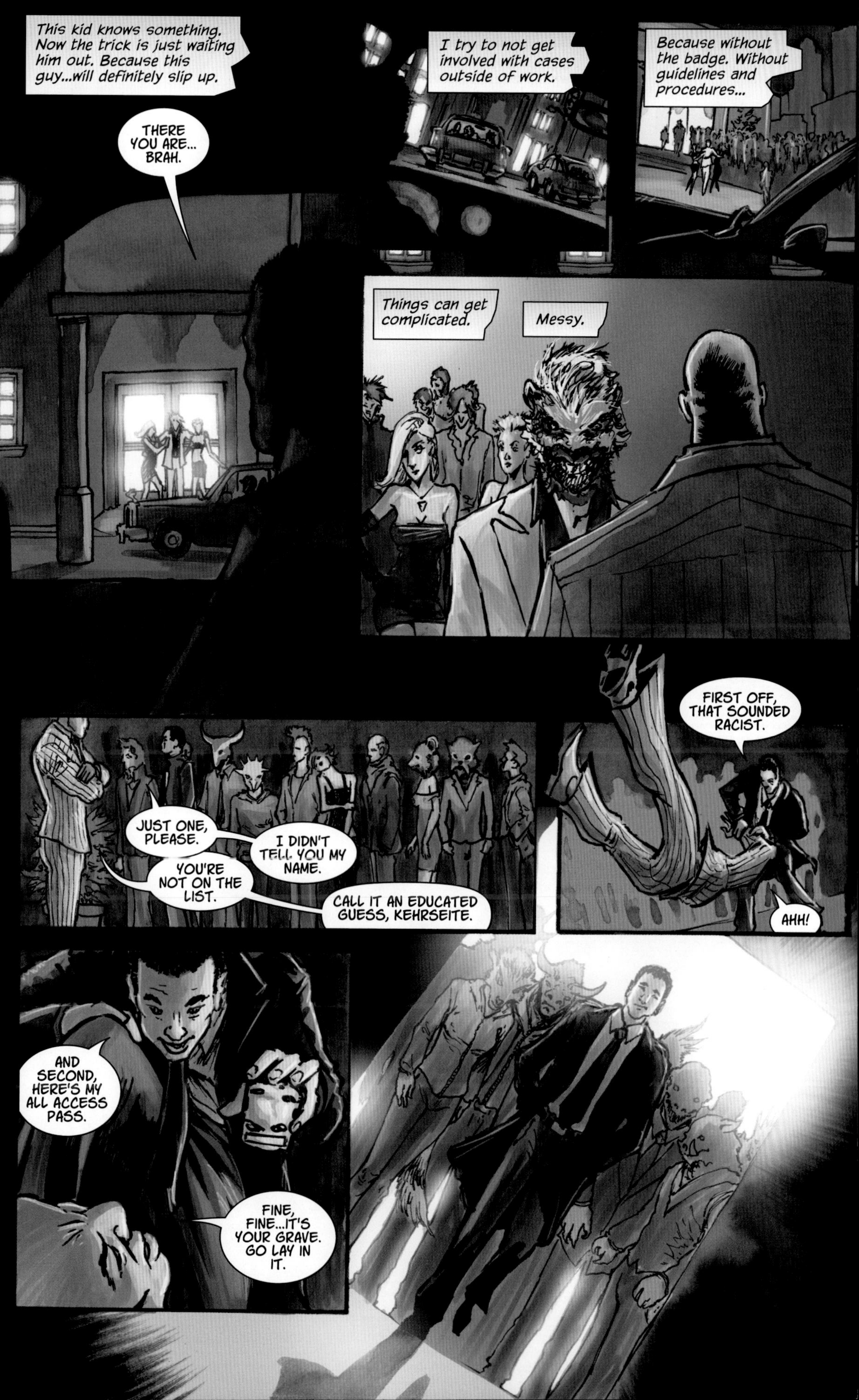
This kid knows something. Now the trick is just waiting him out. Because this guy...will definitely slip up.
THERE YOU ARE... BRAH.
I try to not get involved with cases outside of work.
Because without the badge. Without guidelines and procedures...
Things can get complicated.
Messy.
JUST ONE, PLEASE.
I DIDN'T TELL YOU MY NAME.
YOU'RE NOT ON THE LIST.
CALL IT AN EDUCATED GUESS, KEHRSEITE.
FIRST OFF, THAT SOUNDED RACIST.
AHH!
AND SECOND, HERE'S MY ALL ACCESS PASS.
FINE, FINE...IT'S YOUR GRAVE. GO LAY IN IT.

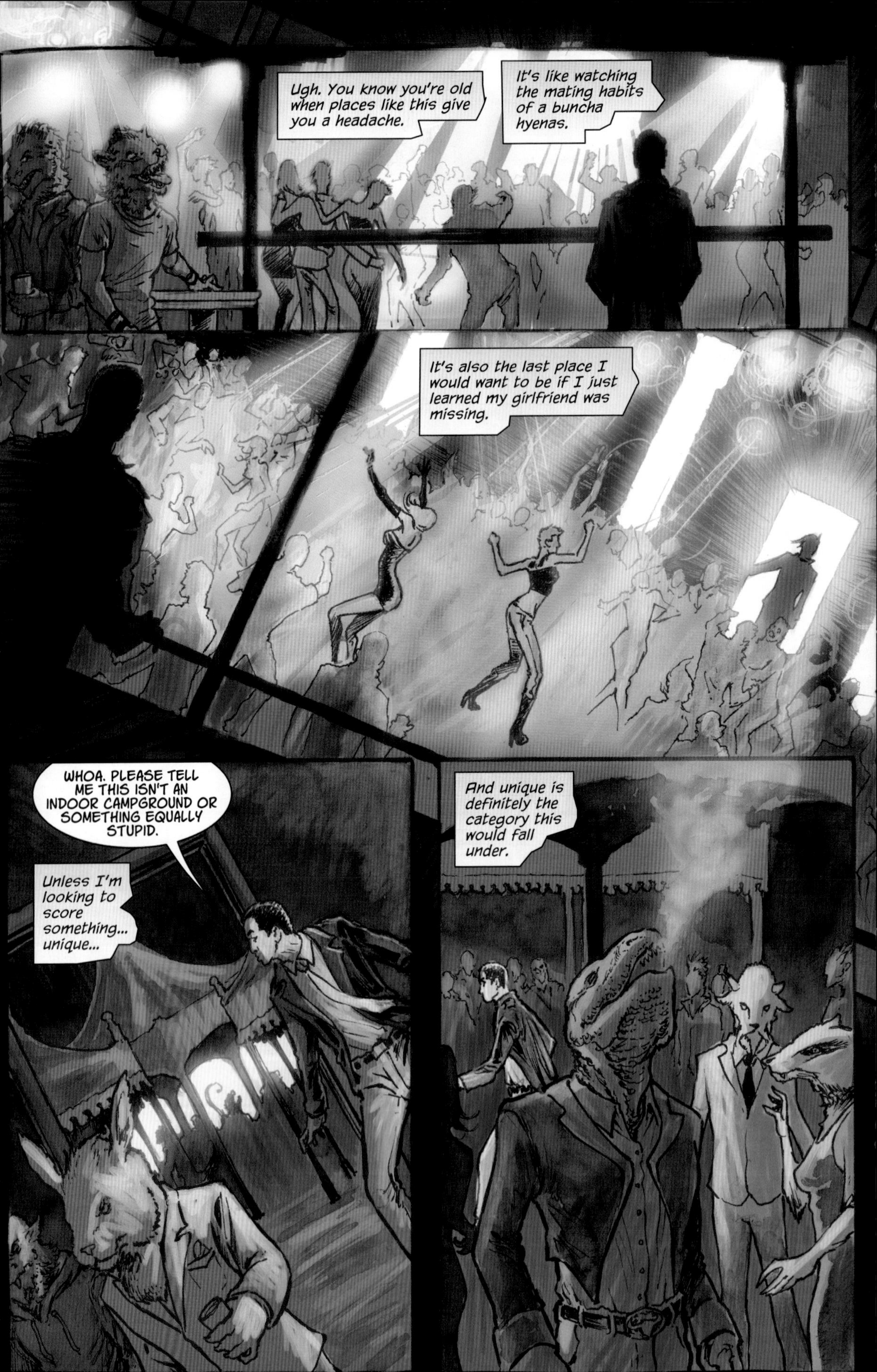
Ugh. You know you're old when places like this give you a headache.
It's like watching the mating habits of a buncha hyenas.
It's also the last place I would want to be if I just learned my girlfriend was missing.
WHOA. PLEASE TELL ME THIS ISN'T AN INDOOR CAMPGROUND OR SOMETHING EQUALLY STUPID.
Unless I'm looking to score something... unique...
And unique is definitely the category this would fall under.

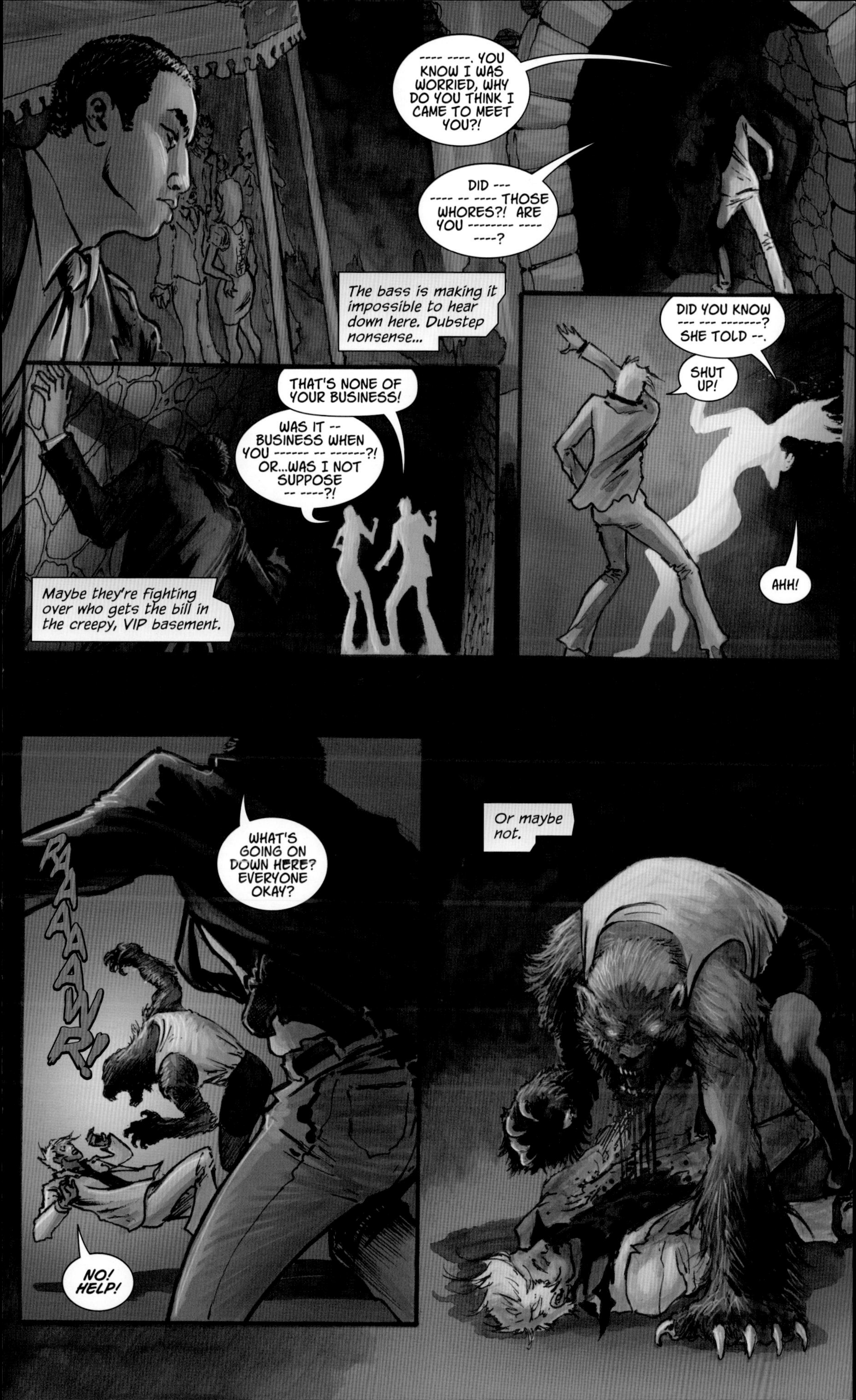
---- ----. YOU KNOW I WAS WORRIED, WHY DO YOU THINK I CAME TO MEET YOU?!
DID --- ---- -- ---- THOSE WHORES?! ARE YOU -------- ---- ----?
The bass is making it impossible to hear down here. Dubstep nonsense...
THAT'S NONE OF YOUR BUSINESS!
WAS IT -- BUSINESS WHEN YOU ------ -- ------?! OR...WAS I NOT SUPPOSE -- ----?!
Maybe they're fighting over who gets the bill in the creepy, VIP basement.
DID YOU KNOW --- --- -------? SHE TOLD --.
SHUT UP!
AHH!
WHAT'S GOING ON DOWN HERE? EVERYONE OKAY?
RAAAAWR!
NO! HELP!
Or maybe not.

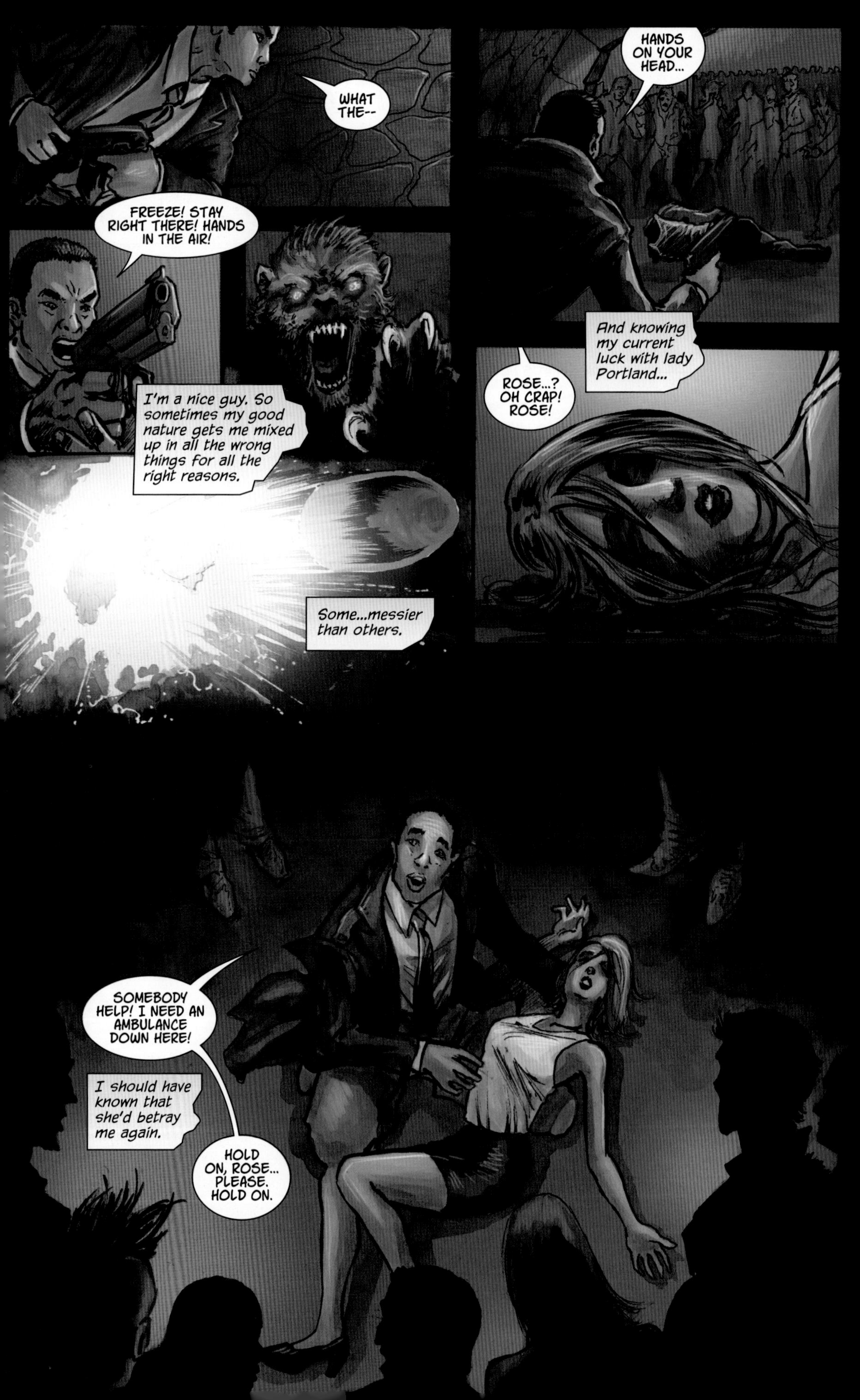
WHAT THE--
HANDS ON YOUR HEAD...
FREEZE! STAY RIGHT THERE! HANDS IN THE AIR!
I'm a nice guy. So sometimes my good nature gets me mixed up in all the wrong things for all the right reasons.
Some...messier than others.
And knowing my current luck with lady Portland...
ROSE...? OH CRAP! ROSE!
SOMEBODY HELP! I NEED AN AMBULANCE DOWN HERE!
I should have known that she'd betray me again.
HOLD ON, ROSE... PLEASE. HOLD ON.

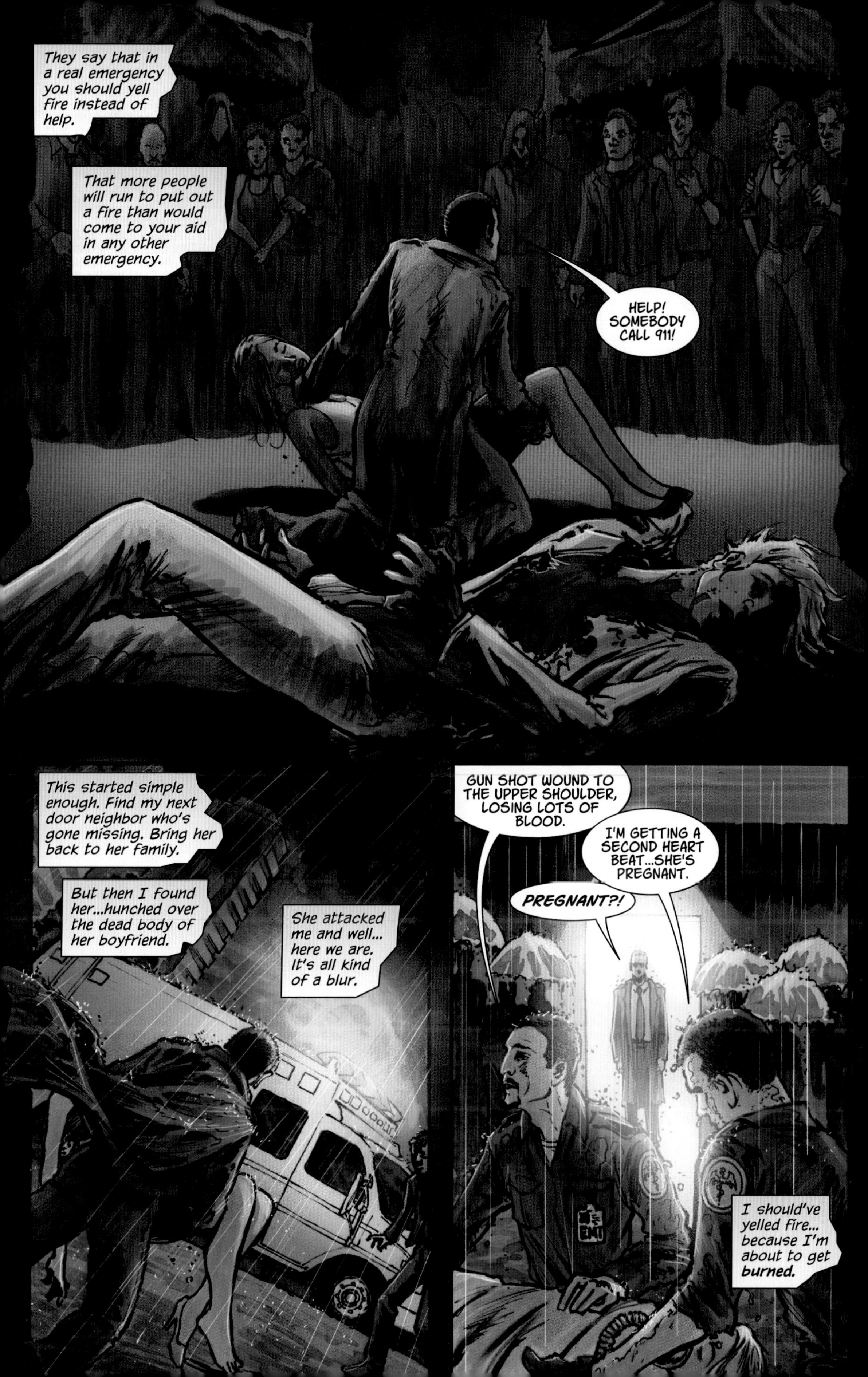

They say that in a real emergency you should yell fire instead of help.
That more people will run to put out a fire than would come to your aid in any other emergency.
HELP! SOMEBODY CALL 911!
This started simple enough. Find my next door neighbor who's gone missing. Bring her back to her family.
But then I found her...hunched over the dead body of her boyfriend.
She attacked me and well... here we are. It's all kind of a blur.
GUN SHOT WOUND TO THE UPPER SHOULDER, LOSING LOTS OF BLOOD.
I'M GETTING A SECOND HEART BEAT...SHE'S PREGNANT.
PREGNANT?!
EMT
I should've yelled fire... because I'm about to get burned.

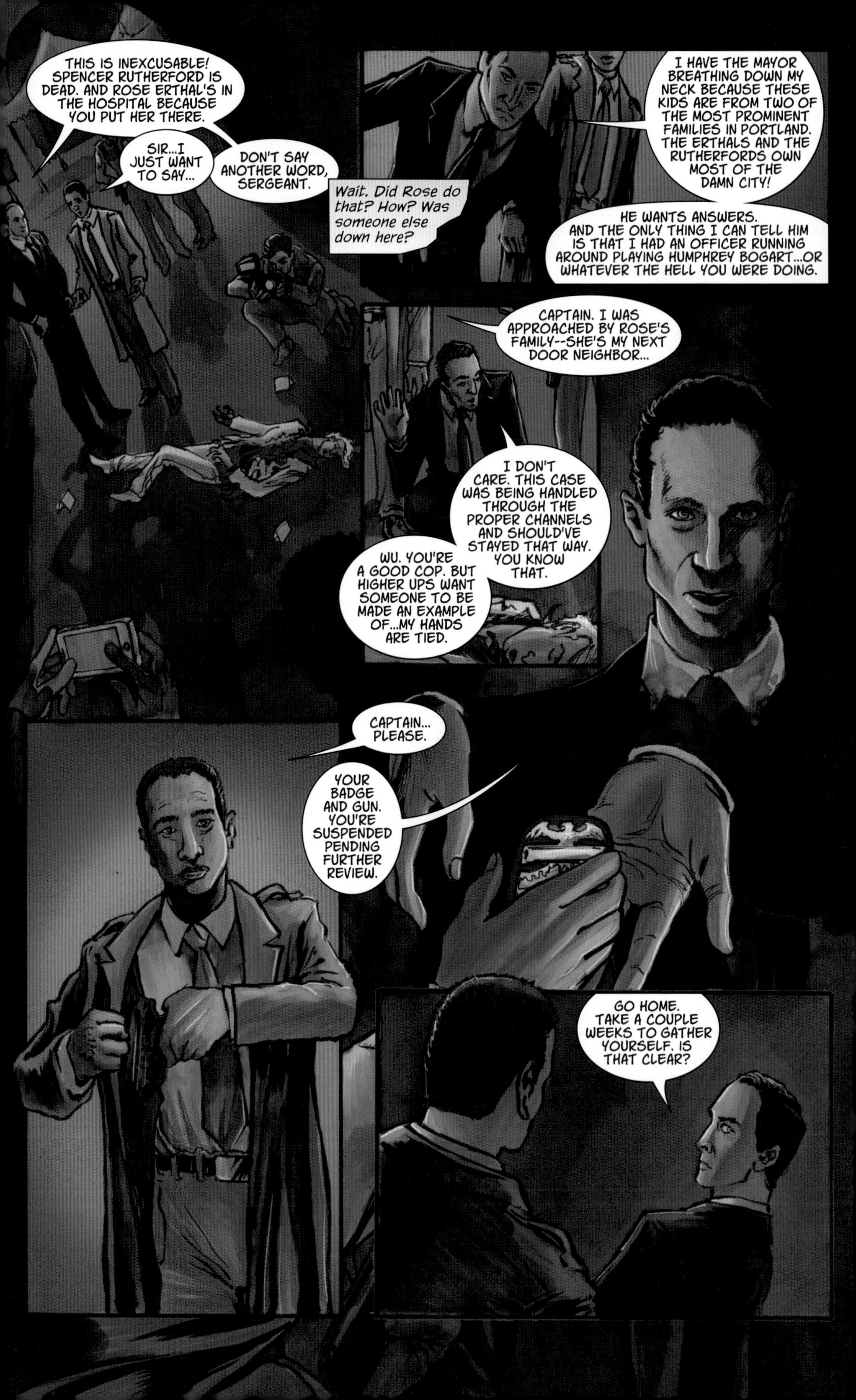
THIS IS INEXCUSABLE! SPENCER RUTHERFORD IS DEAD. AND ROSE ERTHAL'S IN THE HOSPITAL BECAUSE YOU PUT HER THERE.
SIR...I JUST WANT TO SAY...
DON'T SAY ANOTHER WORD, SERGEANT.
Wait. Did Rose do that? How? Was someone else down here?
I HAVE THE MAYOR BREATHING DOWN MY NECK BECAUSE THESE KIDS ARE FROM TWO OF THE MOST PROMINENT FAMILIES IN PORTLAND. THE ERTHALS AND THE RUTHERFORDS OWN MOST OF THE DAMN CITY!
HE WANTS ANSWERS. AND THE ONLY THING I CAN TELL HIM IS THAT I HAD AN OFFICER RUNNING AROUND PLAYING HUMPHREY BOGART...OR WHATEVER THE HELL YOU WERE DOING.
CAPTAIN. I WAS APPROACHED BY ROSE'S FAMILY--SHE'S MY NEXT DOOR NEIGHBOR...
I DON'T CARE. THIS CASE WAS BEING HANDLED THROUGH THE PROPER CHANNELS AND SHOULD'VE STAYED THAT WAY. YOU KNOW THAT.
WU. YOU'RE A GOOD COP. BUT HIGHER UPS WANT SOMEONE TO BE MADE AN EXAMPLE OF...MY HANDS ARE TIED.
CAPTAIN... PLEASE.
YOUR BADGE AND GUN. YOU'RE SUSPENDED PENDING FURTHER REVIEW.
GO HOME. TAKE A COUPLE WEEKS TO GATHER YOURSELF. IS THAT CLEAR?

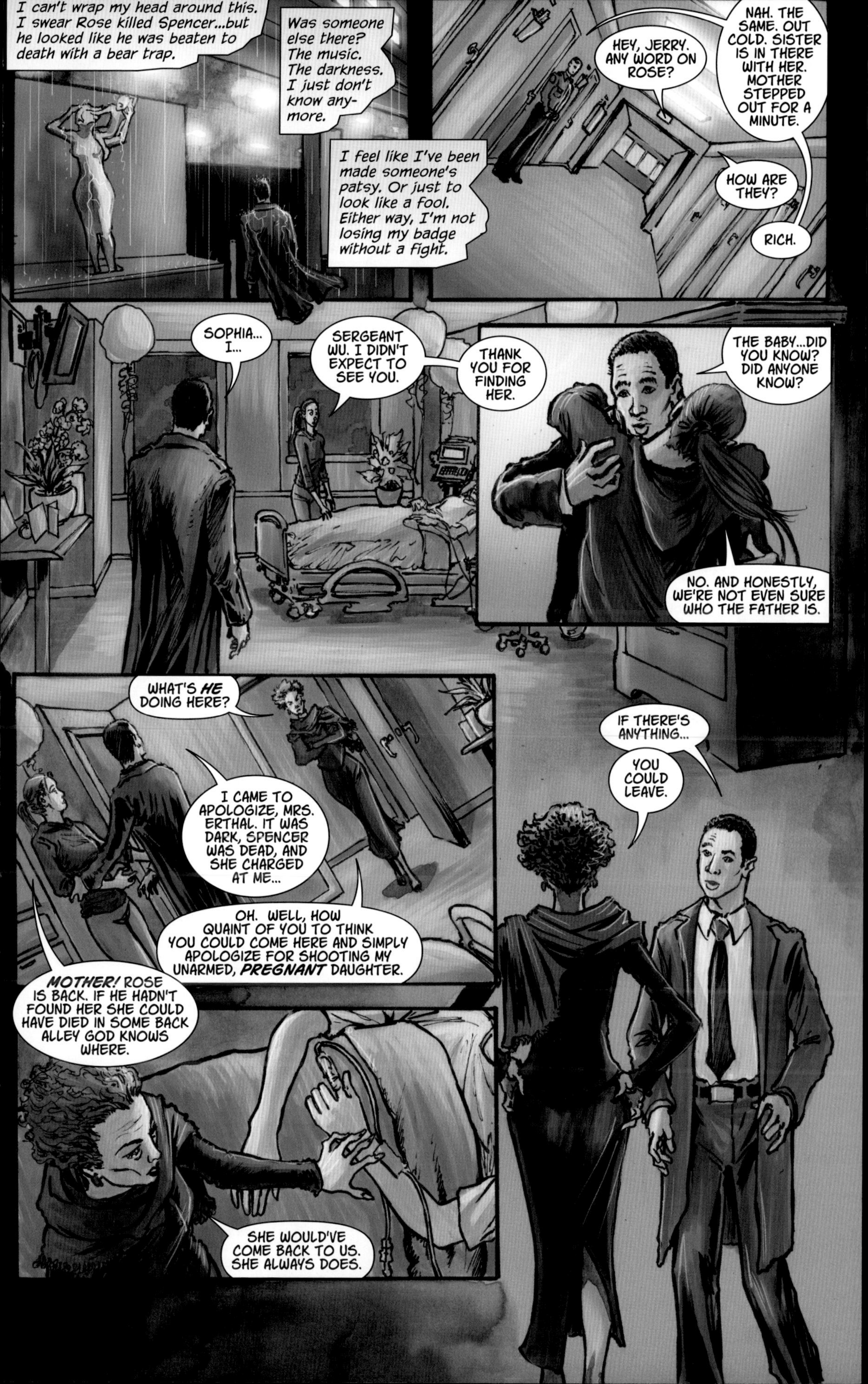
I can't wrap my head around this. I swear Rose killed Spencer...but he looked like he was beaten to death with a bear trap.
Was someone else there? The music. The darkness. I just don't know any-more.
I feel like I've been made someone's patsy. Or just to look like a fool. Either way, I'm not losing my badge without a fight.
HEY, JERRY. ANY WORD ON ROSE?
NAH. THE SAME. OUT COLD. SISTER IS IN THERE WITH HER. MOTHER STEPPED OUT FOR A MINUTE.
HOW ARE THEY?
RICH.
SOPHIA... I...
SERGEANT WU. I DIDN'T EXPECT TO SEE YOU.
THANK YOU FOR FINDING HER.
THE BABY...DID YOU KNOW? DID ANYONE KNOW?
NO. AND HONESTLY, WE'RE NOT EVEN SURE WHO THE FATHER IS.
WHAT'S *HE* DOING HERE?
I CAME TO APOLOGIZE, MRS. ERTHAL. IT WAS DARK, SPENCER WAS DEAD, AND SHE CHARGED AT ME...
OH. WELL, HOW QUAINT OF YOU TO THINK YOU COULD COME HERE AND SIMPLY APOLOGIZE FOR SHOOTING MY UNARMED, *PREGNANT* DAUGHTER.
MOTHER! ROSE IS BACK. IF HE HADN'T FOUND HER SHE COULD HAVE DIED IN SOME BACK ALLEY GOD KNOWS WHERE.
SHE WOULD'VE COME BACK TO US. SHE ALWAYS DOES.
IF THERE'S ANYTHING...
YOU COULD LEAVE.

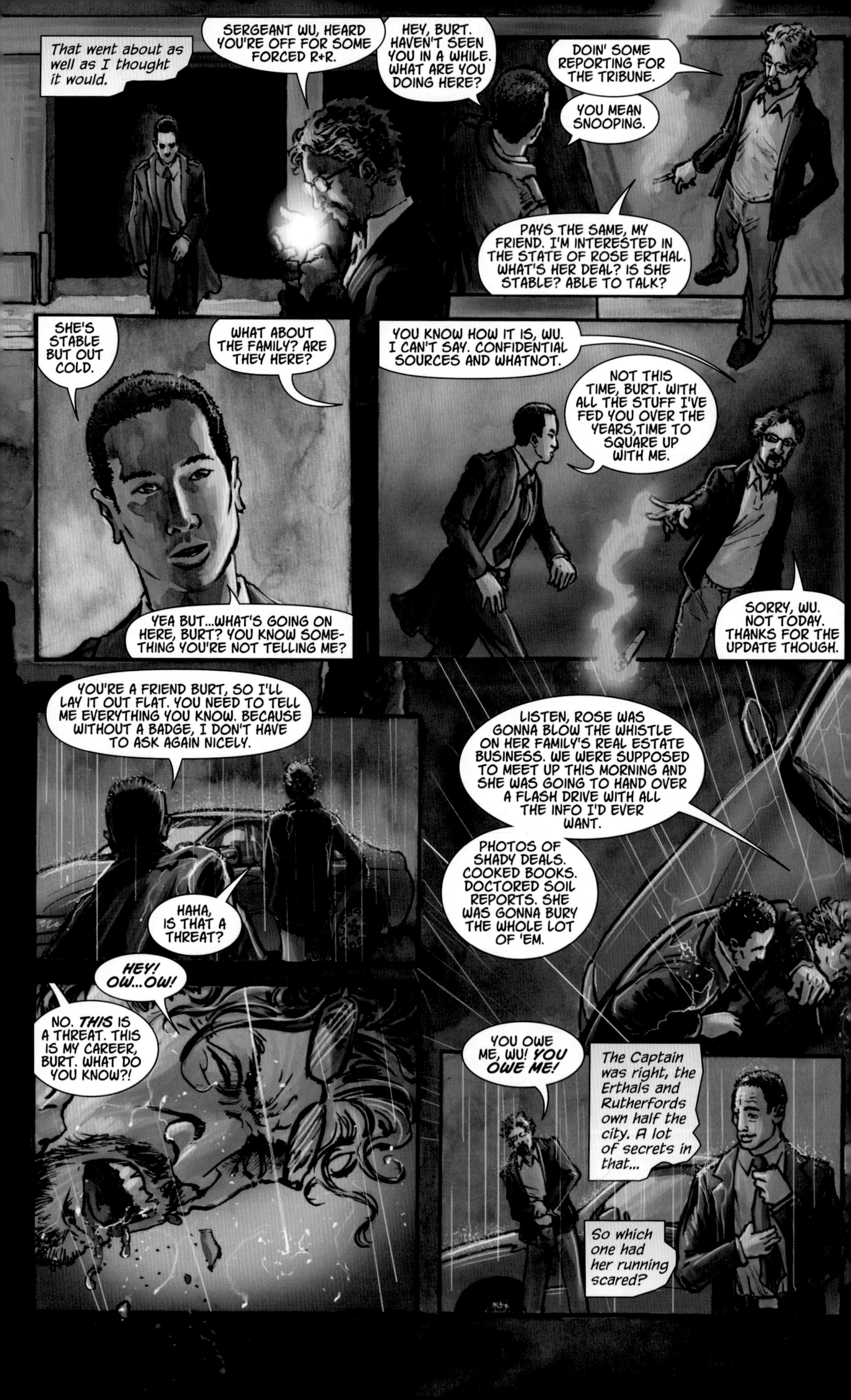

That went about as well as I thought it would.
SERGEANT WU, HEARD YOU'RE OFF FOR SOME FORCED R+R.
HEY, BURT. HAVEN'T SEEN YOU IN A WHILE. WHAT ARE YOU DOING HERE?
DOIN' SOME REPORTING FOR THE TRIBUNE.
YOU MEAN SNOOPING.
PAYS THE SAME, MY FRIEND. I'M INTERESTED IN THE STATE OF ROSE ERTHAL. WHAT'S HER DEAL? IS SHE STABLE? ABLE TO TALK?
SHE'S STABLE BUT OUT COLD.
WHAT ABOUT THE FAMILY? ARE THEY HERE?
YEA BUT...WHAT'S GOING ON HERE, BURT? YOU KNOW SOME-THING YOU'RE NOT TELLING ME?
YOU KNOW HOW IT IS, WU. I CAN'T SAY. CONFIDENTIAL SOURCES AND WHATNOT.
NOT THIS TIME, BURT. WITH ALL THE STUFF I'VE FED YOU OVER THE YEARS,TIME TO SQUARE UP WITH ME.
SORRY, WU. NOT TODAY. THANKS FOR THE UPDATE THOUGH.
YOU'RE A FRIEND BURT, SO I'LL LAY IT OUT FLAT. YOU NEED TO TELL ME EVERYTHING YOU KNOW. BECAUSE WITHOUT A BADGE, I DON'T HAVE TO ASK AGAIN NICELY.
HAHA, IS THAT A THREAT?
HEY! OW...OW!
NO. THIS IS A THREAT. THIS IS MY CAREER, BURT. WHAT DO YOU KNOW?!
LISTEN, ROSE WAS GONNA BLOW THE WHISTLE ON HER FAMILY'S REAL ESTATE BUSINESS. WE WERE SUPPOSED TO MEET UP THIS MORNING AND SHE WAS GOING TO HAND OVER A FLASH DRIVE WITH ALL THE INFO I'D EVER WANT.
PHOTOS OF SHADY DEALS. COOKED BOOKS. DOCTORED SOIL REPORTS. SHE WAS GONNA BURY THE WHOLE LOT OF 'EM.
YOU OWE ME, WU! YOU OWE ME!
The Captain was right, the Erthals and Rutherfords own half the city. A lot of secrets in that...
So which one had her running scared?

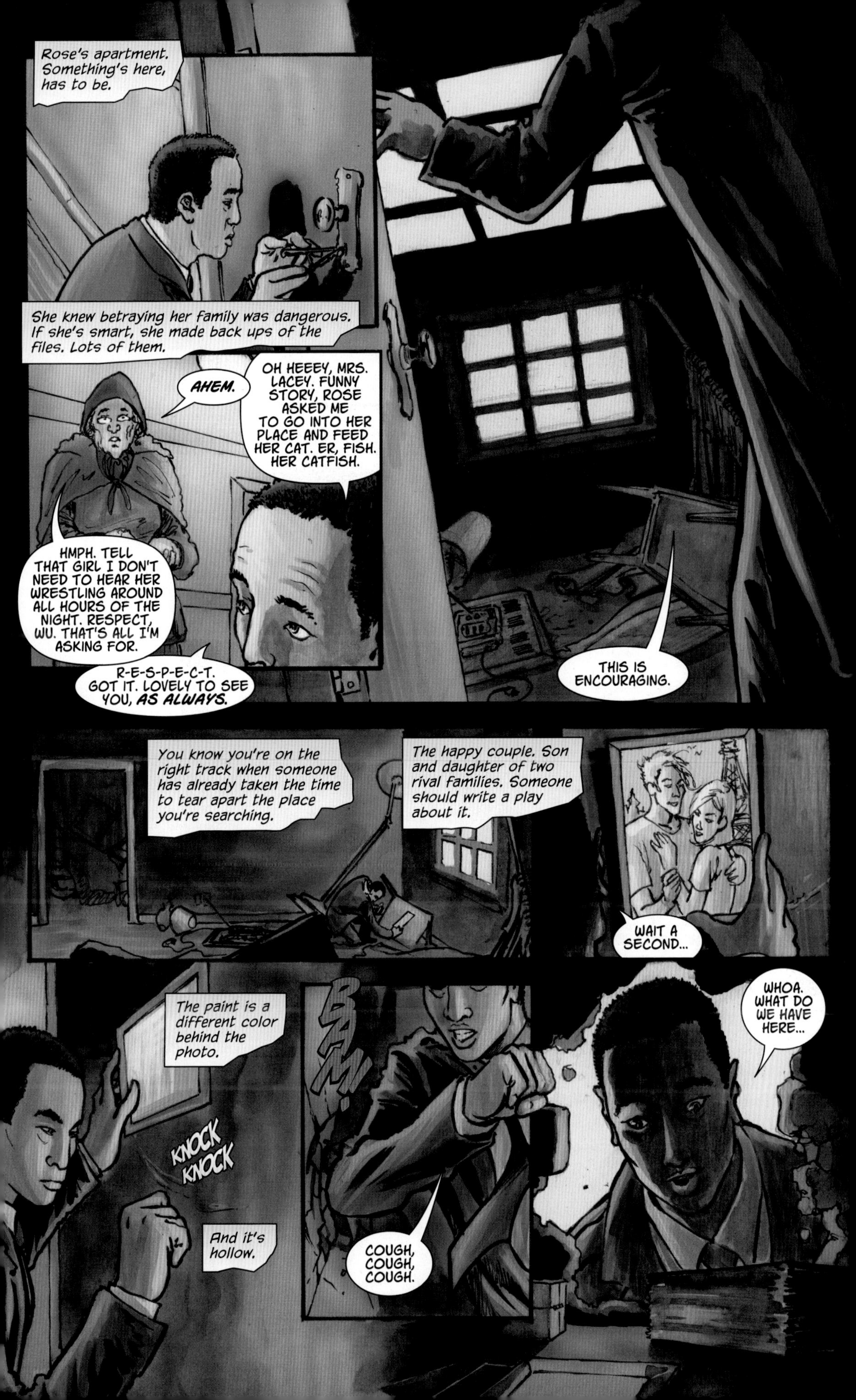
Rose's apartment. Something's here, has to be.
She knew betraying her family was dangerous. If she's smart, she made back ups of the files. Lots of them.
AHEM.
OH HEEEY, MRS. LACEY. FUNNY STORY, ROSE ASKED ME TO GO INTO HER PLACE AND FEED HER CAT. ER, FISH. HER CATFISH.
HMPH. TELL THAT GIRL I DON'T NEED TO HEAR HER WRESTLING AROUND ALL HOURS OF THE NIGHT. RESPECT, WU. THAT'S ALL I'M ASKING FOR.
R-E-S-P-E-C-T. GOT IT. LOVELY TO SEE YOU, AS ALWAYS.
THIS IS ENCOURAGING.
You know you're on the right track when someone has already taken the time to tear apart the place you're searching.
The happy couple. Son and daughter of two rival families. Someone should write a play about it.
WAIT A SECOND...
The paint is a different color behind the photo.
KNOCK KNOCK
And it's hollow.
BAM!
COUGH, COUGH, COUGH.
WHOA. WHAT DO WE HAVE HERE...

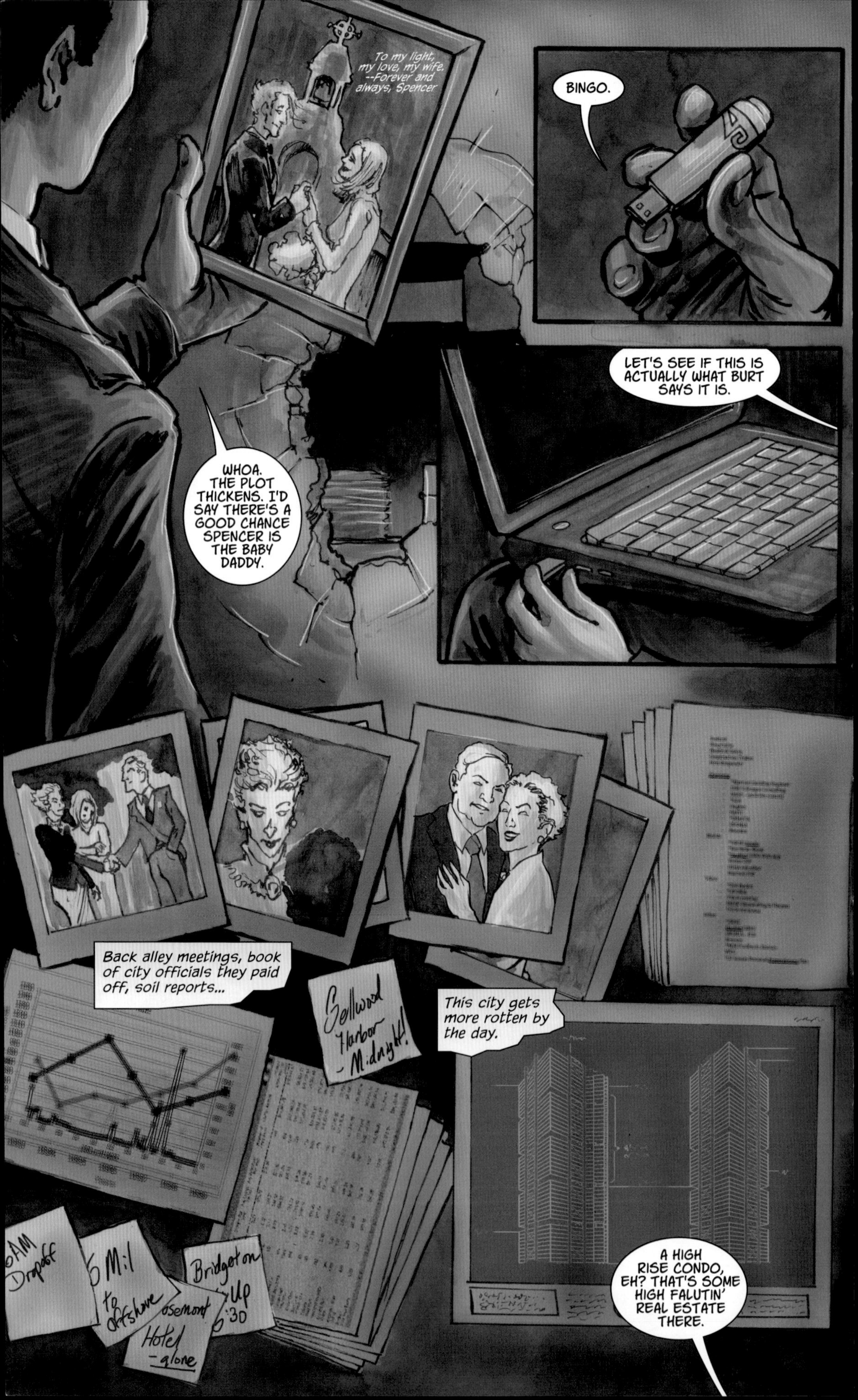
To my light, my love, my wife. --Forever and always, Spencer
BINGO.
LET'S SEE IF THIS IS ACTUALLY WHAT BURT SAYS IT IS.
WHOA. THE PLOT THICKENS. I'D SAY THERE'S A GOOD CHANCE SPENCER IS THE BABY DADDY.
Back alley meetings, book of city officials they paid off, soil reports...
Sellwood Harbor - Midnight!
This city gets more rotten by the day.
A HIGH RISE CONDO, EH? THAT'S SOME HIGH FALUTIN' REAL ESTATE THERE.

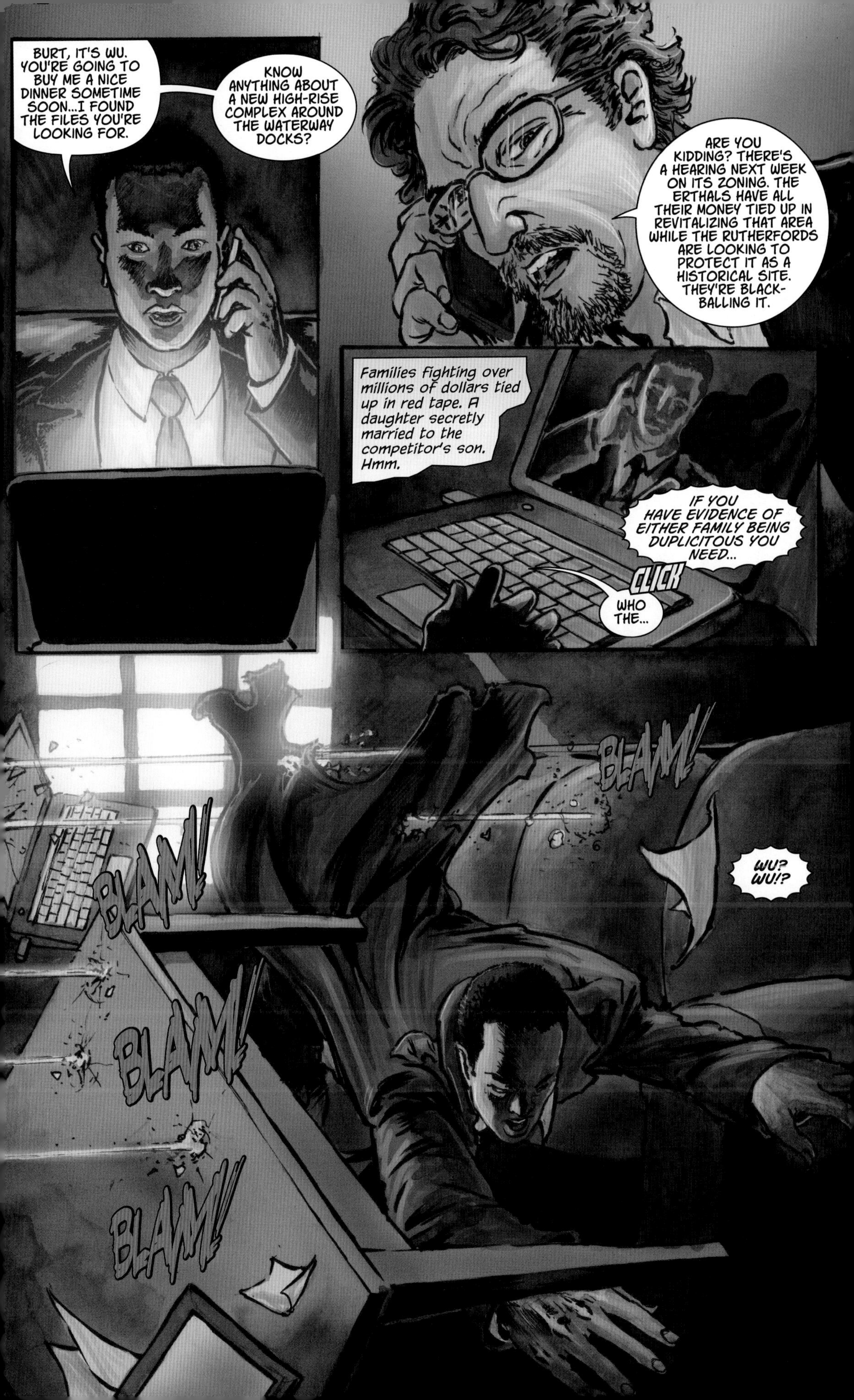
BURT, IT'S WU. YOU'RE GOING TO BUY ME A NICE DINNER SOMETIME SOON...I FOUND THE FILES YOU'RE LOOKING FOR.
KNOW ANYTHING ABOUT A NEW HIGH-RISE COMPLEX AROUND THE WATERWAY DOCKS?
ARE YOU KIDDING? THERE'S A HEARING NEXT WEEK ON ITS ZONING. THE ERTHALS HAVE ALL THEIR MONEY TIED UP IN REVITALIZING THAT AREA WHILE THE RUTHERFORDS ARE LOOKING TO PROTECT IT AS A HISTORICAL SITE. THEY'RE BLACK-BALLING IT.
Families fighting over millions of dollars tied up in red tape. A daughter secretly married to the competitor's son. Hmm.
IF YOU HAVE EVIDENCE OF EITHER FAMILY BEING DUPLICITOUS YOU NEED...
CLICK
WHO THE...
BLAM!
WU? WU!?
BLAM!
BLAM!
BLAM!

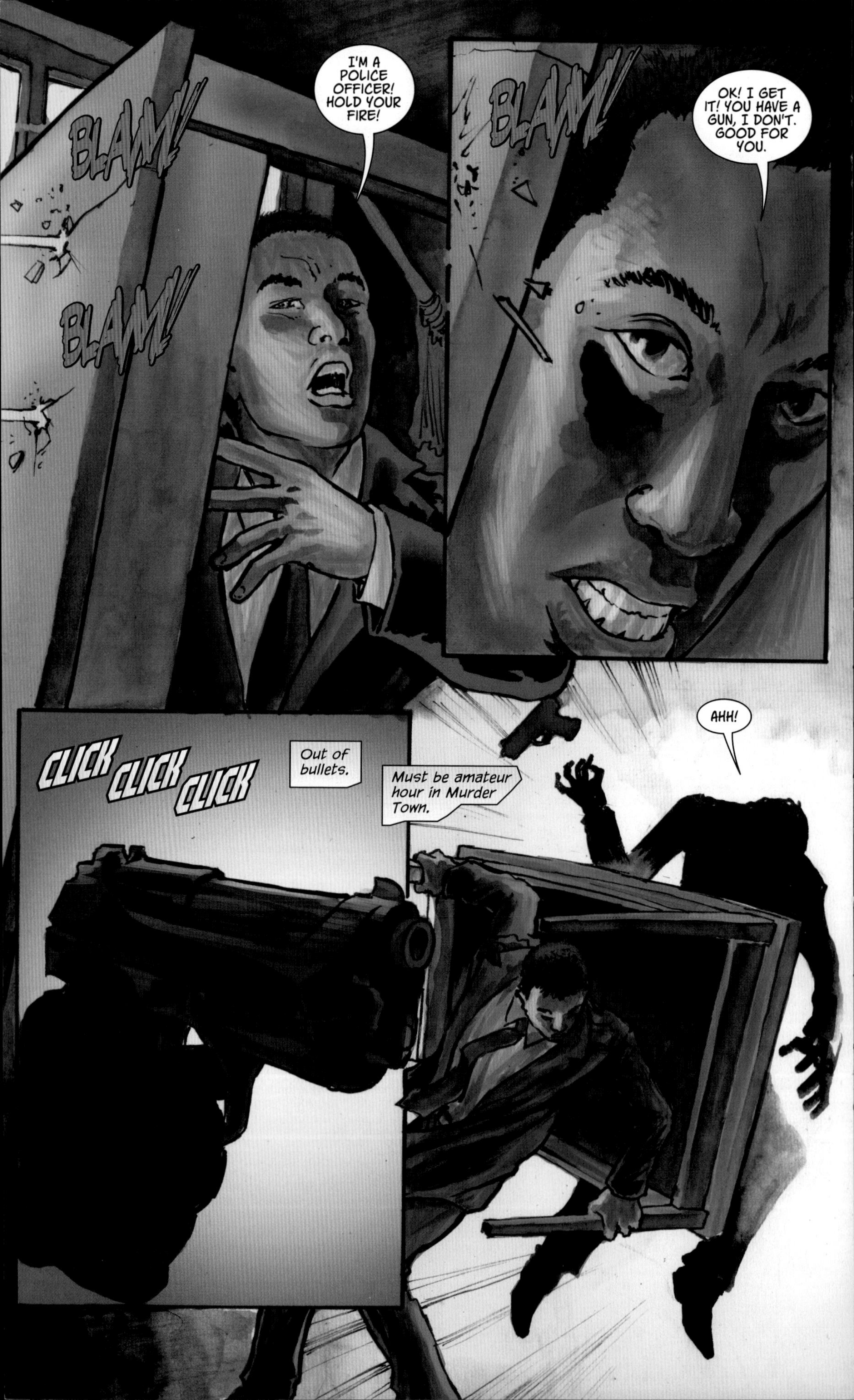
BLAM!
BLAM!
I'M A POLICE OFFICER! HOLD YOUR FIRE!
BLAM!
OK! I GET IT! YOU HAVE A GUN, I DON'T. GOOD FOR YOU.
CLICK CLICK CLICK
Out of bullets.
Must be amateur hour in Murder Town.
AHH!

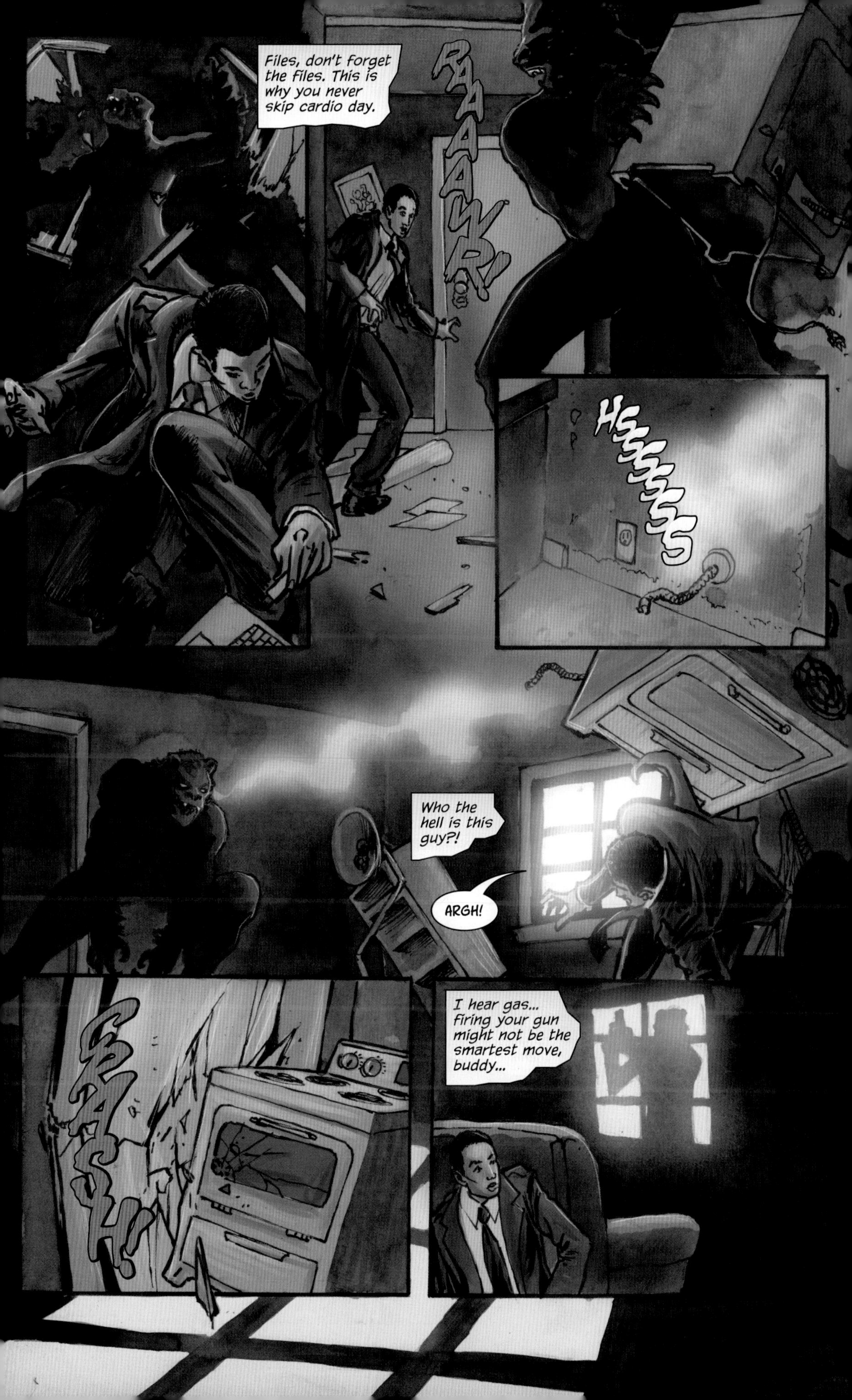

Files, don't forget the files. This is why you never skip cardio day.
RAAAWR!
HSSSSSS
Who the hell is this guy?!
ARGH!
CRASH!
I hear gas... firing your gun might not be the smartest move, buddy...

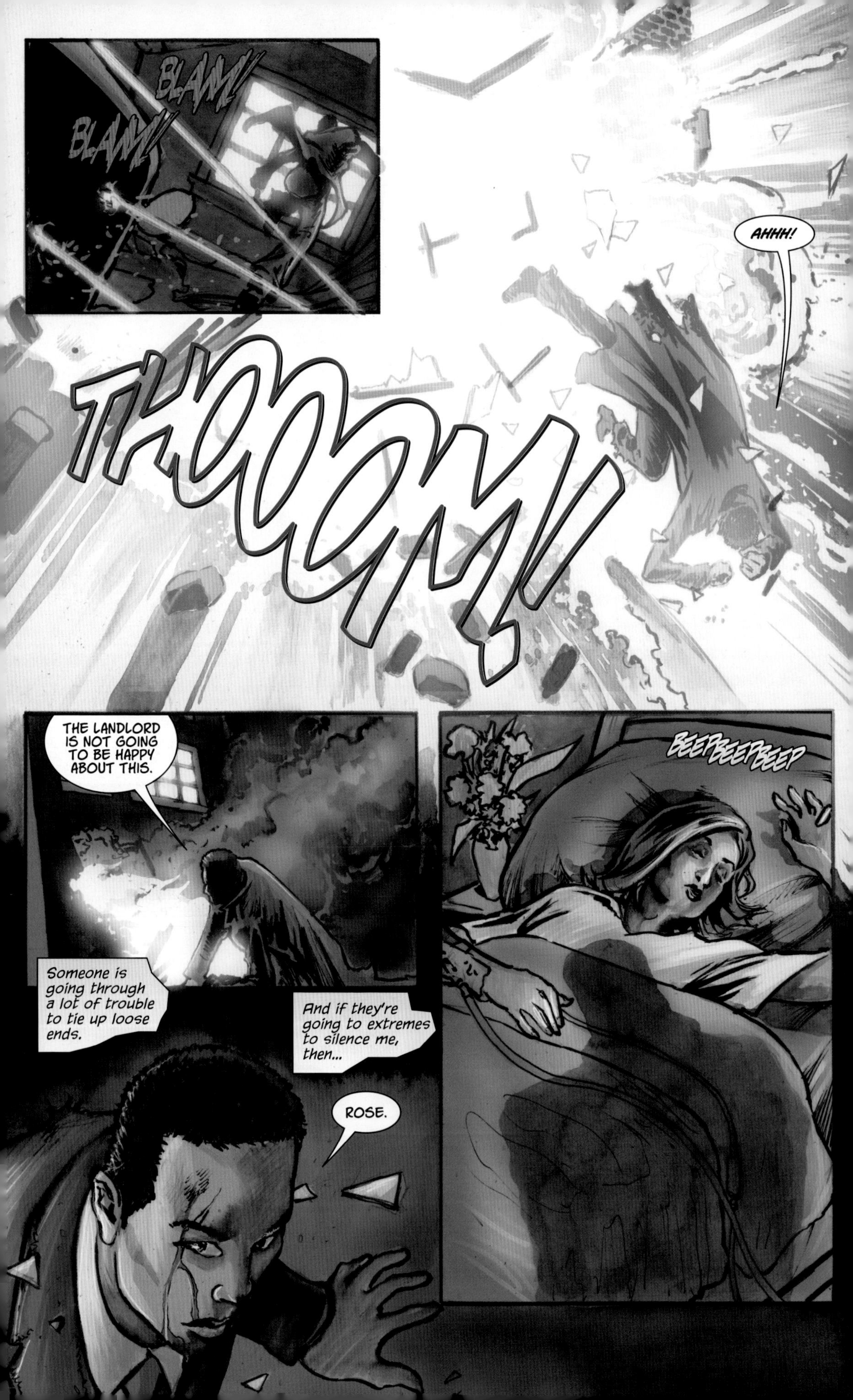
BLAM!
BLAM!
THOOOM!
AHHH!
THE LANDLORD IS NOT GOING TO BE HAPPY ABOUT THIS.
BEEPBEEPBEEP
Someone is going through a lot of trouble to tie up loose ends.
And if they're going to extremes to silence me, then...
ROSE.

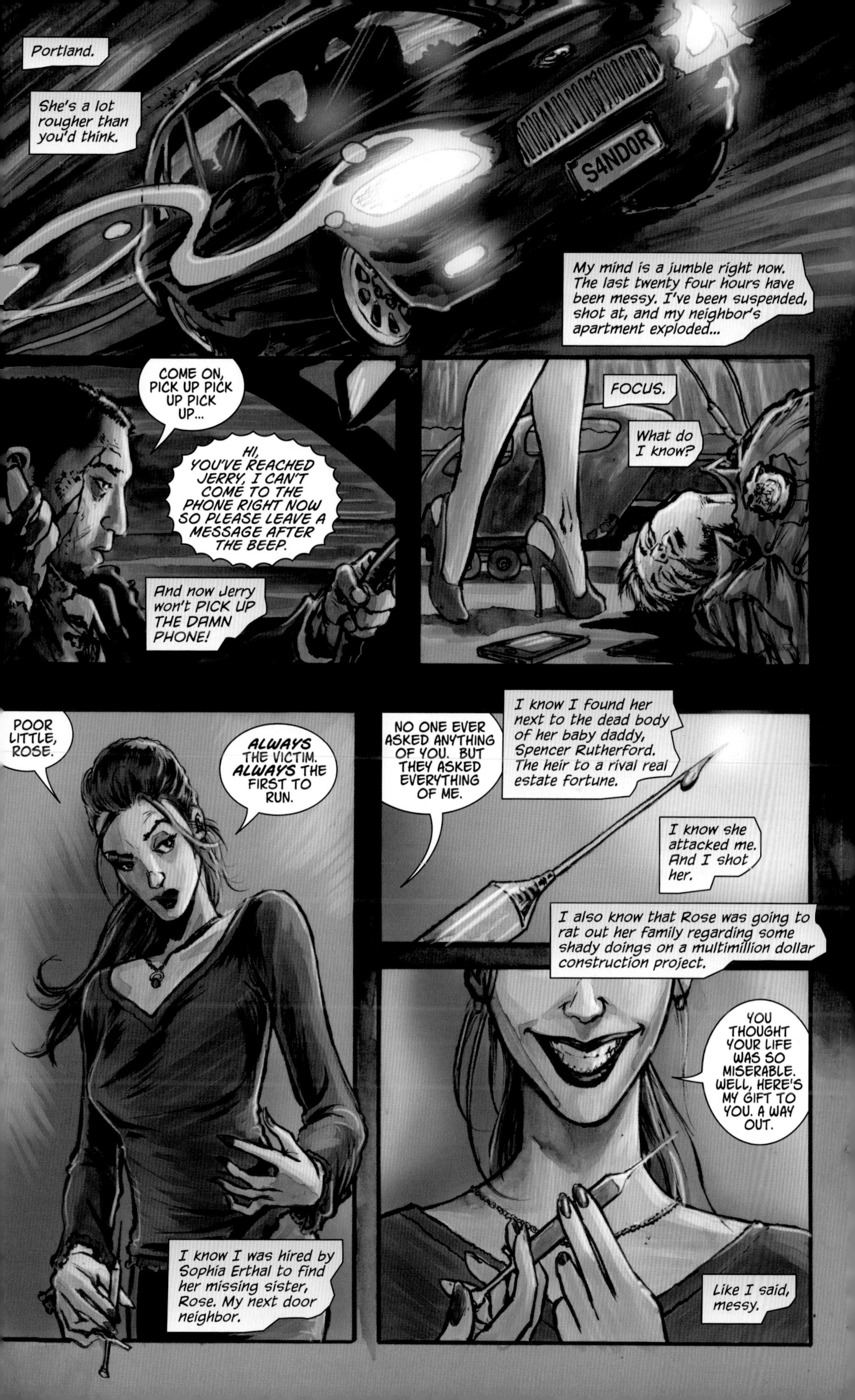

Portland.
She's a lot rougher than you'd think.
S4NDOR
My mind is a jumble right now. The last twenty four hours have been messy. I've been suspended, shot at, and my neighbor's apartment exploded...
COME ON, PICK UP PICK UP PICK UP...
HI, YOU'VE REACHED JERRY, I CAN'T COME TO THE PHONE RIGHT NOW SO PLEASE LEAVE A MESSAGE AFTER THE BEEP.
And now Jerry won't PICK UP THE DAMN PHONE!
FOCUS.
What do I know?
POOR LITTLE, ROSE.
ALWAYS THE VICTIM. ALWAYS THE FIRST TO RUN.
I know I was hired by Sophia Erthal to find her missing sister, Rose. My next door neighbor.
NO ONE EVER ASKED ANYTHING OF YOU. BUT THEY ASKED EVERYTHING OF ME.
I know I found her next to the dead body of her baby daddy, Spencer Rutherford. The heir to a rival real estate fortune.
I know she attacked me. And I shot her.
I also know that Rose was going to rat out her family regarding some shady doings on a multimillion dollar construction project.
YOU THOUGHT YOUR LIFE WAS SO MISERABLE. WELL, HERE'S MY GIFT TO YOU. A WAY OUT.
Like I said, messy.

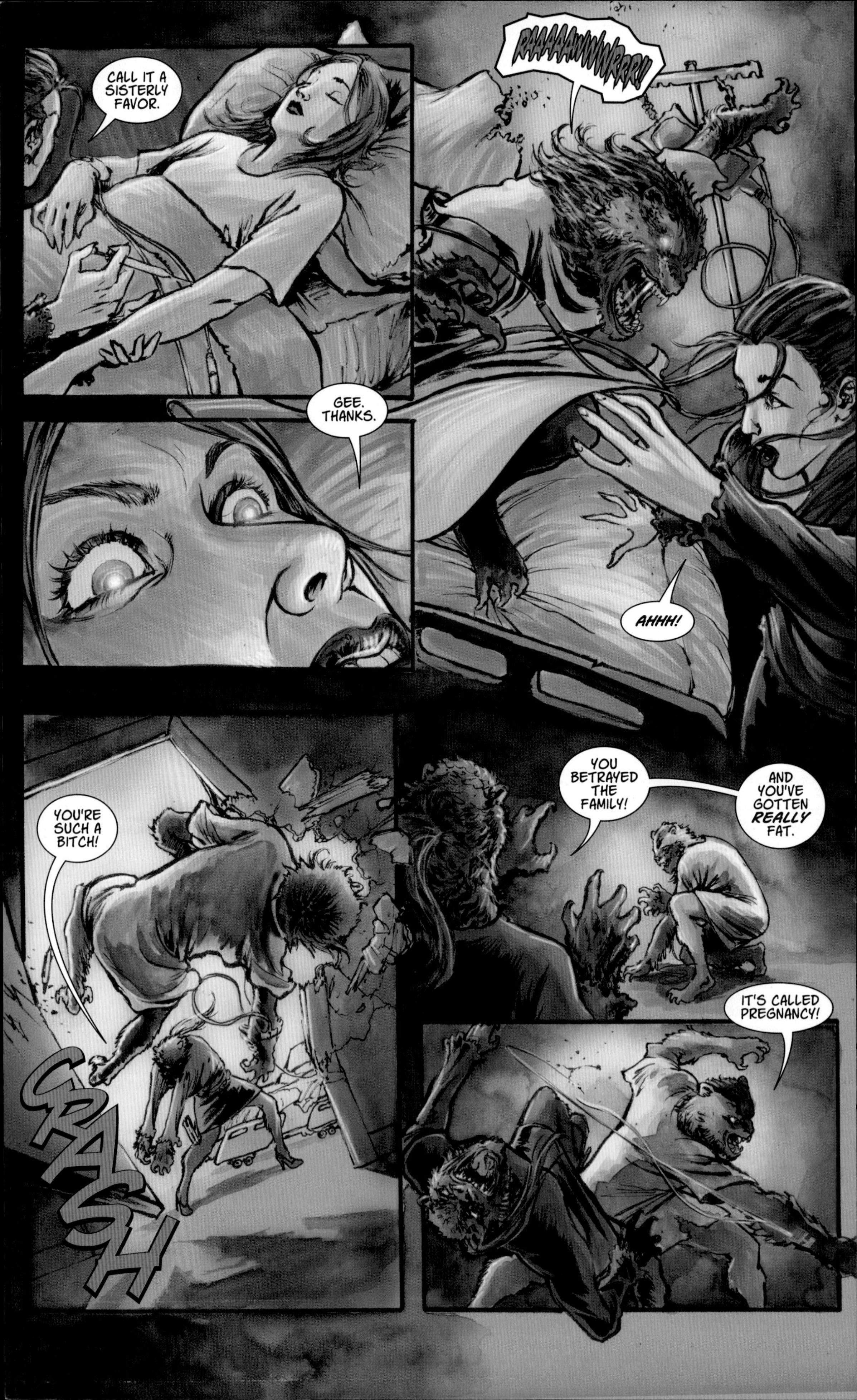
CALL IT A SISTERLY FAVOR.
RAAAAAWWRRR!!
GEE. THANKS.
AHHH!
YOU'RE SUCH A BITCH!
CRASH
YOU BETRAYED THE FAMILY!
AND YOU'VE GOTTEN *REALLY* FAT.
IT'S CALLED PREGNANCY!

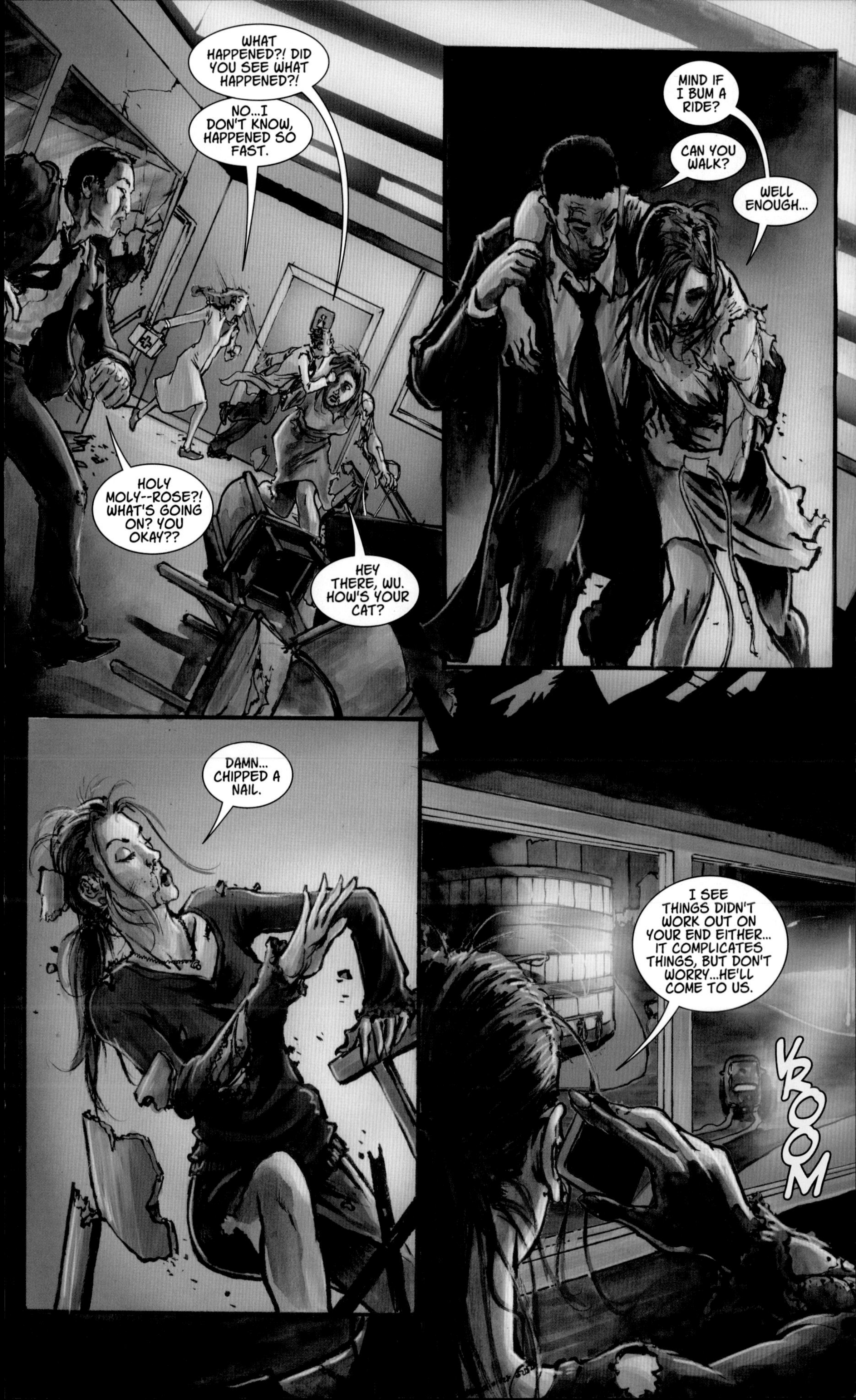
WHAT HAPPENED?! DID YOU SEE WHAT HAPPENED?!
NO...I DON'T KNOW, HAPPENED SO FAST.
HOLY MOLY--ROSE?! WHAT'S GOING ON? YOU OKAY??
HEY THERE, WU. HOW'S YOUR CAT?
MIND IF I BUM A RIDE?
CAN YOU WALK?
WELL ENOUGH...
DAMN... CHIPPED A NAIL.
I SEE THINGS DIDN'T WORK OUT ON YOUR END EITHER... IT COMPLICATES THINGS, BUT DON'T WORRY...HE'LL COME TO US.
VROOOM

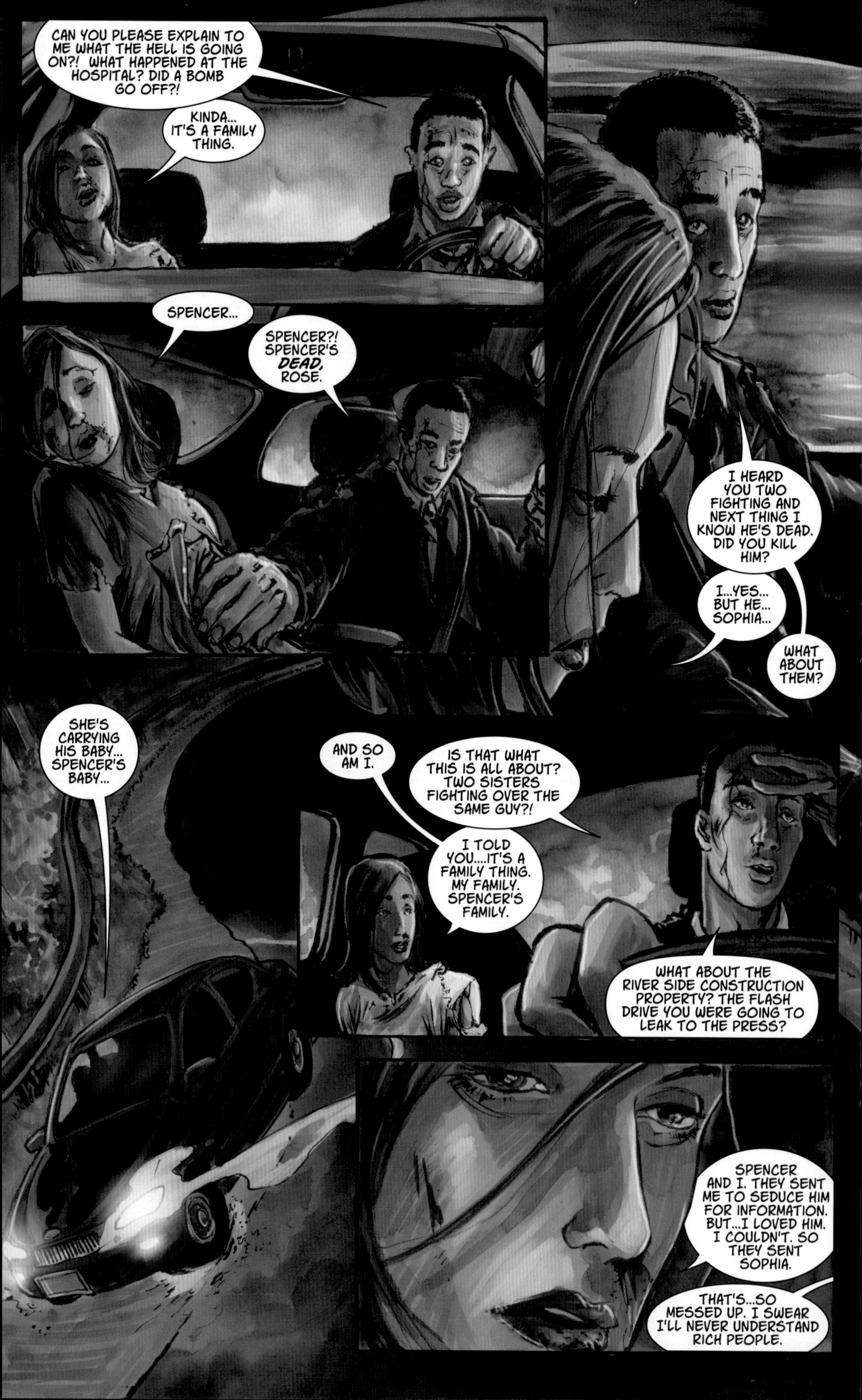
CAN YOU PLEASE EXPLAIN TO ME WHAT THE HELL IS GOING ON?! WHAT HAPPENED AT THE HOSPITAL? DID A BOMB GO OFF?!
KINDA... IT'S A FAMILY THING.
SPENCER...
SPENCER?! SPENCER'S *DEAD,* ROSE.
I HEARD YOU TWO FIGHTING AND NEXT THING I KNOW HE'S DEAD. DID YOU KILL HIM?
I...YES... BUT HE... SOPHIA...
WHAT ABOUT THEM?
SHE'S CARRYING HIS BABY... SPENCER'S BABY...
AND SO AM I.
IS THAT WHAT THIS IS ALL ABOUT? TWO SISTERS FIGHTING OVER THE SAME GUY?!
I TOLD YOU....IT'S A FAMILY THING. MY FAMILY. SPENCER'S FAMILY.
WHAT ABOUT THE RIVER SIDE CONSTRUCTION PROPERTY? THE FLASH DRIVE YOU WERE GOING TO LEAK TO THE PRESS?
SPENCER AND I. THEY SENT ME TO SEDUCE HIM FOR INFORMATION. BUT...I LOVED HIM. I COULDN'T. SO THEY SENT SOPHIA.
THAT'S...SO MESSED UP. I SWEAR I'LL NEVER UNDERSTAND RICH PEOPLE.

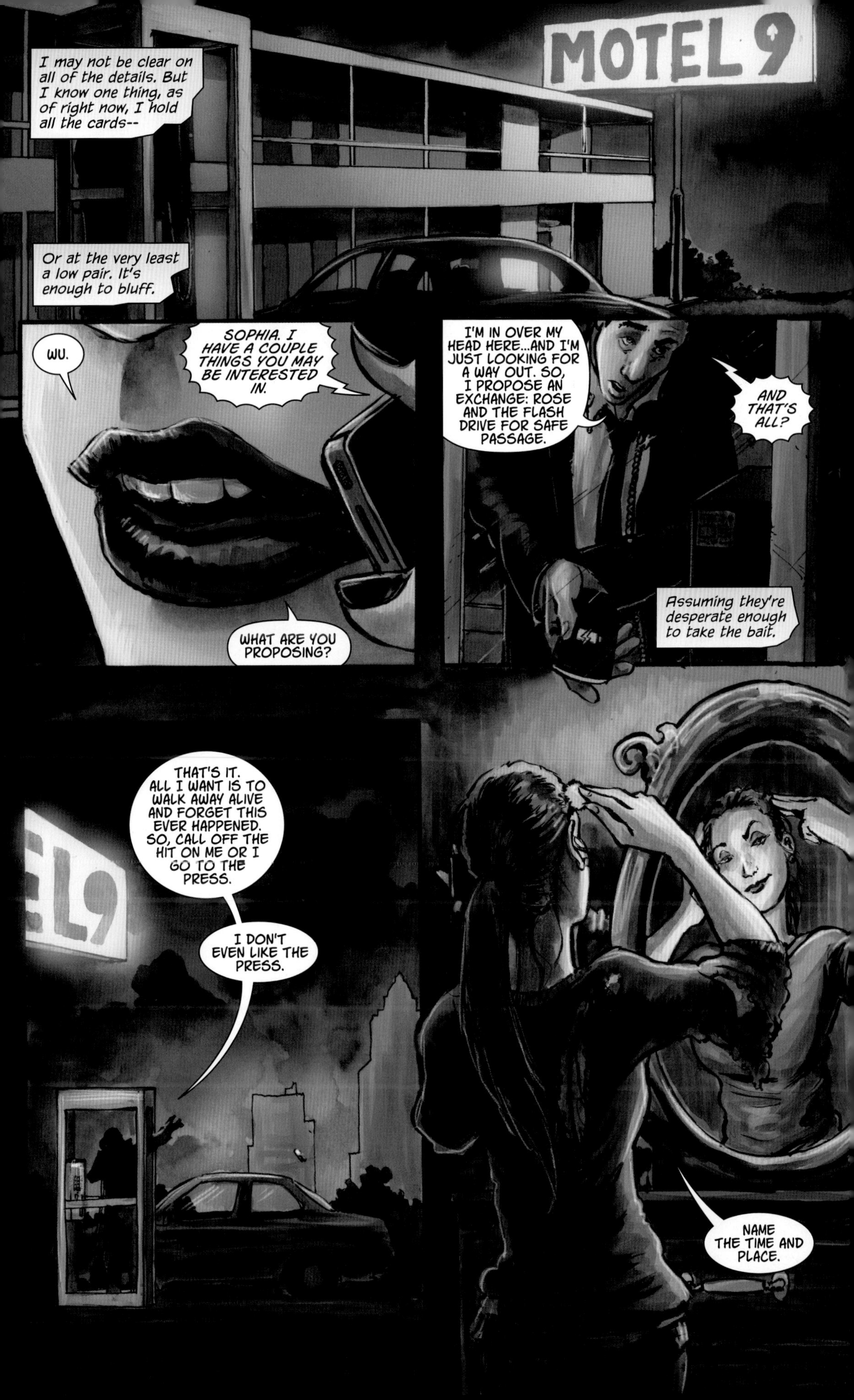
MOTEL 9
I may not be clear on all of the details. But I know one thing, as of right now, I hold all the cards--
Or at the very least a low pair. It's enough to bluff.
WU.
SOPHIA. I HAVE A COUPLE THINGS YOU MAY BE INTERESTED IN.
WHAT ARE YOU PROPOSING?
I'M IN OVER MY HEAD HERE...AND I'M JUST LOOKING FOR A WAY OUT. SO, I PROPOSE AN EXCHANGE: ROSE AND THE FLASH DRIVE FOR SAFE PASSAGE.
AND THAT'S ALL?
Assuming they're desperate enough to take the bait.
EL9
THAT'S IT. ALL I WANT IS TO WALK AWAY ALIVE AND FORGET THIS EVER HAPPENED. SO, CALL OFF THE HIT ON ME OR I GO TO THE PRESS.
I DON'T EVEN LIKE THE PRESS.
NAME THE TIME AND PLACE.

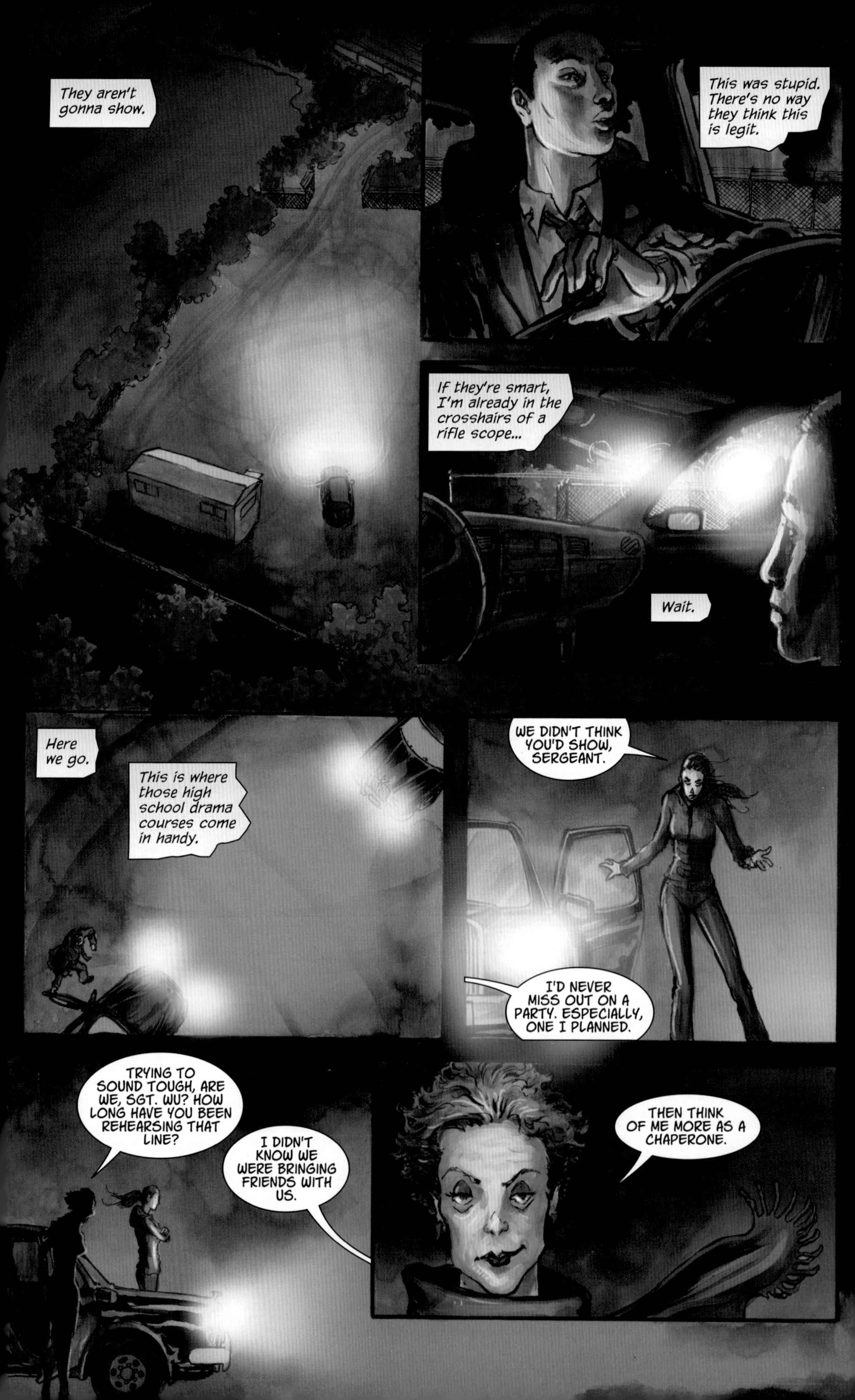
They aren't gonna show.
This was stupid. There's no way they think this is legit.
If they're smart, I'm already in the crosshairs of a rifle scope...
Wait.
Here we go.
This is where those high school drama courses come in handy.
WE DIDN'T THINK YOU'D SHOW, SERGEANT.
I'D NEVER MISS OUT ON A PARTY. ESPECIALLY, ONE I PLANNED.
TRYING TO SOUND TOUGH, ARE WE, SGT. WU? HOW LONG HAVE YOU BEEN REHEARSING THAT LINE?
I DIDN'T KNOW WE WERE BRINGING FRIENDS WITH US.
THEN THINK OF ME MORE AS A CHAPERONE.

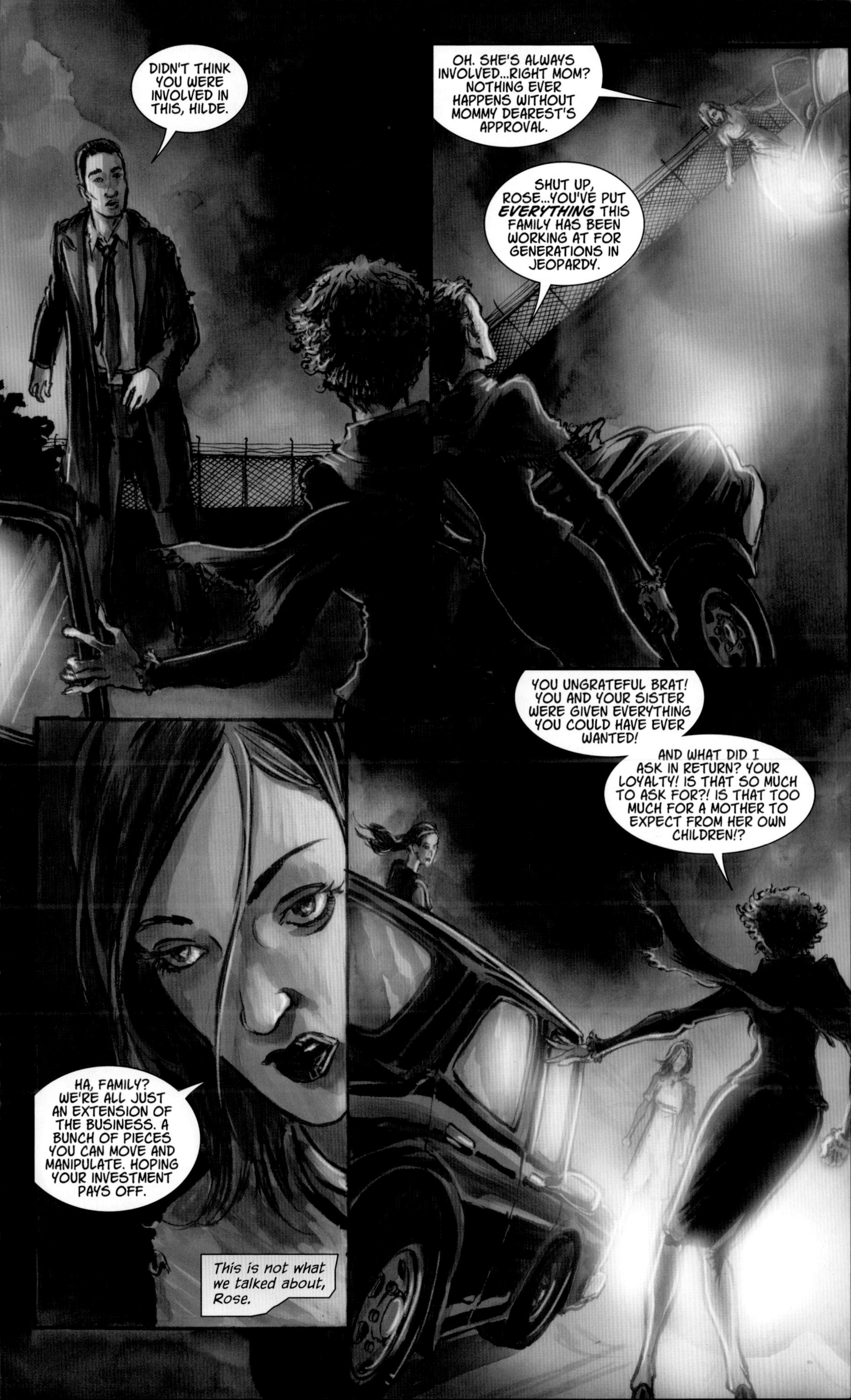
DIDN'T THINK YOU WERE INVOLVED IN THIS, HILDE.
OH. SHE'S ALWAYS INVOLVED...RIGHT MOM? NOTHING EVER HAPPENS WITHOUT MOMMY DEAREST'S APPROVAL.
SHUT UP, ROSE...YOU'VE PUT **EVERYTHING** THIS FAMILY HAS BEEN WORKING AT FOR GENERATIONS IN JEOPARDY.
YOU UNGRATEFUL BRAT! YOU AND YOUR SISTER WERE GIVEN EVERYTHING YOU COULD HAVE EVER WANTED!
AND WHAT DID I ASK IN RETURN? YOUR LOYALTY! IS THAT SO MUCH TO ASK FOR?! IS THAT TOO MUCH FOR A MOTHER TO EXPECT FROM HER OWN CHILDREN!?
HA, FAMILY? WE'RE ALL JUST AN EXTENSION OF THE BUSINESS. A BUNCH OF PIECES YOU CAN MOVE AND MANIPULATE. HOPING YOUR INVESTMENT PAYS OFF.
This is not what we talked about, Rose.

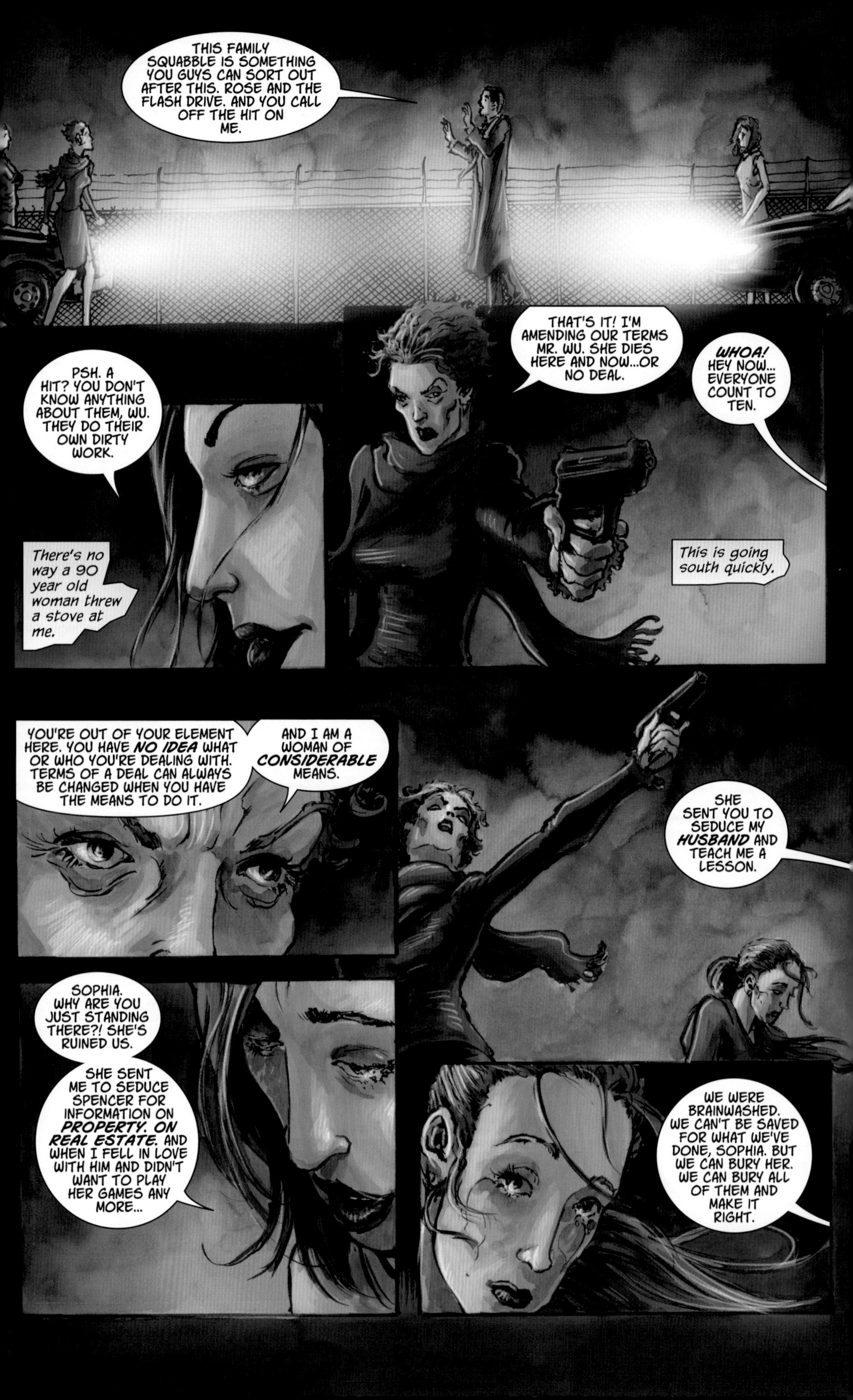

THIS FAMILY SQUABBLE IS SOMETHING YOU GUYS CAN SORT OUT AFTER THIS. ROSE AND THE FLASH DRIVE. AND YOU CALL OFF THE HIT ON ME.
PSH. A HIT? YOU DON'T KNOW ANYTHING ABOUT THEM, WU. THEY DO THEIR OWN DIRTY WORK.
There's no way a 90 year old woman threw a stove at me.
THAT'S IT! I'M AMENDING OUR TERMS MR. WU. SHE DIES HERE AND NOW...OR NO DEAL.
WHOA! HEY NOW... EVERYONE COUNT TO TEN.
This is going south quickly.
YOU'RE OUT OF YOUR ELEMENT HERE. YOU HAVE NO IDEA WHAT OR WHO YOU'RE DEALING WITH. TERMS OF A DEAL CAN ALWAYS BE CHANGED WHEN YOU HAVE THE MEANS TO DO IT.
AND I AM A WOMAN OF CONSIDERABLE MEANS.
SHE SENT YOU TO SEDUCE MY HUSBAND AND TEACH ME A LESSON.
SOPHIA. WHY ARE YOU JUST STANDING THERE?! SHE'S RUINED US.
SHE SENT ME TO SEDUCE SPENCER FOR INFORMATION ON PROPERTY. ON REAL ESTATE. AND WHEN I FELL IN LOVE WITH HIM AND DIDN'T WANT TO PLAY HER GAMES ANY MORE...
WE WERE BRAINWASHED. WE CAN'T BE SAVED FOR WHAT WE'VE DONE, SOPHIA. BUT WE CAN BURY HER. WE CAN BURY ALL OF THEM AND MAKE IT RIGHT.

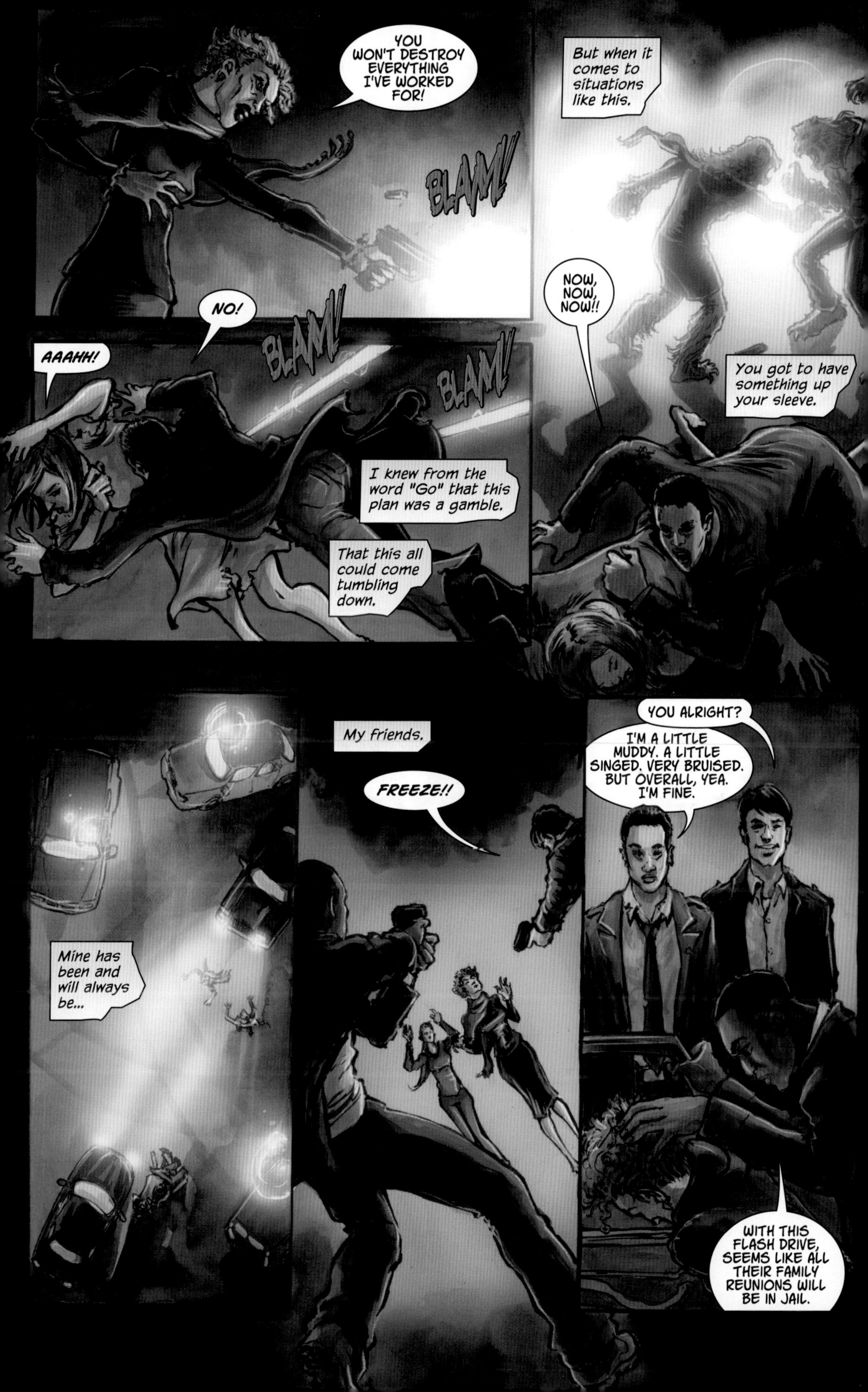
YOU WON'T DESTROY EVERYTHING I'VE WORKED FOR!
BLAM!
But when it comes to situations like this.
NOW, NOW, NOW!!
NO!
AAAHH!
BLAM!
BLAM!
I knew from the word "Go" that this plan was a gamble.
That this all could come tumbling down.
You got to have something up your sleeve.
My friends.
FREEZE!!
Mine has been and will always be...
YOU ALRIGHT?
I'M A LITTLE MUDDY. A LITTLE SINGED. VERY BRUISED. BUT OVERALL, YEA. I'M FINE.
WITH THIS FLASH DRIVE, SEEMS LIKE ALL THEIR FAMILY REUNIONS WILL BE IN JAIL.

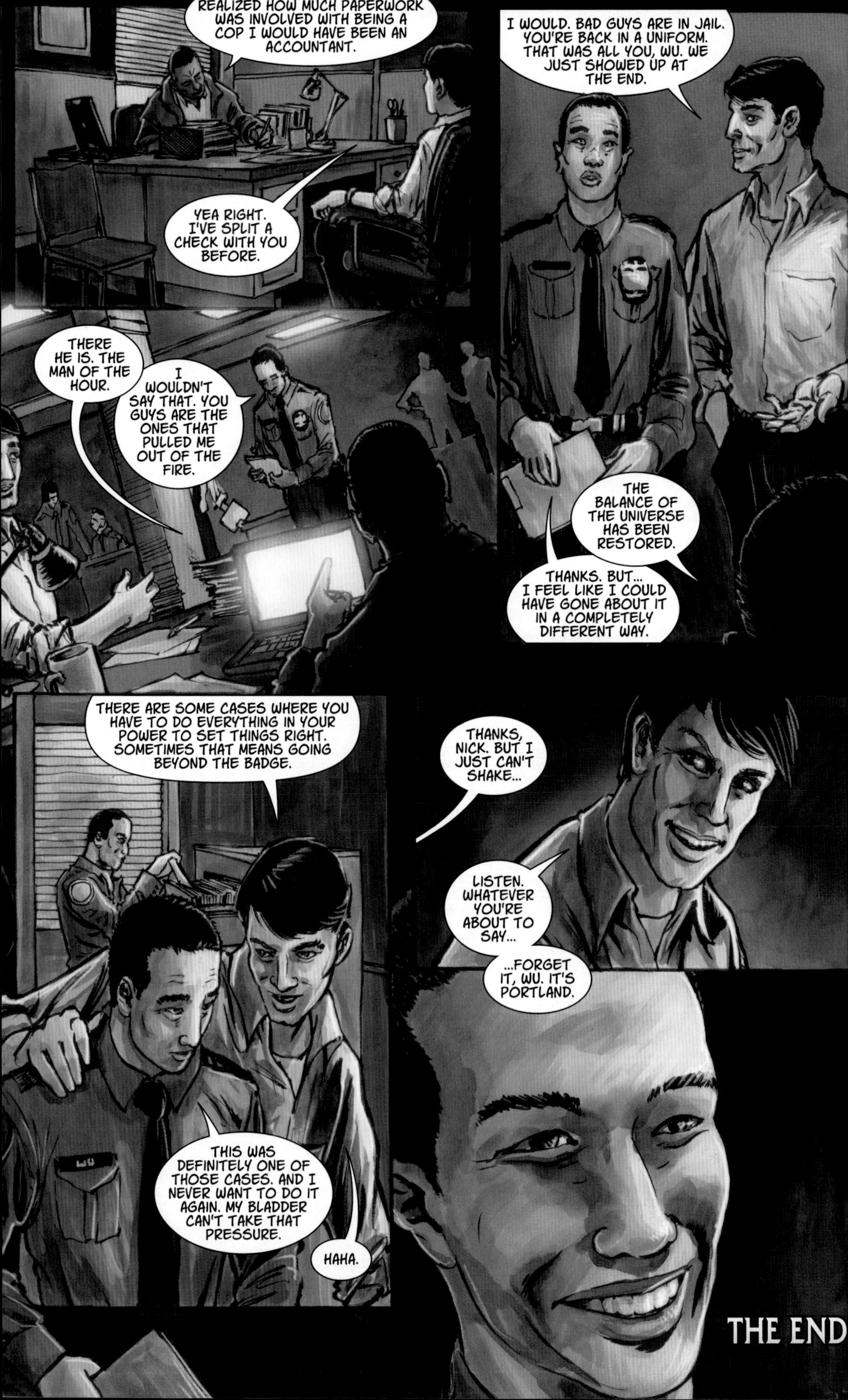
YA KNOW, IF I'D HAVE REALIZED HOW MUCH PAPERWORK WAS INVOLVED WITH BEING A COP I WOULD HAVE BEEN AN ACCOUNTANT.
YEA RIGHT. I'VE SPLIT A CHECK WITH YOU BEFORE.
I WOULD. BAD GUYS ARE IN JAIL. YOU'RE BACK IN A UNIFORM. THAT WAS ALL YOU, WU. WE JUST SHOWED UP AT THE END.
THERE HE IS. THE MAN OF THE HOUR.
I WOULDN'T SAY THAT. YOU GUYS ARE THE ONES THAT PULLED ME OUT OF THE FIRE.
THE BALANCE OF THE UNIVERSE HAS BEEN RESTORED.
THANKS. BUT... I FEEL LIKE I COULD HAVE GONE ABOUT IT IN A COMPLETELY DIFFERENT WAY.
THERE ARE SOME CASES WHERE YOU HAVE TO DO EVERYTHING IN YOUR POWER TO SET THINGS RIGHT. SOMETIMES THAT MEANS GOING BEYOND THE BADGE.
THIS WAS DEFINITELY ONE OF THOSE CASES. AND I NEVER WANT TO DO IT AGAIN. MY BLADDER CAN'T TAKE THAT PRESSURE.
HAHA.
THANKS, NICK. BUT I JUST CAN'T SHAKE...
LISTEN. WHATEVER YOU'RE ABOUT TO SAY...
...FORGET IT, WU. IT'S PORTLAND.
THE END

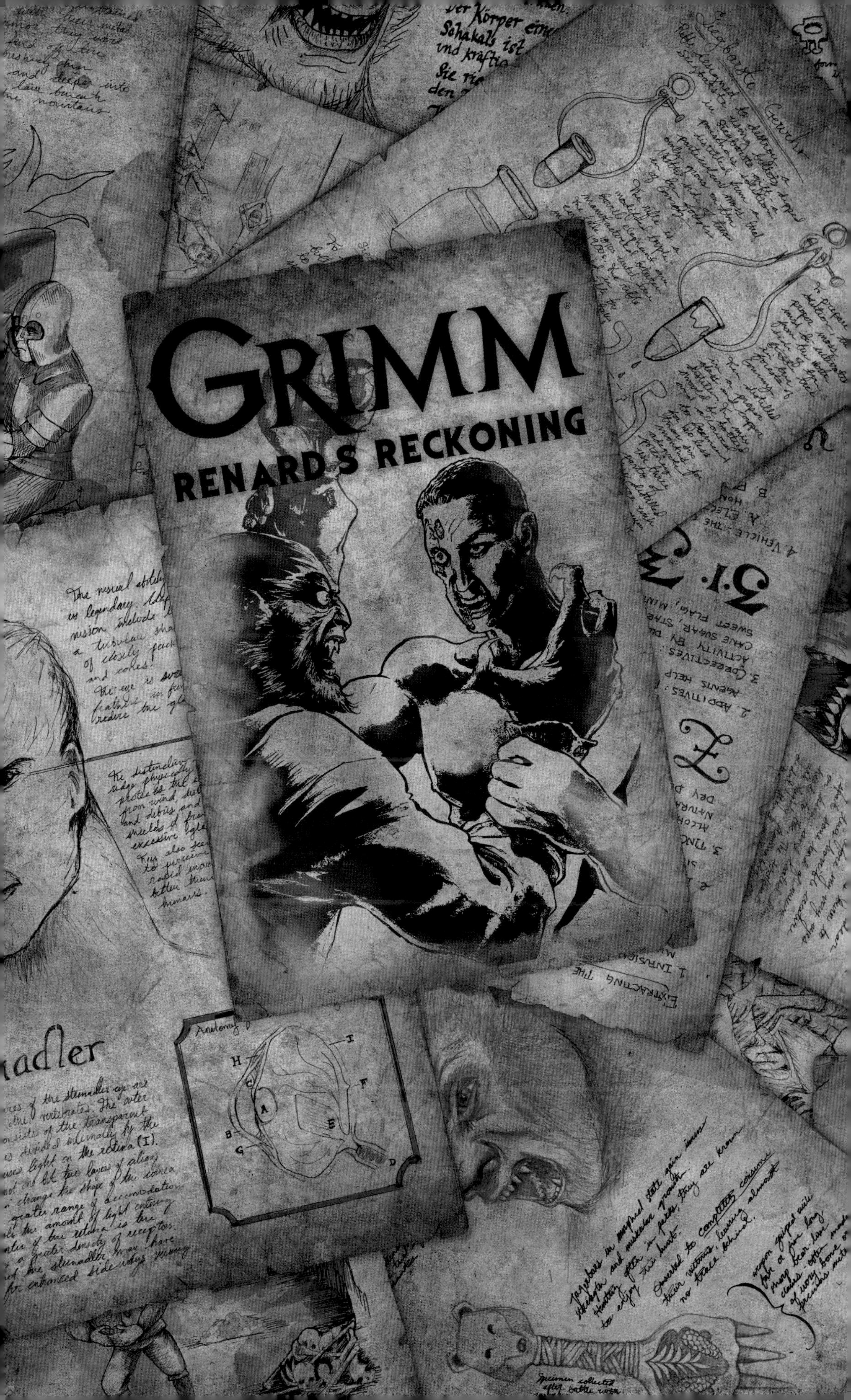
GRIMM
RENARD S RECKONING

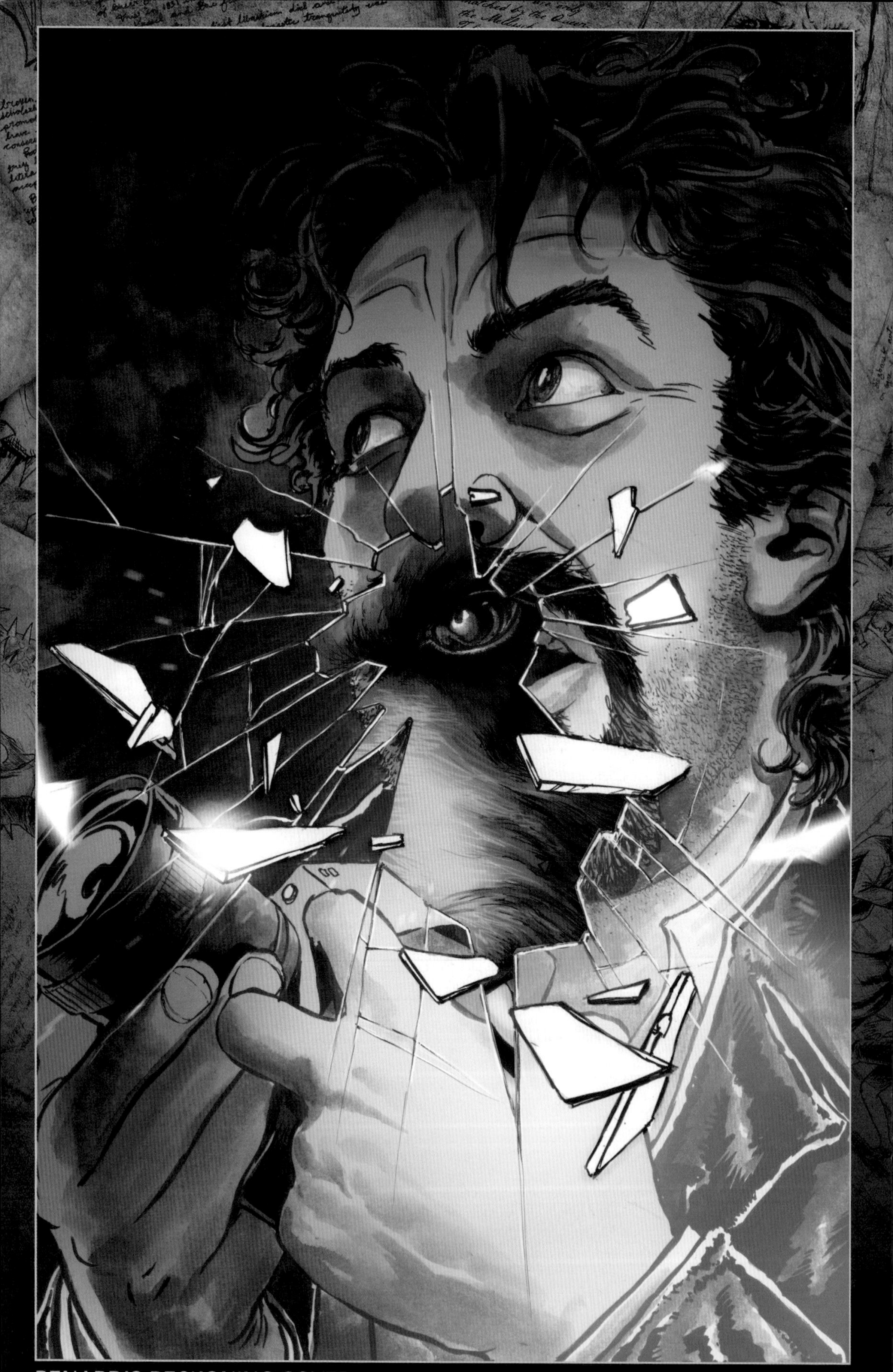

RENARD'S RECKONING COVER

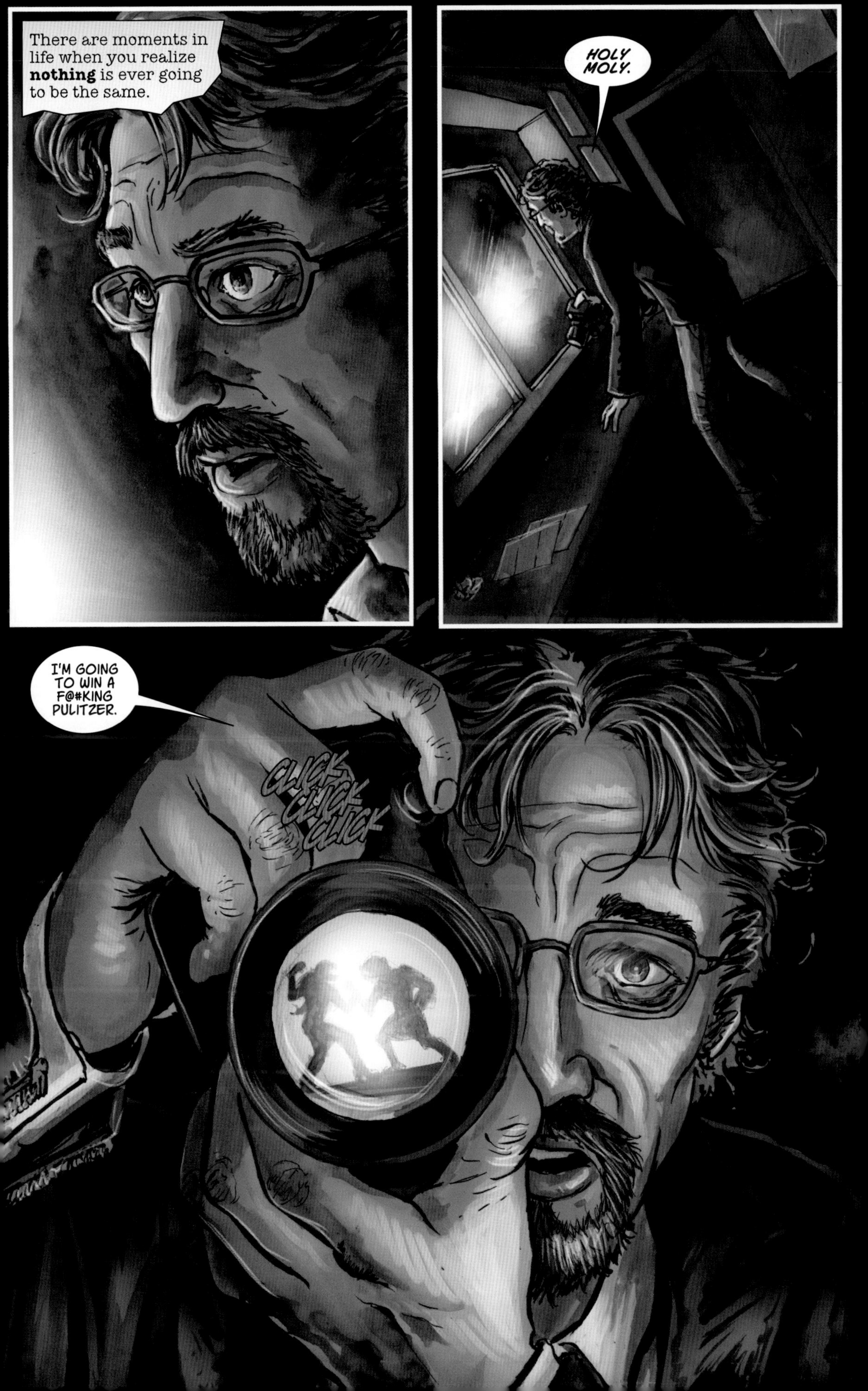
There are moments in life when you realize **nothing** is ever going to be the same.
HOLY MOLY.
I'M GOING TO WIN A F@#KING PULITZER.
CLICK CLICK CLICK

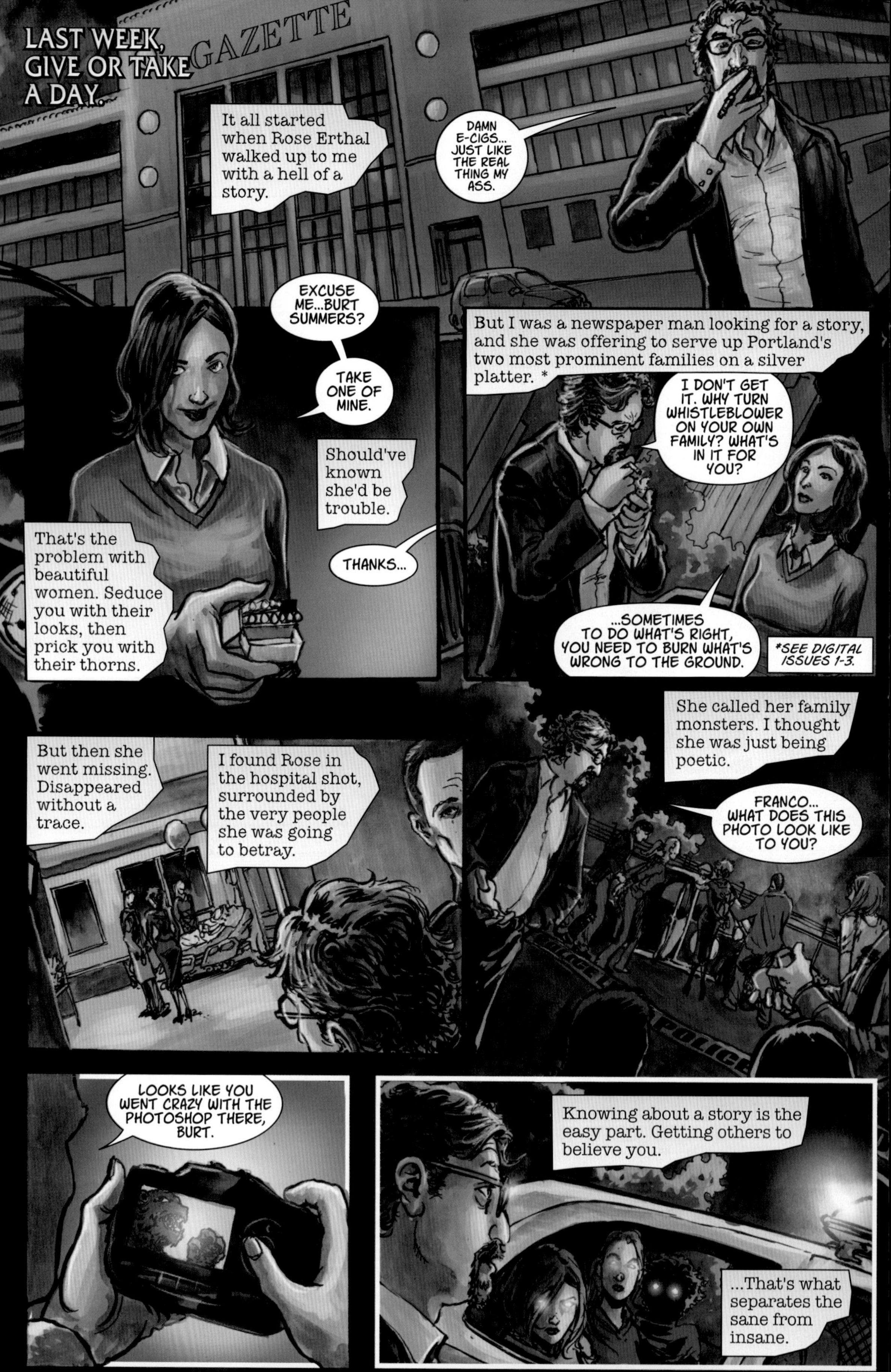

LAST WEEK, GIVE OR TAKE A DAY.
GAZETTE
It all started when Rose Erthal walked up to me with a hell of a story.
DAMN E-CIGS... JUST LIKE THE REAL THING MY ASS.
EXCUSE ME...BURT SUMMERS?
TAKE ONE OF MINE.
Should've known she'd be trouble.
That's the problem with beautiful women. Seduce you with their looks, then prick you with their thorns.
THANKS...
But I was a newspaper man looking for a story, and she was offering to serve up Portland's two most prominent families on a silver platter. *
I DON'T GET IT. WHY TURN WHISTLEBLOWER ON YOUR OWN FAMILY? WHAT'S IN IT FOR YOU?
...SOMETIMES TO DO WHAT'S RIGHT, YOU NEED TO BURN WHAT'S WRONG TO THE GROUND.
*SEE DIGITAL ISSUES 1-3.
But then she went missing. Disappeared without a trace.
I found Rose in the hospital shot, surrounded by the very people she was going to betray.
She called her family monsters. I thought she was just being poetic.
FRANCO... WHAT DOES THIS PHOTO LOOK LIKE TO YOU?
POLICE
LOOKS LIKE YOU WENT CRAZY WITH THE PHOTOSHOP THERE, BURT.
Knowing about a story is the easy part. Getting others to believe you.
...That's what separates the sane from insane.

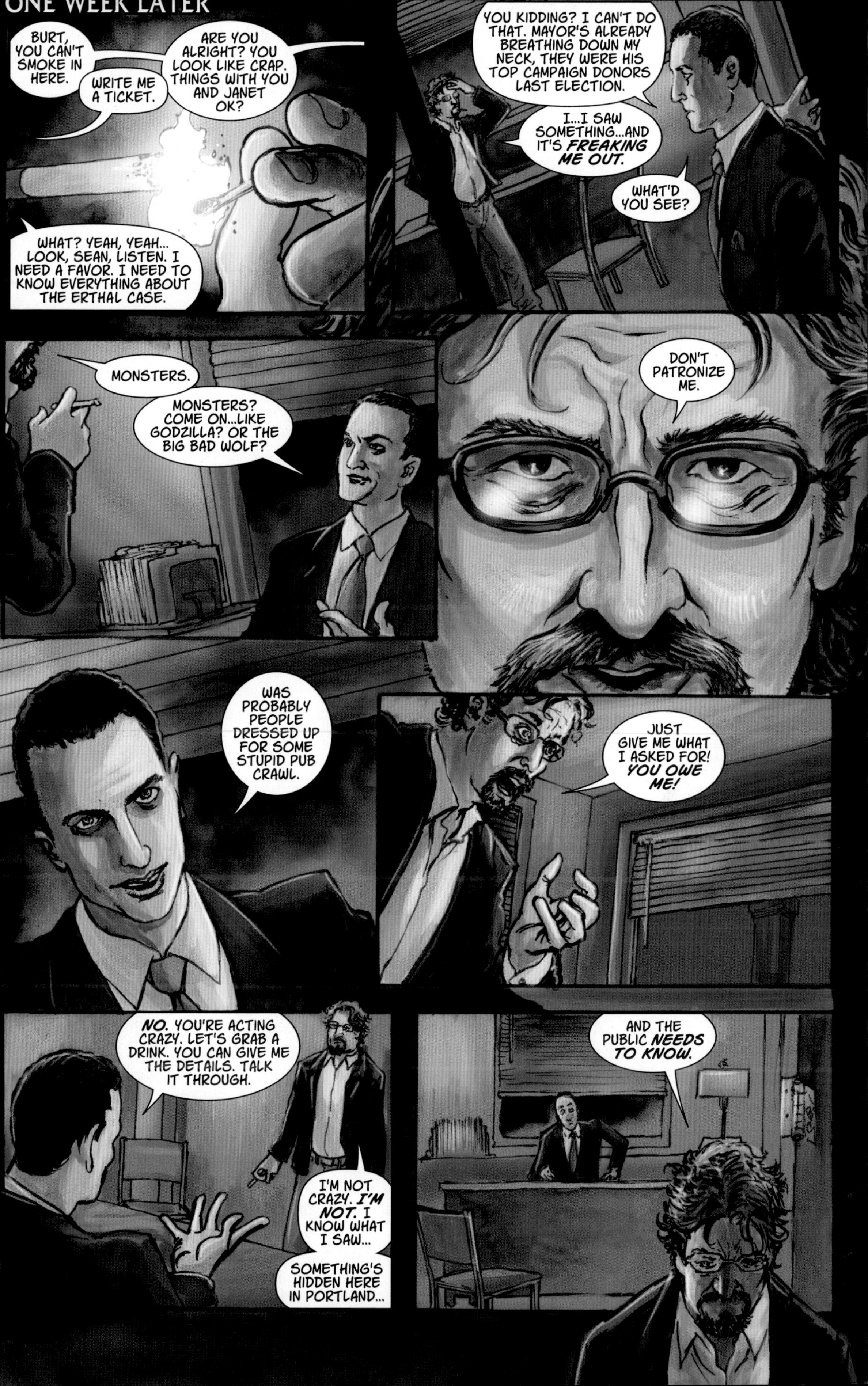
ONE WEEK LATER
BURT, YOU CAN'T SMOKE IN HERE.
WRITE ME A TICKET.
ARE YOU ALRIGHT? YOU LOOK LIKE CRAP. THINGS WITH YOU AND JANET OK?
WHAT? YEAH, YEAH... LOOK, SEAN, LISTEN. I NEED A FAVOR. I NEED TO KNOW EVERYTHING ABOUT THE ERTHAL CASE.
YOU KIDDING? I CAN'T DO THAT. MAYOR'S ALREADY BREATHING DOWN MY NECK, THEY WERE HIS TOP CAMPAIGN DONORS LAST ELECTION.
I...I SAW SOMETHING...AND IT'S FREAKING ME OUT.
WHAT'D YOU SEE?
MONSTERS.
MONSTERS? COME ON...LIKE GODZILLA? OR THE BIG BAD WOLF?
DON'T PATRONIZE ME.
WAS PROBABLY PEOPLE DRESSED UP FOR SOME STUPID PUB CRAWL.
JUST GIVE ME WHAT I ASKED FOR! YOU OWE ME!
NO. YOU'RE ACTING CRAZY. LET'S GRAB A DRINK. YOU CAN GIVE ME THE DETAILS. TALK IT THROUGH.
I'M NOT CRAZY. I'M NOT. I KNOW WHAT I SAW...
SOMETHING'S HIDDEN HERE IN PORTLAND...
AND THE PUBLIC NEEDS TO KNOW.

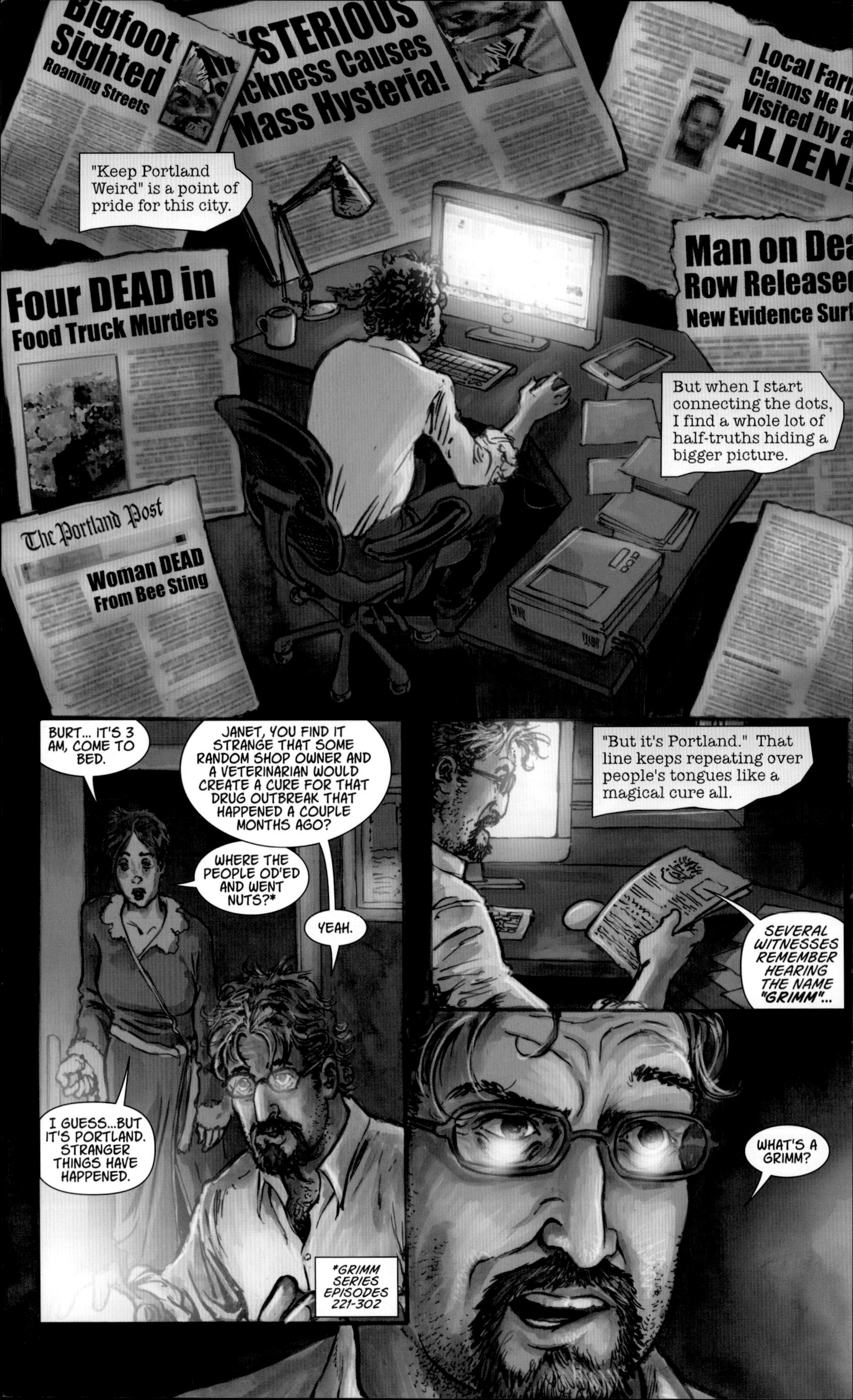
Bigfoot Sighted
Roaming Streets
STERIOUS
ckness Causes
Mass Hysteria!
Local Farm
Claims He W
Visited by a
ALIEN!
"Keep Portland Weird" is a point of pride for this city.
Four DEAD in
Food Truck Murders
Man on Dea
Row Released
New Evidence Surf
But when I start connecting the dots, I find a whole lot of half-truths hiding a bigger picture.
The Portland Post
Woman DEAD
From Bee Sting
BURT... IT'S 3 AM, COME TO BED.
JANET, YOU FIND IT STRANGE THAT SOME RANDOM SHOP OWNER AND A VETERINARIAN WOULD CREATE A CURE FOR THAT DRUG OUTBREAK THAT HAPPENED A COUPLE MONTHS AGO?
WHERE THE PEOPLE OD'ED AND WENT NUTS?*
YEAH.
I GUESS...BUT IT'S PORTLAND. STRANGER THINGS HAVE HAPPENED.
*GRIMM SERIES EPISODES 221-302
"But it's Portland." That line keeps repeating over people's tongues like a magical cure all.
SEVERAL WITNESSES REMEMBER HEARING THE NAME "GRIMM"...
WHAT'S A GRIMM?

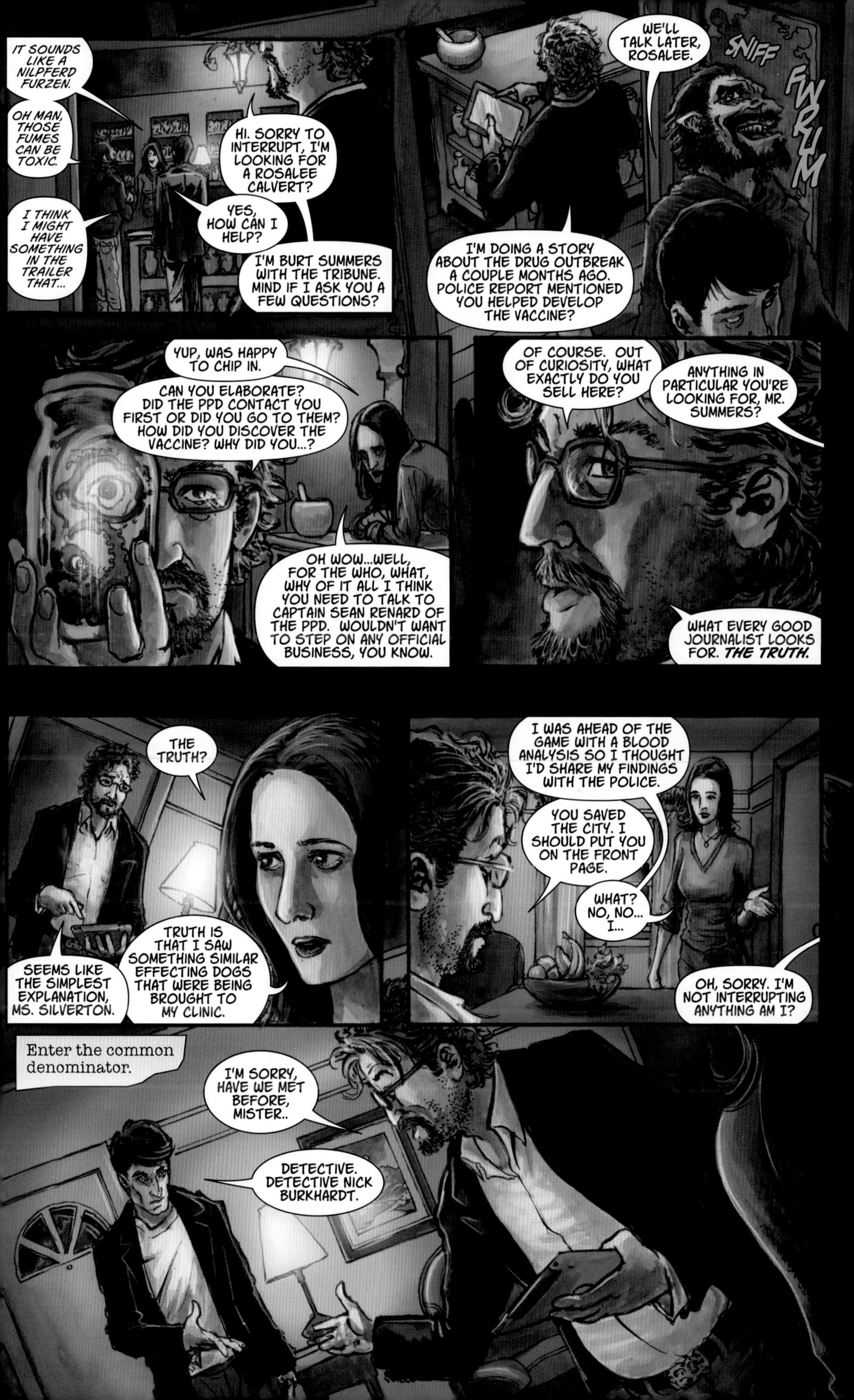
IT SOUNDS LIKE A NILPFERD FURZEN.
OH MAN, THOSE FUMES CAN BE TOXIC.
I THINK I MIGHT HAVE SOMETHING IN THE TRAILER THAT...
HI. SORRY TO INTERRUPT, I'M LOOKING FOR A ROSALEE CALVERT?
YES, HOW CAN I HELP?
I'M BURT SUMMERS WITH THE TRIBUNE. MIND IF I ASK YOU A FEW QUESTIONS?
WE'LL TALK LATER, ROSALEE.
SNIFF
FWRUM
I'M DOING A STORY ABOUT THE DRUG OUTBREAK A COUPLE MONTHS AGO. POLICE REPORT MENTIONED YOU HELPED DEVELOP THE VACCINE?
YUP, WAS HAPPY TO CHIP IN.
CAN YOU ELABORATE? DID THE PPD CONTACT YOU FIRST OR DID YOU GO TO THEM? HOW DID YOU DISCOVER THE VACCINE? WHY DID YOU...?
OH WOW...WELL, FOR THE WHO, WHAT, WHY OF IT ALL I THINK YOU NEED TO TALK TO CAPTAIN SEAN RENARD OF THE PPD. WOULDN'T WANT TO STEP ON ANY OFFICIAL BUSINESS, YOU KNOW.
OF COURSE. OUT OF CURIOSITY, WHAT EXACTLY DO YOU SELL HERE?
ANYTHING IN PARTICULAR YOU'RE LOOKING FOR, MR. SUMMERS?
WHAT EVERY GOOD JOURNALIST LOOKS FOR. THE TRUTH.
THE TRUTH?
SEEMS LIKE THE SIMPLEST EXPLANATION, MS. SILVERTON.
TRUTH IS THAT I SAW SOMETHING SIMILAR EFFECTING DOGS THAT WERE BEING BROUGHT TO MY CLINIC.
I WAS AHEAD OF THE GAME WITH A BLOOD ANALYSIS SO I THOUGHT I'D SHARE MY FINDINGS WITH THE POLICE.
YOU SAVED THE CITY. I SHOULD PUT YOU ON THE FRONT PAGE.
WHAT? NO, NO... I...
OH, SORRY. I'M NOT INTERRUPTING ANYTHING AM I?
Enter the common denominator.
I'M SORRY, HAVE WE MET BEFORE, MISTER..
DETECTIVE. DETECTIVE NICK BURKHARDT.

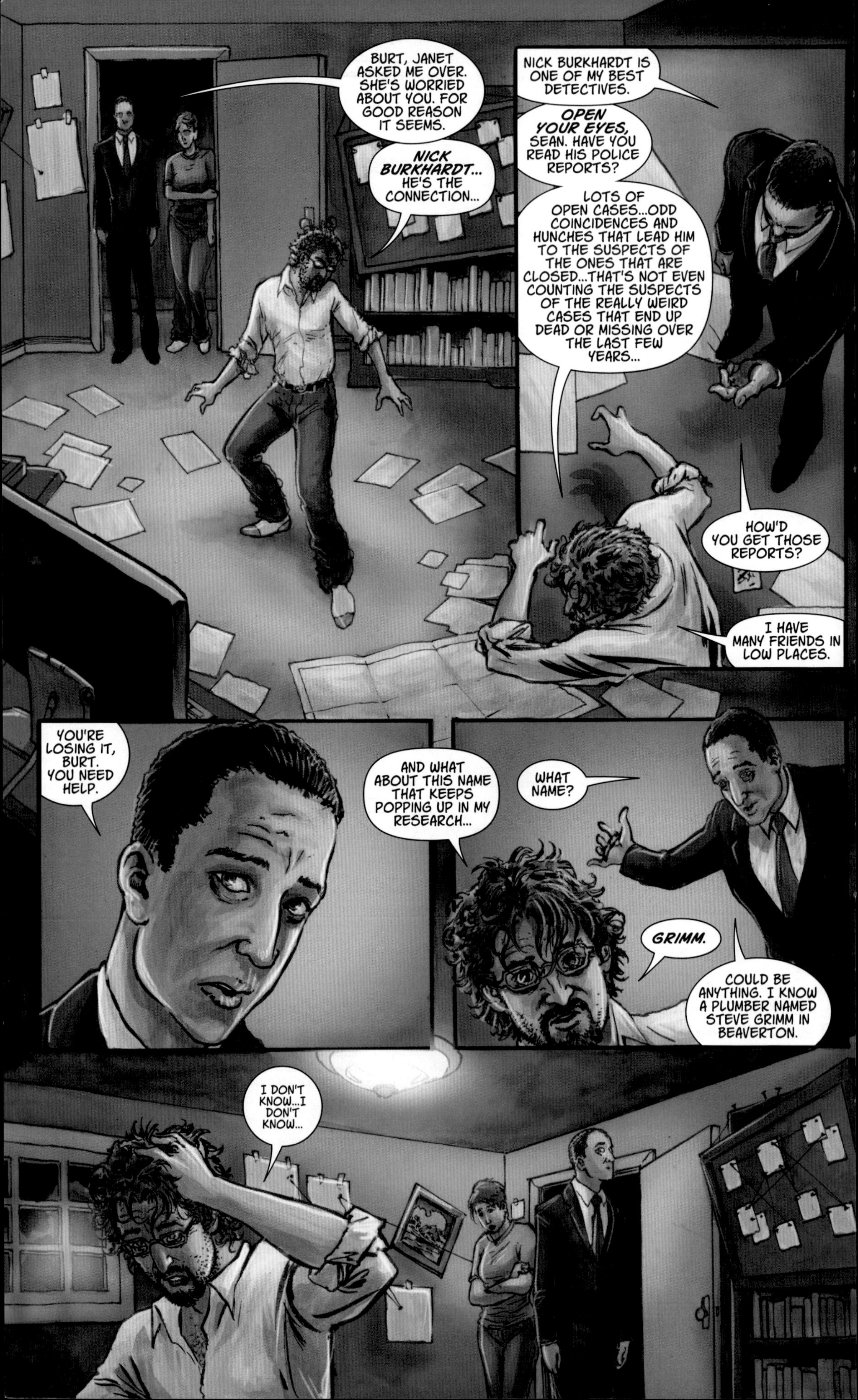
BURT, JANET ASKED ME OVER. SHE'S WORRIED ABOUT YOU. FOR GOOD REASON IT SEEMS.
NICK BURKHARDT... HE'S THE CONNECTION...
NICK BURKHARDT IS ONE OF MY BEST DETECTIVES.
OPEN YOUR EYES, SEAN. HAVE YOU READ HIS POLICE REPORTS?
LOTS OF OPEN CASES...ODD COINCIDENCES AND HUNCHES THAT LEAD HIM TO THE SUSPECTS OF THE ONES THAT ARE CLOSED...THAT'S NOT EVEN COUNTING THE SUSPECTS OF THE REALLY WEIRD CASES THAT END UP DEAD OR MISSING OVER THE LAST FEW YEARS...
HOW'D YOU GET THOSE REPORTS?
I HAVE MANY FRIENDS IN LOW PLACES.
YOU'RE LOSING IT, BURT. YOU NEED HELP.
AND WHAT ABOUT THIS NAME THAT KEEPS POPPING UP IN MY RESEARCH...
WHAT NAME?
GRIMM.
COULD BE ANYTHING. I KNOW A PLUMBER NAMED STEVE GRIMM IN BEAVERTON.
I DON'T KNOW...I DON'T KNOW...

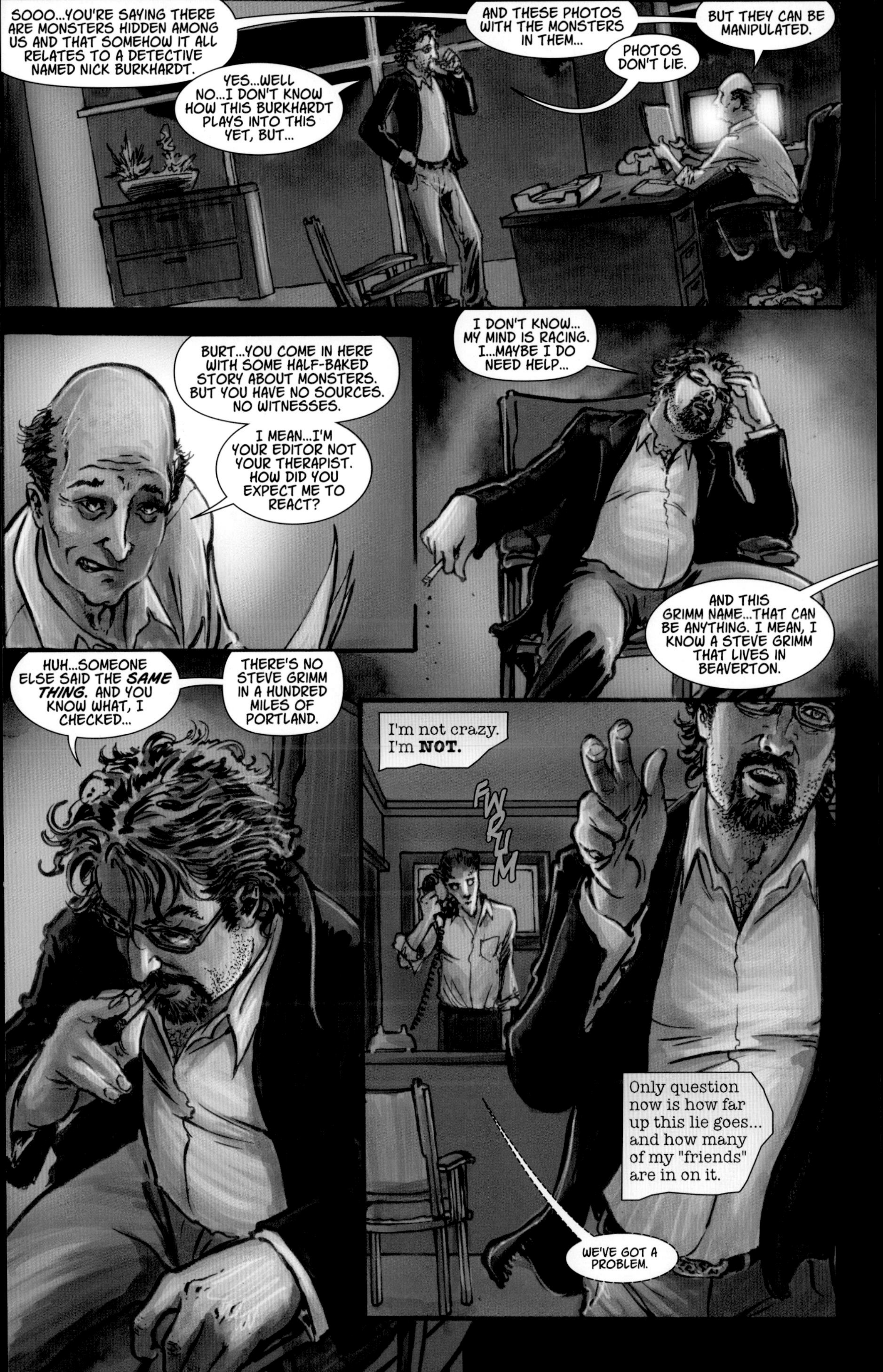
SOOO...YOU'RE SAYING THERE ARE MONSTERS HIDDEN AMONG US AND THAT SOMEHOW IT ALL RELATES TO A DETECTIVE NAMED NICK BURKHARDT.
YES...WELL NO...I DON'T KNOW HOW THIS BURKHARDT PLAYS INTO THIS YET, BUT...
AND THESE PHOTOS WITH THE MONSTERS IN THEM...
PHOTOS DON'T LIE.
BUT THEY CAN BE MANIPULATED.
BURT...YOU COME IN HERE WITH SOME HALF-BAKED STORY ABOUT MONSTERS. BUT YOU HAVE NO SOURCES. NO WITNESSES.
I MEAN...I'M YOUR EDITOR NOT YOUR THERAPIST. HOW DID YOU EXPECT ME TO REACT?
I DON'T KNOW... MY MIND IS RACING. I...MAYBE I DO NEED HELP...
AND THIS GRIMM NAME...THAT CAN BE ANYTHING. I MEAN, I KNOW A STEVE GRIMM THAT LIVES IN BEAVERTON.
HUH...SOMEONE ELSE SAID THE SAME THING. AND YOU KNOW WHAT, I CHECKED...
THERE'S NO STEVE GRIMM IN A HUNDRED MILES OF PORTLAND.
I'm not crazy. I'm NOT.
FWRUM
Only question now is how far up this lie goes... and how many of my "friends" are in on it.
WE'VE GOT A PROBLEM.

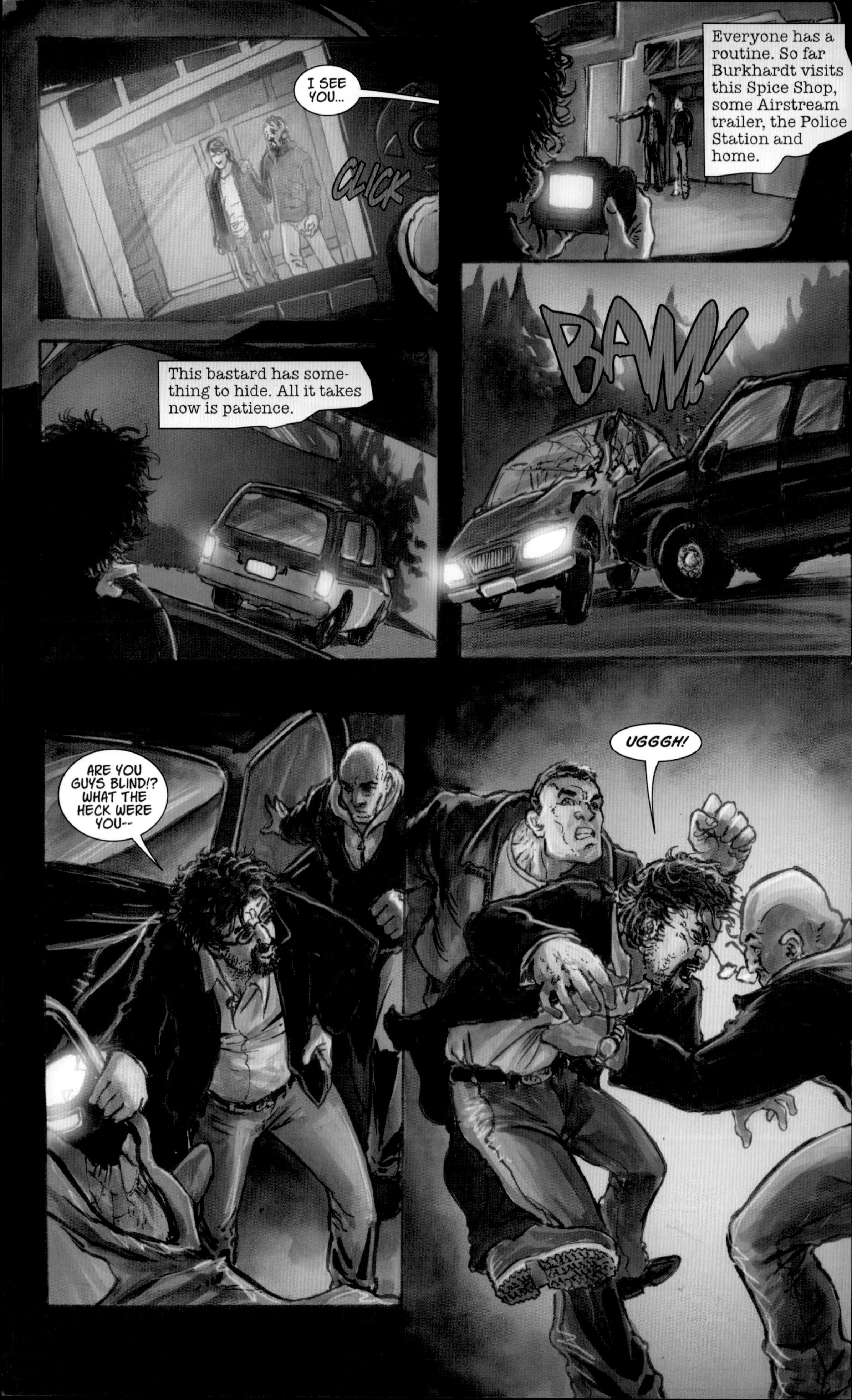
I SEE YOU...
CLICK
Everyone has a routine. So far Burkhardt visits this Spice Shop, some Airstream trailer, the Police Station and home.
This bastard has something to hide. All it takes now is patience.
BAM!
ARE YOU GUYS BLIND!? WHAT THE HECK WERE YOU--
UGGGH!

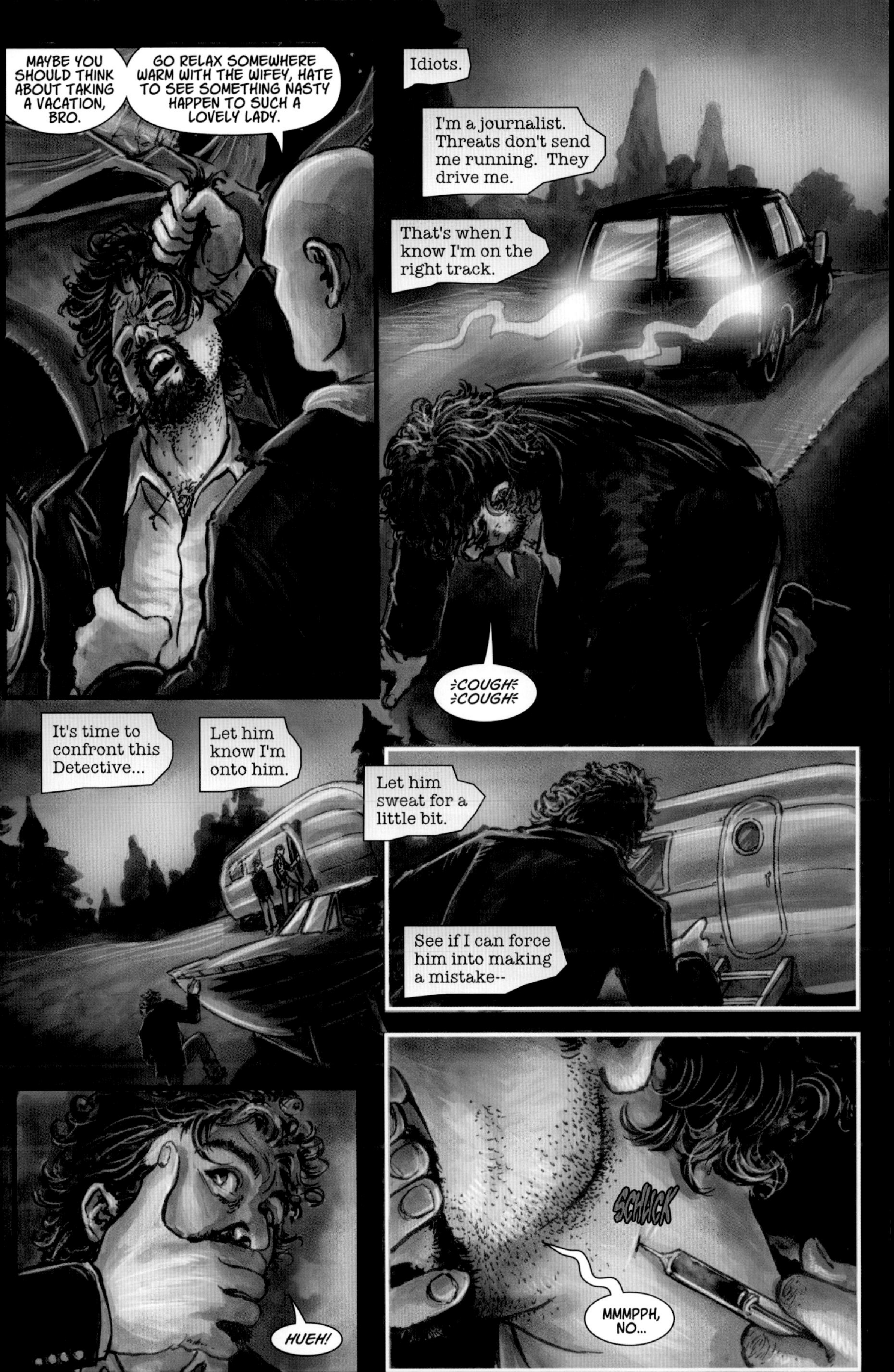
MAYBE YOU SHOULD THINK ABOUT TAKING A VACATION, BRO.
GO RELAX SOMEWHERE WARM WITH THE WIFEY, HATE TO SEE SOMETHING NASTY HAPPEN TO SUCH A LOVELY LADY.
Idiots.
I'm a journalist. Threats don't send me running. They drive me.
That's when I know I'm on the right track.
COUGH COUGH
It's time to confront this Detective...
Let him know I'm onto him.
Let him sweat for a little bit.
See if I can force him into making a mistake--
HUEH!
SCHLICK
MMMPPH, NO...

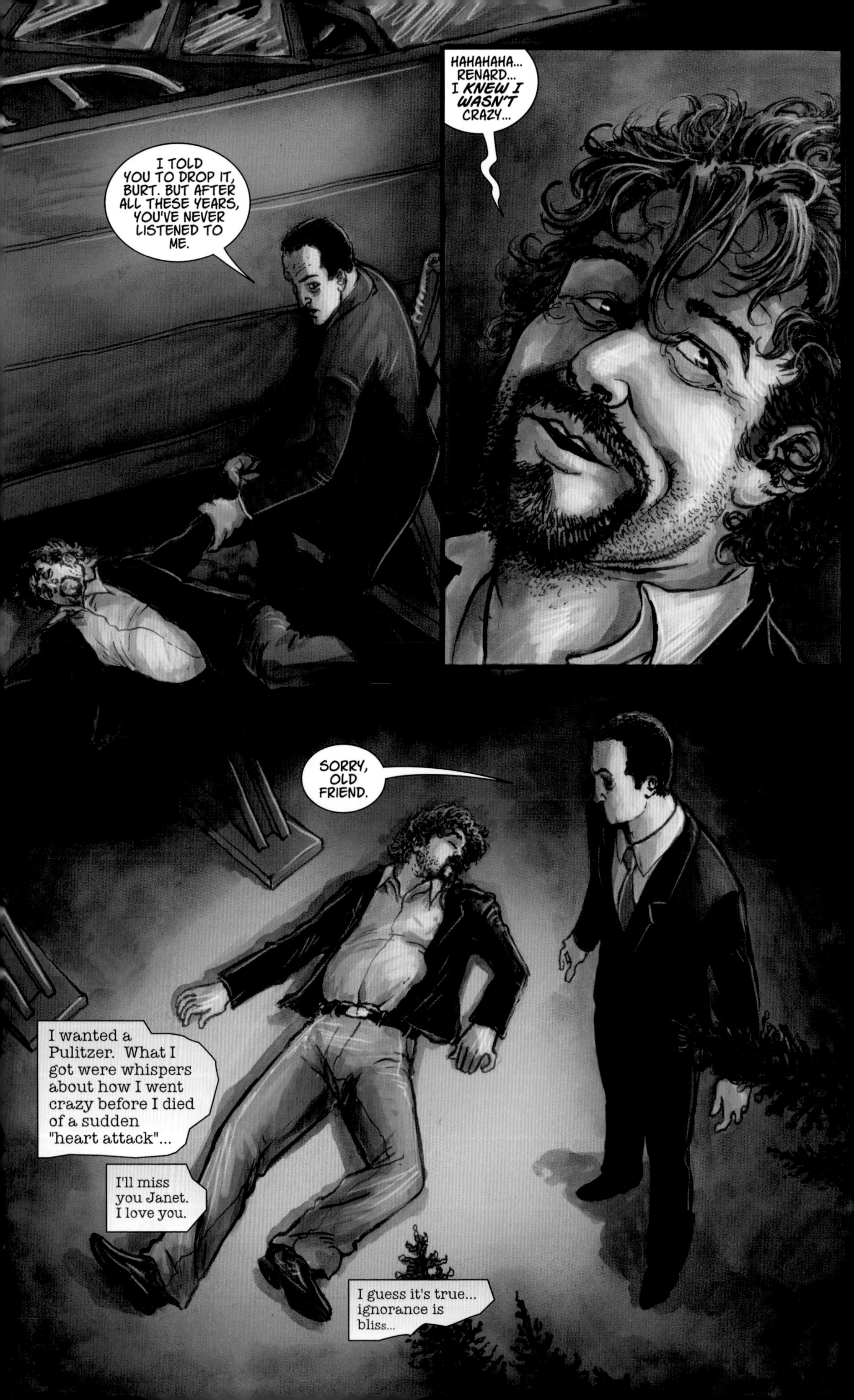
I TOLD YOU TO DROP IT, BURT. BUT AFTER ALL THESE YEARS, YOU'VE NEVER LISTENED TO ME.
HAHAHAHA... RENARD... I *KNEW I WASN'T* CRAZY...
SORRY, OLD FRIEND.
I wanted a Pulitzer. What I got were whispers about how I went crazy before I died of a sudden "heart attack"...
I'll miss you Janet. I love you.
I guess it's true... ignorance is bliss...

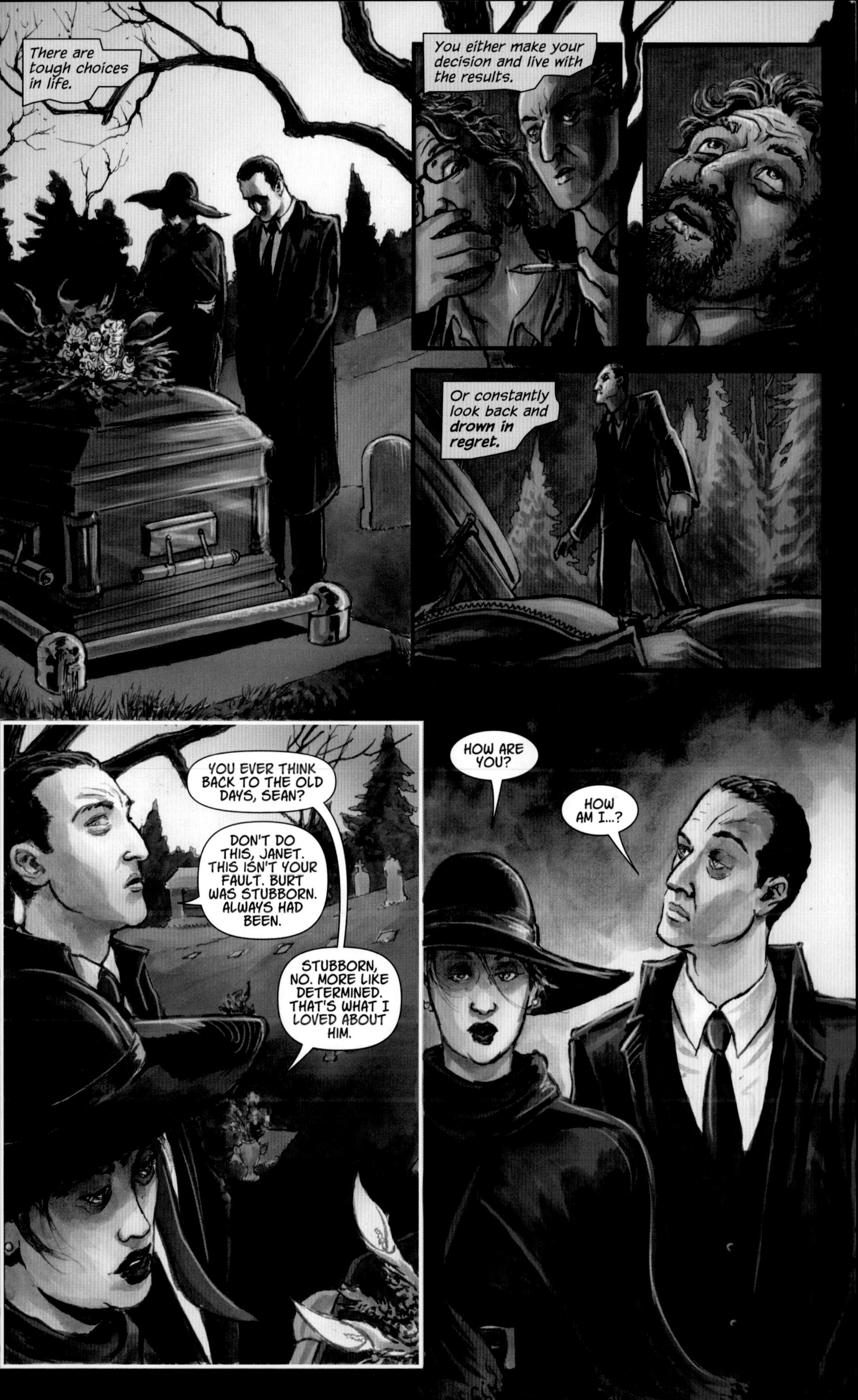
There are tough choices in life.
You either make your decision and live with the results.
Or constantly look back and **drown in regret.**
YOU EVER THINK BACK TO THE OLD DAYS, SEAN?
DON'T DO THIS, JANET. THIS ISN'T YOUR FAULT. BURT WAS STUBBORN. ALWAYS HAD BEEN.
STUBBORN, NO. MORE LIKE DETERMINED. THAT'S WHAT I LOVED ABOUT HIM.
HOW ARE YOU?
HOW AM I...?

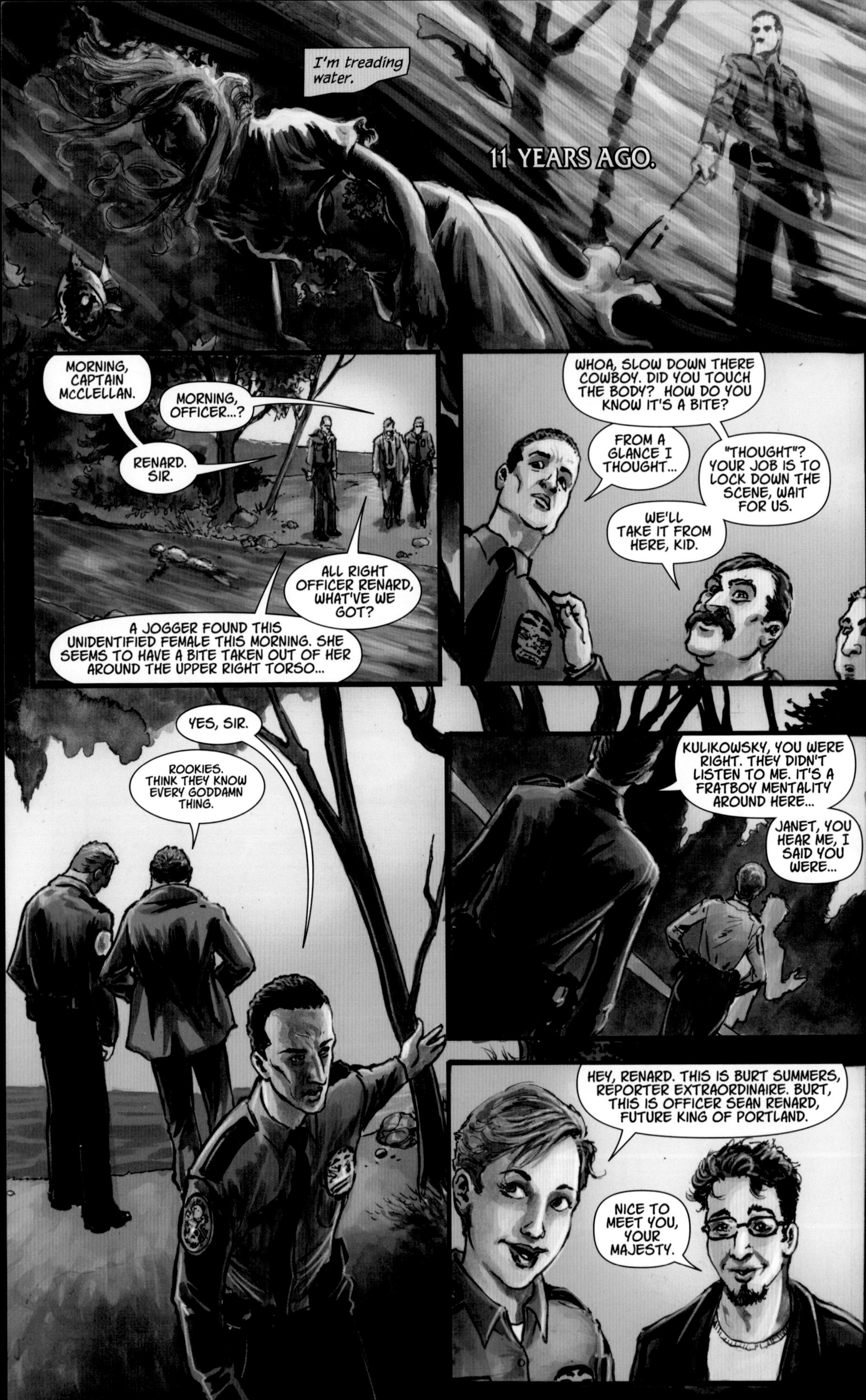
I'm treading water.
11 YEARS AGO.
MORNING, CAPTAIN MCCLELLAN.
MORNING, OFFICER...?
RENARD. SIR.
ALL RIGHT OFFICER RENARD, WHAT'VE WE GOT?
A JOGGER FOUND THIS UNIDENTIFIED FEMALE THIS MORNING. SHE SEEMS TO HAVE A BITE TAKEN OUT OF HER AROUND THE UPPER RIGHT TORSO...
WHOA, SLOW DOWN THERE COWBOY. DID YOU TOUCH THE BODY? HOW DO YOU KNOW IT'S A BITE?
FROM A GLANCE I THOUGHT...
"THOUGHT"? YOUR JOB IS TO LOCK DOWN THE SCENE, WAIT FOR US.
WE'LL TAKE IT FROM HERE, KID.
YES, SIR.
ROOKIES. THINK THEY KNOW EVERY GODDAMN THING.
KULIKOWSKY, YOU WERE RIGHT. THEY DIDN'T LISTEN TO ME. IT'S A FRATBOY MENTALITY AROUND HERE...
JANET, YOU HEAR ME, I SAID YOU WERE...
HEY, RENARD. THIS IS BURT SUMMERS, REPORTER EXTRAORDINAIRE. BURT, THIS IS OFFICER SEAN RENARD, FUTURE KING OF PORTLAND.
NICE TO MEET YOU, YOUR MAJESTY.

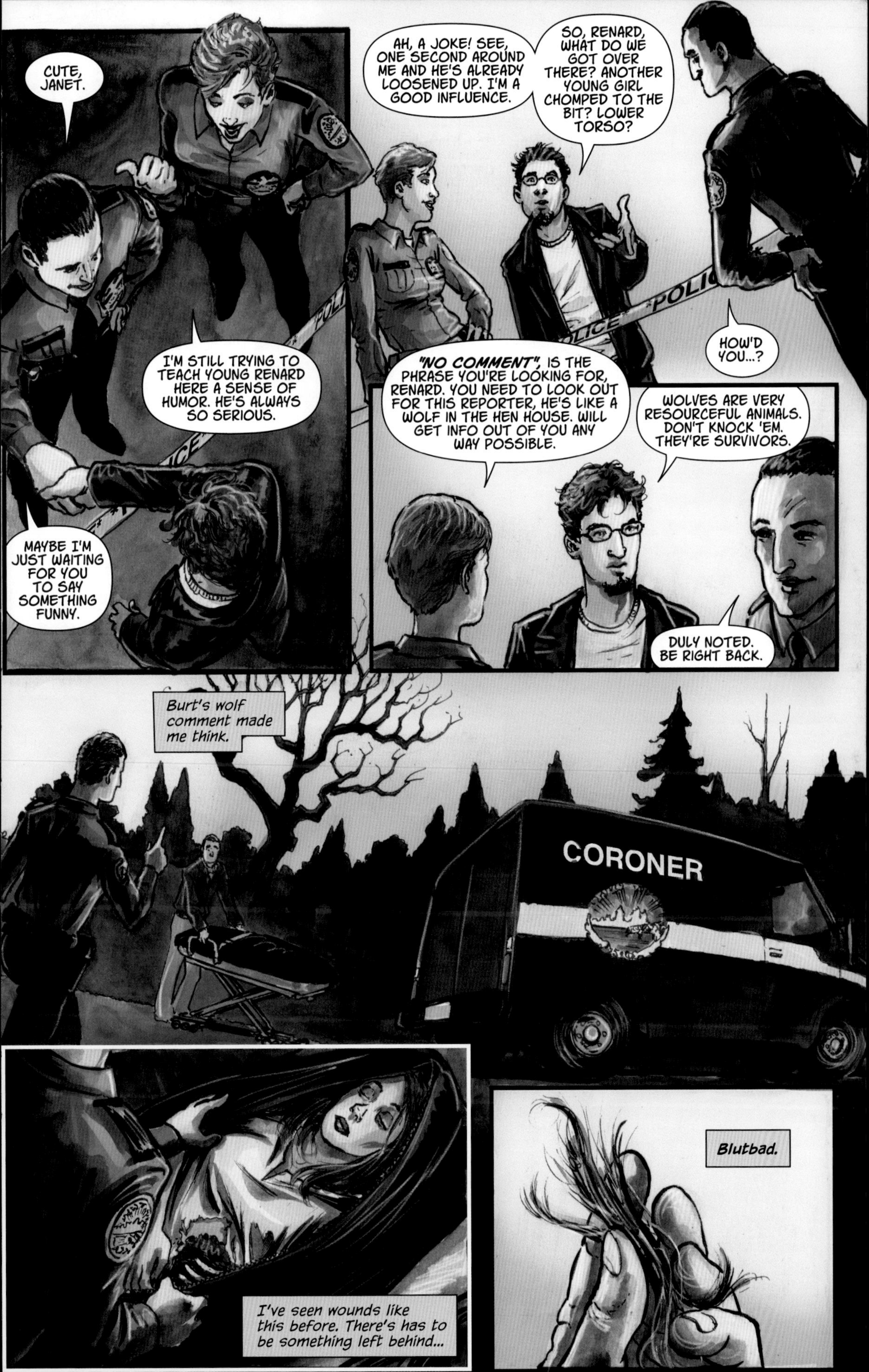
CUTE, JANET.
I'M STILL TRYING TO TEACH YOUNG RENARD HERE A SENSE OF HUMOR. HE'S ALWAYS SO SERIOUS.
MAYBE I'M JUST WAITING FOR YOU TO SAY SOMETHING FUNNY.
AH, A JOKE! SEE, ONE SECOND AROUND ME AND HE'S ALREADY LOOSENED UP. I'M A GOOD INFLUENCE.
SO, RENARD, WHAT DO WE GOT OVER THERE? ANOTHER YOUNG GIRL CHOMPED TO THE BIT? LOWER TORSO?
HOW'D YOU...?
POLICE
"NO COMMENT", IS THE PHRASE YOU'RE LOOKING FOR, RENARD. YOU NEED TO LOOK OUT FOR THIS REPORTER, HE'S LIKE A WOLF IN THE HEN HOUSE. WILL GET INFO OUT OF YOU ANY WAY POSSIBLE.
WOLVES ARE VERY RESOURCEFUL ANIMALS. DON'T KNOCK 'EM. THEY'RE SURVIVORS.
DULY NOTED. BE RIGHT BACK.
Burt's wolf comment made me think.
CORONER
I've seen wounds like this before. There's has to be something left behind...
Blutbad.

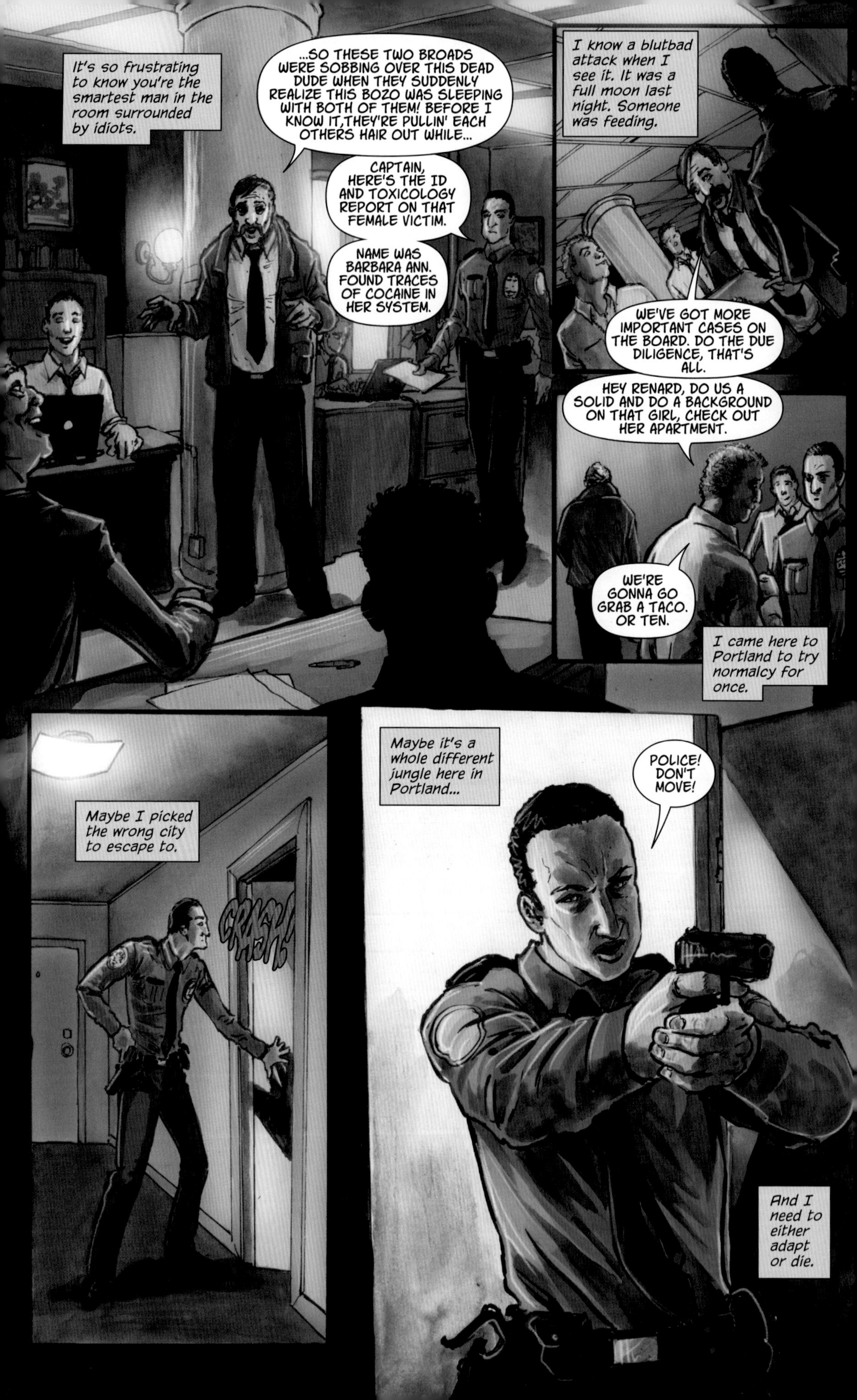
It's so frustrating to know you're the smartest man in the room surrounded by idiots.
...SO THESE TWO BROADS WERE SOBBING OVER THIS DEAD DUDE WHEN THEY SUDDENLY REALIZE THIS BOZO WAS SLEEPING WITH BOTH OF THEM! BEFORE I KNOW IT, THEY'RE PULLIN' EACH OTHERS HAIR OUT WHILE...
CAPTAIN, HERE'S THE ID AND TOXICOLOGY REPORT ON THAT FEMALE VICTIM.
NAME WAS BARBARA ANN. FOUND TRACES OF COCAINE IN HER SYSTEM.
I know a blutbad attack when I see it. It was a full moon last night. Someone was feeding.
WE'VE GOT MORE IMPORTANT CASES ON THE BOARD. DO THE DUE DILIGENCE, THAT'S ALL.
HEY RENARD, DO US A SOLID AND DO A BACKGROUND ON THAT GIRL, CHECK OUT HER APARTMENT.
WE'RE GONNA GO GRAB A TACO. OR TEN.
I came here to Portland to try normalcy for once.
Maybe I picked the wrong city to escape to.
CRASH!
Maybe it's a whole different jungle here in Portland...
POLICE! DON'T MOVE!
And I need to either adapt or die.

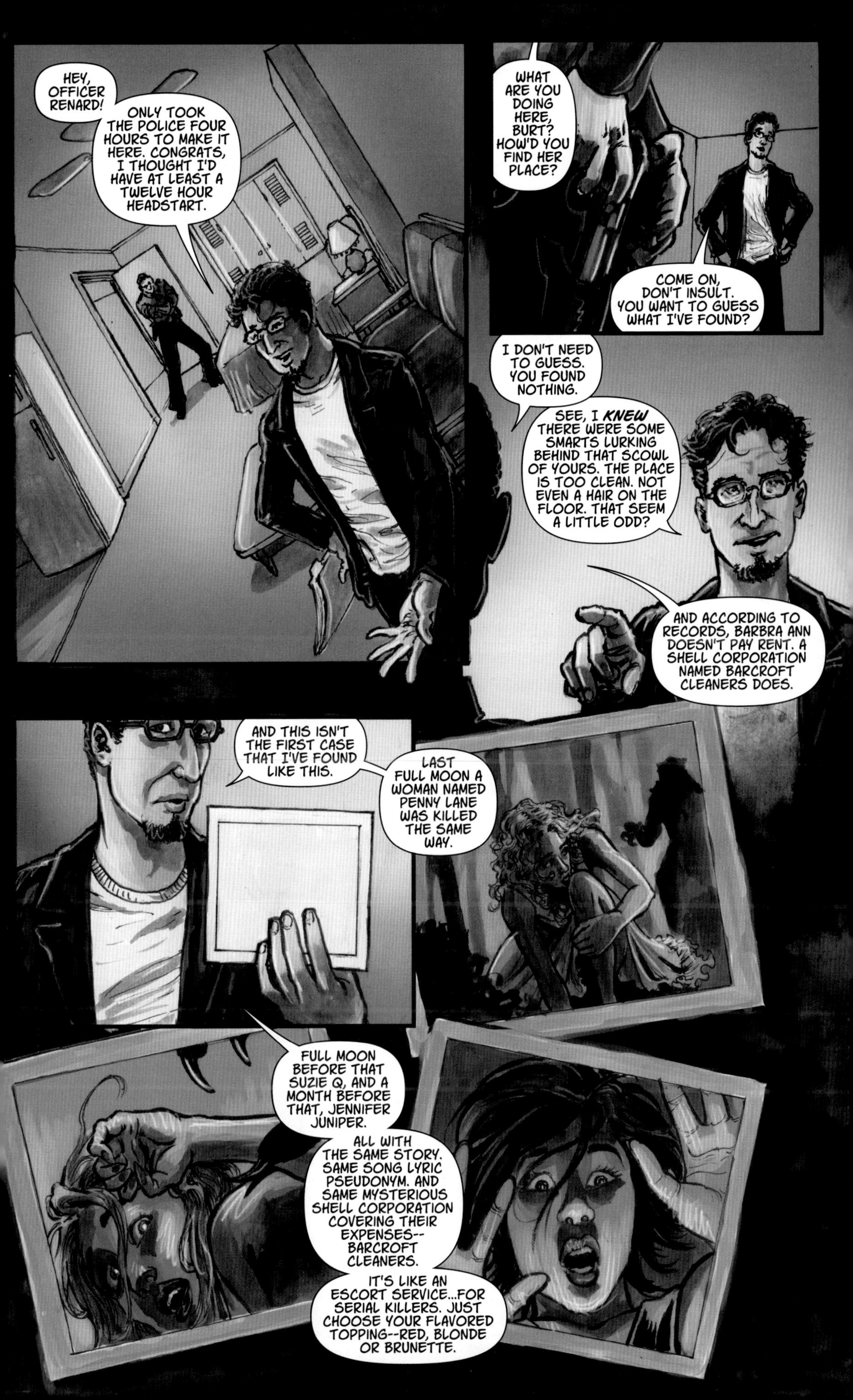
HEY, OFFICER RENARD!
ONLY TOOK THE POLICE FOUR HOURS TO MAKE IT HERE. CONGRATS, I THOUGHT I'D HAVE AT LEAST A TWELVE HOUR HEADSTART.
WHAT ARE YOU DOING HERE, BURT? HOW'D YOU FIND HER PLACE?
COME ON, DON'T INSULT. YOU WANT TO GUESS WHAT I'VE FOUND?
I DON'T NEED TO GUESS. YOU FOUND NOTHING.
SEE, I KNEW THERE WERE SOME SMARTS LURKING BEHIND THAT SCOWL OF YOURS. THE PLACE IS TOO CLEAN. NOT EVEN A HAIR ON THE FLOOR. THAT SEEM A LITTLE ODD?
AND ACCORDING TO RECORDS, BARBRA ANN DOESN'T PAY RENT. A SHELL CORPORATION NAMED BARCROFT CLEANERS DOES.
AND THIS ISN'T THE FIRST CASE THAT I'VE FOUND LIKE THIS.
LAST FULL MOON A WOMAN NAMED PENNY LANE WAS KILLED THE SAME WAY.
FULL MOON BEFORE THAT SUZIE Q, AND A MONTH BEFORE THAT, JENNIFER JUNIPER.
ALL WITH THE SAME STORY. SAME SONG LYRIC PSEUDONYM. AND SAME MYSTERIOUS SHELL CORPORATION COVERING THEIR EXPENSES--BARCROFT CLEANERS.
IT'S LIKE AN ESCORT SERVICE...FOR SERIAL KILLERS. JUST CHOOSE YOUR FLAVORED TOPPING--RED, BLONDE OR BRUNETTE.

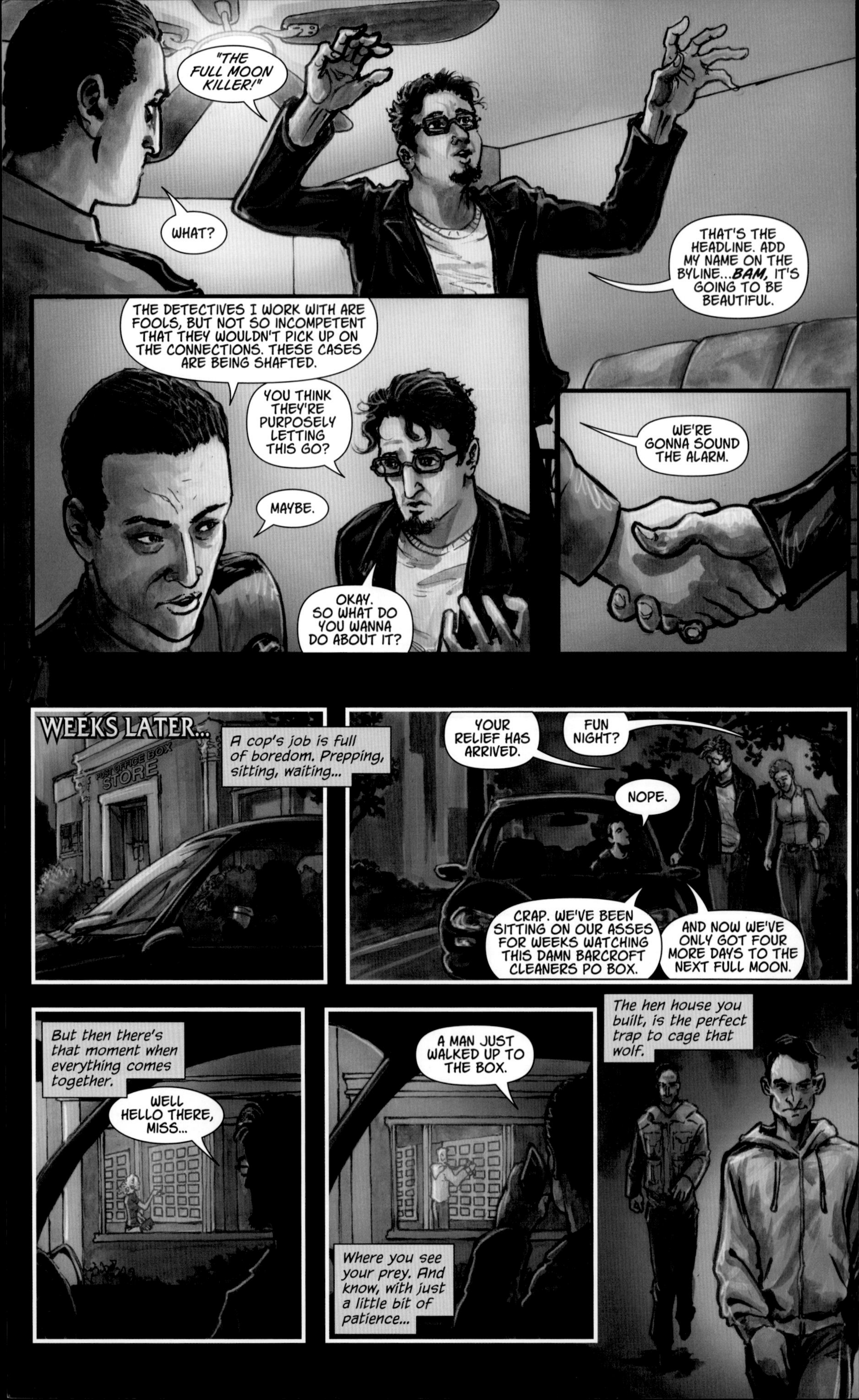

"THE FULL MOON KILLER!"
WHAT?
THAT'S THE HEADLINE. ADD MY NAME ON THE BYLINE...BAM, IT'S GOING TO BE BEAUTIFUL.
THE DETECTIVES I WORK WITH ARE FOOLS, BUT NOT SO INCOMPETENT THAT THEY WOULDN'T PICK UP ON THE CONNECTIONS. THESE CASES ARE BEING SHAFTED.
YOU THINK THEY'RE PURPOSELY LETTING THIS GO?
MAYBE.
OKAY. SO WHAT DO YOU WANNA DO ABOUT IT?
WE'RE GONNA SOUND THE ALARM.
WEEKS LATER...
A cop's job is full of boredom. Prepping, sitting, waiting...
POST OFFICE BOX
STORE
YOUR RELIEF HAS ARRIVED.
FUN NIGHT?
NOPE.
CRAP. WE'VE BEEN SITTING ON OUR ASSES FOR WEEKS WATCHING THIS DAMN BARCROFT CLEANERS PO BOX.
AND NOW WE'VE ONLY GOT FOUR MORE DAYS TO THE NEXT FULL MOON.
But then there's that moment when everything comes together.
WELL HELLO THERE, MISS...
A MAN JUST WALKED UP TO THE BOX.
Where you see your prey. And know, with just a little bit of patience...
The hen house you built, is the perfect trap to cage that wolf.

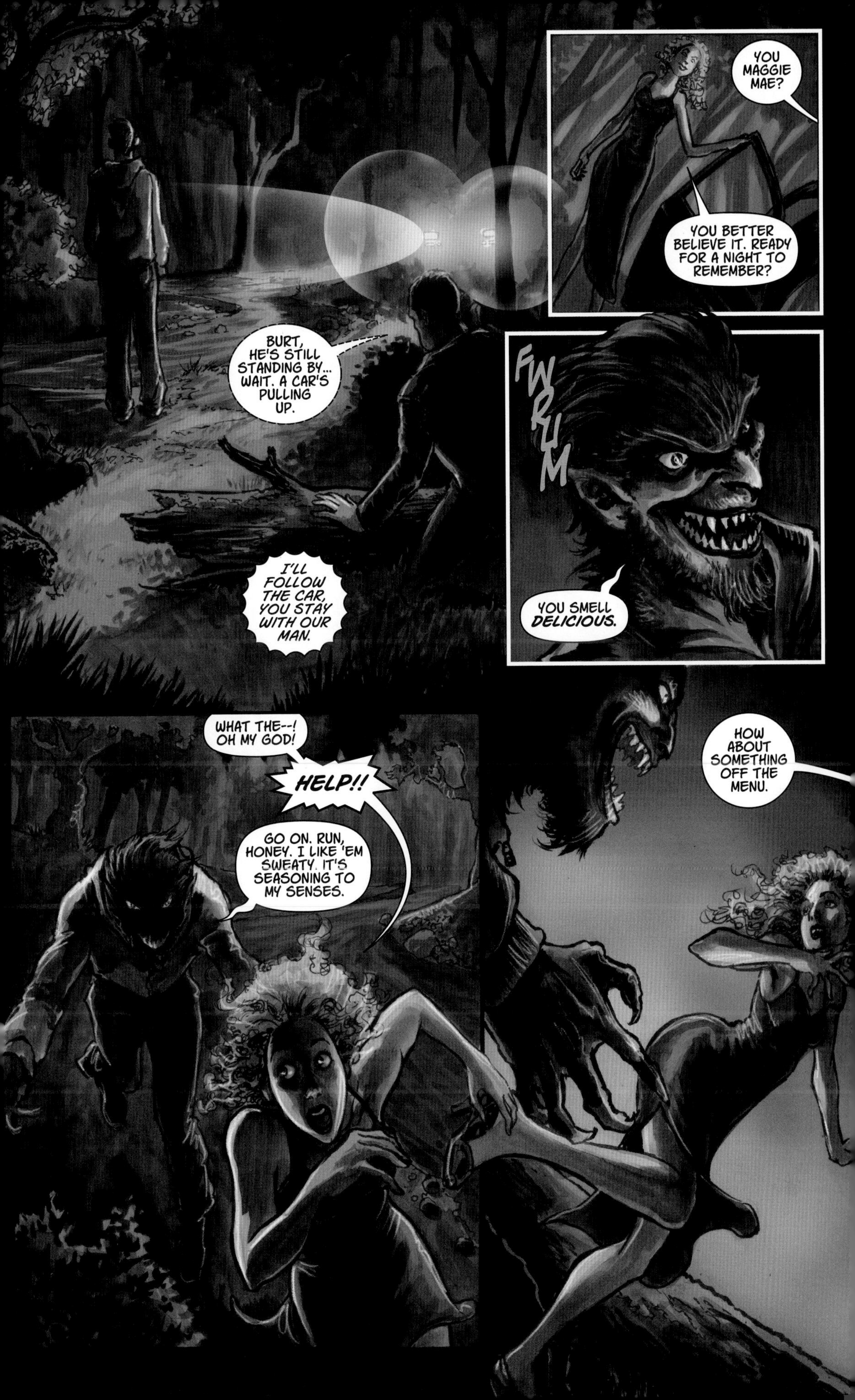
YOU MAGGIE MAE?
YOU BETTER BELIEVE IT. READY FOR A NIGHT TO REMEMBER?
BURT, HE'S STILL STANDING BY... WAIT. A CAR'S PULLING UP.
FWRUM
YOU SMELL DELICIOUS.
I'LL FOLLOW THE CAR, YOU STAY WITH OUR MAN.
WHAT THE--! OH MY GOD!
HELP!!
GO ON. RUN, HONEY. I LIKE 'EM SWEATY. IT'S SEASONING TO MY SENSES.
HOW ABOUT SOMETHING OFF THE MENU.

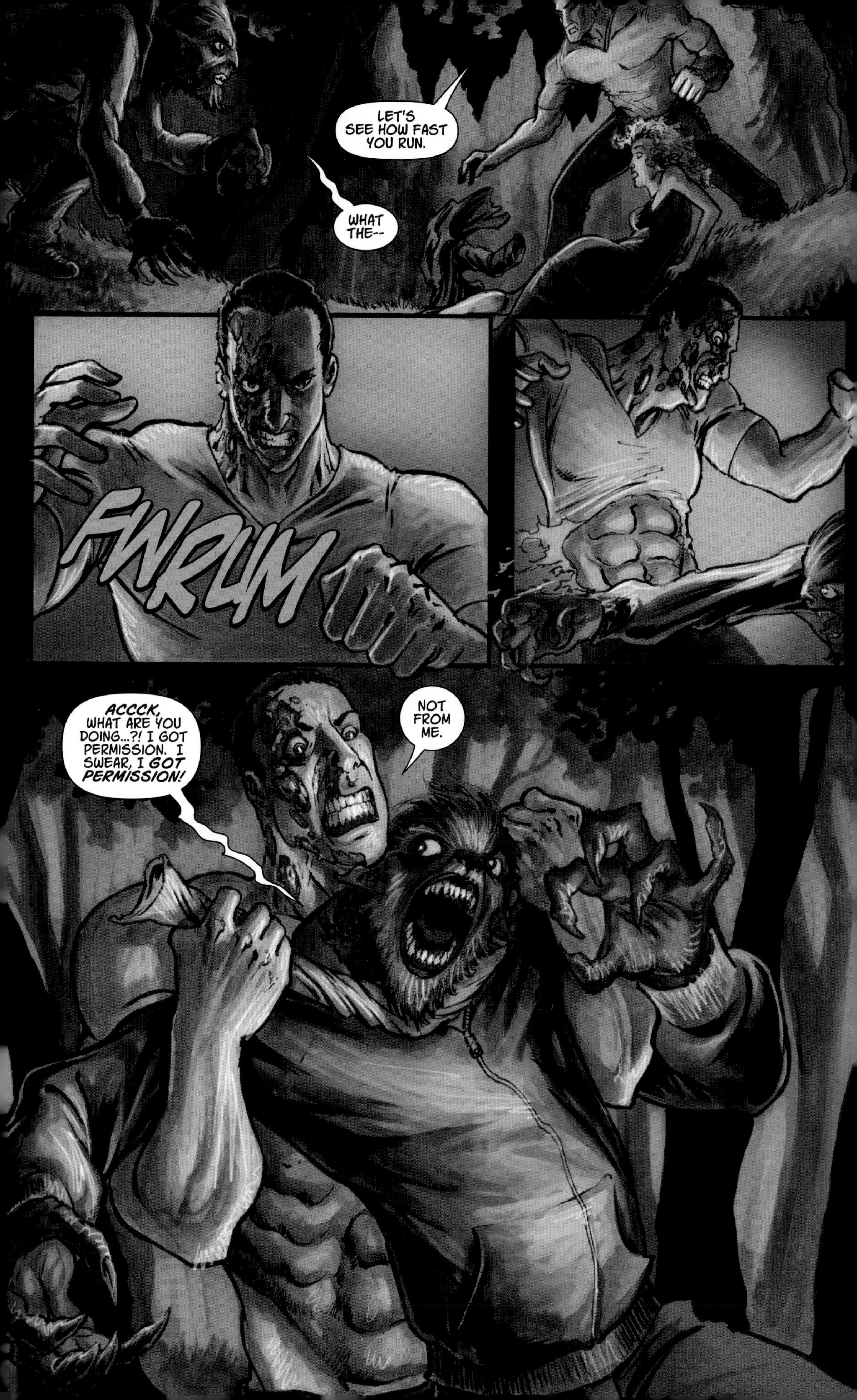
LET'S SEE HOW FAST YOU RUN.
WHAT THE--
FWRUM
ACCCK, WHAT ARE YOU DOING...?! I GOT PERMISSION. I SWEAR, I GOT PERMISSION!
NOT FROM ME.

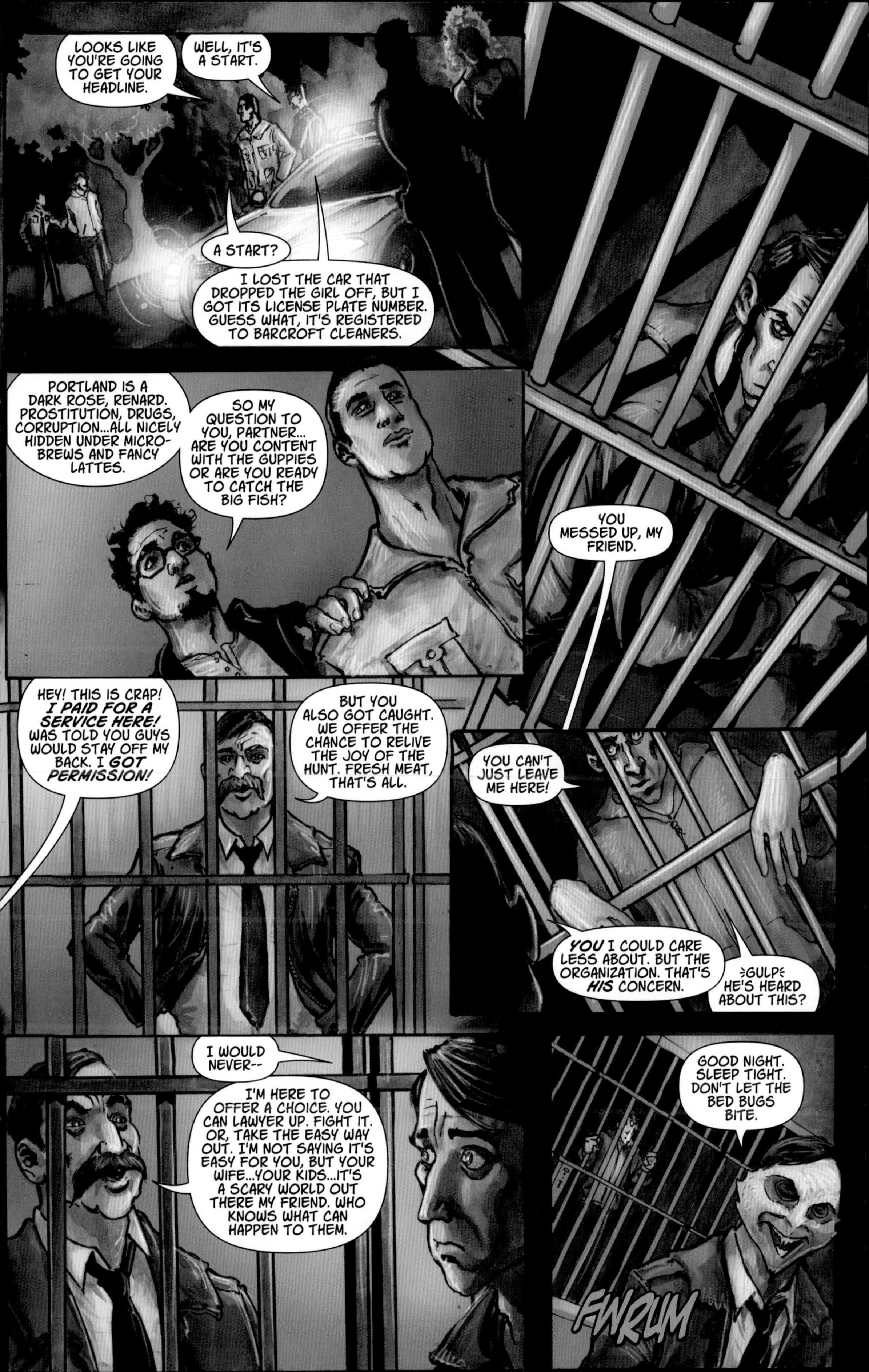
LOOKS LIKE YOU'RE GOING TO GET YOUR HEADLINE.
WELL, IT'S A START.
A START?
I LOST THE CAR THAT DROPPED THE GIRL OFF, BUT I GOT ITS LICENSE PLATE NUMBER. GUESS WHAT, IT'S REGISTERED TO BARCROFT CLEANERS.
PORTLAND IS A DARK ROSE, RENARD. PROSTITUTION, DRUGS, CORRUPTION...ALL NICELY HIDDEN UNDER MICRO-BREWS AND FANCY LATTES.
SO MY QUESTION TO YOU, PARTNER... ARE YOU CONTENT WITH THE GUPPIES OR ARE YOU READY TO CATCH THE BIG FISH?
YOU MESSED UP, MY FRIEND.
HEY! THIS IS CRAP! I PAID FOR A SERVICE HERE! WAS TOLD YOU GUYS WOULD STAY OFF MY BACK. I GOT PERMISSION!
BUT YOU ALSO GOT CAUGHT. WE OFFER THE CHANCE TO RELIVE THE JOY OF THE HUNT. FRESH MEAT, THAT'S ALL.
YOU CAN'T JUST LEAVE ME HERE!
YOU I COULD CARE LESS ABOUT. BUT THE ORGANIZATION. THAT'S HIS CONCERN.
GULP HE'S HEARD ABOUT THIS?
I WOULD NEVER--
I'M HERE TO OFFER A CHOICE. YOU CAN LAWYER UP. FIGHT IT. OR, TAKE THE EASY WAY OUT. I'M NOT SAYING IT'S EASY FOR YOU, BUT YOUR WIFE...YOUR KIDS...IT'S A SCARY WORLD OUT THERE MY FRIEND. WHO KNOWS WHAT CAN HAPPEN TO THEM.
GOOD NIGHT. SLEEP TIGHT. DON'T LET THE BED BUGS BITE.
FWRUM

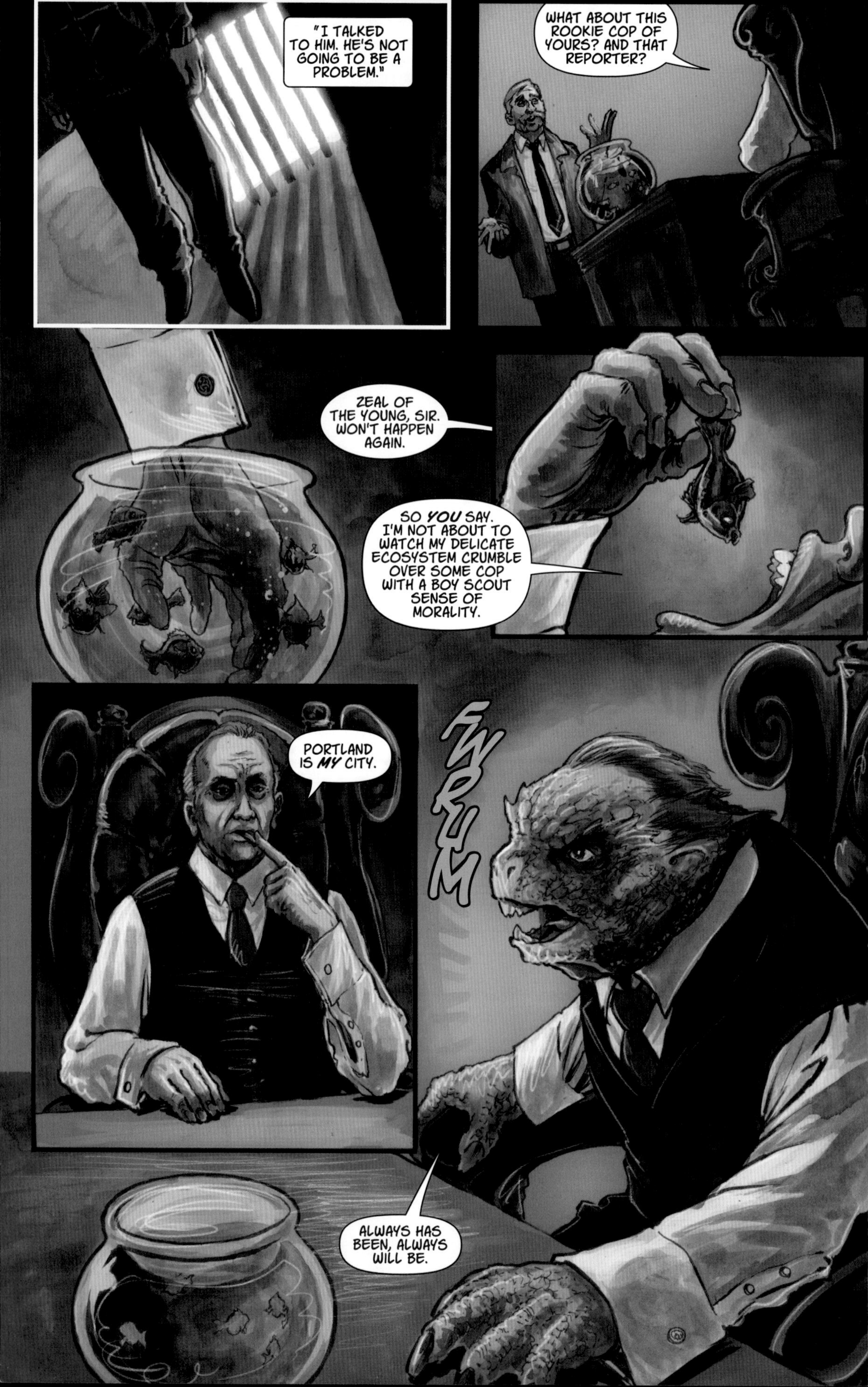
"I TALKED TO HIM. HE'S NOT GOING TO BE A PROBLEM."
WHAT ABOUT THIS ROOKIE COP OF YOURS? AND THAT REPORTER?
ZEAL OF THE YOUNG, SIR. WON'T HAPPEN AGAIN.
SO *YOU* SAY. I'M NOT ABOUT TO WATCH MY DELICATE ECOSYSTEM CRUMBLE OVER SOME COP WITH A BOY SCOUT SENSE OF MORALITY.
PORTLAND IS *MY* CITY.
FWRUM
ALWAYS HAS BEEN, ALWAYS WILL BE.

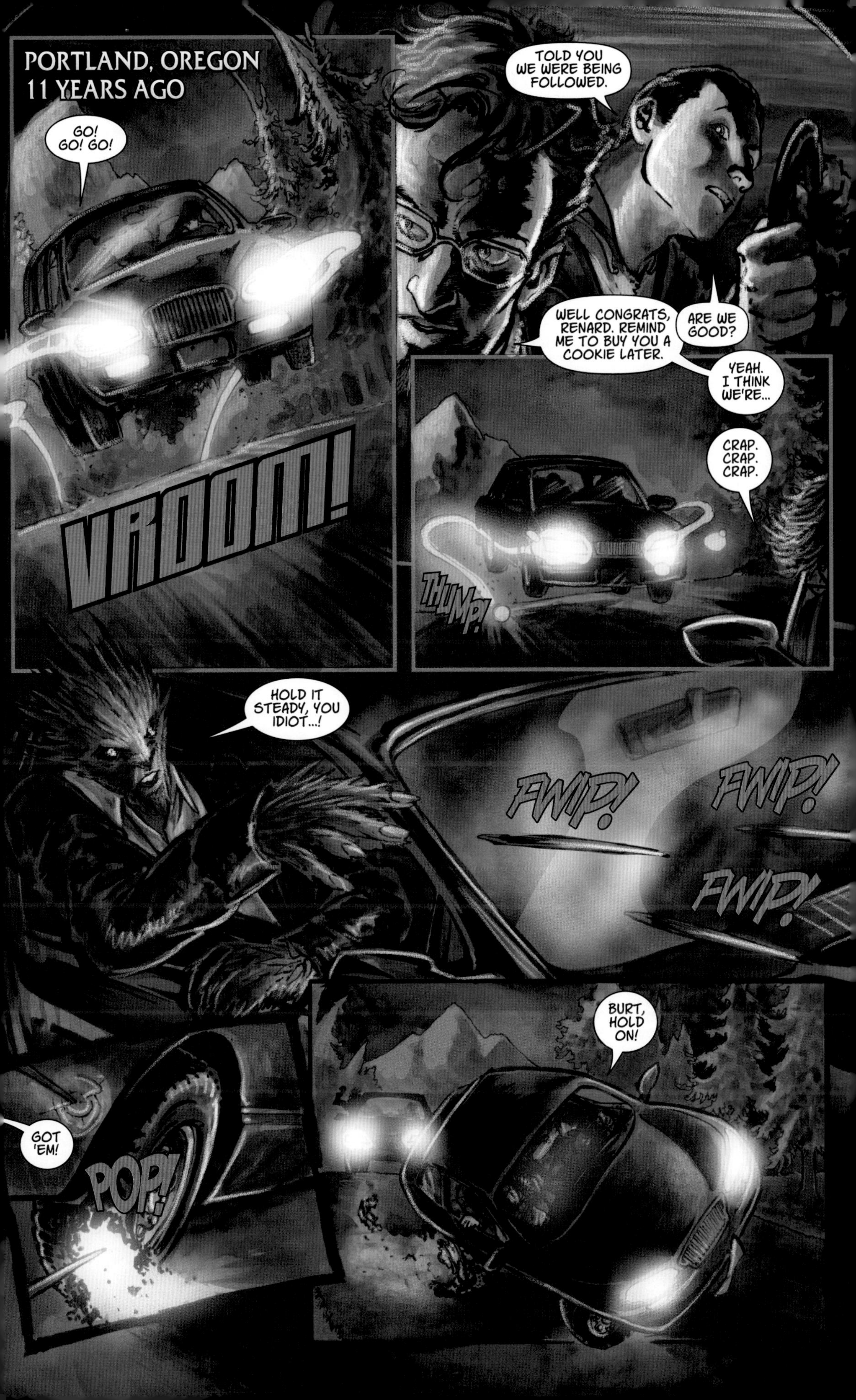
PORTLAND, OREGON
11 YEARS AGO
GO! GO! GO!
VROOM!
TOLD YOU WE WERE BEING FOLLOWED.
ARE WE GOOD?
WELL CONGRATS, RENARD. REMIND ME TO BUY YOU A COOKIE LATER.
YEAH. I THINK WE'RE...
CRAP. CRAP. CRAP.
THUMP!
HOLD IT STEADY, YOU IDIOT...!
FWIP!
FWIP!
FWIP!
BURT, HOLD ON!
GOT 'EM!
POP!

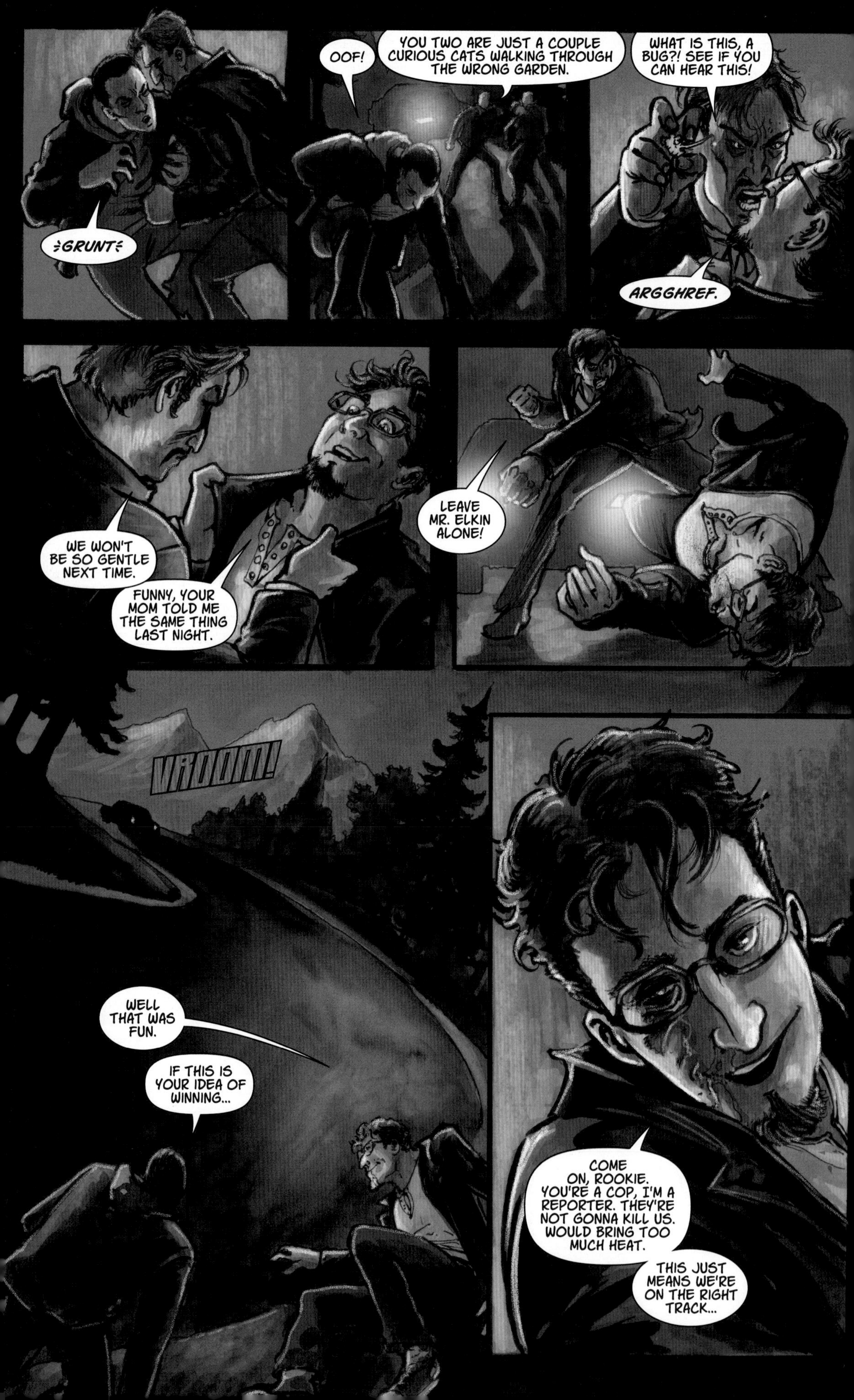
GRUNT
OOF!
YOU TWO ARE JUST A COUPLE CURIOUS CATS WALKING THROUGH THE WRONG GARDEN.
WHAT IS THIS, A BUG?! SEE IF YOU CAN HEAR THIS!
ARGGHREF.
WE WON'T BE SO GENTLE NEXT TIME.
FUNNY, YOUR MOM TOLD ME THE SAME THING LAST NIGHT.
LEAVE MR. ELKIN ALONE!
VROOM!
WELL THAT WAS FUN.
IF THIS IS YOUR IDEA OF WINNING...
COME ON, ROOKIE. YOU'RE A COP, I'M A REPORTER. THEY'RE NOT GONNA KILL US. WOULD BRING TOO MUCH HEAT.
THIS JUST MEANS WE'RE ON THE RIGHT TRACK...

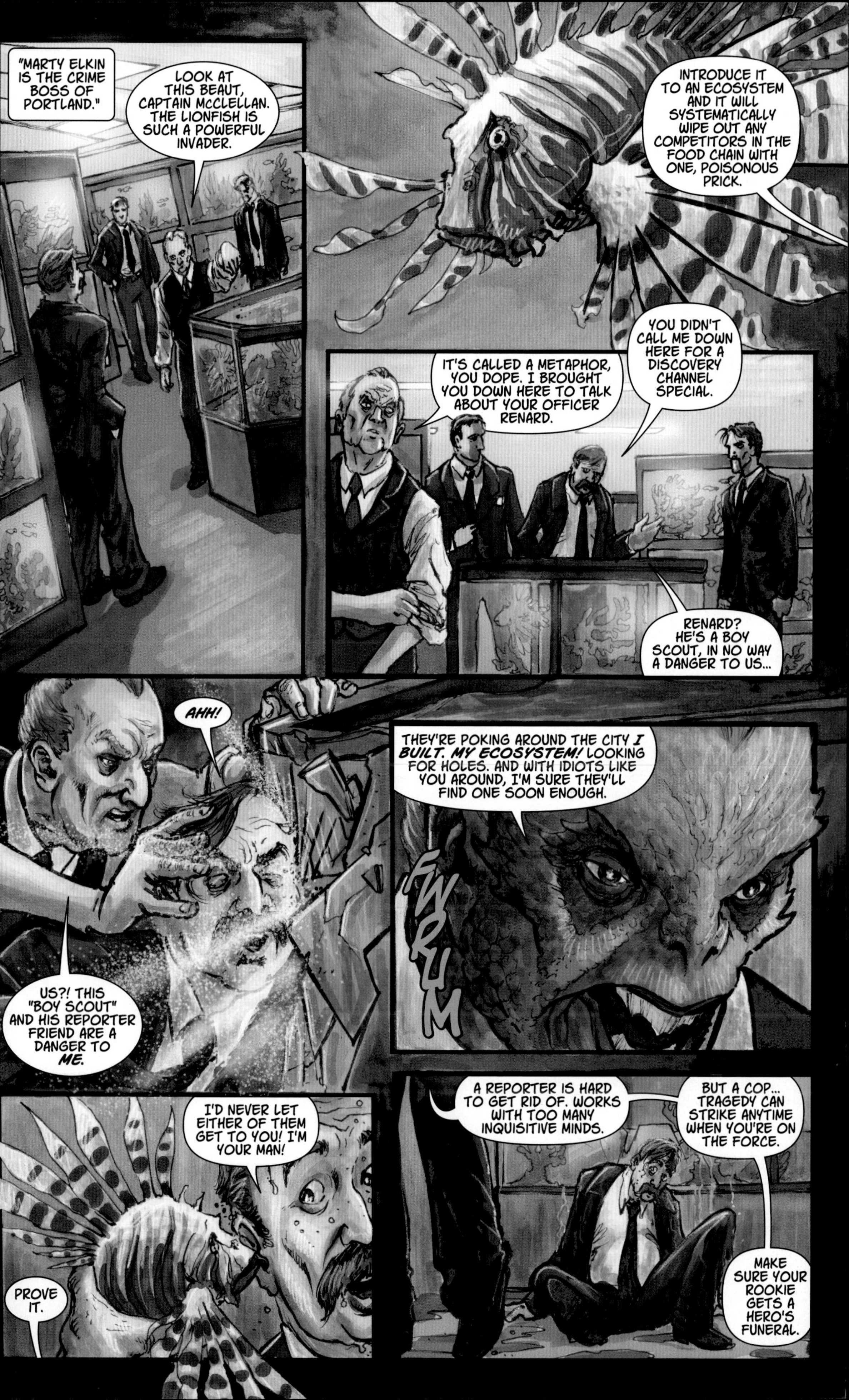
"MARTY ELKIN IS THE CRIME BOSS OF PORTLAND."
LOOK AT THIS BEAUT, CAPTAIN McCLELLAN. THE LIONFISH IS SUCH A POWERFUL INVADER.
INTRODUCE IT TO AN ECOSYSTEM AND IT WILL SYSTEMATICALLY WIPE OUT ANY COMPETITORS IN THE FOOD CHAIN WITH ONE, POISONOUS PRICK.
YOU DIDN'T CALL ME DOWN HERE FOR A DISCOVERY CHANNEL SPECIAL.
IT'S CALLED A METAPHOR, YOU DOPE. I BROUGHT YOU DOWN HERE TO TALK ABOUT YOUR OFFICER RENARD.
RENARD? HE'S A BOY SCOUT, IN NO WAY A DANGER TO US...
AHH!
US?! THIS "BOY SCOUT" AND HIS REPORTER FRIEND ARE A DANGER TO ME.
THEY'RE POKING AROUND THE CITY I BUILT. MY ECOSYSTEM! LOOKING FOR HOLES. AND WITH IDIOTS LIKE YOU AROUND, I'M SURE THEY'LL FIND ONE SOON ENOUGH.
FWRUM
I'D NEVER LET EITHER OF THEM GET TO YOU! I'M YOUR MAN!
PROVE IT.
A REPORTER IS HARD TO GET RID OF. WORKS WITH TOO MANY INQUISITIVE MINDS.
BUT A COP... TRAGEDY CAN STRIKE ANYTIME WHEN YOU'RE ON THE FORCE.
MAKE SURE YOUR ROOKIE GETS A HERO'S FUNERAL.

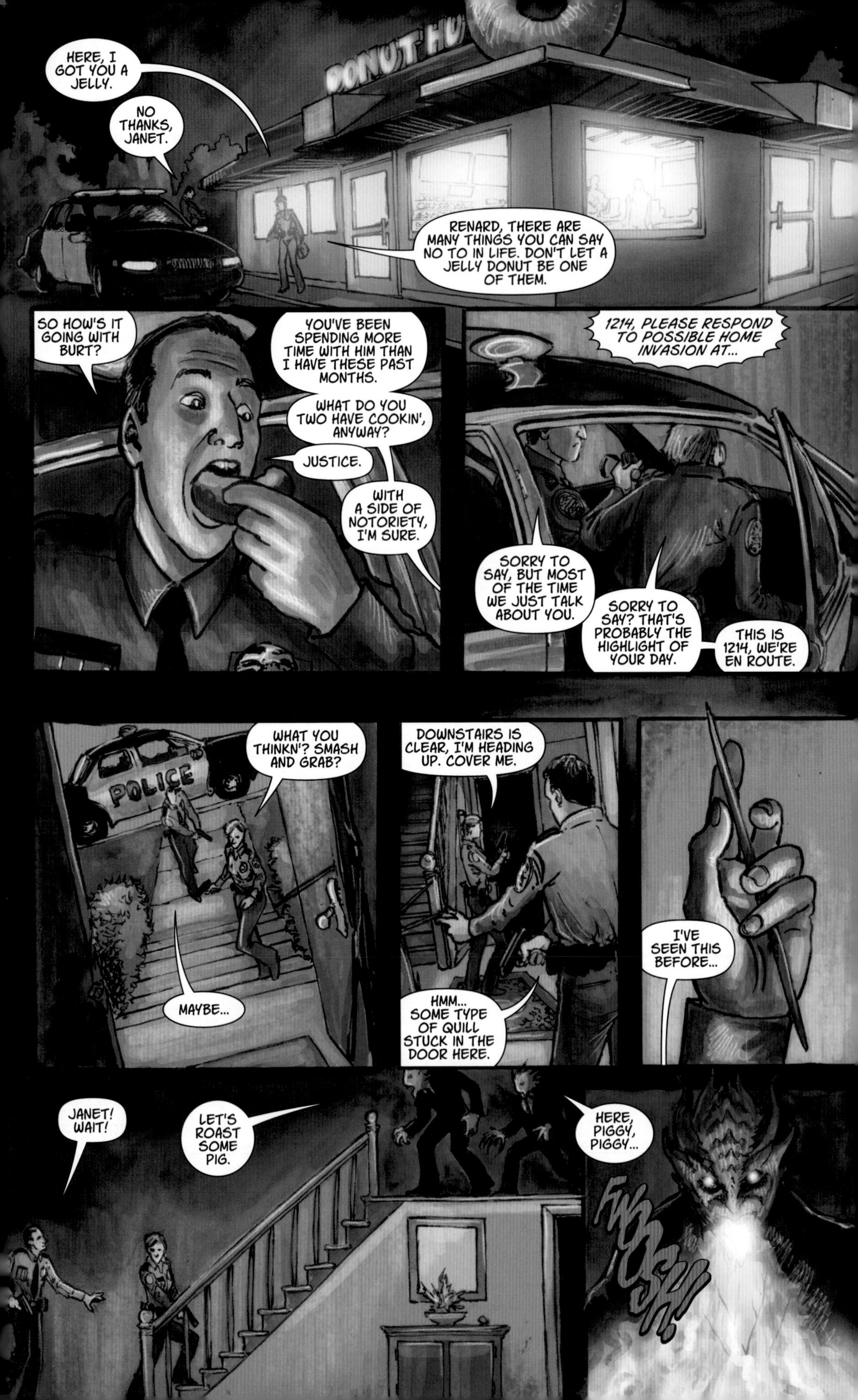
DONUT HU
HERE, I GOT YOU A JELLY.
NO THANKS, JANET.
RENARD, THERE ARE MANY THINGS YOU CAN SAY NO TO IN LIFE. DON'T LET A JELLY DONUT BE ONE OF THEM.
SO HOW'S IT GOING WITH BURT?
YOU'VE BEEN SPENDING MORE TIME WITH HIM THAN I HAVE THESE PAST MONTHS.
WHAT DO YOU TWO HAVE COOKIN', ANYWAY?
JUSTICE.
WITH A SIDE OF NOTORIETY, I'M SURE.
1214, PLEASE RESPOND TO POSSIBLE HOME INVASION AT...
SORRY TO SAY, BUT MOST OF THE TIME WE JUST TALK ABOUT YOU.
SORRY TO SAY? THAT'S PROBABLY THE HIGHLIGHT OF YOUR DAY.
THIS IS 1214, WE'RE EN ROUTE.
POLICE
WHAT YOU THINKN'? SMASH AND GRAB?
MAYBE...
DOWNSTAIRS IS CLEAR, I'M HEADING UP. COVER ME.
HMM... SOME TYPE OF QUILL STUCK IN THE DOOR HERE.
I'VE SEEN THIS BEFORE...
JANET! WAIT!
LET'S ROAST SOME PIG.
HERE, PIGGY, PIGGY...
FWOOSH!

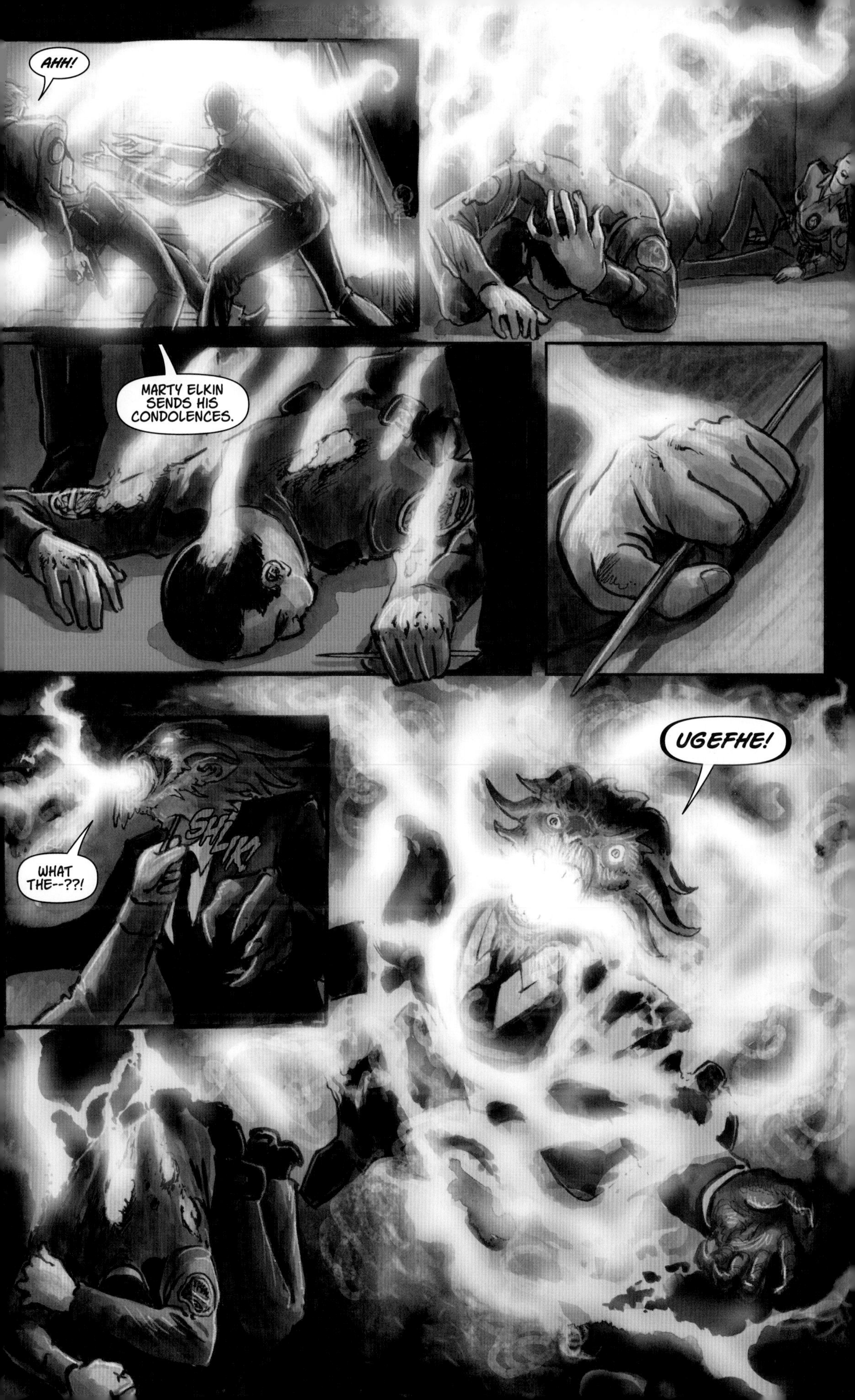
AHH!
MARTY ELKIN SENDS HIS CONDOLENCES.
WHAT THE--??!
UGEFHE!

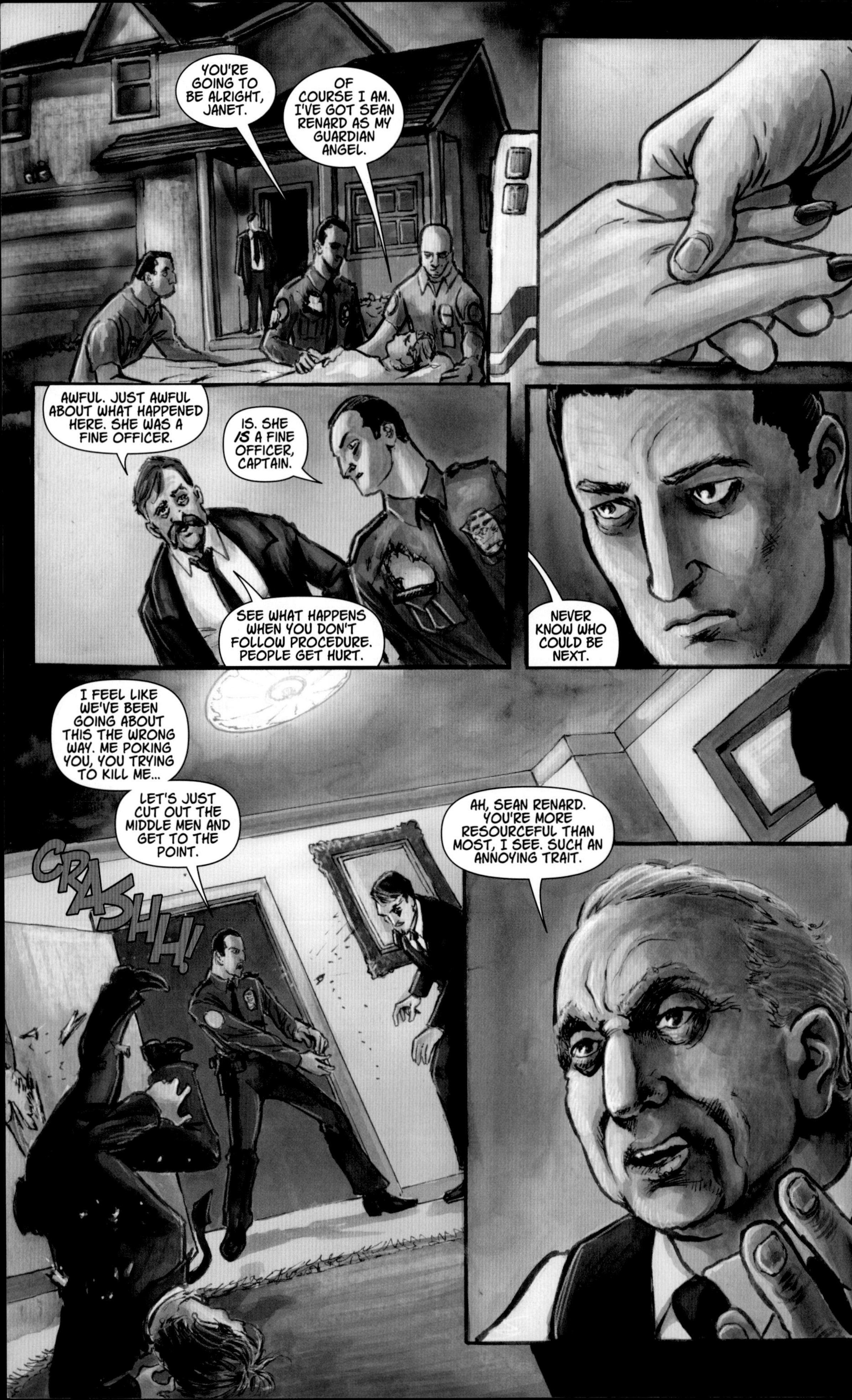
YOU'RE GOING TO BE ALRIGHT, JANET.
OF COURSE I AM. I'VE GOT SEAN RENARD AS MY GUARDIAN ANGEL.
AWFUL. JUST AWFUL ABOUT WHAT HAPPENED HERE. SHE WAS A FINE OFFICER.
IS. SHE *IS* A FINE OFFICER, CAPTAIN.
SEE WHAT HAPPENS WHEN YOU DON'T FOLLOW PROCEDURE. PEOPLE GET HURT.
NEVER KNOW WHO COULD BE NEXT.
I FEEL LIKE WE'VE BEEN GOING ABOUT THIS THE WRONG WAY. ME POKING YOU, YOU TRYING TO KILL ME...
LET'S JUST CUT OUT THE MIDDLE MEN AND GET TO THE POINT.
CRASHH!
AH, SEAN RENARD. YOU'RE MORE RESOURCEFUL THAN MOST, I SEE. SUCH AN ANNOYING TRAIT.

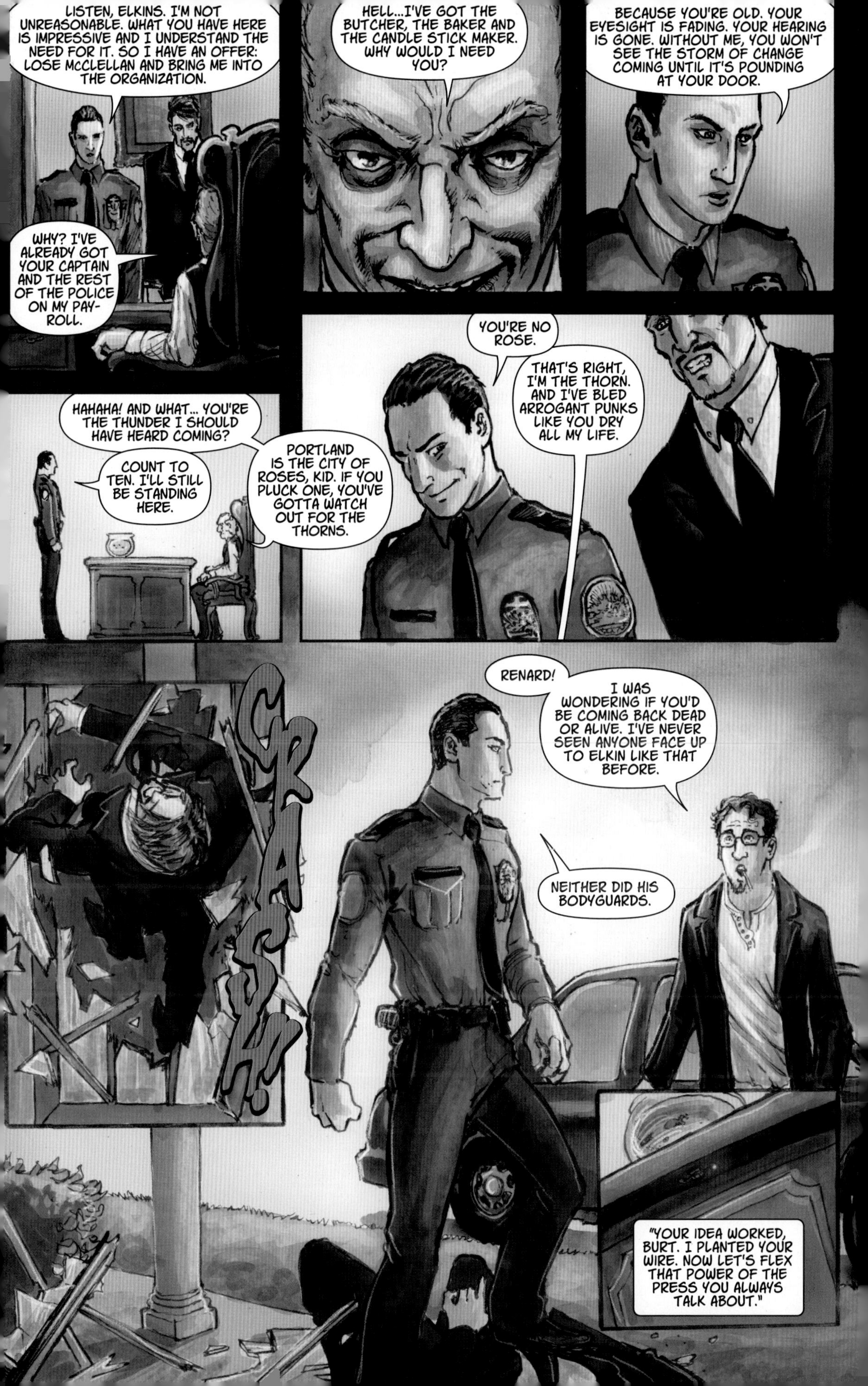
LISTEN, ELKINS. I'M NOT UNREASONABLE. WHAT YOU HAVE HERE IS IMPRESSIVE AND I UNDERSTAND THE NEED FOR IT. SO I HAVE AN OFFER: LOSE McCLELLAN AND BRING ME INTO THE ORGANIZATION.
WHY? I'VE ALREADY GOT YOUR CAPTAIN AND THE REST OF THE POLICE ON MY PAY-ROLL.
HELL...I'VE GOT THE BUTCHER, THE BAKER AND THE CANDLE STICK MAKER. WHY WOULD I NEED YOU?
BECAUSE YOU'RE OLD. YOUR EYESIGHT IS FADING. YOUR HEARING IS GONE. WITHOUT ME, YOU WON'T SEE THE STORM OF CHANGE COMING UNTIL IT'S POUNDING AT YOUR DOOR.
HAHAHA! AND WHAT... YOU'RE THE THUNDER I SHOULD HAVE HEARD COMING?
COUNT TO TEN. I'LL STILL BE STANDING HERE.
PORTLAND IS THE CITY OF ROSES, KID. IF YOU PLUCK ONE, YOU'VE GOTTA WATCH OUT FOR THE THORNS.
YOU'RE NO ROSE.
THAT'S RIGHT, I'M THE THORN. AND I'VE BLED ARROGANT PUNKS LIKE YOU DRY ALL MY LIFE.
CRASH!
RENARD!
I WAS WONDERING IF YOU'D BE COMING BACK DEAD OR ALIVE. I'VE NEVER SEEN ANYONE FACE UP TO ELKIN LIKE THAT BEFORE.
NEITHER DID HIS BODYGUARDS.
"YOUR IDEA WORKED, BURT. I PLANTED YOUR WIRE. NOW LET'S FLEX THAT POWER OF THE PRESS YOU ALWAYS TALK ABOUT."

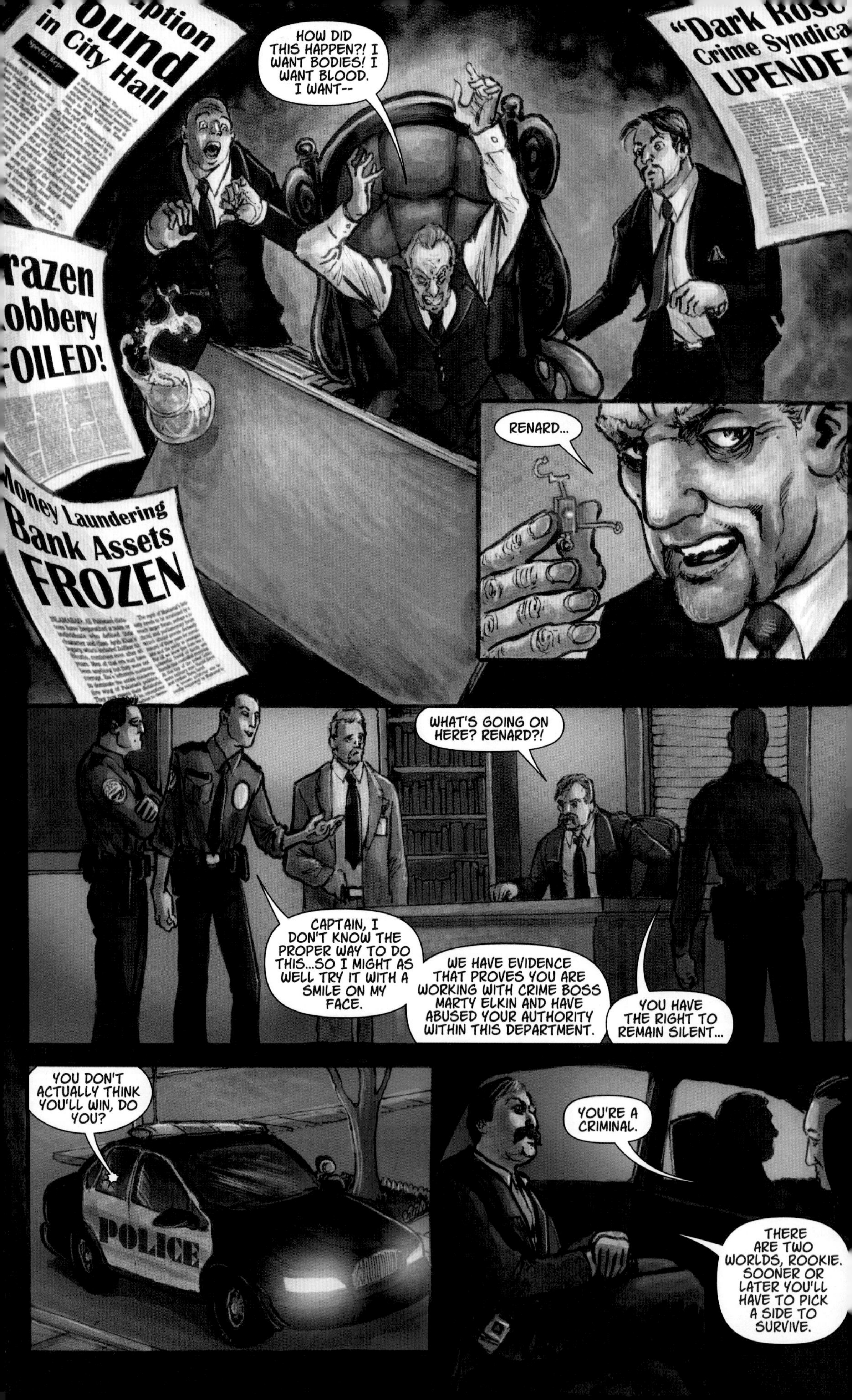
Corruption Found in City Hall
"Dark Rose" Crime Syndicate UPENDED
HOW DID THIS HAPPEN?! I WANT BODIES! I WANT BLOOD. I WANT--
Brazen Robbery FOILED!
Money Laundering Bank Assets FROZEN
RENARD...
WHAT'S GOING ON HERE? RENARD?!
CAPTAIN, I DON'T KNOW THE PROPER WAY TO DO THIS...SO I MIGHT AS WELL TRY IT WITH A SMILE ON MY FACE.
WE HAVE EVIDENCE THAT PROVES YOU ARE WORKING WITH CRIME BOSS MARTY ELKIN AND HAVE ABUSED YOUR AUTHORITY WITHIN THIS DEPARTMENT.
YOU HAVE THE RIGHT TO REMAIN SILENT...
YOU DON'T ACTUALLY THINK YOU'LL WIN, DO YOU?
POLICE
YOU'RE A CRIMINAL.
THERE ARE TWO WORLDS, ROOKIE. SOONER OR LATER YOU'LL HAVE TO PICK A SIDE TO SURVIVE.

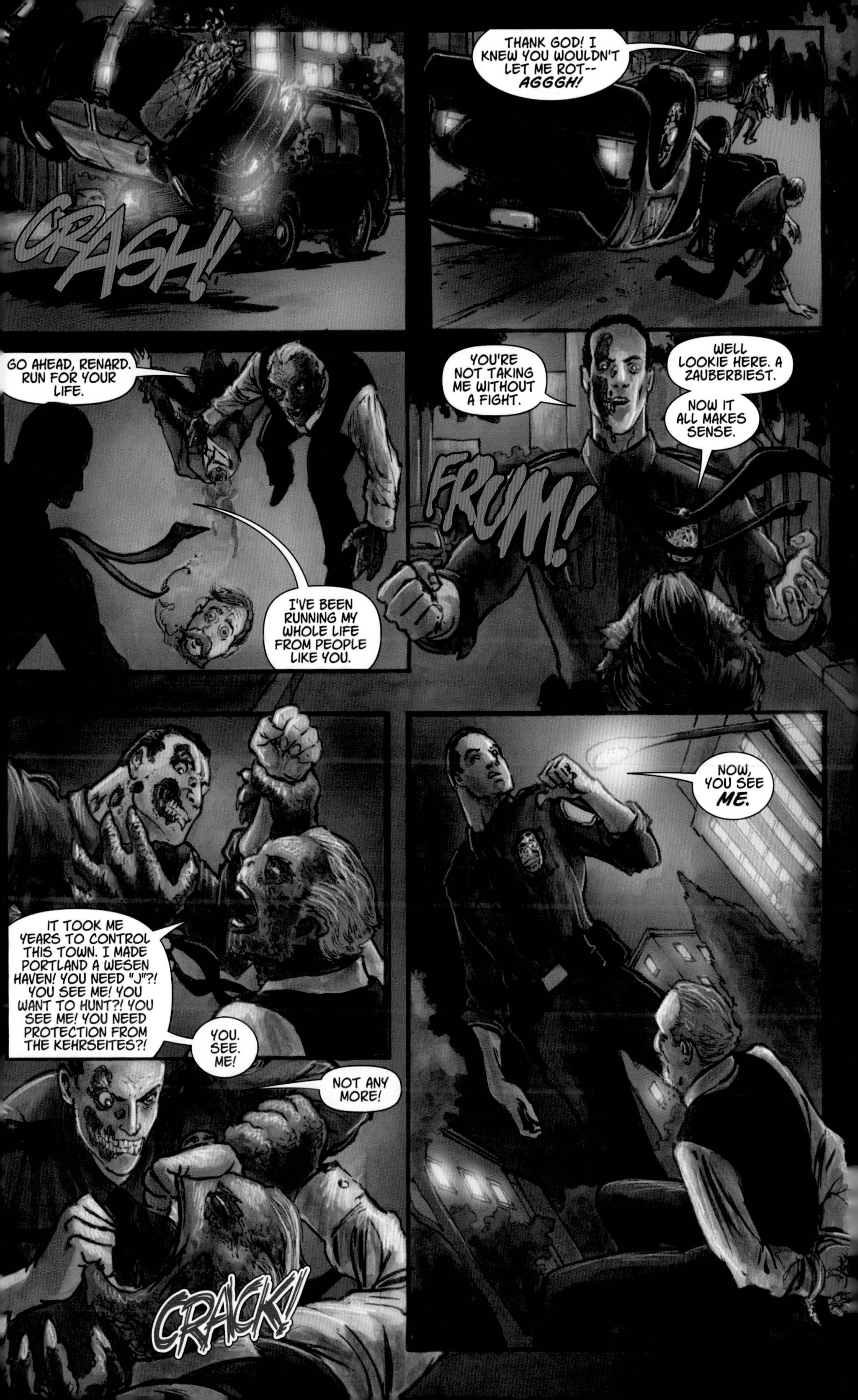
CRASH!
THANK GOD! I KNEW YOU WOULDN'T LET ME ROT-- AGGGH!
GO AHEAD, RENARD. RUN FOR YOUR LIFE.
I'VE BEEN RUNNING MY WHOLE LIFE FROM PEOPLE LIKE YOU.
YOU'RE NOT TAKING ME WITHOUT A FIGHT.
WELL LOOKIE HERE. A ZAUBERBIEST.
NOW IT ALL MAKES SENSE.
FRUM!
IT TOOK ME YEARS TO CONTROL THIS TOWN. I MADE PORTLAND A WESEN HAVEN! YOU NEED "J"?! YOU SEE ME! YOU WANT TO HUNT?! YOU SEE ME! YOU NEED PROTECTION FROM THE KEHRSEITES?!
YOU. SEE. ME!
NOT ANY MORE!
CRACK!
NOW, YOU SEE ME.

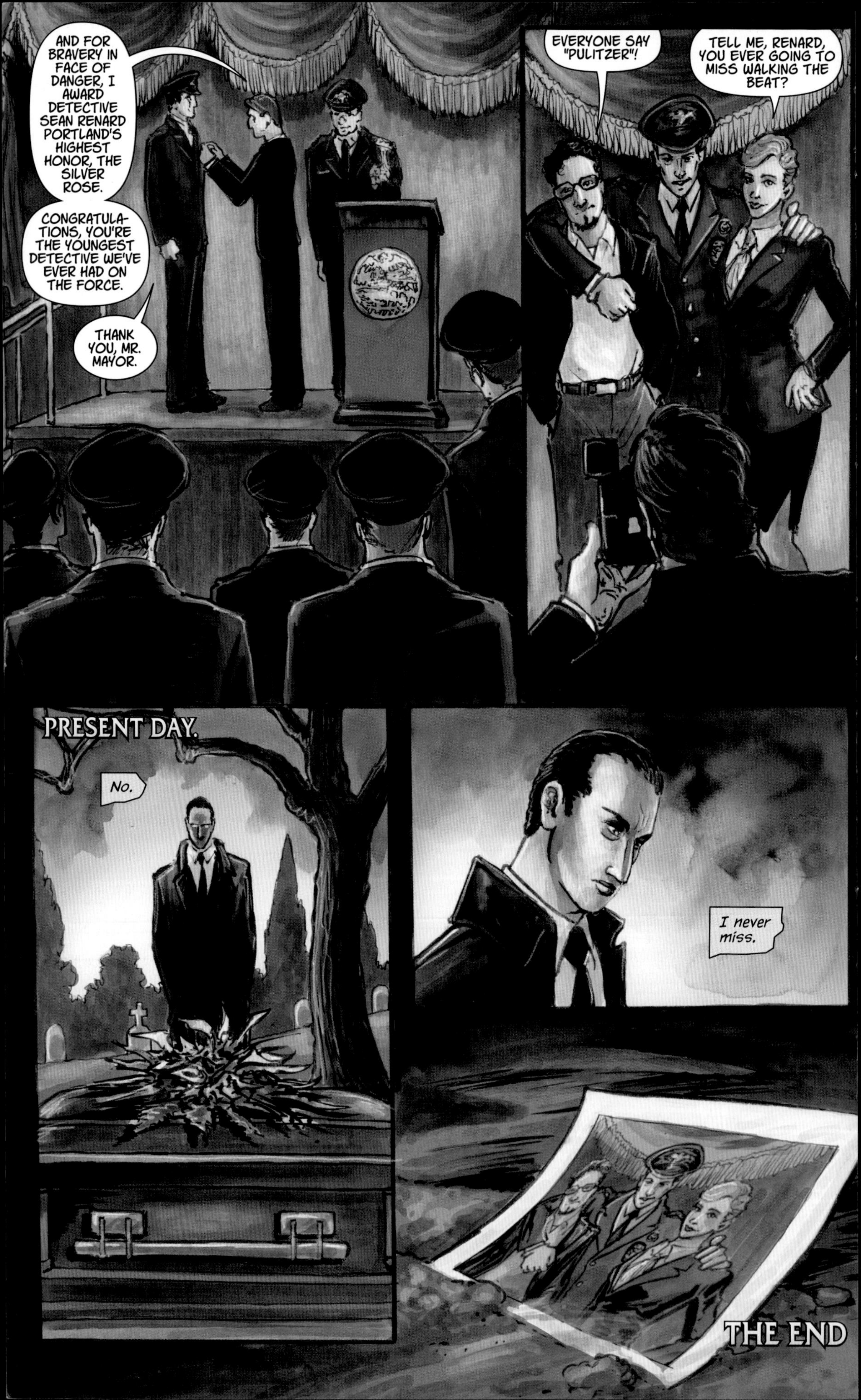
AND FOR BRAVERY IN FACE OF DANGER, I AWARD DETECTIVE SEAN RENARD PORTLAND'S HIGHEST HONOR, THE SILVER ROSE.
CONGRATULATIONS, YOU'RE THE YOUNGEST DETECTIVE WE'VE EVER HAD ON THE FORCE.
THANK YOU, MR. MAYOR.
EVERYONE SAY "PULITZER"!
TELL ME, RENARD, YOU EVER GOING TO MISS WALKING THE BEAT?
PRESENT DAY.
No.
I never miss.
THE END

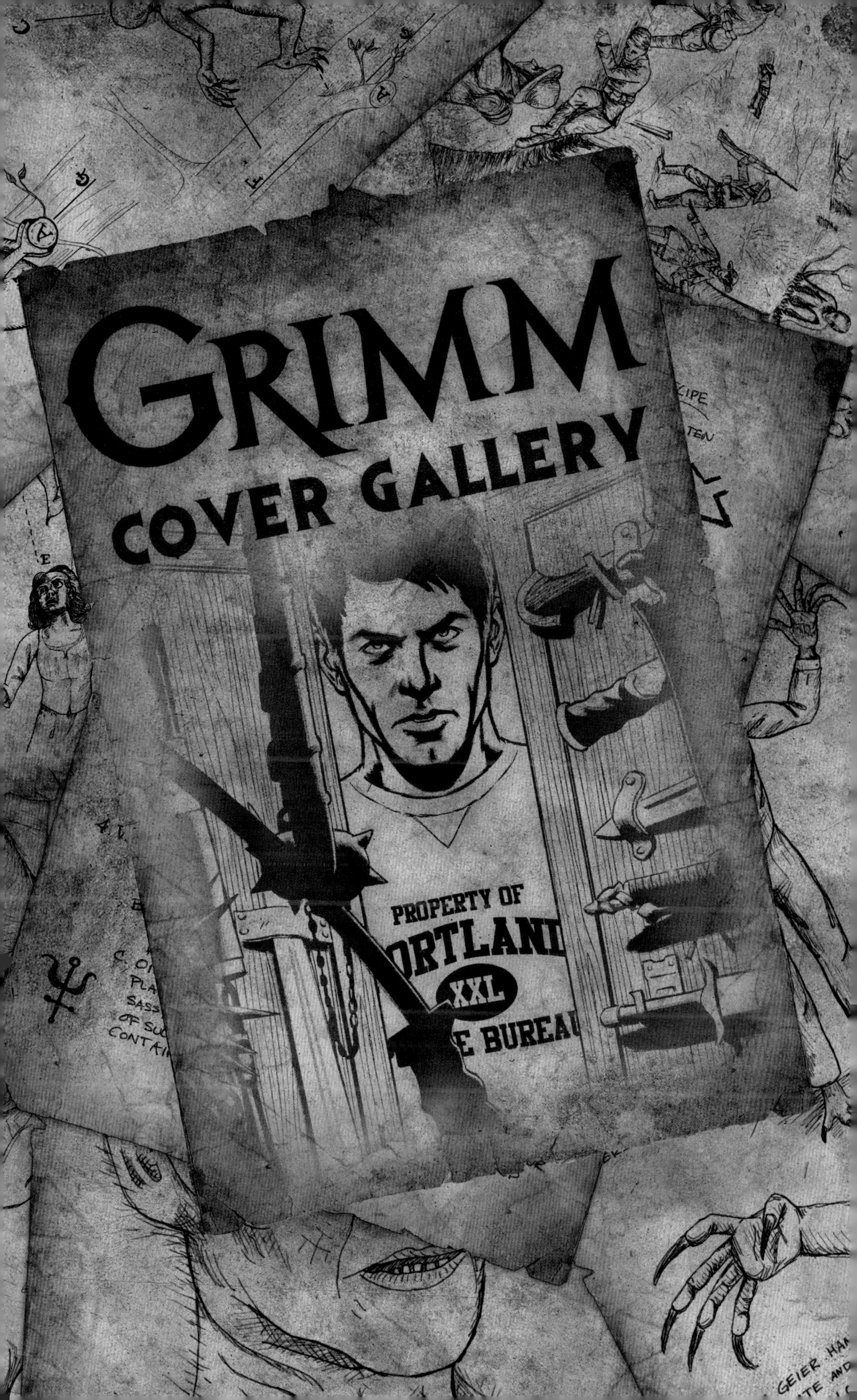
GRIMM
COVER GALLERY
PROPERTY OF
ORTLAND
XXL
E BUREAU

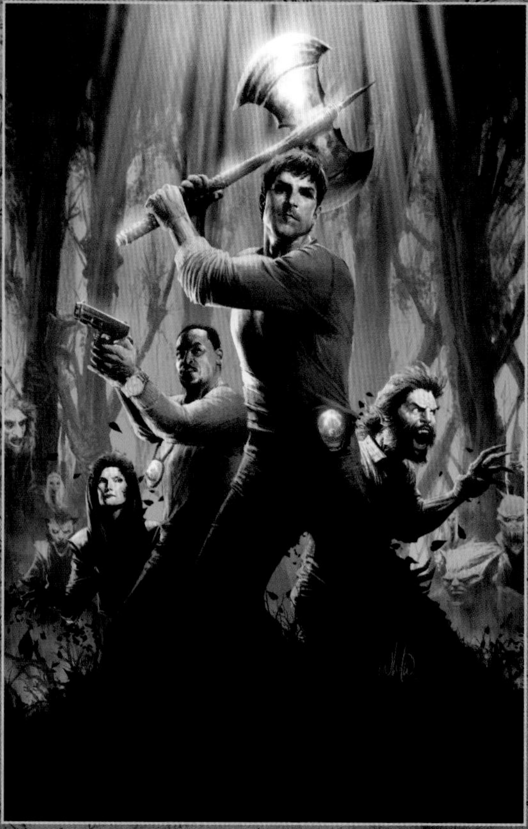

GRIMM #0 COVER
BY WHILCE PORTACIO

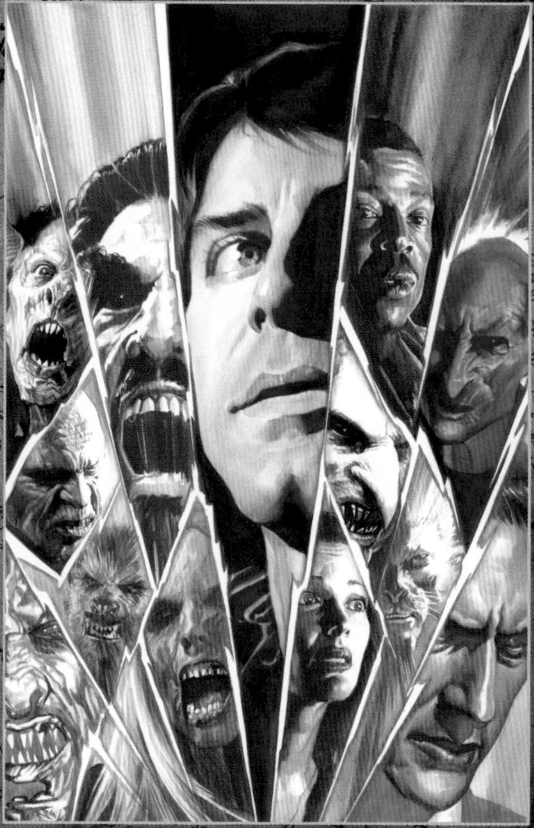

GRIMM #1 COVER
BY ALEX ROSS

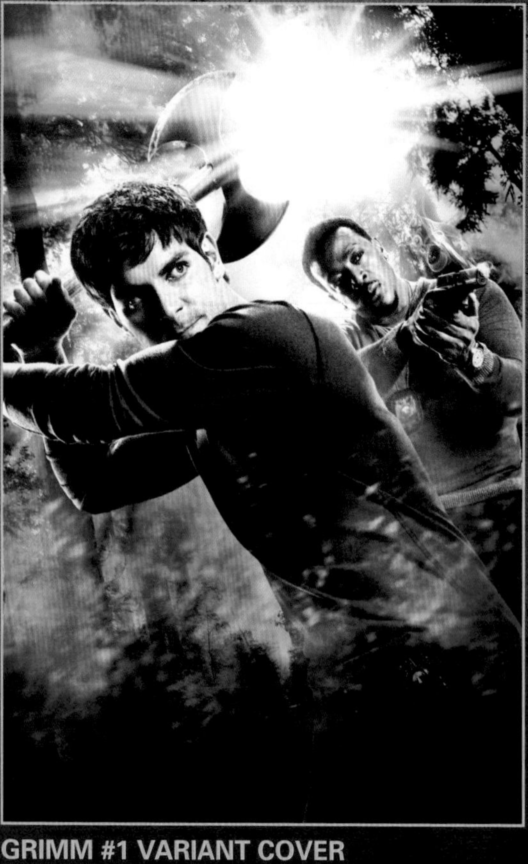

GRIMM #1 VARIANT COVER
SUBSCRIPTION EXCLUSIVE

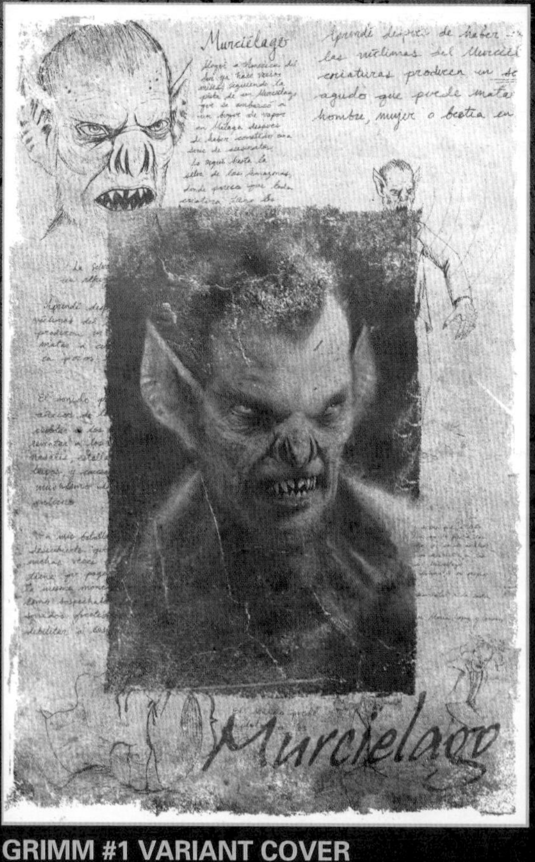
Murciélago
Murcielago

GRIMM #1 VARIANT COVER
MIDTOWN EXCLUSIVE

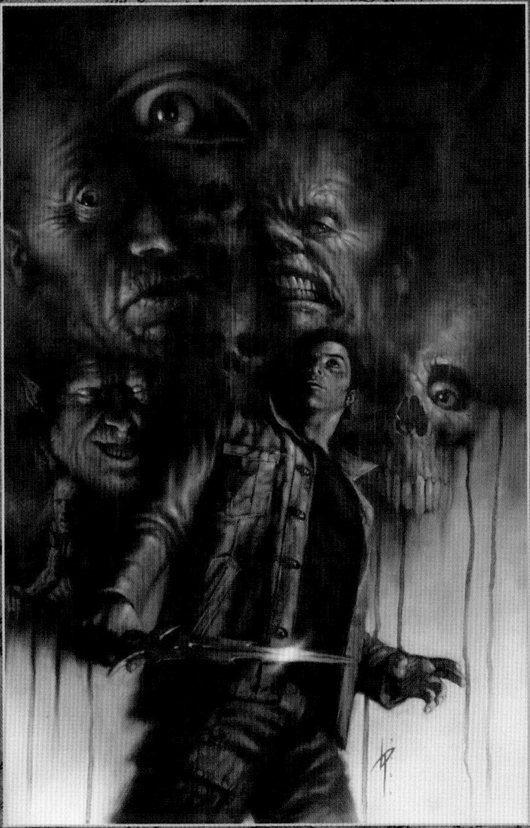

GRIMM #2 COVER
BY LUCIO PARRILLO

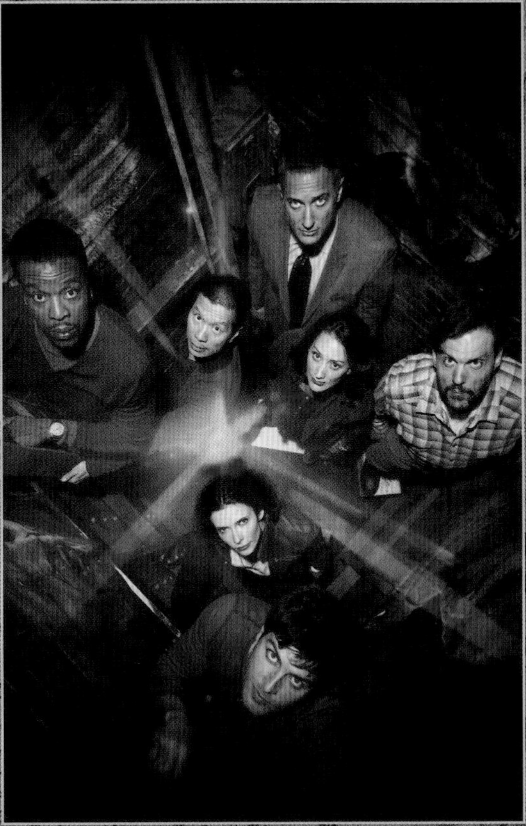

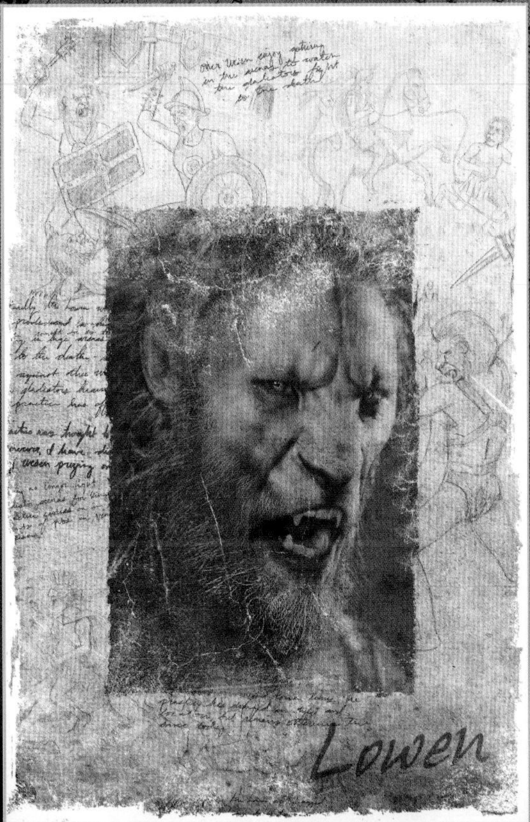
Lowen

GRIMM #2 VARIANT COVER
MIDTOWN EXCLUSIVE

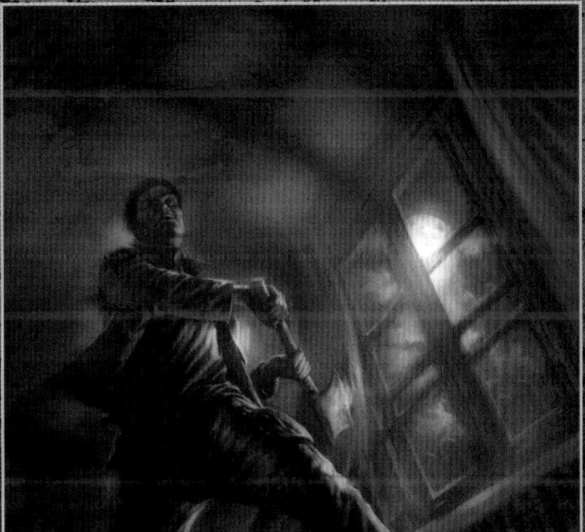

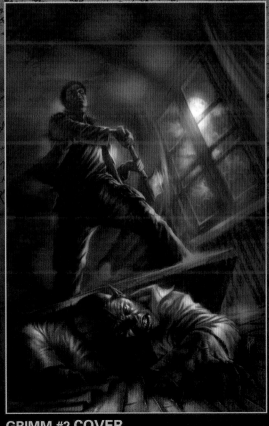

GRIMM #2 COVER
BY LUCIO PARRILLO

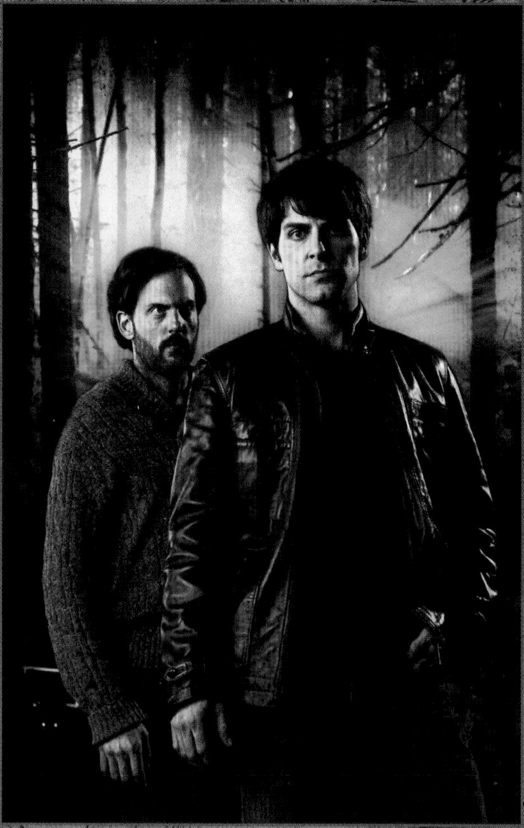

GRIMM #3 VARIANT COVER
SUBSCRIPTION EXCLUSIVE

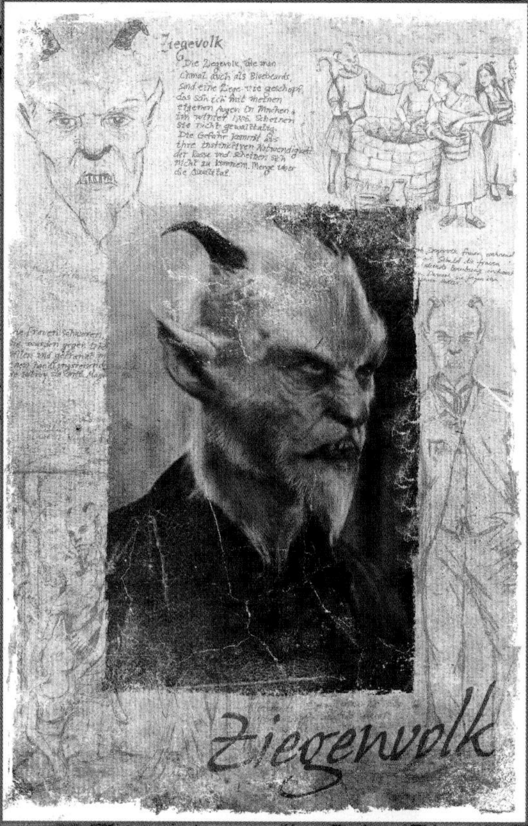
Ziegevolk
Ziegenvolk

GRIMM #3 VARIANT COVER
MIDTOWN EXCLUSIVE

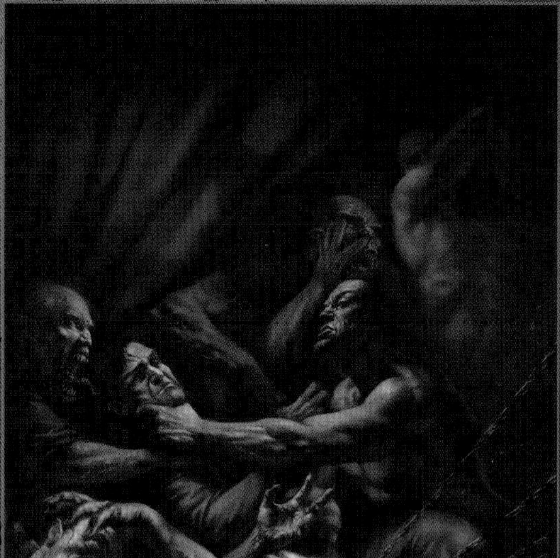

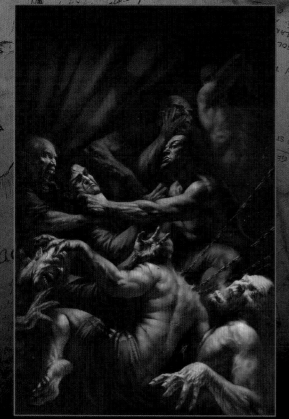

GRIMM #4 COVER
BY LUCIO PARRILLO

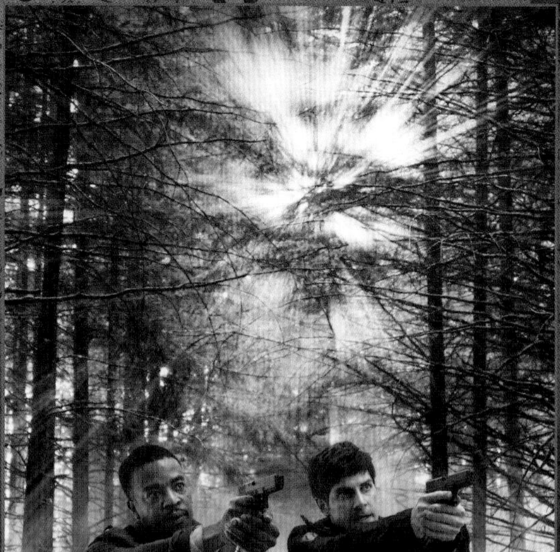

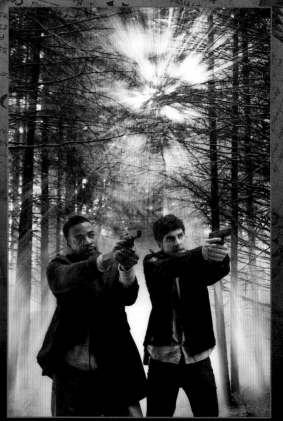

GRIMM #4 VARIANT COVER
SUBSCRIPTION EXCLUSIVE

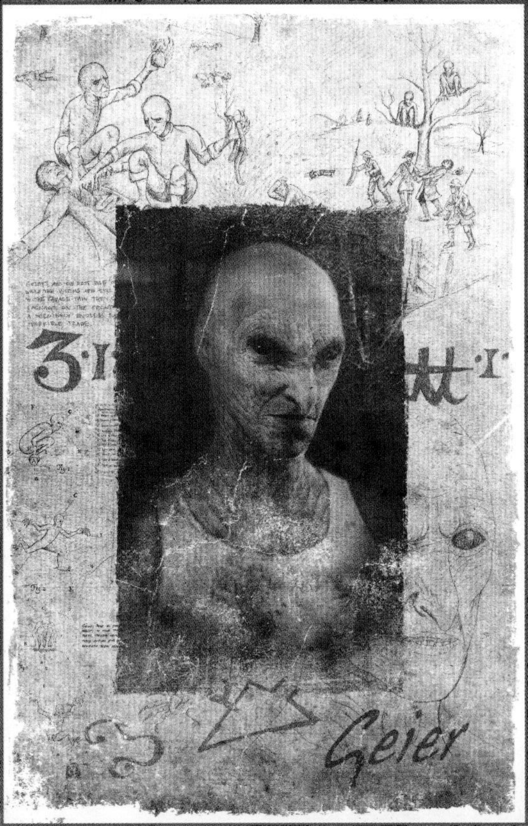
Geier

GRIMM #4 VARIANT COVER
MIDTOWN EXCLUSIVE

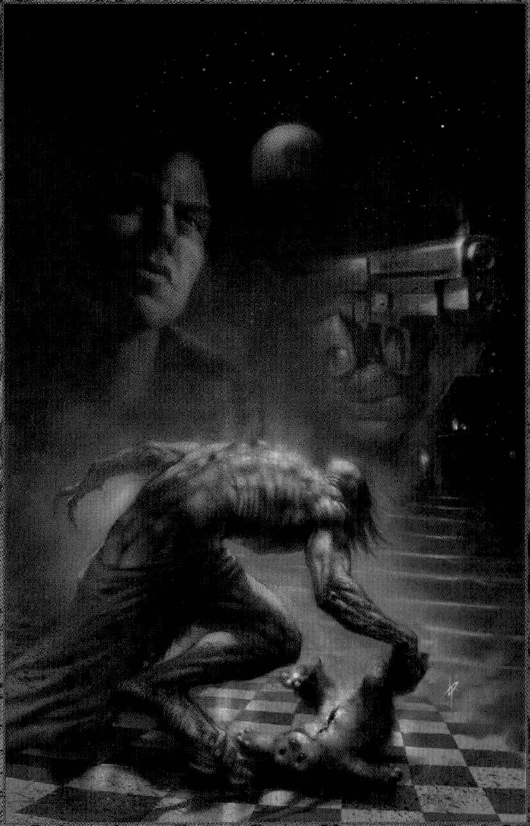

GRIMM #5 COVER
BY LUCIO PARRILLO

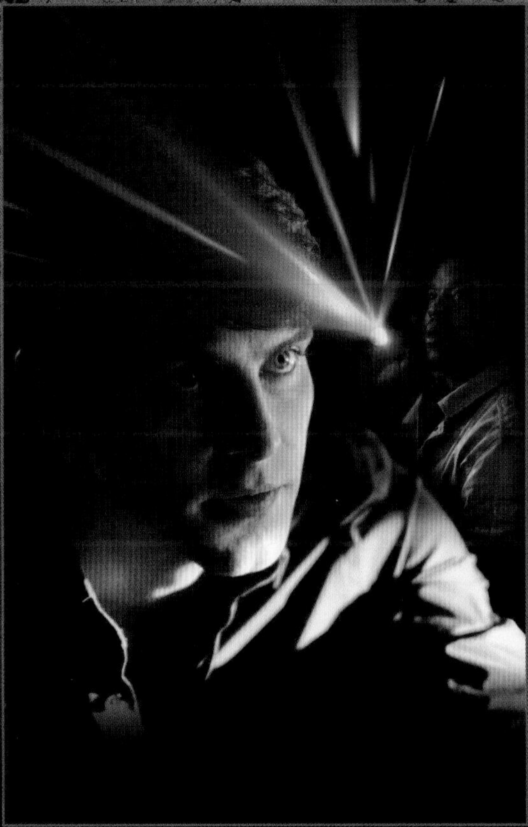

GRIMM #5 VARIANT COVER
SUBSCRIPTION EXCLUSIVE

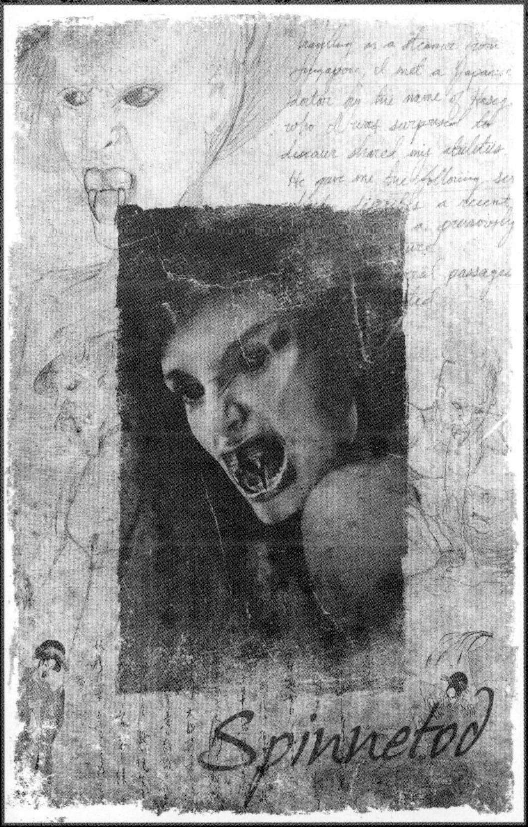
Spinnetod

GRIMM #5 VARIANT COVER
MIDTOWN EXCLUSIVE

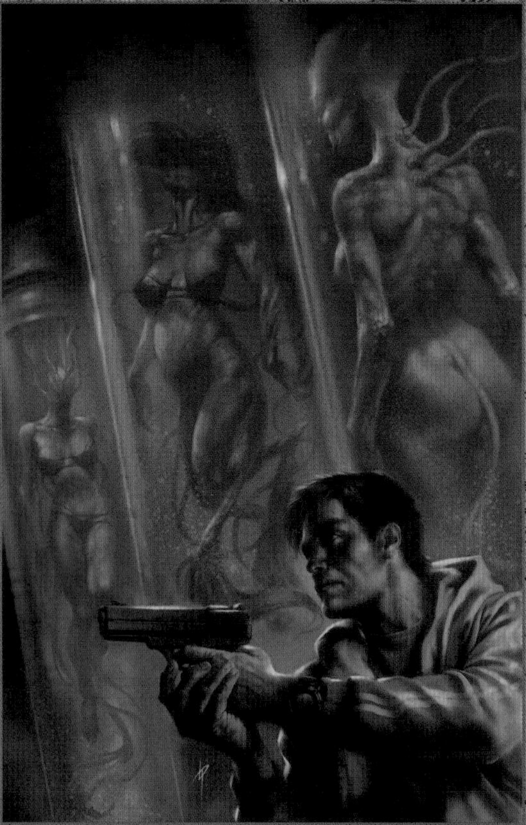

GRIMM #6 COVER
BY LUCIO PARRILLO

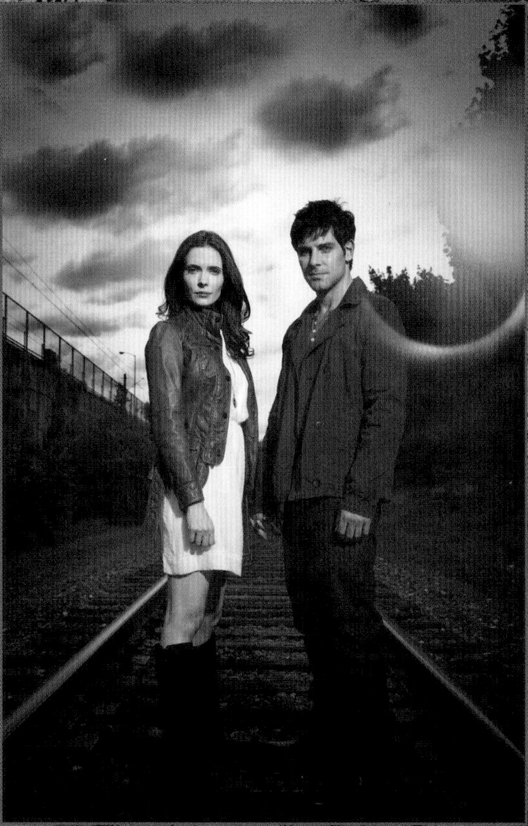

GRIMM #6 VARIANT COVER
SUBSCRIPTION EXCLUSIVE

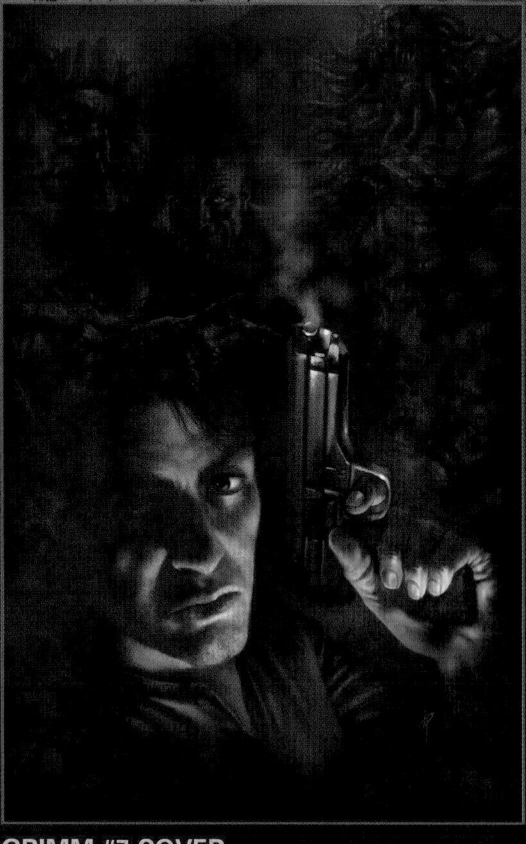

GRIMM #7 COVER
BY LUCIO PARRILLO

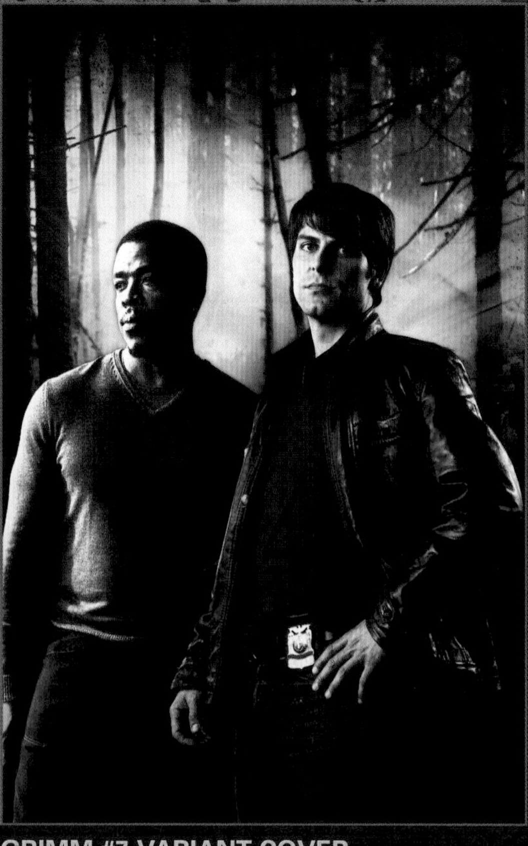

GRIMM #7 VARIANT COVER
SUBSCRIPTION EXCLUSIVE

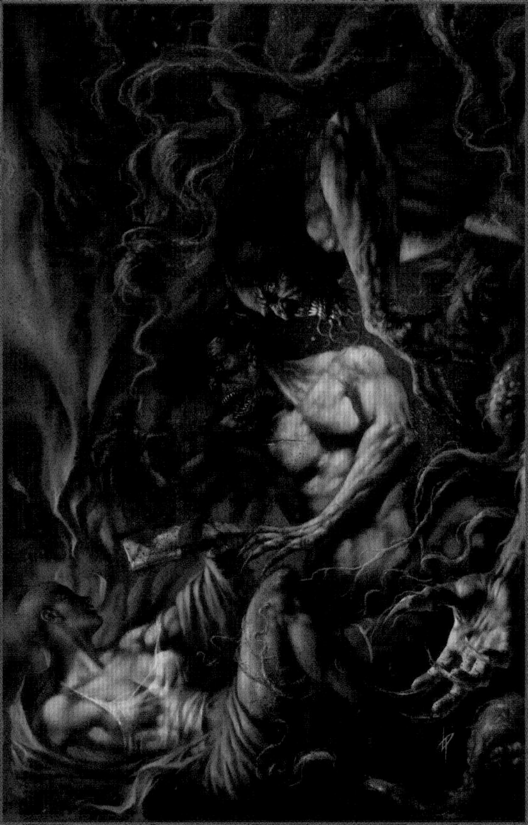

GRIMM #8 COVER
BY LUCIO PARRILLO

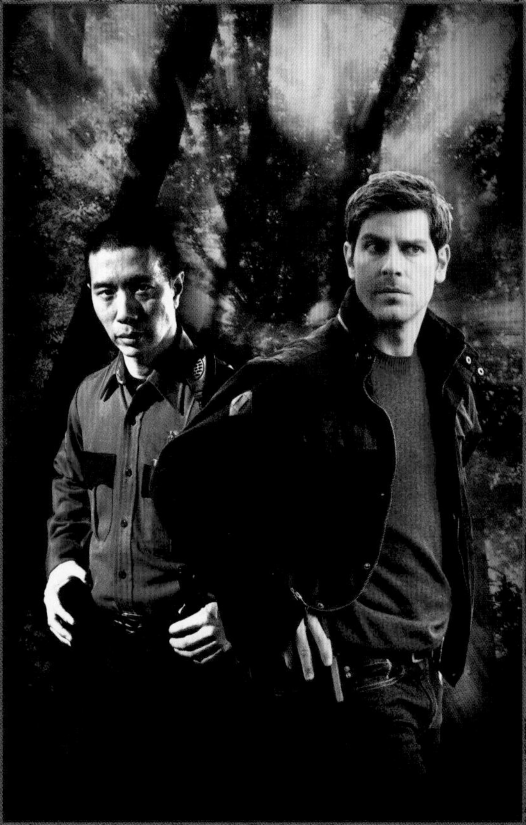

GRIMM #8 VARIANT COVER
SUBSCRIPTION EXCLUSIVE

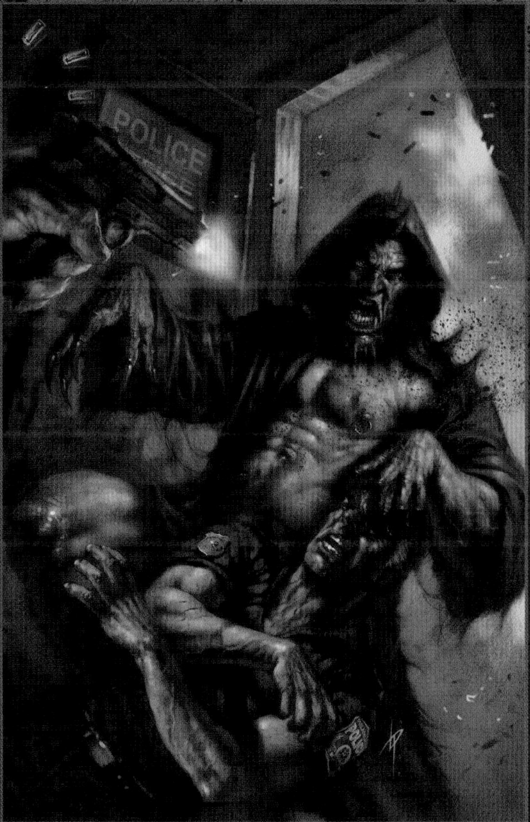
POLICE

GRIMM #9 COVER
BY LUCIO PARRILLO

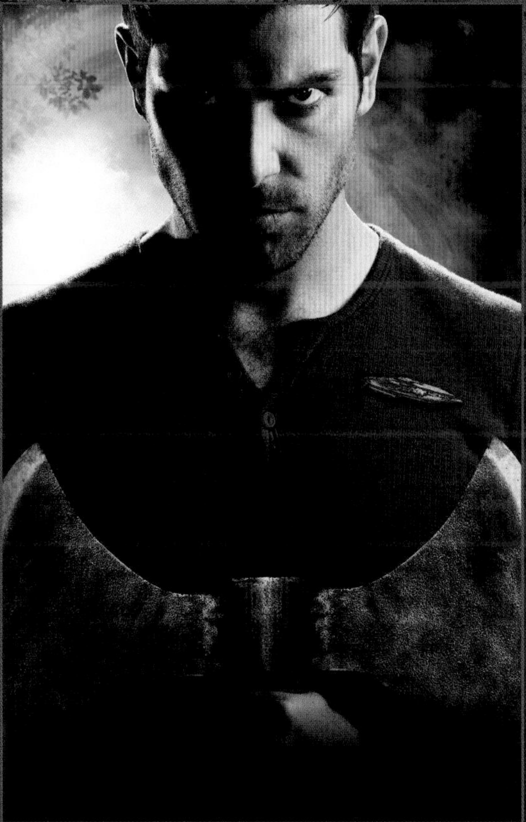

GRIMM #9 VARIANT COVER
SUBSCRIPTION EXCLUSIVE

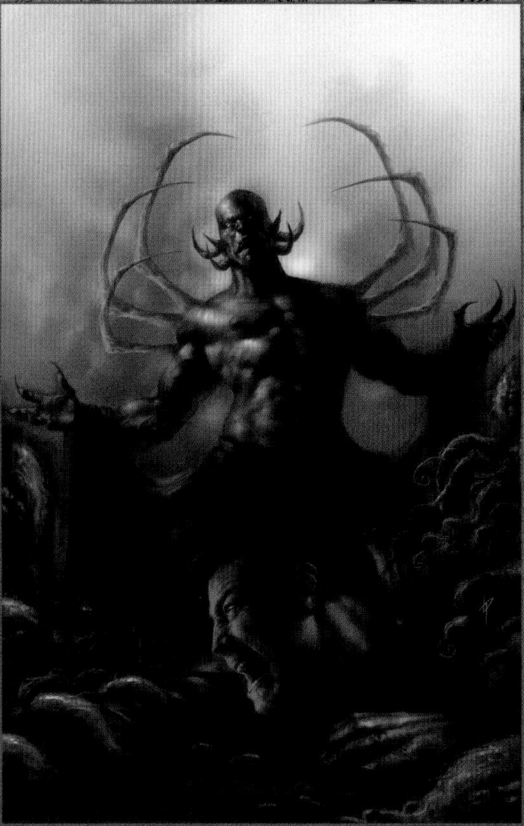

GRIMM #10 COVER
BY LUCIO PARRILLO

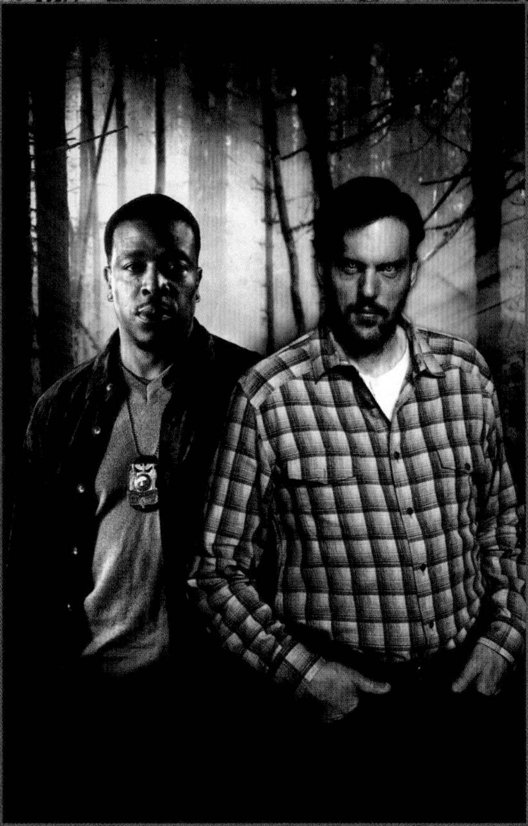

GRIMM #10 VARIANT COVER
SUBSCRIPTION EXCLUSIVE

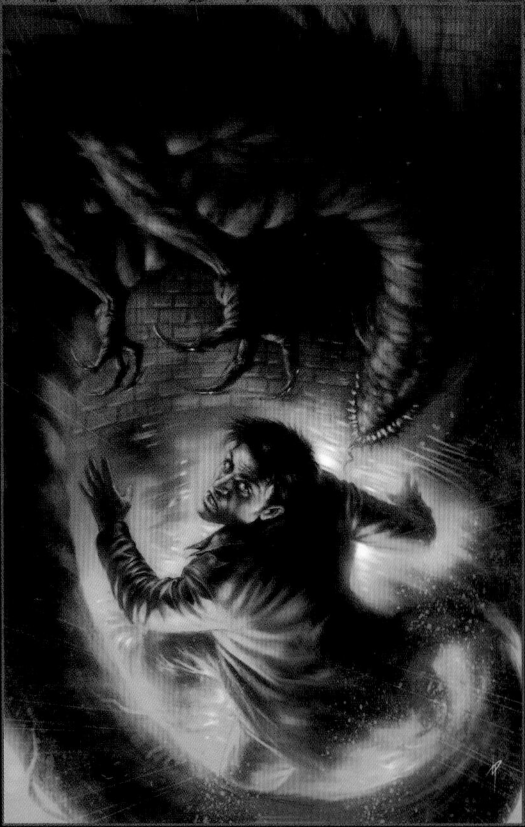

GRIMM #11 COVER
BY LUCIO PARRILLO

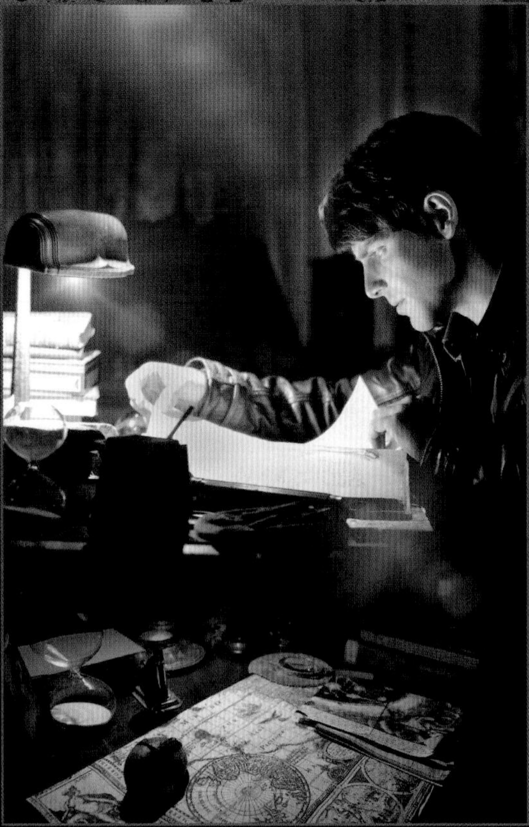

GRIMM #11 VARIANT COVER
SUBSCRIPTION EXCLUSIVE

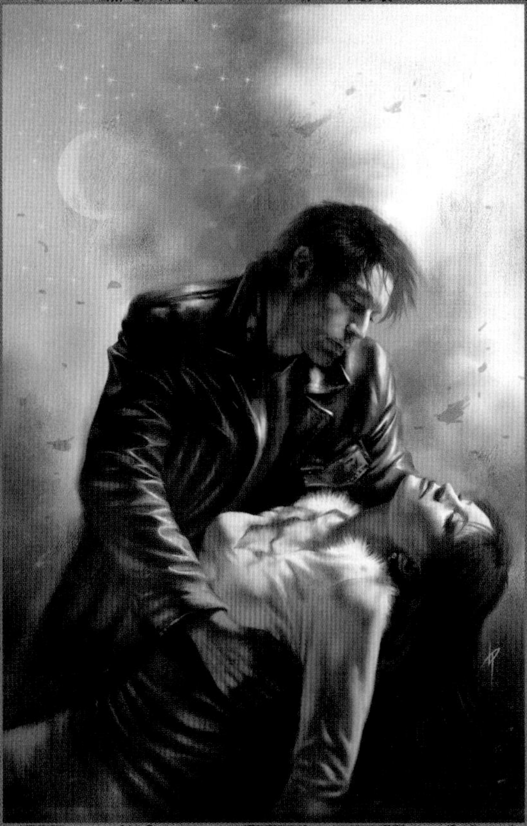

GRIMM #12 COVER
BY LUCIO PARRILLO

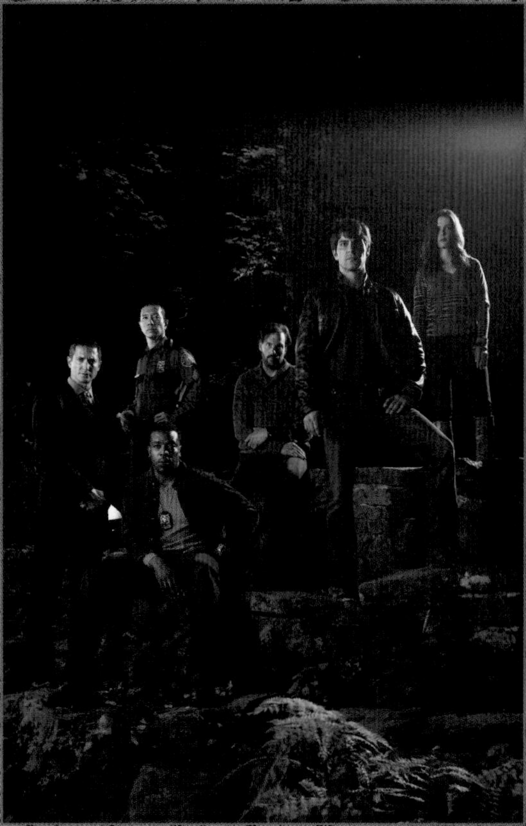

GRIMM #12 VARIANT COVER
SUBSCRIPTION EXCLUSIVE

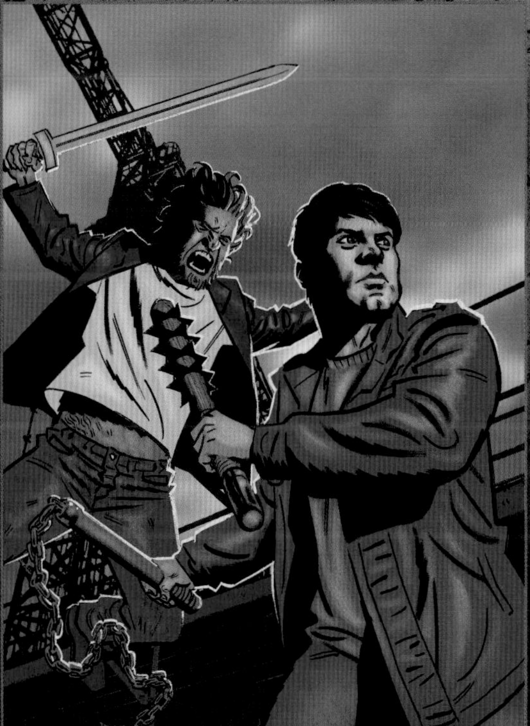

GRIMM: THE WARLOCK #1 COVER
BY GREG SMALLWOOD

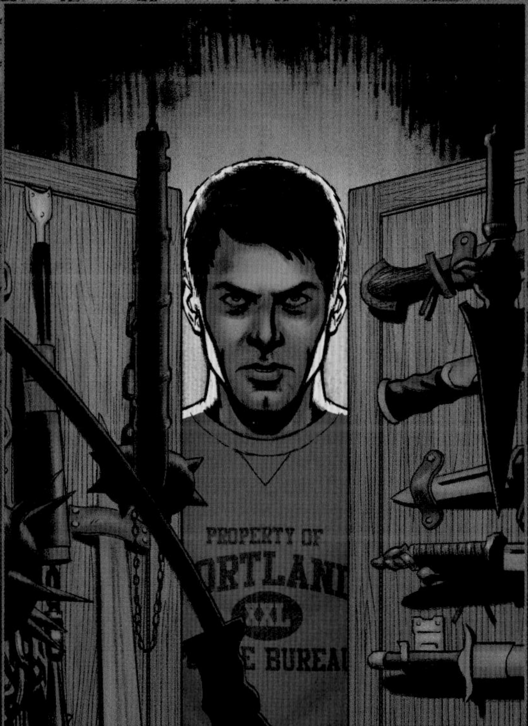
PROPERTY OF

GRIMM: THE WARLOCK #2 COVER
BY GREG SMALLWOOD

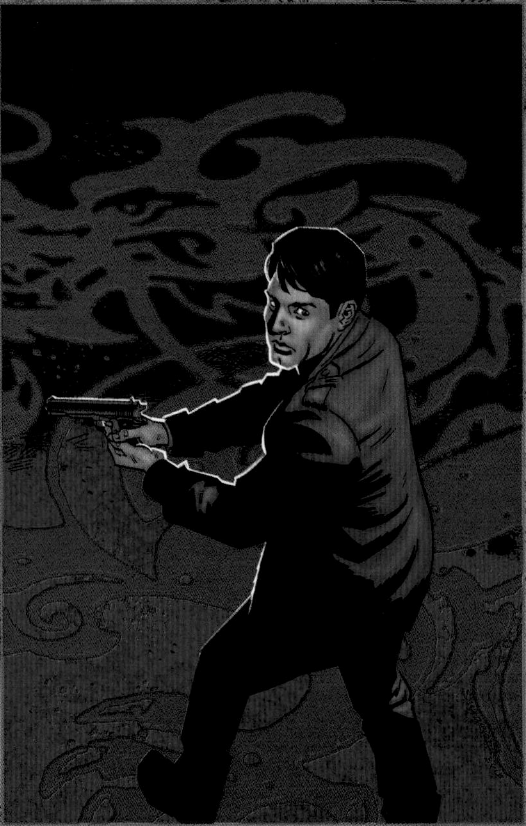

GRIMM: THE WARLOCK #3 COVER
BY GREG SMALLWOOD

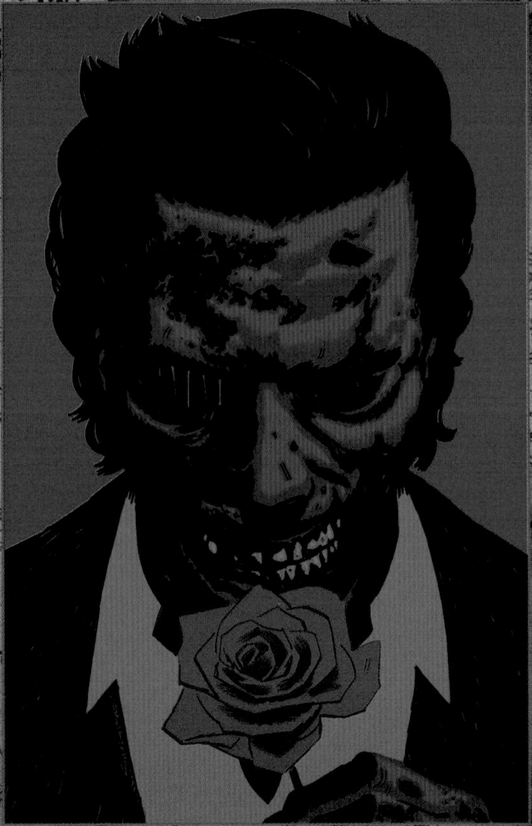

GRIMM: THE WARLOCK #4 COVER
BY GREG SMALLWOOD

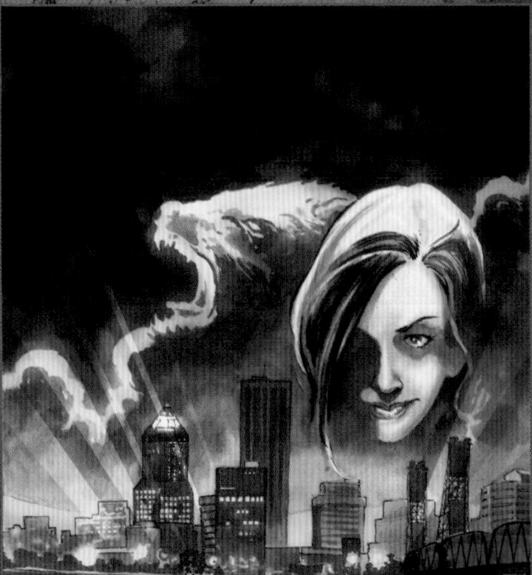

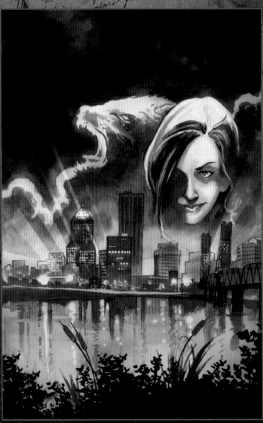

GRIMM: PORTLAND, WU #1 COVER
BY DANIEL GOVER

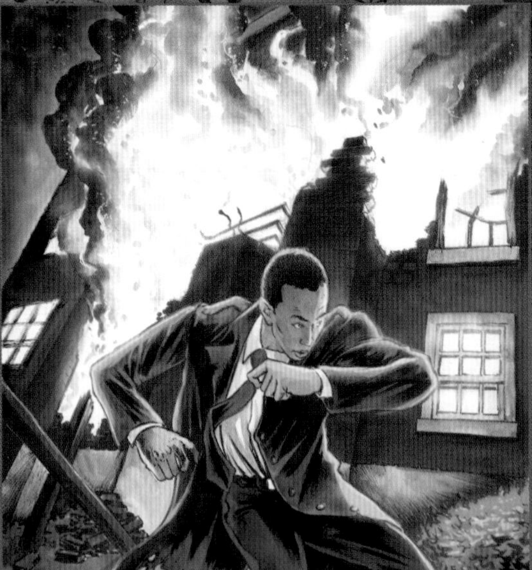

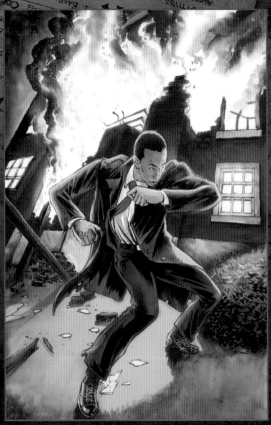

GRIMM: PORTLAND, WU #2 COVER
BY DANIEL GOVER

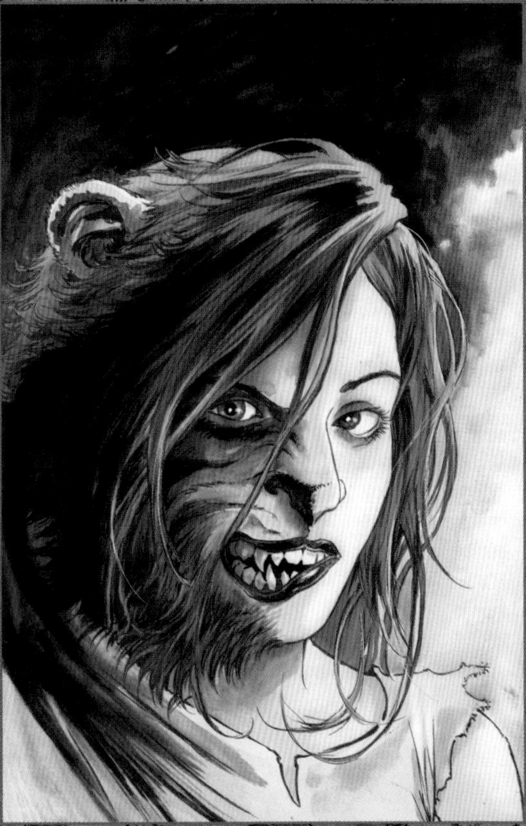

GRIMM: PORTLAND, WU #3 COVER
BY DANIEL GOVER

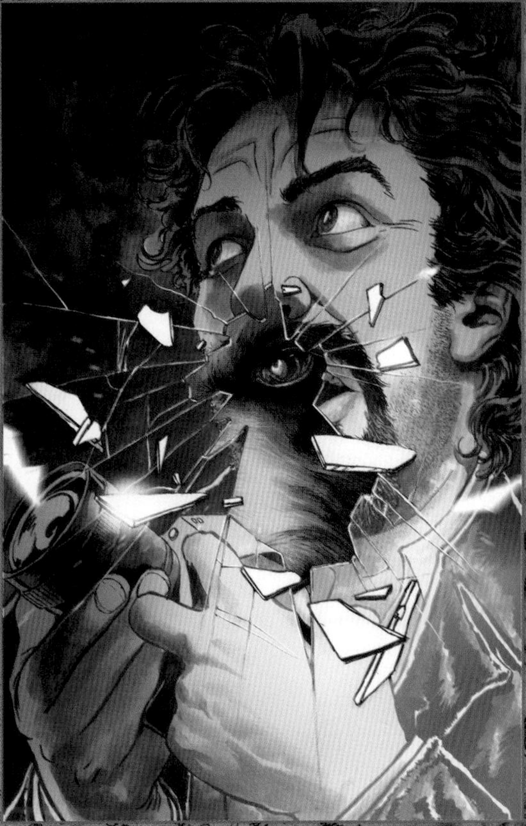

GRIMM: PORTLAND, WU #4 COVER
BY DANIEL GOVER

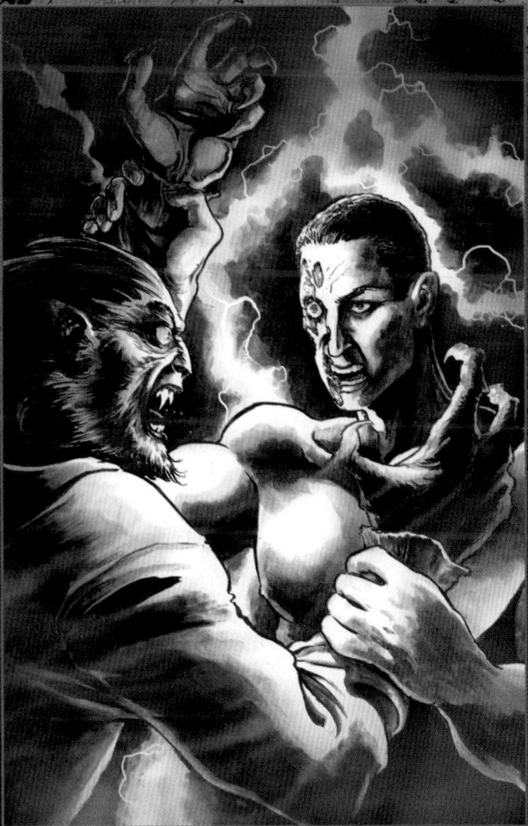

GRIMM: PORTLAND, WU #5 COVER

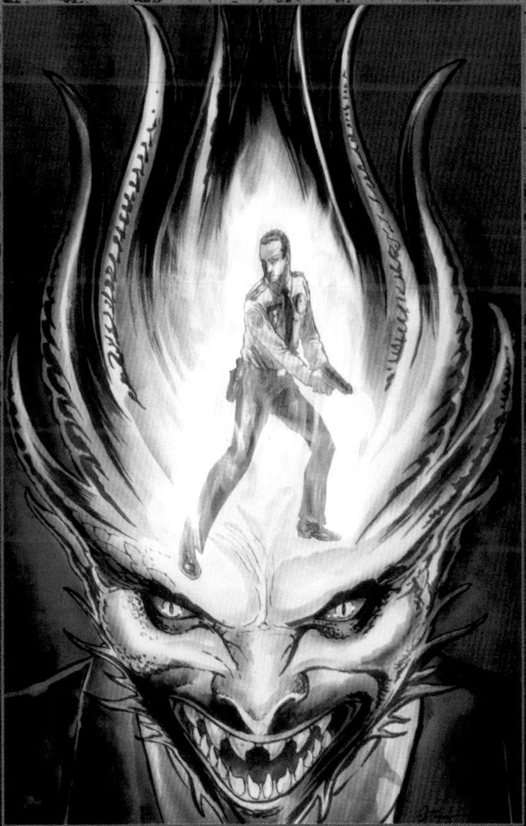

GRIMM: PORTLAND, WU #6 COVER

BEST OF ARMY OF DARKNESS™ COLLECTIONS

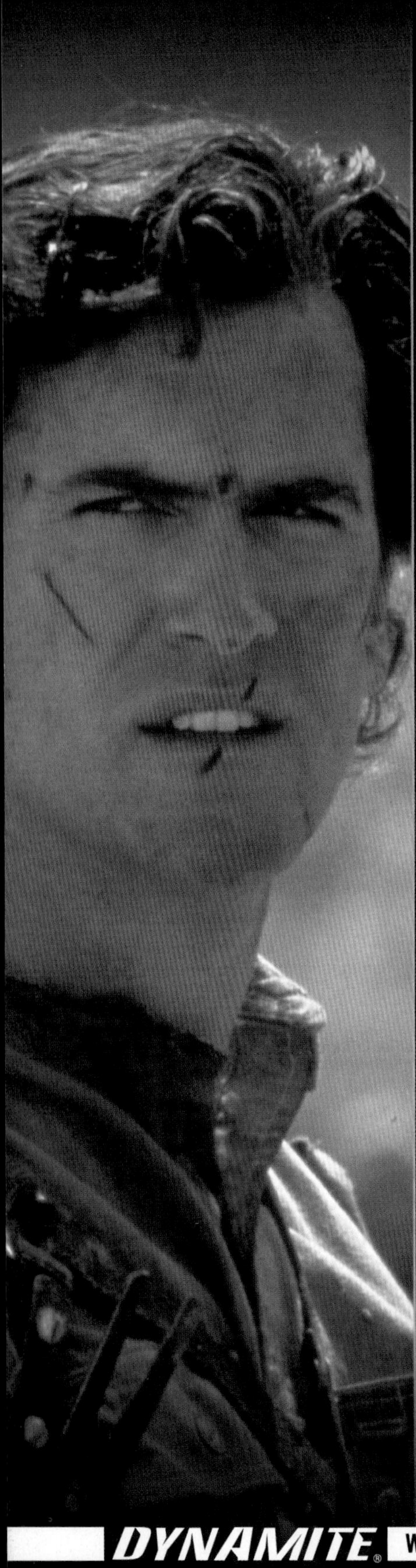

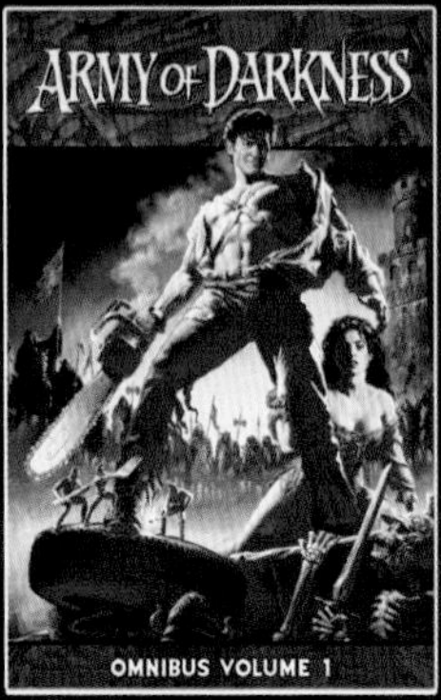
ARMY OF DARKNESS
OMNIBUS VOLUME 1

OMNIBUS VOL. 1

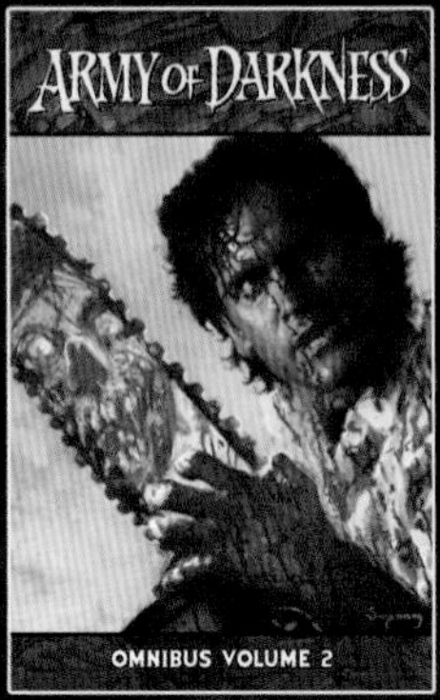
ARMY OF DARKNESS
OMNIBUS VOLUME 2

OMNIBUS VOL. 2

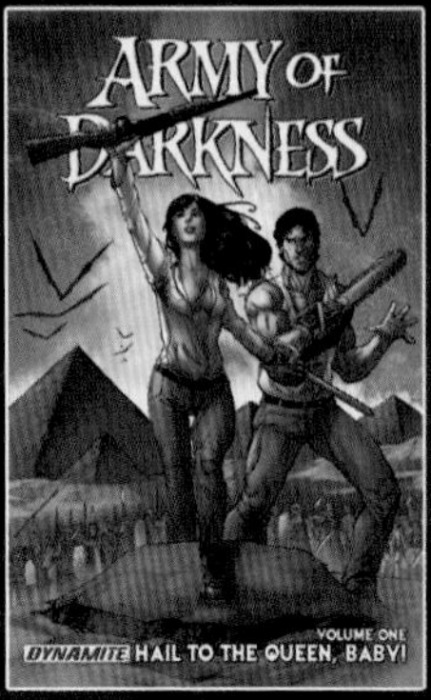
ARMY OF DARKNESS
DYNAMITE
VOLUME ONE
HAIL TO THE QUEEN, BABY!

VOL. 1: HAIL TO THE QUEEN, BABY! TPB

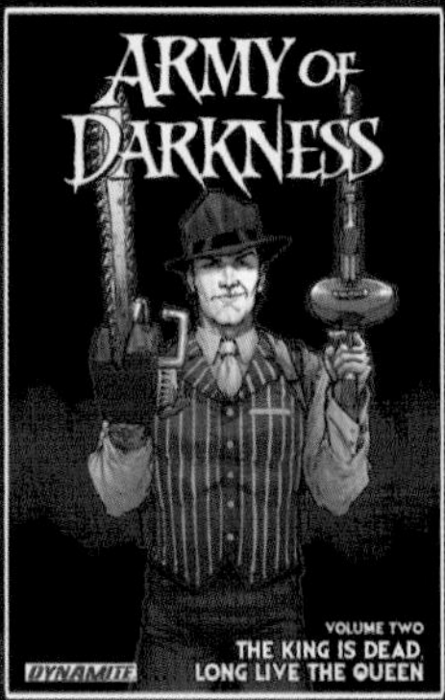
ARMY OF DARKNESS
VOLUME TWO
THE KING IS DEAD, LONG LIVE THE QUEEN
DYNAMITE

VOL. 2: THE KING IS DEAD, LONG LIVE THE QUEEN TPB

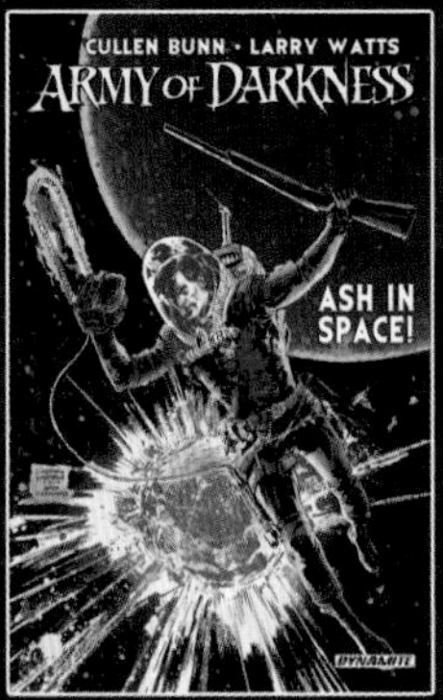
CULLEN BUNN · LARRY WATTS
ARMY OF DARKNESS
ASH IN SPACE!
DYNAMITE

ASH IN SPACE TPB

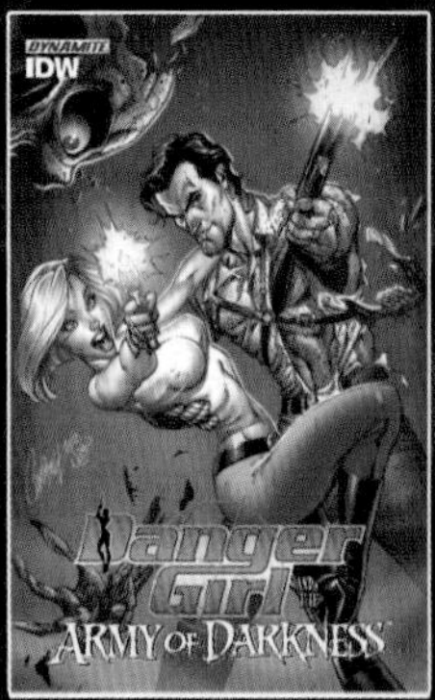
DYNAMITE
IDW
Danger Girl
ARMY OF DARKNESS

DANGER GIRL AND THE ARMY OF DARKNESS TPB

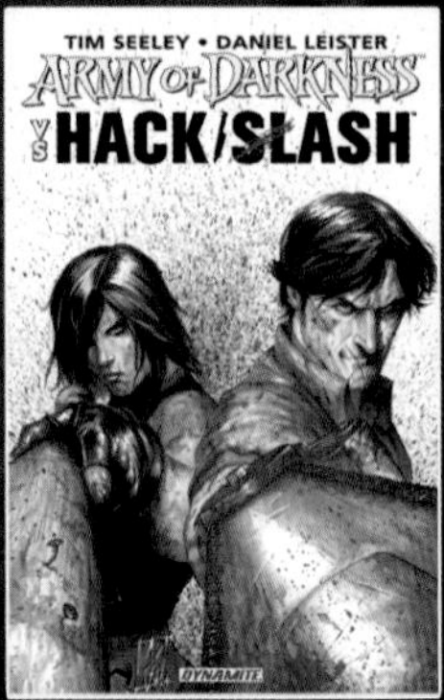
TIM SEELEY • DANIEL LEISTER
ARMY OF DARKNESS
VS
HACK/SLASH
DYNAMITE

ARMY OF DARKNESS VS HACK/SLASH

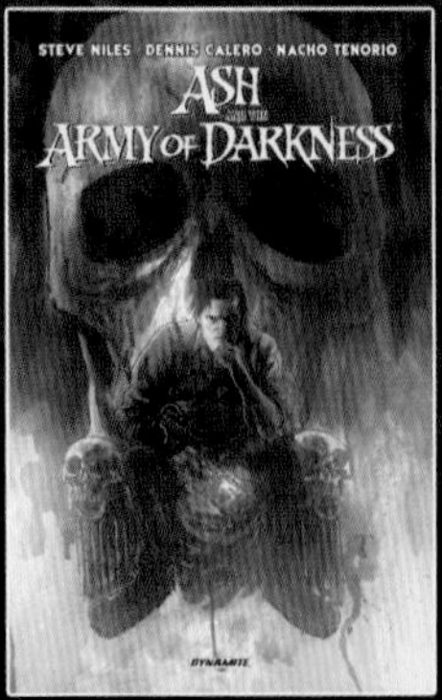
STEVE NILES · DENNIS CALERO · NACHO TENORIO
ASH
AND THE
ARMY OF DARKNESS

ASH AND THE ARMY OF DARKNESS TPB

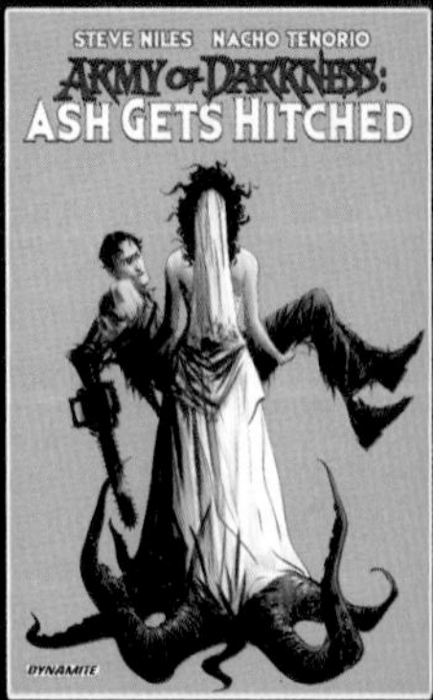
STEVE NILES · NACHO TENORIO
ARMY OF DARKNESS:
ASH GETS HITCHED
DYNAMITE

ASH GETS HITCHED TPB

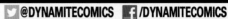

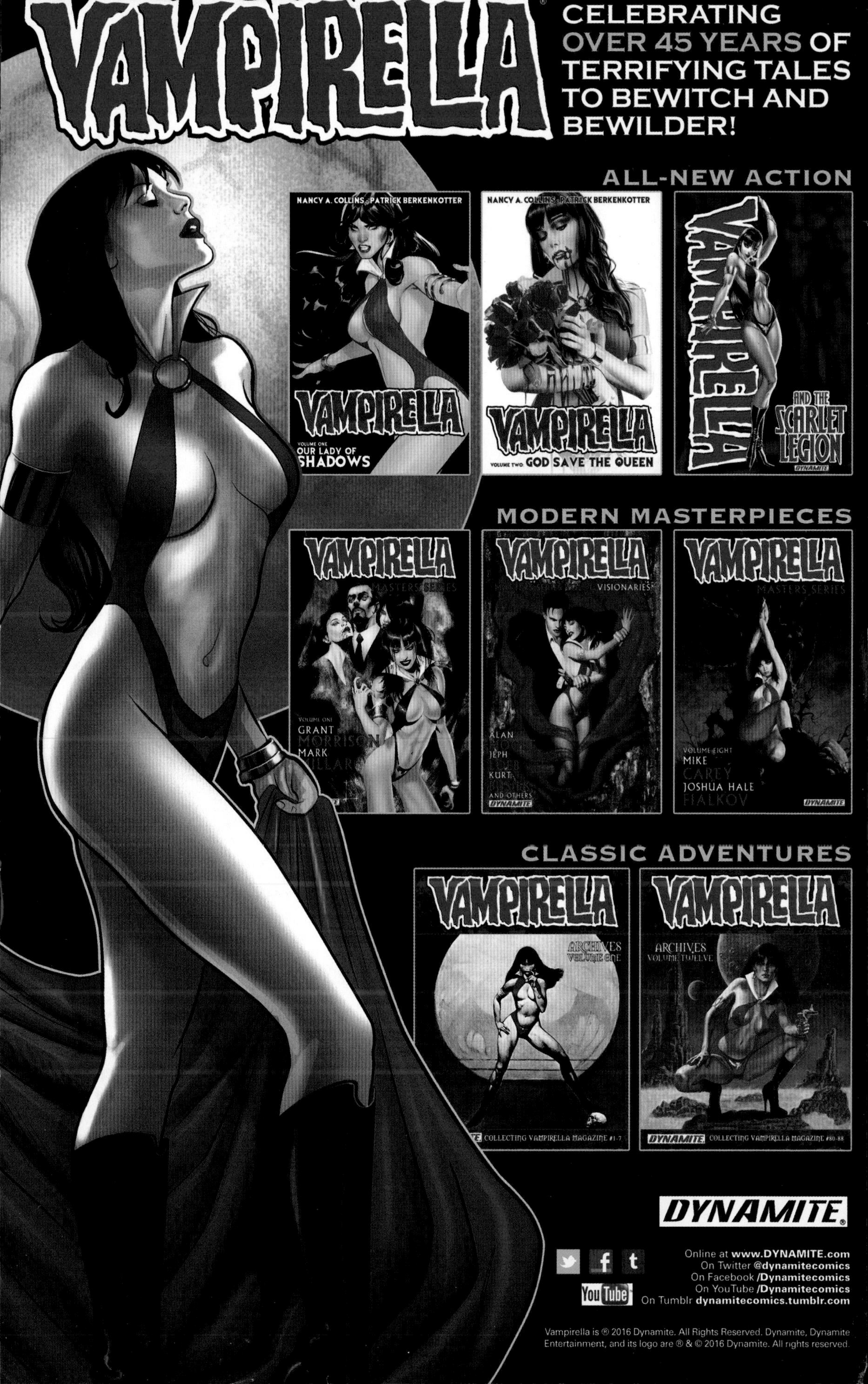
VAMPIRELLA®
CELEBRATING OVER 45 YEARS OF TERRIFYING TALES TO BEWITCH AND BEWILDER!
ALL-NEW ACTION
NANCY A. COLLINS · PATRICK BERKENKOTTER
VAMPIRELLA
VOLUME ONE OUR LADY OF SHADOWS
NANCY A. COLLINS · PATRICK BERKENKOTTER
VAMPIRELLA
VOLUME TWO GOD SAVE THE QUEEN
VAMPIRELLA AND THE SCARLET LEGION
MODERN MASTERPIECES
VAMPIRELLA MASTERS SERIES
VOLUME ONE GRANT MORRISON MARK MILLAR
VAMPIRELLA VISIONARIES
ALAN MOORE JEPH LOEB KURT BUSIEK AND OTHERS
VAMPIRELLA MASTERS SERIES
VOLUME EIGHT MIKE CAREY JOSHUA HALE FIALKOV
CLASSIC ADVENTURES
VAMPIRELLA ARCHIVES VOLUME ONE
COLLECTING VAMPIRELLA MAGAZINE #1-7
VAMPIRELLA ARCHIVES VOLUME TWELVE
DYNAMITE COLLECTING VAMPIRELLA MAGAZINE #80-88
DYNAMITE®
Online at www.DYNAMITE.com
On Twitter @dynamitecomics
On Facebook /Dynamitecomics
On YouTube /Dynamitecomics
On Tumblr dynamitecomics.tumblr.com
Vampirella is ® 2016 Dynamite. All Rights Reserved. Dynamite, Dynamite Entertainment, and its logo are ® & © 2016 Dynamite. All rights reserved.